Published by
Time Out Guides Limited
Universal House
251 Tottenham Court Road
London W1T 7AB
Tel +44 (0)20 7813 3000
Fax +44 (0)20 7813 6001
email guides@timeout.com
www.timeout.com

Editorial
Editor Cath Phillips
Consultant Editor Guy Dimond
Deputy Editor Phil Harriss
Copy Editor Ros Sales
Researchers Jill Emeny, Cathy Limb
Proofer John Pym
Subject Index Jacqueline Brind

Editorial/Managing Director
Peter Fiennes
Series Editor Sarah Guy
Deputy Series Editor Cath Phillips
Business Manager Gareth Garner
Guides Co-ordinator Holly Pick
Accountant Kemi Olufuwa

Design
Art Director Scott Moore
Art Editor Pinelope Kourmouzoglou
Senior Designer Josephine Spencer
Graphic Designer Henry Elphick
Digital Imaging Dan Conway
Ad Make-up Jenni Prichard

Picture Desk
Picture Editor Jael Marschner
Deputy Picture Editor Tracey Kerrigan
Picture Researcher Helen McFarland

Advertising
Sales Director & Sponsorship
Mark Phillips
Sales Manager Alison Wallen
Advertising Sales Ben Holt, Ali Lowry,
Jason Trotman
Advertising Assistant Kate Staddon
Copy Controller Amy Nelson

Marketing
Group Marketing Director John Luck
Marketing Manager Yvonne Poon
Marketing & Publicity Manager, US
Rosella Albanese

Production
Group Production Director Mark Lamond
Production Manager Brendan McKeown
Production Coordinator
Caroline Bradford

Time Out Group
Chairman Tony Elliott
Managing Director Mike Hardwick
Financial Director Richard Waterlow
Director/Group General Manager
Nichola Coulthard
Director/TO Magazine Ltd MD & TO
Communications Ltd MD David Pepper
Director/TO Guides Ltd MD
Peter Fiennes
Group Art Director John Oakey
Group IT Director Simon Chappell

Sections in this guide were written by
African & Caribbean Kevin Gould, Fiona McAuslan, Nana Ocran, Ken Olende, Franka Philip, Sejal Sukhadwala; **The Americas** (North American) Christi Daugherty; (Latin American) Chris Moss, Christi Daugherty, Ruth Jarvis; **British** Sarah Guy; **Chinese** Antonia Bruce, Guy Dimond, Fuchsia Dunlop, Ian Fenn, Phil Harriss, Tim Luard; **East European** Tom Masters, Janet Zromczek; **Fish** Guy Dimond, Jan Fuscoe, Tom Lamont, Sally Peck, Cath Phillips, Lisa Ritchie; **French** Ismay Atkins, Tom Coveney, Guy Dimond, Fuchsia Dunlop, Peter Fiennes, Will Fulford-Jones, Viv Groskop, Ruth Jarvis, Tom Masters, Nick Rider, Ethel Rimmer, Sejal Sukhadwala, Caro Taverne, Simon Tillotson; **Gastropubs** Simon Coppock, Guy Dimond, Kevin Ebbutt, Jan Fuscoe, Ruth Jarvis, Cath Phillips, Patrick Marmion, Chris Moss, Jenni Muir, Nana Ocran, Nick Rider, Ethel Rimmer, Veronica Simpson, Gordon Thomson, Pete Watts, Janet Zmroczek; **Global** Roopa Gulati; **Greek** Alexia Loundras; **Hotels & Haute Cuisine** Helen Barnard; **Indian** Guy Dimond, Roopa Gulati, Phil Harriss, Sejal Sukhadwala; **International** Kevin Ebbutt, Claire Fogg, Cath Phillips; **Italian** Elena Berton, Patrick Marmion, Tom Masters, Jenni Muir, Sally Peck, Nick Rider, Ethel Rimmer, Yolanda Zappaterra; **Japanese** Terry Durack, Tim Jackson, Kei Kikuchi, Susan Low, Rebecca Taylor; **Jewish** Judy Jackson; **Korean** Joe Bindloss, Sejal Sukhadwala; **Malaysian, Indonesian & Singaporean** Terry Durack, Jenny Linford, Simon Richmond; **Middle Eastern** Andrew Humphreys, Vanessa Kendell, Ros Sales, Janet Zmroczek; **Modern European** Ismay Atkins, Tom Coveney, Guy Dimond, Kevin Ebbutt, Richard Ehrlich, Claire Fogg, Will Fulford-Jones, Sarah Guy, Ruth Jarvis, Susan Low, Fiona McAuslan, Lesley McCave, Anna Norman, Sally Peck, Cath Phillips, Ros Sales, Caro Taverne, Simon Tillotson, Janet Zmroczek; **North African** Andrew Humphreys, Janet Zmroczek; **Oriental** Antonia Bruce, Tim Jackson; **Portuguese** Gareth Evans; **Spanish** Elizabeth Carter, Andrew Staffell; **Thai** Joe Bindloss; **Turkish** Ken Olende; **Vegetarian** Sejal Sukhadwala; **Vietnamese** Joe Bindloss, Simon Richmond, Lam Vo; **Budget** Guy Dimond, Natasha Polyviou, Jenny Rigby; **Cafés** Helenka Bednar, Guy Dimond, Eli Dryden, Roopa Gulati, Sarah Guy, Ronnie Hayden, Pendle Harte, Cathy Limb, Jenni Muir, Cathy Phillips, Jenny Rigby; **Fish & Chips** Amanda Smith; **Wine Bars** James Aufenast; **Eating & Entertainment** Alexi Duggins, Jill Emeny, Cathy Limb; **Food Shops** Sejal Sukhadwala; **Drink Shops** David Furer; **Courses** Jenni Muir (Cookery), Alice Lascelles (Wine, beer & cocktails).

Interviews by Jenni Muir, except Shao Wei (Fuchsia Dunlop).

Additional reviews by Ismay Atkins, James Aufenast, Helen Barnard, Antonia Bruce, Glynn Christian, Simon Coppock, Simon Cropper, Guy Dimond, Eli Dryden, Fuchsia Dunlop, Kevin Ebbutt, Richard Ehrlich, Jill Emeny, Peter Fiennes, Claire Fogg, Jan Fuscoe, Will Fulford-Jones, Roopa Gulati, Sarah Guy, Elaine Hallgarten, Ronnie Haydon, Tim Jackson, Ruth Jarvis, Vanessa Kendell, Tom Lamont, Alice Lascelles, Cathy Limb, Sharon Lougher, Susan Low, Patrick Marmion, Lesley McCave, Jenny McIvor, Kathryn Miller, Chris Moss, Jenni Muir, Anna Norman, Nana Ocran, Ken Olende, Sally Peck, Cath Phillips, Holly Pick, Natasha Polyviou, Jenny Rigby, Nick Rider, Ethel Rimmer, Lisa Ritchie, Veronica Simpson, Amanda Smith, Derryck Strachan, Caro Taverne, Susie Theodorou, Yolanda Zappaterra.

The Editor would like to thank Katy Attfield, Guy Dimond, Sarah Guy, Mike Harrison, Phil Harriss, Jenni Muir, and our sponsor, Leffe.

Cover photography by Michael Franke taken at Plateau (7715 7100/ www.conran-restaurants.co.uk)
Photography by pages 2, 21, 29, 41, 114, 159, 228, 242, 247, 328 Alys Tomlinson; pages 3, 4, 6, 21, 44, 53, 58, 59, 82, 94, 103, 119, 120, 135, 141, 152, 161, 170, 181, 193, 205, 220, 232, 233, 235, 277, 296 Britta Jaschinski; pages 3, 4, 5, 8, 21, 22, 23, 24, 39, 49, 61, 62, 66, 67, 68, 72, 74, 77, 80, 86, 87, 100, 131, 186, 188, 216, 217, 210, 211, 239, 251, 258, 259, 267, 298, 299, 304, 309, 311, 319, 322, 332, 333, 343 Ming Tang Evans; pages 5, 35, 52, 55 Martin Daly; pages 22, 24, 27, 97, 122, 123, 126, 190, 198, 200, 218, 224, 253, 271, 272, 273, 280, 291, 317, 345, 346, 348, 349 Heloise Bergman; pages 89, 107, 175, 287 Tricia de Courcy Ling; pages 91, 109, 173 Andrew Lynch; pages 93, 285, 306, 323 Michael Franke; pages 104, 105 Sam Bailey; pages 110, 111, 133, 169, 295 Rob Greig; pages 113, 149, 263 Oliver Knight; pages 145, 165 Nuno Miranda; pages 178, 179, 326 Scott Wishart; pages 289, 292 Thomas Skovsende; page 339 Anthony Webb; page 342 Haris Artemis; page 354 Gemma Day.
The following images were provided by the featured establishment: pages 57, 71, 99, 155, 227, 240, 257, 335.

Maps JS Graphics (john@jsgraphics.co.uk). Maps 1-18 & 24 are based on material supplied by Alan Collinson and Julie Snook through Copyright Exchange.

Reprographics Wyndeham Prepress, 3 & 4 Maverton Road, London, E3 2JE
Printers Copper Clegg Ltd, Shannon Way, Tewkesbury Industrial Centre, Tewkesbury, Gloucestershire GL20 8HB

ISBN 1 905042 086
ISSN 1750-4643

Distribution by Seymour Ltd (020 7396 8000)
Distributed in USA by Publishers Group West

Introduction
How we compile the Time Out Eating & Drinking Guide

The restaurants, gastropubs, cafés, bars and pubs included in this guide are picked by the editors as the best of their type in London. Time Out always pays the bill; restaurants do not pay to be included in the guide, and can exert no pressure on us as to the content of their reviews.

Although our reviewers are often experts in their field, they are in one sense no different from other members of the public: they always visit restaurants anonymously. This is why the reviews here are more likely to match your own experience than reviews you might read elsewhere. Recognised critics receive preferential treatment, so it is much harder to trust their judgment. They get better treatment from the staff and more attention from the kitchen, which invariably colours their impressions of a restaurant. However, when Time Out reviews restaurants for either this guide or the Food & Drink pages of the weekly magazine, we do so anonymously. There is no hob-nobbing with PRs, no freebies and no launch parties. We feel our readers have a right to know what eating at that restaurant might be like for them.

Our reviewers are journalists who have a passion for food, and for finding the best places to eat and drink. Many of them also have extraordinary expertise in specialist areas; a few are trained chefs, but most are just enthusiasts. For example, the two principal authors of the Indian chapter are recognised experts in north Indian and Indian vegetarian cookery (they are also, respectively, Hindi and Gujarati speakers). The principal authors of the Chinese chapter are also experts in regional Chinese cooking (and also speak Mandarin and/or Cantonese).

For the weekly *Time Out* magazine alone, our reviewers visit around 200 new places every year. The better discoveries are then included in this guide. On top of that, reviewers also check other new openings, as well as revisit all the places included in the previous edition. As a result, at least 2,000 anonymous visits were made in the creation of this guide. We also pay attention to recommendations and feedback from readers and from users of our website. We then eliminate the also-rans to create the annual list of London's best eateries that this guide represents.

RESTAURANTS

CHEAP EATS

DRINKING

SHOPS & COURSES

Eating & Drinking 2007
Contents

100% INDEPENDENT
The reviews in the *Time Out Eating & Drinking Guide* are based on the experiences of Time Out restaurant reviewers. All restaurants, bars, gastropubs and cafés are visited anonymously, and Time Out pays the bill. No payment of any kind has secured or influenced a review.

FEATURES

The year that was

Guy Dimond takes a look at the openings, closures, movings and shakings in London's restaurant scene over the past 12 months.

For more than two decades we've had a crack team of food and drink experts roving London to seek out the most authentic regional cooking, the most welcoming service, and best-value eating and drinking on offer. You'd think we'd get blasé about it, but nothing could be further from the truth – the first whiff of a new Afghan restaurant in Middlesex, and we're fighting over who gets to go there and review it. The reason being, London now has one of the world's most dynamic and exciting food and drink scenes. Of course, the capital still has its share of dowdy restaurants with indifferent food and sullen service, but you have to be very complacent when choosing where to eat (there are no excuses now you've got this guide), or very unlucky to eat badly in London these days. What our city has to offer is barely recognisable from the first Eating Guides we published in the early 1980s, and we've seen trends come (and go) that no-one could have anticipated.

Perhaps the most welcome trend is the resurgence of pride in British ingredients and cooking. Of course, this was was always there if you looked, but was given a fillip and a welcome reinterpretation by St John restaurant, which opened in 1994. Over the past few years St John alumni have left to set up their own places, from gastropubs (Anchor & Hope) to DJ bars (Medcalf), all serving modern versions of British cooking. But in the last year alone we've seen the excellent **Roast** and **National Dining Rooms** open, as well as **Canteen** and the **Butcher & Grill**. We never thought we'd see the day, but over the past year, British food and restaurants have become cool.

Other recent trends have been the surge of interest in steakhouses and bistros; a clutch of excellent pâtisseries and wine bars; and a huge growth in the number of low-budget Korean restaurants in central London. Asian food in general continues to improve and move steadily upmarket, particularly Indian restaurants, which have seen some dramatic improvements. Some of the best Indian restaurants in the world are now in London, not India; if you haven't tried one of the upmarket new-wave ones, it's time you did.

The drift away from hyped West End mega-eateries is continuing, with neighbourhood restaurants becoming increasingly sophisticated (helped, no doubt, by monied people buying property in previously down-at-heel neighbourhoods). In the past year we've been particularly impressed by **Upstairs** in Brixton, and **Sam's Brasserie & Bar** and **High Road Brasserie** in Chiswick.

After what appears to be a levelling-off of new openings, we're pleased to see that some excellent new gastropubs are still emerging. North and east London seem to be particularly good breeding grounds for them at the moment, with the **Charles Lamb** and **Marquess Tavern** being two particularly fine examples.

2005

SEPTEMBER

Chiswick, a suburb as well known for chain restaurants as being on a bend in the river, sat up and took notice when **Sam's Brasserie & Bar** (*see p227*) opened in the autumn. Stylish looks! Great cocktails! Food just like the West End! Lucky Chiswick; Sam's won the Time Out Eating & Drinking Award 2006 for Best Local Restaurant. But this action was upstaged by goings-on in the West End. **Galvin Bistrot de Luxe** (*see p93*) became one of the most written-about restaurants of the year, partly because Chris Galvin and his brother Jeff captured the zeitgeist: critics, in particular, had been pining for less fusion and better cooking, less pomp and more attention to getting the details right. Galvin's retro-French cooking is hard to fault.

The most ambitious venture to open in September was **China Tang** (*see p69*). Originally conceived as a collaboration between Alan Yau (of Hakkasan fame) and David Tang (of the Shanghai Tang fashion label), this would have been the restaurant equivalent of Oasis and Blur doing duets. However, the perpetually busy Yau pulled out, but

fish! kitchen

Canteen

the result – an independent David Tang restaurant tucked inside the Dorchester – is still a wow of a place, stunningly designed to evoke 1930s Shanghai, but serving an essentially conservative (and good) Cantonese menu. The biggest surprise of autumn 2005 had to be **Hummus Bros** (*see p290*). It's a fast-food café with no alcohol licence and bench seating, specialising in houmous. That's right, chickpea paste, but served with various toppings, breads and dips. We can't keep away, and neither can half of Soho, judging by way it's busy every time we visit. It has the makings of a really successful chain. You read it here first.

OCTOBER

Remember wine bars? Those smoky places propped up by claret-quaffing soaks trying to get off with their secretaries? **Vinoteca** (*see p331*) dragged the wine bar into the 21st century with some truly extraordinary wines by the glass, some great food, a no-smoking policy and the option of taking home bottles at off-licence prices, Italian enoteca-style. Marvellous, and it won the Time Out Eating & Drinking Award 2006 for Best Wine Bar. A rather less original idea was bringing a 'real' French steakhouse to London from Paris, in the shape of **Le Relais de Venise l'entrecôte** (*see p93*). It's still going strong, but a rival restaurant (Entrecôte de Café de Paris) did the same thing a few months later (by coincidence, it seems), and then closed after less than a year. Steak-frites, you're not dead yet.

Korean restaurants have been opening at the rate of one a month for the last couple of years, but mostly they have been small, unambitious cafés catering mainly for oriental students. Not so with **Asadal** (*see p204*), a large and impressive-looking Korean restaurant next to Holborn tube station. Most of the UK's best Korean food is found around New Malden in Surrey, but this second branch of a New Malden original made us wonder how long it will be before good Korean restaurants start popping up everywhere, just as Japanese restaurants did a decade ago.

Perhaps the longest-anticipated opening of 2005 was **Roast** (*see p59*). Announced more than a year previously, its launch was delayed because of problems with the construction. If you see the building, it's easy to see why: a glass and concrete edifice perched aloft over Borough Market, startling in its use of modern materials in a Victorian setting, but not incongruous. And best of all, the menu is a showcase of the best of British produce, intelligently put together. We like Roast so much we chose it as the venue for our 2006 Time Out Eating & Drinking Awards. A toast to Roast!

British seemed to be flavour of the month, as **Canteen** (*see p51*) also opened in the new development that has arisen in the shadow of Old Spitalfields Market. As the name suggests, it's far removed from the stuffy, old school of British restaurants; it's sleek and modern with smiling service, and an appealing retro menu. Bacon sandwiches and toasted crumpets anyone?

NOVEMBER

Richard Corrigan became a familiar name in 2006, helped along by his appearances on the BBC's now-defunct *Full On Food* series. Very well established in Soho at British restaurant Lindsay House, the smooth-talking Irish chef re-opened **Bentley's** fish restaurant (*see p83*) to immediate applause.

Ladurée

Hugely camp Loungelover was one of the most influential bars to open in London in recent years, so a second branch was bound to arouse lots of interest; when it finally came, **Annex 3** (*see p322*) proved to be less than the eye-candy expected. The cocktails are fabulous, but couldn't the three boys who run it have stretched to more than car-boot sales and wallpaper shop bin-ends to decorate the place? **Ladurée** (*see p298*), in contrast, pulled out all the stops, as you might expect of a top Parisian pâtisserie opening a showcase branch inside Harrods. It's a confection that appeals to all the senses, and has become a must-see for food- and drink-lovers passing through Knightsbridge. Not all in-store launches take off in quite the way Ladurée did. **Obika** (*see p171*), a new 'mozarella bar' inside Selfridges, is a perfectly nice Italian deli that replaced the former in-store Momo. Despite offering journalists a free trip to Milan to try the original, Obika garnered little press, but we liked it for the spectacular people-watching – it's right in the centre of the 'Superbrands' section of women's fashion.

A world away from Chloé and Stella McCartney's frocks, a tequila bar stirred in Shoreditch. **Green & Red** (*see p326*) might not look like much, but it stocks a blinding range of tequilas of all ages, styles and persuasions. The Mexican food accompanying this is also far better than it needs to be. All together now: one tequila, two tequila, three tequila, floor…

National Dining Rooms

DECEMBER

Fine-dining restaurants and hotels go together like expense accounts and business class. **Addendum** (*see p125*) is a jolly fine restaurant in a slightly dull City hotel; chef Tom Ilic is a master of his art. Conran Restaurants' latest French restaurant **Sauterelle** (*see p191*) would have brought the number of Conran restaurants in the Square Mile into double figures, were it not for the end of Conran's collaboration with the Great Eastern Hotel, which decimated his presence in the area. Away from the cut and thrust of the City in the rather more genteel environs of St ▶

Hello

As the guide went to press, scores of new restaurant openings were planned. Dates may change – as may many other details.

2006 SEPTEMBER

The Hoxton Grille
81 Great Eastern Street, EC2 (7550 1000/ www.grille restaurants.com).
A combination of French bistro and American steakhouse, located in the new Hoxton Hotel (www.hoxtonhotel.co.uk).

L'Atelier du Joël Robuchon
13-15 West Street, WC2.
A celebrated French chef's return from retirement resulted in one of the most acclaimed Parisian restaurants of recent years, L'Atelier. This London branch – now one of several around the world – will fuse Japanese-style presentation with French flavours.

The Wallace
Wallace Collection, Manchester Square, W1 (7637 5555).
What used to be Café Bagatelle in the courtyard of the Wallace Collection of fine art will be a brasserie serving classic and contemporary French food, from restaurateur Oliver Peyton of **National Dining Rooms** fame (*see p57*). Open daily from 10am to 5pm, except on Friday and Saturday when it will also open for dinner.

Upper Glas
The Mall Building, 359 Upper Street, N1 (7359 1932/ www.glasrestaurant.co.uk).
Lola's has closed to make room for Upper Glas, the relocated Swedish restaurant Glas, formerly at Borough Market. Chef Patric Blomquist left in February 2006, but his menu will continue via chef Andreas Arberg.

Meals
Heal's, 196 Tottenham Court Road, W1.
The restaurant on the first floor of Heal's department store has been taken over by Oliver Peyton, and will be a 60-cover British restaurant with an interior that acknowledges Heal's Arts and Crafts heritage.

Tom's Kitchen
27 Cale Street, Chelsea Green, SW3.
Tom Aikens' second restaurant, after the haute cuisine **Tom Aikens** (*see p133*), will be a larger and much more casual dining experience, with a 90-seat brasserie serving Modern British food on the ground floor and a bar on the floor above.

Odette's
130 Regent's Park Road, NW1.
Tales of its demise were exaggerated as Odette's reopens in Primrose Hill after refurbishment under new owner, music and club impresario Vince Power.

Tamarai
167 Drury Lane, WC2 (www.tamarai.co.uk).
A pan-Asian bar and restaurant from the owners of Indian outfit Chor Bizarre. Chefs will include Chinese dim sum specialists and an Indian master chef from Chettinad, Tamil Nadu.

OCTOBER

Chelsea Brasserie
Sloane Square Hotel, Sloane Square, SW1 (7896 9988/ www.sloanesquarehotel.co.uk).
The Sloane Square Hotel is opening a French brasserie under David Karlsson Möller, former head chef of French restaurant **Racine** (*see p92*).

Bumpkin
209 Westbourne Park Road, W11 (7243 7818).
A mulit-floored brasserie, fine dining room and 'whisky room' with a bias towards food that is British and traceable.

Mocoto
145 Knightsbridge, SW1.
Huge Brazilian bar and restaurant on the site where Isola used to be.

Fortnum & Mason wine bar
181 Piccadilly, W1 (7734 8040/ www.fortnumandmason.com).
Designed by David Collins, F&M's new wine bar will be one of the first elements of the department store's £24 million refurbishment to open.

Rex
Rex House, corner of Regent Street & Piccadilly, SW1.

▶

James's, the decades-old Italian restaurant **Franco's** (*see p173*) reopened after refubishment and we were wowed by its elegance. Refurbishment and reinvention seemed to be flavour of the month, with long-established Indian restaurant **Veeraswamy** (*see p137*) relaunching yet again with a new and hugely improved menu under the same owners.

2006

JANUARY

One of the most fumbled restaurant launches we've witnessed was **Yakitoria** (*see p193*), located in a new development north of Paddington. For the first few weeks, the hapless waiting staff and kitchen didn't appear to be speaking the same language – and this, of course, was when the critics descended, resulting in some blistering reviews. However, we returned several weeks later, by which time things had smoothed over; it now appears to be running with model efficiency, and the design is striking enough to merit winning the Time Out Eating & Drinking Award 2006 for Best Design. An altogether different design approach was used in the two-year refurbishment of **Brown's Hotel** in Mayfair (*see* **The Grill**, *p132*); it looks as if time has stood still in this splendid hotel, and the bar and dining room are reassuringly old-fashioned. If paying £100 per head for dinner at Brown's isn't your kind of thing, **Imli** (*see p140*) in Soho was more likely to be the discovery of the month. An offshoot of upmarket Tamarind, it's a low-priced fast-food joint that serves a carefully prepared array of Indian street food dishes.

Some of the most interesting new developments were well away from the West End. **Upstairs** (*see p233*) is entered by a buzzer on a nondescript door in a Brixton side street, but word of mouth keeps the place buzzing; the fine Modern European cooking in the tiny dining room is some of the best ever seen in Brixton.

We've been waiting patiently for a wave of interesting bars and eating places to open to the east of Shoreditch as the artists and other trendsetters have migrated there, but it's been slow in coming – east of Brick Lane is largely uncharted territory for decent, mid-range pubs and restaurants. So we were delighted that the **Camel** (*see p329*) had been saved from destruction and refurbed by pub enthusiasts. Now we just need a few more like that.

FEBRUARY

We're used to seeing unusual interiors in London, but **Saran Rom** (*see p263*), a Thai restaurant on the river in Fulham, is something else. Based on the design of an Edwardian-era teak temple in Bangkok, it has a historical-style interior juxtaposed inside a brand-new development; the effect is a bit like stepping through a time portal.

Retro 1970s food pops up from time to time on London menus, but we've never seen such a complete Glam Rock-era menu in a restaurant until the arrival of bar-restaurant **Velvet Lounge** (*see p164*) in Earlsfield. It merits a journey for nostalgia's sake alone; it's the only place we know of serving prawn cocktail, stroganoff and chocolate fondue.

Roast

CANARY WHARF
...there's so much more on the menu

From light - hearted lunches to fine dining, Canary Wharf has a wide range of
restaurants offering food to suit all tastes.

With over 200 shops, bars and restaurants, open seven days a week and accessible
by car, train, underground and river, Canary Wharf is always close to you.

Far from ordinary, close to you

shops & restaurants
CANARY WHARF

www.mycanarywharf.com

Hello (continued)

Rex is the working title of a new Modern European venue from Chris Corbin and Jeremy King, the force behind the **Wolseley** (see p225).

National Café
National Gallery, Trafalgar Square, WC2.
An all-day self-service café from Oliver Peyton inside the National Gallery.

Pearl Liang
Sheldon Square, Paddington Central, W2.
A (much delayed) Chinese dim sum and oriental seafood restaurant in the new Paddington Central development.

Not Automat
33 Dover Street, W1 (7499 3033).
Carlos Almada, the architect behind **Automat** (see p34), is planning a more upscale restaurant in adjacent premises.

St Germain
89 Turnmill Street, EC1.
French-style brasserie located in a 19th-century printing works. Run by former Will Ricker Restaurants director Neil Walkington.

'AUTUMN'

Theo Randall at the InterContinental
InterContinental London Hotel, 1 Hamilton Place, W1 (7318 8577).
The InterContinental hotel is currently undergoing a £60 million refurbishment, but will reopen with chef Theo Randall, head chef at the **River Café** (see p176) for the past 15 years, cooking a regional Italian menu for the restaurant, bar and private dining room.

Haiku
15 New Burlington Place, W1.
South African restaurant group Bukhara is planning a branch in Mayfair, serving pan-Asian food. Diners will be able to watch Chinese dim sum, wok and barbecue dishes, Japanese robata grills and sushi being prepared.

NOVEMBER

Bincho
The Strand, WC2.
Dominic Ford, the man behind **Tamesa@oxo** (see p49) and the **Butcher & Grill** (see p59), is opening a 150-seater Japanese-style yakitori bar, complete with five charcoal grills and a saké sommelier from Japan.

Barrafino
54 Frith Street, W1.
Brothers Sam and Eddie Hart are opening a second Spanish tapas bar, in Soho, which will be cheaper than the first, **Fino** (see p252). It is inspired by Cal Pep, the iconic tapas bar in Barcelona, and will have counters rather than more formal tables and chairs.

Scott's
20 Mount Street, W1 (www.caprice-holdings.co.uk).
The reopening of this Mayfair restaurant has been much delayed, but the new owner – Caprice Holdings, which also runs **The Ivy** (see p223), **J Sheekey** (see p83), **Le Caprice** (see p226) and **Daphne's** (see p179) – is reinventing it as another modern classic. The chef will be Kevin Gratton, formerly head chef at Le Caprice.

DECEMBER

XO
29 Belsize Lane, NW3 5AS.
Will Ricker is turning the Belsize Tavern pub into a bar-restaurant, serving a similar menu to his other pan-oriental restaurants, such as **E&O** (see p243). XO is, of course, the name of a Chinese cooking sauce.

Blackwood
21-24 Cockspur Street, SW1.
A steak and lobster place with an Indian-themed club in the basement, from Iqbal Wahhab, of **Roast** (see p59). The intention is to open before Christmas – but Wahhab projects have a tendency to run late.

2007

Cha Cha No Hana
23 St James's Street, SW1.
The unlucky site that used to be Shumi and before that Che is now in the capable hands of Alan Yau, who is turning it into an upscale Japanese izakaya, supposedly in February.

MARCH

A spring-clean at the National Gallery had restaurateur Oliver Peyton championing jammy dodgers, toad-in-the-hole and pork belly with pease pudding at the terribly British **National Dining Rooms** (see p57). Down on the edge of Clapham Common, **Macaron** (see p302) is anything but common. A delightful pâtisserie that fulfils every fantasy of a frou-frou France, it's quite a picnic, and scooped the Time Out Eating & Drinking Award 2006 as London's Best Pâtisserie. That other green space on the other side of London, Primrose Hill, also got lucky with the opening of **La Collina** (see p189) – The Hill, in Italian – which immediately ranked as one of the best Italian restaurants in the capital.

Afghan food has been available in London for many years, but Afghan restaurants tend to be little hole-in-the-wall places. The opening of **Masa** (see p117) changed all that – it's smart, the food is really interesting, and it's even worth a journey to the terminus of the Bakerloo line (Harrow & Wealdstone), assuming you don't live there already.

New wine bars kept popping up like mad March hares, exemplified by the **Ambassador** (see p221) in Exmouth Market. Except, in this case, the food is so good that it merited inclusion as a finalist in the Time Out Eating & Drinking Awards 2006 in our Best New Restaurant category. Don't let that scare you off: it's still a fine place to pop in for a glass of wine.

Battersea has a tradition of groovy bars (only just exceeded by its tradition of predictable chain bars), but we think **Lost Society** (see p326) is special: winner of the Time Out Eating & Drinking Award 2006 for Best Bar, it offers good cocktails, friendly staff and great food.

APRIL

Bistros are back in and, as if we needed any more evidence of this, John McClements – an established restaurateur in Twickenham – converted his upmarket McClements restaurant into a deluxe French bistro called **La Brasserie Ma Cuisine Bourgeoise** (see p101) – not to be confused with his other bistro, just next door, which really is just an ordinary bistro. Good restaurants surfaced in the most unlikely locations, such as a residential street in Kensal Rise – **The Island** (see p236) does feel cut adrift from Notting Hill or even Queen's Park, but it reflects the growing gentrification of the neighbourhood.

Press and media coverage play a huge role in the early success or failure of new restaurants, something presumably understood by Oliver Rowe of **Konstam at the Prince Albert** (see p53). Even before opening his new place, he enlisted the help of a well-known restaurant PR firm, and became the subject of the BBC2 series *Urban Chef*. It was one of the most hyped openings of the year, but this couldn't prevent it being given a critical panning. The moral: make sure you hire a

La Noisette

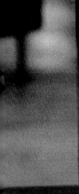

"She's not going to believe you.
I don't believe you and I was there."

"Why is the paint
never the same colour
as on the tin?"

"How about a reality show
where contestants are tricked
into thinking they're making
an interesting, relevant programme?"

"It wasn't a nightmare,
it just wasn't a very nice dream…"

"Remember the
last time we got
together like this?"

"It's like that old adage
about boiling a frog."

"Dreams are like emails
from your subconscious."

"A brontosaurus could
kill a stegosaurus…easily."

"Why is it that now
I'm getting married,
everyone starts
flirting with me?"

With an Abbey brewing heritage dating back over
750 years, Leffe is a beer that demands to be savoured.

Savour Life. Savour Leffe

Planning a function?

Fuller's have more venues than you can shake a cocktail stick at!

We have an unrivalled selection of pubs and bars across the Square Mile and throughout London. Let us know what you are planning and we will provide the venue solution and all the help you need to make your function a success.

Contact us at: functions@fullers.co.uk
or ask for our function organiser on 020 8996 2000

▶ great cook before pushing your restaurant into the limelight. In contrast, some other restaurants open with almost no publicity at all, and immediately shine. **Papillon** (*see p95*) was one of these, a very polished and upmarket French brasserie in Brompton Cross. **Bar Shu** (*see p69*) is considerably less conventional: it's London's first full-blown Sichuan restaurant, with chefs from Cheng Du in China. As if that wasn't enough of a shock, another excellent Chinese restaurant, **Dragon Castle** (*see p73*), opened at the Elephant & Castle – a neighbourhood with no track record whatsoever of fine-dining restaurants.

MAY

Windows on the World at the Hilton hotel on Park Lane has always had spectacular high-rise views, but in May it also gained spectacular cooking to match the setting with the arrival of **Galvin at Windows** (*see p130*), headed by Chris Galvin – a far more polished operation than Galvin Bistrot in Baker Street, opened only months before. May also seemed to be the month when dinner dance, cabaret and burlesque was hitting the headlines, helped along by the opening of Vince Power's high-profile **Pigalle Club** (*see p339*), though other less ambitious clubs include **Volupté** (*see p341*). The busy team behind the Green & Red tequila bar found time to open the **Marquess Tavern** (*see p114*), the Islington gastropub that won the Time Out Eating & Drinking Award 2006 for Best Gastropub.

JUNE

Sketch in Mayfair was previously considered to be the most expensive restaurant launch in London – but this was topped by **Gilgamesh** (*see p327*), which some estimates put at up to £12 million. It's certainly not understated, with a retractable roof, huge wood carvings imported from India, and a pan-Asian menu masterminded by Ian Pengelley.

A more modest attempt to soak up the drinkers of Covent Garden is **Bedford & Strand** (*see p332*), a retro-styled wine bar with a thoughtfully compiled wine list. Shoreditch, of course, has a plethora of new bars – new ones seem to open every week – but **Hawksmoor** (*see p320*) is the first bar with a really serious cocktail list to open since Loungelover. It's also a great little steakhouse, and was shortlisted in both the Best Bar and Best Steak Restaurant categories of the Time Out Eating & Drinking Awards 2006.

JULY

Not content with rejigging to create room for the new China Tang a few months previously, the Dorchester hotel also refurbished and relaunched its bar; the **Dorchester Bar** (*see p323*) immediately created a frisson among London's glitterati. Another high-profile opening was **La Noisette** (*see p127*), Gordon Ramsay Holdings' valiant attempt to rescue its unlucky Sloane Street site by putting (another) top chef in place. Further west, another key player on a roll is Nick Jones of the Soho House Group, whose latest project was the conversion of Foubert's Hotel in Chiswick to High Road House – a new brasserie, hotel and private members' club. **High Road Brasserie** (*see p47*) is a stunning-looking place, and was an instant hit. **Garni** (*see p76*), London's first real Armenian restaurant, also opened in Chiswick. Across the river in Battersea, the **Butcher & Grill** (*see p59*) does

what it says on the label: a butcher at the front, a British restaurant at the back; it's the second of three restaurants opened by restaurateur Dominic Ford in just one year.

As we went to press in late August there were lots of other exciting new openings to look forward to; you'll find these listed in the **Hello** box, which starts on page 6.

> **See the latest restaurant and bar reviews at...**
> www.timeout.com/restaurants

Goodbye

We bid farewell to all the restaurants that have changed hands or turned in their lunch pail since the last edition. The following is just a small selection of the dearly departed.

Allium
Dry your eyes – Dolphin Square Hotel in Pimlico has closed, taking Anton Edelmann's last restaurant with it.

Atlantic Bar & Grill
Not so much a lock-in as a lock-out: the landlords repossessed Oliver Peyton's most famous project – but he's the sort who will swim, not sink.

Chair
You have dinner, try out the designer chair, then take it home – right? Little surprise this new concept store and restaurant folded faster than a deck chair.

Christopher's in the City
The original in Covent Garden is one of the West End's best, but this branch was a disaster. It barely lasted three months.

The Crown
Victoria Park's organic gastropub, now converted into a Spanish tapas bar.

Cotto
Modern European near Olympia that failed to reach Olympian heights.

Entrecôte de Café de Paris
The French have the best cuisine in the world, *non*? So why didn't Londoners want a no-choice menu of steak-frites?

Fina Estampa
London's smartest Peruvian restaurant had a lifespan that most guinea pigs would aspire to, but the time came for the pan pipes to pipe down.

La Galette
This pancake place had a flippin' hard time, so the owners moved from Marylebone in search of richer pastures.

Glas
The Swedish chefs were moved on in August 2006 from their Borough Market premises, but are reopening in Islington soon (**Upper Glas**; *see p6* Hello).

Grocer on Warwick Avenue
A reinvention of the Sugar Club from the same owners that was never as sweet.

Lomo
New-wave Spanish tapas bar in Chelsea that was a ham actor compared to London's old-guard Spanish places.

Manzi's
Almost 80 years old, this fish restaurant on the edge of Leicester Square had become a living fossil.

Momo at Selfridges
Moroccan? *So* last year.

Number 10
Cocktail bar, club, Modern European, oriental... butterfly.

Pengelley's
Former E&O chef resurfaced with the backing of Gordon Ramsay, but his place closed within a year. He's now at **Gilgamesh** (*see p245*).

Taman Gang
Park Lane oriental that was more bling than Paris Hilton's knicker drawer. We just wonder: what happened to the kama sutra carvings that used to line the walls?

Without reservation

Guy Dimond looks at the windows of opportunity that let you slip into London's most sought-after restaurants – without the hassle of long waits and booking.

ILLUSTRATION I Alice Stevenson

Would you like to be able to walk into Nobu without making a reservation and be served right away? Or book the same day for the Ivy? Incredibly, you can – if you know what to do. But if you go about things the wrong way – that is, by ringing ahead to make a booking, like most of us would – you can be kept on hold, asked to call back later, be told you can't have a table for months, be slotted in at an absurd time, or even have your credit card details taken so the restaurant can charge you if you cancel at short notice. So if you want to dine at London's most popular restaurants, here are our top tips, and the pitfalls to beware.

GORDON RAMSAY

It's little wonder that the flagship restaurant of a celebrity chef is very busy, but Gordon Ramsay (his original restaurant, at Royal Hospital Road) wins the prize for sheer cheek. The restaurant has only just reopened (in September 2006) following extensive refurbishment, and bookings are now taken precisely two months in advance for the day in question (previously, it was one month). So if it's 21 November you want, you need to phone on the morning of 21 September – and no other day will do. The phone line opens at 9am, and you are advised to call as soon as possible after that. Despite there being four phone receptionists specifically answering these calls, it's very likely you will then have problems getting to speak to someone. In our recent experience, the phone line is engaged almost solidly from 9am for up to two hours; this means you have to keep calling until you get through.

A spokesperson for Gordon Ramsay Holdings claims they receive an average of 330 calls per day for only 13 tables (45 covers). Then, there is the problem that you have only two possible times for dinner reservations, as Ramsay's restaurants turn tables – they have two sittings per evening – so you are likely to be given the choice of either 6.45pm or 9.30pm. Credit card details are taken, so you will still be charged in the event of a no-show; cancellations must be made a minimum of 24 hours in advance of the reservation, otherwise you run the risk of incurring a cancellation charge of £150 *per person*. The day before the booking, you will be rung to confirm – not unreasonable, as the reservation was made two months before. Then – you're in! For your two and a half hour slot. Don't even think about attempting a 'walk-in' without booking, unless you have a proven track record at working miracles. This is one restaurant where we have never had any success with this method (and this year we tried five times, three times at lunch and twice in the evening).

Gordon Ramsay's other restaurants are also hugely popular, but at least they have more capacity, and therefore more flexibility. This year, the reservations team insisted on the phone that Gordon Ramsay at Claridges had nothing free for weeks, but in reality our reviewers – unrecognised, of course, and treated just like anyone else – were able to get in without booking on the same day just by showing up. We suggest the best way to do this is to arrive early in the week – ideally on Monday or Tuesday, at 5.45pm when the restaurant's doors open. Getting a later slot is much trickier. And if you do try this method, make sure you have a good plan B, because it's a far from infallible way of getting a table.

THE IVY

The Ivy allegedly has a two-track booking system: one for favoured customers and celebrities, the other for the rest of us. This was according to journalist AA Gill nearly a decade ago in his uncharacteristically fawning book about the restaurant, *The Ivy*, published in 1997. We tried to verify this with more up-to-date information by calling the Ivy, but a spokesperson refused to comment.

So unless you are AA Gill, an A-list (or B-list) celebrity, or a high-spending regular, you still have to submit to ordeal by automated phone response. Eventually, after a wait (sometimes of several minutes) you get through to one of four or five receptionists, who between them handle – or so one of them told us – up to 1,400 phone calls per day, between 9.30am and 5.30pm. Ringing in late June, for example, we were offered dinner tables in late November or early December – unless you are prepared to eat at 5.30pm-7.30pm, or after 10.30pm, in which case they might be able to squeeze you in in a matter of, ooh, weeks. So the Ivy's probably not the best place to spontaneously take a new date.

Alternatively, when going through the automated phone system, you will hear the option 'for today's lunch availability, dial 3'. Now, as every luvvie knows, lunch is the *only* way to do the Ivy. So try your luck on the day you want to go. This year, this method worked on our first attempt – a good table on a Monday lunchtime, at a mere three hours' notice.

The other method we tried – three times, before the manager started to get suspicious – was to turn up on spec in the evening, looking suitably glamorous. But this didn't work (for us, at least); the charming manager explained the restaurant was fully booked. Next time, we'll turn up mid-evening with Nicole Kidman on one arm to meet our mates Posh and Becks, and see if this works – because the Ivy does, in fact, always keep a few tables back for the right faces.

THE RIVER CAFE

This one's a surprise. London's best-known Italian restaurant is, as you would expect, very popular, but the phone was answered immediately by a real person on our calls this year. There were dinner tables free for the following week, and a better choice the week after that. A two-sittings policy is applied to most tables: 7-9pm, or 9-11pm. However, the River Café has space for 15 outdoor tables (which, despite the name, do not have a good view of the river). On warm and sunny evenings, extra tables are added for outdoor diners – but the restaurant will only book the usual number of indoor tables, just in case the weather changes. So, effectively, on hot days there are 15 free tables inside for walk-ins. Hallelujah!

TOM AIKENS

Six or seven years ago, several haute cuisine restaurants in London started taking customers' credit card details when booking tables, so that no-shows could still be charged for lost earnings. Although this protects the restaurateur's interests and is understandable in very popular places, it also puts potential diners on the defensive. There was a well-publicised case a few years ago at one particular establishment, when a death in the family prevented a group of diners being able to make their booking. Despite calling to cancel, the restaurant went ahead and 'fined' the organiser £40 per head for loss of earnings. Soon after the publicity surrounding this unfortunate event, the procurement of credit card details fell out of favour with many restaurants – though not with Gordon Ramsay's restaurants – or at Tom Aikens.

On several visits to Tom Aikens' flagship venture, we haven't just found the credit card business irritating, we've also found the general booking policy most discouraging. Customers are told the times they can dine at, with little room for negotiation; more than once we've had to eat very early just to get a table, then been unimpressed to find the restaurant virtually empty for the first hour. Once credit card details are taken, a £55 charge is made per person not turning up, unless a full 48 hours' notice is given. A dress code is decreed – 'smart', meaning no trainers or sportswear, and a jacket is preferred – which, to add insult, then doesn't appear to be observed by all diners. In its favour, Tom Aikens is one of the easiest haute cusine restaurants to get into: bookings are not needed for lunch, and you can make dinner reservations just days in advance. Our advice would be to go for lunch – or be very confident that your dinner date won't cancel.

around 150 seats, it typically caters for around 1,100 people every day (said a spokesperson) – so each seat is likely to be occupied by seven or eight people during that time. It has five receptionists handling around 1,200 phone calls daily, but booking is not really a huge problem; tables for the same or next day are often available, as long as you don't mind being a bit flexible about the timing. Better still, the Wolseley has an encouraging walk-in policy: it sets aside a remarkable one-third of all the dinner tables for people who have not reserved, so if you just show up you're quite likely to be seated right away. Marvellous.

But in contrast to this, if you try phoning in advance to book, you may run into a far more regimented system. Ring for even the most modest slot (say, a Monday lunch) several weeks in advance and you're likely to be told you can come at 12.15pm but need to leave by 1.45pm. Our advice? Save yourself the hassle and just show up at the door.

THE WOLSELEY

The Wolseley is a hugely popular restaurant, but its popularity is ameliorated by its size. Open all day and with

NOBU

Still one of the most sought-after restaurants in London, the original branch of Nobu (in the Metropolitan hotel) has three receptionists receiving between 500 and 550 calls a day – and the phone lines are open only from 9am to 5pm Monday to Friday, and 10am to 5pm on Saturday and Sunday, so don't bother calling in the evening. As at other very popular restaurants, you need to time your call just right to be assured of a booking – you can only reserve up to one calendar month in advance, and the larger tables go within a few days. The standard waiting time is between two and three weeks for lunch or dinner, so if you intend to book for Nobu, call them precisely one month before going.

The good news is that if all this still sounds like a lot of faff, Nobu's sushi bar does not accept bookings for either lunch or dinner – just arrive and you'll almost certainly be seated. Better still, the restaurant does try to accommodate walk-ins if possible, though you may have to wait in the bar for between half an hour and an hour – which sounds just fine to us, as you can spend that long on the phone just trying to get through to some other busy restaurants. In short: as with many of London's hard-to-get-into restaurants, it's best just turn up and try your luck, unless you're a larger group or have a specific occasion to celebrate and want to be assured of a decent table.

Alternatively...

We polled our own panel of critics to see if they felt it was worth the hassle of being made to jump through hoops to get a table in London's most popular restaurants. The unanimous response was 'no'. It's worth remembering that if you want a really good dining experience, there are many outstanding chefs and restaurants that will not make you phone at specific times, take your credit card details or expect you to disappear after two and a half hours while leaving you £150 worse off per head.

In the Hotels & Haute Cuisine chapter of this guide (starting on p125), we list a score of places that are much easier to get into – and are also better value. Even at top restaurants such as **Le Gavroche**, **Foliage** or the **Greenhouse**, you can get a table for a Friday or Saturday night with just one or two days' notice. Additionally, the **Square** and the **Capital** are excellent bets, even for walk-ins early in the week or at lunchtime. Remember, if you don't like the attitude of a restaurant before you've even set foot there, then you can always act on first impressions and decide to eat somewhere else – somewhere where the customer really does come first.

10 YEARS OF DINING AT OXO TOWER WHARF

Oxo Tower Wharf offers plenty choice for eating and drinking with breathtaking views across the River Thames to St Paul's and the City of London

Grilled haloumi with figs and pomegranate dressing and chicken piri piri with coleslaw are some of the delicious dishes on the a la carte menu at **TAMESA@OXO BAR & BRASSERIE** on Oxo Tower Wharf's second floor. Special lunch and pre/post theatre menu is offered at £12.50 for two courses, £15.50 for three.

◆

The eighth floor **OXO TOWER RESTAURANT & BRASSERIE'S** menu features many game dishes including calves liver, crispy pig's ear, pheasant and foie gras.

◆

XIANG@OXO offers a wide variety of traditional Dim Sum and an extensive a la carte menu created by specialist chefs from Hong Kong.

◆

EAT
Sandwiches, soups and pies, desserts, breakfast, hot and cold drinks to take away or eat in
Tel 020 7928 8179

Tamesa@oxo bar and brasserie (& private dining)
Funky bar and contemporary brasserie on second floor
Tel 020 7633 0088

Xiang@oxo
Traditional Dim Sum and extensive a la carte menu on second floor.
Tel 020 7261 9388

OXO Tower Restaurant Brasserie & Bar
Luxurious dining on eighth floor
Tel 020 7803 3888

Oxo Tower Wharf
Bargehouse Street
London SE1 9PH
www.oxotower.co.uk

Ruba

Ruba Bar offers a truly unique experience when drinking, or sampling the fashionable world of finger food

020 3002 4300

5 More London Place, Tooley Street
London, SE1 2BY

THE
LARDER
RESTAURANT

A menu of the freshest ingredients with simplicity and great flavours. The Larder - Bold Inspired Surprising

020 3002 4300

5 More London Place, Tooley Street
London, SE1 2BY

NIPPON TUK

Thai Japanese Fusion Cookery - a sophisticated yet informal dining and bar venue with fabulous views of London

hiltonlondonmet.com/nippontuk

020 7616 6496

23rd Floor, Hilton London Metropole
225 Edgware Road, London, W2 IJU

---

plum
BAR & GRILL

Spacious loft style restaurant awash with natural light, overlooking High Street Kensington

020 7856 1980

380 Kensington High Street, London, W14 8NL

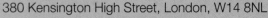

AWARDS 2006
Eating & Drinking

Rounding up the capital's most impressive new restaurants, gastropubs and bars, Time Out honoured the very best in ten categories in its 17th annual awards.

Here at Time Out we're proud of our reputation for championing the best of London's eating and drinking places. Not just those with the grandest credentials, either, but the little places too, the ones you're not likely to read about anywhere else, which are, in their own field, exceptional. This is the ethos behind our broad coverage of London's gastronomic delights – from weekly reviews in *Time Out* London magazine to our numerous guides. And this is why our annual Eating & Drinking Awards take in not only London's restaurant élite, but also representatives from neighbourhood restaurants, gastropubs and bargain eateries as independently selected by a panel of Time Out judges.

With a fresh crop of new reviews appearing each week in *Time Out* magazine (and on our website, www.timeout.com/restaurants), the list of potential candidates can seem dauntingly long, but our panel of independent (and strictly anonymous) reviewers is able to whittle them down to a shortlist of 50 – five nominations in each of ten categories. These categories, which vary each year, reflect the diverse needs and tastes of London's diners and drinkers: this year we included new categories for Best Wine Bar, Best Pâtisserie and Best Steak Restaurant, to reflect the recent emergence of several outstanding new places in all these categories. We then ask readers of the magazine and website for their feedback, which helps inform our judges' choices.

It doesn't end there. We then send our judges out to revisit every shortlisted establishment as normal paying punters (we never accept PR invitations or freebies of any kind), so that a final decision can be reached. The results were announced on 18 September 2006 in a glittering ceremony at Roast restaurant (*see p59*) in Borough Market.

AND THE
WINNERS ARE...

BEST PATISSERIE
Winner
Macaron *See p302.*
Runners-up
Hummingbird *See p301.*
Ladurée *See p298.*
The Wolseley (also Modern European) *See p300 and p225.*
Yauatcha (also Chinese) *See p301 and p70.*

BEST WINE BAR
Winner
Vinoteca *See p331.*
Runners-up
Cellar Gascon *See p331.*
Green & Blue *See p335.*
Vivat Bacchus *See p331.*
Wine Wharf *See p335.*

BEST STEAK RESTAURANT
Winner
Gaucho Piccadilly (Argentinian) *See p40.*
Runners-up
Hawksmoor (North American, Bars) *See p33 and p320.*
Notting Grill (British) *See p58.*
Santa María del Buen Ayre (Argentinian) *See p40.*
Top Floor at Smiths (British) *See p52.*

BEST FAMILY RESTAURANT
Winner
Benihana (Japanese) *See p196.*
Runners-up
Frankie's Italian Bar & Grill (Pizza & Pasta) *See p311.*
Inn The Park (British) *See p55.*
Jo Shmo's (North American) *See p39.*
Marco Polo (Italian) *See p181.*

BEST CHEAP EATS
Winner
The Table (Cafés) *See p302.*
Runners-up
fish! kitchen (Fish & Chips) *See p310.*
Hummus Bros (Budget) *See p290.*
Imli (Indian) *See p140.*
Masa (Afghani) *See p117.*

Gaucho Piccadilly

Vinoteca

Yakitoria

in association with

Leffe
Bière d'Abbaye - Abdijbier

LEFFE BEST GASTROPUB
Winner
Marquess Tavern See p114.
Runners-up
Charles Lamb See p113.
Inn at Kew Gardens See p117.
Phoenix See p104.
Queens Pub & Dining Room See p112.

BEST DESIGN
Winner
Yakitoria (Japanese) See p193.
Runners-up
Canteen (British) See p51.
China Tang (Chinese) See p69.
Ladurée (Cafés) See p298.
The Table (Cafés) See p302.

BEST BAR
Winner
Lost Society See p326.
Runners-up
Annex 3 See p322.
Donovan Bar See p322.
Gilgamesh (also Oriental) See p327 and p245.
Hawksmoor (also North American) See p320 and p33.

BEST LOCAL RESTAURANT
Winner
Sam's Brasserie & Bar (Modern European) See p227.
Runners-up
Dylan's (Modern European) See p236.
Inside (Modern European) See p234.
The Island (Modern European) See p236.
Upstairs (Modern European) See p233.

BEST NEW RESTAURANT
Winner
Arbutus (Modern European) See p226.
Runners-up
Ambassador (Modern European) See p221.
Bar Shu (Chinese) See p69.
La Collina (Italian) See p183.
Papillon (French) See p95.

This year's judges: Jessica Cargill Thompson, Jan Fuscoe, Roopa Gulati, Sarah Guy, Ronnie Haydon, Ruth Jarvis, Tom Lamont, Susan Low, Cath Phillips, Gordon Thomson.

Where to...

Looking for something more specific? Then see the **Subject Index**, starting on p392.

GO FOR BREAKFAST

Breakfast is offered every day unless stated otherwise. *See also* **Cafés** and **Brasseries**.

Automat *The Americas p34*

The Capital
Hotels & Haute Cuisine p127

Carluccio's Caffè *Italian p171*

Cinnamon Club (Mon-Fri) *Indian p141*

Le Coq d'Argent (Mon-Fri)
French p89

Corney & Barrow (Mon-Fri)
Wine Bars p330

Curve *The Americas p39*

Dorchester Grill Room *British p54*

Eagle Bar Diner *The Americas p34*

Engineer (Trattoria) *Gastropubs p112*

Fifteen *Italian p183*

Fifth Floor (Café, Mon-Sat)
Modern European p223

Flâneur Food Hall (Mon-Fri)
Brasseries p46

Franco's (Mon-Sat) *Italian p174*

La Fromagerie *Cafés p298*

Goring Hotel *British p57*

High Road Brasserie
Brasseries p47

Inn The Park *British p55*

Nicole's (Mon-Sat)
Modern European p225

1 Lombard Street (Brasserie, Mon-Fri) *French p89*

The Place Below (Mon-Fri) *Vegetarian p283*

The Providores & Tapa Room *International p161*

Quality Chop House (Mon-Fri) *British p52*

Refuel *International p162*

Rex Whistler Restaurant at Tate Britain (Sat, Sun)
Modern European p226

Roast *British p59*

Royal Exchange Grand Café & Bar (Mon-Fri) *Global p119*

St John Bread & Wine
British p52

S&M Café *Budget p296*

Simpson's-in-the-Strand (Mon-Fri) *British p57*

Smiths of Smithfield (Café) *Modern European p221*

Sotheby's Café (Mon-Fri) *Modern European p225*

Story Deli *Budget p294*

The Table *Cafés p302*

The Terrace (WC2) (Mon-Fri)
Modern European p223

The Wolseley *Modern European p225*

Zetter *Italian p169*

WATERSIDE

Blueprint Café
Modern European p235

Butlers Wharf Chop House
British p59

Canyon *The Americas p39*

Curve *The Americas p39*

Elephant Royale *Thai p267*

Grapes *Pubs p329*

Gun *Gastropubs p110*

Just The Bridge *Brasseries p46*

Lightship Ten *International p165*

Marco Polo *Italian p181*

Oxo Tower Restaurant, Bar & Brasserie *Modern European p234*

Le Pont de la Tour
Modern European p235

The Portrait Restaurant
Modern European p227

Saran Rom *Thai p263*

Ship *Gastropubs p106*

Stein's *Budget p297*

Thai Square *Thai p265*

TAKE THE KIDS

See also **Cafés, Brasseries, Fish & Chips, Pizza & Pasta.**

Benihana
Japanese p196

Blue Elephant
Thai p263

Blue Kangaroo
Brasseries p48

Boiled Egg & Soldiers
Cafés p302

Brilliant Kids Café *Cafés p304*

Bush Garden Café
Cafés p301

Cibo *Cafés p300*

The Depot *Brasseries p48*

Dexter's Grill *The Americas p38*

fish! *Fish p86*

Frankie's Italian Bar & Grill
Pizza & Pasta p311

Frizzante@City Farm *Cafés p303*

Giraffe *Brasseries p49*

Gracelands *Cafés p305*

Inn The Park *British p55*

Jo Shmo's *The Americas p39*

Marco Polo *Italian p181*

Marine Ices *Budget p295*

Nando's *Portuguese p250*

Planet Hollywood *The Americas p38*

Rainforest Café
Eating & Entertainment p341

Smollensky's on the Strand
The Americas p37

Tootsies Grill *The Americas p37*

Victoria *Modern European p231*

Wagamama *Oriental p241*

ENJOY THE VIEW

Babylon *Modern European p229*

Blueprint Café
Modern European p235

Butlers Wharf Chop House British p59

Le Coq d'Argent French p89

Galvin at Windows Hotels & Haute Cuisine p130

Oxo Tower Restaurant, Bar & Brasserie Modern European p234

Plateau Modern European p235

Le Pont de la Tour Modern European p235

The Portrait Restaurant Modern European p227

Roast British p59

Rhodes Twenty Four British p51

Searcy's Modern European p219

Tamesa@oxo Brasseries p49

The Tenth Eating & Entertainment p342

Thai Square Thai p265

Top Floor at Smiths British p52

Vertigo 42 Eating & Entertainment p342

TRY UNUSUAL DISHES

See also **Global**.

Archipelago International p160

Asadal Korean p204

Bar Shu Chinese p69

Esarn Kheaw Thai p263

Garni East European p76

Hunan Chinese p61

Mandalay Global p118

Nahm Thai p260

The Providores & Tapa Room International p161

Rong Cheng Chinese p69 (Regional cooking box)

St John British p52

Tbilisi East European p77

DO BRUNCH

See also **Cafés** and **Brasseries**.

The Avenue (Sun) Modern European p226

Bermondsey Kitchen (Sat, Sun) Modern European p235

Bluebird (Sat, Sun) Modern European p231

Brasserie de Malmaison (Sun) Brasseries p46

Butlers Wharf Chop House (Sat, Sun) British p59

Canyon (Sat, Sun) The Americas p39

Christopher's (Sat, Sun) The Americas p34

Clarke's (Sat) Modern European p229

Cru Restaurant, Bar & Deli (Sat, Sun) Modern European p236

The Farm (Sat, Sun) Modern European p232

Fifth Floor (Sat, Sun) Modern European p223

Flâneur Food Hall (Sat, Sun) Brasseries p46

High Road Brasserie (Sat, Sun) Brasseries p47

Inside (Sat) Modern European p234

Joe Allen (Sat, Sun) The Americas p34

Lundum's (Mon-Sat) Global p120

Manna (Sun) Vegetarian p284

Notting Grill (Sat, Sun) British p58

Penk's (Sat) International p167

Ransome's Dock (Sun) Modern European p233

The Rapscallion (Sat, Sun) International p164

Rivington Bar & Grill (Sun) British p60

Roast (Sat) British p59

Sam's Brasserie & Bar (daily) Modern European p227

The Sequel (Sat, Sun) International p164

Tea Palace Cafés p301

The Terrace (WC2) (Sat) Modern European p223

The Terrace (W8) (Sat, Sun) Modern European p229

Wapping Food (Sat, Sun) Modern European p236

Zetter (Sat, Sun) Italian p169

DINE ALFRESCO

See also p305 **Park cafés**.

Babylon Modern European p229

Bank Westminster Modern European p227

Bull Gastropubs p112

Butlers Wharf Chop House British p59

Café Bohème Brasseries p47

Café des Amis Brasseries p46

Le Coq d'Argent French p89

Corney & Barrow Wine Bars p330

Curve The Americas p39

Dollar Grills & Martinis The Americas p34

Drapers Arms Gastropubs p113

Ealing Park Tavern Gastropubs p104

Electric Brasserie Brasseries p48

Frederick's International p167

Garden Café Cafés p299

Gun Gastropubs p110

High Road Brasserie Brasseries p47

Hoxton Apprentice Modern European p236

Inn The Park British p55

The Island Modern European p236

Manicomio Italian p179

Notting Grill British p58

Ognisko Polskie East European p78

Orrery Modern European p225

Petersham Nurseries Café Modern European p237

Phoenix Bar & Grill Modern European p232

Plateau Modern European p235

Le Pont de la Tour Modern European p235

Queens Pub & Dining Room Gastropubs p112

Raoul's Cafés p301

Roka Japanese p185

Royal China Docklands Chinese p74

Rye Hotel Gastropubs p110

Saran Rom Thai p263

Ship Gastropubs p106

Spoon+ at Sanderson International p161

The Terrace (WC2) Modern European p223

Victoria Modern European p231

Wapping Food Modern European p236

Westbourne Gastropubs p105

▶

About the guide

LISTED BY AREA

The restaurants in this guide are listed by cuisine type: British, Chinese, Indian, etc. Then, within each of chapter, they are listed by geographical area: ten main areas (in this example, Central), then by neighbourhood (Fitzrovia). If you are not sure where to look for a restaurant, there are two indexes at the back of the guide to help: an **A-Z Index** (starting on page 417) listing restaurants by name, and an **Area Index** (starting on p398), where you can see all the places we list in a specific neighbourhood.

STARS

A red star ★ means that a restaurant is, of its type, very good indeed. A green star ★ identifies budget-conscious eateries – expect to pay an average of £15 (for a three-course meal or its equivalent, *not* including drinks or service).

AWARD NOMINEES

Winners and runners-up in Time Out's Eating & Drinking Awards 2006. For more information on the awards, *see p20*.

OPENING HOURS

Times given are for *last orders* rather than closing times (except in cafés and bars).

MAP REFERENCE

All restaurants that appear on our street maps (starting on p357) are given a reference to the map and grid square on which they can found.

Central
Fitzrovia

★ ★ **Pipe & Slippers** NEW
2006 RUNNER-UP BEST DESIGN
1 Matronly Mews, WC1 3AB (7654 3210).
Euston tube/rail. **Lunch served** noon-3pm, **dinner served** 6-11pm daily. **Main courses** £8-£13. **Set meal** (6-7.30pm Mon-Sat) £12 2 courses, £16 3 courses. **Cover** £1. **Credit** AmEx, DC, MC, V.
Giving modern chaps the sympathy they deserve,' is the mission statement that adorns the entrance to this men-only eaterie – and it's a mission they take very seriously indeed. The entire restaurant is done up like a 1950s kitchen, complete with pies cooling on Formica counters and the sound of the Everly Brothers piped through discreetly positioned wireless sets. Every diner is assigned his own individual waitress or 'little lady' for the evening, and she fusses around him from the moment he walks in: his coat is spirited away to a closet, he is shooed into a comfortable chair; a jug of Martini, a footstool and a freshly ironed newspaper are delivered lovingly to his side. 'You poor dear!' coo the waitresses to their drowsy charges. 'You must be simply famished,' they say. And while there is no menu, the cooking has a predictably comforting quality (on a recent visit, we enjoyed fish pie and a glass of porter followed by swiss roll with ice-cream). 'All we hear about is these career women with their soya milk and *Cosmopolis* magazine,' declares owner Bertram Bunter. 'But what about the bachelors? Who will take care of them?' Well, look no further: Pipe & Slippers will.
Babies and children welcome: crayons; high chairs; toys. Disabled: toilet. No-smoking tables. Tables outdoors (10, garden). Vegetarian menu. **Map 11 O6**.

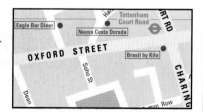

NEW ENTRIES

The NEW symbol means new to this edition of the *Eating & Drinking Guide*. In most cases, these are brand-new establishments; in other instances we've included an existing restaurant for the first time, or reviewed a different branch.

PRICES

We have listed the cheapest and most expensive main courses available in each restaurant. In the case of many oriental restaurants, prices may seem lower – but remember that you often need to order more than one main course to have a full meal.

COVER CHARGE

An old-fashioned fixed charge may be imposed by the restaurateur to cover the cost of rolls and butter, crudités, cleaning table linen and similar extras.

SERVICES

These are listed below the review.

Babies and children We've tried to reflect the degree of welcome extended to babies and children in restaurants. If you find no mention of either, take it that the restaurant is unsuitable.

Disabled: toilet means the restaurant has a specially adapted toilet on the premises, which implies that customers with walking disabilities or wheelchairs can get into the restaurant. However, we always recommend phoning to double-check.

No smoking 'No-smoking tables' means that the restaurant has made some attempt to separate smokers and non-smokers. 'No smoking' means it is banned throughout the venue.

Vegetarian menu Most restaurants claim to have a vegetarian dish on the menu. We've highlighted those that have made a more concerted effort to attract and cater for vegetarian (and vegan) diners.

Anonymous, unbiased reviews

The reviews in the *Eating & Drinking Guide* are based on the experiences of Time Out restaurant reviewers. Restaurants, pubs, bars and cafés are always visited anonymously, and Time Out pays the bill. No payment or PR invitation of any kind has secured or influenced a review. The editors select which places are listed in this guide, and are not influenced in any way by the wishes of the restaurants themselves. Restaurants cannot volunteer or pay to be listed; we list only those we consider to be worthy of inclusion. Advertising and sponsorship has no effect whatsoever on the editorial content of the *Eating & Drinking Guide*. An advertiser may receive a bad review, or no review at all.

LOVE EATING & DRINKING IN LONDON?

Visit timeout.com/restaurants

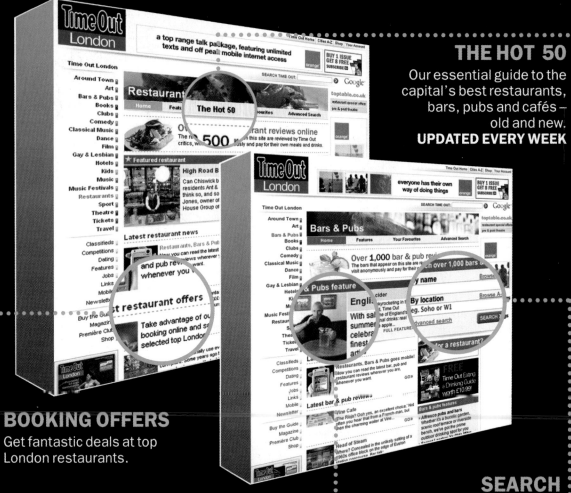

THE HOT 50

Our essential guide to the capital's best restaurants, bars, pubs and cafés – old and new.
UPDATED EVERY WEEK

BOOKING OFFERS

Get fantastic deals at top London restaurants.

SEARCH

More than 3,000 restaurant, bar, pub and café reviews.
NEW REVIEWS ADDED EVERY WEEK

FEATURES

Everything from a behind-the-scenes look at a Michelin-starred restaurant to the top 50 cheap eats.
Plus, discover where to get the best fish and chips, breakfast and Sunday roast.
NEW FEATURES ADDED EVERY WEEK

Time Out Online

Restaurants

African & Caribbean

Bob Marley has a lot to answer for. Because he was a musician instead of a celebrity chef, the Caribbean will forever by associated with reggae and rastafarianism, rather than exotic island dishes or the finesse of French-based seafood cookery. Caribbean restaurants in London tend to rely on their convivial feel and rum cocktails to get the party swinging, though a couple of great Caribbean restaurants show how it should be done: **Cottons** and **Mango Room**. Sub-Saharan African food, on the other hand, remains unexplored terrain to most Londoners just as the African continent did to David Livingstone. Yet Ethiopean restaurants such as **Queen of Sheba** are worth crossing town for, as is **Mosob**, which serves the similar cuisine of Ethiopia's neighbour, Eritrea. Of London's several Nigerian restaurants, only a couple merit inclusion here, most notably the smart **805 Bar Restaurant**.

AFRICAN

Central

Covent Garden

★ Calabash

The Africa Centre, 38 King Street, WC2E 8JR (7836 1976). Covent Garden or Leicester Square tube.
Bar **Open** 6-11pm Mon-Sat.
Restaurant **Lunch served** 12.30-2.30pm Mon-Fri. **Dinner served** 6-10.30pm Mon-Sat.
Main courses £6.95-£8.10.
Both **Credit** MC, V. Pan-African
The Africa Centre has become rather run-down of late, and the ground-floor bookshop has closed. It would be a great pity if its decline led to problems for the lively bar or for the long-established restaurant hidden away in the basement, which still serves a wonderful range of dishes from around the continent. The large room has cream walls decorated with pictures, a faded red carpet and colourful fabric tablecloths. Starters showed the style of the place: not spectacular, perhaps, but intriguing and endearing. Alaco was slices of plantain in rich sauce. A deep-fried meat sambusa was a lightly spiced and crisp parcel, not unlike a samosa. A main course of Calabash chicken was filling and robust. Two fried chicken legs were served with chips of sweet potato and a slightly stodgy fried plantain. West African groundnut stew had a lovely thick nutty sauce and contained a tasty but bony fish; it came with a dish of doughy sticky yam. Service was knowledgeable and quietly efficient. Calabash is remarkably cheap and deserves its popularity with lovers of African food. *Babies and children admitted. Booking advisable. Separate room (in Africa Centre) for parties, seats 150. Takeaway service. Vegetarian menu.* **Map 18 L7.**

Euston

★ African Kitchen Gallery

102 Drummond Street, NW1 2HN (7383 0918). Euston Square tube/Euston tube/rail. **Lunch served** noon-3.30pm Tue-Sun. **Dinner served** 6-11pm Mon; 5.30-11pm Tue-Sun. **Main courses** £6.50-£9. **Credit** MC, V. African & Caribbean
Offering a fusion of African and Caribbean food, this tiny restaurant decked out with crafts, artefacts and jewellery (much of it for sale) is a little African-Caribbean enclave among Drummond Street's mainly Indian restaurants. The benevolent owner takes pleasure in discussing the menu and offering his recommendations. A starter of diced and fried peppered plantain with chilled pepper sauce was a gorgeously spicy dish. Jerk chicken tasted great too. Unfortunately, we made a slight mistake in choosing spicy jollof to accompany it, instead of (as recommended) rice and peas, a dryer option that would have better absorbed the pepper and hot sauce from the chicken. Own-made ginger beer mixed with fresh mango juice was a perfect refresher, and suited the food well. If you want a proper lunch away from the plethora of sandwich outlets, then AKG is a good choice: it's usually quiet enough for you to bag one of the few tables. *Babies and children admitted. Booking advisable. No smoking. Tables outdoors (4, garden; 1, pavement). Takeaway service. Vegetarian menu. Vegan dishes.* **Map 3 J3.**

King's Cross

★ Addis

42 Caledonian Road, N1 9DT (7278 0679/ www.addisrestaurant.co.uk). King's Cross tube/rail/17, 91, 259 bus. **Meals served** noon-midnight Mon-Fri; 1pm-midnight Sat, Sun. **Main courses** £5.95-£8.50. **Credit** AmEx, JCB, MC, V. Ethiopian
A usually buzzing restaurant serving a wide range of Ethiopian food to those who love it, both Ethiopians and others. The walls are decorated with words in the Amharic script, and the restaurant has a choice of western-style tables and traditional low seating. A starter of selata aswad – delicious fried aubergine with tahini – showed the potential. Samak sire (sardine stuffed with herbs and spices) was also lovely. Main courses are served in the traditional manner, on a tray covered in a large pancake of tangy injera bread – a roll of injera is supplied for every diner. The taste is light, but the bread is filling. We tried doro wot – chicken and boiled egg served in a very hot sauce – and derek tibs – delightfully crispy, diced lamb fried with onion. As a vegetarian alternative, there's fuul musalah: crushed fava beans with feta sprinkled over spicy slices of falafal. The friendly atmosphere and wide range of dishes make this a good place for novices of Ethiopian cooking. *Babies and children welcome: high chairs. Book weekends. No-smoking tables. Takeaway service.* **Map 4 L2.**

★ Merkato Restaurant

196 Caledonian Road, N1 0SL (7713 8952). King's Cross tube/rail/17, 91, 259 bus. **Meals served** noon-midnight daily. **Main courses** £5-£10. **Credit** MC, V. Ethiopian
This light and welcoming high-ceilinged café is a hangout for local Ethiopians. Brightly coloured cloths cover the walls and ceiling and there is a small fenced-off seating area on the wide pavement outside. Though it looks like a café, Merkato is licensed and serves a full range of Ethiopian dishes. On to a traditional bed of tangy injera bread was added yebeg wot, a very spicy lamb stew; the house special, kitfo (traditionally made with marinated raw minced beef); and ystsome beye-aynetu, a kind of vegetable 'mixed meze'. This was poured out in neat stripes; we particularly enjoyed the lentils and a mix of carrot and green beans. Portions were, if anything, too large; we had to leave food. Staff were exceptionally helpful, giving advice and tips on what was available and what is recommended – Merkato is a hospitable place for newcomers to the cuisine as well as Ethiopian regulars. *Babies and children welcome: high chairs. Booking advisable Fri, Sat. Tables outdoors (2, pavement). Takeaway service.* **Map 4 M1.**

West

Westbourne Park

Angie's

381 Harrow Road, W9 3NA (8962 8761/ www.angies-restaurant.co.uk). Westbourne Park tube. **Meals served** noon-11pm Mon-Sat; 1-10pm Sun. **Main courses** £10-£15. **Set buffet** (Sun) £12.50. **Credit** AmEx, DC, JCB, MC, V. African & Caribbean
Angie's has established a big reputation for authentic Nigerian food. The space is white and wide, and our welcome from the staff was warm. We ordered a tableful of meaty dishes; some were marvellous. We loved suya, flavoursome beef barbecued with dried chilli. Plantain with gizzards was a marriage of sweet, yielding plantain and mysterious bits of chewy chicken innards. Moimoi was as good as you get: African beans mashed with fish and bits of egg, then steamed to a subtle lightness. The next dish was snail. Nothing like a French escargot, this African snail had a shell the size of a small coconut, flesh the shape of a helix and all the texture of a rubber tyre. Just one snail per serving, but one was enough. As a contrast, jollof rice was delightfully, elegantly soft and full of flavour. To drink, there's everything from Mateus Rosé to palm wine through to Star Lager and non-alcoholic Malta Guinness. Sundays are all about mountaineous buffets, served from 2pm, for under £13 a head. *Babies and children admitted. Booking advisable. Disabled: toilet. No-smoking tables. Takeaway service; delivery service.* **Map 1 A4.**

★ ★ Mosob

339 Harrow Road, W9 3RB (7266 2012/ www.mosob.co.uk). Westbourne Park tube. **Meals served** 6-11pm Mon-Fri; 3pm-midnight Sat, Sun. **Main courses** £5-£9. **Credit** AmEx, MC, V. Eritrean
Mosob is enchanting, and as accessible to non-Eritreans as it is authentic. The atmosphere is warm and welcoming, the dining room and small lounge unselfconsciously chic. Mum is in the kitchen, her three charming boys serve, soft loungey sounds fill the air, and food comes beautifully presented on mosobs (woven patterned stands). Sambusas (similar in appearance to

Cottons. See p32.

Indian samosas, or Middle Eastern sambusak) were a perfect combo of taste and texture – crisp, fresh, with a chilli bite. Main-course qulwa was a mound of juicy, flavourful scraps of lamb, rich and bright with spice. We also tried ajibo mes hamli, spinach flecked with cottage cheese, tomato and spiced butter; and shiro, a comforting paste of pounded chickpeas. All were served with fresh salad on wonderful injera bread, with more provided on the side. There are bottles of wine for a tenner, me'iss honey wine for special occasions, and sweetish, refreshing Asmara beer. Desserts are not a strong suit. As Eritrean ladies drift in then out clutching takeaway injera and the boys flash their smashing smiles, you realise that Mosob has woven its spell on you too.
Babies and children welcome: high chairs. Booking advisable. Separate room for parties, seats 22. Takeaway service. **Map 1 A4.**

South
Brixton

★ Asmara
386 Coldharbour Lane, SW9 8LF (7737 4144). Brixton tube/rail. **Dinner served** 5.30pm-midnight daily. **Main courses** £4-£7.50. **Set meals** £25 (vegetarian) 6 courses, £27 (meat) 7 courses. **Credit** MC, V. Eritrean
Asmara restaurant is an East African enclave on Brixton's relentlessly active Coldharbour Lane. The food is authentic Eritrean cuisine, along with a few pasta dishes, a nod to Italy's one-time colonial influence on the country. But it's the spiced beef, lamb or chicken stews that are most popular, along with huge platters of injera for mopping up. We tucked into green lentil stew, with dullet (fried liver and lamb) and alicha (tender stewed lamb). We enjoyed the lentils and the stewed lamb the most – the liver and lamb combination was fine, but a little on the dry side. Best of all was the Eritrean coffee.

The freshly roasted, still smoking beans are presented for infusion at each table and served with an incongruous but endearing bowl of warm salted popcorn. Asmara is a budget restaurant, but with staff in traditional dress, serene and benevolent service, banks of traditional seating, and the coffee ceremony, it's definite step up from your average cut-price venue.
Babies and children welcome: high chairs. Booking advisable. Separate room for parties, seats 40. Takeaway service. Vegan dishes. Vegetarian menu. **Map 22 E2.**

South East
Peckham

★ 805 Bar Restaurant NEW
805 Old Kent Road, SE15 1NX (7639 0808/ www.805restaurant.com). Elephant & Castle tube/rail then 21 bus/53 bus. **Meals served** 2pm-midnight daily. **Main courses** £6-£15. **Credit** MC, V. Nigerian
Considered by the capital's Nigerian community to be London's best Nigerian restaurant, this smart, spacious establishment on an insalubrious stretch of the Old Kent Road is an undiscovered gem for the rest of us. It opened in 2001 with the look and feel of a continental brasserie, the two vanilla-hued dining rooms decorated with plants and pictures. It's constantly abuzz with a dressed-up crowd of affluent Nigerians. The signature dish, Monika (the chef's own creation), comprises a whole marinated grilled fish drizzled with chilli sauce: it was impressive to look at, and exquisitely succulent. The popular accompaniment of moyin moyin (slabs of wobbly bean pudding flecked with dried fish and meat) was a good foil for the fish. Mashed Nigerian brown beans with chilli sauce, fried plantain and yam chips sounds pretty basic, but it was a hearty and flavoursome dish. Specialising in the cooking of southern Nigeria, the menu also includes a range of porridges, pottages (Nigerian-style stews), jollof rice, goat meat soups and grills. Service from staff in black and white uniforms was efficient and swift. If you arrive by car – probably the best way to get here, unless you're arriving by limo – parking is no problem.
Babies and children welcome: high chairs. Disabled: toilet. No smoking. Tables outdoors (6, pavement). Takeaway service.

North East
Dalston

Suya Obalende NEW
523 Kingsland Road, E8 4AR (7275 0171/ www.obalendesuya.com). Dalston Kingsland rail/ 38, 67, 76, 149 bus. **Dinner served** 3pm-midnight Fri, Sat; 2-10pm Sun. **Main courses** £7.95-£8.95. **Set buffet** (Sun) £9.95. **Credit** MC, V. Nigerian
The slogan in the window of this long-established restaurant reads: 'We don't serve fast food. We serve good food fast.' But it's easy to miss that this place houses a restaurant as well as a takeaway. Hidden behind a door at the back lies a sizeable area where grills can be eaten in. The menu is limited, but dishes are hearty and filling – variations on suya grills with chicken, lamb, beef, goat, fish and, apparently, the occasional appearance of crocodile. A buffet is sometimes also available. Grills are served with jollof rice or pounded yam and potato. Several, such as the kirikiri grill, are offered with 'notorious' chilli sauces. We tried suya chicken with jollof rice, which came in a great mound, along with a thick gravy. Asaro lamb was a well-grilled portion with a satisfying mix of yam and potato. Good food, and Obalende is a good local café. Our only complaints were that the room was windowless, and the air-conditioning too powerful.
Babies and children admitted. No smoking. Restaurant available for hire. Takeaway service. **Map 25 B5.**
For branch (Suya Express) see index.

North
Finsbury Park

★ Senke
*1B-1C Rock Street, N4 2DN (7359 7687).
Finsbury Park tube/rail.* **Meals served** noon-midnight daily. **Main courses** £5-£7.50.
Tasting plate £14. **No credit cards.** Ethiopian
Senke shelters in the shadow of the Arsenal
Emirates Stadium and serves crowd-pleasing
Ethiopian meals. It was pretty deserted when we
visited in the early evening. It wasn't quiet, though;
a French gladiator B-movie blasted from the
widescreen TV. One wall is taken up by the bar,
from which we ordered a snorter of Ethiopian
araki, the aniseed-flavoured spirit that guarantees
an out-of-body hangover. Chasers of good crisp St
George's Ethiopian beer were apt. The menu is
extensive, affordable and written in language
tantalisingly close to English. Take derek tibs, for
example: not someone who played for the Gunners
in a dim and distant past, but cubes of meat
sautéed with onion and spices (derek means 'dry'
and tibs means 'fry'). We ordered the £14 tasting
plate, and the two of us ate like Ethiopian royalty.
On a bed of really good injera were chicken and
lamb stews, both delicious and sinus-clearing; split
peas cooked with chilli; mild rich chickpeas; very
fresh green beans; and smooth soft spinach.
Portions are big (we needed a take-home bag). All
flavours were bright, true and as loud as the movie.
Go in a crowd, take pot luck from the menu and
you too are likely to have a blast.
*Babies and children admitted. Booking advisable
weekends. Takeaway service.*

Kentish Town

★ Lalibela
*137 Fortess Road, NW5 2HR (7284 0600).
Tufnell Park tube/134 bus.* **Dinner served**
6pm-midnight daily. **Main courses** £7.50-£8.95.
Credit JCB, MC, V. Ethiopian
The capital's most beautiful Ethiopian restaurant,
bedecked with East African artefacts, is set over
two floors. From a lengthy menu, we chose doro
wot – a classic hot and spicy stew that in Ethiopia
would be made with a chicken and its own eggs.
This version was unlikely to be quite so authentic,
but was very tasty. We also liked gomen (stir-fried
spring greens) and mushroom shiro (spicy stew
thickened with ground chickpeas). Tibs are strips
of marinated items, sautéed with peppers, onions,
tomatoes and chillies; the fish and tofu versions
here were beautifully flavoured. Rice isn't eaten in
Ethiopia, except by Muslims. Here, there is
delicious turmeric rice for those who don't enjoy
the flannel-like texture and sharp, sour tang of
injera. Although Lalibela's cooking is very
accomplished, dishes tend to be too oily and are not
as hot and spicy as they could be – the flavours
seem toned down for the restaurant's
predominantly western customers. Service too can
be a little terse. However, if you've never tried
Ethiopian food before, this is a good place to start.
*Babies and children welcome: high chairs. Booking
advisable. No-smoking tables. Takeaway service.
Vegetarian menu. Vegan dishes.* **Map 26 B3.**

★ ★ Queen of Sheba
*12 Fortess Road, NW5 2EU (7284 3947/
www.thequeenofsheba.co.uk). Kentish Town
tube/rail.* **Meals served** 1-11.30pm Mon-Sat;
1-10.30pm Sun. **Main courses** £5-£10.50. **Set
lunch** £7.50 2 dishes. **Credit** MC, V. Ethiopian
A contemporary venue, Queen of Sheba is a small,
cream-coloured room decorated with Ethiopian
masks and other knick-knacks, and graced by
stunningly beautiful, statuesque Ethiopian
waitresses. Every item we tried was distinctly and
individually spiced, a combination of great tastes.
Minced beef stew was aromatic with garlic, ginger
and cardamom, and laced with rich, spiced, aged
butter – one of the main flavouring agents in
Ethiopian cookery. Vegetables stews made from
spinach, lentils, mushrooms and butter-soft, own-
made yoghurt cheese were simply amazing. Injera
in British restaurants is usually made from a

batter that hasn't been fermented long enough; as
a result the flatbread often tastes bland. Not so
here, where it had notably deep, sour tang, which
made it a perfect foil to the robustly flavoured
food. The only let-down was the coffee ceremony,
which wasn't as theatrical and elaborate as it
should be. This was our only gripe; this is one of
London's best Ethiopian restaurants.
*Babies and children welcome: high chairs. Booking
advisable. Tables outdoors (2, patio). Takeaway
service. Vegetarian menu.* **Map 26 B4.**

North West
Cricklewood

Abyssinia NEW
*9 Cricklewood Broadway, NW2 3JX (8208 0110).
Kilburn tube.* **Dinner served** 6pm-midnight
Mon-Fri. **Meals served** 2pm-midnight Sat,
Sun. **Main courses** £4.50-£10. **Credit** MC, V.
Ethiopian
One of the best restaurants in the Kilburn/
Cricklewood area, this well-established venue is
popular with Ethiopians and other locals. It's a
compact space that was once furnished with
mosobs (traditional low seating), but is now
smartly but simply decked out with plants, framed
pictures and linen-dressed tables. The cooking is
reliably and consistently good. We enjoyed
sprightly spring greens cooked with ginger; the
complex flavours of red lentils in hot berbere
sauce; whole green chillies stuffed with tomatoes
and onions; and bulgar wheat dressed simply in
Ethiopian aged butter (similar to Asian ghee).
Spiced lamb with rosemary and white wine (a
contemporary Ethiopian dish) was served very
cold, so we had to send it back. Once heated
through, though, it was tasty, and we enjoyed
scooping it up with injera (a bread freshly made
from an imported grain called tef, which is now
widely available in north London's Ethiopian food
shops). Service was perhaps rather too leisurely,
but was good-natured.
*Babies and children admitted. Booking advisable.
No-smoking tables. Tables outdoors (6, garden).
Takeaway service.*

CARIBBEAN

Central
Soho

★ Mr Jerk
*189 Wardour Street, W1F 8ZD (7287 2878/
www.mrjerk.co.uk). Tottenham Court Road tube.*
Meals served 9am-11pm Mon-Sat; 10am-8pm
Sun. **Main courses** £5-£7.50. **Credit** MC, V.
Caribbean
Mr Jerk has built a reputation for serving hearty
Jamaican food. With staples like patties, jerk
chicken, ackee and saltfish, and brown stew fish,
the menu is just like that in a quality restaurant in
downtown Kingston. The small and awkwardly
shaped Wardour Street branch attempts to be both
a takeaway and a restaurant. Space is at a
premium: if you're unlucky in your choice of
seating you'll find yourself in a tight squeeze. But
if you can cope with that, and with the slightly
abrupt service, you'll be in for a culinary treat.
Portion sizes are extremely generous, so try not to
over-order. Starters include jerk chicken wings,
fried fish, saltfish dumplings and fried plantain.
Our choice of Jamaican patties and coco bread
turned out to be enough for a small meal. Mains of
succulent braised oxtails with rice and peas, and
tender peppered steak with ground provisions
(root vegetables) were delicious, but heaped so high
they were hard to finish. Dishes are mainly
Jamaican, but the Trinidadian-styled rotis – flat
breads filled with a choice of curried fillings – are
deservedly popular.
*Babies and children welcome: high chairs.
No smoking. Takeaway service.* **Map 17 J6.**
For branch see index.

West
Ealing

BB's
*3 Chignell Place, off Uxbridge Road, W13 0TJ
(8840 8322/www.bbscrabback.co.uk). Ealing
Broadway tube/rail/West Ealing rail.* **Lunch**
served 11.30am-2.30pm Mon-Fri. **Dinner**
served 6.30-11.30pm Mon-Fri; 6.30pm-12.30am
Sat. **Main courses** £9.50-£12.95. **Credit** MC, V.
Grenadian
BB's menu reflects the diversity of Caribbean
cuisine with a definite nod to Grenada, the native
land of chef Brian Benjamin. There are staples
like callaloo, ackee and saltfish, and curried goat
as well as modern interpretations of less well-
known regional dishes. 'Bathway Express', an
appetising curried split pea risotto served with
mild mint and yogurt sauce, is clearly based on
split peas and rice, a dish that's widely cooked in
the southern Caribbean. The excellent king
prawns seretse (cooked in butter with lobster
sauce and served with pimentos and mango) was
matched by a perfect rum punch made with
Jamaican white rum. Rum lovers will be heartened
by an extensive list that includes Cockspur, Vat 19
and Clarke's Court. Passionfruit sorbet or bananas
flamed in rum and lemon were tempting options
for dessert, but we decided to sample some bush
tea, a delicious and soothing infusion of Grenada's
finest spices: West Indian bay leaves (which is a
relative of allspice), lemongrass and cinnamon. It
turned out to be a great end to a satisfying meal.
BB's setting is homely and the service was easy
but attentive – not unlike many places in the
Caribbean where simple surroundings can belie
the high standard of the food.
*Babies and children welcome; high chairs.
Booking essential Thur-Sat. Disabled: toilet.
No-smoking tables. Tables outdoors (4, pavement).
Vegan dishes.*

South
Brixton

★ Bamboula
*12 Acre Lane, SW2 5SG (7737 6633).
Brixton tube/rail.* **Meals served** 11am-11pm
Mon-Fri; noon-11pm Sat; 1-8pm Sun. **Main
courses** £7-£9.50. **Credit** MC, V. Caribbean
A bijou restaurant with a big character,
Bamboula's bright interior, lush foliage and regular
playing of old-school reggae make it a Brixton
favourite, drawing a wide range of customers from
council workers to business people. One thing that
attracts them is value for money. The dish named
Satisfaction (a quarter of jerk chicken with rice and
peas, plantain and a soft drink) makes a good all-
in-one bumper-sized meal for a mere £5.50. For an
extra quid you can have Walkerswood jerk lamb
with the same rice and plantain combination.
Lighter dishes include a gorgeous red pea soup
with pumpkin, yam and potato; and Bamboula
salad, with lettuce, tomato, mango, avocado and
soft cheese. In fact, the menu is extensive and
versatile, with ample room to mix and match – you
can have curried chicken with callaloo, for
example, instead of the usual rice. Desserts are
super-sweet and a challenge after the generous
mains. Coconut, rum and raisin or vanilla ice-
cream is the most modest option; those with
gargantuan appetites can go for a heavyweight
bread pudding or tropical crumble with cream.
*Babies and children admitted. Booking advisable
Fri, Sat (£5 deposit required). No smoking.
Tables outdoors (2, garden). Takeaway service.*
Map 22 D2.

South East
Herne Hill

Brockwells
*75-79 Norwood Road, SE24 9AA (8671 6868).
Herne Hill rail/3, 68, 196 bus.* **Open** 6pm-1am
Mon, Wed; 6pm-2am Tue; 6pm-3am Thur-Sat;
2.30pm-1am Sun. **Dinner served** 6-10pm

Menu

AFRICAN

Accra or **akara**: bean fritters.

Aloco: fried plantain with hot tomato sauce.

Asaro: yam and sweet potato porridge.

Ayeb or **iab**: fresh yoghurt cheese made from strained yoghurt.

Berbere: an Ethiopian spice mix made with many hot and aromatic spices.

Cassava, manioc or **yuca**: a family of coarse roots that are boiled and pounded to make bread and various other farinaceous dishes. There are bitter and sweet varieties (note that the bitter variety is poisonous until cooked).

Egusi: ground melon seeds, added to stews and soups as a thickening agent.

Enjera, enjerra or **injera**: a soft, spongy Ethiopian and Eritrean flatbread made with teff/tef (a grain originally from Ethiopea), wheat, barley, oats or cornmeal. Fermented with yeast, it should have a distinct sour tang.

Froi: fish and shrimp aubergine stew.

Fufu: a stiff pudding of maize or cassava (qv) flour, or pounded yam (qv).

Gari: a solid, heavy pudding made from ground fermented cassava (qv), served with thick soups.

Ground rice: a kind of stiff rice pudding served to accompany soup.

Jollof rice: like a hot, spicy risotto, with tomatoes, onions and (usually) chicken.

Kanyah: a sweet snack from Sierra Leone made from rice, peanuts and sugar.

Kelewele or **do-do**: fried plantain.

Kenkey: a starchy pudding that's prepared by pounding dried maize and water into a paste, then steaming inside plantain leaves. Usually eaten with meat, fish or vegetable stews.

Moi-moi, moin-moin or **moyin moin**: steamed beancake, served with meat or fish.

Ogbono: a large seed similar to egusi (qv). Although it doesn't thicken as much, it is used in a similar way.

Pepper soup: a light, peppery soup made with either fish or meat.

Shito: a dark red-hot pepper paste from Ghana, made from dried shrimps blended with onions and tomatoes.

Suya: a spicy Nigerian meat kebab.

Tuo or **tuwo**: a stiff rice pudding, sometimes served as rice balls to accompany soup.

Ugali: a Swahili word for bread made from cornmeal and water.

Ugba: Nigerian soy beans; also called oil beans.

Waakye: a dish of rice and black-eyed beans mixed with meat or chicken in gravy.

Waatse: rice and black-eyed beans cooked together.

Wot: a thick, dark sauce made from slowly cooked onions, garlic, butter and spices – an essential component in the aromatic stews of East Africa.

Doro wot, a stew containing chicken and hard-boiled eggs, is a particularly common dish.

CARIBBEAN

Ackee: a red-skinned fruit with yellow flesh that looks and tastes like scrambled eggs when cooked; traditionally served in a Jamaican dish of salt cod, onion and peppers.

Bammy or **bammie**: pancake-shaped, deep-fried cassava bread, commonly served with fried fish.

Breadfruit: this football-sized fruit has sweet, creamy flesh that's a cross between sweet potato and chestnut. Eaten as a vegetable.

Bush tea: herbal tea made from cerese (a Jamaican vine plant), mint or fennel.

Callaloo: the spinach-like leaves of either taro or malanga, often used as a base for a thick soup flavoured with pork or crab meat.

Coo-coo: a polenta-like cake of cornmeal and okra.

Cow foot: a stew made from the foot of the cow, which is boiled with vegetables. The cartilage gives the stew a gummy or gelatinous texture.

Curried (or **curry**) **goat**: more usually lamb in London; the meat is marinated and slow-cooked until tender.

Dasheen: a root vegetable with a texture similar to yam (qv).

Escoveitched (or **escovitch**) **fish**: fish fried or grilled then pickled in a tangy sauce with onions, sweet peppers and vinegar; similar to escabèche.

Festival: deep-fried, slightly sweet dumpling often served with fried fish.

Foo-foo: a Barbadian dish of pounded plantains, seasoned, rolled into balls and served hot.

Jerk: chicken or pork marinated in chilli spices, slowly roasted or barbecued.

Patty or **pattie**: a savoury pastry snack similar to a pasty, made with turmeric-coloured short-crust pastry, usually filled with beef, saltfish or vegetables.

Peas or **beans**: black-eyed beans, black beans, green peas and red kidney beans (the names are interchangeable).

Pepperpot: traditionally a stew of meat and casserep, a juice obtained from cassava; in London it's more likely to be a meat or vegetable stew with cassava.

Phoulorie: a Trinidadian snack of fried doughballs often eaten with a sweet tamarind sauce.

Plantain or **plantin**: a savoury variety of banana that is cooked like potato.

Rice and peas: rice cooked with kidney or gungo beans, pepper seasoning and coconut milk.

Roti: the Indian flatbread, usually filled with curried fish, meat or vegetables.

Saltfish: salt cod, classically combined with ackee (qv) or callaloo (qv).

Sorrel: not the European herb but a type of hibiscus with a sour-sweet flavour.

Soursop: a dark green, slightly spiny fruit; the pulp, blended with milk and sugar, is a refreshing drink.

Yam: a large tuber, with a yellow or white flesh and slightly nutty flavour.

Mon-Sat. **Meals served** 2.30-10pm Sun. **Main courses** £8.50-£10.95. **Set buffet** (Sun) £9.95. **Credit** JCB, MC, V. Caribbean

There's an undeniable air of the 1980s about the design of this wine bar and restaurant. Dark floors, black leather sofas, a neon-lit bar and plenty of chrome are the main culprits. Added quirks include splashes of graffiti and some well-worn stools with seats shaped like open-palmed hands: novelty touches that have outstayed their welcome. We visited on a Sunday lunchtime when an all-you-can-eat menu is available for £9.95, but fish or vegetarian options were limited, so we decided to order from the main menu instead. This featured well-known dishes such as jerk chicken, oxtail stew, snapper, and brown fish stew. An expected 20-minute wait turned into 40 minutes, which was fairly bewildering as we were initially the only customers in the place. But ackee and saltfish with rice and salad was a good rendition of a traditional dish, with fresh flavours and a fine portion of fried plantain. Steamed salmon steak with garlic mash was also successful. A slow but steady stream of diners shows that Brockwells does have a loyal following, but despite the good food, there's a sense that the venue relies more on its popular club nights and birthday parties, which makes the daytime service suffer.
Babies and children welcome (until 8pm); children's buffet. Booking advisable. Disabled: toilet. Dress: smart casual; no caps or trainers. Entertainment: DJs 9pm Tue, Fri-Sun; open microphone 7pm Wed, Thur. **Map 23 A5**.

East
Shoreditch

★ Anda de Bridge
42-44 Kingsland Road, E2 8DA (7739 3863/ www.andadebridge.com). Old Street tube/rail/26, 48, 55, 67, 149, 242, 243 bus. **Meals served** 11am-midnight Mon-Sat; noon-11pm Sun. **Main courses** £7-£10. **Credit** AmEx, DC, MC, V. Caribbean

Anda de Bridge was undergoing a refurbishment when we last visited. New leather sofas were positioned under the windows, while the bar had been moved a few feet to create unity between the previously separate front and back rooms. Despite the fresh look, our meal wasn't as convivial as it might have been. The thundering ragga music was extremely intrusive and our request to turn it down (not unreasonable as we were the only customers) was ignored. The food, ordered at the bar, was serviceable. Starters were limited, but olives and good-quality bread sufficed. For mains, tasty ackee and saltfish was well seasoned and served with a generous slide of rice and peas, while brown chicken curry was succulent, the meat sliding from the bone. The bar is well stocked with a variety of rums and Caribbean beers, including imported bottled Guinness. Busiest at weekends, Anda de Bridge best serves drinkers who fancy a quick bite, rather than anyone looking for a gastronomic experience.
Babies and children admitted. Disabled: toilet. Entertainment: DJs 8pm Fri, Sat. Separate room for parties, holds 200. Takeaway service. **Map 6 R3**.

North
Camden Town & Chalk Farm

★ Cottons
55 Chalk Farm Road, NW1 8AN (7485 8388/ www.cottons-restaurant.co.uk). Chalk Farm tube. **Lunch served** noon-4pm Sat. **Dinner served** 6pm-midnight Mon-Thur; 6pm-1am Fri, Sat. **Meals served** noon-midnight Sun. **Main courses** £10.25-£14.50. **Set meal** £18.50 2 courses, £21.50 3 courses. **Credit** AmEx, MC, V. Caribbean

There are two ways to approach Caribbean cuisine: one is to create new dishes from indigenous ingredients; the other is to do the classic dishes well. Cottons falls mainly into the former camp, but occasionally dips into the latter. A starter of whitebait featured little fish that were cleanly fried and perfectly crispy. A tangy papaya coulis gave a welcome zesty edge to king prawn and pineapple kebabs. Large portions meant we struggled to do justice to the mains: a superb traditional curried goat with rice and peas, and a less successful salmon fillet with spicy black beans, pickled red onions and sweet soy dressing, which we found a mite too sweet. Cocktails, on the other hand, were excellent. The wood-lined interior is comfortable; most of the tables are at the rear, providing plenty of scope for cosy evenings. If you're dining à deux, try to bag the lone window table, quite the nicest spot in the place, particularly in summer. *Babies and children welcome: high chairs. Booking advisable; essential weekends. Entertainment: DJ 9pm Fri, Sat; jazz 7pm Sun. No-smoking tables. Separate rooms for parties, seating 20 and 35. Tables outdoors (2, pavement). Vegetarian menu. Vegan dishes.* **Map 27 B1**. **For branch see index.**

★ Mango Room
10-12 Kentish Town Road, NW1 8NH (7482 5065/www.mangoroom.co.uk). Camden Town tube. **Lunch served** noon-5pm, **dinner served** 5-11pm Mon-Sat. **Meals served** noon-11pm Sun. **Main courses** £9-£13. **Credit** AmEx, MC, V. Caribbean
The main dining area at Mango Room is a spacious room that in summer opens on to busy Kentish Town Road. For more intimacy, head to the smarter space off to the side, bedecked with bright colours and modern artworks. Cocktails are always a hit here, and include some non-alcoholic punches. Food was superb on a recent visit: a starter of salt fish fritters was fluffy and light and well complemented by an apple chutney, while rum jelly added a kick to a smooth duck and pheasant parfait on toast. For mains, okra, spinach and coconut risotto was as flavoursome as it was original, and beautifully presented; snapper with mango and green peppercorn sauce was satisfyingly fresh and tangy. A side of potatoes showed simple flair by mashing white and sweet varieties together. Rich desserts, such as chocolate rum torte, looked appealing but were just too much. Shame about the service, though. Staff seemed inattentive and overstretched, and service was scrappy throughout. We hope it was a one-off. *Babies and children welcome: high chairs. Booking advisable weekends. No smoking. Separate room for parties, seats 30. Takeaway service.* **Map 27 D2**.

Stroud Green

Hummingbird
84 Stroud Green Road, N4 3EN (7263 9690/ www.thehummingbird.co.uk). Finsbury Park tube/rail. **Meals served** noon-midnight Mon-Sat; 1-11pm Sun. **Main courses** £6.50-£19.95. **Set dinner** £12 3 courses. **Credit** MC, V. Trinidadian
With an impressive pan-Caribbean menu that reflects the diversity of the region's cuisine it's easy to see why the Hummingbird has long been a favourite with Caribbean food fans. Lovers of Barbadian food, for example, will appreciate coo-coo and stewed fish. The dish of creamy polenta with okra and coconut milk, with red fish cooked in a rich tomato, pepper and red herb stew, was sumptuous and near perfect. Curry lovers will be impressed by the dhalphouri rotis, delicate Trinidadian flatbreads stuffed with ground split peas and served with fillings such as curried chicken, goat, fish or vegetables. And it's refreshing to visit a Caribbean restaurant where underrated dishes like fried spratts (commonly known as 'fry dry'), Tobagonian curried crab and dumplings, and St Lucian lobster are at the heart of the menu. So that's top marks for the food, but the Hummingbird didn't do so well in other areas. Service was not unfriendly, but it was quite slow. The bar is cluttered and untidy, and the white minimalist decor, which must have been chic several years ago, is now in urgent need of updating. *Babies and children welcome: high chairs. Booking essential weekends. Takeaway service. Vegetarian menu.*

The Americas

NORTH AMERICAN

The North American dining genre has been changing lately, as newer restaurants (**Hawksmoor**, **The Bar & Grill**, **Dollar Grill & Martinis**, **Curve**) roar on to the scene, and old favourites (**Christopher's**, **Smollensky's**) go under the knife for a bit of a nip and tuck. **The Bar & Grill** is a classic American steakhouse, with a mix of sophisticated decor and laid-back attitude, while **Curve** is just fabulous, with a creative approach to seafood, and sunny waterfront tables. Lunch at the wonderfully authentic **Arkansas Café** will dazzle those who have fond memories of dining on barbecue in the American South, but may puzzle those who have not shared this experience. The very latest American-style bar and grill is **Hawksmoor**, a steakhouse that is also an excellent cocktail bar for those seeking the full US-style dining and drinking experience without any overt American flag-waving. This is an increasingly varied and exciting sector, as restaurants become more willing to vary from the straight and narrow steaks-and-burgers formula, and bring over more cutting-edge US cooking, influenced by the international cuisine of the country's immigrant population. The result is intriguing, entertaining and welcome. As George W Bush said, in more controversial circumstances, 'Bring it on.'

Central
City

★ ★ Arkansas Café
Unit 12, Old Spitalfields Market, E1 6AA (7377 6999). Liverpool Street tube/rail. **Lunch served** noon-2.30pm Mon-Fri; noon-4pm Sun. **Main courses** £7-£16. **Credit** MC, V.
If it's real barbecue you're after, this is where to go. The Arkansas is not a stylish place. Seating is whatever Bubba – the gregarious Arkansan owner, usually found tending the grill – has put out that week (folding chairs, church pews). The walls are chiefly covered with pictures of farmyard animals scavenged from heaven knows where. Service can be abrupt, but that's part of this café's personality. (As is the painted mirror reading, 'Nice girls don't spit'.) Frankly, we would walk through fire to eat here, so bring on the bad mood. We don't care. We're here for the food. Specifically, steaming plates of well-sourced, freshly grilled meats. Options to tickle your smoky fancy include huge platters of pork ribs: glistening, juicy, perfectly cooked. Or how about steaks of Irish beef so tender they fall apart under the fork? All platters are served (on plastic plates) with potatoes, coleslaw, purple cabbage salad, and beans (cooked from scratch). If you want more than that, go to Soho. As Bubba always says when he has to get back to cooking: 'Talk to y'all later!' *Babies and children admitted. Booking advisable; not accepted Sun. No-smoking tables. Separate room for parties, seats 50. Tables outdoors (30, terrace inside market, Sun only). Takeaway service.* **Map 12 R5**.

★ Hawksmoor NEW
2006 RUNNER-UP BEST STEAK RESTAURANT
2006 RUNNER-UP BEST BAR
157 Commercial Street, E1 6BJ (7247 7392). Liverpool Street tube/rail. **Meals served** 5pm-1am Tue-Sat; 5pm-midnight Sun. **Main courses** £14-£22. **Credit** AmEx, DC, MC, V.
Named after the architect responsible for nearby Christ Church in Spitalfields, this excellent cocktail bar and restaurant is also simple, classic and timeless. From a brief menu, a starter of 'shrimp cocktail' was three monstrous, juicy Madagascan black tiger prawns perched on a chiffonade of pert green lettuce. The selection of sandwiches – 'Po'boys' – includes crisp soft-shell crab, with a side dish of excellent tartare sauce. Other side dishes such as coleslaw or chips were also exemplary, but the steaks are the focus. A huge ribeye slab of 28-day-aged Longhorn beef was cooked slightly more medium than the rare requested – but, hey, this isn't the US, where 'rare' can mean still twitching. If you're not eating beef, other grills include poussin, pork chop, veal chop, sea bass and stuffed zucchini. If you still have any appetite – portion sizes are generous – the only puddings are a choice of three ice-cream sundaes. *Babies and children admitted. Disabled: toilet. Restaurant available for hire. Separate room for parties, seats 30.* **Map 6 R5**.

Missouri Grill
76 Aldgate High Street, EC3N 1BD (7481 4010/ www.missourigrill.com). Aldgate tube. **Meals served** noon-11pm Mon-Fri. **Main courses** £10-£19.50. **Set dinner** £12 2 courses, £16 3 courses. **Credit** AmEx, MC, V.
This small restaurant is geared towards business diners. On our weeknight visit, it was particularly favoured by businessmen, who occupied every other table in the place. We were the only people not wearing dark wool-blend suits with white button-down shirts. Such a clientele is no surprise given Missouri Grill's location in a kind of corporate wasteland – a flat, forgettable gap between office buildings. The room is a bit chain-hotel chic, with a few anonymous framed posters the only decoration, but tables are smoothly draped in nice linens, and both the food and the service are top-notch. Starters such as creamy clam

chowder and crisp crab cakes are of ample proportions and cooked with a light touch. Mains include a divine peppered New York strip that melts on the tongue, and a robust rack of lamb that yields tenderly to the fork. Sides of steamed spinach and crisp skinny fries add to meals that could not be described as frugal. To finish, a moreish, cold chocolate soufflé will put paid to that diet once and for all.
Babies and children welcome: children's menu; high chairs. Booking essential lunch. No-smoking tables. Separate room for parties, seats 14. **Map 12 R6**.

Clerkenwell & Farringdon

The Bar & Grill

2-3 West Smithfield, EC1A 9JX (7246 0900/ www.barandgrill.co.uk). Farringdon tube/rail. **Meals served** noon-11pm daily. **Main courses** £6.75-£50. **Credit** AmEx, MC, V.

The Bar & Grill opened in 2005 with a rush of publicity for its 'Kobe' beef, and big steaks served with a vast array of marinades and rubs. Then it dropped the marinades and rubs. And some of the steaks. The menu is longer and more varied now, roving from wine bar-like starters through several salads via lobster, sausages, burgers and fajitas, with good salad and seafood sections. Some are good, with great-quality ingredients (lovely smoked salmon); some are not so good, without them (cakey apple in the crab salad). But it still loves its steaks, offering all the usual cuts plus the fabled wagyu steak (£50 for 8oz) for the guys with really big wallets (you can cheat, as we did, and try the wagyu steak burger for £16.95, whose flavour we will dream about). We can confidently recommend the ribeye too; but our steak experience stumbled a little on the T-bone special. For there was no T-bone, nor any clear differentiation in the meat (T-bones have sirloin on one side and fillet on the other); and it was gristly too. The aimiable manager couldn't help us in our bewilderment, but he did dock 20% from our bill. We hope this was a one-off experience, because the attractive, cream-clad Bar & Grill was becoming one of our favourite American restaurants.
Babies and children welcome: high chairs. Booking advisable. Disabled: toilet. Separate area for parties, seats 10. **Map 11 O5**.

★ Dollar Grills & Martinis NEW

2 Exmouth Market, EC1R 4PX (7278 0077). Angel tube/Farringdon tube/rail/19, 38 bus. *Bar* **Open** 6pm-1am Mon-Sat; 6pm-midnight Sun. **Meals served** 6-11pm Mon-Sat; 6-10pm Sun. **Main courses** £4.50-£9.
Restaurant **Meals served** noon-11pm Mon-Sat; noon-10pm Sun. **Main courses** £7.50-£16.75. *Both* **Credit** MC, V.

If the Scissor Sisters owned a restaurant, it would look like this place. The spectacular restaurant-as-work-of-art design of Dollar comes courtesy of its actual owners, who also run the exotically styled Beach Blanket Babylon in Notting Hill. With dim lighting, lots of mirrors, draped fabrics, elaborate

artworks and rows of windows overlooking Exmouth Market, it looks more Moroccan brothel than US-style grill – but don't be fooled. Steaks are juicy and tender, chips are skinny and crisp, side orders are fresh and tasty. Our burger was piled so high we literally couldn't get our mouth around it. Other mains include the likes of salmon with new potatoes and caper butter, and roast leg of lamb with aubergine and pesto-stuffed tomato. Starters vary from a crisp endive salad with roquefort, pear and walnut to creamy foie gras with sweet peach chutney. We had raspberry Martinis for pudding, but you might prefer the passionfruit cheesecake or tiramisu. The cocktails are certainly a selling point – they're excellent, and well priced at between £6.50 and £8. Staff were friendly and professional, despite their crazy shin-length trousers.
Babies and children admitted. Bar available for hire. Entertainment: DJs 8pm Fri, Sat. Tables outdoors (10, pavement). **Map 5 N4**.

Covent Garden

Christopher's

18 Wellington Street, WC2E 7DD (7240 4222/ www.christophersgrill.com). Covent Garden tube. *Bar* **Open/snacks served** noon-midnight Mon-Sat; noon-10.30pm Sun.
Restaurant **Brunch served** 11.30am-3pm Sat, Sun. **Lunch served** noon-3pm Mon-Fri. **Dinner served** 5-11pm Mon-Sat. **Main courses** £12-£32. **Set meal** (5.30-7pm, 10-11.15pm Mon-Sat) £14.50 2 courses, £17 3 courses.
Both **Credit** AmEx, DC, MC, V.

The builders have been busy at this Wellington Street stalwart, giving the bar a successful makeover (it's now a dark and soothing candlelit space) and sprucing up the big upstairs dining room. The menu writers have been industrious too, raising the prices. Expense-account diners now dominate Christopher's; the families who once frequented it seem to have been replaced by men in suits complaining indiscreetly over scotch and prime rib. The food is excellent: lobster cobb salad was rich with chunks of lobster tail and chilled quail eggs; the fillet steak was big and perfectly prepared (it ought to be for £24 with no side dishes). But the 'surf 'n' turf' burger at £22 seemed pure expense-account padding: a hamburger served with half a lobster. Want fries with that? It'll cost you £2.95 extra. Puddings were great – the poached pear with caramelised ginger cream was gorgeous, and the pecan tart tasted like cold candy – but so they should be for £6.50 each. Perhaps Christopher's should learn from having opened a City branch that didn't last.
Babies and children welcome: children's menu; high chairs. Booking advisable. Separate room for parties, seats 10. **Map 18 L7**.

Joe Allen

13 Exeter Street, WC2E 7DT (7836 0651/ www.joeallen.co.uk). Covent Garden tube. **Brunch served** 11.30am-4pm Sat, Sun. **Meals served** noon-12.45am Mon-Fri; 11.30am-12.45am Sat; 11.30am-11.30pm Sun. **Main courses** £8-£16. **Set brunch** £18.50 2 courses, £20.50 3 courses incl drink. **Set meal** (noon-3pm Mon-Fri, 5-6.45pm Mon-Sat) £15 2 courses, £17 3 courses incl coffee. **Credit** AmEx, MC, V.

A true West End institution – one of the prime spots for pre- and post-theatre dining – Joe Allen comfortably rests on its laurels, and the theatre crowd just keeps on coming. Not just audience members, but cast and crew all gather here nightly to eye up each other amid posters memorialising past hit shows. That's what this place is all about. Food is such an afterthought that, frankly, it's no surprise it's not particularly good. The menu hugs 1978 as if it were yesterday. For example, starter options include chopped calf's liver; anchovy, green bean and olive salad; and grilled garlic mushrooms. Among the main courses you'll find grilled lamb cutlets with broccoli, pan-fried pork loin with baby aubergine, and grilled sirloin with 'steak fries'. Service can be hectic and uneven; our waiter seemed merely to be finding time for us between auditions. On our visit, the kitchen played fast and loose with the vegetables; you were as likely to get broccoli with your pork, and

mangetouts with your lamb, but who's counting? After all, nobody comes here for the food.
Babies and children welcome: booster seats. Booking advisable. Entertainment: pianist 9pm-1am Mon-Sat. No-smoking tables. **Map 18 L7**.

Fitzrovia

★ Eagle Bar Diner

3-5 Rathbone Place, W1T 1HJ (7637 1418/ www.eaglebardiner.com). Tottenham Court Road tube. **Meals served** noon-11pm Mon-Wed; noon-midnight Thur, Fri; 10am-midnight Sat; 10am-6pm Sun. **Main courses** £5.95-£12.95. **Credit** MC, V.

This funky hamburger joint is increasingly enamoured of the club crowd. These days it has a DJ spinning loud jammin' tunes at dinner time. Um, yay? Is it better to get that repetitive beat slamming into your ear than to hear a word anybody at your own table has to say? Conversation must be *so* last year. Lunches, thankfully, are safe from this aural assault – for now. So that's when we chose to visit. The food remains reliably good. The main attraction is the burgers. There are fish burgers, steak burgers, chicken burgers, ostrich burgers… you name it, they'll grill it and serve it with fries. And the burgers are still perfect. You get to choose your meat, your sauces, whether you want your fries fat or skinny, you can have cocktail or milkshake, and cokes are served in old-fashioned bottles with straws. Along with burgers there are big, hearty sandwiches (the salt beef is excellent) and fresh salads, as well US-style breakfasts served all day. The Eagle is a worthwhile option, but the DJ fetish is tiresome.
Babies and children admitted (until 9pm if dining). Booking advisable. Disabled: toilet. Entertainment: DJs 7.30pm Wed-Sat. Takeaway service. **Map 17 K6**.

Marylebone

Black & Blue

90-92 Wigmore Street, W1V 3RD (7486 1912/www.blackandblue.biz). Bond Street tube. **Meals served** noon-11pm Mon-Thur, Sun; noon-11.30pm Fri, Sat. **Main courses** £8-£25. **Credit** MC, V.

With branches all over town, this little chain of steak restaurants is a real success story. Our favourite is the Wigmore Street outlet, which has the big spacious booths characteristic of all Black & Blues, plus a long central bar for those just popping in for a starter and a glass of wine. The menu is short and sweet: starters are a standard US selection of friendly dips and crispy nibbles; mains consist of steaks (with a scant handful of alternatives); and there are three or four puddings. We dived into the artichoke and spinach dip like it was a swimming pool on a hot day – cheesy, spinachy goodness on a tortilla chip. We also nibbled on butterfly prawns in a ladylike fashion. They were as good as they are in just about every other restaurant in London. Which is quite good. The steaks are the thing here, of course, and our ribeye was cooked precisely to order, and served with nice chips and a big, fresh salad. Our only complaint was the cut of meat; it could have been more tender. Still, for the price: not bad.
Babies and children admitted. Bookings not accepted. No-smoking tables. Tables outdoors (2, pavement). **Map 9 G6**.
For branches see index.

Mayfair

Automat

33 Dover Street, W1S 4NF (7499 3033/ www.automat-london.com). Green Park tube. **Meals served** noon-midnight Mon-Fri; 11am-midnight Sat; 11am-5pm Sun. **Main courses** £7-£24. **Credit** AmEx, DC, JCB, MC, V.

Knowingly kitsch, the trendy Automat deals in American comfort food. Its interior is based on US roadside diners: one long, narrow room with an open kitchen. On our visit, the first strike was the service, which verged on snobby. The second strike was the layout; putting the kitchen in the dining room raises the noise level and makes the dining

RESTAURANTS

The Bar & Grill

room smell... well, like a kitchen. We hoped the food would set us right, and a bowl of flavourful and cheesy french onion soup made a promising start, while another starter of golden beet salad with mozzarella and endive was bland but fresh. Mains were a setback, though. Black cod served with a prawn cake was enjoyable, but the prawn cake was overloaded with dill; a huge pot of chicken casserole arrived in a rich reduction, but the chicken was dry. Sides were a catastrophe: creamed spinach was flavourless and overloaded with cream; and the same fate befell the macaroni cheese, which was drowned in milky sauce and buried in greasy cheese. In contrast, lemon meringue pie arrived as a piece of tangy perfection, and a vast portion of chocolate mousse didn't disappoint either. File under 'uneven'.

Babies and children admitted. Booking advisable. Disabled: toilet. No-smoking tables. Takeaway service. **Map 9 H7**.

Soho

Bodean's

10 Poland Street, W1F 8PZ (7287 7575/ www.bodeansbbq.com). Oxford Circus or Piccadilly Circus tube.
Deli **Open** noon-11pm Mon-Sat; noon-10.30pm Sun.
Restaurant **Lunch served** noon-3pm, **dinner served** 6-11pm Mon-Fri. **Meals served** noon-

11pm Sat; noon-10.30pm Sun. **Main courses** £6-£16. **Set meal** (minimum 8) £16.95 2 courses, £19.95 3 courses.
Both **Credit** AmEx, MC, V.
The terse treatment we received from the stern gatekeeper here (a woman ticking customers off her fully booked list) was a bad start. We had arrived ten minutes early; she tapped her watch disapprovingly and told us to come back in precisely ten minutes, yet when we were finally admitted to the inner sanctum the place was half empty. But the service downstairs was so friendly, and the food so good, that we soon forgot our irritation and simply enjoyed another excellent Bodean's meal. This place is deservedly popular; its barbecue reputation stretches far and wide. You can order ribs by the half rack or the mighty full rack (which fills a platter end to end); they are always smoky and well marinated. If you feel like a starter, be warned: portions are big, and although the chicken wings are juicy and fiery, you risk filling up on them or on the divine chicken gumbo, thus leaving little room for the excellent ribs, the tender steaks and the tasty pulled pork. Note that Bodean's is a no-go area for vegetarians. Sides are worthwhile – particularly the barbecue beans and the crisp fries – but puddings are forgettable. Still, who has space for them?

Babies and children welcome: children's area; children's menu; high chairs. Booking advisable

(restaurant). No smoking (restaurant). Restaurant & deli available for hire. Tables outdoors (4, pavement). Takeaway service. **Map 17 J6**. **For branches see index.**

★ Ed's Easy Diner

12 Moor Street, W1V 5LH (7434 4439/ www.edseasydiner.co.uk). Leicester Square or Tottenham Court Road tube. **Meals served** 11.30am-midnight daily. **Main courses** £4.40-£5.75. **Minimum** (6pm-midnight Fri-Sun) £4.55.
Credit MC, V.
This chain of 1950s-style diners – all shiny chrome and determinedly cheerful red and white colour schemes – is where to find fast food done well. Stepping straight out of TV's *Happy Days*, each branch is more or less the same: bar stools at the counter around the open kitchen, a scattering of booths and tables, mini-jukeboxes playing hits of the 1970s, and a menu devoted almost exclusively to burgers and 'dogs. The formula is solid and successful, although quality can vary based on how busy the place is. Most of the time, we have good experiences at Ed's. Burgers are reliably fresh and piled high with onions, pickles and lettuce. The fries and onion rings are crisp, and portions are generous. The milkshakes and malts are dangerously delectable and arrive in copious amounts. What's more, the waiters are almost relentlessly perky, despite listening to that old pop music all day long.

Babies and children welcome: children's menu. No smoking. Tables outdoors (2, pavement). Takeaway service; delivery service (within 1-mile radius). **Map 17 K6.**
For branches see index.

South Kensington

PJ's Grill
52 Fulham Road, SW3 6HH (7581 0025/ www.pjsgrill.net). South Kensington tube.
Meals served noon-midnight Mon-Fri; 11am-midnight Sat; 10.30am-11.30pm Sun.
Main courses £9.95-£18.95. **Credit** AmEx, MC, V.
PJ's is all about good food, good times and polo, apparently (its name stands for 'Polo Joe's'). The decor at this branch is men's clubby, with plenty of polished wood dominated by a massive ceiling fan above the bar. There's also polo memorabilia: polo photos, polo paintings, polo jerseys, polo mallets… Frankly, the theming is peripheral to the fine menu of upmarket American cuisine on offer. The house special raw oysters on the half shell got us going even better than the ice-cold G&T we picked up from the bar while waiting for a seat on a very busy Sunday night (this place is always crowded). The fresh, salty molluscs slid down in satisfying fashion. For mains we sampled the ribeye; it wasn't the most tender cut, but well cooked and served with perfect chips and rich béarnaise sauce. We also ordered shepherd's pie. The vast serving arrived piping hot, with a tangy, well-balanced flavour. We had no room for puddings, but they looked good – crumbles, pies and cheesecakes. Service was flatteringly attentive. We approve.
Babies and children welcome: high chairs. Booking advisable. **Map 14 E11.**
For branch see index.

Tootsies Grill
107 Old Brompton Road, SW7 3LE (7581 8942/www.tootsiesrestaurants.co.uk). South Kensington tube. **Meals served** noon-11pm Mon-Thur; noon-11.30pm Fri; 10am-11.30pm Sat; 10am-11pm Sun. **Main courses** £6.25-£13.50. **Credit** AmEx, MC, V.
You'd be hard-pressed to find a parent in London who doesn't know about and sing the praises of the Tootsies chain. Staff at its family-friendly restaurants don't wince when the bottle falls, the kids choose to have a sing-song, or parents have to dash across the room to pry junior off the plate-glass window. Most branches have elements of their decor in common: round wooden tables, bistro-style chairs, lots of windows and light. At this restaurant, big windows look out over leafy Holland Park Avenue. The menu promises the 'best burger you've ever eaten'. While that might not be the case (the gourmet burger market is fiercely competitive), the burgers aren't bad, and the selection is massive, ranging from the usual beef and vegetarian versions to thai chicken burgers, pork and apple burgers, and lamb and rosemary burgers. Further options include baby-back ribs (tender and juicy), steaks and other grills, salads (two caesars and a house mixed version, all fresh and crisp), and a wide choice of sandwiches. Shakes and malts vie with wine and beer on the drinks list; if you choose alcohol over a creamy malt, you're more of an adult than us. Expect to see more Tootsies in London as the new parent company expands the brand.
Babies and children welcome: children's menu; crayons; high chairs. Booking advisable; not accepted lunch Sat & Sun. No smoking. Tables outdoors (3, pavement). Takeaway service. **Map 14 D11.**
For branches see index.

Strand

Smollensky's on the Strand
105 Strand, WC2R 0AA (7497 2101/ www.smollenskys.co.uk). Covent Garden, Embankment or Temple tube/Charing Cross tube/rail.
Bar **Open** noon-11pm Mon-Thur; noon-1am Fri, Sat; noon-5.30pm, 6.30-10.30pm Sun.

Restaurant **Meals served** noon-11pm Mon-Sat; noon-10pm Sun. **Main courses** £8.95-£21.95.
Set meal (noon-6.30pm, after 10pm Mon-Fri) £10.95 2 courses, £12.95 3 courses.
Both **Credit** AmEx, DC, MC, V.
It's all change in this basement steakhouse. Everything, from the floors to the ceilings, has been replaced. The new look is cool and modern, with dark colours predominating and candles glittering everywhere. Attractive, yes, but there are some problems in practice: the tables are up against the waiters' station, which had our nerves jangling along with the clashing silverware; and the bar has encroached on the dining room, which can make you feel on display. The food is as straightforward as ever, with the emphasis (as always) on steaks. Ours were big and juicy, yet cooked unevenly – blue in places, medium in others. The steaks all arrive with good chips and a choice of sauces, making the price (£15.95 for a 285g/10oz ribeye) something of a bargain. Starters have always been hit and miss: goat's cheese with salad and vinaigrette was fine, but honey-grilled prawns were dry and overcooked. We've no complaints about the puddings, though: chocolate mousse was moreish, and the mississippi mud pie memorable. The place might look fancy now, but it's the same old Smollensky's. The company has also launched a burgers and cocktails fast-food version, Smollensky's Metro (currently there are three branches in outer London).
Babies and children welcome: booster seats; children's menu; entertainment (noon-3pm Sat, Sun); high chairs; toys. Booking advisable. Entertainment: blues 7.30-10.30pm Mon-Sat; DJ 11pm-12.30am Fri, Sat; jazz 8.15-10.30pm Sun. No-smoking tables. **Map 18 L7.**
For branches see index.

West

Acton

The Coyote
100-102 Churchfield Road, W3 6DH (8992 6299/www.thecoyote.co.uk). Acton Town tube/ Acton Central rail. **Dinner served** 5-11pm Mon-Fri. **Meals served** 11am-11pm Sat; 11am-10.30pm Sun. **Main courses** £8.25-£15.50.
Credit AmEx, MC, V.
The popular Chiswick-based Coyote Grill has sprouted an attractive branch, with lots of dark wood and candles glowing on the tables. Customers are a mix of couples and groups of friends, producing a lively buzz above the blues, which floats out at polite levels from the speakers. As at the Chiswick home base, the well-priced food speaks with a Southwestern US twang. A large list of starters includes old favourites such as gooey nachos and tangy chicken wings alongside more novel options like the cool tuna ceviche marinated in lime juice, or baby-back ribs crusted in smoky spices. Most are big enough to share. The mains list ranges from the exotic (peppered ostrich steak) to the mundane (burgers), but the best food is to be found in dishes that use smoky Southwestern spices; the lamb marinated in dried Central American spices and crusted in pecans is a prime example, as is the ribeye: a tender steak served with distinctively flavoured chipotle gravy. Service is sharp and the mood relaxed – the Coyote is a fine choice way out west.
Babies and children welcome: children's menu; high chairs. Booking advisable. Tables outdoors (7, garden). Takeaway service.
For branch see index.

Bayswater

Harlem
78 Westbourne Grove, W2 5RT (7985 0900/ www.harlemsoulfood.com). Bayswater or Notting Hill Gate tube. **Open** 9am-2am Mon-Fri; 10am-2.30am Sat, Sun. **Meals served** 9am-1am Mon-Fri; 10am-1.30am Sat, Sun. **Main courses** £6.50-£29.95. **Set meal** (noon-6pm) £5 1 course.
Credit AmEx, DC, MC, V.
This Notting Hill eaterie started well when it opened a few years ago, but since then has foundered. The idea – bringing American soul food

to London – is a good one, and the menu looks enticing, but somehow betwixt the concept and the reality, something slipped. It's an attractive space – with lots of dark polished wood, a marvellously out-of-place chandelier above the bar, and glittering gold touches – and filled with attractive people. The most coveted seats are those by the window looking out over busy Westbourne Grove. The problems lie with the food and the service, neither of which has been particularly good on our recent visits. The best options are the char-grilled jumbo prawns (huge and meaty) and the salads, which are fresh; however, the salad dressing tasted cheap, and turned all that it touched to mush. Of the main courses that we tried, the hamburger was big and tasty, but the catfish was so heavily battered it was hard to tell there was any fish in there at all. Then there was the service. This is one of those places where the waiters seem to forget you exist at a certain point, and become much more interested in one another than the customers – very frustrating.
Babies and children welcome: children's menu; high chairs. Entertainment: DJs 10pm Thur-Sat (£10 after 11pm). Takeaway service.
Map 7 B6.

Hammersmith

Pacific Bar & Grill **NEW**
320 Goldhawk Road, W6 0XF (8741 1994). Stamford Brook tube. **Meals served** noon-11.30pm Mon-Sat; noon-11pm Sun. **Main courses** £9.95-£16.50. **Set lunch** (noon-5pm Mon-Fri) £10.50 2 courses, £12.50 3 courses. **Credit** AmEx, MC, V.
Changing name but not ownership, this airy space used to be a Café Med; it now looks smart in an understated, New England way. On a frosty night, the open fire threw welcome warmth our way; service was laid-back and friendly. The owners have kept the Café Med formula – a good-value set-price lunch, grills at dinner, desserts built for comfort – but tweaked the specifics, now providing a 'greatest hits' of American bistro food. Choices run the East/West Coast gamut from New England clam chowder to Californian chardonnay risotto with enoki mushrooms, plus a few Southwestern dishes. Blue claw crab cake didn't stint on crab meat and came with a citrus mayo. Char-grilled West Coast calamares were seared on the 'rod iron' grill and arrived just-cooked and tender, although the accompanying chilli jam was overpowering. An 8oz ribeye steak was tender and flavourful, yet the chips (a massive bowlful) seemed a bit flaccid. Cheesecake was a Yank-sized, calorific triangle of tangy creaminess, even if its crust was undercooked. At weekends the usual menu gives way to brunch dishes such as New York steak and eggs or buttermilk pancakes with bacon, eggs and maple syrup.
Babies and children welcome: children's menu; crayons; high chairs; magician (1-3pm Sun). No smoking. Tables outdoors (12, terrace).
Map 20 A3.

Kensington

Sticky Fingers
1A Phillimore Gardens, W8 7QG (7938 5338/ www.stickyfingers.co.uk). High Street Kensington tube.
Bar **Open** noon-10pm Mon-Sat.
Restaurant **Meals served** noon-11pm Mon-Sat; noon-10.30pm Sun. **Main courses** £9.25-£17.95.
Both **Credit** AmEx, JCB, MC, V.
A kind of British answer to the Hard Rock Café, Sticky Fingers is sleek, loud and approachable. It's co-owned by former Rolling Stone Bill Wyman, so the rock 'n' roll soundtrack and decor of Stones memorabilia are inevitable. The menu is a middle-of-the-road list of salads, sandwiches, steaks, ribs and burgers, and the cooking is similarly MOR. You will have neither the best meal of your life here, nor the worst. In recent years the focus has shifted from rock kids to those who were rock kids in the 1970s and '80s. Consequently, the venue is a huge favourite with west London yummy mummies who pack it with their pricey prams and pampered offspring during the day. All are

RESTAURANTS

Chain gang

For many Londoners the only thing they know about American dining comes courtesy of its loudest, brightest, dizziest chains. These themed, kid-friendly, often celebrity-oriented establishments have been spreading confusing messages about American cuisine for years. And they're not about to stop now, so here's a basic rundown of four of the most popular options.

Cheers

72 Regent Street, W1R 6EL (7494 3322/ www.cheersbarlondon.com). Piccadilly Circus tube.
Bar **Open/snacks served** noon-3am Mon-Sat; noon-12.30am Sun. **Snacks** £6-£8.
Restaurant **Meals served** noon-10pm daily. **Main courses** £6.95-£12.90. **Minimum** £7. **Set meal** (noon-5pm Mon-Fri) £2.95 1 course.
Both **Credit** AmEx, MC, V.
The lesser of the chains, Cheers is a dark, warehouse-sized space, loosely based on the US TV show of the same name. The menu borrows liberally from the television series, with salads, burgers and other dishes named after characters. Over the years, this place has become hugely popular with sports fans who pack in to watch games on the numerous screens, so it's more blokey than family-oriented.
Babies and children welcome (until 6pm in restaurant): children's menu; crayons; high chairs. Disabled: toilet. Dress: smart casual. No-smoking tables. **Map 17 J7**.

Hard Rock Café

150 Old Park Lane, W1K 1QZ (7629 0382/ www.hardrock.com). Green Park or Hyde Park Corner tube. **Meals served** 11.30am-midnight Mon-Thur, Sun; 11.30am-1am Fri, Sat. **Main courses** £8.50-£15. **Credit** AmEx, MC, V.
Arguably the most famous American restaurant in London, and a classic example of the Hard Rock chain, with rock memorabilia covering the walls, music blasting at impressive levels (more pop than rock, if you ask us) and the trademark hamburgers, nachos and salads piled high on plates carried by wafer-thin waitresses in teeny-tiny uniforms. This place is ideal for children, as nobody can hear them scream, and the ice-cream sundaes are excellent. Prices are, however, outrageous.
Babies and children welcome: children's menu; high chairs; toys. Booking advisable. No smoking. Tables outdoors (18, pavement). **Map 9 H8**.

Planet Hollywood

Trocadero, 13 Coventry Street, W1D 7DH (7287 1000/www.planethollywood.com). Piccadilly Circus tube. **Meals served** 11.30am-1am Mon-Sat; 11.30am-12.30am Sun. **Main courses** £9.95-£19.95. **Credit** AmEx, DC, MC, V.
The Hollywood version of the Hard Rock, with movie memorabilia floor to ceiling, swinging klieg lights (just like in LA!) and blasting film soundtracks. It's ideal for open young minds, eager to be

inculcated into the Hollywood cabal. The food is slightly more adventurous than at the Hard Rock: fewer burgers, more rôtisserie chickens, fajitas and steaks. But don't worry, there's still plenty for the kids to choose from.
Babies and children welcome: children's menu; high chairs; nappy-changing facilities. Booking advisable. Disabled: toilet. No-smoking tables. Separate room for parties, seats 80. **Map 17 K7**.

TGI Friday's

6 Bedford Street, WC2E 9HZ (7379 0585/ www.tgifridays.co.uk). Covent Garden tube/Charing Cross tube/rail.
Bar **Open** noon-11pm Mon-Sat; noon-10.30pm Sun.
Restaurant **Meals served** noon-11.30pm Mon-Sat; noon-11pm Sun. **Main courses** £7.95-£17.95.
Both **Credit** AmEx, MC, V.
The most child-centred of all the US chains, despite the fact that the entire restaurant is focused on a big noisy bar. Kids are decked out with balloons, given crayons to colour with, and generally encouraged by waiters in cheery 1980s-style red braces covered in 1980s-style badges. The food is arguably the most varied, with an emphasis on sticky barbecues and tasty Tex-Mex dishes, as well as the inevitable burgers and fries.
Babies and children welcome: children's menu; crayons; high chairs. Disabled: toilet. No smoking. Takeaway service. **Map 18 L7**. **For branches see index.**

---

cheerfully welcomed by the youthful international staff. Evenings are less kid-oriented, and the cocktail menu tends to take the lead. Prices, which reached silly levels a few years ago, have gradually dropped to the point where we'll stop complaining about them. Starters (buffalo wings, crab cakes) cost around £5. Half-pound burgers go for £9. The steaks are the best bargains – a 16oz ribeye is £15. And the blueberry cheesecake is downright good.
Babies and children welcome: children's menu; entertainment (face-painting & magician 1.30-3.30pm Sat, Sun); high chairs. Booking advisable. No smoking (noon-5pm Sat, Sun). Takeaway service. **Map 7 A9**.

Westbourne Park

★ Lucky 7

127 Westbourne Park Road, W2 5QL (7727 6771). Royal Oak or Westbourne Park tube. **Meals served** 10am-11pm Mon-Thur; 9am-11pm Fri, Sat; 9am-10.30pm Sun. **Main courses** £5.45-£12.95. **Credit** MC, V.
Tom Conran's take on the American diner theme, Lucky 7 is a small, low-key joint. Within you'll find big booths (which must be shared with others when the place gets crowded), lots of mirrors, and a short but solid menu of burgers, sandwiches, salads and shakes. The tantalising smell of sizzling burgers and steaming fries will surely lure you to the unhealthiest items on the menu. The burgers are big and heavy, with all the fixings. The fries are skinny, and served hot and crisp. But it's the milkshakes that separate the men from the boys. They're served in three levels of thickness, starting at £4 for a regular, with prices climbing rapidly the thicker they get. The thinnest version is thick enough for most. Breakfasts are big and fresh, with eggs and pancakes leading the way. Lucky 7 is generally a commendable option, but the food seems to get greasier the busier it is. One more niggle: sharing a booth with strangers feels weirdly intimate, so try to visit in between rush hours.

Babies and children welcome: booster seats. Bookings not accepted. Separate room for parties, seats 35. Tables outdoors (2, pavement). Takeaway service. **Map 7 A5**.

South West
Chelsea

Big Easy

332-334 King's Road, SW3 5UR (7352 4071/ www.bigeasy.uk.com). Sloane Square tube then 11, 19, 22 bus.
Bar **Open** noon-11pm Mon-Fri; 11am-11pm Sat; 11am-10.30pm Sun. **Main courses** £7.95-£14.95.
Restaurant **Meals served** noon-11.30pm Mon-Thur; noon-12.30am Fri; 11am-12.30am Sat; 11am-11.30pm Sun. **Main courses** £9.95-£22.95.
Set lunch (noon-5pm Mon-Fri) £7.95 2 courses.
Both **Credit** AmEx, DC, JCB, MC, V.
With all the raucous conviviality of its namesake city (New Orleans), this somewhat unlikely Chelsea restaurant packs in crowds of twentysomethings and families every night for huge steaks, massive seafood platters, racks of ribs and cold, long-neck American beers. The decor would be a complete cliché were it not for the fact that thousands of restaurants in the US look just like it, with rough wood panelling, old adverts and faux street signs as art, gingham tablecloths and dark wood floors. A band plays downstairs, and the overall volume can be ear-splitting, but it's all good clean fun. In the midst of all the ruckus, the food can get a bit lost, but it need not. Steaks are tender and well priced, Alaskan king crab and lobster are house specialities, side dishes are carefully done. Consider the chicken wings as a hearty, spicy starter, or try the thick, rich clam chowder, and then dive into one of those huge plates of food.
Babies and children welcome: children's menu; crayons; high chairs. Entertainment: musicians 8.30pm daily. No-smoking tables. Tables outdoors (5, pavement). Takeaway service. **Map 14 D12**.

Fulham

Sophie's Steakhouse & Bar

311-313 Fulham Road, SW10 9QH (7352 0088/ www.sophiessteakhouse.com). South Kensington tube then 14, 211, 414 bus. **Meals served** noon-11.45pm Mon-Fri; 11am-11.45pm Sat; 11am-10.45pm Sun. **Main courses** £6.95-£16.50. **Set meal** (noon-6pm Mon-Fri) £9.95 2 courses. **Credit** AmEx, MC, V.
With plenty of polished wood and trendy light fixtures, Sophie's certainly has the look of a hip, South Kensington steakhouse. The waiting staff all seem preternaturally tall and slim, while the clientele are a mix of old Kensington money and new American cash. The chill-out music is kept to a low repetitive beat and, in general, the place pushes all the right buttons. Tables are a bit too close together, meaning it's impossible not to hear the neighbouring party's conversation about their hedge fund or their kid's private tutor, but the food is excellent, straightforward cooking. Steaks are big and juicy: good cuts of meat well cooked. The peppered steak salad seems to be one of the most popular dishes; it comes with lots of fresh greens and beautifully grilled slices of beef. Even the puddings are large and freshly made, although not particularly creative (think brownies with ice-cream). The kitchen has a better grasp of detail than the waitresses (who forgot our beer for 45 minutes, despite being reminded, and then forgot our salad dressing, and then forgot our cutlery).
Babies and children welcome: children's menu; high chairs. Disabled: toilet. **Map 14 D12**.

Wandsworth

Dexter's Grill & Bar

20 Bellevue Road, SW17 7EB (8767 1858). Wandsworth Common rail/319 bus. **Meals served** noon-11pm Mon-Fri; 11am-11pm Sat; 11am-10.30pm Sun. **Main courses** £7.25-£14.50. **Credit** AmEx, MC, V.

This small branch of the Tootsies tree on the edge of Wandsworth Common is a good choice for families – and families certainly take advantage of the fact. During the day, the spacious dining room, with its exposed brick walls, wood beams and polished wooden floors, is virtually given over to mothers, pushchairs and toddlers. So child-friendly is Dexter's there's a kind of kiddie heaven in the back devoted to sweets and ice-cream. Nobody's going to complain if you set up a crayon colouring station at your table, and nobody will glare at your pram. In the evening, the lights dim and the venue becomes more grown up. Day and night the menu is the same: basic Americana that veers from the healthy (big mix-and-match salads, where you can add the meat and dressing of your choice from a wide selection), to the unhealthy (burgers and divine ice-cream desserts), via somewhere in between (steaks). The atmosphere is casual and relaxing, and the staff are eager to help.
Babies and children welcome: children's menu; crayons; face painting (noon-3pm Sun); high chairs; toys. Booking advisable weekends. No-smoking tables. Separate room for parties, seats 40. Tables outdoors (9, patio). Takeaway service.

Wimbledon

★ Jo Shmo's
2006 RUNNER-UP BEST FAMILY RESTAURANT
33 High Street, SW19 5BY (8879 3845/ www.joshmos.com). Wimbledon tube/rail then 93 bus. **Meals served** noon-11pm Mon-Thur, Sun; noon-11.30pm Fri, Sat. **Main courses** £6.95-£13.50. **Credit** AmEx, MC, V.
Proving that family restaurants can be slick and attractive too, Jo Shmo's smoothly offers the best of both worlds – families with kids by day, and couples and groups of friends at night. The restaurant is large enough for waiting staff to seat people with children away from the mainstream clientele of troughing couples, and everyone is happy. On a weekend lunchtime, it positively embraced the onslaught, with a sensibly compiled children's menu, high chairs and a tolerant attitude to roving toddlers. The menu helps make it versatile, with nearly as many milkshakes as cocktails among the options. The food is good value and substantial. For starters, crayfish popcorn arrived hot, if less crisp than the name implied, while rib fingers were tender and smoky. Mains include burgers (thick and juicy), steaks, grilled chicken dishes and plenty of good salad options. Children can have a scaled-down burger, a proper hot dog, salmon steak and salad, pasta or chicken, as well as a drink, for £4.45. Puds, which may be their excellent shakes or malts, are £1.80. The presence of liquorice and caramel ice-cream on the pudding menu was a bonus – it's delightful.
Babies and children welcome: children's menu; high chairs. Disabled: toilet. No-smoking tables. Tables outdoors (2, pavement).
For branch see index.

East
Docklands

★ Curve
London Marriott, West India Quay, 22 Hertsmere Road, E14 4ED (7093 1000 ext 2622). Canary Wharf tube/DLR/West India Quay DLR. **Breakfast served** 6.30-11am Mon-Fri; 7-11am Sat, Sun. **Lunch served** noon-2.30pm, **dinner served** 5-10.30pm daily. **Main courses** £10-£22. **Credit** AmEx, DC, JCB, MC, V.
Opened in 2004, this sleekly appointed waterfront restaurant has maintained its high standards while racking up a devoted following. It makes the most of its Docklands location – on sunny days there are plenty of tables outside for a pre-dinner cocktail and some people-watching. The clientele is largely fuelled by their expense accounts, but the place still manages a bit of romance. The menu focuses on modern American cuisine with an emphasis on steaks and seafood. All the fish is purchased each morning from nearby Billingsgate Market; our calamari, flash-fried in a light tempura

batter, was among the best we've ever had – if it had been any fresher it would have wiggled. Another starter of New England clam chowder was delicately seasoned, with a light hand on the cream. For mains, surf and turf skewers mixed big, tender chunks of fillet steak with enormous char-grilled prawns and crisp fries, while dover sole was light and lemony, and moreish mussels marinier (sic) featured a delicate white wine sauce. The beautifully presented food, friendly service and lovely views make this one of our favourites.
Babies and children welcome: children's menu; crayons; high chairs. Booking advisable. Disabled: toilet (in hotel). No smoking. Tables outdoors (12, terrace).

North East
South Woodford

Yellow Book Californian Café
190 George Lane, E18 1AY (8989 3999/ www.theyellowbook.co.uk). South Woodford tube. **Lunch served** noon-2.30pm Mon-Fri. **Dinner served** 6-10pm Mon; 6-11pm Tue-Fri. **Meals served** noon-11pm Sat; noon-10pm Sun. **Main courses** £6.95-£15.45. **Set lunch** £6.75 1 course incl drink. **Credit** AmEx, MC, V.
Tucked away in far east London at the edge of Essex, this place has grown in our estimation over time. Its sunny decor of golden walls and rustic wooden tables is welcoming, the prices are fair, and the waiting staff may be young but they're helpful and friendly – we visited on a busy Friday night and they never dropped the ball. The menu is gratifyingly varied. Starters of nachos were crisp and cheesy, while the houmous plate was beautifully served with angular flatbread nicely arranged in the lemony chickpea dip. A main of goat's cheese quesadilla was big and surprisingly hearty, packed with salty cheese and flavoured with well-balanced spices. The thin-crust pizzas are baked in a wood-fired oven, which gives them a great smoky taste. The margherita pizza was an enjoyable variation on the theme, with a tangy, thick tomato sauce lightly kissed with soft cheese. Puddings were the only drawback; the options were limited, and although the brownies

and ice-cream we settled on were fine, the brownies didn't taste own-made. Nevertheless, the Yellow Book is a reliable choice.
Babies and children welcome: high chairs. Bookings not accepted Fri, Sat or for parties of less than 5. No-smoking tables. Tables outdoors (8, patio). Takeaway service (pizza only).

Outer London
Richmond, Surrey

Canyon
The Towpath, nr Richmond Bridge, Richmond, Surrey TW10 6UJ (8948 2944/www.jamies bars.co.uk). Richmond tube/rail. **Brunch served** 11am-3.30pm Sat, Sun. **Lunch served** noon-3.30pm Mon-Fri. **Dinner served** 6-10.30pm daily. **Main courses** £11-£19. **Set lunch** £12.50 2 courses, £15 3 courses. **Credit** AmEx, JCB, MC, V.
This handsome restaurant on the banks of the Thames in Richmond owes that river a great debt. The quality of the food here has been variable for years, and the service can be hit and miss as well, but the sweeping riverside views from the plentiful outdoor tables on the attractive terrace keep the crowds flocking. And it is undeniable that the overall atmosphere is one of seductive, elegant relaxation. The menu changes regularly, but often features uninspired Modern European-influenced American dishes, such as gazpacho soup or endive pear and gorgonzola salad for starters, and roast duck breast with glazed apricots or rump of lamb with greek salad for mains. Even the side dishes (new potatoes, cherry tomato salad) tend to be unambitious and dull. We have been here on several occasions when we have not seen one thing on the menu that made us hungry. Still, the simple fact remains that there are few better places to sit on a sunny evening with a glass of chilled white wine watching the world float by, so Canyon keeps plugging along.
Babies and children welcome: children's menu; high chairs. Booking advisable. Disabled: toilet. Entertainment: jazz 8.30pm Wed. No-smoking tables. Tables outdoors (12, courtyard; 16, terrace).

Pacific Bar & Grill. See p37.

LATIN AMERICAN

While Latin America has cultural cachet for its music and dance, its culinary contribution to London is considerably more low-key. The Argentine parrilla **Santa María del Buen Ayre** continues to wow diners with its no-nonsense offering of mixed grills and friendly waiters, and we're delighted to hear that there are plans to open a second branch in Battersea in late 2006. Another Argentine success story is the long-established Gaucho Grill chain, which successfully revamped its Swallow Street flagship in 2006 – now called **Gaucho Piccadilly**. Both restaurants were contenders for the Best Steak Restaurant category of the 2006 Time Out Eating & Drinking Awards.

Fina Estampa has closed, which means there's only one Peruvian eaterie (Tito's) left in London. Otherwise, **Sabor** remains vivacious, **El Vergel** is as bustling as ever and **Armadillo** seems to be back on track. Real Mexican food (as opposed to Tex-Mex) is a gourmet delight and is deservedly popular in the southern US, but it's just never caught on over here. An attempt to fill the gap is the new **Green & Red**, a stylish tequila bar in east London; despite being more bar than restaurant, we think the food merits a visit too. Green & Red came hot on the heels of **Mestizo** and **Taqueria**, which opened in 2005. Could they be part of a new Mexican wave?

Argentinian

Central
Piccadilly

★ Gaucho Piccadilly
2006 WINNER BEST STEAK RESTAURANT
25 Swallow Street, W1B 4QR (7734 4040/ www.gaucho-grill.com). Piccadilly Circus tube.
Bar **Open** noon-3pm, 5-11pm Mon-Fri; noon-11pm Sat; noon-10.30pm Sun.
Shop **Open** 10am-6pm Mon-Sat.
First-floor restaurant **Lunch served** noon-5pm, **dinner served** 5-11pm Mon-Fri. **Meals served** noon-midnight Sat; noon-10.30pm Sun. **Main courses** £8.50-£32.
Top-floor restaurant **Dinner served** 8pm-1am Wed-Sat. **Main courses** £8.50-£32.
All **Credit** AmEx, DC, MC, V.
This Argentinian steakhouse, the flagship of the Gaucho Grill chain, has gone up in the world – literally: out of its basement and into the handsome upper floors of the building next door. It clearly needed the extra capacity: the house was full on our lunchtime visit, and if there were nine men to every woman, that spoke to the lure of a good steak rather than a macho atmosphere. Also good: the less-camp-than-you'd-think cowhide decor, the easy professionalism of every staff member and the centrality of the chef station/grill. Steaming balls of cheese bread prefaced delicious if not particularly authentic puff-pastry empanadas, and a terrific, tangy hake and prawn ceviche (from a list of six ceviches). Then the steak: rump, sirloin, fillet, ribeye and churrasco de lomo. In lieu of an explanation of the latter we received a demo: the chef deftly opened out a fillet, the better to soak up its olive oil and garlic marinade. We had one he'd prepared earlier, and, like our ribeye, it was wonderfully flavoursome and so tender you could have cut it with a spoon (no steak knives were ever offered). Great thin chips and spicy sweetcorn accompanied, along with a bang-on budget malbec produced for the restaurant. You can also get seafood, burgers, a pasta and a couple of chicken grills, but you'd be missing the point of a restaurant passionate about its speciality. And considering the quality of the food, prices are very keen. The ground floor houses an Argentine wine shop, which turns into a private dining area by night, while the top floor offers a supper lounge with Latino musicians.
Babies and children welcome: high chair. Booking advisable. Entertainment: band/musician 10pm Wed-Sat (top floor restaurant). Top-floor restaurant available for hire (Mon, Tue, Sun). Wine cellar available for hire, seats 100. Wine tastings; phone for details. **Map 17 J7.**
For branches (The Gaucho Grill) see index.

South Kensington

El Gaucho
30B Old Brompton Road, SW7 3DL (7584 8999/ www.elgaucho.co.uk). South Kensington tube.
Meals served 5-11.30pm Mon-Sat; noon-11.30pm Sun. **Main courses** £15-£20.
Set lunch £7.90 1 course. **Credit** AmEx, MC, V.
There's a theme-park feel to this basement bistro, with posters of Evita, Che Guevara and cartoon gauchos splashed on the walls. Yet, the bottled water is Italian, the beers Mexican and Spanish. Post-modern or just sloppy? Perhaps it doesn't matter, as most of the food, from the tasty dips presented with the menu to the classic Latin American mains, is pretty fine. Big beef is the central theme. The rump was sweet and tender, while the massive milanesa (breaded veal cutlet, highly popular in Argentina) was lean, tasty, tender and cooked right through as ordered. To finish, flan (crème caramel) tasted rather sweet and came with dulce de leche as well as bland, unnecessary strawberries. Fairly priced Trapiche wines are on the drinks list, but while these are decent imports from Mendoza, any serious Argentinian restaurant should be importing a wider selection of bottles, including some boutique wines. The venue is warm and cosy, with flamenco and Spanish tunes kept to a chat-friendly volume. The waitresses are jovial too. There's little wrong with El Gaucho, it just needs to smooth the rough edges and be more adventurous.
Babies and children admitted. Booking advisable. Takeaway service. **Map 14 D10.**
For branch see index.

South
Battersea

La Pampa Grill
4 Northcote Road, SW11 1NT (7924 1167). Clapham Junction rail. **Dinner served** 6-11pm Mon-Thur; 6-11.30pm Fri, Sat. **Main courses** £8.50-£16.50. **Credit** MC, V.
In Buenos Aires the whole point of parrillas (steakhouses) is that they never change. In this sense, Clapham's two ranch-style outlets of La Pampa Grill keep the flame burning. They continue to deliver steaks of reasonable girth, red wines of woody elegance and an atmosphere of carnal conviviality. By 9pm tables are invariably full of well-to-do locals (such steaks don't come cheap; it's £14.95 for a medium-sized rump) and there's a buzz in the air. Meat empanadas were juicy and tasty, if costly at £3.75. Side orders of vegetables are well prepared and generous enough to share. Main courses are dominated by steaks; these are grilled with care, but you should err on the side of rare if you like some blood on your plate. Note that there's no choice if you don't eat meat: a miserly situation – even in Argentina hake and squid are common offerings. Desserts are also uninspired, with little but heavyweight dulce de leche pancakes and plain ice-cream. We found the music a mite frantic for winding down, but enjoyed talking to a waiter enthusiastic about cumbia music. In all, this was a variable experience – and the menu certainly needs a tweak.
Booking advisable Fri, Sat. Tables outdoors (7, pavement). **Map 21 C4.**
For branch see index.

North East
Hackney

★ Santa María del Buen Ayre
2006 RUNNER-UP BEST STEAK RESTAURANT
50 Broadway Market, E8 4QJ (7275 9900/ www.buenayre.co.uk). Liverpool Street tube/ rail then 26, 48 or 55 bus/London Fields rail.
Dinner served 6-10.30pm Mon-Fri. **Meals served** noon-10.30pm Sat, Sun. **Main courses** £7-£19. **Credit** AmEx, MC, V.
When *Time Out* gave a glowing review to London's first parrilla grill back in spring 2005, six months after it had opened, we triggered a wave of publicity that made it briefly the restaurant du jour. It became perma-packed, and we were concerned that it might have its head turned and its kitchen overtaxed by all the attention. We needn't have worried. Santa María remains an unpretentious local for Hackneysiders and Argentinians from all over town along with their British friends. The menu remains sensibly straightforward, with little cooking undertaken off-grill. There are snacks for drinkers and Broadway Market visitors (£6 for a great steak sandwich), cold starters and hearty empanadas, a decent vegetarian trio, and then the reason you're here: five Argentinian beef steaks, one veal, some sausages and a variety of parilladas – mini table

BEST LATIN AMERICAN

Best for steak and wine
Gaucho Piccadilly. *See left.*

Best for a neighbourhood vibe
Santa María del Buen Ayre. *See above.*

Best for a long lunch
El Vergel. *See p45.*

Best for cocktails
Floridita. *See right.*

Best for fab fusion
Sabor. *See p45.*

Gaucho Piccadilly

grills bearing an assortment of the above, plus a choice of black pudding, sweetbreads, kidneys and ribs. We've not had a duff dish here, and this time round our ribeye was full of flavour, and our fillet tender without being bland. We also like the authentically sweet deserts and the reasonably priced wine list. The room is long and butter-yellow, with contemporary Argentine pictures and photos on the wall.
Babies and children welcome: high chairs. Booking advisable. Disabled: toilet. No-smoking tables. Tables outdoors (5, garden).

Brazilian

Central
Oxford Street

★ Brasil by Kilo
First floor, 17 Oxford Street, W1D 2DJ (no phone/www.brasilbykilo.co.uk). Tottenham Court Road tube. **Open** 11am-9pm daily. **Buffet** 99p per 100g. **Unlicensed. No credit cards.**
We've never been able to connect how Brazilians walk, dress, look and dance – that's to say, with effortless style – and how they eat. The 'by kilo' system, prevalent throughout urban Brazil, involves diners (often smart office workers) going round vats of pre-prepared rice, beans, vegetables, croquettes and salads and scooping them on to a plate before queuing to weigh the lot and pay for each gram of their grub. Somehow such a system seems to suit this manic, style-devoid corner of London, and, fortunately, the food on show is mostly fresh, tasty and filling. It's homely fare forged by a mixing of African and Portuguese palates. Highlights include the frango ensopado (chicken sautéed with spices), deep-fried banana and

roast pork, alongside the staple accompaniments of rice, beans, cheesy bread and salad. Brazil's 'national dish', feijoada (slow-cooked pork and bean stew) is often available and is not to be missed. If all this seems heavy and you need some vitamins and fibre, try some stimulating guaraná or one of the fruit juices, made from cupuaçu, cashew flower, and passionfruit, imported as frozen purées from Brazil. Desserts are quite sugary; the lightest and most subtle is probably the classic pudim caramel.
Babies and children welcome: high chairs. No smoking. Takeaway service. **Map 17 K6.**

West
Westbourne Grove

Rodizio Rico
111 Westbourne Grove, W2 4UW (7792 4035). Bayswater tube. **Lunch served** noon-4.30pm Sat. **Dinner served** 6-11.30pm Mon-Sat. **Meals served** 12.30-10.30pm Sun. **Set buffet** £11.90 vegetarian, £18 barbecue. **Credit** MC, V.
Before you get meat at a Brazilian buffet, you must serve yourself rice, feijão (beans) and farofa (manioc flour), as well as drab salads, and perhaps some fried seafood. On a Friday night at Rodizio Rico, this first stage can become an ordeal. Booking for 8.30pm we beat the worst of the rush, but by 9.30pm there were people smashing into each other just to scoop a few stewed beans. Then came the waiters with their 'swords' – long skewers bearing trophies of tender meat. Best were the pork and chicken sausages, the chicken hearts and a minty lamb kebab. Less interesting was the silverside, which was dry, and the supposedly nobler cuts of beef. Worse was the sheer breathlessness of the outing. Swords came in volleys, so you had barely digested another little birdy heart before a hot, sweating skewer laden with pork appeared.

Desserts were glass bowls of luridly coloured goo. For a brash, lively night of decent-quality fast food, this is great; but don't bring a date. The Notting Hill branch is warm and wooden in style, and cosier than the newer Islington outlet – or more claustrophobic, depending on your point of view.
Babies and children welcome: high chairs. Booking advisable; essential dinner. Separate room for parties, seats 55. Tables outdoors (6, pavement). **Map 7 B6. For branch see index.**

Cuban

Central
Soho

Floridita
100 Wardour Street, W1F 0TN (7314 4000/ www.floriditalondon.com). Tottenham Court Road tube. **Meals served** 5.30pm-1am Mon-Wed; 5.30pm-1.30am Thur-Sat. **Main courses** £13.50-£35. **Admission** (after 6.30pm Thur-Sat) £10. **Credit** AmEx, DC, MC, V.
The Cuban original, in Old Havana, is a gorgeous bar with a stuffy restaurant at the back. This Conran-run franchise is a much more glitzy affair that strives to combine restaurant, private members' club, smoking den, cabaret and cocktail bar. It only partially succeeds and the vast open space (which once housed Mezzo) – and live music – means there's much background noise if you come for dinner. That said, chef Andrew Rose has done his homework and serves the kind of dishes Cubans used to eat in the 1940s, including salt cod and parsley croquettes, sweet Cuban lobster, a wonderful suckling pig dish, and immense steaks (from Argentina). The red snapper comes charred

with a spicy coating, but just isn't very fishy once you peel back the onions and garlic. As an accompaniment, ask for 'Moors and Christians' (black beans and rice) and a side salad. The tres leches chocolate cake looked awesome, but didn't really deliver. Staff are quite attentive and very attractive, as you'd expect, and the Mojitos and Daiquiris are among the best in London. Floridita can't replicate the glamour of Cuba, but it's great for a night of dancing and drinking – with eating as an option.

Booking advisable. Disabled: toilet. Entertainment: DJ/band 8pm Mon-Sat. Separate rooms for parties, seating 6 and 56. **Map 17 K6**.

Mexican & Tex-Mex

Central

Fitzrovia

Mestizo

103 Hampstead Road, NW1 3EL (7387 4064/ www.mestizomx.com). Warren Street tube/Euston tube/rail. **Lunch served** noon-4pm Mon-Sat. **Dinner served** 6-11.30pm Mon-Sat; 6-10.30pm Sun. **Main courses** £9.50-£14.50. **Credit** MC, V.
This friendly little place is a true rarity, a genuine Mexican restaurant – not Tex-Mex, Flori-Mex, Cali-Mex or any of the other variations on the Mex theme. With a few exceptions, the menu sticks to classic Mexican cooking like an iguana clings to a stone wall on a hot day. Service can be slow and laid-back, but be patient, as you'll be rewarded. To start, the flautas (finely chopped chicken and spices rolled in corn tortillas and fried crisp) were served with a bit too much tangy green tomatillo sauce for our taste, but were fresh and delicious. The ensalada de nopales (salad of lettuce and pickled cactus) was sour and tangy: strangely appealing. Sopa de tortilla, a clean smoky chicken broth, was served with creamy avocado, salty Mexican cheese and dried chillies – and tasted incredible. For mains, we tried a moreish enchiladas pollo (spiced chicken wrapped in tortillas and drizzled with another amazing sauce). There's also a long, addictive menu of tacos, which you dress to your taste, along with plenty of Mexican beer and pricey pitchers of Margaritas. This is the real deal.
Babies and children welcome: high chairs. Booking advisable weekends. Disabled: toilet. No-smoking tables. Separate room for parties, holds 150. Takeaway service. **Map 3 J3**.

La Perla

11 Charlotte Street, W1T 1RQ (7436 1744/ www.cafepacifico-laperla.com). Goodge Street or Tottenham Court Road tube. **Bar Open** 5-11pm Mon-Sat. **Restaurant Meals served** noon-10pm Mon-Sat; 5-9pm Sun. **Main courses** £7.95-£13.95. **Both Credit** AmEx, MC, V.
Tex-Mex food with a touch of sophistication is what this compact little place aims to offer – along with a strong emphasis on Margaritas. You can have Margaritas gold, have them silver, on the rocks, frozen, with salt, without it… the options are virtually limitless. And these cocktails are, indeed, very tasty. The food menu is not as long or innovative as the drinks list, which gives you an idea of what's the priority here. Still, the dishes are flavourful and interesting, so if you can find the time between your frosty pitchers of tequila-based goodness, you might want to try the 'street tacos': big platters of half a dozen tacos, each with a different filling ranging from smoky prawns to spicy chicken to rich shredded pork, served with a large bowl of refried beans. Another option, the tostadas, resemble flat tacos: a crispy corn tortilla piled high with beans, grilled chicken or beef, salad and creamy sour cream. There are also sizzling fajitas (always reliable), which, for many people, will be big enough to share.
Babies and children admitted (restaurant). Booking advisable. **Map 9 J5**.
For branches see index.

Trafalgar Square

Texas Embassy Cantina

1 Cockspur Street, SW1Y 5DL (7925 0077/ www.texasembassy.com). Charing Cross tube/rail. **Meals served** noon-11pm Mon-Wed; noon-midnight Thur-Sat; noon-10.30pm Sun. **Main courses** £7.50-£16.95. **Credit** AmEx, DC, MC, V.
A big, boisterous barn of a restaurant, the Texas Embassy is brazenly staked out at the edge of Trafalgar Square. Here it puzzles tourists who didn't know that American states got their own embassies in London (they don't, though Texas was independent for ten years from 1836). In the past, this place has dazzled us with its country music and sexy tomato salsa, but on this visit… not so much. The food seemed to be thrown together carelessly, the waiters were kind but didn't appear to be particularly content, and the mood was, in all, a little cool. We started with chile con queso (chillies and cheese dip), which arrived as a soup bowl filled with melted cheese but no visible chillies; it was too large a portion, lacking in finesse. A main course fajita salad featured plenty of crisp greens, but the chicken was abysmally tough and dry; to liken it to shoe leather would be both clichéd and accurate. Combination fajitas were fresher and tastier, but we were still not ready to forgive the Embassy for that chicken. Improvement needed.
Babies and children welcome: children's menu; crayons; high chairs. Booking advisable. Disabled: toilet. Separate room for parties, seats 120. Tables outdoors (8, pavement). **Map 17 K7**.

West

Notting Hill

★ Taqueria

139-143 Westbourne Grove, W11 2RS (7229 4734). Notting Hill Gate tube. **Meals served** noon-11pm Mon-Thur; noon-11.30pm Fri, Sat. **Main courses** £2.50-£5.50. **Set lunch** £5.50-£7.50 1 course. **Credit** MC, V.
Taqueria is a small, casual eaterie with white walls, polished dark wood and cool light fixtures that manages, somehow, to look very Latin American. It's loosely based on the corner taco shops that pack in lunchtime crowds in Florida, California and Texas. It opened with great promise in 2005, but almost immediately began attracting bad reviews. The service was rubbished as slow, the food condemned as strange, the queues lined up outside dismissed as clueless. The criticism is unnecessarily harsh. Yes, the service can be amateurish, and yes, sometimes the tacos arrive colder than we might have hoped, but in general Taqueria provides good, cheap food. Tacos are the house special – as the name implies – and most use soft corn tortillas made fresh in-house (a rarity in London), topped with what seems like everything in the kitchen: marinated tuna, spicy chicken, black beans, roast peppers, potatoes and cheese… you name it. Regular specials, to have with or instead of the tacos, include huevos rancheros (fried eggs with beans and salsa) and enchiladas (corn tortillas, filled, rolled up and baked). There are also side salads, rice and beans, and (relatively) cold Mexican beers.
Babies and children welcome: high chairs. Bookings not accepted. No smoking. **Map 7 A6**.

South

Clapham

★ Café Sol

56 Clapham High Street, SW4 7UL (7498 9319/ www.cafesol.net). Clapham Common or Clapham North tube. **Meals served** noon-midnight Mon-Thur, Sun; noon-1am Fri, Sat. **Main courses** £5.95-£10.95. **Credit** AmEx, DC, MC, V.
This Clapham stalwart is a classic Tex-Mex restaurant. The vast dining room has been decorated to look like a Mexican restaurant in Texas, with sunny paintings, arched doorways, and wooden tables and chairs shoved close

together. It's ideal for groups of friends, which explains why most tables are packed with large parties. The menu may be basic by-the-book burritos 'n' tacos fare, but it's consistently well done, and service is friendly. Join the throngs for big plates of cheesy nachos with beans, salsa, sour cream and plentiful jalapeño chillies. Then you can move on to the enchiladas (chicken, with a tart creamy sauce, beef with a tangy tomato salsa, or tasty mixed veg) with heaps of rice and beans. Or dive into the beef or chicken fajitas, which are served steaming up a storm with a large plate of salad, salsa and extras to pile on top and roll into a tasty hand-held sandwich. There are also tacos, and a genuinely good taco salad, which arrives in a 'bowl' made of a fried flour tortilla, filled to the brim with crisp greens and fresh fajita chicken. This place gets seriously packed as the night goes on, so arrive early to avoid the crowds.
Babies and children welcome: high chairs. Booking essential dinner Fri, Sat. Disabled: toilet. Entertainment: DJ 11pm Fri, Sat. No-smoking tables. Tables outdoors (6, pavement). Takeaway service. **Map 22 B1**.

East

Bethnal Green

★ Green & Red NEW

51 Bethnal Green Road, E1 6LA (7749 9670/ www.greenred.co.uk). Liverpool Street tube/rail. **Open** 5.30pm-midnight Mon-Fri; noon-midnight Sat; noon-11.30pm Sun. **Lunch served** noon-5pm daily. **Dinner served** 6-11pm Mon-Sat; 6-10.30pm Sun. **Main courses** £9.40-£14.50. **Credit** AmEx, MC, V.
If tequila is the ultimate no-brainer party drink, then Green & Red – with a choice of over 100 dangerous-looking tequilas – should be the ultimate no-brainer party venue. But it's more considered than that. Inspired by the Jalisco region of coastal Mexico, this wood-slatted proposition makes most bar-cantinas look as authentic as a pasty holiday-maker arriving in a sombrero at Heathrow. Dishes deploy everything from the mild smokiness of chipotles to hotly fruity habaneros, but none could be called intensely fiery. For that pleasure, add the house salsas. Plump, char-grilled shrimps made a good starter, as did the 'chile relleno' stuffed with herby ewe's milk cheese. All mains arrive with mini rounds of hand-pressed tortillas, plus dinky pots of refried beans, shredded cabbage salad and salsas: fodder for sharing. Slow-roasted pork belly seemed better suited to the tortilla treatment than did the baked sea bream, but as stand-alone dishes each fared well. In the basement is a DJ bar. A monthly Tequila Club helps you say *adios* to slammers by savouring the distinctive flavours of anything from earthy lowland tequilas to ones that have been wood-aged for up to five years.
Babies and children welcome: high chair. Disabled: toilet. Entertainment: DJs 8pm Fri, Sat. Tables outdoors (6, terrace). **Map 6 S4**.

Pan-American

South West

Fulham

1492

404 North End Road, SW6 1LU (7381 3810/ www.1492restaurant.com). Fulham Broadway tube. **Dinner served** 6pm-midnight Mon-Fri. **Meals served** 12.30pm-midnight Sat; 12.30-11pm Sun. **Main courses** £8.50-£19. **Credit** AmEx, MC, V.
It was hot and noisy on a Friday night at this conquistador-tribute restaurant. Many customers were Latinos. The staff seemed to be having more fun than their guests, as if work was a (minor) inconvenience. The kitchen comes up with ostensibly inventive ideas, but we didn't get the feeling that spices and sauces were fine-tuned. Our ribeye steak was satisfactory, but the fish curry

RESTAURANTS

Green & Red. See p43.

was nothing like the moqueca you might find in Salvador. Yes, it seemed pungent and looked plentiful, but the taste was monotonous and the fishiness was almost completely drowned by a yellowish goo. The mixed salad wasn't very mixed and the 'chimmichurri' simply wasn't the genuine Argentinian herby dip we'd hoped for. The Tierra del Fuego wine was fine, and the passionfruit mousse was probably the best thing we ate all night – but it arrived rather too late to salvage a very ordinary meal. The 'Latin fusion' ambitions of 1492 deserve praise, but the owner, cooks and waiters need to work much harder to deliver it. *Babies and children welcome: children's menu; high chairs. Booking advisable. No-smoking tables. Separate room for parties, seats 30.* **Map 13 A13**.

South East
London Bridge & Borough

★ El Vergel
8 Lant Street, SE1 1QR (7357 0057/ www.elvergel.co.uk). Borough tube. **Meals served** 8.30am-3pm Mon-Fri. **Main courses** £3.80-£6. **No credit cards**.
Those of us not fortunate enough to live in Borough are still waiting for El Vergel to branch out and become a citywide chain. But apart from the catering arm, it's unlikely you could replicate this charming snack bar and its highly personalised attention to detail. For the perfect lunch here, arrive late – when most of the local office workers have moved on. Armed with a magazine or book, indulge in a tortilla crammed with refried beans, spring onion, coriander and guacamole. There's even some feta cheese in there, proving the Chilean owners aren't bent on a purist Latino recipe but only believe in tasty food. If you want a larger lunch, try one of the tender steaks smeared with avocado and tomato. Or a stew: the chicken broth is the light option, but the lamb stew is bolder and packs a peppery punch. There's also the Chilean signature dish, pastel de choclo (corn pie), which is sweet and creamy, but probably needs some aji (hot sauce) to liven it up. The waitresses are among the sweetest and chattiest in town, and the coffee is strong enough to get you on your feet if you don't have the option of a siesta. *Babies and children admitted. No smoking. Tables outdoors (10, pavement). Takeaway service.* **Map 11 P9**.

North East
Hackney

Armadillo
41 Broadway Market, E8 4PH (7249 3633/ www.armadillorestaurant.co.uk). Liverpool Street tube/rail then 26, 48 or 55 bus/London Fields rail. **Meals served** 6.30-10.30pm Tue-Sat. **Main courses** £7.50-£11. **Credit** AmEx, DC, JCB, MC, V.
After an up-and-down 2004-05, Armadillo is back with a vengeance, and Brazilian-born chef/owner Rogerio David has livened up the service as well as the kitchen. The menu changes regularly, though a few faves – steaks, spicy dips, vegetable pickles – remain in place. You can explore about five countries during one dinner here, taking in the likes of fanesca (Ecuadorian salt cod soup with dumplings), Andean sweet corn humitas (wraps), and Peruvian ceviche (lime-marinated raw fish: rather like sushi with character and the best starter). Some dishes are highly novel, including quail smoked in maté, the bitter tea Argentinean gauchos suck on. Both our duck breast and rice with sultanas and pea guacamole, and roast suckling pig were outstanding. As well as Argentinean and Chilean wines (and a spirited Mexican syrah) the bar makes mean Margaritas and Pisco Sours, and also serves tequilas, rums and imported beers – so you needn't stray once to the Old World. Guava ice-cream, quince jelly and manchego cheese round off this bud-tingling experience. The restaurant – subdued in style, with tasteful artwork – is intimate verging on cramped,

with a little garden at the back for hot evenings and a bookable room for groups upstairs. *Babies and children welcome: high chairs. Booking advisable; essential Fri, Sat. Separate room for parties, seats 30. Tables outdoors (1, balcony; 4, garden).*

North
Islington

Sabor
108 Essex Road, N1 8LX (7226 5551/ www.sabor.co.uk). Angel tube/Essex Road rail/ 19, 38, 73 bus. **Lunch served** noon-2.30pm, **dinner served** 5-11pm Mon-Sat. **Main courses** £8-£15.50. **Set lunch** £10 2 courses, £12.50 3 courses. **Credit** MC, V.
You rarely see the words 'Latin American cuisine' alongside the term 'experimental', but Sabor takes fusion into the realms of culinary science fiction. Empanadas are usually stuffed with cheese or minced beef, but here they get fillings of crab, plantain, mint and garlic. Escabeche pickles are soaked in a sherry vinaigrette; ginger adds verve to the clam chowder. Among the newfangled mains are rabbit in chocolate sauce, lamb with healthy quinoa, and even the steak is paired with plantain instead of the usual salad or fries. It's as if the chef has decided to stay almost faithful to the ingredients, but be wanton in their exploitation. Combine the gusto and good humour of the menu with personable waiters, chilled music and some fair-priced set menus and you can see why Sabor is thriving in Islington. For drinks, choose between New World wines (including an Argentinean champaña) and nourishing, fresh cupuaçu, acerola and cashew juices. Desserts include all the chocolate cakes, sorbets and dulce de leche biscuits so beloved of Latino diners, but there are also some great Iberian cheeses and a Luigi Bosca dessert wine. The decor is bright, bubbly and full of pinks and yellows – eating here feels a bit like dining inside one of Del Boy's cocktails. *Babies and children welcome: high chairs. Booking advisable. Disabled: toilet.* **Map 5 P1**.

Peruvian

South East
London Bridge & Borough

★ Tito's
4-6 London Bridge Street, SE1 9SG (7407 7787). London Bridge tube/rail. **Lunch served** noon-3pm Mon-Fri. **Dinner served** 6-11pm Tue-Fri. **Meals served** noon-11pm Sat, Sun. **Main courses** £7.90-£13.50. **Set lunch** £7.90 3 courses. **Credit** AmEx, MC, V.
Very much a cantina, Tito's is designed to offer London Bridge's office workers a break from chilled sandwiches and crisps. It's a bit basic for an evening excursion, unless you've spent months in Lima and have got used to zero-atmosphere dining and hearty food. Nonetheless, we gave it a go, and the combination of traditional ceviche (fresh raw fish marinated in lime, with onions and sweet potato) followed by rice, yucca, pumpkin and fried prawns was impressive. The vegetables and fish were carefully spiced, and tastier than the maize-heavy dishes served in many Colombian cantinas. Both items were vast, so it's best to share. We even managed a fruit cocktail and ice-cream and a glass of Inca Kola between the beers. With the waitresses more relaxed and caring than at lunch, the place even managed to be a bit romantic in a lovers-down-at-heel kind of way. It's an ideal spot to down a Pisco Sour and enjoy an authentic experience, and now that nearby Fina Estampa has closed, Tito's is London's surviving temple of Peruvian reality – rather like the Machu Picchu ruin that adorns its menu. *Babies and children welcome: high chairs. Booking advisable weekends. Entertainment: samba class 6.30pm Thur; salsa class 6.30pm Fri. Separate room for parties, seats 60.* **Map 12 Q8**.

Interview
HUW GOTT

Who are you?
Co-owner, with Will Beckett, of **Green & Red** (see p43), **Hawksmoor** (see p33), the **Marquess Tavern** (see p114), and DJ bar the **Redchurch** (107 Redchurch Street, E2 7DL, 7729 8333). We also have Underdog, a consultancy and accountancy firm for independent bars and restaurants.
Eating in London: what's good about it?
Diversity. Turn left out of my flat and there's a cluster of great Vietnamese places, turn right they're Turkish, and straight on Bengali and Pakistani. And there are lots of small independents doing interesting, original things.
What's bad about it?
The high churn rate. Lots of good independents go bust because they don't fully get to grips with the business side of things. They don't have the skills or support to deal with planning, licensing, accounting, payroll, hiring and firing regulations and general government red tape. Especially with the rise of chains that nab the best sites, push up rents and put pressure on pricing.
Which are your favourite London restaurants?
For a cheese fix, the back room at **La Fromagerie** (see p298). **Huong Viet** (see p287), my local Vietnamese: they do a great sweet tofu dessert. For something a bit more upmarket, **Roka** (see p185) or **Yauatcha** (see p70).
What single thing would most improve London's restaurant scene?
Using better ingredients. My mum has got a great café in Shropshire (Berry's, Church Stretton), where they source all their ingredients locally, cook them simply and don't charge a fortune.
Any hot tips for the coming year?
I think we'll see less fusion and things prefixed by the word 'modern', and more straightforward, regional food – British, Chinese and east European.

RESTAURANTS

Brasseries

Compared to most European cities, London is now a great place to be if you're feeling peckish and thirsty at 3pm. Most central London pubs stay open all afternoon, and so do many of the capital's cheaper pit-stops: Japanese noodle bars, Middle Eastern kebab specialists, home-grown pie and mash shops and caffs, and Chinatown's dim sum specialists. Nevertheless, since the licensing laws were relaxed in the 1990s, brasseries – whose aim is to provide drinks plus casual, speedy dining (from snacks to a full meal), throughout the day – have grown increasingly popular. There are now some excellent examples of the genre, including **Flâneur Food Hall** and the **Depot**, where expert sourcing of ingredients has produced rich dividends. Newcomer **High Road Brasserie** is a welcome addition to the west London dining scene.

Central
City

Just The Bridge
1 Paul's Walk, Millennium Bridge North Side, EC4V 3QQ (7236 0000/www.justthebridge.com). St Paul's tube/Blackfriars tube/rail.
Bar **Open** *Easter-Sept* 11am-10pm Mon-Fri; 6-11pm Sat. *Oct-Easter* 11am-10pm Mon-Fri. **Main courses** £4-£7.
Restaurant **Lunch served** noon-3pm Mon-Fri. **Dinner served** *Easter-Sept* 6-10pm Mon-Sat. *Oct-Easter* 6-10pm Mon-Fri. **Main courses** £10.50-£15.
Both **Credit** AmEx, DC, JCB, MC, V.
This light, spacious room with its slightly dated 1990s decor is just across the Millennium Bridge from Tate Modern, which explains the mix of City office groups and London visitors dining here. The menu is mostly a mixture of westernised Thai, Italian and the odd British dish (such as Aberdeen Angus steak or char-grilled calf's liver). Oriental breast of duck arrived well done, yet was still tender, with a curious mixture of pickled ginger (the pink sushi variety) plus a few large slices of mango in the accompanying noodles. The desserts were much better. Classic British choices included sticky toffee pudding or summer berries with clotted cream. Our waitress recommended the eton mess, which was perfectly presented with a disc of crunchy meringue on the base, topped with a gentle mound of whipped cream folded with blueberries, raspberries, chopped strawberries and more crushed-up meringue; this was surrounded by two syrups, of tangy lemon, and strawberry. The lemon syrup was perfect for the richness of the cream and sweet meringue. At £7, it was the most expensive dessert, but worth it. Familiar wine countries make up the wine list, with bottle prices mainly in the £15-£25 range.
Babies and children admitted. Booking advisable Wed-Sat. Disabled: toilet. Restaurant and bar available for hire. Tables outdoors (11, terrace). **Map 11 O7.**

Clerkenwell & Farringdon

Brasserie de Malmaison
Malmaison, 18-21 Charterhouse Square, EC1M 6AH (7012 3700/www.malmaison.com). Barbican tube/Farringdon tube/rail. **Brunch served** 11am-3pm Sun. **Lunch served** noon-2.30pm Mon-Sat. **Dinner served** 6-10.30pm daily. **Main courses** £12-£20. **Set lunch** £14.50 3 courses (minimum 2). **Set dinner** £15.95 2 courses, £17.95 3 courses. **Credit** AmEx, DC, JCB, MC, V.

What initially looks like a rather dark (though groovy) basement bar opens out to reveal a reasonably illuminated, modern restaurant. True, the furniture and wall colours are best suited to winter months, but it's not a gloomy setting. During the week the place does a brisk trade with local business people and nearby residents; weekends see more mini-breakers. And the brasserie deserves to be busy: the food is much better than hotel food often is, and the set lunch is a really great deal. £12.50 bought a very decent two courses – roast cod with crushed potatoes followed by mango, payaya and pineapple salad with a dollop of lemon sorbet. The main menu is a user-friendly mix of classics tweaked just enough to make them interesting; the shrimp cocktail, for example, is very prettily arranged. There are salads (seared tuna niçoise scored highly), a variety of oysters, steaks and burgers, plus the likes of charcuterie plates, spinach and ricotta cannelloni, and lemon sole goujons with fat chips. French bread comes on a board with butter and tapanade; coffee comes with little glasses of chocolate mousse. Service is attentive and the vibe relaxed – shame it's not open true brasserie hours.
Babies and children welcome: high chairs. Booking advisable. Disabled: toilet. No smoking. Separate rooms for parties, seating 16 and 30. **Map 3 O3.**

★ Flâneur Food Hall
41 Farringdon Road, EC1M 3JB (7404 4422/ www.flaneur.com). Farringdon tube/rail. **Open** 8.30am-10pm Mon-Sat; 10am-6pm Sun. **Breakfast served** 8.30-10.30am, **lunch served** noon-3pm Mon-Fri. **Brunch served** 9am-4pm Sat, Sun. **Dinner served** 6-10pm Mon-Sat. **Main courses** £8.50-£15.50. **Set menu** £18 2 courses, £21 3 courses. **Credit** AmEx, JCB, MC, V.
This slightly unassuming storefront on an entirely unprepossessing stretch of Farringdon Road may not look like much from the outside, but don't be deterred. Behind the plain frontage lie two related enterprises, each well worthy of investigation. As you enter, the most obvious of the pair is the capacious food hall, its towering shelves lined tidily with gourmet goodies and artisanal delights. Tucked away towards the back are around 15 tables; together they comprise a restaurant that, almost casually, manages to be terrific. The kitchen staff are kept on their toes by a pair of menus that often change: one lists appetising breakfasts; the other encompasses lunches and dinners that, on the whole, either acknowledge a Mediterranean influence or nod at gastropub culture. There's also a weekend brunch, very welcome in a city with surprisingly few decent brunch options. Sweetcorn

fritters and bacon was delicious, but overshadowed by a positively awesome full english breakfast that really showed just how well Flâneur sources its ingredients. Before ordering desserts, take a sneaky peek at them in the cabinet display; you'll find it impossible to resist the banana walnut cake with toffee sauce.
Babies and children admitted. Booking advisable. No smoking. Takeaway service. **Map 5 N5.**

Covent Garden

Café des Amis
11-14 Hanover Place, WC2E 9JP (7379 3444/ www.cafedesamis.co.uk). Covent Garden tube.
Bar **Open** 11.30am-1am Mon-Sat.
Restaurant **Meals served** 11.30am-11.30pm Mon-Sat. **Main courses** £13.50-£20.50. **Set meal** (11.30am-7pm, 10-11.30pm Mon-Sat) £14.50 2 courses, £16.50 3 courses.
Both **House wine** £15.75 bottle, £4.05 glass. **Credit** AmEx, DC, MC, V.
Perhaps it's the location (just off Long Acre) that ensures this place is always busy. The setting is nice enough – an open-plan dining room on the ground floor, swanky wine bar downstairs – and the atmosphere is lively. But the food on our last visit was pretty disappointing. A starter of grilled tiger prawns with garlic, chilli and gremolata – which arrived just as the bread was being brought to the table – was OK, but the prawns were verging on mushy and the sauce was chilli-hot yet bland. A main of roast rack of new season lamb with spinach, artichoke hearts and thyme arrived slightly pink, even though we'd asked for it well done; while the quality of the meat was impressive, there was little else of note about it. The dish seemed to sum up the whole meal: lukewarm and boring. One of the simpler fish dishes – mussels marinière – was equally unmemorable. Indeed, the highlights were a zingy herb salad with garlic vinaigrette, and a stunning raspberry crème brûlée – and if that's as good as it gets, we're at a loss to explain this place's popularity. Ah, it'll be the location, then.
Babies and children admitted. Booking advisable Thur-Sat. No-smoking. Separate room for parties, seats 80. Tables outdoors (12, terrace). **Map 18 L6.**

Fitzrovia

RIBA Café
66 Portland Place, W1B 1AD (7631 0467/ www.riba.org). Great Portland Street or Oxford Circus tube. **Meals served** 8am-6pm Mon-Fri; 9am-4pm Sat. **Main courses** (noon-3pm Mon-Fri; 9am-4pm Sat) £5.50-£12.95. **Set meal** (Mon-Fri) £12.95 1 course, £16.95 2 courses, £20.95 3 courses. **Credit** AmEx, DC, MC, V.
Not your average office canteen, this – unless your office happens to be the Royal Institute of British Architects. The listed 1930s building retains its lovely interior, right down to the detail on the signage. The café shares the first floor with exhibitions, pillars and a lot of space and light. With unobtrusive but stylish design (we love those semi-circular couches), smart and respectful service and generous spacing between tables, this is a serene and rather special place: particularly good for long catch-ups or business lunches (though there's an express menu if you need it). Set against the flawless background, our food was a tad disappointing on a recent visit, although still pretty good for the price bracket. The menu eschews red meat, proffering seared, smoked and roasted fish, along with poultry and veg dishes in simple modern presentations. Roasted sea bream with a bean and tomato salad was punchy and satisfying; char-grilled baby plaice seemed a bit overwhelmed by its own treatment; and marinated strawberries were nicely accented by a champagne granita. We ate on the spacious terrace with its designer fountain and purple plantings: one of London's best summer secrets.
Babies and children welcome: high chairs. Booking advisable. Disabled: lift; toilet. No smoking. Tables outdoors (20, terrace). Separate rooms for parties, seating 280. **Map 3 H4.**

Mayfair

Truc Vert

42 North Audley Street, W1K 6ZR (7491 9988/ www.trucvert.co.uk). Bond Street tube. **Meals served** 7.30am-9.30pm Mon-Sat; 9.30am-3pm Sun. **Main courses** £12.50-£17. **Credit** AmEx, MC, V.

Alfresco diners at this Mayfair brasserie/deli needn't worry about handbag-snatching while they eat, thanks to the Uzi-toting cops on view outside the US Embassy opposite. Light, inviting and with a rustic beach-hut feel, Truc Vert is commendably convenient for deli staples (Spanish cheeses, Italian charcuterie, French honey, preserves, smoked meats and fish) and as a venue for pleasant all-day dining or weekend brunch, although prices reflect its location. Simple home-style cooking (everything is own-made on site; the menu changes daily) has a Gallic-Mediterranean slant: seared wild boar medallions, fish soup, merguez sausage, grilled lamb cutlets. Vegetarian choices are limited. Buffalo mozzarella with marinated peppers and courgettes was fresh, flavoursome and light on oil; we also ordered a bowl of plentiful but unremarkable chunky chips. Our Gressingham duck breast, served with wilted spinach and roast butternut squash, was nicely roasted although slightly overseasoned. Desserts include chilled lemon soufflé (too sweet and more like shop-bought mousse), tarts and ice-cream. The young French staff are pleasant enough once you've gained their attention, but on our visit concentrated on chatting among themselves.
Babies and children welcome: high chairs. Booking advisable. No smoking. Tables outdoors (6, pavement). Takeaway service. **Map 9 G6.**

Piccadilly

Zinc Bar & Grill

21 Heddon Street, W1B 4BG (7255 8899). Piccadilly Circus tube. **Bar Open** noon-midnight Mon-Sat. *Restaurant* **Meals served** noon-11pm Mon-Sat; noon-4pm Sun. **Main courses** £9.50-£15.50. *Both* **Credit** AmEx, DC, JCB, MC, V.

Bought by Bank Restaurant Group from Conran Restaurants in 2005, Zinc doesn't seem to have improved since the handover. The name suggests the order of priorities; a zinc bar spans almost the length of the big warehousey space. The menu is laid out like a snacks list, encompassing antipasti, charcuterie, ciabatta sandwiches and sharing dishes such as dips – as well as conventional starters and mains. We enjoyed the over-generous helping (enough for two) of Norwegian prawns, served in a mini bucket, even though they had a metallic thawed-from-frozen flavour. The Loch Fyne smoked salmon was excellent, as you'd expect. Main dishes were less of a hit. The Scottish sirloin steak was a good cut, but arrived barely cooked despite our request for medium rare, and the accompanying béarnaise sauce was overseasoned. Crab with canestrini (little pieces of pasta often used in soup) was a stodgy dish, skimpy on the seafood and with little evidence of the advertised chilli oil; the recipe seemed designed as a pre-binge stomach liner. Still, the outside tables in the cobbled pedestrian street are a find in summer.
Babies and children welcome: high chairs. Booking advisable. Disabled: toilet. No-smoking tables. Separate room for parties, seats 40. Tables outdoors (9, pavement). **Map 17 J7.**
For branch see index.

Soho

Balans

60 Old Compton Street, W1D 4UG (7437 5212/ www.balans.co.uk). Leicester Square or Piccadilly Circus tube. **Meals served** 8am-5am Mon-Thur; 8am-6am Fri, Sat; 8am-2am Sun. **Main courses** £8-£17.50. **Credit** AmEx, MC, V.

Balans has excellent service, a capacious interior (a throwback to the 1980s) and an adventurous and varied menu that is served into the small hours – which all adds up to a competitive edge in Old Compton Street's packed restaurant scene. Very popular with Soho's gay men, it also offers smokers the street-facing front, and non-smokers the cooler, quieter back rooms. Arriving early for dinner on a scorching summer day, we ordered excellent cocktails which we were left to enjoy for as long as we wanted. Around us, people happily tucked into beetroot gravadlax and roast monkfish, chickpea and potato curry, and lamb and pine nut samosas. We opted for pan-fried scallops with sautéed endive, pancetta and sesame soy; and buffalo mozzarella and vine-tomato salad – both were fresh and beautifully presented. Mains matched the quality of presentation, but were otherwise disappointing: haddock fish cakes consisted of stodgy, floury patties of potato and barely there haddock; sea bass was a mean, thin slice of overcooked fish that was dry and tasteless. We passed on the tempting-looking dessert menu and left five hours after we arrived, nicely chilled out thanks to the cool interior and the attentive but unobtrusive service.
Babies and children admitted (until 6pm). Bookings not accepted Fri, Sat. No-smoking tables. **Map 17 K6.**
For branches see index.

Café Bohème

13 Old Compton Street, W1D 5JQ (7734 0623/ www.cafeboheme.co.uk). Leicester Square tube. **Open** 8am-3am Mon-Sat; 8am-10.30pm Sun. **Meals served** 8am-2.30am Mon-Sat; 8am-10pm Sun. **Main courses** £6-£15. **Set meal** (noon-7pm) £11.50 2 courses, £13.50 3 courses. **Cover** (Fri, Sat) £3 10-11pm, £4 after 11pm. **Credit** AmEx, DC, MC, V.

Café Bohème may not be the kind of place you make a special trip to, but if you're looking for somewhere to eat in the West End, it passes muster. A traditional brasserie menu served in a Toulouse-Lautrec-style café is initially appealing, but a restaurant in Old Compton Street filled exclusively with heterosexual couples just feels wrong – and without the Gauloise, so does the Gallic decor. The food's another matter. Leaving aside the fact that a steak frites with béarnaise sauce had to go back because it was stone cold, the flavour and texture of the replacement, and a huge fillet steak with creamy roquefort sauce, couldn't be faulted. The chips and (mixed green) salad panachée served in pretty aluminium pots were crisp and fresh. A pot of moules marinière was equally delicious, as was the bourbon vanilla crème brûlée. A strength of Café Bohème is its wide menu; lots of petits plats and salads mean you don't need to linger. With so many dating couples crammed in around you, that may be just as well.
Babies and children admitted (before 7pm). Entertainment: jazz 4-6pm Thur, Sun. Tables outdoors (9, pavement). **Map 17 K6.**

Randall & Aubin

14-16 Brewer Street, W1F 0SG (7287 4447). Piccadilly Circus tube. **Meals served** noon-11pm Mon-Sat; 4-10.30pm Sun. **Main courses** £7-£18. **Credit** AmEx, DC, JCB, MC, V.

Retaining the original tiled walls, ceiling racks and venetian blinds from its previous incarnation (a much-loved French grocer), R&A throws chandeliers, a mirrorball, haughty staff and uncomfortably loud music into the mix. High stools at cramped counters do little to encourage lingering, and yet R&A is always packed despite plentiful local competition. Seafood is a speciality: a fellow diner raved about the roasted langoustine; our grilled tuna, while not quite cooked to spec, was fresh and flavoursome. Lobster, rock oysters and fruits de mer platters are further options. Meaty choices include beef and spit-roasted chicken from the rotisserie, plus steak, lamb shank and filled baguettes. Vegetarians are limited to starters and side dishes (grilled goat's cheese en croûte was fine, but its accompanying mango and pear chutney was far too sweet, and at £9.50 the dish was pricey). Is it just the Soho location that makes this boisterous brasserie so popular? When a fifth of our bill consisted of service and non-optional cover charges (for unimpressive olives and bread), we resented being selectively ignored by monosyllabic waiters who messed up orders, then sulked. Bad service does not equal 'atmosphere', and certainly not at these prices.
Babies and children admitted. Bookings not accepted. Takeaway service. **Map 17 K6.**

South Kensington

Aubaine

260-262 Brompton Road, SW3 2AS (7052 0100/www.aubaine.co.uk). South Kensington tube. **Meals served** 8am-10.30pm Mon-Sat; 9am-10pm Sun. **Main courses** £9.95-£19.50. **Set dinner** £17.50 2 courses, £21 3 courses. **Credit** AmEx, MC, V.

It's rumoured that the stretch of road by this Kensington honey-pot is a summer traffic blackspot, due to the number of drivers who are distracted by the beautiful women sitting outside. The interior is a cool, industrial grey, with distressed wooden furniture and glass cabinets displaying myriad brightly coloured sweets. A bakery offers freshly baked goodies, while the adjoining restaurant serves classic French brasserie food. Our green bean salad starter was a generous pile of crunchy beans slicked with tangy vinaigrette. Less delightful was a dish of baby aubergines stuffed with bland and undercooked goat's cheese. A juicy fillet of sea bass was delicious, but poorly partnered by an overly sweet carrot purée and orange juice dressing. Most unsatisfying was our coq au vin: chicken joints smothered in a thick, gelatinous gravy that was over-reduced and sour rather than savoury. Salvation came in the form of a lovely sweet-sour tarte citron and a tiny but moreish tarte tatin. Aubaine is wonderful for breads and pastries: we suggest you stick to those.
Babies and children welcome: high chairs. Booking advisable. Disabled: toilet. No smoking. Restaurant available for hire. Tables outdoors (5, pavement). Takeaway service. **Map 14 E10.**

West

Chiswick

★ High Road Brasserie NEW

162-166 Chiswick High Road, W4 1PR (8742 7474/www.highroadhouse.co.uk). Turnham Green tube. **Open** 7am-midnight Mon-Thur; 7am-1am Fri; 8am-1am Sat; 8am-11pm Sun. **Breakfast served** 7am-noon Mon-Fri; 8am-noon Sat, Sun. **Brunch served** noon-5pm Sat, Sun. **Dinner served** 5pm-midnight Mon-Sat; 5-10pm Sun. **Meals served** noon-11pm Mon-Thur; noon-midnight Fri. **Main courses** £10-£22. **Set lunch** £12 2 courses, £15 3 courses. **Credit** AmEx, MC, V.

Nick Jones, owner of the Soho House Group of clubs, bars and restaurants, opened High Road House – a mix of brasserie, private members' club and boutique hotel – in July 2006, and it's been rammed ever since. With its pillars and mirrors, french windows and canopied pavement seats, it's a stunning-looking place; the pewter-topped tables, leather banquettes, marble bar and patchwork-coloured floor tiles are the work of interior designer Ilse Crawford. You can eat lighter options such as club sandwiches or salads, through a good seafood list, to roasted and grilled meats, most of the dishes in the European brasserie mould. This is complemented by a good cocktail list (£5.50-£7.50) and an alluring selection of wine bottles with sufficient choice below £20. The cheapest seafood platter at £25 was still enough oysters whelks, tiger prawns, Dorset crab and half lobster to make two generous starter portions. Choucroute alsacienne is a hard dish to get right, but ours would bring a smile to the lips of a sceptical Strasbourg sourpuss. The dessert menu is a tempting mix of French and English, from caramelised lemon tart to summer pudding. Service was very professional, attentive and charming on our visit – no mean feat in a brasserie that's an instant hit.
Babies and children welcome: children's menu; crayons; high chairs; toys. Booking advisable. Disabled: toilet. Tables outdoors (14, terrace).

Ladbroke Grove

Electric Brasserie

191 Portobello Road, W11 2ED (7908 9696/ www.the-electric.co.uk). Ladbroke Grove tube. **Open** 8am-12.30am Mon-Wed; 8am-1am Thur-Sat; 8am-11.30pm Sun. **Meals served** 8am-11pm Mon-Fri; 8am-5pm, 6-11pm Sat; 8am-5pm, 6-10pm Sun. **Main courses** £9.50-£17.50. **Credit** AmEx, DC, MC, V.
The Electric is all things to all Notting Hillbillies. Next door to the listed art deco Electric cinema, it boasts mosaic floor tiles and chrome finishes in its cavernous interior. The all-day menu offers a European spin to a New York diner theme. This means starters from eggs benedict to grilled scallops, sandwiches from burgers to crayfish on rye, and mains from pork chop to lobster and chips. The salads aren't just for weight-watchers, and the seafood selection offers substantial, sophisticated nibbles. Then there's the trolley dish of the day (suckling pig on Friday) and sundry roasted fish and meats for two (from turbot to chateaubriand). The menu can be bemusing, but a set lunch is mercifully simpler. From a choice of three in each course, smoked haddock fish cakes were more fish than cake, and a good fresh monkfish came with braised roast carrots. Pork chop, sage and onion stuffing with braised cabbage was a hearty repast, and eton mess (strawberries, meringue, cream) made a tidy finish. The long global wine list is divided into user-friendly categories, with good house wines and some available in 500ml carafes. The four-year-old Electric may have lost its novelty, but it still has plenty of voltage.
Babies and children welcome: high chairs. Disabled: toilet. No-smoking tables. Tables outdoors (8, pavement). **Map 19 B3**.

Notting Hill

★ Notting Hill Brasserie

92 Kensington Park Road, W11 2PN (7229 4481). Notting Hill Gate tube. **Lunch served** noon-3pm daily. **Dinner served** 7-11pm Mon-Sat. **Main courses** £18.50-£23.50. **Set lunch** (Mon-Sat) £14.50 2 courses, £19.50 3 courses; (Sun) £25 2 courses, £30 3 courses. **Credit** AmEx, MC, V.
NHB's casual-posh style remains in line with Notting Hill's ever-more chi-chi bohemianism. The cosy design features mini armchairs at the tables, soothing stone colours all about, and higgledy-piggledy pictures on the walls. It's all finessed with light, live jazz in the bar. Prices discourage riff-raff, but the elegant cuisine lassoes the discriminating. The eight starters (almost entirely over £10) include crispy seared scallops on a bed of subtle herb gnocchi and shallots. There's always an excellent selection of sensitively cooked fish main courses, but among the meats, roast duck with caramelised onion purée, crisp potato and warm salad of crispy duck confit was a marvel. Likewise, a perfectly hung chateaubriand served with a Stonehenge pile of fat chips and béarnaise sauce was the last word on fillet steak. Cheesecake seemed an over-indulgent finish, but was an ethereally light confection with cinnamony poached pear. The wine list is pitched at a discriminating, well-travelled palate in an environment where a 1998 Pomerol at £73.50 doesn't even make it on to the fine wine appendix. Don't worry: the house wines at £14.50 are good. If service seems obsequious, seek out the sardonically seasoned French waiter who's worth well over 12.5%.
Babies and children welcome: entertainer (Sun lunch); high chairs. Booking advisable. Entertainment: jazz and blues musicians 7pm daily. Separate rooms for parties, seating 12 and 32. **Map 7 A6**.

South West

Barnes

★ The Depot

Tideway Yard, 125 Mortlake High Street, SW14 8SN (8878 9462/www.depotbrasserie.co.uk). Barnes, Barnes Bridge or Mortlake rail/209 bus. **Open** noon-11pm Mon-Sat; noon-10.30pm Sun.

Lunch served noon-3pm Mon-Fri; noon-4pm Sat, Sun. **Dinner served** 6-11pm Mon-Sat; 6-10.30pm Sun. **Main courses** £8.95-£17.50. **Set meal** (noon-7.30pm Mon-Fri) £13.50 2 courses. **Credit** AmEx, DC, JCB, MC, V.
This ever-popular restaurant has softened its looks with the introduction of banquette seating around the walls and a more comfortable bar area. Otherwise, all remains the same: polished wooden furnishings, cordial and efficient staff, and accomplished cooking. The location, in a courtyard adjacent to the Thames, is a big draw; the best seats are along the window overlooking the towpath and the river – perfect for sunset viewing. Expect the likes of charcuterie, asparagus or foie gras for starters, and grilled swordfish, roast duck leg and lamb chump for mains, marked by the judicious use of high-quality seasonal ingredients. Smoked haddock with mash and soft-boiled egg was a fine example of that brasserie classic, while strongly flavoured sea trout matched well with creamy spinach, and tarragon risotto speckled with crayfish. A starter of seared yellowfin tuna with shallot and ginger dressing could have done with less cautious spicing, though the fish was spot-on. Party-style puddings included eton mess (with banana, pineapple and mango instead of the more usual strawberries) and that 1970s fave, baked alaska, which was marred by runny, uncooked meringue. A well-priced wine list, with plenty of choices by the glass, adds to the appeal.
Babies and children welcome: children's menu; crayons; high chairs. Booking advisable. No-smoking tables. Tables outdoors (10, patio).

Chelsea

Blue Kangaroo

555 King's Road, SW6 2EB (7371 7622/ www.thebluekangaroo.co.uk). Fulham Broadway tube/Sloane Square tube then 11, 22 bus. **Meals served** 11.30am-6.30pm daily. **Main courses** £8.50-£12.50. **Credit** AmEx, MC, V.
It might be looking a little dog-eared from sterling service in the field of children's eating and entertainment, but the Blue Kangaroo formula is still a winner. The basement playground is the main attraction for under-eights. You can eat alongside it, but grown-ups would perhaps prefer a table in the crisper restaurant upstairs, where there's white linen and less taxing noise levels. Wherever you eat, the food is presented with care, and children are served first. The minors' menu (£5.45 including drink) consists of tasty, own-made burgers, chicken goujons, scrambled eggs (meat, poultry and eggs are organic), spaghetti carbonara or penne pasta or one of the Kangaroo's splendid salmon fishcakes. Big portions of chicken breast, fish cakes, pumpkin risotto or specials such as tagliatelle with beef ragu for the adults arrive with large, mixed leaf salads or seasonal vegetables. Our plate of creamy toasted goat's cheese on olive oil-drenched bread with salad was terrific; cod in beer batter with plenty of chips was satisfying, although the batter seemed a bit flat. You certainly wouldn't come here without young children, but if you fancy lingering over a decent meal in the adult tradition, with wine, not whine, the Kangaroo will do for you.
Babies and children welcome: children's menu; high chairs; toys. Booking advisable weekends. Disabled: toilet. No smoking. Restaurant available for hire. **Map 13 C13**.

The Market Place

Chelsea Farmers' Market, 125 Sydney Street, SW3 6NR (7352 5600). South Kensington tube/ 11, 19, 22, 49 bus. **Meals served** Apr-Sept 9.30am-5pm Mon-Fri; 9.30am-7pm Sat, Sun. Oct-Mar 9.30am-4.30pm daily. **Main courses** £8-£12. **Credit** AmEx, MC, V.
Somewhat at odds with its posh address, this largely outdoor eaterie in the boho shopping enclave that is Chelsea Farmers' Market, has a beach-café feel due to its umbrella-shaded picnic tables (some of which are wonky) and Virgin radio blasting from the speakers. The vaguely shambolic air that began on our arrival with confusion about whether we should wait to be seated, was

reinforced by the friendly but dippy staff. But on a sunny day, Market Place has a laid-back holiday atmosphere that seems to appeal to a young neo-Sloaney crowd. A browse through the menu reveals Mediterranean-influenced salads, burgers and pasta, plus ciabatta sandwiches: the latter inexplicably served only on weekdays. Our expectations for the food weren't high, but we were pleasantly surprised. A seasonally correct seared asparagus salad with rocket, parmesan and sun-dried tomato relish was attractively presented, the vegetables fresh and firm. Grilled tuna niçoise, while cooked right through, remained tender and there wasn't a wilted salad leaf in sight. Salmon fish cakes featured reassuring chunks of fish and a tangy chilli dip. A convenient shopping pit-stop.
Babies and children welcome: high chairs. Bookings not accepted. Tables outdoors (35, patio). **Map 14 E12**.

South

Balham

Balham Kitchen & Bar

15-19 Bedford Hill, SW12 9EX (8675 6900/ www.balhamkitchen.com). Balham tube/rail. **Open** 8am-midnight Mon-Thur; 8am-1am Fri, Sat; 8am-10.30pm Sun. **Meals served** 8am-11pm Mon-Thur; 8am-11.45pm Fri, Sat; 8am-10.15pm Sun. **Main courses** £9.50-£16. **Set lunch** (noon-4pm Mon-Fri) £10 2 courses, £13 3 courses. **Credit** AmEx, MC, V.
A new top-class deli, monthly farmers' market, and Waitrose replacing the Safeway – all are sure signs that Balham is not merely on the up, but has arrived. BK&B was one of the first of Balham's many watering holes that now cater for the Can't-Afford-Notting-Hill classes. It remains one of the best, attracting a cool neighbourhood crowd with its modern good looks, intriguing layout, extensive drinks list and bistro-style menu. There are the expected salads, good sandwiches, and dishes grilled in the open kitchen next to the central bar, but there's also a seafood counter with oysters, and special-occasion treats such as chateaubriand (the roasted thick end of beef fillet) or whole sea bass for two people. The simple dishes are done well: linguini with artichoke, pesto and pea shoots, for example. Mackerel with a potato and beetroot salad was also enjoyable, though it would have been better still if the skin had been crisped on that ever-ready grill. Puddings centre around comfort food such as sticky toffee pudding or chocolate fudge cake. Service is cheerful and smiling, though not always terribly efficient.
Babies and children welcome: high chairs. Disabled: toilet. Entertainment: DJ 10pm Fri, Sat. No-smoking tables. Separate rooms for parties, seating 20 and 40. Tables outdoors (6, pavement).

Clapham

Newtons

33-35 Abbeville Road, SW4 9LA (8673 0977/ www.newtonsrestaurants.co.uk). Clapham South tube. **Lunch served** noon-4pm daily. **Dinner served** 7-10.30pm Mon-Thur, Sun; 7-11pm Fri, Sat. **Main courses** £9.50-£16. **Set lunch** (noon-3pm Mon-Sat) £8 2 courses, £10.50 3 courses; (Sun) £16.50 3 courses. **Set dinner** £15 2 courses; (Sat, Sun) £18.50 3 courses. **Credit** AmEx, MC, V.
This reliable, elder statesman of Abbeville Road offers Modern European cooking with a twist of Thai. It's a friendly, relaxed establishment that caters for all ages. The bare-bricked interior has an airy, French feel and there's room for eight tables on the terrace during balmier days. Newtons is a popular place on Sundays for roasts. On our most recent visit, starters of asparagus and calamares were fresh and well presented. Sea bass came without the potatoes advertised on the menu, but the manager immediately admitted his mistake and rectified the situation quickly and with charm. Our Thai curry lacked zest, begging the question: why bother with the Asian slant to the menu when the European food is so good? The dessert menu jokingly claims to help with calorie

Pumphouse Dining Bar. See p50.

control – the cheesecake is popular. Lovely touches such as (cheap) handmade truffles to accompany your coffee add to the homely feel. Another bonus is the quaffable French house wine, which costs less than a tenner.
Babies and children welcome: crayons; high chairs. Booking advisable. No-smoking tables. Tables outdoors (8, terrace). **Map 22 A3**.

Waterloo

Giraffe
Riverside, Royal Festival Hall, Belvedere Road, SE1 8XX (7928 2004/www.giraffe.net). Embankment tube/Waterloo tube/rail. **Meals served** 7.45am-10.45pm Mon-Fri; 9am-10.45pm Sat; 9am-10.30pm Sun. **Main courses** £6.95-£12.95. **Set meal** (5-7pm Mon-Fri) £6.95 2 courses; (7-11pm Mon-Fri) £8.95 2 courses. **Credit** AmEx, MC, V.
Giraffe's successful formula of familiar global menu favourites and unobtrusive world music in relaxed surroundings has been embraced by Londoners; the South Bank makes a great location for this fast-expanding, family-friendly chain. The balance is just right – not too gimmicky or nappy-happy – mixing families during the day and, later, groups gathering for post-work, two-for-one drinks. Weekend queues are standard. Pancakes with banana and blueberries, fry-ups and french toast are popular for weekend brunch, and the Surf Skewer Bar offers the likes of fiery tiger prawns, BBQ chicken wings and teriyaki salmon. Mains include Vietnamese curries, Tex-Mex burritos, salads, steaks and burgers (the veggie falafel with grilled pepper, rocket, halloumi and harissa is recommended). Children's options are healthy and tasty; grilled salmon fingers with baby carrots and peas, for example. The varied drinks list takes in smoothies (the Giddy Giraffe, with papaya, mint, banana, orange and lime juice is an invigorating alternative to coffee) and flavoured lattes via cocktails and wine (largely South African and

Antipodean). Desserts can't fail to please: rocky road ice-cream sundae, white chocolate and crushed Toblerone cheesecake, and – our favourite – lime and mascarpone tiramisu. Staff are smiley, unflappable and efficient.
Babies and children welcome: children's menu; crayons; high chairs. Disabled: toilets. No smoking. Tables outdoors (34, terrace). Takeaway service. **Map 10 M8**.
For branches see index.

Tamesa@oxo NEW
Second floor, Oxo Tower Wharf, Barge House Street, SE1 9PH (7633 0088/www.coinstreet.org). Blackfriars or Waterloo tube/rail. **Lunch served** noon-3.30pm, **dinner served** 5.30-11.30pm Mon-Fri. **Meals served** noon-11.30pm Sat; noon-10.30pm Sun. **Main courses** £8.95-£13.50. **Set meal** (lunch Mon-Sat; 5.30-7pm, 10-11.30pm Mon-Sat) £12.50 2 courses, £15.50 3 courses. **Credit** AmEx, MC, V.
The windows of Oxo Tower's second-floor dining area provide an intimate view of the Thames that is arguably better than the panoramic, waterless scenes to be found in the restaurant/brasserie on the eighth floor. Yet three businesses have failed to make this place work. Let's hope Tamesa@oxo fares better. The space is attractive – bright aqua rear wall, neat red chairs, white tables – and was buzzing with customers on our visit. Some were in for cocktails at the circular bar or on the orange designer chairs by the riverwalk entrance; others had arrived for dinner. The wide-ranging menu (hot-and-sour and hoi sin, niçoise and caesar, a spot of pub grub, a bit of Italian) was cooked and presented nicely, but suffered from underripe produce. We loved the brightly coloured chilled green pea soup: it was thick and richly flavoured, like spring in a bowl. New season lamb was cooked perfectly to order, and a side dish of green beans with shallots and rosemary was a lovely balance of well-melded flavours and crisp textures. The sweet potato fries were gorgeous too. We drank

Sequoit tempranillo, an inexpensive quality quaffing wine from Valencia. Service was slow, despite plenty of staff bustling around the tables.
Babies and children welcome: children's menu; crayons; high chairs. Booking advisable. Disabled: lift; toilet. No smoking. Separate room for parties, seats 28. **Map 11 N7**.

South East

Bankside

Tate Modern Café: Level 2
Second floor, Tate Modern, Sumner Street, SE1 9TG (7401 5014/www.tate.org.uk). Southwark tube/London Bridge tube/rail. **Breakfast served** 10-11.30am, **lunch served** 11.30am-3pm, **afternoon tea served** 3-6pm daily. **Dinner served** 6-9.30pm Fri. **Main courses** £9.95. **Credit** AmEx, DC, MC, V.
Tate Modern's contemporary feel continues in this light, spacious café, which has a long, sleek bar, well-spaced tables and wall-hung art. Floor-to-ceiling windows overlook the Thames. The prices are rather high, but the view is great and the food is a cut above usual museum-café cooking. The menus (breakfast, lunch, afternoon tea, plus dinner on late-closing nights) have a Modern European/ Mediterranean leaning – roast Loch Duart salmon with pesto, or white bean cassoulet and pancetta, for example. A tapas-style light lunch of spiced chickpeas, houmous and aubergine salad with grilled flatbread was bursting with rich Med flavours: simple and delicious. Desserts are tempting too; elderflower sorbet melting into warm poached rhubarb with shortbread was a glorious mix of flavours and textures. Drinks include top-notch smoothies, English and Aussie beers, and a decent wine list. Given the queues, the table service was impressively attentive, efficient and child-friendly.
Babies and children welcome: crayons; high chairs. Bookings not accepted Sat, Sun. Disabled: toilets. No smoking. **Map 11 O7**.

Crystal Palace

Joanna's

56 Westow Hill, SE19 1RX (8670 4052/
www.joannas.uk.com). Crystal Palace or Gipsy
Hill rail. **Open** 10am-11pm Mon-Sat; 10am-
10.30pm Sun. **Brunch served** 10am-6pm
Mon-Sat. **Meals served** noon-11pm Mon-Sat;
noon-10.30pm Sun. **Main courses** £5-£19.
Credit AmEx, MC, V.
This spacious, classy brasserie has impressed us
on several occasions with great service from its
attentive, crisply dressed staff and a consistently
satisfying, mostly British menu. The tables are
attractively laid and well spaced, although the
railway carriage towards the back makes a quirky
alternative for a special occasion. Brunch is
reasonably priced and mixes well-known oriental
dishes like salmon teriyaki alongside such solid
British fodder as cottage pie and cumberland
sausages. The à la carte menu follows a similar
theme, embracing several fish dishes and a choice
of meaty platters including succulent, char-grilled
rump steak served simply with frites. The
traditional roast dinners on Sundays shouldn't be
missed. They arrive crowned with a crispy-edged
giant yorkshire pudding and a decent portion of
seasonal vegetables. Mains are hefty, so opt for an
ice-cream for dessert; moreish, high-quality
flavours include vanilla bean, cinnamon and honey,
and pistachio. Joanna's attracts a mixed crowd –
from ladies-who-lunch to young couples.
Babies and children welcome (before 6pm):
children's menu; high chairs. No-smoking tables.
Separate room for parties, seats 6. Tables outdoors
(4, patio).

East Dulwich

The Green

58-60 East Dulwich Road, SE22 9AX (7732
7575/www.greenbar.co.uk). East Dulwich rail/
37, 484 bus. **Open** 10am-11pm daily. **Breakfast**
served 10am-noon, **lunch served** noon-5pm,
dinner served 6-11pm daily. **Main courses**
£8.95-£13.95. **Set lunch** (noon-3.30pm Mon-
Sat) £8.50 2 courses, £11.50 3 courses; (Sun)
£13.95 2 courses, £16.95 3 courses. **Credit**
AmEx, MC, V.
The Green (next to Goose Green) aims to be
something of a neighbourhood all-rounder for the
young families of gentrified East Dulwich, offering
breakfast, lunch and dinner in the restaurant, and
various in-between-snacks in the bar. The spacious
but anonymous restaurant (cream walls hung with
colourful but uninspiring contemporary artworks)
usually accommodates low-key jazz duos on
Tuesday and Thursday evenings. From the
unimaginative yet fairly well-balanced à la carte,
we enjoyed a flavourful starter of coriander, ginger
and salmon fish cakes served with a zingy chilli
jam (usefully, all starters can be taken as mains).
Haddock, to follow, was lightly poached, topped
with a poached egg and then smothered by a heavy
hollandaise sauce. A ribeye steak was char-grilled
and served with peppercorn and red onion butter.
Both dishes were reasonably well executed, but not
as fresh-tasting as we'd have wished. The set lunch
menu – which includes the likes of mussels
marinière and baked salmon fillet – is good value.
Better still are the breakfast choices; the generous
set menus (continental, full english, vegetarian and
so on) all cost around £5. The affected over-
politeness of the staff is a little unconvincing.
Babies and children welcome: children's menu;
high chairs. Disabled: toilet. Entertainment: jazz
8pm Tue, Thur. Booking advisable. No-smoking
tables. Separate room for parties, seats 39. Tables
outdoors (12, terrace). **Map 23 C3.**

Greenwich

Bar du Musée

17 Nelson Road, SE10 9JB (8858 4710/
www.bardumusee.com). Cutty Sark DLR. **Open**
noon-1am Mon-Thur; noon-2am Fri; 11am 2am
Sat; 11am-midnight Sun. **Lunch served** noon-
3pm Mon-Fri; 11am-5pm Sat, Sun. **Dinner**
served 6-10pm daily. **Main courses** £10.50-
£16.50. **Credit** MC, V.

Bar du Musée is much loved locally, busy on
weeknights and hard to get into at weekends when
Greenwich Market is in full swing. It's a
comfortable place of many spaces and moods,
branching out from a homely Left Bank frontage
into atmospheric bar areas with a rough-hewn
maritime feel and then a large, quite chic patio. The
menu too speaks of familiar comforts: winter and
summer, food is flavoursome, buttery, unaffected
and unchallenging, in bistro mode. It's quite nice,
but a little hit and miss: butternut squash ravioli
had a tasty filling, but was so dry it curled up at
the edges; endive salad was fine; roast duck was
served so pink it was a little cold and tough inside.
The wine list offers only four choices per colour by
the glass, and lacks explanation, which the well-
meaning but generally inexpert staff were unable
to provide. This is a homely place, with a certain
charm, but we found the shabby chic just a little
too shabby and the relaxed vibe extending a little
too far into the kitchen and service.
Babies and children welcome: high chairs.
Separate room for parties, seats 15. Tables
outdoors (20, garden).

North
Crouch End

Banners

21 Park Road, N8 8TE (8348 2930/www.banners
restaurant.co.uk). Finsbury Park tube/rail then W7
bus. **Meals served** 9am-11.30pm Mon-Thur;
9am-midnight Fri; 10am-4pm, 5pm-midnight Sat;
10am-4pm, 5-11pm Sun. **Main courses** £6.95-
£14.75. **Credit** MC, V.
A crazy cartoon-painted wall greets you outside
this lively venue. The supersized noticeboard
advertising events from holistic fairs to the
Woodcraft Folk provides further clues to the nature
of Banners' customers – as do the menus
decorated with children's drawings. You'll find
much that kids will love to eat, along with plenty
of fun items for grown-ups, from candy bars to
tobacco and a complimentary bowl of popcorn.
This is where hungry Crouch Enders come
throughout the day, for portions of food as
generous as the ambience. The 'world food'
encompasses Mexican, Greek, Thai and
particularly Caribbean cuisines (jerk being a
favourite sauce). Cornmeal-coated calamares with
own-made tartare sauce, and a creamy celery soup
made excellent starters. To follow, tender venison
steak, almost swamped by a mass of delicious
sweet potato and chorizo mash, nearly defeated us.
Jerk sea bass, with rice and black beans and a crisp
salad, was cooked to perfection. A massive portion
of the daily crumble – pineapple and passionfruit
smothered in custard – finished us (and the meal)
off. Banners also has a fine house wine, a viognier
at £12.85; Lappland beer and tropical cocktails
continue the global theme.
Babies and children welcome: high chairs. Booking
advisable. No-smoking tables (9am-7pm Mon-Fri).
Takeaway service.

Camden Town &
Chalk Farm

The Roundhouse NEW

Roundhouse, Chalk Farm Road, NW1 8EH
(0870 389 9920). Chalk Farm tube. **Meals**
served 11am-11pm Tue-Sat; 11am-5pm Sun.
Main courses £8-£14. **Credit** JCB, MC, V.
The revitalised Roundhouse theatre houses a
colourful modern café of glass and metal, which
curls around the performance centre, itself housed
in an old brick structure originally built in 1846.
Part-Mediterranean, part-Caribbean, part-British,
the menu seems designed to reflect multicultural
London. Deliciously fresh-tasting Scottish lobster
came on a buttery cholla roll with an invigorating
dill-flavoured coleslaw. The addictive chips were
from new season potatoes, with some of the skin
left on for extra flavour. Roast rack of lamb was
served with new potatoes, wilted spinach and a
feta cheese dressing. There's also a choice of six
(six!) chocolate desserts. The signature Round

Brownie served with a shot of cranberry gin may
be too sweet for some; deeper chocolate flavour
was to be found in the squidgy chocolate pudding.
A fruit plate and Lincolnshire Poacher cheese are
also available. Outside show times the café is fairly
quiet, but on our visit it was completely full – this
is one restaurant that has a ready-made audience
after all. It's run by the Company of Cooks, which
also operates the Brew House in Kenwood, among
other ventures.
Babies and children welcome: high chairs. Booking
advisable. Disabled: toilet. No smoking. Separate
room for parties, seats 40. Tables outdoors (14,
terrace). Vegan dishes. **Map 27 B1.**

Hornsey

Pumphouse Dining Bar

1 New River Avenue, N8 7QD (8340 0400/
www.mosaicarestaurants.com). Turnpike Lane
tube/Hornsey rail.
Bar Open 11.30am-11pm Mon-Sat; noon-
10.30pm Sun.
Restaurant **Lunch served** noon-3pm Mon-Fri.
Dinner served 6-9.30pm Mon-Wed; 6-10pm
Thur, Fri. **Meals served** noon-10pm Sat;
noon-9.30pm Sun. **Main courses** £10-£16.
Both Credit AmEx, DC, JCB, MC, V.
'Dining bar' is a particularly apt description for
what the Pumphouse offers. Lots of 'zones' lend a
cool, clubby atmosphere to this beautifully
converted building. A long cocktail list and a well-
chosen wine list, as well as brasserie-style eating,
mean all comers are catered for. Food is
Mediterranean-influenced, with a seasonally
based, daily changing menu. A starter of grilled
polenta with chorizo, red pepper and rocket was a
corker – a fabulous balance of flavours and
textures. Summer spiced lentil soup was pleasantly
piquant. Among the main courses, asparagus, pea
and mint risotto was a competent version of a
classic dish and came in a generous serving,
though it could have been creamier. Sea bass with
'vanilla pots and confit toms' was another
competent rendition at a fair price. Puddings of the
sticky toffee/vanilla brûlée variety didn't tempt,
but moving indoors to those leather sofas and the
digestifs was a smart move. Thankfully, the
extensive range of wines and beers are shown with
their alcohol percentage. Service was sweet.
Babies and children welcome (restaurant and
patio only): high chairs. Booking advisable.
Disabled: toilet. Tables outdoors (10, patio).
For branch see index.

Muswell Hill

Café on the Hill

46 Fortis Green Road, N10 3HN (8444 4957/
www.cafeonthehill.com). Highgate tube then 43,
134 bus. **Meals served** 8am-4pm Mon, Sun;
8am-10pm Tue-Sat. **Main courses** £6.95-£12.95.
Credit MC, V.
For locals this could be an extension of their own
homes – they pop in for coffee, rock up for
breakfast, bring the babies while they schmooze
over salad or chicken skewers, dine informally.
White brick walls are almost hidden by the Jack
Vettriano prints. There's nothing too demanding
here, and that includes the ambience and the food.
The dinner menu is short, offering predictable
brasserie fare. Duck liver pâté (with yellow
chutney of no discernible provenance) tasted
better than its charcoal-grey colour promised. Crab
mousse was more dressed crab than mousse. Our
request for bread meant a long wait (aggravated
by being charged £2.25 for 'bread and oil' that, it
turned out, was boring bread and no oil). Things
improved with the main courses. We relished a
thick, perfectly grilled piece of tuna topped with
avocado salsa. Spinach pancakes stuffed with
ratatouille and feta were tasty enough, though the
pancakes were a bit dry around the edges and the
ratatouille slightly undercooked. There's no
agonising necessary over the choice of wine; the
list contains just four each of red and white, with
large (250ml) glasses at a third of the bottle price.
Babies and children welcome: high chairs; toys.
Entertainment: jazz 8pm Fri, Sat. No smoking.
Tables outdoors (4, pavement).

British

London's British restaurants number some long-celebrated haunts, and a growing band of forward-looking, innovative ones too, but there remain some real shockers, charging cynical prices for food that perpetuates the tourist impression that food in Britain sucks. The best places offer a strong rebuttal to this notion: particular pleasures are well-kept cheese boards, good own-made breads, and seasonal ingredients used in revitalised dishes by interested chefs, all sourced from suppliers who care about their produce.

Chef Fergus Henderson is rightly lauded for dragging British food out of the doldrums, and his two restaurants (**St John** and **St John Bread & Wine**) are still going strong. Gary Rhodes (**Rhodes Twenty Four**, **Rhodes W1**) and Richard Corrigan (**Lindsay House**) have done their bit too, as has Terence Conran (especially at **Bluebird Dining Rooms**), but this year special mention must go to Oliver Peyton. He deserves a medal for bringing good British food to a general public more used to settling for substandard fare in park and museum catering. Other London galleries and museums should look at the **National Dining Rooms** and **Inn the Park** and learn – most of them rely on big catering companies to deliver identikit, plastic-wrapped fare. Other new places (**Butcher & Grill**, **Canteen**, **Konstam at the Prince Albert**, **Roast**) demonstrate that the revival is ongoing, and happily the trend is for a more casual, unstuffy style.

A few gripes: old-style British restaurants seem to be the last refuge of the cover charge, and also of sexism – at many of the older restaurants, any woman making a booking is assumed to be the secretary. Wine lists are a bugbear too – many places have amazing wine lists that are out of reach except for the wealthy; we'd love to see a wider range of prices and more lists featuring at least one English wine producer.

Central

City

Boisdale Bishopsgate

Swedeland Court, 202 Bishopsgate, EC2M 4NR (7283 1763/www.boisdale.co.uk). Liverpool Street tube/rail.
Bar **Open** 11am-11pm Mon-Fri.
Restaurant **Lunch served** noon-3pm, **dinner served** 6-9.30pm Mon-Fri. **Main courses** £12.15-£21.95. **Set meal** £17.80 2 courses.
Both **Credit** AmEx, MC, V.
All the fuss made over jazz, whisky and cigars at the two Boisdale London branches can't disguise that the food isn't really up to scratch. This year we ate at the City branch, and although the place has a comforting cellar bar ambience, we failed to fall under its tartan spell. From the set menu, gravadlax followed by a fish cake with poached egg was good comfort food. Less satisfying were dishes from the main menu – crab served with russian salad was lacklustre, and cost £9.95; more disappointing was venison fillet (£21.50), a special that was anything but. Perhaps one of the steaks – 'finest matured beef from the glens of Scotland' – would have been a better bet. After this we didn't have the heart to try the likes of raspberry cranachan or 'Scottish tart' (walnuts, raisin and whisky with malt ice-cream and toffee sauce), but we're sure they go down a treat with the mostly male diners – as, no doubt, does the waitress in a mini-kilt. On this showing, Boisdale is useful for the City, but not worth a journey.
Booking essential. Dress: smart casual. Entertainment: jazz 7pm Mon-Thur; blues 7pm Fri. **Map 12 R5.**
For branch see index.

Canteen NEW

2006 RUNNER-UP BEST DESIGN
2 Crispin Place, off Brushfield Street, E1 6DW (0845 686 1122/www.canteen.co.uk). Liverpool Street tube/rail. **Meals served** 11am-10pm Mon-Fri; 9am-10pm Sat, Sun. **Main courses** £7-£12.50. **Credit** AmEx, MC, V.
Neat, functional and streamlined, Canteen's corporate branding suggest the possibility of a chain to be rolled out. Communal oak tables are both utilitarian and elegant, booths with upholstered banquettes and ceramic table lamps have a diner-like feel, while a glazed canopy outside allows a busy alfresco space. So it looks a treat, plus the staff are lovely and the menu is a splendid read: all-day breakfasts (bacon sandwiches and toasted crumpets), light dishes (potted duck with piccalilli and toast, leek and Lancashire cheese tart), and an array of cakes alongside some great-sounding mains. But that's where the rave review stops. The food doesn't live up to all this promise. Fried fish of the day was smoked haddock; it seemed like a strange idea, and

it was. Smoked and fried made an uneasy mix and we ended up leaving most of it (though the chips were fine). Conversely, gammon and potatoes with parsley sauce went in the other direction; the gammon was bland. The best dish was potted shrimps with cress salad and toast – the butter to shrimp ratio was wrong (too much butter), but it was a decent version. Still, there are enough encouraging touches to make us try again – the glasses of sparkling Nyetimber wine from Sussex, for instance – and prices are very reasonable. Ribeye steak with anchovy butter is one of the more expensive dishes at £12.50, and stomach fillers such as macaroni cheese cost £7. And it's in a great location – the new bit of Spitalfields Market – ideal for City workers and market trawlers.
Babies and children welcome: children's portions; high chairs. Disabled: toilet. No smoking. Tables outdoors (5, plaza). **Map 12 R5.**

Paternoster Chop House

Warwick Court, Paternoster Square, EC4M 7DX (7029 9400/www.conran.com). St Paul's tube. **Meals served** 10.30am-10pm Mon-Fri; noon-5pm Sun. **Main courses** £12.50-£26.50. **Set lunch** (Sun) £19.50 2 courses, £23.50 3 courses. **Credit** AmEx, DC, MC, V.
There's lots to like at PCH. It's nice and airy for a start, a bright, white room with patches of colour coming from a few modern still lifes, and red banquettes along one wall; plus lots of outdoor tables on Paternoster Square. It's also very laid-back for a Conran City establishment, with a big open kitchen at one end and a busy bar round the corner of the L-shaped space. What's more, men don't outnumber women too outrageously. And the menu is a great scamper through the best of British: Cornish cod with seaweed and wild mussel cream, or wild boar and apple sausages with mash and gravy. The downsides are that it's noisy, and service was erratic on the night of our visit – when it was good it was very good, but at times we were just… left. And dishes were variable too. Breaded fish cake with tartare sauce and Devon crab were 'more please' starters, but the much heralded Beast of the Day, roast middle white pig, was a bit underwhelming; ditto the cottage pie. And it's expensive: many of the main courses are closer to £20 than £15, and a Keen's cheddar rarebit costs £7.50 – though, to be fair, you can get a pickled egg for a quid.
Babies and children welcome: children's menu; games; high chairs. Booking advisable. Disabled: toilet. Tables outdoors (25, courtyard). **Map 11 O6.**

Rhodes Twenty Four

24th floor, Tower 42, Old Broad Street, EC2N 1HQ (7877 7703/www.rhodes24.co.uk). Bank tube/Liverpool Street tube/rail. **Lunch served** noon-2.15pm, **dinner served** 6-8.30pm Mon-Fri. **Main courses** £17.50-£45. **Credit** AmEx, DC, MC, V.
The view apart, Rhodes Twenty Four is a rather sterile, plain restaurant. And depending on where you're sitting, the view isn't that exciting considering it's 24 floors up – the restaurant faces east, so there aren't too many real landmarks – though diners on one side do get up close and personal with the Gherkin. No doubt the landscape twinkles away more prettily in the evening. At lunch, inevitably, the atmosphere is dictated by office diners. Starters run from light dishes, such as asparagus three-ways, to cumberland sausage with warm pickled cabbage and damson jelly. Mains are similarly diverse. A buttered potato filled with soft cheese and morels, served with a light summer vegetable casserole was a fine choice on a sunny day; but against the odds, the best dish was a trencherman-sized suet pudding, filled with steamed oxtail and kidney, served with carrots and beef gravy. This rendered the likes of bread and butter pudding or vanilla rice pudding with rhubarb and ginger shortbread an impossibility. Service was as attentive as it could be given the long gaps between courses. As we left, the lack of expected pzazz was exemplified by the sight of a waiter unashamedly ironing a tablecloth in full view of diners.

Babies and children admitted. Booking essential, 2-4 weeks in advance. Disabled: toilet. Dress: smart casual. **Map 12 Q6**.

St John Bread & Wine

94-96 Commercial Street, E1 6LZ (7251 0848/ www.stjohnbreadandwine.com). Aldgate East tube/Liverpool Street tube/rail. **Meals served** 9am-10.30pm Mon-Fri; 10am-10.30pm Sat; 10am-5pm Sun. **Main courses** £11-£14. **Credit** AmEx, MC, V.

You either appreciate the pared-down nature of the St John aesthetic or you don't. The airy white-painted room, with large windows streetside and an open-plan kitchen and bakery at the back, leaves the focus on the diners and, of course, the food. Patrons of this restaurant are usually an interesting bunch, but it's the food that delivers time after time. The menu is also without frills: what's listed in the brief dish description is what you get on the plate. Beetroot, sorrel and boiled egg was perfection: full of flavour and sporting a beautifully orange yolk. Grilled sprats with horseradish, though more monochrome, scored highly, as did a blood orange trifle, a delightful combination of sweet and tart. When there are no extra flourishes on the plate, though, what's there has to be spot-on, and skate, served with a small parsley salad, was fractionally undercooked on one side. Cauliflower cheese was slightly the wrong side of al dente, and cheekily priced at £11. Maybe we should have gone with the duck offal salad instead. Still, there's no pressure to spend money here – you can have just one dish and a glass of wine. Staff are professional but unponcey. There's a great (French) wine list – not too long but nicely priced; as with the baked goods, you can buy these to take away.

Babies and children welcome: high chairs. Booking advisable. Takeaway service. **Map 12 S5**.

Clerkenwell & Farringdon

Medcalf

40 Exmouth Market, EC1R 4QE (7833 3533/ www.medcalfbar.co.uk). Angel tube/Farringdon tube/rail/19, 38 bus. **Open** noon-11pm Mon-Thur, Sat; noon-12.30am Fri; noon-5pm Sun. **Lunch** served noon-3pm Mon-Fri; noon-4pm Sat, Sun. **Dinner served** 6-10pm Mon-Thur; 6-10.30pm Sat. **Main courses** £9.50-£14.50. **Credit** MC, V.

Ramshackle in a good way, Medcalf occupies long thin premises that used to be a butcher's. Slightly wonky tables and chairs, rather over-casual service and the atmosphere of a bar (which it partly is) mean that the standard of the cooking comes as a bit of a surprise. A short, regularly changing menu is not always thought through – for example, on one visit all the vegetarian choices featured cheese (feta in a salad with romesco peppers, parmesan with spinach in a tart, Cropwell Bishop stilton in the soup, welsh rarebit). But an otherwise very focused kitchen turns out quality dishes: sirloin steak with chunky chips was a fine piece of meat, and the (huge) welsh rarebit was a zinger. Do save room for dessert: plum syllabub with shortbread; bramley apple and rhubarb charlotte; chocolate cheesecake and the like. Coffee comes with a delicious little biscuit; mint tea is the real thing. Don't be deceived by the laid-back vibe – it really is best to book now that Exmouth Market has become a gastro destination, and Medcalf's reputation is growing steadily.

Babies and children admitted (until 7pm). Disabled: toilet. Entertainment: DJs 7pm Fri. Tables outdoors (5, garden; 6, pavement). **Map 5 N4**.

Quality Chop House

92-94 Farringdon Road, EC1R 3EA (7837 5093). Angel tube/Farringdon tube/rail/19, 38 bus. **Breakfast served** 7.30-10am, **lunch served** noon-3pm Mon-Fri. **Dinner served** 6-11.30pm Mon-Sat. **Meals served** noon-10pm Sun. **Main courses** £6.95-£18.95. **Set meal** (lunch Mon-Fri, 6-7.30pm Mon-Sat) £9.95 2 courses. **Credit** AmEx, JCB, MC, V.

There was less of the 'quality' about this Chop House that we'd have liked. Original owner Charles Fontaine left a couple of years ago, and we'd heard reports that standards had dropped since the glory days, but we have great fondness for this place so our hopes remained high. The evening started badly: watercress soup had an artificial taste, with none of the expected vibrancy, while anchovy and tomato salad (usually one of our favourites on the QCH menu) seemed a much coarser dish than we remembered, with an ocean of gloopy dressing swamping the ingredients. Mains redeemed the evening somewhat – haddock and chips, and a sirloin steak were both fine, if not glorious, versions. We didn't have the heart for dessert (not even the rice pudding), and regretted ordering coffee (it tasted as though it had come from a vending machine). Perhaps breakfast – grilled kippers with poached egg, or a full english featuring cumberland sausage and back bacon – is a more satisfying affair; or maybe the early evening 'tapas' selection of dishes such as devilled whitebait or steak tartare is the answer. Either way, it would be a shame not to experience this sensitively restored chop house, with its etched glass, tiles and wooden settles, while fervently hoping for a return to form.

Babies and children admitted. Booking advisable. **Map 5 N4**.

★ St John

26 St John Street, EC1M 4AY (7251 0848/ 4998/www.stjohnrestaurant.com). Farringdon tube/rail. **Bar** **Open/meals served** 11am-11pm Mon-Fri; 6-11pm Sat. **Main courses** £4-£15. *Restaurant* **Lunch** served noon-3pm Mon-Fri. **Dinner served** 6-11pm Mon-Sat. **Main courses** £12.70-£21.50. **Credit** AmEx, MC, V.

We had a bit of a hiccup at the start of our most recent evening here: beware the new centralised booking system, as you may be booked in at the branch (St John Bread & Wine; *see above*). Otherwise, our latest visit to this bastion of new-Brit cooking resembled all the others – that is, pretty much satisfaction all round. There are certain quibbles: such as, why are the puddings so expensive? Admittedly, gooseberry jelly with a few gooseberries and biscuits was heavenly, but so it should be when it costs £6.70. And though we like the stark whiteness of the decor, some first-timers may be surprised that such an internationally renowned restaurant is quite so basic. This is all in keeping with the ethos of the menu; dish descriptions are short (peas in the pod being literally that) and you won't find too many ingredients on any one plate. Tomato, anchovy and little gem salad was a great example: melded tomato and anchovy draped over perky lettuce leaves. Also summer-fresh was cured sea trout with a dressed cucumber accompaniment. Lentils and curd with watercress offered richly flavoured comfort; a good sized skate with chunks of fried bread and capers also pleased. An even more relaxed time can be had in the affable ground-floor bar, where the full range of drinks is served alongside a more snacky version of the menu.

Babies and children welcome: high chairs. Disabled: toilet (bar). No cigars or pipes (restaurant). Separate room for parties, seats 18. **Map 5 O5**.

☆ Top Floor at Smiths

2006 RUNNER-UP BEST STEAK RESTAURANT

Smiths of Smithfield, 67-77 Charterhouse Street, EC1M 6HJ (7251 7950/www.smithsofsmithfield. co.uk). Farringdon tube/rail. **Lunch served** noon-3pm Mon-Fri; noon-3.45pm Sun. **Dinner served** 6.30-10.45pm Mon-Sat; 6.30-10.30pm Sun. **Main courses** £17-£28. **Credit** AmEx, DC, MC, V.

Top Floor sits above the two other Smiths of Smithfield restaurants, literally and metaphorically. Respected chef John Torode oversees the cooking in all three, but this is where he invests his reputation. He's known for simple, expert treatments that allow the first-rate ingredients – meats, particularly – to shine through. Salt and pepper squid with chilli dressing was exceptional, almost impossibly fresh and with a flavour that changed enjoyably on the palate; subtle bresaola was complemented rather than overwhelmed by its olive oil and white truffle accompaniments. The steaks are billed as 'fine meats' and accorded the status of ageing and sourcing details on the menu, except, surprisingly, the 'rare breed fillet', which at £28.50 for 7oz we felt was the one that most deserved an explanation. All steaks are offered grilled but recommended pan-fried. Welsh Black sirloin and rare breed fillet were cooked respectfully,

National Dining Rooms. See p57.

Canteen. See p51.

the flavour to be sought out and savoured rather than leaping at you from char-marks. Both were very good indeed. The experience merited concentration, even contemplation, but on our Friday evening visit, the rest of the packed house seemed more interested in chatting than in their food. Perhaps they were distracted by the dramatic views over Smithfield meat market, the dominant feature of the otherwise suave decor.

Babies and children welcome: high chairs. Booking advisable. Disabled: lift; toilet. Tables outdoors (8, terrace). **Map 11 O5.**

Covent Garden

Rules

35 Maiden Lane, WC2E 7LB (7836 5314/ www.rules.co.uk). Covent Garden tube. **Meals served** noon-11.30pm Mon-Sat; noon-10.30pm Sun. **Main courses** £15.95-£19.95. **Credit** AmEx, JCB, MC, V.

There's so much history attached to Rules (described in detail in their brochure) that it seems churlish not to have had an unreservedly good time here. And the groups of tourists, couples on celebratory dates and lone male diners working their way through the wine list all seemed to be enjoying themselves. And we loved parts of it – Forman's excellent smoked salmon is served with great ceremony, with finely chopped shallots, capers and a lemon half (wrapped in muslin, naturally), and lobster bisque is lovingly ladled out at table by formally attired waiters. And the cheese board is a generous spread for £8.95: five British specimens, plus celery and an impressive silver container with all manner of biscuits. Other dishes – for example, Morecambe Bay potted shrimps, and a special of sea bream with Cornish scallops, spring veg and truffle sauce – were OK, but nothing to write home about. And the interior is

looking a little tired: all the stuffed animals, oil paintings and stained glass can't quite disguise this. For the price, London's oldest restaurant should try a little harder.

Babies and children welcome: high chairs. Booking advisable. Dress: smart casual. No smoking. Separate rooms for parties (7379 0258), seating 10, 12, 16 and 20. **Map 18 L7.**

King's Cross

Konstam at the Prince Albert `NEW`

2 Acton Street, WC1X 9NA (7833 5040/ www.konstam.co.uk). King's Cross tube/rail. **Lunch served** 12.30-3pm, **dinner served** 7-10.30pm Mon-Sat. **Main courses** £10.50-£15.50. **Credit** AmEx, MC, V.

A big PR push and the TV series *Urban Chef* made sure Oliver Rowe's new venture attracted a lot of attention before opening in spring 2006. His gimmick is that nearly all the food served is produced within Greater London, taking the 'locally grown' mantra to a new level. The menu changes daily, but ingredients include mushrooms from polytunnels in East Ham, potted crab from – er – Canvey Island, chicken from Waltham Abbey, and Norbury Blue cheese, which is from Dorking, not Norbury. All of which is admirable, except we found the standard of cooking a bit lacklustre. Nettle 'pierogi' were more like tortelloni, with a filling that was too moist and vegetal; coq au vin was tough, making the meat hard to separate from the bone or skin. Mutton chops with a caper sauce suffered from a similar excess of bone and fat, but the flavour was good. The desserts were better, such as the crisp honey snaps served with lavender ice-cream. The drinks list 'cheats' by reaching beyond the M25 to areas such as Chablis, but the

bottled beers – from the Meantime Brewery in Greenwich – are excellent. Konstam at the Prince Albert is an attractive-looking restaurant inside a former pub, and is not to be confused with the Konstam café, Rowe's humbler operation just around the corner.

Babies and children admitted. Booking advisable. Disabled: toilet. No smoking. Tables outdoors (2, pavement). **Map 4 M3.**

Knightsbridge

Rib Room & Oyster Bar

Jumeirah Carlton Tower, 2 Cadogan Place, SW1X 9PY (7858 7053/www.jumeirahcarlton tower.com). Knightsbridge tube. **Lunch served** 12.30-2.45pm daily. **Dinner served** 7-10.45pm Mon-Sat; 7-10.15pm Sun. **Main courses** £22-£37. **Set lunch** (Sun) £45 3 courses incl coffee. **Credit** AmEx, DC, MC, V.

You need deep pockets to enjoy the Rib Room. You also need a liking for American steak houses and a tolerance for erratic service. Sometimes there were lots of waiters, sometimes none; we had to wait an age to be seated and only ever got one menu between us, but no sooner had a cigar been produced than it was lit. Still, there's an easy-going vibe in this spacious room; decor is red upholstery and lots of dark wood, lighting is low and there's a happy buzz of conversation. Even the dress code is relaxed – diners are either wearing suits, or leisurewear (favoured by tourists staying in the Jumeirah Carlton Tower hotel above). Prices are eye-poppingly high: grilled New York strip loin with mushrooms and béarnaise was a big portion, and a decent steak, but it cost £34. Salmon and haddock fish cakes with spinach and sorrel sauce were fine, but there are many better to be had elsewhere, for a lot less than £22. There are no bargains to be had from the Oyster Bar either – the

cheapest oysters are six Loch Fyne specimens costing £15. But, of course, this is beside the point – if you're at all worried about value for money, you won't be dining here.
Babies and children welcome: high chairs. Booking advisable. Disabled: toilet. Dress: smart casual; no shorts or trainers. Entertainment: pianist 7-11pm Mon-Sat. Separate room for parties, seats 18. **Map 14 F9**.

Marble Arch

★ Rhodes W1

The Cumberland, Great Cumberland Place, W1A 4RF (7479 3838/www.garyrhodes.co.uk). Marble Arch tube.
Bar Open/snacks served 11am-11pm Mon-Sat; 11am-10.30pm Sun.
Restaurant Lunch served noon-2.30pm, **dinner served** 6-10pm daily. **Main courses** £11.90-£23. **Set lunch** £15 2 courses, £18.50 3 courses. **Set dinner** £34 2 courses, £39.95 3 courses. **Credit** AmEx, MC, V.
The lobby at the Cumberland is a resolutely modern space, and its dining room, Rhodes W1, follows suit. There's a great sense of space, and the use of dark furnishings and blue lighting gives an effect that's almost oriental. The looks won't be to everyone's taste, but the food is a more certain bet. Everything we tried – from a salad starter of mango, orange beetroot and red endive with a mango mayo and citrus dressing, to a champagne jelly with summer fruits and warm orange cakes – left us wanting more. Green minestrone broth with summer vegetables, pasta and mozzarella was sunshine in a bowl. Bread-crumbed plaice with a zingy lime-infused guacamole was enhanced by first-rate chunky chips. Beautifully cooked leg and breast of duck came with baby turnips and peaches, in a tangy jus. And unlike many upmarket British restaurants, it's an egalitarian place – there's no dress code or stiff atmosphere, and the young staff are smiley. Note that the large light-filled bar is a useful spot in this

part of town. The opening of a planned fine dining annexe appears to have been put on permanent hold. Gary Rhodes's other London venture is Rhodes Twenty Four (*see p51*).
Babies and children welcome: high chairs. Booking advisable. Disabled: toilet. Restaurant available for hire. **Map 9 G6**.

Mayfair

Dorchester Grill Room

The Dorchester, 53 Park Lane, W1A 2HJ (7317 6336/www.dorchesterhotel.com). Hyde Park Corner tube. **Breakfast served** 7-11am Mon-Sat; 8-11am Sun. **Lunch served** noon-2.30pm Mon-Sat; 12.30-3pm Sun. **Dinner served** 6-11pm Mon-Sat; 7-10.30pm Sun. **Main courses** £14-£30. **Set lunch** (Mon-Sat) £25 2 courses incl coffee, £27.50 3 courses incl coffee; (Sun) £32.50 3 courses. **Credit** AmEx, DC, JCB, MC, V.
Redecoration has left the Grill Room a riot of red and green tartans. They're a striking sight, only overshadowed by the larger-than-life murals of rugged Highlanders. Whether you like the effect or not, it makes for an unstuffy room. Staff are more soberly dressed, but they too are welcoming. Lunch or dinner here is a serious business (and there's a wine list to match), but the menu has moved with the times: Denham Estate venison burger with quail's egg, griottine cherries, parsnips and port might be followed by ragout of john dory, lobster and mussels with crème fraîche and chives. More traditional are the grills: ribeye steak say, or calf's liver and bacon. Finish with strawberry ripple ice-cream or a selection of fine cheeses. On our most recent visit, we plumped for breakfast. The full english costs £25.50, but this brought a generous basket of dainty pastries and a vast plate of sausage, bacon, 'blood' (ie black) pudding, tomato, mushrooms, and poached eggs on muffins, plus juice and coffee. Other choices run from toast and top-notch preserves to a moreish smoked haddock kedgeree. Our only quibbles were that the bacon was slightly dry and that the handsome silver pots

don't keep the coffee hot for long. But they don't detract from the fact that this is a very agreeable place for a lingering meal, especially in winter.
Babies and children welcome: high chairs. Booking advisable; essential weekends. Disabled: toilet. Dress: smart casual. **Map 9 G7**.

Guinea Grill NEW

30 Bruton Place, W1J 6NL (7499 1210/www. theguinea.co.uk). Bond Street or Green Park tube. **Bar Open** 11am-11pm Mon-Fri; 6-11pm Sat. **Restaurant Lunch served** 12.30-3pm Mon-Fri. **Dinner served** 6-10.30pm Mon-Sat. **Main courses** £12.50-£34. **Cover** £1.50. *Both* **Credit** AmEx, DC, MC, V.
The Grill makes so much fuss about the award-winning steak pies here that they're almost bound to be an anti-climax. There's a choice of steak and kidney or steak and mushroom; both cost £12.50 and are a decent size, but neither scored better marks for us than a well-known supermarket's 'gastropub' range. An accompanying baked potato was close to cremated. We rated a starter of Cornish crab tart with watercress salad, and a main of chump of lamb with garlic-roasted aubergine higher. Pan-seared salmon with chive mash and sauce vierge wasn't bad either, and a green salad was beautifully varied and fresh. But there was nothing to make the heart sing – not even the deluxe chocolate pudding platter – and at these prices (£17.95 for the lamb, £3 a portion of veg, plus a £1.50 per head cover charge), there should be. The Grill is two tightly packed rooms at the back of a small, old-fashioned Mayfair pub. Service is jovial and solicitous, but not super-professional (there was a lot of 'who's having the lamb?'), and the furnishings have seen better days. On the plus side, it's a Young's pub, and no one is rushing you along; it's obviously popular with a mixed bag of office workers, but its particular charms were lost on us.
Children over 12 years admitted (restaurant). No-smoking tables. Separate room for parties, seats 28. **Map 9 H7**.

Piccadilly

Fortnum & Mason

181 Piccadilly, W1A 1ER (7734 8040/
www.fortnumandmason.co.uk). Green Park
or Piccadilly Circus tube.
Fountain (ext 2492) **Breakfast served** 8.30-
11.30am, **meals served** 11.30am-7.45pm Mon-
Sat. **Main courses** £11-£24.
St James's (ext 2241) **Lunch served** noon-2pm
Tue-Sat. **Tea served** 10am-5.30pm Mon; 3-
5.30pm Tue-Sat. **Set lunch** £20-£32 2 courses,
£25-£37 3 courses.
Patio (ext 2491) **Meals served** 10am-5.30pm
Mon-Sat; noon-5pm Sun. **Main courses** £10-
£24.50.
All **Credit** AmEx, DC, JCB, MC, V.
Fortnum & Mason celebrates its 300th anniversary
in 2007 – no wonder it's a tourist attraction. To
mark the occasion, a substantial refurbishment is
under way (to be completed in 2007), which, F&M
is keen to stress, will not alter the 'essential
character' of the place. Let's hope they're right –
the Fountain restaurant (currently one of three in
the store, along with the Patio on the lower ground
floor and the St James's on the fourth) has long
been an agreeable escape from the rigours of
modern life. At the time of writing it's pleasantly
decorated in soft shades, enlivened by murals
portraying Messrs Fortnum and Mason, and
staffed by a solicitous crew of uniformed
waitresses. This is a comfort zone like no other, and
all tastes are catered for. At breakfast there's
wheat-free muesli with own-made fruit purée,
kippers, pastries or the english breakfast (eggs,
two sausages, back bacon, black pudding – a
choice of English or Irish – tomato, portobello
mushroom and toast). Highland scramble was a
rich combo of quality smoked salmon tucked next
to beautifully yellow scrambled eggs on sourdough
toast. After 11.30am the likes of lobster bisque,
macaroni cheese, steak and chips and pie of the
day join a handful of the breakfast dishes to carry
diners through to last orders at 7.45pm. By the
afternoon most people are here for the sweet stuff
– ice-cream sundaes being a speciality.
Babies and children welcome: high chairs.
Booking advisable. No-smoking tables
(Fountain). Separate room for parties,
seats 32. **Map 17 J7**.

St James's

Inn The Park

2006 RUNNER-UP BEST FAMILY RESTAURANT
St James's Park, SW1A 2BJ (7451 9999/
www.innthepark.co.uk). St James's Park tube.
Breakfast served 8-11am Mon-Fri; 9-11am
Sat, Sun. **Lunch served** noon-3pm Mon-Fri;
noon-4pm Sat, Sun. **Tea served** 3-5pm Mon-
Fri. **Dinner served** 5-9.45pm daily. **Main
courses** £13.50-£22. **Credit** AmEx, MC, V.
This is one of the best-located restaurants in
London – and it's a looker too. The modern wooden
structure fits perfectly into a lakeside slot in St
James's Park, with every table having a water view.
We've a real soft spot for this place – good for
families (staff are charming with young diners),
it's also a romantic night-time haunt, and whatever
the occasion, it's affordable. Breakfasts might be a
full english or a bowl of granola with yoghurt and
pomegranate; at lunch there's a choice of
sandwiches or a full meal. Star turns on a summer
lunch menu were asparagus with morels, peas and
mint in a butter-rich broth, and Devonshire Bronze
chicken breast with braised fennel; beautifully tan
chips were a nice side order. We made fast work of
treacle tart with clotted cream, but special mention
has to go to the British cheese plate: £7.50 bought
goat's cheese, stilton and cheddar, a shiny apple,
chutney and plenty of biscuits. All this is
buttressed by a global wine list, and a fine batch
of cocktails. A park café par excellence. Owner
Oliver Peyton is also behind the National Dining
Rooms (see p57).
Babies and children welcome: children's menu;
high chairs. Booking advisable. Disabled: toilet.
No smoking (indoors). Tables outdoors (23,
terrace). Takeaway service. **Map 10 K8**.

Konstam at the Prince Albert. See p53.

Wiltons

55 Jermyn Street, SW1Y 6LX (7629 9955/
www.wiltons.co.uk). Green Park or Piccadilly
Circus tube. **Lunch served** noon-2.30pm,
dinner served 6-10.30pm Mon-Fri. **Main
courses** £19-£40. **Credit** AmEx, DC, MC, V.
Push open the door of Wiltons (est. 1742) and give
yourself over to its charms. The food is good –
very good in places – but there's so much more to
it than that. The furnishings are old-fashioned but
delightfully so, all cosy booths, upholstered chairs
and a hotch-potch of paintings. Napkins are whiter
than white and heavy cutlery gleams; service is
impeccable but not intimidating. Fish is a
speciality – there's an oyster bar – but not to the
exclusion of meat dishes (there are grills, and
game in season). The hefty wine list provides
stalwart support. A very trad menu produced sure-
fire starters in lightly spiced potted shrimps and
asparagus with hollandaise sauce. Then came beef
rossini (a melting plateful of indulgence) and cold
poached wild salmon – a fine fish hampered by the
accompanying russian salad. An alcohol-drenched
sherry trifle, coffee and petits fours rounded off a
very pleasing meal. You'll be brought back to earth
with a bang though when the bill arrives: the
salmon alone cost £30. One to cherish, but only
when funds permit.
Babies and children admitted. Booking advisable.
Disabled: toilet. Dress: jacket; no jeans or trainers.
Separate room for parties, seats 18. **Map 17 J7**.

Soho

Lindsay House

21 Romilly Street, W1D 5AF (7439 0450/
www.lindsayhouse.co.uk). Leicester Square
tube. **Lunch served** noon-2.30pm Mon-Fri.
Dinner served 6-11pm Mon-Sat. **Set lunch**
£52 3 courses. **Set meal** (12-2.30pm Mon-Fri,
6-6.45pm Mon-Sat) £27 3 courses. **Set dinner**
£52 3 courses, £62 tasting menu. **Credit** AmEx,
DC, MC, V.
Ignore the raffish Soho location; the neat townhouse
premises sets the tone for what is a pretty formal
dining experience. There are waiting staff galore,
some of whom seem intent on reinforcing the
already stiff atmosphere. We can't really
understand it: Richard Corrigan seems a jovial
presence on TV, and the food is good (often very
good) – possibly the geography of several different
small dining rooms puts a dampener on
proceedings. From the £27 set menu, duck liver
parfait with pickled figs and melba toast (served
fussily at table), followed by roast fillet of cod with
asparagus and clam vinaigrette, were pleasing but
unmemorable; and nice though apricots with lemon
curd and stem ginger ice-cream was, it seemed a
slightly wintery pudding on a hot day. Pan-roasted
sea trout with a fennel emulsion and a few prawns
(from the £52 lunch menu) just wasn't special
enough either. In fact, the only dish that made the
taste buds sing was a starter from the same menu
– roast scallops and pea gnocchi with crispy bacon
and pork – a brilliant mix of tastes and textures.
More of that, please, and a few more diners out to
enjoy themselves, and Lindsay House will be back
among our favourites.
Babies and children admitted. Booking advisable.
Dress: smart casual. Separate rooms for parties,
seating 6, 12 and 18. Vegetarian menu.
Map 17 K6.

Strand

Savoy Grill

The Savoy, Strand, WC2R 0EU (7592 1600/
www.gordonramsay.com). Embankment tube/
Charing Cross tube/rail. **Lunch served** noon-
2.45pm Mon-Fri; noon-4pm Sat. **Dinner served**
5.45-10.45pm Mon-Sat. **Meals served** noon-
10pm Sun. **Set meal** (lunch, 5.45-6.45pm Mon-
Fri) £30 3 courses; (Sun lunch) £18 2 courses,
£25 3 courses. **Set dinner** £55 3 courses;
(7-10.45pm Mon-Sat) £65 tasting menu.
Credit AmEx, MC, V.

Understated, sombre elegance is what you get at the Savoy Grill. Sensitively refurbished under the new management of Gordon Ramsay Holdings in 2003, the art deco room is quite dark, even on the sunniest of days, and the only touch of frivolity is the beautiful displays of white lilies. It's the perfect haven for men in suits. They need to be wealthy men, obviously – you pay for three courses even if you only order two (except on Sunday), so that's at least £30 at lunch before you've even considered drinks. For the price you get near-impeccable food from a kitchen run by Joss Stone but managed by Marcus Wareing, faultlessly served by personable staff. The sure-fire hits came from the carte – an amazing omelette Arnold Bennett made with lobster, followed by roast sea bass with glazed baby beetroot and red wine dressing, and pecan tart with cream (from the impressive pudding trolley). From the set lunch menu, caramelised shallot tarte tatin topped by goat's cheese and chive salad with a balsamic reduction was very good but very sweet, while pavé of roast salmon with white onion purée, wild asparagus and chervil broth was fine, apart from the mild disappointment at seeing salmon as the fish option. It's worth noting that the only view is of the Savoy hotel forecourt.
Babies and children welcome: high chairs. Booking essential. Disabled: toilet (in hotel). Dress: jacket; no denim, sportswear or trainers. Vegetarian menu. Vegan dishes. **Map 18 L7.**

Simpson's-in-the-Strand
100 Strand, WC2R 0EW (7836 9112/ www.simpsons-in-the-strand.com). Embankment tube/Charing Cross tube/rail. **Breakfast served** 7.15-10.30am Mon-Fri. **Lunch served** 12.15-2.30pm Mon-Sat; noon-3pm Sun. **Dinner served** 5.45-10.45pm Mon-Sat; (Grand Divan) 6-9pm Sun. **Main courses** £15.95-£24.95. **Set breakfast** £15.50-£17.50. **Set meal** (5.45-6.45pm Mon-Fri) £22.50 2 courses, £27.75 3 courses. **Credit** AmEx, DC, JCB, MC, V.
The Grand Divan room is very handsome; ignore the peach-coloured tablecloths and focus on the chandeliers and splendid wood panelling. But the decor turned out to be the only impressive thing about breakfast here. The atmosphere was mellow, which was nice, but it seemed to have spread to the staff, who certainly weren't rushing to clear the breakfast detritus from vacated tables. Coffee was lukewarm, pastries unappealing and the Great British Breakfast was no better than many a caff fry-up (limp bacon being the worst crime). Smoked salmon and scrambled eggs was a better choice, and both were generous portions. Considering what a fuss Simpson's makes about its breakfasts, this was a poor performance. In the past we've had better experiences at lunch and dinner, when stalwarts such as potted shrimps or lobster soup precede grills (sirloin steak, veal cutlet), pies (beef and kidney or fish) and, the pièce de résistance, roasts wheeled in on trolleys and carved in front of you. Simpson's has many loyal fans, but judging by this outing it will have to try harder to win any new ones – especially as prices are considerable.
Babies and children admitted. Booking advisable. Disabled: toilet. Dress: smart casual. Separate rooms for parties, seating 15 and 120. **Map 18 L7.**

Trafalgar Square

Albannach
66 Trafalgar Square, WC2N 5DS (7930 0066/ www.albannach.co.uk). Charing Cross tube/rail. **Bar Open/snacks served** noon-1am Mon-Wed; noon-3am Thur-Sat. *Restaurant* **Lunch served** noon-3pm Mon-Sat. **Dinner served** 5-10pm Mon-Thur; 5-10.30pm Fri, Sat. **Main courses** £15-£25. **Set lunch** £15 2 courses, £18 3 courses. **Set dinner** £27.50 2 courses, £32.50 3 courses. *Both* **Credit** AmEx, DC, MC, V.
The dining room at the Albannach seems a bit of an afterthought, as it's perched up a flight of stairs at the back of the bar-heavy premises. And even though it's just off Trafalgar Square, views are limited to the occasional glimpse of a red bus through white muslin drapes. The style is modern

Scottish (typified by illuminated stag sculptures and waiters in kilts) and the cooking follows suit. Drink, especially whisky, plays a large part, though food hasn't been ignored. A starter of cos lettuce, mustard leaves and grilled asparagus with Dunsyre Blue cheese and port wine dressing was a nicely bitter salad, but was eclipsed by tempura black pudding with a soft poached egg – the pudding, made on the premises, was wonderful melt-in-the mouth stuff. Mains were less lip-smacking: cassoulet of white beans with spring veg and poached egg was tasty but salty, while roast ribeye of Buccleuch beef with onion confit, spring veg and morel sauce was let down by overcooked, too-dry meat. A sweet hit of orange cheesecake with dark chocolate crumble (served in a cocktail glass and far runnier than a regular cheesecake), followed by coffee with tablet (a Scottish dry fudge), redeemed matters. A reliable business lunch spot.
Babies and children admitted. Disabled: toilet. Separate room for parties, seats 20. Tables outdoors (3, pavement). **Map 17 K7.**

★ National Dining Rooms **NEW**
Sainsbury Wing, National Gallery, Trafalgar Square, WC2N 5DN (7747 2525/www. nationalgallery.co.uk). Charing Cross tube/rail. *Bakery* **Snacks served** 10am-5.30pm Mon, Tue, Thur-Sun; 10am-8.30pm Wed. *Restaurant* **Lunch served** noon-3.30pm daily. **Dinner served** 5-7.15pm Wed. **Main courses** £13.50-£18.50. **Set meal** £23.50 2 courses, £29.50 3 courses. **Credit** AmEx, JCB, MC, V.
Hurrah for Oliver Peyton (who also runs Inn the Park; *see p55*) – and for the National Gallery for being brave enough to choose him over some corporate catering option. This is fine British food, in a modern (David Collins-designed) setting, at a reasonable price – especially in the café area, where a raised pork pie is £4.50 and scones with Cornish clotted cream cost £3.50. From the restaurant menu, heritage tomato salad was a warm plate of loveliness to start. Next, roast beetroot and wensleydale tart on mustard leaves was a little more liquid than expected, but tasted fabulous, while plaice was a generous portion of excellent fish. The best was yet to come: wonderful eccles cakes with Lancashire cheese and first-class eton mess with splendidly chewy meringue. It was a difficult choice, as the British cheeses looked so alluring. There's an interesting drinks list (though why no English wines?), with a good choice of teas (over 20), plus ales and ciders. A children's menu includes boiled eggs with soldiers and macaroni cheese. The only shame is the limited opening times. We wish every museum café had the same commitment to good food.
Babies and children welcome: children's menu; high chairs. Booking advisable. Disabled: lift; toilet. No smoking. **Map 18 K7.**

Victoria

★ Goring Hotel
Beeston Place, Grosvenor Gardens, SW1W 0JW (7396 9000/www.goringhotel.co.uk). Victoria tube/rail. **Breakfast served** 7-10am Mon-Sat; 7.30-10.30am Sun. **Lunch served** 12.30-2.30pm Mon-Fri, Sun. **Dinner served** 6-10pm daily. **Set lunch** £27 2 courses, £29.75 3 courses; (Sun) £32.50 3 courses. **Set dinner** £37.50 2 courses, £44 3 courses. **Credit** AmEx, DC, MC, V.
Refurbished in summer 2005, this old stager now looks a treat. The dining room makeover has resulted in a very pretty, light-filled room, with beautiful yellow-gold curtains and branch-like Swarovski crystal chandeliers in pink. The professional, smiley staff have uniforms to match (though only the ties are pink). The food has a lot to live up to, and mostly succeeds. Avocado salad with watercress, pine kernels and Lincolnshire Poacher cheese crisps was delightfully unctuous. The Goring fish cake with spinach and a lobster sauce was more solid and fish-packed than many, but all the better for it, and the deluxe sauce was a perfect match. A generous helping of pert raspberries was paired with an intensely flavoured vanilla ice-cream. The wine list comes in book form, but is clearly laid out, plus there's a sommelier eager

Interview
JESSE DUNFORD WOOD

Who are you?
Head chef at the **National Dining Rooms** (*see left*).
Eating in London: what's good about it?
Having worked in Australia, the US and Scotland, I think we get good real food here in London. I know everyone harps on about **St John** (*see p52*), **Moro** (*see p252*) and the **River Café** (*see p176*), but they are great landmark London restaurants: no messing around with the food, just really lovely produce simply cooked. In Australia and America there's lots of fusion and all that jazz, but we have a spread of fairly traditional, real restaurants with real food.
What's bad about it?
You do feel the pinch in your pocket. In the States they have amazing mid-market, accessibly priced food – you can eat very well for not much money. The other problem is European snobbery, such as being refused entry to a restaurant for not wearing a jacket.
Which are your favourite London restaurants?
I like **St John** (*see p52*). **Canteen** (*see p51*) is wonderful – great food, not snobbish, and it's a beautiful restaurant. I used to work at **Kensington Place** (*see p229*), and like that you can go for a bowl of soup, or an omelette, or a four-course meal.
What single thing would most improve London's restaurant scene?
American service is fantastic, even if it's a tiny bit fake sometimes. English service is appalling a lot of the time. We need waiters who are interested in serving people, interested in the job, interested in the industry.
Any hot tips for the coming year?
The continuation of the British food revolution. People like foragers will become more widely used to put interesting things on menus, such as chickweed and unusual herbs.

RESTAURANTS

Roast

to help. We watched the roast of the day (loin of pork) make stately progress round the room and vowed to return soon to sample it. The hotel was opened in 1910 and is still run by the Goring family, and this personal touch is evident at every level. Here's to the Goring remaining out of corporate hands for many years to come.
Babies and children admitted (lounge area). Disabled: toilets (in hotel). Separate rooms for parties, seating 6, 12 and 40. Tables outdoors (9, terrace). **Map 15 H10**.

Westminster

Shepherd's
Marsham Court, Marsham Street, SW1P 4LA (7834 9552/www.langansrestaurants.co.uk). Pimlico or Westminster tube. **Lunch served** 12.30-2.45pm, **dinner served** 6.30-11pm Mon-Fri. **Main courses** £22. **Set meal** £29 2 courses, £33 3 courses. **Credit** AmEx, DC, JCB, MC, V.
Shepherd's doesn't have to try very hard – and it doesn't. There are almost no other restaurants in the immediate area, and the parliamentary workers, lobbyists and government officials who eat here almost certainly aren't paying with their own money anyway. The kitchen turns out a tired succession of dishes at prices that would buy you an amazing meal in some of the capital's best restaurants. Starters of stilton and onion tart with apple chutney, and a smoked fish platter came adorned with the same salad leaf selection; the tart was flaccid and oily, the chutney a sweet jam; the platter run-of-the-mill apart from the smoked eel. Mains – duck confit with decent mash, and sea bass with a freshly made tomato and olive combo – were better, but that's not saying much; and it wasn't enough to persuade us to spend money on pudding (eton mess, trifle or similar). A short wine list produced a tart Rioja. The place has a cosy buzz about it (it was packed), the decor is designed to offend no one (apart from the design-conscious) and the staff were much the best thing about the place, being welcoming and attentive. There's no explaining the tastes of a certain type of middle-aged English bloke – but Shepherd's caters to them, exclusively.
Babies and children admitted. Booking advisable. No-smoking tables. Separate room for parties, seats 32. **Map 16 K10**.

West

Holland Park

Notting Grill
2006 RUNNER-UP BEST STEAK RESTAURANT
123A Clarendon Road, W11 4JG (7229 1500/ www.awtonline.co.uk). Holland Park tube. Bar **Open** 6.30-11pm Mon-Thur; 6.30pm-midnight Fri, Sat; noon-10pm Sun. *Restaurant* **Brunch served** noon-4pm Sat, Sun. **Lunch served** noon-2.30pm Tue-Fri. **Dinner served** 6.30-10.30pm Mon-Thur; 6.30-11.30pm Fri, Sat. **Meals served** noon-10pm Sun. **Main courses** £12.50-£34.95.
Both **Credit** AmEx, DC, JCB, MC, V.
This is an Antony Worrall Thompson restaurant, though you'll realise that the minute you clock the assortment of promotional material by the door. As a marketing strategy it's not particularly refined, but then neither are the cheerful surroundings nor the full-on food. And we wouldn't want them to be. The two comfortable and appealing storeys of exposed brickwork, lots of cushions and random prints and paintings, plus a large terrace, are invitingly relaxing, and the food is all about big tastes and good ingredients cooked straight-up. It's a meaty menu, with a decent choice of seafood but little for vegetarians. We started with fried prawns with chilli and garlic, which were enormous, tasty and good value for their £9.95, and avocado and crab cocktail, both singing with flavour. Steaks – a ribeye and a fillet, served with jars of Taylor's relishes – were tender and full of flavour, with big and quite lovely chips. So far, so good, but the whole experience was undermined by the juvenile antics of the staff, who may have been charming but also forgot about the basics (bread, bill, mentioning the terrace on a hot day), and were prone to indulging in boisterous games with the kitchen boys. The most recent addition to this small chain is the Barnes Grill, opened in summer 2006.
Babies and children welcome: high chairs. Booking advisable. No-smoking tables. Separate room for parties, seats 80. Tables outdoors (6, terrace; closes 10pm). **Map 19 A4**.
For branches (Barnes Grill, Kew Grill) see index.

Kensington

Maggie Jones's
6 Old Court Place, Kensington Church Street, W8 4PL (7937 6462). High Street Kensington tube. **Lunch served** 12.30-2.30pm daily. **Dinner served** 6.30-11pm Mon-Sat; 6.30-10.30pm Sun. **Main courses** £7-£19.50. **Set lunch** (Sun) £16.50 3 courses. **Cover** £1 (dinner). **Credit** AmEx, DC, JCB, MC, V.
Come to Maggie Jones's to experience a 1970s time-warp. The decor, over three floors, is country kitchen meets wine bar. Copper pans, baskets and enamelware hang from walls and ceilings; willow pattern plates sit on dressers, and candles drip wax on to wine bottles at scrubbed pine tables. You'll be in the company of multinational couples on dates, and Japanese and American tourists. Either they have more money than sense, or they're just enjoying the kitsch (and the camp service). A short wine list produced a sharp house wine. A long menu is supplemented by a roster of blackboard specials. Out of nostalgia we ordered avocado vinaigrette; perfectly ripe but with an acidic dressing – in the circumstances it was lucky that the onion tart (more of a quiche) that followed was so bland. The best bit was the red cabbage on the side. Globe artichoke was an uncontroversial starter, followed by saddle of lamb (a special) that was OK but fairly taste-free. Given the mismatch between quality and price (the lamb cost £18; sides are £3-£3.50) we gave desserts (burnt cream, bread and butter pudding) a miss. The name? – supposedly the one Princess Margaret used whenever she booked a table. Why is it full every night? We have no idea.
Babies and children welcome: high chairs. Booking advisable. **Map 7 B8**.

Olympia

Popeseye Steak House
108 Blythe Road, W14 0HD (7610 4578). Kensington (Olympia) tube/rail. **Dinner served** 7-10.30pm Mon-Sat. **Main courses** £9.95-£45.95. **No credit cards.**
Do you like steak, simplicity and an ample array of condiments? Then this is the place for you. Popeseye takes the classic meal of steak and chips

and focuses solely on that. Sure, you can order a side salad, but other than that the only choice to make is what cut of meat to have, how big you want it, and how bloody it should be. This is carnivore territory. 'Popeseye' (rump), sirloin and fillet are offered, in sizes ranging from 6oz to 30oz; the quality of the meat is excellent. As well as chips, a tray of nine mustards and condiments arrives with each order. This is a simple shack, a little grubby-looking from the street, but perfectly nice inside with its stripped wooden floor and open kitchen in the corner – you can hear the sizzle as your steak cooks. The wine list is ample, far larger than the food menu itself, with bottle prices extending up to £145. A little incongruous considering the surroundings, maybe, but if you're pushing the boat out for a 30oz fillet steak, why not go the whole way?

Babies and children admitted. Booking advisable. **For branch see index.**

South West
Chelsea

★ Bluebird Dining Rooms

350 King's Road, entrance in Beaufort Street, SW3 5UU (7559 1129/www.conran.com). Sloane Square tube then 11, 19, 22, 49, 319 bus. **Dinner served** 7-10.45pm Mon-Sat. **Set dinner** £30 3 courses. **Credit** AmEx, DC, JCB, MC, V.
The Bluebird Dining Rooms is a vision of 1930s masculine glamour, right down to the bar filled with leather armchairs. It's a pleasure to eat here, though whenever we've visited the place has been quiet – unlike the more boisterous parts of this dining complex (Mod Euro restaurant Bluebird). Perhaps the £30 set meal (if you only want two courses, you still pay for three) deters people. If so, it's a shame, because the seasonally based menu devised by executive chef Mark Broadbent is an assured, inventive roam around the country. Smoked salmon on potato cake topped with herby crème fraîche was a big-hearted starter, but Ragstone goat's cheese savoury custard (aka panna cotta), Cheltenham beetroot and land cress was an inspired one. Pearl barley risotto with penny bun mushrooms, globe artichokes, lemon and parsley was full of flavour, as was an

intriguingly spiced Goosnargh chicken with colcannon, baby turnips, baby onions and yellow leg mushrooms. The regional British cheeseboard, with Bath Oliver biscuits, apple, celery and chutney carries a £3 supplement, but was worth it; and made a fine contrast with a bowl of plump English cherries lightly dusted with icing sugar. Service was impeccable throughout. A shining example of ambitious British cooking.
Babies and children welcome: high chairs. Disabled: toilet. Separate room for parties, seats 30. **Map 14 D12**.

South
Battersea

The Butcher & Grill NEW

39-41 Parkgate Road, SW11 4NP (7924 3999/ www.thebutcherandgrill.com). Clapham Junction or Queenstown Road rail/49, 319, 345 bus. **Bar Open** 9am-11pm Mon-Sat; 9am-4pm Sun. **Snacks served** 9-11am daily. **Lunch served** noon-11pm Mon-Sat; noon-4.30pm Sun. **Main courses** £4.95-£9.
Restaurant **Lunch served** noon-3.30pm Mon-Sat; noon-4.30pm Sun. **Dinner served** 6-11pm Mon-Sat. **Main courses** £8.50-£25.
Both **Credit** MC, V.
At the new Butcher & Grill you're presented with a wide-bladed French Trappeur knife that looks like it should have been handed in to police during the recent amnesty. But such macho affectations rather suit this egalitarian grill restaurant and bar with a butcher's shop at the front. The retail area gives way to the spacious bar, where you could turn up in the morning for pastries or a sandwich. Up a short flight of stairs lies the main dining area, which boasts some patio tables overlooking the dock. The decor is all open brickwork, dark blue wood panelling and high-backed banquettes. We liked the simplicity of the menu. After a short list of starters – salads, terrines and so on – comes a list of cuts. You pick the one you want, and a free sauce (onion gravy, hollandaise, horseradish, red wine, green peppercorn, burnt chilli salsa and more) to be served alongside. Then choose extras such as beautifully crisp fine green beans, succulent chips served in a little terracotta flower pot, or spinach. The terrine of the day – a juicy jellied ham number – had a delightful caper piquancy, but a barnsley chop was disappointingly smaller than the sirloin, though cooked as ordered and delicious with its side pot of salsa verde. Service was prompt and friendly.
Babies and children welcome: children's menu; high chairs. Disabled: ramp; toilet. No smoking. **Map 21 C1**.

South East
East Dulwich

Franklins

157 Lordship Lane, SE22 8HX (8299 9598/ www.franklinsrestaurant.com). East Dulwich rail/40, 176, 185 bus. **Open** noon-11pm Mon-Wed; noon-midnight Thur-Sat; noon-10.30pm Sun. **Lunch served** noon-4pm Mon-Sat. **Dinner served** 6-10.30pm Mon-Sat. **Meals served** 1-10pm Sun. **Set lunch** (Mon-Fri) £9 2 courses, £12 3 courses. **Credit** AmEx, MC, V.
Conversion of these corner-pub premises into a restaurant with small bar at the front has worked a treat. The small dining room is daintily attractive, with flowers on each table, gilt-edged mirrors and a view of the kitchen at the back. The place has been going for a few years now, and has settled nicely into its role as a top neighbourhood haunt. A decent wine list and a menu that has more flair than most helps a lot, and service comes with a smile. We gave brawn and chicory a miss in favour of some excellent Colchester oysters and a too-large helping of borlotti beans with flatbread; asparagus soup would have been a lighter option. Monkfish with broad beans was a good-looking plateful; more monochrome but equally tasty was a dish of girolles, coolea cheese, lovage and potato. To follow, there are savouries, cheese or puds such as lemon curd ice-cream or rhubarb fool. Prices are slightly higher than the location would suggest – starters £5-£7.50, mains £11.50-£16.60 – but the weekday set lunch is an absolute steal for food of this quality and interest.
Babies and children welcome: high chairs. Disabled: toilet. Separate room for parties, seats 30. Tables outdoors (3, pavement). **Map 23 C4**. **For branch see index.**

London Bridge & Borough

★ Roast NEW

The Floral Hall, Borough Market, Stoney Street, SE1 1TL (7940 1300/www.roast-restaurant. com). London Bridge tube/rail. **Breakfast served** 7-9.30am Mon-Fri; 8-10.30am Sat; 9-11am Sun. **Lunch served** noon-2.30pm Mon-Fri; noon-3.30pm Sun. **Brunch served** 11.30am-3.30pm Sat. **Dinner served** 5.30-10.30pm Mon-Fri; 6-10.30pm Sat. **Main courses** £13.50-£25. **Set meal** (lunch Mon-Fri; 5.30-6.30pm, 9-10.30pm Mon-Sat) £18 2 courses, £21 3 courses. **Credit** AmEx, MC, V.
Roast opened with great fanfare late in 2005, not least because it is gastro-destination Borough Market's first proper fine dining establishment. It's a great use of space (upstairs in a new mezzanine level looking down on the market), and while the views may not be the most beautiful in the world, they're certainly arresting, especially if you like trains, markets or a glimpse of St Paul's Cathedral. Lunch on a sunny day showed the big airy room to its best advantage, though it was too hot to appreciate anything from the spit-roast. Moreish bread was followed by Lincolnshire spring leeks with mustard dressing and boiled egg (delicious), and pickled octopus with beetroot, carrots and white beans (an acquired taste). Wholehearted enthusiasm greeted mains of roast hake with creamed leeks, and pan-fried halibut with mussels and asparagus, plus a side of minted Cornish new potatoes. Custard tart with rhubarb was an old-fashioned treat. Roast gets points too for an intriguing range of drinks, many of them British. Breakfast here – the Ayrshire smoked streaky bacon, cumberland sausages, fried bread, black pudding, grilled tomatoes, field mushrooms and eggs (the Full Borough, £12) – is a real treat in a near-empty restaurant with crisp linen and relaxed staff.
Babies and children welcome: high chairs. Booking advisable. Disabled: toilets. No smoking. **Map 11 P8**.

Tower Bridge

Butlers Wharf Chop House

Butlers Wharf Building, 36E Shad Thames, SE1 2YE (7403 3403/www.conran.com). London Bridge tube/rail/Tower Gateway DLR.

Bar **Open** noon-3pm, 6-11pm Mon-Fri; noon-4pm, 6-11pm Sat; noon-4pm Sun. **Brunch served** noon-4pm Sat, Sun. **Set brunch** (Sat, Sun) £13.95 2 courses, £16.95 3 courses. **Set meal** (noon-3pm, 6-11pm Mon-Fri; 6-11pm Sat, Sun) £10 2 courses, £12 3 courses.
Restaurant **Lunch served** noon-3pm, **dinner served** 6-11pm daily. **Main courses** £13.50-£26. **Set lunch** £22 2 courses, £26 3 courses.
Both **Credit** AmEx, DC, JCB, MC, V.
The riverside terrace really makes this place; the interior is pretty plain (sort of Scandinavian-kitchen chic), with not much difference in decor between bar and restaurant (indeed, the main distinction seems to be that in the restaurant you pay more for very similar food). You have to show steely resolve in order to bag one of the outdoor tables; you can request one when you book, but be prepared to wait when you get there. Efficient bar staff make this more of a pleasure than a chore, but the pace here is hectic and it's a relief finally to be settled and watching the boats and people go by. Best dishes on an attractive menu – which has grilled steaks as the centrepiece (16oz T-bone, £26) – were some very perky potted shrimps, and delicious but sinfully double-battered fish and fat chips, served with mushy peas. Watercress and lovage soup was fine, but just too earthy to finish; meringue with summer fruits and vanilla ice-cream looked prettier than it tasted. The least successful dish was beetroot and pickled walnuts with a stilton sauce – the ingredients just didn't do anything for each other. There are savouries or cheese as alternatives. A comprehensive drinks list includes English beers and wines. In short – food six out of ten; setting nine and a half.
Babies and children welcome: high chairs. Booking advisable; essential dinner. Dress: smart casual. Tables outdoors (12, terrace). **Map 12 R8.**

East

Shoreditch

Rivington Bar & Grill

28-30 Rivington Street, EC2A 3DZ (7729 7053/www.rivingtongrill.co.uk). Liverpool Street or Old Street tube/rail/55, 243 bus.
Bar **Open/snacks served** noon-midnight Mon-Sat; noon-11pm Sun.
Restaurant **Breakfast served** 8-11am Mon-Fri. **Brunch served** noon-4.30pm Sun. **Lunch served** noon-3pm Mon-Sat. **Dinner served** 6.30-11pm daily. **Main courses** £9.75-£21.25.
Credit AmEx, DC, MC, V.
Now owned by Caprice Holdings (owners of the Ivy, J Sheekey and Le Caprice, among others), but less glamorous than that association might suggest, the Rivington is low-key and comfortable. A solid-looking bar has all the day's newspapers spread out on it, a good selection of wine by the glass, and a tempting blackboard menu of down-home dishes. Off to one side is the restaurant, where between starters and mains on an interesting menu there's a cheery middle section of things on toast (own-made beans, herring roes, potted Morecambe Bay shrimps). Decent bread comes as a small loaf on a board – just the right side of cute. Next came beetroot salad with smoked anchovy (the dish of the evening) and steamed sprouting broccoli with pickled walnuts and rape seed oil (good, but no contest). Mains of grilled sea bass with herbs and a large helping of scallops slipped down nicely enough. But the evening failed to ignite: the tables are very close together and we suffered the fallout from a group of loudmouths; the staff weren't very smiley; and the atmosphere was a little strained. Still, there's an alluring breakfast menu (bacon sandwich, in either a bap or a muffin, plus boiled duck's egg with soldiers, or fruit and oats with yoghurt), and a nice-looking deli next door. There's now a branch in Greenwich too.
Booking advisable. Takeaway service (deli). Vegetarian menu. **Map 6 R4.**
For branch see index.

Chinese

Gone are the days when Chinese dining in London simply meant cheap takeaways, roast duck on rice or predictable Anglo-Cantonese food. A new generation of Chinese residents is demanding more sophisticated food and more authentic regional flavours, and newcomers such as China Tang and Bar Shu (a contender for Best New Restaurant in the 2006 Time Out Eating & Drinking Awards) are riding the wave of a growing general interest in all things Chinese. Chinatown in the West End remains the centre of the Chinese community, with its bustling groceries, casual restaurants and travel agents specialising in cheap flights to the East. But it's also alive with tourists, which is why you're best off looking elsewhere for more sophisticated dining.

China Tang, the new restaurant in the super-posh Dorchester hotel, serves deftly prepared Chinese favourites in surroundings that make you feel you're starring in a film about 1930s Shanghai. Don't expect to see as many Chinese people there as glamorous westerners splashing out on Krug champagne, lobster and peking duck. **Bar Shu** in Soho has set a new standard for Sichuanese cuisine in the capital, employing six chefs from Sichuan province and importing key seasonings like chilli bean paste and weird, lip-tingling sichuan pepper. Non-Chinese diners go there for unusually authentic versions of classic Sichuan dishes, food critics for wild offal dishes, and Chinese diners for a taste of modern mainland dining-out.

In the unlikely location of Elephant & Castle, newcomer **Dragon Castle** has been creating a stir with its fine dim sum and expertly cooked Cantonese dishes. Like Bar Shu, it has attracted unusual attention for a Chinese restaurant, with prominent reviews in mainstream magazines and newspapers. Dim sum continues to grow in popularity, served in bars and pubs as well as Chinese restaurants; arrivals this year include **Old China Hand** and **Royal China Club** (an offshoot of the Royal China chain). It's not surprising, perhaps, given the fashion for tapas-style dining, but this would have seemed unlikely just five years ago. Truly, Chinese cooking has jumped out of the ghetto.

A FEW TIPS

Most set menus in Chinese restaurants pander to outdated western stereotypes of Chinese food, yet main menus can be daunting if you're unused to the cuisine. Here are a few pointers.

The art of ordering a Chinese meal lies in assembling a variety of dishes, differing from one another in terms of ingredients, cooking methods and flavours. Thus, if you're dining with a group, it's best to coordinate your ordering; if each guest insists on a personal favourite you may end up with a lopsided meal. Starters are easy: just order as you please and remember there is life beyond the usual deep-fried snacks (a cold-meat platter or steamed seafood can make a delicious beginning to the meal).

For main courses, aim to order about one dish for every person in your party, and then one or two extra, and share everything. Make sure you choose a variety of main ingredients so that things don't get repetitive. Then try to balance dry, deep-fried dishes with slow hot-pots and crisp stir-fries; rich roast duck with fresh vegetables; gentle tastes with spicy flavours. And ask your waiter about seasonal greens; you may find the restaurant has pak choi, gai lan (chinese broccoli), pea shoots, water spinach and other marvellous Chinese treats.

Most Chinese fill up on plain steamed rice, which makes a good foil to the flavours of the other food and is much more comfortable than that old takeaway staple, egg-fried rice. Desserts aren't a forte of Chinese cuisine, and you rarely find much beyond the old clichés of red-bean paste pancakes and toffee bananas – **Hakkasan** and **Yauatcha** are notable exceptions, as is **Mr Chow**, where French pastries are brought-in from a pâtisserie. Better, in most cases, to order an extra savoury dish and stop at a café afterwards if you want something sweet.

Central

Belgravia

★ Hunan

51 Pimlico Road, SW1W 8NE (7730 5712).
Sloane Square tube. **Lunch served** 12.30-2pm,
dinner served 6-11pm Mon-Sat. **Set meal**
£33-£150 per person (minimum 2). **Credit**
AmEx, DC, MC, V.

As the name suggests, this smart Pimlico
restaurant derives culinary inspiration from
Hunan, the central Chinese province south of
Sichuan. Although the dishes the Peng family
serve here come via Taiwan and have mutated
considerably, they are recognisably different from
the Cantonese cooking found elsewhere in London.
The best approach is to let the chef assemble a
succession of small dishes. These are likely to
include bamboo cups holding a gingery stock
containing pieces of guinea fowl, chicken, pork
and egg white; beef with three types of chilli and
sichuan pepper; and green beans deep-fried in a
garlicky batter. Other surprises might include a
salad of minced chicken and vegetables served in
a lettuce leaf, or strips of lamb with a Laotian-style
chilli-spiked dressing. Some ingredients can be
more international than Chinese, such as turkey,
or stuffed mushrooms. Be warned that if you visit
more than once you might find the chef's selection
doesn't vary much from one visit to the next.
Despite this, Hunan is a charming restaurant, with
food like no other and a wine list to match.
Babies and children admitted. Booking
essential. No smoking. Vegetarian menu.
Map 15 G11.

Chinatown

Chinese Experience

118 Shaftesbury Avenue, W1D 5EP (7437
0377/www.chineseexperience.com). Leicester
Square or Piccadilly Circus tube. **Meals served**
noon-11pm Mon-Thur; noon-11.30pm Fri, Sat;
noon-10.30pm Sun. **Main courses** £6-£22.
Set meal £19-£23 per person (minimum 2).
Credit AmEx, MC, V.

A highly enjoyable experience it is too, if bursting
with bustle. This simply furnished venue remains
immensely popular with Chinese diners (from
students to grandmothers), despite frenzied
competition. High-quality dim sum at unfeasibly
low prices is the lunchtime draw; on our visit a
50%-off deal meant that most snacks cost less
than £1.50 before 4.30pm. There are plenty of
enticements on the dim sum list, including 'pork
dumpling topped crispy custard' (little char siu
buns with a crunchy-sweet covering) and springy
steamed 'cuttlefish and sweetcorn balls'. We also
enjoyed the profoundly earthy 'steamed tripe with
black pepper sauce' (chitterling, in fact), the
delicately constructed 'peking ravioli in chilli
sauce', the subtle stock in the 'dumpling with
supreme soup' (the dumplings fried and served
separately), and the soothing blancmange-like
dessert of green tea pudding. Only the thinly filled
crispy seafood and egg roll was prosaic. We've also
had fine meals from the full menu (which includes
a notable vegetarian list) since the restaurant's
2005 opening. Arrive early if you want one of the
smaller tables in the left-hand section; otherwise,
grab a space at the communal tables to the right.
Babies and children welcome: high chairs.
Booking advisable. Separate room for parties,
seats 30. Takeaway service. Vegetarian menu.
Map 17 K6.

Feng Shui Inn

6 Gerrard Street, W1D 5PG (7734 6778/
www.fengshuiinn.co.uk). Leicester Square or
Piccadilly Circus tube. **Meals served** noon-
11.30pm daily. **Main courses** £6.80-£24.80.
Set lunch (noon-4.30pm) £3.90 1 course incl
tea, £5.90-£10.90 2 courses incl tea. **Set meal**
£12.80-£26.80 per person (minimum 2). **Credit**
AmEx, MC, V.

This isn't your average Chinatown eaterie. The
brightly lit dining room is broken into a warren of
intimate spaces chock-full of Chinese goodwill

tokens, including imitation firecrackers and
Chinese lanterns. The result is a fun and friendly
environment that seems to attract predominantly
young Chinese as well as westerners. Most of the
menu consists of Anglo-friendly dishes, but there
are also some less-common choices including the
restaurant's signature dish, 'kam sha' chicken. At
first, this seems nothing special – deep-fried
chicken covered with freshly deep-fried flakes of
garlic – but the combination of moist flesh and
crisp skin won us over. Stir-fried chinese mushroom
and seasonal greens (pak choi) was competently
stir-fried, but both Cantonese-style pork chop, and
sweet and sour king prawn were less impressive.
The key ingredients were cooked well, but both
were doused in wishy-washy sauces that tasted
similar and lacked flavour. Service is much
improved since the restaurant's opening in 2003;
our waitresses, dressed in red sweatshirts, were
friendly and attentive throughout.
Babies and children admitted. Booking
essential weekends. Entertainment: karaoke
(call for details). Separate rooms for parties,
seating 12, 20 and 40. Vegetarian menu.
Map 17 K7.

★ Fook Sing

25-26 Newport Court, WC2H 7JS (7287 0188).
Leicester Square or Piccadilly Circus tube. **Meals**
served 11am-10.30pm daily. **Main courses**
£3.90-£4.30. **Unlicensed. No credit cards**.

Head for the Fujianese specials at Fook Sing, a
rudimentary tiled caff featuring easy-wipe tables
and cheerful, kind staff. There's plenty for the
adventurous. Chewy fried snails arrived spiced up
with chilli and bulked up with mushrooms and
carrots; hotchpotch soup contained nigh-on all
edibles known to humankind (from tripe to
mussels, from ham to yam); and pork and cabbage
stew was a warming broth featuring tender meat
and a stock to savour. Portions are immense and
prices modest; three dishes plus rice for £14.50 is
the best deal. The enticing menu (which also
includes a long list of Cantonese-style stir-fries)
attracts Chinese diners, both young and old. Unlike
many Chinatown cafés, there's a relaxed feel to
proceedings, especially in the left-hand side of the
two-room interior; some regulars read the paper
here, mid-afternoon. Our advice is to come early
for lunch before the delectable oyster cakes run out.
Babies and children admitted. Takeaway service.
Map 17 K6.

Golden Dragon

28-29 Gerrard Street, W1D 6JW (7734 2763).
Leicester Square or Piccadilly Circus tube.
Meals served noon-11.30pm Mon-Thur; noon-
midnight Fri, Sat; 11am-11pm Sun. **Dim sum**
served noon-5pm Mon-Sat; 11am-5pm Sun.
Dim sum £2.10-£4. **Main courses** £6-£25.
Set meal £12.50-£35 per person (minimum 2).
Credit AmEx, MC, V.

Old China Hand. See p66.

A prime site on Gerrard Street makes Golden Dragon an easy choice for tourists (both Chinese and otherwise), and we can't help feeling the place is now taking things a little for granted as a result. The occasionally slapdash service and the slightly worn decor lack the lustre of the elaborate wall-carving of a golden dragon, which dominates the main dining area. But the cooking is fine, if not exceptional. A dish of braised belly pork may have looked like thick bacon yet it was meltingly tender, served on preserved vegetables. Stuffed beancurd consisted of big blocks of the stuff with single prawns embedded in them, in a slithery sauce with gai lan (chinese broccoli). More interesting was the dish of pallid chinese leaves, with threads of fragmented, orange-coloured dried scallops in the sauce. The classic hot and sour soup was correctly gloopy, with lots of flavour and colourful titbits to savour. However, the loud noise levels and brusque feel of Golden Dragon don't make it a relaxing spot for a meal.

Babies and children welcome: high chairs. Booking advisable. Separate rooms for parties, seating 20 and 40. Takeaway service. **Map 17 K7**.

Harbour City

46 Gerrard Street, W1D 5QH (7287 1526/7439 7859). Leicester Square or Piccadilly Circus tube. **Meals served** noon-11.30pm Mon-Thur; noon-midnight Fri, Sat; 11am-10.30pm Sun. **Dim sum served** noon-5pm Mon-Sat; 11am-5pm Sun. **Dim sum** £1.90-£5.50. **Main courses** £5.50-£20. **Set meal** £13.50-£15.50 per person (minimum 2); £15.50-£16 per person (minimum 4); £16.50-£21.50 per person (minimum 6). **Credit** AmEx, JCB, MC, V.

Several of Chinatown's dim sum stalwarts have sharpened their act since the arrival of Yauatcha (*see p70*) – serving dumplings into the night, or inventing modish specials. Not Harbour City. But despite a menu and furnishings that have changed little over the years, standards remain reliably high. Try for a table on the airy first floor, rather than the cramped ground level, which has little natural light. We did, and were comfy enough in a room sporting wood-laminate or pastel yellow walls, white linen, and windows looking out at Gerrard Street's Chinatown arch. Most diners were Chinese. Staff, competent if not congenial, delivered the snacks. Best of these were the crisp taro croquettes enclosing juicy minced pork, though we also relished the gelatinous meat in the five-spice beef tendon, and the juxtaposition of sponginess and springiness in the fish maw with minced prawn paste. Throw in some steamed whelks in curry sauce, and the odd glutinous rice roll (doughy roll, chewy filling) and we left happy. Nothing disappointed, though nothing scintillated either. The lengthy full menu majors in seafood: lobster, crab, eel, oyster and abalone receiving star billing. *Babies and children welcome: high chairs. Booking advisable; essential weekends. Separate room for parties, seats 60-70. Takeaway service. Vegetarian menu.* **Map 17 K7**.

Royal China Club. See p69.

Hong Kong

6-7 Lisle Street, WC2H 7BG (7287 0352/
www.london-hk.co.uk). Leicester Square or
Piccadilly Circus tube. **Meals served** noon-
11.30pm Mon-Thur; noon-midnight Fri, Sat;
11am-11pm Sun. **Dim sum served** noon-5pm
daily. **Dim sum** £2-£3.50. **Main courses**
£6-£9. **Set meal** £11.80-£15.80 per person
(minimum 2). **Credit** AmEx, JCB, MC, V.
The menus at Hong Kong are plasticky, the style
tacky, and the photographs of dim sum titbits so
small and dim you have to peer at them. Decor is
modern Chinese, with plastic-covered chairs and
the odd bizarre knick-knack (like the water wheel
installation on the wall over the stairs). Service
on our visit came with a smile, and willingness.
Our dim sum lunch was a mixed experience.
Steamed dumplings came stuffed with scallop;
with prawn and chives; and with pea shoots – all
nicely done. The deep-fried lobster dumplings
were pleasant enough too, though a tad
overcooked. Pan-fried cheung fun was finely
textured, yet only meanly studded with the
promised dried shrimp, and the slabs of turnip
paste were greasy. Worse, the 'crispy' vietnamese
spring rolls were shockingly rubbery, and our
first bite into the stodgy pork stuffing discovered
a nugget of gristle, so we set them aside and took
comfort instead in a bowlful of silken congee
with pieces of fish and dried scallop. We left
feeling vaguely dissatisfied.
Babies and children welcome: high chairs.
Booking advisable. Separate room for parties,
seats 60. Takeaway service. Vegetarian menu.
Map 17 K7.

Imperial China

White Bear Yard, 25A Lisle Street, WC2H
7BA (7734 3388/www.imperial-china.co.uk).
Leicester Square or Piccadilly Circus tube.
Meals served noon-11.30pm Mon-Sat; 11.30am-
10.30pm Sun. **Dim sum served** noon-5pm
daily. **Dim sum** £2.20-£3.50. **Main courses**
£6-£24. **Set meal** £14.95-£30 per person
(minimum 2). **Minimum** £10. **Credit** AmEx,
JCB, MC, V.
Imperial China has fully translated its menus in
the past year, revealing some interesting dishes
hitherto hidden from diners unversed in Chinese.
These include steamed scallop with rice
vermicelli and dong choi (preserved chinese
leaves); and baked lobster with salted duck egg-
yolk, which we chose to start a recent lunchtime
meal. Small, harshly cut and coated with the
bright, gooey orange egg, the lobster was
awkward to eat but worth the effort. Glancing
across the short dim sum menu, we noticed
several items marked as 'not recommended'. Be
wary of such advice; these are simply dishes
considered popular only with Chinese diners.
Congee with sliced fish, for example, wasn't too
challenging – just comforting rice porridge
studded with tender pieces of fish fillet. Most of
our other dim sum choices were equally good.
Only prawn and pork dumpling in broth
disappointed; the meat was tough and the stock
tasteless. Hong Kong-style beancurd pudding
(also 'not recommended') proved a cold and
refreshing finale. Smarter than most Chinatown
eateries, Imperial China attracts business people
on weekdays and Chinese diners at weekends.
Regrettably, service was shambolic compared to
previous enjoyable experiences: staff kept
bringing dishes intended for other tables.
Babies and children welcome: high chairs.
Booking advisable. Disabled: toilet. Entertainment:
pianist 7.30-10.30pm Thur-Sat. No-smoking
tables. Separate rooms for parties, seating 10-70.
Tables outdoors (5, courtyard). Vegetarian menu.
Map 17 K7.

Joy King Lau

3 Leicester Street, WC2H 7BL (7437 1132/
1133). Leicester Square or Piccadilly Circus tube.
Meals served noon-11.30pm Mon-Sat; 11am-
10.30pm Sun. **Dim sum served** noon-4.45pm
Mon-Sat; 11am-4.45pm Sun. **Dim sum** £1.90-
£2.90. **Main courses** £6.50-£20. **Set meal**
£9.80-£35 per person (minimum 2). **Credit**
AmEx, DC, MC, V.

In true Chinatown style, you might find yourself
seated on the second floor next to a huge pile of
dirty dishes awaiting the dumbwaiter, as we
invariably seem to at Joy King Lau. But this
shouldn't distract you too much from the excellent
dim sum, which makes the clatter of plates
perfectly tolerable. Prawn fun gwor were very
proper and correct, like tiny cornish pasties with
the minced filling visible through the translucent
wheat-starch casing. Har gau prawn dumplings
had been made with an equally delicate touch.
'Deep-fried squids' were an unexpected treat, like
white marshmallows inside but with golden skin.
Traffic cone-orange chickens' feet weren't as spicy
as we'd expected, but had an interesting texture to
compensate for the lack of flavour. The only dish
that puzzled us was the deep-fried shrimp cheung
fun. The filled pasta sheets of the cheung fun were
fine, but why serve them with a plum sauce that
overpowered the dish; was it a mistake? Still, with
a reliably good dim sum lunch for two coming in
at under £20, we weren't complaining.
Babies and children welcome: high chairs.
Booking advisable weekend. Takeaway service.
Map 17 K7.

Laureate

64 Shaftesbury Avenue, W1D 6LU (7437
5088). Leicester Square or Piccadilly Circus
tube. **Meals served** noon-11.30pm Mon-Sat;
11am-10.30pm Sun. **Main courses** £6.50-£15.
Set meal £9.50-£14.50 per person (minimum 2).
Credit AmEx, MC, V.
One of the more recent arrivals in Chinatown, the
Laureate has a lot going for it. Blessed with a prime
corner location and smart, bright and airy good
looks, it also steals a march on some of its older,
dowdier neighbours with its friendly and obliging
service. The chefs are no slouches either. The menu
isn't as adventurous or innovative as at some other
newcomers, preferring to stick to standard
Cantonese food, with a good selection of seafood,
but it also offers some northern dishes. Steamed
sea bass with ginger and spring onion couldn't be
faulted, even if its delicate whiteness and the
solicitous way in which it was deboned for us did
make us feel rather like hospital invalids. Mandarin
(or capital) spare ribs were much more robust:
thick and meaty in a dark orange, almost treacly
sauce. Seasonal greens (garlicky gai lan) were
nicely al dente. We found the dim sum first-rate:
vibrantly slithery cheung fun bursting with
prawn; and siu mai neatly topped with crab coral
and tightly packed with pork. Only jasmine tea
was allowed; we were told the darker and more
interesting bo lei was 'too strong'.
Babies and children admitted: high chairs.
Booking advisable. **Map 17 K7.**

Mr Kong

21 Lisle Street, WC2H 7BA (7437 7341/9679).
Leicester Square or Piccadilly Circus tube.
Meals served noon-2.45am Mon-Sat; noon-
1.45am Sun. **Main courses** £5.90-£26.
Set meal £10 per person (minimum 2); £16-
£22 per person (minimum 4). **Minimum** £7
after 5pm. **Credit** AmEx, DC, JCB, MC, V.
The menu at this Chinatown old-hand bears
careful scrutiny – demands it, even, such is the
long, confusing list of 'chef's specials', 'manager's
recommendations' and 'miscellaneous dishes'.
These three categories contain the majority of the
most alluring dishes. Start, perhaps, with steamed
razor clam with glass noodles, the tender bivalve
presented in its shell, covered with noodles and
sprinkled with browned garlic; a soy, coriander and
chilli dip adds some oomph. Next there's plenty of
classic and more innovative dishes. From the
former camp, braised belly pork with preserved
vegetables was an admirable hot-pot, the juicy fat
the consistency of butter (as it should be). 'Boiled
cuttlefish fillet' was nothing of the sort, being fried
slices of springy cuttlefish cake, but the
accompanying gai lan (chinese broccoli) was
delectably crunchy and fresh. Furnishings on all
three floors here are very much old-school: pink
linen tablecloths, worn green carpet, shrubbery in
the window and Chinese paintings on the walls.
Service improves markedly if you order proper

Chinese food, so avoid the set meals. Tourists
(especially Americans) eat here, yet so too do
Chinese Londoners, who know how to winkle out
some of Chinatown's best food from the menu.
Babies and children welcome: high chairs.
Booking advisable. Separate room for parties,
seats 30. Takeaway service. Vegetarian menu.
Map 17 K7.

New China NEW

48 Gerrard Street, W1D 5QL (7287 9889).
Leicester Square or Piccadilly Circus tube.
Meals served 10.30am-11.30pm Mon-Thur,
Sun; 10.30am-midnight Fri, Sat. **Main courses**
£5-£25. **Set meal** £11-£21 per person (minimum
2). **Credit** AmEx, MC, V.
We were excited by the opening of New China in
December 2005. Everything we saw suggested a
novel approach to Chinese food in Chinatown. The
former pub exterior had been transformed, with
Chinese-style bamboo roofing, while the
previously grimy interior had become decidedly
cool, with dark wood and purple tones. The menu
was different too, featuring expertly prepared
Hong Kong-influenced dishes rare to London.
Unfortunately, things have already changed,
primarily in the kitchen where a new brigade
reigns. The menu has become mainstream, with
the most interesting dishes now on a separate
Chinese language list. While we deciphered it, lai
tong (house soup) arrived unrequested. It was a
disappointing and overseasoned broth of pork
bones that set the tone for the rest of our meal.
Capital spare ribs arrived tough; cantonese roast
duck had been ruined through deep-frying. Even
the stir-fried chinese spinach was overcooked.
Fellow diners seemed to be young mainland
Chinese attracted by a heavily promoted selection
of Sichuan-style dishes. We tried the double-
cooked pork and wished we hadn't; the slices of
meat were dry and tasteless. Service was friendly

Chinatown cafés

Chinatown may be slipping somewhat in the Chinese haute cuisine stakes, but it remains the top destination for a casual, swift Chinese snack. The cafés roughly divide into two: old and new school. One-plate meals (roast meats served over rice, steaming bowls of noodle soups) are the mainstay of the old guard – venues such as **Hing Loon** and **Canton**. For decades such places have dealt in speedy, low-priced stomach-fillers. Comforts are often minimal and surroundings cramped, but the food can be very good. We've also included the traditional Chinese bakery and café **Far East**, where buns are the raison d'être.

During the past few years, a new breed of café has developed around Chinatown's edges. These places – including **Café TPT**, **HK Diner** and **Café de HK** – sport modern, light decor and attract cosmopolitan young Asian students, especially those originating from China and Malaysia. The food mimics that of Hong Kong's trendy snack joints and often includes Chinese-style takes on western dishes (barbecued meat and scrambled egg sandwiches, for instance). Drinks of choice are Taiwanese-style 'bubble teas': frothy, icy concoctions filled with gelatinous globes of starch that have to be sucked up through large straws in a reverse-peashooter operation – darned good fun.

★ Café de HK
47-49 Charing Cross Road, WC2H 0AN (7534 9898). Leicester Square or Piccadilly Circus tube. **Meals served** 11am-11pm daily. **Main courses** £4.80-£12. **Credit** (over £10) AmEx, MC, V.
Chinese teenagers in baseball hats favour this bright funky venue, tucking into meal-in-one plates of rice or noodles while watching Hong Kong pop videos. There's a ground-floor canteen plus two further floors for dining, though lingering is discouraged by hard blond-wood benches and the abrupt staff. Avoid the 'Russian borsht soup' (like packet tomato) and plump for a hawker soup noodle meal (choice of toppings, noodles in beef or curry stock). Ice pearl bubble tea is a popular thirst-quencher.

Bookings not accepted. No-smoking tables. Takeaway service. Vegetarian menu. **Map 17 K6.**

★ Café TPT
21 Wardour Street, W1D 6PN (7734 7980). Leicester Square or Piccadilly Circus tube. **Meals served** noon-1am daily. **Main courses** £6.50-£24. **Set meal** £9.50-£11 per person 2 courses; £16.50 per person 4 courses (minimum 2); seafood £19.50 per person 3 courses (minimum 2). **Credit** MC, V.
New and old marry well at the bustling little TPT. Clued-up staff sport orange sweatshirts and keep the pace cranked up, while the chef chops succulent roast meats in his kiosk by the window. Roast duck (on the bone) is juicy indeed – and tender. Good too are the Malaysian-style cold drinks; black tea with milk and pearl tapioca is fun to try, full of ice and chewy balls to be sucked up with a straw. Babies and children welcome: high chair. Takeaway service. Vegetarian menu. **Map 17 K7.**

★ Canton
11 Newport Place, WC2H 7JR (7437 6220). Leicester Square or Piccadilly Circus tube. **Meals served** noon-11.30pm Mon, Sun; noon-midnight Tue-Thur; noon-12.30am Fri, Sat. **Main courses** £5.20-£9. **Set meal** £9-£15 per person (minimum 2). **Credit** AmEx, JCB, MC, V.
Yes, there are paper tablecloths and a tiled floor, but new spotlights have produced an airier, more modern feel behind the glistening brown ducks that dangle in Canton's window. Food is resolutely old-school, as are the customers. Roast meats are the pick of the lengthy menu, chopped with flair by the chef. Juicy roast pork comes with crisp skin, gravy, a mound of rice and the odd leaf of chinese cabbage. Dab on a spot of chilli oil for good measure. Babies and children admitted. Booking advisable. Separate room for parties, seats 22. Takeaway service. **Map 17 K6.**

★ Far East Chinese Bakery NEW
13 Gerrard Street, W1D 5PS (7437 6148). Leicester Square or Piccadilly Circus tube. Bakery **Open** 10am-7pm daily. **No credit cards.** Restaurant **Dinner served** 6pm-4am Mon-Thur, Sun; 6pm-5am Fri, Sat. **Main courses** £5-£20. **Set meal** £8-£21 per person (minimum 2). **Credit** AmEx, MC, V.

Chinese Londoners like to take a break at this little café-bakery, lured by the thought of a chat, some tea and one of the splendid array of cakes. Buns come in savoury and sweet varieties, so you could start with a doughy ham and spring onion roll before embarking on a deep-fried red bean cake. An iced soya bean drink will complete the bean-feast. Babies and children admitted. Bookings not accepted. Takeaway service. Vegetarian menu. **Map 17 K7.**

★ Hing Loon
25 Lisle Street, WC2H 7BA (7437 3602/7287 0419). Leicester Square or Piccadilly Circus tube. **Meals served** noon-11.30pm Mon-Thur; noon-midnight Fri, Sat; noon-11pm Sun. **Main courses** £3.70-£7.50. **Set lunch** £4.50 2 courses. **Set dinner** £5.80-£9.50 per person (minimum 2). **Credit** AmEx, JCB, MC, V.
Long-lived but remarkably spruce, this tiny two-floor diner goes about its business without any fuss. A collection of the world's banknotes, and service that is polite as well as swift, mark out Hing Loon from the pack. So too does its pricing – a marvellous nourishing soup of tender brisket of beef with plentiful noodles in the most beefy of stocks costs just £3.80. The menu's huge, but the single-plate 'economic meals' are the savvy choice. Babies and children admitted. Takeaway service. Vegetarian menu. **Map 17 K7.**

★ HK Diner NEW
22 Wardour Street, W1D 6QQ (7434 9544). Leicester Square or Piccadilly Circus tube. **Meals served** 11am-2am daily. **Main courses** £5-£22. **Set meal** £10-£30 per person (minimum 2). **Credit** AmEx, MC, V.
A snazzily designed modern café, HK has a traditional roast meat counter by the window, and a variety of seating to suit its all-encompassing menu. Slurp noodles or meal-in-one rice dishes while sitting on stools by the counter; dine on monk's vegetarian hot-pot at a round wooden table to the rear; or venture into the adjacent room where Chinese students share wooden benches and suck honey peach pearl bubble tea. Babies and children welcome: high chairs. Bookings not accepted. Disabled: toilet. Takeaway service. Vegetarian menu. **Map 17 K7.**

---

and professional, but this was little consolation for a poor-quality meal. Babies and children welcome: high chairs. Booking advisable. Disabled: lift; toilet. No-smoking tables. Separate room for parties, seats 20. Takeaway service. Vegetarian menu. **Map 17 K6.**

New Diamond
23 Lisle Street, WC2H 7BA (7437 2517/7221). Leicester Square or Piccadilly Circus tube. **Meals served** noon-2.30am daily. **Main courses** £5.50-£20. **Set meal** £12-£19 per person (minimum 2). **Minimum** £10 after 5pm. **Credit** AmEx, DC, MC, V.
The parchment colour scheme, apparent spaciousness and absence of bustle set New Diamond apart from many Chinatown restaurants. Most customers are non-Chinese. The menu kicks off with boring set meals, then lists mainstream Cantonese dishes in English and Japanese, before leaving the specials list (around 100 of them) to the end in untranslated Chinese. Choose carefully, though, and you can avoid dull dishes such as fried ho fun with beef (which was no better than high street takeaway fare, with its gristly meat and pieces of uncooked noodles mixed into the beansprouts). A much better choice was the crab meat and fish maw soup, which had a wonderful viscous texture – you could wallpaper with it – and delicate briny flavour. Better still was the stewed eel and roast pork dish, in a sauce redolent of braising juices, with succulent boneless eel and squishy skin-on pork chunks. At the next table, Chinese diners were relishing the dishes they had ordered from the Chinese menu; next time, we'll ask for some translations. Babies and children welcome: high chairs. Booking advisable. Takeaway service. Vegetarian menu. **Map 17 K7.**

New Mayflower
68-70 Shaftesbury Avenue, W1D 6LY (7734 9207). Leicester Square or Piccadilly Circus tube. **Meals served** 5pm-4am daily. **Main courses** £6.80-£45. **Set meal** £9.50-£22 per person (minimum 2). **Minimum** £8. **Credit** MC, V.
Not even a booking can ensure you slip past the perpetual queue just inside New Mayflower. But the ebb and flow of diners is fast-moving, and service is eager and attentive once you're seated. The restaurant is constantly packed with Chinese people, here for the excellent and interesting Cantonese cooking. There are effectively three menus – English, the specials, and one in Chinese. We took the middle path of the specials list. An order for clams in black bean sauce produced a mound of tiny shells, but the bivalves were tasty enough to merit the fuss of seeking out the little blighters with chopsticks. Fish head soup didn't

contain any visible fish heads peering at us; it was a gingery fish stock with chunks of narrow bony fish among the straw mushrooms and green preserved vegetables. The menu is full of surprises, from a type of egg custard with pieces of halibut set in it, to a Malay-style coconutty lamb dish. A service charge had already been added to our bill in indecipherable Chinese, but when the waiter brought the credit card machine he asked if we wanted to leave a gratuity before conceding we'd already been charged for service.
Babies and children welcome: high chairs. Booking essential. Separate room for parties, seats 30. Takeaway service. **Map 17 K7**.

New World
1 Gerrard Place, W1D 5PA (7734 0396). Leicester Square or Piccadilly Circus tube. **Meals served** 11am-11.45pm Mon-Sat; 11am-11pm Sun. **Dim sum served** 11am-6pm daily. **Dim sum** £2-£5. **Main courses** £4.90-£10.50. **Set meal** £9.50-£50 per person (minimum 2). **Minimum** £5 evening. **Credit** AmEx, DC, MC, V.
Dining successfully at this huge, well-worn restaurant, noted for serving dim sum from trolleys, requires forethought and patience. First, time your visit well. Turning up when the doors first open works best as you're guaranteed the freshest dim sum: it won't have been on the trolleys for long. This is less critical at weekends when three full dining rooms guarantee a rapid turnover – and queues in the street of half an hour or more. Second, be patient: you'll be interrupted constantly by trolley dollies desperate for sales. Following our own advice, we turned up one weekday morning to find the ground-floor dining room empty and the waitresses impersonating terracotta warriors. This momentary pause didn't last for long. Within seconds they'd circled our table and were stationary once again. We glanced down. There was enough food to feed an army. Among the highlights were tender slices of cantonese roast duck and soft cheung fun filled with firm prawn. We also enjoyed har gau (prawn dumplings) which were uncharacteristically shaped like money bags,

but filled with minced prawn and a little bamboo shoot for crunch. Not the best dim sum in the (new) world, but certainly worth trying.
Babies and children welcome: high chairs. Bookings not accepted lunch Sun. No-smoking tables. Separate rooms for parties, seating 5-200. Takeaway service. **Map 17 K7**.

Royal Dragon
30 Gerrard Street, W1D 6JS (7734 1388). Leicester Square or Piccadilly Circus tube. **Meals served** noon-3am daily. **Dim sum served** noon-5pm Mon-Fri. **Dim sum** £2.10-£3. **Main courses** £6.50-£15. **Set meal** £12.50-£25 per person (minimum 2). **Credit** AmEx, MC, V.
In 2005 Royal Dragon emerged from a lengthy refurbishment completely transformed. The previously well-worn and unassuming interior is now almost trendy, with comfy seating, exposed air-conditioning tubes and plentiful dark wood. A new karaoke room upstairs isn't the only indication that the proprietors are trying to attract a younger crowd; the new menu includes such culinary delights as minestrone soup, cheese burgers, mixed sausage spaghetti, instant noodles and bubble teas – popular with Chinese yoof. Dropping by for a lunchtime bite we found the place, like last year pre-refit, empty. Tasting the food, it wasn't obvious why. 'Pan-fried pork chop with salted fish' also featured squid and was generously portioned, with plenty of salted fish. 'Egg tofu with minced pork served in pot' bubbled away on arrival, rich with oyster sauce and Chinese wine. Dim sum was reasonably well executed too. Har gau (prawn dumplings) were filled with moist prawn, though the wrappers were a little soft. Shredded chicken cheung fun was better: a good, slithery rice roll packed with succulent chicken pieces, shredded carrot and coriander. Staff are no longer resplendent in sparkly green waistcoats and ties; service is now cool, efficient and dressed in black.
Babies and children welcome: high chairs. Booking advisable. Entertainment: karaoke room (call for details). No-smoking tables. Takeaway service. Vegetarian menu. **Map 17 K7**.

Clerkenwell & Farringdon

Old China Hand **NEW**
8 Tysoe Street, EC1R 4RQ (7278 7678/ www.oldchinahand.co.uk). Angel tube/19, 38, 341 bus. **Open** noon-midnight Mon-Thur, Sun; noon-1am Fri, Sat. **Lunch served** noon-3pm, **dinner served** 6-10pm Mon-Sat. **Main courses** £6-£7.50 **Credit** MC, V.
There's an urban myth that Alan Yau's Hakkasan (*see below*) was the first UK Chinese restaurant to gain a Michelin star. In fact, this honour went to the Dorchester's Oriental restaurant, which closed in 2004. Dim sum chef Ngan Tung Cheung, who was part of the award-winning team, has resurfaced in this unassuming and atypical corner pub, producing a monthly changing menu. It's clear from the moment the dumplings arrive that this is no ordinary pub food; they could be mistaken for works of art rather than mere nourishment. Taste-wise, however, chef Tung still seems to be finding his feet in new (and more modest) surroundings. It was not until our fourth visit that we felt the flavours got close to matching the brilliant presentation. Gum sook jein gai beng (chicken and corn cakes) were perfectly fried, soft and sweet; gum yue kau (steamed prawn 'goldfish' dumplings) were beautiful and contained firm, fresh prawn and diced water chestnut for crunch. Prices are slightly higher than elsewhere, but most dumplings arrive in fours, not threes. Staff are friendly. A welcome addition to an area otherwise devoid of decent dim sum.
Bar available for hire. No-smoking tables. Separate room for parties, seats 30. Tables outdoors (4, pavement). Takeaway service. **Map 5 N3/4.**

Fitzrovia

★ Hakkasan
8 Hanway Place, W1T 1HD (7907 1888). Tottenham Court Road tube. *Bar* **Open** noon-12.30am Mon-Wed; noon-1.30am Thur-Sat; noon-midnight Sun. *Restaurant* **Lunch/dim sum served** noon-3pm

Mon-Fri; noon-4pm Sat, Sun. **Dinner served** 6-11.30pm Mon, Tue, Sun; 6pm-12.30am Wed-Sat. **Dim sum** £3.50-£16. **Main courses** £12.50-£48. *Both* **Credit** AmEx, MC, V.

We love Hakkasan. It's still one of London's most glamorous restaurants, and the beauty of it can startle. The low lighting, dark oriental screens (seemingly stretching into infinity), and general buzz of this big basement are like nothing else in London. There's fantastic attention to design detail, from the flattering staff costumes to the embroidered leather seats in the Ling Ling lounge bar. We like the place best for weekday lunch, when it's quieter (there's rarely need to book). Then you can explore the innovative dim sum menu, yet still spend a mere £15 per head on a meal that might comprise baked venison puffs, steamed dumplings topped with flying-fish roe, or perfectly slithery cheung fun. For dinner, you need to book well in advance, and might only get a two-hour slot at an awkward time; and the à la carte prices vary from steep to exorbitant. But at least you're guaranteed interesting dishes, such as slivers of mango sandwiching rare roast duck in a sharp lemon sauce, or steamed fish paste and tofu stuffed into pepper skins. Hakkasan gets almost everything right, from the dishes (of course), to the cutting-edge cocktail list mixed by friendly barmen, to in-house DJs who play music that's cool yet listenable. It's a seminal London experience. *Babies and children admitted. Disabled: toilet. Entertainment: DJs 9pm daily. Restaurant available for hire. Separate room for parties, seats 65.* **Map 17 K5.**

Holborn

Shanghai Blues

193-197 High Holborn, WC1V 7BD (7404 1668/www.shanghaiblues.co.uk). Holborn tube. *Bar* **Open/dim sum served** noon-11.30pm daily. *Restaurant* **Meals served** noon-11.30pm, **dim sum served** noon-5pm daily. **Main courses** £7-£40. **Set lunch** £16 per person (minimum 2). *Both* **Dim sum** £3-£20. **Credit** AmEx, JCB, MC, V.

Sultry style meets superb service in this unexpectedly delicious City restaurant serving modern Chinese cuisine. What was once St Giles' library has been converted to create a gorgeous den of black wood tables with pale blue leather chairs, glowing lantern lamps and dark red screens decorated with a floral motif. The menu is Cantonese, with enticing new takes offered alongside more classic choices. When we visited, seasonal specials included tender slices of ostrich fillet with young garlic served in a 'bird's nest' of crisp fried noodles. Other highlights were the 'new style' dim sum offered as appetisers. These included hot, moist Chilean sea bass wrapped in a crisp blanket of pastry; and delectable steamed vegetable dumplings in a bright orange casing made with carrot juice. Desserts were also a hit, with sticky 'yuan-yang delights' made of coconut-coated glutinous rice with sweet fillings of custard or red bean paste; and a delightfully wobbly green-tea pudding. The waiters were exceptionally courteous and obliging. Private rooms are available for hire and come with the bonus of a secluded mezzanine lounge bar for pre-dinner drinks. *Booking essential dinner. Disabled: toilet. Dress: smart casual. Entertainment: jazz 6.30-9.30pm Fri, 9pm-late Sat. No-smoking tables. Separate room for parties, seats 25. Takeaway service.* **Map 18 L5.**

Knightsbridge

★ Mr Chow

151 Knightsbridge, SW1X 7PA (7589 7347/ www.mrchow.com). Knightsbridge tube. **Lunch served** 12.30-3pm, **dinner served** 7pm-midnight daily. **Main courses** £12.50-£25. **Set lunch** £22 2 courses, £26 3 courses. **Set dinner** £35-£39 3 courses. **Credit** AmEx, DC, MC, V.

Back in the 1960s, Mr Chow had a stroke of genius: combine Chinese food with Italian service, and put it in a smart Knightsbridge setting. The formula worked then, and it works now, attracting the area's many deep-pocketed folk who think nothing of spending £50 per head on a boozy lunch. And this is easy to do: a single glass of wine adds around £10 to the bill, while wines by the bottle start dear and get dearer. Still, the cooking's good, and the service exemplary; on the whole, you get what you pay for. The menu is structured in the style of an Italian ristorante, into starters, pasta, fish, and so on. The homage to Italy doesn't stop there; the signature Mr Chow noodles resemble elastic spaghetti, with a minced pork sauce that looks like bolognese. The 'pink prawns' (£18.50) are huge beasts, split and served shell-on like grilled lobsters, but with a sweet and sour sauce. Shanghai soup dumplings were our only disappointment; they contained little liquid and the pasta cases were quite thick. Nevertheless, Mr Chow is an extraordinary place, with an old-school glamour and steady pace that makes newcomers such as Hakkasan (with its two-hour time-slots) appear somewhat nouveau riche. *Babies and children admitted. Booking advisable lunch; essential dinner. Separate rooms for parties, seating 20, 50 and 75.* **Map 8 F9.**

Marylebone

★ Phoenix Palace

5 Glentworth Street, NW1 5PG (7486 3515). Baker Street tube. **Meals served** noon-11.30pm Mon-Sat; 11am-10.30pm Sun. **Dim sum served** noon-5pm Mon-Sat; 11am-5pm Sun. **Dim sum** £2-£3.80. **Main courses** £6.50-£25. **Set meal** £14 2 courses per person (minimum 2), £24 3 courses per person (minimum 2) **Credit** AmEx, JCB, MC, V.

Tucked away in a backstreet near Baker Street underground station, Phoenix Palace is one of the capital's premier locations for Cantonese dining. Less well-known than the Royal China chain, it's a hot favourite for Chinese celebrations, and was packed on our visit with smartly dressed family groups. The decor and atmosphere are pure Hong Kong, with latticework panels, patterned carpets and vigorous cosmopolitan chatter. The menu is particularly intriguing, with bilingual specials lists featuring many unusual ingredients. Dim

Bar Shu. See p69.

China Tang

sum are seriously good. Standout dishes were the 'mini onion pancakes' (rings of melt-in-the-mouth pastry with a silky spring onion filling), the delicate prawn and chive dumplings, and the rolls of crisp batter encasing a succulent melange of mango, scallop and prawn. Barbecue pork puff pastries were a little too sweet, and the chicken dumplings rather stodgy, but these were minor quibbles in a generally excellent meal. A fresh, bouncy stir-fry of delicious venison with yellow chinese chives and other vegetables from the main menu was nicely cooked too. Service was pleasant and efficient, if a little hectic, but that was understandable because of the crowds.
Babies and children welcome: high chairs.
Booking advisable. Separate rooms for parties, seating 10 and 20. Takeaway service; delivery service (over £10 within 1-mile radius).
Map 2 F4.

★ Royal China
24-26 Baker Street, W1U 3BZ (7487 4688/ www.royalchinagroup.co.uk). Baker Street tube.
Meals served noon-11pm Mon-Thur; noon-11.30pm Fri, Sat; 11am-10pm Sun. **Dim sum served** noon-5pm daily. **Dim sum** £2.30-£4.60. **Main courses** £7-£30. **Set meal** £30-£38 per person (minimum 2). **Credit** AmEx, MC, V.
The Royal China restaurants can excel at dinnertime, although satisfaction is not guaranteed. Dim sum, however, rarely disappoint. On our last visit to the Baker Street branch, we grazed our way through an indecently large selection of snacks, and every single one was superb. The cheung fun was caressingly soft, each roll cradling a trio of very fresh prawns, and the accompanying sauce was delicately spiced. The steamed chinese chive dumplings were bursting with the fragrance of chives, enlivened by crunchy water chestnut and tiny morsels of shiitake mushroom. One special of pan-fried lamb and black pepper dumplings (pot-stickers) was unusual and delicious. Another – translucent, wobbly spheres stuffed with roast duck, cucumber, spring onion whites and a sweet bean sauce – was a witty variation on the crispy duck theme. Sadly, the standard of service on our visit didn't match the food. Waitresses with blank faces and don't-give-a-damn attitude did their best to freeze us out, and we needed to ask pointedly for our teapot to be refilled. After this, we had to raise an eyebrow when a waitress smiled as she encouraged us to add a tip on the credit card machine; service was already included in the bill.
Babies and children welcome: high chairs. Booking essential. Separate room for parties, seats 15. Takeaway service. Vegetarian menu. **Map 9 G5**.

Royal China Club NEW

40-42 Baker Street, W1U 7AJ (7486 3898/ www.royalchinaclub.co.uk). Baker Street or Marble Arch tube. **Meals/dim sum served** noon-11pm Mon-Thur, Sun; noon-11.30pm Fri, Sat. **Dim sum** £2.60-£8. **Main courses** £8-£38. **Set lunch** £15 3 courses. **Set meal** £36 per person (minimum 2). **Credit** AmEx, DC, JCB, MC, V.

This new venture by the Royal China chain – whose Baker Street branch is just down the road – is, rather too obviously, a response to Alan Yau's innovations at Yauatcha (*see p70*) and Hakkasan (*see p66*). So, dark bamboo lattices over burnished gold walls, low lighting and background cool beats replace the usual RC lacquer. Service, by black-clad young staff, is different too. One lad was charm itself, but two waitresses subjected us to the hard sell: touting expensive seafood around the tables, butting in to our ordering to suggest pricier alternatives. Such annoyances are a pity, as the food is great. Exquisite dim sum included meaty lobster dumplings in a sweet yellow wine sauce, slippery fresh cheung fun packed with plump prawns and chives, featherweight char siu puff pastries, and creamy cakes of dried scallop turnip paste with wind-dried meat. To follow, don't miss the ginseng and cream custard puff pastries (cleverly constructed to resemble the entire ginseng root), nor the exciting choice of teas. The full menu features banquet luxuries (roast suckling pig), skilfully made delicacies (such as hard-to-handle steamed glass ho fun noodles) and a few fusion dishes (sautéed prawns in cream and butter sauce). *Babies and children welcome: high chairs. Booking advisable. Sat, Sun. Disabled: toilet. No-smoking tables. Separate room for parties, seats 24. Takeaway service. Vegetarian menu.* **Map 9 G5**.

Mayfair

China Tang NEW

2006 RUNNER-UP BEST DESIGN

The Dorchester, Park Lane, W1K 1QA (7629 9988/www.thedorchester.com). Green Park or Hyde Park Corner tube. *Bar* **Open/dim sum served** 11am-1am Mon-Sat; 11am-midnight Sun. *Restaurant* **Meals/dim sum served** 11am-midnight Mon-Sat; 11am-11pm Sun. **Main courses** £10-£45. *Both* **Dim sum** £4-£22. **Credit** AmEx, DC, MC, V.

Tucked in the depths of the Dorchester hotel, China Tang will seduce you with its 1930s Shanghai opulence, pepped up with revolutionary memorabilia and funky modern art. There are some beautiful touches, such as the long fish murals, birdcage lanterns and delicate wallpaper design. It is gorgeous, decadent, and seriously expensive. The menu makes some attempt to be authentically Chinese, with dishes like chicken's feet and shark's fin soup scattered among the lemon chickens and peking ducks, but this isn't a restaurant aimed at the Chinese. Though the wine list is splendid, no attempt has been made to offer good Chinese teas (the Iron Buddha was dreadful). Our pork and watercress soup, typically Cantonese, was tasty, but had been strained of meat and watercress. More appealing were the sticky barbecued ribs: an expertly cooked version of a Chinese restaurant favourite. We deliberately ordered a couple of the more unusual main courses, which were delicious: a tangle of soft-shelled crabs, fried with 'egg-yolk' (actually crab coral), and a beautiful platter of steamed chicken interleaved with slices of yunnan ham and shiitake mushrooms. Despite the marble-topped tables, heavy crystal wine glasses, and generally magnificent ambience, service was surprisingly amateurish. Waiting staff forgot our requests for toothpicks, and for ginger in our stir-fried greens, and the spicy sauces we were offered never materialised. But the glittering atmosphere won us over; we had a wonderful evening. *Babies and children welcome: high chairs. Disabled: toilet. Separate rooms for parties, seating 18-50. Vegetarian menu.* **Map 9 G7**.

Kai Mayfair

65 South Audley Street, W1K 2QU (7493 8988/ www.kaimayfair.com). Bond Street or Marble Arch tube. **Lunch served** noon-2.30pm Mon-Fri; 12.30-3pm Sat, Sun. **Dinner served** 6.30-11pm Mon-Sat; 6.30-10.30pm Sun. **Main courses** £13-£39. **Set lunch** £22 3 courses. **Credit** AmEx, DC, JCB, MC, V.

Chinese cuisine offers plenty of scope for showing off, and what better place to show off than Mayfair? The menu at this sumptuous-looking restaurant lists dishes with names like 'Parcels of Prosperity' and 'Union of Land and Sea'. Not forgetting 'Buddha Jumps over the Wall', a bowl of shark's fin and abalone soup that costs £108. But does a deliciously simple green vegetable like gai lan need to be treated to a 'white truffle jus reduction'? So dense were the sauce and batter covering our chang sah prawns that it was hard to identify any of the promised 15 ingredients, let alone taste the prawns. Clay pot Chinese bacon, with dried chillies and whole cloves of garlic, was a much better bet. The unlikeliest item on the menu was chop suey, which turned out to be tender cubes of finest Scotch beef in a soy, plum and honey sauce on a nest of beansprouts. After so much that was on the sweet and heavy side, we hardly needed the complimentary chocolates that were served dramatically steaming with dried ice. However, there's plenty of quality here, not all of it outrageously expensive. A refit is likely during the coming year. *Babies and children welcome: high chairs. Booking advisable. Separate rooms for parties, seating 6 and 12.* **Map 9 G7**.

Princess Garden NEW

8-10 North Audley Street, W1K 6ZD (7493 3223/www.princessgardenofmayfair.com). Bond Street tube. **Lunch served** noon-4pm Mon-Fri; noon-4.30pm Sat, Sun. **Dinner served** 6pm-midnight Mon-Sat; 6-11pm Sun. **Dim sum served** noon-4pm daily. **Dim sum** £2.50-£3.80. **Main courses** £8.50-£12. **Set lunch** £12 per person (minimum 2). **Set dinner** £30-£45 per person (minimum 2). **Credit** AmEx, DC, JCB, MC, V.

For a stress-free Sunday lunch, avoid Chinatown and head to Princess Garden. The dim sum is of a high standard, and lower volumes of diners allow for a more leisurely meal. Our prawn and scallop steamed dumplings were fresh and light, and the roast pork buns were wonderful. Dinner was a more mixed affair, with a menu of mainly standard Anglo-Chinese dishes interspersed with a few unusual Cantonese home-cooking choices. A daily special of double-boiled soup was delicious, but other dishes failed to reach the same standard. Pork casserole with preserved vegetables was tough and could have done with more cooking, while steamed egg with dried scallops and preserved and salted duck eggs was overcooked. More successful was a starter of minced game wrapped in lettuce leaves, which was a little coarsely chopped but full of pleasing textures and tastes, and a rustic dish of stir-fried spinach with chilli and fermented beancurd sauce. The light and airy interior is smartly decorated (with antiques displayed in glass cabinets), providing a suitable setting for business dining. *Babies and children welcome: high chairs. Booking advisable. Separate rooms for parties, seating 6-50. Takeaway service. Vegetarian menu.* **Map 9 G6**.

Soho

★ Bar Shu NEW

2006 RUNNER-UP BEST NEW RESTAURANT

28 Frith Street, W1D 5LF (7287 6688). Leicester Square tube. **Meals served** noon-11am daily. **Main courses** £7-£30. **Credit** AmEx, MC, V.

Bar Shu isn't London's first Sichuan restaurant, but it's the first to have recreated Sichuan food so successfully – with six chefs from Sichuan – and with such style. The smart three-storey site is decorated in an appealing mix of dark stone, carved wood, blue lighting and bold graphics using Sichuan opera masks. The menus are glossy

Regional cooking

Chinese cuisine is conventionally divided into four major schools: the fresh Cantonese cooking of the south; the sweeter, oilier food of Shanghai and the east; the strong spicy cuisine of western China (especially Sichuan and Hunan provinces); and northern cookery, which is typified by a reliance on breads and noodles, and by famous dishes such as mongolian hot-pot and peking duck, rather than by any dominant flavouring style. Beyond these four great culinary regions, many provinces, not to mention cities and towns, have their own special dishes.

London's restaurant scene is still dominated by the Cantonese, many of whom originated in Hong Kong. Cantonese tastes have inevitably influenced the whole development of British Chinese cooking (Cantonese people don't, for example, much like spicy food, and they tend to tone down the flavours of the Sichuanese specialities on their menus).

A growing number of restaurants, however, are offering genuine regional specialities. New **Bar Shu** (*see left*) has attracted widespread attention for its authentic Sichuan flavours; **Angeles** (*see p75*) and **Sichuan Restaurant** (*see p71*) also offer spicy Sichuan dishes, though in more functional surroundings. There's a modest but real Hunanese venue, the **Shangri-La Hunan Cuisine Restaurant** in the Oriental City shopping complex in Colindale (399 Edgware Road, NW9 0JJ, 8200 9838), and **Hunan** (*see p61*) and **Taiwan Village** (*see p72*) serve a sophisticated, Taiwanese version of Hunanese cuisine.

ECapital (8 Gerrard Street, W1D 5PJ, 7434 3838, map 17 K7) offers Shanghainese specialities such as 'vegetarian goose' and 'lion's head' meatballs. **North China** (*see p71*) serves a great cold-meat platter and a fine peking duck (prepared in three courses, including not only the familiar duck skin with pancakes, but also a duck-and-vegetable stir-fry and a final duck soup). **Mr Chow** (*see p67*) serves hand-pulled pasta (well loved by the Muslims of northern China) in spectacular fashion; watch as a chef comes out of the kitchen to whack a ball of dough into a delicate skein of noodles. Visit **Rong Cheng** (72 Shaftesbury Avenue, W1D 6NA, 7287 8078, map 17 K7) and **Fook Sing** (*see p61*) for Fujianese food.

and beautifully illustrated, with photographs of the dishes. Two of the most distinguishing features of Sichuan cooking are chilli heat (rare in Cantonese food) and sichuan pepper. Sichuan pepper has an extraordinary tingling and numbing effect on the palate; after a while, it proves addictive. 'Numbing and hot dried beef' lived up to the name, but a dish called 'man and wife offal slices' (made with slivers of ox heart, tripe and

RESTAURANTS

tongue, garnished with roasted peanuts, coriander leaves and sesame seeds) was even more zingy and hot. The best dish was the 'fire-exploded kidney flowers'. Pigs' kidneys are cut and cross-hatched before being stir-fried at a high temperature so they 'flower'; they are then served with mixed vegetables including wood-ear mushrooms. If you're a true fan of Chinese food, or simply keen to try something different, then Bar Shu is a must-visit. Service can become chaotic, especially when the restaurant is full.
Babies and children welcome: high chairs. Booking advisable. Disabled: toilet. Separate room for parties, seats 10. **Map 17 K6.**

★ Ping Pong
45 Great Marlborough Street, W1F 7JL (7851 6969/www.pingpongdimsum.com). Oxford Circus tube. **Dim sum served** noon-midnight Mon-Sat; noon-10.30pm Sun. **Dim sum** £2.80-£3.90. **Set dim sum** (noon-6pm) £9.90-£11.90. **Credit** AmEx, MC, V.

It hasn't been open much more than a year, but Ping Pong already has a keen following among the young and fashionable. This is the first branch of what looks like becoming a chain of 'designer dim sum' joints. There's no booking and queues can stretch almost to Liberty's down the road. Inside, the dramatic decor is very 21st century, with stools ranged around curving counters and a huge glass wall looking on to a Japanese-style garden. Service is friendly, but can slow as things get busy. The dim sum looks nice, yet tastes and textures lack a certain Chinese pungency and earthiness – just as the entire restaurant (apart from the cooking area) lacks Chinese faces. Chilli squid cakes were good in a mildly bouncy sort of way. But the squidgy paste in the delicately crested har gau wasn't very prawn-like; the shanghai siew long bun fell apart on first touch; and the crispy duck fried rolls left a lingering flavour of cloying hoi sin sauce. Cocktails are the drink of choice; the only tea is jasmine, served in a theatrical long glass, complete

with budding flower inside. Prices are reasonable, but go for the vibe rather than the food.
Babies and children welcome: high chairs. Bookings not accepted. Disabled: toilet. No smoking. Takeaway service. **Map 17 J6.**

★ Yauatcha
2006 RUNNER-UP BEST PÂTISSERIE
15 Broadwick Street, W1F 0DL (7494 8888). Leicester Square, Oxford Circus or Tottenham Court Road tube.
Tea house **Tea/snacks served** noon-11pm Mon-Fri; 11.45am-11pm Sat; 11.45am-10.30pm Sun. **Set tea** £19-£26.50.
Restaurant **Meals served** noon-midnight Mon-Sat; noon-10.30pm Sun.
Both **Dim sum served** noon-midnight Mon-Sat; noon-10.30pm Sun. **Dim sum** £3-£14.50. **Main courses** £3.50-£24. **Credit** AmEx, JCB, MC, V.

Two years into its reign, Yauatcha remains a smash hit with fashionable thirtysomethings content to wolf down dim sum in the allotted 90 minutes. Few are Chinese. Style over content? Perhaps, but the style is so slinky. Inside Richard Rogers' classy, glassy Ingeni building, designer Christian Liagre has created a ground-floor tea room (where exquisite cakes are displayed like museum exhibits) and a large, buzzing basement restaurant. Down here, lights twinkle from a black ceiling, a fish tank runs the length of the bar, and fastidious staff – trained for speed – flit among the plain wooden tables and turquoise banquettes. Alan Yau's latest enterprise has transformed dim sum dining in London by serving the snacks into the night. The choice is wide and innovative, backed up by some enticing vegetable dishes (try the delectable baby pak choi given punch by salted fish). Our recommendations: three-style mushroom cheung fun (diverting textures, stunning fungi flavours), scallop and kumquat dumplings (fruitiness married with springiness), baked venison puffs (gorgeous pastry, peppery filling). Our criticisms: prawn and date dumplings

(dates masking the minced prawns' sweetness), and the steamed pastry (we've known lighter). Prices are about double those of Chinatown, and there's little under £25 on the wine list; try instead the delicate huang jin gui tea, from a long list of teas arranged by region.
Babies and children admitted. Booking advisable (restaurant). Disabled: toilet. No smoking. Takeaway service (tea house). **Map 17 J6.**

Yming
35-36 Greek Street, W1D 5DL (7734 2721/ www.yminglondon.com). Leicester Square, Piccadilly Circus or Tottenham Court Road tube. **Meals served** noon-11.45pm Mon-Sat. **Main courses** £5-£10. **Set lunch** (noon-6pm) £10 3 courses. **Set meal** £15-£20 per person (minimum 2). **Credit** AmEx, DC, JCB, MC, V.

Yming has built up a loyal following of western regulars over the years. Located just outside Chinatown, the restaurant has a bustling atmosphere yet retains the feel of a 'best-kept secret'. The menu offers several unusual entries that stray from the expected Cantonese staples; look at the specialities section in particular. On a previous visit, we were bowled over by a sublime braised pork hot-pot comprising slices of unctuous melt-in-the-mouth meat, laid over preserved vegetables and cloaked in a rich savoury sauce. This time we opted for 'village duck', a dish from the nomadic Hakka people of China; it was full of tender meat, with a hint of the earthy flavour of fermented beancurd. Beijing-style sautéed white cabbage was also very good, with the spicy hot and sour leaves providing a refreshing contrast to the rest of the meal. Not everything was up to scratch – chicken in hot sesame sauce was dry and bland; and our fish-fragrant aubergine was burnt – but Yming definitely executes some of its repertoire extremely well.
Babies and children admitted. Booking essential weekends. No-smoking tables. Separate rooms for parties, seating 10 and 18. Takeaway service. **Map 17 K6.**

West

Acton

★ North China

305 Uxbridge Road, W3 9QU (8992 9183/
www.northchina.co.uk). Acton Town tube/207 bus.
Lunch served noon-2.30pm, **dinner served**
6-11pm daily. **Main courses** £5-£12.80.
Set meal £14-£21 per person (minimum 2).
Credit AmEx, MC, V.

There are surprisingly few places in London specialising in northern Chinese cuisine. This smart, intimate restaurant in Acton Town is a 30-year-old treasure. It is evidently appreciated by the locals, so we were glad we'd reserved a table. At the same time as booking, we'd ordered our peking duck. This was duly presented to us in its golden-glazed glory, then whisked away to be carved into moist slices of meat and skin, ready for us to wrap – along with plum sauce, cucumber and spring onion – into immaculate, handmade, wafer-thin pancakes. Like many fun activities, this can all get a bit messy, so the water-bowl proved a useful prop. If you prefer things drier and crispier, opt for the 'aromatic' duck served in most other restaurants. Rather than over-indulging on the two final stages of the duck ritual (stir-fry and soup), we turned our attention to other regional delights. Highlights (from the owner's home province of Shandong) include green beans in a deliciously sticky garlic sauce, gungbao prawns and various own-made dumplings and noodles. Service was as charming as the old Peking Opera photos lining the apricot-coloured wall.
Babies and children welcome: high chairs.
Booking advisable; essential dinner Fri, Sat.
Separate room for parties, seats 36. Takeaway
service; delivery service (within 2-mile radius).
Vegetarian menu.

Sichuan Restaurant

116 Churchfield Road, W3 6BY (8992 9473).
Acton Central tube. **Meals served** 5.30-10.30pm
Tue-Sat. **Main courses** £5-£15. **Set meal**
£12.95-£19.95 per person (minimum 2). **Credit**
(over £10) AmEx, DC, JCB, MC, V.

This homely local still seems to be coming to terms with its suburban location. Students from mainland China tuck into fiery Sichuan dishes, while waiters offer non-Chinese diners free prawn crackers and steer them towards more lacklustre Cantonese fare. Persevering, we headed to the rear of the menu where most of the Sichuan options are listed. Our best dish by far was the pork tripe and tongue; served cold, the offal had been shredded and skilfully dressed with chilli oil and sesame seeds. A very generous helping of Sichuan-style beancurd (mapo tofu) was similarly pleasing, but lacked the characteristic zing of sichuan pepper. Other choices were equally well prepared, but the spice seemed toned down; requesting more chilli heat may be a good idea. Still, stir-fried green beans were agreeably crunchy, and the diced chicken with Sichuan sauce (gong bao chicken), while slightly too sweet, was nicely fragrant. This is a small and simple restaurant with affable, if occasionally clumsy, staff. The short Chinese language menu advertises 'steamboat', otherwise known as Sichuan hot-pot, a communal dish where diners cook their own thinly sliced meat, seafood and vegetables in hot, spicy broth.
Babies and children welcome: high chairs.
Booking advisable. No-smoking tables. Takeaway
service; delivery service (over £10 within
1-mile radius).

Bayswater

Magic Wok

100 Queensway, W2 3RR (7792 9767).
Bayswater or Queensway tube. **Meals served**
noon-11pm daily. **Main courses** £6-£14.
Set meal £11.50-£24 per person (minimum 2).
Credit AmEx, MC, V.

In contrast to the queues and brusque service of some other Queensway restaurants, the service at Magic Wok is organised, on-the-ball and efficient. The room is comfortable (cream walls, peach tablecloths, traditional Chinese art on the walls) without being trendy or smart. The most interesting dishes are marked at the front of the menu, in red ink; the more pedestrian listed at the back. The red 'specials' section includes braised winter melon, cut into slices and braised with threads of dried scallops to give a gelatinous sauce. Chunks of eel are cooked – bones, skin and all – in a hot-pot with pork to give a stew that's rich and savoury; the eel is best sucked from the bone. Equally dramatic dishes include strips of deboned chicken breast, served with a mustardy sesame sauce and topped with thin strips of jellyfish (very chewy and best not attempted if you have dentures). Even simple vegetable stir-fries might be pepped up, perhaps with the addition of two types of preserved eggs. Although Magic Wok is a cut above its rivals, lingering isn't encouraged; the manager signalled it was time for us to leave by the unbidden arrival of carved oranges and fortune cookies.
Babies and children admitted. Booking advisable
dinner. Separate room for parties, seats 30.
Takeaway service. **Map 7 C6.**

★ Mandarin Kitchen

14-16 Queensway, W2 3RX (7727 9012).
Bayswater or Queensway tube. **Meals served**
noon-11.30pm daily. **Main courses** £5.90-£28.
Set meal £10.90 per person (minimum 2).
Credit AmEx, DC, JCB, MC, V.

Vehemently of the old guard of Chinese restaurant – complete with vast menu, hectoring service and decor that's somewhere between Baker Street underground station (Circle line) and a 1970s wine bar – Mandarin Kitchen nevertheless thrives. The reason? First-rate seafood, cooked with an uncommonly light touch. Such finesse was best exhibited in our meal by a dish named 'stewed king prawns and crispy squid': the prawns plump, resilient and barely cooked (let alone stewed), the squid in tender rolls coated in gossamer-light batter. Exquisite timing was also evident in some crunchy-fresh gai lan (chinese broccoli) and a starter of deep-fried beancurd (the crisp coating still radiating heat, the interior luscious and wobbly). Another starter, XO jellyfish with smoked chicken and arctic clam wrap (the shreds served cold on a lettuce leaf, pepped up with the chilli-hot oil-based XO sauce), was a pleasing jumble of flavours and textures, while a dish of oysters with ginger and spring onions was most notable for the generous portion of little bivalves. All this with rice, a drink and service cost only £41 for two – though it's easy to spend more. Chinese come here in large parties to feast on lobster.
Babies and children welcome: high chair. Booking
essential dinner. Takeaway service. **Map 7 C7.**

Royal China

13 Queensway, W2 4QJ (7221 2535/
www.royalchinagroup.co.uk). Bayswater or
Queensway tube. **Meals served** noon-11pm
Mon-Thur; noon-11.30pm Fri, Sat; 11am-10pm
Sun. **Dim sum served** noon-5pm Mon-Sat;
11am-5pm Sun. **Dim sum** £2.20-£4.50. **Main**
courses £7-£10. **Set meal** £28-£36 per person
(minimum 2). **Credit** AmEx, MC, V.

Has this popular dim sum destination discovered its wild side? We couldn't help wondering as we sampled a new menu of earthy 'oriental delicacies'. Skipping over the 'pig's blood jelly', we tried crispy fried fish skin. It had a highly unfishy taste of smoky salt and pepper, and seemed like a garnish rather than a serving in its own right. Another choice from the same menu, pig's liver with ginger and spring onion, also failed to impress; there was no subtle ginger fragrance to the liver, just a coating of salty oyster sauce. Switching to the main 'chef specialities' menu, which we've enjoyed in the past, disappoointment continued. 'Tender ribs in chef's special barbecue sauce' arrived dry and tough with an overly sweet chilli sauce. Crispy golden king prawns stuffed with, er, minced king prawn, weren't as bad, just bland. The poshest Chinese in Bayswater, Royal China is renowned for superb dim sum. It remains popular with American tourists, but several Chinese regulars are on first-name terms with staff. They ordered more

Interview
SHAO WEI

Who are you?
Owner of **Bar Shu** (*see p69*).
Eating in London: what's good
about it?
It's such a cosmopolitan city, with people from all over the world, and you can find so many different kinds of food here.
What's bad about it?
There are too many cheap takeaways selling junky, industrialised food – this isn't food culture, it's rubbish. And I find most Chinese food in London very disappointing. I'm used to eating Chinese food in China, where the restaurant scene is amazing these days, not only in terms of food, but also design and service. Most Chinese restaurateurs in Britain simply want to make money. And the cheap, eat-all-you-can buffets give Chinese food a bad name. The diversity of Chinese cuisine, with all its regional variations, is poorly represented too: most people only have experience of Cantonese food.
Which are your favourite London
restaurants?
I like the Korean restaurants in New Malden that serve spicy barbecues – delicious. And in terms of design and environment, **Hakkasan** (*see p66*) is fantastic, although the food isn't authentically Chinese enough for my tastes.
What single thing would most
improve London's restaurant scene?
With so many nationalities here, I think we should see more emphasis on authenticity. In particular, I'd like to see more authentic Chinese restaurants. That's what we try to do at Bar Shu, to give people a glimpse not only of Sichuanese cuisine but also of Sichuanese culture.
Any hot tips for the coming year?
We're planning to open another Sichuanese restaurant in London, so watch this space!

simple dishes: steamed fish, hot-pots, stir-fried vegetables. Next time we'll do likewise.
Babies and children welcome: booster chairs. Booking essential Fri, dinner Sat; bookings not accepted lunch Sat, Sun. Separate room for parties, seats 40. Takeaway service. Vegetarian menu. **Map 7 C7**.

South West

Barnes

Chinoise NEW

190 Castelnau, SW13 9DH (8222 8666/8748 3437). Hammersmith tube then 33, 72, 209 or 283 bus. **Lunch served** noon-2.30pm, **dinner served** 6-11pm Mon-Sat. **Meals served** noon-10pm Sun. **Main courses** £5.80-£14. **Set meal** £15.50-£19.50 per person (minimum 2). **Credit** AmEx, MC, V.
A smart restaurant just over Hammersmith Bridge, Chinoise has already done better than its predecessors, which only managed to stay open a year or less. It's off to a good start though, complementing all-too-familiar Cantonese standards with a small but unique selection of dishes described as north-eastern Chinese. Simplicity and clear flavours seem characteristic of this little-known subsection of northern cuisine, along with the clever use of pork and vinegar. The kitchen adds no MSG to dishes. Tomato and egg soup made a refreshing starter – slices of tomato and cucumber supported by a light, peppery broth of chicken stock. We also enjoyed the crisp, thinly battered slices of 'guo bao' pork, which came coated in a wonderfully sticky sweet vinegar sauce. Another highlight was a gently sour hot-pot of tender slices of belly pork with chinese leaves and potato noodles. Culinary adventurers will certainly want to try the 'liufeichang' (pig's intestine) or 'hongshao dupian' (pig's stomach). Both arrived skilfully stir-fried with capsicum pepper and onion in a slightly spicy oyster sauce. Oily, thick, spring onion pancakes proved a tasty alternative to rice. Service is friendly, giving the place the feel of a family-run restaurant. A new chef specialising in seafood dishes should be arriving from China by the end of 2006.
Babies and children welcome: high chairs. Booking advisable weekend. Tables outdoors (2, pavement). Takeaway service; delivery service (within 2-mile radius).

Chelsea

Yi-Ban

5 The Boulevard, Imperial Wharf, Imperial Road, SW6 2UB (7731 6606/www.yi-ban.co.uk). Earls Court tube then C3 bus. **Meals served** 6-11pm Mon-Sat. **Credit** AmEx, MC, V. **Main courses** £5-£30
Yi-Ban's Docklands branch is a thoroughly Chinese restaurant serving fine dim sum, so we had high expectations of the food at their newer branch in Chelsea. A smart place in a swanky riverside development, its long dark dining room is divided by muslin screens and lit alluringly by a modern take on traditional red lanterns. The waiters who served us were charming. Despite the high prices and fancy garnishes, however, the dishes we tried would barely have passed muster in cheaper Chinatown restaurants. The dumplings on the dim sum platter were elegantly made but tasted a little jaded, while the deep-fried soft-shell crab, though nicely seasoned, was only limply crisp. 'Walnut prawns' turned out to be a bizarre concoction of deep-fried prawns soused in a kind of thousand island dressing and scattered with walnuts – a disaster. Duck with ginger and spring onions was cut into unappetisingly large chunks and came with chewy spring onion greens; and the beancurd in the ma po dou fu seemed untouched by the flavours of the sauce around it. The general lack of Chinese customers was telling.
Babies and children welcome: high chairs. Booking advisable. Disabled: toilet. Entertainment: jazz 8pm Thur. No-smoking tables. Tables outdoors (8, pavement). Takeaway service; delivery service (within 5-mile radius). **Map 21 A1**.
For branch see index.

The art of dim sum

The Cantonese term 'dim sum' can be translated as 'touch the heart'. It is used to refer to the vast array of dumplings and other titbits that southern Chinese people like to eat with their tea for breakfast or at lunchtime. This eating ritual is simply known as 'yum cha', or 'drinking tea' in Hong Kong. Many of London's Chinese restaurants have a lunchtime dim sum menu, and at weekends you'll find them packed with Cantonese families. A dim sum feast is one of London's most extraordinary gastronomic bargains: how else can you lunch lavishly in one of the capital's premier restaurants for as little as £15 a head?

Dim sum are served as a series of tiny dishes, each bearing two or three dumplings, perhaps, or a small helping of steamed spare ribs or seafood. Think of it as a Chinese version of tapas, served with tea. You can order according to appetite or curiosity; a couple of more moderate eaters might be satisfied with half a dozen dishes, while *Time Out*'s greedy reviewers always end up with a table laden with little snacks. Some people like to fill up with a plateful of stir-fried noodles, others to complement the meal with stir-fried greens from the main menu. But however wildly you order, if you stick to the dim sum menu and avoid more expensive specials that waiting staff may wave under your nose, the modesty

of the bill is sure to come as a pleasant surprise. The low price of individual dishes (most cost between £1.80 and £3) makes eating dim sum the perfect opportunity to try more unusual delicacies: chicken's feet, anyone?

Two London restaurants serve dim sum Hong Kong-style, from circulating trollies: the cheerful **New World** (*see p66*) and the less-cheerful **Chuen Cheng Ku** (17 Wardour Street, W1D 6PJ, 7437 1398, map 17 K7). Some of the snacks are wheeled out from the kitchen after being cooked; others gently steam as they go or are finished on the trolley to order. The trolley system has the great advantage that you see exactly what's offered, but if you go at a quiet lunchtime some of the food may be a little jaded by the time it reaches you. Other places offer snacks à la carte, so everything should be freshly cooked.

Dim sum lunches at the weekend tend to be boisterous occasions, so they are great for children (take care, though, as adventurous toddlers and hot dumpling trollies are not a happy combination). Strict vegetarians are likely to be very limited in their menu choices, as most snacks contain either meat or seafood – honourable exceptions include **Golden Palace** and **Local Friends** (for both, *see p75*), which have generous selections of vegetarian snacks.

Fulham

Taiwan Village NEW

85 Lillie Road, SW6 1UD (7381 2900/ www.taiwanvillage.com). West Brompton tube/rail. **Lunch served** noon-2.30pm Tue-Fri; 12.30-3pm Sat, Sun. **Dinner served** 6.30-11.30pm Mon-Sat; 6.30-10.30pm Sun. **Main courses** £6.50-£25. **Set meals** £17.90-£21 per person (minimum 2). **Credit** AmEx, MC, V.
Like Hunan in Pimlico (*see p61*), where the chef here used to work, Taiwan Village offers a 'leave-

it-to-us feast', so you can cast aside the menu, sit back and let the staff bring it on, which we did. The kitchen specialises in the robust, spicy flavours of Sichuanese and Hunanese cuisines (as interpreted on the island of Taiwan), which makes a refreshing change from the Cantonese mainstream. Our dishes owed much to the menu of Pimlico's Hunan, though the cooking was executed with less finesse. A 'minced pork soup', served in a bamboo tube, was delicately scented with lemon, ginger and coriander; our barbecued ribs slid sexily off the bone; and 'pepper fish' was

HOW TO EAT DIM SUM

Restaurants used to cease serving dim sum at 4pm or 5pm, when the rice-based evening menus took over. These days, however, since dim sum became fashionable outside the Chinese community, it's more common to find them served all day long, and into the night. Dim sum specialists always list the snacks on separate, smaller menus, which are roughly divided into steamed dumplings, deep-fried dumplings, sweet dishes and so on. Try to order a selection of different types of food, with plenty of light steamed dumplings to counterbalance the heavier deep-fried snacks. If you are lunching with a large group, make sure you order multiples of everything, as most portions consist of about three dumplings.

Tea is the traditional accompaniment. Some restaurants offer a selection of teas, although they may not tell you this unless you ask. Musty bo lay (pu'er in Mandarin Chinese), grassy Dragon Well (long jing) or fragrant Iron Buddha (tie guan yin) are delicious alternatives to the jasmine blossom that is usually served by default to non-Chinese guests. Waiters should keep teapots filled throughout the meal; leave the teapot lid tilted at an angle or upside down to signal that you want a top-up.

London's best dim sum are found at **Hakkasan** (see p66) and **Yauatcha** (see p70), which offer a sublime selection of unusual dumplings in glamorous settings; and the impeccable **Royal China** restaurants in Bayswater (see p71), Baker Street (see p68), St John's Wood (see p75) and Docklands (see p74), which have particularly exciting specials. The new **Dragon Castle** (see right) has been wowing diners with its dim sum since opening in 2006, and the snacks served at **Phoenix Palace** (see p67) and **Royal Dragon** (see p66) are also impressive. Outside central London, try friendly **Shanghai** in Dalston (see p75), **Yi-Ban** in Chelsea (see left), **Local Friends** in Golders Green (see p75), **Royal China** in Putney (see below), **Golden Palace** in Harrow (see p75) and **Mandarin Palace** (see p75) in Gants Hill.`

Below is a a guide to the basic canon of dim sum served in London.

Char siu bao: fluffy steamed bun stuffed with barbecued pork in a sweet-savoury sauce.

Char siu puff pastry or **roast pork puff:** triangular puff-pastry snack, filled with barbecued pork, scattered with sesame seeds and baked in an oven.

Cheung fun: slithery sheets of steamed rice pasta wrapped around fresh prawns, barbecued pork, deep-fried dough sticks, or other fillings, splashed with a sweet soy-based sauce. Some non-Chinese dislike the texture.

Chiu chow fun gwor: soft steamed dumpling with a wheat-starch wrapper, filled with pork, vegetables and peanuts. Chiu chow is a regional Chinese cooking style popular in Hong Kong.

Chive dumpling: steamed prawn meat and chinese chives in a translucent wrapper.

Har gau: steamed minced prawn dumpling with a translucent wheat-starch wrapper.

Nor mai gai or **steamed glutinous rice in lotus leaf:** lotus-leaf parcel enclosing moist sticky rice with chicken, mushrooms, salty duck-egg yolks and other bits and pieces, infused with the herby fragrance of the leaf.

Paper-wrapped prawns: tissue-thin rice paper enclosing plump prawn meat, sometimes scattered with sesame seeds, deep-fried.

Sago cream with yam: cool, sweet soup of coconut milk with sago pearls and morsels of taro.

Scallop dumpling: delicate steamed dumpling filled with scallop (sometimes with prawn) and vegetables.

Shark's fin dumpling: small steamed dumpling with a wheaten wrapper pinched into a frilly cockscomb shape on top, stuffed with a mix of pork, prawn and slippery strands of shark's fin.

Siu loon bao: Shanghai-style round dumpling with a whirled pattern on top and a juicy minced pork filling.

Siu mai: little dumpling with an open top, a wheat-flour wrapper and a minced pork filling. Traditionally topped with crab coral, although minced carrot and other substitutes are common.

Taro croquette or **yam croquette:** egg-shaped, deep-fried dumpling with a frizzy, melt-in-your mouth outer layer, made of mashed taro with a savoury minced pork filling.

Turnip paste: a heavy slab of creamy paste made from glutinous rice flour and white oriental radishes, studded with fragments of wind-dried pork, sausage and dried shrimps and fried to a golden brown on either side.

Babies and children admitted. Booking advisable. Separate room for parties, seats 15. Takeaway service. Map 13 A12.

Putney

Royal China
3 Chelverton Road, SW15 1RN (8788 0907). East Putney tube/Putney rail/14, 37, 74 bus. **Lunch served** noon-3.30pm Mon-Sat; noon-4pm Sun. **Dinner served** 6.30-11pm Mon-Sat; 6.30-10.30pm Sun. **Dim sum served** noon-3.30pm daily. **Dim sum** £1.80-£5. **Main courses** £5.50-£40. **Set meal** £23-£35 per person (minimum 2). **Credit** AmEx, DC.
Despite the name, this Royal China has long been disconnected from the Royal China chain that's renowned for dim sum. While the dim sum here is perfectly adequate, the forte is the à la carte, dinner menu. Chunks of lamb are stewed (on the bone) in a hot-pot with sheets of dried beancurd sticks that resemble the smooth connective-tissue attached to the meat; bamboo shoots give crunch, and chinese leaves add extra texture to an already intriguing dish. Vegetables such as morning glory (tung choi) might be stir-fried in a salty beancurd sauce with shredded chillies. There are occasional luxury ingredients too, such as geoduck (giant clams), and XO sauce (a chilli-hot oil with pungent dried seafood) is used to flavour strips of perfectly tender sautéed squid. You'll also find several more familiar dishes, but the menu tends towards the interesting rather than the predictable. Royal China's smooth, courteous service, and the dining room's extraordinary appearance – it's gloss-black, lacquered and a bit art deco in places, evocative of 1930s Shanghai – make this one of the best places to eat out in Putney.
Babies and children admitted. Booking advisable; bookings not accepted lunch Sun. Takeaway service; delivery service (within 3.5-mile radius).

South East
Elephant & Castle

★ Dragon Castle NEW
114 Walworth Road, SE17 1JL (7277 3388/ www.dragoncastle.co.uk). Elephant & Castle tube/rail. **Meals served** noon-11pm Mon-Thur; noon-11.30pm Fri, Sat; 11.30am-10.30pm Sun. **Main courses** £4.50-£90. **Set meals** £13.50-£22.50 per person (minimum 2). **Credit** AmEx, JCB, MC, V.
Located on the ground floor of a smart new development, this Cantonese restaurant sticks out proudly among the ugly buildings and traffic jams of the Walworth Road. Diners enter to the side of a magnificent Chinese armoured door. Inside, crystal chandeliers light a vast dining room that, while opulent, is restrained (by Chinese standards), with white walls, dark floor tiles and only the occasional oriental flourish. The kitchen produces superb Cantonese food featuring fresh ingredients, uncluttered flavours and contrasting textures. Wun tun soup comprised large pork and prawn wun tuns and a little pak choi in a flavourful chicken broth. Tasty dried scallop starred in the winter melon soup, while Chinese ham to rival the best from Italy or Spain helped flavour braised tien tsin cabbage (chinese leaf). Daytime dim sum is skilfully produced: fresh scallops filled the soft and silky cheung fun; har gau (prawn dumpling) included traditional white fungus rather than the common (and cheaper) bamboo shoot. Staff are friendly too. In terms of food, service and decor, Dragon Castle compares favourably with anything available in the West End. We expect it to become a much-loved feature of this area's regeneration.
Babies and children welcome: high chairs. Booking advisable Fri, Sat. Disabled: toilet. No-smoking tables. Separate room for parties, seats 60. Takeaway service. Vegetarian menu. Map 24 O11.

Greenwich

Peninsula
Holiday Inn Express, Bugsby's Way, SE10 0GD (8858 2028/www.mychinesefood.co.uk). North Greenwich tube. **Meals served** noon-11pm Mon-Fri; 11am-11.30pm Sat; 11am-11pm Sun. **Dim sum served** noon-5pm Mon-Fri; 11am-5pm Sat, Sun. **Dim sum** £2-£3.80. **Main courses** £5-£15. **Set meal** £15-£19 per person (minimum 2). **Credit** AmEx, MC, V.
At the weekend crowds of Chinese families and friends flock to this large dining room, a stone's throw from the Millennium Dome, to drink tea, feast on dim sum and catch up on gossip. While the cooking is not up to the refined standards of

fabulously sizzly with chilli, garlic and sichuan pepper. Other specialities, however, were disappointing. Scallops came suffocated in a heavy sweet-sour sauce; deep-fried green beans were greasy and oversalted; and three out of four main courses were served in similar sauces, all of them variations on the sweet-sour-salty theme. Still, the meal was excellent value: 14 little dishes with rice for just £21.50 a head. Staff were sweet and helpful, though had limited English. The place is decked out in sleek, dark wood, with nice lighting and some romantically secluded tables.

London's premier Chinese establishments, it is competent and very reasonably priced. The bustling atmosphere and cheerfully tacky surroundings are reminiscent of similar places in Hong Kong. Our lunch was a mixture of hits and misses. Successes included steamed half-moon dumplings filled with crunchy prawns and water chestnuts; and the 'three kinds of cheung fun' (silky steamed rice-wrapper rolls with fillings of prawn, beef and roast pork). Less successful were some underfried savoury meat croquettes, which contained a bland, nondescript filling; and shanghai dumplings that had leaked the stock which should have been filling them. Never mind: some hot flaky egg-custard tarts provided a sweet finish to the meal.

Babies and children welcome: high chairs. Bookings not accepted before 5pm. Disabled: toilet. Separate rooms for parties, seating 40 and 60. Takeaway service. Vegetarian menu.

East
Docklands

★ Royal China

30 Westferry Circus, E14 8RR (7719 0888/ www.royalchinagroup.co.uk). Canary Wharf tube/ DLR/Westferry DLR. **Meals served** noon-11pm Mon-Thur; noon-11.30pm Fri, Sat; 11am-10pm Sun. **Dim sum served** noon-5pm daily. **Dim sum** £2.20-£4.50. **Main courses** £7-£40. **Set meal** £28-£36 per person (minimum 2). **Credit** AmEx, JCB, MC, V.

Lunching here is consistently more congenial than at any other Royal China branch. Perhaps it's the stunning location, on the brink of the glittering Thames. Perhaps it's the sense of detachment from the frenzy of central London, making the staff and the atmosphere kinder and less harried. Perhaps it's knowing that even at weekends you rarely have to queue for long. The food, of course, is top-notch, and tastes even more delicious on a sunny day if you manage to bag a table under the trees outside. Seasonal specials on our last visit included batons of juicy cod in marvellously flaky pastry, superb crab meat 'siu loon' buns that burst open in a flush of savoury stock (served with the requisite ginger-and-vinegar dip), and delicate grilled dumplings stuffed with watercress. Dim sum from the regular menu were as good as ever: luxuriantly textured turnip paste; steamed dumplings stuffed with scallop, and crisp, deep-fried prawn dumplings served with fruity salad cream. Dinner can be pretty good too, although it's the dim sum that shines.

Babies and children welcome: high chairs. Booking advisable; essential lunch Mon-Fri. Disabled: toilet. Separate room for parties, seats 40. Tables outdoors (26, terrace). Takeaway service; delivery service (within 1-mile radius).

Dragon Castle. See p73.

North East

Dalston

★ Shanghai

*41 Kingsland High Street, E8 2JS (7254 2878).
Dalston Kingsland rail/38, 67, 76, 149 bus.*
Meals served noon-11pm, **dim sum served**
noon-5pm daily. **Dim sum** £2-£3.90. **Main
courses** £5.20-£7.20. **Set meal** £13.50-£15.20
per person (minimum 2). **Credit** AmEx, MC, V.
In recent years we've found the food at this local
Chinese opposite Ridley Road Market quite patchy,
but two recent visits impressed. A well-executed
broth of shark's fin and crab meat was thick with
crab and comforting egg white. We also enjoyed
the braised stuffed scallops with crab meat sauce;
tasty medallions of minced prawn were generously
sandwiched between slices of fresh scallop.
'Shanghai devil' brought tender, sweetly fragrant
pieces of lamb with a deceptive spiciness that took
a few moments to hit. The dim sum is generally
good too, and absurdly cheap during late
afternoons. The pretty scallop dumplings with
their spinach-green wrappers are definitely worth
trying. Cheung fun wrappers can be a bit thick and
heavy, but ours were packed with firm, succulent
prawn. Prawn balls with crispy shredded pastry
were nicely deep-fried, though we found them a
little rubbery, featuring more squid than prawn.
Dating from 1862, the front dining room was once
a pie and mash shop; now listed, it still boasts the
original art nouveau features. A rear dining room
is more conventional, with private rooms for
karaoke. Service, from staff in red sweatshirts, is
friendly and informal but occasionally too hurried.
*Babies and children welcome: high chairs.
Booking advisable. Disabled: toilet. Separate
rooms for parties, both seating 45. Takeaway
service.* **Map 25 B5.**

North West

Golders Green

★ Local Friends

*28 North End Road, NW11 7PT (8455 9258).
Golders Green tube.* **Meals served** noon-11pm,
dim sum served noon-10pm daily. **Dim sum**
£2.20-£6. **Main courses** £5.50-£8. **Set meal**
£11-£19 per person (minimum 2). **Credit** AmEx,
JCB, MC, V.
As the name suggests, this little local is indeed
very friendly. The interior is simple and white, with
dark wooden furniture, and Chinese paintings on
the walls. The menu has few surprises, but there's
a list of dim sum available until 10pm (instead of
the usual 5pm cut-off). which includes a selection
of tasty-sounding vegetarian options. On the
evening of our visit we opted for the main menu.
Shredded roast duck with celery and pickles was
a nice balance of soft meat, crunchy celery and
mildly piquant carrot slivers. We also enjoyed
tender aubergine, crisp red peppers and soft
beancurd stuffed with well-seasoned, freshly
minced prawns. Less successful were a bland dish
of thick rice noodles, stir-fried with chewy pork
and shredded dried scallops; and a fish-fragrant
aubergine that lacked spiciness and was too oily.
If you're in the area, pop in for a quick bite with
friends and enjoy the warm welcome.
*Babies and children welcome: booster chair.
Booking advisable weekends. Separate room
for parties, seats 45. Takeaway service.
Vegetarian menu.*

Kilburn

Angeles NEW

*405 Kilburn High Road, NW6 7QL (7625 2663).
Kilburn tube.* **Meals served** noon-10.30pm daily.
Main courses £5-£8.50. **Set meal** £19.50-£23
per person (minimum 2); £32-£44 per person
(minimum 3); £49-63 per person (minimum 4).
No credit cards.
This modest-looking restaurant is far more than
just a neighbourhood Chinese. Standard Anglo-
Cantonese fare is available, but this pales in
comparison to the enticing, spicy and authentic

Sichuanese menu. Angeles' devoted Chinese fans
gather for lively steamboats (here called hot-pots),
a rarity in the UK, in which diners cook vegetables,
noodles, seafood and meat – from lamb to spam –
in a bubbling pot of fiery broth. A main course of
twice-cooked pork combined the richness of belly
pork with the sharpness of whole spring onions
and chilli oil to pleasing effect. We also enjoyed a
spectacular dish of la zi ji: small pieces of stir-fried
fragrant chicken (on the bone) served in a fiery pile
of shiny dried red chillies. Angeles was a pioneer
of Sichuanese cuisine in London, yet has toned
down the chillies and sichuan peppercorns a little
since opening in 2003. Dishes like ma po tofu and
dry-fried green beans, while flavourful, lack the
heat and mouth-numbing effect generally found in
China. Nevertheless, this is the closest you'll get,
for the money, to the taste of Sichuan in London.
*Babies and children welcome: high chairs.
Booking advisable. Disabled: toilet. No-smoking
tables. Takeaway service.*

St John's Wood

Royal China

*68 Queen's Grove, NW8 6ER (7586 4280/
www.royalchinagroup.co.uk). St John's Wood tube.*
Meals served noon-11pm Mon-Sat; 11am-10pm
Sun. **Dim sum served** noon-4.45pm Mon-Sat;
11am-4.45pm Sun. **Dim sum** £2.20-£4.50. **Main
courses** £6-£50. **Set lunch** (noon-5pm Mon-Fri)
£14 2 courses. **Set dinner** £28-£36 per person
(minimum 2). **Credit** AmEx, MC, V.
This north-western outpost of the Royal China
Group serves great daytime dim sum but only
reasonable fare in the evening. The room is richly
appointed, with gold panels decorated with lotus
leaves, birds in flight and other oriental motifs in
trademark Royal China style. On the night of our
visit, most diners were westerners. Staff helpfully
provided suggestions of what to choose from the
classic Cantonese menu. Chilli salt baby squid were
tender and crisp, but the batter was a little too thick
for the delicate cephalopods and their flavour was
further overwhelmed by too much salty spicy
seasoning. Steamed chilli pork dumplings were
savoury and soft, but let down by stodgy pastry
and another overly salty sauce. Most disappointing
was the aubergine stuffed with minced prawns in
black bean sauce; the filling was bland, white and
spongy. Things improved with the Royal China
lotus leaf rice: fragrant and full of tender duck and
crunchy prawns. Given the choice, we would stick
to the dim sum here any day.
*Babies and children welcome: high chairs.
Booking advisable dinner Mon-Fri; bookings
not accepted lunch Sat, Sun. Separate rooms for
parties, seating 14 and 21. Takeaway service.
Vegetarian menu.* **Map 2 D1.**

Swiss Cottage

★ Green Cottage

*9 New College Parade, Finchley Road, NW3
5EP (7722 5305/7892). Finchley Road or
Swiss Cottage tube.* **Meals served** noon-11pm
daily. **Main courses** £5.80-£25. **Set meal**
£12.50-£25 per person (minimum 2). **Credit**
(over £10) AmEx, MC, V.
If loyal fans of this old-style Cantonese family
restaurant were worried by its lengthy closure for
rebuilding work, they can relax. It's back in
business, with the same old homely tiled floor and
dark wooden ceiling – and, more importantly, the
same old roast meat kiosk by the window, turning
out truly delicious barbecued duck and pork. The
rich dark flesh of the duck and the succulent pale
fat of the belly pork contrast perfectly with their
respective sweet and salty crackly skins. If you're
a purist, you might say that serving such delicacies
with the sauce already added makes them a little
over-moist, but then the sauce is good too. The
steamed fish could hardly have been fresher,
slipping easily off the bone and on to the
chopsticks, looking and tasting spectacular in its
black bean sauce. Complementing this were a
simple dish of dou miao (pea shoots) with garlic,
and a delightfully complex creation of minced
pork, preserved greens and braised beancurd.

True, the staff were as curt as ever, but as we were
told by the manager (whose father opened the
place 34 years ago), you can't get this sort of food
at a takeaway.
*Babies and children admitted. Booking advisable;
essential dinner. Restaurant available for hire.
Takeaway service. Vegetarian menu.* **Map 28 B4.**

Outer London

Harrow, Middlesex

★ Golden Palace

*146-150 Station Road, Harrow, Middx HA1
2RH (8863 2333). Harrow-on-the-Hill tube/rail.*
Meals served noon-11.30pm Mon-Sat; 11am-
10.30pm Sun. **Dim sum served** noon-5pm
Mon-Sat; 11am-5pm Sun. **Dim sum** £2.30-£3.20.
Main courses £5.20-£8.50. **Set meal** £18-
£24.50 per person (minimum 2). **Credit** AmEx,
DC, MC, V.
Such is the popularity of this large suburban
restaurant that the recently painted dining room is
already showing signs of wear and tear. In
contrast, the dim sum remain as fresh as ever. Soft
beef belly (tripe) with preserved cabbage woke us
up with its spirited covering of cracked black
pepper. Cuttlefish with 'dried garlic and fresh
garlic' then blew us away; served with rice
vermicelli, it had a taste and texture similar to
(much more expensive) steamed razor clam.
Steamed crystal prawn dumplings (har gau) were
attractively handmade and sensitively seasoned,
while oven-baked roast pork puff pastries arrived
flaky and bursting with sweet filling. Thrilled by
the meal, we ordered more. Taro croquettes were
crisp outside and filled with tasty pork. A dim sum
special, 'grilled chicken lemongrass flavour', was
beautifully tender and aromatic. This wonderful
meal was blighted only by hasty and abrupt
service straight out of Chinatown. Dim sum aside,
the lengthy à la carte menu is equally well prepared
and includes a large vegetarian selection with
several dishes made from tofu or wheat gluten. A
small Chinese language menu (which staff will
usually willingly translate) is now accompanied by
a short selection of Sichuan specialities.
*Babies and children welcome: high chairs.
Booking advisable dinner. Disabled: toilet.
Separate rooms for parties, seating 60 and 100.
Takeaway service. Vegetarian menu.*

Ilford, Essex

★ Mandarin Palace

*559-561 Cranbrook Road, Gants Hill, Ilford,
Essex IG2 6JZ (8550 7661). Gants Hill tube.*
Lunch served noon-4pm, **dinner served** 6.30-
11.30pm Mon-Sat. **Meals served** noon-midnight
Sun. **Dim sum served** noon-4pm Mon-Sat; noon-
5pm Sun. **Dim sum** £2-£3.80. **Main courses**
£2.50-£22. **Set dinner** £19.50-£39 per person
(minimum 2). **Credit** AmEx, DC, MC, V.
The gaudy, faux-antique Chinese decor that greets
diners here belies the mastery in the kitchen.
Mandarin Palace provides a good example of what
Chinese food should be like. The menu claims to
offer Cantonese, Peking and Sichuan cuisine, but
in reality the food is predominantly Cantonese.
Even the chef's speciality section is entitled 'Hong
Kong Sizzlers'. We went for dim sum and were
delighted by our meal. Prawn dumplings were
fresh and full of bouncy flavour, while pork puff
pastries were a mouth-watering combination of
tender sweet-savoury roast meat and the lightest
layers of delicate pastry. Taro croquettes had meat
and mushrooms wrapped in softly mashed taro,
deep-fried to produce an exterior as fragile as lace:
crisp, comforting and delicious. Fried turnip cake
contained little dried sausage, but was otherwise
well-seasoned and tasty. The only disappointment
was a chilli salt and pepper squid (ordered from
the main menu); it was chewy and uninspiring.
Nonetheless, the quality of the dim sum here is
among the best in London.
*Babies and children welcome: high chairs.
No-smoking tables. Separate room for parties,
seats 30. Takeaway service; delivery service
(within 2-mile radius). Vegetarian menu.*
For branch see index.

East European

You can't fail to have noticed it: London has experienced a rapid rise in the number of Polish and east European grocery stores. What's more, many existing corner shops now compete to sell the widest range of kielbasa (sausage) and Polish beers. This is great news for those of us who want to try our hand at making pierogi, but indicates a problem for the capital's east European restaurants. The core customers for stockists of this hearty fare are members of the new Polish and east European communities, who have settled here since the 2004 enlargement of the European Union. Most of these arrivals must be staying at home to eat their barszcz, as London's east European restaurant scene is pretty static. Let's hope that, as the new communities become more economically secure, there will be a flowering of restaurants dedicated to their cuisine.

The main news this year is the resurgence of two old-timers that have been rejuvenated by the influx of younger customers. Welcome back the **Polish White Eagle Club** and the **Czech Restaurant**. Otherwise, **Baltic** remains the glamorous star in the Polish firmament, while **Daquise**, **Patio** and **Polanka** provide potato pancakes and herrings just like grandma used to make. **Bar Polski** (formerly Na Zdrowie) continues to offer a first-rate bar experience, with an impressive list of beers and vodkas – and great 'drinking food' to match.

Of the restaurants from other nationalities that contribute to this cuisine, **Tbilisi** (Georgian) is still a favourite of ours, offering little-known and exotic dishes in stylish surroundings at reasonable prices. Newcomer **Garni** specialises in ancient Armenian recipes, while the venerable **Gay Hussar** (Hungarian) continues to draw those in search of a more old-school dining experience. Surprisingly, we still lack a really great Russian restaurant – **Potemkin**, **Erebuni** and the eccentric **Rasputin** leading an otherwise disappointing pack. When will that hungry bear awake?

Armenian

Central

Gloucester Road

Jakob's
*20 Gloucester Road, SW7 4RB (7581 9292).
Gloucester Road tube.* **Meals served** 8am-10pm daily. **Main courses** £6.50-£14. **Credit** AmEx, MC, V.
It can get frenetic here on a busy lunchtime as well-heeled locals popping in for takeaway tabouleh and olives get entangled with the eat-in crowd. The system of staking claim to a table, ordering drinks from the staff, then rejoining the throngs to order food at the counter can be challenging. Once this is negotiated, however, the superior quality of the café shines through. Choose from half a dozen hot dishes such as grilled halibut, Armenian-style dolma (the owner's Armenian roots evidenced also by old photos of goatherds in mountainous landscapes) or chicken and pepper stew served with two veg. We particularly rate the wide choice of fresh salads; intense blistered grilled red peppers, houmous, delectable grated carrots with cumin and cinnamon, and chewy brown rice with lentils are among our favourites. Great puds such as rich Russian chocolate cake seem quite permissible after such wholesome low-cal fare. Even the drinks are top-notch: own-made lemonade, fresh juices and seriously strong espressos. House wine by the glass slips down nicely too. Given the Gloucester Road location, all this doesn't come cheap, but for a leisurely Sunday lunch with the papers, Jakob's is a winner.
Babies and children welcome: high chairs. Booking advisable. No smoking. Takeaway service. **Map 7 C9.**

West

Chiswick

Garni NEW
472 Chiswick High Road, W4 5TT (8995 5129/ www.garni.co.uk). Chiswick Park tube. **Meals served** 7am-11pm daily. **Main courses** £7.50-£9.50. **Set lunch** £8.95 2 courses, £11.95 3 courses. **Credit** MC, V.
Garni is the only restaurant in London that specialises in ancient Armenian cooking. Armenian food is a cross between Turkish and Russian, with influences from neighbouring Georgia, Iran, Iraq and Syria. So you'll find aromatic spices, aubergines and an abundance of fresh verdant herbs, as in Turkish cookery, combined with the dumplings, dried fruit and walnut pastes of Russia and Georgia. We tried the eponymous 'garni' – a delicious combination of baked aubergines stuffed with herbed minced veal and bulgur, topped with grated carrot and tomatoes. We also liked buttery pilaf accompanied by charcoal-grilled aubergines, peppers, tomatoes and green beans, whose musky, burnished smokiness was underscored by a sharp, refreshing lemon tang. The bread basket came with warm, crisp lavash (thin 'cracker bread'), and soft, round pillows of sesame-studded churek. Proprietor Larissa Arakelyan previously ran Libation wine bar on the same site. It's a cosy and attractive venue, with a glass frontage that opens on to the street, where a few tables are laid out for alfresco eating. An intimate dining space at the back leads to a small garden with covered seating; in good weather you might find the barbecue chef here cooking on charcoal.
Babies and children welcome: high chairs. Booking advisable. No smoking. Tables outdoors (4, garden). Takeaway service; delivery service.

Czech

North West

West Hampstead

★ **Czech Restaurant**
Czech & Slovak House, 74 West End Lane, NW6 2LX (7372 1193/www.czechoslovak-restaurant.co.uk). West Hampstead tube. **Dinner served** 5-11pm Tue-Fri. **Meals served** noon-11pm Sat; noon-10.30pm Sun. **Main courses** £4.50-£12. **No credit cards.**
Dating back far into the Cold War era (though under new management since late 2004), this is London's only Czech restaurant and bar. It forms part of a social club for Czech and Slovak expats, hidden on a residential strip in West Hampstead. Our lunch coincided with the Dvořák Society's annual dinner, and we found ourselves squeezing into the last remaining table amid a furore of chatter. The main dining room is decorated in typical Czech café style, complete with heavy chandeliers, red velvet curtains and tiny tables. Sleek, efficient staff serve a varied mix of authentic dishes: roast pork with dumplings, goulash and even street food snacks such as sausage, mustard and rye bread. Specials looked mouth-wateringly good: goose breast, venison steak and roasted wild boar, all with dumplings as standard. We began with a flavourful sauerkraut soup flecked with ham, and a satisfyingly greasy potato pancake. Portions are, as you might expect, generous. Main courses saw us wading through svickova na smetane (sirloin of beef in sour cream sauce) and vepro knedlo zelo (pork with sauerkraut and dumplings), both served with dumplings the size of door-stoppers. If you have room after such fare, you can round off the meal (and yourself) with such belt-busting puddings as strudel, fruit pancakes and fruit dumplings.
Babies and children welcome: high chairs. Booking advisable weekends. Disabled: toilet. No smoking. Separate room for parties, seats 25. Tables outdoors (4, terrace). Takeaway service. Vegetarian menu. **Map 28 A3.**

Georgian

West

Kensington

Mimino NEW
197C Kensington High Street, W8 6BA (7937 1551/www.mimino.co.uk). Kensington High Street tube. **Lunch served** noon-3pm, **dinner served** 6pm-midnight daily. **Main courses** £10-£12. **Set meal** £20 3 courses incl glass of wine. **Credit** AmEx, MC, V.

Polish White Eagle Club. See p79.

We welcomed the news that Tbilisi was to be joined by a new Georgian restaurant: Mimino (the Falcon). But this low-ceilinged basement resembling an old hotel restaurant (brown velveteen chairs and all) is devoid of atmosphere. Waiters are friendly but serious in their mission to guide the uninitiated through what is a standard Georgian menu. Georgian choral music added more gravity. Meze was a choice of three starters with khachapuri bread – a vast portion for two. Lobio was superlative: tender black beans with the walnut and spice mix also present in badrijani (succulent roast aubergines). However, loko (catfish with garlicky coriander) was far too vinegary. Our main course of chicken tabaka (spatchcocked roast chicken, with matchstick chips and chilli sauce) was exceedingly plain, while the chef's special of gently spiced roast beef with mushrooms, sour cream and sour cucumber was a daunting, overly rich grey-hued heap. Dessert (Georgian cakes or fruit) was impossible after all this. Georgia's winemaking tradition is well-represented here; our classic Kindzmarauli was gorgeous: a semi-sweet, dark blueish red from the Kaheti region. Mimino is worth a visit to experience such excellent Georgian wines, along with classic warmly spiced vegetable dishes – but it's all too heavy.
Babies and children admitted. No smoking. Tables outdoors (2, pavement). **Map 7 A9.**

North

Holloway

★ ★ Tbilisi

91 Holloway Road, N7 8LT (7607 2536). Highbury & Islington tube/rail. **Dinner served** 6-11pm Mon-Fri; 6pm-midnight Sat, Sun. **Main courses** £6.95-£8.45. **Credit** MC, V.
We've always loved Tbilisi's relaxing, rather glam red decor, dark furniture and clever lighting; the strikingly fresh and subtly warm spicing, typical of Georgian cuisine; and the chance to savour heavy, semi-sweet Georgian wines (hard to come by in London). Yet in the past we've lamented the venue's emptiness and resulting lack of atmosphere. This time, sparkling cut-glassware gave everything a cheering gleam, enjoyed by an

eclectic stream of happy diners. Starter plates are irresistible, combining dishes themed by region. Our kolheti, ample for two, comprised two salads (exquisite spicy walnut and spinach, and beetroot), accompanied by khachapuri – the typical yeasty bread filled with crumbly soft cheese. Walnut, ubiquitous in the Georgian kitchen, features heavily in main courses too; try that most famous of Georgian dishes, chicken satsivi, the creamy ground walnut sauce countered by the blandness of satisfying, polenta-like ghomi (made from cornmeal). Walnut also figures in the tarragon-infused soupy lamb stew, kharcho. Tbilisi's exotic cooking – using high-quality fresh ingredients, and served in smart surroundings – remains a genuine bargain, and a well-kept secret.
Babies and children admitted. Booking advisable Fri, Sat. Restaurant available for hire. Separate room for parties, seats 40. Takeaway service.

Hungarian

Central

Soho

Gay Hussar

2 Greek Street, W1D 4NB (7437 0973). Tottenham Court Road tube. **Lunch served** 12.15-2.30pm, **dinner served** 5.30-10.45pm Mon-Sat. **Main courses** £9.50-£16.50. **Set lunch** £16.50 2 courses, £18.50 3 courses. **Credit** AmEx, DC, JCB, MC, V.
Traditional yet not fusty, the Gay Hussar has for decades been a favourite with politicians. The small downstairs room – tightly packed with tables, its walls saturated with old political cartoons – feels cosy rather than claustrophobic. Service is old-school, with the maître d' warmly welcoming regulars and newcomers alike. We were encouraged to try several wines before plumping for the famous Egri Bikavér (Bull's Blood). The menu is described in English as well as Hungarian. Asparagus and bacon salad and surprisingly light fish dumplings in a creamy dill and mushroom sauce got the meal off to a good start. We also

loved the brassó érmék: succulent grilled medallions of fillet steak on a bed of pepper and tomato ragout richly spicy with Hungarian paprika. Kacsa sült (roast duck with red cabbage and apple sauce) was a touch dry. This is hearty cooking, but if you've the appetite, try a scrumptious pud such as sweet-cheese pancakes or poppyseed strudel. We've heard Hungarians cast doubts over the authenticity of some dishes, but this place certainly does the trick for us.
Babies and children welcome: children's portions; high chairs. Book dinner. Separate rooms for parties, seating 12 and 24. **Map 17 K6.**

Polish

Central

Holborn

★ Bar Polski

11 Little Turnstile, WC1V 7DX (7831 9679). Holborn tube. **Meals served** 4-10pm Mon; 12.30-10pm Tue-Fri; 6-10pm Sat. **Main courses** £5-£7.50. **Credit** MC, V.
We love the new look at this popular bar, formerly called Na Zdrowie. Cool, blond wood is decorated with the hippest folk motifs this side of the Vistula: colourful cockerels, storks and delicate black filigree work in wycinianki style (traditional paper-cuttings). Bar Polski is best enjoyed early in the week when it's quieter after the post-work drinks rush. Then, you're more likely to get a seat to sample the tasty home-style food, the impressive choice of Polish bottled beers and the huge selection of vodkas. Tender herring, served alone or as part of a beetroot and mixed salad; potato pancakes with mushroom sauce; garlicky Polish sausage with mustard and mash; and pleasingly light pierogi stuffed with meat, cabbage or cheese – all these dishes marry perfectly with the drinks. Alcohol includes lesser-known Polish dark beers as well as the increasingly ubiquitous Zywiec, Okocim (try it with raspberry syrup) and so on, along with a stunning array of over 60 vodkas (sweet, clear, dry: you name it) carefully arranged

and described. Try Ziota Woda with real gold leaf and anise, or Jarzebiak (rowanberry). All this, an eclectic crowd and friendly, chatty staff too. *Babies and children admitted. Booking not accepted. Tables outdoors (3, pavement). Takeaway service.* **Map 18 L5.**

South Kensington

★ Daquise

20 Thurloe Street, SW7 2LP (7589 6117). South Kensington tube. **Meals served** noon-11pm daily. **Main courses** £5.50-£12.50. **Set lunch** (noon-3pm Mon-Fri) £7.50 2 courses incl glass of wine, coffee. **Credit** MC, V.

Need an antidote to over-hyped dining? Then repair to Daquise. With over 50 years' experience, this venerable South Ken institution knows what it's doing. Everything is highly retro: from the plastic tablecloths and worn leatherette banquettes, to the unreconstructed homely waiting staff serving up a little of what does you good (or, in some cases, a great deal of it). Robust, beetrooty barszcz with uszka; tender herrings with apple, smothered in sour cream; and fluffy blini with smoked salmon – all are here, just like *babcia* used to make. We're big fans of the mixed Polish platters: ideal if you can't make up your mind between all the calorific delights. Both meat and vegetarian versions offer a great combination of pierogi, golabki and bigos – and potato pancakes to die for. We also love the zrazy and nutty kasza gryczana (roasted buckwheat). After all this, you'll need a heroic appetite to manage a pud. These include szarlotka (apple-cake), makowiec and sernik (cheesecake), along with plump, sweet-cheese pancakes. Quaff a reasonably priced house wine, or down a Polish beer with a vodka or two before and after. For home-style Polish food, Daquise is great value.
Babies and children admitted. Booking advisable. No-smoking tables. Separate room for parties, seats 25. **Map 14 D10.**

Ognisko Polskie

55 Exhibition Road, Prince's Gate, SW7 2PN (7589 4635/www.ognisko.com). South Kensington tube.
Bar **Open** noon-11pm daily.

Restaurant **Lunch served** 12.30-3pm, **dinner served** 6.30-11pm daily. **Main courses** £9-£14. **Set meal** £11 3 courses.
Both **Credit** AmEx, DC, MC, V.

It's easy to picture dashing Polish airmen enjoying an evening's respite from perilous wartime missions in the bar of Ognisko Polskie (the Polish Hearth Club). Adorned with portraits of military heroes and English royals, the cosy, pink-pillared dining room is rather Home Counties, but correct yet friendly service from smart young Poles dispels any snobbishness. The food, though, just isn't up to scratch; our Polish choices from the international menu cried out for a lighter hand. Barszcz was fine, but a pile of high-quality smoked salmon rested on top of a soggy buckwheat blini smothered in sour cream. Golonka (pork knuckle) was enough to make us, and a succession of fellow diners who also ordered it, gasp. Of gargantuan proportions, the pork was deliciously succulent but buried in an obscenely quivering mountain of fat – too much even for devotees of robust country-style fare. Fillet of beef Czartoryski-style consisted of a decent lean steak overwhelmed by tooth-achingly sweet caramelised onion gravy. With its romantic garden terrace open in summer, we can't fault Ognisko for the delightful retro atmosphere, but with these prices, the chef needs to do better.
Babies and children welcome: children's portions; high chair. Booking advisable. Separate room for parties, seats 150. Tables outdoors (10, terrace). **Map 8 D9.**

West

Bayswater

Antony's

54 Porchester Road, W2 6ET (7243 8743/ www.antonysrestaurant.com). Royal Oak tube. **Dinner served** 6-11pm Mon-Sat. **Main courses** £7.50-£13.80. **Cover** 70p. **Credit** MC, V.

With its welcoming Polish hostess and mellow atmosphere, Antony's glows with all the cosy old-style charms of Mittel Europa. The smart dark red decor brightened by gilt-framed mirrors, subtle lighting, cool jazzy music and proper but friendly service seem to please an older local crowd and bright young things in equal measure. Polish classics – with a gratifyingly light hand evident in the kitchen – are supplemented by an international list of steaks, fish dishes and suchlike. Barszcz with uszka and sour cream was first-rate: intensely beetrooty, peppery and topped with pungent fresh dill. Other successful starters included potato pancakes, meltingly tender herring, leniwe (cheese and potato dumplings) and even juicy prawns flambéed in vodka. So good are the starters we're prone to have several in lieu of mains. These don't disappoint, though. Generous portions of such treats as spicy hunter's-style lamb and fillet of venison à la Radziwill (pungent with juniper) came with good veg: coarsely grated beetroot, carrot surowka, rough mashed potato. Nalesniki are always a hit with us, but good fruity desserts such as baked apples and caramelised peaches are also available. A reliable, reasonably priced favourite, just right for a romantic dinner à deux.
Babies and children welcome: high chairs. Booking advisable weekends. Restaurant available for hire. **Map 7 C5.**

Hammersmith

Lowiczanka Polish Cultural Centre

First floor, 238-246 King Street, W6 0RF (8741 3225). Ravenscourt Park tube.
Café **Open** 9.30am-9pm daily.
Bar/restaurant **Lunch served** 12.30-3pm daily. **Dinner served** 6.30-11pm Mon-Thur, Sun; 7pm-midnight Fri, Sat. **Main courses** £7.30-£14.50. **Set lunch** (Mon-Sat) £8.50 3 courses; (Sun) £9.90 3 courses.
Both **Credit** AmEx, MC, V.

Functioning like a portal into a different country and another time, Lowiczanka is housed in a concrete cultural centre that seems airlifted-in from Warsaw. Indeed, the Soviet-style welcome (dour security guards instruct you to check-in your bag, whether you want to or not) begins immediately. The restaurant, tucked away on the second floor, resembles a Travelodge breakfast room. It will be familiar to anyone who stayed in Polish hotels during the Communist era. Céline Dion and the theme tune to *Friends* serenaded us

Menu

Dishes followed by (Cz) indicate a Czech dish; (G) Georgian; (H) Hungarian; (P) Polish; (R) Russian; (Uk) Ukrainian. Others have no particular affiliation.

Bigos (P): hunter's stew made with sauerkraut, various meats and sausage, mushrooms and juniper.
Blini: yeast-leavened pancake made from buckwheat flour, traditionally served smothered in butter and sour cream; **blinchiki** are mini blinis.
Borscht: classic beetroot soup. There are many varieties: Ukrainian borscht is thick with vegetables; the Polish version (**barszcz**) is clear. There are also white and green types. Often garnished with sour cream, boiled egg or little dumplings.
Caviar: fish roe. Most highly prized is that of the sturgeon (**beluga, oscietra** and **sevruga,** in descending order of expense), though **keta** or salmon caviar is underrated.
Chlodnik (P): cold beetroot soup, bright pink in colour, served with sour cream.
Coulebiac (R): see koulebiaka.
Galabki, golabki or **golubtsy:** cabbage parcels, usually stuffed with rice or kasha (qv) and sometimes meat.

Golonka (P): pork knuckle, often cooked in beer.
Goulash or **gulasz (H):** rich beef soup.
Kasha or **kasza:** buckwheat, delicious roasted: light and fluffy with a nutty flavour.
Kaszanka (P): blood sausage made with buckwheat.
Khachapuri (G): flatbread; sometimes called Georgian pizza.
Kielbasa (P): sausage; Poland had dozens of widely differing styles.
Knedliky (Cz): bread dumplings.
Kolduny (P): small meat-filled dumplings (scaled-down pierogi, qv) often served in beetroot soup.
Kotlet schabowy (P): breaded pork chops.
Koulebiaka or **kulebiak (R):** layered salmon or sturgeon pie with eggs, dill, rice and mushrooms.
Krupnik (P): barley soup, and the name of a honey vodka (because of the golden colour of barley).
Latke: grated potato pancakes, fried.
Makowiec or **makietki (P):** poppy seed cake.
Mizeria (P): cucumber salad; very thinly sliced and dressed with sour cream.
Nalesniki (P): cream cheese pancakes.

Paczki (P): doughnuts, often filled with plum jam.
Pelmeni (R): Siberian-style ravioli dumplings.
Pierogi (P): ravioli-style dumplings. Typical fillings are sauerkraut and mushroom, curd cheese or fruit (cherries, apples).
Pirogi (large) or **pirozhki** (small) **(R):** filled pies made with yeasty dough.
Placki (P): potato pancakes.
Shashlik: Caucasian spit-roasted meat.
Shchi (R): soup made from sauerkraut.
Stroganoff (R): beef slices, served in a rich sour cream and mushroom sauce.
Surowka (P): salad made of raw shredded vegetables.
Uszka or **ushka:** small ear-shaped dumplings served in soup.
Vareniki (Uk): Ukrainian version of pierogi (qv).
Zakuski (R) or **zakaski (P):** starters, traditionally covering a whole table. The many dishes can include pickles, marinated vegetables and fish, herring, smoked eel, aspic, mushrooms, radishes with butter, salads and caviar.
Zrazy (P): beef rolls stuffed with bacon, pickled cucumber and mustard.
Zurek (P): sour rye soup.

through the meal. Yet while this eccentric establishment won't win any design awards, it is made far more appealing by the rich, homely Polish cooking. Barszcz with mushroom dumplings, and a rich wild boar pâté were both great starters. To follow, the shared Polish 'meze' for two showcased some of the best of the menu: delicious smoked sausage, golabki, potato balls with minced meat, hunter's stew and a superb carrot salad. The food, combined with a decent Châteauneuf-du-Pape and very good service, left us full and satisfied by the time we re-emerged into present-day London.
Babies and children welcome: high chairs. Book lunch Sat, Sun. Disabled: toilet. Entertainment: gypsy band 8pm-midnight Fri, Sat. No-smoking tables. Separate rooms for parties, seating 60 and 200. Tables outdoors (5, patio). Takeaway service (café). **Map 20 A4.**

★ Polanka
258 King Street, W6 0SP (8741 8268). Ravenscourt Park tube. **Meals served** noon-10pm Mon-Sat; noon-8pm Sun. **Main courses** £4-£11.50. **Unlicensed. Corkage** £3 wine; £5 spirits. **Credit** AmEx, MC, V.
You'll find Polanka tucked away at the back of a Polish deli. Jars of gherkins and packets of dumpling mix give way to a small informal room sporting blond wood, paper tablecloths and bright lighting. Straw dolls and bric-a-brac festoon the walls. Service was slow and a little haphazard on our visit, despite few diners. Our soup and wine orders were mixed up, but all was taken in good humour – why grumble when the house red is only £8? Cooking is a homely affair: comfort food rather than anything more ambitious. Borscht, herrings and meatballs all feature, but there's little on the meat-heavy list for vegetarians. We started with wonderfully savoury cabbage soup, and a tangy bowl of red borscht. To follow, Hussar's roast beef with potatoes was hearty and filling, while the golabki (cabbage leaves stuffed with rice and meat, in a tomato and mushroom sauce) was pure comfort. The only disappointment came from the pierogi (stuffed with cheese and potato), which were a little overdone and flavourless. For dessert, choose from a shelf of Polish cakes.
Babies and children welcome: high chairs. Booking advisable. No-smoking tables. Separate room for parties, seats 8. Takeaway service. **Map 20 A4.**

Kensington

Wódka
12 St Alban's Grove, W8 5PN (7937 6513/ www.wodka.co.uk). High Street Kensington tube. **Lunch served** noon-3pm Mon-Fri. **Dinner served** 6.30-11.15pm daily. **Main courses** £12.50-£15. **Set lunch** £11.50 2 courses, £14.50 3 courses. **Credit** AmEx, MC, V.
We've always had a soft spot for Wódka, long before its showier younger sister Baltic (*see below*) burst on to the scene. This is a more intimate venue, with a pleasing menu of eastern European classics (given a light touch) and well-executed Modern European dishes. The pared-down decor and mellow background jazz add to the unique appeal. An older crowd, primarily of well-heeled locals, comes to enjoy the calmer, more personal approach. But on a busy Saturday night we felt rather uncared for; service was haphazard and too casual. To begin, smoked salmon blinis were a little greasy. Lamb shashlik with couscous salad was a disappointment too – made of minced lamb, not the expected chunks. Much better was the full-on flavour of hearty char-grilled ribeye steak with sautéed potato and (somewhat superfluous) leafy salad. Roasted sea bream with a crunchy fennel salad was moist and delicious, but left us hungry. There's a great range of vodkas, clear (Belvedere, Królewska) and flavoured (rose petal, angelica), sold by the glass or carafe, or mixed into winning cocktail combinations. Yes, Wódka has all the right ingredients, but we needed more cosseting.
Babies and children admitted. Booking advisable. Separate room for parties, seats 30. Tables outdoors (3, pavement). **Map 7 C9.**

Shepherd's Bush

★ Patio
5 Goldhawk Road, W12 8QQ (8743 5194). Goldhawk Road tube. **Lunch served** noon-3pm Mon-Fri. **Dinner served** 6-11.30pm daily. **Main courses** £7.50-£9. **Set meal** £14.90 3 courses incl vodka shot. **Credit** AmEx, DC, JCB, MC, V.
Patio is a cosy, reassuring place: a home-from-home that locals use regularly, sure of a welcome from the charming Polish owner. They are also attracted by one of London's best bargain set meals. Heavy velvet drapes, an eclectic mix of artworks and a piano topped with cut-glass vases of flowers conjure up the feel of an elderly Polish relative's apartment. The quality of the home-style cooking can be variable, but it's a steal at £14.90 for three courses (four really, as pre-dessert chewy coconut cake and fruit are always proffered), with a shot of vodka to boot. Herrings, bigos and peppery barszcz (topped with sour cream and dill) are dependable starters; if you've a delicate appetite, beware the heavy, torpedo-like blini with smoked salmon. It's the main courses that sometimes disappoint. Our hunter's-style lamb was bony and fatty; and the duck arrived overcooked and dry. The accompanying fresh vegetables (red cabbage, roast potatoes and surowka of raw grated carrot) saved the day. Desserts – the usual calorie-fest of cheesecake, sweet-cheese pancakes and so on – are pretty good. Although it's great value, Patio's kitchen needs to take a touch more care.
Book dinner Fri, Sat. No-smoking tables. Separate room for parties, seats 45. Takeaway service. **Map 20 C2.**

South

Balham

★ Polish White Eagle Club
211 Balham High Road, SW17 7BQ (8672 1723). Tooting Bec tube/Balham tube/rail/49, 155, 181, 319 bus. **Bar Open** noon-3pm, 6-11pm Mon-Fri; noon-2am Sat; 11am-10.30pm Sun. *Restaurant* **Lunch served** 11.30am-3pm, **dinner served** 6-10pm Mon-Sat. **Meals served** 11.30am-10pm Sun. **Main courses** £5.95-£14.95. **Set lunch** £7 2 courses incl coffee. **Set dinner** £9.90 2 courses incl coffee. *Both* **Credit** MC, V.
The recent influx of young Polish émigrés to SW17 has improved the fortunes of this long-established social club. The dining room has had a *Changing Rooms*-style makeover, moving it on from Soviet-era decor to the Solidarity era. Don't let the colour-sponged walls, mirrors and gilded cherubs put you off – or even the builders' radio, tuned to Mindless Muzak FM – as a meal here is a real Polish feast. The menu is quite long, and includes all the classics, such as brine-pickled herrings and light, fluffy blinis topped with lashing of sour cream and smoked salmon. Portions are huge. The platter of mixed Polish specialities for one person could serve two. It included a stunningly flavoured bigos, breaded pork chop, stuffed cabbage, Polish sausage and more besides. The only disappointment was a separate order of pierogi. Although these dumplings were of good quality, their reheating was a failure; on the first attempt they arrived lukewarm, on the second they were dry and not an appealing consistency. But at only £25 or so per head, it's small wonder the Club is so popular with Polish family groups.
Babies and children welcome: high chairs. Booking advisable. No smoking (restaurant). Separate rooms for parties, seating 30 and 120. Takeaway service.

Clapham

★ Café Wanda
153 Clapham High Street, SW4 7SS (7738 8760). Clapham Common tube. **Meals served** noon-11pm Mon-Fri; 11am-11pm Sat; 11am-7pm Sun. **Main courses** £6.55-£14.95. **Set lunch** £7.25 2 courses. **Credit** AmEx, MC, V.

An unexpected find amid the bland gastropubs and bars of Clapham High Street, Café Wanda can rustle up anything from a takeaway cake to a full meal of Polish home cooking. It's an informal spot, furnished with potted plants and eastern European art, and is populated by a steady stream of Polish diners, all of whom seem to know the staff by name. The small menu of Polish staples and mainstream European dishes allows diners to pick and mix; vegetarians are well looked after. To start, the mixed vegetarian platter (goat's cheese bruschetta, roasted aubergine and courgette) was excellent, if about as untypical of Polish cuisine as you can get. This was followed by the two cornerstones of any Polish restaurant: pierogi and blini. Both were faultless: the pierogi succulent and flavoursome; the two large blini (with smoked salmon and sour cream) wonderfully calorific and comforting. Our waiter's comedic patter was relentless, despite our cringing, but service overall was tip-top. Café Wanda makes a fine venue for a quiet supper during the week and is an even better choice for a raucous group dinner at the weekend.
Babies and children admitted. Booking advisable. Entertainment: pianist 8.30-11pm Fri, Sat. Tables outdoors (2, pavement). Takeaway service. Vegetarian menu. **Map 22 B2.**

Waterloo

★ Baltic
74 Blackfriars Road, SE1 8HA (7928 1111/ www.balticrestaurant.co.uk). Southwark tube/rail. **Bar Open/meals served** noon-11pm Mon-Sat; noon-10.30pm Sun. **Main courses** £3-£8. *Restaurant* **Lunch served** noon-3.30pm daily. **Dinner served** 6-10.45pm Mon-Sat; 6-10.30pm Sun. **Main courses** £9-£15. **Set meal** (noon-3pm, 6-7pm) £11.50 2 courses, £13.50 3 courses. *Both* **Credit** AmEx, MC, V.
Jan Woroniecki's Baltic remains the east European destination restaurant for discerning Londoners. We never cease to gasp at the spectacular chandelier set against red brickwork and dripping with golden shards of Baltic amber, which hangs at one end of the vaulted white room. The amber-walled cocktail bar is also impressive; here, a lively mixed crowd enjoys superior bar food and a great selection of beers, vodkas (35 of 'em, including own-made infusions such as mint, dill and caramel) and fab cocktails. The scrumptious Zuberek (Zubrówka with white peach purée and ginger beer) really hits the spot. We were briefly forgotten in the bar while waiting for our table, but otherwise found the service much better and friendlier than on previous visits. Food was top-notch too, a sea-fresh Swedish salad of prawns, crab and fine gravadlax setting the tone. Main courses were exemplary: char-grilled rump of lamb with Georgian-style aubergines; and a robust roast monkfish with fennel and white beans. With wódka cherry ice-cream and warm chocolate sauce for pud, we were in heaven.
Babies and children admitted. Disabled: toilet. Entertainment: jazz 7pm Sun. Separate room for parties, seats 30. Tables outdoors (6, terrace). **Map 11 N8.**

Russian

Central

Clerkenwell & Farringdon

Potemkin
144 Clerkenwell Road, EC1R 5DP (7278 6661/ www.potemkin.co.uk). Farringdon tube/rail. **Meals served** noon-10.30pm Mon-Fri; 6-10.30pm Sat. **Main courses** £9.50-£17. **Set lunch** £10 2 courses. **Credit** AmEx, DC, MC, V.
Glamorous and fun, Potemkin is decked out in sumptuous reds and purples. Its wine list is good (especially the Georgian house red), but the vodka list is better. The food menu manages to be both adventurous and traditional; Potemkin has long been one of London's best Russian restaurants, if not the best. This time, however, service was a let-

Potemkin. See p79.

down and the food was under-par given the high prices. Aubergine caviar with blinis looked tired: a pile of puréed veg and three tiny miserable pancakes, no garnish. Solyanka (sturgeon soup) was authentically fishy, but horribly greasy. Mains of shashlik chicken, marinated chicken with a piquant tomato sauce, and baked rabbit were fine but unimpressive. Illy coffee dessert – a shot of coffee liqueur, an espresso and a petit-four – was OK, but oddly corporate in character. We enjoyed the atmosphere, enhanced by Cossack music and Russian pop, but a mix-up with the bill sent things crashing down again. At least the staff deducted the service charge without having to be asked. We hope Potemkin isn't resting on the laurels of its (excellent) vodka bar upstairs.

Booking advisable. No smoking (restaurant). Takeaway service. **Map 5 N4**.

West
Acton

Rasputin

265 High Street, W3 9BY (8993 5802). Acton Town tube/70, 72, 207, 266 bus. **Meals served** 6pm-midnight daily. **Main courses** £7.50-£12.95. **Credit** MC, V.

Bathed in the yellow neon light of a giant Morrisons store on insalubrious Acton High Street, Rasputin stands out as one of the more interesting establishments in the area. On a Tuesday evening only one other group was eating, leaving the cavernous light-blue room feeling rather melancholy. But the warm Montenegrin hostess didn't allow that feeling to last long, giving us honest recommendations from a wide menu that encompasses Balkan and Polish staples as well as more recognisably Russian food. Her Russian might have been cracked, but the blinis with smoked salmon and smetana (like thick sour cream) were greasy comfort food from the heavens, and breaded whitebait with tartar sauce was melt in the mouth. Mains were just as assured; the house speciality, golubtsy (cabbage-wrapped ground beef) was some of the spiciest – and best – we've had, while the venison steak sautéed in cranberry and red wine sauce was full of flavour and cooked just as ordered. After the restaurant's delightful matriarch joined us for a vodka to round off the meal, we left wonderfully full and impressed by the quality of food at this offbeat place in the least likely of locations.

Babies and children admitted. Booking advisable. Separate room for parties, seats 40.

Bayswater

Erebuni

London Guards Hotel, 36-37 Lancaster Gate, W2 3NA (7402 6067/www.erebuni.ltd.uk). Lancaster Gate tube. **Dinner served** 4pm-midnight Mon-Sat. **Main courses** £6.50-£18.50. **Set dinner** (Mon-Thur) £15 2 courses. **Credit** MC, V.

Erebuni seems intent on hiding its light under a bushel. We've eaten here before, so weren't put off on approaching the London Guards Hotel to find no obvious sign that a Russian-Armenian-Georgian hotspot lurked within. Inside, a plastic sign points down a shabby staircase to a 'breakfast room and restaurant'. This dining room, decked out in red and green, resembles a provincial hotel restaurant circa 1975, save for Fauvist-style Armenian artworks on the walls. We felt like aged interlopers, as our few fellow diners were all Russians in their early twenties. The unrelenting beat of Russian pop and satellite TV at the bar clearly targets this audience. Despite all this, the food isn't bad. Tender herring with dill and potatoes and Russian salad were as good as you'd find in Moscow. Next, our Georgian-style mains of chicken tabaka (spatchcocked baby chicken) and chahohbili (chicken stew with tomatoes, garlic and coriander) were also well executed, if quite plain. Alternatives include Armenian-style kebabs, and dolma. Drinks are pricey; we balked at ordering a Georgian wine for an astonishing £40, opting for ice-cold Viru Estonian beer. Somewhere to sample a unique slice of London Russian life.

Babies and children admitted. Booking advisable. Entertainment: karaoke 7pm Mon-Thur; musicians 7pm Fri, Sat. Restaurant available for hire. Takeaway service. **Map 8 D6**.

South West
Earl's Court

Nikita's
65 Ifield Road, SW10 9AU (7352 6326/ www.nikitasrestaurant.com). Earl's Court tube. **Dinner served** 7-11.30pm Mon-Sat. **Main courses** £10.50-£15.50. **Set meals** £22.50-£36.50 4 courses incl coffee. **Cover** (Fri, Sat) £1.50. **Credit** JCB, MC, V.

Below the gorgeous, icon-adorned street-level bar at Nikita's is a convivial, exotic, red-painted basement. The lack of windows quickly produces a surreal feeling of cultural dislocation – you could be in a fin-de-siècle Siberian *traktir* were it not for the oddly chosen Russian house music. The menu ranges from babushka's home cooking to tsarist feast. We combined both: borscht, slightly over-sweet but full of flavour, would have done any Russian grandmother proud; and blini with raw onion, chopped egg, sour cream and beluga caviar was divine, the unusually thick and crispy blini more like warm, fresh bread than a pancake. Mains were less of a highlight; a good steak wrapped in pancake was a mite overcooked at the edges but still delicious, while the stuffed pepper (one of only two vegetarian main courses) was very unexciting. We accompanied these with a light, fruity cabernet sauvignon, and finished off with an excellent shot of ice-cold raspberry vodka. For the pure Russian atmosphere alone, Nikita's is worth a visit. But the incredibly slow service needs improvement.

Booking advisable; essential Thur-Sat. Dress: smart casual. Entertainment: gypsy music 8.30-11.30pm Fri, Sat. Separate rooms for parties, seating 6, 15 and 45. **Map 13 C12**.

North
Camden Town & Chalk Farm

★ Trojka
101 Regent's Park Road, NW1 8UR (7483 3765/www.troykarestaurant.co.uk). Chalk Farm tube. **Meals served** 9am-10.30pm daily. **Main courses** £6-£9.50. **Set lunch** (noon-4pm) £9.95 2 courses. **Corkage** £3 wine; £15-£25 spirits. **Credit** AmEx, MC, V.

We've been disappointed by off-hand service at Trojka on occasion, but this time, on a cold, wet Sunday afternoon, the place was an oasis of warm fuggy hospitality. A diverse crowd, from lone grannies to babes in arms, was enjoying the easy-going atmosphere. Red decor and dark wood furniture relieved by bold artwork create an appropriately Mittel Europa vibe. A full menu of east European cuisine is served all day, along with grills, breakfasts, coffees and the like – all easy on the wallet, given the chic Primrose Hill location. The usual herrings, blini, russian salad and borscht make reliable starters. Koulebiaka (puff pastry and salmon pie), bigos, golubtsy and latkes feature among the mains. It's all quite plain, but hearty and tasty. Trojka works well for big parties on a budget; you can bring your own drink (though beware the expensive corkage on vodka) and by night a gypsy violinist is sometimes on hand to lure customers to polka round the tables. For afters, there's an enticing selection of cakes, including a gooey Hungarian chocolate torte.

Babies and children welcome: high chair. Book dinner Fri, Sat. Entertainment: Russian folk music 8-10.30pm Fri, Sat. No-smoking tables. Tables outdoors (3, pavement). Takeaway service. **Map 27 A1**.

Fish

The huge success of the likes of the rapidly expanding **FishWorks** chain emphasises the current popularity of fish as a prime, and healthy, source of protein. So too does the number of new fish restaurants opening. This year we welcome Borough Market seafood bar **Wright Brothers**, upmarket Italian operation **Hosteria del Pesce**, and stylish Wanstead newcomer **Applebee's** – as well as the spectacular relaunch of the age-old Piccadilly oyster bar **Bentley's**. In contrast, closures have been few, but we must note (and lament) the passing of Wheeler's, a fixture in St James's since the late 1920s; and of Manzi's, just off Leicester Square.

Central
City

Chamberlain's
23-25 Leadenhall Market, EC3V 1LR (7648 8690/www.chamberlains.org). Bank tube/DLR/ Liverpool Street tube/rail.
Bar **Open** noon-11pm Mon-Fri.
Restaurant **Meals served** noon-9.30pm Mon-Fri. **Main courses** £17-£27. **Set dinner** £16.95 3 courses.
Both **Credit** AmEx, DC, MC, V.

The three levels of this establishment in Leadenhall Market are very different: the basement bar is a rather dingy brick-walled space; the ground-floor restaurant is a brasserie-style room, with a nice view over the market; and the first floor hides a classier dining room, with deep leather chairs and a smarter feel. Essentially, it gets better as you climb the stairs. At lunchtime the place heaves with business lunchers, while in the evening it empties and some sections of the restaurant are roped off (annoying when you're seated within inches of another party, despite all the available space). The menu is large and varied, with plenty of options for those not interested in fish. Those that are will be rewarded with produce brought in daily from Billingsgate market. We enjoyed a fresh-tasting piece of sea bass in an olive and pine nut sauce, as well as a perfectly fine dish of seared tuna with crunchy vegetables. Smoked salmon to start was flavourful and amply portioned. Some of the prices are high, perhaps because of the preponderance of business lunchers charging their meals to expenses. We noticed a price-tag of £21.50 for 'speciality' fish and chips – at that price, it had better be special, expense account or not.

Babies and children admitted. No-smoking tables. Restaurant available for hire. Tables outdoors (18, pavement). **Map 12 Q7**.

Sweetings
39 Queen Victoria Street, EC4N 4SA (7248 3062). Mansion House tube. **Lunch served** 11.30am-3pm Mon-Fri. **Main courses** £10.50-£25.50. **Credit** AmEx, JCB, MC, V.

In business since 1830 and occupying its current premises for more than 100 years, Sweetings can rightly claim to be a City institution. Open only for lunch, it's exceedingly popular with Square Mile suits (mainly male), so arrive early or late if you don't want to have to wait – you can't book. The slightly shabby interior, with its mosaic floor and cricketing prints, is a charmer, though cramped. Seating is mainly on stools at high counters covered in white linen, behind which the amiable serving staff (trapped for the duration) dole out plates of potted shrimps and dressed crab, followed by fish pie or whole fish grilled, poached or fried. Buttered brown bread plugs any gaps.

Drinks include Pimms, draught Guinness and bitter (served in pint or half-pint silver tankards) and lashings of white wine and champagne. Cooking can be plain – witness whole smoked haddock, of good quality but unadorned save for a poached egg (still whiffy with vinegar) balanced on top. And there's more than an air of public-school dinners about the watery spinach and defiantly retro puddings (spotted dick, steamed syrup sponge). But we wouldn't have it any other way: may Sweetings last another 100 years.

Babies and children admitted. Bookings not accepted. Restaurant available for hire, seats 30 (dinner only). Takeaway service. **Map 11 P6**.

Clerkenwell & Farringdon

Rudland & Stubbs
35-37 Greenhill Rents, Cowcross Street, EC1M 6BN (7253 0148/www.rudlandstubbs.co.uk). Farringdon tube/rail.
Bar **Open** noon-11pm Mon-Fri.
Restaurant **Meals served** noon-3pm, 6-10.30pm Mon-Fri. **Main courses** £10.50-£23.
Both **Credit** AmEx, MC, V.

Although under new ownership, this long-standing restaurant hasn't changed greatly. The dark wooden bar is still there, as are the original tiled floors from the building's former incarnation as a sausage factory. To be honest, this aspect of the operation didn't need much of a makeover; the open-plan, platformed space is attractive enough, and pleasantly breezy when the front bay doors are open, even if it could do with a touch of that liveliness brought only by more customers. No, what really needed attention was the menu and this, thankfully, has improved significantly. We were very impressed by our mains: fleshy scallops atop miniature mounds of mash, touched with a dark salty sauce; and a big ol' fillet of sea bass served with just-still-crunchy pak choi. We didn't need a pudding after a deliciously creamy compote of crab to start; this was almost dessert-like in itself, coming in a tall glass with long sundae spoons. Management seem to have made improvements in the right places, without altering R&S's character unnecessarily. A good job.

Booking advisable lunch. Tables outdoors (3, pavement). No-smoking tables. **Map 5 O5**.

Fitzrovia

Back to Basics
21A Foley Street, W1W 6DS (7436 2181/ www.backtobasics.uk.com). Goodge Street or Oxford Circus tube. **Lunch served** noon-3pm, **dinner served** 6-10.30pm Mon-Sat. **Main courses** £12.75-£17.95. **Credit** AmEx, DC, MC, V.

On sunny days, this little neighbourhood restaurant moves its tables out on to the pavement to become a prime alfresco dining spot. And this

Bentley's Oyster Bar & Grill

little neighbourhood being Fitzrovia, it can charge prices that make denizens of less flush districts wince. Even on weekday lunchtimes, local office workers have to shell out around £7 for starters and £13-£16 for a main course, so you'd hardly pop here as an alternative to the sandwich shop. Such prices might be fairly standard in smart seafood restaurants, but this is no smart seafood restaurant – if it wasn't for the neat linen napkins and wine glasses, you could mistake it for a caff, especially with the rather brusque service. In the restaurant's favour, the fish and seafood were fresh, such as the gilthead bream served on fat asparagus stalks with a tomato salsa scattered with pieces of crayfish. Veg costs extra. The BTB seafood salad consisted of clams, mussels, tiger prawns and some huge crab claws and crab meat scattered on a bed of lettuce. These were both decent enough dishes, but the arrival of some loud buskers (ignored by the staff) had us asking for the bill. If you do stay for desserts, you'll find the likes of bread and butter pudding for a fiver.
Babies and children welcome: high chair. Booking essential. Tables outdoors (17, pavement). Takeaway service. **Map 3 J5**.

Leicester Square

Café Fish
36-40 Rupert Street, W1D 6DW (7287 8989/ www.santeonline.co.uk/cafefish). Leicester Square or Piccadilly Circus tube.
Bar Open noon-11pm Mon-Sat; 2-9pm Sun.
Canteen Meals served noon-11pm Mon-Sat; 2-9pm Sun. **Main courses** £9.95-£18.95.
Set meal £11.50 2 courses, £13.95 3 courses.
Both **Credit** AmEx, DC, MC, V.
This two-level restaurant (part of the Chez Gérard group, like Livebait – *see p86*), located on the edge of Chinatown, pulls in plenty of tourists and theatre-goers. Part of the appeal is the good-value set menu and bargain-priced fish and chips (£5.95, noon-5pm). Black and white tiling and dark-green paintwork decorate the rather cramped front area; better is the high-ceilinged smokers' area at the back with its rustic bench seating, skylight and faux rusty ship wall. The long menu is in English and French: the latter to add an air of sophistication, we suppose, rather than because there's anything especially Gallic about the food. After all, Thai, Cajun and oriental flavours appear, along with shellfish platters, salads, fish pie, kedgeree and straightforward grilled fish. To start, a trio of rock oysters were briny and fresh, but crab, avocado and grapefruit salad was a collection of (mediocre) ingredients waiting to be assembled rather than a completed salad. A main of Thai fish and shellfish curry used too much coconut milk and had none of the depth of flavour of authentic Thai food. Seared sea bass fillet with bubble and squeak, glazed shallots and port jus was also rather clumsily executed, though the fish was fine. Staff were pleasant, yet hard to find come bill time.
Babies and children welcome: children's menu; high chairs. Booking advisable. Disabled: toilet. Entertainment: pianist 6.30-10pm Mon-Sat. No-smoking tables. **Map 17 K7**.

★ J Sheekey
28-32 St Martin's Court, WC2N 4AL (7240 2565/www.caprice-holdings.co.uk). Leicester Square tube. **Lunch served** noon-3pm Mon-Sat; noon-3.30pm Sun. **Dinner served** 5.30pm-midnight Mon-Sat; 6pm-midnight Sun. **Main courses** £10.75-£35. **Set lunch** (Sat, Sun) £23.75 3 courses. **Cover** £2. **Credit** AmEx, DC, MC, V.
Although it could coast on its reputation alone these days (rather like, some would argue, sister operation Le Caprice), London's most renowned fish restaurant remains a winner, its star quality relatively undimmed by the passing years. Once ushered inside by the top-hatted doorman and led to your table in one of several immaculately maintained restaurant rooms (if there are no tables, there's often room at the very handsome bar), you'll be confronted with a pleasingly plain-speaking and unflashy menu, egalitarian enough to sit beluga caviar alongside (admittedly poshed-up) jellied eels. We started with potted shrimps and

crab pâté; both were even more buttery than is usual, but by no means the worse for it. Mains were calmer: the Cornish fish stew, something of a house speciality, remains a generous jumble of flavours (everything from scallops to salmon), while a special of red mullet with saffron potatoes was a simpler, more delicate affair. Save room for the near-legendary honeycomb ice-cream, one of London's must-scoff desserts. Service throughout strikes the perfect balance between formality and friendliness, helping make this a destination restaurant par excellence.
Babies and children welcome: colouring books; high chairs. Booking essential. Vegetarian menu. Vegan dishes. **Map 18 K7**.

Piccadilly

★ Bentley's Oyster Bar & Grill `NEW`
11-15 Swallow Street, W1B 4DG (7734 4756/ www.bentleysoysterbarandgrill.co.uk). Piccadilly Circus tube.
Oyster Bar **Meals served** noon-midnight Mon-Sat; noon-10pm Sun. **Main courses** £12.75-£28.
Restaurant **Lunch served** noon-3pm daily.
Dinner served 6-11pm Mon-Sat; 6-10pm Sun.
Main courses £15-£29.95.
Both **Credit** AmEx, MC, V.
Chef Richard Corrigan, of Lindsay House fame, has done a grand job in breathing new life into this Piccadilly oyster bar. In centre stage on the ground floor is a swanky, marble-topped bar lined with deep-red, studded leather chairs, where diners can sample half a dozen native or rock oysters, langoustine mayonnaise or lobster and fennel cocktail. Smaller tables with banquette seating line the walls, perhaps more suited to consumption of the mains on the classic-with-a-twist menu – whether creamy fish pie, cooked to order, or deliciously fresh and fragrant tiger prawns partnered with lemony chickpeas and lentils. The whole place has a slightly clubby feel, reinforced by the discreet yet friendly service and (at lunchtime) a mostly business clientele. On the first floor is an airy, more formal dining room where a lengthier (and pricier) modern grill menu offers the likes of hot foie gras with apple and lime, monkfish with ceps, or red mullet with roast pumpkin, plus a set of sophisticated puddings (clementine and medjool date salad with lemon curd and cinnamon waffles). With a wine list that features plenty of choices by the glass, as well as a number of sherries – perfect chilled partners to shellfish – Bentley's is well on its way to becoming a cool favourite.
Booking essential. Disabled: toilet. Dress: smart casual; no shorts. No smoking. Separate room for parties, seats 60. **Map 17 J7**.

St James's

★ Green's
36 Duke Street, SW1Y 6DF (7930 4566/ www.greens.org.uk). Green Park or Piccadilly Circus tube. **Lunch served** *Sept-Apr* 11.30am-3pm Mon-Sat; noon-3pm Sun. *May-Aug* 11.30am-3pm Mon-Sat. **Dinner served** *Sept-Apr* 5.30-11pm Mon-Sat; 5.30-9pm Sun. *May-Aug* 5.30-11pm Mon-Sat. **Main courses** £11-£40.
Cover £2. **Credit** AmEx, DC, MC, V.
Surrounded by the gentlemen's clubs of London (the kind found off Piccadilly, not Old Compton Street), this place has the power to intimidate those who think black balls belong in a pool hall. Leather banquettes of racing green, mahogany panelling, a marble oyster bar with cigar box hidden away... despite opening in the 1980s, Green's harks back to an older era. As you'd expect, service is respectful, though also surprisingly warm considering the formal surrounds. Yes, we were almost rebounded into the street on entry (by a running maître d' who insisted there was 'absolutely no space' and stood aside only when convinced we'd made a reservation), but the floor staff were friendly and helpful throughout. They explained, for example, the details of a main course called smoked haddock 'Parker Bowles' (named after owner Simon PB) with such

Interview
RICHARD CORRIGAN

Who are you?
Chef-patron of **Lindsay House** (*see p55*) and **Bentley's Oyster Bar & Grill** (*see left*).
Eating in London: what's good about it?
Complete variety, from Alan Yau's Chinese restaurants **Hakkasan** (*see p66*) and **Yauatcha** (*see p70*) to simple, wonderful bistro food at **Kensington Place** (*see p229*), to the best service in London at **Le Gavroche** (*see p131*). It's never boring, and something brilliant is forever opening.
What's bad about it?
It's extraordinarily expensive when you compare sterling to the euro. A lot of my European friends, even those from Ireland, think London is a bit 'ouch'. But there's the rents, rates, costs – we're not putting millions in the bank opening restaurants in central London, believe me. The good side is that interesting things are happening in cheaper parts of town as well, such as around Hoxton Square.
Which are your favourite London restaurants?
I'm not going pull your leg. **Le Gavroche** is my favourite. If you want to be treated well and swooned over, I don't know anywhere like it. I like to eat at the bar at **Kensington Place**, and I love having the fish pie in my own **Bentley's**. It costs £12.50 and with a £3.50 glass of wine, you don't need to bring your chequebook.
What single thing would most improve London's restaurant scene?
Coming up with a better system with the Inland Revenue regarding service charge. For example – increase it to 15% of the bill and make that go straight to the staff.
Any hot tips for the coming year?
The middle ground serving excellent food is going to thrive – those at the top end will have to be more distinct than they are now just to survive.

RESTAURANTS

enthusiasm that we had to give it a try: rich smoked fish offset by creamy herb mash and a runny poached egg on top. Starters were just as successful: an ample half-lobster with green salad, and a satisfying platter of rock oysters (hulking, flavourful brutes). Meat lovers have plenty of choice too; we enjoyed a main of rare Perthshire steak as much as the fish.

Babies and children admitted. Booking advisable. Dress: smart casual; no jeans or trainers. Separate room for parties, seats 36. **Map 17 J7.**

Soho

Zilli Fish

36-40 Brewer Street, W1F 9TA (7734 8649/ www.zillialdo.com). Piccadilly Circus tube. **Meals served** noon-11.30pm Mon-Sat. **Main courses** £8.70-£28. **Credit** AmEx, MC, V.

Most restaurants are content to brag about one or two house specialities. The menu at Zilli Fish lists a mighty ten dishes under the heading 'What we are famous for.' Well, why hide your light under a bushel? Besides, as this is the flagship operation of celebrity chef and restaurateur Aldo Zilli (he still occasionally rattles pots and pans in the kitchen), we came expecting a little brass. We got it. Expressive waiters glide around the compact dining room, navigating tight spaces between the tables, ever attentive and charming the pants off diners right and left. Slide-back glass doors open on to the mayhem of what is probably Soho's most chaotic street. A varied customer base (on our visit, a suited business group and an even bigger Italian family group) makes for a constant hubbub of loud conversation. Food is just as unrestrained. A generous mound of crisp and meltingly tender calamares to start established a vein of richness; salmon in a powerful Thai dressing continued it. And what of the dishes that Zilli is 'famous for'? We tried the lobster spaghetti: a marvellous mound of own-made pasta in a tomato sauce, loaded with meaty lobster, served atop its empty half-shell – an absolute triumph.

Babies and children welcome: high chairs. Booking advisable. No-smoking tables. Tables outdoors (2, patio). Takeaway service. **Map 17 J7.**

For branch (Zilli Café) see index.

South Kensington

Bibendum Oyster Bar

Michelin House, 81 Fulham Road, SW3 6RD (7589 1480/www.bibendum.co.uk). South Kensington tube. **Meals served** noon-10.30pm Mon-Sat; noon-10pm Sun. **Main courses** £13-£31. **Credit** AmEx, DC, MC, V.

Forget the rule about there being an 'r' in the month: oysters are available all year round at this seafood specialist on the ground floor of the lovely 1911 Michelin building. It's a great setting for an informal light lunch. You can sit in the foyer (which is a thoroughfare for customers to Bibendum restaurant above, or the Conran Shop next door), in a room to one side, or at the front of the building, sandwiched between the oyster stall and flower stand – best for keeping an eye on the street action. Tiled floor and walls (decorated with images of Bibendum, aka the Michelin Man) mean it can be a noisy and clattering dining experience. There's plenty of crustacea – crab salad, lobster mayonnaise, a fruits de mer platter for two – plus salads, daily specials and even sevruga caviar (a cool £86 for 30g). A half-dozen mixed rock oysters were super-fresh, followed by (from the specials list) high-quality gravadlax with pickled cucumber, and fabulously sweet-sour roll mop herrings with onion salad and crème fraîche. Simple summery puds included strawberries and cream, and crème brûlée. The house wines are, usefully, available in 450ml pot size, and there's plenty of champagne if you're in celebrating.

Babies and children welcome: high chairs. Bookings not accepted. Disabled: lift; ramp; toilet. Dress: smart casual. Tables outdoors (5, pavement). **Map 14 E10.**

Poissonnerie de l'Avenue

82 Sloane Avenue, SW3 3DZ (7589 2457/ www.poissoneriedelavenue.co.uk). South Kensington tube. **Lunch served** noon-3pm, **dinner served** 7-11.30pm Mon-Sat. **Main courses** £12.50-£25. **Set lunch** £16 1 course, £22 2 courses, £28 3 courses. **Cover** £1.50. **Credit** AmEx, DC, JCB, MC, V.

'You serve the best turbot in the world,' the elderly American gent gushed to the maître d'. While we're not sufficiently well travelled to know, the fish was indeed excellent, served in a light champagne sauce that respected its delicate flavour. This Chelsea fixture, opened in 1964, has an adjoining fishmonger, La Marée, to ensure a super-fresh catch. The predominantly French menu flirts with Italian elements; alongside the escargots are such starters as pumpkin ravioli and lobster penne, while mains major in classic fish dishes such as sole véronique (with white wine sauce and grapes) and bouillabaisse. A few meat dishes cater to fish-phobes. Everything we sampled was delicious, from Mediterranean prawns sautéed with a hint of chilli, to a non-cloying tarte tatin and the superior house white (a fairly priced sauvignon blanc from the Loire). No wonder the Poissonnerie has been a favourite with the likes of Mary Quant and Mick Jagger. Don't expect a trendy hotspot, though. The nautical-themed, panelled dining room has the feel of a corporate hotel restaurant and, if our experience is anything to go by, most diners are in the same age bracket as Mary and Mick.

Booking advisable dinner. Children admitted (babies admitted lunch only). Disabled: toilet. Dress: smart casual. Separate room for parties, seats 20. Tables outdoors (6, pavement). **Map 14 E10.**

West

Chiswick

Fish Hook [NEW]

8 Elliott Road, W4 1PE (8742 0766/ www.fishhook.co.uk). Turnham Green tube. **Lunch served** noon-2.30pm Tue-Fri; noon-3.30pm Sat, Sun. **Dinner served** 6-10.30pm Tue-Sat; 6.30-10pm Sun. **Main courses** £12-£16. **Set meal** (lunch, 6-7pm) £12.50 1 course, £16.50 2 courses, £18.50 3 courses. **Credit** AmEx, JCB, MC, V.

Fish Hook occupies the same premises as Fish Hoek, which specialised in South African fish. It's an all-new team, though – headed up by chef-proprietor Michael Nadra – and a new menu too with, usefully, most dishes available in starter or main course size. The only South African fish offered on our visit was kingklip, which has firm white flesh in large flakes; it was served with slightly nutty-flavoured potatoes, broad beans and the chopped garlic and lemon zest that is gremolata, and was quite a catch. Ceviche consisted of slivers of marinated salmon, tuna and swordfish with a garnish of diced scallops and salmon roe that were all reassuringly fresh. Dark brown fish soup had a concentrated flavour and was packed with mussel shells, baby clams, octopus, shrimps and squid – plenty to interest. Side dishes included surprise options such as roasted salsify with dice of bacon. Familiar desserts include panna cotta, here served with poached peaches. The space is simply decorated, with cream paintwork, wooden tables and fishy-themed monochrome screenprints. The friendly service and relaxed atmosphere are a big part of the appeal. Most of our fellow diners were satisfied-looking locals, clearly pleased that the site hadn't been taken over by a restaurant chain.

Babies and children admitted (lunch). Booking advisable. No smoking.

South West

Earl's Court

Lou Pescadou

241 Old Brompton Road, SW5 9HP (7370 1057). Earl's Court tube. **Lunch served** noon-3pm daily. **Dinner served** 7pm-midnight Mon-Fri; 6.30pm-midnight Sat, Sun. **Main courses** £8.90-£18. **Set lunch** (Mon-Fri) £10.90 3 courses. **Set meal** (until 8pm Sat, all day Sun) £14.50 3 courses. **Credit** AmEx, DC, MC, V.

On a Tuesday night, this Earl's Court favourite was packed with a mixed crowd: quiet couples, single men avoiding cooking at home, and a trio of girls in black cocktail dresses. Defiantly untrendy, Lou Pescadou is a fair replica of a Riviera bistro, with woven café chairs, Dufy-esque prints and young French staff bearing massive platters of fruits de mer. The place is justifiably popular. For starters, gambas à la provençale were enormous, with a buttery garlic and fennel sauce that deserved to be mopped up with the excellent fresh bread, while smoky grilled baby squid needed no more embellishment than a squeeze of lemon. We ordered mains from the 'fish of the day' menu; dover sole was perfectly cooked and well-priced at £19.50, including accompanying veg. A selection of classic meat dishes is also offered. Unsurprisingly, the wine list is almost exclusively Gallic. Do try a dessert – we aren't chocoholics, but the warm moelleux au chocolat was a melting experience. We've heard the restaurant may relocate later in 2006, but the management won't be drawn on that matter.

Babies and children welcome: children's menu; high chairs. Booking advisable. Tables outdoors (8, terrace). Takeaway service. **Map 13 B11.**

For branch (Chez Patrick) see index.

Fulham

Deep

The Boulevard, Imperial Wharf, SW6 2UB (7736 3337/www.deeplondon.co.uk). Fulham Broadway tube then 391, C3 bus. **Bar Open/snacks served** noon-11pm Tue-Fri; 5-11pm Sat; noon-5pm Sun. **Snacks** £4-£11.50. *Restaurant* **Lunch served** noon-3pm Tue-Fri; noon-4pm Sun. **Dinner served** 7-11pm Tue-Sat. **Main courses** £15-£24. **Set lunch** £12.50 1 course, £15.50 2 courses, £19.50 3 courses. *Both* **Credit** AmEx, JCB, MC, V.

Located in the rather soulless (and out-of-the-way) Imperial Wharf development, this capacious modern space was almost empty on a Tuesday night, bar a large group who had come specially for the crayfish menu. Deep is run by Swedish husband and wife team Christian and Kerstin Sandefeldt, so August's crayfish season is a big deal, the centrepiece of the three-course feast being an array of crustacea accompanied by smooth cheese pie, nutty cheddar and dry toast. It was a messy job pulling the blighters apart, but the meat was delicious, fresh-tasting and scented with dill. Not cheap, though, at £37, which also included a dull starter of creamy mushrooms on toast, and a pretty dessert of (English) berries with chantilly cream. Otherwise, Scandinavian influences were disappointingly scarce: herrings, gravadlax and a topping of prawns, chopped egg and (barely discernible) horseradish on a main of halibut. But the fish was overcooked and inadequately deboned. Still, the drinks list features 19 akvavits, along with fish-friendly wines, including a good grüner veltliner for £20. Staff were friendly but inattentive and surprisingly uninformed about their Swedish specialities. There's also an extensive bar area, with suede-covered seating in rather queasy colours, and a large outdoor terrace.

Babies and children welcome: high chairs. Booking advisable. Disabled: toilet. Dress: smart casual. Entertainment: DJ 7pm Fri (bar). No smoking (restaurant). Tables outdoors (16, terrace). **Map 21 A2.**

Hosteria del Pesce [NEW]

84-86 Lillie Road, SW6 1TL (7610 0037/ www.hosteriadelpesce.com). West Brompton tube. **Dinner served** 7.30-11.30pm Tue-Sun. **Main courses** £20-£120. **Credit** AmEx, MC, V.

During our visit to this classy new restaurant, many people came to the door, read the menu and left quickly, suggesting they (like us) appreciate the stylish look of the place, like the idea of an Italian seafood restaurant, but find the menu's format and price structure a deterrent. Plates of pasta cost

FishWorks. See p88.

£20, the 'hot and cold antipasto' for two to share is £35. Main-course fish dishes are priced by weight. The cheapest bottle of white wine is £30. You need to be sitting in the restaurant, attended by the friendly and enthusiastic staff, before you appreciate that it is reasonable value. That hot and cold antipasto is a veritable banquet of eight separate dishes; you'd do well to fit in half a plate of pasta after it, let alone a main course and dessert. Highlights included a simple dish of steamed shellfish that emphasised why langoustine is sometimes described as sweet, and a sauté of tender baby cuttlefish and asparagus. We were less impressed by the chewy gnocchi and undercooked aubergine that accompanied the swordfish steak, and floury ciabatta bread. And while there was no denying the superlative freshness of the fish, we were a little uncomfortable with the idea that it is flown in daily from Italy. A gully pleasure in more ways than one.
Babies and children admitted. Booking advisable. No smoking tables. Tables outdoors (3, terrace). Restaurant available for hire.
Map 13 A12.

South
Kennington

★ The Lobster Pot
3 Kennington Lane, SE11 4RG (7582 5556/ www.lobsterpotrestaurant.co.uk). Kennington tube. **Lunch served** noon-2.30pm, **dinner served** 7-10.45pm Tue-Sat. **Main courses** £14.50-£19.50. **Minimum** (8-10pm) £23. **Set lunch** £11.50 2 courses, £14.50 3 courses. **Set meal** £21.50 3 courses, £39.50 8 courses. **Credit** AmEx, JCB, MC, V.
The Lobster Pot's seaside soundtrack (on permanent repeat) of seagulls crying and boats sounding horns, and its wood-lined dining room (chequered with portholes revealing aquariums with real fish swimming by), conspire to make the innocent newcomer believe the owner is mad. Upon tasting the authentic French fare, however, the diner realises the kitsch effects merely serve to transport you from grimy Elephant & Castle to an elegant world of fish, butter, garlic and cream. The moustachioed chef and owner, M Hervé, emerges periodically from the kitchen to make sure everyone is strong enough to crack the crab shells

on the popular seafood platter, which also includes fresh oysters and sweet tiny brown shrimps to be dipped in own-made mayonnaise. A special gratin featured lumps of lobster swimming with wild mushrooms in butter, garlic and a dash of Pernod. Skate wing with capers and brown butter, and bouillabaisse with a host of sea life, were both divine. The set menus are limited and vegetables scarce, but that's not why you're here. The French wine list has all the fish favourites, though a Picpoul de Pinet would make a nice addition.
Babies and children admitted: high chairs. Booking advisable. Dress: smart casual. Separate rooms for parties, seating 20 and 28. **Map 24 O11.**

Waterloo

Livebait
43 The Cut, SE1 8LF (7928 7211/www.sante online.co.uk/livebait). Southwark tube/Waterloo tube/rail. **Meals served** noon-11pm Mon-Sat, 12.30-9pm Sun. **Main courses** £9.95-£36. **Set meal** (noon-7pm) £14.50 2 courses, £18.50 3 courses. **Credit** AmEx, DC, JCB, MC, V.
Livebait's overly bright, completely tiled interior, evocative of a fishmonger's or a cheery public loo, does nothing to dissuade diners from the suspicion that this is a slick chain operation without much soul. Perfunctory service adds to the feeling that you've entered a bit of a factory line – which could be promising for work lunches or for people rushing to the Old Vic. Given the name, it was a great disappointment to find only one fish dish among the main courses on the set menu. From the à la carte, moules marinière featured plump mussels swimming in a garlic wine broth – but don't try anything more exotic than that. Cornwall crab salad with grapefruit, avocado and chilli was stingy on the crab and heavy on the vinegar. A special of grilled whole dover sole was an example of what Livebait should be doing: preparing quality fish in a simple manner. Stick to the grilled menu, which offers generous portions of perfectly cooked fish with a choice of one side order, and you won't be disappointed. The back-of-the-menu wine list is predictable but adequate.
Babies and children admitted: high chairs. Booking advisable. Disabled: toilet. No-smoking tables. **Map 11 N8.**
For branch see index.

South East
London Bridge & Borough

fish!
Cathedral Street, Borough Market, SE1 9AL (7407 3803/www.fishdiner.co.uk). London Bridge tube/rail. **Meals served** 11.30am-11pm Mon-Thur; noon-11pm Fri, Sat; noon-10.30pm Sun. **Main courses** £9.95-£19.95. **Credit** AmEx, DC, MC, V.
A gleaming, glass and steel building surrounded by London at its most grimy and Dickensian, fish! nonetheless does very well out of the affluent food shoppers of Borough Market. A large noticeboard informs diners of the provenance of their dinner (the cod's Icelandic, the salmon organic, and the veg is from across the road). For starters, a toasted cheese-topped piece of smoked haddock was a savoury treat, while calamares and rocket provided a fresh, lemony lead in to a main of cod and chips. Lovely crunchy batter surrounded nice firm cod; chips were golden and chunky, the mushy peas pleasantly starchy. However, at £13.95, we'd say you're paying a bit extra for this increasingly fashionable location. Sea bass on a pad of wilted spinach, tomatoes and carrot, was less comforting, being slightly translucent; we were obliged to order extra chips to make it go further. To follow, bread and butter pudding with custard is a little much if you've had chips, but was deliciously sweet and creamy. The warm chocolate fondant is another favourite. Service can slow at busy times (notably weekend lunches), but remains good-natured. The child in our party was fed with alacrity and a smile, which endeared the staff to us.
Babies and children welcome: children's menu; crayons; high chairs. Booking advisable. Disabled: toilet. No smoking (indoors). Tables outdoors (35, pavement). **Map 11 P8.**

Wright Brothers NEW
11 Stoney Street, SE1 9AD (7403 9554/ www.wrightbros.eu.com). Borough tube/London Bridge tube/rail. **Meals served** noon-11pm Mon-Thur; 10am-11pm Fri; 9am-11pm Sat; 11am-5pm Sun. **Main courses** £8-£22. **Credit** AmEx, DC, MC, V.
From the edge of Borough Market, this seafood bar catches your attention with its bustle of upbeat

Wanstead

★ Applebee's NEW

*17 Cambridge Park, E11 2PU (8989 1977).
Wanstead tube.* **Lunch served** noon-3pm
Tue-Fri. **Dinner served** 6.30-10.30pm Tue-Sat;
noon-9pm Sun. **Main courses** £13-£17.50.
Set lunch £14.50 2 courses. **Set dinner**
£21.50 3 courses. **Credit** AmEx, JCB, MC, V.
Forget the day-trips to Southend, the tide seems to
have come in as far as Wanstead, so fresh is the
catch served up at this stylish seafood restaurant.
Having previously sold fish at Borough Market,
the owners clearly have the wherewithal to source
quality produce and develop a loyal customer base.
What's more, they don't overdo it. Plates aren't
overcrowded, flavours don't compete, the
ingredients are left to speak (never shout) for
themselves. Crab meat salad was lifted with a
delicate ginger marinade, which suited the baby
carrots and apple slices. An octopus and new
potato salad was artfully assembled. The mixed
fish platter for two gives your taste buds the run
of the menu: chunks of sea bream, red snapper,
salmon, tuna and halibut – all simply grilled and
delicious, with seasonal vegetables and a ramekin
of piquant caper sauce. Decor is crisply modern
with just a hint of retro in the form of orange-
flecked mosaic tiling. Given this level of
professionalism, it's less a case of Wanstead-on-
Sea and more a case of W1 in Wanstead.
*Babies and children welcome: children's
portions; high chairs. Booking advisable dinner.
No smoking. Tables outdoors (5, courtyard).*

North

Finsbury Park

Chez Liline

*101 Stroud Green Road, N4 3PX (7263 6550).
Finsbury Park tube/rail.* **Lunch served** 12.30-
2pm Tue-Sat. **Dinner served** 6.30-10.30pm daily.
Main courses £10.95-£17.75. **Set meal** £15
3 courses. **Credit** AmEx, MC, V.
The key dishes at Chez Liline involve super-fresh
fish with delicate Mauritian spicing, alongside
successful nods to French and other cuisines. A
starter of a duo of tunas was Japanese in influence
and presentation, with barely seared tranches of
tuna on one side of the plate and raw slivers on the
other. Soy sauce, daikon and salad leaves worked
well with this dish, though the french dressing was
unnecessary. A special of blue crab with ginger
and spring onions was robust and substantial:
three crab halves in a tasty, spicy sauce. Of the
main courses, braised monkfish with spiced butter
beans was delicious, with a moistness often lost in
other treatments. Fricassée des Îles featured
grouper, snapper and swordfish in a sauce of
tomatoes, chilli and parsley. Side orders aren't
strictly necessary given the generous servings, but
we enjoyed a portion of achard (raw vegetable
pickle). Puds were French classics with a twist:
papaya tarte tatin or banana sorbet.
*Babies and children welcome: high chairs.
Booking advisable. Restaurant available for hire.*

Islington

The Fish Shop

*360-362 St John Street, EC1V 4NR (7837 1199/
www.thefishshop.net). Angel tube/19, 38, 341 bus.*
Lunch served noon-3pm, **dinner served**
5.30-11pm Tue-Sat. **Meals served** noon-8pm
Sun. **Main courses** £10-£44. **Set meal** (noon-
3pm, 5.30-7pm Tue-Sat) £13.50 2 courses, £17
3 courses. **Credit** AmEx, DC, MC, V.
Once an excellent neighbourhood restaurant – and
admirable replacement for the much-loved Upper
Street Fish Shop formerly operated by the owners
– the Fish Shop has declined a jot in recent years.
The corner building is still an attractive spot, with
a bright mezzanine floor at the rear, and stools in
the front looking out over the expansive alfresco
dining space. And the staff are very friendly. It's
the food that does the team no favours. Of the four
dishes we ordered on our visit, only one had us
licking our lips: a richly flavoured starter of split

---

punters. The temptation to join them is hard to
resist. Staff greet you warmly, and invite you to
perch on a bar stool or at the equally lofty shared
dining table. Wright Brothers – actually Ben
Wright and business partner Robin Hancock – are
oyster importers, wholesalers and growers who
supply many of London's top restaurants, but this
is their own place. The day's oyster list is written
on a blackboard: Duchy of Cornwall No.1, wild
Colchester rocks, spéciales de claires, and so on. As
at most other seafood bars, the prices can be high,
but the oysters we tried were sensational: the meat
sweet and with the aroma of fresh rock pool, and
so fresh they winced when lemon juice was added.
The black winkles, verdigris-coloured whelks,
pink Atlantic prawns and grilled lobster were also
beyond reproach. In our experience the cooked
dishes can be far more haphazard, but Wright
Brothers is shuckingly good for the simple stuff.
*Babies and children admitted. Booking
advisable. Disabled: toilet. No smoking. Tables
outdoors (3, pavement). Takeaway service.*
Map 11 P8.

East

Bethnal Green

Winkles

*238 Roman Road, E2 0RY (8880 7450/
www.winklesseafood.com). Mile End tube/
Bethnal Green tube/rail/8 bus.* **Dinner served**
6-10.30pm Mon. **Meals served** noon-10.30pm
Tue-Sat; noon-9pm Sun. **Main courses** £8.50-
£20. **Set lunch** £12.50 3 courses. **Set dinner**
£24.50 3 courses incl glass of wine. **Credit**
AmEx, MC, V.
What a peculiar place Winkles is. Stuck in a
frankly grim part of the Roman Road, it exudes a
bistro chic that tries gamely to attract clientele into
an airy and nicely understated space. Fish is the
draw, but the subtle fish-themed decor and art
don't scream it out; that's left to the counter, where
shellfish from winkles and whelks to oysters and
live lobsters can be bought to take away or selected
for your à la carte meal. It's not a cheap meal, but
a large assiette de mer of oysters, langoustine,
winkles, whelks, shrimp and prawns was fresh and
filling, while pan-fried halibut was firm, thick and
delicate without being bland. Starters too were
generous, though crab claws were a little colder

---

than we would have liked, and clams in a marinière
sauce were slightly too salty. Still, you'll come out
paying around half what you would at some other
places, and if you opt for the set meals (listed on
the door as you go in, but not on the menu), you'll
have plenty left for the trad English desserts and
a bottle of the crisp Jacques Veritier white house
wine. And a cab to a nicer part of town.
*Babies and children welcome: children's portions;
high chairs. Booking advisable weekends. Disabled:
toilet. No-smoking tables. Tables outdoors
(3, pavement). Takeaway service.*

North East

South Woodford

Ark Fish Restaurant

*142 Hermon Hill, E18 1QH (8989 5345/
www.arkfishrestaurant.com). South Woodford
tube.* **Lunch served** noon-2.15pm Tue-Sat.
Dinner served 5.30-9.45pm Tue-Thur;
5.30-10.15pm Fri, Sat. **Meals served** noon-
8.45pm Sun. **Main courses** £8.75-£22.50.
Credit MC, V.
You can't book and it's always packed, but since
some of the best fish in town is served at the Ark,
it's worth the wait (up to 40 minutes). Starters
include rock oysters, smoked salmon, whitebait or
(our choice), a deliciously chunky prawn and crab
timbale served with a capery dip. There are plenty
of excellent main-course options, including
monkfish, lobster, crab, and fisherman's pie, as well
as a couple of specials. On our visit the specials
included rock eel: a superb, perfectly cooked chunk
wrapped in golden batter and served with big
chips and mushy peas. Another was a fine sea bass
accompanied by a well-dressed salad and new
potatoes. In our experience, the simpler the dish,
the better the result; the fried fish and chips are
invariably excellent. Desserts are school-dinner in
style, but no less enjoyable for that. Trifle was a
big hit: a retro ice-cream dish filled with custard,
cream and – could it be? – tinned mandarins. Apart
from the wait, the other drawback is that the light,
airy room filled with excited diners can get noisy.
Service is always prompt, friendly and helpful. The
wine list is short, but fairly priced.
*Babies and children welcome: children's menu;
high chairs. Bookings not accepted. No-smoking
tables.*

---

langoustine in Pernod butter. The others – a starter of smoked salmon atop curried potato; a whole roast sea bass, badly gutted, covered in an unmatched tomato salsa; and an over-large wedge of turbot harmed by too much oil – were all disappointing. It's a real shame: the produce is clearly fresh (there's plenty of unvarnished seafood available if you want to go off-menu and mix and match with a platter), and the continental ambience makes this a nice spot for a linger. If only the food matched the rest of the package.

Babies and children welcome: children's portions. Booking advisable dinner Fri, Sat. Disabled: toilet. Tables outdoors (10, terrace). **Map 5 O3.**

Outer London
Barnet, Hertfordshire

Loch Fyne Restaurant
12 Hadley Highstone, Barnet, Herts EN5 4PU (8449 3674/www.loch-fyne.com). High Barnet tube/Hadley Wood rail. **Meals served** 9am-10pm Mon-Fri; 10am-10.30pm Sat; 10am-9pm Sun. **Main courses** £7.95-£15.95. **Set lunch** £10 2 courses incl side dish. **Credit** AmEx, MC, V.

This branch of the popular fish chain has all the trademark elements: large windows, scrubbed pine and piles of oysters on ice. A weekend lunch visit saw the place positively bustling, with the kitchen rather stretched as a result, and the arrival of dishes not timed quite as they might be. The fixed price lunch is excellent value. A starter of fish soup was thick and tasty, though lacked the usual croûton goodies we have come to expect. Whole arctic char ('trout-like' was the accurate description from our waitress) with chilli and coriander butter was perfectly cooked. From the carte, Loch Fyne ashet was a simple and tasty plate of the company's own smoked fish. Puddings of the banoffi pie school are only for the truly dedicated. A surprise hit was the kids' menu, with excellent sea bass, mash and mixed veg. There is a 'cooking by numbers' feel to some of the combinations, but fresh ingredients and friendly staff make Loch Fyne a reliable and popular choice.

Babies and children welcome: children's menu; high chairs. Booking advisable. No-smoking tables. Tables outdoors (7, terrace).
For branches see index.

Richmond, Surrey

★ FishWorks
13-19 The Square, Old Market, Richmond, Surrey TW9 1EA (8948 5965/www.fishworks. co.uk). Richmond tube/rail. **Lunch served** noon-3.30pm, **dinner served** 6-10.30pm Mon-Fri **Meals served** 9.30am-10.30pm Sat, Sun. **Main courses** £9.50-£25. **Credit** AmEx, DC, MC, V.

Mitchell Tonks' FishWorks chain is growing at a phenomenal rate. From one branch in London in 2003, it now has ten – six of which opened in 2006 alone – with plans for more. There are also three outside London, including Bath (the original). Each branch combines fishmonger, restaurant and cookery school. The royal blue and white decor, with colourful seaside pictures, is light and bright. The atmosphere is casual – and particularly appealing to women, it seems, if the customers on a visit to the Richmond branch are typical. This is the biggest outlet to date, housed in an ex-market building with a soaring roof and huge skylight: a lovely spot. The menu offers 'classic' dishes (many in starter or main-course sizes), such as smoked salmon, Dartmouth crab, and skate with black butter and capers, along with seasonal crustacea (oysters, lobster, langoustines, winkles, cockles). There are also salads large and small, and a blackboard list of specials that varies according to the day's catch. Zuppa del pescatore, a generous stew in a thyme and garlic broth, was a good choice, though the fish and shellfish in the simple mixed grilled platter were slightly overcooked.

Babies and children welcome: children's menu; high chairs. Booking essential Thur-Sat. Cookery school. Disabled: toilet. Fishmonger. No smoking. Tables outdoors (6, terrace).
For branches see index.

French

A flurry of interest was created by the opening of two rival steak-frites joints in Marylebone at the end of 2005 – **Le Relais de Venise l'entrecôte** and Entrecôte de Café de Paris. Both claiming to be the original no-choice formula, and both with long pedigrees to prove it, they were both greeted with yawns of critical disappointment; the latter lasted less than a year. Simply being 'authentically French' isn't good enough any more, because Londoners expect much better than that – and we got it when **Galvin Bistrot de Luxe** opened, also in Marylebone. Although it got off to sticky start – service could be a problem during the first few months – it now seems to have settled into a steady stream of critical praise, and has proved to be one of the most talked-about openings of the year, heralding a return to bistro-style cooking that became one of the trends of 2006.

Another restaurant getting back to its roots was **La Brasserie Ma Cuisine Bourgeoise** in Twickenham, which changed from fancy-pants McClements restaurant to a simpler bistro style. The Club Gascon boys have consolidated their hold on Clerkenwell by converting their traiteur to **Le Comptoir Gascon**. At the other end of the spectrum, London still does smart French very well indeed. **Papillon** is slicker than a Charles Aznavour comb-over, and has proved as popular with Brompton Cross locals as a Manolo Blahnik sale. Terence Conran's love of French dining continues unabated, and he opened **Sauterelle** in the City to some indifference; but it's quite good, really.

Central
Belgravia

Le Cercle
1 Wilbraham Place, SW1X 9AE (7901 9999). Sloane Square tube.
Bar **Open/snacks served** noon-midnight Tue-Sat.
Restaurant **Lunch served** noon-3pm, **tea served** 3-5.30pm, **dinner served** 6-11pm Tue-Sat. **Set lunch** £15 3 dishes incl tea or coffee, £19.50 4 dishes. **Set dinner** (6-6.45pm Tue-Sat) £17.50 3 dishes incl tea or coffee, £21.50 4 dishes. **Tapas** £4-£16. **Credit** AmEx, JCB, MC, V.

A discreet entrance hidden among mansion blocks leads you down into this bright, airy basement restaurant, which is owned by the Club Gascon people (*see p91*). Le Cercle is furnished simply but attractively in wood and leather, with drifty curtains marking off the bar and cosy private booths. The atmosphere is smart but unpretentious. The menu, divided into unconventional categories such as 'terroirs' (French farmhouse dishes) and 'plaisirs' (foie gras and other luxuries), offers small and appealing dishes, tapas-style. Our mousseron St George's mushrooms, brewed with cream and garlic, were served in a tiny cast-iron cocotte, while a sweet roasted scallop came on a piece of dark slate with a spring-like asparagus bavarois. Chunks of pig's cheek served with cabbage were especially appetising, and we enjoyed a delicious but somewhat chewy piece of beef with dreamily liquescent bone marrow. The savoury dishes tended to be a little oversalted for our tastes, but nonetheless were pretty good. Desserts were magnificent: a casually artful rhubarb millefeuille, and a crisp, flaky tart topped with vanilla cream (accompanied, bizarrely, by a sharp grapefruit

granita). The drinks menu includes an interesting selection of fairly priced wines by the glass or bottle. Our waiter was assiduous and enthusiastic.

Babies and children admitted. Booking advisable. No-smoking tables. **Map 15 G10.**

La Poule au Pot
231 Ebury Street, SW1W 8UT (7730 7763). Sloane Square tube. **Lunch served** 12.30-2.30pm Mon-Fri; 12.30-3pm Sat, 12.30-3.30pm Sun. **Dinner served** 6.45-11pm Mon-Sat; 6.45-10pm Sun. **Main courses** £14-£21. **Set lunch** £15.75 2 courses, £17.75 3 courses. **Credit** AmEx, DC, MC, V.

Famous for its cosy nooks and crannies, this Belgravia institution proved on our last visit that it also excels at alfresco ambience – its candlelit tables spilling on to the leafy streets outside. We ordered a punchy cabernet franc and settled down for the fullest fat splurge the fiercely traditional menu could offer. The meal kicked off in style with foie gras poêlé (a whole liver pan-fried) that was a melt-in-the-mouth mainline to gluttonous heaven; and an irresistible plate of plump, flavoursome scallops. Main courses include a wide choice of fish, poultry and meat. We tried a couple of the daily specials – whole roast pigeon, and medallions of venison in a red wine jus. The pigeon's tender pink meat made it the pick of the two, while the char-grilled venison was lovely and rare but a little lacking in flavour. For pudding, crème brûlée was a bit too eggy, but flambéed banana came satisfyingly drenched in caramel and vanilla ice-cream. Service is energetic, so dining at La Poule au Pot will always be fun. But prices reflect the Chelsea postcode.

Babies and children welcome: high chairs. Booking essential. Separate room for parties, seats 16. Tables outdoors (12, terrace).
Map 15 G11.

★ Roussillon

16 St Barnabas Street, SW1W 8PE (7730 5550/www.roussillon.co.uk). Sloane Square tube. **Lunch served** noon-2.30pm Mon-Fri. **Dinner served** 6.30-10.30pm Mon-Sat. **Set lunch** £35 3 courses incl half bottle of wine, water and coffee. **Set dinner** £48 3 courses. **Set meal** £65 tasting menu. **Credit** AmEx, MC, V.

Does the chic Roussillon, stylishly decorated in cream and browns, serve one of the best-value lunches in town? A few brightly coloured paintings have been added to this long-time favourite, and a new children's menu was introduced in 2006, which seems to have been a success with smart Chelsea families. (We heard a precocious six-year-old say, 'Daddy, I've finally managed to tackle eight courses.') Executive chef Alexis Gauthier's imaginative three-course £35 set lunch includes canapés, pre-starter, pre-dessert, coffee, petits fours, half a bottle of wine, and mineral water – making this an ideal venue not just for lunching ladies, but for everybody else too. Everything we tried was carefully prepared, with due attention to detail. The food was beautifully presented, and boasted deep and intense, yet fresh, light flavours: the perfect cooking for our times. Parmesan-rolled potato gnocchi came with crisp courgette-flower tempura. Grilled trout was coral-pink, flaky and meaty. Open ravioli comprised featherlight, wafer-thin sheets of own-made pasta atop jewel-coloured summer vegetables, including fennel, artichokes and black truffle. Zingy lime sorbet accompanied crunchy lemon crème brûlée. Service was exemplary too.

Children over 8 years admitted; children's menu. Booking advisable. Dress: smart casual. No smoking. Restaurant available for hire. Separate room for parties, seats 26. Vegetarian menu. **Map 15 G11.**

City

Le Coq d'Argent

No.1 Poultry, EC2R 8EJ (7395 5000/ www.conran.com). Bank tube/DLR. *Bar & Grill* **Lunch served** 11.30am-3pm Mon-Fri. **Main courses** £12-£16. *Restaurant* **Breakfast served** 7.30-10am Mon-Fri. **Lunch served** 11.30am-3pm Mon-Fri; noon-3pm Sun. **Dinner served** 6-10pm Mon-Fri; 6.30-10pm Sat. **Main courses** £15-£23. **Set lunch** £23 2 courses, £27 3 courses. *Both* **Credit** AmEx, DC, JCB, MC, V.

James Cagney would enjoy this Conran restaurant if only for its top-of-the-world potential. The skyline views are splendid, particularly from the mini lawn that juts out over one end of this City high-rise. You arrive by lift, into a circular bar that's lush with greenery – a popular spot for after-work drinks and light lunches. The restaurant is unstuffy, with comfortable club chairs, acres of white linen and a lovely shaded terrace. It's very much a City affair (the clientele is largely male and besuited). The drinks list, a 45-page book, is crammed with vintage French wines at expense-account prices (the costliest bottle is a 1921 Château d'Yquem for a mind-blowing £5,170). There's plenty of caviar, oysters, crustacea and classic French dishes (snails, chateaubriand), and prices reflect the location – so the prix-fixe menu is good value. Sea bass came with a swirl of olive mash, a single razor clam and lemony spinach; the fish was perfect, but the spinach tasted vinegary. Chicken supreme was rather dull, but was lifted by a tarragon sauce. Desserts, such as a delicate, creamy wedge of passionfruit tart, are huge and excellent. Staff are poised and friendly. This being a Conran joint, smoking is positively encouraged, with an annotated list of cigars on the menu.

Babies and children welcome: high chairs. Booking advisable. Disabled: lift; toilet. Entertainment: noon-4pm Sun. Restaurant available for hire. Tables outdoors (13, restaurant terrace; 25, bar terrace). **Map 11 P6.**

★ 1 Lombard Street

1 Lombard Street, EC3V 9AA (7929 6611/ www.1lombardstreet.com). Bank tube/DLR. *Bar* **Open** 11am-11pm, **tapas served** 5.30-10.30pm Mon-Fri. **Tapas** £3.50-£14.50. *Brasserie* **Breakfast served** 7.30-11am, **meals served** 11.30am-10.30pm Mon-Fri. **Main courses** £14.50-£27.50. **Set dinner** (6-10.30pm) £19.50 5 courses. *Restaurant* **Lunch served** noon-3pm, **dinner served** 6-10pm Mon-Fri. **Main courses** £27.50-£29.50. **Set lunch** £34 2 courses, £36 3 courses. **Set dinner** £36 3 courses. *All* **Credit** AmEx, DC, MC, V.

1 Lombard Street is by no means the only former City banking hall to have been remodelled into a restaurant and/or bar: walking along nearby Cornhill, you can't swing a fiver without hitting similar conversions. However, it's unique among its rivals in one crucial regard: under executive chef Herbert Berger, the food has won a Michelin star. A calm, secluded space at the rear of the building holds the 50-seat restaurant favoured by the Michelin men; at the front sits a larger, more approachable brasserie, anchored by a circular bar beneath a glorious domed skylight. You'll pay slightly less out here, but the food is still terrific: we followed an immaculate gazpacho and an agreeably simple asparagus starter with a crunchy confit of duck, served over butter beans, parsley mash and pristine chorizo slices, and a deeply moreish square of smoked haddock, with creamed leeks and a trio of clams. Given the location (a coin's toss from the Bank of England), it's not

Sauterelle. See p91.

surprising that both brasserie and restaurant draw a monied crowd keen on keeping the receipt at meal's end. However, to their credit, staff are careful to treat the handful of interloping scruffs with grace and equanimity. An excellent experience, all told.

Children over 10 years admitted (brasserie). Booking advisable lunch. Disabled: lift; toilet. Entertainment: pianist and singer 6.30pm Fri. No smoking (restaurant). Restaurant available for hire. Separate room for parties, seats 40. **Map 12 Q6.**

Rosemary Lane

61 Royal Mint Street, E1 8LG (7481 2602/ www.rosemarylane.btinternet.co.uk). Tower Hill tube/Fenchurch Street rail/Tower Gateway DLR. **Lunch served** noon-2.30pm, **dinner served** 5.30-10pm Mon-Fri. **Dinner served** 6-10pm Sat. **Main courses** £13-£19. **Set meal** £14 2 courses, £17 3 courses. **Set dinner** (Sat) £30 tasting menu. **Credit** AmEx, MC, V.

The trendy gentrification (trendification?) that has swallowed up much of the East End has yet to spread to run-down Royal Mint Street – until, that is, you get inside this organic 'French fusion' restaurant. Hush-inducing curtains, flickering tea lights and friendly service set the scene for unusual combinations of French basics and enthusiastic New World experimentation, with a globalised wine list to match. We ordered an elegant Californian pinot noir and tucked into amuse-bouches of Irish cheese and peaches in anticipation of what was to come. Chilled asparagus salad was a heady plateful of crunchy green stems, rocket, red onion and bacon, topped with delicious Belgian baby white asparagus stalks. Chicken liver pâté came with onion chutney, dijon sauce and an exquisite citric celeriac remoulade. For mains, a fleshy fillet of sea bream was served with cherry tomatoes, white beans and shimeji mushrooms; and a huge hunk of Gloucester belly pork was cooked in chardonnay with three different types of tomato. If anything, both dishes were a little too fussy, overpowering excellent basic ingredients with too many flavours. A shared pudding of mandarin orange cheesecake was a disappointment – an over-gelatinous ending to an otherwise exciting and enjoyable meal.

Booking advisable lunch. Dress: smart casual. Restaurant available for hire. **Map 12 S7.**

Sauterelle NEW

Royal Exchange, EC3V 3LR (7618 2483/ www.conran.com). Bank tube/DLR. **Lunch served** noon-2.30pm, **dinner served** 6-9.30pm Mon-Fri. **Main courses** £16.50-£19. **Credit** AmEx, DC, MC, V.

A cosy, understated restaurant in the Royal Exchange, Sauterelle snakes round the first-floor arcade of the building, giving a nice view of the courtyard. It's a tricky space for a restaurant, and the folk from Conran ran risks in taking it on. But they've done it proud: our meal here was a nearly unbroken pleasure. The menu consists of bistro classics gently modernised. Choosing was agonising because everything looked so good – but we picked well. Lobster bisque and fritot (fritters) of salt cod, both among the cheaper starters, were exemplary. Beautifully roasted suckling pig served on a rösti with spinach was heavenly down to the last detail. Grilled calf's liver with bacon was slightly overcooked, but excellent nonetheless; the kitchen staff know how to assemble the right ingredients in just the right way. A well-focused wine list gives acceptable choice under £30, including intelligent selections from outside France (even the New World); our Juliénas, one of the cheapest on the list, was excellent. As was a shared dessert of mango and passionfruit mousse and some delectable petits fours that came even without coffee. The cost can mount, especially if you order drinks before dinner. But this was a highly successful meal, and not expensive for the quality and the location.

Babies and children admitted. Disabled: toilet. No smoking. **Map 12 Q6.**

Clerkenwell & Farringdon

Café du Marché

22 Charterhouse Square, Charterhouse Mews, EC1M 6AH (7608 1609). Barbican tube/ Farringdon tube/rail. **Lunch served** noon-2.30pm Mon-Fri. **Dinner served** 6-10pm Mon-Sat. **Set meal** £29.95 3 courses. **Credit** MC, V.

With a menu geared towards familiar bistro-style comfort food, exposed brickwork and smoochy candlelight, Café du Marché offers a perennially reliable respite from the bustle of the city outside. Our last visit got off to a good start with an old favourite – a bisque-y fish soup accompanied by croûtons, garlic mayonnaise and cheese; and a more experimental offering – an appetite-whetting bowl of thin pasta and crab meat topped with a pile of juicy clams. Mains, however, were a little disappointing: 'catch of the day' was a fillet of brill that was meaty enough, but hardly enhanced by a bland sauce of white beans and beetroot; while tender spatchcock quail 'à la Marocaine' disappeared under too much barbecue-style glaze with only an uninspiring mound of couscous for support. Happily, dessert restored the gastronomic order with a melt-in-the-mouth white chocolate mousse, and a pear tart laden with fruity chunks and sweet crumbly pastry. With a great atmosphere, impeccable service and a well-stocked Francophile wine list (we had a very good bottle of white Burgundy for £24.50), Café du Marché is always good fun even if the food is sometimes a little hit and miss.

Babies and children admitted. Booking advisable. Entertainment: jazz duo 8pm Mon-Thur; pianist 8pm Fri, Sat. Separate rooms for parties, seating 30 and 70. Tables outdoors (4, pavement). **Map 5 O5.**

★ Club Gascon

57 West Smithfield, EC1A 9DS (7796 0600). Barbican tube/Farringdon tube/rail. **Lunch served** noon-2pm Mon-Fri. **Dinner served** 7-10pm Mon-Thur; 7-10.30pm Fri, Sat. **Main courses** £8.30-£20. **Tapas** £6-£16.50. **Set lunch** £35 3 courses. **Set meal** £39 5 courses (£60 incl wine). **Credit** AmEx, MC, V.

Quietly, with dignity, and eschewing celebrity, Club Gascon has become one of London's consistently great restaurants. Sure, it has spun off a bar (Cellar Gascon) and a deli-restaurant (Le Comptoir Gascon; *see below*), but it remains low key and expert, with the customer very definitely king. Service is well judged and egalitarian. The room – marble-lined, dimly lit, with statement flowers – is clubbily atmospheric, but the feeling of luxurious well-being that Gascon engenders probably stems from the sensual effect of its artistically conceived, beautifully presented food. The speciality is foie gras, which accounts for one section of the six on the menu. Dishes are deliberately small: even light eaters will need three; four or five are recommended (there's also an amuse-gueule). Seasonal produce (samphire, summer truffle, 'hay jus', on our July visit) speckles the menu. So too do high-end ingredients: truffle, caviar, lobster (which work well in the small servings). Of six dishes we sampled, one was perhaps not entirely successful (raw tuna with too-dry veal), one slightly odd (raspberry and cherry gazpacho, but with a blinding almond ice-cream) and four quite exquisite. The five-course set menu is a good way to go, particularly the with-wine option, given the complexity of choices and multiplicity of courses.

Babies and children admitted. Booking essential. No smoking. Restaurant available for hire. **Map 11 O5.**

Le Comptoir Gascon NEW

61-63 Charterhouse Street, EC1M 6HJ (7608 0851). Farringdon tube/rail. **Lunch served** noon-2pm, **dinner served** 7-11pm Tue-Sat. **Main courses** £7.50-£13.50. **Credit** AmEx, MC, V.

The laid-back sister to Club Gascon (*see above*) makes clever use of a sliver of a site in Smithfield. The tiny interior is all industrial chic, with lots of exposed brick and steel; there's a cut-down deli/bistro menu to go with the casual surroundings.

Interview
PHILIPPE MESSY

Who are you?
General manager and sommelier at **Papillon** (*see p95*).

Eating in London: what's good about it?
The vast choice of styles of food and restaurants at different prices.

What's bad about it?
Turns. When you are paying the amount of money that restaurants are charging, you should have your table for more than two hours.

Which are your favourite London restaurants?
The service and food at **Racine** (*see p92*) and **Aubergine** (*see p133*) are great. I also like **Roka** (*see p185*).

What single thing would most improve London's restaurant scene?
I would get rid of the service charge and make the waiters really work for their money. It would probably improve the service.

How could London's diners and sommeliers enjoy a more mutually rewarding relationship?
I think fewer sommeliers are inclined to rip off customers. A guest maybe should ask the sommelier: 'I am used to drinking this wine – have you got something in the same style to help me discover something new?'

What do people who usually buy New World wines need to know about choosing French wine?
Start with wines from the South of France. The style is frequently rich and opulent – closer in style to wines from the New World – and they are quite good value. Those on a budget should try not to choose the cheapest wine on a list. Choose wines that cost £18-£25. Entry-level wines are too often nondescript and a bit boring.

Any hot tips for the coming year?
I feel customers are more and more inclined to go back to more simple and traditional food and drink, whether it is Asian, British, French or Italian.

You can sit at the bar or at one of a handful of tables, and sample dishes listed under 'mer', 'terre' or 'végétal', with 'humble beginnings' to start and 'sweet things' to finish. Despite this, the food is mercifully simple, unpretentious and generally pretty good. We tried some textbook-perfect duck confit with lovely, fat french fries and a salad of curly leaves on the side. Smoky grilled squid came with a sweet tomato confit and creamy pearl barley. Homage to the grander Club Gascon up the road can be found in a starter of creamy foie gras flavoured with Sauternes – as well as in the tendency to serve dishes on flint, stone or other bewildering forms of crockery. A short list of Gallic wines, available by the bottle or glass, as well as several aperitifs and digestifs, completes the picture. A worthwhile, reasonably priced bet in a busy area.
Babies and children welcome: high chairs. Booking advisable. No smoking. Tables outdoors (4, pavement). **Map 11 O5.**

Covent Garden

Incognico
117 Shaftesbury Avenue, WC2H 8AD (7836 8866/www.incognico.com). Leicester Square or Tottenham Court Road tube. **Lunch served** noon-3pm, **dinner served** 5.30-11pm Mon-Sat. **Main courses** £11.50-£25. **Credit** AmEx, DC, MC, V.
The well-appointed dark wood interior and the fleet of efficient staff may scream Paris, but, alas, Incognico's food and prices certainly do not. The simple menu (no cappuccino of aubergine here) is refreshingly straightforward, heavy on fish but with a good selection of meat dishes. Our starters materialised within seconds of ordering and both were underwhelming: a serrano ham, buffalo mozzarella, fig and rocket salad was all ham and no cheese; and an endive, gorgonzola and pear salad was watery and bland. Mains were better, but were astonishingly priced given their quality and size. Monkfish was overpowered by the accompanying artichokes and tomatoes, while the rack of lamb was surprisingly small for £18.50 and thoroughly unexciting. Were the food half the price, this would be a great refuge from Cambridge Circus and a fine place to grab an efficiently served meal in the centre of town. As it is, Incognico offers more of the same – another expensive West End restaurant for out-of-towners.
Babies and children admitted. Booking essential. Dress: smart casual. Restaurant available for hire. **Map 17 K6.**

Mon Plaisir
19-21 Monmouth Street, WC2H 9DD (7836 7243/www.monplaisir.co.uk). Covent Garden tube. **Lunch served** noon-2.15pm Mon-Fri. **Dinner served** 5.45-11.15pm Mon-Sat. **Main courses** £13.95-£22. **Set lunch** £13.95 2 courses, £15.95 3 courses. **Set meal** (5.45-7pm Mon-Sat; after 10pm Mon-Thur) £12.50 2 courses, £14.50 3 courses incl glass of wine and coffee. **Credit** AmEx, MC, V.
Claiming to be 'London's oldest French restaurant', Mon Plaisir caters to tourists and Francophiles pining for the ramshackle charms of Montmartre. Dining rooms packed with bric-a-brac are bordered by a lovingly polished zinc bar. Thick-accented staff flit unfussily between the tables. As well as traditional bistro food (foie gras, escargots, steak tartare), the menu includes more imaginative interpretations of classic French flavours. So, 'déclinaison gourmande' (literally 'greedy line-up') was a tantalising plate of crunchy asparagus spears, pots of hollandaise sauce and lobster soup, and creamy smoked ham mousse. Another starter, rillettes lapereaux (potted meat of young rabbit) matched layered buttery meatiness to our basket of fresh warm bread. To follow, a thick fillet of monkfish came with rich ginger sauce and pea ravioli, while a satisfyingly pink roast rack of lamb was deliciously offset by a saffron-infused jus. Old favourites pack the dessert list, from clafoutis to crème caramel, but we plumped for 'contraste chocopassionnément' – warm moist chocolate cake topped with tangy passionfruit sorbet. Throw in

a wine list crammed with reliable French favourites and you'll find yourself humming *La Vie en Rose* all the way home.
Babies and children admitted. Booking advisable. **Map 18 L6.**

Fitzrovia

Elena's L'Étoile
30 Charlotte Street, W1T 2NG (7636 7189). Goodge Street or Tottenham Court Road tube. **Lunch served** noon-2.30pm Mon-Fri. **Dinner served** 6-10.45pm Mon-Sat. **Main courses** £14.75-£20.75. **Credit** AmEx, DC, JCB, MC, V.
London's 'institution restaurants' roll on through the decades by creating an unmistakeable, unchanging identity. At Elena's, it's a combination of a circa-1900 Parisian bistro look (dark woods, glittering lamps), with an air of raffish, theatre-world bohemia (emphatically indicated by the signed photos of all the famous names, from Ingrid Bergman to Stephen Fry via Maria Callas, who have graced the tables over the years). The reasons for coming are just as unchanging: service, still sometimes presided over by venerable owner Elena Salvoni herself, that's idiosyncratic yet ever-professional, and old-fashioned comforts like the plush red banquettes, ideal for expansive lunches. The food, mostly classic French with a few Italian touches, is comforting too, without being anything special. A feuilleté of crisp fresh asparagus with a light hollandaise sauce was excellent, but croquettes of salt cod, prawn and crab brandade were a bit crude, and overpowered by the cod. A salmon and leek fish cake came in a deliciously herby crust – and with exceptional mushy peas, a menu tradition – but the salmon was dull. Confit of lamb with spring onion mash and caper sauce would have been nicer had the meat not been overcooked. The wine list is heavy on classic French labels, which seems only right.
Babies and children admitted. Booking advisable; essential lunch. Separate rooms for parties, seating 10, 16 and 32. **Map 9 J5.**

Knightsbridge

Brasserie St Quentin
243 Brompton Road, SW3 2EP (7589 8005/ www.brasseriestquentin.co.uk). Knightsbridge or South Kensington tube/14, 74 bus. **Lunch served** noon-3pm daily. **Dinner served** 6-10.30pm Mon-Sat; 6-10pm Sun. **Main courses** £12.50-£23.50. **Set meal** (noon-7.30pm) £15.50 2 courses, £17.50 3 courses. **Credit** AmEx, DC, JCB, MC, V.
Opposite the Brompton Oratory and a block from Harrods, this convincing French brasserie attracts a wealthy Knightsbridge clientele. It was humming to the strains of well-heeled laughter when we last visited. Despite the annoying mirrors (how can watching yourself eat be considered desirable?), St Quentin is very well designed. In appearance it could quite conceivably be a brasserie on the Rue de Rivoli. Our meal was of sound quality: a feuilleté d'escargots in garlic sauce provided fine, meaty snails and a flavourful sauce; soupe de poisson, aïoli and croûtons was velvety and equally powerful. We followed this with an excellent breast of Brittany chicken that was slightly overpowered by a lemon and thyme jus, but perfectly cooked and served with delicious chorizo potatoes. Another main, halibut, was less punchy, but was complemented well by lemon and parsley butter. St Quentin's wine list is excellent, with 20 bottles under £20; our choice of a light and summery Touraine sauvignon (£19.75) was a good one. Service, which began as supremely efficient, descended to the downright uninterested by the end of the meal – our only complaint with this enjoyable and convivial establishment.
Babies and children welcome: high chair. Booking advisable. Separate room for parties, seats 20. **Map 14 E10.**

Drones
1 Pont Street, SW1X 9EJ (7235 9555/ www.whitestarline.org.uk). Knightsbridge or Sloane Square tube. **Lunch served** noon-2.30pm Mon-Fri; noon-3.30pm Sun. **Dinner served**

6-11pm Mon-Sat. **Main courses** £13.50-£24.50. **Set lunch** (Mon-Fri) £14.95 2 courses, £17.95 3 courses; (Sun) £22.50 3 courses. **Credit** AmEx, DC, MC, V.
A thoroughly confident and clubbish Anglo-French restaurant, Drones is best remembered for its luxurious atmosphere, supremely professional French staff and occasionally wonderful dishes. It was set up in the 1970s by David Niven Jr and Dave Gilmour, but is now under the wing of Marco Pierre White. The space has a brown, leathery feel, with monochrome portraits of old British film stars (David Niven, Diana Dors), display cases with phallic coral, and aspidistras. Tellingly, the menu advises that, for private parties, there's the 'elegant Michael Winner room'. A quick scan revealed that our fellow diners were reassuringly well-heeled and, on the whole, couples. Starters reflected the entente cordiale theme: parfait of foie gras sat in a sticky pool of caramel gelée, while a comforting omelette Arnold Bennett (a Savoy hotel supper dish from the early 20th century) had been baked in a blini pan with smoked haddock and gruyère. The best moment was the arrival of a fantastic tournedos rossini topped with fresh truffles and more foie gras - gout on a plate, maybe, but worth the visit alone for its flavour. Summing up the Anglo leanings of Drones, the cheeses were all English farmhouse and arrived with Bath Olivers and Carr's water biscuits.
Babies and children admitted. Booking essential. Restaurant available for hire. Separate room for parties, seats 45. **Map 15 G10.**

★ Racine
239 Brompton Road, SW3 2EP (7584 4477). Knightsbridge or South Kensington tube/14, 74 bus. **Lunch served** noon-3pm Mon-Fri; noon-3.30pm Sat, Sun. **Dinner served** 6-10.30pm Mon-Sat; 6-10pm Sun. **Main courses** £12.50-£20.75. **Set meal** (lunch, 6-7.30pm) £16.50 2 courses, £18.50 3 courses. **Credit** AmEx, JCB, MC, V.
Enter through curtains into the convivial surroundings of one of London's most consistently enjoyable restaurants. Lighting is subdued, and smoked mirrors are set above the brown leather seating. Tables, placed close together (too close, according to one of our group), are filled with families, bon vivants from the French Embassy, and fathers treating their student daughters. Service comes from upright and focused French staff. The food is a mix of modern and retro bistro classics. Six fines claires oysters were a godsend on a hot night: slightly out of season but still fat and wet, theatrically presented on a tray of crushed ice, with juicy spiced lamb sausages in a dish to the side. Strips of squid sautéed with chorizo in manzanilla sherry and thick black ink were topped with paper-thin slices of browned garlic: a delightful dish to taste and to see. Mains were just as assured. Buttery, fresh skate wing was partnered by brown shrimps and tiny croûtons; lamb rump was pink and tender inside its crisp skin, baby artichokes and black olives making a

BEST FRENCH

Tongue-in-chic
Gastro (see p98), **Les Trois Garçons** (see p99).

For vegetarians
The Admiralty (see p97), **Morgan M** (see p100), **Roussillon** (see p89).

French polish
Galvin Bistrot de Luxe (see p93), **The Ledbury** (see p98), **1 Lombard Street** (see p89), **Papillon** (see p95), **Racine** (see above), **La Trompette** (see p98).

Where the clock stands still
L'Aventure (see p101), **Le Bistro** (see p100), **Mon Plaisir** (see left), **La Poule au Pot** (see p88).

Sidebar: RESTAURANTS

Le Relais de Venise l'entrecôte

slightly sour counterbalance. Chef Henry Harris is sometimes teased for creating a place too retro even for France; to our mind, though, this is a thoroughly vibrant restaurant that knows how to innovate and delight.

Babies and children welcome: high chairs. Booking advisable. Dress: smart casual. No-smoking tables. **Map 14 E10**.

Marylebone

★ Galvin Bistrot de Luxe NEW

66 Baker Street, W1U 7DH (7935 4007/ www.galvinbistrotdeluxe.co.uk). Baker Street tube. **Lunch served** noon-2.30pm daily. **Dinner served** 6-11pm Mon-Sat; 6-10.30pm Sun. **Main courses** £10.50-£21. **Set lunch** £15.50 3 courses. **Set dinner** (6-7pm) £17.50 3 courses. **Credit** AmEx, MC, V.

It's no surprise that this smartly corporate take on a modern French brasserie has been wowing most of the critics since it opened autumn 2005. Teething problems with the service appear to have been put aside, and during a recent lunch the front-of-house team worked like clockwork. The clientele of local business diners (almost entirely men in suits) appreciatively tucked into the Galvin brothers' impeccable Gallic fare. Chris and Jeff Galvin share an impressive culinary pedigree, including stints at the Orrery, Wolseley and Savoy – and Chris Galvin recently opened haute-cuisine operation Galvin at Windows, in the Hilton hotel. Here, they've chosen to concentrate on serving classic bistro dishes at fair prices. Choices such as terrine of foie gras, velouté of asparagus with poached duck egg, escargots bourguignonne, tête de veau with piquant sauce ravigote, or roast rump of lamb with flageolet beans and thyme, are all in the traditional mould. And there's tarte tatin, crème brûlée or baba au rhum to finish. The immaculate execution and perfect balance of simple yet intense flavours is a delightful reminder of just how good these bourgeois classics can be. Recommended.
Babies and children welcome: high chairs. Booking advisable. Disabled: toilet. **Map 9 G5**.

Le Relais de Venise l'entrecôte NEW

120 Marylebone Lane, W1U 2QG (7486 0878/ www.relaisdevenise.com). Bond Street tube. **Lunch served** noon-2.30pm Mon-Fri; 12.30-3.30pm Sat, Sun. **Dinner served** 6-10.45pm

Mon-Fri; 6.30-10.45pm Sat; 6.30-10.30pm Sun. **Set meal** £17 2 courses, £22 3 courses. **Credit** MC, V.

An outpost of the venerable Parisian brasserie of the same name, the Relais de Venise emphasises gastronomic simplicity with a £17 menu of salad and steak-frites. It thus offers a welcome alternative to the indulgent foodcentricity of Marylebone and has been packing in the crowds since opening in 2005. Unfortunately, success seems to be taking its toll on the staff, who abandoned all attempts at social niceties during our visit. Walnut-covered salads were shoved in front of us, the wine (a decent vin de pays d'Oc) was dumped without being poured, and our chairs were repeatedly clattered as the meal got off to an inauspicious start. The arrival of plates stacked with steak and chips raised our spirits; the meat was tender and juicy and the chips satisfyingly crunchy. If only the dish hadn't been drenched in 'secret' sauce: a taste-smothering, mustard-inflected goo. Things improved with a delicious plate of cheeses, before the arrival of a 'tulipe de framboise melba': an extravagant heap of biscuit, ice-cream and raspberries. Decor is modelled on the original, all banquette seating, white paper tablecloths, mirrored walls and colourful pictures.
Babies and children welcome: children's portions; high chairs. Bookings not accepted. Disabled: toilet. No-smoking tables. Tables outdoors (10, pavement). **Map 9 G5**.

Mayfair

Mirabelle

56 Curzon Street, W1Y 8DN (7499 4636/ www.whitestarline.org.uk). Green Park tube. **Lunch served** noon-2.30pm Mon-Sat; noon-3pm Sun. **Dinner served** 6-11pm daily. **Main courses** £16.50-£27.50. **Set lunch** (Mon-Sat) £17.50 2 courses, £21 3 courses; (Sun) £23.95 3 courses. **Credit** AmEx, MC, V.

Noël Coward, Liz Taylor and all the froth of Mayfair society gathered at Mirabelle in its first heyday, from the 1930s to the 1960s. Its loving 1998 restoration under Marco Pierre White went all out to recapture the retro glamour, with a dining room in rather fey '30s-style pastel shades, a spectacular bar with giant mirror ball, and explosions of fresh lilies on all sides. You feel there should be a 'black tie and cocktail number' dress code, but the crowd we saw were a more casual, varied bunch. The food

too has a full-on, old-fashioned opulence. A signature dish, tarte tatin of scallops and endives with orange butter, was a wonderfully bitter-sweet combination, balanced with great skill. Bayonne ham was a more simple starter, but still came with truffle and delicate celeriac remoulade. There's almost an element of overkill in some of the cooking: peppered ribeye had a superb oyster on top; lovely caramelised skate was showered with winkles – both came with a potato purée that was far too buttery. The wine list is vast and expensive, but there's an able sommelier on hand. Staff throughout are charming and obliging. For a special splurge, Mirabelle also has two highly opulent private dining rooms.
Babies and children welcome: high chair. Booking advisable. Dress: smart casual. Entertainment: pianist dinner Fri, Sat, lunch Sun. Restaurant available for hire. Separate rooms for parties, seating 33 and 48. Tables outdoors (14, patio). **Map 9 H7**.

Patterson's

4 Mill Street, W1S 2AX (7499 1308/ www.pattersonsrestaurant.co.uk). Oxford Circus or Bond Street tube. **Lunch served** noon-3pm Mon-Fri. **Dinner served** 6-11pm Mon-Sat. **Main courses** £13-£17. **Set lunch** £15 2 courses, £20 3 courses. **Credit** AmEx, MC, V.

You get the impression at Pattersons that the owners pay attention to every aspect of the meal. This is a family affair, with father in the kitchen and son front of house. Together they have created a special, hospitable feel to the place. Even on a Monday night, the white-walled room was packed (mainly with affluent local business people), though it still felt cool with tables well spaced. The service was good, the food exceptional. Dover sole and crab soufflé had wonderful freshness, texture and subtlety; a civet of rabbit (cooked in red wine) with a foie gras mousse was a treat too. Yet the real stars were the main courses. A loin of lamb wrapped in soft filo pastry was a revelation (though the curried crab mousse to the side of the plate was jarring); and caramelised suckling pig with foie gras sausage delighted us. Every dish looked great – with bright coloured jewels of fruit and vegetables on each – at least, until the lights became so romantically low that everything started to look brown. Sadly, this compromised the visual impact of the desserts and, as each cost £11, it killed off our desire to try them.

Papillon

Babies and children welcome: high chair. Booking advisable. Separate room for parties, seats 30. **Map 9 H/J6**.

St James's

Brasserie Roux

Sofitel St James, 8 Pall Mall, SW1Y 5NG (7968 2900/www.sofitelstjames.com). Piccadilly Circus tube. **Lunch served** noon-3pm Mon-Fri; 12.30-3pm Sat, Sun. **Dinner served** 5.30-11pm Mon-Fri; 5.30-10.30pm Sat, Sun. **Main courses** £9.50-£21.50. **Set meal** £24.50 3 courses incl 2 glasses of wine, water and coffee. **Set dinner** (5.30-7pm Mon-Sat) £15 3 courses. **Credit** AmEx, DC, JCB, MC, V.

With its rather sterile decor enlivened only by a few neo-colonial flounces, Brasserie Roux resembles the hotel restaurant that it is. This is a shame, as the food is a cut above any you'd find in an average hotel, and isn't badly priced either. Salade niçoise was surprisingly non-traditional; succulent chicken slices topped a wonderfully fresh salad bursting forth with aubergine, asparagus and various leaves. Another starter, remoulade of cured pork with a poached egg, was well conceived and tasty. Next, skirt of beef was perfectly cooked, flavoursome and pleasantly chewy without being tough (quite a feat with skirt). Sea bass en croûte was just assured; beautifully presented, it was rather bland and not complemented by a tomato and pepper sauce. Staff were well intentioned, but service was fussy and the succession of different servers led to a lack of continuity. Despite this, we managed to pour our own excellent bottle of Alsace pinot blanc a full three times, each time causing consternation. At the end, we were given a blank gratuity slip despite service being included in the bill. The management needs work, but the kitchen is in fine fettle.
Babies and children welcome: children's menu; high chairs. Booking advisable. Disabled: toilet (hotel). Dress: smart casual. No-smoking tables. **Map 17 K7**.

Soho

Astor Bar & Grill NEW

20 Glasshouse Street, W1B 5DJ (7734 4888/ www.astorbarandgrill.com). Piccadilly Circus tube.
Bar **Open** 5pm-1am Mon-Wed; 5pm-3am Thur-Sat.
Restaurant **Dinner served** 6-11pm Mon-Sat. **Main courses** £17-£27.50. **Set dinner** £32.50-£50 3 courses incl coffee. **Admission** £10 after 10pm Thur; £15 after 10pm Fri, Sat.
Both **Credit** AmEx, MC, V.

What used to be the Atlantic Bar & Grill has a new name and new tenants. The accountants now running the place have wisely done little to change the classic ballroom-era look of this huge basement, with its dark dining booths and decadent feel, but they have greatly simplified kitchen operations. The menu steers you towards expensive steak, averaging over £20 each. But the examples we tried were of excellent quality: air-dried, hung for 35 days. Both a rare and well-done steak were cooked as requested, and the chips were excellent. Prices throughout are high; bread and butter pudding, although a fine, custardy version, hardly justifies an £8 price tag. Our bottle of Crozes-Hermitage, £35 on this list (not including 12.5% service), can be bought online for around £10: just one example of hefty mark-ups. Despite a dizzying array of events and the still-strong emphasis on the cocktail-bar side of the business (Dick's Bar remains one of London's best, when not hired out for a private function), Astor lacks the glamour that defined the Atlantic in its early days.
Entertainment: musicians 10.30pm Thur; DJs 10.30pm Thur-Sat. Separate rooms for parties, seating 60 and 80. **Map 17 J7**.

Circus

1 Upper James Street, W1F 9DF (7534 4000/ www.egami.co.uk). Piccadilly Circus tube.
Bar **Open** 5pm-1am Mon-Wed; 5pm-3am Thur-Sat.
Restaurant **Lunch served** noon-3pm, **dinner served** 5.45pm-midnight Mon-Sat. **Main courses** £6-£18.80. **Set lunch** £14.50 2 courses, £16.50 3 courses. **Credit** AmEx, DC, MC, V.

Modern European restaurant Circus closed briefly in the summer of 2006, to reopen as a French bistro and bar under head chef Rowley Leigh and working chef Richard Lee. In fact, the food is more French-lite, or even modern Soho French, and not necessarily the worse for that. A starter of hot asparagus was wonderfully fresh, even though the hollandaise was over-fluffed. Better was the pea, celery and lovage soup, which we tried chilled (nicely tart, that lovage) and hot with a poached egg (the cannier choice). The best main course was black bream niçoise, which came with a lovely crispy skin and a crafty melange of capers, chopped tomatoes and coriander. But grilled onglet steak (strips of red meat with shallots) was also well executed. Puddings are the most French of all: profiteroles, rum baba and so on. Service was spot-on, except when trying to provide cream for the strawberries (English, bland). The decor now includes an eye-catching chandelier, banquette seating, white-clothed tables, a fabulous butcher's block in the middle, huge windows, French posters and a zinc bar. All of which is enjoyed by a youthful Soho crowd, who must also appreciate the lowish prices (note the set lunch menu) and the late-opening bar.
Babies and children admitted. Booking advisable. Entertainment (bar): DJ 9pm-3am Thur-Sat. Separate room for parties, seats 16. **Map 17 J6**.

L'Escargot Marco Pierre White

48 Greek Street, W1D 4EF (7437 2679/ www.whitestarline.org.uk). Leicester Square or Tottenham Court Road tube.
Ground-floor restaurant **Lunch served** noon-2.15pm Mon-Fri. **Dinner served** 6-11.30pm Mon-Fri; 5.30-11.30pm Sat. **Main courses** £12.95-£14.95. **Set meal** (lunch, 6-7pm Mon-Fri) £15 2 courses, £18 3 courses.
Picasso Room **Lunch served** 12.15-2pm Tue-Fri. **Dinner served** 7-11pm Tue-Sat. **Set lunch** £20.50 2 courses, £25.50 3 courses. **Set meal** £42 3 courses.
Both **Credit** AmEx, DC, JCB, MC, V.

L'Escargot's first-floor Picasso Room is closed on Mondays, so we were limited to the ground-floor restaurant with a menu that seemed less adventurous. Nevertheless, our meal left us happy – the food was excellent. First impressions of the place were less positive. While the room has style (cut-glass mirrors, grey and tan banquettes), on this occasion the waiting staff did not; we were chased for our orders by several in turn. Other diners seemed to be here because of the convenient location, rather than a sense of excitement or occasion. In all, the atmosphere was surprisingly soulless, perhaps due in part to very hot weather. The cooking, though, was celebratory: the ingredients fresh, the flavours clear, the presentation enticing. A crab tian came with tangy lemon sauce; roast foie gras looked wonderful, caramel-crisp on the outside, pink and almost runny within. To follow, tenderloin of pork was a triumphant dish, wrapped in pancetta, with sage polenta and skinned broad beans; duck with puy lentils was tender and fragrant, with a sharp vinegar edge to the sauce. With its long history, L'Escargot has become an institution, yet food such as this keeps the place vital.
Babies and children admitted (ground-floor restaurant). Booking essential weekends. Dress: smart casual. Separate rooms for parties, seating 24 and 60. Vegetarian menu. **Map 17 K6**.

La Trouvaille

12A Newburgh Street, W1F 7RR (7287 8488/ www.latrouvaille.co.uk). Oxford Circus tube.
Lunch served noon-3pm, **dinner served** 6-11pm Mon-Sat. **Set lunch** £15.50 2 courses, £18 3 courses. **Set dinner** £27.50 2 courses, £33 3 courses. **Credit** AmEx, MC, V.

We were big fans of La Trouvaille's quirkily cosy look, so it was with a degree of trepidation that we approached its 2006 revamp. The fantastic location – tucked away down a narrow cobbled street off Carnaby Street – and the superbly rendered French menu remain unchanged. The decor, meanwhile, has shifted up several gears with a new whiter-than-white aesthetic, featuring perspex chairs (we've sat on comfier), crystal-edged mirrors and starched white tablecloths. But the food's the thing here. A starter of leg of quail with ravioli, spring carrots and leeks with juniper sauce was beautifully crafted, with the pasta perfectly judged and the quail prepared with a delicate hand. A skirt of Galloway beef, with crunchy haricots verts and celeriac purée, was fantastically juicy. Less memorable – though perfectly enjoyable – was the vegetarian option of courgette flower stuffed with cottage cheese, spinach and basil. Now, as before, we find the waiters' sporadic use of French a tad pretentious, but in general the service is excellent, demonstrating a rare energy and knowledge. We're not totally sold on the new look – some of the romance of the place has been sacrificed – but we heartily recommend La Trouvaille for its reliably excellent food and wine.
Babies and children admitted. Booking advisable. Separate room for parties, seats 30. Tables outdoors (10, pavement). **Map 17 J6**.

South Kensington

Le Colombier

145 Dovehouse Street, SW3 6LB (7351 1155). South Kensington tube/14 bus. **Lunch served** noon-3pm Mon-Sat; noon-3.30pm Sun. **Dinner served** 6.30-10.30pm Mon-Sat; 6.30-10pm Sun. **Main courses** £13.50-£23.30. **Set lunch** (Mon-Sat) £16 2 courses; (Sun) £19 2 courses. **Credit** AmEx, JCB, MC, V.

Located in the backstreets of South Ken, Le Colombier has great style and clearly fills a local niche as the trusted neighbourhood brasserie. The tight seating and small round tables with rattan chairs are French to a fault, along with uniformed staff who clearly have right of way when moving around the restaurant. There's definitely a buzz factor here, which is the principal attraction; we found the food to be good, but not dazzling. Goat's cheese salad was fine, if stingy on the tomato. The crab in a crab salad tasted as if it had been frozen, but this was hard to tell due to the salad being heavily dressed and overburdened with cucumber. Next, steak tartare was decent, although, bewilderingly, it was served with two types of tabasco sauce (is this a South Ken thing?). Our other main course, duck confit, was faultless. In all, the meal was pleasant enough, especially when coupled with an enjoyable Burgundy. Service wasn't without slips, though, and we were initially overcharged (a mistake that was rectified immediately). As we left, the sound of braying old money was still ringing in our ears.
Babies and children admitted. Booking advisable; essential Sun. Dress: smart casual. Separate room for parties, seats 30. Tables outdoors (10, terrace). **Map 14 D11**.

★ Papillon NEW

2006 RUNNER-UP BEST NEW RESTAURANT
96 Draycott Avenue, SW3 3AD (7225 2555/ www.papillonchelsea.co.uk). South Kensington tube. **Lunch served** noon-3pm Mon-Sat; noon-4pm Sun. **Dinner served** 6-11.30pm Mon-Sat; 7-10pm Sun. **Main courses** £14.50-£25. **Set lunch** £14.50 2 courses, £16.50 3 courses. **Credit** AmEx, DC, MC, V.

Wine takes centre stage at this sleek South Kensington newcomer. There are almost 600 wines on the list, and more than 20 of them can be had by the glass. Sommelier Philippe Messy is on hand to help if these facts alarm rather than delight you. The emphasis on wine should not detract from the menu, which has plenty to please too. There's even a short vegetarian menu, from which provençal tart followed by pea risotto with rocket made a satisfying lunch. Other simple options include a range of salads (savoyard, niçoise), which is sensible, given that this neighbourhood is a honeypot for monied shoppers. Where the kitchen really shines is in dishes such as foie gras terrine with onion and cherry chutney and toasted brioche: rich perfection. And in classic styles such as fillet of cod meunière with shellfish, served with a baby potato ragout. French desserts include a melon soup with basil sorbet (very pretty, very

refreshing), but the cheese plate with walnut and raisin bread and frisée salad is a must-order. The chic, proficient staff also smile a lot, and the room is a study in muted elegance.

Babies and children welcome: high chairs. Booking advisable. Dress: smart casual. Separate room for parties, seats 16. Tables outdoors (6, pavement). **Map 14 E10**.

Strand

The Admiralty

Somerset House, Strand, WC2R 1LA (7845 4646/www.somerset-house.org.uk). Embankment or Temple tube/Charing Cross tube/rail. **Lunch served** noon-2.30pm daily. **Dinner served** 6-10.30pm Mon-Sat. **Set lunch** £17.50 2 courses, £19.50 3 courses. **Set dinner** £29.50 2 courses. **Credit** AmEx, DC, JCB, MC, V.

The main approach to the Admiralty – through the gorgeous fountain-filled courtyard of neo-classical Somerset House – creates a magnificent first impression. Located in the high-ceilinged, Thames-side wing that was once home to the Naval Operations Office, the restaurant (which has no river views) makes gently playful nods to its maritime heritage with ship-shaped chandeliers and seaside turquoise leather banquettes – but diners' eyes are more likely to be drawn to the stuffed gharial (Indian croc) mounted on the wall. Everything about the Admiralty experience oozes class, from the formal service and setting to the startlingly formal prices. On the whole, the food does a sterling job of living up to the surroundings. Successes on our latest visit included a starter of crab tortellini, a beautifully fragrant citrus soufflé, and a main course of venison (loftily priced at £23), which arrived medium rare as requested. Less impressive were a slightly mushy risotto of butternut squash and girolle mushrooms, and a dry roast saddle of rabbit. Minus points are also dished out for the over-zealous refilling of glasses. The Admiralty offers good food in a fantastic location – but really, at these prices, you should expect excellence all round.

Babies and children admitted. Booking advisable. Disabled: toilet. Dress: smart casual. No-smoking tables. Restaurant available for hire. Separate room for parties, seats 30. **Map 10 M7**.

West

Chiswick

★ La Trompette

5-7 Devonshire Road, W4 2EU (8747 1836/ www.latrompette.co.uk). Turnham Green tube. **Lunch served** noon-2.30pm Mon-Sat; 12.15-3pm Sun. **Dinner served** 6.30-10.30pm Mon-Sat; 7-10pm Sun. **Set lunch** (Mon-Fri) £23.50 3 courses; (Sat) £25 3 courses; (Sun) £29.50 3 courses. **Set dinner** £35 3 courses, £45 4 courses. **Credit** AmEx, JCB, MC, V.

La Trompette continues to be a big noise in Chiswick. With links to Chez Bruce, the Ledbury (for both, *see p98*) and the Glasshouse (Modern European), it is super-chic with parquet floors and a broad glass frontage opening on to a neat terrace. Even the loos cradle you in stylish luxury. And there's the cooking. A fixed dinner menu of £35 or £45 will preclude some, but if you're looking for a reliably good dining experience, this is it. To start, a divinely refreshing gazpacho was beautifully presented with trails of bright green basil oil, while a nicoise salad ascended into heaven with grilled tuna stacked with fine chopped beans and crowned with oozing quail eggs. From eight mains, daube of veal provençale served with artichokes and olive oil mash was rich yet exquisitely light. Moreover, dishes are served express from the pan, as was clear from the piping hot, crispy yet soft-centred potato pancakes accompanying steaming guinea fowl breast, broad beans, morels and Rizla-thin pancetta. Nor can desserts be resisted when mascarpone cheesecake with tropical fruits and passionfruit sorbet is such a taste sensation, and Valrhona chocolate fondant and chocolate chip ice-cream delivers you direct to Valhalla. Finally, a word of

The Food Room. See p98.

praise for the sommelier who patiently guided us through a galactic wine list. Maintaining such high standards is no mean feat, and La Trompette deserves a fanfare.

Babies and children welcome: high chairs. Booking advisable. Disabled: toilet. No smoking. Tables outdoors (7, terrace).

★ Le Vacherin

76-77 South Parade, W4 5LF (8742 2121/ www.levacherin.co.uk). Chiswick Park tube/rail. **Lunch served** noon-3pm Tue-Sun. **Dinner served** 6-10.30pm Mon-Thur; 6-11pm Fri, Sat; 6-10pm Sun. **Main courses** (lunch) £9.95; (dinner) £12.50-£19. **Credit** MC, V.

This much-praised restaurant (opened 2004) has progressed smoothly under the guidance of chef-patron Malcolm John. Named after the Alpine cheese (available here in numerous guises from October to March when it's in season), Le Vacherin brings an authentic French flavour to leafy Chiswick. Even the wine list is entirely French, with bottles starting at a very reasonable £13. The look is right too, with brown banquette seating, white linen and a narrow mirror running around the edge of the room to bring light into the darker corners. For starters, we enjoyed a pot of creamy, mustardy smoked haddock – of impeccable quality – with a baked egg served separately, and a delicate salad of pink lambs' tongues atop beetroot and ratte potatoes. Traditionalists could opt for steak tartare, charcuterie, snails or frogs' legs. Meat-eaters do well, as you might expect (rabbit leg, chateaubriand, veal tongue and stuffed pig's ear), but there's plenty of fish too, including a bouillabaisse thick with tomatoes, peppers and big hunks of fish in a strong yet delicate broth. Sides of haricots verts and tomato salad were spot-on. In fact, it was hard to fault the food (perhaps the Valrhona chocolate mousse was too large?). Staff were low key but a little unobservant, especially as the room wasn't full.

Babies and children welcome: high chairs. Booking advisable. No smoking. Separate room for parties, seats 20.

Hammersmith

★ Chez Kristof

111 Hammersmith Grove, W6 0NQ (8741 1177/www.chezkristof.co.uk). Goldhawk Road or Hammersmith tube.
Deli **Open** 8am-8pm Mon-Fri; 8.30am-7pm Sat; 9am-6pm Sun.
Restaurant **Lunch served** noon-3pm Mon-Fri; noon-4pm Sat, Sun. **Dinner served** 6-11.15pm Mon-Sat; 6-10.30pm Sun. **Main courses** £12.50-£17.
Both **Credit** AmEx, JCB, MC, V.

When we visited on a Thursday evening, Chez Kristof was phenomenal. Owner Jan Woroniecki

had taken a pavement table by the entrance, greeting friends and radiating pleasure at the success of this, his third venture after east European restaurants Baltic and Wódka. Dining as a social event is what's offered here – from informal staff who could easily have been customers, to the buzzy, party atmosphere. Food gives diners the splendid opportunity to get messy. We sampled (and loved) sea bream en papillote, which arrived wrapped in a large paper pasty that our waitress had to cut open, slopping out the contents on to a plate. A pot au feu came in a copper pot with an almost indecent amount of salty, sticky stock; the sausage, pork belly and ham hock retained their individual flavours without being greasy. We also relished a huge jar of buttery chicken liver parfait: light and strong, and helped by rhubarb chutney. Another starter – warm ham hock salad with fried quails' eggs, lentils and mixed leaves – was addictive. Light and airy by day, intimate at night (table lights sparkling through the wine glasses), Chez Kristof has a magical quality.

Babies and children welcome: children's menu; high chairs; films. Booking advisable. Disabled: toilet. No-smoking tables. Separate room for parties, seats 45. Tables outdoors (24, terrace). Takeaway service (deli). **Map 20 B3**.

Holland Park

The Belvedere

Holland House, off Abbotsbury Road, in Holland Park, W8 6LU (7602 1238/www.whitestar line.org.uk). Holland Park tube. **Lunch served** noon-2.30pm Mon-Sat. **Dinner served** 6-10pm Mon-Sat. **Main courses** £10-£18. **Set lunch** (Mon-Fri) £14.95 2 courses, £17.95 3 courses; (Sat, Sun) £24.95 3 courses. **Credit** AmEx, MC, V.

We were relishing a return to the grand surrounds of the Belvedere, located in the former summer ballroom of Holland House that gives Holland Park its name, for an evening of well-executed cuisine. A starter of game terrine served with tangy marmalade had a perfectly firm bite and clearly defined flavours, which counted in our book as a flying start. What a shame, then, that our main courses were underwhelming. Red mullet, which is potentially one of the tastiest fish in British waters, was one of the specials. By the time it had reached our plate, however, it was tired-tasting and a touch too salty, served with an uninspiring cylinder of mash. Breast of pheasant was also dry and salty, but redeemed in part by beautifully sweet and crispy green beans. Pear and cinnamon crumble, though pleasant, hardly counted as a grand finale: the crumble was too doughy, the fruit too mushy and the whole struggled to justify its £6.50 price tag. On the plus side, the setting is as gorgeous as

ever (think opulence, high ceilings and generously spaced tables); service is flawless; a pianist creates a romantic mood; and our red Côtes du Rhône (£30) was pleasantly peppery yet restrained.
Babies and children welcome: high chairs. Booking essential. Restaurant available for hire. Tables outdoors (5, terrace).

Notting Hill

★ The Ledbury

127 Ledbury Road, W11 2AQ (7792 9090/ www.theledbury.com). Westbourne Park tube. **Lunch served** noon-2pm Mon-Fri; noon-2.30pm Sat, Sun. **Dinner served** 6.30-10.15pm daily. **Set lunch** (Mon-Sat) £24.50 2 courses, £29.50 3 courses; (Sun) £30 3 courses. **Credit** AmEx, JCB, MC, V.

Everything about the Ledbury is delightful. The staff are unfailingly pleasant and helpful. The dining room is smart without being pretentious or intimidating. And the food, cooked by Australian Brett Graham, is exceptional. Think fine seasonal ingredients; a few dashes of Ferran Adria-style technology; ravishing presentation; sublime tastes and textures. On a summer's day, we began with a refreshing tomato 'consommé' served with avocado, tomato sorbet and tiny coriander shoots; and a magnificent raviolo stuffed with tender kid, mushroom and celery, accompanied by artichoke purée and generous shavings of black truffle. The breast of our roast pigeon came pink and juicy, with soft sweetcorn 'pancakes' and a smooth sweetcorn sauce; the legs had been confit and deep-fried so they were meltingly tender. For dessert, a spoonful of honey ice-cream slid sexily into the heart of a hot fig soufflé. Passionfruit tart with lime ice-cream and the various amuse-bouches and petits fours were equally impressive. The only dish that didn't sing was john dory with borlotti beans, chorizo and baby squid – the fish seemed a little dry. But this was a minor fault in an otherwise fabulous lunch.
Babies and children admitted. Booking advisable; essential dinner. Disabled: toilet. No smoking. Tables outdoors (8, pavement). **Map 7 A5/6.**

South West

Putney

L'Auberge

22 Upper Richmond Road, SW15 2RX (8874 3593/www.ardillys.com). East Putney tube. **Dinner served** 7-10pm Tue-Sat. **Main courses** £11.95-£15.75. **Set dinner** £12.95 2 courses, £16 3 courses. **Credit** MC, V.

Sometimes this gem of a restaurant is so full you get turned away. Sometimes, as when we arrived, you're the only customers. The location is awkward, and neighbouring eateries come and go frequently. The owners, M and Mme Ardilly, are professional and welcoming enough to make sure even a solitary diner has a relaxed and enjoyable time. Settle down in the pleasant dining room, and look forward to the prospect of reliable starters and mains, outstanding desserts, and a personal touch from the Ardillys (thoroughly French, sourcing ingredients on their cross-Channel shopping trips). We liked the textures and flavours of a snail and pesto tart, a rabbit casserole with tarragon and lemon, and a thick slice of calf's liver with Muscat jus. We loved, though, the lavender and honey crème brûlée: warm and crisp at the first bite, and one of the best we've tasted anywhere. A creamy, sharp lemon tart was thoroughly impressive too. This blend of hospitality and some star dishes is good reason why L'Auberge succeeds where others nearby do not. We keep returning.
Babies and children admitted. Booking advisable for large parties.

Wandsworth

★ Chez Bruce

2 Bellevue Road, SW17 7EG (8672 0114/ www.chezbruce.co.uk). Wandsworth Common rail. **Lunch served** noon-2pm Mon-Fri; 12.30-2.30pm Sat; noon-3pm Sun. **Dinner served** 6.30-10.30pm Mon-Sat; 7-10pm Sun. **Set lunch** (Mon-Fri) £23.50 3 courses; (Sat) £27.50 3 courses; (Sun) £32.50 3 courses. **Set dinner** £37.50 3 courses. **Credit** AmEx, DC, JCB, MC, V.

Plaudits and prizes rain down on Bruce Poole's place, and with good reason. It's remarkable to find such a quality, Michelin-starred restaurant acting as a local in one of London's leafier outposts. OK, so locals can include venture capitalists, but many others also throng to Chez Bruce's light, buzzing rooms. Big bow windows overlook Wandsworth Common, big art covers the clean white walls. There's also a perfectly pleasant overflow room upstairs. In short, it's a happy place, further blessed by a wondrous sommelier who presides, unpretentiously, over one of London's finest lists. The classy modern French cuisine, from a prix fixe menu, hits the heights. We've returned more than once to the roast cod with olive oil mash and provençal sauce, while the chateaubriand (for two, £4 extra) is gorgeously weighty. A delicate, cold pea soup was a recent special starter; there was a non-Gallic influence in the ceviche of tuna with a lovely, fluffed prawn tempura and lime and coriander. We had a slightly dud main course – flaccid fillet of bream was unhappily paired with a crab-stuffed courgette flower – but that's a rare occurrence. Puddings are nicely done, but ignore them, because you must try the cheeseboard. A lovely place, and relatively good value.
Babies and children welcome (lunch): high chairs. Booking essential. No smoking. Separate room for parties, seats 16.

South

Battersea

Le Bouchon Bordelais

5-9 Battersea Rise, SW11 1HG (7738 0307/ www.lebouchon.co.uk). Clapham Junction rail/ 35, 37 bus.
Bar **Open** 10am-1am Mon-Sat; 10am-11pm Sun. **Breakfast served** 10am-2pm, **meals served** 12.30-10pm daily. **Main courses** £4.50-£16. **Set meal** £5.50 1 course.
Restaurant **Lunch served** noon-3pm, **dinner served** 6-11pm Mon-Fri. **Meals served** noon-11pm Sat; 12.30-11pm Sun. **Main courses** £14.50-£19.50. **Set lunch** £10 2 courses, £13 3 courses.
Both **Credit** AmEx, MC, V.

There's a Gallic, sporty vibe to the thriving bar rooms of BB – manifested in TVs for both rooms, and rugby shirts and cycling memorabilia on the walls. Almost everything has the whiff of a Gauloise-rich, old-style French brasserie: heavy accents at the zinc bar, whirring fans on the ceiling, loud music, Ricard ashtrays, a serious coffee-machine, dark wood chairs and a competent bar menu. Not quite so Gallic is the downstairs crèche, but this is the northern border of Nappy Valley. To one side (and at the back when needed) is the more staid restaurant, which dispenses digestifs and brasserie fare to an older clientele; mirrors and white tablecloths provide the backdrop. A starter of terrine of ham in parsley jelly, tipped on to an exquisite baguette, was quite the best we've had for a while – but such results aren't guaranteed. A risotto of undercooked cod with a dominating squid ink sauce was less successful: certainly less so than a very fine, very plain fillet steak. Most of the classics are compressed on to the short menu, and French dessert lovers will be thrilled to explore the tarte tatin, crème brûlée, profiteroles and mousses. We can vouch for all these. Service is as you'd expect: supercilious and/or charmingly knowledgeable.
Babies and children welcome: children's menu; crèche (Sat, Sun); high chairs. Separate room for parties, seats 80. No-smoking tables. Tables outdoors (4, terrace). **Map 21 C5.**
For branch (Le Bouchon Lyonnais) see index.

The Food Room

123 Queenstown Road, SW8 3RH (7622 0555/ www.thefoodroom.com). Battersea Park or Queenstown Road rail/137, 156 bus. **Lunch served** noon-2.30pm Wed-Fri. **Dinner served** 7-10.30pm Tue-Sat. **Set lunch** £13.50 2 courses, £16.50 3 courses. **Set dinner** £19.50 2 courses, £24.50 3 courses. **Credit** MC, V.

Located on a quiet stretch of Queenstown Road, this usually outstanding local was empty on our visit. Entertainment consisted of watching our own reflections in the large mirrors, and listening to a Phil Collins CD playing over and over again. Sad news indeed for a place that was runner-up in the Best New Restaurant category of the 2005 Time Out Awards. The food, though, made us happy: a light and well-balanced meal of Mediterranean-leaning French cuisine, with portions ideally sized for three courses. An asparagus soup with mussel soufflé was interesting and appetising, as was stuffed, rolled rabbit with ground chicken liver. Better still was a main of grilled salmon with a musky truffle risotto, tomato sorbet and lobster sauce, while best of all were the grilled strawberries in a champagne sabayon, caramelised and eggy. Personable French staff increased our enjoyment. In all, the Food Room is still much more than a local – though its sister restaurant, the French Table in Surbiton *(see p101)*, is a more tantalising prospect.
Babies and children admitted. Booking advisable. Disabled: toilet. No-smoking tables.

Clapham

Gastro

67 Venn Street, SW4 0BD (7627 0222). Clapham Common tube. **Breakfast served** 8am-3pm, **meals served** noon-midnight daily. **Main courses** £12.95-£16.75. **Set lunch** (noon-3pm Mon-Fri) £9.95 2 courses incl coffee. **Credit** MC, V.

Gastro, a long-standing Clapham hangout, doesn't need to resort to faux-Frenchness. Those nicotine-stained walls aren't a paint effect, and those French accents haven't been copied from Antoine de Caunes. The menu is uncompromisingly French (veggies beware), with a selection of pork preserves (cochonailles) based on rillons, pâtés and andouilles galore, plus seafood platters for the *minceurs*. Tartiflette, from Savoy, is a dish you don't often see this side of La Manche: fried pork belly plus potatoes and onions, all covered in molten reblochon cheese. Our steak-frites comprised a nice cut of meat, cooked rare, with lumpy béarnaise sauce. Frites have to be ordered separately; ours were undercooked. Swordfish, served with sautéed red and orange peppers, was very small and needed a side salad to bulk it up. The short, all-French wine list is nothing extraordinary, but we wish more London restaurants would offer wines by the pichet as well as the glass, as here. Desserts include a selection from Gastro's equally Gallic neighbour, Macaron pâtisserie. Our passionfruit tart, though lovely to look at, tasted of the freezer. 'Could try harder' is our verdict. They now accept credit cards.
Babies and children admitted. Booking advisable. No-smoking tables. Separate area for parties, seats 25. Tables outdoors (4, pavement). **Map 22 A2.**

Waterloo

Chez Gérard

9 Belvedere Road, SE1 8YL (7202 8470/ www.santeonline.co.uk/chezgerard). Waterloo tube/rail. **Meals served** noon-11pm Mon-Sat; noon-5pm Sun. **Main courses** £9.95-£25.95. **Set meal** £13.95 2 courses, £16.95 3 courses. **Cover** £1.50. **Credit** AmEx, DC, JCB, MC, V.

The sleek dining area in the South Bank branch of Chez Gérard, evoking a chic French brasserie, made for pleasant surroundings in which to have some fairly average food. Gravadlax Norvegien was thick, dry and salty; it came with something billed as dill and cucumber salad, which was in fact a pile of mayonnaise with only rare appearances by either green item. The snails, in escargots de bourgogne, were drowned in a garlic butter sauce, just as they would be in Paris. To follow, we enjoyed confit of duck with prunes and Armagnac. However, repeated helpings of English mustard and a pleasant Lamothe-Cissac 2002 claret were required to coax any flavour out of a nicely cooked but woefully bland entrecôte. At least the frites served with the steak were nice and crisp. The convenient locations of the various Chez Gérard branches mean the chain should continue to be well patronised. The food isn't so dull as to be a waste of money, but the complete lack of personality here means you're unlikely to feel the urge to make a special trip.

Babies and children welcome: high chairs. Booking advisable. Disabled: toilet. Separate rooms for parties, seating 20 and 40. Tables outdoors (5, pavement). **Map 10 M8**. **For branches see index.**

★ RSJ

33A Coin Street, SE1 9NR (7928 4554/ www.rsj.uk.com). Waterloo tube/rail. **Lunch served** noon-2pm Mon-Fri. **Dinner served** 5.30-11pm Mon-Sat. **Main courses** £12-£17. **Set meal** £15.95 2 courses, £17.95 3 courses. **Credit** AmEx, DC, MC, V.

The serene first-floor dining room at RSJ betrays no sign of the eponymous rolled steel joists, and the bland design in no way reflects the overall dining experience at this Waterloo treasure. The menu is an ideal balance of seasonal modern French dishes. What sets RSJ apart from London's other quality French restaurants is its uniquely Loire-centred wine list. You'll rarely find such strength in Loire reds: fresh, light but structured wines (the antithesis of heavy Australian shiraz) that go beautifully with food. In addition to its phenomenal binder of bottles, RSJ has a separate, constantly changing, 12 wines-by-the-glass menu. A 2004 Saumur Champigny was excellent with a smoked haddock starter. Our other choice, crab risotto, was subtly rich and arrived with a well-chosen mint garnish. To follow, pan-fried plaice was perfectly cooked and went beautifully with Domaine de la Perrière-Chinon 2004, which had wonderful fruit and a long finish. Desserts shouldn't be missed, and demand pairing with the quality dessert wines; refreshing apricots in white wine with mascarpone sorbet were wonderfully matched with a 2001 Vouvray Moelleux 'Cuvée Moelleuse'. A real find.

Babies and children admitted. Booking advisable. Separate room for parties, seats 25. **Map 11 N8**.

East

Bethnal Green

Bistrotheque

23-27 Wadeson Street, E2 9DR (8983 7900/ www.bistrotheque.com). Bethnal Green tube/rail/ Cambridge Heath rail/55 bus. **Bar Open** 5.30pm-midnight Mon-Sat; 1pm-midnight Sun. *Restaurant* **Lunch served** 11am-4pm Sat, Sun. **Dinner served** 6.30-10.30pm daily. **Main courses** £10-£21. **Set lunch** £21 3 courses. **Set dinner** (6.30-7.30pm Mon-Fri) £12 2 courses, £15 3 courses. *Both* **Credit** AmEx, MC, V.

For all that it's a landmark of Hackney's new-found chic, Bistrotheque has an unaffected warehouse charm. Downstairs is an agreeable bar, with an eccentric baronial ambience, and a cabaret room that's a prime mover in the burgeoning east London scene (you get a discount in the restaurant if you see a show; mention it when you book). Upstairs is the restaurant: a large white-painted space rising right into the apex of the roof, simply styled with marble-topped tables, soft hanging lights and statement flowers. The food is Anglo-French, but kept simple; every taste speaks for itself. Starters are relatively luxurious, with razor clams, foie gras and scallops making an appearance on our last visit. The mains generally have a more direct appeal: fish and chips (with a lovely pea purée), steak tartare, chicken and garlic, and lobster and chips, for example. We can speak particularly highly of the barnsley chop (if not its potato salad accompaniment) and the twice-cooked chips. The only disappointment was a flaccid rhubarb pie. Enjoyable food, a choice of cheaper quick dishes, spot-on staff and good-value house wines on a well-chosen list: no wonder Bistrotheque was nearly full on a Sunday night. *Babies and children admitted. Booking advisable. Disabled: toilet. Entertainment: cabaret 10pm Wed-Sat. Separate room for parties, seats 50.*

Brick Lane

★ Les Trois Garçons

1 Club Row, E1 6JX (7613 1924/www.lestrois garcons.com). Liverpool Street tube/rail/8, 388 bus. **Dinner served** 7-10.30pm Mon-Thur; 7-11pm Fri, Sat. **Main courses** £18-£32. **Set dinner** (Mon-Thur; 7-8pm Fri, Sat) £24 2 courses, £28 3 courses. **Credit** AmEx, DC, JCB, MC, V.

When you enter this former corner pub, it's difficult not to suspect that the set-up is a case of style over content. After all, there's no way that the content churned out by the kitchen could possibly match the style of the room itself – a stupendously theatrical mix of antique bar fittings, vintage handbags (dangling from the ceiling) and ornamental taxidermy – could it? Well, to our surprise and delight, the kitchen continues to live up to its side of the bargain, delivering an immaculate French-slanted menu to Shoreditch sophisticates (and couples of every sexual inclination) and the occasional bigger party. Torchon of foie gras was beautifully silky, but was matched by sweet corn velouté, poured at the table (with no little ostentation) over a crumbled black truffle. The mains, if anything, were better: a generous confit of smoked salmon went perfectly with white asparagus; and the beef fillet, requested and served medium-rare with a delicate sweet potato purée and a trio of baby carrots, was close to perfection. Tarte tatin rounded things off immaculately. Les Trois Garçons isn't cheap, but from the dazzling decor to the fabulous food, you get what you pay for.

Booking advisable. Restaurant available for hire. Separate room for parties, seats 10. **Map 6 S4**.

North

Crouch End

Les Associés

172 Park Road, N8 8JT (8348 8944/ www.lesassocies.co.uk). Finsbury Park tube/rail then W7 bus. **Lunch served** by appointment Wed-Fri; 1-3pm Sun. **Dinner served** 7.30-10pm Tue-Sat. **Main courses** £12.50-£17. **Set dinner** (Tue-Fri) £10.50 2 courses, £14.50 3 courses. **Credit** AmEx, MC, V.

A lovable eccentric, Les Associés is a piece of eternal France snuck into a London terrace. There's a leafy little front garden for summer dining; inside, you find the unchanging, rather chintzy look of a classic French provincial restaurant. The two 'associates' (one in the kitchen, one front-of-house) preside with unmistakeably Gallic, slightly dry charm. The classic French cuisine is put together with skill, individuality and panache, and admirable attention to sourcing the best ingredients. Prices have been kept down, so lately the food's become a bargain too. The daily specials are a highlight: langoustines à la provençal was an eye-catching platter of juicy, first-rate seafood, served with wonderfully fresh herbs; roast camembert with salad was less spectacular, but still highly enjoyable. There's no shying away from bold flavours, as demonstrated by a luxuriously rich duo of quails and foie gras with a powerful port sauce. Halibut fillet aux petits légumes was prepared with uninhibited amounts of butter, yet was still beautifully delicate, and based, again, on top-quality fish. Enticing desserts, fresh bread, wines and other details are all very properly done, *comme il faut*. Not a restaurant for food fashionistas, but one that knows what it's doing and does it well. Deservedly popular.

Babies and children admitted. Booking advisable. No-smoking tables. Restaurant available for hire. Tables outdoors (8, garden).

Interview
CHRIS GALVIN

Who are you?
Chef-patron (with brother Jeff) of **Galvin at Windows** (see p130) and **Galvin Bistrot de Luxe** (see p93).
Eating in London: what's good about it?
We're very lucky to have such diversity and good examples of most cuisines.
What's bad about it?
Prices, and not enough flexibility regarding people's dietary needs. We are getting many more requests for dishes that are dairy-free, wheat-free and so on. I wish restaurants could make things easier for those customers.
Which are your favourite London restaurants?
The Square (see p132) is always a fantastic treat. Phil Howard's food has great flavours and technically it's fireworks, but he makes it seem so simple. **Racine** (see p92) has beautiful flavours, fabulous service and good prices. And I like **Le Gavroche** (see p131) – it just has a lovely feeling of grandeur and celebrated haute cuisine. I'm excited every time I go and eat there.
What single thing would most improve London's restaurant scene?
Maybe to spread dining times and avoid the 1pm and 8pm rush. In Spain, for example, people eat out much later. Restaurants here tend to lose atmosphere between 6pm and 8pm, and from 9.30pm onwards.
Any hot tips for the coming year?
Have better entry points for wine. My wife doesn't drink, so I hate being ripped off on half bottles, and wines by the glass are often not good. I like what they're doing with carafes at **Arbutus** (see p226). At **Galvin Bistrot**, we offer eight whites and eight reds by the carafe, and I love to see our customers sharing them. I also love offering unusual wines by the glass to introduce people to new things.

RESTAURANTS

Bistro Aix

54 Topsfield Parade, Tottenham Lane, N8 8PT (8340 6346/www.bistroaix.co.uk). Finsbury Park tube/rail then W7 bus/91 bus. **Lunch served** noon-3pm, **dinner served** 6.30-11pm Tue-Sun. **Main courses** £8.50-£17. **Set lunch** (Tue-Sat) £10 1 course incl drink, £11.50 2 courses. **Set meal** (dinner, all Sun) £15 3 courses. **Credit** AmEx, DC, MC, V.

Bistro Aix opened in 2002, just ahead of the bistrot de luxe trend. Now, four years later, it seems right in tune with the zeitgeist. Chef/proprietor Lynne Sanders trained with Alain Ducasse. Her menu features bourgeois classics like soupe de poisson, as well as some newer spins and the odd rogue Italian dish (osso bucco or wild mushroom risotto). We couldn't get enough of one starter: a silky, own-cured goat's cheese with walnut bread (baked on site) and date chutney. The other first course – a roquefort, pear and watercress salad – was handicapped by what seemed to be the total absence of roquefort. A good fillet of sea bass came with mashed Jersey royal potatoes and a butter sauce (though not, apparently, the promised clams), and a side dish of carrots was boiled, not roasted, as billed. Steak-frites, however, was a textbook version, as was the crème brûlée. Service was charming, and our food was none the worse for deviating from the menu. The set lunch hovers at around a tenner, but à la carte prices are just the high side of offering value for money.

La Brasserie Ma Cuisine Bourgeoise

Babies and children admitted. Booking advisable weekends. Restaurant available for hire. Separate room for parties, seats 24.

Hornsey

Le Bistro

36 High Street, N8 7NX (8340 2116). Turnpike Lane tube/Hornsey rail/41, W3 bus. **Brunch served** 12.30-5pm Sun. **Dinner served** 6.30-11pm Mon-Sat; 5-10pm Sun. **Main courses** £10.95-£16. **Set meal** £10.95 2 courses, £12.95 3 courses. **Credit** MC, V.

Restaurants come and go along this stretch, but after 20 years Le Bistro has worked out what a neighbourhood bistro should deliver. French artefacts and signs jostle for position in a cosy interior (topped up with extra heaters on our winter's visit), with simple red tea lights on tables. The regularly changing menu is resolutely French (as are the staff), featuring some nice twists on the usual repertoire, reflecting seasonality and thoughtful sourcing of ingredients. Among à la carte starters, traditional fish soup with all its trimmings was tasty and authentic, and celeriac soup had a fabulous velvety texture, enlivened by the addition of mini poached herb ravioli. A sautéed monkfish medallion – with chive oil, wild mushrooms and celeriac mash – was well-presented, though the fish chunks were a bit thin. Bargain-hunters select from the set menu, with mains such as perfectly cooked beef steak au poivre with frites. Puds include lavender and vanilla crème brûlée, and an assortment of French cheeses from La Fromagerie. Vegetables cost no extra, house wines are reasonable, and with Edith Piaf crooning away in the background, this place has the feeling of *le vrai bistro*.

Babies and children welcome: high chairs. Booking advisable. Tables outdoors (18, garden).

Islington

Almeida

30 Almeida Street, N1 1AD (7354 4777/ www.conran.com). Angel tube/Highbury & Islington tube/rail. **Lunch served** noon-2.30pm Mon-Fri; noon-3pm Sat, Sun. **Dinner served** 5.30-10.45pm Mon-Sat; 5.30-9.30pm Sun. **Set lunch** £20 2 courses, £22 3 courses. **Set dinner** £22 2 courses, £27 3 courses. **Set meal** (lunch, 5.30-7pm daily; 10-10.45pm Mon-Sat) £14.50 2 courses, £17.50 3 courses. **Credit** AmEx, DC, MC, V.

This Conran spot shares with the Almeida Theatre opposite an ethos rather than an entrance. It is cultured and contemporary, with a luxury warehouse feel and upper arts-class clientele. Locals say it's Islington's best restaurant, but also comment on less than lavish portions and high prices. They'll be pleased to know, then, that Almeida has abandoned its à la carte in favour of two moderately priced set menus, one served at lunch and dinner, and a cheaper option served at lunch and pre- and post-theatre. Did the quality hold up? A barely qualified 'yes' on our visit. The main menu offers around ten choices per course, none radical but all pleasingly conceived. Exquisite baked scallops arrived in a shell with a puff-pastry coddling and a beurre blanc poured at table; roast rack of pork was accompanied by deeply tasty girolles and broad beans. From the pre-theatre menu, the options were a little more rustic: a light pissaladière and an intense daube de boeuf. Desserts disappointed slightly: an oversweet raspberry sorbet and a chilled charentais melon soup whose base ingredient wasn't up to it. Portions were not, it is true, enormous, but they were certainly sufficient, given the rich food. The bar, a cosier space, serves tapas from south-western France.

Babies and children welcome: high chairs. Booking advisable. Disabled: toilet. No-smoking tables. Restaurant available for hire. Separate room for parties, seats 20. Tables outdoors (8, pavement). **Map 5 O1**.

Morgan M

489 Liverpool Road, N7 8NS (7609 3560/ www.morganm.com). Highbury & Islington tube/ rail. **Lunch served** noon-2.30pm Wed-Fri, Sun. **Dinner served** 7-10pm Tue-Sat. **Set lunch** £19.50 2 courses, £23.50 3 courses. **Set dinner** £32 3 courses. **Set meal** £36 (vegetarian), £39 (non-vegetarian) tasting menu. **Credit** DC, MC, V.

Chef-proprietor Morgan Meunier's ambitious venture is renowned for its vegetarian food – and on our visit it was the vegetarian dishes that worked best. From a five-course spring/summer tasting menu, the highlight was an intensely flavoured chilled gazpacho in which swam a solitary crouton topped with gorgeously flavoured aubergine pâté, accompanied by a scoop of sparklingly summery tomato and olive oil sorbet. We also liked the verdant, grassy, 'just picked' flavour of steamed English asparagus capped with shaved truffles, served in a pool of sprightly, dense broad bean velouté. A ragout of light potato gnocchi, cherry tomatoes and basil was as lively and flamboyant as summertime jazz. Disappointing dishes included foie gras and artichoke terrine that tasted a little stale, and squab pigeon that was overgrilled, burnt and therefore bitter. Fluffy, perfectly cooked fresh apricot soufflé was lingering and memorable as a kiss. The hushed cream and green decor, a grown-up wine list, and seriously accented and attired staff added to a somewhat reverential dining experience.

Babies and children admitted (lunch). Booking essential. Dress: smart casual. No smoking. Separate room for parties, seats 12. Vegetarian menu.

Palmers Green

Café Anjou

394 Green Lanes, N13 5PD (8886 7267/ www.cafeanjou.co.uk). Wood Green tube then 329 bus/Palmers Green rail. **Lunch served** noon-2.30pm, **dinner served** 6.30-10.30pm Tue-Sun. **Main courses** £8.55-£11.45. **Set lunch** (noon-2pm Tue-Sat) £7.45 1 course incl coffee. **Set meal** (Tue-Fri, lunch Sat) £12.95 2 courses, £14.45 3 courses. **Credit** AmEx, MC, V.

With its relaxed dining room, friendly staff and appetising seasonal menu, this family-run restaurant is a perennial hit with the residents of Palmers Green. The unfussy card menu is packed with choices that reflect both the best of regional France (périgordais magret de canard, for instance) and influences from further afield (chicken supreme flavoured with coconut curry). We started our latest meal with delicious tender chicken livers that arrived stacked on toast and drizzled in a tangy red wine jus. Hearty mushroom salad was perked up by thick shavings of parmesan. To follow, halibut with crunchy green asparagus and sun-blushed tomatoes was a plate of tantalising summery goodness. Fillet of lamb came with merguez sausages: an interesting combination, although the spiciness slightly overpowered the rest of the dish. From the varied pudding list, we stuck to basics: icy lemon sorbet was the perfect palate cleanser, and crème brûlée the epitome of reliable French simplicity.
Babies and children welcome: children's portions (Sun); high chairs. Booking essential dinner Fri, Sat. Restaurant available for hire.

North West

St John's Wood

L'Aventure

3 Blenheim Terrace, NW8 0EH (7624 6232). St John's Wood tube/139, 189 bus. **Lunch served** 12.30-2.30pm Mon-Fri. **Dinner served** 7.30-11pm Mon-Fri; 7-11pm Sat. **Set lunch** £15 2 courses, £18.50 3 courses incl coffee. **Set dinner** £27.50 2 courses, £32.50 3 courses. **Credit** AmEx, MC, V.

A potential bidder to be the most-French French restaurant in London, L'Aventure seems to fit its well-heeled, international, comfortably middle-aged clientele perfectly. Tapestries, ornate but soft-cushioned seating, dried flowers and gleaming table settings create the cosy opulence of a traditional French provincial restaurant, and there's a shaded front terrace for summer dining. Service is professional, slightly dry, in a proper French way, and regulars clearly appreciate the personal attention they receive. At its best the cuisine too is a first-rate demonstration of traditional French culinary virtues, of skill and care for detail. A summer salad of foie gras with green beans and lentils was both refreshing and deliciously, unreservedly, old-fashioned rich. In a main, brochette of quail in rosemary with polenta, the perfect, deeply savoury poultry was delicately offset by a couple of raspberries. Desserts could almost have a fan club: seductive all-time French faves like bavarois with red berries, parfait glacé à la nougatine or assorted crèmes brûlées. The set-price formula makes it excellent value for lunch, much more expensive for dinner. Wines (classic French, naturally) are also excellent, but pricey.
Babies and children admitted. Booking advisable dinner. Tables outdoors (6, terrace). **Map 1 C2.**

Outer London

Richmond, Surrey

Chez Lindsay

11 Hill Rise, Richmond, Surrey TW10 6UQ (8948 7473/www.chez-lindsay.co.uk). Richmond tube/rail. **Crêperie Meals served** noon-11pm Mon-Sat; noon-10pm Sun. **Main courses** £3.30-£9.45. **Restaurant Meals served** noon-11pm Mon-Sat; noon-10pm Sun. **Main courses** £11.75-£15.75. **Set lunch** (noon-3pm Mon-Sat) £9.75-£14.50

2 courses, £17.50 3 courses. **Set dinner** (after 6.30pm) £16.50 2 courses, £19.50 3 courses. *Both* **Credit** MC, V.

This charming Richmond restaurant, with its simple furnishings and yellow walls, provides a welcome slice of regional France in the heart of south-west London suburbia. Lindsay's menu focuses in on the 'twin glories of Breton cooking', which is to say that seafood and traditional galettes (thin, crêpe-like pancakes made with buckwheat flour) figure large. A starter of mussels à la St Malo, served with white wine, cream, shallots and thyme, was incredibly moreish. The pancake menu runs from the classic (ham and cheese, egg and ham, cheese and onion) to the more culinarily complex, such as a decadent option with onion and roquefort sauce, celery and walnuts. Seafood enthusiasts will have plenty to get their teeth into with the mighty *cotriade*, a hearty Breton casserole of red gurnard, sea bream, mackerel, lobster, mussels and langoustines. The carefully considered wine list emphasises lesser-known wine producers, with plenty of Loire vintages. But to accompany galettes, the drink of choice has to be one of the selection of superior French sparkling ciders. Chez Lindsay is very popular, particularly at weekends – and it's a pleasure to see an independent restaurant thriving on a high street dominated by chain restaurants.
Babies and children welcome: high chairs. Booking advisable. No cigars or pipes. Separate room for parties, seats 36.

Surbiton, Surrey

★ The French Table

85 Maple Road, Surbiton, Surrey KT6 4AW (8399 2365/www.thefrenchtable.co.uk). Surbiton rail. **Lunch served** noon-2.30pm Tue-Fri, Sun. **Dinner served** 7-10.30pm Tue-Sat. **Main courses** £10.50-£15.50. **Set lunch** (Tue-Fri) £14.50 2 courses, £17.50 3 courses; (Sun) £17.50 3 courses. **Credit** MC, V.

We visited for Sunday lunch and would happily have stayed all day. The walls are lilac, the French staff friendly and efficient, and the other diners were mainly local. Customers dress up to eat at the French Table, enjoying the sense of occasion and the remarkably good value of the set lunch menu. The food is more complex and flamboyant than at the sister restaurant, Battersea's the Food Room (*see p98*), and is French/East Asian fusion in style. Standards are consistently high, with fresh and intense flavours. The own-baked bread is enticing, especially with chunks of melted gruyère or saucisson. A starter of pan-fried salmon (cut almost through into sushi-like strips) with plum sauce and sliced black radishes (white on the plate) was sharp and fresh, while another of rolled, cut rabbit stuffed with chorizo was pleasingly savoury. Roast cod on a bed of pea and asparagus risotto was delightful, enhanced by a lobster mousseline. Smoked pork fillet came with a croustillant of shredded pork and black pudding, puréed celeriac and port sauce: a great mix of textures and flavours. Some local restaurants are for locals; this one is well worth a detour.
Babies and children welcome: children's portions; high chairs. Booking advisable; essential weekends. No smoking.

Twickenham, Middlesex

La Brasserie Ma Cuisine Bourgeoise NEW

2 Whitton Road, Twickenham, Middx TW1 1BJ (8744 9598/www.labrasserietw1.co.uk). Twickenham rail. **Lunch served** noon-2.30pm, **dinner served** 6.30-10.30pm Mon-Sat. **Main courses** £14-£18. **Set lunch** £18.50 3 courses. **Credit** AmEx, MC, V.

This replaces McClements restaurant, and is a modernised but simplified version of the same (the slightly cheaper and much more rustic Ma Cuisine Le Petit Bistrot is only two doors away and shares the same kitchen – *see below*). It now looks 'modern French' – nothing too showy, just simple and elegant. Chef John McClements' fondness for offal is evident in dishes such as a starter of pig's trotter

boned and braised for 12 hours in port, then finely chopped, breadcrumbed and fried into a patty shape. It had an intense meaty flavour, and was paired with sauce gribiche. Riz de veau (calf's sweetbreads, in this case the pancreas) has deliciously earthy, feral flavours once it's blanched, skinned then caramelised in a frying pan, and served with cubes of celeriac and some braised little gem lettuce. Tarte tatin is an apple dish that takes a minimum of half an hour to bake in the oven, but chef McClements gets around this by keeping a few warm in a slow oven; if no one in the Brasserie orders them, they go on special in the Bistrot. The individual tarte portion here (flipped over, with the pastry lid underneath) would make the Tatin sisters proud.
Babies and children admitted. Disabled: toilet. No smoking. Separate rooms for parties, seating 25 and 40.

★ Brula

43 Crown Road, Twickenham, Middx TW1 3EJ (8892 0602/www.brulabistrot.co.uk). St Margaret's rail. **Lunch served** noon-3pm, **dinner served** 6-10.30pm daily. **Main courses** £12.75-£17.50. **Set lunch** £11.50 2 courses, £14 3 courses. **Credit** MC, V.

The residents of St Margaret's must be counting their blessings. This gem of a brasserie is straight out of the little black book of the most pedantic Parisian gastronome. Kitted out as a charming and romantic bistro, Brula has a menu that manages to be both aspirational and unpretentious, offering fabulous French urban cuisine. On a weekday evening, the atmosphere changed from reverential to raucous as tables of couples and friends realised they had struck gold. Seared scallops with a fennel salad were barely tampered with – simply perfect. Potted shrimps were excellent: not too buttery, shrimps just the right size. Everything is carefully sourced; both the onglet steak (with garlic and fries) and the fillet of beef were sublime examples of meat, lavishly garnished (although decent-sized portions of vegetables cost £2.75 extra). A textbook crème brûlée and a good selection of cheeses rounded off a flawlessly simple meal. The wine list is extensive and competitively priced, with a variety of wines by the glass. Service is friendly and discreet. With effortless brilliance, Brula manages to combine a sense of occasion with the feeling of being an everyday treat.
Babies and children admitted. Booking advisable. Separate room for parties, seats 24. Tables outdoors (6, pavement).
For branch (La Buvette) see index.

Ma Cuisine Le Petit Bistrot

6 Whitton Road, Twickenham, Middx TW1 1BJ (8607 9849/www.macuisinetw1.co.uk). Twickenham rail. **Lunch served** noon-2.30pm Mon-Sat. **Dinner served** 6.30-10.30pm Mon-Thur; 6.30-11pm Fri, Sat. **Main courses** £11.50-£14.50. **Set lunch** £12.95 2 courses; £15.50 3 courses. **Credit** MC, V.

This is the rustic branch of the newer La Brasserie Ma Cuisine Bourgeoise (*see above*), just two doors away. While La Brasserie aims high, Le Petit Bistrot serves cuisine de grand-mère in a clichéd bistro setting: old-fashioned, classic staples such as onion soup, coq au vin, cassoulet and tarte au citron. Huge portions of rabbit and ham-hock terrine were spooned on to a starter plate; 'portion control' is clearly not a phrase in the jolly waiter's vocabulary. The meat was suitably flavourful, while the Chablis jelly in which it was set was delicate and melted at body temperature. Bouillabaisse was another impeccable dish, stained with saffron and laden with firm chunks of fresh fish and mussels, plus a rouille, croûton and roasted garlic clove garnish. It's great to see hearty cooking done well; the ox cheeks must have been slowly braising since France embraced the euro, they were so tender. Flavour-packed, their rich Madeira sauce was foiled by some peas in a white onion sauce and some dauphinoise potatoes.
Babies and children admitted. Booking advisable: essential weekends. Separate room for parties, seats 25. Tables outdoors (4, terrace).
For branch see index.

Gastropubs

The gastropub boom that occurred during the 1990s seems to have reached something of a plateau. It's still a dynamic area, with vibrant new ventures opening up in all areas of London; newcomers such as the **Charles Lamb**, **Horseshoe**, **Norfolk Arms** and **Marquess Tavern** have all upped the stakes in an already very competitive field. But we've noticed a slipping of standards too, and for this edition have dropped quite a few previously reliable operations. The biggest shift in recent years has been the increased gentrification of the gastropub scene, to the extent that many are more like restaurants than pubs – and prices reflect this. Gastropubs do, however, still offer a far more relaxed and informal dining environment than many restaurants, with the bonus that it's usually not essential for everyone in the group to order food: some can just drink, while others eat.

Central
Belgravia

★ Ebury
11 Pimlico Road, SW1W 8NA (7730 6784/ www.theebury.co.uk). Sloane Square tube/Victoria tube/rail/11, 211, 239 bus. **Open** noon-11pm Mon-Sat; noon-10.30pm Sun. **Lunch served** noon-3.30pm Mon-Fri; noon-4pm Sat; noon-3pm Sun. **Dinner served** 6-10.30pm Mon-Sat; 6-10pm Sun. **Main courses** £9.50-£16.95. **Set lunch** (Mon-Fri) £18.50 3 courses. **Credit** AmEx, MC, V.
To call this place a pub is a little misleading – but if we must, we have it down as the Rolls-Royce of London gastropubs. No carefully battered sofas or scuffed floorboards here; this slick bar-brasserie-restaurant, nestled between the suitably monied quarters of Pimlico and Chelsea, has a tangibly ritzy feel, from the loaded crustacea bar and modishly low-slung seating on the ground floor to the glittery pink chandeliers and crisp white linen of the more formal upstairs dining room. Fortunately, the kitchen – now in the capable hands of head chef James Holah, previously of Claridges – is more than a match for the decor. The menu is short but a fine read, peppered with enticing ingredients and the odd subtly original twist (pomegranate syrup with goat's cheese mousse, say, or peanut ice-cream). On our latest visit, every dish delivered on its promises: from extremely succulent saddle of lamb with sautéed artichokes and confit potatoes to a starter of chunky slices of organic salmon gravadlax cured (to pretty effect) in beetroot, and served with a fantastically creamy horseradish sauce. But it was a cleverly simple dessert – fresh yet soothing lemongrass crème brûlée with candied chilli and coconut sorbet – that really stole the show.
Babies and children admitted. Disabled: toilets. Restaurant available for hire. Separate room for parties, seats 60. **Map 15 G11**.

Bloomsbury

★ Norfolk Arms [NEW]
28 Leigh Street, WC1H 9EP (7388 3937/ www.norfolkarms.co.uk). Russell Square tube/ King's Cross tube/rail. **Open** 11am-11pm Mon-Sat; noon-10.30pm Sun. **Lunch served** 12.30-3.30pm, **dinner served** 6.30-10.15pm daily. **Main courses** £3.75-£12.50. **Credit** AmEx, MC, V.
The Norfolk Arms has gone so seriously gastro that there's no real vestige of the 'pub' that ought to complete the epithet. All the tables inside are set with rudimentary tea towels and cutlery; there's no obvious non-dining area. It's almost (but not quite) a restaurant. The menu pays no heed to traditional course divisions (except dessert). Instead it's divided into 'Snacks', 'From the bar' and 'From the kitchen', all of which contain dishes of varying sizes. So you just order and share until you're full. Dishes might include a lovely octopus and squid salad with wild rocket and cherry tomatoes; the squid was stuffed with mozzarella, and came with a really good, sweet and subtle lemon dressing. Pork belly with leeks and lentils was also terrific. Haddock, black pudding and cabbage were cooked together like a luxury bubble and squeak, stylishly topped with a fried egg. Cold dishes – such as own-made scotch egg, or chicken liver and pancetta pâté with toast – were equally good. The wine list is quite small, but it's well chosen. Staff are sensitive to their own (rare) lapses in service, and have been very helpful and attentive on our visits.
Babies and children admitted. No smoking. Separate room for parties, seats 25. Tables outdoors (10, pavement). **Map 4 L3**.

Perseverance
63 Lamb's Conduit Street, WC1N 3NB (7405 8278). Holborn or Russell Square tube. **Open** 12.30-11pm Mon-Thur; 12.30pm-midnight Fri, Sat; 12.30-10.30pm Sun. **Lunch served** 12.30-3pm Mon-Fri; 12.30-5pm Sun. **Dinner served** 6.30-10pm Mon-Fri. **Main courses** £11.50-£14. **Credit** MC, V.
Drinkers spill out from the smoky ground floor of this pub on to the traffic-free street in good weather. Inside, it's usually rammed with a cool young crowd enjoying the ear-splitting playlist of diverse music, the slightly baronial look of the bare-boarded room, and the real ales on tap (most recently, Deuchars IPA and Courage Directors). Upstairs is the small dining room, which is an altogether quieter experience; we were one of only three tables taken on a Thursday evening. The menu offers the usual gastropub fare: fish cakes (curiously made with mackerel, giving them a very 'fishy' smell), or tagliatelle with tomatoes and rather rubbery mozzarella cheese scattered with salad leaves. A sliver of chocolate tart was slightly dry, but at least it was dense and rich in cocoa solids, served with a chocolate sauce. While the dish quality was adequate, the prices charged seem a little steep. Service, although smiling, was sporadic and rushed. We had to switch off a skipping CD ourselves – three times – before our waitress reappeared from the busy pub below to switch it back on again.
Babies and children admitted (Sun). Booking advisable. Tables outdoors (3, pavement). No-smoking tables. Restaurant available for hire. **Map 4 M4**.

City

White Swan Pub & Dining Room
108 Fetter Lane, EC4A 1ES (7242 9696/ www.thewhiteswanlondon.com). Chancery Lane or Holborn tube.
Bar Open 11am-midnight Mon-Thur; 11am-1am Fri. **Lunch served** noon-3pm Mon-Fri. **Dinner served** 6-10pm Tue-Fri. **Main courses** £10-£15.
Restaurant **Lunch served** noon-3pm, **dinner served** 6-10pm Mon-Fri. **Set lunch** £20 2 courses, £25 3 courses. **Main courses** £14-£22.
Both **Credit** AmEx, MC, V.
The mirrored and panelled dining room of the White Swan, perched above the ground-floor pub and mezzanine, lacked conviviality even on a Friday night. Yet the short menu was full of temptations. Both starters were admirable: potted shrimps with pickled cucumber and brown bread, and smoked haddock and bacon risotto with a poached egg. So too was a main of venison carpaccio with baby cress, black truffle and sherry vinaigrette. Only the rolled 'Baillet' mountain pig with fondant potato, sage and apple crumble disappointed, with the pork rather overwhelmed by its crumble accompaniment. Afters saw an oversweet passionfruit crème brûlée outpaced by a fine selection of ripe British Isles cheeses, proportioned to match a £9.50 price tag. The atmosphere became boisterous with the arrival of a hen party, causing prodigious schmoozing. Our waitress, entirely forgetting the red wine we'd asked to accompany our mains, was assiduous in pouring our white whenever a glass was rested. We were also unhappy to have ordered a side of spinach, only to find the same served unannounced with the pork. Downstairs, the bar has three tiny outside tables, three guest ales and a stuffed white swan in a case. Next time, that's where we'll eat.
Babies and children admitted (restaurant). No-smoking tables. Tables outdoors (4, pavement). Restaurant available for hire. **Map 11 N5**.

Clerkenwell & Farringdon

★ Coach & Horses
26-28 Ray Street, EC1R 3DJ (7278 8990/ www.thecoachandhorses.com). Farringdon tube/rail. **Open** 11am-11pm Mon-Fri; 6-11pm Sat; noon-4pm Sun. **Lunch served** noon-3pm Mon-Fri, Sun. **Dinner served** 6-10pm Mon-Sat. **Main courses** £10-£14. **Credit** AmEx, MC, V.
There's a gastropub on virtually every street in this part of town, but this congenial and thoughtfully updated old corner boozer (a former winner of a Time Out Eating & Drinking Award) remains a cut above the competition. It does so by being careful to cater for both eaters and drinkers. The pub is usually as popular with after-work beer-hounds (including some you might recognise from byline photos in the *Guardian*, the offices of which are just a short stagger up the hill) tucking into Timothy Taylor Landlord and a short list of bar snacks, as it is with diners sampling the daily changing, always-appetising full menu. Nothing we ate was especially complicated, but nor was it anything other than excellent. King prawns with chilli oil and cherry tomatoes were appealing, yet were outdone by a pristine starter of gently warmed beetroot served with creamy St Tola goat's cheese from Ireland. Tender slices of Goosnargh chicken breast came with a deliciously crispy skin, served over spinach and baby leek vinaigrette. The Highland short ribs, meanwhile, were implausibly soft and utterly irresistible. The only let-down? Some bizarrely greasy bread. All things considered, though, this is a terrific little operation.
Babies and children welcome: high chairs. No-smoking tables. Restaurant available for hire. Tables outdoors (16, courtyard). **Map 5 N4**.

Phoenix. See p104.

Eagle

159 Farringdon Road, EC1R 3AL (7837 1353). Farringdon tube/rail. **Open** noon-11pm Mon-Sat; noon-5pm Sun. **Lunch served** 12.30-3pm Mon-Fri; 12.30-3.30pm Sat, Sun. **Dinner served** 6.30-10.30pm Mon-Sat. **Main courses** £8-£15. **Credit** MC, V.

Though it's the grandaddy of all gastropubs, there's no suggestion that the Eagle is shuffling into retirement. The place still buzzes with energy (and noise – if you want a quiet chat, come here during the day), and the chefs manning the tiny kitchen area behind the bar are kept busy. A short blackboard menu lists hob- and grill-based Med dishes such as napoli sausages with white beans and salsa verde, linguine with pesto, and yellowfin tuna with sauce romesco. There are also tapas, including olives, manchego with membrillo and toast, gazpacho and (on a hot night) watermelon. Dishes aren't always perfect – the tuna was a little overcooked – but most give no cause for complaint. The ribeye was a class act, for example, with juicy pieces of steak nicely offset by intensely peppery rocket. Add to this a good beer selection (draught Bombardier), lots of decent wines by the glass and bottle, plus the laid-back but civilised vibe, and the enduring popularity makes perfect sense.
Babies and children welcome: children's portions. Tables outdoors (4, pavement). **Map 5 N4**.

Easton

22 Easton Street, WC1X 0DS (7278 7608/ www.theeaston.co.uk). Farringdon tube/rail/19, 38 bus. **Open** noon-11pm Mon-Thur; noon-1am Fri; 5.30pm-1am Sat; noon-10.30pm Sun. **Lunch served** 12.30-3pm Mon-Fri; 1-4pm Sun. **Dinner served** 6.30-10pm Mon-Sat; 6.30-9.30pm Sun. **Main courses** £9-£13. **Credit** MC, V.

The pub on this site was once the Queen's Head, a murky hangout for strippers and gangsters (or so we're told). Under its new Aussie owners (who also run the Princess – *see p111*) it has been thoroughly scrubbed up and is now in favour with a trendy local set. The large open room has a cosy boho feel, with flamingo flock wallpaper, long velvet banquettes and a scattering of pub tables. These fill up quickly on most nights, but you can also eat comfortably at the bar. Food is of the hearty, unfussy gastropub variety, with six or seven main choices, including one or two veggie numbers, chalked up each day. Risotto with smoked aubergine and taleggio was lovely: the cheese still melting as it was served, the rice perfectly al dente and the aubergine with subtle charcoal undertones, all set off by peppery fresh basil. A pork belly salad came with lashings of new potatoes; the meat was delicious, but the spuds were somewhat smothered in a mayonnaise dressing. Puddings are simple but gluttonous; the night we visited, giant, squishy meringues were paraded on a bed of strawberries, blueberries and thick cream. Unshowy wines are available by the bottle or glass; the beer selection contains all the usual suspects.
Babies and children admitted. Entertainment: DJs 9pm Fri. Restaurant available for hire. Tables outdoors (4, pavement). **Map 5 N4**.

Peasant

240 St John Street, EC1V 4PH (7336 7726/ www.thepeasant.co.uk). Angel tube/Farringdon tube/rail/19, 38 bus. *Bar* **Open** noon-11pm daily. **Meals served** noon-10.45pm Mon-Sat; noon-10pm Sun. **Main courses** £6.50-£11.50. *Restaurant* **Dinner served** 6-11pm Tue-Sat. **Main courses** £9.70-£15.70. *Both* **Credit** AmEx, MC, V.

By sidestepping the formula, the Peasant shows how homogeneous gastropubs have become. The light first-floor dining room, enlivened by circus posters and broad Islington views, leaves the pub firmly downstairs, and the menu dares to break several cardinal rules. Dishes mix a long list of elements, flavours and styles. The ingredients are not always seasonal; some are sourced from unfashionably far away (step forward, kangaroo). We feared the worst but tasted the best. There was barely a misstep. Grilled prawns on lotus root purée, with ginger and coriander salsa and a tamarind dressing, was subtle and surprising. Kholrabi, roast apple, mustard-orange yoghurt and

rocket set a fine piece of venison off nicely. Points too for the celeriac, spinach and truffle-mushroom stack with crisp soba noodles: a vegetarian dish that involved no compromise and plenty of taste. We were also impressed with the puddings, which eschew the nursery but still indulge. The gastro-tag is misleading: this is a very enjoyable restaurant (charging, it should be said, restaurant prices). There's a more conventional, tapas-like bar menu downstairs, where the drinks include a couple of ales on tap, and ciders and Belgian beers in the bottle.
Babies and children admitted. No-smoking tables. Restaurant available for hire. Tables outdoors (4, garden terrace; 5, pavement). **Map 5 O4**.

Well

180 St John Street, EC1V 4JY (7251 9363/ www.downthewell.com). Farringdon tube/rail. **Open** 11am-midnight Mon-Thur; 11-1am Fri; 10.30-1am Sat; 10.30am-11pm Sun. **Lunch served** noon-3pm Mon-Fri; 10.30am-4pm Sat, Sun. **Dinner served** 6-10.30pm Mon-Sat; 6-10pm Sun. **Main courses** £9.95-£15.95. **Credit** AmEx, MC, V.

It's easy to spot the blue awnings of this corner pub on the northern, less fashionable end of St John Street. It's a breezy spot with huge windows, de rigueur battered wooden furniture, and a cluster of tables on the pavement. The basement is more lounge-like: all low brown sofas, dim lighting and wall-set fish tanks (also visible from the toilets). The menu is short and not particularly inspiring – more the kind of fare that a competent home cook could produce than restaurant standard. Roast cod came with puy lentils, chorizo and salsa verde; the lentils were earthy and satisfying, but the fish was overcooked and the chorizo unpleasantly strong. The pricing seems a bit askew. A starter of buffalo mozzarella with provençal vegetables, rocket and pesto cost £7.50, but was merely OK, and ingredients weren't premium quality. The sole veggie main (pasta) was £11.50, and you're charged extra for side dishes. Rich desserts included lemon and plum posset and an excellent treacle tart with clotted cream, plus Neal's Yard cheeses. There are no draught ales, only lager. In short: useful if you're in the neighbourhood, but not worth a trek.

Babies and children welcome: high chairs. Booking advisable. Entertainment: DJ 7.30pm Fri. Restaurant available for hire. Separate room for parties, seats 70. Tables outdoors (6, pavement). Vegan dishes. **Map 5 O4.**

Marylebone

Queen's Head & Artichoke

30-32 Albany Street, NW1 4EA (7916 6206/ www.theartichoke.net). Great Portland Street or Regent's Park tube. **Open** 11am-11pm Mon-Sat; noon-10.30pm Sun. **Meals served** 12.30-10pm daily. **Main courses** £9-£13.50. **Credit** AmEx, MC, V.

This thoughtfully restored Victorian tavern, near Regent's Park, provides a good choice of Modern European classic dishes as well as an extensive tapas menu. With its name and licence dating back to good Queen Bess, the Queen's Head is a fine choice whether you're after a sit-down meal or just a drink and snack. The wooden ground-floor bar, with large windows and leather sofas, has a relaxed feel but gets packed with the after-work crowd. To escape, seek refuge in the pleasant walled garden. There's real ale on tap (Marston's Pedigree, Adnams Bitter) and tapas to share: order a few dishes, as portions can be quite small. For a quieter experience, head upstairs to the dining room, with its fresh flowers, chandeliers and golden-framed pictures. We sampled an inventive starter of mango, halloumi, mint and olives: a surprisingly successful combination. Gazpacho with basil oil was light and flavoursome, a perfect summer dish. For mains, we enjoyed well-prepared, organic, crispy-skin salmon, with mash, watercress, tomato and leek; and seared scallops with carrot and pea purée, pancetta and chervil. Tempting desserts included panna cotta and caramel with almond shavings; or blueberry, Cointreau and custard tartlet. A great find near the culinary desert that is the Euston Road.

Babies and children admitted. Booking advisable. Disabled: toilet. No-smoking tables. Separate room for parties, seats 50. Tables outdoors (4, garden; 8, pavement). **Map 3 H4.**

Soho

Endurance

90 Berwick Street, W1F 0QB (7437 2944). Leicester Square, Oxford Circus or Tottenham Court Road tube. **Open** noon-11pm Mon-Sat; noon-10.30pm Sun. **Lunch served** 12.30-4pm Mon-Sat; 12.30-4.30pm Sun. **Main courses** £7.95-£11.50. **Credit** AmEx, MC, V.

A spot of New Soho in the only street in the area to retain the manor's old sinful flavour, the Endurance is gastropub by day, trendy bar at night. Located at the bottom end of Berwick Street, 'twixt record shops, market stalls and porn emporiums, the daylight Endurance offers a menu that fits nicely between standard pub fare and gastro-pretension. Goat's cheese and tomato tart on a bed of rocket with pesto sauce was an ample starter, while smoked salmon with asparagus spears was simplicity itself. For mains, we followed a trad route: beer-battered cod, peas and fat chips for one, grilled gammon steak with poached egg for the other. A brief wine list contains three whites and four reds by the glass, plus sundry ales and lagers. With tables well spaced, laid-back service and the jukebox set to soothe, it's all a far cry from the Endurance's evening incarnation, when the place gets rammed with fancy hairstyles shouting to be served above classic cuts from the jukebox. We know which version we prefer.

Babies and children welcome (before 5pm): children's portions. Tables outdoors (9, garden). **Map 17 J6.**

Victoria

★ Phoenix NEW

2006 RUNNER-UP BEST GASTROPUB
14 Palace Street, SW1E 5JA (7828 8136/ www.geronimo-inns.co.uk). Victoria tube/rail. **Open** 11am-11pm Mon-Sat; noon-11pm Sun.

Lunch served noon-3pm Mon-Fri; noon-4pm Sat, Sun. **Dinner served** 6-10pm daily. **Main courses** £9-£14. **Set lunch** (Mon-Fri) £7.50 2 courses, £10 3 courses. **Credit** AmEx, MC, V.

A big, busy refurbed bar with a small dining room, the Phoenix (part of the Geronimo Inns stable) does things differently from other gastropubs. Lunchtime diners must choose two or three courses from two wildly eclectic menus. These are served all at once in small dishes: perfect for the discerning but time-stretched diner. We put the 'ten-minute express lunch' claim to the test, ordering tomato, basil and feta soup; cider and sausage casserole; and strawberries with vanilla custard and sugared puff pastry. Incredibly, the three dishes arrived with two minutes to spare. The 'main course' casserole was kept warm inside a dinky orange Le Creuset while we attacked the reassuringly tomatoey soup. All three dishes were excellent: fresh, perfectly seasoned and adequately proportioned. A businessman nearby was happily polishing off a green bean and shallot salad with balsamic dressing, toasted cumin and vegetable curry, and banana and rhubarb cheesecake, before scooting back to the office. There are also some tempting hot sandwiches and a salad bar. The evening menu includes the likes of potted truffle duck with crostini and capers; and crispy pork belly seasoned with lemon and thyme. Service is friendly if a little hectic. There's also a tempting array of drinks, including Deuchars IPA, Adnams and Sharp's Doom Bar.

Babies and children admitted. No-smoking tables. Separate room for parties, seats 40. Tables outdoors (5, garden; 4, pavement).

West

Ealing

★ Ealing Park Tavern

222 South Ealing Road, W5 4RL (8758 1879). South Ealing tube. **Open** 6-11pm Mon; noon-11pm Tue-Sat; noon-10.30pm Sun. **Lunch served** noon-3pm Mon-Sat; noon-3.45pm Sun. **Dinner served** 6-10pm Mon-Sat; 6-9.30pm Sun. **Main courses** £10-£12. **Credit** AmEx, MC, V.

Pig's Ear. See p106.

A chateau of a place, this is a magnificent pub with a massive bar area, large back garden and echoing high-ceilinged dining room with exposed beams and wooden panelling. Big though the eating area is, it's also very popular: even on a Tuesday evening we only just managed to snag an unreserved table. It's easy to see why business is thriving. This is a highly professional operation: the all-male staff attend tables like their lives depend on it – swift, precise and clued-up on the menu. What's more, the food is terrific. There was a pronounced fishy slant on our visit: starters included a spicy shellfish bisque, wonderfully fresh pan-fried sardines, and gravadlax. Pan-roasted skate wing, fillet of red mullet and saltimbocca of monkfish accounted for half the mains. Even so, it was the juicy ribeye in a pepper sauce that was really flying off the grill. (Vegetarians get a very raw deal: just the one dish of butternut squash, pea and parmesan risotto.) The wine list is extensive, and the range of beers is noteworthy – including, if you're lucky, fruity Twickenham Golden Ale, a particularly good match for pork or duck.
Babies and children admitted: children's portions. No-smoking tables. Restaurant available for hire. Tables outdoors (25, garden).

Hammersmith

Anglesea Arms
35 Wingate Road, W6 0UR (8749 1291). Goldhawk Road or Ravenscourt Park tube. **Open** 11am-11pm Mon-Sat; noon-10.30pm Sun. **Lunch served** 12.30-2.45pm Mon-Sat; 12.30-3.30pm Sun. **Dinner served** 7-10.30pm Mon-Sat; 7-10pm Sun. **Main courses** £8.95-£12.95. **Credit** MC, V.
Drinkers occupy the low-lit front of this small corner pub. Diners eat at the back, next to the open kitchen and beneath a skylight (it can get stuffy on warm evenings), or at the cluster of umbrella-shaded pavement tables next to the street; you can't book. The marriage between drinking and dining is a fruitful one, and the Anglesea is an exceedingly popular spot. Deservedly so: the cooking shows flair, good use of seasonal produce, and is more ambitious than at many gastropubs. Dishes do run out, though, and the balance can go

awry; there was no choice for vegetarians among the five mains, and only two fish dishes (one of which was whole lobster at an eye-opening £28). Standouts included a starter of organic gravadlax tartare with caviar crème fraîche, surrounded by a pool of pale green avocado cream; and a main of roast gilthead bream with samphire, mussels and cucumber – a great combination of tastes and textures (if a tad salty). Less successful was poached spiced pineapple with mascarpone and black pepper sorbet; the fruit was far too sweet and the sorbet too creamy. A varied drinks list includes more than 20 wines by the glass, plus a couple of real ales. Service is casual but efficient.
Babies and children welcome: high chairs. No-smoking tables. Tables outdoors (5, pavement). Map 20 A3.

Olympia

Cumberland Arms
29 North End Road, W14 8SZ (7371 6806/ www.thecumberlandarmspub.co.uk). West Kensington tube/Kensington (Olympia) tube/rail. **Open** noon-11pm Mon-Sat; noon-10.30pm Sun. **Lunch served** 12.30-3pm Mon-Sat; 12.30-3.30pm Sun. **Dinner served** 7-10.30pm Mon-Sat; 7-10pm Sun. **Main courses** £7-£13.50. **Credit** MC, V.
The Cumberland remains true to the original gastropub blueprint. Its formula of unfancy, well-priced food and decent drinks (three real ales and a globetrotting wine list), served by convivial staff in low-key surroundings, remains unaffected by fashion. You can sit inside at the haphazard collection of wooden tables (the front is the airiest spot), or outside, along the side of the pub, beneath tumbling hanging baskets and window boxes. The short Mediterranean-slanted menu isn't divided into starters and mains, so price is the best indication of the size of a dish – though portions tend towards the substantial regardless. Baked goat's cheese bruschetta atop strips of grilled courgette, roast figs and a mound of rocket, all slathered in a strong pesto sauce, was far bigger than its £7 suggested, while a slab of nicely grilled tuna almost overflowed its plate. Expect full flavours and homely presentation and you won't be disappointed, though there's the occasional duff dish (chicken and broad bean risotto was dull). Finally, we give thanks to Donald, whose chocolate and almond cake always makes a great finish.
Babies and children admitted (until 7pm). Tables outdoors (9, pavement).

Shepherd's Bush

Havelock Tavern
57 Masbro Road, W14 0LS (7603 5374/ www.thehavelocktavern.co.uk). Hammersmith or Shepherd's Bush tube/Kensington (Olympia) tube/rail. **Open** 11am-11pm Mon-Sat; noon-10.30pm Sun. **Lunch served** 12.30-2.30pm Mon-Sat; 12.30-3pm Sun. **Dinner served** 7-10pm Mon-Sat; 7-9.30pm Sun. **Main courses** £8.50-£14. **No credit cards.**
Nestled in a villagey set of Shepherd's Bush streets, the Havelock is a relaxed, unpretentious gastropub beloved of a young, well-spoken crowd. Even on an early weeknight it was oversubscribed, with loud, smoky, garrulous chatter filling the assorted wood tables squeezed around the main bar. The interior has had a refurb, but is still a simple affair of cream walls and aubergine cornicing, with the odd jar of flowers to add decoration. A starter of chorizo-braised octopus with piquillo peppers, kalamata olives and roast lemon was tasty if a little salty; it needed a zestier dressing to lift the heavy, meaty octopus. The main course was much better: roast cod fillet with peas, broad beans and new potatoes. The cod had a beautifully crisp skin, and the greens a lovely, just-podded freshness, enhanced by a tangy mint and olive tapenade. Vegetarians are not neglected, with dishes such as own-made ravioli filled with goat's cheese, sweet potato and swiss chard. Delicious, fresh-made bread is served with every meal. Puds are of the waist-expanding variety: banoffi pie, raspberry crème brûlée,

chocolate mousse. Our main quibble was with the lack of technology behind the bar – it's cash or cheques only.
Babies and children welcome: children's portions. Tables outdoors (6, garden; 2, pavement). Map 20 C3.

Westbourne Park

★ Cow
89 Westbourne Park Road, W2 5QH (7221 0021). Royal Oak or Westbourne Park tube. **Open** noon-11pm Mon-Thur; noon-midnight Fri, Sat; noon-10.30pm Sun. **Lunch served** noon-3.30pm daily. **Dinner served** 6-10.30pm Mon-Sat; 6-10pm Sun. **Main courses** £15.50-£19. **Credit** MC, V.
We can't fault the Cow, which is still among the most popular noshing shops in its field. Upstairs from one of the best pubs in London (for drinks and bar food), the dining room has a menu that's always simple, inventive and deftly dispatched. Like the bar, the restaurant is compact, squeezing barely ten tables into an awkward trapezium-shaped room that has a 1950s, retro feel right down to Irish lace curtains. Oysters are a speciality, although there are only two varieties. Thereafter it's six starters, six mains and five desserts. Don't fill up on the excellent fresh breads, as there's plenty of enticements on the steadily evolving menu, which may cover toasted scallops, catalan potato and almond stew, or simply an excellent salad of chicken livers. Mains may be a good juicy duck breast with poached pear and lettuce, or tender leg of Elwy lamb served on a summer salad of broad beans, shallots, goat's curd and mint. Standard sides of spuds, salad or greens cost £3 extra. Be sure to leave space for desserts, which range from rich raspberry brûlée to fresh figs and sherry syllabub. The world-covering wine list is strong too, and wisely doesn't exceed £50 a bottle.
Babies and children admitted (lunch). Restaurant available for hire. Tables outdoors (4, pavement). Map 7 A5.

Westbourne
101 Westbourne Park Villas, W2 5ED (7221 1332). Royal Oak or Westbourne Park tube. **Open** 5-11pm Mon; noon-11pm Tue-Sat; noon-10.30pm Sun. **Lunch served** 12.30-3pm Tue-Thur; 12.30-3.30pm Sat, Sun. **Dinner served** 7-10pm Mon-Thur; 7-9.30pm Fri-Sun. **Main courses** £10.50-£15. **Credit** MC, V.
The Westbourne gets packed on hot summer nights. We had booked, but encountered barely organised chaos on arrival, with no seat to be spotted or waitress to be found in the throng. Eventually a table came free and was grabbed. Ordering food is problematic. We queued at the bar for 15 minutes only to find that all our choices – from bavette of beef and pork belly to an appetising

(sounding) scallop, broad bean and pea risotto – were no longer available. It was only 8.30pm. We had to settle for trout and mackerel salad, and tuna steak. Then pork loin with mustard suddenly appeared on the menu and we switched. The pork was overpowered by whole-grain mustard, and drew a 'someone's just bought their first cookbook' comment. The salad was a competent combination of fish and leaves, but again uninspiring. Other people's food looked reasonably good. For dessert, we plumped for pear and almond tart. Guess what? It had run out. Our buttermilk pudding alternative was a little bitter, but a luscious, rich brownie and crème fraîche helped assuage our disappointment. The Westbourne has a decent wine and beer selection and is a better bet for drinks rather than destination dining.
Babies and children welcome: high chairs. Tables outdoors (14, terrace). **Map 7 B5**.

South West
Chelsea

★ Lots Road Pub & Dining Room
114 Lots Road, SW10 0RJ (7352 6645/ www.thespiritgroup.com). Fulham Broadway tube then 11 bus/Sloane Square tube then 11, 19, 22 bus. **Open** 11am-11pm Mon-Thur; 11am-midnight Fri, Sat; noon-10.30pm Sun. **Lunch served** noon-3pm, **dinner served** 5.30-10pm Mon-Fri. **Meals served** noon-10pm Sat, Sun. **Main courses** £8.50-£14. **Credit** JCB, MC, V.
It's a tribute to the diplomatic qualities of the staff and the skill in the kitchen that, despite being seated beside a table of obnoxiously drunk Chelsea fans (Stamford Bridge is five minutes away), we still thoroughly enjoyed a recent meal here. The food is terrific. Even basic dishes such as cod or steak are cooked with precision, inventiveness and flair. The fish, a wonderfully flaky slab, came on a rack of fennel and garnished with three plump dumplings, while the steak was settled on an autumnal mound of wild mushrooms and parsnips and drizzled with a thin garlic sauce. Such is the presentation you feel like photographing the dishes before you tuck in. As for dessert, we're almost willing to concur with the blackboard behind the bar that reads, 'You haven't lived until you've tried our sticky toffee pud.' Other pluses include well-kept real ales and a commendably broad range of wines by the glass. When the blue-shirted specimens behind us started singing, 'Oh it's all gone quiet over there,' we could only agree. We had our mouths full and were far too blissed out to respond.
Babies and children welcome: high chairs. Disabled: toilet. No-smoking tables. Restaurant available for hire. **Map 13 C13**.

★ Pig's Ear
35 Old Church Street, SW3 5BS (7352 2908/ www.thepigsear.co.uk). Sloane Square tube. **Bar Open** noon-11pm Mon-Sat; noon-10.30pm Sun. **Lunch served** 12.30-3pm Mon-Fri; 12.30-4pm Sat, Sun. **Dinner served** 7-10pm Mon-Sat; 7-9.30pm Sun.
Dining room **Lunch served** 12.30-3pm Sun. **Dinner served** 7-10pm Mon-Sat.
Both **Main courses** £3.50-£20. **Credit** AmEx, MC, V.
Pig's ears on the menu aren't the only surprise in this popular pub, occupant of a prime corner site in a quiet Chelsea backwater. The real shock is how reasonable the prices are, in both the nicely decorated downstairs boozer and the upstairs dining room ('formal but not stuffy,' we were told). You can fill yourself for as little as £15, which is slightly miraculous in such a well-heeled area. And it's not just pub-fodder, but expert, sophisticated cooking with a strong emphasis on seasonality (menus change frequently) and big flavours. The pigs' ears are a crunchy mouthful, prepared over five days before getting battered and expertly fried. A chilled pea and mint soup was masterfully executed, if slightly too salty. Crab salad was cleverly served on a disc of watermelon (perfect summer food), and potted shrimps were spicy and filling. Breads are awe-inspiring. Upstairs, the

choice is larger, the cooking somewhat more elaborate, and the prices slightly higher. The wine list offers good choice under £20, and great bargains for £40-£50. Service was genuinely warm without venturing into 'have a nice day' territory. Weekday lunch gave us the place practically to ourselves; at weekends, you'd better book. But do go. This place is a silk purse, not a sow's ear.
Babies and children welcome: high chairs. Booking advisable (dining room). No smoking (dining room). Restaurant available for hire. **Map 14 E12**.

Putney

Spencer Arms NEW
237 Lower Richmond Road, SW15 1HJ (8788 0640). Putney Bridge tube. **Open** 10am-midnight daily. **Lunch served** noon-2.30pm Mon-Fri, Sun; noon-3pm Sat. **Dinner served** 6.30-10pm Mon-Sat; 6.30-9.45pm Sun. **Main courses** £7-£15.50. **Credit** MC, V.
Occupying a prime site on the edge of Barnes Common and a few minutes from the river, the Spencer Arms answers many needs. Dog walkers, drinkers, dining couples, groups of mates: all were in evidence on a recent visit. You can read the papers, have a pint (it's a proper pub with draught beers that include London Pride and Adnams, as well as a longish wine list), sun yourself on one of the pavement tables or settle inside for some food. The space is attractive, flooded with light, with sage and burgundy paintwork and an appealing array of polished wooden furniture and sofas. There's even a bookshelf and board games. As for the food, it's an odd mix of old-fashioned pub grub and more gastro-like fare, with 'British tapas' (sausage toasty with HP sauce, boiled egg with pork crackling soldiers), 'staples' such as ploughman's, fancier titbits (guinea fowl terrine), plus more conventional dishes (roast leg of lamb, bavette steak and chips). Cooking can be a bit basic – macaroni cheese was actually penne, covered in rich cheese sauce, with no garnish whatsoever – but also quite sophisticated: a dessert of cider granita, cider jelly and two chunks of roast apple was a striking-looking, delicately flavoured creation. A convivial atmosphere reigns, helped along by charming staff.
Babies and children admitted (until 9pm): children's menu; high chairs. Disabled: toilet. Entertainment: jazz duo 9pm occasional Tue-Thur. No-smoking tables. Restaurant available for hire. Tables outdoors (8, pavement).

Southfields

Earl Spencer
260-262 Merton Road, SW18 5JL (8870 9244/ www.theearlspencer.co.uk). Southfields tube. **Open** 11am-11pm Mon-Sat; noon-10.30pm Sun. **Lunch served** 12.30-2.30pm Mon-Sat; 12.30-3pm Sun. **Dinner served** 7-10pm Mon-Sat; 7-9.30pm Sun. **Main courses** £8-£12.50. **Credit** AmEx, MC, V.
Young's pubs have a (rightful) reputation for quality, and the Earl Spencer is a case in point. It was 'done up' in 2003 and was a runner-up in Time Out's Best Gastropub category that same year. A few years on, the place has retained its winsome ways. There's a selection of well-kept ales (Hook Norton and Shepherd Neame Spitfire on our visit), plus some good wines by the glass – and a hugely appealing menu that combines best of British with continental influences. A half-pint of oak-smoked prawns was served with a gutsy, chunky tartare sauce. For mains, roast neck of pork arrived with flavourful new potatoes, carrots and green beans, surrounded by a tasty, mushroomy broth. Grilled sea bass, cooked until the skin crisped, came with divine chunky chips, salad and a chilli- and saffron-spiked rouille. For afters, choose from a cheese plate or sturdy-sounding desserts. If you don't want to eat, no one will mind if you come in, browse the weekend papers or look through the selection of well-thumbed cookery books on display.
Babies and children welcome: high chairs; children's portions. No-smoking tables. Separate room for parties, seats 70. Tables outdoors (10, patio).

Wandsworth

Freemasons
2 Wandsworth Common Northside, SW18 2SS (7326 8580). Clapham Junction rail. **Open** noon-11pm Mon-Sat; noon-10.30pm Sun. **Lunch served** noon-3pm Mon-Fri; 12.30-3.30pm Sat; 12.30-4pm Sun. **Dinner served** 6.30-10pm Mon-Sat; 6.30-9.30pm Sun. **Main courses** £9.50-£12.50. **Credit** AmEx, MC, V.
The Freemasons has been open a couple of years, so seems to be staying the course at this appealing but once-troubled site (there has been a clutch of openings and closures here over the past decade). That's probably because a competent, unpretentious gastropub is exactly what's needed in this residential area on the edge of Wandsworth Common, a comfortable distance from the hustle and boom of Northcote Road. The big, circular room ticks all the right boxes: chunky wooden tables, big screens when necessary, a great sweep of bar space and, up a couple of steps at the back, a small restaurant area (hardly any different from the bar, except that the overstretched waiter will pay you slightly more attention). The food is well-executed gastro fare: an enjoyable, high-stacked burger comes with chunky chips; a lavish pork steak is drenched in a wine-rich sauce and sautéed potatoes; the bruschetta is fresh; tempura chicken is light and oil-free. All well done, in other words, without fuss or slip-up – just the way a gastropub should operate. And the good news for this otherwise restaurant-free stretch is that the crowds seem to be coming.
Babies and children welcome (restaurant): children's menu; high chairs. No-smoking tables. Tables outdoors (11, patio). **Map 21 B4**.

Ship
41 Jew's Row, SW18 1TB (8870 9667). Wandsworth Town rail. **Open** 11am-11pm Mon-Wed; 11am-midnight Thur-Sat; noon-11pm Sun. **Meals served** noon-10.30pm Mon-Sat; noon-10pm Sun. **Main courses** £7.50-£14.95. **Credit** AmEx, DC, MC, V.
Right on the Thames, yet sited close to a rather industrial patch of SW18 (complete with cement works), this hidden-away pub is a bit of a find if you're unfamiliar with the area. The indoor pub and dining area is more than decent enough, with big windows, a huge skylight and banks of sturdy dark wood tables. There's an adjoining marquee at the back. Barbecues are often held in the sunken garden in summer (weekends only in winter) and are very popular with families. The daily changing menu encompasses a varied choice of well-executed gastropub hits such as seared tuna, fish cakes, and spiced aubergine. Subtly herbed sausages came with creamy mushroom mash and a generous helping of thick onion gravy – all for a very reasonable £8.95. Chicken breast with vegetables on a bed of sweet potato mash was excellent too, and a healthy enough option to warrant an order of sweet and tangy apple crumble with custard. A great summer spot for outdoor dining, with an accompanying view of the river.
Babies and children admitted (before 7pm). Booking advisable. No-smoking tables. Separate room for parties, seats 16. Tables outdoors (30, riverside garden). **Map 21 A4**.

South
Battersea

Greyhound
136 Battersea High Street, SW11 3JR (7978 7021/www.thegreyhoundatbattersea.co.uk). Clapham Junction rail/49, 319, 344, 345 bus. **Open** noon-11pm Tue-Sat; noon-5pm Sun. **Lunch served** noon-3pm Mon-Sun. **Dinner served** 7-10pm Mon-Sat. **Main courses** £7.50-£12.50. **Set dinner** £27 2 courses, £31 3 courses. **Credit** AmEx, MC, V.
A pub with a sommelier and a 30-page wine list isn't really a pub, gastro or otherwise. The Greyhound may be set on a pretty sidestreet, but you can't even get real ale here, and prices are those of a nobby restaurant. Paying £27 for two courses,

RESTAURANTS

you might expect more attentive service from the casual staff (attired in Fred Perrys and jeans). You might also like your table wiped between courses. But the cooking is as good as the woody interior is smart. Rustic breads come with butter that's made in-house with West Country cream and flavoured with dandelion. All the starters show a touch of invention (smoked eel and fried eel served with horseradish mousse; calf's tongue with salsa verde and quail's egg). Main courses are similarly sophisticated and typified by a gorgeous calf's liver served with spinach, pancetta and garlic purée; or a fairly fresh grilled tuna steak arriving with asparagus, red chard and celeriac purée. Deserts are pan-European and included a deconstructed apple crumble (apple and crumble on different parts of the plate). As for that 30-page wine list, the affable sommelier jokes that the Greyhound likes to make life difficult – but it also makes life fascinating if you're up for splashing out in casual surroundings.

Disabled: toilet. No-smoking tables. Restaurant available for hire. Separate room for parties, seats 25. Tables outdoors (6, garden; 6, patio). **Map 21 B2**.

Matilda

74-76 Battersea Bridge Road, SW11 3AG (7228 6482/www.matilda.tv). Clapham Junction rail then 319 bus. **Lunch served** noon-3pm Mon-Fri; noon-4pm Sat, Sun. **Dinner served** 6-10.30pm daily. **Main courses** £6.50-£12.95. **Credit** AmEx, MC, V.

A neon sign outside this unusual corner venue proclaims it as a pub-diner. On our visit a wedding party was making the most of the property's function rooms, while a raucous group of young people lay around, sang and laughed too loudly in a corner of the restaurant area. We retreated to the front bar, where eventually a guy we'd seen enjoying a beer announced himself as our waiter. Once you clock the laid-back, rather Australian mood, this place, fitted out with a ramshackle collection of wooden furniture, is fun. An open kitchen near the front window produces hearty dishes to a generally high standard. A Middle Eastern platter of dips, fried halloumi and olives was let down only by dry bread. Fritto misto of sea bass, salmon and squid featured impressively fresh fish, perfectly fried, while Moroccan spiced fish cakes had a tasty flavour that belied their slightly offputting luminous orange colour. Refreshing Veneto rosé from Alpha-Zeto (one of three on the wine list) was terrific value; beer drinkers could choose from Adnams Bitter, San Miguel, Fosters and Carling on tap.

Babies and children admitted. Disabled: toilet. No-smoking tables. Separate room for parties, seats 40. Tables outdoors (5, garden; 5, pavement). **Map 21 B1**.

Brixton

Hive NEW

11-13 Brixton Station Road, SW9 8PA (7274 8383/www.hivebar.net). Brixton tube/rail. **Open** noon-midnight Mon-Wed; noon-2am Thur; noon-3am Fri; 10am-3am Sat; 10am-midnight Sun. **Lunch served** noon-4pm, **dinner served** 6-10pm Mon-Fri. **Meals served** noon-10pm Sat, Sun. **Main courses** £4.50-£8.50. **Credit** MC, V.

Although not a true gastropub, this bar and diner at the edge of Brixton Market straddles these two functions and as a result defies easy categorisation. It serves breakfast, lunch, dinner and drinks, and has become a one-stop shop for lounging, live music and exhibitions. The Hive also manages to maintain a high standard on the food front. Decor is light and bright, with stencilled bees on sage green walls. Sit downstairs at large wooden tables, or upstairs, on the first floor, where soft sofas make everything seem a little more laid-back. Daytime snacks include glorious sandwiches with salad or own-made fries, roast organic beef ploughman's, and pasta dishes. The evening menu offers an enticing range of well-thought-out dishes. Prawn and pea risotto was excellent, with bumper-sized crustacea and smooth, creamy rice. Also enjoyable was vegetarian tagliatelle with red onions, sun-

dried tomatoes and green olives. Service was efficient and friendly. To drink, there's a wide range of wine, plenty of champagne, plus contemporary and classic cocktails (passionfruit Margarita, London Mojito, Raspberry Collins), but no real ales; it's a 'gastrobar', really.

Babies and children admitted (restaurant). Entertainment: DJs 8pm Thur-Sat. Restaurant available for hire. Tables outdoors (7, pavement). **Map 22 E1**.

Waterloo

★ Anchor & Hope

36 The Cut, SE1 8LP (7928 9898). Southwark or Waterloo tube/rail. **Open** 5-11pm Mon; 11am-11pm Tue-Sat. 12.30-5pm Sun. **Lunch served** noon-2.30pm Tue-Sat; noon-2pm Sun. **Dinner served** 6-10.30pm Mon-Sat. **Main courses** £9.80-£12.80. **Credit** MC, V.

There are two problems with the A&H: it doesn't take bookings, and it's always full. But persist: the place is full because, in an area bereft of decent restaurants, the food is extremely good. The pub isn't the most attractive building from the outside, but it's handsome indoors, with nursery-style furniture, aubergine walls, an open kitchen and a healthily populated bar that treats real ales and classic cocktails with due respect. Progress into the dining room and you'll be given excellent bread,

tap water if you want it, and a short menu of seasonal (largely) British classics. We were disappointed on our visit that several dishes had run out, and a couple of others (lancashire hot-pot, steak and kidney pie) required two or more to share. But though our choices were limited, they didn't disappoint. Garlic soup was deeply flavoursome; crab on toast featured quality meat with good textural contrasts; and cod on white beans was melt-in-the-mouth tender. In fact, everything from side dishes to (buttermilk and rhubarb) pudding was pretty special. So, a meal's worth the wait. Note that the pub is popular with business diners, so come at 2pm or after 8.30pm and the crowds should have thinned (and become a little more laid-back).

Babies and children admitted: children's portions; high chairs. No smoking tables. Tables outdoors (4, pavement). **Map 11 N8**.

South East

Bermondsey

Garrison

99-101 Bermondsey Street, SE1 3XB (7089 9355/ www.thegarrison.co.uk). London Bridge tube/rail. **Open** 8am-11pm Mon-Fri; 9am-11pm Sat; 9am-10.30pm Sun. **Breakfast served** 8-11.30am

Charles Lamb. See p113.

DUKEONTHEGREEN

"Welcome to the Duke on the Green, a truly stylish & elegant yet relaxed place to eat, drink & enjoy, right on Parson's Green.

The menu at the Duke on the Green offers the very best in quality & choice, complimented by our exclusive drinks list including fabulous wines, a selection of beers from around the world & Young's unique cask conditioned ales.

Heard about our Privilege card? Sign up online and receive fantastic exclusive monthly offers - Just another reason to come & visit us.

We look forward to entertaining you here at the Duke!"

235 New Kings Road, Fulham, London SW6 4XG
t: 020 7736 2777 e: dukeonthegreen@youngs.co.uk

Mon-Fri; 9-11.30am Sat, Sun. **Lunch served** 12.30-3.30pm Mon-Fri; 12.30-4pm Sat, Sun. **Dinner served** 6.30-10pm Mon-Sat; 6-9.30pm Sun. **Main courses** £8.90-£14.50. **Credit** AmEx, MC, V.

While the music here is a bit loud, this suits the lively youngish crowd at the Garrison. They wait for tables while enjoying a range of beers, wines and appealing bar snacks, including Japanese seaweed nuts and own-made root vegetable crisps. On a recent night, the specials board had many enticing seasonal dishes, and was notably strong on vegetarian choices. Girolle and shropshire blue risotto, while slightly dry and suspiciously quick to the table, was nonetheless highly enjoyable due to the freshness of the mushrooms and sharpness of the dill and chives. Sweetbreads with chutney and watercress were smooth and rich. To follow, the pastry on beef wellington was slightly undercooked, and the portion size of the butternut squash and sage dumplings was far too big. We finished with a divine own-made mango sorbet, and a faultless warm chocolate pudding with milk ice-cream. A stylish medley of shabby-chic decor, the Garrison is lively and cosy, but has a hip edge. Service is unusually cheerful, helping make this a great venue for a relaxing meal. Note that the whole place is now no-smoking.
Babies and children admitted (lunch Sat, Sun). Booking essential. Disabled: toilet. No smoking. Separate room for parties, seats 25. Vegan dishes. **Map 12 Q9.**

Hartley

64 Tower Bridge Road, SE1 4TR (7394 7023/ www.thehartley.com). Borough tube/London Bridge tube/rail. **Open** noon-midnight Mon-Thur; noon-2am Fri; 11-2am Sat; noon-11pm Sun. **Lunch served** noon-3pm Mon-Fri; 11am-4pm Sat. **Dinner served** 6-10pm Mon-Sat. **Meals served** noon-7pm Sun. **Main courses** £7.50-£15. **Credit** AmEx, MC, V.

There's not much competition nearby for the Hartley, but the pub has gained many plaudits for its 'traditional food with a twist'. The place is as much a pub as pub, fairly relaxed and spacious with a zinc bar and hardy furniture. The no-smoking tables don't offer much protection from the puffers. Service is friendly and on the case – on quiet nights, anyway. The menu's 'twists' include adding truffle to macaroni cheese, foie gras to lamb burgers, and lavender to crème brûlées. Yet we struggled to identify the flavours of the added ingredients. Still, all the food was well cooked and presented, and the chunky chips got a big thumbs up. Most of the ambitious dishes on the blackboard cost over a tenner but under £15. Anyone for braised pig's head, honey-roast pork belly, scallops, champ and cabbage? Desserts are all around £5. The small wine list is reasonably priced too, and there's a decent choice by the glass. The Hartley's a fair bet if you're in the area, but needs to raise its game to justify the praise heaped on it.
Babies and children admitted: children's portions; high chairs. Entertainment: musicians 8pm Tue, alternate Fri. No-smoking tables. Separate room for parties, seats 50.

Camberwell

Castle NEW

65 Camberwell Church Street, SE5 8TR (7277 2601). Denmark Hill rail/12, 36, 68, 68A, 171, 176, 345 bus. **Open** noon-midnight Mon-Thur, Sun; noon-2am Fri, Sat. **Meals served** noon-10pm Mon-Sat; noon-9.30pm Sun. **Main courses** £4-£9. **Credit** AmEx, DC, MC, V.

This is the best place to eat in Camberwell (a bit of an egg and spoon race, we'll admit). It's a pretty standard gastropub in many respects – bare boards, cream walls, two real ales on tap (Adnams Broadside and a golden ale, Itchen Valley's Godfather, on our visit), plus a good wine list and varied menu. A few things make the Castle stand out from the norm, and the most obvious is the music playlist: an iPod mix of great tunes from early Roxy Music through seminal world music to contemporary cult stuff, not the usual muzak you hear in pubs. Another big plus is the wine list: short, well chosen and keenly priced. You can drink well here without resort to dull brands. The

food's not bad either. A grilled aubergine 'burger' in a good bun was a well-made vegetarian dish, but was upstaged by a carefully marinated lamb brochette and lamb burger served with greek salad. A side portion of fat chips was excellent, with real potato flavour. The only disappointment was the summer pudding, a small portion so dry that the bread was still white. Cheery, efficient service compensated for any shortcomings.
Babies and children welcome: high chairs. Booking advisable. Entertainment: DJs 10pm Fri, Sat. Separate room for parties, seats 30. **Map 23 B2.**

Dulwich

★ Palmerston

91 Lordship Lane, SE22 8EP (8693 1629/ www.thepalmerston.co.uk). East Dulwich rail/185, 176, P13 bus. **Open** noon-11pm Mon-Thur; noon-midnight Fri, Sat; noon-10.30pm Sun. **Lunch served** noon-2.30pm Mon-Fri; noon-3pm Sat; noon-4pm Sun. **Dinner served** 7-10pm Mon-Sat. **Main courses** £12-£15.25. **Credit** MC, V.

As competition in East Dulwich intensifies, so Palmerston chef Jamie Younger has raised his game, bringing premium produce and greater inventiveness to his menu. This may have raised his prices a little, but every visit is a treat, the menu a mouth-watering array inducing agonies of decision-making. In early summer, a special starter of deep-fried courgette flowers (stuffed with ricotta, sultanas and mint, and served with chilli jam) was just flying off the menu. The finest British produce is imaginatively garnished with European delicacies: roast quails served with chorizo, pine nuts, sherry and sage; fillet of wild halibut with pickled girolles, pea-shoots and chives. The gastropub staples (steak, lamb) are executed with flair; we greedily used our chips to soak up the remaining lamb gravy, which was tinged with rosemary, garlic and artichoke juice. The drinks menu has also gone up a notch, and now offers classic cocktails, a fine whisky selection and well-picked wines (from £12 to £50 a bottle) – all of which helps to keep trade at the bar steady, with an appreciative, mainly local crowd.
Babies and children welcome: children's portions; high chairs. Booking advisable. Entertainment: jazz/soul 7pm Sun. No smoking tables. Restaurant available for hire. Tables outdoors (6, pavement). **Map 23 C4.**

Herne Hill

Prince Regent NEW

69 Dulwich Road, SE24 0NJ (7274 1567). Herne Hill rail/3, 196 bus. **Open** noon-11pm Mon-Wed; noon-midnight Thur-Sat; noon-10.30pm Sun. **Lunch served** noon-3pm Tue-Sat; noon-6pm Sun. **Dinner served** 7-10pm Mon-Sat. **Main courses** £5-£14. **Credit** MC, V.

The Prince Regent was in urgent need of an overhaul. Usually empty, this Victorian-style pub had been filled with a melancholy fug dispersed only by quiz nights and the occasional summer breeze blowing in from Brockwell Park. The transformation duly happened. Now, there's nothing novel about the low-key brownish decor or the imported beers, but the short, savvy menu is packing the place out evenings and weekends. The light dishes (chicken and bacon salad with poached egg; salmon fish cakes; soups of the day) are flawless. Veggie and cumberland sausages were herb-tinged and gently charred, with either mash or hand-cut chips coming as sides – though sausage and chips need greens too, and you shouldn't have to pay another £3.50 for them. Cod, onglet and lamb are also on the menu. Lemon tart was tangy but not sour; pear tatin with ice-cream is a melt-in-the-mouth alternative should you need something sweet. Wines are rarely obvious (Bouchon from Chile, Alsatian rieslings, a La Linda malbec), but always classy. This is why gastropubs were invented, and Herne Hill is better for the revamped Regent.
Babies and children welcome (until 7pm): high chairs. Disabled: toilet. No-smoking tables. Separate room for parties, seats 50. Tables outdoors (12, pavement). **Map 22 E3.**

Interview
TOM MARTIN

Who are you?
Joint owner, with brother Ed, of gastropubs the **Gun** (*see p110*) in Docklands, and the **White Swan Pub & Dining Room** (*see p102*) and the **Well** (*see p103*), both in Clerkenwell.

Eating in London: what's good about it?
The fact that you can eat very good quality food from anywhere in the world at most times of the day.

What's bad about it?
Too many mundane corporate chains only in it for the money, serving up bland, uninspired food with basic drinks offerings to match.

Which are your favourite London restaurants?
Every element of the **Cow** (*see p105*) is really well done, from the welcoming service, to the lovely restaurant upstairs, the simple but ever-changing menus and, in particular, their shellfish, which is always of the highest standard. **Galvin Bistrot** (*see p93*) has one of those menus that has so many excellent dishes, you just don't know what to choose. And I like **Viet Hoa** (*see p286*) on the Kingsland Road, because they make the best won ton noodle soup I've ever had.

What single thing would most improve London's restaurant scene?
More investment in catering colleges to encourage more talented people to train as chefs. There are too few chefs of a decent standard around.

Any hot tips for the coming year?
Look east! With the influx of money being poured into east London, it will be a particularly interesting time, not only for residential and retail developments, but also restaurant and bars. I predict particular hotspots will be Victoria Park and London Fields – both brimming with character, oozing with charm and just waiting for a leading eating-out destination.

RESTAURANTS

Lewisham

Dartmouth Arms

7 Dartmouth Road, SE23 2NH (8488 3117/ www.thedartmoutharms.com). Forest Hill rail/122, 176, 312 bus. **Open** noon-midnight Mon-Sat; noon-11.30pm Sun. **Lunch served** noon-3.30pm, **dinner served** 6.30-10pm Mon-Sat. **Meals served** noon-9pm Sun. **Main courses** £10.50-£14. **Credit** MC, V.

Just off the South Circular Road, the Dartmouth Arms has the smart, spare, sophisticated air of a classy country gastropub. Both lunch and dinner menus aren't particularly extensive, but the dishes we tried were all top-notch, including some nicely charred king prawns and moreish salmon fish cakes for starters. Next, free-range chicken came with sage puntalette (rice-shaped pasta), which made a pleasant, lightweight change from rice or chips. Pea and mushroom risotto was nutty, creamy and generously laced with pungent thyme. Steaks here are slender affairs, but come with marvellous chunky hand-cut chips that taste of spud. Only the desserts seemed uninspired, as two were stodgy, one was off and the only temptation, a rhubarb fool, was poorly presented and not zingy enough. The wines come from across the world, but on the recommendation of our friendly waitress, we tested a British wine, the Chapel Down Bacchus. At 11% ABV it was a perfect, light lunchtime white with hints of apple and nettles. In all, a highly enjoyable *rus in urbe* experience.
Babies and children welcome: high chairs. Disabled: toilet. No-smoking tables. Restaurant available for hire. Tables outdoors (10, garden).

Peckham

Rye Hotel NEW

31 Peckham Rye, SE15 3NX (7639 5397). Peckham Rye rail/12, 37, 63 bus. **Open** noon-11pm Mon-Thur, Sun; noon-midnight Fri, Sat. **Lunch served** noon-4pm Mon-Fri; noon-5pm Sat, Sun. **Dinner served** 6-10pm Mon-Sat; 6-9pm Sun. **Main courses** £6.50-£11.50. **Credit** MC, V.

More than two years after opening, this bohemian drinking den is still holding up well, balancing the pub/restaurant elements expertly and evenly. The menu, though unvarying, has proved a consistent crowd puller, thanks to the quality of the cooking. The choice favours meat-eaters, with expertly cooked rye burgers, or sirloin steak served with rocket, caramelised onions, chips and black pepper mayonnaise. Sunday lunch specials may include roast corn-fed chicken breast with lemon and herb stuffing, roast potatoes, courgettes, carrots and red-wine gravy (with a kids' version for a fiver). South-east Asian dishes (thai green chicken curry, massaman curry, crispy duck with noodles) are superb, thanks to a Thai head chef. Puds – warm treacle tart or 'squidgy choc brownie', accompanied by vanilla bean ice-cream – are not to be missed. Good beers (Young's plus guest ales), enthusiastic bar staff and a varied wine list keep the bar buzzing throughout the week. A family-friendly crowd fills up the big back garden on summer weekends, especially when the Sunday barbecue season starts.
Babies and children admitted (until 6pm). Separate room for parties, seats 40. Tables outdoors (40, garden). **Map 23 C3**.

East

Bow

Morgan Arms

43 Morgan Street, E3 5AA (8980 6389/ www.geronimo-inns.co.uk). Mile End tube. **Open** noon-11pm Mon-Thur, Sun; noon-midnight Fri, Sat. **Lunch served** noon-3pm Mon-Sat; noon-4pm Sun. **Dinner served** 7-10pm Mon-Sat. **Main courses** £12.50-£18. **Credit** MC. V.

The highly popular Morgan has a firm no-booking policy, so we welcome the roofed extension despite it halving the space outdoors. Our recent visit was rather late (9pm at a weekend), but we were still surprised to find three starters and two mains off. Of the starters, twice-baked roquefort soufflé with rocket and spiced pear was an unqualified success (the perfect combination of airiness and big flavour); wild mushroom and mascarpone tart was let down only by an underpowered piccalilli; but the flaccid devilled whitebait tried to make up in quantity what it lacked in crispiness. Mains all comfortably made the grade: grilled sea bream fillet with mediterranean vegetable tart, rocket and pesto; char-grilled pavé steak, minted pea purée, spring greens, garlic butter and red wine jus; and roast chump of lamb, dauphinois potatoes, french beans and lamb jus. From the half-dozen puddings, the 'oranges and lemons' platter of five mini desserts proved a good wheeze; the lemon meringue pie, crème brûlée, polenta marmalade cake, and Cointreau and Grand Marnier ice-cream with ginger biscuit and honey each found an advocate, leaving only the ginseng and orange-blossom jelly unloved. Staff remained accommodating even as closing time loomed.
Bookings not accepted. Disabled: toilet. No-smoking tables. Restaurant available for hire. Tables outdoors (4, pavement; 3, garden).

Docklands

★ Gun

27 Coldharbour, Docklands, E14 9NS (7515 5222/www.thegundocklands.com). Canary Wharf tube/DLR/South Quay DLR. **Open** 11am-midnight Mon-Sat; noon-11pm Sun. **Lunch served** noon-3pm Fri; noon-4.30pm Sat, Sun. **Dinner served** 6-10.30pm Mon-Sat; 6-9.30pm Sun. **Main courses** £9.50-£21.50. **Credit** AmEx, MC, V.

The Isle of Dogs' extraordinary skyline contrasts barren industrial land with the latest glass and steel skyscrapers, and the pretty little residential area in which this pub is secreted. Welcoming rows of linen-covered tables and a few stools feature in the bright front bar, but many customers walk straight out the back where terrace tables and riverside rooms (one with a jokey naval mural) offer an intimate view of the Dome. Bottled lager and buckets of rosé are favoured by the braying suits who arrive from nearby Canary Wharf in a procession of black cabs, but there's a fine choice of proper beers including Adnams Broadside,

Marquess Tavern. See p114.

Brakspear Honeycomb and Young's Bitter. The Gun doesn't quite forget it's a pub, but the kitchen offers better food than many others with the gastro tag. Pints of prawns with mayonnaise, well-made fresh fish pie with mornay sauce, and sandwiches of roast beef and Gloucester Old Spot bacon are ideal lunchtime fare for hungry workers. Gooseberry crumble made the best use of seasonal produce. Friendly, practised service was not as prompt as diners who need to head back to the office might wish, but the Gun makes every day feel like Friday.
Babies and children welcome: high chairs. Disabled: toilet. No-smoking tables. Separate rooms for parties, seating 14 and 24. Tables outdoors (11, terrace).

Shoreditch

Fox
28 Paul Street, EC2A 4LB (7729 5708). Old Street tube/rail. **Open** noon-11pm Mon-Fri. **Lunch served** 12.30-3pm, **dinner served** 6.30-10pm Mon-Fri. **Set meal** £16.50 2 courses, £21.50 3 courses. **Main courses** £11.50-£13.50. **Credit** MC, V.
Wrestle your way through the crowds that fill the busy ground-floor bar and head upstairs to a quiet (midweek at least) haven of dark wood, mirrors, chandeliers and wax candles. There's also a small, leafy terrace, perfect for warm summer evening dining. The regularly changing fixed-price menu is short but confident. Starters included brawn, razor clams, and tender asparagus with a perfect soft-boiled egg and nicely tart hollandaise. Chef Trish Hilferty is renowned for her expertise with fish, so next we chose a chunky serving of cod with buttery oven potatoes and aïoli. A dish of flatbread with caponata (a flavoursome pile of tomato and aubergine stew) would have benefited from something more – a green salad or a chunk of feta or halloumi, perhaps. Dessert included a chocolate and almond cake, and lemon posset, but a creamy honeyed semifreddo was the sweetest choice. Service was distracted (possibly due to our position out of eye-shot), yet friendly and efficient. With a

dozen reds and whites on the list (and a couple of rosés), ranging from £12 to £30, choosing a wine won't be a problem either.
Babies and children admitted (restaurant). Restaurant available for hire. Tables outdoors (6, terrace). **Map 6 Q4**.

Princess
76-78 Paul Street, EC2A 4NE (7729 9270). Old Street tube/rail. **Open** noon-11pm Mon-Fri; 5.30-11pm Sat; 12.30-5.30pm Sun. **Lunch served** 12.30-3pm Mon-Fri; 1-4pm Sun. **Dinner served** 6.30-10.30pm Mon-Sat. **Main courses** £11.95-£14.95. **Credit** AmEx, MC, V.
We raved about the Princess last year, and it was a finalist in the Best Gastropub category of the 2005 Time Out Eating & Drinking Awards. Twelve months on, however, a lunchtime visit left us disappointed. Sure, the rooms themselves are hard to fault (pub downstairs, restaurant upstairs, both with friendly serving staff and a relaxed, retro vibe), but the food wasn't up to its usual stellar standard. A perfect pairing of plump seared scallops with lively harissa and lemon rocket got things off to a great start. A main course of pan-fried sea bream fillet with a warm salad of beetroot, almonds and pancetta, and sorrel aïoli also worked well, though the presence of several moderately sized fish bones was offputting. More of a let-down was slow-roast leg of kid with potatoes, wild oregano and lemon – a dull, unrelenting mound of meat and spuds. Of the (only) four desserts, the most tempting one was off (the charming waitress at least smiled as she broke the news), though a meringue with fresh strawberries and mascarpone was a perfect second choice. Certainly not a bad meal, and perhaps our expectations were too high, but the Princess needs to raise her game if she's to retain her crown.
Babies and children admitted. Restaurant available for hire. **Map 6 Q4**.

Royal Oak
73 Columbia Road, E2 7RG (7729 2220/ www.royaloaklondon.com). Bethnal Green tube/Old Street tube/rail/26, 48, 55 bus. **Open** 6-11pm Mon-Thur; noon-midnight Fri, Sat;

noon-11pm Sun. **Lunch served** noon-4pm Sat, Sun. **Dinner served** 6-10pm Mon-Sat; 6-9pm Sun. **Credit** AmEx, MC, V.
This vibrant corner pub found a home crowd pretty swiftly after a spring 2005 refit; it's packed with diners and drinkers most evenings. Some locals find the place too fashiony, and we can't disagree; this is the only pub we know with a magnifying mirror in both the ladies and gents. For all that, there's a great atmosphere, and it looks good too: still a proper boozer with old brewery insignia, a central bar with attendant barflys, and light pouring in from the wraparound windows. Food, from a surprise-free gastro menu, isn't at all bad, with top marks for fresh artichokes in a summer salad, watercress with actual buds, and tasty lamb and ratatouille. But prices aren't low, especially considering that table service in the bar involves diffident staff plonking the food down in front of you, no questions asked. We didn't much like the stale nuts or untended toilets, either. You can get Timothy Taylor Landlord and Adnams on tap, plus capably mixed cocktails and wines from a so-so list with seasonal sections. There's a pleasant dining room upstairs, open Thursday to Saturday evenings and for Sunday lunch, when the Royal Oak is enlivened by the flower market's flotsam clientele (and you'd do well to book).
Babies and children welcome: high chairs. Booking advisable. No-smoking tables. Restaurant available for hire. Separate room for parties, seats 40. Tables outdoors (4, yard). **Map 6 S3**.

Stratford

King Edward VII **NEW**
47 Broadway, E15 4BQ (8534 2313/www.king eddie.co.uk). Stratford tube/rail/DLR. **Open** noon-11pm Mon-Wed; noon-midnight Thur-Sat; noon-11.30pm Sun. **Meals served** noon-10pm daily. **Main courses** £7.50-£14. **Credit** MC, V.
Opening a gastropub in Stratford six years before the 2012 Olympics? Now that takes some vision. Head chef Kerwin Browne's CV takes in Gordon Ramsay and Lindsay House as well the Hartley gastropub near Tower Bridge. Though there are

RESTAURANTS

some Mediterranean-inspired dishes (such as prosciutto with preserved lemon and goat's curd), British produce seems to be the focus at King Eddie's, a claim reinforced by the rear dining room's educational 'What's Coming In, What's Going Out' board listing seasonal produce. Fat, fleshy pilchards and tomatoes on toast (bread is made on the premises) and a borlotti bean salad were tasty starters, but way too large. Main courses (breadcrumbed plaice, and ribeye, both served with thick-cut chips cooked in duck fat) were gargantuan. Good desserts included a nicely textured cranachan and a moist, well-flavoured chocolate cake served with poached cherries and ice-cream. Drinks include English bottles from Chapel Down winery, and Scottish brews such as Fraoch heather ale and Innis & Gunn's oak-aged beer with its flavours of vanilla, toffee and whisky. Service in the restaurant was a little slow, but friendly. If you're just looking for a drink and a chat, head to the rear bar or courtyard. The front bar is welcoming but terribly noisy.
Babies and children admitted. Entertainment: acoustic/open mic 8pm Thur. No-smoking tables. Separate room for parties, seats 32. Tables outdoors (7, yard).

North East
Hackney

Cat & Mutton
76 Broadway Market, E8 4QJ (7254 5599/ www.catandmutton.co.uk). Liverpool Street tube/rail then 26, 48 or 55 bus/London Fields rail. **Open** 6-11pm Mon; noon-11pm Tue-Thur, Sun; noon-midnight Fri, Sat. **Lunch served** noon-3pm Tue-Sat; noon-5pm Sun. **Dinner served** 6-10pm Mon-Sat. **Main courses** £9-£16.50. **Set lunch** (Mon) £12.50 2 courses, £15 3 courses. **Credit** AmEx, MC, V.
This corner boozer has come on since its 'bare-brick-and-girders' refurb a few years back. Mismatching wooden chairs and tables are filled with hungry punters ordering simple, well-cooked food from the daily-changing blackboard menu. On the downside, plenty of other customers come in for a pint and a fag – and might be sitting (and chuffing) beside you if you don't choose your table carefully. Upstairs is quieter (but buzz-free). A tasty starter of crab and salmon fish cakes came with own-made tartare sauce and a small dressed salad. Chunky pieces of crab were combined, not unpleasantly, with carrot. Other options included asparagus with hollandaise sauce and rock oysters. Mains of poussin, and herb-crusted salmon were overlooked in favour of a huge rump steak (well-done rather than medium as ordered) served in a bowl with a rather watery red wine gravy (meaning the chips became soggy). Better was a good-sized mackerel in herb and garlic butter, served with Cornish new potatoes and a pile of tasty samphire. Desserts included eton mess with kirsch, and British cheeses with plum chutney. The extensive wine list has a Klippenkop chenin blanc and a quaffable house red.
Babies and children welcome (until 8pm): high chairs. Disabled: toilet. No-smoking tables. Separate room for parties, seats 50. Tables outdoors (5, pavement).

North
Archway

St John's
91 Junction Road, N19 5QU (7272 1587). Archway tube. **Open** 5-11pm Mon-Thur; noon-11pm Fri, Sat; noon-10.30pm Sun. **Lunch served** noon-3pm Fri; noon-4pm Sat, Sun. **Dinner served** 6.30-11pm Mon-Sat; 6.30-9.30pm Sun. **Main courses** £10.50-£15. **Credit** AmEx, MC, V.
Entering St John's on the pub side, we were immediately impressed by its high-ceilinged airiness. Yet this didn't prepare us for the huge restaurant at the back, absolutely heaving on a Saturday night with an older north-London crowd. Stylistically it's a quirky mix: mossy green

paintwork; a long, gleaming bar; a high, vaulted bronze ceiling; and a wall crammed with macabre artwork. All this sits oddly with the vibrant buzz of happy diners. Overstretched staff valiantly provided good-humoured service. The wine list offers great variety at a range of prices. But our high expectations weren't quite met by the food. To start, seared squid with chorizo and grilled peppers was delectably tender, but an undressed salad of endive, frisée, broad beans, tomato and feta was redolent of a supermarket chiller cabinet. Next, charred ribeye steak with superlative chunky chips would please any meat-eater. We also loved our moist pan-fried hake, but found the intensity of the accompanying rice (in rich, gloopy squid ink, rimmed with creamy garlic aïoli) overwhelming. A velvety chocolate, date and orange ice-cream saved the day. Always fully booked at weekends, St John's is obviously getting things right most of the time – we'll certainly try again.
Babies and children welcome: high chairs. Booking essential. Restaurant available for hire. Tables outdoors (6, patio). **Map 26 B1**.

Camden Town & Chalk Farm

Engineer
65 Gloucester Avenue, NW1 8JH (7722 0950/ www.the-engineer.com). Chalk Farm tube/31, 168 bus. **Open** 9am-11pm Mon-Sat; 9am-10.30pm Sun. **Breakfast served** 9-11.30am Mon-Fri; 9am-noon Sat, Sun. **Lunch served** noon-3pm Mon-Fri; 12.30-4pm Sat, Sun. **Dinner served** 7-11pm Mon-Sat; 7-10.30pm Sun. **Main courses** £12.50-£16.75. **Credit** MC, V.
The Engineer isn't the hot table that it used to be, but the place is still popular enough to feel it can impose two-hour time slots for diners. The menu remains international and experimental, although anyone with a conservative palate will still find things to appeal, including a beautiful char-grilled organic sirloin steak served with chips the size and shape of Mars bars. All the food is well executed and beautifully presented, but the highlight for us was a chicken breast rubbed with pesto and stuffed with pumpkin, ricotta and sage, and served on a mound of risoni pasta. It's worth leaving room for dessert, as some of these are even more intriguing than the mains – what, for instance, to expect from 'warm gingerbread, chilli grilled pineapple, coconut ice-cream'? We sampled three puddings and all were gorgeous, although you should steer clear of the whisky fruit cake if you're driving (especially if you had the tequila-cured salmon and miso-marinated cod as your previous courses). The atmosphere is convivial, and the service prompt and friendly.
Babies and children welcome (restaurant): children's menu; high chairs. Disabled: toilet. No-smoking tables (lunch Sun). Separate rooms for parties, seating 20 and 32. Tables outdoors (15, garden). **Map 27 B2**.

★ Lansdowne
90 Gloucester Avenue, NW1 8HX (7483 0409). Chalk Farm tube/31, 168 bus. **Bar Open** noon-11pm Mon-Fri; 9.30am-11pm Sat; 9.30am-10.30pm Sun. **Breakfast served** 9.30-11.30am Sat, Sun. **Lunch served** noon-3pm Mon-Fri; 12.30-3.30pm Sat; noon-4pm Sun. **Dinner served** 7-10pm Mon-Sat; 7-9.30pm Sun. *Restaurant* **Lunch served** 1-3pm Sat, Sun. **Dinner served** 7-10pm daily. *Both* **Main courses** £10-£16.50. **Credit** MC, V.
Getting a table isn't easy in the downstairs bar of this perennially popular pub. The favoured technique seems to be to stand with folded arms staring at anyone with a table, trying to will them away. We shared for a while on an outsized round table scattered with newspaper supplements, until the waitress sweetly bagged us seats near the back door. Quite a contrast to the off-hand, 'I'm too cool to speak to you' chap behind the bar, from whom we ordered Deuchars IPA and a nicely chilled glass of gamay. The scrawled blackboard menu is difficult to read, but contains a short, gutsy list that's not afraid to indulge in premium ingredients like foie gras. Near the bar you'll find other

possibilities including pizzas (a very popular choice) and bar nibbles. Lamb chops came with grainy tabouleh and harissa dressing to make a satisfying main course; whole red snapper with sausage, tomato and romanesco was even more generously proportioned and the fish beautifully cooked. Own-cured salmon with beetroot pickle and Jersey royals tempted too. To finish: chocolate biscuit cake with cashew cream, apple crumble with custard, or vanilla panna cotta with strawberries and white balsamic vinegar. No wonder families bring children and grandparents here: there's something for everyone.
Babies and children welcome: high chairs. Booking advisable (restaurant). Disabled: toilet. Restaurant available for hire. Tables outdoors (5, pavement). **Map 27 B2**.

Crouch End

★ Queens Pub & Dining Room **NEW**
2006 RUNNER-UP BEST GASTROPUB
26 Broadway Parade, N8 9DE (8340 2031). Finsbury Park tube/rail then W3, W7 bus. **Open** noon-midnight daily. **Meals served** noon-10.30pm Mon-Sat; noon-9pm Sun. **Main courses** £8.50-13.50. **Credit** MC, V.
A bona fide classic of Victoriana, the Queens has been quietly brought up to date with glossy red paint (on the ornate plasterwork ceilings), planters (cool zinc things in the entrance) and posh food, but otherwise retains its might and majesty. The gastropub fare is first rate. Chef Torren Lewis, who heads up the open-plan kitchen at the back of the (no-smoking) dining room, has created a enticing mix of restaurant-style dishes and informal pub classics. You could go for ham hock and smoked chicken terrine, or calamari with green bean and beetroot salad; or perhaps simpler fare, such as battered cod and chips with mushy peas, or bacon and cheeseburger. Desserts – banana panna cotta, white chocolate mousse – were solid too, if missing a few British numbers. Much of the crowd were young, though a few old regulars clung defiantly to the bar (and weren't eating). Service was good if a tad haphazard come settling-up time, but by then we were past caring, having sampled several of the wines on a decent list (tempranillo from Navarra was great value at £13.50) and some flavour-busting pints (Greene King IPA and Bombardier).
Babies and children welcome (until 6pm): children's menu; high chairs. Booking advisable. Disabled: toilet. No-smoking tables. Tables outdoors (10, garden).

Highgate

Bull
13 North Hill, N6 4AB (0845 4565 033/ www.inthebull.biz). Highgate tube. **Open** 5-11pm Mon; 11am-11pm Tue-Sat; 11am-10.30pm Sun. **Lunch served** noon-2.30pm Tue-Fri; noon-3.30pm Sat, Sun. **Dinner served** 6-10.30pm Mon-Sat; 6.30-9.30pm Sun. **Main courses** £13.50-£24.50. **Credit** MC, V.
The Bull makes the most of its position on leafy North Hill with a stylish front terrace (a prime summer destination), and an upstairs dining area with tree-framed views. The drinking and eating aspects of the operation sit awkwardly together – if you just want a beer, you'd be better off at one of the many pubs up the road – but the lack of good places to eat in the area make this a welcome destination. Prices are premium, but standards are generally high, and there are discount options such as the express lunch menu. A special of pork fillet and a superb shepherd's pie maintained the kitchen's reputation for fine meat cookery. The own-made bread is excellent, and is proffered generously. Apple pie was good enough for a prize at a county fair and, like the chocolatey 'gateau opera' with espresso syrup and ice-cream, was enthusiastically passed around for sampling. The wine list is rather sophisticated, but aims to help with occasionally descriptive categories such as 'light red with a twist' and 'for the passionate and mad about riesling'. There's also Leffe on tap, and Fentiman's ginger beer for the designated drivers.

Babies and children welcome: children's menu; high chairs. Disabled: toilet. No-smoking tables. Separate room for parties, seats 70. Tables outdoors (16, terrace).

Islington

★ Charles Lamb NEW

2006 RUNNER-UP BEST GASTROPUB

16 Elia Street, N1 8DE (7837 5040/ www.thecharleslambpub.com). Angel tube. **Open/meals served** 4-11pm Mon-Wed; noon-11pm Thur-Sun. **Main courses** £8-£11. **Credit** MC, V.

This gorgeous, little-known corner pub is well worth a trip across London. Tucked away off the hideous City Road on a noiseless sidestreet, the Charles Lamb feels like it has been plucked from a village green in Somerset, and indeed the inspiration for its food and drink is noticeably bucolic. On a warm Friday lunchtime we were welcomed by the cheery young landlord who was busy chalking up a mouth-watering summer menu: whole crab with new potatoes, mayonnaise and salad; smoked salmon and potato salad; chilled beetroot and apple soup with crème fraîche and dill. On his recommendation we plumped for a bowl of the latter and were rewarded with a mouthful of flavours: raspberry lollipops oddly being the most prominent. The salmon was fresh, simply prepared and generously portioned: perfect for a June lunch. The interior – split into main bar, cosy lounge and the kind of snug that can snatch away whole afternoons – has been carefully modernised, while retaining its quirks and charms. On the quiet pavement there's a handful of benches for eating; the exterior is festooned with flowers. Timothy Taylor Landlord, Fuller's Honeydew, Leffe and Amstel are on tap, while pleasingly murky bottles of Breton cider fill the fridges.
Babies and children welcome: children's portions. Bookings not accepted. No-smoking tables. Restaurant available for hire. Tables outdoors (6, pavement). **Map 5 O2.**

★ Drapers Arms

44 Barnsbury Street, N1 1ER (7619 0348/ www.thedrapersarms.co.uk). Angel tube/ Highbury & Islington tube/rail. **Open** noon-11pm Mon-Sat; noon-10.30pm Sun. **Lunch served** noon-3pm Mon-Sun. **Dinner served** 7-10pm Mon-Sat; 6.30-9.30pm Sun. **Main courses** £11-£15. **Credit** AmEx, MC, V.

The Drapers is several cuts above your average gastropub. It's not just the secluded location on a leafy sidestreet that sets it apart from tawdry Upper Street: the service is spot on, the food terrific and the ambience one of cool professionalism. You can eat downstairs in the pub proper, in the lovely garden out back, or upstairs in a large, airy dining room that seems lifted from a glossy magazine feature on 'elegantly understated interiors' – a classic but slightly raffish look echoed in the waiters' smart attire. Dishes come from the safer, more solid end of the gastro menu, but are beautifully executed. We enjoyed a splendid parfait of chicken livers and foie gras the size, shape and consistency of a block of room-temperature butter; a massive inch-thick pork chop on baked beetroot and spinach; and a fillet of sea bream on feisty crab mash. Flavours are intense (the pork chop was set off by a smear of melted goat's cheese) and well defined, with no mucking about. There are other nice touches too, such as the pot of own-made garlicky houmous that arrives with the complimentary bread. Prices may be a quid or two more than elsewhere, but it's money well spent.
Babies and children admitted (until 7pm unless dining). No-smoking tables. Tables outdoors (20, garden). **Map 5 N1.**

Duchess of Kent

441 Liverpool Road, N7 8PR (7609 7104/ www.geronimo-inns.co.uk). Highbury & Islington tube/rail. **Open** noon-11pm Mon-Thur, Sun; noon-midnight Fri, Sat. **Lunch served** noon-3pm Mon-Fri; noon-4pm Sat. **Dinner served** 7-10pm Mon-Thur; 7-10.30pm Fri, Sat.

Horseshoe. See p115.

Meals served noon-10pm Sun. **Main courses** £6-£14. **Credit** MC, V.

The Duchess, a corner pub in an off-the-beaten-track residential neighbourhood, does an excellent job of serving the locals, but is less exemplary when it comes to providing a fine-dining experience. The menu is decent enough, with standards of steamed mussels, smoked duck salad or tomato and shallot tart for starters, and the likes of veal burger, baked sea bass and rump steak as mains, supplemented by a board of daily specials. However, the execution is patchy. On a recent Sunday visit, starters were fine, very good even, but a bland pork chop came accompanied by some horribly glutinous rice; and the fish cakes, which arrived glistening with oil, were hugely stodgy. There's no real separation between diners and drinkers, so an intimate dinner à deux may take place against a background of lads on the lash after an afternoon on the five-a-side pitch. The route to the toilets meanders through the tables, so your meal is accompanied by bracing blasts of urinal cake as the door to the gents swings back and forth every few minutes. Drinks are better, with a couple of real ales on tap, a decent Bloody Mary (free with Sunday lunch) and an estimable number of wines by the glass.
Babies and children admitted (until 6pm). Disabled: toilet. No-smoking tables. Tables outdoors (10, pavement).

★ Duke of Cambridge

30 St Peter's Street, N1 8JT (7359 3066/ www.dukeorganic.co.uk). Angel tube. **Open** noon-11pm Mon-Sat; noon-10.30pm Sun. **Lunch served** 12.30-3pm Mon-Fr; 12.30-3.30pm Sat, Sun. **Dinner served** 6.30-10.30pm Mon-Sat; 6.30-10pm Sun. **Main courses** £10-£18. **Credit** AmEx, MC, V.

Contented diners come back time and again to the Duke of Cambridge for its tasty organic food, great wines and beers, and friendly, laid-back yet efficient service. There's nothing po-faced about the commitment to provide only the freshest seasonal organic delights. On our visit the blackboard menu changed frequently throughout the evening. We were mightily impressed by the extensive and informative list of over 50 organic wines, many served by the glass. Feeling enlightened and emboldened, we chose an Austrian bio-dynamic wine (grown according to a holistic farming system based on lunar and cosmic rhythms) completely new to us – a great zesty, peppery Meinklang Grüner Veltliner, Neusiedler See, full of citrus fruit tones. This sat perfectly with robust starters of roast butternut squash with mozzarella; and smoked mackerel and salmon with beetroot and horseradish cream. Our taste buds were singing. Mains of darne of pollock with chorizo and cannellini bean stew and swiss chard, and a rich coq au vin with artichoke mash hit all the right spots. Eyeing our neighbours' puds, we were full of regret not to have room for semolina and blackcurrant pudding or banana cake with rum and raisin ice-cream. Never has healthy eating been more fun.
Babies and children welcome: children's portions; high chairs. No-smoking tables. Tables outdoors (5, pavement). **Map 5 O2.**

House

63-69 Canonbury Road, N1 2DG (7704 7410/ www.inthehouse.biz). Highbury & Islington tube/rail. **Open** 5-11pm Mon; noon-11pm Tue-Sat; noon-10.30pm Sun. **Lunch served** 12.30-2.30pm Tue-Fri; 12.30-3.30pm Sat, Sun. **Dinner served** 6.30-10.30pm Mon-Sat; 6.30-9.30pm Sun. **Main courses** £13.50-£23. **Credit** MC, V.

Blurring the lines between a bar and restaurant, the triangular House – white walls, dark wood and beautiful floral displays – keeps drinkers and diners happy. Move from the cosy bar space to the more formal dining area and check the blackboard for specials; these usually include a couple of fish and vegetarian dishes. Friendly service is neither over-attentive nor lackadaisical, adding to the relaxed ambience. Sashimi of wild sea bass, yuzu and pickled ginger was super-delicate, light and flavourful. Fritto misto of

vegetables with chive mayonnaise started better than it finished (serving it in a bowl meant the batter was pretty soggy halfway down). Tuna with niçoise arrived à point, with a sauce ravigote and parmesan crisp. Equally impressive was lamb imam bayildi: wonderfully tender meat pressed with cracked coriander seeds, served in a rich jus. Portions were ample and a side order of chips couldn't be finished. Desserts included a Valhrona chocolate pudding with espresso ice-cream, and La Fromagerie cheeses with own-made walnut bread. From Tuesday to Friday there's a bargain express-lunch available.
Babies and children welcomed: children's menu; high chairs. Disabled: toilet. No-smoking tables. Restaurant available for hire. Tables outdoors (4, garden).

★ Marquess Tavern NEW

2006 WINNER BEST GASTROPUB
32 Canonbury Street, N1 2TB (7354 2975). Angel tube/Highbury & Islington tube/rail. **Open** noon-11pm Mon-Thur, Sun; noon-midnight Fri, Sat. **Meals served** 12.30-10pm daily. **Main courses** £8-£18. **Credit** AmEx, MC, V.

Approach the bar at the Marquess and it will immediately become clear this is a serious gastropub. The fridges in the gorgeous, meandering bar area (battered leather sofas, rickety chairs, nice little nooks and – get this – a bar billiards room) are stuffed not with Red Bulls and Irish cider, but exotic bottled ales. A 9th-century Pictish nettle beer from Scotland is a classic example of the 40-odd ales offered (there are 40 malt whiskies too). Food, served in the airy and attractive open dining room at the rear, is, we are told, based on '1940s English cuisine'. So, there's potted salmon and pickled cucumber; sardines and tomatoes on toast; whole crab, mayonnaise and raspberry salad (a feast); and duck leg, potatoes, bacon and carrots. All this is superb, clearly explained by the knowledgeable and charming waiter, and cooked beautifully without fuss or frippery by kitchen staff drawn from the Ivy and St John. The wine list is inspiring too, the highlights being some English sparkling wines (Camel Valley Brut 2004 from Cornwall, anyone?). The only quibble was with the cheese: no doubt about the quality of the beenleigh blue, Cornish yarg or waterloo, but the plate needed a good hour longer out of the fridge.
Babies and children welcome (until 6pm): high chairs. No-smoking tables. Restaurant available for hire. Tables outdoors (4, patio). **Map 5 O2.**

Northgate

113 Southgate Road, N1 3JS (7359 7392). Essex Road rail/38, 73 bus. **Open** 5-11pm Mon-Thur; 5pm-midnight Fri; noon-midnight Sat; noon-10.30pm Sun. **Lunch served** noon-4pm Sat, Sun. **Dinner served** 6.30-10.30pm Mon-Sat; 6.30-9.30pm Sun. **Main courses** £9.50-£14. **Credit** MC, V.

What looks from outside like an unreconstructed corner boozer hides a handful of post-rave photographs and a back dining room that's handsome in the accepted mode (red candles, dark-wood tables). On a hot evening we dined alfresco at a slightly ratty trestle table that had clearly done some service over the day. To start, tequila-cured salmon on corn blini with dill crème fraîche was so bland we wished we'd essayed the king prawns with papaya and wasabi. In contrast, baby potato salad with prosciutto, a zingy sprig of shiso cress and a fruity/sweet lemon dressing was a real hit. The roast beef with giant (and pleasantly doughy) yorkshire pudding was disappointingly pub grade, ingratiating itself with the Sunday family trade by portion size, though the meaty jus and quality roast veg (tatties enhanced by turnip and swede) get an honourable mention. The mascarpone would have made our butternut squash risotto too rich for some, but was spot on for us. For pudding we could have had Kahlúa tiramisu or some cheeses from La Fromagerie, but did we mention the portion sizes? Good drinking options include three real ales on tap, and two dozen wines.

Inn at Kew Gardens. See p117.

Babies and children admitted (patio, restaurant). Booking advisable weekends. No-smoking tables. Tables outdoors (10, patio). **Map 6 Q1.**

Social

33 Linton Street, Arlington Square, N1 7DU (7354 5809/www.thesocial.com). Angel tube. **Open** 5-11pm Mon-Fri; noon-11pm Sat; noon-10.30pm Sun. **Meals served** 5-10.30pm Mon-Fri; 12.30-10.30pm Sat; 12.30-9.30pm Sun. **Main courses** £7.50-£14. **Credit** MC, V.

Hidden in the backstreets south of Essex Road, the Social isn't conveniently located, but there was a warm welcome from the unaffectedly friendly waitress. We settled in the dining section, separated by a bar counter and open hot-plate from the main pub. The rather limited menu did little to engage our enthusiasm, with only one veggie main, a lot of heavy meat, and frequent recurrence of certain ingredients (balsamic vinegar, lemon, stilton). Worse, the cooking was inattentive. Roast asparagus arrived wrapped in crispy parma ham on a bed of little gem lettuce, with an overdone poached egg and a balsamic reduction that was far too sweet. The balsamic char-grilled lamb cutlets, with minted mashed peas, spinach and minty yoghurt sauce, were closer to well-done than the pink we'd been offered; the dish was presented in a careful pyramid to a table of regulars, but to us as a jumble slathered with yoghurt sauce. Even the char-grilled Argentinian rump steak came less than rare and with a stilton butter not especially blessed with stilton. The cheese selection was short on surprises; the house red was a decent vin de pays rather than the listed tempranillo. Comfortable and relaxed, but disappointing.

Babies and children welcome (until 6pm Sat, Sun): high chairs. Entertainment: DJs 7pm Fri, Sat, 4pm Sun. No-smoking tables. Restaurant available for hire. Separate room for parties, seats 40. Tables outdoors (2, pavement). **Map 5 P2.**

Kentish Town

Junction Tavern

101 Fortess Road, NW5 1AG (7485 9400/www.junctiontavern.co.uk). Tufnell Park tube/Kentish Town tube/rail. **Open** noon-11pm Mon-Sat; noon-10.30pm Sun. **Lunch served** noon-3pm Mon-Fri; noon-4pm Sat. **Dinner served** 6.30-10.30pm Mon-Sat; 6.30-9.30pm Sun. **Main courses** £10.50-£14.50. **Set lunch** (Sun) £15 2 courses. **Credit** MC, V.

The garden (little statuary included) at the back of the Junction Tavern is a very pleasurable place to relax for an afternoon. It is accordingly popular: so much so that on a summer Sunday, some of the food seemed to be running out. Never fear, though, for staff dealt with last-minute menu changes with friendly aplomb. As refreshers, the imaginative salads were right on the money, the quality of fresh ingredients being highly impressive: goat's cheese, asparagus and dried prosciutto (more like bacon), and a lovely, delicately flavoured mix of roquefort, celery, apple and toasted almonds. After such a start we feared the mains might feel a bit heavy, but a generous braised duck leg with peas, spinach and a tapenade jus, and poached salmon with a dill sauce, asparagus and more peas – the kitchen seems to like them – showed the same nicely balanced, distinctive mix of flavours and textures. You can also eat in the big, old, wood-lined bar area, or in the slightly comfier dining room. Wines from an enterprising list are properly served, and there's a changing, high-quality beer selection. A worthy contender in the gastropub stakes.

Babies and children admitted (restaurant). Booking advisable. Tables outdoors (15, garden). **Map 26 B4.**

Oxford

256 Kentish Town Road, NW5 2AA (7485 3521/www.realpubs.co.uk). Kentish Town tube/rail. **Open** noon-11.30pm Mon-Thur; noon-midnight Fri, Sat; noon-10.30pm Sun. **Lunch served** noon-3.30pm Mon-Fri; noon-5pm Sat. **Dinner served** 6-10pm Mon-Sat. **Meals served** noon-9pm Sun. **Main courses** £9-£13. **Credit** MC, V.

A big old Victorian pub, the Oxford hits all the gastropub buttons with a high-ceilinged dining area painted black, leather seats in the bar, an imaginative menu, and tables on a wide pavement outside. Certain things help the place stand out from the crowd: friendly and very able service; and a genuinely welcoming, easy-going buzz, in both bar and dining space. There's a big fiery range in the open kitchen, so char-grilling features strongly in the cooking – a bit too strongly in a starter of squid with black bean and ginger salsa, which was a tad sooty. Things picked up with a great pork chop in rosemary, cider and apple jus with bubble and squeak: an ultra-generous slab of good meat delicately flavoured, with slices of baked apple for an extra touch of freshness. For something lighter, there are original fish and vegetarian dishes, and moreish sandwiches at lunchtime. The drinks range shows the same blend of care and generosity as the food menu, with excellent bitters as well as superior lagers, and a bargain list of quality wines.

Booking advisable. Children admitted. Entertainment: jazz 8.30pm Mon. Disabled: toilet. Separate room for parties, seats 18. Tables outdoors (6, pavement). **Map 26 B5.**

Tufnell Park

Lord Palmerston

33 Dartmouth Park Hill, NW5 1HU (7485 1578/www.geronimo-inns.co.uk). Tufnell Park tube. **Open** noon-11pm Mon-Sat; noon-10.30pm Sun. **Lunch served** 12.30-3pm Mon-Sat; 1-4pm Sun. **Dinner served** 7-10pm Mon-Sat; 7-9pm Sun. **Main courses** £9-£14. **Credit** AmEx, JCB, MC, V.

Prime seats at this laid-back pub are the front pavement benches and the stools by the central bar. There are many other options, though, as the premises seem to stretch endlessly at the back and upstairs, with large, high-ceilinged rooms confidently decorated in floral wallpaper and bright colours. The good choice of draught beers includes Deuchars IPA and Bitburger. Belgian raspberry beer, Frambozenbier, is available by the bottle, and there are 16 wines by the glass including Yalumba viognier and Nautilus sauvignon blanc. Service on our visit was friendly and well meaning, though not helped by the difficult-to-read blackboard menu that caused confusion between availability of salmon and sirloin steaks. There was a tendency for long gaps between dishes arriving. Thai smoked fish cakes had a nice flavour but were unattractively presented on a salad with unripe tomato, and the advertised 'chilli jam' was just thai sweet chilli sauce. Curried mussels were bizarrely served with a side dish of veg but no starch. Confit duck was OK, but sat on a massive bed of salsa verde-flavoured green lentils, making the dish heavy-going. Turkey escalope with garlic jus was tough and dry. The kitchen needs to raise standards considerably to remain competitive.

Babies and children admitted. Bookings not accepted. Separate room for parties, seats 60. Tables outdoors (7, garden; 13, pavement). **Map 26 B3.**

North West

Belsize Park

Hill

94 Haverstock Hill, NW3 2BD (7267 0033). Belsize Park or Chalk Farm tube. **Open** noon-11pm Mon-Wed; 11am-midnight Thur-Sat; 12.30-11pm Sun. **Lunch served** noon-3pm, **dinner served** 7-10pm Mon-Sat. **Meals served** 12.30-9pm Sun. **Main courses** £11-£18. **Credit** MC, V.

A large potted cactus by the door has to be bad feng shui, but there was nothing spiky about the service here. Smiley, chatty staff did their best to accommodate us on a heavily booked night, even though we arrived on spec and an influx of people wanting to watch football on the smallish TV kept them busy. Blackboards above the bar advertise 'divine smoothies and Bloody good Marys'.

Draught beers include Honey Dew Organic and Amstel, and wines such as a pleasing Chilean sauvignon blanc are available by the small or large glass. Food was only just OK – a yellow curry contained fresh, succulent swordfish steak, but the sauce had the harsh taste of uncooked spices. We liked the crisp green beans accompanying it, though. Steak was correctly medium-rare, served with a grilled tomato, chips, béarnaise and too much gravy. Desserts weren't an improvement: weedy lemon tart, and a banoffi pie with too much cream and not enough toffee. Still, the Hill's a jolly place and its feminine decor – dusky green walls, gold stencilling, pink-striped love seat, and chandeliers – puts customers in a fun mood.

Babies and children admitted. No-smoking tables. Separate rooms for parties, seating 25 and 60. Tables outdoors (20, garden). **Map 28 C4.**

Hampstead

Horseshoe NEW

28 Heath Street, NW3 6TE (7431 7206). Hampstead tube. **Open** 10am-11pm Mon-Sat; 10am-10.30pm Sun. **Lunch served** 12.30-3.30pm Mon-Sat; noon-4.30pm Sun. **Dinner served** 6.30-10pm Mon-Sat; 6.30-9.30pm Sun. **Main courses** £8-£15. **Set lunch** (Mon-Fri) £7 1 course incl glass of wine and coffee. **Credit** MC, V.

This new dining pub has a microbrewery in the basement, which is a bit of a surprise in the heart of Hampstead. Landlord McLaughlin's own brews change but might include a summer beer and a bitter – when these run out, there are always other real ales (such as Adnams or Sharps). A split-level dining area has been created at the back of the pub, with tables shaped from old floorboards. The main bar would be spacious if it wasn't already so popular. 'Quality produce from farm to fork' is the headline on the menu, with lots of carefully sourced English ingredients. The roast of Red Poll beef had a light coating of black pepper and intensely flavoured gravy that made the large portion very moreish. Loin of lamb had a nice crust to its fatty layer and came with a refreshing sauté of courgettes, pine nuts and mint. We enjoyed a lovely crème brûlée with fresh blackberries, but a fruit trifle was too heavy on cream. This, and the exhausted service, were the only low points of an otherwise very enjoyable evening. The horseshoe is a traditional symbol of luck, and NW3 is doubly lucky to have this one.

Babies and children welcome: high chairs. Booking advisable. No-smoking tables. Tables outdoors (4, pavement). **Map 28 B2.**

Wells

30 Well Walk, NW3 1BX (7794 3785/www.thewellshampstead.co.uk). Hampstead tube. **Open** noon-11pm Mon-Sat; noon-10.30pm Sun. **Lunch served** noon-3pm Mon-Fri; noon-4pm Sat, Sun. **Dinner served** 5-10pm Mon-Fri; 7-10pm Sat; 7-9.30pm Sun. **Main courses** £12-£18. **Set lunch** (Sun) £20 2 courses, £25 3 courses. **Credit** MC, V.

A slight reshuffle of tables and sofas in the ground-floor bar has improved the layout and ambience of this trendy Hampstead village pub. More for locals than tourists, the bar offers games such as chess. In good weather, the tables outside this imposing Georgian structure are hugely popular. On our visit several potential diners left disappointed that they couldn't snare a table, some of which are covered with linen and reserved for dining. Service was willing but suffered from a language barrier and lack of training; our waitress struggled to explain the specials and couldn't tell the difference between ginger beer and ginger ale. For real ale fans there's Black Sheep and Adnams Broadside; other options include draught Grolsch and Stella Artois. We shared a plate of decent Spanish nibbles, and a moreish bowl of roast almonds. A burger, served with purple coleslaw, had a good char-grilled flavour. The pasta special made the most of seasonal asparagus and wild mushrooms. Desserts of rhubarb and apple crumble with custard, a rich and sizeable chocolate pot, and crunchy-topped crème brûlée

RESTAURANTS

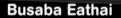

busaba

Busaba Eathai

Wardour Street
Phone 020-7255-8686
106-110 Wardour Street
London W1T 0TR

Store Street
Phone 020-7299-7900
22 Store Street
London WC1E 7DF
Pre-booking available
for groups of 12+
Take away available

Bird Street
Phone 020-7518-808
8–13 Bird Street
London W1U 1BU
Take away available

were ace, though lemon tart disappointed. While downstairs was buzzing, the restrained upstairs restaurant was quiet.

Babies and children welcome: children's menu; colouring books; high chairs. Disabled: toilet. Entertainment: jazz 8.30pm Mon (winter). No-smoking tables. Separate room for parties, seats 12. Tables outdoors (8, patio). **Map 28 C2.**

Queen's Park

Salusbury
50-52 Salusbury Road, NW6 6NN (7328 3286). Queens Park tube/rail. **Open** 5-11pm Mon; noon-11pm Tue-Sat; noon-10.30pm Sun. **Lunch served** 12.30-3.30pm Tue-Sun. **Dinner served** 7-10.15pm Mon-Sat; 7-10pm Sun. **Main courses** £11-£14.50. **Set lunch** (Tue-Fri) £5 1 course incl drink. **Credit** MC, V.

It's in the nature of gastropubs to have their ups and downs, and recently the Salusbury, hub of Queen's Park's trendy/gentrified enclave, has been on a high. The food is a touch more expensive than the pub norm, but in return is more imaginative and sophisticated than the routine char-grills and sausage-and-mash mix. Octopus salad with red onion and chickpeas is an original regular on the menu; it was beautifully done on our last visit, with first-rate ingredients freshly put together. Mozzarella, aubergine and tomato bruschetta had plenty of zest too. Seared tuna with sweet-and-sour onions and cannellini beans was the star of our mains: a generous piece of excellent fish cooked exactly right. Moist, richly flavoured pan-fried duck breast with braised chicory didn't lag far behind. Decor is classic gastropub, with stripped-down and battered old wood, and mirrors; the relaxing dining area is separate from the bar, which has kept a nicely unfussy, real pub feel. The temptation to settle in and hang around was increased by service that was charming and on the ball, and by our Côtes de Provence rosé (from a substantial, well-varied wine list) served chilled.
Babies and children welcome (until 7pm): high chairs. No smoking (restaurant). Tables outdoors (4, pavement).

Outer London
Kew, Surrey

★ Inn at Kew Gardens NEW
2006 RUNNER-UP BEST GASTROPUB
292 Sandycombe Road, Kew, Surrey TW9 3NG (8940 2220/www.theinnatkewgardens.com). Kew Gardens tube. **Open** 11am-11pm Mon-Thur, Sun; 11am-midnight Fri, Sat. **Lunch served** noon-3pm Mon-Fri; noon-4pm Sat, Sun. **Dinner served** 6-10pm Mon-Sat; 6-9pm Sun. **Main courses** £9.50-£13.50. **Credit** AmEx, MC, V.

A rustic bistro feel dominates the main dining room at the back of this tastefully refurbished boozer (cream wooden panelling, antique mirrors). A jump up the spiral staircase reveals an altogether more modern, clubby area: empty on a Saturday lunchtime. Still, food is the main draw. The menu features confidently executed gastropub classics (juicy ribeye, chips and grain mustard aïoli; toulouse sausages, olive oil mash and slow-roast plum tomatoes). We enjoyed a pair of sensational shared platters. The fish platter was crammed with goodies: plump prawns, smoked salmon, crab, salty anchovies, eel and a colourful saffron and garlic aïoli. The shared charcuterie arrived with slices of perfectly pink roast beef, smooth duck pâté, ham on the bone, smoked gammon and excellent horseradish and piccalilli. For pudding, chocolate fudge cake was served with banana ice-cream; and a moist, delicious cherry and almond tart with clotted cream. Well-kept Greene King IPA and Adnams Bitter are on draught. The wine list is also notable. Service is polite but too laid-back. At the rear is an attractive, small patio.
Babies and children welcome: children's portions. Disabled: toilet. No-smoking tables. Separate room for parties, seats 40. Tables outdoors (2, pavement; 8, terrace).

Global

It's like going on holiday without crossing the M25. You can discover representatives from a startling array of the world's cultures within London's boundaries: from large communities long associated with a particular district to tiny enclaves of national or religious groupings occupying otherwise mundane suburban backstreets. The rest of this guide celebrates the major culinary cultural influences on our city, but in this section you'll find the enticing rarities: oases of a treasured national cuisine such as Harrow's new Afghan venture, **Masa** – a Best Cheap Eats contender in the 2006 Time Out Eating & Drinking Awards – and the Edgware Road's stupendous Burmese, **Mandalay**. Iberian/Mediterranean stalwart **Eyre Brothers** in Shoreditch remains as enticing as ever. Hone your appetite, grab a travel pass and start exploring. You shouldn't miss it for the world.

Afghan

North
Islington

★ Afghan Kitchen
35 Islington Green, N1 8DU (7359 8019). Angel tube. **Lunch served** noon-3.30pm, **dinner served** 5.30-11pm Tue-Sat. **Main courses** £5-£6.50. **No credit cards**.

A tiny little place next to Islington Green, Afghan Kitchen has just a few tables at ground level and the same on the first floor. Nevertheless, it's surprisingly easy on the eye, with soothing pastel colours and blond-wood furnishings making best use of the confined space. Homespun Afghan cooking is the attraction for Islington locals, college students and office workers. The menu offers a limited range of pre-prepared dishes, akin to Indian curries, but milder and sweeter in nature. Banjon borani (squidgy fried baby aubergines, spiced with garlic and cumin) married well with the chill of a beaten yoghurt topping: marvellous for mopping up with hot flatbreads. Chicken curry also received the thumbs-up; we especially liked its soupy yoghurt-based masala spiked with dried mint and lemon juice. To accompany the food, try the doga, an Afghan take on Indian lassi made from churned yoghurt whisked with crushed mint and nutty-tasting toasted cumin – it's seriously thirst-quenching.
Babies and children admitted: high chairs. Booking advisable. Takeaway service. **Map 5 O2.**

Outer London
Harrow, Middlesex

★ ★ Masa NEW
2006 RUNNER-UP BEST CHEAP EATS
24-26 Headstone Drive, Harrow, Middx HA3 5QH (8861 6213). Harrow & Wealdstone tube/rail. **Meals served** noon-11pm daily. **Main courses** £4.95-£12. **Unlicensed. Corkage** no charge. **Credit** MC, V.

Trek to London's own north-western frontier to discover this source of appetising, well-priced Afghan home cooking. The menu at Masa incorporates a medley of flavours from the region. Expect meaty kebabs with strains of Middle Eastern character, central Asian dumplings, Indian-inspired curries, and a selection of pastas and flatbreads. On our visit, the pasta chef hadn't yet joined the kitchen team, so we plumped for a delectably smoky platter of well-marinated kebabs. Kobeda (minced chicken kebab) was milder than its Indian counterpart, and deliciously subtle with coriander and ginger spicing. Similarly, seared lamb chops, devoid of cloying masala, scored highly for simplicity; we mopped up the flavoursome juices with a super-sized naan. Next, quabili palow (spiced basmati rice, studded with tender lamb morsels) won plaudits for its fragrant seasoning of toasted cumin, cinnamon and cloves. A generous accompaniment of fiery chicken curry came spiked with the bite of red chillies and richness of fried onion paste; it overwhelmed our sweetly scented rice. Masa looks smart and showy with its sparkling open kitchen, oriental carpets, glossy granite flooring, and heavy wood panelling. Prices are low, and there's a BYO policy. Worth crossing zones for.
Babies and children welcome: high chairs. No-smoking tables. Takeaway service; delivery service (within 3-mile radius).

Southall, Middlesex

Kabul
First floor, Himalaya Shopping Centre, 65-67 The Broadway, Southall, Middx UB1 1LB (8571 6878). Southall rail. **Meals served** noon-midnight daily. **Main courses** £4.99-£9.99. **Credit** AmEx, MC, V.

Sited in a Southall shopping centre, this community café is kitted out in royal blue upholstery, fake greenery and an assortment of Afghan artefacts. Peaceful it isn't – expect blasts of Bollywood beats alongside golden oldie hits. In the past, we've been impressed with the calibre of cooking, which embraces a medley of earthy flavours from central Asia, India and the Middle East. A shame, then, that over the past year, standards seem to have slipped. On our latest visit, only the potato burani (deep-fried puffed bread, filled with lightly spiced mashed potato and diced onions) was memorable for its freshness. Quabli pulao, although scented with toasted cumin and garnished with plump raisins and shreds of carrot, was let down by leathery mutton pieces. Do pyaza lamb curry was just as lacklustre, poor-quality meat and oily onion masala adding to our disappointment. We can only hope for a return to past glories here.
Babies and children welcome: high chairs. No-smoking tables. Takeaway service; delivery service (within 3-mile radius).

Belgian

North
Belsize Park

Belgo Noord
72 Chalk Farm Road, NW1 8AN (7267 0718/ www.belgo-restaurants.com). Chalk Farm tube. **Lunch served** noon-3pm Mon-Fri. **Dinner served** 6-11pm Mon-Thur; 6-11.30pm Fri. **Meals served** noon-11.30pm Sat; noon-10.30pm Sun. **Main courses** £8.95-£17.95. **Set lunch** £5.95 1 course incl drink. **Credit** AmEx, DC, JCB, MC, V.
Descend into Belgo Noord's expansive cellar-like basement, and you'll find a fine selection of steamed mussels, crisp french fries and one of London's best Belgian beer lists. This is a popular spot with office workers and families with kids (making good use of special offers). Exposed metal pipes and concrete walls lend it an industrial vibe, which is softened by colourful posters and chunky wooden tables. Service is swift, friendly and knowledgeable. We gave top marks to a first course of juicy mussels, topped with silky-smooth creamed spinach, snippets of smoked bacon, and deliciously molten gruyère cheese. This dish comes with a mountain of golden fries and a pot of mayonnaise – it's not one for calorie-counters. Lamb carbonade, a hearty casserole simmered with beer and nutty-tasting browned onions, won our approval for its additional fruity twist of squishy plums and caramelised apple wedges. Less appealing was the waterzooi – a melange of seafood and sea bass fillets tossed in a sharply discordant lemon sauce. Despite the occasional slip, the food's generally decent, and the relaxed atmosphere makes this branch a more peaceable option than its busy Covent Garden sister.
Babies and children welcome: children's menu; colouring books; high chairs. **Map 27 B1.**

For branches (Belgo Centraal, Bierodrome) see index.

Burmese

Central
Edgware Road

★ ★ Mandalay
444 Edgware Road, W2 1EG (7258 3696/ www.mandalayway.com). Edgware Road tube. **Lunch served** noon-2.30pm, **dinner served** 6-10.30pm Mon-Sat. **Main courses** £3.90-£6.90. **Set lunch** £3.90 1 course, £5.90 3 courses. **Credit** AmEx, DC, JCB, MC, V.
Edgware Road isn't known for its tropical landscape, but it does contain a gem of a Burmese restaurant – London's one and only. Located amid a drab line of shops close to the incessant traffic, Mandalay is a small, family-run set-up. The easy-wipe tablecloths and touristy prints aren't much to write home about, but the cooking certainly is. Sharing influences with Thailand, India and China, Burmese cuisine celebrates contrasting flavours to great effect. Expect plenty of fish and seafood, fragrant bowls of rice and noodles, and light aromatic curries. We started with crisp-fried savoury fritters: a tasty, batter-coated tangle of shredded onions, broccoli florets and shrimps. They were similar to Indian bhajis but of almost tempura-like lightness. Twice-cooked fish curry (lime-steeped talapia fillets, fried and simmered in sweet-sour tomato and tamarind masala) was equally satisfying. If you enjoy healthy broths, opt for bottle gourd soup. Scented with toasted garlic slivers and containing shrimps, rice noodles and strips of the gourd, it makes a superb palate cleanser. Staff are passionate about their craft and happy to take curious customers on a guided tour of the menu.

Babies and children welcome: high chairs. Booking essential. No smoking. Takeaway service. Map 2 D4.

Irish

Central
Marylebone

O'Conor Don
88 Marylebone Lane, W1U 2PY (7935 9311/ www.oconordon.com). Bond Street tube. *Bar* **Open** noon-11pm Mon-Wed, Fri; noon-1am Thur. **Meals served** noon-3pm, 5-10pm Mon-Fri. *Restaurant* **Lunch served** noon-2.30pm, **dinner served** 6-10pm Mon-Fri. **Main courses** £9.95-£16. *Both* **Credit** AmEx, MC, V.
Rooted in Irish tradition, the O'Conor Don pub is a popular watering hole with nearby office workers. Upstairs, its restaurant is a favourite with Americans, especially those with Emerald Isle connections. Large windows flanked by weighty drapes, an abundance of Irish-themed pictures, and dark wood flooring add to the homespun feel. Although the menu includes modern interpretations of classic dishes, the best bets are simply executed Irish staples. Sea-fresh oysters, deliciously salty and astringent, made a perfect match with a pint of Guinness. Fried black pudding slices didn't rate as highly; a bit dry, they were marooned by a moat of sweet Calvados and cream sauce. Hearty Irish stew brought everything back on track. Crammed with meltingly tender lamb (cooked on the bone) and studded with pearly white potatoes and carrots, this classic rendition was comfort cooking at its best. An impressive beef casserole was just as satisfying, its glossy Guinness-based sauce working wonders with a mound of champ (buttery mash, flecked with

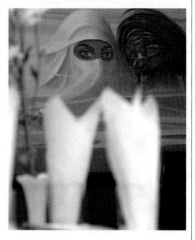

Masa. See p117.

sliced spring onions). We had no space for puddings, so the treacle tart and steamed sponge will have to wait until our next visit.
Babies and children admitted. Booking advisable. Restaurant available for hire; all areas available for hire. Separate bar for parties. **Map 9 G5**.

Mediterranean

Central

City

Royal Exchange Grand Café & Bar

The Royal Exchange, EC3V 3LR (7618 2480/ www.conran.com). Bank tube/DLR. **Breakfast served** 8-11am Mon-Fri. **Meals served** 11.30am-10pm Mon-Fri. **Main courses** £6.50-£14.50. **Credit** AmEx, DC, MC, V.
Hidden from the street and surrounded by bijou shops aimed firmly at City salaries, this Conran venture mutates from calm breakfast haunt (grilled bacon focaccia, croissant, muesli) through to buzzing cocktail bar. Seats aplenty are dotted about the Royal Exchange's grand hall concourse and the mezzanine areas. We chose the latter at lunch, all the better to look down on the action below, centred round a large oval bar. Service comes with a smile in this upmarket location. Indeed, the least satisfactory part of the experience was the food. Grilled chicken noodle salad was good, with succulent bird and punchy dressing, but penne with rocket pesto, sun-blush tomato and olive was workaday, with a slightly too bitter tang – all for £11.50. Perhaps we should have gone for the seafood (oysters galore, langoustine mayonnaise,

or even toasted lobster sandwich). It's worth having at least have a coffee here, in what is possibly the grandest premises in London. Conran's new French restaurant Sauterelle is also based here.
Babies and children admitted (restaurant). Bookings not accepted. Disabled: toilet. Dress: smart casual. **Map 12 Q6**.

West

Hammersmith

Snow's on the Green

166 Shepherd's Bush Road, W6 7PB (7603 2142/ www.snowsonthegreen.co.uk). Hammersmith tube. **Lunch served** noon-3pm Mon-Fri. **Dinner served** 6-11pm Mon-Sat. **Main courses** £10.50-£16. **Set meal** £13.50 2 courses, £17.50 3 courses. **Credit** AmEx, DC, MC, V.
This long-standing restaurant opposite Brook Green was rammed on a midweek evening. The indifferent decor (mushroom walls, black floorboards) and subdued lighting meant that all attention was focused on the food. Rightly so. The menu is long – and quite expensive, with most mains hovering around £16, although there's a good-value set menu too – but the kitchen didn't falter, churning out a stream of successful dishes. Marinated swordfish garnished with cubes of tomato and potato, capers and olives made a zingy starter, while a mini soufflé of smoked haddock and cheddar atop just-so spinach was fluffy and comforting (both dishes from the set menu). There's no stinting on portion size, so choosing two starters instead of a starter and main is an option. Open ravioli with crab, salt cod, coconut and chilli was an unctuous delight, with each flavour distinct (no mean feat). Puds included a light almond, lemon and ricotta cake with a nicely tart currant compote. The only dud dish was an oily

starter of goat's cheese, broad bean and pancetta gratin. Other pluses: lots of by-the-glass choices on the New World-oriented wine list; and on-the-ball service that only wobbled when it came to calling for the bill.
Babies and children welcome: high chair. Booking advisable. Separate room for parties, seating 28. Tables outdoors (2, pavement). **Map 20 C3**.

South East

Gipsy Hill

Numidie

48 Westow Hill, SE19 1RX (8766 6166/ www.numidie.co.uk). Gipsy Hill rail. **Bar Open** 6pm-midnight Tue-Sun. *Restaurant* **Lunch served** noon-3pm, **dinner served** 6-10.30pm Tue-Sun. **Main courses** £9.50-£13. **Set dinner** (Tue-Thur) £13 2 courses. *Both* **Credit** MC, V.
A compact, Parisian-style bistro, Numidie is understandably popular, especially on weekend evenings. When things get busy, the tables can feel crammed-in and service becomes slow. Don't worry: the great food and ambience more than compensate. The friendly French staff and authentic vibe – oil paintings and faded newspaper clippings decorate the walls – managed to sweep us away from the reality of Crystal Palace for a few enjoyable hours. The concise menu of Mediterranean and North African dishes includes plenty of vegetarian options. Juicy beef fillet topped with truffle butter came with a good pile of hand-cut chips, while sea bream with new potatoes and spring vegetables (a special) was flaky and succulent. Fish is a highlight, including traditional bouillabaisse, and grilled red mullet with chekchouka (a tomato and pepper dish). For dessert we shared a very pleasing crème brûlée au

cognac. The candle-lit basement bar stays open until late and is perfect for an after-dinner cocktail. *Babies and children welcome: booster seats. Bar available for hire (Tue-Thur). No-smoking (restaurant).*

East
Shoreditch

★ Eyre Brothers
70 Leonard Street, EC2A 4QX (7613 5346/ www.eyrebrothers.co.uk). Old Street tube/rail. **Lunch served** noon-3pm Mon-Fri. **Dinner served** 6.30-11pm Mon-Sat. **Main courses** £13-£22. **Credit** AmEx, DC, MC, V.
Eyre Brothers is entirely contemporary – sleek dark woods, deep-brown leather banquettes – and yet (unlike many modern restaurants) feels so comfortable you instantly know you can settle in and unwind. Essential to this is the service: friendly, knowledgeable and attentive. The food – a changing, essentially Spanish-Portuguese-based mix, reflecting David and Robert Eyre's upbringing in Mozambique – has just the right blend of strength and subtlety. Very superior pan-fried scallops came with a deliciously smooth chickpea purée and grelot onion salad, while grilled chorizo with broad beans, garlic, coriander and sweet vinegar was a lovely mixture of tastes and textures. Of our mains, coelhos caçadora – a Portuguese 'hunter's casserole' of rabbit, ham, red wine and Jersey potatoes – sounded ruggedly peasanty, but had a distinct fragrance of cardamom; gammon-like grilled fillet of Ibérico pork was finely marinated in garlic and paprika. Ingredients are first rate, and the Eyres' attention to detail is also seen in the list of enticing, unusual, mostly Iberian wines at eminently reasonable prices. Even the coffee is above average. Glitches? We looked, honest, but couldn't find any.
Babies and children admitted. Booking advisable. Disabled: toilet. No-smoking tables. Restaurant available for hire. **Map 6 Q4.**

Scandinavian
Central
Marylebone

Garbo's
42 Crawford Street, W1H 1JW (7262 6582). Baker Street or Edgware Road tube/Marylebone tube/rail. **Lunch served** noon-3pm Mon-Fri, Sun. **Dinner served** 6-11pm Mon-Sat. **Main courses** £6.50-£17. **Set lunch** £10.95 2 courses, £11.95 3 courses; £12.95 smörgåsbord. **Set buffet lunch** (Sun) £13.95. **Cover** £1 (à la carte only). **Credit** AmEx, MC, V.
The decor is a trifle dated, and the Scandinavian dishes are presented with a touch of 1970s kitsch – but we're not complaining. Garbo's old-fashioned charm and extended warm welcome is a big draw for Swedish corporate types and nostalgic expats. The walls are adorned with a smörgåsbord of knick-knacks: black and white photos of movie stars, a well-weathered elk's head, and even a shelf stocked with crispbread. First courses made for a promising start to the meal. Jansson's temptation (a baked patty of grated potato, chopped anchovies, softened onions and a dash of cream) was perfectly cooked and served piping hot; we were particularly impressed with its golden crust, which gave way to a creamy well-seasoned layer below. Equally stimulating, a Baltic-inspired pickled herring salad worked well with the bite of crisp apple chunks, verdant dill, and surprisingly light mayonnaise dressing. Main courses were more mundane. A dish of dense meatballs, dunked in bland cream sauce, was a very lacklustre choice. Bright, breezy service made some recompense for any failings on the culinary front. Next time, we'll probably pick and choose from the cold spread.
Babies and children welcome: high chair. Booking advisable. Separate room for parties, seats 35. **Map 8 F5.**

South Kensington

Lundum's
117-119 Old Brompton Road, SW7 3RN (7373 7774/www.lundums.com). Gloucester Road or South Kensington tube. **Brunch served** 9am-noon, **dinner served** 6-11pm Mon-Sat. **Lunch served** noon-4pm Mon-Sat; noon-1.30pm Sun. **Main courses** £13.50-£27.25. **Set lunch** (Mon-Sat) £14.50 2 courses, £18.50 3 courses; (Sun) £21.50 buffet. **Set dinner** £19.50 2 courses, £24.50 3 courses. **Credit** AmEx, DC, MC, V.
Exuding an almost rarefied atmosphere, Lundum's boasts a loyal clientele of monied professionals who favour simply prepared Scandinavian dishes executed with a light touch. There's a cosy lounge by the entrance, alcoves for secluded eating, and spacious dining areas furnished in shades of cream and beige. Chefs are renowned for their fish dishes, and for good reason. We were impressed by the freshness of a trio of salmon morsels for our first course – smoked salmon wisps, herby gravadlax topped with a chilled froth of dill foam, and sublime-tasting salmon tartare. Plaice skagen, sautéed and served on the bone, made a delicious main course, its buttery surface shielding succulent white flesh below. Simple accompaniments to this dish – warmed clarified butter, cranberry compote and plain boiled potatoes – were a testament to understated elegance. Sadly, a dish of fried sea bass fillets, although flavoursome, was undone by a stodgy salsify salad and excessively buttery potato rösti. Non-piscine choices on the menu include meatballs, stroganoff and cured roast duck. Service is slick but a little austere. For buffet buffs, the Sunday brunches are a big draw. The wine list, although pricey, is impressive too.
Babies and children welcome: high chairs. Booking advisable. Tables outdoors (8, patio). Separate room for parties, seats 18. **Map 14 D11.**

Seychelles
North
Camden Town & Chalk Farm

Kaz Kreol [NEW]
St Martin's Tavern, 35 Pratt Street, NW1 0BG (7485 4747). Camden Town tube. **Lunch served** 11.30am-3.30pm, **dinner served** 7-11pm Mon-Sat. **Main courses** £6.99-£14.99. **Set buffet** (lunch) £7.99. **Credit** MC, V.
The Seychelles kitchen is celebrated here, with aromatic spices, lush tropical produce and fabulous fish from the Indian Ocean. French, African, Indian and Chinese cuisines are influences; it's Creole food, with an extra chilli kick. The restaurant looks like a traditional boozer from the outside, but inside it's bright and modern, embellished with black granite table-tops and an occasional dinky seashell. We started dinner with sliced smoked king fish fillets sharpened by lemon juice and capers: top marks for simplicity. To follow, whole sea bass, grilled then veiled in a tongue-tingling ginger, chilli and tomato sauce, was a triumph of perfectly cooked fish, well matched with steamed rice and mildly spiced dahl-like lentils. An equally agreeable beef sauté – sliced fillet flash-fried with onions and shredded red chillies – was deliciously saucy in a French way, yet with a fiery, robust African character. Other gems include coconut-based curries with octopus and crab, French-inspired grills and steamy mussels with chillies. There's little for vegetarians except aubergine fritters and vegetable curry. But don't miss the relishes; mashed pumpkin 'chutney', sweetened and fried with toasted garlic and lime juice was marvellous. With its friendly staff, homely meals and reasonably priced menu, Kaz Kreol is a real asset for local diners.

Babies and children welcome: high chairs. No smoking. **Map 27 D2.**

South African
South West
Putney

Chakalaka
136 Upper Richmond Road, SW15 2SP (8789 5696/www.chakalakarestaurant.co.uk). East Putney tube. **Dinner served** 6-10.45pm Mon-Fri. **Meals served** noon-10.45pm Sat, Sun. **Main courses** £9.95-£16.95. **Credit** MC, V.
The menu at Chakalaka is inspired by African culinary tradition and modern cooking styles. As such, it offers a flavour of back home to well-heeled South Africans. This is an informal, friendly place, with brightly painted brick walls, colourful prints and tribal artefacts. Its striking zebra-striped frontage sets the scene for big-game dining, but vegetarians get a look in too. We began with seared crocodile tail in a garlicky chilli sauce, served with spiced couscous. Tasting like a cross between chicken and fish, the succulent crocodile meat worked well with the spike of chillies and the sweetness of a sticky balsamic dressing. A homely butternut soup had been subtly infused with aromatic cinnamon and toasted curry powder, but was thick and cloying. Bobotie (lightly curried lamb mince baked under a layer of savoury egg custard) was a triumph of Cape Malay cooking, providing a tasty blend of Asian flavours and western influences. We can also vouch for the spare ribs steeped in tongue-tingling peri peri sauce; portions are enormous. An affordable South African wine list coupled with cheerful service add to the appeal.
Babies and children welcome: children's portions; high chairs. Booking advisable. No-smoking tables. Separate room for parties, seats 30.
For branch (The Boom Bar) see index.

Swiss
Central
Soho

St Moritz
161 Wardour Street, W1F 8WJ (7734 3324/ www.stmoritz-restaurant.co.uk). Tottenham Court Road tube. **Lunch served** noon-3pm Mon-Fri. **Dinner served** 6-11.30pm Mon-Sat. **Main courses** £10.95-£18.90. **Credit** AmEx, DC, MC, V.
A one-stop destination for all things cheesy, St Moritz might well have been fashioned from a 1970s pantomime set. Chalet-like in looks, it is kitted out with dark wood fittings, glorious gingham curtains, rustic pans on the walls, and an assortment of tinkling cow bells. No one's ringing any changes here, though: food, like the decor, remains rooted in Swiss tradition. Over the past three decades, this cosy den has built up a loyal following of fondue-loving aficionados. Not wanting to miss out, we opted for a large pot of cheese fondue complete with dunks of crusty bread cubes and new potatoes. Our choice – a blushing-pink combination of gruyère and vacherin cheese, warmed with tomato sauce, white wine and hints of garlic – was decadently rich, but deliciously intense. As the cheese bubbled and thickened over the spirit flame, the more mellow its flavour became. Vegetable rösti didn't fare so well; our crisp-fried shredded potato cake, topped with tired-looking broccoli florets, was stodgy and oily. Equally disappointing, an overly chilled first course of chicken liver pâté exhibited a boozy bitterness. Staff seemed grumpy too.
Babies and children welcome: high chair. Book dinner. Separate room for parties, seats 28.
Map 17 K6.

Greek

A sk a Greek where to find the best Greek food and you'll invariably be directed to their mother's kitchen. Hellenic cuisine is not complicated. It's about simple foods that taste as though their secrets have been handed down the generations: slow-roasted lamb, grilled fresh fish, and hearty oven-baked soul-pleasers like moussaká. Among the best London tavernas – **Vrisaki**, **Aphrodite**, **Hellenic** – this certainly seems to be the case. Generally speaking, the Greeks don't tamper with their beloved recipes. However, there are exceptions. **The Real Greek** and **Café Corfu** specialise in giving Mama's – or as the Greeks would say, *Mana*'s – venerable recipes modern makeovers, to varying degrees of success. But even at these establishments, the universal rule applies: the ingredients must be allowed to speak for themselves.

Nevertheless, a truly great Greek dining experience is about more than just food. Traditionally, meal times are family gatherings: social occasions to be enjoyed with close ones. London's Greek restaurants for the most part reflect this, providing ample measures of buzzing, laid-back conviviality. As the standard of the capital's tavernas continues to improve, so too does their selection of native social lubricants. Greek wines are on the up, with producers such as Katogi-Strofilia coming into their own. There's also an increased availability of Greek spirits – from ouzo and Metaxa brandy to rarer, home-grown treats such as the grappa-like tsipouro. What better way to accompany this simple but sumptuous soul food?

Central
Covent Garden

★ The Real Greek Souvlaki & Bar
60-62 Long Acre, WC2E 9JE (7240 2292/ www.therealgreek.com). Covent Garden tube. **Meals served** 11.30am-11pm daily. **Main courses** £4.85-£6.25. **Credit** MC, V.
This hip younger sister to the upmarket Hoxton originals is one of the newest additions to the Real Greek franchise (no longer owned by its creator, Theodore Kyriakou; outlets are cropping up all over the city). It occupies the shell of an old Victorian pub, but while the wood panelling hardly evokes images of Greece, the food – and ethos – is satisfyingly Hellenic. There's a healthy selection of mezédes; the creamy gigandes (served cold) and tender bite-sized dolmádes were excellent. But these were bettered by a faultless souvláki: the centrepiece of the simple menu. Chunks of chicken (lamb, pork, haddock and vegetarian alternatives are available) were perfectly char-grilled, wrapped in flatbread with a herby sauce (a modern twist on the traditional tzatziki) and served in greaseproof paper, just as they should be. Other main courses include a meaty and flavoursome grilled country-style sausage. Desserts (baklavá, yoghurt and honey) are basic, but the choice of Greek wines (available by the carafe) and beers is vast and includes the criminally underrated Mythos lager. There's a boisterous feel to this place, though service is professional, if a little slow.
Babies and children admitted. Bookings not accepted. Disabled: toilet. No-smoking tables. Takeaway service. **Map 18 L6.**
For branches see index.

West
Bayswater

Aphrodite Taverna
15 Hereford Road, W2 4AB (7229 2206). Bayswater, Notting Hill Gate or Queensway tube. **Meals served** noon-midnight Mon-Sat. **Main courses** £8.50-£27.50. **Set mezédes** £17 vegetarian, £19.50 meat, £27.50 fish. **Cover** £1. **Credit** AmEx, DC, JCB, MC, V.
It's hard not to feel at ease in this homely Cypriot taverna, run by the effervescent Rosana. It's a charming haven of quirky clutter amid the ordered, posh, west London terraces. Replica statues, gourds, copper pots and mismatched paintings hang from the ceiling and decorate the walls. Service is friendly and relaxed but professional. The food – from an extensive menu that pretty much covers the Greek-Cypriot culinary repertoire – seems designed to hit all the comfort zones. Starters are impeccable: creamy grilled halloumi served on slices of deliciously ripe tomato was delectable; and the huge portion of light, fresh, fried kalámari would have done us as a main course. Monkfish kebab, the regulars' favourite, was fleshy and flavoursome, but this was outdone by a perfect, almost buttery, grilled sea bass, served decapitated. Old and New World wines are available, along with a selection of trusty Greek dependables (from producers such as Hatzimichalis and Tsantali). Desserts are fairly traditional, but you'll never manage them. Aphrodite is quirky and a little chintzy, but blissfully lacking in pretension: a wonderfully welcoming treat. It's popular locally, so do book.
Babies and children welcome: high chairs. Booking advisable dinner. Tables outdoors (12, terrace). Takeaway service. Vegetarian menu. **Map 7 B6.**

Notting Hill

★ Greek Affair
1 Hillgate Street, W8 7SP (7792 5226). Notting Hill Gate tube. Oct-Apr **Lunch served** noon-3pm, **dinner served** 5.30-11pm Tue-Sun. *May-Sept* **Meals served** noon-11pm daily. **Main courses** £7-£12. **Unlicensed. Corkage** £1.80. **Credit** AmEx, MC, V.
This charming, laid-back restaurant is a welcoming spot: bright and airy on the first floor, where diners share a huge wooden table, and intimate downstairs. The emphasis is on mezédes and the selection, both hot and cold, is extensive. A simple dish of revithósalata mé spanáki (warm salad of chickpeas and spinach, served with a subtle drizzle of lemony olive oil) had been excellently prepared. The melitzanosaláta was rich and creamy enough to balance its powerful garlic kick. But in contrast to this flavoursome dip, the kalámari, cooked in a soupy tomato sauce, tasted somewhat flat. Of the mains, a huge slab of hearty moussaká was gorgeously satisfying. But a plate of garides mesogion (prawns in a tomato and pepper sauce, served over a mound of rice) proved dull; the underwhelming sauce and the slippery, awkward-to-peel prawns were something of an appetite suppressant. Never mind: the decadent honey-soaked kataïfi, which arrived with the bill, was a lovely sweetener. A little hit and miss perhaps, but Greek Affair is still worth a visit for its atmosphere and its starters alone.
Babies and children welcome: high chairs. Booking advisable. No-smoking tables. Separate room for parties, seats 30. Tables outdoors (5, roof garden). Vegetarian menu. **Map 19 C5.**

Shepherd's Bush

★ ★ Vine Leaves
71 Uxbridge Road, W12 8NR (8749 0325/ www.vineleavestaverna.co.uk). Shepherd's Bush tube. **Lunch served** noon-3pm, **dinner served** 5pm-midnight Mon-Thur. **Meals served** noon-1am Fri, Sat; noon-11.30pm Sun. **Main courses** £6.95-£15.95. **Set meal** (Mon-Thur, Sun) £9.95 3 courses incl coffee. **Set mezédes** £9.95 mini, £13.95 mixed, £16.95 fish. **Credit** AmEx, JCB, MC, V.
Like the bustling multicultural street on which it stands, what this small neighbourhood taverna lacks in intimacy it makes up for with a buzzy, down-to-earth vibe. Service is friendly and the food is satisfying. The extensive menu covers all Greek culinary bases – from soutzoukákia (spicy meatballs in tomato sauce) and moussaká to grilled fish and lamb chops. From the large list of hot and cold meze, both the tzatziki (creamy with a hint of mint) and the houmous (rich and granular) were faultless. Fat fingers of hot dolmádes, served in a tomato sauce, were herby and hearty. Only the tiropitákia (small filo triangles filled with feta) let down the high standard: too much filo, not enough feta, but the addition of chillies with the crumbly cheese was inspired. Even the chips were perfect: crisp on the outside, fluffy within. To follow, a main course of inch-thick grilled king prawns cooked in chilli and coriander, though succulent, defeated us. The wine list is short and the dessert menu shorter still (yogurt and honey, ice-cream), but no matter: we were happily sated.
Babies and children welcome: children's menu. Booking advisable weekends. No-smoking tables. Takeaway service. Vegetarian menu. **Map 20 B2.**

South West
Earl's Court

★ As Greek As It Gets
233 Earl's Court Road, SW5 9AH (7244 7777/ www.asgreekasitgets.com). Earl's Court tube. **Lunch served** noon-3pm, **dinner served** 6-11pm Mon-Fri. **Meals served** noon-11pm Sat, Sun. **Main courses** £6.50-£9. **Credit** AmEx, MC, V.

Mezedopolio

As the tables full of young Greeks suggest, this brightly lit souvlaki joint is pleasingly authentic. It specialises in an array of meaty treats served with genuine souvlaki flatbread, but also offers traditional favourites such as pastitsio (an oven-cooked dish of mince, macaroni and béchamel sauce). The fun, modern outlook of the place is typified by its novel mix-and-match souvlaki menu, whereby you combine any of five meats with a variety of fillings and sauces. The drinks list is rudimentary (retsina wine, Alfa beer), and the food is simple but, on the whole, decent. Staff are friendly and efficient. A square slice of spinach pie struck a good balance between feta creaminess and spinachy richness. A hearty portion of creamy moussaká featured a sweet, cinnamon twist. We also sampled the Mixed Greek: a giant's feast of a mixed grill that included a rich, succulent country sausage of particular note. Desserts – thick greek yoghurt with honey, and custardy milk pies – left us happy and satisfied, as did the modest bill.
Babies and children welcome: high chairs.
No-smoking tables. Tables outdoors (2, pavement).
Takeaway service.

East

Shoreditch

★ Mezedopolio

14 Hoxton Market, N1 6HG (7739 8212/
www.therealgreek.co.uk). Old Street tube/rail/
26, 48, 55, 149, 243 bus. **Meals served**
noon-10.30pm Mon-Sat. **Mezédes** £2.10-£6.75.
Credit MC, V.
It might be set in an old mission hall and feature chandeliers styled on Greek Orthodox church lighting, but the sister restaurant to the Real Greek next door (*see below*) buzzes with bar-like conviviality. Like the Greek equivalent to a tapas joint, Mezedopolio is a drink and nibble sort of place, offering a menu of small seasonal mezédes that give a funky twist to a traditional meal. The emphasis is on sharing; six to eight dishes are about right for two diners. But while the portions seem to have got smaller, prices haven't. Two small

fingers of battered, flaky salt cod on a tiny mound of skordaliá cost a princely £6.25. Still, the food is delightful. Fáva (puréed split peas) was rich, the tzatziki was thick, and the fluffy gígandes were comforting. Though inaccurately described as tirópitakia (small cheese pies), the bite-sized spinach and feta filo triangles were pleasingly delicate. The selection of Greek beers and wines from boutique producers is unrivalled; a light red Mikri Strofilia made a perfect accompaniment. Desserts are imaginative; though the baklavá was dense and a little dry, the accompanying cardamom ice-cream was inspired. Service can be pushy, but this is a fun venue.
Babies and children welcome: high chairs. Booking advisable; essential weekends. Tables outdoors (6, pavement). Takeaway service. **Map 6 Q/R3.**

The Real Greek

15 Hoxton Market, N1 6HG (7739 8212/
www.therealgreek.com). Old Street tube/rail/
26, 48, 55, 149, 243 bus. **Lunch served** noon-
3pm, **dinner served** 5.30-10.30pm Mon-Sat.
Main courses £13.25-£16.55. **Credit** MC, V.
Founder Theodore Kyriakou has moved on, but the original Real Greek – bustling even on a Monday night – remains as popular as ever. The blond wood and glazed brickwork decor is understatedly swish, service is courteous (if on the slow side) and each dish comes well presented. The restaurant also deserves praise for creatively melding Mediterranean flavours. A meze combination of spicy soutzouki (beef sausage), tangy tirokeftedes (fried cheese dumplings) and tomatoey warm chickpeas worked well, though the latter was somewhat bland. Bougiourndi meze (a small slab of feta baked with chilli, tomato and olive oil) was a triumph of complementary flavours. There were no vegetarian choices on the changing menu, but the light, char-grilled fillet of sea bass from the 'fagakia' (small second courses) was superb. In contrast, stewed mutton from the heftier mains was disappointing: the meat tough, the gravy overpowering. And a side order of warm courgettes was too bitter to eat. The all-Greek wine list remains impeccable and the inspired desserts

(warm fig pie with mavrodaphne cream) bring a modern twist to traditional recipes. Despite its culinary vision and accompanying high prices, the Real Greek sometimes falls short of the mark.
Babies and children welcome: high chairs. Booking advisable. Disabled: toilet. Separate rooms for parties, seating 8 and 20. Tables outdoors (12, pavement). Takeaway service. **Map 6 Q/R3.**

North

Camden Town & Chalk Farm

Andy's Taverna

81-81A Bayham Street, NW1 0AG (7485 9718).
Camden Town or Mornington Crescent tube.
Lunch served noon-2.30pm, **dinner served**
6pm-midnight Mon-Fri. **Meals served** noon-
midnight Sat, Sun. **Main courses** £8.95-£14.
Set mezédes £13.95 per person (minimum 2).
Credit AmEx, DC, JCB, MC, V.
Run by amiable Greek proprietors, and dotted with regulars, this unassuming taverna bustles with life. The beamed interior has a subtle blue and white colour scheme, and there's a whitewashed courtyard out back. The food, like the decor, is simple yet inviting. Warm, moreish pide bread is served with cheerful banter alongside the usual olive and chilli nibbles that account for the cover charge. Meze starters were faultless: tzatziki featured crisp chunks of cucumber suspended in the thickest yoghurt, the melitzanosaláta was heady and rich, and the spinach-rich spanakópittas were smooth and buttery. Mains were similarly satisfying. Chunky dolmádes arrived in a smooth tomato-based sauce that complemented the moist meaty rice wrapped in young vine leaves. The gently grilled sea bass – flown in from the Greek islands – was light and delicately flavoured. Only a side order of slightly undercooked chips disappointed, but crunchy salads, which accompanied each main (complete with slabs of creamy feta), made up for the shortfall. The wine list is modest yet more than adequate, and the Keo beer is an assured thirst-quencher.

Babies and children welcome: crayons; high chairs. Booking advisable Fri, Sat. Separate rooms for parties, seating 30 and 40. Tables outdoors (7, garden). Takeaway service. **Map 27 D2.**

Café Corfu

7 Pratt Street, NW1 0AE (7267 8088/ www.cafecorfu.com). Camden Town or Mornington Crescent tube. **Meals served** noon-11pm Mon-Thur; noon-midnight Fri-Sun. **Main courses** £7.95-£12.95. **Set meal** £16.75 3 courses, £20 4 courses. **Credit** MC, V.

With a solid reputation for applying creative twists to traditional dishes, this stylish, family-run establishment has become a standard bearer for innovative modern Greek cuisine. An excellent starter of dolmádes didn't disappoint: the vine leaves were young and supple, and the plump, squishy rice within was imbued with a delicate lemony flavour. But as the meal progressed, cracks in Café Corfu's spotless veneer became apparent. The pistachio-encrusted psári plaki (baked fish) was a victim of false advertising: unless 'encrusted' means three or four nuts crushed and sprinkled on top. And the accompanying sticky spanakórizo (spinach rice) was neither sticky nor particularly spinachy – just rather ordinary. Thankfully, the slow-roasted lamb shank served with kritharáki (rice-shaped pasta) fared better. However, a side order of gigandes was bland and undercooked, the beans served in a watery chopped-tomato sauce. The desserts and Hellenic-inspired cocktails are inventive and the Greek wine list remains top-notch, but the usual courteous service was abrupt. The back room, laid-out for a function later that evening, might explain these lapses. Café Corfu is still capable of being London's best modern Greek restaurant, but needs to keep its eye on the ball.

Babies and children welcome: high chairs. Booking advisable; essential weekends. Entertainment: belly dancer, DJ, dancing 9pm Fri, Sat; musicians 8pm Sun. No-smoking tables. Separate rooms for parties, seating 50-150. Tables outdoors (6, forecourt). Takeaway service. **Map 27 D2.**

Daphne

83 Bayham Street, NW1 0AG (7267 7322). Camden Town or Mornington Crescent tube. **Lunch served** noon-2.30pm, **dinner served** 6-11.30pm Mon-Sat. **Main courses** £7.50-£13.50. **Set lunch** £6.75 2 courses, £8.25 3 courses. **Set mezédes** £13.50 meat or vegetarian, £17.50 fish. **Credit** MC, V.

Time seems to stand still in this homely, bustling little bolt-hole. Vintage black and white photos of the old country dot the walls, the bubbly proprietress welcomes diners from the bar, and Greek and Cypriot regulars chat loudly in the booths at the back. Even the daily specials board hardly seems to change. The food, as ever, is pleasingly old school. Lovely fresh kalámari were fried in a light, crispy batter. A portion of revithia (warm chickpeas with spinach, cooked in a smooth tomato sauce), ordered on the recommendation of the amiable waiter, was excellent. A main course of hearty moussaká – a hefty portion, served in its own pot – was pure comfort food: rich and herby and topped with an inch of thick, fluffy mash. Giant prawns had run out, but a handful of large tiger prawns, lightly marinated and grilled to flavourful perfection, made a fine alternative. The Greek wine list is short (disappointingly, the house white is Italian), but desserts such as rice pudding are reassuringly traditional.

Babies and children welcome: high chairs. Booking essential Fri, Sat. Disabled: toilet. Separate room for parties, seats 50. Tables outdoors (8, roof terrace). **Map 27 D2.**

Lemonia

89 Regent's Park Road, NW1 8UY (7586 7454). Chalk Farm tube. **Lunch served** noon-3pm Mon-Fri; noon-3.30pm Sun. **Dinner served** 6-11.30pm Mon-Sat. **Main courses** £7.75-£12.95. **Set lunch** (Mon-Fri) £7.75 2 courses incl coffee, £8.95 3 courses. **Set mezédes** £17 per person (minimum 2). **Credit** MC, V.

With a blue glass eye hanging by the front bar (warding off evil spirits), and an elegant window-lined front room, this long-standing eaterie manages to feel both pleasingly traditional and effortlessly modern. But it's not the airy decor or the alfresco feel of the vine-draped conservatory-style back room that draws a well-to-do crowd every night – it's the food. The daily specials don't seem to change, but the quality of cooking remains consistently high: a starter of golden brown, grilled halloumi was smooth and almost buttery; gigandes plaki, cooked in a delicate tomato sauce, were soft and pillow-like. From the robust selection of mains – which includes stalwarts like stifádo, grilled meats and fish, as well as the rarely seen gemistá (vegetables stuffed with rice) – chunks of chicken shishlik were tender and moist and served with a side of fluffy roast potatoes. Vegetarian moussaká (hearty layers of tomatoes, aubergines and courgettes interspersed with a creamy béchamel) was simply gorgeous. This sumptuous food was well matched with a decent wine list and professional service. As upmarket as its Primrose Hill location, the enduringly popular Lemonia continues to impress.

Babies and children admitted. Booking advisable. Separate room for parties, seats 40. Tables outdoors (6, pavement). **Map 27 A1.**

Limani

154 Regent's Park Road, NW1 8XN (7483 4492). Chalk Farm tube. **Lunch served** noon-3pm Sat. **Dinner served** 6-11.30pm Tue-Sat; 3.30-10.30pm Sun. **Main courses** £8.75-£16.50. **Set mezédes** £16 meat or vegetarian, £18 fish, per person (minimum 2). **Credit** MC, V.

With its terrace-like top floor and rustic basement, the older sister to Lemonia (*see above*) has a characterful setting. A steady stream of regulars attests to the enduring popularity of this Greek-Cypriot taverna. The food (from a traditional, grilled meats and fish-dominated menu) and the service haven't always lived up to expectations, but on this visit Limani delivered. The warm pitta bread tasted as if it had been heated from frozen, but a starter of pleasingly plump black-eyed peas with spinach had been doused in a delicate, lemony oil; and the grilled halloumi was tender and flavourful. Mains arrived a little too quickly, but were hard to fault. Portions are healthy: a door-stop of moist, meaty swordfish steak fell away in chunks; and a good-sized grilled sea bass, from the specials, was gloriously fresh and remarkably fleshy. Only the chips, served with the swordfish and tasting refried, were disappointing. The Greek wine selection is uninspiring compared to the choice of non-Greek bottles, but desserts (from baklavà to crème caramel) please the sweet tooth. Limani's food easily passes muster, though it's the service that we found most improved this time: attentive and courteous.

Babies and children admitted. Booking essential weekends. Separate room for parties, seats 30. Takeaway service. **Map 27 A1.**

Wood Green

★ Vrisaki

73 Myddleton Road, N22 8LZ (8889 8760). Bounds Green or Wood Green tube. **Lunch served** noon-4pm, **dinner served** 6-11.30pm Mon-Sat. **Meals served** noon-6pm Sun. **Main courses** £10-£18. **Set mezédes** £18 per person (minimum 2). **Credit** AmEx, MC, V.

For a taverna to remain popular in an area brimming with Greeks implies a level of authenticity. And once you've gained access via its unorthodox entrance (through a kebab shop), you'll find Vrisaki imbued with old-school charm. Trompe l'oeil pastoral scenes make the windowless room feel airy, while friendly service lends the bustling restaurant a laid-back vibe. The menu is succinct yet covers all bases. Keo beer and standard Greek wines are served, while food includes grilled meats and fish, along with specialities seemingly prepared from age-old recipes. The starters, which arrived with five complimentary meze, were impeccable. Thick slices of grilled halloumi were moreishly salty, and the tzatziki was zingy with a hint of mint. Mains were similarly satisfying. A club-sized kléftiko, served with roast potatoes as well as saffron rice, was falling off the bone. Two large skewers of chicken kebabs, with rice, came nicely char-grilled. In the misplaced fear we might go hungry, staff also brought a huge bowl of complimentary greek salad. It's a wonder they ever sell any of the baklavàs and cream desserts on the sweets trolley. A wholeheartedly traditional bolt-hole.

Babies and children admitted. Booking advisable; essential weekends. Takeaway service (8881 2920).

North West

Swiss Cottage

★ Hellenic Restaurant NEW

291 Finchley Road, NW3 6ND (7431 1001/ www.gonumber.com/hellenic). Swiss Cottage tube. **Lunch served** noon-3pm, **dinner served** 5.30pm-midnight daily. **Main courses** £8.50-£12.50. **Set lunch** £7.95 2 courses. **Set mézedes** £15.50 per person (minimum 2). **Credit** MC, V.

This family-run restaurant comes recommended by the Hellenic Centre – and rightly so. The decor, featuring blue and white tablecloths and nostalgic photos of the old country under a starlit ceiling, is simple and welcoming, as are the service and the food. The Hellenic specialises in huge portions of homely nourishment (leftovers are graciously wrapped in doggy bags), rustled up by Greek women gossiping in the kitchen. Starters were fresh and satisfying: kalámari were lightly fried and tender, and the spinach pie – wrapped in fine filo – was oven-baked, as they should be. Grilled meats and fish are well represented, but traditional home-cooking dominates the authentic menu. Chicken pilaff with mixed mushrooms, courgettes and peas was hearty and rich, underscored with the warm tang of white wine. The ladera was excellent: a medley of melt-in-the-mouth aubergine, potatoes and courgettes in a olive oil-rich tomato sauce. There's a modest but adequate wine list, and desserts of baklavá and halvas to satisfy the sweet of tooth. On Friday and Saturday evenings, a bouzouki band adds to the congenial atmosphere.

Babies and children welcome: high chairs. Entertainment: band 8.30pm Fri, Sat. Separate room for parties, seats 60. Takeaway service. **Map 28 B3.**

Menu

Dishes followed by (G) indicate a specifically Greek dish; those marked (GC) indicate a Greek-Cypriot speciality; those without an initial have no particular regional affiliation. Spellings often vary.

Afélia (GC): pork cubes, ideally from filleted leg or shoulder, stewed in wine, coriander and other herbs.

Avgolémono (G): a sauce made of lemon, egg yolks and chicken stock. Also a soup made with rice, chicken stock, lemon and whole eggs.

Baklavá: a pan-Middle Eastern sweet made from sheets of filo dough layered with nuts.

Dolmádes (G) or **koupépia (GC):** young vine leaves stuffed with rice, spices and (usually) minced meat.

Fasólia plakí or **pilakí:** white beans in a tomato, oregano, bay, parsley and garlic sauce.

Garídes: prawns (usually king prawns in the UK), fried or grilled.

Gígantes or **gígandes:** white haricot beans baked in tomato sauce; pronounced 'yígandes'.

Halloumi (GC) or **hallúmi:** a cheese traditionally made from sheep or goat's milk, but increasingly from cow's milk. Best served fried or grilled.

Horiátiki: Greek 'peasant' salad of tomato, cucumber, onion, feta and sometimes green pepper, dressed with ladolémono (oil and lemon).

Hórta: salad of cooked wild greens.

Houmous, hoúmmous or **húmmus (GC):** a dip of puréed chickpeas, sesame seed paste, lemon juice and garlic, garnished with paprika. Originally an Arabic dish.

Htipití or **khtipíti:** tangy purée of matured cheeses, flavoured with red peppers.

Kalámari, kalamarákia or **calamares:** small squid, usually sliced into rings, battered and fried.

Kataïfi or **katayfi:** syrup-soaked 'shredded-wheat' rolls.

Keftédes or **keftedákia (G):** herby meatballs made with minced pork or lamb (rarely beef), egg, breadcrumbs and possibly grated potato.

Kléftiko (GC): slow-roasted lamb on the bone (often shoulder), flavoured with oregano and other herbs.

Kopanistí (G): a cheese dip with a tanginess that traditionally comes from natural fermentation, but is often boosted with chilli.

Koukiá: broad beans.

Loukánika or **lukánika:** spicy coarse-ground sausages, usually pork and heavily herbed.

Loukoúmades: tiny, spongy dough fritters, dipped in honey.

Loukoúmi or **lukúmi:** 'turkish delight' made with syrup, rosewater and pectin, often studded with nuts.

Loúntza (GC): smoked pork loin.

Marídes: picarel, often mistranslated as (or substituted by) 'whitebait' – small fish best coated in flour and flash-fried.

Melitzanosaláta: purée of grilled aubergines.

Meze (plural mezédes, pronounced 'mezédhes'): a selection of either hot or cold appetisers and main dishes.

Moussaká(s) (G): a baked dish of mince (usually lamb), aubergine and potato slices and herbs, topped with béchamel sauce.

Papoutsáki: aubergine 'shoes', slices stuffed with mince, topped with sauce, usually béchamel-like.

Pastourmá(s): dense, dark-tinted garlic sausage, traditionally made from camel meat, but nowadays from beef.

Pourgoúri or **bourgoúri (GC):** a pilaf of cracked wheat, often prepared with stock, onions, crumbled vermicelli and spices.

Saganáki (G): fried cheese, usually kefalotyri; also means anything (mussels, spinach) made in a cheese-based red sauce.

Sheftaliá (GC): little pig-gut skins stuffed with pork and lamb mince, onion, parsley, breadcrumbs and spices, then grilled.

Skordaliá (G): a garlic and breadcrumb or potato-based dip, used as a side dish.

Soutzoúkákia or **soutzoúki (G):** baked meat rissoles, often topped with a tomato-based sauce.

Soúvla: large cuts of lamb or pork slow-roasted on a rotary spit.

Souvláki: chunks of meat quick-grilled on a skewer (known in London takeaways as kebab or shish kebab).

Spanakópitta: small turnovers, traditionally triangular, stuffed with spinach, dill and often feta or some other crumbly tart cheese.

Stifádo: a rich meat stew (often rabbit) with onions, red wine, tomatoes, cinnamon and bay.

Taboúlleh: generic Middle Eastern starter of pourgoúri (qv), chopped parsley, cucumber chunks, tomatoes and spring onions.

Tamará, properly **taramósalata:** fish roe pâté, originally made of dried, salted grey mullet roe (avgotáraho or botárgo), but now more often smoked cod roe, plus olive oil, lemon juice and breadcrumbs.

Tavás (GC): lamb, onion, tomato and cumin, cooked in earthenware casseroles.

Tsakistés (GC): split green olives marinated in lemon, garlic, coriander seeds and other optional flavourings.

Tyrópitta (G): similar to spanakópitta (qv) but usually without spinach and with more feta.

Tzatzíki, dzadzíki (G) or **talatoúra (GC):** a dip of shredded cucumber, yoghurt, garlic, lemon juice and mint.

RESTAURANTS

Hotels & Haute Cuisine

It has been a gradual process – about 20 years – but food in Britain is finding a place to call home, a place where it can be itself, develop with confidence and not be scared of its own shadow. In London's best hotels and restaurants, where the cream of the country's chefs work against a backdrop of beautiful landmark buildings, a clearer style of cooking is emerging that's fresh, distinct and decidedly British. Two decades ago London chefs did nothing but emulate their French counterparts, who were happy to bask in the glory the rest of the world gave them. Even ten years back the only break from our tradition of copying the French was that we copied Italy and the Far East. But now, scattered liberally throughout the menus of our lovely home-grown restaurants, we see lovely home-grown food. Standards were raised even higher this year with the opening of **Addendum** in the City, **Galvin at Windows** in Park Lane, **The Grill** in Mayfair and **La Noisette** in Knightsbridge. They joins a stellar line-up that ranges from the supreme **Le Gavroche** to the newly reopened **Pied à Terre**, not to mention the bevy of beauties already in the Gordon Ramsay stable. Every restaurant in this section offers gems plucked from British land and sea, delivered with haste, cooked with reverence and served with celebration. Hallelujah!

Central

City

★ Addendum NEW

Apex City of London Hotel, 1 Seething Lane, EC3N 4AX (7977 9500/www.addendum restaurant.co.uk). Tower Hill. **Lunch served** noon-2.30pm, **dinner served** 6-9.30pm Mon-Fri. **Main courses** £18.50-£24.50. **Credit** AmEx, DC, MC, V.

Addendum. Boring office extra, last minute add-on, useful Scrabble word? Probably. But does it suggest a fine dining experience? Probably not. Ignore the jobsworth connotations of this dull moniker and get yourself to Tom Illic's latest venture after Bonds. Tucked along Seething Lane, just a zebra-crossing away from a fine vista of the Thames, this contemporary bar and restaurant joined to the Apex hotel is cleverly lit and sharply decorated with lots of walnut, slate, black leather and ikebana. It's a far cry from the lavishly draped environs of most hotel restaurants. Illic grew up in Yugoslavia and it shows in his robust country cooking, which doesn't shy away from big flavours and less popular cuts of meat. Yet the food is highly refined in its delivery, a point illustrated perfectly by a dish of braised pig's cheeks with chorizo and garlic and parsley mash: an outstanding assemblage of melting, sticky tenderness charged with full-throttle flavours. Similarly, another starter featured sea trout three-ways (cured, pan-fried and tartare), its related flavours caught up in the radiant juiciness of an orange, carrot and cardamom salad. Handmade linguine – light, buttery, beautifully presented and shot through with mushrooms, truffle and artichokes – was equally masterful. Ditto some exceptional lamb: loin and cutlet joined by baby turnips, spinach and spiced aubergine cannelloni. Desserts were absolutely faultless too (it's not often we rave about every dish in an entire meal). Service was French, correct and intelligent (note the setting out of cutlery with gloved hands to avoid smudges, which we've seen elsewhere only at Le Gavroche), and the wine list is succinct and priced with plenty of beguiling choice for under £35. One for all restaurant nutters to watch.
Disabled: lift; toilet (in hotel). No smoking. Separate rooms for parties, seating 10-50. Tables outdoors (12, terrace). **Map 12 R7**.

Bonds

Threadneedles, 5 Threadneedle Street, EC2R 8AY (7657 8088/www.theetongroup.com). Bank tube. **Lunch served** noon-2.30pm, **dinner served** 6-10pm Mon-Fri. **Main courses** £15.50-£25. **Set lunch** £20 2 courses, £25 3 courses. **Credit** AmEx, MC, V.

The razor-edged chic and tempo of London's financial pulse, the dizzying dimensions and echoes of a past banking hall, the frenetic talk of pensions and relocations… this is what to expect of Bonds restaurant and bar. The venue is hidden within Threadneedles hotel, itself camouflaged against dozens of other 19th-century architectural masterpieces in the City. Many more people were eating, wheeling and dealing here than we've found on previous occasions, so the head chef must be doing something right. Although Barry Tonks only began cooking ten years ago, he aimed high and started at the Dorchester, then continued to tread a steady path through high-quality joints under big-name chefs, impressing critics along the way. His passion for tapas can be witnessed in the funky bar, while more serious sit-down meals are 'modern' French, whatever that is. Certainly, there are plenty of fine British ingredients in the line-up,

with Colchester crab turning up in a truly sensational à la carte starter: a plate of perfect white crab meat faintly tinged with lemon juice, a streak of creamy brown crab meat, a sliver of smoked salmon, a spoonful of chilled crème fraîche and the freshest, fluffiest blinis around. The set lunch menu features simpler combinations, such as stilton, pear and pine nut salad or vanilla crème brûlée and rhubarb sorbet. From the carte came a richer assembly of Elwy Valley Welsh lamb, the best end of this tender and flavour-packed meat served pink, and the slow-cooked shoulder layered with potato slices in a melting boulangère, joined by vivid crushed peas, shiny roasted vine tomatoes and a healthy whiff of marjoram. Worth a detour into City-slicker territory.
Disabled: lift; toilet. Dress: smart casual. No smoking. Separate rooms for parties, seating 9, 12 and 20. **Map 12 Q6**.

Embankment

Jaan

Swissôtel London, The Howard, 12 Temple Place, WC2R 2PR (7300 1700/http://london. swissotel.com). Temple tube. **Lunch served** noon-2.30pm Mon-Fri. **Dinner served** 5.45-10.30pm Mon-Sat. **Set lunch** £19 2 courses, £22 3 courses. **Set dinner** £33 2 courses, £38 3 courses, £45 6 courses. **Credit** AmEx, DC, JCB, MC, V.

You have to admire the efforts of the Howard's sales staff for the volume of press releases recently spewing from their office. The gist of these is that a new chef has arrived, a new menu is in place, a delightfully opulent black and fuchsia bar has replaced a beige abyss in the hotel foyer, and no new decorating has been done elsewhere (they don't mention the last bit, but the coffee-coloured restaurant could do with a perk up). Australian Simon Duff's last post was at the posh Hanbury Manor in Hertfordshire and, before that, Sydney and Melbourne hotels and London's Oak Room of old under Marco Pierre White. As a result, chef Duff brings a refreshing pan-Asian-French style to this establishment on the banks of the Thames (there isn't a riverside view from the restaurant, but a fecund, three-tier water garden suffices). Aussie chefs can generally cook fish exceptionally well, and barramundi is on the menu at Jaan: not from halfway around the world, as you might expect, but from the New Forest, where a revolutionary and environmentally friendly fish farm is rearing them. The tasting menu is genuinely good value and runs a gamut of excellent flavours, many with subtle sweet/sour/spicy elements, along with dainty presentation and sensible portion sizes. Enjoyably morphing the flavours of several continents were a mussel and clam marinière infused with laksa leaf (sometimes called Vietnamese mint, although not really a mint); beautiful sea trout infused with coriander and port served on fennel mousse; and rabbit and lobster roulade with warmly fragrant vanilla bean potato mash. Unusual, stylish and satisfying food.
Book ahead. Children welcome: high chairs. Disabled: ramp; toilet. Dress: smart casual. Restaurant available for hire. Tables outdoors (28, garden). **Map 10 M7**.

Fitzrovia

★ Pied à Terre

34 Charlotte Street, W1T 2NH (7636 1178/ www.pied-a-terre.co.uk). Goodge Street or Tottenham Court Road tube. **Lunch served** 12.15-2.30pm Mon-Fri. **Dinner served** 6.15-11pm Mon-Sat. **Main courses** £32. **Set lunch** £24.50 2 courses, £30 3 courses. **Set dinner** £49.50 2 courses, £60 3 courses, £75 8 courses (£127 incl wine). **Credit** AmEx, MC, V.

Following a serious fire, tiny Pied à Terre has undergone a complete reconstruction and change of decor, from deep purple and brown tones to creamy cappuccino, which lightens the space considerably. Even so, some large and novel doughnut-like seating bays and a curvaceous wall still can't disguise the corridor confines of this

Addendum. See p125.

building. Staff congregate, duck and dive in a central section, leaving either end free for a mere handful of tables. You'll need to book a few days ahead, but there are no tedious month-long waiting lists to endure. The restaurant layout means that intimate conversation is best uttered elsewhere, but that's no bad thing since Shane Osborn's glorious food deserves your undivided attention. A deceptively simple-sounding lunch menu effortlessly and cleverly managed to satisfy all imaginable flavour fantasies, with quirky touches such as a starter of crispy chicken wings – boned, of course, and stuffed with foie gras – or confit cod cheeks (which probably took longer to coat in basil breadcrumbs than they took to confit), plus the constant feature of canapés, angelic in delicacy and genius. Another sure-footed combination took the form of pan-fried plaice fillets with creamed trompettes de mort, shelled baby broad beans and almond foam. Extra pennies lavished on the carte or tasting menus are well spent, providing an exciting array of ingredients arranged in mouth-teasing and sometimes challenging compositions. Wine is big here too, and £52 per person will see some cracking and unusual choices made on your behalf to accompany all eight courses for the gustatory carnival that is the tasting menu. The set lunch is excellent value.

Babies and children admitted. Booking advisable; essential weekends. Dress: smart casual.
No smoking. Separate room for parties, seats 12. Vegetarian menu. **Map 9 J5.**

Holborn

★ Pearl Bar & Restaurant

Chancery Court Hotel, 252 High Holborn, WC1V 7EN (7829 7000/www.pearl-restaurant. com). Holborn tube.
Bar **Open** 11am-11pm Mon-Fri; 6-11pm Sat.
Restaurant **Lunch served** noon-2.30pm Mon-Fri.
Dinner served 6-10pm Mon-Sat. **Set lunch** £23.50 2 courses, £26.50 3 courses. **Set dinner** £45 3 courses, £55 5 courses (£100 incl wine).
Both **Credit** AmEx, DC, MC, V.
It has taken a while to catch on, but this vast glossy venue, redesigned by the team behind Nobu and the Metropolitan hotel, is finally alive with folk who lunch, drink on the way home from work, eat alone on business, and dine in style with friends of an evening – all the punters that a swanky restaurant could wish for. Pearl was very quiet two years ago, but chef Jun Tanaka has steered the food from a fusion course to one heading firmly for France, giving Londoners what they really seem to want: understandable food. Nothing is dull, though, as Tanaka's history at heavenly abodes such as the Oak Room (Marco Pierre White), the Square (Phil Howard), the Capital, Chavot and Les Saveurs has given him an expert touch and shrewd eye for risk taking. So, the seared scallops with parsley purée and garlic foam are there all right, but accompanied by crusted frogs' legs; and the classic raviolo of turbot and langoustine stands not alone but on the same plate as braised oxtail

and horseradish. The result is a menu to keep traditionalists happy, yet goad the daring too. Just one of these novel combinations didn't work, an own-made coffee yoghurt with lemon foam that was truly nasty – but this was a complimentary pre-dessert so no lasting harm occurred. The packaging around the real desserts also seemed more substantial than their flavour, as in an elaborately presented tiramisu of fluffy nothingness. Mostly, Pearl offers a fabulous mix of hip surroundings, stunning food and an excellent wine and bar menu.
Babies and children welcome (if dining). Disabled: toilet. Music (pianist 6pm daily). No smoking (restaurant). **Map 10 M5.**

Knightsbridge

Boxwood Café

The Berkeley, Wilton Place, SW1X 7RL (7235 1010/www.gordonramsay.com). Hyde Park Corner or Knightsbridge tube. **Lunch served** noon-4pm Mon, Fri-Sun; noon-3pm Tue-Thur. **Dinner served** 6-11pm daily.
Main courses £12.50-£25. **Set lunch** £21 3 courses. **Set meal** £55 6 courses. **Credit** AmEx, MC, V.
Boxwood Café is so popular that the draughty, hard-floored corridor at street level, previously in service as a waylaying-with-drinks area, has been crammed with tables. That's where we were seated, on a night to freeze the ears off a brass monkey. Someone clearly more authoritative than us was

seen to a table alongside, but, on loudly declaring that he usually sat downstairs when he ate at Boxwood, was subsequently escorted down through the bar and into the cosier confines of the main restaurant. Dark and with a vaguely colonial-cum-oriental feel, modernised by quirky black and white photography, this branch of the Gordon Ramsay empire started out with casual café-like airs. However, the introduction this year of a tasting menu, smaller portions of more complex food, and an accompanying price increase all take the experience into decidedly classic restaurant territory. A proper à la carte menu with independent prices for each dish is available at both lunch and dinner. The choice is wide and tempting. At its simplest, a starter might be fried oysters with fennel and lemon, or a fusion-style boudin blanc of foie gras with poached spiced quince and sichuan pepper. Saddle of Dornoch lamb with pine nut crust, baby artichokes and celeriac purée demonstrates the unmistakable Ramsay influence, which winningly combines familiar British ingredient familiarity with hints of sunnier Mediterranean climes. Char-grilled Saudi prawns with blood orange hollandaise, and another main course of seared tuna with black pepper sauce were completely delicious, those giant shell-on prawns the very thing Marco Polo raved about en route to China.
Babies and children welcome: children's menu; high chairs. Booking essential. Disabled: toilet (in hotel). No smoking. Separate room for parties, seats 12-16. **Map 9 G9.**

★ The Capital

22-24 Basil Street, SW3 1AT (7589 5171/7591 1202/www.capitalhotel.co.uk). Knightsbridge tube.
Bar **Open** noon-1am daily.
Restaurant **Breakfast served** 7-10.30am Mon-Sat; 7.30-10.30am Sun. **Lunch served** noon-2.30pm daily. **Dinner served** 7-11pm Mon-Sat; 7-10.30pm Sun. **Set breakfast** £14 continental, £18.50 full English. **Set lunch** £29.50 3 courses. **Set dinner** £55 3 courses, £68 tasting menu.
Both **Credit** AmEx, DC, MC, V.
If a restaurant's quality could be measured in 'mmms', the Capital's diners would be delivering one of London's loudest murmurs of collective satisfaction. Chef Eric Chavot dishes out increasingly gorgeous food year after year. Rather than being a slave to fickle culinary fashions, he deliberately concentrates on hallowed French favourites with their traditional garnishes à la grandmère, barigoule and the like. But don't let that conjure up visions of stews stuck in the Dark Ages, or fading bistros offering thin crème caramels. Treacle-cured Scottish salmon served with a tangle of tempura-crisped soft-shell crab, dabs of chilli and spring roll prove that Chavot is a master of subtlety and divine presentation, and shows he refuses to let his style be pigeonholed. Strength in the kitchen is mirrored front of house (where some of London's best waiting staff glide around like guardian angels), and in the decor (a lesson in restrained expense and lustre). No fault could be found with any of our chosen dishes: the salmon starter described above; a smoky, sultry haddock risotto; and main courses of slow-cooked daube of beef with silky pommes purée; and an exciting melange of sweet and savoury pork delights. Manjari molleux is the last word in single-variety chocolate chic, the natural fruity character of the bubbly molten chocolate emphasised by a jazzy lime and ginger sorbet. If that isn't enough for you, log on to the website to book a place on one of pastry chef Andrew Gravett's 'passion for chocolate' master classes.
Booking advisable; essential weekends. Children over 12 admitted. Dress: smart casual. Restaurant available for hire. Separate rooms for parties, seating 10, 12 and 24. **Map 8 F9.**

Foliage

Mandarin Oriental Hyde Park Hotel, 66 Knightsbridge, SW1X 7LA (7201 3723/ www.mandarinoriental.com). Knightsbridge tube.
Lunch served noon-2.30pm, **dinner served** 7-10.30pm daily. **Set lunch** £25 3 courses (£32 incl wine). **Set meal** £47.50-£50 3 courses. **Credit** AmEx, DC, JCB, MC, V.
Split-level seating and floor-to-tall-ceiling windows ensure everyone eating at Foliage, or its little sister restaurant the Park next door, has a fabulous view of Hyde Park in all its sun-kissed (if you're lucky) greenery, complete with joggers, wedding parties and dog walkers. This lovely backdrop for Chris Staines' exciting and accomplished menu guarantees Foliage is constantly awash with suits, shoppers, tourists, retired Chelsea folk and ladies-who-lunch, yet the feel is never too busy, too casual or too formal. The food similarly manages the formidable achievement of being both slick and inviting, cunningly orchestrated and artistically presented with no sacrifice of honest-to-goodness flavour and seasonality. Successfully bridging two seasons, a competitively priced three-course lunch encompassed both comfort food and lighter options in the form of a soft-boiled egg, bacon and herbed toast assembly with a distinctly Sunday-morning-in-bed appeal, although the rich Burgundian wine sauce would be a tad beyond most DIY breakfasters. Dispensing a dash of sophisticated cauliflower velouté, a waiter nattily scattered a fairy ring of tiny diced salmon, cucumber, parsley and caviar in its bowl. Main courses were of equal contrast; Welsh lamb had real mountain-reared flavour and bite, rather than the innocent insubstantiality of much restaurant lamb, while a waistline-conscious plate of john dory on lightly spiced lentils came garnished with enticingly aromatic basil and green apple mousse. There was a long wait for both dessert and coffee, and staff were clearly exercised but unable to prevent whatever delay was unfolding in the kitchen. Glitches in service, however, happen rarely at Foliage. A very grown-up experience.
Babies and children welcome: high chairs. Booking advisable. Disabled: toilet. Dress: smart casual. **Map 8 F9.**

Mju

The Millennium Knightsbridge, 16-17 Sloane Street, SW1X 9NU (7201 6330/www. millenniumhotels.com). Knightsbridge tube.
Lunch served noon-2.30pm Fri. **Dinner served** 6.30-10.30pm Mon-Sat. **Main courses** £18-£26. **Set lunch** £39 3 courses incl champagne. **Set dinner** £39 2 courses, £42 3 courses, £46 5 courses (£71 incl wine); £62 tasting menu (£97, £132, £162 incl wine). **Credit** AmEx, DC, JCB, MC, V.
If someone asked you to direct them to Mju, it's unlikely that the black granite-clad façade of the Millennium Knightsbridge hotel would immediately spring to mind, followed by a clear mental picture of the shimmering artwork, secluded snugs and sleek oriental good-looks in the first-floor restaurant and bar. You probably don't know its whereabouts (between Fendi and Gucci, as it happens) because folk have yet to discover Mju. And, unfortunately, the bargain set lunch price of last year has been sacrificed on the voracious altar of economy, leaving only pricier options; how the management thinks this is going to entice in more customers is anybody's guess. At least Friday sees an opportunity to drink as much champagne as you want from the dubiously named Friday Fish & Fizz menu – fizz included at no extra charge. Food is genuinely good and described as 'not fusion, but French with an Asian twist'. The bar is a genuinely good place to hunker down with cracking cocktails and a few mates. A three-course meal kicked off with sweet and succulent beetroot, papaya, pine nut and toasted halloumi cheese salad. This was followed by a deconstructed fricassée of lobster and chicken, fragrant with saffron and carefully spaced on a capacious platter with a prawn dumpling and too-thick dribble of thai green curry sauce. Desserts balance hot and cold, sweet and spicy, dense and ethereal, and should not be missed. Hot chocolate fondant is getting a bit old hat, but continues to draw all but the most disciplined to its dark, molten, bittersweet loveliness, especially when a touch of spiced fig ice-cream and vanilla mousse is thrown in. Come now, lest there be further downsizing.
Babies and children welcome: high chairs. Booking advisable. Disabled: lift; toilets. No smoking. Restaurant available for hire. **Map 8 F9.**

La Noisette NEW

164 Sloane Street, SW1X 9QB (7750 5000/ www.gordonramsay.com). Knightsbridge or Sloane Square tube. **Lunch served** noon-2.30pm Mon-Fri. **Dinner served** 6-11pm Mon-Sat. **Set meal** £55-£65 tasting menu. **Credit** AmEx, MC, V.
Bjorn van der Horst has moved from the Greenhouse and, with backing from Gordon Ramsay Holdings, is now chef-patron of La Noisette. This first-floor site owned by the adjacent Jumeirah Carlton Tower hotel was most recently known as Pengelley's; it's an 'unlucky site' that has changed name and chefs as often as Gordon Ramsay changes Ferraris, but this new enterprise appears to be the most serious yet. The new decor features lots of wood veneer, crisp heavy linens, a bold Mediterranean landscape painting, and palest pink roses on the table. Van der Horst's choice of menus includes à la carte, a six-course seasonal tasting menu and the 'Inspirational Tasting Menu' – an offer to 'take you on a culinary adventure' inspired by the day's market produce. Almond gazpacho was poured by the waiter into a dish of shrimp flavoured with smoked paprika and a little tomato sorbet. With tiny peeled green grapes bobbing in the dish as well, this was a savvy balance of sweet and bitter. Sharing is encouraged in dishes such as lemon and thyme roast chicken with meze and persian rice, and rib of beef with mash and condiments. Like the roasted john dory with plump razor clams among the accompanying shellfish, these are carved tableside by smartly dressed yet friendly waiters. A little chocolate baba came with gorgeous chocolate ice-cream and poached cherries. Fromage blanc soufflé was given oomph with a hint of thyme, and served on rich-tasting poached apricots with toasted almond ice-cream. The wine list inexcusably begins around the £20 mark, but the charming sommelier otherwise won us over; staff were eager to please throughout, and highly welcoming. Let's hope this one lasts longer than its predecessors.
Babies and children welcome: high chairs. Booking advisable. Disabled: toilet. No smoking. Restaurant available for hire. **Map 14 9F.**

One-O-One

101 William Street, SW1X 7RN (7290 7101). Knightsbridge tube. **Lunch served** noon-2.30pm, **dinner served** 7-10.30pm daily. **Main courses** £22-£28. **Set lunch** £25 3 courses. **Set dinner** £48 5 courses, £79 tasting menu. **Credit** AmEx, DC, JCB, MC, V.
Some say this is the best fish restaurant in London and certainly Breton chef Pascal Proyart is serious about seafood. Dishes are pretty, generous and on the right side of adventurous, with plenty of novel combinations that you probably won't have eaten elsewhere. Meat is available, but mostly it's woven carefully into other fish ingredients, such as a dish of pan-fried john dory garnished with slow-cooked pork belly. Desserts don't really match the quality of the fish dishes; in fact, if you aren't of a piscivorous nature, you may be fed more joyously elsewhere. If you are, you'll enjoy a fresh, delicious and sustainably sourced meal starting with the likes of a surprisingly delicate ravioli of Norwegian king crab risotto. Yes, rice wrapped in pasta, but both were light as a feather and profoundly tasty, served with a smidgen of parmesan sauce and sharp, lemony sorrel salad. A set lunch continued with red fish goujonettes, deep fried in an exemplary light beer batter but not drained before hitting the plate and therefore too greasy. These were accompanied by tartare sauce and gruyère cheese mashed potato (repeating the cheesiness of the first course and served almost cold: a shame, because this could have been a great combo). Such inconsistencies in otherwise lovely food drag One-O-One some way short of being the best. The furnishings and service need attention too. The cool aquamarine decor would be better suited to Brittany's bracing coastline than a city centre, and staff, while genuinely nice, bumbled about too much to be taken seriously. Still, there's no denying the appeal of a cool glass of riesling with some damn fine seafood.

Homage

Inspired by the grand cafés of Europe, indulge in the majestic Grand Salon, Homage Bar or the intimate Homage Patisserie for the traditional Waldorf Afternoon Tea

homagerestaurant.co.uk

020 7759 4080

Aldwych, London, WC2B 4DD

A mouth watering journey around the South Pacific

tradervics.com

020 7208 4113

London Hilton on Park Lane, 22 Park Lane, W1K 4BE

Chef's tables

Just as reality TV series now require an element of jeopardy to keep the viewers' attention, fine dining also seeks to lure customers by inviting them into the kitchen to see the temper tantrums and pot-boiler dramas. The 'chef's table' originated overseas (probably first in the US, then in Australia), where it meant a table inside the kitchen where diners can watch the chefs in action while having their meal. However, the term is now used very loosely for any booth or table with a view of the kitchen – available often at a premium price, and usually seating a group of between four and 12 people. In theory, you are close enough to the kitchen to feel the heat, sense the concentration and hear the banter of a real commercial kitchen in full swing – though, in reality, the chef's tables that we have tried have offered a much more cossetted experience.

Gordon Ramsay Holdings have been the most enthusiastic takers of the concept in London, as you might expect from a company that is never slow in promoting its chefs as celebrities. And the concept is proving popular, especially for corporate entertaining. Restaurants currently offering chef's tables include **Angela Hartnett at the Connaught**, **Gordon Ramsay at Claridge's**, **Maze**, **Pétrus** and the **Savoy Grill** (in the British section). Don't forget, though, that countless other London restaurants also allow you to experience a fine view of the chefs at work, from Dalston's Turkish grill restaurants to many gastropubs to nearly every sushi bar in London – and for a fraction of the price you'll be paying for one of Mr Ramsay's hallowed tables.

Babies and children welcome: high chairs. Booking advisable Thur-Sun. Disabled: toilet (in hotel). Dress: smart casual. No-smoking tables. **Map 8 F9.**

★ Pétrus

The Berkeley, Wilton Place, SW1X 7RL (7235 1200/www.petrus-restaurant.com). Hyde Park Corner or Knightsbridge tube. **Lunch served** noon-2.30pm Mon-Fri. **Dinner served** 6-10.45pm Mon-Sat. **Set lunch** £30 3 courses. **Set dinner** £60 3 courses, £80 tasting menu. **Credit** AmEx, MC, V.

A meal here is a treat to be savoured. Such food, combined with sumptuous decor and smooth, somewhat theatrical service, makes Pétrus a fantastic venue for any kind of celebration. The look is dark and sophisticated, with purple velvet (Gordon Ramsay's signature hue, although the kitchen is Marcus Wareing's domain) padding the walls from floor to ceiling. Dazzlingly beautiful lights and an abundance of silverware create a visual stir against the soft plummy backdrop. Guests tend to be plummy too, elegantly dressed and often on their way to or from shows, private gallery openings and book signings. The cuisine is firmly in the style of Ramsay, with elegant, carefully balanced menus, slow-cooked this, luxury-topped that and plenty of mirror-finish sauces poured at table around precisely prepared squares of faultless meat and fish. From the à la carte, a starter of seared tuna was dramatically blood-red in colour with just the bare rim seared golden brown, sharpened by a touch of pink grapefruit and served atop cool melon carpaccio: good looks with subtle flavours. Punchier was a square of red mullet 'confit', soft and pliant on silky fennel purée. Main courses were sliced veal with pommes anna, rounded out by a tasty grain mustard sauce and morels; and an unusually poached and glazed duck breast with madeira jus, baby veg and little else. Earl grey-scented cream, wittily capped with milk foam, was followed by supercharged espresso and the matchless bonbon trolley, which is wheeled tantalisingly around the room, goodies being dispensed for instant delectation, or a box provided for takeaway indulgence later. Very civilised.
Babies and children welcome: high chairs. Booking essential. Dress: smart; jacket preferred. No smoking. Separate room for parties, seats 16. Vegetarian menu. **Map 9 G9.**

Mayfair

Angela Hartnett at the Connaught

The Connaught, 16 Carlos Place, W1K 2AL (7592 1222/www.gordonramsay.com). Bond Street or Green Park tube. **Breakfast served** 7-10.30am Mon-Fri; 7-11am Sat, Sun. **Lunch served** noon-2.45pm Mon-Fri; noon-3.30pm Sat, Sun. **Dinner served** 5.45-11pm Mon-Sat; 7-10.30pm Sun. **Set lunch** £30 3 courses. **Set dinner** £55 3 courses, £70 6 courses. **Credit** AmEx, DC, MC, V.

With a fabulous luxury setting, opening hours that stretch lengthily into each day of the week, and pedigree by the bucket-load, the Connaught ticks many of the right boxes for folk with money and time on their hands. The elegantly original and beautifully decorated dining room is usually full (although it's worth trying your luck for a midday sojourn sans booking). Most customers – foreign visitors, business people and regulars – follow suit, with their ageing but carefully tended patinas. They are dedicated foodies all, so Angela Hartnett has an appreciative audience upon which to shower her considerable culinary talent. Overall, dishes on each menu have settled into a comfortable Modern British-cum-Mediterranean partnership. A few surprises sneak through the back door (duck gizzard in a salad, for example, or soft-shelled crab and chilli spaghetti), but these are tamed so as not to shock the core clientele. Hartnett conducts tours of the kitchen and dining room, signing menus to keep everybody in touch with celebrity. Bread, tapenade, olive oil and a fresh-faced cup of pea shoot velouté made a deliciously promising start to a meal, which continued through a salad of summery artichoke, semi-dried tomato and sweet, fresh sairass ricotta, dressed with 2005 Manni olive oil. For the main courses, Castle Mey beef (sadly, no further info is offered about these intriguing ingredients) – was a slab of fillet pan-fried, sliced and stacked around a soothing cake of braised oxtail – was spectacularly good, while roasted moulard duck breast, cooked and cut the same way, was boldly treated with mustard, pears and orange-glazed chicory. Charming earl grey tea bavarois (similarly served at Pétrus) with Sprite granita rounded off a gorgeous meal.
Babies and children welcome: high chairs. Booking essential. Disabled: lift; toilet. No smoking. Separate rooms for parties, seating 14 and 22. Vegetarian menu. **Map 9 H7.**

Brian Turner Mayfair

Millennium Hotel Mayfair, 44 Grosvenor Square, W1K 2HP (7596 3444/www.millenniumhotels.com). Bond Street tube.
Bar **Open** noon-midnight Mon-Fri; 6.30-11.30pm Sat.
Restaurant **Lunch served** 12.30-2.30pm Mon-Fri. **Dinner served** 6.30-10.30pm Mon-Sat. **Main courses** £13.50-£28. **Set lunch** £23.50 2 courses, £26.50 3 courses.
Both **Credit** AmEx, DC, MC, V.

More thought has gone into the menu construction here recently, with sensible dishes and their key components straightforwardly stated. There's also a clear definition between the appealingly British à la carte and a pared-to-the-bone lunch menu, which lists just three options for each of three courses. Brian Turner's restaurant isn't pretending to be anything other than a relaxed, down-to-earth, pleasingly kitted out place for a bite to eat and a tipple, minus the heart-stopping prices charged by Turner's TV-obsessed compatriots. It's a refreshingly low-key take for a hotel restaurant, particularly given the location and sheer upper-crustiness of Grosvenor Square. Home-grown dishes may include braised ox cheeks with celeriac mash, smoked bacon and shallots; grilled dover sole with hollandaise; or Brixham crab mayonnaise, with egg custard tart to finish – all carefully sourced, generously portioned and competently cooked. Familiar ingredients make for an approachable meal, so this is a good place to bring your less adventurous friends, and grandma on her 80th. Salad of baby spinach, red chard, green beans, sliced asparagus, pine nuts, sun-blushed raisins (and the kitchen sink), was pretty much as you'd make it yourself at home with a bag of supermarket salad leaves and nuts tipped straight from the packet (and no noticeable suntan on the raisins). So, no fireworks, but a fish main course was bang on target: monkfish, served on the bone, perfectly fresh and perfectly cooked, its snowy white flesh moist and well married to exotically infused cardamom basmati rice with a smattering of lobster and crab running through it, all surrounded by coriander cream sauce. A concise but well-chosen wine list won't break the bank and adds a welcome dimension of luxury.
Babies and children admitted. Booking advisable. Disabled: toilet (in hotel). Dress: smart casual. No-smoking tables. Separate room for parties, seats 45. Tables outdoors (5, terrace). **Map 9 G7.**

Galvin at Windows NEW

28th Floor, The London Hilton, Park Lane, W1K 1BE (7208 4021). Green Park or Hyde Park Corner tube.
Bar **Open** noon-1am Mon-Thur; noon-3am Fri; 5.30-3am Sat; noon-10.30pm Sun. **Admission** £7 after 11pm.
Restaurant **Breakfast served** 7-10.30am daily. **Lunch served** noon-2.30pm Mon-Fri; noon-3pm Sun. **Dinner served** 6-10.30pm Mon-Sat. **Main courses** £15-£28. **Set lunch** £28 3 courses. **Set dinner** £65 6 courses (£95 incl wine).
Both **Credit** AmEx, DC, MC, V.

Galvin at Windows' sumptuous views over Hyde Park and across south London, from the 28th floor of the Hilton, are worth at least one visit. The kitchen is headed by Chris Galvin, who produced haute cuisine to acclaim at Orrery before helping open the Wolseley and then, with brother Jeff, Galvin Bistrot de Luxe on Baker Street. Galvin at Windows sees him back in full posh-dinner mode, and it's a pleasure. Working with head chef André Garrett (also ex-Orrery), he presents a modern French menu with dishes such as a chunky cutlet of Limousin veal with broad beans and fresh morels, and roast langoustine with slow-cooked pork belly and cauliflower purée. Our fillet of john dory, with tender, juicy braised fennel, jerusalem artichoke and pinot noir sauce, was slightly overcooked and dry, but the freshness of the fish remained clear. It was all we could find to criticise in an exquisite procession of dishes. Marinated scallops were thinly sliced and presented with alternating discs of Jersey royal potatoes in a beautifully simple yet luxurious starter. Fresh basil was cleverly employed to enliven crème brûlée, topped with a strawberry ice-cream of pure fruit flavour. Yes, this is where to come for a special occasion. Apart from an ungracious woman at the front desk, service was excellent too. We have gripes about the starting prices for wine (the cheapest glass of red is £11.25), but the bottles aren't poor value; our Carmenère La Poda Corta, a red from Chile's Rapel Valley, was fabulous. The bar is stylish, not too trendy, but a little small. A singer-guitarist in Jack Johnson mode hit the right note of late-evening entertainment. But £10.50 plus service for a small Martini (and no nibbles) is, well, a bit rich.

Babies and children welcome (restaurant).
Disabled: toilet (in hotel). No smoking.
Map 9 G8.

★ Le Gavroche

43 Upper Brook Street, W1K 7QR (7408 0881/
www.le-gavroche.co.uk). Marble Arch tube.
Lunch served noon-2pm Mon-Fri. **Dinner**
served 6.30-11pm Mon-Sat. **Main courses**
£27-£40. **Minimum** (dinner) £60. **Set lunch**
£46 3 courses incl half bottle of wine,
mineral water, coffee. **Set dinner** £90 tasting
menu (£140 incl wine). **Credit** AmEx, DC, JCB,
MC, V.

If you're scanning menu prices in this illustrious
section of the guide, you'll have noticed that Le
Gavroche is top of the pops. Those who've eaten
here before will know exactly why that is, and
those who haven't might press on to another venue.
Don't. Brothers Michel and Albert Roux opened the
'Urchin' or 'Ragamuffin' (named after a painting)
in 1967, offering food previously experienced only
in France. Ever since, Le Gavroche has not just
dominated the London restaurant scene, but has
drawn food lovers from across the globe. Michel
Roux Jnr (Albert's son) took over the kitchen in
1991 and lightened things up a little, but not one
iota of prestige has faded in the process. Attention
to detail is unequalled, from the moment of
booking to the moment of your cruel release back
on to the street afterwards. The food is full of
gentle surprises, carefully considered temperature
differentials and sublime tapestries of taste. Worth
every penny is the seven-course menu exceptionnel,
which, after canapés and appetiser, kicked off
feistily with rare peppered tuna on mouth-tingling
ginger and chilli. Sensational too was a crisp-cased,
molten-middled, sizzling hot slab of foie gras with
warm duck and cinnamon pastilla. Nobody here
shouts about this fusion aspect of Michel Roux's
food, unlike other chefs who just love to label and
fanfare their individuality, and yet his style
positively glows with brilliance. Milky new lamb
from the Pyrenees (along with a profound sun-
baked thyme jus, garlic and flageolets) marked the
passing of the main course. It was followed by
another romp over French mountains via the
cheeseboard, on to divine desserts – bitter
chocolate, steeped pears, salted caramel and so on,
crowned by simply the best coffee and petits fours.

Children admitted. Booking essential. Dress:
jacket; no jeans or trainers. No smoking.
Restaurant available for hire. **Map 9 G7.**

★ Gordon Ramsay
at Claridge's

Claridge's, 55 Brook Street, W1K 4HR (7499
0099/www.gordonramsay.com). Bond Street tube.
Lunch served noon-2.45pm Mon-Fri; noon-
3pm Sat, Sun. **Dinner served** 5.45-11pm Mon-
Sat; 6-11pm Sun. **Set lunch** £30 3 courses.
Set dinner £60 3 courses, £75 6 courses. **Credit**
AmEx, DC, JCB, MC, V.

Sneaking into Claridge's at lunchtime, without a
booking but laden with shopping bags, has to be
one of London's matchless little nuggets of
indulgence. Arrive shortly after midday on a
Monday to Thursday and you're more than likely
to secure a precious table, although the tedious
telephone booking system is unavoidable at any
other time. For such a glamorous venue – the entire
hotel basks in a vintage-luxe league of its own –
the restaurant is a happy, buzzy place and more
relaxed than other GR enterprises such as Royal
Hospital Road, the Connaught or Pétrus. The menu
is exciting without resorting to whimsy, and
satisfyingly, mood-enhancingly seasonal. A few of
the more unusual offerings on this trip included
salmon with pan-fried watermelon and ginger
velouté, and the day's appetiser which consisted of
frothy creamed celeriac soup boldly punctuated by
the tart and hot flavours of diced granny smith
apple and horseradish. Counteracting the cold wet
weather, succour came from the à la carte menu in
the form of crisp oxtail pancakes marooned in a
pool of brown onion consommé in which a few
slices of winter truffle bobbed, adding to an overall
theme of steaming, sticky, rustic intensity. Also
bang on the nose was a dish of west country pork
cheeks, the meat braised to short, loose luscious
threads, charged with honey, clove and cinnamon
braising juices and served on a silky, buttery,
grain-mustard pommes mousseline (which really
can't be described as mashed potato). Desserts run
from the familiar, perfectly executed type (lemon
tart/parfait/syllabub) to the more dashing tropical
and fusion type: the gold dust on an exceptional
restaurant experience.

Babies and children welcome: high chairs.
Booking essential. Disabled: toilet. Dress: smart;

jacket preferred; no jeans or trainers. Separate
rooms for parties, seating 6, 10 and 30.
Vegetarian menu. **Map 9 H6.**

★ Greenhouse

27A Hay's Mews, W1J 5NY (7499 3331/www.
greenhouserestaurant.co.uk). Green Park tube.
Lunch served noon-2.30pm Mon-Fri. **Dinner**
served 6.45-11pm Mon-Sat. **Set lunch** £28
2 courses, £32 3 courses. **Set meal** £60 3 courses,
£75 tasting menu. **Credit** AmEx, DC, MC, V.

Tucked down a quaint mews, this fabulous
restaurant feels more like a very secret garden
serving exceptional food to a select number of
special guests, rather than anything remotely
linked to a greenhouse (but that's what it was
called years ago under Gary Rhodes). The booking
system is painless and a table usually available just
when you want it. Your credit card details are not
taken hostage to confirm the arrangement, and no
ludicrous cancellation charges are threatened
(Ramsay and Aikens, take note). Staff are genned
up on the most minute food details, go about their
work expertly and don't harrumph at customers
not spending lavishly on wine or extras. There's
no turning of tables, the entrance is amazing and
the colour scheme of paprika, cappuccino and
walnut is beautifully stylish. As for the food, chefs
manipulate your senses like magicians, yet the
showmanship is never at the expense of your
enjoyment. Stand-outs from the pricey but worthy
tasting menu were sea urchin and butternut soup
with silken tofu and mussels; and moist Limousin
veal and salsify gratin seasoned with two praline
elements (a bitter caramel and nut sauce
contrasting with a separate, sweet, warm hazelnut
foam, both of which came together and focused
attention like a searchlight on the meat). Also
splendid were a mini dessert of dark chocolate
sorbet and soft milk chocolate espuma, hiding a
cheeky crunch of salted butter popcorn; and a
spellbinding granita served at the end to cleanse
the palate, raking across the tongue in an icy blast
of celery, followed by a prickle of salt and a vodka
and lime fillip, which lurked in the base of the
glass. A fun, crest-of-a-wave experience no self-
respecting foodies should deny themselves.

Babies and children admitted. Booking essential.
Dress: smart casual. No smoking. Separate room
for parties, seats 10. **Map 9 H7.**

RESTAURANTS

The Grill. See p132.

The Grill NEW

Brown's Hotel, 33-34 Albemarle Street, W1S 4BP (7493 6020/www.roccofortehotels.com). Green Park tube. **Lunch served** 12.30-2.30pm daily. **Tea served** 2-5.45pm daily. **Dinner served** 6-10.30pm daily. **Set tea** £25, £30 (extra £11 for champagne). **Main courses** £16.50-£32. **Set meal** (lunch, 6-7pm Mon-Sat) £25 2 courses, £30 3 courses. **Credit** AmEx, DC, MC, V.

Brown's became a hotel in 1837 and has been in the hands of Rocco Forte since 2003. The Georgian building (originally 11 townhouses) has recently emerged from a two-year mega-million refit. Exquisite features remain, thankfully, and the restaurant has undergone sensitive transformation: oak panelling faintly lightened, sash windows complemented by gauzy drapes, delicious lighting, and the introduction of subtle earthy green colours in 1930s furniture. So, it impresses the eye, but how about the tongue? Executive chef Laurence Glayzer's name may not be familiar, but his previous time at the Savoy Grill, Harry's Bar and the Ritz gives a clue to his traditional leanings. The Grill panders to tourists and old-school types with its nursery timetable of daily specials from the carving trolley or, from the carte, rib of beef, rump of beef, beef rossini, steak and kidney pie, calf's liver and bacon… a meaty, British bulldog kind of menu where fish or vegetarian dishes get barely a look in. Morecambe Bay potted shrimps, and pea and ham soup, were as good as they could have been, but a main of calf's liver and bacon was curiously pungent and furry, and an excellent slab of char-grilled Scottish beef came with unpleasantly tepid pan-fried foie gras. Once this was mentioned, staff were most apologetic and offered a replacement or free desserts, but such fundamental errors are unacceptable in a top-flight kitchen. There are more nursery comforts for afters, where pastry, cream and custard abound, but that's no bad thing: the Grill is proudly British without influences of here, there and everywhere clouding the mixture. Service let the place down on this occasion, staff making great attempts to look busy rather than wait on tables and then making mistakes aplenty. A very British experience all round.
Children over 12 years admitted (lunch). Disabled: toilet (in hotel). No smoking. **Map 9 J7.**

Maze

10-13 Grosvenor Square, W1K 6JP (7107 0000/ www.gordonramsay.com). Bond Street tube. **Bar Open** noon-midnight daily. **Restaurant Tapas** £6-£9. **Main courses** £14-£20. **Both Lunch served** noon-3pm, **dinner served** 6-11pm daily. **Credit** AmEx, DC, MC, V.

In a bid to tempt younger diners into fine-dining rooms and keep pace with the trend for smaller portions of more daring food combinations, Maze has repackaged Ramsay for the hip. Head chef Jason Atherton has inside knowledge of Spain's famous El Bulli. The blurb prefacing the menu trumpets the Asian-French influence he brings, but the food here tastes pure Ramsay. Expensively reared protein is prepared and cooked to perfection, flavours are intense, sauces essence-like, the presentation finely tuned. Perhaps Maze is slightly victim to its own media hype, because we expected the buzz and spontaneity of a tapas bar, we found instead classic haute cuisine, served course by course. Asian interest was restricted to mere trimmings on plates and uniforms. Outstanding among our selection were Cornish crab mayonnaise with avocado, sweetcorn sorbet and caviar; jerusalem artichoke velouté with duck ragout and cep brioche; Orkney scallops roasted with spices, raisin purée and cauliflower; and slow-cooked beef tongue and cheek with gingered carrots. Portions are tiny, not listed under traditional starter and main course headings, and priced at around £8 each – the idea being that you select anything you fancy in quantities to suit. The menu's recommendation of eight-plus courses per person would result in complete overload. Five or so plates including a mini dessert means you can experience a Ramsay-style meal on quite a modest budget: an opportunity to be celebrated. Decor is coffee, cream and lime-splashed sleek, the cocktails free-flowing and fabulous. Many staff didn't speak good English or know what to do with the constant cutlery changes on our visit, but don't let such details put you off.
Babies and children welcome: high chairs. Booking advisable. Disabled: toilet. No smoking. Separate room for parties, seats 10. **Map 9 G6.**

Sketch: The Lecture Room

9 Conduit Street, W1S 2XZ (0870 777 4488/ www.sketch.uk.com). Oxford Circus tube. **Lunch served** noon-2.30pm Tue-Fri. **Dinner served** 7-10.30pm Tue-Sat. **Main courses** £45-£59. **Set lunch** £35 3 courses. **Set dinner** £80-£140 3 courses. **Credit** AmEx, DC, MC, V.

Surprises flow thick and fast at Sketch, starting with the *Alice in Wonderland* entrance. Greeters lead you down to the Gallery (Louis XIV meets IMAX theatre) or up to the Lecture Room ('Pierre Gagnaire's fine dining experience,' we were told), along with a history of the building. Remember to specify which venue you want when booking. A pâtisserie, the Parlour, resides on the ground floor and there is also a new less costly lunch restaurant, the Glade. The Lecture Room is light, colourful, high ceilinged and quirky. Waiting staff are strictly schooled, which sometimes interferes with customers' desires. There seemed to be a problem with the wine list and menu being on the table at the same time, and although we were allowed to keep the menu for reference during the meal, it clearly disturbed staff, so a separate side table was produced for it to perch on. Food is overtly designed to challenge culinary preconceptions. Technically brilliant nibbles (all the pastry work is superb) gave way to tasting menus, highlights of which included featherweight foie gras chantilly with crab and smoked eel; sea bass on sweet dried fruits, apple and riesling; and quinoa, spelt and bulgar risotto with turnip. On the scarier side of unusual were a shot glass of ewe's milk velouté and chestnut honey (nice flavours, but have you ever tried sucking honey through a straw?), and a quadruplet of desserts that overstepped the unspoken law that the end of a meal should caress and soothe instead of clash with confused fruit flavours and bolshie textures. The bill is slipped into the pages of a visitors' book, with comments that edit down to 'amazing', 'memorable', 'different', 'interesting', 'expensive'. Nevertheless, prices are down on last year.
Babies and children admitted. Booking essential. Dress: smart casual. Restaurant available for hire. **Map 9 J6.**

★ The Square

6-10 Bruton Street, W1J 6PU (7495 7100/ www.squarerestaurant.com). Bond Street or Green Park tube. **Lunch served** noon-2.45pm Mon-Fri. **Dinner served** 6.30-10.45pm Mon-Sat; 6.30-9.45pm Sun. **Set lunch** £25 2 courses, £30 3 courses. **Set dinner** £60 3 courses, £75 8 courses. **Credit** AmEx, DC, JCB, MC, V.

Post-refit, the Square has assumed a more refined air, eschewing the worn oak parquet for a sleeker, darker floor, buff polished plaster walls, silvery blinds and elegant mocha lampshades. Once the place had filled up, staff looked less glum and deftly got on with the job of waiting on tables rather than just waiting around. Chef Philip Howard remains on delectable form. Although set lunch prices are exceptionally good value for such delicious food, the choice of just two dishes for each course failed to fire the anticipatory appetite on this occasion, so we plumped for the more luxurious à la carte option of main course and dessert for £50. Line-caught cod with crisp and piquant beaufort cheese crust was accompanied by vivid crushed broad beans, with morels and uplifting bay leaf emulsion. Fabulously chunky and meaty saddle of lamb came encrusted with Mediterranean herbs, shallot purée, artichoke hearts, dangerous whole garlic cloves, balsamic vinegar and olive oil. Good as these were, it was the desserts that stole the show: a lush salted caramel mousse with poached pear, honeycomb tuiles and an amber droplet of cashew praline; and eton mess. Devised, supposedly, by public school boys vigorously stirring strawberries, cream and meringue together, this really is a mess to look at – usually. Served with humour and purity but none of the prepubescent presentation skills, the Square's version of eton mess consists of no less than five mini strawberry-themed desserts: the aforementioned meringue combo delicately folded together, with strawberry syrup on top; a hot fresh doughnut filled with strawberry jam; a dinky kilner jar of creamy panna cotta and strawberry compote; an amazingly refreshing champagne flute of strawberry juice; and a mini strawberry ice-cream cone. Form an orderly queue, boys.
Babies and children admitted. Booking essential. Disabled: toilet. Dress: smart. No smoking. Restaurant available for hire. Separate room for parties, seats 18. **Map 9 H7.**

Piccadilly

The Ritz

150 Piccadilly, W1J 9BR (7493 8181/ www.theritzhotel.co.uk). Green Park tube. **Bar Open** 11.30am-11pm Mon-Sat; noon-10.30pm Sun. *Restaurant* **Breakfast served** 7-10.30am Mon-Sat; 8-10.30am Sun. **Lunch served** 12.30-2.30pm daily. **Tea served** (reserved sittings) 11.30am, 1.30pm, 3.30pm, 5.30pm, 7.30pm daily. **Dinner served** 6-10.30pm Mon-Sat; 7-10pm Sun. **Main courses** £25-£40. **Set tea** £35. **Set dinner** (6-7pm, 10-10.30pm) £45 3 courses; Mon-Thur £65 4 courses; Fri, Sat £80 4 courses. *Both* **Credit** AmEx, MC, V.

If you like your meals to include pomp and flounce, then the Ritz will be right up your Piccadilly. If you don't like being told how to dress, or dislike evening dances and piano music, then you might not appreciate this bells-and-whistles dining experience. Gilding, drapes, buttonholes and starch still form the bedrock of César Ritz's hotel, much as they have done since it opened in 1906. Gaze in awe at the trompe l'oeils and cherub-encrusted cornicing. Wonder at the time it must take the morning-suited waiters to set the tables three times a day. Expect cruets, cloches and chargers, rose bowls, butter dishes and bread baskets, plus numerous changes of cutlery and elaborate trolleys groaning with a hundred loaves or Roast of the Day – all the accoutrements gleaming in that solid, self-assured way that only antique silver can. Prices don't smart quite as much this year as they did last, with a few pounds here and there off the resolutely traditional menu. Lunch is on the lighter side, possibly opening with smoked trout and celeriac remoulade dressed with a dash of passionfruit, followed by a modest slice of lamb saddle 'belle epoch' (which refers to an inoffensive if bland stuffing), and a wild dessert of green apple jelly with creamy cold tapioca and caramel ice-cream. Yes, we chose this last option for a dare, but it turned out to be the star of the show. Roll up, roll up for a ride at the Ritz.
Babies and children welcome: children's menu; high chairs. Disabled: toilet. Booking advisable restaurant; essential afternoon tea. Dress: jacket and tie; no jeans or trainers. Entertainment: dinner dance Fri, Sat (restaurant); pianist daily. Separate rooms for parties, seating 22 and 55. Tables outdoors (8, terrace). **Map 9 J7.**

St James's

L'Oranger

5 St James's Street, SW1A 1EF (7839 3774/ www.loranger.co.uk). Green Park tube. **Lunch served** noon-2.30pm Mon-Fri. **Dinner served** 6-10.30pm Mon-Sat. **Main courses** £24-£29 (lunch); £22-£29 (dinner). **Set lunch** £27 2 courses, £32 3 courses. **Set dinner** £40 3 courses, £70 6 courses. **Credit** AmEx, DC, MC, V.

L'Oranger is one of those laudable venues that manages to feel both intimate and local, as well as smart and special: a seldom-found ambience that most restaurants would practically kill for. It's one of the reasons there's a full house here for lunch and dinner. You'll be lucky to get a table without

phoning ahead, unless you turn up at midday Monday to Wednesday. Expect classic decor with mirrors and oak panelling, and light bouncing through a central atrium – all enhanced by tables of blinding white linen and sparkling, fishbowl-sized wine glasses. The food, care of Frenchman Laurence Michel, isn't half bad either. Challenging the straitlaced aesthetic of St James's more conservative suits, dishes are attractively spread-eagled across spacious plates, wafting the goodly scent of reduced cooking juices, fresh herbs and sizzled meat under your nose. Both appetite and taste buds are satisfied with the innovative, vaguely French combinations. Negligibly smaller but distinctly cheaper than the à la carte, the 'business lunch' doesn't suffer from inferior content or cooking skills, and is thus excellent value; £27 gives you two courses, as opposed to one main course from the carte (our dover sole was £28). One menu produced a delicately spiced, slow-cooked calamares pie with thin, crisp, buttery pastry, 'market garden' salad and tomato salsa, while the other gave us a few fine fillets of dover sole with intense wild mushrooms and fresh grapes in classic cream sauce. So difficult to choose between them… Service is impeccable too, in a restaurant that deserves more publicity – although perhaps that would spoil it for the regulars.
Children over 7 years admitted. Booking essential. Dress: smart casual; no trainers. Separate room for parties, seats 32. Tables outdoors (6, courtyard). Map 9 J8.

South Kensington

Tom Aikens

43 Elystan Street, SW3 3NT (7584 2003/ www.tomaikens.co.uk). South Kensington tube. **Lunch served** noon-2.30pm, **dinner served** 6.45-11pm Mon-Fri. **Set lunch** £29 3 courses. **Set meal** £60 3 courses, £75-£100 7 courses. **Credit** AmEx, JCB, MC, V.
Light and airy by day, dark and sombre by night, this stand-alone restaurant needs to earn its keep through pure enticement of customers, as opposed to having a hotel full of captive businessmen attached. Consequently, it should always be on top and most welcoming form. After several phone calls booking, handing over credit card details, being told what not to wear and how much a cancellation would cost (a staggering £55 per person), then having to reconfirm on the day… it was all a rather unwelcoming performance. Besides, we were the only people who had obeyed the dress code, so what's the point in having one? Still, the food is good and the set lunch, although limited to just two choices per course, includes sensational petits fours and coffee – at £29 a head it's well worth pitching up for. Said sweet frivolities came in the form of fruit twizzlers and lollipops coated in chocolate and space dust (remember that?), spiced truffles and tiny bowls of crème brûlée, lemon posset and the like – better, in fact, than the dessert of the day, which was an unadventurous mango assembly. Cheese proved a more preferable option, despite the set lunch choice restricted to a pre-selected four specimens, and crackers and bread having to be practically begged for. Main courses were superb, less pretentious than of late and majoring in the flavour department rather than the art department. Succulent, long-roasted and caramelised pork belly came with strips of unnecessary squid, but on funky spiced chickpeas and intense bacon jus. John dory was also fine, crisply edged and lightly accompanied by hot sliced cucumber, pea shoots and buttery asparagus sauce. Slick, but could be more customer-friendly.
Children over 7 years admitted. Booking essential dinner. Disabled: toilet. Dress: smart casual. No smoking Map 14 E11.

South West
Chelsea

★ Aubergine

11 Park Walk, SW10 0AJ (7352 3449/ www.auberginerestaurant.co.uk). Bus 14, 345, 414. **Lunch served** noon-2.15pm Mon-Fri.

Dinner served 7-11pm Mon-Sat. **Set lunch** £34 3 courses incl half bottle of wine, mineral water, coffee. **Set dinner** £64 3 courses, £77 7 courses. **Credit** AmEx, DC, JCB, MC, V.
Listening in (a bit cheekily but not without cause) to the opinions of other diners in restaurants is particularly revealing. In this case, a couple next to us first argued over which of their main courses was the best – the roast skate with capers, lemon and beurre noisette, or roast cod with lentils and bacon – before collaring the sommelier and voicing their incredulity that Michelin has bestowed a single paltry star upon Aubergine when they had eaten their way around Britain and found it to be one of the very best restaurants in the country. We agree that this small, welcoming and gold-hued venue is underrated. From the start, the service – nay, hospitality – compares perhaps with only Le Gavroche for professionalism. Maître d' Thierry Tomasin is one of those rare people with eyes in the back of his head yet the charm of Humphrey Bogart as he works the room. He knows his food and wine too, and conversed with genuine enthusiasm about some exceptionally lovely 2001 L'Esprit de Chevalier Pessac-Leognan served with lunch, and the sustainably sourced ingredients, 97% of which are British. The fish, for example, is caught off the Dorset coast by a father-and-son team, who fax details of the night's catch to the restaurant by breakfast time and deliver it by 11am, where a chef and hot pan are waiting, followed an hour or so later by the hungry and appreciative diner. How good is that? Seafood comes from the west coast of Scotland, meat from Cumbria. Cooking is talented yet allows the true character of the food to shine. Go today (unless today happens to be Sunday, when it's closed).
Children over 5 years admitted. Booking advisable; essential weekends. Dress: smart casual. No pipes or cigars. No-smoking tables. Map 14 D12.

Gordon Ramsay

68 Royal Hospital Road, SW3 4HP (7352 4441/ www.gordonramsay.com). Sloane Square tube. **Lunch served** noon-2pm, **dinner served** 6.30-11pm Mon-Fri. **Set lunch** £40 3 courses. **Set meal** £70 3 courses, £90 tasting menu. **Credit** AmEx, DC, JCB, MC, V.
News this year that Gordon Ramsay is one of Channel 4's highest paid presenters means that even his most ardent fans cannot help but ask what GR actually does for a living. Is he a chef, or a presenter? Is it possible to do both? Come to that, is he not also an author, columnist, businessman, entrepreneur, tableware designer? Still, no one can blame him for making hay while the sun shines, and there doesn't appear to be any imminent threat of rainfall for Gordon Ramsay Holdings. A New York restaurant is planned for late 2006, to be followed by ventures in Miami and Los Angeles in 2007, adding to those already thriving in London, Dubai and Tokyo. More TV series seem likely in addition to *Kitchen Nightmares*, *Hell's Kitchen* and *The F-Word*, along with all those yummy associated books and merchandise. Thank goodness for the regular staff in Royal Hospital Road, then, who keep the hallowed place humming along nicely in the great man's absence. Executive chef Mark Askew and restaurant director Jean-Claude Breton have been here, and with Ramsay, for years and know a great deal more than most about sublime food and subliminal service. Booking a table will be nigh-on impossible (get your secretary to do it, most diners here obviously have one or two), and eventually you will be rewarded with amazing examples of British ingredients and French know-how at their best. Perhaps roast fillet and braised belly of pork with baby langoustines; or pan-fried john dory with Cromer crab and caviar; or creamed strawberries with champagne and coriander. Prices are up even more on last year, but, hey, that's the cost of celebrity. As we went to press the restaurant closed for another David Collins refurbishment, but should have reopened by the time you read this.
Booking essential. Children admitted. Dress: smart; jacket preferred; no jeans or trainers. No smoking Map 14 F12.

Interview
BJORN VAN DER HORST

Who are you?
Chef-patron of **La Noisette** (see p127).
Eating in London: what's good about it?
The extraordinary variety of ethnic and eclectic types of food available. At the ethnic level, London rates very highly.
What's bad about it?
Poor quality at the mid range. The bottom range is very good, the top range is very good, but in the middle there's not enough restaurants like **Galvin Bistrot de Luxe** (see p93) that do good-quality food for not too much money.
Which are your favourite London restaurants?
I think the food at the **Square** (see p132) is great, but my favourite London restaurant is **Umu** (see p188). The chef is fantastic and the food is like nowhere else in the UK. It's straightforward Japanese food, not rearranged for the British public.
What single thing would most improve London's restaurant scene?
People are already starting to be more interested in quality produce and will become more so. Whether you like them or not, TV stars like Jamie Oliver and Gordon Ramsay have exposed the public to ideas they previously never thought about, and it will be good for the industry in the long term.
Any hot tips for the coming year?
Back to basics: roasts, carving, tableside work – everything we're doing at La Noisette. We've gone full circle, tasted it all, and in the end mature people interested in food want to see simple food cooked well. The molecular gastronomy thing's going to wear off. The shame is that it's done very well by a few people, but a lot of people (particularly young chefs) are not doing it very well.

RESTAURANTS

Indian

We've seen this process before. A cuisine that had long been undervalued asserts itself. Where once it was generally perceived as fit only for low-budget belly filling, created by unskilled cooks using factory-made ingredients, it starts to be treasured. The parallels between British food's journey from the transport caff to the Modern European gastronomic temple, and the long trek of Indian cuisine (as found in Britain) from the curry house to the glitzy fine-dining establishment, are striking. The process breaks down into several stages: the rediscovery of culinary history, especially as regards regional recipes; the experimentation with fusion cooking; the promotion of talented chefs; the move to more lavish premises; the (usually justifiable) rise in prices; and the move away from the worst excesses of fusion food towards an updated version of traditional regional cuisine. This transformation in British perceptions of Indian cuisine – by which we mean the cooking to be found in Pakistan, Bangladesh, Nepal and Sri Lanka as well as the modern state of India – needed to happen. The proper preparation of traditional Indian food requires much skill and can be laborious: think, especially, of the work involved in grinding, mixing and frying of complicated blends of spices. At such venues as **Café Spice Namaste**, **Chutney Mary**, **Painted Heron** and **Red Fort**, you'll find the apotheosis of this process: first-rate (and expensive) restaurants where the traditions of the cuisine are treasured, even as its boundaries are stretched.

But there are many options available in London. Most exciting for culinary adventurers are the modest enterprises that serve properly prepared regional cuisine to customers largely from the Asian community, at startlingly low prices. **Dadima** (Gujarati), **Five Hot Chillies** (Punjabi), **Nauroz** (Pakistani), **Ram's** (Gujarati) and **Sagar** (South Indian) offer some of the best examples of this approach. There are also, of course, restaurants that seek to take advantage of Indian cuisine's rise to prominence by cutting corners in the hope of swift profits. Beware of plush venues serving dreadful Indo-Mediterranean amalgams (using the same curry pastes beloved of high street tandooris) at highly inflated prices. Thankfully, though, such charlatans are in a minority, and London in 2007 is a terrific place to eat Indian food.

Central

Belgravia

Salloos
62-64 Kinnerton Street, SW1X 8ER (7235 4444). Hyde Park Corner or Knightsbridge tube. **Lunch served** noon-2.15pm, **dinner served** 7-11pm Mon-Sat. **Main courses** £13.50-£16.50. **Credit** AmEx, DC, MC, V. Pakistani
For 30 years, Salloos has been London's poshest Pakistani restaurant. Situated on the first floor of small premises in a select backstreet, it is the haunt of affluent local couples, high-ranking Pakistani officials and, on our visit, a couple of earnestly smoking pop star types. The setting is serene: white walls decorated with modern art; geometrically patterned grilles over the windows; crisp table-linen; a flock of polite waiting staff (men of bank-manager demeanour, well-spoken women). Tandoori food has long been renowned here and rightly so. Perfectly weighted nans and well-marinated chunks of lamb (tender, juicy) were brought forth from the oven, helping ease our disappointment at the non-availability of the famous lamb chops. Main courses included a remarkably light dish of gurda masala, with the most tender of kidneys diced in a spiced tomato and onion sauce. Chicken kofte (two dense meatballs in copious gravy) seemed mundane in comparison. Large portions of mousse-like spinach and delectable dahl (topped with browned onions) together with superb rice (cooked in lamb stock; Salloos is no place for vegetarians)

emphasised the quality at this old-school, buttoned-up, high-class establishment.
Booking advisable. Children over 8 years admitted. Dress: smart casual. Takeaway service. **Map 9 G9.**

Covent Garden

Mela NEW
152-156 Shaftesbury Avenue, WC2H 8HL (7836 8635/www.melarestaurant.co.uk). Leicester Square tube. **Meals served** noon-11.30pm Mon-Thur; noon-11.45pm Fri, Sat; noon-10.30pm Sun. **Main courses** £8.95-£14.95. **Set lunch** £2.95-£5.95 1 course. **Set dinner** (vegetarian) £25.95 serves 2, (non-vegetarian) £36.95 serves 2. **Set meal** (5.30-7pm, 10-11pm) £10.95 3 courses. **Credit** AmEx, DC, MC, V. Pan-Indian
Popular with the theatre crowd, tourists, students and minor Bollywood celebrities, this centrally located venue was livelier than ever on our visit. Several embroidered wall-hangings with mirror-work have been added to the empty spaces around the brightly hued pictures and murals that hang on the walls. The result is a riot of festive colours, indeed a 'mela'. Delectable grilled tuna, flaky and meaty, was marinated in lime, ginger, garlic, honey, yellow chilli powder and concentrated yoghurt. Delicious aloo tikki stuffed with dates and cashews came with wonderful coriander-mint and tamarind sauces. You rarely see rabbit on Indian menus; here, it was cooked in yoghurt-based gravy beautifully flavoured with dried red chillies, coriander seeds and dried mango powder. We'd heard that Mela's kadhi pakodi (spicy North Indian 'yoghurt soup' with dumplings) is a big hit with Indian expats, and we could see why: it had lively hot and tangy flavours. Roomali roti wasn't as wafer-thin and soft as it should be, so we'd suggest sticking to the nans. Many of the curries, like baby aubergines in peanut sauce, are too oily and soupy in texture, but for food so robustly flavoured and imaginative, prices are very fair.
Babies and children welcome: children's menu; high chairs. Booking advisable. No-smoking tables. Restaurant available for hire. Separate room for parties, seats 40. Takeaway service. Vegetarian menu. **Map 18 K6.**

Fitzrovia

★ Indian YMCA
41 Fitzroy Square, W1T 6AQ (7387 0411/ www.indianymca.org). Great Portland Street or Warren Street tube. **Lunch served** noon-2pm Mon-Fri; 12.30-1.30pm Sat, Sun. **Dinner served** 7-8.30pm daily. **Main courses** £2-£5. **Credit** AmEx, JCB, MC, V. Pan-Indian
The Indian YMCA allows the public to partake in its meals. There can be few better places for culinary tourism in London. True, the surroundings are prosaic: the ground-floor canteen of an office block, recently cheered up with blue banquettes and wooden chairs. True also, the food is liable to be lukewarm if you arrive more than ten minutes after kick-off. Long-simmered curries are the best bet. At lunch, simply take a tray, point to what you'd like, and pay at the till; then take your booty to a table, which you might share with office workers (Indians and others). At dinner, the process is still more gloriously Indian (though there's no choice and quality can be basic): pay for your set meal in the entrance hall, then hand your chitty to the cooks; communal bowls of rice and dahl are at the table; most diners are Indian students. Set dinners change daily. Our Friday evening repast was centred around egg curry, with side helpings of mixed veg (seemingly from a freezer pack, but boosted by fried mustard seeds), a highly savoury chickpea curry, and pitta bread. Pud was tinned pineapple.
Babies and children admitted. No smoking. Separate rooms for parties, seating 20, 30 and 200. Takeaway service. Vegetarian menu. **Map 3 J4.**

Rasa Samudra
5 Charlotte Street, W1T 1RE (7637 0222/ www.rasarestaurants.com). Goodge Street tube. **Lunch served** noon-3pm Mon-Sat. **Dinner served** 6-10.45pm daily. **Main courses**

£6.25-£12.95. **Set meals** (vegetarian) £22.50, (seafood) £30. **Credit** AmEx, JCB, MC, V.
South Indian

The Rasa flagship has ridden the crest of London's new wave of Indian dining since opening in 1999 – despite being devoted to the seafood and vegetarian cuisines of Kerala, rather than any Modern Indian shenanigans. It's a plush, relaxing spot occupying several small rooms over the ground and first floors of a Charlotte Street townhouse. Behind the trademark pink frontage, Keralite artefacts and wooden carvings provide decoration. Start a meal with popadom-like snacks and relishes (highlight: shrimp pickle), all made in-house. This time, though, our pickles seemed dried-out in their ramekins. The 'seafood feast' set meal is the best choice for first-timers, ideally alongside a companion's 'vegetarian feast'. After the crispy titbits, our feast continued with a wonderful assembly of snacks, plus delightful seafood-packed samudra rasam soup. Then followed a thali-like selection of main courses, the pick of which were koyilandi konju masala (prawns with a zesty sauce of ginger, curry leaves and onions) and the humble but heavenly spicy potatoes (stir-fried with peas, peppers, cloves, black peppers and tomatoes). An à la carte main course of konju manga curry was let down by combining too-ripe mango with prawns, depriving the dish of tanginess. So, two squalls amid a sea of treasures: Samudra just missed a red star.
Babies and children welcome: high chairs. Booking advisable. No smoking. Separate rooms for parties, seating 15, 20 and 40. Takeaway service. Vegetarian menu. **Map 9 J5**.
For branches (Rasa Express, Rasa Travancore, Rasa E1) see index.

Gloucester Road

Bombay Brasserie
Courtfield Road, SW7 4QH (7370 4040/ www.bombaybrasserielondon.com). Gloucester Road tube. **Lunch served** 12.30-3pm, **dinner served** 7.30-11.45pm daily. **Main courses** £16-£21. **Minimum** (dinner) £25. **Set buffet** (lunch) £18.95 incl tea or coffee. **Credit** AmEx, DC, JCB, MC, V. Pan-Indian

Has any restaurant rested on its laurels as long as the Bombay Brasserie? Its look was much copied in the 1980s, when the place had good claim to be London's best Indian restaurant. A grand cocktail lounge leads to a grander dining room (with palms, ceiling fans, photos of the Raj, and a mural of the Red Fort in Delhi); a light conservatory leavens the mix. Our buffet lunch was a dismal experience, despite the generally acceptable food. Courteous waiters drifted around bored, the vast room being all-but empty save for two middle managers from Harmondsworth, plotting over the peas pilau. Stars of the lunchtime carousel were a meaty fish curry, a gingery sweetcorn soup and a rich lamb and vegetable curry. Less appealing were the tired-looking chicken wings, pallid chicken korma, the dull salads, and the final bill (over £30 a head). Next time we'll sample the new dinner menu – at night the restaurant becomes livelier (with tourists) and an altogether better prospect. Mumbai beach snacks are listed alongside Goan, Moghul and tandoori food plus a few 'specialities' (including fish malabar from Kerala, and the Modern Indian-styled chilgoza murg – chicken grilled with pine nuts in a creamy mint sauce). But on this showing, the BB has much to do to reclaim its panache.
Babies and children welcome: high chairs. Booking advisable; essential weekends. Dress: smart casual. No-smoking tables. Restaurant available for hire. Separate conservatory for parties, seats 150. Vegetarian menu. **Map 13 C10**.

Knightsbridge

Amaya
Halkin Arcade, SW1X 8JT (7823 1166/ www.realindianfood.com). Knightsbridge tube. **Lunch served** 12.30-2.15pm Mon-Fri; 12.30-2.30pm Sat; 12.45-2.45pm Sun. **Dinner served** 6.30-11.15pm Mon-Sat; 6.30-10.15pm Sun. **Main courses** £8.50-£25. **Credit** AmEx, DC, JCB, MC, V. Modern Indian

RESTAURANTS

Imli. See p140.

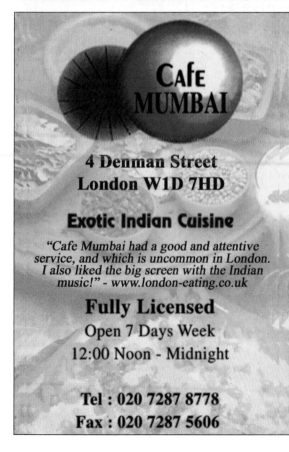

Amaya opened in 2004 in a blaze of publicity due to its innovative grazing menu of kebabs and birianis, and its beautiful decor of rosewood panels, terracotta ornaments and twinkling chandeliers. An open kitchen makes the most of the awkward layout. Gushing reviews and several awards followed. So does the food still live up to its early promise? Our dining experience was a mixed one. Kebabs are cooked on the tandoor (clay oven), sigri (charcoal grill) and tawa (griddle), and we ordered one of each variety. Rock oysters in ginger-flecked coconut sauce were so stunning they left us speechless. Tender chicken tikka, and baby lamb shanks were less dazzling, but still scrumptious. Yet three vegetable dishes were disappointing: bland paneer tikka, with own-made organic paneer; somewhat leathery grilled baby aubergines sprinkled with dried mango powder; and flavourless tinda (Indian baby gourd) filled with soya mince. In contrast, spinach tikki stuffed with figs was packed with verdant, mineral flavours. Vegetable biriani tasted fine, but lacked the characteristic complexity. There's a notable list of sugar-free desserts, from which pomegranate sorbet, looking like crushed velvet studded with rubies, was fabulous. A problem with one dish was dealt with swiftly and appropriately by the staff. *Babies and children admitted. Booking advisable. Disabled: toilet. Dress: smart casual. No-smoking tables. Separate room for parties, seats 14.* **Map 9 G9.**

Haandi
7 Cheval Place, SW3 1HY (7823 7373/ www.haandi-restaurants.com). Knightsbridge tube. **Lunch served** noon-3pm daily. **Dinner served** 5.30-11pm Mon-Thur, Sun; 5.30-11.30pm Fri, Sat. **Main courses** £6-£16. **Set lunch** £8-£12 incl soft drink. **Credit** AmEx, DC, JCB, MC, V. North Indian
The long, dark dining room of Haandi – reached down a couple of steps from the front bar on this select, mewsy street – was made darker still on our visit by some dud light bulbs. The back, windowless overflow room seemed sunny in comparison. Such intimate surrounds were improved by the fiery display in the open-view kitchen, the smart, considerate service and the alluring menu. Though Haandi has branches in Nairobi and Kampala (as well as Edgware), there's scant African influence on the menu, which is dominated by North Indian cuisine. And jolly good it is too, judging by the creamy lassi, the deeply flavoursome kake-di-lamb curry (on-the-bone lamb in a rich tomato sauce), and the exquisitely cooked South Indian samundri khazana (tender calamares, haddock, tuna and plump king prawns in a lemony green masala). Less pleasing were the high levels of salt in some dishes and the tasty yet under-seared minced chicken kebabs. Overall, though, this was a solid performance, notable for skilful spicing. Prices aren't extortionate for such a monied district, especially given the large portions (we'd suggest skipping starters). Wealthy locals, couples and tourists (some Indian) eat here. *Babies and children welcome: high chairs. Booking advisable weekends. Restaurant available for hire. Takeaway service; delivery service (within 1-mile radius).* **Map 14 E9. For branch see index.**

Marble Arch

Chai Pani
64 Seymour Street, W1H 5BW (7258 2000/ www.chaipani.co.uk). Marble Arch tube. **Lunch served** noon-2.30pm Mon-Fri; noon-4.30pm Sat, Sun. **Dinner served** 6-10.30pm daily. **Main courses** £5-£7. **Set buffet** (lunch Mon-Fri) £8. **Thalis** £8-£20. **Credit** AmEx, JCB, MC, V. Rajasthani vegetarian
We applauded this Rajasthani vegetarian restaurant when it first opened. Not only was the food delicious, but the menu showcases dishes rarely seen even in India. However, over the years, standards have slipped. For a start, the menu is too long. On our visit, it listed 24 starters, snacks and salads; 26 curries and dahls; 14 breads; 12 rice dishes; around ten accompaniments (like pickles and relishes); 14 own-made desserts (plus a

separate list of bought-in desserts); 14 types of thalis to cater for every dietary need – plus other items. More dishes, including a tea-time menu, have been introduced since. No kitchen (unless it has a large battalion of chefs) can cope with this number of dishes. As a result, almost every item we tried was badly made, rushed or simply wrong. White marrow pakoras, for instance, were burnt and greasy, and pakodi kadhi (spicy yoghurt 'soup' with dumplings) was so overwhelmed with asafoetida we couldn't eat it. A Rajasthani wedding-style thali came without many of the items advertised. In trying to please a wide variety of customers, this colourful, smartish venue (which is now looking a little scuffed) seems to have lost its focus. *Babies and children welcome: high chairs. Booking advisable weekends. Disabled: toilet. Takeaway service. Vegetarian menu. Vegan dishes.* **Map 8 F6.**

Deya
34 Portman Square, W1H 7BH (7224 0028/ www.deya-restaurant.co.uk). Bond Street or Marble Arch tube. **Lunch served** noon-2.45pm Mon-Fri. **Dinner served** 6.30-10.45pm Mon-Sat. **Main courses** £12-£15.50. **Set lunch** £14.95 2 courses. **Set meal** £27.50-£32.50 5 courses. **Credit** AmEx, JCB, MC, V. Modern Indian
The high ceilings, expansive windows and sizeable mirrors at Deya are softened by a colourful mural and lots of silk furnishings. This spacious, swish set-up is let down only by an incongruous bar, plonked in the middle of the dining area. Sanjay Dwivedi oversees kitchen affairs and has reproduced a few dishes found at his former restaurant, Zaika (*see p142*), where he worked as sous chef. We were impressed by the freshness of seared tuna steak, cooked to juicy excellence and crowned with popped mustard seeds. But an accompaniment of stir-fried cabbage and ground-lentil dumplings was marred by a copious amount of astringent mustard seeds. Each dish had its highs and lows. Deliciously creamy upma, made from savoury cream of wheat semolina flecked with curry leaves and broccoli florets, would have made an ideal match with fried sea bass fillets had the fish not been overcooked. Overly complex dishes and fussy flourishes tend to mask simple, clean flavours – best to order simple classics. Service, although well meaning, became chaotic when the restaurant filled up. Deya has potential, but needs more passion in its cooking and slickness in service if it is to continue attracting corporate suits on expense accounts. *Babies and children welcome: high chairs. Booking advisable. Dress: smart casual. Vegetarian menu.* **Map 9 G6.**

Mayfair

Benares
12A Berkeley Square House, Berkeley Square, W1J 6BS (7629 8886/www.benaresrestaurant. com). Green Park tube. **Lunch served** noon-2.30pm Mon-Fri, Sun. **Dinner served** 5.30-10.30pm Mon-Sat; 6-10pm Sun. **Main courses** £15-£40. **Set meal** (noon-7.30pm) £20 3 courses. **Credit** AmEx, DC, MC, V. Modern Indian
With such prosperous neighbours as a Bentley showroom, it's hardly surprising that Benares positively sighs with sumptuousness and attracts big spenders. Seductively swathed in glossy black granite, the restaurant and glamorous cocktail bar are at the top of a flight of stairs. Expect colonial-look seating arrangements, weighty antiques and decorative water tanks adorned with flowers. Chef-patron Atul Kochhar was the first Indian chef to be awarded a Michelin star, during his time at Tamarind (*see below*). His creative cooking style combines contemporary influences alongside classic Indian favourites. The forte is seafood, and we were impressed by a scrumptious starter of battered soft-shell crab, served atop flash-fried chilli squid and accompanied by dark-hued Peruvian potato salad in a sublime passionfruit dressing. Similarly, a winsome combination of seared paneer cubes, steeped in lime juice and ginger, worked well with garlicky mushrooms, creamy avocado chunks and an intensely flavoured blue cheese dressing. Grilled lamb chops, scented with pounded fennel and cardamom seeds, married well with a green salad scattered with pomegranate kernels and dates, but lost succulence through overcooking. Our main gripe was with the inconsistent, slack service; a restaurant of this calibre should deliver better. *Booking advisable. Dress: smart casual. No smoking. Restaurant available for hire. Separate rooms for parties, seating 12, 16 and 22.* **Map 9 H7.**

Tamarind
20-22 Queen Street, W1J 5PR (7629 3561/ www.tamarindrestaurant.com). Green Park tube. **Lunch served** noon-3pm Mon-Fri, Sun. **Dinner served** 6-11.30pm Mon-Sat; 6-10.30pm Sun. **Main courses** £14.50-£26. **Set lunch** £16.95 2 courses, £18.95 3 courses. **Set meal** (6-7pm) £24 2 courses. **Credit** AmEx, DC, MC, V. North Indian
This established fine-dining restaurant is especially popular with the deep-pocketed and well-travelled business set. Good use is made of an awkward basement space by clever placement of mirrors across walls, creating a more spacious feel. Tables face an open kitchen, offering a peek at chefs in action in front of clay ovens. Celebrating authenticity over new-wave presentations, head chef Alfred Prasad focuses on the earthy appeal of mainly North Indian dishes. No meal would be complete without trying the makhani dahl – it's probably the best in London. Slow-cooked black lentils, simmered with an infusion of garlic, ginger and green chillies, are emboldened by dollops of butter, ladlefuls of cream and puréed tomatoes: a perfect match for hot nans. Hariyali chicken curry also received top marks for its garden-fresh masala featuring a silky-smooth base of pounded mint leaves, coriander and green chillies. Not all the food was as memorable; lacklustre paneer cubes cooked with squishy tomatoes, peppers and onions was a shade too homespun. Equally disappointing, potato tikkis (savoury griddle cakes) were made from dry, powdery mashed potatoes, filled with equally bland creamed spinach. Stick with the aromatic curries, creamy dahl and superb breads for best results. *Babies and children welcome: high chair. Booking advisable; essential dinner. Dress: smart casual. Takeaway service; delivery service (within 1-mile radius).* **Map 9 H7.**

Veeraswamy
Mezzanine, Victory House, 99-101 Regent Street, W1B 4RS (7734 1401/www.realindianfood.com). Piccadilly Circus tube. **Lunch served** 12.30-2.15pm Mon-Fri; noon-2.30pm Sat, Sun. **Dinner served** 5.30-10.30pm Mon-Sat; 6-10pm Sun.

RESTAURANTS

Main courses £14-£27. **Set meal** (lunch, 5.30-6.30pm, after 10pm Mon-Sat) £16 3 courses; (Sun) £20 3 courses. **Credit** AmEx, DC, JCB, MC, V. Pan-Indian

Billed as London's oldest surviving Indian restaurant (established 1926), Veeraswamy hopes to revive past glories with its latest refurbishment. The look and feel of a maharaja's palace has been recreated with chandeliers, coloured glass shades and silvery grilles. On our visit, starters were outstanding. Plump tandoori oysters scented with ginger were deliciously smoky, making a perfect match with the tart bite of red onion slices pickled in lime and beetroot juice. Just as tasty, raj kachori – a puffed, wafer-thin wheat disc, filled with soft lentil dumplings, sweet tamarind chutney and dollops of mint chutney – delivered an explosion of contrasting flavours. Good news over, main courses weren't such a big hit. Chingri malai prawns (a Bengali speciality of king prawns simmered in a coconut-based masala) was let down by a bland, turmeric-heavy sauce. Nihari (a slow-cooked lamb curry) scored highly for meaty succulence, but was marred by a heavy dose of synthetic-tasting floral essence. Pineapple curry won our gold star for its spike of popped mustard seeds and chilli. Service is as smooth as Indian silk. Owners Camellia and Namita Panjabi (also of Amaya, *see p135*, and Chutney Mary, *see p142*, fame) have given this upmarket restaurant a new lease of life.

Babies and children welcome: high chairs. Booking advisable weekends. Disabled: lift. Dress: smart casual. Restaurant available for hire. Separate room for parties, seats 36. Map 17 J7.

Piccadilly

Mint Leaf NEW

Suffolk Place, SW1Y 4HX (7930 9020/ www.mintleafrestaurant.com). Embankment or Piccadilly Circus tube/Charing Cross tube/rail. Bar **Open/meals served** noon-midnight Mon-Wed; noon-1am Thur-Sat. **Set meal** £30-£48 tandoori platter. *Restaurant* **Lunch served** noon-3pm Mon-Fri. **Dinner served** 5.30-11pm Mon-Sat. **Main courses** £9-£24. **Set lunch** £15 2 courses, £22 3 courses. **Set meal** (noon-3pm Mon-Fri; 5.30-7.30pm, 9.30-11pm Mon-Sat) £15 2 courses, £22 3 courses.
Both **Credit** AmEx, DC, MC, V. Pan-Indian

This trendy restaurant and bar has a gorgeous dark-wood interior, with several dining rooms lit with flickering lights. We started with excellent cocktails at the bar, which, on a Friday night, featured a saxophonist and DJs. Curiously, on our visit all the Indian diners were directed to one dining room and the non-Indian diners to the other rooms. To start, grouper steamed in pandan leaves was marvellous because the fish had retained its meaty taste while taking on the subtle but distinctive fragrance of the leaves. 'Medley of vegetables' was, in fact, sweet potato patties served with own-made pineapple chutney. Lamb kofta were tasty, but too large: the size of tennis balls, when they should be walnut-sized. They were coated, unusually, in breadcrumbs, but tasted fine. A dish of grilled, mashed aubergines was tasty, as were the nan and cumin rice. Lotus stem dumplings stuffed with dried figs, cashews and paneer were more mundane than they sounded, and other dishes such as vegetable-stuffed courgettes and black lentil dahl were merely OK. All the dishes arrived very quickly, and didn't seem freshly made to order. Our verdict: Mint Leaf works better as a bar than a restaurant.
Booking advisable. Disabled: lift; toilet. Restaurant available for hire. Separate room for parties, seats 60. Map 17 K7.

St James's

Quilon

41 Buckingham Gate, SW1E 6AF (7821 1899/ www.thequilonrestaurant.com). St James's Park tube. **Lunch served** noon-2.30pm Mon-Fri. **Dinner served** 6-11pm Mon-Sat. **Main courses** £8.50-£23. **Set lunch** £12.95 2 courses, £15.95 3 courses. **Credit** AmEx, DC, MC, V. South Indian

Pan-Indian menu

Spellings of Indian dishes vary widely; dishes such as gosht may appear in several versions on different menus as the word is transliterated from (in this case) Hindi. There are umpteen languages and several scripts in the Indian subcontinent, the most commonly seen on London menus being Punjabi, Hindi, Bengali and Gujarati. For the sake of consistency, however, we have tried to adhere to uniform spellings. The following are common throughout the subcontinent.

Aloo: potato.
Ayre: a white fish much used in Bengali cuisine.
Baingan: aubergine.
Balti: West Midlands cooking term for karahi cooking (qv, North Indian menu), which became all the rage a decade ago. Unfortunately, many inferior curry houses now apply the name to dishes that bear little resemblance to real karahi-cooked dishes.
Bateira, batera or **bater**: quail.
Bengali: Bengal, before Partition in 1947, was a large province covering Calcutta (now in India's West Bengal) and modern-day Bangladesh. 'Bengali' and 'Bangladeshi' cooking is quite different, and the term 'Bengali' is often misused in London's Indian restaurants.
Bhajia or **bhaji**: vegetables dipped in chickpea-flour batter and deep-fried; also called pakoras.
Bhajee: vegetables cooked with spices, usually 'dry' rather than sauced.
Bhindi: okra.
Brinjal: aubergine.
Bulchao or **balchao**: a Goan vinegary pickle made with small dried prawns (with shells) and lots of garlic.
Chana or **channa**: chickpeas.
Chapati: a flat wholewheat griddle bread.

Chat or **chaat**: various savoury snacks featuring combinations of pooris (qv), diced onion and potato, chickpeas, crumbled samosas and pakoras, chutneys and spices.
Dahi: yoghurt.
Dahl or **dal**: a lentil curry similar to thick lentil soup. Countless regional variations exist.
Dhansak: a Parsi (qv) casserole of meat, lentils and vegetables, with a mix of hot and tangy flavours.
Dhaniya: coriander.
Ghee: clarified butter used for frying.
Gobi: cauliflower.
Gosht, josh or **ghosh**: meat, usually lamb.
Gram flour: chickpea flour.
Kachori: crisp pastry rounds with spiced mung dahl or pea filling.
Lassi: a yoghurt drink, ordered with salt or sugar, sometimes with fruit. Ideal to quench a fiery palate.
Machi or **machli**: fish.
Masala or **masaladar**: mixed spices.
Methi: fenugreek, either dried (seeds) or fresh (green leaves).
Murgh or **murg**: chicken.
Mutter, muter or **mattar**: peas.
Nan or **naan**: teardrop-shaped flatbread cooked in a tandoor (qv, North Indian menu).
Palak or **paalak**: spinach; also called saag.
Paan or **pan**: betel leaf stuffed with chopped 'betel nuts', coconut and spices such as fennel seeds, and folded into a triangle. Available sweet or salty, and eaten at the end of a meal as a digestive.
Paneer or **panir**: Indian cheese, a bit like tofu in texture and taste.
Paratha: a large griddle-fried bread that is sometimes stuffed (with spicy mashed potato or minced lamb, for instance).
Parsi or **Parsee**: a religious minority

based in Mumbai, but originally from Persia, renowned for its cooking.
Pilau, pillau or **pullao**: flavoured rice cooked with meat or vegetables. In most British Indian restaurants, pilau rice is simply rice flavoured and coloured with turmeric or (rarely) saffron.
Poori or **puri**: a disc of deep-fried wholewheat bread; the frying makes it puff up like an air-filled cushion.
Popadom, poppadom, papadum or **papad**: large thin wafers made with lentil paste, and flavoured with pepper, garlic or chilli. Eaten in the UK with pickles and relishes as a starter while waiting for the meal to arrive.
Raita: a yoghurt mix, usually with cucumber.
Roti: a round, sometimes unleavened, bread, thicker than a chapati and cooked in a tandoor or griddle. Roomali roti (literally 'handkerchief bread') is a very thin, soft disc of roti.
Saag or **sag**: spinach; also called palak.
Tamarind: the pods of this East African tree, grown in India, are made into a paste that imparts a sour, fruity taste – popular in some regional cuisines, including Gujarati and South Indian.
Thali: literally 'metal plate'. A large plate with rice, bread, containers of dahl and vegetable curries, pickles and yoghurt relishes.
Vadai or **wada**: a spicy vegetable or lentil fritter; dahi wada are lentil fritters soaked in yoghurt, topped with tamarind and date chutneys.
Vindaloo: originally, a hot and spicy pork curry from Goa that should authentically be soured with vinegar and cooked with garlic. In London restaurants, the term is usually misused to signify simply very hot dishes.
Xacuti: a Goan dish made with lamb or chicken pieces, coconut and a complex mix of roasted then ground spices.

RESTAURANTS

Quilon recreates South Indian flavours for western palates and well-heeled tourists. It forms part of the Taj Hotel Group's St James's Court Hotel. Here you'll find the joys of coconut-based curries, saucer-shaped rice-flour pancakes and a medley of seafood dishes, though little in the way of genuine tropical heat. The restaurant's bland decor isn't likely to win awards for innovative design. No matter, our main aim was to devour the chef's marvellous mango curry. We weren't disappointed; popped mustard seeds, curry leaves and sliced chillies, simmered in tart whipped yoghurt, provided a deliciously sweet-sour base for fresh mango chunks. If you order only one dish here, make it this one. Standards varied in our other dishes. Peppery, ginger-flecked seafood broth, although crammed with scallops, prawns, mussels and clams, was lukewarm and had an oily sheen across its surface. Spicing is generally timid; even rasam, usually a fiery broth laced with chillies, lacked bite. In contrast, roast duck breast did deliver the heat of its marinade (pounded chillies and toasted fennel seeds), but was marred by a stodgy 1970s-style presentation. Service too needs to sharpen its act if this pricey restaurant is to pull in new punters.
Babies and children welcome: high chair. Booking advisable. No smoking. Takeaway service. Vegetarian menu. **Map 15 J9**.

Soho

★ Chowki

2-3 Denman Street, W1D 7HA (7439 1330/ www.chowki.com). Piccadilly Circus tube. **Meals served** noon-11.30pm Mon-Sat; noon-10.30pm Sun. **Main courses** £6-10.95. **Set meal** £12.50 3 courses. **Credit** AmEx, DC, MC, V. Pan-Indian

Among the throng of low-budget curry houses just off Piccadilly Circus, Chowki stands out not for its rather basic and perfunctory looks, but for its intriguing dishes. The menu changes every few weeks, always highlighting three regional cuisines of India, with excellent-value set meals that allow you to try a selection of small dishes. On our most recent visit, Parsi, Benarasi and Bengali dishes were the theme. Highlights included samosas with a nice crumbly shell that resembled Mexican empanadas, a subtly spiced Bengali fish curry simmered in coconut milk, and a Parsi prawn curry rich with the sweetness of jaggery but also sour with the tang of tamarind and lime juice. The details were excellent; two unusually flavoured rotis and the khichadi rice were perfect. Only the desserts disappointed: a type of laddoo (gram flour 'biscuit') that was too dry, and a sweetmeat that was a bit so-what. To drink, avoid the plonk-like house wine (General Bilimoria); the other wines are fine. Also be warned that the jal jeera, often drunk as a digestif in India, has a strong sulphurous smell from 'black salt'; it can be a shock if you're not expecting it.
Babies and children welcome: high chairs. Booking advisable. Vegetarian menu. **Map 17 K7**.

★ Imli NEW

2006 RUNNER-UP BEST CHEAP EATS
167-169 Wardour Street, W1F 8WR (7287 4243/www.imli.co.uk). Tottenham Court Road tube. **Meals served** noon-11pm daily. **Tapas** £3.95-£6.95. **Set tapas** £10.75. **Credit** MC, V. Pan-Indian

Popular with young office types, Soho newcomer Imli focuses on tapas-style light bites for sharing, rather than weighty Indian stalwarts. It's a very different offshoot of fine-dining restaurant Tamarind (*see p137*). A spacious venue, it blends contemporary fittings with Indian antiques and vibrant splashes of orange across the walls. Punjabi-style samosas made a promising start to our meal, with richer, more crumbly pastry than the usual filo, and a filling of potatoes spiced with toasted coriander seeds. Fruit chaat (a spicy sweet-sour salad of diced guavas, apples and pears, sharpened with lime juice, crushed black rock salt, and tamarind chutney) was as authentic as those sold from Indian street stalls. But masala grilled beef fillet, though tender, was disconcertingly bland, and the buttery mashed potato was too close to nursery grub for our liking. On a brighter note, makhani dahl was a dream dish; made with black lentils, it was as creamy and indulgent as that of Tamarind – at a fraction of the price. On the whole, Imli's curries are adequate, but need bolder, more confident spicing to deliver the goods. Gripes aside, this spot has great potential.
Babies and children welcome: children's menu; high chairs. Disabled: toilet. No smoking. Separate room for parties, seats 45. Takeaway service; delivery service (over £15 within W1). **Map 17 J/K6**.

★ Red Fort

77 Dean Street, W1D 3SH (7437 2115/ www.redfort.co.uk). Leicester Square or Tottenham Court Road tube. **Lunch served** noon-2.15pm Mon-Fri. **Dinner served** 5.45-11pm Mon-Sat; 5.30-10pm Sun. **Main courses** £12.50-£20. **Set lunch** £12 2 courses. **Set meal** (5.45-7pm) £16 3 courses incl tea or coffee. **Credit** AmEx, MC, V. North Indian

Providing rich pickings for monied tourists and smart young media types, Red Fort exudes an almost Zen-like calm, enhanced by its sandstone walls, sleek water feature and antique artefacts. Although Mohammad Rais has long since left the kitchen, his famed legacy for blending spices continues. Kicking off with a fabulously fruity warm salad of grilled apples, pineapple chunks and ruby-hued pomegranate kernels, we were impressed with the dish's tart lime-juice dressing, speckled with red chillies and crushed dried mint. Savoury griddle cakes, made from mustard-green purée and spinach paste, encased a delectable filling of molten cheese: top marks for the silky-smooth texture and light peppery spicing. Ringing the changes, a South Indian-style duck curry had its tender meat boosted by a tease of South-east Asian lemongrass, and warming star anise. Lamb

biriani unleashed a fragrant puff of steam as its pastry-lid seal was broken at our table, leaving us to the pleasures of tender morsels of Welsh lamb and lightly spiced basmati rice. Side dishes are executed with as much precision as main courses and starters. A welcoming service team adds to the attraction of this classy venue.
Babies and children admitted. Booking advisable. Disabled: toilet. Dress: smart casual. Entertainment: DJ 8pm Thur-Sat (bar). Vegetarian menu. Vegan dishes. **Map 17 K6.**

Strand

★ India Club
Second floor, Strand Continental Hotel, 143 Strand, WC2R 1JA (7836 0650). Covent Garden, Embankment or Temple tube/Charing Cross tube/rail. **Lunch served** noon-2.30pm, **dinner served** 6-10.50pm daily. **Main courses** £3.50-£7.80. **Set meal** £12-£15 per person (minimum 2) 4 courses. **Unlicensed. Corkage** no charge. **No credit cards.** Pan-Indian
More at home in a Delhi backstreet than on the Strand, the India Club has notched up half a century of service. The location is unpromising: up two flights of dingy stairs. And though the restaurant's walls received a lick of lemon paint a few years back, its cracked red lino flooring, wobbly tables and mismatched seating look as if they haven't had a makeover for decades. Nevertheless, the Club exudes faded charm. Chefs, in contrast to their surroundings, wear gleaming white jackets and provide meals for a clientele of old India hands, office workers and the backpacker brigade. Our top marks went to fried minced lamb, cooked with heaps of ginger and garlic, and studded with garden peas. Less impressive was the tandoori chicken, which tasted like an Indian-inspired rendition of deep-fried battered chicken. Lamb pilao, although hardly authentic, made a tasty dish with its robust masala base of fried onions, ginger, garlic and chillies working well with tender meat morsels and fluffy rice grains. Portions aren't huge, but prices are rock bottom, and service is sweetness itself. Remember to buy beer from the first-floor bar on your way to the restaurant.
Babies and children admitted. Booking advisable. No-smoking tables. Takeaway service. Vegetarian menu. **Map 10 M7.**

Victoria

★ Sekara
3 Lower Grosvenor Place, SW1W 0EJ (7834 0722/www.sekara.co.uk). Victoria tube/rail. **Lunch served** noon-3pm, **dinner served** 6-10pm daily. **Main courses** £9.95-£12.95. **Set lunch** (Mon-Sat) £4.95 1 course. **Set buffet** (Sun) £9. **Credit** AmEx, MC, V. Sri Lankan
Everything about this intimate, primrose-coloured eaterie is suspended in a time-warp hammock that swings gently between this century and times past: the softly spoken, exceedingly polite service; the brightly coloured framed paintings of scenes from a bygone era; and the sort of thick patterned carpet you'll want to sink your feet into. To start, vegetable pancake rolls and mutton rolls looked similar, and were both spikily spiced and flavoursome. Next, meaty, robustly flavoured seerfish curry came with a tangle of expertly created string hoppers made from roasted Sri Lankan red rice. Vegetable kothu roti – stir-fried with shredded leeks, red and green chillies, peppers, carrots, fennel seeds and curry leaves – was more substantially flavoured and lighter in texture than the versions you'll find in lesser Sri Lankan restaurants. Aubergine curry was aromatic and gorgeously spiced with cinnamon, cardamom, cloves and star anise, while a delicately flavoured white curry (cooked in coconut milk) turned the humble potato into a thing of wonder, with the addition of green chillies, curry leaves and wisps of freshly grated coconut. An ideal place for a relaxed, unhurried meal.
Babies and children welcome: high chair. Booking advisable. Restaurant available for hire. Takeaway service. Vegetarian menu. **Map 15 H9.**

Veeraswamy. See p137.

Westminster

Cinnamon Club
The Old Westminster Library, 30-32 Great Smith Street, SW1P 3BU (7222 2555/www.cinnamon club.com). St James's Park or Westminster tube. **Breakfast served** 7.30-9.30am, **lunch served** noon-2.30pm Mon-Fri. **Dinner served** 6-10.45pm Mon-Sat. **Main courses** £12-£26. **Set dinner** £65 5 courses (£105 with wine). **Credit** AmEx, DC, MC, V. Modern Indian
Housed in a spacious former Victorian library, the Cinnamon Club makes much of its colonial club atmosphere and proximity to Parliament. It's a prime destination for politicians and power brokers. Executive chef Vivek Singh's menu isn't for timid palates – expect fiery flavours and robust masalas rather than delicate notes, along with innovation aplenty. Indian breakfasts (uthappams, spicy scrambled eggs) are also offered. Our starters of steamed crab and cod cakes worked well with the tang of a dipping sauce that combined herby coriander and South-east Asian fish sauce with lively chillies. But although deliciously succulent, fried scallops, encrusted with crunchy fennel seeds, were let down by bland add-ons of fried mushrooms and insipid cardamom froth. Lal maas (an earthy mutton curry) would win the approval of Rajasthani truck drivers for its authentic fried onion base, pepped up with red chillies and toasted peppercorns. Side dishes failed to impress, being akin to high-street offerings. South Indian prawn masala raised the standard, with lemony king prawns complementing a clinging sauce of nutty-tasting pounded coriander seeds and garlic. With such majestic surroundings, it was a shame about the service. For most of the evening, the waiters seemed to be everywhere but at our table.
Babies and children welcome: high chairs. Booking advisable. Disabled: toilet. Separate rooms for parties, seating seating 30 and 50. **Map 16 K9.**

West

Hammersmith

★ ★ Sagar
157 King Street, W6 9JT (8741 8563). Hammersmith tube/266 bus. **Lunch served** noon-2.45pm Mon-Fri. **Dinner served** 5.30-10.45pm Mon-Thur; 5.30-11.30pm Fri. **Meals served** noon-11.30pm Sat; noon-10.45pm Sun. **Main courses** £5-£10. **Thalis** £8.95-£11.45. **Credit** AmEx, DC, JCB, MC, V. South Indian vegetarian

Since our first visit to this soothing, minimally decorated restaurant when it opened in 2002, we've had consistently fabulous meals. Our most recent trip didn't disappoint. Crisp, fluffy masala dosa came with a beautifully spiced filling of roughly mashed potatoes; opt, as South Indian connoisseurs do, for the delicate rava (semolina) version, rather than that made from ordinary wheat flour. The accompanying sambar, and coconut and coriander chutney, were sparklingly fresh and vibrantly flavoured. Idli wasn't as soft as it should be, but delicate lemon rice was so delicious we could have eaten a large bowlful on its own. Sagar specialises in Udupi cuisine, the natural, additive-free, vegetarian temple-style cooking from Karnataka, a coastal region in southern India. The flavours are subtle, sophisticated, understated, yet clear and distinctive, and the food is light and healthy. Udupi curries are often based on pumpkins and marrows, and Sagar's vegetable kootu (yoghurt-and coconut-based curry) and sukee bhaji (pan-fried vegetables) are made from daily changing veg. On our visit, the former was made from chow-chow (a type of gourd), and the latter from baby aubergines: both were exquisite. Service was friendly and professional. A new branch has opened in Twickenham, but this one is the bigger, buzzier flagship.
Babies and children welcome: high chairs. Booking advisable. No-smoking tables. Takeaway service. Vegetarian menu. **Map 20 B4. For branch see index.**

Kensington

Zaika

1 Kensington High Street, W8 5NP (7795 6533/ www.zaika-restaurant.co.uk). High Street Kensington tube. **Lunch served** noon-2.45pm Mon-Fri, Sun. **Dinner served** 6.30-10.45pm Mon-Sat; 6.30-9.45pm Sun. **Main courses** £12.50-£19.50. **Set lunch** £15 2 courses, £18 3 courses, £19 4 courses. **Set meal** £38-£60 tasting menus. **Credit** AmEx, DC, JCB, MC, V. Modern Indian

Zaika's substantial antiques, sweeping silken drapes and artful flower arrangements help transform this former bank. The dining hall makes an almost theatrical setting, and is favoured by a mix of wealthy tourists, business groups and occasional couples. There's plenty of drama on the plates too. Our meal began with a selection of chicken tikkas: deliciously smoky, yet delicately spiced, the best being cloaked in a tangy marinade of lime juice, spinach, mint and coriander. Sweet and sour potatoes made for an equally scrumptious first course; dressing up a popular Indian street snack, chef Sanjay Dwivedi takes crisp-fried diced potatoes and douses them in tart tamarind sauce and perky mint chutney – delectable. Main courses weren't as convincing. A complicated concoction of fried cod fillet, couscous cooked with black squid ink, and soupy tomato sauce, was further confused with a tangle of greasy fried squid rings. Fried sea bass fillets and crushed potatoes, spiced with curry leaves and mustard seeds, restored our faith with a happy melange of South Indian flavours. Service was decidedly tardy. Despite our grumbles, we reckon Zaika is a better choice than its lesser-known sister concern, Deya (*see p137*).
Babies and children welcome: high chair. Booking advisable. Dress: smart casual. Restaurant available for hire. Vegetarian menu. **Map 7 C8.**

Paddington

Jamuna

38A Southwick Street, W2 1JQ (7723 5056/ www.jamuna.co.uk). Edgware Road tube/ Paddington tube/rail. **Lunch served** noon-2.30pm Mon-Fri. **Dinner served** 6-11pm Mon-Sat. **Main courses** £11-£27. **Credit** AmEx, DC, JCB, MC, V. Modern Indian

This sleek little Modern Indian has many things going for it. Pricing isn't among them. How does a two-course meal with a glass of the cheapest wine and a lassi for over £57 a head grab you? Small

wonder the sheepish staff chucked in a couple of gulab jamun gratis. The kebab platter delivered a petite lamb cutlet and two types of chicken tikka – all expertly marinated, juicy and seared to perfection. But it wasn't an immense portion for £12. Then came sea bass: two ultra-fresh fillets of modest size, pan-fried just so, resting on daintily sliced, still-crunchy courgette. Yet the dish was swamped in a sauce that, though zesty with mustard and singing with fresh fennel, was of an indelicate, thick, oily consistency. A side dish of makka palak porial (one of several interesting-looking vegetable dishes) combined spinach with overcooked sweetcorn to dull effect. The surroundings are plush – wooden flooring, mustard walls, bright-orange modern art, background chamber music – the long thin space looking every inch the smart neighbourhood restaurant. There's obvious culinary talent (those kebabs were memorable), but the Modern Indian cuisine needs a surer hand, and pricing needs urgent attention. We dined alone on a Friday lunchtime.
Babies and children admitted. Booking advisable. No smoking. Separate room for parties, seats 25. **Map 8 E5.**

South West
Chelsea

★ Chutney Mary

535 King's Road, SW10 0SZ (7351 3113/ www.realindianfood.com). Fulham Broadway tube/11, 22 bus. **Lunch served** 12.30-2.30pm Sat; 12.30-3pm Sun. **Dinner served** 6.30-11pm Mon-Sat; 6.30-10.30pm Sun. **Main courses** £16-£29.75. **Set lunch** £17 3 courses. **Credit** AmEx, DC, JCB, MC, V. Pan-Indian

Though no longer London's most fashionable Indian restaurant, Chutney Mary remains firmly tucked into the top drawer. It was among the first ventures of the Panjabi sisters, who also run Amaya (*see p135*) and Masala Zone (*see p150*). The kitchen began by specialising in Anglo-Indian food, then regional dishes and now Modern Indian cuisine (along with elements of the previous two). To start, tender, tangy Cochin-style squid was outshone by tokri chaat, a beautifully composed symphony of vegetarian snacks presented in a just-cooked basket of potato sticks. Main courses include luxury ingredients like lobster, but we recommend the tasting curry platter, the star of which was narangi murg (chicken with blood oranges and kashmiri chilli). The Punjabi vegetable selection was an equally fine vegetarian thali; care with textural pairings was exhibited in such dishes as bhindi and water-chestnut dopiaza. Neither should puddings be overlooked: try the dark chocolate fondant with orange blossom lassi. These large premises consist of a ground-floor reception and party venue, and a large, lavish split-level basement restaurant, lit by candles and including a conservatory. On a Saturday night, celebrating parties and couples dine here; business suits dominate during the week. Service was impeccable: staff standing sentinel discreetly throughout.
Babies and children welcome: high chairs. Booking advisable dinner. Dress: smart casual. Entertainment: jazz 12.30pm Sun. No-smoking tables. Separate room for parties, seats 24. **Map 13 C13.**

★ Painted Heron

112 Cheyne Walk, SW10 0TJ (7351 5232/ www.thepaintedheron.com). Sloane Square tube/11, 19, 22, 319 bus. **Lunch served** noon-2.30pm Mon-Fri. **Dinner served** 6-11pm daily. **Main courses** £11-£16. **Thalis** £11-£14. **Credit** AmEx, JCB, MC, V. Modern Indian

Some Indian chefs chase Michelin stars; others are busy penning cookery books or being on the telly. Chef Yogesh Datta, on the other hand, has been quietly making culinary waves at this upmarket venue. We had one of our most thrilling Indian meals of the year here. Smoked duck, alphonso mango and holy basil salad sparkled with a well-judged balance of flavours, as did a dish of duvet-

soft paneer tikka. Imaginative garnishes like khandvi (savoury Gujarati chickpea flour rolls – an elaborate dish in its own right) accentuated their beautiful presentation. To follow, Goan-style black tiger prawn curry was flavoured with an extraordinarily delicious mixture of freshly ground spices and roasted coconut. Yellow lentil dahl studded with slices of baby turnips was earthiness married with exquisite sophistication. Strawberry curry worked surprisingly well as the rich, subtle tomato and onion sauce complemented, rather than dominated, the fruit. A stir-fry of asparagus and sugar-snap peas topped with curry leaves and shredded coconut is a dish we've encountered in many top Indian restaurants – but nowhere does it work as well as here. With a stylishly stark decor of cream walls festooned with gorgeous monochrome contemporary art, Painted Heron is a seriously impressive venue.
Babies and children admitted. Booking advisable weekends. No-smoking tables. Separate room for parties, seats 25. Tables outdoors (5, garden). Vegetarian menu. **Map 14 D13.**

★ Rasoi Vineet Bhatia

10 Lincoln Street, SW3 2TS (7225 1881/ www.vineetbhatia.com). Sloane Square tube. **Lunch served** noon-2.30pm Mon-Fri. **Dinner served** 6-10.30pm Mon-Sat. **Main courses** £14-£36. **Set meal** £58-£69 tasting menus. **Credit** AmEx, JCB, MC, V. Modern Indian

For over a decade, Vineet Bhatia has been one of London's top Indian chefs. In 2006 this latest venture was awarded a Michelin star (to follow the star he earned in 2001 at Zaika; *see above*). The restaurant, located within a swish Chelsea townhouse, is well suited to the tastes of wealthy local residents. The fancy new-wave cooking comes at startling prices. Guests ring the doorbell to enter. The decor favours elegant restraint over grand opulence, and is softened by Rajasthani antiques, South Indian masks, and wispy silken drapes. We were bowled over by a memorable platter of tandoori treats. Presented on a banana leaf, this outstanding medley of smoky morsels included juicy scallops topped with pounded fennel seeds; succulent ginger-scented lamb seekh kebabs; and deliciously herby chicken tikka. Main courses also impressed. Seafood biriani had been steamed under a pastry lid that was opened with aplomb at table. It was a touch rich for our taste, but we appreciated the cardamom-laced fragrance and lightly cooked selection of seafood. Portions are lavish, so pace yourself and be prepared for a feast. Take a deep breath before scrutinising the wine list; although seriously pricey, it contains an inspiring selection. Service, as you'd expect, is professional and attentive.
Babies and children admitted. Booking advisable. Dress: smart casual. No smoking. Separate rooms for parties, seating 8 and 15. Vegetarian menu. **Map 14 F11.**

Vama

438 King's Road, SW10 0LJ (7351 4118/ www.vama.co.uk). Sloane Square tube then 11, 22 bus. **Lunch served** 12.30-3pm Sat, Sun. **Dinner served** 6.30-11.30pm Mon-Sat; 6.30-10.30pm Sun. **Main courses** £9.50-£15.50. **Set buffet** (noon-3pm Sun) £14.99. **Credit** AmEx, DC, MC, V. North Indian

With peach-coloured drapes flanking its light, stylish interior, Vama bears passing resemblance to a marquee at a posh wedding. Flagstoned flooring and a conservatory add a sense of permanence. Well-groomed Chelsea folk dine here. Andy Varma's expensive restaurant was once among London's best Indians, but we feel it may now be treading water. There's little Modern Indian innovation here, and the exhilarating spicing of authentic regional food is sometimes lacking. North-western cuisine is the speciality, and the tandoori food can be terrific. Masala chaap delivered three tangy, tender lamb chops (marinated in yoghurt, chilli and garlic) – for £13.95. Vegetarian starters cost about half this, but both aloo katlangi (potato skins with stuffed with grated potato and paneer) and pudina aloo

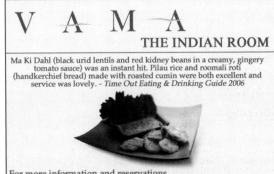

North Indian menu

Under the blanket term 'North Indian', we have included dishes originating in the Punjab (the region now straddling the political divide separating India and Pakistan), Kashmir and all points down to Hyderabad. Southall has some of London's best Punjabi restaurants, where breads cooked in the tandoor oven are often preferred to rice, marinated meat kebabs are popular, and dahls are thick and buttery.

Bhuna gosht: a dry, spicy dish of lamb.
Biriani or **biryani**: a royal Moghul (qv) version of pilau rice, in which meat or vegetables are cooked together with basmati rice, spices and saffron. It's difficult to find an authentic biriani in London restaurants.
Dopiaza or **do pyaza**: cooked with onions.
Dum: a Kashmiri cooking technique where food is simmered slowly in a casserole (typically a clay pot sealed with dough), allowing spices to permeate.
Gurda: kidneys.
Haandi: an earthenware or metal cooking pot, with handles on either side and a lid.
Jalfrezi: chicken or vegetable dishes cooked with fresh green chillies – a popular cooking style in Mumbai.

Jhingri, **jhinga** or **chingri**: prawns.
Kaleji or **kalezi**: liver.
Karahi or **karai**: a small iron or metal wok-like cooking dish. Similar to the 'balti' dish made famous in Birmingham.
Kheema or **keema**: minced lamb, as in kheema nan (stuffed nan).
Kofta: meatballs or vegetable dumplings.
Korma: braised in yoghurt and/or cream and nuts. Often mild, but rich.
Magaz: brain.
Makhani: cooked with butter (makhan) and sometimes tomatoes, as in murgh makhani.
Massalam: marinated, then casseroled chicken dish, originating in Muslim areas.
Moghul, **Mogul** or **Moglai**: from the Moghul period of Indian history, used in the culinary sense to describe typical North Indian Muslim dishes.
Nihari or **nehari**: there are many recipes on the subcontinent for this long-simmered meat stew, using goat, beef, mutton or sometimes chicken. Hyderabadi nihari is flavoured with sandalwood powder and rose petals. North Indian nihari uses nutmeg, cloves, dried ginger and tomato. In London, however, the dish is made with lamb shank (served on the bone).
Pasanda: thin fillets of lamb cut from the leg and flattened with a mallet. In

British curry houses, the term usually applies to a creamy sauce virtually identical to a korma (qv).
Paya: lamb's feet, usually served on the bone as paya curry (long-cooked and with copious gravy); seldom found outside Southall.
Punjabi: Since Partition, the Punjab has been two adjoining states, one in India, one in Pakistan. Lahore is the main town on the Pakistani side, which is predominantly Muslim; Amritsar on the Indian side is the Sikh capital. Punjabi dishes tend to be thick stews or cooked in a tandoor (qv).
Roghan gosht or **rogan josh**: lamb cooked in spicy sauce, a Kashmiri speciality.
Seekh kebab: ground lamb, skewered and grilled.
Tak-a-tak: a cooking method – ingredients (usually meat or vegetables) are chopped and flipped as they cook on a griddle.
Tandoor: clay oven originating in north-west India in which food is cooked without oil.
Tarka: spices and flavourings are cooked separately, then added to dahl at a final stage.
Tikka: meat, fish or paneer cut into cubes, then marinated in spicy yoghurt and baked in a tandoor (qv).

tikki (mint and potato fritters with chickpeas) lacked zest and came with oily salad garnishes. To follow, gosht sag combined tender lamb and spinach boosted with fresh ginger – but would have benefited from assertive Punjabi spicing. Scallop masala was much better: a generous portion of perfectly cooked shellfish in a delicate, herby sauce. Puddings are imaginative; gajjerella (gajjar halva with cardamom ice-cream and saffron sauce) was warm, light and moist. Swift, professional staff are keen to pour wine, but overall we expected more flair at these prices.
Babies and children welcome: high chairs. Booking essential weekends. Separate room for parties, seats 35. Tables outdoors (2, patio). Takeaway service. **Map 14 D12.**

Norbury

Mirch Masala
1416-1418 London Road, SW16 4BZ (8679 1828/8765 1070). Norbury rail. **Meals served** noon-midnight daily. **Main courses** £3-£10. **Set buffet** (noon-4pm Mon-Sat) £6.99. **Unlicensed. Corkage** no charge. **Credit** AmEx, JCB, MC, V. East African Punjabi
Mirch Masala (meaning 'chilli and spice') has had a refurb. But fans of this no-frills canteen needn't worry: the tables are still wipe-clean, the stainless-steel kitchen is still visible through the back, and the service is still brusque. Popadoms arrive unbidden, but they're complimentary. The menu has changed not one jot, and the secret to a successful meal here is to order carefully. Give the pilao rice a swerve, unless you like added traffic-light colours; there's no need for rice when the nan breads are sublime. The 'fresh passion' juice is also artificially coloured. People come here for the karahis and the 'deigi' dishes, both of which can be spiced to taste (mild or hot). The deigi karela dahl birji had a pleasant tartness because of the slow-cooked karela (bitter gourd) and a good firm texture, courtesy of the toor dahl used and the relatively dry style of the dish. The best dish was

a starter of Mirch Masala fish: boneless, even chunks from a large fillet of coley, rubbed with spices then fried. There's a laminated card of bought-in desserts to catch out the unwary.
Babies and children welcome: high chairs. Booking advisable. Takeaway service; delivery service (within 2-mile radius). Vegetarian menu.
For branches see index.

Putney

Ma Goa
242-244 Upper Richmond Road, SW15 6TG (8780 1767/www.ma-goa.com). East Putney tube/Putney rail/74, 337 bus. **Lunch served** noon-2.30pm Tue-Fri; 1-4pm Sun. **Dinner served** 6.30-11pm Mon-Sat; 6-10pm Sun. **Main courses** £7.50-£12. **Set dinner** (6.30-8pm) £10 2 courses. **Set buffet** (Sun lunch) £10. **Credit** AmEx, DC, JCB, MC, V. Goan
Visiting Goa is now as easy as booking a week's package holiday with Monarch Airlines. This has fuelled interest in Goan food, which brings central and South Indian flavours together with Christian Portuguese influences (vinegar and pork are both common in this former Portuguese colony). London's leading Goan restaurant does the classics well: flavourful pork vindaloo with its sour-spice contrasts; the pleasing spice after-rush of a prawn balchao; and fish caldine, made with top-quality, expertly deboned, chunky white fish. Dish presentation is also exquisite, from the tiny white bowls of low-fat curries and side dishes on geometric serving plates, to the extraordinary east-west fusion desserts made exclusively for Ma Goa by a pâtissier (try the traditional bebique or bibenca – a layered confection of coconut milk, egg and jaggery – or the lime cheesecake topped with rosewater jelly). The service at this stylishly modern restaurant also takes some beating: polite, attentive, and cheery. The rare problems are dealt with swiftly and gracefully; on our most recent visit, a single substandard dish was immediately replaced, yet taken off the bill.
Babies and children welcome: children's menu; high chairs. Booking advisable; essential weekends.

Dress: smart casual. No smoking. Restaurant available for hire. Separate room for parties, seats 35. Takeaway service; delivery service (within 3-mile radius).
For branch see index.

Southfields

Sarkhel's
199 Replingham Road, SW18 5LY (8870 1483/www.sarkhels.com). Southfields tube. **Lunch served** noon-2.30pm Tue-Sun. **Dinner served** 6-10.30pm Tue-Thur, Sun; 6-11pm Fri, Sat. **Main courses** £6.95-£9.95. **Set lunch** £5 2 courses. **Thali** £9.95. **Credit** MC, V. Pan-Indian
Although still highly popular with locals, the cooking at this pan-Indian restaurant (with contemporary furnishings and intimate corners) seems a shadow of its early glory days. We started with mini popadoms topped with freshly grated coconut and coriander; they arrived with chutneys and pickles that appeared to have come straight from a jar. Chicken lollipops is a contemporary Indian dish (allegedly invented to appeal to a visiting English cricket team). Here, the chicken nuggets were batter-fried and cooked for too long, resulting in a too-dark appearance and a dull, overcooked flavour. Shinghara chaat was much better: small Bengali vegetable samosas made from wonderfully dense, crumbly shortcrust pastry, topped with gustily spiced chickpeas and drizzled with soothing yoghurt and piquant tamarind chutney. In contrast, lagan nu sabzi (Parsi wedding vegetable curry) was indistinctly flavoured and mundane. Kolmi nu patia (Parsi black tiger prawn curry with pumpkin and aubergines) was much livelier. Peripherals were a little disappointing: dhansak rice was overwhelmed with over-roasted spices; and onion kulcha was stuffed with what tasted like onion pakora batter. To finish, payesh (Bengali rice pudding) and carrot and sweet-potato halwa were a little thin, but mercifully not too sweet.

Babies and children welcome: high chairs. Book Fri, Sat. Disabled: toilet. No-smoking tables. Takeaway service (8871 0808). Vegetarian menu. **For branch see index.**

South

Battersea

Swayam Ruchi NEW

2 Battersea Rise, SW11 1ED (7738 0038). Clapham Junction rail. **Lunch served** noon-3pm, **dinner served** 6-11pm daily. **Main courses** £5.95-£12.95. **Set lunch** £4.99 2 courses. **Set dinner** £18.50-£20 4 courses. **Credit** AmEx, MC, V. South Indian

This family-run Keralite restaurant has replaced an earlier South Indian venue on the same site. The interior looks much the same as before, apart from the addition of kasuvu fabric (Keralite gold-striped cotton) as improvised seat covers; it remains a cool, quiet place to eat. Chef-proprietor Ajit Kumar used to be the head chef at Rasa (*see p149*) in the early days – something evident in the menu, which recreates many of Rasa's greatest hits. Unusually, seafood and meat dishes are given the most prominent billing, but it's the vegetarian food that provides a better test of most Keralite restaurants. The cooking lacks the finesse of London's best South Indian restaurants; for example, the lemon rice was claggy, when the grains should be distinct. Other dishes were of a high standard, such as a pert and succulent cabbage thoran, and the cheera parippu (a wet lentil curry made with toor dahl and spinach, flavoured with garlic). Snacks such as the banana boli were a little heavy, but tasted just fine. Although Swayam Ruchi would benefit from more attention to detail in the kitchen, it's a welcoming, relaxing restaurant with a good menu and attentive service. Next time, we'll try the seafood dishes.

Babies and children welcome: high chairs. No-smoking tables. Separate room for parties, seats 25. Takeaway service; delivery service (over £15 within 3-mile radius). **Map 21 C4**.

Tooting

In the past 20 years, Tooting has become one of the prime destinations for anyone seeking 'real' South Asian food in London. There has long been a significant Asian population in the neighbourhood, mostly a result of the South West London College, which attracted well-educated students to its accountancy and business courses during the 1960s. Some of these immigrants came from Kerala, Gujarat, Pakistan, Sri Lanka – areas of the subcontinent with excellent educational systems. The first South Indian restaurant, Sree Krishna, opened in 1973, but it was during the 1970s and '80s that Tooting took on the visible Asian identity you can see today.

A wave of black nationalism swept through East Africa in the 1970s, forcing many white-collar Asians to flee their adopted countries (Uganda, Tanzania, Kenya); some of these refugees made Tooting their new home. A second wave of immigration occurred in the late 1980s, when a civil war between Tamil separatists in the north of Sri Lanka and the Sinhalese government intensified. The Tooting and Colliers Wood area is now home to about 30,000 Tamil people, of the 100,000 estimated to be in London.

The result of this mixture is that, unlike Punjabi Southall, Gujarati Wembley or Bangladeshi Brick Lane, Tooting has an unusually rich and diverse Asian population, reflected in its growing number of excellent cafés, food shops and restaurants. Prices are remarkably low. There is nowhere else in the UK where you will find Keralite seafood dishes, Sri Lankan sambols, Gujarati East African ingredients and Lahori-style deigi dishes within a ten-minute walk of one other.

★ Apollo Banana Leaf

190 Tooting High Street, SW17 0SF (8696 1423). Tooting Broadway tube. **Meals served** noon-11pm daily. **Unlicensed. Corkage** no charge. **Main courses** £3.50-£6.25. **Credit** AmEx, MC, V. Sri Lankan

'Banana leaf restaurants' (serving food on banana leaves) are currently very trendy all over Asia; it's a pity this compact, no-frills caff has stopped following the practice. A new menu lists generic pan-Indian dishes alongside Sri Lankan specialities. Idlis and vadais are a good test of Sri Lankan and South Indian chefs' skills; they should be marshmallow-soft and featherlight, but rarely are. Here, the urid lentil fritters soaked in well-spiced sambar were silky smooth and soft as a baby's cheek. Vegetable kothu was a fiery stir-fry of veechu roti (a type of Sri Lankan flatbread) and what appeared to be frozen mixed vegetables, distinctly flavoured with cloves, cinnamon, fennel seeds and curry leaves. Red rice string hoppers were stir-fried with eggs, onions and green chillies in another dish with full-on flavours. No alcohol is served, but on our visit, a happy mix of customers who looked liked they'd stepped out of a Hanif Kureishi novel were enjoying Sri Lankan cream soda-like drinks such as Necto and Portello. Service, from a giggling waitress, was charming. *Babies and children welcome: high chairs. Booking advisable weekends. No smoking. Takeaway service.*

Painted Heron. See p142.

★ Kastoori

188 Upper Tooting Road, SW17 7EJ (8767 7027). Tooting Bec or Tooting Broadway tube. **Lunch served** 12.30-2.30pm Wed-Sun. **Dinner served** 6-10.30pm daily. **Main courses** £4.75-£6.25. **Thalis** £8.50-£16.25. **Minimum** £7. **Credit** MC, V. East African Gujarati vegetarian

Vegetarians and, in particular, vegans come from miles to eat at this sparklingly clean, long-established restaurant. East African Gujarati food is the specialism, cooked with lots of tomatoes, and African ingredients such as cassava, peanuts, sweetcorn and green bananas. The venue is strikingly decorated, with a deep-blue carpet and matching padded chairs, bright yellow table linen, and cream walls hung with stone reliefs of a devadasi (female temple dancer). The menu lists chaats, curries and a wide variety of little-seen speciality dishes, from which only one is available daily. Robustly flavoured masala kachori was served like a chaat: crumbled and topped with yoghurt and tamarind sauces and vivid red chilli powder. Fresh tomato curry was vibrantly flavoured, but green pepper curry in peanut and sesame sauce was too oily. Together with chowri (aduki bean) curry, all the dishes tasted rather similar with their cinnamon-laced tomato sauce. Moreover, the onions used in the sauce base were undercooked. Gujarati dishes are usually made only with a pinch of sugar to round out the flavours; the dishes here are way too sweet, with sugar proving to be a predominant (rather than a background) flavour.
Babies and children admitted. Booking essential. Takeaway service. Vegan dishes.

★ Radha Krishna Bhavan

86 Tooting High Street, SW17 0RN (8682 0969/www.mcdosa.com). Tooting Broadway tube. **Lunch served** noon-3pm daily. **Dinner served** 6-11pm Mon-Thur, Sun; 6pm-midnight Fri, Sat. **Main courses** £1.95-£6.95. **Thalis** (Sun) £5.95-£7.95. **Minimum** £5. **Credit** AmEx, DC, MC, V. South Indian

Most Indian restaurants – heck, most restaurants these days – have a generic decor of cream walls and wooden floors. Not here: this Keralite venue dares to be different. Its walls are covered with bold, brightly coloured photographic wallpaper of palm-fringed beaches and sunsets, and strewn with kathakali masks. There's also a life-size statue of a kathakali (temple) dancer. The look, in other words, is individual. A long menu contains much that is standard curry-house fare, but stick to the Keralite dishes and you won't go far wrong. Idli vadai sambar was a large bowl of mellow lentil broth crammed with vegetable drumsticks; in it floated a chunky idli and a hefty urid lentil fritter, neither of which was as tender as it should have been, but the dish was tasty and substantial. Adai should be a small, crumpet-like pancake made from rice, three or four varieties of lentils and split peas, vegetables and whole spices. Here, it's a large, thin pancake made fiery and fragrant with cracked black pepper, hot chilli powder and curry leaves. On our visit, good-looking twenty- and thirty-somethings were having fun tackling the enormous 'ghee roast' masala dosas.
Babies and children admitted. Booking advisable. Takeaway service; delivery service (within 3-mile radius). Vegetarian menu.
For branch (Sree Krishna Inn) see index.

South East

Herne Hill

3 Monkeys

136-140 Herne Hill, SE24 9QH (7738 5500/ www.3monkeysrestaurant.com). Herne Hill rail/ 3, 37, 68 bus. **Lunch served** noon-2.30pm, **dinner served** 5.30-10.30pm Mon-Sat. **Meals served** noon-10.30pm Sun. **Main courses** £8.95-£10.95. **Set lunch** (Mon-Thur, Sun) £7.95 2 courses. **Set dinner** (Mon-Thur, Sun) £12.95 2 courses. **Credit** AmEx, DC, JCB, MC, TC, V. Pan-Indian

Our meal at this smart venue didn't start well. Despite booking and being the only customers on an early evening visit, we were shown to a tiny table behind a pillar (one of many; despite the slick cream and purple decor, the layout remains awkward). The manager insisted that all other tables had been reserved. It was only by persisting that we were moved to a better table (we subsequently noticed other diners being given the dud seats, despite their protestations). The restaurant remained mostly empty until closing time. From an ambitious North Indian menu, fig-stuffed, fennel-flecked green banana kebabs were delicious; as was paneer and fresh fenugreek curry, flavoured, Kashmiri-style, with dried ginger. Disappointing dishes included bland batter-fried soft-shell crab with insipid crab meat, and pot-roasted lamb tikka that was tough and dry. Wonderful own-made kulfi had an appropriately layered texture and clotted cream flavour. The food here is good – but unless the management treats customers more appropriately, 3 Monkeys won't make it into the top league.
Babies and children welcome: high chairs. Booking advisable. Disabled: toilet. No-smoking tables. Separate rooms for parties, seating 16 and 40. Takeaway service; delivery service (7738 5550). **Map 23 A5**.

East

Looking for good Indian food in east London? Then avoid Brick Lane. Although it's still famous for curries – especially among tourists – the 'Indian' food here is nothing like the real thing. What's more, the dish quality is sometimes questionable, and you risk being hassled by the curry touts that pounce on bemused passers-by. The best reason to visit Brick Lane is to buy mouth-watering, authentic Bengali sweets, and little-seen Bangladeshi vegetables, fruit, meat, fish and groceries. The numerous *melas* (Indian festivities) held in Brick Lane throughout the year are another good reason to come here.

For wonderful Indian food, head to nearby **Café Spice Namaste** (*see p149*), a contemporary, slickly run Indian venue where the cooking, though pricey, is rooted firmly in tradition. It's also worth travelling further east to the long, snaking Green Street outside Upton Park tube station, and the High Street outside East Ham

South Indian menu

Much South Indian food consists of rice-, lentil- and semolina-based dishes (semolina being small grains of crushed wheat). Fish features strongly in non-vegetarian establishments, and coconut, mustard seeds, curry leaves and red chillies are widely used as flavourings.

If you want to try South Indian snacks like dosas, idlis or uppama, it's best to visit restaurants at lunchtime, which is when these dishes are traditionally eaten, and they're more likely to be cooked fresh to order. In the evening, we recommend you try the thalis and rice- and curry-based meals, including South Indian vegetable stir-fries like thorans and pachadis. For the tastiest Tamil food, try **Sanghamam** in Wembley (*see p159*). **Satya** in Uxbridge (*see p157*) offers some of the liveliest, most colourful Keralite specialities. **Sagar** (*see p141*) is best for Udupi vegetarian cooking from Karnataka.

Adai: fermented rice and lentil pancakes, with a nuttier flavour than dosais (qv).
Avial: a mixed vegetable curry from Kerala with a coconut and yoghurt sauce. Literally, 'mixture' in Malayalam (the language of Kerala).
Bonda: spiced mashed potatoes, dipped in chickpea-flour batter and deep-fried.
Dosai or **dosa:** thin, shallow-fried pancake, often sculpted into interesting shapes; the very thin ones are called **paper dosai**. Most dosais are made with fermented rice and lentil batter, but variants include **rava dosai**, made with 'cream of wheat' semolina.
Masala dosais come with a spicy potato filling. All variations are traditionally served with sambar (qv) and coconut chutney.
Gobi 65: cauliflower marinated in spices, then dipped in chickpea-flour batter and

deep-fried. It is usually lurid pink due to the addition of food colouring.
Idli: steamed sponges of ground rice and lentil batter. Eaten with sambar (qv) and coconut chutney.
Kadala: black chickpea curry.
Kalan: a thin curry from the southern states made from yoghurt, coconut and mangoes.
Kancheepuram idli: idli (qv) flavoured with whole black peppercorns and other spices.
Kappa: cassava root traditionally served with kadala (qv).
Kootu: mild vegetable curry in a creamy coconut and yoghurt sauce.
Kozhi varutha: usually consists of pieces of chicken served in a medium-hot curry sauce based on garlic and coconut; it is very rich.
Moilee: Keralite fish curry.
Pachadi: spicy vegetable side dish cooked with yoghurt.
Rasam: consommé made with lentils; it tastes both peppery-hot and tamarind-sour, but there are many regional variations.
Sambar or **sambhar:** a variation on dahl made with a specific hot blend of spices, plus coconut, tamarind and vegetables – particularly drumsticks (a pod-like vegetable, like a longer, woodier version of okra; you strip out the edible interior with your teeth).
Thoran: vegetables stir-fried with mustard seeds, curry leaves, chillies and fresh grated coconut.
Uppama: a popular breakfast dish in which onions, spices and, occasionally, vegetables are cooked with semolina using a risotto-like technique.
Uthappam: a spicy, crisp pancake/ pizza made with lentil- and rice-flour batter, usually topped with tomato, onions and chillies.
Vellappam: a bowl-shaped, crumpet-like rice pancake (same as appam or hoppers, qv, Sri Lankan menu).

tube station. Both are lined with numerous Pakistani, Gujarati and South Indian eateries that offer cheap, filling and tasty meals. You'll also be able to buy inexpensive meat, fish and vegetables in the many shops and markets to be found in the area.

Upton Park

★ Vijay's Chawalla
268-270 Green Street, E7 8LF (8470 3535). Upton Park tube. **Meals served** 11am-9pm daily. **Main courses** £4-£7. **Thalis** £6-£7. **Unlicensed. Corkage** no charge. **Credit** JCB, MC, V. Gujarati vegetarian

We've enjoyed the food at this popular Green Street stalwart for years, but our most recent visit disappointed. The venue looks tired (despite a new lick of burnished orange paint), the worn crockery needs replacing, and service from staff who were more interested in watching Bollywood films on plasma screens was slow and inattentive. The venue is essentially a Gujarati takeaway snack shop with a few tables for eating-in. Pani poori should feature hollowed-out pooris filled with lots of goodies such as diced potatoes, onions, chickpeas and sprouted beans. Here it's a simplified version that comes with only one sauce (rather than the more usual two to four varieties). Flavoured with fresh mint and black salt, the sauce was nonetheless piquant and tasty. Special bhel featured ribbons of crisp pooris mixed with potatoes, onions and chickpeas, topped with yoghurt and tamarind sauce and chickpea-flour vermicelli. The day's special was sandwich pakora: bread sandwiched with potatoes, sweetcorn and cauliflower, fried in chickpea-flour batter. It would have been tasty, save for the undercooked pieces of cauliflower. Next time we'll stick to the thalis and the rarely seen Gujarati specialities.
Babies and children welcome: high chairs. Disabled: toilet. No smoking. Takeaway service. Vegetarian menu.

Whitechapel

★ Café Spice Namaste
16 Prescot Street, E1 8AZ (7488 9242/ www.cafespice.co.uk). Aldgate East or Tower Hill tube/Tower Gateway DLR. **Lunch served** noon-3pm Mon-Fri. **Dinner served** 6.15-10.30pm Mon-Fri; 6.30-10.30pm Sat. **Main courses** £11.25-£18.95. **Set meal** £30 3 courses; £60 tasting menu. **Credit** AmEx, DC, JCB, MC, V. Pan-Indian

On the night we visited this bright, cheery, colourful pan-Indian venue – which has had a fresh lick of paint – the owner, Cyrus Todiwala, was away launching his new café inside Asia House, and his hospitable, on-the-ball son was running the show. We ordered from a chatty, eccentrically written tenth-anniversary menu (the only one available, for a limited period, at the time of our visit) in which all the dishes were named after regular customers. To start, black prawn shashlik was assertively spiced with hot red chillies. Burmese food is enormously popular in Mumbai – here, cold Burmese rice noodles came with numerous accompaniments (including chickpea flour, which, for this dish, should have been toasted). It was a DIY assembly job, and not a success as the dish tasted raw. Goan vegetable curry was made with potatoes and what appeared to be frozen mixed vegetables, but boasted a truly outstanding sauce layered with roasted spices and fresh coconut. Also scrumptious was Parsee-style festive pumpkin curry, but the real show-stopper was the astonishingly flavoursome duck and venison tikka. Puddings, including rose kulfi (made from syrup distilled from fresh rose petals) and Parsee apricot toffee ice-cream, were memorable. An exceptional meal.
Babies and children welcome: high chairs. Booking advisable. Disabled: toilet. Tables outdoors (8, garden). Takeaway service; delivery service (within 2-mile radius). **Map 12 S7.**

Aanya Wine Lounge. See p150.

Kasturi
57 Aldgate High Street, EC3N 1AL (7480 7402/ www.kasturi-restaurant.co.uk). Aldgate tube. **Meals served** 11am-11pm Mon-Sat. **Main courses** £6.95-£10. **Set buffet** (11am-3pm Mon-Fri) £9.99. **Credit** AmEx, MC, V. Pan-Indian

In contrast to the cacophonous traffic on the High Street, Kasturi offers an oasis of calm that goes down well with busy City types. It's a more upmarket restaurant than nearby venues on Brick Lane, with wooden flooring, modern art and mirrors producing a bright and airy vibe. Chefs have a tendency to overstretch themselves when celebrating little-known culinary gems; their strengths lie in delivering simple kebabs and curries from the north-west frontier. We had no complaints about a first course of adraki lamb chops: well-steeped with ginger, yoghurt and lime juice, and cooked to succulent perfection. Just as satisfying, meltingly soft griddle cakes, made from sweet potato and plantain mash, were enlivened with heaps of fresh dill and hints of toasted cumin. Main courses were disappointing, comprising a confusing mix of discordant dishes. A vegetarian thali contained sweetish lentils, overly aromatic rice, and

an undistinguished potato and green pea curry. Service, although well-meaning, tends to be bumbling.
Babies and children welcome: high chairs. Booking advisable. Disabled: toilet. No-smoking tables. Separate rooms for parties, seating 20 and 40. Takeaway service; delivery service (over £15 within 3-mile radius). Vegetarian menu. **Map 12 S6.**

North East
Stoke Newington

Rasa
55 Stoke Newington Church Street, N16 0AR (7249 0344/www.rasarestaurants.com). Stoke Newington rail/73, 243, 393, 426, 476 bus. **Lunch served** noon-3pm Sat, Sun. **Dinner served** 6-10.45pm Mon-Thur, Sun; 6-11.30pm Fri, Sat. **Main courses** £3.95-£6. **Set meal** £16 4 courses. **Credit** AmEx, DC, JCB, MC, V. South Indian vegetarian

The original restaurant of a six-strong chain, Rasa is a hit with well-travelled local residents blessed with adventurous tastes. Its striking cochineal-pink frontage leads to a traditional interior complete with lit joss sticks, hanging lamp stands

Gujarati menu

Most Gujarati restaurants are located in north-west London, mainly in Wembley, Sudbury, Kingsbury, Kenton, Harrow, Rayners Lane and Hendon, and they tend to be no-frills, family-run eateries.

Unlike North Indian food, Gujarati dishes are not normally cooked in a base sauce of onions, garlic, tomatoes and spices. Instead they're tempered; whole spices such as cumin, red chillies, mustard seeds, ajwain (carom) seeds, asafoetida powder and curry leaves are sizzled in hot oil for a few seconds. The tempering is added at the start or the end of cooking, depending on the dish. Commonplace items like grains, beans and flours – transformed into various shapes by boiling, steaming and frying – are the basis of many dishes. Coriander, coconut, yoghurt, jaggery (cane sugar), tamarind, sesame seeds, chickpea flour and cocum (a sun-dried, sour, plum-like fruit) are also widely used.

Each region has its own cooking style. Kathiyawad, a humid area in western Gujarat, and Kutch, a desert in the north-west, have spawned styles that are less reliant on fresh produce. Kathiyawadi food is rich with dairy products and grains such as dark millet, and is pepped up with chilli powder. Kutchis make liberal use of chickpea flour (as do Kathiyawadis) and their staple diet is based on khichadi. In central Gujarat towns such as Baroda and Ahmedabad, grains are widely used; they appear in snacks that are the backbone of menus in London's Gujarati restaurants.

The gourmet heartland, however, is Surat – one of the few regions with heavy rainfall and lush vegetation. Surat boasts an abundance of green vegetables like papadi (a type of broad bean) and ponk (fresh green millet). A must-try Surti speciality is undhiyu. Surti food uses 'green masala' (fresh coriander, coconut, green chillies and ginger), as opposed to the 'red masala' (red chilli powder, crushed coriander, cumin and turmeric) more commonly used in western and central regions.

The standard of Gujarati food available in restaurants has improved since the last edition of this guide. **Dadima** (see p158) serves excellent Ahmedabadi food; authentic Surti food is now available at **Ram's** (see p155); and **Sakonis** (see p159) offers good Kenyan-Gujarati versions of Mumbai street snacks. The best time to visit Gujarati restaurants is for Sunday lunch, which is when you'll find little-seen regional specialities on the menu – but be warned, you will almost certainly need to book.

Bhakarvadi: pastry spirals stuffed with whole spices and, occasionally, potatoes.
Bhel poori: a snack originating from street stalls in Mumbai, which contains crisp, deep-fried pooris, puffed rice, sev (qv), chopped onion, tomato, potato and more, plus chutneys (chilli, mint and tamarind).
Farsan: Gujarati snacks.
Ganthia: Gujarati name for crisply fried savoury confections made from chickpea flour; they come in all shapes.
Ghughara: sweet or savoury pasties.
Kadhi: yoghurt and chickpea flour curry, often cooked with dumplings or vegetables.
Khichadi or **khichdi**: rice and lentils mixed with ghee and spices.
Mithi roti: round griddle-cooked bread stuffed with a cardamom-and-saffron-flavoured lentil paste. Also called puran poli.
Mogo: deep-fried cassava, often served as chips together with a sweet and sour tamarind chutney. An East African Asian dish.
Pani poori: bite-sized pooris that are filled with sprouted beans, chickpeas, potato, onion, chutneys, sev (qv) and a thin, spiced watery sauce.
Patra: a savoury snack made of the arvi leaf (colocasia) stuffed with spiced chickpea-flour batter, steamed, then cut into slices in the style of a swiss roll. The slices are then shallow-fried with sesame and mustard seeds.
Pau bhajee: a robustly spiced dish of mashed potatoes and vegetables, served with a shallow-fried white bread roll.
Puran poli: see mithi roti.
Ragda pattice or **ragada patties**: mashed potato patties covered with a chickpea or dried-pea sauce, topped with onions, sev (qv) and spicy chutney.
Sev: deep-fried chickpea-flour vermicelli.
Thepla: savoury flatbread.
Tindora: ivy gourd, a vegetable resembling baby gherkins.
Undhiyu: a casserole of purple yam, sweet potatoes, ordinary potatoes, green beans, Indian broad beans, other vegetables and fenugreek-leaf dumplings cooked with fresh coconut, coriander and green chilli. A speciality of Surat.

and statues of Hindu deities. You'll find no modern interpretations on the menu; Rasa is resolutely true to its Keralite culinary heritage. Tempting own-made crunchy snacks work particularly well with the array of tongue-tingling relishes; shredded garlic pickle flecked with chillies, and a coconut and coriander chutney were our favourites. Mysore bonda (deep-fried dumplings of mashed potato, spiced with mustard seeds and curry leaves) were all the more delicious for their crisp chickpea-flour batter. But idlis (steamed rice cakes) didn't measure up to expectation, having a dense (rather than light and spongy) texture. Masala dosa (lentil and rice pancake) was another let-down, losing points for its flaccid texture and tepid temperature. Our mood perked up with a marvellously fruity mango and green banana curry; sweet with ripe mango halves, and astringent with warm whipped yoghurt and slit green chillies, this dish made a fabulous partner to lemon rice. Service, like the cooking, is homely.
Babies and children welcome: high chairs. Booking essential weekends. No smoking. Takeaway service. Vegetarian menu. Vegan dishes. **Map 25 B1**. **For branches see index.**

North
Archway

The Parsee
34 Highgate Hill, N19 5NL (7272 9091/ www.theparsee.com). Archway tube. **Dinner served** 6-10.45pm Mon-Sat. **Main courses** £9.95-£12.95. **Set dinner** £25 3 courses, £30 4 courses. **Credit** AmEx, MC, V. Parsi

Restaurateur Cyrus Todiwala celebrates Parsee traditions with confidence and creative flair, championing a blend of Middle Eastern and coastal Indian flavours. His restaurant's glass frontage looks a little frayed from the outside, but its interior remains cheerfully modern, if a touch austere. Black and white photographs across the walls highlight a Parsee connection, but it's the cooking that provides a passport to an authentic culinary heritage. Patrani machi (baked pomfret, smothered in herby coconut chutney) was a feast of tropical flavours, its banana-leaf wrapping adding to the authentic appeal. Parsees moved from Persia to India in the first century AD, and their cooking style reflects a love of sweet and sour flavours. Prawn patio (juicy prawns, coated with a saucy tamarind and jaggery masala) was milder than expected, but tasty nevertheless. Chefs can also whip up a delectable lassi and excellent fresh lime soda – a lot more refreshing than wine. The cooking here isn't in the premier league occupied by Todiwala's flagship restaurant, Café Spice Namaste (see p149), but it's certainly a cut above regular curry-house offerings.
Babies and children admitted. Booking advisable weekends. No-smoking tables. Separate rooms for parties, seating 18-35. Takeaway service; delivery service (over £25 within 3-mile radius). **Map 26 B1.**

Crouch End

Aanya Wine Lounge NEW
29 Park Road, N8 8TE (8342 8686/www.aanya. co.uk). Finsbury Park tube/rail then W7 bus. **Lunch served** 11am-3pm, **dinner served** 5.30-10.30pm Mon-Fri. **Meals served** 11am-10.30pm Sat; noon-10.30pm Sun. **Main courses** £2.95-£7.95. **Set lunch** £6 1 course incl soft drink. **Credit** MC, V. North Indian

Although Aanya is a wine bar not a restaurant, it deserves inclusion here for the impressive selection of North Indian snack food; it's the sort of fare you might find at a smart cocktail party in Mumbai. Reshmi ('silken') chicken kebab and lamb chops were tender and vibrantly spiced, while paneer parcels were expertly made filo pastry bags stuffed with spiced cheese. We also liked the bread-based canapés topped with sweetcorn and peppers, but succulent tandoori prawns were somewhat overwhelmed by their coriander, mint and chilli marinade. Artisan-made Italian ice-cream, served on a block of ice embedded with rose petals, pleased both the eye and the palate. The menu can seem short and repetitive if you're planning a full meal. 'Vegetarian bites' are based primarily on paneer and potatoes, rendering the snacks somewhat stodgy. The non-vegetarian versions are mostly variations on chicken and lamb; there's also an over-reliance on frying and grilling. On our visits Aanya has always been packed with beautiful young people having a good time, which goes a long way to making up for its limitations as a destination dining venue.
Babies and children admitted (daytime). Booking advisable dinner Thur-Sat. Restaurant available for hire. Takeaway service.

Islington

★ Masala Zone
80 Upper Street, N1 0NU (7359 3399/ www.realindianfood.com). Angel tube. **Lunch served** 12.30-3pm, **dinner served** 5.30-11pm

Satya. See p157.

Mon-Fri. **Meals served** 12.30-11pm Sat; 12.30-10.30pm Sun. **Main courses** £6.50-£9. **Thalis** £7-£11.55. **Credit** MC, V. Pan-Indian

'We serve more customers than any other Indian cuisine restaurants within the M25,' boasts Masala Zone. Certainly on our visit, this branch was abuzz with gorgeous, hip twentysomethings. It's a spacious venue decorated with colourful tribal-style murals, an open kitchen, outside seating and, in fine weather, a barbecue at the front. We started with two signature dishes: gosht (lamb) dabalroti and chana (chickpea) dabalroti. These are classic Sindhi Sunday lunch dishes in which the lamb/chickpeas are cooked in spicy gravy, combined with cubes of bread, and topped with tamarind sauce, minced onions, fresh coriander and chickpea-flour vermicelli. Both dishes were tangy, aromatic and deeply savoury. Creamy chicken curry subtly laced with cardamom and mace was tasty, but the accompanying rice was undercooked. Vegetable 'burger' hot off the barbecue was a mush of sautéed vegetables slathered inside a sesame seed bun. It had a sharp, slightly odd taste of cloves mixed with boiled cabbage, and wasn't a success. Masala Zone tries to make more accessible the Indian snacks and street food that are widely available in the restaurants of Wembley and Southall – but the results are hit and miss.

Babies and children welcome: high chair.
Bookings not accepted. No smoking. Separate
area for parties, seats 40. Takeaway service.
Map 5 O2.
For branches see index.

North West
Hampstead

Woodlands
102 Heath Street, NW3 1DR (7794 3080).
Hampstead tube. **Dinner served** 6-11pm Mon-Thur. **Meals served** noon-11pm Fri-Sun. **Main courses** £4.25-£16.95. **Set thali** (noon-3pm Fri-Sun) £7.50. **Credit** MC, V. South Indian vegetarian
This burgeoning restaurant chain, with close to three dozen branches in India, has recently opened another London outlet in the genteel setting of Hampstead. It's a modern, glass-fronted restaurant, embellished with a soothing water feature near the entrance, and wispy drapes across windows. A Zen-like calm prevails. Unlike the decor, the South Indian menu is traditional, eschewing new-wave flavour combinations. Idlis were as good as they get: light, spongy, and a perfect complement to sambar (mouth-watering lentils, sharpened with tamarind and tomatoes and incorporating squishy aubergines). Other dishes weren't quite as confident; we felt authenticity had been compromised to suit apprehensive western palates. Masala dosa was dense in texture, rather than light and crisp; its potato filling was little more than plainly seasoned mash. Uppama – a classic breakfast dish and anytime snack, made from creamed wheat cooked with chillies, vegetables, curry leaves and mustard seeds – was equally meek. Let's hope this branch can raise the heat and spices things up without delay.

Babies and children welcome: high chairs. Booking
advisable. No-smoking tables. Takeaway service.
Map 28 C1.
For branches see index.

Kilburn

Kovalam
12 Willesden Lane, NW6 7SR (7625 4761/
www.kovalamrestaurant.co.uk). Kilburn tube/
98 bus. **Lunch served** noon-2.30pm daily.
Dinner served 6-11pm Mon-Thur, Sun; 6pm-midnight Fri, Sat. **Main courses** £4.95-£8.95.
Set meal (vegetarian) £18-£35 serves 2-4, (non-vegetarian) £26-£48 serves 2-4. **Credit** AmEx, JCB, MC, V. South Indian
Across the road from two South Indian old-stagers, Kovalam is the newest, and we reckon the best, of the bunch. Service is quiet and engaging, and the long thin dining room (white walls, maroon carpet) is cheered up by chintzy chandeliers and groovy uplights in purple and lime green. There's little to distinguish the place from the curry house norm, and indeed, much of the menu is of the 'kebab followed by tikka masala' ilk. But look to the 'vegetarian starters' and 'South Indian specialities' for some enticing Keralite cuisine. The Kovalam platter for two gives a good idea of the range of vegetarian snacks: five filling titbits each, from crunchy, lentil-filled parippu vada, to various pakodas and tiny samosas. These we enjoyed much more than the lacklustre main courses of lamb malabar (tender meat in a thick, barely seasoned coconut sauce), sambar (insipid and watery) and green banana thoran (great textural mix of pulse-like banana and crunchy fried coconut and mustard seeds, but again quite bland). Only the squid masala (in a thick, sweetish tomato, onion and ginger sauce) had zest. We hope for a return to form next year.

Babies and children admitted. Booking advisable.
No-smoking tables. Takeaway service; delivery
service (over £15 within 3-mile radius).
Vegetarian menu. **Map 1 A1.**

Kingsbury

★ Tandoor
232-234 Kingsbury Road, NW9 0BH (8205
1450/www.tandoorrestaurant.co.uk). Kingsbury
tube/83, 183, 302, 204 bus. **Lunch served** noon-3.30pm, **dinner served** 6-11.30pm daily.
Main courses £5-£7.50. **Set lunch** £6.99
1 course. **Credit** AmEx, MC, V. North Indian
Hurrah! A pub with a curry house attached. Yet this is no mundane tandoori joint, but a modestly priced, high-quality source of North Indian cuisine. Test its mettle by ordering the tandoori non-veg platter: a glorious ensemble (15 pieces) of juicy, fiercely seared chunks of cod, lamb, tandooried chicken drumsticks (one of ours was a mite undercooked) and chicken tikka. This huge helping left us nearly full before main courses, but we couldn't miss the likes of lal maas (a rich dark-red Rajasthani dish of strongly spiced tender lamb), creamy dahl makhani or mellow murgh shahi korma (properly prepared with ground cashew nuts). Yes, we ordered too many rich dishes, and yes, the (creamy) methi matar malai (fenugreek leaves, peas and shreds of paneer) was slightly gritty, but this was food of a high order. Staff are gracious and prompt, swiftly bringing a pint of cider from the bar, which went a treat with the food. The venue, the former lounge bar of this big 1930s boozer, is a comfortable split-level spot with yellow walls, wooden flooring and attractive Indian artefacts. It beats the pants off the rather downmarket saloon bar in the next room.

Babies and children welcome: high chairs.
Booking advisable weekends. Disabled: toilet.
No-smoking tables. Separate room for parties,
seats 60. Takeaway service. Vegetarian menu.

Swiss Cottage

Cumin
02 Centre, 255 Finchley Road, NW3 6LU (7794
5616). Finchley Road tube. **Meals served** noon-11pm Mon-Wed, Sun; noon-midnight Thur-Sat.
Main courses £6-£9.95. **Credit** MC, V. Pan-Indian

RESTAURANTS

When we tried to reserve a table for a Friday evening, we were told that booking wasn't required. Why is this contemporary venue mostly empty? Is it the garish purple, turquoise and lime lighting? Or the too-loud Bollywood soundtrack? Or perhaps it's the food? No, the food was fine: we liked the mild, creamy chicken malai tikka; and hara bhara kebab ('kebab filled with greens') were tasty spinach and pea patties flecked with coriander and mint. Both arrived within seconds of ordering, though, and lacked just-made freshness. Slow-cooked tender lamb curry was flavoured with screw pine essence – just as is currently done in Mumbai's smart kitchens. Chana masala, palak paneer and baingan bhartha (grilled, mashed aubergines) were all beautifully cooked. Desserts like carrot halwa were moreish, and the soft, pillowy nan was notable. Cumin's food was impressive when it first opened, then standards slipped, but now the kitchen is back on form with a new menu – although dishes are a little under-seasoned and timidly spiced. Our meal for two with house wine cost around £80, which is a lot for a venue located in a shopping mall. Perhaps that's why it's often (and undeservedly) empty.
Babies and children welcome: children's menu; crayons; high chairs. Booking advisable weekends. Disabled: toilet. No smoking. Tables outdoors (2, balcony). Takeaway service; delivery service (within 3-mile radius). Vegetarian menu. Vegan dishes. **Map 28 A/B3.**

★ Eriki

4-6 Northways Parade, Finchley Road, NW3 5EN (7722 0606/www.eriki.co.uk). Swiss Cottage tube. **Lunch served** noon-3pm Mon-Fri, Sun. **Dinner served** 6-11pm daily. **Main courses** £7.95-£11.95. **Set lunch** £12.95 2 courses. **Credit** AmEx, JCB, MC, V. Pan-Indian

We're consistently impressed with the standard of cooking at this agreeable neighbourhood restaurant, and so too are local north Londoners. When we visited (a weekday evening), Eriki was crowded with customers tucking into delectable pan-Indian choices. Brightly decked out in vibrant Bollywood colours, chunky wooden antiques and traditional carved screens, the restaurant exudes a relaxed vibe, complemented by an utterly charming service team. The food rivals, and indeed betters, that served at many top-end restaurants. The reasonable prices also score highly with punters. A first course of haryali scallops won our gold star for quality. Juicy scallops were cloaked in a creamy sauce exhibiting delicate garlic and coriander tones: a marvellous rendition of Indian coastal flavours. More contemporary in nature, a dish of flash-fried slices of duck breast, simmered in pounded pink peppercorn and tangy tamarind masala, was notable for its sweet yet tart sauce (a perfect match with steamed rice). Vegetarian dishes were also a triumph; own-made paneer, meltingly soft to the touch, worked particularly well with a clinging masala of cooked-down tomatoes, peppers and onions. With its exciting blend of classic and Modern Indian dishes, Eriki is one of London's unsung champions.
Babies and children admitted. Booking advisable. Restaurant available for hire. Takeaway service. Vegetarian menu. **Map 28 B4.**

Outer London

Eastcote, Middlesex

★ ★ Nauroz NEW

219 Field End Road, Eastcote, Middx HA5 1QZ (8868 0900). Eastcote tube. **Meals served** noon-midnight Tue-Sat. **Main courses** £3-£9. **Set meal** (vegetarian) £4, (meat) £5. **Unlicensed. Corkage** no charge. **Credit** MC, V. Pakistani

Nauroz means 'new day' or 'new beginnings' in Parsee, Afghani and Persian, and is also the name of the New Year's Day festival in these cultures. This Pakistani restaurant is hardly a new beginning for its owners, however; they've been in the business for more than 20 years, and were the original owners of Karahi King in Wembley (*see p158*), Mirch Masala in Norbury (*see p144*) and Five Hot Chillies in Sudbury (*see p157*), before selling each venue in turn and moving on. The curries, freshly cooked to order, come in fiery sauces flavoured with onions, garlic, ginger, tomatoes and green chillies. We liked the robustly spiced deigi gosht (lamb curry cooked on the bone), Punjabi tinda (Indian baby squash), and butter beans with fresh fenugreek. Moong makhani wasn't a cheeky twist on the classic murgh makhani (butter chicken) made with moong beans, but a scrumptious version of maa ki dahl – traditional Punjabi black urid and kidney bean dahl. Nan was soft, crisp and enormous; and malai kulfi was own-made. Portions are huge, prices rock-bottom and service excellent, which may explain why this cosy BYO eaterie (with tasteful framed pictures on pastel walls, and an open kitchen) is packed with raucous crowds.
Babies and children welcome: high chairs. Booking advisable. No-smoking tables. Takeaway service.

Harrow, Middlesex

Blue Ginger

383 Kenton Road, Harrow, Middx HA3 0XS (8909 0100/www.vijayrestaurant.com). Kenton tube/rail. **Lunch served** noon-3pm Tue-Sat. **Dinner served** 6-11pm daily. **Meals served** noon-10.30pm Sun. **Main courses** £5.25-£9.95. **Credit** AmEx, MC, V. North Indian

A big hit with the affluent British Asian set, Blue Ginger combines a sports bar vibe with club-like atmosphere. A glossy black granite bar, a plethora of flat-screen televisions, and an assortment of comfy sofas and seating arrangements are easily accommodated at this spacious venue. A selection of classic North Indian kebabs and curries is served, alongside Indo-Chinese choices. Amritsari fish, a popular Punjabi bar snack, raised battered fried fish to a different level with a delectable chilli-speckled batter hiding lemon-steeped white fish fillets. North Indian main courses and accompaniments also delivered the goods. Yellow lentils, simmered with spinach paste and ginger,

Sri Lankan menu

Sri Lanka has three main groups: Sinhalese, Tamil and Muslim. Although there are variations in the cooking styles of each community and every region, rice and curry form the basis of most meals, and curries are usually hot and spicy.

The cuisine has evolved by absorbing South Indian, Portuguese, Dutch, Arabic, Malaysian and Chinese flavours over the years. Aromatic herbs and spices like cinnamon, cloves, nutmeg, curry leaves and fresh coriander are combined with South-east Asian ingredients such as lemongrass, pandan leaves, sesame oil, dried fish and rice noodles. Fresh coconut, onions, green chillies and lime juice (or vinegar) are also used liberally, and there are around two dozen types of rice – from short-grained white varieties to several long-grained, burgundy-hued kinds.

Curries come in three main varieties: white (cooked in coconut milk), yellow (with turmeric and mild curry powder) and black (with roasted curry powder, normally used with meat). Hoppers (saucer-shaped pancakes) are generally eaten for breakfast with kithul palm syrup and buffalo-milk yoghurt, while string hoppers (steamed, rice-flour noodles formed into flat discs) usually accompany fiery curries and sambols (relishes).

Sri Lankan restaurants in Tooting, Southall, Wembley and Harrow are becoming increasingly popular, and contemporary venues such as **Eastern Fire** (*see p155*) have also sprung up.

Ambul thiyal: sour fish curry cooked dry with spices.
Appam or **appa**: see hoppers.
Badun: black. 'Black' curries are fried; they're dry and usually very hot.
Devilled: meat, seafood or vegetable dishes fried with onions in a sweetish sauce; usually served as starters.
Godamba roti: flaky, thin Sri Lankan bread, sometimes wrapped around egg or potato.

Hoppers: confusingly, hoppers come in two forms, either as saucer-shaped, rice-flour pancakes (try the sweet and delectable milk hopper) or as string hoppers (qv). Hoppers are also known as appam.
Idiappa: see string hoppers.
Katta sambol: onion, lemon and chilli relish; fearsomely hot.
Kiri: white. 'White' curries are based on coconut milk and are usually mild.
Kiri hodi: coconut milk curry with onions and turmeric; a soothing gravy.
Kuttu roti, kottu or **kothu roti**: strips of thin bread (loosely resembling pasta), mixed with mutton, chicken, prawns or vegetables to form a 'bread biriani'; very filling.
Lamprais or **lumprice**: a biriani-style dish where meat and rice are cooked together, often by baking in banana leaves.
Lunnu miris: a relish of ground onion, chilli and maldives fish (qv).
Maldives fish: small, dried fish with a very intense flavour; an ingredient used in sambols (qv).
Pittu: rice flour and coconut steamed in bamboo to make a 'log'; an alternative to rice.
Pol: coconut.
Pol kiri: see kiri hodi.
Pol sambol: a mix of coconut, chilli, onions, maldives fish (qv) and lemon juice.
Sambols: strongly flavoured relishes, often served very hot; they are usually chilli-hot too.
Seeni sambol: sweet and spicy, caramelised onion relish.
Sothy or **sothi**: another name for kiri hodi.
String hoppers: fine rice-flour noodles formed into flat discs. Usually served steamed (in which case they're dry, making them ideal partners for the gravy-like kiri hodi, qv).
Vellappam: appams (qv) served with vegetable curry.
Wattalappan or **vattilapan**: a version of crème caramel made with kithul palm syrup.

RESTAURANTS

made an earthy and wholesome treat – ideal for mopping up with a stack of rotis. In comparison, Indian interpretations of Chinese dishes didn't get off the starter's block and were akin to mundane takeaway offerings. For best results, order chilled lagers and tuck into North Indian staples. If you fancy giving the crowds a miss, visit at lunchtimes rather than weekend evenings. Service tends to be harried when the place fills up, but the staff remain friendly throughout.
Babies and children welcome: high chairs. Booking essential. Disabled: toilet. Dress: smart casual. No-smoking tables. Restaurant available for hire (Mon-Thur). Tables outdoors (7, terrace). Takeaway service.

★ ★ Ram's
203 Kenton Road, Harrow, Middx HA3 0HD (8907 2022). Kenton Road tube. **Lunch served** noon-3pm, **dinner served** 6-11pm daily. **Main courses** £3.50-£5. **Thalis** £4.99 (lunch), £8.99 (dinner). **Set meal** £15 (unlimited food and soft drinks). **Credit** AmEx, DC, JCB, MC, V. Gujarati vegetarian
After despairing of the cooking here in recent years, we were impressed on our latest visit. Ram's specialises in Surti food from Surat – a famously food-obsessed city located in the heart of Gujarat. The venue has been refurbished with purple and lilac walls, large, colourful portraits of Hindu gods, and torans (festive wall and doorway hangings). Many authentic Surti specialities have been added to the very long, revamped menu. Kand (purple yam fritters) and khandvi (steamed chickpea-flour spirals topped with mustard seeds and finely grated coconut) were scrumptious. Val ni dahl (spicy split field beans) was authentically mushy, but vengan na ravaiya was nothing like the real thing; instead of the classic dish of baby aubergines stuffed with fresh coriander, coconut and ground peanuts, it was little more than standard aubergine curry in tomato sauce – nonetheless, the sauce was extremely tasty. Kadhi, prettily presented in a copper pail, was overwhelmed with the tongue-numbing heat of black pepper. Shrikhand and poori is a quintessential festive accompaniment to Surti dishes; here, both items had a satisfyingly rich, dense texture. Own-made pickles, and chutneys added to a highly enjoyable experience. Let's hope Ram's much-improved standards are maintained.
Babies and children welcome: high chairs. Booking advisable weekends. Disabled: toilet. No smoking. Restaurant available for hire (Mon-Thur). Takeaway service.

Rayners Lane, Middlesex

★ Eastern Fire
430 Alexandra Avenue, Rayners Lane, Middx, HA2 9TW (8866 8386/www.easternfire online.co.uk). Rayners Lane tube. **Meals served** 6-11.30pm daily. **Main courses** £3.75-£6.50. **Credit** AmEx, MC, V. South Indian
This contemporary, sparklingly clean, cream-coloured venue has had a makeover and is now under new management. The owners are Sri Lankans from Malaysia, and the head chef is South Indian. Consequently, the very long and ambitious menu offers an extensive selection of Sri Lankan, South Indian and Indian-Malaysian 'mamak' dishes (spicy Indian-influenced food that's unique to Malaysia's roadside stalls). South Indian sambar vadai was a substantial dish; urid lentil fritter (a little too hard) was soaked in an extraordinarily flavoursome sambar crammed with fresh tropical vegetables such as yams, bottle gourd and vegetable drumsticks. A hearty dish of crushed pittu was also packed with flavour and colour: scrambled with paneer cubes and vegetables such as aubergines, leeks, carrots and potatoes. Malaysian roti canai stuffed with eggs, green chillies and red onions was hefty, but lip-smackingly tasty. The only dull dish was fried aubergine curry, which came in a lacklustre sauce. The cooking here is hot and fiery, and there's a large choice of meat and fish dishes rarely seen on the menus of other Sri Lankan-owned restaurants.

Babies and children welcome: high chairs. Booking advisable. Disabled: toilet. No smoking. Restaurant available for hire. Takeaway service; delivery service (over £20 within 2-mile radius).

Papaya
15 Village Way East, Rayners Lane, Middx HA2 7LX (8866 5582/www.papayauk.com). Rayners Lane tube/H10, H12 bus. **Meals served** noon-midnight Mon-Sat; noon-11pm Sun. **Main courses** £6-£10. **Credit** MC, V. Sri Lankan
After a recent refit, Papaya has attempted to raise its profile. We're not sure this works. Candles on tables, flowers in vases, and polished granite flooring are all very well, but we miss the rough homespun street-credibility of the original restaurant. Judging by the lack of customers on our Sunday evening visit, we're not alone in this sentiment. Catering to Sri Lankan and South Indian residents, the menu offers meals with a focus on coconut-based curries and rice staples. Culinary stars included a hearty shrimp curry, sharpened with the tang of tamarind and softened with creamy coconut milk. This marvellous curry, tempered with slit green chillies, made a super match with some saucer-like appams (spongy rice and lentil pancakes). On the downside, sambar – soupy lentils with softened aubergines and onions – was bland. Even the chutneys lacked punch, and could have done with a chilli hit. We've been loyal fans of Papaya, but the kitchen staff need to regain their old form if the restaurant is to retain custom.
Babies and children welcome: high chairs. Booking essential weekends. No-smoking tables. Restaurant available for hire. Takeaway service; delivery service (over £15 within 3-mile radius). Vegetarian menu.

Southall, Middlesex

Colourful and at times chaotic, Southall provides a snapshot of Punjabi market life, right in the heart of Middlesex. Honking car horns, blaring Bollywood music and shimmering saris in shop windows are the backdrop to the Broadway's boisterous street life, but it's the aroma of fried samosas, kebabs and curries that's the area's real calling card.

New-wave restaurant decor, helped along by the first flush of conspicuous wealth, may have changed the look of many venues, but most menus remain resolutely Punjabi – we're talking stacks of nans, black creamy dahls and deliciously smoky skewered meats. For a taster of the best kebabs and yoghurt-based snacks, take a brisk walk away from the Broadway, down South Street, and head for **New Asian Tandoori Centre** (*see p157*). We recommend its butter chicken curry, and nans stuffed with spiced ground lamb: all accompanied by a tall glass of icy, cumin-scented lassi.

Yes, Southall is cursed with maddening traffic; if you're driving, leave your motor at the main car park behind the Broadway's Himalaya Centre. Better still, take the train or bus: shops are close by and there's plenty to see on the way. Check out **Kwality Foods** (47-61 South Road, 8917 9188) for groceries and fresh vegetables pegged at rock-bottom prices: gourds, leafy greens and a brilliant display of chillies.

For local residents going about their business, Old Southall still has its well-worn charm. **Glassy Junction** (97 South Road, 8574 1626), a Punjabi pub, has the vibe of a working men's club, with its patterned carpet and pints of beer – but here you can also buy hot parathas. Down the road is the more upmarket **Madhu's** (*see p157*); this dressy restaurant, with its black granite floors and stylish Indo-Kenyan menu, is

---

Interview
ATUL KOCHHAR

Who are you?
Chef-patron of **Benares** (*see p137*) and author *Indian Essence* (Quadrille).
Eating in London: what's good about it?
The variety of food – we're spoiled for choice. Every Sunday, the only day I can go out to eat, I argue with my wife about which two or three restaurants we should go to.
What's bad about it?
Restaurants that are quite posh yet their food is disappointing and the service appalling.
Which are your favourite London restaurants?
I really enjoy the concept of sharing dishes and tasting a variety of things. For that, at the basic level, I like **Busaba Eathai** (*see p260*); for more upmarket dining, **Maze** (*see p132*).
How do top Indian restaurants in London compare to those in India and New York?
Indian restaurants in London are great. It's a very competitive market, and they serve top-notch food. I try not to eat in Indian restaurants in New York because, to be honest, I'd struggle to name more than three decent ones. In India most of the top-quality Indian restaurants are in five-star hotels, with access to zillions of workers as the cost of labour is so cheap. This can produce a less sophisticated result, often with low, or no, size and quality regulations. I can proudly say that Indian restaurants in London are even better than in India.
What single thing would most improve London's restaurant scene?
I wish we could charge less. High rates and the high demand for sites makes it difficult to keep prices down. London is too expensive, and I'm the first to moan about it.
Any hot tips for the coming year?
Stay local, stay with British produce, and use more of it.

RESTAURANTS

PREEM RESTAURANT & BALTI HOUSE

If you fancy a bit of a change and don't want to pile on the pounds, then head down to the Preem restaurant and Balti House in the East End of London. The food tastes just as good, if not better than other restaurants but the secret is in the way it's cooked. Most of the curries are cooked in the oven and oil is kept to a minimum. The natural fat of the meat is used to enhance the flavour. The pimento chicken is a specially selected Turkish green pepper stuffed with finely chopped, Chicken and fresh coriander. Carefully packaged into a neat parcel - it's a must if you want to be different. Then there's the lemon chicken channa is an aromatic dish which is cooked using freshly chopped lemon, fragrant mixed herbs and chick peas. A tangy dish, it's best eaten with naan. Ultimately the ambience of a place is its main attraction. Preem's service is fantastic. The waiters and manager recommend dishes to customers who have no idea about Asian food and they even offer cooking lessons!

Eastern Eye Magazine

120 Brick Lane, London E1 6RL
Tel: 020 7247 0397   Fax: 020 7247 0397
www.preembricklane.com

where well-heeled Asian locals like to hang out. For more down-to-earth munchies, grab a bag of samosas from **Ambala** (107 The Broadway, 8843 9049) – they're a bargain at 40p small/50p large. If you'd rather chill out with an ice, cross the road and pick up a creamy khoya (dried milk) kulfi from the stand outside **Moti Mahal** (94 The Broadway, 8571 9443).

★ Delhi Wala NEW

11 King Street, Southall, Middx UB2 4DG (8574 0873). Southall rail. **Meals served** 8.30am-10pm daily. **Main courses** £2-£4.50. **Credit** MC, V. Punjabi vegetarian

Although there are many vegetarians in northern India, vegetarian Indian food in the UK is (erroneously) associated mainly with Gujarati and South Indian cuisines. In truth, the subject is much more complex. The fact remains, however, that there are few Punjabi vegetarian establishments in London. Delhi Wala is a light, airy, spacious restaurant and snack shop, which sells a mixture of everyday dishes that you'd find in Delhi households, the rustic fare of the Punjabi countryside, and unpretentious grub of dhabas (roadside pit-stops for truck drivers – renowned for extraordinary home-style food, low prices and warm hospitality). We liked the paneer samosas stuffed with finely diced paneer, peas and cumin seeds. The thin filo-like pastry betrayed the fact that a few of the chefs here are Gujarati (Gujarati 'patti samosas' are made with wafer-thin pastry, Punjabi ones with thick shortcrust). Chana bhatura was dark chickpea curry pepped up with cinnamon, cloves and shredded ginger, accompanied by impossibly fluffy fried bread. Makki roti aur sarson saag (cornmeal flatbread with curried mustard greens: Southall's signature dish) was also delicious.
Babies and children welcome: high chairs. No alcohol allowed. No smoking. Separate room for parties, seats 70. Takeaway service.

★ Madhu's

39 South Road, Southall, Middx UB1 1SW (8574 1897/www.madhusonline.com). Southall rail. **Lunch served** 12.30-3pm Mon, Wed-Fri. **Dinner served** 6-11.30pm Mon, Wed-Sun. **Main courses** £6-£12. **Set meal** £17.50-£20 16 dishes incl tea or coffee. **Credit** AmEx, DC, MC, V. East African Punjabi

Outshining its surroundings on a scruffy shopping parade, Madhu's is one of Southall's best – and poshest – restaurants. It was set up by the Kenyan-Asian Anand family over 25 years ago, but a major refurb a few years back has produced two stylish floors (ground and first) with stylish black leather chairs, uplit glass wall panels and blond wood or black-tiled flooring. Highly presentable young staff are professional if a mite over-attentive; customers are a well-turned-out multicultural bunch. The African heritage can be seen on a menu that contains mogo (cassava) chips and tilapia fish, and accommodates the tradition for shared starters (an entire butter chicken, say). Bold spicing and expert char-grilling characterise the cooking. Tandoori salmon was beautifully executed: succulent chunks, marinated in lemon and given a thyme-like edge with carom seeds. To follow, king prawn masala featured big meaty crustaceans in a sauce zingy with fresh ginger; karela aloo juxtaposed the slightly chewy skin of the bitter gourd with chunks of potato in a rather too salty, dryish spice blend; but dahl makhani was splendidly creamy. Puddings are notable too: delicate mounds of gajjar halwa left us smiling.
Babies and children welcome: high chairs. Booking advisable. Disabled: toilet. Dress: smart casual. Separate room for parties, seating 35. Takeaway service.

★ New Asian Tandoori Centre (Roxy)

114-118 The Green, Southall, Middx UB2 4BQ (8574 2597). Southall rail. **Meals served** 8am-11pm Mon-Thur; 8am-midnight Fri-Sun. **Main courses** £3-£7. **Credit** MC, V. Punjabi

There are two must-try dishes that every visitor to Southall restaurants should order. The first is nan kebab: spicy kebab slathered in sauces, relishes and salad, rolled in freshly cooked nan. The second is makki di roti aur sarson ka saag, which translates as maize-flour flatbread with a curry of fresh mustard greens. And the best example of both dishes is found at Roxy – a cream-and-terracotta coloured restaurant that has become even buzzier since its refurbishment. The paneer kebab rolled in soft nan was smoky and substantial. The maize bread and mustard greens combo, a traditional Punjabi winter dish, was robustly flavoured with fresh ginger and green chillies. Lamb kebab was also tasty, if a little too glowingly red. We also enjoyed the chicken and spinach curry, and a dahl made from chunky black urid lentils and split Bengal gram. Roxy showcases the rich, rustic, earthy fare of the Punjabi countryside. However, some dishes seem pre-prepared and standards are inconsistent. On a second visit a couple of days later, all the curries (lamb, chickpeas, palak paneer, and so on) were insipid and watery, and appeared to have been cooked by a different chef.
Babies and children welcome: high chairs. Booking advisable. Disabled: toilet. No smoking. Separate room for parties, seats 60. Takeaway service. Vegetarian menu.

★ Palm Palace

80 South Road, Southall, Middx UB1 1RD (8574 9209). Southall rail. **Lunch served** noon-3pm daily. **Dinner served** 6-11pm Mon-Thur; 6-11.30pm Fri-Sun. **Main courses** £4-£6.95. **Credit** AmEx, JCB, MC, V. Sri Lankan

Southall is best known for its Punjabi restaurants, but in recent years a sizeable Sri Lankan community has been making inroads. As a result, several Sri Lankan and South Indian eateries have sprung up in the area. This long-established venue, with polished wooden floor, biscuit-coloured wallpaper, and smart, high-backed wood, metal and maroon suede chairs, appears to be a popular meeting place for young Sri Lankan men. A long menu lists Sri Lankan, South Indian and North Indian dishes, chef's specials, seafood delicacies and a variety of thalis. Devilled paneer was more like that contemporary Indian classic, chilli paneer; tender cubes of paneer were slathered in oriental-style sweet chilli sauce, rather than the more traditional chilli and vinegar combo, but the dish was tasty nonetheless. Egg hopper was served cold and had a brittle, dried-out texture; string hoppers made from Sri Lankan red rice were much tastier. Potato ceylon had been deliciously laced with fennel seeds and curry leaves, but Jaffna-style aubergines were too oily and lacked the complex layering of spices for which this classic dish is renowned. Portions were hearty, and service was warm and chatty.
Babies and children welcome: high chairs. Booking advisable weekends. Takeaway service. Vegetarian menu.
For branch see index.

Sudbury, Middlesex

★ ★ Five Hot Chillies

875 Harrow Road, Sudbury, Middx HA0 2RH (8908 5900). Sudbury Hill or Sudbury Town tube. **Meals served** noon-midnight daily. **Main courses** £3.50-£9. **Unlicensed**. **Corkage** no charge. **Credit** MC, V. Punjabi

Welcome to Sudbury's best-known culinary destination. Five Hot Chillies is as much a magnet for local Pakistani and Punjabi residents as for London's far-flung curry aficionados. It's a no-frills community café decked out with plastic seating, functional easy-wipe tables and faded melamine tableware. Kebabs and hearty curries are what to order. We've yet to taste a more impressive seared fish tikka; the firm-fleshed chunks of white cod, cloaked with yoghurt, red chilli flecks and thyme-like carom seeds, delivered a perfect balance of intensely smoky flavours and tart lemony bite. Next, a generous helping of saag gosht had a beguiling aroma of pounded cardamom seeds

and ginger: a fabulous base for meltingly tender lamb. The admirable breads go better with the curries than rice dishes. Vegetarians aren't quite as lucky with their choices. An oily jeera aloo (crushed potatoes with cumin and tomatoes) and an overly thick dahl didn't measure up to the high standards set by our meat curries. The restaurant is noisy, but no matter: the boisterous, feel-good vibe only adds to its charm.
Babies and children welcome: high chairs. Booking advisable. Takeaway service. Vegetarian menu.

Twickenham, Middlesex

Tangawizi

406 Richmond Road, Richmond Bridge, East Twickenham, Middx TW1 2EB (8891 3737/ www.tangawizi.co.uk). Richmond tube/rail. **Dinner served** 6.30-11pm daily. **Main courses** £6.95-£12.95. **Credit** AmEx, MC, V. Modern Indian

This contemporary venue is owned by a friendly young Indian couple from Kenya. Decked out in glowing midnight purple and sunset oranges, with backlit panels and tables inlaid with colourful sari fabrics, the two-room Tangawizi (which means 'ginger' in Swahili) is immensely popular with locals. Our starters were light: tandoori paneer had been marinated in piquant pickling spices and was served with a drizzle of freshly pulped alphonso mangoes; red snapper in crispy, snowflake-like tempura batter was also a success. Next, chicken curry came in a pool of delicate coconut sauce with wedges of fresh lime to perk it up. Spinach curry was a forest of rich, grassy flavours enlivened with hot red chillies and shredded coconut. We also liked a beguilingly smoky dish of smashed, charcoal-grilled aubergines, and a garlicky yellow lentil dahl. Chilli and garlic nan and pilau rice were also expertly made. We finished with a refreshingly tangy passionfruit sorbet. It's a pity that – in common with most Indian restaurants – more of the desserts aren't made in-house, but otherwise we had no complaints. In addition to the imaginative, though fairly conventional, à la carte, there's also an ambitious monthly changing list of innovative specials.
Babies and children welcome: high chairs. Booking advisable Fri, Sat. No smoking (before 10pm). Restaurant available for hire. Takeaway service; delivery service (over £15 within 3-mile radius). Vegetarian menu.

Uxbridge, Middlesex

★ Satya NEW

33 Rockingham Road, Uxbridge, Middx UB8 2TZ (01895 274250). Uxbridge tube. **Lunch served** noon-3pm, **dinner served** 6-11pm daily. **Main courses** £4-£9. **Set buffet** (lunch) £6.50. **Credit** AmEx, MC, V. South Indian

Owned by the family who run Ram's (see p155) as well as Vijay in Kilburn, Satya ('truth') is a spacious, smartly decorated venue, with two dining rooms, bare floorboards and a lively cream, maroon and purple colour scheme. The menu includes some interesting Keralite dishes, something you don't see a lot of in Uxbridge. Masala dosa was a crisp pancake filled with assertively spiced soya mince (popular in contemporary Indian home cooking), accompanied by a light tamarind-tart sambhar (lentil broth) and creamy fresh coconut chutney. Keralan fish curry featured succulent pieces of pomfret in rich gravy suffused with cloves, cumin and coriander. Mathanga erissery (festive pumpkin curry, here cooked with black eye beans) is rarely seen on restaurant menus, and even prosaic dishes like sizzling chilli paneer, vegetable pilau and coconut rice were notably fresh and sparkled with flavour, colour, texture and spice. We gave the bought-in desserts a wide berth, though – they're a missed opportunity when Keralite desserts are far more interesting. Service from smiling Keralan waiters was efficient, if a little languorous.
Babies and children welcome: high chairs. Booking advisable. Disabled: toilet. No-smoking tables. Separate room for parties, seats 10. Takeaway service.

Wembley, Middlesex

This bustling, buzzy area of London is home to many of the capital's Gujarati, South Indian and Sri Lankan residents. The stretch of Ealing Road close to Wembley Central station is where you'll find some of the capital's best Tamil restaurants, plus a few Sri Lankan eateries and Sri Lankan grocers and butchers.

Walk further down Ealing Road, towards Alperton tube station, and you'll come across family-run Gujarati cafés, grocery stores, greengrocers, aromatic shops selling sweets and snacks, kitchenware and cookery book shops, pavement stalls selling many varieties of Indian and Pakistani mangoes, and ice-cream vans that offer a range of kulfis and faloodas. At its busiest, Ealing Road looks like an Indian bazaar. Don't miss the fashionable vada pau (Indian-style burgers), and freshly pressed sugar-cane and coconut juices.

In recent years, second-generation Gujarati businessmen and their young families have moved out to more affluent parts of London such as Sudbury, Kingsbury, Harrow, Rayners Lane and Hendon. As a result, you'll find a similar mix of Gujarati cafés and food shops in these areas, particularly outside the tube stations.

★ ★ Dadima

228 Ealing Road, Wembley, Middx HA0 4QL (8902 1072). Alperton tube/79, 83, 297 bus. **Lunch served** noon-3pm, **dinner served** 5-10pm Mon, Wed-Fri. **Meals served** noon-10pm Sat, Sun. **Main courses** £3-£4.50. **Thalis** £2.99-£5.99. **Credit** MC, V. Gujarati vegetarian

All over Asia, restaurants that pay homage to old-fashioned cooking and lost recipes have been springing up. If Dadima (meaning 'grandmother') had a PR company to speak on its behalf, no doubt much more would be made of the three varieties of dadi ni thali ('grandma's thali') and little-seen items that are central to its menu. However, Dadima is an unassuming family-run restaurant, with cream walls and bright red and yellow furniture. It specialises in the traditional home cooking of Ahmedabad in central Gujarat that's rapidly disappearing – even in Gujarati homes. We've enjoyed the thalis on previous visits, so this year decided to try the snacks. Khichi (two substantial steamed lentil flour dumplings) came with a separate container of oil (to keep the dumplings lubricated) and dried red chilli chutney. The dumplings weren't as soft as they should be, but were still fabulous. Samosa chaat was a dramatic combination of hot miniature samosas, cooling yoghurt and fruity tamarind sauce. Best of all was methi bhajiya (fenugreek fritters); impossibly soft, fluffy and ungreasy, they were authentically flavoured with whole coriander seeds and topped with fried green chillies – just as they would be in the famous khaada (fast-food pit) of Ahmedabad.

Babies and children welcome: high chairs. Booking essential weekends. Disabled: toilet. No smoking. Takeaway service. Vegetarian menu. Vegan dishes.

Karahi King

213 East Lane, North Wembley, Middx HA0 3NG (8904 2760/4994). North Wembley tube/ 245 bus. **Meals served** noon-midnight daily. **Main courses** £3.50-£12. **Unlicensed. Corkage** no charge. **Credit** AmEx, DC, JCB, MC, V. Punjabi

Asian families with kids in tow love Karahi King. The darkened glass frontage doesn't look terribly tempting, and the decor isn't scintillating, but a warm welcome extended by staff soon puts newcomers at ease. Grab a ringside seat by the open kitchen and admire cooks as they swirl sizzling masalas around capacious karahis, turn kebabs over glowing charcoal, and slap rotis into the tandoor. Meat kebabs are the best bets. We can recommend the garlicky lamb chops and the deliciously smoky tandoori chicken – both were succulent and bore witness to full-flavoured marinades. Keema methi (lamb mince fried with mustard greens, green chillies, and heaps of ginger) was a resounding success, every bit was mopped up with an obliging mint-speckled paratha. Curries, unlike the kebabs, tend to be variable. An underwhelming butter chicken was little more than an oily offering of boiled and shredded boneless fowl, simmered in insipid tomato and onion masala. Vegetarians had better look elsewhere; it's the kebabs and hot breads that get top marks.

Sweets menu

Even though there isn't a tradition of serving puddings at everyday meals in South Asia, there is much ceremony associated with distributing sweetmeats at auspicious events – especially weddings and religious festivals. Many of these delicacies are rarely found in the West: shahi tukra (nursery-like bread and butter pudding); nimesh (rose-scented creamy froth, scooped into clay pots); and misti dhoi (jaggery-flavoured set yoghurt from Calcutta).

Desserts served at many Indian restaurants in London include the likes of gulab jamun (deep-fried dumplings in a rosewater-flavoured syrup), cardamom scented rice pudding, creamy kulfi, and soft, syrup-drenched cheese dumplings. Home-style family meals don't often include a dessert; you're more likely to be treated to a platter of seasonal fruit. Even in Britain, thousands of miles away from mango groves, the onset of India's mango season in May is a date for the calendar. To appreciate this lush fruit at its best, look out for boxes of alfonso mangoes in Asian stores.

Winter warmers also have their place, including comforting, fudge-like carrot halwa, a Punjabi favourite and popular street snack. In Punjabi villages, a communal cauldron is often simmered for hours on end, sending out wafts of aromatic cardamom and caramelised carrots as the halwa cooks down into an indulgent treat. Winter is also the season for weddings, where other halwas, made with semolina, wholewheat flour, lentils and pumpkin might be served. These sweetmeats aren't for the health conscious, but they do taste good.

Most 'sweets' take a long time to make, which is why people prefer to visit sweetmeat shops, the best known of which is **Ambala**'s flagship store near Euston station (112 Drummond Street, NW1 2HN, 7387 3521). Here, an impressive array of eye candy for the seriously sweet-toothed includes soft cheese-based dumplings immersed in rose-scented syrup, cashew nut fudgy blocks, toasted gram-flour balls, and marzipan-like rolls. Expect floral flavours, shed-loads of sugar and a good whackof calorie-laden ghee (clarified butter). It's hard to believe that with all the varieties offered, specialist sweet-makers (known as halwais) cook with so few ingredients; milk products, dried fruit, sugar and ghee are the key constituents.

However, more adventurous flavours are starting to appear. Chefs at leading Modern Indian restaurants are boldly combining fresh fruity flavours with hints of Asian spice: raspberry and black-salt sorbet at **Imli** (see p140). Others are giving British stalwarts a makeover; check out the sticky toffee pudding steeped in cardamom sauce at **Zaika** (see p142). But the flamboyant desserts at **Amaya** (see p135) take the cake – chilli-flecked custard, anyone?

Barfi: sweetmeat usually made with reduced milk, and flavoured with nuts, fruit, sweet spices or coconut.
Bibenca or **bibinca**: soft, layered cake from Goa made with eggs, coconut milk and jaggery.
Falooda or **faluda**: thick milky drink (originally from the Middle East), resembling a cross between a milkshake and a sundae. It's flavoured with either

rose syrup or saffron, and also contains agar-agar, vermicelli, nuts and ice-cream. Very popular with Gujarati families, faloodas make perfect partners to deep-fried snacks.
Gajar halwa: grated carrots, cooked in sweetened cardamom milk until soft, then fried in ghee until almost caramelised; usually served warm.
Gulab jamun: brown dumplings (made from dried milk and flour), deep-fried and served in rose-flavoured sugar syrup, best served warm. A traditional Bengali sweet, now ubiquitous in Indian restaurants.
Halwa: a fudge-like sweet, made with semolina, wholewheat flour or ground pulses cooked with syrup or reduced milk, and flavoured with nuts, saffron or sweet spices.
Jalebis: spirals of batter, deep-fried and dipped in syrup, best eaten warm.
Kheer: milky rice pudding, flavoured with cardamom and nuts. Popular throughout India, where there are countless regional variations.
Kulfi: ice-cream made from reduced milk, flavoured with nuts, saffron or fruit.
Payasam: a South Indian pudding made of reduced coconut or cow's milk with sago, nuts and cardamom. Semiya payasam is made with added vermicelli.
Rasgullas: soft paneer cheese balls, simmered and dipped in rose-scented syrup, served cold.
Ras malai: soft paneer cheese patties in sweet and thickened milk, served cold.
Shrikhand: hung (concentrated) sweet yoghurt with saffron, nuts and cardamom, sometimes with fruit added. A traditional Gujarati favourite, eaten with pooris.

Sanghamam

Babies and children welcome: high chairs.
Separate room for parties, seats 60. Takeaway
service. Vegetarian menu.

★ Sakonis

*129 Ealing Road, Wembley, Middx HA0
4BP (8903 9601). Alperton tube/183 bus.*
Breakfast served 9-11am Sat, Sun. **Meals
served** noon-10pm daily. **Main courses**
£3.50-£7. **Set buffet** (breakfast) £3.99, (noon-
4pm) £6.99, (7-9.30pm) £9.99. **Credit** MC, V.
South Indian
Although the Green Street branch has closed, this
chain of Gujarati vegetarian chaat houses (snack
bars) is doing very well, having opened new
branches in Leicester and Dubai. Gujarati families
often travel for miles to eat here; for many Gujarati
housewives from neighbouring counties, a
monthly food shopping trip to Wembley combined
with a visit to Sakonis is a must. So why, then, the
grim-faced, tight-lipped service? The black and
white decor is largely unmemorable, so it's best to
focus on the colourful food. Aloo papdi chaat is a
typically vibrant dish; here, pastry-like strips of
pooris were combined with diced potatoes, fresh

chickpeas and onions, drizzled with sweet yoghurt,
tangy tamarind and green coriander chutneys, and
topped with hot red chilli powder and coriander
leaves. Sakonis' crispy bhajiya is famous: wafer-
thin potato slices fried in garlicky, herby,
flavoursome chickpea-flour batter (the recipe is a
well-guarded secret). Fluorescent pink, turkish
delight-like falooda, and freshly pressed melon
juice made a perfect foil to the fried, intensely
flavoured food. Sakonis also offers Indian-Chinese
dishes. Its buffets featuring Gujarati specialities
are legendary.
*Babies and children welcome: high chairs.
No smoking. Takeaway service.*
For branches see index.

★ Sanghamam NEW

*531-533 High Road, Wembley, Middx HA0
2DJ (8900 0777). Wembley Central tube.*
Meals served 11am-11pm daily. **Main courses**
£4.95-£6.95. **Set thali** £6.95. **Credit** MC, V.
South Indian
When we first visited this spacious eaterie with its
large glass frontage, it was a franchise of the
Saravanna Bhavan chain. We were blown away by

the food, but shortly afterwards the restaurant
changed its name to Sanghamam because the
management (which has remained the same) had
decided to go it alone. The menu is almost identical
to the original, but a wide selection of chaats and
a Gujarati thali have been added to appeal to the
local Gujarati community. This is still primarily a
South Indian restaurant, though, with new chefs
flown in from that region. The decor – polished
tiled floor, a vertical kitchen hatch, fresh juice bar
– hasn't changed. We loved the South Indian
thali, which at £4.95 must be one of the best-value
meals in the capital. It contained 13 items,
including fluffy rice, poori (soft and crumbly
though slightly greasy), sambar, rasam, split
pigeon-pea dahl, suran (a variety of Indian yam
with a nutty taste), black chickpea curry, spinach
and bengal-gram curry, moong dahl (featuring
slightly undercooked onions) and somewhat
runny payasam. The cooking was extraordinary
on our original visit, and although it's now less
distinctive, it remains excellent.
*Babies and children welcome: high chairs.
No smoking. Separate room for parties, seats 60.
Takeaway service.*

International

Fusion cuisine, wrought by the wrong hands, can be grim: some ingredients should never, ever appear on the same plate. Yet an inspired chef can create novel dishes from unlikely components with exhilarating results. At the top of this multinational tree is New Zealander Peter Gordon of the **Providores & Tapa Room** who brings Asian spicing to bear on Antipodean ingredients with surprisingly harmonious effect. This year we found the food at **Ottolenghi** similarly accomplished, and also enjoyed the inventive menu at the new **Sketch: The Glade**. Other restaurants have chefs whose culinary repertoire strays across national boundaries, perhaps incorporating classic Caribbean and European dishes on the same menu (as at the **Abingdon**), or serving dishes originating from, say, Japan, Italy and India that – in multicultural, 21st-century London – have simply become fashionable (try **The Collection**). Special mention should also go to the **Vincent Rooms**, whose trainee chefs produce high-class food in a variety of culinary styles at enticingly low prices.

Central
Clerkenwell & Farringdon

Vic Naylor Restaurant & Bar
38-42 St John Street, EC1M 4AY (7608 2181/ www.vicnaylor.com). Barbican tube/Farringdon tube/rail.
Bar **Open** 5pm-1am Tue, Wed; 5pm-2am Thur-Sat.
Restaurant **Meals served** noon-midnight Mon-Sat. **Dinner served** 5pm-midnight Sat.
Main courses £8-£17.50. **Credit** AmEx, MC, V.
When a gang of Al Capone lookalikes swaggered out of the back room, we momentarily feared the worst. Then they took up strategic places behind the bar. In reality, of course, nothing sinister was afoot. It was just a ruse to get the party started. Where others have often failed, Vic's successfully walks the line between club, bar and restaurant. Burnished ochre walls lit by towering mock torches create a hedonistic ambience, but rather than being ridiculously OTT, it's offset by starched table linen and unaffected service. The menu is fresh and simple, but changes regularly. Crispy shredded duck with watercress, blood orange and walnut pieces had pleasing textures, but was slightly sour. Creamy egg taglierini with peas, broad beans and asparagus used seasonal ingredients to strong effect; while the meatiness of pan-fried swordfish withstood punchy sweet-and-sour mixed vegetables. An exception to the usual rule, Vic Naylor's plays up the goodtime vibe and produces lush food. Film buffs might know it as a location for *Lock, Stock and Two Smoking Barrels*. *Babies and children admitted. Booking advisable. Separate room for parties, seats 35.* **Map 5 O5**.

Covent Garden

Asia de Cuba
45 St Martin's Lane, WC2N 4HX (7300 5588/ www.asiadecuba-restaurant.com). Leicester Square tube. **Breakfast served** 6.30-11am Mon-Fri; 7am-noon Sat, Sun. **Lunch served** noon-2.30pm daily. **Tea served** 3-4.30pm daily. **Dinner served** 5pm-midnight Mon-Wed; 5pm-12.30am Thur-Sat; 5-10.30pm Sun.
Main courses £16.50-£48. **Set meal** (noon-7pm daily) £22.50-£30 bento box.
Credit AmEx, DC, MC, V.

Sister restaurant of Spoon+ at Sanderson (*see p161*), Asia de Cuba shares the family penchant for Philippe Starck's quirky modernist schema. Solitary exposed lightbulbs dangle low over the tables, while the standing bar area has regimented tables of preposterous Alice in Wonderland-style proportions – tiny steel tops perched on spindly legs. Of the two siblings, it is Asia de Cuba that inherited the cooking gene. And it doesn't wear its name lightly, mixing Asian inspiration (lotus root chips, wasabi mash, hot and sour dressing) and home-style Cuban favourites (fried plantain, black beans, dulce de leche). Mains are intended for sharing, which helps justify price-tags of up to £48, though most hover around £25. Calamari salad, the house appetiser, was a supersized helping of shredded leaves, cashews, banana slices and crispy calamari in a sesame orange dressing. Miso-cured black cod was perfect, with a lovely blackened glaze, but the accompanying black bean and edamame salad contained just three edamame beans (less good for sharing). Strong desserts include lengkong – a Malaysian jelly not unlike coconut blancmange – while cocktails such as lychee and apple mojito should help you fulfill your recommended five a day. Loud music enhances the clubby vibe.
Babies and children welcome: high chairs. Booking advisable. Disabled: toilet. No-smoking tables. Separate rooms for parties, seating 48 and 96. Vegetarian menu. **Map 18 L7**.

Le Deuxième
65A Long Acre, WC2E 9JH (7379 0033/ www.ledeuxieme.com). Covent Garden tube.
Lunch served noon-3pm, **dinner served** 5pm-midnight Mon-Fri. **Meals served** noon-midnight Sat; noon-11pm Sun. **Main courses** £11.50-£16. **Set meal** (noon-3pm, 5-7pm, 10pm-midnight Mon-Fri; noon-11pm Sun) £10.95 2 courses, £14.50 3 courses. **Credit** AmEx, MC, V.
This place is a curious mix. The name is French – and indeed the crisp table linen, restrained decor and suave service lend a formality that feels French – but the menu dips and dives from continent to continent. Clam and sweetcorn chowder is, of course, Boston's signature dish; wild mushroom risotto with white truffle oil couldn't be more quintessentially Italian; while the likes of Scotch beef and freshwater shrimp tempura with sweet Thai dressing are thrown in for multicultural measure. The cooking of chef Geoffrey Adams is

invariably competent. Plump seared scallops had a creamy Danish caviar beurre blanc, while the rare-grilled tuna steak was glistening and ruddy, complemented by wilted choi sum, water chestnuts and a sticky sesame glaze. Only quality fish could have successfully succumbed to such a fleeting meeting with the grill. A slickly run operation in a prime Covent Garden location, Le Deuxième holds its own in a part of London where competition is fierce and often touristy. We're not alone in this observation, though, so booking is advisable. French sister restaurant Café du Jardin is nearby. *Babies and children admitted. Booking advisable.* **Map 18 L6**.

Fitzrovia

Archipelago
110 Whitfield Street, W1T 5ED (7383 3346). Goodge Street or Warren Street tube. **Lunch served** noon-2.30pm Mon-Fri. **Dinner served** 6-10.30pm Mon-Sat. **Main courses** £13.50-£19.50. **Set lunch** £12.50 per person (minimum 2) tasting menu. **Credit** AmEx, DC, JCB, MC, V.
With its riot of exotic memorabilia from across the globe, Archipelago is a playful antidote to contemporary minimalism. We counted at least three uninvited guests at our table: an African fertility idol, a wooden pelican and a Mandarin figurine, plus countless peacock feathers and the like. What would a feng shui expert make of it? In fact, the clutter is entirely by design: the eclectic decor befits the food, which also demands a traveller's eye for novelty and exploration. Dining here is a little like eating your way through the cast of a safari holiday: crocodile, peacock and kangaroo are among the wildest offerings, with tamer dishes given outlandish names such as Hungarian Chilli Pig (flash-fried honey and chilli pork loin). Quality varies: the seared crocodile fillet in vine leaves with plum dipping sauce was splendidly succulent, but the ground Ethiopian lamb was so fiery that a minuscule salad of cubed papaya and pineapple failed to soften the sting. That said, the unique menu certainly throws down the gauntlet for the adventurous – and a £25 per person late-cancellation charge will stop anyone from bailing out at the last minute. *Babies and children admitted. Booking advisable. No smoking. Tables outdoors (2, patio).* **Map 3 J4**.

Mash
19-21 Great Portland Street, W1W 8QB (7637 5555/www.mashbarandrestaurant.co.uk). Oxford Circus tube.
Bar **Open** 11am-2am Mon-Sat.
Restaurant **Breakfast served** 8-11.30am, **lunch served** noon-3pm Mon-Fri. **Dinner served** 6-11pm Mon-Sat. **Main courses** £11-£17.50. **Set meal** £24-£28 3 courses. **Admission** £5 after 9pm Fri; £5 after 9pm, £10 after 10pm Sat.
Both **Credit** AmEx, DC, MC, V.
Pie lovers take heed: Mash does not serve mash. Instead, the name comes from the hops it pummels in its on-site microbrewery. With good own-brews on tap, the plasticky ground-floor bar with curvy red sofas and lozenge-shaped lighting is the main attraction, beloved by the Soho Square brigade. Heading upstairs to the more laid-back restaurant means navigating a sea of square-rimmed specs, each pair swivelling to size you up. The food, however, is less subject to seasonal trends than the clientele. Little has changed since last year's revamp, and it's still a gastropubby mix of deluxe burgers (beef with red pepper relish, Elwy Valley lamb burger with goat's cheese, tuna with guacamole, houmous and salsa), mains such as Norfolk mussels, fish cakes and steak, plus a few pizzas. Thai chicken curry proved adequate, while the tuna burger was a monster portion, with crisp if oversalted chips. Culinary ambition crept into the apple and blackberry crumble, which arrived moulded into a fussy circle. Expect some Pinter-esque pauses between courses, but it's all a touch inconsequential: mostly the food comes second to the drinking experience.

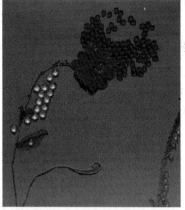

Sketch: The Glade. See p162.

Babies and children welcome: high chairs. Bar available for hire. Disabled: toilet. Dress: smart casual. Entertainment: DJs 9pm Thur-Sat. Separate room for hire, seats 28. Tables outdoors (4-8, pavement). **Map 9 J6**.

Spoon+ at Sanderson

The Sanderson, 50 Berners Street, W1T 3NG (7300 1444/www.spoon-restaurant.com). Oxford Circus or Tottenham Court Road tube. **Breakfast served** 6.30-11.45am, **lunch served** noon-2.30pm, **tea served** 3-5pm daily. **Dinner served** 6-11pm Mon-Sat; 6-10pm Sun. **Main courses** £21-£49. **Set dinner** £50-£88 tasting menu. **Credit** AmEx, DC, MC, V.

Burly men dressed in black usually open the door, inviting you past the plate-glass windows and white drapes into an elongated bar with dining tables beyond. If the spaceship in Stanley Kubrick's *2001* had a social club, this would be it.

So much gleaming white feels clinically precise, except for the occasional ornate mirror and images of kohl-rimmed eyes peeping out from chair backs. Detractors think the Philippe Starck design contrived, but Spoon+ has a legion of fans. Daytime diners favour the kind of impractical outfits that denote a life of leisure – pastel linens and fine Merino knits – layered over angular figures. By night, the party gear would make a bird of paradise look demure. The food? Obsequious waiters volunteer to cater for your allergies; dressings are typically on the side; a whole section of the menu is steamed. At lunch there is SpoonSum – mini dishes such as spicy shrimp brochette, duck foie gras and chicken wings, ideal for grazing. By night, Alain Ducasse's mix-and-match menu enables you to customise your meal, but in practice such recommendations as chicken breast with 'devil' marmalade and a potato nest, or pan-seared salmon, béarnaise and tomatoes confit,

suffice. It tastes good, not amazing – and is terrifyingly expensive. You're paying for the image as well as the food.

Babies and children welcome: high chairs. Booking advisable. Disabled: toilet (hotel). Separate room for parties, seats 50. Tables outdoors (15, terrace). **Map 17 J5**.

Marylebone

★ The Providores & Tapa Room

109 Marylebone High Street, W1U 4RX (7935 6175/www.theprovidores.co.uk). Baker Street or Bond Street tube.
The Providores **Lunch served** noon-2.45pm daily. **Dinner served** 6-10.30pm Mon-Sat; 6-10pm Sun. **Main courses** £18-£24.50. **Cover** (lunch Sat & Sun) £1.50.
Tapa Room **Breakfast served** 9-11.30am Mon-

Fri; 10am-3pm Sat, Sun. **Meals served** noon-10.30pm Mon-Fri; 4-10.30pm Sat; 4-10pm Sun. **Tapas** £2-£13.40.
Both **Credit** AmEx, MC, V.
An exhaustive list of premium Kiwi wines and such ingredients as seared kangaroo and New Zealand venison should alert you to the main inspiration at work here. But Peter Gordon brings Asian and Middle Eastern spices to the mix, creating a rarefied fusion that usually impresses and often excels. At street level is the buzzy Tapa Room, combining casual dining with utter professionalism, with crowds attracted by the exquisite global tapas. Upstairs is the Providores: a dining room so classic it takes a reserved backseat to the lip-smacking dishes. The menu is frequently adjusted – a new twist here, a seasonal ingredient there – and though the results sound complicated, all are a delight. Thai-style soft-shell crab salad with Cape gooseberries, green mango, young coconut, cucumber and toasted karengo, for instance, was a harmonious feast of crispy-fried crab and hyper-fresh salad. Likewise, the pan-fried sea bass on red cabbage with sautéed squid, shaved fennel and pink grapefruit salad presented a united front, the squid a tasty bit player next to the plump sea bass. Consistently delicate of touch, this place costs a premium, but is difficult to fault.
Babies and children welcome: high chairs. Booking advisable (Providores); bookings not accepted (Tapa Room). Disabled: toilet. No smoking. Tables outdoors (2, pavement). **Map 9 G5.**

Mayfair

Sketch: The Gallery
9 Conduit Street, W1S 2XG (0870 777 4488/ www.sketch.uk.com). Oxford Circus tube. **Dinner served** 7-11pm Mon-Sat. **Main courses** £12-£24. **Credit** AmEx, DC, MC, V.
Be prepared for hassle when booking. You're put on hold, the phone is answered by someone who says you can have the table for two hours only, and that without leaving a credit card number you can't make a reservation. Once you've agreed to all this, the table is yours. On this year's showing, we're not sure it was worth it. There's a lot to look at: white padded sofas at white melamine tables, silver candelabras, decorative arches covered in wallpaper and a great black sphere hanging under the domed ceiling, with little moving dots of red light and cine-films by fashion fave Guy Bourdin projected on all four walls. (And the loos – housed in white egg-shaped pods – are fabulous.) What's on the plate is decorative too, but less entertaining. Ravioloni filled with tomato concassé, rocket and ricotta, and served with nectarine beurre blanc, was bland. Better was pan-seared swordfish steak with béarnaise, steamed radishes and pak choi. A selection of treats from Parlour (Sketch's café; the premises also house the haute cuisine Lecture Room and the Glade; *see below*) seemed a safe bet for dessert, but wasn't; basil sorbet was the worst offender, yet even the chocolate slice was left unfinished. We guess the multinational crowd aren't here for the food; the place was packed.
Booking essential. Entertainment: DJs 11pm-2am Wed-Sat. Restaurant available for hire. **Map 9 J6.**

★ Sketch: The Glade NEW
9 Conduit Street, W1S 2XG (0870 777 4488/ www.sketch.uk.com). Oxford Circus tube. **Lunch served** noon-3.30pm Mon-Sat. **Main courses** £9-£24. **Set lunch** £19.50 2 courses, £24 3 courses. **Credit** AmEx, DC, JCB, MC, V.
The one thing everyone knows about Sketch is that it's outrageously expensive. But not everyone realises that Sketch houses three restaurants: the infamously pricey Lecture Room; the mid-range Gallery (*see above*); plus the Glade, opened in autumn 2005, which is comparatively proletarian in its pricing. It might only be open to the public at lunchtimes, but it does allow a taste of the inventive menu of Pierre Gagnaire, the celebrated chef who oversees the kitchen from his HQ in, er, Paris. The menu goes in for some daft names. We tried 'Hommage à M. L'Ambassadeur, 33 Faubourg St Honoré'. It was a remarkable dish: a rice pilaf

decorated with the bright colours of green peas, salmon, salmon roe, grapes and fried duck egg; it tasted good too. Portion sizes are on the small side – fashionable people don't eat much, after all – but the prices are fair, with this large starter or small main course costing £9. The flavour combinations are imaginative, such as a foamed horseradish cream served on an onion tartlet. Tamer, but also a good dish, was smoked haddock with creamed potatoes and olives. Glade is fun, quirky, amusingly pretentious – and puts the cost of a meal at Sketch within the reach of almost anyone.
Babies and children welcome: high chairs. Booking advisable. Disabled: ramp; toilet. Separate room for parties, seats 50. **Map 9 J6.**

Soho

Refuel
The Soho Hotel, 4 Richmond Mews, W1D 3DH (7559 3007/www.refuelsoho.com). Tottenham Court Road tube.
Bar **Open** 11am-midnight Mon-Sat; 11am-10.30pm Sun.
Restaurant **Meals served** 7am-11pm Mon-Fri; 7am-11am, 5.30-11pm Sat; 8am-10.30pm Sun. **Main courses** £16.50-£29. **Set meal** (noon-3pm, 5-10pm Mon-Fri) £19.95 3 courses; (noon-3pm Sun) £24.95 3 courses.
Both **Credit** AmEx, JCB, MC, V.
You might once have parked your car on this very spot, as the Soho Hotel, where Refuel is located, was formerly a multistorey car park. Its transformation into stylish hideaway, however, has been thorough. A narrow partition of rustic amphoras barely divorces restaurant from bar, so if the former is slow, as it was on a recent visit, it can feel like being a timid guest eavesdropping on a lively party. The dining room mixes gently distressed kitchen tables with more formal furniture, and further adds personality with a queue of glass-droplet lights by the plate-glass window. Service was variable – with drinks being muddled up and brought at the wrong time – which we attributed to new staff, but the food mostly delivered. Goat's cheese ravioli with sweet pepper dressing needed another, sharper flavour, but the pasta had bite. Plum tomato and pesto tart tasted OK despite overflaky pastry. Slow-roast pork belly with bubble and squeak was superb, while the tarte tatin confounded expectation by using caramelised banana instead of apple. Prices are reasonable, with a three-course set menu offering good value at £19.95.
Babies and children welcome: high chairs. Booking advisable. Disabled: toilet. No-smoking tables. Separate room for parties, seats 45. Takeaway service (breakfast until 11am). **Map 17 K6.**

South Kensington

The Collection
264 Brompton Road, SW3 2AS (7225 1212/ www.the-collection.co.uk). South Kensington tube.
Bar **Open** 5pm-midnight daily.
Restaurant **Dinner served** 6-11.30pm Mon-Sat. **Main courses** £13-£22. **Set dinner** (6-7.15pm Mon-Fri) £12 2 courses, £18 3 courses. **Credit** AmEx, MC, V.
Entering the Collection involves walking back in illuminated purple-floored time. On busy nights this epitome of 1990s-cool still throbs with house music and beautiful party people, but its interior (bare brick warehouse meets South-east Asia) is showing signs of wear and tear. A crowd-pleaser menu offers everything from salmon sashimi to steak and chips, plus a frequently changing list of specials. Our order was executed with varying degrees of success. Wok-fried scallops with coconut and chilli were small, overcooked and too lemony. Fried oysters were a touch doughy but otherwise crisp; they were accompanied by a moreishly tangy hot-sour sauce. Mains differed wildly in portion size. A seasonal special of tender ostrich slices paired with saffron-scented cabbage was surprisingly successful, but half the size of our other two mains: rump steak with three sauces; and a comforting, mildly cumin-spiced chicken curry. Desserts were also familiar favourites; we liked our gooey, warm chocolate fondant. The food here is fine, but the people-watching is even better.

Babies and children admitted (restaurant). Booking advisable. Disabled: toilet. Separate room for parties, seats 70. Entertainment: DJ 8pm daily. Vegetarian menu. **Map 14 E10.**

Westminster

The Atrium
4 Millbank, SW1P 3JA (7233 0032/www.atrium restaurant.com). Westminster tube. **Lunch served** noon-3pm, **dinner served** 6-9.45pm Mon-Fri. **Main courses** £9-£17.95. **Set lunch** £17.95 2 courses. **Set dinner** £14.95 2 courses. **Credit** AmEx, DC, MC, V.
Seen any well-nourished politicos lately? Chances are they've been enjoying some of those famously long lunches at the Atrium. Restaurant of choice for the nearby Houses of Parliament, this secluded one-off has improved immeasurably of late. Dishes are modern and consistently good; the waiters knowledgeable. An ample starter of glazed salmon and potato terrine with gruyère and pancetta made the most of country-style chunky ingredients, served warm. Fillet of beef was a robust main, topped with wild mushrooms and parmesan, while the more subtle wild trout came with a dainty fish cake and a piquant chilli and poached fennel dressing. Good own-baked bread rolls too, some sweetened with the food world's seed du jour: toasted black sesames. In terms of ambience, little has changed. It's still an unusual affair, tucked into the basement of a towering building otherwise inhabited by a health club and the offices of broadcasters who rely on this spot for their news scoops. The best tables are 'outside', which means in the spacious central courtyard with a skylight many metres above. Evenings are invariably quiet; lunchtimes busier.
Booking advisable lunch. Disabled: lift; toilet. No-smoking tables. Separate rooms for parties, seating 12 and 24. **Map 16 L10.**

★ The Vincent Rooms
Westminster Kingsway College, Vincent Square, SW1P 2PD (7802 8391/www.westking.ac.uk). St James's Park tube/Victoria tube/rail. **Lunch served** noon-1.15pm Mon-Fri. **Dinner served** 6-7.15pm Tue-Thur. Closed 2 wks Apr, July-Sept, 2wks Dec-Jan. **Main courses** £6.25-£9.50. **Set meal** *Escoffier Room* £18 2 courses, £20 3 courses incl coffee. **Credit** MC, V.
It's a great idea: this restaurant serves the day's lesson from the college that has trained chefs of the calibre of Jamie Oliver and Ainsley Harriott. The menu changes according to the skills being taught, and food can veer in style from the likes of paupiettes of sole stuffed with a salmon mousse with chilled Cointreau grapes to braised belly of pork on black pudding mash with cider jus. There aren't many establishments offering dishes like that for under a tenner. The quality of ingredients is immediately evident, and the execution exceptional. Spinach and gorgonzola ravioli was moreishly fresh, while Moroccan lamb was a fabulous cut accompanied by subtly spiced apricot and almond couscous. Desserts were dreamy: the airy white chocolate cheesecake could convert a vegan, and was presented as professionally as the sophisticated raspberry millefeuille. The space is a pleasure to dine in: the high ceiling, bay windows overlook a leafy square, and widely spaced tables create a calm, elegant atmosphere. The students serving can be sweetly shy, though in keeping with the refined surroundings they are well turned out in stylish black. Note that the restaurant is closed during college holidays and half-term breaks.
Babies and children welcome: high chair. Booking advisable. Disabled: toilet. No smoking. Separate room for parties, seats 30 (7802 8383). **Map 15 J10.**

West

Kensington

Abingdon
54 Abingdon Road, W8 6AP (7937 3339). Earl's Court or High Street Kensington tube.
Bar **Open** 12.30-11pm Mon-Sat; 12.30-10.30pm Sun.

The Gallery at sketch

a gastro-brasserie with an edge

mad but cleverly thought through

Fay Maschler Evening Standard February 22nd 2006

reservations 0870 777 4488
www.sketch.uk.com
sketch 9 conduit street london
W1S 2XG

Restaurant **Lunch served** 12.30-2.30pm Mon-Fri; 12.30-3pm Sat, Sun. **Dinner served** 6.30-10.30pm Mon, Sun; 6.30-11pm Tue-Sat. **Main courses** £11.95-£18.50. **Set lunch** (daily) £15.95 2 courses; (Sun) £18.95 3 courses. *Both* **Credit** AmEx, MC, V.

When does a made-over pub cease to be a pub? The current decor at the Abingdon is nothing like a pub: light, jaunty, quirkily retro – including intimate booths straight from a 1940s American bar – and suitably elegant for its Kensington setting. It does maintain a separate drinking area, however. The lengthy menu is mostly Modern European-Mediterranean, with a few Pacific Rim and Caribbean touches; dishes tend to be quite busy, and feature enjoyable combinations of flavours ahead of great culinary subtlety. A summer salad of apple, beetroot and goat's cheese with pecans, rocket, and maple and balsamic dressing was a case in point – lots to like, but there would have been still more if the main ingredients had been better. Jamaican jerk chicken with sweet potato purée and tomato and ginger chutney was rich and sweet rather than spicy, while pan-fried sea bass with celeriac mash, tomato relish and dill dressing was the best of our choices, and very nicely balanced. To finish, there are some fun desserts, such as Irish coffee semifreddo with praline shards. Service is friendly, and a well-priced, global wine list helps things along.
Babies and children welcome: high chairs. Booking essential. No-smoking tables. Tables outdoors (4, pavement). **Map 13 A9.**

Ladbroke Grove

Food@The Muse
269 Portobello Road, W11 1LR (7792 1111/ www.foodatthemuse.co.uk). Ladbroke Grove tube. **Meals served** 11am-11pm Tue-Thur; 10am-11pm Fri, Sat; 10am-6pm Sun. **Main courses** £9.50-£14. **Set lunch** (noon-4pm) £6 1 course. **Credit** MC, V.

A sanitised white-on-white restaurant that doubles as an art gallery by day in so-cool Portobello Road. Even the hunky minimalist built-in tables shriek potential. But on a recent visit we found that the signature sharp, deep, often Thai-inspired flavours had been blunted. A first-course chicken salad included cos lettuce, cherry tomatoes and pistachio nuts in a creamy garlic dressing and looked comfortably rustic. But vegetable ravioli was tough, the filling unidentifiable and the added shards of highly salted ham seemed wilful. The tea for the tea-smoked Barbary duck breast must still have been in China, for we detected no smokiness. The damp-tasting flesh of the duck was grey. It did come with excellent, generous accompaniments, though pumpkin purée and a toffee-coated plum salad. Someone in the kitchen had messed up red mullet stuffed with Thai curry vegetables in a light coconut sauce too. The promised fragrance was only a few thin gratings of fresh ginger, something Thais never use in curry. Where was the kaffir lime, the lemongrass, the galangal? At least, the French provincial house wine was excellent, and available in a choice of glass sizes.
Babies and children admitted. Disabled: toilet. No smoking. **Map 19 B2.**

South West
Chelsea

Foxtrot Oscar
79 Royal Hospital Road, SW3 4HN (7352 7179). Sloane Square tube/11, 239 bus. **Lunch served** 12.30-2.30pm Mon-Fri; 12.30-3.30pm Sat; 12.30-4pm Sun. **Dinner served** 7-11pm Mon-Sat. **Main courses** £8.95-£15.50. **Credit** MC, V.

Take a trip back in time at this pleasantly scruffy haunt. The eras are a bit muddled – it looks like a 1970s wine bar, but the waitresses are pure '80s (black lycra, big blonde hair) and the soundtrack to a Sunday brunch was classic '60s. There's a TV in one corner. Service is a bit sloppy (we had to stop a waitress replacing the mineral water bottle cap after it had rolled on the floor), but very willing (she happily made another coffee after a super-weak

first attempt). The food is better than all this leads you to expect. The menu is retro too, and not in an ironic way – witness deep-fried emmenthal with mango chutney, and avocado with prawns – but there are times when a bacon cheeseburger or an omelette are all you want. The best dishes this time around were the burger (ignoring the sorry-looking lettuce garnish) and a very moreish kedgeree, though salmon fish cakes weren't bad either. Fillet steak costs £15.50, but that's as expensive as it gets, and lots of dishes are available in two sizes. The wine list is only just longer than the cocktail list. A very Chelsea local, with a loyal clientele.
Babies and children welcome: high chairs. Booking advisable. Separate room for parties, seats 30. **Map 14 F12.**

Earlsfield

Velvet Lounge **NEW**
394 Garratt Lane, SW18 4HP (8947 5954). Earlsfield rail/44, 77 bus. **Dinner served** 6-10pm Tue-Fri. **Meals served** noon-10pm Sat, Sun. **Main courses** £8.95-£14.95. **Credit** AmEx, MC, V.

There's a retro feel to both the decor and food at this small neighbourhood operation on Earlsfield's main street. Velvet Lounge looks more like a bar than a restaurant (though most people were eating on our visit), with purple and dark green paintwork, swirly wallpaper and spangly bar area. The menu reads like a list of dinner-party favourites from the 1970s: garlic mushrooms, toad in the hole (vegetarian and meat versions), shepherd's pie, mushroom stroganoff. But good-humoured staff and a tongue-in-cheek air keep bad taste at bay. Prawn cocktail ('served 70s style') comprised a large pile of prawns in a seafood dressing-drenched Martini glass of mixed leaves. Toad in the hole was served Desperate Dan style, with three fat sausages (veggie, in this case) poking out of a huge yorkshire pudding that was nicely crisp on the outside, but too soft and doughy in the middle. Good-quality salmon and haddock fish cakes were surrounded by a lake of pleasant but overly thick parsley sauce. It's old-fashioned comfort food in gargantuan portions; each main could easily feed two. Cocktails, beers (bottled and draught), a short wine list and easy-listening music add to the feel-good factor, though we have doubts as to whether the Lounge would survive in a smarter part of town.
Babies and children welcome: high chairs. Booking advisable Thur-Sat. Disabled: toilet. No smoking. Tables outdoors (3, pavement).

South
Battersea

Cinnamon Cay
87 Lavender Hill, SW11 5QL (7801 0932/ www.cinnamoncay.co.uk). Clapham Junction rail then 77A, 156, 345 bus. **Dinner served** 6-10.30pm Mon-Sat. **Main courses** £9.95-£14.95. **Set dinner** (Mon-Wed) £13.50 2 courses. **Credit** AmEx, DC, MC, V.

Cinnamon Cay brings a neighbourly feel and an exotic slant to Lavender Hill. Outside, the front seating area is ideal for summer dining. Inside, the decor is modern, with bright, sea-inspired pictures along the rich red walls. The small open kitchen is towards the back; on our visit, despite what looked like a shortage of staff, it coped admirably. Service was slick and professional. There are some intriguing choices on the fusion menu, such as a starter of crocodile-on-a-skewer with noodles; ginger and lemon brought out the best in this unusual meat. Shredded crispy duck with crispy wun tun and sweet red chilli jam worked well too. A main of steamed lemon sole with pak choi, mash and fried quail egg was delicious, with subtle flavourings and fleshy, fresh fish. A large rack of lamb had rather tough meat, but the pumpkin and rosemary mash was excellent. Chocolate salami and brandy cream just edged out chocolate cake with vanilla ice-cream (from local specialists Judes) in a quality finale. The small list of mainly French and Australian wines starts at £11.95.

Babies and children welcome: high chairs. Booking advisable. Tables outdoors (5, patio).

Clapham

The Rapscallion
75 Venn Street, SW4 0BD (7787 6555/ www.therapscalliononline.com). Clapham Common tube/35, 37, 355 bus. **Breakfast served** 10.30am-3.30pm, **lunch served** noon-3.30pm Mon-Fri. **Brunch served** 10.30am-4pm Sat, Sun. **Dinner served** 6-11pm Mon-Sat; 6-10.30pm Sun. **Main courses** £8-£14. **Credit** AmEx, DC, JCB, MC, V.

This smaller, younger sister of the Sequel (*see below*) could easily be mistaken for a bar. It's as popular with Claphamites for brunches and/or late-night cocktails as for restaurant dining. Space is at a premium, with elbow room difficult to find and neighbouring conversations hard to ignore. The regularly changing fusion menu offers such concoctions as tea-smoked duck breast with cardamom cherry compote, and lobster cannelloni on courgettes. Our deep-fried squid starter arrived very quickly, with an overdose of sweet chilli sauce. Mains followed swiftly afterwards – turnover has to be rapid in such a tight and popular spot. Lamb rump was fatty and chewy, but cod with sweet-potato mash and green beans was a well-balanced dish in both flavour and texture. Desserts can often be a highlight, but our dull cheesecake wasn't a patch on certain supermarket versions. The wine choice is large, although the selection available by the glass is limited. Beware the mixed toilets with insecure locks.
Babies and children admitted. Booking advisable. Tables outdoors (4, pavement). **Map 22 A2.**

The Sequel
75 Venn Street, SW4 0BD (7622 4222/ www.therapscalliononline.com). Clapham Common tube/35, 37, 355 bus. *Bar* **Open** 5pm-midnight Tue-Thur; 5pm-2am Fri; 11am-2am Sat; 11am-midnight Sun. *Restaurant* **Brunch served** 11am-4pm Sat; 11am-6pm Sun. **Dinner served** 6-11pm Tue-Thur; 6pm-midnight Fri, Sat; 6-10.30pm Sun. **Main courses** £11-£17. *Both* **Credit** AmEx, DC, JCB, MC, V.

The larger, older sibling of the Rapscallion (on the opposite side of the road; *see above*), the Sequel is next door to the Clapham Picturehouse and ideal for a meal before or after a movie. It has two levels, decked out in shades of brown and caramel, with suedette banquettes and a large but unobtrusive bank of screens above the bar showing classic films. This is the perfect place for relaxed weekend brunching, offering soothing music and a menu that includes excellent smoothies, eggs benedict and combinations of bacon, egg, sausage and muffin – plus proper Bloody Marys. The menu is fairly priced and relatively reliable: just occasionally, the chef tries too hard to 'fuse'. On our last visit, a chilli-salt squid starter was fresh and not overloaded with chilli; seafood spaghetti had a lovely, rich moreish sauce. Most of the desserts cost under a fiver, with the chocolate tart a particular favourite. The wine list offers a fair choice, though there aren't many bottles under £20. Staff are friendly, on the case (sometimes too much), and have a cheery smile for regulars.
Babies and children admitted. Booking advisable. Tables outdoors (5, pavement). **Map 22 A2.**

Waterloo

Laughing Gravy
154 Blackfriars Road, SE1 8EN (7721 7055/ www.thelaughinggravy.com). Southwark or Waterloo tube/rail. *Bar* **Open** noon-11pm Mon-Fri; 7-11pm Sat. *Restaurant* **Meals served** noon-10pm Mon-Fri; 7-10pm Sat. **Main courses** £7.25-£14.95. *Both* **Credit** MC, V.

Laughing Gravy's atmosphere hovers between that of a gastropub (though it has only Heineken on tap) and eccentric, casual restaurant. An eclectic mix of amateur oils and watercolours dots the walls. The menu, which includes favourites like bangers and mash and hearty hamburgers, also

Cantaloupe

branches out into fusion dishes that often feature exotic meats. A stir-fried ostrich salad owed much in its marinade and sprinkled peanuts to Thai cuisine. Dorset crab with brown shrimps and melba toast was wonderfully sweet and simple. Next, wild boar rubbed in jerk spices was perfectly tender and moist, but the accompanying fruit salsa was tired, and the sweet-potato fries were soggy and undercooked. As often happens with fusion attempts, many of the dishes at Laughing Gravy left us wanting the real thing. We were divided on whether the menu was quirky, or directionless and too long. Nevertheless, the friendly and relaxed service, the complete lack of pretension and the promise of something a little different for a work lunch or quiet dinner will inspire us to return.
Babies and children welcome: high chairs. Booking advisable. Disabled: toilet. Restaurant available for hire. Tables outdoors (2, pavement). **Map 11 O9**.

South East
Tower Bridge

Lightship Ten
5A St Katharine's Way, St Katharine's Dock, E1W 1LP (7481 3123/www.lightshipx.com). Tower Hill tube. **Lunch served** noon-3pm Tue-Fri. **Dinner served** 6-10pm Mon-Sat. **Main courses** £11-£18.50. **Credit** AmEx, MC, V.
The setting – aboard a 1877 Danish lightship moored among the fancy yachts of St Katharine Dock – is the main appeal here. Eat outside on the top deck if you can; the lower deck, although

romantic and cosy with its portholes and glossy oak timbers, is possibly too intimate, with barely enough room for the waiting staff to manoeuvre between the closely packed tables. The tourist draw of the location means that the Mod European/Scandinavian menu is not cheap (starters at dinner cost around £8, most mains over £15) but the cooking doesn't really justify the pricing. Even the side orders are expensive: haricots verts for £4.25 anyone? A Scandinavian fish platter (a starter, for two) comprised small portions of gravadlax, marinated herring and the like: decent enough, but the quality of the ingredients was certainly not up to the standard of London's Scandinavian specialists. Pan-fried sea bream with roasted vegetables millefeuille and pepper coulis was equally underwhelming. The young staff were willing but inept. The interior was full on our evening visit (mainly canoodling couples and out-of-towners, it seemed), but we feel the kitchen has some way to go to live up to the surroundings.
Booking advisable. Entertainment: jazz 7-10pm Mon, Wed. Separate room for parties, seats 30. Tables outdoors (23, top deck). **Map 12 S8**.

East
Shoreditch

Cantaloupe
35-42 Charlotte Road, EC2A 3PB (7613 4411/ www.cantaloupe.co.uk). Old Street tube/rail/55 bus.
Bar **Open** 11am-midnight Mon-Fri; noon-midnight Sat; noon-11.30pm Sun. **Meals served**

noon-11.30pm Mon-Sat; noon-5pm, 5.30-10.30pm Sun. **Main courses** £3.50-£7.95.
Restaurant **Lunch served** noon-3pm Thur, Fri. **Dinner served** 6-11pm Mon-Fri; 7-11pm Sat. **Main courses** £9.50-£19.95.
Both **Credit** AmEx, DC, MC, V.
This bustling DJ bar and restaurant succeeds on many levels: the relaxed and friendly vibe, great music, the excellent drinks list, and the cosy dining room with its red padded booths through the back. The menu has taken a few more steps towards Latin culture of late, but our most recent visit revealed a kitchen that had lost its groove. Ceviche had a taste and texture as if the raw cod and salmon had only just met their marinade, and the lime juice, chilli, coriander and spring onion made a crude assault on the senses. Vegetable empaniditas were made with delicate pastry, but the undersides were slightly burnt. Moqueca is a Brazilian seafood stew, but this version was like a Thai seafood soup. Its liquid was rich in coconut milk, there were only small pieces of meat and seafood, and none of the advertised cashew nuts; overwhelmed by the coconut milk, we left most of it uneaten. The best dish was the Uruguayan fillet steak, aged, tender, and cooked perfectly medium-rare as requested. Standards in the kitchen appeared to be at a low point on this visit, but we'll be happy to return for the fabulous selection of wines by the glass and the cool, easy vibe.
Bar available for hire. Disabled: toilet. Entertainment: DJ 8pm Fri-Sun. Restaurant available for hire. **Map 6 R4**.

Shish
313-319 Old Street, EC1V 9LE (7749 0990/ www.shish.com). Liverpool Street or Old Street tube/rail.
Bar **Open** 5pm-midnight Mon-Sat; 5-10.30pm Sun.
Restaurant **Meals served** 11.30am-11.30pm Mon-Fri; 10.30am-11.30pm Sat; 10.30am-10.30pm Sun. **Main courses** £3.95-£10.95. **Set meal** (until 7pm Mon-Fri) £6.95-£8.65 2 courses.
Both **Credit** AmEx, DC, JCB, MC, V.
This small chain markets itself as serving Silk Road cuisine, with food hailing from points along the old trading route, all the way from Turkey to China and Japan. This concept does make room for some strengths. Alongside the Middle Eastern-style starters (falafel, tabouleh, borek) are the likes of Tashkent dumplings. Steamed, then pan-fried, the dumplings had a delicate flavour and came with a sweet soy sauce dip. Chinese beans – green beans dressed in soy, ginger and sesame – are another eastern variant on a Middle Eastern theme. As one might guess from the place's name, main courses are kebabs, offered with a choice of accompaniments – rice, couscous, chips or salad – and as wraps. All are made fresh with good meat, but occasionally can taste rather bland. Szechuan chilli beef, for example, was supposed to be marinated in spices, though any chilli flavour was indiscernible. The accompanying couscous was a large portion, with a small garnish of what was mostly onion – quite a lot of couscous for a dish without sauce. A nice touch is the sparkling or still mineral water on tap for a fixed price, along with spectacular fresh fruit juice cocktails.
Babies and children welcome: children's menu; high chairs. Bookings not accepted for parties of less than 8 (restaurant). Disabled: toilet. Entertainment: DJs 8pm Fri. No smoking (restaurant). Tables outdoors (6, pavement). Takeaway service. Vegetarian menu. Vegan dishes. **Map 6 R4**.
For branches see index.

Victoria Park

Frocks
95 Lauriston Road, E9 7HJ (8986 3161/ www.frocks-restaurant.co.uk). Mile End tube then 277 bus. **Lunch served** noon-4pm Sat. **Dinner served** 6.30pm-midnight Mon-Sat. **Meals served** noon-9pm Sun. **Main courses** £11-£17. **Credit** MC, V.
Midway along a leafy Hackney road seldom frequented by hoodies, Frocks has been serving traditional nosh to genteel diners since before local

estate agents started disingenuously calling this area 'Victoria Park village'. Dark wood panelling betrays its gastropub leanings, as do demure cream walls intermittently splashed with famous quotes, and a lone chunk of exposed brickwork. But it's not just the decor that seems risk-averse. The menu could have been assembled by a designated first-aider, so safe are its offerings. Where a case can be made for simplicity, it usually rests on the fine provenance of ingredients. Regrettably, Frocks let us down. Deep-fried soft-shell crab had weighty fish and chip shop-style batter. Pan-fried ribeye steak with peppercorn sauce, typically a reliable option, proved a fatty cut. Better was the chicken liver parfait with fig jam. Icelandic cod fillet with softly stewed cumin aubergine displayed more abandon, but was topped by an unappealing-looking brown shrimp vinaigrette. Bipolar service flipped between brusque and charming, yet other customers seemed undaunted. Our previous visits have been better than this, and perhaps loyal regulars aren't usually so disappointed.
Babies and children welcome: high chair. Booking advisable weekends. Separate room for parties, seats 40. Tables outdoors (6, pavement; 6, walled garden).

North East

Wanstead

Hadley House

27 High Street, E11 2AA (8989 8855). Snaresbrook or Wanstead tube. **Breakfast served** 10-11.30am Mon-Fri; 10am-noon Sat, Sun. **Lunch served** noon-2.30pm, **dinner served** 6.30-10pm Mon-Sat. **Meals served** 12.30-9pm Sun. **Main courses** £9-£17.50. **Set dinner** (Mon) £19.95 3 courses. **Credit** MC, V.
If Hadley House were to have a role model, it would be Jordan, her pink wedding dress and perma-tan translated here into the fuchsia drapes and sunshine-yellow walls. Besides, there's an Essex kind of charm about the place. For this thriving restaurant, with its self-assured air, is like a local kid who's done good. It's constantly busy, thanks to a multifaceted approach (lots of blackboard specials, Monday's three-course set menu at £19.95, breakfasts, hearty Sunday lunches) that offers something for couples, groups and families alike. Such popularity is impressive when you consider that most mains are at West End prices (£17 or so). Goat's cheese on roast veg with red pesto dressing was a predictable starter, nicely done. Chicken breast with fresh herb and mushroom arancini with dauphinoise potatoes proved full-on comfort nosh. The gargantuan salmon and prawn fish cake was a little soggy, albeit freshly made. If the proof lies in the pudding, though, cherry chocolate brownie with chocolate sauce and vanilla ice-cream should confirm beyond doubt that the cooking here isn't subtle. It is, however, deliciously in-your-face.
Babies and children welcome (lunch and Sun): high chairs. Booking advisable. Tables outdoors (7, patio). Takeaway service (lunch).

North

Islington

Frederick's

Camden Passage, N1 8EG (7359 2888/ www.fredericks.co.uk). Angel tube.
Bar **Open** 11am-11pm Mon-Sat.
Restaurant **Lunch served** noon-2.30pm, **dinner served** 5.45-11.30pm Mon-Sat. **Main courses** £11.50-£19.50. **Set meal** (lunch, 5.45-7pm) £14 2 courses, £17 3 courses.
Both **Credit** DC, JCB, MC, V.
A first glimpse suggests a clientele of cravat-wearing businessmen, but venture beyond the bar area to the spacious restaurant – with vaulted glass ceiling, Kandinsky-esque paintings, white tablecloths and lovely garden – and the vibe freshens up. Here, expense-accounters and smart couples enjoy a well-balanced menu offering

sophisticated yet unpretentious dishes with strong Italian, French and British undercurrents and a propensity for seasonal ingredients. Chilled watercress soup, accompanied by smoked salmon on dry blinis, made a bland start; main courses (from the carte; there's also a set menu) were better. Fresh pappardelle pasta with mushrooms, crème fraîche and truffle oil was perfectly al dente and full of flavour, with a generous supply of wild mushrooms. Steamed sea bass fillet was spanking fresh, served with asparagus and new potato salad. Portion sizes are designed to sate rather than stuff, so there was room for dessert. Knickerbocker glory looked ashamed to be sharing menu space with the more respectable tarte tatin/panna cotta/cheese choices. We plumped for raspberry crème brûlée, and weren't disappointed. Frederick's is popular with wine lovers; there's a varied, 200-plus list (strong on champagne) and free tastings on the last Thursday of every month.
Babies and children welcome: children's menu (lunch Sat); high chairs. Booking advisable weekends. No-smoking tables. Separate rooms for parties, seating 18 and 32. Tables outdoors (12, garden). **Map 5 O2.**

★ Ottolenghi

287 Upper Street, N1 2TZ (7288 1454/ www.ottolenghi.co.uk). Angel tube/Highbury & Islington tube/rail. **Meals served** 8am-11pm Mon-Sat; 9am-7pm Sun. **Main courses** (breakfast) £4.90-£7.50; (lunch) £7.50-£11.50. **Meze** (dinner) £5.50-£9. **Credit** MC, V.
Ottolenghi is the restaurant of choice for Islington's discerning diners who are more interested in good food than fuss and furbelows. Not that it's plain or dreary: far from it. The long, brightly white room looks stunning, with long shared tables, white Panton chairs, clever art and nice design details. The entrance area doubles as a bakery shop and deli, with big, puffy meringues, colourful salads and sublime breads to take away or eat in. In the evening, Ottolenghi shifts emphasis from café to restaurant, with a daily changing menu of small dishes 'from the counter' or 'from the kitchen' (the latter are served hot). Imaginative combinations are Ottolenghi's trademark: a plate of tender, marinated beef fillet with zaatar (a Middle Eastern herb mix) crust and a smoky tomato sauce; or a salad of beetroot with red chard leaves, slivers of red onion and a fig relish. There is a modern Mediterranean slant in dishes such as pan-fried halibut on a dahl and sweet potato mash with minted yoghurt and pitta bread, while other dishes defy categorisation – such as pork belly on a purée of potato and salt cod. Ottolenghi is more than just somewhere for terrific food; even a dull date can become fun here, as the shared tables encourage cross-party chat.
Babies and children welcome: high chairs. Booking advisable evening; not accepted lunch. No smoking. Takeaway service. **Map 5 O1.**
For branches see index.

North West

Queen's Park

Hugo's

21-25 Lonsdale Road, NW6 6RA (7372 1232). Queen's Park tube/rail. **Meals served** 9.30am-11pm daily. **Main courses** £10.50-£15.80. **Set lunch** £11.50 2 courses. **Credit** MC, V.
Amazing what you can do with two mews houses in a distinctly unglamorous street. Don't be misled by Hugo's quirky location and offbeat decor – the multi-generational clientele look happy enough. This place covers all bases: from all-day brunch to dinner; from burgers to tempura; from steaks to fish and chips, with daily specials of pasta and risotto. There is Soil Association-certified organic food (the cod is apparently 'so well treated they have toys to play with') and some organic wines and beers on the fairly priced list. Our sweet potato, yoghurt and honey mint soup was pretty and subtly flavoured; and a starter of Mediterranean fish stew with garlic bread was suitably appetising. A generous hunk of the finest smoked haddock with poached egg, new potatoes

and plenty of hollandaise was a winner, as was the equally impressive chicken breast on chorizo mashed potatoes – both served with wilted spinach. Desserts are irresistible. Mango tart – a wedge of creamy Alphonso mango semifreddo – was utterly divine. Friendly and efficient service and crisp white napkins add to the experience.
Babies and children welcome: high chairs. Booking advisable dinner. Entertainment: jazz 8pm occasional Thur, 8-10.30pm Sun. No smoking. Tables outdoors (7, pavement). **Map 1 A1.**
For branch see index.

Penk's

79 Salusbury Road, NW6 6NH (7604 4484/ www.penks.com). Queen's Park tube/rail. **Brunch served** 10.30am-3pm Sat. **Lunch served** noon-3pm Mon-Fri. **Dinner served** 7-11pm Mon-Thur; 7-11.30pm Fri, Sat. **Meals served** 10.30am-11pm Sun. **Main courses** £9.95-£15.95. **Credit** MC, V.
A great place for Queen's Park eavesdropping, Penk's tables are squeezed into a seriously tiny space. It could be claustrophobic or intimate, depending on your mood. From a rather expensive wine list, we chose a glass of the 'wine of the month' (an accurately described Sicilian) and a house white of no great distinction. The food, all beautifully presented, with plenty of interesting, strong flavours, wasn't entirely satisfactory. Game terrine, served with candied fruit chutney, had too much gristle; soup of the day (fish), while perfectly acceptable, with good aioli replacing traditional rouille, wasn't too fishy. But rack of lamb, served pink, with delicious dauphinois potatoes, was spot on. The daily grilled fish – halibut – came with a delicately spiced yoghurt sauce, which detracted from the (overcooked) fish. The accompanying heap of wonderful vegetable fritters and crisp fresh salad helped redress the balance. The weekend brunch, with muesli, kedgeree and a full English breakfast (with vegetarian options), is a local favourite. We'll go back because Penk's is a comfortable place with charming service and the menu, happily not overlong, is worth exploring further.
Babies and children admitted. Booking advisable. No-smoking tables. Separate room for parties, seats 20. **Map 1 A2.**

Swiss Cottage

Globe

100 Avenue Road, NW3 3HF (7722 7200/ www.globerestaurant.co.uk). Swiss Cottage tube/13, 31 bus. **Lunch served** noon-3pm Mon-Fri. **Dinner served** 6-11pm Mon-Sat. **Main courses** £12.50-£16.50. **Set dinner** (6-7pm, 10-11pm Mon-Sat) £12 2 courses, £15 3 courses. **Credit** MC, V.
Don't be put off by the fact that Globe is in the middle of the nightmarish Swiss Cottage traffic island – it's well worth getting to, even if you're not going to the Hampstead Theatre next door. Situated in a high, airy conservatory, the restaurant offers an odd mix of modern international cuisine with the occasional touch of high camp (witness the 9ft-tall over-the-top wing chairs). This reaches its zenith every Thursday night when the Globe Girls drag show cabaret. On other nights things are quieter, but the food and quality of service still shine. Watercress soup with lime crème fraîche was just the right side of peppery and tangy, while tagliatelle with green beans, peas, mangetout and pesto captured the early summer sunshine perfectly. An imaginative selection of salad starters made equally good use of seasonal vegetables, while mains concentrated on simple food, well cooked and lovingly presented. Fish – grilled tuna and pan-fried sea bass or salmon – is a strong feature, but meat and the sole vegetarian option offer the same high quality of food, all featuring nicely balanced ingredients and accompaniments – and all for just £15 in a three-course set dinner.
Babies and children welcome: high chairs. Booking advisable. Entertainment: cabaret 8.30pm Thur (also Sat July & Aug). No smoking. **Map 28 B4.**

Italian

It's been a year of consolidation for London's Italian restaurants. Celebrities seem to be leading the increasingly confident dining public to glamorous Japanese venues; gastropubs are the hip alternative to outdated trattorias with their supermarket-level pastas and grills; and anyone can boil a pack of spaghetti and stir pesto through it – so why go out for the same? But there's much to please. It's often said that fine seasonal produce is the foundation of good Italian cooking, that the best chefs will take excellent ingredients and do little to them. A few are experimenting with the molecular gastronomy trend, but the best cooking (and raw materials) are generally found at classic, high-end venues. Don't worry: not all have stuffy service to match their premium prices, and when it comes to sexy interior design, well, the Italians are up with the best. Newcomers worthy of mention include **La Collina**, **Franco's**, **Mooli** and **Via Condotti**.

Central

Belgravia

Il Convivio
143 Ebury Street, SW1W 9QN (7730 4099/ www.etruscagroup.co.uk). Sloane Square tube/ Victoria tube/rail. **Lunch served** noon-2.45pm, **dinner served** 7-10.45pm Mon-Sat. **Set lunch** £15.50 2 courses, £19.50 3 courses. **Set dinner** £26.50 2 courses, £32.50 3 courses, £38.50 4 courses. **Credit** AmEx, DC, JCB, MC, V.
Though we were 30 minutes late arriving for our lunch at Il Convivio, the friendly staff were gracious and accommodating. High levels of comfort, the relaxed tones of Ray Charles, Aretha Franklin and Joss Stone, and a rear glass ceiling that makes every day seem like spring, soften the starched elements of this smart Belgravia restaurant. Wine is a preoccupation, and our waiter seamlessly attempted to increase our order of just one glass, bringing the bottle to the table to show the label. Dishes are inventive but astutely judged. Meat cookery is a particular strength, with boxes such as Salt Marsh and Black Angus carefully ticked. Lean, crisp and tender roast Gressingham duck came with a sauce of molasses and cobnuts, and a basket of ruby chard and mushrooms. Preserved lemon brought verve to grilled prawns and sprout salad. Other temptations included citrusy deboned baby chicken cooked in a clay pot, and a grilled veg and goat's cheese lasagne with pea sauce. Presentation tends to be carefully conceived too. Finish with a simple dish of white espresso ice-cream if the likes of nougat semifreddo with passionfruit sauce don't appeal. *Babies and children admitted. Booking advisable dinner. Restaurant available for hire. Separate room for parties, seats 14.* **Map 15 G10.**

Olivo
21 Eccleston Street, SW1W 9LX (7730 2505). Sloane Square tube/Victoria tube/rail. **Lunch served** noon-2.30pm Mon-Fri. **Dinner served** 7-11pm Mon-Sat; 7-10.30pm Sun. **Main courses** £14.50-£16. **Set lunch** £17.50 2 courses, £19.50 3 courses. **Cover** £1.50. **Credit** AmEx, DC, JCB, MC, V.
Tall olive trees in chest-high terracotta planters mark out the simple wooden frontage of this delightful perennial near Victoria rail station. Inside, cooling cement walls are boldly decorated in island-holiday colours, and tables are swathed in jute cloths and paper. The menu is a single sheet offering dishes that this Sardinian set-up has perfected over the years, with prices at lunchtime especially good value given the high standard of cooking. Olivo's concise wine list cherry-picks from all Italy, but best value and interest is to be found in the Sardinian selection. Waiters dressed in pristine white shirts and brightly coloured neckties usually have a few specials to reveal: swordfish steak with tomatoes and rocket, perhaps, or marinated vegetables. Grilled courgette salad with fine white shavings of salted ricotta was a winning starter, so too tuna carpaccio featuring a lovely lemony dressing and finely snipped chives. Main courses may include chicken thigh casserole fragrant with rosemary, or grilled calf's liver. Bootylicious plates of pasta – one with Sardinian bottarga (grey mullet roe), another with plenty of fresh crab and a judicious hint of chilli – were moist and satisfying. We also managed to squeeze in dessert of properly wobbly panna cotta with crushed raspberry sauce, and white peaches marinating in red wine. *Children admitted. Booking advisable.* **Map 15 H10.**
For branch (Olivetto) see index.

City

Caravaggio
107 Leadenhall Street, EC3A 4DP (7626 6206/ www.etruscagroup.co.uk). Aldgate tube/Bank tube/DLR. **Lunch served** 11.45am-3pm, **dinner served** 6.30-10pm Mon-Fri. **Main courses** £14-£22.50. **Set meal** £19.50 2 courses, £23.50 3 courses. **Cover** £1.50. **Credit** AmEx, DC, JCB, MC, V.
Caravaggio appears to be extremely popular with City movers and shakers – and their expense accounts. We suspect this is the reason why it can get away with charging sky-high prices for well-presented, but unspectacular modern Italian food. A minute plate of paper-thin vitello tonnato, a classic summer dish of sliced veal with a tuna mayonnaise dressing, cost an eye-watering £8.20, but was still a bargain compared with other starters. Sea bass with poached asparagus and a light olive oil sauce was pleasant and well executed, but its £18 price tag was far more difficult to stomach. Even the tangy combination of tagliolini with courgette, courgette flowers and lemon (costing £4.50 extra as a main course) failed to impress as there was only one tiny flower hidden among the pasta. Although the mirrored, art deco-inspired dining room can get packed at lunchtime, service remains efficient and crisp. The wine list is extensive and, on the plus side, includes a short selection of half bottles for folk who have to head back to work on the next multi-million-pound deal after their power lunch. Try the set menu if your expense account doesn't stretch too far. *Babies and children admitted. Booking advisable. Disabled: toilet. Dress: smart casual; no shorts. Restaurant available for hire.* **Map 12 R6.**

1 Blossom Street
1 Blossom Street, E1 6BX (7247 6530/ www.1blossomstreet.com). Liverpool Street tube/rail. **Bar Open/snacks served** noon-11pm Mon-Fri. *Restaurant* **Lunch served** noon-3pm, **dinner served** 6-9pm Mon-Fri. **Main courses** £12.50-£17.
Both **Credit** AmEx, DC, JCB, MC, V.
The outdoor dining area in a secluded courtyard (open only at lunchtimes), is a real asset on warm days; when it's not in use, you descend into a large, bland basement. The mostly Italian wine list is excellent, listing not just the great, good and hugely expensive (super-Tuscans, Barolos and the like), but also plenty of interesting and well-chosen bottles at City prices. Dish prices are also high, and although the cooking is good, it's not first class. Medallions of beef arrived well-done (we weren't given the option of how we'd like the meat cooked), with roast potatoes and a full-flavoured gorgonzola and mustard sauce topped with truffle shavings. Lemon sole was perfect, but the fat fingers of asparagus it came with were overdone. Other details are carefully considered, from the excellent Italian cheeseboard to a trolley loaded with grappas. Desserts are relatively straightforward, from pears poached in red wine to amaretto parfait with chocolate sauce. Service from the smiling staff was variable: no one greeted us on arrival, and when we pointed out we had been undercharged for a forgotten glass of wine, the amount was added back into the bill without so much as a measly thank you. *Babies and children admitted. Booking advisable. Disabled: lift; toilet. Dress: smart. Restaurant and bar available for hire. Separate rooms for parties, seating 8, 12 and 26. Tables outdoors (16, garden; lunch only).* **Map 6 R5.**

Refettorio
Crowne Plaza Hotel, 19 New Bridge Street, EC4V 6DB (7438 8052/www.tableinthecity.com). Blackfriars tube/rail. **Lunch served** noon-2.30pm Mon-Fri. **Dinner served** 6-10.30pm Mon-Sat. **Main courses** £11.50-£22. **Credit** AmEx, MC, V.
Refettorio feels like the diffusion line of a luxury fashion label. While it's not the real thing in terms of quality or price, you can distinctly sense the influence of Giorgio Locatelli, who acts as consultant. As a result, food is classy but unstuffy, and skewed toward Mediterranean-inspired dishes. Attention is paid to detail, so the fresh pasta and bread is own-made. At lunchtime, Refettorio lives up to its name, turning into an upmarket refectory for the financial community. But unlike many City restaurants, where robotic service tends to be the norm, staff on our visit remained friendly and accommodating despite being super-busy. Imaginative starters included marinated baby artichoke salad with mixed leaves and shaved parmesan. There were several fish and seafood main courses, such as pan-fried red mullet. Refettorio's major draw is its extensive selection of Italian cheese and cured meats, featuring lesser-known regional delicacies such as fresh squacquerone cheese, goat salami and cured goose breast, to share for a convivial lunch. The bread basket that complements such bounty is spectacular and well worth the extra £3.50. It's also worth keeping an eye out for Refettorio's regional-themed dégustation events, which offer the chance to sample unusual dishes. *Babies and children admitted. Booking advisable. Separate room for parties, seats 30.* **Map 11 06.**

Clerkenwell & Farringdon

Zetter

86-88 Clerkenwell Road, EC1M 5RJ (7324 4455/www.thezetter.com). Farringdon tube/rail. **Breakfast served** 7-10.30am Mon-Fri; 7.30-11am Sat, Sun. **Brunch served** 11am-3pm Sat, Sun. **Lunch served** noon-2.30pm Mon-Fri. **Dinner served** 6-10.30pm Mon-Wed, Sun; 6-11pm Thur-Sat. **Main courses** £12-£20. **Credit** AmEx, MC, V.

The Zetter is one of those few hotels that succeed in attracting both guests and locals to its restaurant and bar – something of a holy grail in the hospitality industry. Many diners probably don't realise it has rooms, though the breakfast and afternoon tea on the menu might tip them off. The ground floor of the corner building, with a sweep of views through its many windows, is entirely given over to eating and drinking. Decor plays to the arcing space, with a long, curved bar, low discs of lampshades and swirly graphic devices: red accents in a handsome sea of browns and buffs. When we visited, a new chef (Diego Jacquet) was bedding-in his menu: still Italian but with international rovings and unusual combinations. The attentive staff were genuinely interested to know how the dishes were received. The answer was very well indeed, though the balance of ingredients didn't always work: orecchiette pasta with parsley and garlic clams, roast fennel and peppers didn't also need lemon cream; the intense celeriac purée with sautéed sea bass could have been more than a smear, as could the chimichurri with the fillet steak. However, flavours were wonderful, particularly in the many vegetables, so expect good things. In summer, eat outside in lovely St John's Square.
Babies and children welcome: children's portions; crayons; high chairs. Booking advisable. Disabled: toilet. Separate rooms for parties, seating 10 and 40. Tables outdoors (14, pavement). **Map 5 O4.**

Covent Garden

Neal Street

26 Neal Street, WC2H 9QW (7836 8368/ www.carluccios.com). Covent Garden tube. **Lunch served** noon-2.30pm, **dinner served** 6-10.45pm Mon-Sat. **Main courses** £12.50-£25. **Set meal** (lunch, 6-7pm, 10-11pm Mon-Sat) £21 2 courses, £25 3 courses. **Credit** AmEx, DC, JCB, MC, V.

Antonio Carluccio's seminal London restaurant remains at the top of its game – the game of fine Italian dining, that is – after more than 30 years in business. Carluccio is a renowned funghi obsessive (an array of foraging sticks adorn the wall, all hand-carved by the man himself), so you can come safely expecting big things from the mushroom dishes. On our latest visit, the sautéed mushrooms of the day with wild garlic and chilli, served with crispy carasau bread, yielded a fantastically varied selection; and beautifully al dente pappardelle with mushrooms and prosciutto was the ultimate in comfort food. Purists should, look no further than the classic hand-cut tagliolini served simply with an unforgettably rich butter and truffle sauce. For an unusual dessert treat, try Campari and passionfruit sorbet, or summery peaches in red wine. The prices at Neal Street can be rather hard to stomach (though there is a more affordable set menu), but the restaurant does show impressive attention to detail, from the own-made artisanal breads and giant pre-prandial olives to the polished but not patronising service.
Babies and children admitted. Booking advisable. Dress: no shorts. No smoking. Separate room for parties, seats 24. **Map 18 L6.**

Fitzrovia

Camerino

16 Percy Street, W1T 1DT (7637 9900/ www.camerinorestaurant.com). Goodge Street or Tottenham Court Road tube. **Lunch served** noon-3pm Mon-Fri. **Dinner served** 6-11pm Mon-Sat. **Main courses** £15-£18. **Set meal** £19.50 2 courses, £22.50 3 courses, £27.50 4 courses. **Credit** AmEx, DC, MC, V.

Prettily decorated in black, white and red, Camerino is conveniently situated for a smart local business crowd and stands as a superior option on a street lined with budget eateries. The welcome is warm and the service gracious, though we've never seen staff pressed for time. Prices are on the high side, given the general standard of cooking. This was highlighted dramatically by the seasonal vegetable soup: a large bowl of chopped vegetables in broth – not good value for £8.50. The daily pasta special was pappardelle with wild boar ragout, but we opted for the appealing risotto of provolone, walnuts and pistachios, and linguine with prawns, garlic, chilli and parsley. Badly washed, gritty spinach ruined a main course of calf's liver with balsamic, pine nuts and raisins. Desserts tempted with a choice of three chocolate puds, including chocolate and banana doughnut with tea ice-cream. Those preferring savouries could choose from gorgonzola, parmigiano reggiano, pecorino sardo and taleggio served with own-made raisin bread. While much here is pleasing, the kitchen needs to up its game if it is to compete with the better-known Italian restaurants in the vicinity.
Babies and children welcome: high chairs. Booking advisable. Restaurant available for hire. Tables outdoors (3, pavement). **Map 10 K5.**

Latium

21 Berners Street, W1T 3LP (7323 9123/ www.latiumrestaurant.com). Oxford Circus tube. **Lunch served** noon-3pm Mon-Fri. **Dinner served** 6.30-10.30pm Mon-Fri; 6.30-11pm Sat. **Main courses** £12.50-£16. **Set meal** £24.50 2 courses, £28.50 3 courses. **Credit** AmEx, JCB, MC, V.

A subtle reworking of the seating and artwork has brought a classier mood to Latium. The kitchen has stepped up a gear, producing decorative dishes to match the striking paintings. Taleggio, chard and walnut ravioli arrived as a picture of sunflowers with chive stems and carrot leaves – delightful. Brill fillet was covered with fine potato 'scales' and set

Obika. See p171.

RESTAURANTS

on a stormy sea of watercress sauce. Other dishes looked more natural but were no less stunning. Gamey-tasting venison was incredibly tender, served with a timbale of chard, chestnuts and polenta. A raft of complimentary appetisers made us feel like we were on a picnic: briny purple olives, big juicy green ones, arancini, pizzette, crisp calzone and several breads (we used the second basket to mop up the luscious sauces of the main courses). The cheese list is impressive. Desserts were less tempting, but the opportunity to try candied artichokes, served as an accompaniment to buffalo ricotta mousse, seemed unmissable; they were surprisingly good. The waiter kept us waiting after depositing the generous plate of petits fours, but was gracious and prompt to process the bill once asked. Latium's a fine choice for an expense-account lunch, with wines by the glass including a lovely cabernet sauvignon from the Veneto.
Babies and children welcome: high chairs.
Booking advisable weekends. **Map 17 J5**.

Passione
10 Charlotte Street, W1T 2LT (7636 2833/ www.passione.co.uk). Goodge Street tube. **Lunch served** 12.30-2.15pm Mon-Fri. **Dinner served** 7-10.15pm Mon-Sat. **Main courses** £14-£22. **Credit** AmEx, DC, JCB, MC, V.
We've had mixed experiences at this long-established venue fronted by Gennaro Contaldo, whose fame rests largely on being mates with

Jamie Oliver. The menu invariably holds some experimental ideas (this time an intriguing bean soup flavoured with coffee), but it is not a place where you can confidently put your taste buds in the hands of the kitchen. And certainly not at these prices: our biggest gripe is that the standard of cooking and service often does not measure up to the size of the bill. On this visit the kitchen was in fine form, producing a winning salad of crab and pearl barley, and lamb stuffed with mint and cheese (a signature dish) that brought groans of pleasure. Service aspires to sophistication, bringing a plate of knobbly raw mushrooms to the table to offer them as a special, but lacks genuine hospitality – when the waitress knocked the tiny (yet still £3) bottle of mineral water over the table, she brought napkins to mop it up but did not replace the water or offer to remove it from the bill. Fortunately, there was fresh mint tea and superb ice-cream to relieve the sour taste left in the mouth.
Babies and children admitted. Booking advisable. Restaurant available for hire. Separate room for parties, seats 18. Tables outdoors (2, patio; 1, pavement). **Map 10 K5**.

★ Sardo
45 Grafton Way, W1T 5DQ (7387 2521/ www.sardo-restaurant.com). Warren Street tube. **Lunch served** noon-3pm Mon-Fri. **Dinner served** 6-11pm Mon-Sat. **Main courses** £8.90-£18. **Credit** AmEx, MC, V.

Although it observes mainstream Italian aesthetics (white walls with the odd Doric feature and sleek wooden floors), there's an air of Sardinian separatism in this charming restaurant at the back of Warren Street. Antipasti are fish-oriented Mediterranean favourites (tuna carpaccio, grilled squid, beef carpaccio). But regionality becomes more evident in the Sardinian classic spaghetti bottarga – a rich dish of fish roe and extra-virgin oil, which is best enjoyed in modest quantities. This and a saffrony octopus starter in white wine sauce made excellent openers to our meal. Main courses are more noticeably Sardinian; the menu is practically Greek in its array of grilled fish and lamb. Lamb cutlets with beans, tomatoes and roast potatoes was a nice simple combination, while Sardinian pork sausage served with greens and roast potatoes was juicier and more exciting than it sounds. Desserts returned to Italian conformism: tiramisu, panna cotta, although there was little sign of ice-cream. There's an intriguing selection of good Sardinian wine, temptingly priced (bottles from £14); the mainland vinos are less notable and more expensive. Despite poor ventilation at the back on a hot summer's evening, Sardo isn't in the least bit stuffy.
Babies and children admitted. Booking advisable. No-smoking tables. Separate area for parties, seats 30. Tables outdoors (3, patio). **Map 3 J4**. **For branch (Sardo Canale) see index**.

Franco's. See p174.

RESTAURANTS

Fitzrovia

Carluccio's Caffè

*8 Market Place, W1W 8AG (7636 2228/
www.carluccios.com). Oxford Circus tube.* **Meals
served** 7.30am-11pm Mon-Fri; 10am-11pm Sat;
10am-10pm Sun. **Main courses** £5.95-£12.95.
Credit AmEx, MC, V.

Carluccio's is not well suited to people with hearing
aids. The New York-style Italian deli chain has
shocking acoustics; clattering cutlery and
cacophonous conversation ricochet around the
light and airy environment, off plain white walls
and stripped wooden floors. Otherwise, the place
is testimony to the fact that you can't keep a good
brand down. Food is of a high quality and service
is impeccable – by café standards. Snacking or
picnicking is half the deal here, with soups,
antipasti, salads and pasta dishes leading the way
by deploying classic combinations. So mozzarella
and tomato salad is good according to the season,
while penne alla luganica (spicy sausage ragout)
and gnocchi al gorgonzola are typically solid
dishes. Daily specials supplement the fixed menu
with fresh fish and other variations on the theme
(although this isn't somewhere to sample more
sophisticated Italian cucina), and there are wines
to match. Desserts too are notable, including a
lemon tart with a rich yet light filling on a crumbly
pastry. Coffee is of the same high standard as you
get in Italy. Also impressive was a congenial
waitress who kept her cool on a sunny weekday
lunch with tables packed inside and out.
*Babies and children welcome: children's menu;
high chairs. Disabled: toilet. No smoking. Tables
outdoors (16, pavement). Takeaway service.*
Map 17 J6.
For branches see index.

Knightsbridge

San Lorenzo

*22 Beauchamp Place, SW3 1NH (7584 1074).
Knightsbridge tube.* **Lunch served** 12.30-3pm,
dinner served 7.30-11.30pm Mon-Sat.
Main courses £15.50-£28.50. **Cover** £2.50.
No credit cards.

Despite the Beauchamp Place gloss, San Lorenzo
is showing a few cracks here and there, and we are
not just referring to its white-tiled floor. The
glitterati and glitterati-watchers still turn up in fair
numbers, but such a glamorous reputation fails to
make up for a kitchen that dishes out indifferent
food, and staff whose degree of attention increases
in proportion of the amount of bling customers
are prepared to flash. Pleasant own-made egg
tagliarini with fresh lobster sauce and prawns
arrived swimming in plenty of tomato sauce, but
the lobster was nowhere to be tasted. Pollo al
dragoncello turned out to be a chicken breast
smothered with a bland creamy sauce speckled
with tarragon. A starter of roast red peppers was
similarly bathed in bagna cauda, a Piedmontese
anchovy and garlic sauce that would usually be
served on the side. Even the ice-cream, supposedly
made using the famed Pernigotti chocolate from
Italy, tasted watery and insipid. Pricey, sloppy food
and a surly attitude may not be endearing, but
there's no bigger disappointment than an Italian
restaurant that serves poor ice-cream.
*Babies and children welcome: children's portions;
high chairs. Booking advisable Fri, Sat. Dress:
smart casual. Restaurant available for hire.
Separate rooms for parties, seats 20 and 40.*
Map 14 F9.
For branch see index.

Zafferano

*15 Lowndes Street, SW1X 9EY (7235 5800/
www.zafferanorestaurant.com). Knightsbridge
tube.* **Lunch served** noon-2.30pm Mon-Fri;
12.30-3pm Sat, Sun. **Dinner served** 7-11pm
Mon-Sat; 7-10.30pm Sun. **Set lunch** £25.50
2 courses, £29.50 3 courses, £34.50 4 courses.
Set dinner £29.50 2 courses, £39.50 3 courses,
£49.50 4 courses. **Credit** AmEx, DC, MC, V.
Polished and classy, with friendly and attentive
service that doesn't falter even at busy times,
Zafferano is highly popular with ladies who lunch

BEST ITALIAN

Regional specialities

La Collina (see p183) – Piedmont; **Olivo**
(see p168), **Pane Vino** (see p184),
Sardo (see p170) – all Sardinian.

New-wave flair

Latium (see p169), **Metrogusto**
(see p184), **Quo Vadis** (see p175),
Rosmarino (see p184).

Family fun

Amici (see p181), **La Famiglia** (see
p179), **Manicomio** (see p179), **Marco
Polo** (see p181), **Philpott's Mezzaluna**
(see p184), **San Lorenzo** (see left).

Dining alfresco

Cantina del Ponte (see p183),
Carluccio's Caffè (see left), **La Collina**
(see p183), **La Famiglia** (see p179),
Manicomio (see p181), **Marco Polo**
(see p181), **The River Café** (see p176),
Zetter (see p169).

---

and well-heeled locals. Its elegant, contemporary
Italian cooking is perfectly executed, and the all-
Italian wine list is outstanding, yet some dishes
seem to be too clinical. A starter of sardine in saor,
a typical Venetian dish of marinated deep-fried
sardines and onions, had been sanitised to the
point that the end result bore little resemblance to
the original recipe either in appearance or flavour.
Other dishes less rooted in regional cooking
worked far better, such as the own-made saffron
pappardelle with pig's cheek, or the moreish calf's
liver with balsamic vinegar, both highlights of
our meal. There's also a separate truffle menu
(in season). Chocoholics are catered for with a
scrumptious chocolate fondant with Gianduia ice-
cream, which is well worth enduring a 12-minute
wait. The lunch and dinner menu is fixed price
(varying with the number of courses), but a few
dishes carry a further £5 or £10 supplement,
which unfortunately tends to raise the final bill to
dizzy heights.
*Babies and children welcome: high chairs.
Booking essential, at least 1wk in advance for
lunch, 4-6 weeks in advance for dinner. Dress:
smart casual; no shorts (dinner). Separate room
for parties, seats 20.* **Map 15 G9.**

Marble Arch

Arturo

*23 Connaught Street, W2 2AY (7706 3388/
www.arturorestaurant.co.uk). Marble Arch tube.*
Lunch served noon-2.30pm Mon-Sat; 12.30-
3.30pm Sun. **Dinner served** 6-10pm Mon-Sat;
6-9.30pm Sun. **Main courses** £12-£16.
Set meal £12.95 2 courses, £15.95 3 courses.
Credit AmEx, MC, V.
Just off the Edgware Road, Arturo provides the
neighbourhood with a ground-floor restaurant and
basement bar. Its design aspires to the stylishness
of Heal's, but service and cooking are not quite up
to the same standard. Small tables line up in front
of an upholstered bench on standard wooden
floors. Piped music proves intrusive in the
otherwise rather naked environment. The antipasti
are dishes you'd expect to find in any decent deli;
grilled squid was perfectly adequate. Among the
vegetable- or fish-oriented pastas, own-made egg
rosemary tagliatelle was a large stodgy number,
not ideal as a main course – although the use of
ginger sauce alongside the artichoke and pancetta
was nothing if not imaginative. A main of fried
veal cutlet was typically Tuscan, arriving with
spinach and sautéed potatoes. More adventurous
dishes include calf's liver with red onion and
dandelion; or chicken with basil, sun-dried
tomatoes and artichoke, served with a Marsala
sauce. Our dessert was most disappointing: a
heavy, catering-quality ricotta chocolate cake.
Although the ambience is amenable, and the Italian

---

wine list is pleasing, there's an unfortunate gap at
Arturo between expectation and result.
*Babies and children admitted. No-smoking tables.
Tables outdoors (3, pavement).* **Map 8 F6.**

Obika NEW

*2nd floor, Selfridges, 400 Oxford Street, W1A
1AB (7318 3620/www.obika.co.uk). Bond Street
tube.* **Meals served** 11.30am-7.30pm Mon-Wed,
Fri, Sat; 11.30am-8.30pm Thur; noon-5.30pm
Sun. **Main courses** £12-£18. **Credit** AmEx,
DC, MC, V.
As the boho look is out, it stands to reason that this
clean-lined Italian 'mozzarella bar' has replaced
Moroccan eaterie Momo in Selfridges' high-fashion
Superbrands section. The operation isn't as slick
as the glass and steel design suggests; it's unclear
whether you should wait to be seated (yes), and
staff are often too busy to assist. Two bars provide
contrasting entertainment for solitary lunchers.
Behind the central bar, tasting plates of buffalo
mozzarella (choose from two regional varieties, one
with a more acidic intensity than the other) are
assembled with such delicacies as wild boar
prosciutto and smoked swordfish. Starting at £12
for three items, they don't come cheap. The other
bar looks out on to the catwalk of shoppers.
Obika's menu also covers salads, antipasti and
pasta dishes. Fresh pappardelle with anchovies,
spinach and tomatoes was pure peasant comfort
food. The wine selection is from Liberty Wines, one
of the top Italian wine importers in the UK.
Desserts (apple pie, chocolate and almond cake) are
rich enough to prevent you buying a body-
skimming number at Gucci opposite.
*Babies and children welcome: high chairs.
Disabled: toilet (in Selfridges). No smoking.
Takeaway service.* **Map 9 G6.**

Marylebone

★ Locanda Locatelli

*8 Seymour Street, W1H 7JZ (7935 9088/
www.locandalocatelli.com). Marble Arch tube.*
Lunch served noon-3pm Mon-Fri; noon-
3.30pm Sat, Sun. **Dinner served** 6.45-11pm
Mon-Thur; 6.45-11.30pm Fri, Sat; 6.45-10pm Sun.
Main courses £19.50-£29.50. **Credit** AmEx,
JCB, MC, V.
The permanently darkened interior of wood
veneer, convex mirrors and expansive tan leather
lounges suggests sleazy Saturday nights rather
than sunny Sunday lunchtimes; however, Locanda
Locatelli is now open on Sunday and it is one of
the easiest times to get a table at this notoriously
popular venue. Pleasant white wine from the
Marche sold for £12 a bottle begs the question why
other top-flight restaurants in central London are
pushing entry-level wine prices way above £20.
The perception of value is not so strong when it
comes to simple dishes of grilled pork chop with
(admittedly delicious) gravy, spinach and a few
wedges of beetroot for £28. However, much
thought and effort clearly goes into the
complimentary bread basket with varieties that
include onion focaccia, cauliflower bread, grissini
and little pastries stuffed with spinach and cheese.
Pasta is always an excellent choice, and our
gnocchi were astonishingly cloud-like pillows,
cloaked with light goat's cheese sauce and black
truffle. There is an exquisite selection of ice-
creams and sorbets (cocoa, prune and armagnac,
and crema catalan among them), plus several more
flamboyant dessert options, including a perfect
chocolate fondant with a boozy kick. Service was
prompt enough, though in wishing not to rush us,
the lack of attention made it hard to get the bill.
*Babies and children welcome: high chairs. Booking
essential. Disabled: toilet (hotel). Dress: smart
casual.* **Map 9 G6.**

2 Veneti

*10 Wigmore Street, W1U 2RD (7637 0789).
Bond Street or Oxford Circus tube.* **Lunch
served** noon-3pm, **dinner served** 6.30-
10.30pm Mon-Sat. **Main courses** £10.50-
£28.50. **Credit** AmEx, MC, V.
As we went to press, Eddalino had friendly new
owners and had begun its transformation into 2
Veneti. First changes: more relaxed though still

formal service, with waiters dressed in smart jeans and shirts rather than the embarrassing waistcoats of yore. And a new wine list: a large card with a contemporary design and fun facts about wine production, such as a comparison of land prices in Tuscany and the Napa Valley. The chef has stayed, and immediately impressed with a sublime special pasta dish of lime-marinated raw tuna with green tomato, green beans, capers, chilli and spaghetti. Also very good was a classic dish of spaghetti with spicy Calabrian sausage, tomatoes, spinach and pecorino. Veal masala featured a luscious sauce but was a little too rare; tuna, on the other hand, was slightly overdone. Main courses featured inventive salads (such as lamb's lettuce and mango), but in both cases the leaves were well past their best. A superb pistachio ice-cream with chocolate biscuit cake saw honour returned. Extra touches such as the crunchy olives, good breads, amuse-bouches and petits fours reinforced the impression of quality. If they can sort out the decor, this promises to be an inviting venue.
Babies and children welcome: high chairs. Booking advisable. No-smoking tables. Restaurant available for hire. Tables outdoors (2, pavement). **Map 9 H5**.

Mayfair

★ Alloro
19-20 Dover Street, W1X 4LU (7495 4768). Green Park tube.
Bar **Open** noon-11pm Mon-Fri; 7-11pm Sat. **Main courses** £8-£16.
Restaurant **Lunch served** noon-2.30pm Mon-Fri. **Dinner served** 7-10.30pm Mon-Sat. **Set lunch** £26 2 courses, £29 3 courses. **Set dinner** £28.50 2 courses, £33 3 courses, £36 4 courses.
Both **Credit** AmEx, DC, JCB, MC, V.
Alloro is an Italian among Italians: typically minimal and stylish. Diners are greeted by chessboard parquet flooring connecting a curvy cocktail bar and the very smart restaurant. The dining room proper is hung with stone artworks in wood-veneer alcoves bordered by fashionable ribbed wallpaper. The set menus aren't cheap, and some dishes carry supplements (a bit rich), but this isn't any old Italian cooking. The execution of primi piatti ranging from cauliflower soup to crab ravioli to crayfish risotto emphasises the point. Perhaps the best testimony to the chef was the delicate simplicity of basil-infused tomato sauce on the tagliatelle. Thereafter, pesce and carne included an exquisite monkfish in saffron sauce seasoned with chorizo sausage, as well as a fine fillet steak on a bed of spinach. There's more experimentation in desserts, including a divine banana mousse. However, the biggest treat is for lovers of Italian wine in a list stewarded by a delightful wine waiter. You can even savour a fine Brunello by the glass (though at £15 it may well be just the one glass). So long as you're flush, you can't go wrong.
Babies and children admitted. Booking advisable. Restaurant and bar available for hire. Separate room for parties, seats 16. Tables outdoors (2, pavement). **Map 9 J7**.

Giardinetto
39-40 Albemarle Street, W1S 4TE (7493 7091/ www.giardinetto.co.uk). Green Park tube.
Lunch served 12.30-3pm Mon-Fri. **Dinner served** 6-10.30pm Mon-Sat. **Main courses** £14-£35. **Set lunch** £18 2 courses, £22 3 courses, £25.50 4 courses. **Credit** AmEx, DC, JCB, MC, V.
A whole lot of design has gone into creating Giardinetto in a tiny Mayfair house, from the push-button doors that let you in through the frosted glass panels, to the sleek, light woodwork. It's a test of the staff's professionalism to keep moving, and stay charming, through the confined spaces. Chef Maurizio Vilona produces highly refined, Ligurian-based cuisine. The full menu offers various intricate possibilities. Presentation is a major feature and is as exquisite as the decor, but we found the execution to be surprisingly irregular for a place with such high ambitions and prices. Cappon magro alla genovese (a traditional seafood salad of lobster, prawns and cod on a kind of

pesto, bean and potato cake) was superb; yet poor-quality, listless shellfish let down a dish of seared scallops with lentil cream and leek froth. In both main courses – roasted monkfish in white wine with mozzarella-filled baby aubergine; and mixed fried fish in tempura-like batter – wonderful fish was skilfully infused with delicate flavours of citrus and saffron. To finish, though, a 'sinfonia di the e nocciola' was a dull hazelnut cream pudding. The imposing wine list has prices to match those of the dinner menu; the lunch menu is more economical, but much shorter.
Babies and children admitted. Booking advisable. No-smoking tables. Separate rooms for parties, seating 10 and 14. **Map 9 J7**.

Sartoria
20 Savile Row, W1S 3PR (7534 7000/ www.conran.com). Oxford Circus or Piccadilly Circus tube.
Bar **Open/snacks served** 9am-midnight Mon-Sat.
Restaurant **Lunch served** noon-3pm Mon-Fri. **Dinner served** 6-10.45pm Mon-Sat. **Main courses** £17-£24. **Set meal** £19.50 2 courses, £24.50 3 courses.
Both **Credit** AmEx, DC, JCB, MC, V.
Japanese and American tourists seem to make up the core custom of this tailor-themed Conran eaterie. Based on the ritzy restaurants of Milan, Sartoria could easily pass for a Japanese venue, thanks to its sliding screen doors and serene yet formal air. The room is so large that even when busy it doesn't seem full. A wide choice of six to eight dishes is offered in each category – antipasti, pasta e risotto, secondi, contorni and dolci – plus a daily set menu. On-message ingredients such as barba di frate and cime di rapa (both greens), and a weighty Italian wine list, ensure there's no comparison with cod-Italian joints on the other side of Regent Street. Kudos to the kitchen for offering eco-friendly fish such as red gurnard and zander (an earthy-tasting river fish that was paired simply with artichokes). Meat lovers will revel in dishes such as calf's tongue with salsa verde, veal kidney with parmigiana, veal milanese and roast fillet of beef. Finish with a selezione di formaggi, or desserts such as raspberry and amaretti panna cotta, or wheat tart with blood orange sorbet. The stiff, ceremonial service revealed itself to be kind and thoughtful as our meal progressed.
Babies and children welcome: high chairs. Booking advisable; essential lunch. Disabled: toilet. Entertainment: pianist 7-10pm Thur-Sat. Restaurant available for hire. Separate rooms for parties, seating 20 and 45. **Map 9 J7**.

★ Via Condotti NEW
23 Conduit Street, W1S 2XS (7493 7050). Oxford Circus tube. **Lunch served** noon-3pm Mon-Fri; 12.30-3pm Sat. **Dinner served** 6.30-11pm Mon-Sat. **Main courses** £9.50-£18.50. **Credit** AmEx, MC, V.
Named after Rome's most famous shopping street, and set on one of London's best, this latest venture from Italian restaurateur Claudio Pulze is co-owned with chef Pasquale Amico and general manager Richard Martinez. Amico is a veteran of London kitchens such as Zafferano, Cecconi's, Refettorio and Sartoria, but hails from Campania, home of buffalo mozzarella and some of the tasty olives that arrived quickly at our table. The menu lists six or seven options in antipasti, primi piatti, secondi and desserts, plus a cheese plate served with polenta bread. From the pastas, tortelli with goat's cheese, hazelnuts and pesto, and ravioli with scamorza, sun-dried tomatoes, and tomato and basil sauce are particularly tempting. Desserts such as Sicilian cannolo, while well executed, are dairy-rich and generously portioned, making them difficult to finish (it's a good idea to share); lighter fruit options would be welcome. Martinez knows much about wine and can advise on the most suitable picks from the Italian list. We were pleased with our Lagrein Gries from the north, near the German border, which neatly bridged disparate main courses of roast lamb with aubergine and red mullet with lemony salad.
Babies and children admitted. Booking advisable. Separate room for parties, seats 18. **Map 9 J6**.

RESTAURANTS

Party central

Italian restaurants are a great choice when it comes to organising a group gathering, whether you need somewhere for work colleagues, old school friends, or are faced with the multi-generational challenges of a family reunion. Kids love pasta and tomato sauce (and Italian waiters love kids). Beef tagliata, roast lamb or grilled chicken will suit the non-foodies, yet the menu will hold treats such as truffles, calf's liver, duck, sheep's milk cheeses and polenta for the gastronauts. Everyone's happy and – when you choose from the centrally located venues below – everyone can get home easily.

Aperitivo
41 Beak Street, W1F 9SB (7287 2057/ www.aperitivo-restaurants.com). Oxford Circus or Piccadilly Circus tube. **Tapas served** noon-11pm Mon-Sat. **Tapas** £2.95-£9.95. **Set tapas** (noon-5pm daily) £9.50-£14. **Credit** AmEx, MC, V.
A great option for vegetarians, Aperitivo's tapas-style menu lists six veggie dishes in addition to meat, fish, salads and a couple of unusual pastas. Downstairs has a private dining room; upstairs there are a couple of sofas for relaxing with cocktails and nibbles. *Babies and children admitted. Booking advisable Wed-Sat. Separate room for parties, seats 35.* **Map 17 J6**.

Bertorelli
19-23 Charlotte Street, W1T 1RL (7636 4174/www.santeonline.co.uk). Goodge Street tube. **Bar Open** 3-11pm Mon-Sat. **Café Meals served** noon-11pm Mon-Sat. **Main courses** £7.50-£14.95. **Restaurant Lunch served** noon-3pm Mon-Fri. **Dinner served** 6-11pm Mon-Sat. **Main courses** £13.75-£24. **Set meals** £15.50 2 courses, £18.50 3 courses. **All Credit** AmEx, DC, MC, V.
Owned by the Chez Gérard group, Bertorelli's has five outlets in London, but the Charlotte Street branch was the first, founded by the Bertorelli family over 90 years ago. The first-floor restaurant has plenty of space for large tables, plus two private rooms, and serves classic Italian dishes with modish presentation. Downstairs is a lively café-bar. *Babies and children welcome: high chairs. Booking advisable. No-smoking tables. Restaurant available for hire. Separate rooms for parties, seating 22 and 44. Tables outdoors (5, terrace).* **Map 9 J5**. **For branches see index.**

St James's

Al Duca
4-5 Duke of York Street, SW1Y 6LA (7839 3090/www.alduca-restaurant.co.uk). Piccadilly Circus tube. **Lunch served** noon-2.30pm Mon-Fri; 12.30-3pm Sat. **Dinner served** 6-11pm Mon-Sat. **Set lunch** £19.50 2 courses, £22.50 3 courses, £25.50 4 courses. **Set dinner** £22.50 2 courses, £24.50 3 courses, £29.50 4 courses. **Credit** AmEx, DC, MC, V.
Fresh and relaxing, Al Duca sports an artful mix of clean modern lines, crisp linen, flowers and subtle Italianate terracotta and stone colourings. Staff seemed nervous at first glance, but got it

Caffè Caldesi
118 Marylebone Lane, W1U 2QF (7935 1144/www.caffecaldesi.com). Bond Street tube. **Bar Meals served** noon-10.30pm Mon-Sat; 9.30am-4pm Sun. **Main courses** £6.50-£14. **Restaurant Lunch served** noon-3pm, **dinner served** 6-10.30pm Mon-Sat. **Main courses** £15-£17. **Both Credit** AmEx, JCB, MC, V.
This useful bar-deli that spills on to the street secretes an airy first-floor restaurant with friendly staff and simple cooking. The menu makes the most of the char-grill and deli counter, and throws in plenty of fresh vegetables. *Babies and children welcome: high chairs; nappy-changing facilities. Booking advisable (restaurant). Disabled: toilet. Restaurant and bar available for hire. Tables outside (8, pavement).* **Map 9 G5**. **For branch (Caldesi Tuscan) see index**.

Orso
27 Wellington Street, WC2E 7DB (7240 5269/www.orsorestaurant.co.uk). Covent Garden tube. **Meals served** noon-midnight daily. **Main courses** £8.50-£17. **Set meal** (5-6.45pm Mon-Sat) £16 2 courses, £18 3 courses incl coffee. **Credit** AmEx, MC, V.
American visitors love this reliable place and no wonder: the Cal-Ital menu is full of good, fresh ingredients used in tempting but not wacky combinations. Classy, yet relaxed and colourful, you can have just a pizza, but the meat dishes, pasta, salads and tart of the day are worth ordering. *Babies and children welcome: booster seats. Booking advisable. No-smoking tables.* **Map 18 L7**.

Signor Zilli
40-41 Dean Street, W1V 5AB (restaurant 7734 3924/bar 7734 1853/www.zillialdo. com). Leicester Square, Piccadilly Circus or Tottenham Court Road tube. **Bar Open** noon-midnight, **meals served** noon-11pm Mon-Sat. **Main courses** £9.50-£16.50. **Restaurant Lunch served** noon-2.30pm Mon-Fri. **Dinner served** 5.30-11.30pm Mon-Sat. **Main courses** £8.50-£20.50. **Both Credit** AmEx, JCB, MC, V.
Come here for big plates of shellfish pastas, hearty antipasto, a few flashy ingredient combinations, and evocative Italian service that's flirtatious and offhand by turns. The small basement dining area is not private, but is a neat choice for large gatherings. *Babies and children welcome: high chairs. Bar available for hire. Booking advisable. Tables outdoors (4, pavement).* **Map 17 K6**.

together pretty quickly. The contemporary Italian food is impressive and highly enjoyable. Dishes are inventive, not stuck in Italian routine. A speciality starter – poached egg with a crispy parmesan wafer, bacon, and potato and spring onion salad – provided an unusual, intricate but lovely mix of flavours and textures. Baby octopus salad with crispy celery and marinated artichokes was nicely put together using excellent ingredients. The menu offers a pasta and a risotto special daily. When we visited, risotto of squid in ink with cherry tomatoes (a difficult dish that needed to be done just right) was a wonderful, rich-but-delicate blend. Grilled swordfish with roast Mediterranean veg was more simple, but just as satisfying, and

beautifully presented. Hard-to-resist desserts are in the same creative style. There's also a huge wine list, with bottles from every Italian region (including an especially good choice from Sardinia) at an equally broad something-for-everyone price range. What's more, the set-price menu formula makes a meal here exceptional value for such high-quality food, particularly in this upmarket district. *Babies and children welcome: high chair. Dress: no shorts. Restaurant available for hire (Sun).* **Map 17 J7**.

Fiore
33 St James's Street, SW1A 1HD (7930 7100/ www.fiore-restaurant.co.uk). Green Park tube. **Lunch served** noon-2.30pm Mon-Fri. **Dinner served** 6-10.30pm Mon-Sat. **Main courses** £14-£16. **Credit** MC, V.
Once a French restaurant called Fleur, the flower logo of this Italian set-up emphasises the joke behind the new name. Inside is a small bar area, then a long dining room lined with abstract art. On our visit it was populated primarily by charming, intelligent, neatly dressed staff. If you were an American or Japanese tourist staying at the nearby Ritz, you'd no doubt be delighted to find this smart, safe joint a short walk from the hotel. Who else it attracts, we're not entirely sure; local competition is tough with long-established hits such as the Avenue and Le Caprice. A sprightly artichoke salad got the meal off to a good start. Scallops in our other starter were beautifully fresh and perfectly seared, though their number (two) was disappointing. A main course of calf's liver with spinach and raisins was a show-stopper: tender chunks of medium-rare meat cut on the bias, and astonishingly pretty to look at. Dessert of three 'emozione' of chocolate did not show the same finesse, but tasted delicious with its three custardy layers of white, milk and dark chocolate. Montepulciano d'Abruzzo from Tollo was the cheapest red at £16 and not bad for the price. Given the area, a meal at Fiore is remarkably good value. *Babies and children welcome: high chairs. Restaurant available for hire.* **Map 17 J7**.

★ Franco's NEW
61 Jermyn Street, SW1Y 6LX (7499 2211/ www.francoslondon.com). Green Park tube. **Breakfast served** 7.30-10.30am, **lunch served** noon-2.30pm, **tapas served** 2.30-11pm, **dinner served** 5.30-11pm Mon-Sat. **Tapas** £7.50-£14. **Main courses** £15-£22. **Set lunch** £25 2 courses, £30 3 courses. **Credit** AmEx, MC, V.
Franco's is the epitome of St James's aspirations: patrician, classy and well-bred. The warm beige, comfortable 1940s-style decor wouldn't look out of place in a gentleman's club. The menu forsakes flashiness for genuine yet refined cooking that could make an Italian feel almost at home. The use of seasonal ingredients ensures the menu changes daily, blending regional dishes with classic touches like chicken broth with tortellini, a Christmas Day tradition in Italy. Pasta dishes are where Franco's comes into its own. Own-made stracci with venison ragù, from the special menu, was cooked to perfection, with the sauce simmered for hours to temper the pungency of the tomatoes. Zitoni with n'duja (a spicy, soft sausage from Calabria), aubergine, fresh tomatoes and hard ricotta cheese was equally flawless, with a just-right hint of chilli. A main course special of sautéed Calabrian sausage with broccoli was big in flavour – if not in quantity – and not too fiery. Desserts include mainstays like tiramisu and panna cotta. The wine list is extensive, with gems like vino novello from Tuscany at £24 a bottle. Apart from the occasional slip-up in the kitchen, service was exemplary. *Babies and children admitted. Disabled: toilet. Dress: smart casual. No-smoking tables. Separate rooms for parties, seating 18 and 50. Tables outdoors (4, pavement).* **Map 17 J7**.

Luciano NEW
72-73 St James's Street, SW1A 1PH (7408 1440/www.lucianorestaurant.co.uk). Green Park tube. **Lunch served** noon-2.30pm, **dinner served** 6-11pm Mon-Sat. **Main courses** £16.50-£26. **Set lunch** (Mon-Fri) £18.95 2 courses, £22.50 3 courses. **Credit** MC, V.

Since opening in October 2005, Marco Pierre White's homage to his Italian roots has rapidly acquired the elegant but sober patina of a gentleman's club – complete with doorman, wall-to-wall artwork and starched white linen. You get the impression women are almost expected to turn up with a male companion. The food is more Milan-meets-St James's rather than traditionally correct Italian fare, yet the combination works and the mostly male clientele appears to appreciate it. A succulent rack of lamb was whole instead of sliced, but pleasantly set off by the distinctly Italian flavour of capers and anchovies. Cornish crab dressed simply with olive oil and served with pane carasau (thin and crispy Sardinian flatbread) made a memorable starter. A classic Milanese risotto with osso bucco was less exciting, due to its runny texture, a heavy-handed use of saffron, and skimpy meat portion. The inventive dessert menu included exquisite cannoli, the fried wafers filled with ricotta cheese that are among the highlights of Sicilian pâtisserie. Service is flawless, but can be a bit stand-offish if customers don't look the part.
Babies and children admitted. Booking advisable. Disabled: toilet. Separate room for parties, seats 22. **Map 9 J8**.

Soho

Quo Vadis

26-29 Dean Street, W1D 6LL (7437 9585/ www.whitestarline.org.uk). Leicester Square, Piccadilly Circus or Tottenham Court Road tube. **Lunch served** noon-2.30pm Mon-Fri. **Dinner served** 5.30-11pm Mon-Sat. **Main courses** £8-£19.95. **Set meal** (lunch, 5.30-6.30pm) £14.95 2 courses, £17.95 3 courses. **Credit** AmEx, DC, JCB, MC, V.
Although Quo Vadis has been around for several years, the decor in the charming arts and crafts building remains startling. 'Is that fancy dried pasta in the display case behind you?' 'No, it's bird skeletons.' These days the menu is similarly wacky, but the media crowd takes this in its stride. Among the starters and mains, we counted 14 references to fruit on our summer visit; peaches seemed to garnish everything. Pasta pairings are a little more traditional, but presentation is still of the

experimental skool. When desserts arrive, you'll encounter such items as beetroot and white chocolate mousse (of course). Nevertheless, we were still surprised to find chocolatey tuiles garnishing a dish of gamey-tasting roast lamb saddle with creamed black rice and beignet of sweet chard and mango (the flavours worked remarkably well together). Apart from a long wait for the main courses, service was prompt and gracious. French bottles predominate on the wine list, but Italy plays a key role, and Prosecco and Bellinis are offered as aperitifs. An eccentric original.
Children admitted. Booking advisable. Dress: smart casual. Separate rooms for parties, seating 12, 14, 30 and 80. **Map 17 K6**.

Vasco & Piero's Pavilion

15 Poland Street, W1F 8QE (7437 8774/ www.vascosfood.com). Oxford Circus or Piccadilly Circus tube. **Lunch served** noon-3pm Mon-Fri. **Dinner served** 6-11pm Mon-Sat. **Main courses** £9.50-£17. **Set dinner** £22 2 courses, £26 3 courses. **Credit** AmEx, DC, JCB, MC, V.
If you were after a typical 1980s Italian restaurant from central casting, you'd be pleased with this Soho stalwart. The Pavilion has distressed orange walls, bronze pineapples, dinky metal chairs packed closely together, and plenty of 'prego, prego'. Such is its popularity with local office workers, a queue often forms by the door. The bread basket wins no prizes, but is replenished during the meal. There are also good fat green olives to nibble while you browse the understated menu. Fish features heavily; even on our Monday night visit there was a choice of four piscine dishes. Shallot dressing gave oomph to grilled fillets of salmon served with green beans that were crisp and brightly coloured from judicious blanching. Roast duck came Umbrian-style (properly well-done) with wild fennel seeds beautifully cutting through the rich taste of the meat. Two slices of buffalo mozzarella were prettily presented with grilled antipasto veg and rocket salad. Pastas are classic, such as tagliatelle with beef ragù. The mainly Italian wine list starts at £14 and includes a good Salice Salentino from Puglia by the glass.
Booking advisable. Children over 6 years admitted. Separate room for parties, seats 36. **Map 17 J6**.

Victoria

Volt NEW

17 Hobart Place, SW1W 0HH (7235 9696/ www.voltlounge.com). Victoria tube/rail. **Meals served** noon-11pm Mon-Fri. **Dinner served** 6-11pm Sat. **Main courses** £12-£18. **Set meal** £17 2 courses, £22 3 courses. **Credit** AmEx, DC, MC, V.
With flat screens showing the latest Roberto Cavalli collection on Fashion TV, and sexy-suited waiters of dark good looks, Volt aims to appeal first to young women and thus attract the men who want to date them. The colourful, flashy decor is good of its type, with extraordinary striped lighting that suddenly switched from bright red to blue halfway through our meal. In such a club-lounge environment, it's curious to see formal dining touches like food brought on trays by porters, careful attention to cutlery and wine service, and complimentary luxuries such as petits fours. Most astonishing, however, is the value. The set menu has so many choices it's hardly worth looking at the carte, and the standard of cooking and presentation is high. A modern take on vitello tonnato (sliced veal with a tuna mayonnaise dressing) was a creamy delight. Seared squid came with a black ink sauce, piquillo peppers and grilled aubergine. Meat cookery was especially good, as exemplified by slow-roasted belly of pork served with vanilla and truffle honey – divine. On our platter of ice-creams, liquorice was the only flavour that disappointed (the others were excellent). There are Italian and New World wines on the list, but France seems to be the priority; a long list of cocktails is offered too.
Babies and children welcome: booster seat. Booking advisable. Separate rooms for parties, seating 14, 18 and 30. **Map 15 H9**.

Westminster

Quirinale

North Court, 1 Great Peter Street, SW1P 3LL (7222 7080). St James's Park or Westminster tube. **Lunch served** noon-2.30pm, **dinner served** 6-10.30pm Mon-Fri. **Main courses** £12.50-£17. **Credit** AmEx, DC, MC, V.

Volt

A creamy stone stairway with strategically placed floorlights leads guests down to this gracious New Labour haunt. Clever interior design, including glass brickwork and neat sliding doors, make the small basement space seem spacious and full of light. We've enjoyed some excellent meals at Quirinale over the years. The menu emphasises seasonal ingredients and tempting combinations. Meals begin with a tasty selection of breads. Pasta courses are generously portioned, and there is a good array of antipasto starters with pretty salads and seafood options such as grilled sardines, plus judicious use of cheese and charcuterie. A dry fillet of john dory with Mediterranean vegetables and pesto was not up to the usual high standard, but another main course of tender quail with figs and pancetta was pure delight. Quirinale's sizeable cheese list is most impressive, taking in specialities from several regions, though well-executed desserts such as chocolate fondant are hard to pass up. The intriguing Italian wine list kicks off with a pleasing Soave Cadoro at £16.50. Service is formal but friendly. If it were in another part of town, Quirinale would be have wider renown.
Babies and children admitted. Booking advisable. **Map 16 L10**.

West

Bayswater

L'Accento
16 Garway Road, W2 4NH (7243 2201). Bayswater or Queensway tube. **Lunch served** noon-2.30pm, **dinner served** 6.30-11.15pm Mon-Sat. **Main courses** £14-£16.50. **Set meal** £13.50 2 courses. **Credit** AmEx, JCB, MC, V.
This Bayswater backstreet venue has the air of a café pretending to be something rather special: a brilliant unknown Italian around the corner. Something, in short, that it clearly isn't. The management attitude is downright sloppy; a bottle of wine was presented to us with half the broken cork floating in it. When we noticed this, the staff agreed (without the necessary alacrity) to replace it, yet the next bottle had the same problem. We settled on a different bottle, and hoped that the meal wouldn't be as haphazard. Starters were fine: rolled aubergine and leek with scamorza cheese in a tomato and basil sauce was choked with flavour and pleasantly smoky; pumpkin ravioli with fresh sage, butter and parmesan was good too, if excessively rich. Sadly, standards slumped for the main courses. The sauce with a lobster dish was too salty, although the lobster itself was fine; but an enticing-sounding grilled monkfish and prawns with chilli was rather thrown together, lacking any subtlety, and featured dry fish and tasteless prawns. Service throughout was uninterested. L'Accento is not the charming venue it could be.
Babies and children admitted. Booking advisable dinner Fri, Sat. No-smoking tables. Separate room for parties, seats 22. Tables outdoors (5, pavement). **Map 7 B6**.

★ Assaggi
First floor, 39 Chepstow Place, W2 4TS (7792 5501). Bayswater, Queensway or Notting Hill Gate tube. **Lunch served** 12.30-2.30pm Mon-Fri; 1-2.30pm Sat. **Dinner served** 7.30-11pm Mon-Sat. **Main courses** £16.95-£19.50. **Credit** MC, V.
A short walk from the highly fashionable clothes and interiors stores of Westbourne Grove, Assaggi is discreetly tucked above a pub on a residential street, yet has become one of London's premier destinations for authentic Italian dining. The colourful first-floor room makes the most of its tall windows and well-kept window boxes. Young, experienced staff are uniformly dressed in black. The menu is purist, offering a brief list of simply cooked dishes using fine seasonal ingredients, and it's always entertaining listening to the manager's translation. A deliciously moist, finely chopped octopus salad with celery came served in a curled leaf of radicchio propped up with thin slices of potato. Crab salad was even simpler: a generous portion of exquisitely fresh shellfish on crisp leaves. The creamy potato purée with nutmeg

backnote is an essential side order to main courses such as roast veal chop, lamb cutlets or our special of grilled turbot dressed with lemon and capers. To finish, two long-standing favourites: creamy vanilla bavarois topped with a shot of hot espresso, and a hearty slice of flourless chocolate cake. Wine prices have edged up, but we were delighted with our bottle of Nuragus, a white wine featuring one of Sardinia's most ancient grape varieties.
Babies and children welcome: high chairs. Booking advisable. **Map 7 B6**.

Hammersmith

★ The River Café
Thames Wharf, Rainville Road, W6 9HA (7386 4200/www.rivercafe.co.uk). Hammersmith tube. **Lunch served** 12.30-3pm daily. **Dinner served** 7-9.30pm Mon-Sat. **Main courses** £23-£32. **Credit** AmEx, DC, MC, V.
High summer must be the best time to visit the River Café. Not only is it easier to get a table, but that table is likely to be in the courtyard, amid trailing raspberry bushes and squash plants. Many customers look vaguely as though they must be in the public eye, but there was no mistaking Chris Martin and Gwyneth Paltrow on our visit. The sensibly priced wine list makes other establishments look greedy, while options such as chilled Valpolicella reinforce the hipper-than-thou reputation. Service was a little confused and disorganised, with the wrong plates being brought to the table and mistakes on the bill, but this is not our usual experience. For a restaurant that attributes its premium prices to exquisite ingredients, a starter of buffalo mozzarella marinated in crème fraîche was rubbery; but accompanied by wilted chard and a lemony dressing, it exhibited a beautiful balance of flavours. Poached Dorset lobster deliciously smeared with wild fennel and chilli had a herby kick reminiscent of Indian cuisine. Desserts include a lush summer pudding, and rich ice-creams of caramel, roast almond and stracciatella, though chocolate fans should opt for the famous Nemesis, at least on a first visit.
Babies and children welcome; high chairs. Booking essential. Disabled: toilet. Dress: smart casual. Tables outdoors (15, terrace). **Map 20 C5**.

Holland Park

Edera
148 Holland Park Avenue, W11 4UE (7221 6090). Holland Park tube. **Coffee served** 10am-noon, **lunch served** noon-2.30pm, **dinner served** 6.30-11pm Mon-Sat. **Meals served** noon-10pm Sun. **Main courses** £11-£18. **Credit** AmEx, MC, V.
While traffic pounds up and down Holland Park Avenue, Edera remains a haven of urbane Sardinian peace. It's a young, minimally styled place with simple, creatively presented cooking – you can't really go wrong. Thick linen napkins add a classical touch to the otherwise austere, white-box surroundings, which are set out on multiple levels stacking up from the pavement. Antipasti are mostly delicatessen fare sold at optimistic prices (£10-£14). Such a charge may be understandable for tuna carpaccio, but mixed cured meats for £14 is taking a chance. Likewise, pasta (though reliably al dente) isn't cheap, with Sardinian spaghetti con bottarga (fish roe) at £14 and lasagne at £15. A fried cod with french beans proved that the chef has a light and sensitive touch. Thankfully, a typical set of meat dishes (veal, calf's liver, steak) remains below the £20 skyline. Desserts are as expected; tiramisu was a worthy example, while pear tart made a light and crisp finale. House wines are well priced and worth trying, with an emphasis on the Sardinian. Recommended is the house rosé – full enough almost to be a light red. Service on our most recent visit was a little sullen, but we've enjoyed happier trips in the past.
Babies and children admitted. Booking advisable dinner. Restaurant available for hire. Separate room for parties, seats 15. Tables outdoors (4, pavement). **Map 19 B5**.

Kensington

Brunello
Baglioni Hotel, 60 Hyde Park Gate, Kensington Road, SW7 5BB (7368 5700/www.baglioni hotellondon.com). Gloucester Road or High Street Kensington tube. **Breakfast served** 7-10.30am Mon-Sat; 7.30-11am Sun. **Lunch served** noon-2.30pm, **dinner served** 7-10.30pm daily. **Set lunch** £20 2 courses, £24 3 courses. **Main courses** £22-£28. **Credit** AmEx, MC, V.
Tucked inside the Baglioni hotel, Brunello couldn't be more removed from the nondescript norm of hotel restaurants. A glamorous, naughty ambience is created by black and bronze drapery, black tablecloths, and an army of black-clad staff whose service is so attentive it verges on the pampering. A cursory glance at the skinny Kensington set that populates the dining room lets you know that this is no place to gorge on huge portions of homely food. Instead, expect refined and rarefied Italian cuisine in diminutive but exquisitely executed portions, artful amuse-bouches and picture-perfect bread baskets laden with a selection of Sardinian carta da musica, focaccia and hand-shaped grissini. Even a trattoria-style dish such as gnocchi with mozzarella and tomato received the glossy treatment, turning up in the guise of thumb-sized dumplings made with aubergines. So creamy was lamb saddle with black truffle and Roman-style artichoke, it was virtually an aphrodisiac. The wine list is extensive and expensive, but even the bottom of the range yields gems like a glass of Dolcetto d'Alba, a fruity red from Piedmont, for £8. If you're looking for a romantic tête-à-tête, book the table for two near the window overlooking Kensington Gardens.
Babies and children welcome: high chairs. Booking essential Fri, Sat. Disabled: toilet (hotel). Tables outdoors (5, terrace). **Map 7 C9**.

Timo
343 Kensington High Street, W8 6NW (7603 3888/www.timorestaurant.net). High Street Kensington tube. **Lunch served** noon-2.30pm Mon-Fri. **Dinner served** 7-11pm Mon-Sat; 7-10.30pm Sun. **Main courses** £13.50-£21.95. **Credit** AmEx, JCB, MC, V.
Someone seemingly forgot to do the shopping prior to our last visit to Timo. There was no beef, no fruit juice apart from cranberry, no amuse-bouches, no specials. It was as if the shine had been taken off what is usually a highly polished operation. Some consolation came in a rich-tasting bottle of Elima Pala Monica di Sardegna 2003. The list of tempting starters included dishes such as lamb carpaccio with basil and celery, deep-fried calamari, and soup of taro and vegetables. One of the simpler pastas, tagliolini with Italian sausage and rosemary, was generously portioned, but too austere to work as a main course. Prime turbot was let down by an accompaniment of underdone potato cubes, green olives and cherry toms, but osso bucco with parmesan risotto was a lip-smacking treat, artfully presented. Chocolate bavarese had an intense flavour and was studded with crunchy chocolate pieces, but the underripe strawberry garnish was detrimental. No complaints, though, about nougat semifreddo with poached pears. The stylish, serene interior looks as good as ever. On a busy Sunday night, two parties of ten hampered the flow of the meal but the staff coped well under the circumstances.
Babies and children admitted. Booking advisable. No smoking. Restaurant available for hire. Separate room for parties, seats 18. **Map 13 A9**.

Ladbroke Grove

Essenza
210 Kensington Park Road, W11 1NR (7792 1066/www.essenza.co.uk). Ladbroke Grove tube. **Meals served** 12.30-11.30pm daily. **Main courses** £15.50-£17.50. **Set lunch** £10 2 courses. **Credit** MC, V.
Essenza is a little smarter than its sister restaurants – Mediterraneo (*see p178*) and Osteria Basilico, a hundred yards up the road – and it's also a little fishier. Fishy, that is, in a good way. The

RESTAURANTS

Feed your imagination. Indian sauces, but in an organic won't glow in the dark kind of way.

SEEDS of CHANGE

jalfrezi

© Seeds of Change 2006

small box dining room is all white plaster with brown leather bench seating; innocuously stylish artworks are dotted here and there. Although you may be rubbing elbows in the small space, be content that those elbows may belong to the rich or famous. Besides, the cooking is entirely reliable. Antipasti hold few surprises, with mozzarella, squid and scallops lining up alongside tuna tartare and beef carpaccio. Pastas also see seafood consorting with bacon or vegetable combinations, but the seafood linguine made a good fresh flavoursome opener. There are the expected meat main courses (veal and the rest), but it's the fish again that catch the eye. Char-grilled squid, chilli rocket and cherry tomatoes transported us directly to the Med, while tuna steak seared rare was delightfully accompanied by crispy fried courgettes. The wine list is a respectable Italian assembly (no great surprises). Service comes with a twinkle. In short: chic and cheerful.
Babies and children welcome: high chairs. Booking essential Fri, Sat. Tables outdoors (2, pavement). **Map 19 B3**.
For branch (Osteria Basilico) see index.

Mediterraneo
37 Kensington Park Road, W11 2EU (7792 3131/www.osteriabasilico.co.uk). Ladbroke Grove or Notting Hill Gate tube. **Lunch served** 12.30-3pm Mon-Fri; 12.30-4pm Sat; 12.30-3.45pm Sun. **Dinner served** 6.30-11.30pm Mon-Sat; 6.30-10.30pm Sun. **Main courses** £8-£16.50. **Set lunch** (Mon-Fri) £12.50 2 courses incl coffee. **Credit** AmEx, JCB, MC, V.
One day, historians of Notting Hill's culinary transformation may debate the differences between the three Italian sister restaurants on Kensington Park Road. Of Mediterraneo they will observe that it doesn't serve pizza like Osteria Basilico, and that it's not as chic as Essenza (*see p176*). In Mediterraneo the tables are as closely packed as in the other two, but the bare floorboards are offset by pretty marble tiles to waist height. The ambience is smart-casual and the cooking is as good as at the others, with a full set of antipasti and primi piatti typified by a Tuscan bean and black cabbage soup, or seafood linguine – just the rich gooey comfort food you need for a wet British summer. The list of specials deserves most attention, even if there's nothing more unusual than classics such as osso bucco. You can be sure it will be done well. The same applies to desserts, although strawberry tiramisu was more like strawberry trifle topped with two inches of mascarpone – a slimmer's nightmare and a heart surgeon's cardinal sin. Service is generally cheerful, and the Italian wine list reasonable. It is unfussy consistency that keeps Mediterraneo and its two sisters popular with fortunate locals.
Babies and children welcome: high chairs. Booking advisable; essential dinner. Tables outdoors (3, pavement). **Map 19 B3**.
For branch (Osteria Basilico) see index.

Notting Hill

The Ark
122 Palace Gardens Terrace, W8 4RT (7229 4024/www.thearkrestaurant.co.uk). Notting Hill Gate tube. **Lunch served** noon-3pm Tue-Sat. **Dinner served** 6.30-11pm Mon-Sat. **Main courses** £10-£18. **Set truffle tasting menu** (autumn only) £55 5 courses. **Credit** AmEx, MC, V.
We've had excellent meals here, but on a recent visit, things were below par. The sumptuously feminine, somewhat oriental interior – dove grey, hot pink, black and white – retains a stylish feel. However, the sheer fabric blinds seemed to need a thorough clean, and the restaurant had very few customers on Saturday night. No complaints about the basket of tangy, chewy, open-textured bread brought by a glamorous skinny waitress. A starter of pumpkin tortelloni with sage, toasted hazelnuts and butter was laughably tiny, and its sauce oversalted. Roast squid, stuffed with potatoes, olives and garlic, wasn't very tender, and the tomatoes in the accompanying salad were under-ripe. It wasn't all bad news; we enjoyed a pleasant dish of gnocchi with red onion, dolcelatte and peas,

and applauded the rich, rounded flavours of osso bucco bianco with saffron risotto. Desserts included a panettone bread and butter pudding with Cointreau, and pear tarte tatin with cinnamon ice-cream. The wine list is well written, with the Nero d'Avola blend from Sicily good value at £13.50. The ticketing system for coats is a good idea; that staff brought the wrong coats when there were only five tables dining shows sloppiness.
Babies and children admitted. Booking advisable. Restaurant available for hire. Tables outdoors (4, terrace). **Map 7 B7**.

Olympia

Cibo
3 Russell Gardens, W14 8EZ (7371 6271/2085/ www.ciborestaurant.co.uk). Shepherd's Bush tube/ Kensington (Olympia) tube/rail. **Lunch served** noon-2.30pm Mon-Fri, Sun. **Dinner served** 7-11pm Mon-Sat. **Main courses** £10.50-£23.50. **Set lunch** (Mon-Fri) £16.50 2 courses; (Sun) £18.95 2 courses, £24.95 3 courses. **Credit** AmEx, DC, JCB, MC, V.
Tucked away in what over-zealous estate agents may soon call Olympia Village, Cibo occupies a prime space on a pleasant strip. Our first impressions weren't good: bafflingly eccentric art decorates the walls; and we were presented with some of the driest olives ever encountered. The long, frequently changing menu eschews Italian simplicity in favour of a more complex fusing of ingredients, which at least makes for some interesting reading. We began with duck ravioli in

artichoke sauce (salty but perfectly pleasant), and deep-fried courgette flowers, which were over-burdened by a rich ricotta stuffing but lacked any of the promised rocket. Mains were similarly average. Osso bucco was wizened and resolutely refused to melt in the mouth, its bone so small that getting the marrow out was impossible. The accompanying 'saffron risotto' was an inedible salty sludge with no saffron in evidence at all. A plate of squid was also disappointing: rubbery and served with a side salad of dull leaves and sliced chicory. Service was friendly and relatively attentive, and the atmosphere was convivial and fun – which made it all the more sad that the food wasn't up to scratch.
Babies and children welcome: high chair. Booking advisable dinner. Dress: smart casual. Restaurant available for hire. Separate rooms for parties, seating 12 and 16. Tables outdoors (4, pavement).

South West

Barnes

Riva
169 Church Road, SW13 9HR (8748 0434). Barnes or Barnes Bridge rail/33, 209, 283 bus. **Lunch served** 12.15-2.15pm Mon-Fri, Sun. **Dinner served** 7-10.30pm Mon-Sat; 7-9pm Sun. **Main courses** £12-£21. **Credit** AmEx, MC, V.
This long-standing restaurant works well in affluent Barnes, where half the population has holiday homes in the Tuscan hills. The understated

decor – shades of green, burnt sienna and beige – is enlivened by dramatic flower arrangements and a mirror along one wall that brings light into the compact space (though it can be disconcerting if you're facing it). It's a lively spot, crammed on our midweek visit with couples, friends, families, young and old. A starter of butter-soft grilled baby squid with a generous pile of lightly braised wild herbs (tarragon, dill, parsley) was simplicity itself, and absolutely gorgeous. Gnocchi with tomato, mozzarella and basil (available as a starter or main) also highlighted premium-quality ingredients, typical of the kitchen's unfussy approach. Mains might include pan-fried calf's liver, grilled tuna steak or roast lamb; and there's always a risotto, pasta, fish and meat dish of the day. Ice-cream and alcohol feature heavily in the long dessert menu, usually to excellent effect, though our sgroppin – lemon sorbet with grappa and prosecco – would have set off a breathalyser at five paces. The all-Italian wine list is a treat, but it helps if you're knowledgeable; staff can be a little abrupt with novices, though are generally charming.
Babies and children welcome (lunch); high chairs. Booking essential dinner. Tables outdoors (3, pavement).

Chelsea

★ Daphne's

112 Draycott Avenue, SW3 3AE (7589 4257/ www.daphnes-restaurant.co.uk). South Kensington tube. **Lunch served** noon-3pm Mon-Fri; noon-3.30pm Sat; 12.30-4pm Sun. **Dinner served** 5.30-11.30pm Mon-Sat; 5.30-10.30pm Sun. **Main courses** £12.25-£22.75. **Set lunch** £18.75 2 courses, £21.75 3 courses. **Credit** AmEx, JCB, MC, V.

Don't be fooled by the old-fashioned name and Brompton Cross location: Daphne's may look like a crusty classic, but this operation is run by Caprice Holdings, who run some of London's most sought-after restaurants (including the Ivy). From a courtyard like entrance with a bar, guests turn right into the three-part dining area: first a soothing split-level section divided by a sculpted stone balustrade, then an airy, simply decorated room with glass ceiling. The rustic cooking makes the best of seasonal produce (there's always some sort of interesting mushroom or leaf on the menu) and in true Italian style the kitchen favours first-rate local (that is, British) ingredients. Service is practised, efficient and usually charming, even when you order the cheapest wine on the list – in this case an excellent Borgo Selenes (£13) from Sicily. Char-grilled lamb cutlets were dainty and delicious, served with caponata, while peas and pancetta accompanied Gressingham duck breast. Creamy cheese sauce oozed over spring vegetable cannelloni. The only slightly duff note was a dessert of mixed berries cloaked with white chocolate sauce: a spell under a high grill had resulted in bitter, charred fruit and a sickly sweet, oily topping. Perfectly gooey-centred soufflé was a much better finale to an otherwise excellent lunch.
Babies and children welcome: high chairs. Booking advisable. Separate room for parties, seats 40.
Map 14 E10.

Manicomio

85 Duke of York Square, SW3 4LY (7730 3366/ www.manicomio.co.uk). Sloane Square tube.
Deli **Open** 8am-7pm Mon-Fri; 10am-7pm Sat; 10am-6pm Sun.
Restaurant **Lunch served** noon-3pm Mon-Fri; noon-5pm Sat, Sun. **Dinner served** 6.30-10.30pm Mon-Sat; 6.30-10pm Sun. **Main courses** £8.50-£25.
Both **Credit** AmEx, JCB, MC, V.
Part of the Duke of York Square shopping centre, Manicomio benefits from plenty of outdoor seating, with glass screens and potted trees to offer protection from sun and wind. Inside there are wide expanses of open brickwork and red banquette seating, but a window table will provide attractive views of the pavement action. Owned by a company that imports and distributes fine Italian foods to the restaurant trade (and with a deli next door), the kitchen has the good sense to let the first-rate ingredients do the talking – though prices seem a little too high for what you get. A simple plate of smoked swordfish dressed with lemon had us swooning with pleasure, but the crab content of another starter was mean. Beef tagliata with rocket was another straightforward dish cooked to perfection, and we enjoyed desserts of chocolate fondant, and cherry and almond tart. The house red is OK at £14 per bottle. We finished with lovely macchiato and cappuccino, but previously good service fell off completely towards the end of the meal and a subsequent shift change made the situation worse. If you need to rush back to the office, you'll have to be proactive.
Babies and children welcome: booster seats. Booking advisable. No-smoking tables. Separate room for parties, seats 30. Tables outdoors (30, terrace). **Map 14 F11**.

Osteria dell'Arancio

383 King's Road, SW10 0LP (7349 8111/ www.osteriadellarancio.co.uk). Fulham Broadway or Sloane Square tube. **Lunch served** noon-2.30pm Mon-Fri; noon-3pm Sat; noon-4pm Sun. **Dinner served** 6-11pm Mon-Sat. **Main courses** £12-£18. **Set dinner** £40 tasting menu. **Credit** MC, V.
Just off the squiggle of Kings Road at World's End, Osteria dell'Arancio sits opposite a council housing estate, but still attracts well-heeled ladies who come to lunch and enjoy a flirt with the macho-Italiano staff. The decor is girly rustic, all pastels and florals with colourful chintz plates and decoupage. Outside are a few pavement tables with metal garden chairs far enough away from the traffic to be pleasant. Staff were welcoming, but otherwise offhand and distracted – we ordered the described asparagus risotto of the day to find it arrived made of peas and heavily laden with saffron. A bowl of pappardelle with courgettes and parma ham was fine, but nothing you could not have made at home. Better were starters, presented in a highly contrived fashion. Crunchy crudités came in an iced bowl with choice of tasty dips, while the Choice platter was a large square glass plate of buffalo mozzarella, anchovies, tomatoes, rocket and bruschetta. The chef apparently hails from the Marche, but we left with the impression that this is a modern trattoria for carefree meals rather than a temple of regional cooking.
Babies and children welcome: high chairs. No-smoking tables. Separate room for parties, seats 30. Tables outdoors (14, terrace).
Map 14 D12.

Fulham

La Famiglia

7 Langton Street, SW10 0JL (7351 0761/7352 6095/www.lafamiglia.co.uk). Sloane Square tube then 11, 22 bus/31 bus. **Lunch served** noon-2.45pm, **dinner served** 7-11.30pm daily. **Main courses** £8.50-£22.50. **Cover** £1.75. **Minimum** £18.50 dinner. **Credit** AmEx, DC, JCB, MC, V.
Feeling nostalgic for that Italian holiday? Head to this old-style restaurant and you'll be whisked from Fulham to Tuscany before you can say 'Chianti'. La Famiglia is the real thing. Its menu incorporates a classic range of pastas and a discerning selection

Marco Polo. See p181.

of meat and fish dishes. It's these that many of the locals in the rustic, crowded garden choose – and understandably so. Our main courses of sautéed liver and grilled sea bass were delicate and uncomplicated. Side dishes are obviously popular too – particularly the plates of crisp and delicious deep-fried zucchini visible everywhere. Not everything is as successful. A T-bone steak was tough and lukewarm; fried broccoli with garlic arrived drowned in oil; a mozzarella and tomato salad was let down by three mean slices of watery tomatos. Desserts, including profiteroles and chocolate mousse, proved better, exhibiting authentic Italian (sweet, nutty and alcoholic) traits. Less charming was the service, from staff keen to capitalise on the balmy weather by regaining our table as quickly as possible. We complied, feeling like we often do on holiday: slightly exploited by the establishment, a little disappointed with the food, yet just about won over by the ambience. *Babies and children welcome: high chairs. Booking advisable dinner and Sun. Tables outdoors (30, garden).* **Map 13 C13**.

Putney

★ Enoteca Turi

28 Putney High Street, SW15 1SQ (8785 4449/ www.enotecaturi.com). Putney Bridge tube/ Putney rail/14, 74, 220, 270 bus. **Lunch served** noon-2.30pm, **dinner served** 7-11pm Mon-Sat. **Main courses** £10.50-£17. **Set lunch** £13.50 2 courses, £16.50 3 courses. **Credit** AmEx, DC, MC, V.
This is one of the few restaurants in London where you can dine and wine the real Italian way – especially the wine bit. Owner Giuseppe Turi's 300 hand-picked bins should satisfy the most fastidious oenophile. At 50 pages the drinks list is rather daunting, but the menu helpfully suggests wines that are suitable for every listed dish, and there's also a small selection of wines by the glass. Although the food menu cannot rival the length of the wine list, it bears the same fastidiousness. Seasonal ingredients are chosen for dishes that are imaginative, yet traditional, and beautifully presented. On our visit, food was clearly inspired by southern Italy, especially minchiareddi, a type of barley pasta from Apulia, dressed with fresh tomato and pungent Sicilian salted ricotta. The chicken with smoked mozzarella-filled aubergine parcels was another appealing dish with a southern twist, as was a starter of octopus salad with colfiorito beans and samphire. The wooden-

floored interior is light and bright. As we left, we couldn't help feeling somewhat jealous of Putneyites for having such a gem in their midst. *Babies and children admitted. Booking advisable. Disabled: toilet. No smoking. Separate room for parties, seats 30.*

Marco Polo NEW
2006 RUNNER-UP BEST FAMILY RESTAURANT
6-7 Riverside Quarter, Eastfields Avenue, SW18 1LP (8874 6800). East Putney tube. **Meals served** noon-11pm Mon-Sat; noon-10pm Sun. **Main courses** £11.95-£16.95. **Set lunch** £8.95 2 courses, £9.95 3 courses. **Credit** MC, V.
The frenzied poncing up of every inch of riverside Wandsworth has resulted in myriad apartment developments – and this modish Italian restaurant on Point Pleasant. There's a useful patch of greensward beside the numerous outdoor tables where parents can safely play with their children away from speeding 4X4s (they're all parked on the single yellows inland). Inside, the restaurant is furnished swishly in dark wood, glass and chrome, with a trendy bar. A grown-up calf's liver on crushed new potatoes was adeptly pink; salmon tagliatelle was creamy, with large lumps of fish, and our comforting little filler of crespolini (pancakes with spinach and ricotta) was nicely seasoned. A swordfish steak was grilled to just-done, with a Sicilian-style dressing of salmoriglio, which is like a light salsa verde, consisting mostly of olive oil, lemon, parsley and mint. Almost all the puddings had been snapped up by early lunchers, but the fudgy profiteroles and sticky toffee pudding assuaged the need for something sweet. A Sunday lunchtime was exceedingly popular with middle-class family groups. The waiters were so harried by the rush they twice forgot our order and their manners – no apologies were forthcoming. *Babies and children welcome: high chairs. Booking advisable. Disabled: toilet. No-smoking tables. Separate room for parties, seats 30. Tables outdoors (60, riverside terrace).*

Wandsworth

Amici NEW
35 Bellevue Road, SW17 7EF (8672 5888/ www.amiciitalian.co.uk). Wandsworth Common rail/319 bus. **Lunch served** 11am-3pm Mon-Fri; 11am-4pm Sat, Sun. **Dinner served** 6-10.30pm daily. **Main courses** £8.50-£15. **Credit** AmEx, MC, V.
The faltering Pomino on Wandsworth Common has been given a boost by a name-change, and by

employing a 'name' chef-consultant to give it improved credibility. The new consultant is prolific food writer Valentina Harris, author of many books on Italian cookery including *100 Perfect Risottos*. However, the mushroom risotto we tried was anything but perfect; it was a bowl of soupy rice that had the right flavours but completely the wrong texture. Risotto apart, our other dishes were made well. Buffalo mozzarella was of excellent quality, good enough to present simply with some cooked beetroot and olive oil. Caponata was near-perfect, served as an accompaniment to swordfish. Torta di mele (Italian apple cake) was a textbook-worthy version, though it arrived with walnut and maple-syrup ice-cream. Many of the desserts shared this Disney-like take on Italian food, more Italian-American than truly Italian. However, there's much else to recommend Amici. It's still a good-looking place – dark wood mixed with an orange and yellow colour scheme – with a very appealing bar area, and the staff are keen to please. *Babies and children welcome: children's menu; crayons; high chairs. Booking advisable. Disabled: toilet. No smoking. Tables outdoors (12, pavement).*

South

Battersea

Osteria Antica Bologna
23 Northcote Road, SW11 1NG (7978 4771/ www.osteria.co.uk). Clapham Junction rail/35, 37, 319 bus. **Lunch served** noon-3pm Mon-Fri. **Dinner served** 6-11pm Mon-Thur; 6-11.30pm Fri. **Meals served** noon-11.30pm Sat; noon-10.30pm Sun. **Main courses** £8.50-£16.90. **Set lunch** (Mon-Sat) £10.50 2 courses, £13 3 courses. **Cover** 90p. **Credit** AmEx, MC, V.
OAB was one of the first of the smarter dining places to colonise Northcote Road, and it continues to thrive despite vigorous competition. There's invariably a crowd packing the benches in the dark, wood-panelled, cellar-like room, filling it with the requisite happy Italian sounds. The youthful, busy and engaged staff also contribute the right atmosphere. While the interior hasn't changed in about 15 years, the cuisine has – from ambitious, regional Italian specialities to a more conventional trattoria menu, albeit one with a few surprises. Generally, you're better off sticking to the mainstream. A starter of (superb) mozzarella with thinly sliced courgette and a thick, sticky balsamic dressing was very pleasantly done, but an ostrich steak was bland and overwhelmed by an avalanche of celery. Better was a salad of spinach, peppers, pine nuts and goat's cheese: only to be followed by a drab slice of lime and passionfruit tart. In short: variable. On warm days you can occupy one of the few outdoor pavement tables that lurk behind a low, plant-filled wall. *Babies and children admitted. Booking essential dinner Fri, Sat. Restaurant available for hire. Tables outdoors (6, pavement).* **Map 21 C4**.

Clapham

Mooli NEW
36A Old Town, SW4 0LB (7627 1166/ www.moolirestaurant.com). Clapham Common tube. **Lunch served** noon-3pm, **dinner served** 6.30-11pm Mon-Fri. **Tea served** 3-6pm Mon-Sat. **Meals served** noon-11pm Sat; 1-11pm Sun. **Main courses** £12.95-£14.50. **Set buffet lunch** (1-4pm Sun) £14.50. **Credit** MC, V.
Bedecked with comfy cushions and painted in crème brûlée hues, Mooli borrows from the current culinary scene in Italy, where a younger generation of restaurateurs is busily reinventing and rejuvenating the traditional neighbourhood trattoria. These pioneers are forsaking allegiances to regional food in favour of dishes inspired by the daily availability of produce from the local market – hence Mooli's eclectic menu, which changes frequently and incorporates flavours from every corner of Italy. A risotto dish of the day featured radicchio, its mild bitterness complemented by the savoury tang of gorgonzola cheese. Among the pasta dishes, the southern-inspired fusilli with

La Collina. See p183.

broccoli and sausage was pleasantly scented with fennel. In contrast, caponata, the traditional Sicilian vegetable stew, lacked its typical vinegary zest and ended up tasting like a bland ratatouille. Much better were the 'pockets' of veal stuffed with sautéed aubergines and rich, pungent taleggio cheese from Lombardy. The addition of a pâtisserie at the rear of the property (not open to the public) has greatly improved the range of desserts, which also includes own-made gelatis and sorbets. As a nod to the latest trend sweeping through London, afternoon tea is also now served from 3pm, while the focus shifts to cocktails from 5pm to 8pm.

Babies and children welcome: high chairs. Booking advisable. No smoking. **Map 22 A1.**

South East
Bermondsey

Arancia
52 Southwark Park Road, SE16 3RS (7394 1751/www.arancia-uk.co.uk). Bermondsey tube/ Elephant & Castle tube/rail then 1, 53 bus/South Bermondsey rail. **Lunch served** 12.30-2.30pm, **dinner served** 7-11pm Tue-Sat. **Main courses** £9-£10.50. **Set lunch** £7.50 2 courses, £10.50 3 courses. **Credit** AmEx, MC, V.

Incongruously nestled between housing estates, this quirky gem uses fresh ingredients to create intelligent flavour combinations after an Italian fashion. We had to wait 30 minutes to order (there was just one server in a busy dining room). It didn't matter: the orange walls, wooden floors, exposed brick and flickering candles created an aura of calm in which we were quite content to sip our wine, eat olives and preserved lemons, and watch the world roll by outside. Our line-up of dishes included rosemary-stuffed sardines; delicate lasagne with own-made pasta and asparagus; belly pork with borlotti beans; and beautifully cooked lamb. Desserts are excellent, and at these prices you'd be silly not to order one. The semifreddo is popular for good reason; it provided a rich end to a lovely meal. Baked ricotta cheesecake with lemon peel was also superb. The all-Italian wine list isn't fancy, but hits the right tone with the food. Arancia is the ideal inexpensive neighbourhood stalwart. It serves food of a higher quality and greater finesse than many places charging twice the price.

Babies and children welcome: high chair. Booking advisable evenings. Separate room for parties, seats 8.

Tower Bridge

Cantina del Ponte
Butlers Wharf Building, 36C Shad Thames, SE1 2YE (7403 5403/www.conran.com). Tower Hill tube/Tower Gateway DLR/London Bridge tube/rail/47, 78 bus. **Lunch served** noon-3pm daily. **Dinner served** 6-11pm Mon-Sat; 6-10pm Sun. **Main courses** £9.50-£16. **Credit** AmEx, DC, JCB, MC, V.

Cantina del Ponte's combination of rustic terracotta decor and heated canopy may easily fool diners into thinking they are enjoying a balmy Mediterranean evening on drizzly, windswept Butlers Wharf. The cooking, however, is more Italianate than Italian. We were looking forward to the panzanella: a delicious *cucina povera* dish made with stale Tuscan bread soaked in water and mixed with ripe tomatoes, herbs and olive oil. What turned up was a plate of designer lettuce leaves, a couple of cherry tomatoes and a few soggy focaccia cubes – 'bread salad' indeed, but calling it panzanella was a bit cheeky, especially at £5.50. Potato gnocchi with basil pesto and pecorino cheese was much closer to the real thing, but inauthentically overwhelmed by a heavy-handed use of the sauce. Much better was roast guinea-fowl breast with grilled fennel, which was delectably juicy. However, more disappointment followed with orange and grappa panna cotta, which tasted little of either flavour. The close-up view of Tower Bridge is truly breathtaking, but not matched by the mediocre and pricey dining experience at this Conran outpost.

Babies and children welcome: children's portions; high chairs. Booking advisable. Dress: smart casual. Restaurant available for hire. Tables outdoors (20, terrace). Takeaway service (pizza only, noon-3pm, 6-10pm daily). **Map 12 S8.**

★ Tentazioni
2 Mill Street, SE1 2BD (7237 1100/ www.tentazioni.co.uk). Bermondsey tube/London Bridge tube/rail. **Lunch served** noon-2.45pm Tue-Fri. **Dinner served** 7-10.45pm Mon-Sat. **Main courses** £17-£20. **Set dinner** £29 4 courses, £38 tasting menu (£60 incl wine). **Credit** AmEx, MC, V.

Hidden in a quiet street near Tower Bridge, Tentazioni is an intimate Italian treat. Sophisticated but classical dishes, changed monthly by the chef-owner, are matched with a modern, European interior and perfectly charming (and subtly flirtatious) staff. Among an appealing selection of starters, we chose cod and salmon carpaccio marinated with chilli and served with the most refreshing and light Tagiasca olive jelly imaginable. Own-made fettuccine with white meat ragù, served with a courgette flower, was beautifully executed if a bit too hearty a portion for a starter. To follow, roasted quail over dried porcini mushroom risotto was delicate, while pan-fried lobster served with saffron-scented pasta ribbons and rocket was divine. The menu offers highly appealing prix fixe options, and has an impressive separate menu for vegetarians. Barring the odd champagne, the wine list is, not surprisingly, all Italian; while not extensive, it is diverse and well chosen. Of particular interest are the often under-represented whites from Trentino, and Le Marche reds. A striking black and white chocolate mousse with pistachio sauce provided the perfect end to a decadent meal.

Babies and children admitted. Booking advisable dinner Fri, Sat. Restaurant available for hire. Separate room for parties, seats 24. **Map 12 S9.**

East
Shoreditch

Fifteen
15 Westland Place, N1 7LP (0871 330 1515/ www.fifteenrestaurant.com). Old Street tube/ rail.
Trattoria **Breakfast served** 7.30-11am Mon-Sat; 9-11am Sun. **Lunch served** noon-3pm Mon-Sat; noon-3.30pm Sun. **Dinner served** 6-10pm Mon-Sat. **Main courses** £11-£18.
Restaurant **Lunch served** noon-2.30pm, **dinner served** 6.30-9.30pm daily. **Main courses** £12-£24. **Set meal** £50-£60 tasting menu.
Both **Credit** AmEx, JCB, MC, V.

Now joined by offshoots in Amsterdam and Cornwall, and with more planned, Fifteen continues as promised in founder Jamie Oliver's ground-breaking TV series: to provide young disadvantaged people with an opportunity to learn the restaurant trade. Tourists from Japan and Germany were making their pilgrimages on our visit. There have been some tweaks in the decor, such as smaller chairs that work better in the upstairs trattoria and bar space. Antipasto ingredients are displayed atop the open kitchen's counter; strings of dried chillies and garlic hang from ceiling racks. Apart from one antipasto plate, starters focus on pasta and rice. There was a choice of accompaniments to 'the lightest potato gnocchi', but our gorgonzola version arrived without the advertised toasted walnuts. Though piled with lovely seafood, the oversized saffron-flavoured risotto was dry and chewy. Mains of pan-fried monkfish with roast fennel and burstingly ripe Isle of Wight tomatoes, and spatchcocked poussin, were delicious yet oversalted. Desserts of mint panna cotta, and drab-looking cakes such as orange and poppyseed, were wholly untempting. The brief Italian wine list offers a few choice bottles below £25, but the entry point is a too-high £20. For such a charitable set-up, the mostly efficient service was surprisingly Oxbridge.

Babies and children welcome: high chairs. Booking essential. Disabled: toilet (trattoria). Dress: smart casual. No smoking. **Map 6 Q3.**

North
Camden Town & Chalk Farm

★ La Collina NEW
2006 RUNNER-UP BEST NEW RESTAURANT
17 Princess Road, NW1 8JR (7483 0192). Camden Town or Chalk Farm tube. **Lunch served** noon-3pm Fri-Sun. **Dinner served** 6.30-11pm daily. **Set meal** £17.50 2 courses, £22.50 3 courses. **Credit** MC, V.

La Collina is a rather small restaurant on two floors, both of which have their pluses – the ground floor is light and airy, but the basement means you can watch the kitchen in action; it's all a bit cramped, though, with tables very close together. The main attraction is the menu of authentic Italian dishes. These are northern Italian, with an emphasis on Piedmont. Grilled baby squid with anchovy sauce was a pretty-looking if surprisingly unpunchy starter; more satisfying was gnocchetti neri (black gnocchi) with baby langoustine, mussels and fresh tomato. From a choice that included roast rabbit with olives and pine kernels, and risotto made with prawns and courgette flowers, grilled sea bream served with a mixed green salad was easily the best main – simple, but bursting with flavour. If you still have room for pudding, try bonet: a dessert made with cocoa and amaretti biscuits that's a good example of Piedmontese pâtisserie. The short, all-Italian wine list is a less vital read than the menu. Staff are unobtrusive but charming. Prices are very reasonable for the quality of the food – though there are more supplements than is ideal, and (admittedly fabulous) bread and olives incur a charge of £1.50.

Babies and children welcome: high chair. Booking advisable. No-smoking tables. Separate room for parties, seats 16. Tables outdoors (14, garden). **Map 27 B2.**

Crouch End

Florians
4 Topsfield Parade, Middle Lane, N8 8PR (8348 8348). Finsbury Park tube/rail then W7 bus/91 bus.
Wine bar **Open/meals served** noon-11pm Mon-Fri; 11am-11pm Sat; 11am-10.30pm Sun. **Main courses** £6.50-£7.50. **Set meal** £6.75 2 courses.
Restaurant **Lunch served** noon-3pm daily. **Dinner served** 7-11pm Mon-Sat; 7-10.30pm Sun. **Main courses** £9-£17.50.
Both **Credit** MC, V.

A charming, reliable local restaurant tucked behind an old-fashioned but popular wine bar of the same name. In the main restaurant (which has a tiny courtyard dining area through the rear glass doors), the decor is cool blue, white and blond wood, with a changing display of local artists' work. The partially open kitchen is shielded by cleverly placed screens of deep coral. On our visit the menu was fashionably chock-a-block with pulses. Cannellini beans featured in a starter with octopus salad, as well as in a special main course of char-grilled tuna with rocket, leeks and tomatoes. Chickpea and sesame salad accompanied a spanking-fresh cod with herb crust. Pastas, whether served as a starter or main course, are generously portioned – maybe too much, as we struggled to finish our mains. So we had no room, unfortunately, for the blackboard desserts such as hot chocolate fondant, strawberry and balsamic mousse, and lemon polenta cake with mascarpone and acacia honey. Some of the wines are available by the small or large glass, and there are 50cl and half-bottles on the list; the cheaper end offers reasonable quality. Our fired-up waitress was so adept at enticing us to buy the more expensive bottles she could have auditioned for *The Apprentice*.

Babies and children welcome: high chairs. Booking advisable dinner. Separate rooms for parties, seats 15 and 40. Tables outdoors (8, patio).

RESTAURANTS

Islington

Casale Franco

Rear of 134-137 Upper Street, N1 1QP (7226 8994). Angel tube/Highbury & Islington tube/ rail. **Lunch served** noon-2.30pm Sat. **Dinner served** 6-11.30pm Tue-Sat. **Meals served** noon-10pm Sun. **Main courses** £8.50-£17.50. **Cover** £1. **Credit** AmEx, JCB, MC, V.

Tucked down an alleyway that opens out to a Citroën forecourt by day and the Casale Franco courtyard by night, this modern Italian restaurant serves food that hits all the right spots. A short menu and handful of specials belie the variety to be had; closer inspection revealed a thoughtful and well-balanced menu that makes choice pleasantly difficult. First up is a small range of pastas and pizzas that sound mouth-wateringly good; handmade tagliatelle with fresh asparagus proved to be rich in substance and flavour. Starters too offer a delightful choice, from scallops and razor clams with Sardinian couscous, to giant gamberoni or more traditional dishes like calamares and antipasto. But it's the mains selection that makes choosing what to eat here really hard: the perfectly succulent porchetta or the beautifully presented rack of lamb in a herb crust? The simple cracked crab, the slab-like filetto steak, or the more adventurous red snapper with samphire and baby aubergines? The latter two turned out to be as good as the starters, and were served in a congenial atmosphere by attentive and pleasant staff.
No-smoking tables. Restaurant available for hire (Mon-Thur, Sun). Separate room for parties, seats 50. Tables outdoors (32, courtyard). **Map 5 O1.**

Metrogusto

13 Theberton Street, N1 0QY (7226 9400/ www.metrogusto.co.uk). Angel tube. **Lunch served** noon-2.30pm Mon-Thur; 6.30-11pm Fri, Sat. **Main courses** £11.50-£17.50. **Credit** AmEx, JCB, MC, V.

A short walk from the high-profile sites of Upper Street, Metrogusto is a well-established local crammed with chunky wooden furniture and unusual paintings. It has a loyal following – surprising, perhaps, given that the cooking is as bold and inventive as the large-scale pictures lining the walls, but results are mixed. Take the liquorice sauce that accompanied pepper-crusted tuna steak, for example. On its own it had a flavour reminiscent of herbal cough mixture, but it worked well with the rich, juicy fish and crunchy pungent peppercorns. Crumbed veal suffered from a lack of technique: it was greasy, and the accompanying leeks almost raw. No complaints about our pasta starters, however. Green parcels of thyme and ricotta were deliciously comforting, and spaghetti with tuna, tomatoes and courgette was a well-executed, classic combo. There was also an intriguing venison risotto on offer. To finish, voluptuous chocolate fondant came with berry sauce and fine mint ice-cream. Salento Rosso San Marzano at £13.50 is one of many reasonably priced wines on the list. Service hits a good balance between formal and casual, though we experienced long waits between courses.
Babies and children welcome: high chairs. Booking advisable; essential weekends. No smoking. Separate room for parties, seats 24. Tables outdoors (4, pavement). **Map 5 O1.**

Kentish Town

Pane Vino NEW

323 Kentish Town Road, NW5 2TJ (7267 3879). Kentish Town tube/rail. **Lunch served** noon-3pm Mon-Sat. **Dinner served** 6.30-11pm daily. **Main courses** £10.80-£16.90. **Credit** AmEx, MC, V.

This is the sort of reliable, fairly priced trattoria most people would like to have near home, but something of an endangered species in London. A Sardinian influence is revealed in ingredients such as bottarga, malloredus and Vernaccia, but this is foremost a friendly neighbourhood joint that has the sense to list 11 pizzas and offer to make other varieties if customers prefer. Monica de Sardegna and Prosecco are served by the glass; Graspello white and red house wines come by the 500ml carafe. Antipasto Sardo featured piles of marinated semi-dried tomatoes, tiny, oily, preserved mushrooms, aubergine, olives, pecorino, bottarga and very good salami on crisp, rosemary-studded flatbread. Lemony ricotta gnocchi were hand-cut, daubed with plenty of tomato and aubergine sauce and topped with crunchy deep-fried onions. This, like our other pasta main of linguine with grainy bottarga and rich butter sauce, were generously portioned. Striped fabric banquettes and classic rustic chairs surround the cramped, linen-covered tables. On busy nights, when it can be extremely noisy, this is not a place to linger. On our visit, however, the restaurant was fairly quiet and the contented customers and easy-going staff took the opportunity to chat.
Babies and children admitted. No-smoking tables. Tables outdoors (3, pavement). Takeaway service. **Map 26 B5.**

North West

Golders Green

Philpott's Mezzaluna

424 Finchley Road, NW2 2HY (7794 0455/ www.philpotts-mezzaluna.com). Golders Green tube. **Lunch served** noon-2.30pm Tue-Fri; noon-3pm Sun. **Dinner served** 7-11pm Tue-Sun. **Set lunch** £12 1 course, £17 2 courses, £20 3 courses, £25 4 courses. **Set dinner** £19.50 1 course, £24.50 2 courses, £29.50 3 courses, £34.50 4 courses, £39.50 5 courses. **Credit** MC, V.

Philpott's Mezzaluna attracts a loyal clientele of monied locals, from sophisticated young families to mature groups of friends. The menu has a strong Italian foundation, but doesn't hesitate to incorporate other influences and proffers occasional wild cards such as black cod with caramelised pineapple salsa. At £24.50 for two courses at dinner, this place isn't cheap; the value increases substantially if you opt for three or four courses, yet huge portions make it hard to manage that much. A main course of roast lamb came with *seven* thick slices of fatty meat. Still, it tasted good, and we enjoyed the penne with mushrooms and tarragon, and foie gras ravioli with peas. Typical desserts include marsala semifreddo and mango brûlée. Exploring the wine list is fun, thanks to occasional limited offers and discounts (one wine was substantially reduced to £100 on our visit). The classy Italian barman brought our bottle of wine and offered us a taste even though we'd only ordered a glass. Staff are on the whole charming and efficient, but the kitchen is prone to tardiness, and the waits can seem interminable when the room is stuffy, as it often is in warm weather.
Babies and children welcome: high chairs. Booking advisable dinner Sat. Restaurant available for hire. Tables outdoors (3, terrace).

Maida Vale

Green Olive

5 Warwick Place, W9 2PX (7289 2469). Warwick Avenue tube/6 bus. **Lunch served** noon-2.30pm Mon-Fri. **Dinner served** 6.30-10.30pm Mon-Fri; 6.30-11pm Sat. **Main courses** £13-£15.50. **Credit** AmEx, JCB, MC, V.

Tucked into a mews in Little Venice, small and so discreet you scarcely see it until you're at the door, the Green Olive is evidently a favourite 'place around the corner' for denizens of this affluent neighbourhood. Decor is understated-modern, with artworks (all for sale) around the walls. Service is smart, eager and sporadically uncoordinated. The modern Italian cuisine is also very prettily presented, although a few of the ingredients could be better. Some very delicate parma ham came with rather unripe melon; and in a dish of scallops and prawns with cherry tomatoes and sweet peppers, the sauce was lovely, smooth and subtle, but the seafood lacked flavour. Of our mains, pan-fried red snapper with caramelised endive, grapes and vernaccia sauce was an inventive combination that would have come alive more if the fish had been better sourced. In the day's pasta special, pappardelle with asparagus and prawns, fine fresh summer veg were paired with the same kind of dullish prawns as in the starter. Desserts are enjoyably indulgent, and the wine list offers a quality Italian range at pretty high prices. This is probably a nice restaurant to have in your locality, but not one worth a journey.
Babies and children admitted. Booking advisable. Restaurant available for hire. Separate room for parties, seats 20. **Map 1 C4.**

St John's Wood

Rosmarino

1 Blenheim Terrace, NW8 0EH (7328 5014). St John's Wood tube. **Lunch served** noon-2.30pm Mon-Fri; noon-3pm Sat, Sun. **Dinner served** 7-10.30pm Mon-Thur; 7-11pm Fri, Sat; 7-10pm Sun. **Main courses** £12.50-£17.50. **Credit** AmEx, JCB, MC, V.

This upmarket local restaurant is mercifully free of the puns that could have littered its menu. We found rosemary only in the intense ice-cream that added a sophisticated flourish to sigh-inducing tortino al cioccolata. Prime seating is in the serene conservatory area of wood and glass that makes the most of the leafy exterior, though all tables benefit from linen cloths, capacious glasses and elegant cutlery. The menu incorporates plenty of creativity, but also classics such as veal scaloppini and crostata di mele. Our seafood risotto was luscious with chunky pieces of fish and shellfish, but tuna was let down by overzealous coating of pungent pink peppercorns – discomforting eaten in quantity. Wines by the glass include a pleasing Rosso Piceno from the Marche at £4.50. Formally attired waiters were sweetly attentive. The crowd at this rather tranquil place (we've rarely seen it packed) tends to comprise Japanese expat families, groups of adult friends who live locally, and extended families with teenagers who almost look as though they'd rather be in a Pizza Express – almost, but not quite.
Babies and children welcome: high chairs. Booking advisable dinner Thur-Sun. Restaurant available for hire. Separate room for parties, seats 20. Tables outdoors (7, terrace). **Map 1 C2.**

Outer London

Twickenham, Middlesex

A Cena

418 Richmond Road, Twickenham, Middx TW1 2EB (8288 0108). Richmond tube/rail. **Lunch served** noon-3pm Tue-Sun. **Dinner served** 7-10.30pm Tue-Sat. **Main courses** £13.75-£19. **Set lunch** (Sun) £22 3 courses. **Credit** AmEx, MC, V.

A Cena's handsome, woody interior off the busy Richmond Road makes for a relaxed venue with the atmosphere of a bistro or wine bar. But cooking is more serious. Set Sunday lunch, with dishes selected from the longer dinner menu, is well worth sampling and reasonably priced. Octopus chopped with potatoes was a weighty but gorgeous starter, while deep-fried courgettes were light and crunchy. Surprisingly, there was only one pasta dish: a rich and reduced composition of rigatoni, balsamic, tomato and pecorino cheese. Although this was included among main courses, it would have made a better starter. There's some repetition across the menu, notably rocket, bruschetta and olive oil mash. However, guinea fowl, fried plaice and roast pork loin were all good homely dishes. Confirmation that the cooking is on the heavy side came with a chocolate mousse cake that was richer than the Sultan of Brunei. An almond meringue torte with strawberries and thick cream was scarcely more cardio-friendly – but that isn't necessarily a criticism. Service was charming and amenable from start to finish, helping us navigate a well-proportioned wine list of which staff are justly proud.
Babies and children welcome: high chairs. Booking advisable. Restaurant available for hire.

Japanese

Confucius would approve of the way Japanese restaurants know their place in London's pecking order. The rarefied top end of the ladder remains the preserve of flash-your-cash **Nobu** (London now has three, including Nobu Berkeley Street and Ubon) and kaiseki specialist **Umu** (the highest prices in the capital), with **Zuma**, **Roka** and **Tsunami** a rung or two below. Hailing from Moscow, newcomer **Yakitoria** could have been a contender with its sleek, chic looks (it was nominated for Best Design in the 2006 Time Out Eating & Drinking Awards), but hasn't quite made the major league. Meanwhile, the budget brigade cheerfully covers the mass market and continues to multiply – some setting a fine example in new territory, such as **Tosa** with its tapas approach in Hammersmith. The bottom line is: if you know what you want and how much you want to pay, you're sure to find it here.

Central

City

Moshi Moshi Sushi
24 Upper Level, Liverpool Street Station, EC2M 7QH (7247 3227/www.moshimoshi.co.uk). Liverpool Street tube/rail. **Meals served** 11.30am-10pm Mon-Fri. **Dishes** £1.70-£3.50. **Main courses** £8-£11. **Credit** MC, V.
Tucked down a corridor behind a Marks & Spencer food shop, Moshi Moshi offers kaiten-zushi that's well above average, plus a menu listing a range of izakaya-style dishes. Customers sit at the counter on high dark stools beneath a big rustic fish painting on washi (handmade paper), or in swooping wooden pods overlooking the platforms of the mainline station, with a playful mini-Ryoanji (Zen garden) of rocks and sand underfoot. As in other conveyor-belt joints, temaki sushi is often a good bet here as it's made freshly to order. The temaki set – a trio of eel, salmon-skin-and-avocado, and fresh crab handrolls – were spankingly fresh and included rice of just the right temperature and moistness. Miso soup and pickles were well flavoured, while the oyako-donburi (chicken pieces, egg and carrots on rice) was full of earthy tastes for a cold day. Green-tea crème brûlée was a mistake; stick to fruit if you need a dessert. An unexpectedly pleasant experience in what amounts to a railway station diner.
Babies and children admitted. Disabled: toilet. No smoking. Takeaway service; delivery service. Vegetarian menu. **Map 12 R5.**
For branches see index.

Clerkenwell & Farringdon

Saki NEW
4 West Smithfield, EC1A 9JX (7489 7033/ www.saki-food.com). Barbican tube/Farringdon tube/rail.
Bar **Open** 6-11pm Mon-Wed; 6pm-midnight Thur-Sat.
Deli **Open** noon-7.30pm Mon-Fri.
Restaurant **Lunch served** noon-2.30pm, **tea served** 2.30-6pm Mon-Fri. **Dinner served** 6-10.30pm Mon-Sat. **Main courses** £8.50-£19.90. **Set lunch** £7.90-£25. **Set dinner** £38-£55.
All **Credit** JCB, MC, V.
The drinks quotient of the menu is significant at this low-ceilinged basement bar and restaurant. Even in the dining area there's a choice of 17 sakés and four shochus, not to mention the extensive cocktail list in the next-door bar. The centre of the dining room is dominated by a shared square table of black marble, its centre filled by white stalagmites rising out of a gravelled well. Beaming staff explained the 'concept' to us: there are tapas-sized portions listed under 'kobachi', then larger dishes arranged into meaningless gimmicky categories such as 'carbo' (as in -hydrate). We couldn't fault our fresh seafood – the uni was so fresh it lacked the pungency many people dislike. Some dishes had an Ascot-hat quality: soft-shell crab had been deep-fried in tempura batter before being up-ended skywards. Western fusion influences creep into many dishes, such as the addition of caperberries in a pork belly and potato casserole. Saki's menu isn't cutting edge (unlike at Nobu or Zuma), but the dishes are unconventional by Japanese standards.
Babies and children admitted. Booking advisable. Disabled: lift; toilet. No smoking. Separate room for parties, seats 12. Takeaway service. Vegetarian menu. **Map 11 O5.**

Covent Garden

Hazuki
43 Chandos Place, WC2N 4HS (7240 2530/ www.hazukilondon.co.uk). Charing Cross tube/rail. **Lunch served** noon-2.30pm Mon-Fri; 12.30-3pm Sat. **Dinner served** 5-10.30pm Mon-Sat; 5-9.30pm Sun. **Main courses** £5.50-£28. **Set meal** £16-£45. **Credit** AmEx, MC, V.
Despite its diminutive stature, Hazuki has a broad-ranging menu. Beginners might want to play safe with one of six set menus, while aficionados will find the specials at the front of the menu too intriguing to pass up. Among these are Japanese-style street snacks such as tuna and tofu balls served with tare on a bamboo skewer, and scallop-shaped pieces of yam topped with light and dark miso, also on little skewers. Horse mackerel sushi came minced in a bowl with grated ginger and fine slivers of dried seaweed. Our waitress looked concerned when we ordered ika natto; the fermented soy beans (served here with squid) are something of an acquired taste – but it's a taste definitely worth acquiring. Nigiri sushi and sashimi, including tender yellowtail, were good if not exemplary. As well as saké and wine, there's a list of shochu cocktails and a (highly recommended) shiso-infused shochu that makes a great foil to this style of food.
Babies and children admitted. Booking advisable; essential dinner. No-smoking tables. Separate room for parties, seats 25. Takeaway service; delivery service (within 2-mile radius). **Map 18 L7.**

Fitzrovia

★ Roka
37 Charlotte Street, W1T 1RR (7580 6464/ www.rokarestaurant.com). Goodge Street or Tottenham Court Road tube.
Bar **Open** 6pm-midnight Mon, Sat, Sun; noon-midnight Tue-Fri.
Restaurant **Meals served** noon-11pm Mon-Fri; 12.30-11pm Sat; 12.30-10.30pm Sun. **Main courses** £3.60-£21.
Both **Credit** AmEx, DC, MC, V.
Roka rocks. What started life as baby Zuma has grown into a confident, buzzy, space serving some of the best modern Japanese food in London. The mood is more casual and easy-going than at Zuma (*see p187*), mixing ten-year-old heiresses with trainer chopsticks, skimpy little designer-clad skinny binnies and bonus-amplified brokers doing lines of soft-shell crab maki. The focus of the restaurant is the central grill kitchen where Kiwi head chef Nic Watts and his team tend the coals surrounded by a broad sweep of brown wooden benching. Hot off the grill come succulent chicken wings, and an expertly charred, thick, moist sea bream fillet. Also worth sampling are the loose and lovely pork and scallop gyoza, the silky, chilled, own-made tofu with fresh wasabi and ginger, and a texturally thrilling rice and king crab hot-pot that arrives at table in its iron cooking pot. Desserts aren't especially Japanese, but they're fun, especially the mocha and honeycomb custard with kumquats and medjool date ice-cream. Party on.
Babies and children welcome: high chairs. Booking advisable. Disabled: toilet. No smoking (restaurant). Tables outdoors (10, pavement). **Map 9 J5.**

Holborn

★ Aki
182 Gray's Inn Road, WC1X 8EW (7837 9281/ www.akidemae.com). Chancery Lane tube. **Lunch served** noon-3pm Mon-Fri. **Dinner served** 6-11pm Mon-Fri; 6-10.30pm Sat. **Main courses** £4.50-£11.50. **Set lunch** £7.80-£14.70. **Set dinner** £18-£40.50. **Credit** AmEx, JCB, MC, V.
With the exception of an unexpectedly stupendous mural in its basement, Aki epitomises shabby izakaya homeliness. Staff wear faded happi coats and sweet smiles; furnishings include a glowing

BEST JAPANESE

For thrills from the grill
Savour charcoal-infused titbits on sticks at **Ikkyu** and **Soho Japan** (*see p190 Bargain central*), **Jin Kichi** (*see p196*), **Roka** (*see above*), **Tosa** (*see p190*) and **Zuma** (*see p187*).

For that old izakaya magic
When you're here for the beer too, try **Aki** (*see above*), **Asakusa** (*see p195*), **Donzoko** (*see p188*) and **Ikkyu** (*see p190 Bargain central*).

For Seoul food side orders
Pursue a new Korea by mixing and matching neighbouring cuisines at **Hana** (*see p195*), **Kyoto** (*see p190 Bargain central*), **Makiyaki** (*see p193*) and **Matsuba** (*see p198*).

For punishing the plastic
Splash out at **Nobu** (*see p187*), **Nobu Berkeley Street** (*see p187*), **Roka** (*see above*), **Sumosan** (*see p187*), **Tsunami** (*see p195*), **Umu** (*see p188*) and **Zuma** (*see p187*).

For going easy on the wallet
See p190 **Bargain central** for cheap, cheery choices in the West End.

Saki. See p185.

red lantern and indigo noren curtains; and the cooking features choice ingredients and thoroughbred techniques. You know you're in safe, traditional hands when your meal is preceded by a complimentary zensai of okara (it's only a humble by-product of tofu-making, but is very tasty and exceedingly nutritious). Equally flavoursome is Aki's scallop and garlic kushiage (deep-fried in breadcrumbs on skewers). Dinner courses are fairly standard, but of a decent quality. Our tempura set (£22) started with a generous platter of sashimi, followed by good yakitori, miso soup, rice, and tempura (prawn, fish and vegetable). It was rounded off with that classic set-meal fresh-fruit ensemble of strawberries and orange segments. There's a remarkably long list of specials too, where you can get a fix of natto, raw quails' eggs, mountain yam, yellowtail jaw and other less mainstream fare. So much to choose from, so little time… repeat visits recommended. *Babies and children admitted. Booking advisable. Separate room for parties, seats 30. Takeaway service.* **Map 4 M4.**

Knightsbridge

Nozomi

14-15 Beauchamp Place, SW3 1NQ (7838 1500/ www.nozomi.co.uk). Knightsbridge tube. **Lunch served** 12.30-3pm, **dinner served** 6.30-11.30pm Mon-Sat. **Main courses** £12-£50. **Credit** AmEx, JCB, MC, V.
Nozomi's not sure what it wants to be. There's a liveried doorman in a top hat, a bar at the front (with a DJ behind the world's smallest DJ booth) and a couple of taupe and cream dining rooms higher up that would please the ladies-who-lunch brigade. The menu might strike fear into those with a suspicion of East-meets-West (con)fusion, listing such dishes as roasted lamb with avocado and soy. This being monied Knightsbridge, there's wagyu beef galore. You'll find sushi, small dishes (the best option here) and meat and fish mains. Our dinner was a mixed bag. The sushi rice was a total failure – overcooked and under-vinegared. A drab seaweed salad remained virtually untouched. Redemption came with two seafood dishes: seared scallops topped with caviar and dressed with yuzu and miso; and halibut 'gratinated' with miso (a gorgeous piece of fish, moist and enhanced by the savoury miso crust). Service was polite but not well informed. We were served the tiniest tumblers of saké for £4 a throw. *Babies and children admitted. Booking essential. Dress: smart casual. Entertainment: DJ 8pm-1am Mon-Sat. No-smoking tables. Separate room for parties, seats 20-25.* **Map 14 F9.**

★ Zuma

5 Raphael Street, SW7 1DL (7584 1010/ www.zumarestaurant.com). Knightsbridge tube. Bar **Open** noon-11pm Mon-Fri; 12.30-11pm Sat; noon-10pm Sun. *Restaurant* **Lunch served** noon-2.15pm Mon-Fri; 12.30-3.15pm Sat; 12.30-2.45pm Sun. **Dinner served** 6-10.45pm Mon-Sat; 6-10.15pm Sun. **Main courses** £3.80-£65. *Both* **Credit** AmEx, DC, MC, V.
Though no longer new, Zuma has retained its glamorous sheen. Seats at the sushi bar, the grill or in the slickly designed main dining area still require a week or two's wait. Then expect to be informed the table is yours for just two hours. We were also required – twice – to confirm our reservation. So, once you've jumped through the flaming hoops, is it worth it? Yes. The Flintstones-chic interior is a hoot and the food is as good as ever. Zuma calls itself a 'contemporary izakaya', which is akin to calling your Manolo Blahniks (de rigueur here for the laydeez) a pair of plimsolls. New-style sushi and sashimi are just the ticket: think seared miso-marinated foie gras or wagyu beef with shoyu and wasabi. High-quality sashimi is served unadorned, evincing a purist ethos at work. The sushi tends to be more innovative. An exotic fruit platter (£12.80 for two) was massive and contained a weird variety of brightly coloured fruits. The saké list is amazing, but make sure you grab the sommelier for guidance. As you might

expect, Zuma is not cheap – a bottle of water costs £4.50 and the service charge is a hefty 13.5%. *Babies and children welcome: high chairs. Booking advisable. Disabled: toilet. No smoking (restaurant). Separate rooms for parties, seating 12 and 14. Tables outdoors (4, garden).* **Map 8 F9.**

Mayfair

Chisou

4 Princes Street, W1B 2LE (7629 3931). Oxford Circus tube. **Lunch served** noon-2.30pm, **dinner served** 6-10.15pm Mon-Sat. **Main courses** £3.50-£22. **Set lunch** £9-£17. **Credit** AmEx, JCB, MC, V.
You are probably not allowed to hire Japanese waitresses for their cheekbones, but if you were, these are the women you would hire. Chisou is a good-looking place with its Japanese screens, rice-paper lamps and cushioned banquettes. By day, the place is fast, efficient and businesslike. At night, groups linger over bottles of Puligny-Montrachet and first-growth Bordeaux, picking and pecking at degustation-style dishes from the daily list of out-there specials, including pan-fried spicy burdock, and monkfish liver with ponzu. More familiar is the black cod with miso (now the Japanese equivalent of Chinese crispy duck), which tasted fine but felt squidgy. All was forgiven with the arrival of the nigiri sushi – beautifully buttery salmon and bright, fresh tuna which literally melted in the mouth. Also good were four plump, mouth-filling Irish rock oysters topped with spicy radish, spring onion and ponzu. Dish of the night was a plate of mixed sashimi and avocado served with a beachcomber salad of mizuna, rocket and seaweed: bliss. *Babies and children admitted. Booking advisable. No-smoking tables. Separate room for parties, seats 12. Takeaway service.* **Map 9 J6.**

★ Miyama

38 Clarges Street, W1Y 7EN (7499 2443). Green Park tube. **Lunch served** noon-2.30pm Mon-Sat, **dinner served** 6-10.30pm daily. **Main courses** £9-£25. **Set lunch** £13-£25. **Set dinner** £30-£35. **Credit** AmEx, DC, JCB, MC, V.
Kimono-clad waitresses greet you at the entrance, signalling that this is formal dining territory. The brightly lit dining room feels like the lobby of a bland business hotel; perhaps the intention is to focus the mind on the menu, where it belongs. The emphasis is on top-quality sushi, traditional and 'new'. New-style sea bass 'carpaccio' had tender slices gracefully draped over a mound of grated daikon with a side of chilli-spiked yuzu sauce. It tasted as good as it looked. If you can judge a Japanese kitchen by the quality of its stock, Miyama's red star is well deserved. Our soup stock was gorgeous – subtly smoky and umami-intense. The teishoku are worth considering as diners can pick and choose dishes; our set included grilled scallop with yuzu (beautifully presented with shards of deep-fried lotus root and served atop deeply flavoured sautéed mushrooms), vegetable tempura and black cod with miso. Less successful were a dull green tea mousse dessert and soft-shell crab maki that fell apart halfway between plate and mouth. Still, Miyama is one of the best places in London for sushi. *Babies and children welcome: high chairs. Booking advisable. Takeaway service.* **Map 9 H8. For branch (City Miyama) see index.**

★ Nobu

First floor, The Metropolitan, 19 Old Park Lane, W1K 1LB (7447 4747/www.noburestaurants. com). Hyde Park Corner tube. **Lunch served** noon-2.15pm Mon-Sat. **Dinner served** 6-10.15pm Mon-Thur; 6-11pm Fri, Sat; 6-9.30pm Sun. **Main courses** £3.50-£27.50. **Set lunch** £25 bento box, £25 sushi box. **Set dinner** £70, £90. **Credit** AmEx, DC, JCB, MC, V.
Ten years on from the opening of this branch, the Nobu chain extends from the US to Paris, Milan, Tokyo and other cities around the globe. There are now three Nobus in London. Sister Ubon (Nobu

backwards) serves the same menu to Docklands denizens, and there's Nobu Berkeley Street (*see below*). Here at the Metropolitan hotel, you still get great views over Hyde Park, as well as substantial waiting lists, but the shine is starting to come off this former celeb magnet. Chef Nobu Matsuhisa's signature dishes – such as rock shrimp tempura with spicy sauce, new-style sashimi and black cod with miso – caused a sensation a decade ago, but no longer hold the same 'wow' factor. That's fashion for you. Dining at Nobu is inevitably expensive, but go at lunchtime and there are relative bargains in the form of a bento or sushi box. For our sashimi set, shrimp tempura and spicy tuna hand rolls were enclosed in crisp nori, accompanied by quality salmon, tuna and sea bass sashimi. A Nobu classic, chicken skewers anti-cucho, were moist and zippy. Servers seem keen to whip plates away before you can eat the final nibble; they aren't so keen to refill teacups or clean up spills – yet charge 15% and leave the credit slip open 'in case you want to add more'. We didn't. *Babies and children welcome: high chairs. Booking essential. Disabled: toilet. No-smoking tables. Separate room for parties, seats 14-40.* **Map 9 H8. For branch (Ubon) see index.**

★ Nobu Berkeley Street

15 Berkeley Street, W1J 8DY (7290 9222/ www.noburestaurants.com). Green Park tube. Bar **Open** 5pm-2am Mon-Fri; 6pm-2am Sun; 6-11pm Sun. *Restaurant* **Lunch served** noon-2pm daily. **Dinner served** 6pm-1am Mon-Sat; 6-10pm Sun. **Main courses** £8.50-£26.60. *Both* **Credit** AmEx, MC, V.
Thankfully, Nobu III has abandoned the no-bookings policy it opened with in 2005. So you can now roll up to its spaceship-cum-womb of a bar on the ground floor, assured of a seat in the first-floor restaurant. Just decide whether you'd like a Tokyo Peach (Bellini with Calpis) first, or head straight up the elegant spiral staircase to your table. We couldn't resist tarrying in the bar with its subdued lighting, tapered stainless-steel pillars and starlit woodland night motif. Bar-room lingering is recommended, as the dining room has an almost claustrophobically low ceiling, limited window space and no view (unless you count the façade of the Mayfair Hotel). Yes, this branch lacks the sense of occasion afforded by the Hyde Park panorama you're treated to at Nobu on Park Lane (*see above*). Never mind – at least here you can pay full and deserved attention to the likes of seared toro and rib-eye anti-cucho (both spicily dressed and from the 'wood oven' section of the menu), or regular Nobu offerings such as new-style scallop sashimi (dressed with oil and chives) and old-style aubergine tempura. The puddings, usually a highlight, were underwhelming. Chestnut brûlée, for example, came with a good dark-chocolate sorbet, but lacked flavour and substance elsewhere. *Babies and children welcome: high chairs. Bookings advisable. Disabled: toilet. Dress: smart casual. Entertainment: DJ 9pm Thur-Sat. No smoking (restaurant). Vegan dishes.* **Map 9 H7. For branch (Ubon) see index.**

Sumosan

26B Albemarle Street, W1S 4HY (7495 5999/ www.sumosan.com). Green Park tube. **Lunch served** noon-2.45pm Mon-Fri. **Dinner served** 6-11.30pm Mon-Sat. **Main courses** £7.50-£25.50. **Set lunch** £22.50; £50 per person 6 courses. **Set dinner** £70 per person 8 courses. **Credit** AmEx, MC, V.
With its pared-down aesthetic of dark wood and glass there's something a little soulless about Sumosan. Sadly, the same can be said of the food. The basement bar is candlelit, presumably so you don't choke on your drink when clocking the cocktail prices. Upstairs, the menu isn't strictly Japanese, with smatterings of Thai-influenced noodles as well as a Chinese-style duck dish. Of the Japanese food, salmon and avocado roll melted in the mouth and sea bream was exquisite. However, vegetable tempura, though impeccably presented, was greasy and undistinguished; a dish of scallops and ginger (£19) was tasteless; and glass noodles

with beef could have come from your local Thai takeaway. Better was the flavourful grilled sea bass, which arrived poised mid-leap as if it had just left the water. And at least the desserts are a treat – in particular, a dorayaki pyramid of cake, berries and custard. Nonetheless, the largely bland offerings and slow service (despite stacks of unctuous staff milling about) don't warrant these prices. Despite a swanky address and a clientele of gilded youth, we reckon Sumosan is all mouth and no trousers.

Babies and children welcome: high chairs. Booking advisable. No-smoking tables. Separate area for parties, seats 30. Takeaway service. **Map 9 H7.**

★ Umu

14-16 Bruton Place, W1J 6LX (7499 8881/ www.umurestaurant.com). Bond Street or Green Park tube. **Lunch served** noon-2.30pm Mon-Fri. **Dinner served** 6-10.30pm Mon-Sat. **Main courses** £12-£45. **Set lunch** £22-£45. **Set dinner** £60-£130. **Credit** AmEx, DC, JCB, MC, V.

Umu is an authentic slice of metropolitan Japan in central Mayfair, from the understated entrance to the sleek wood panelling to the unstinting detail paid to the serving plates and all that goes on them. Yes, this is one of the most expensive places to eat in the capital; you could easily spend £300-plus for two if not careful. And yes, it does take itself rather seriously. But we were won over by the enthusiasm of the staff, particularly the sommelier, who presides over the lengthiest saké list in Europe. Umu specialises in the haute cuisine of Kyoto. The food is impeccably sourced (with many ingredients imported from Japan) and artfully prepared. We'd recommend one of the multi-course kaiseki sets (£60-£130 per person). Even the simplest-sounding dishes, such as sesame tofu with fresh wasabi, or saké-flavoured clear soup (from the Special Kaiseki, £90), display a clarity and purity of flavour. As well as the set menus, there's sushi in both 'classic' and 'modern' forms. Of the latter, blue crab with courgette, pine nuts and red ichimi (a kind of chilli), and scallop with lemon confit, were among the more curious (yet successful) combinations. Only one dish – an overcooked toro teriyaki – disappointed. Unless you're a millionaire, Umu is special-occasion territory, but for Japanophiles, it's a must-try.

Babies and children welcome: high chairs. Booking advisable dinner. Disabled: toilet. Dress: no shorts. No smoking. **Map 9 H7.**

St James's

Matsuri

16 Bury Street, SW1Y 6AL (7839 1101/ www.matsuri-restaurant.com). Green Park tube. **Lunch served** noon-2.30pm Mon-Sat; noon-3pm Sun. **Dinner served** 6-10.30pm Mon-Sat; 6-10pm Sun. **Main courses** £10-£25 lunch, £20-£50 dinner. **Set lunch** £15-£45. **Set dinner** £35-£85. **Credit** AmEx, DC, JCB, MC, V.

If you didn't know that a matsuri is a traditional festival in Japan, you'd figure it out from the hangings and papier-mâché models that decorate the staircase leading down to this basement restaurant in St James's. Food snobs may dismiss teppanyaki as the inauthentic johnnie-come-lately of Japanese cuisine, promoted by an enterprising Kobe restaurant chain as the occupying GIs arrived. But Matsuri reminds you how good it can be, even if your wallet can't run to Kobe beef. Sirloin steak came off the hot-plate in richly textured rare cubes, delicious dipped in a sweet sesame sauce. Salmon teriyaki was crusty outside, moist inside. Mixed sashimi arrived fresh and skilfully cut. Mango and tropical fruit outshone the more traditional ice-creams and desserts. The teppan counters may need updating, but the kimono-clad staff are attentive. Our waitress was charmingly mystified that we wanted to add a tip to the included service charge. Choosing with care at lunchtime, you can eat for £14; at dinner, letting yourself go, be prepared for St James's pricing.

Babies and children welcome: high chairs. Booking advisable. Disabled: stair lift; toilet. No-smoking tables. Separate rooms for parties

(teppanyaki), seating 8-18. Takeaway service. Vegetarian menu. **Map 17 J7.**
For branches see index.

Soho

Donzoko

15 Kingly Street, W1B 5PS (7734 1974). Oxford Circus or Piccadilly Circus tube. **Lunch served** noon-2.30pm Mon-Fri. **Dinner served** 6-10.15pm Mon-Sat. **Main courses** £6.50-£28. **Set lunch** £12-£30. **Credit** AmEx, DC, JCB, MC, V.

During the latter part of the week, expect a cacophonous, smoky and fast-paced experience at Donzoko: it's an enduringly popular spot among visiting Japanese business folk and local Japanese food aficionados. There's a great drinks list – 17 sakés and nine shochus – and the gutsy cooking follows suit. A list of garlic-based dishes is intended to soak up the alcohol. Our grilled whelk with garlic was excellent. Similarly, 'bonito guts pickled in salt' pulled no punches. We love Donzoko for its honest, earthy approach to food, but, as you might expect in an izakaya, the cooking can be patchy. Tsukune (minced chicken balls on a skewer) was disappointingly dry, and the nigiri sushi was less than technically perfect. Still, the variety is usually wide; our selection of surf clam, black sea bream and scallop was excellent, as was a salmon-skin maki. The high point was a cockle-warming hot-pot of belly pork simmered in sweet

soy and served with a smear of fiery mustard – just the thing to chase away a wintry chill.
Babies and children admitted. Booking advisable. Disabled: toilet. Takeaway service. **Map 17 J6.**

★ Ten Ten Tei

56 Brewer Street, W1R 3PJ (7287 1738). Piccadilly Circus tube. **Lunch served** noon-2.30pm Mon-Fri; noon-4pm Sat. **Dinner served** 5-10pm Mon-Sat. **Main courses** £5.80-£7. **Set lunch** £6.50-£12. **Set dinner** £14.80-£18.80. **Credit** JCB, MC, V.

It ain't pretty, but for generously proportioned well-made sushi at a streetwise price, Ten Ten Tei is hard to beat. This Soho stalwart has the look of a back-lane noodle bar and the ethics of a British caff, with its plain wooden tables ready-loaded with napkins, chopsticks, toothpicks, pepper pots, togarashi sprinkles, soy and tonkatsu sauce. The location behind Piccadilly Circus makes it perfect for a low-cal lunch for media fat cats from Golden Square, and an easy pre-theatre and pre-club refuelling point. Some dishes may lack finesse, but they're great value, and the sweet service means that a table of My First Sushi novices and another of old hands receive equal treatment. Crisp-skinned grilled mackerel (packed with omega-3) was a treat; salt-grilled squid legs were chewy but clean-tasting; and hiyayakko (refreshing, chilled beancurd with bonito flakes) was the Japanese

Nobu Berkeley Street. See p187.

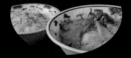

Bargain central

Kyoto

They might not win awards for culinary excellence, and their seating may discourage lingering, but these reliable spots in the West End, Mayfair and Fitzrovia offer all the mainstream options (sushi, sashimi, noodles, yakitori, teriyaki, tempura, katsu and bento combinations) at purse-pleasing prices.

THE ALL-ROUNDERS

Centrepoint Sushi (Hana)

20-21 St Giles High Street, WC2H 8JE (7240 6147/www.cpfs.co.uk). Tottenham Court Road tube. **Meals served** noon-10pm Mon-Sat. **Main courses** £7.50-£15. **Set lunch** £8-£13.50. **Credit** MC, V.
Tucked away above a spick and span Korean-Japanese food shop, Hana uses high-quality ingredients and offers unexpectedly plush seating.
Best for Decent rice and eager-to-please service.
Babies and children welcome: high chairs. Booking advisable. Takeaway service. Vegetarian menu. **Map 17 K6**.

Ikkyu

67A Tottenham Court Road, W1T 2EY (7636 9280). Goodge Street or Tottenham Court Road tube. **Lunch served** noon-

2.30pm Mon-Fri. **Dinner served** 6-10.30pm Mon-Fri, Sun. **Main courses** £6-£13. **Set lunch** £6.20-£9.60. **Set dinner** £6.10-£13.50. **Credit** AmEx, MC, V.
A long-standing all-rounder in an easy-to-miss basement, where the decor is shabby and the service brisk (especially come the end of lunchtime) – but the food is genuine.
Best for Treats from the grill and authentic bustle.
Babies and children admitted. Booking essential dinner. No-smoking tables. Separate room for parties, seats 12. Vegetarian menu. **Map 4 K5**.

Japan Centre (Toku)

212 Piccadilly, W1J 9HG (7255 8255/ www.japancentre.com). Piccadilly Circus tube.
Shops Open 10am-7pm Mon-Fri; 10.30am-8pm Sat; 11am-7pm Sun.
Restaurant Meals served noon-10pm Mon-Sat; noon-8pm Sun. **Main courses** £2.50-£14. **Set lunch** £6.90-£14.30. **Set dinner** £7.90-£14.80. **Credit** JCB, MC, V.
Packed at 1pm, deserted at 8pm (midweek), Toku offers the real deal and, unusually, brown rice as well as white.
Best for Proper noodles and lip-smacking dressings.

Babies and children welcome: high chairs. Booking advisable. Disabled: toilet. No smoking. Vegetarian menu. **Map 17 J7**.

Kyoto

27 Romilly Street, W1D 5AL (7437 2262). Leicester Square or Piccadilly Circus tube. **Lunch served** noon-3pm, **dinner served** 5-11pm Mon-Sat. **Main courses** £6-£12. **Set lunch** £7.99. **Credit** JCB, MC, V.
The calligraphy-covered tables and Ultramen models in display cabinets give this quiet Korean-run place a bit of character.
Best for Sweet service and savoury steamed gyoza (but give the katsudon a miss).
Babies and children admitted. Booking advisable. No smoking. Tables outdoors (2, pavement). Takeaway service. **Map 17 K6**.

Ramen Seto

19 Kingly Street, W1B 5PY (7434 0309). Oxford Circus tube. **Meals served** noon-9.30pm Mon-Sat; 1-8pm Sun. **Main courses** £5.70-£6.50. **Set meals** £6-£8.80. **Credit** JCB, MC, V.
There's much more than decent ramen to be had here. Top-value sets include salmon sashimi and pork gyoza.

---

equivalent of a between-course sorbet. But the best order here is the sushi – of tuna, salmon, red snapper, scallop and mirin-sweetened omelette. Before sushi restaurants started buying in ready-made tamago, it was considered the ultimate litmus test. Here, at least, the old rule still works.
Babies and children admitted. Bookings not accepted Fri, Sat. Takeaway service. **Map 17 J7**.

West
Ealing

★ ★ Sushi-Hiro

1 Station Parade, Uxbridge Road, W5 3LD (8896 3175). Ealing Common tube. **Lunch served** 11am-1.30pm, **dinner served** 4.30-9pm Tue-Sun. **Sushi** 60p-£2.20. **Set meal** £5-£14. **No credit cards.**

The frosted white shopfront on Uxbridge Road doesn't look promising for sushi. But Sushi-Hiro, run by a friendly husband-and-wife team, occupies a prime position to intercept hungry office workers on their way home from the tube to the Japanese expatriate enclaves of Ealing. The restaurant's busy take-out trade explains both the biggish waiting area, with plastic sushi displays by the cash desk, and the small-town decor, with its Hello Kitty touches. Eating at the well-lit counter or the half-dozen scrubbed tables, you get no gimmicks or frills but straightforward sushi made with fine ingredients and faultless technique. The £12 ten-piece tokujo set includes startlingly fresh scallop and sweet prawn, plus melting chu-toro and sea eel. The kampyo (pickled gourd) maki and the inari (sushi rice wrapped in deep-fried tofu) were delicious too. Expect to pay three times more ordering piece by piece. This restaurant can be

busy even on weekday lunchtimes; and you should note the early closing time, which suits its primarily Japanese clientele.
Babies and children welcome: high chair. Booking advisable. Disabled: toilet. Takeaway service.

Hammersmith

Tosa NEW

332 King Street, W6 0RR (8748 0002/ www.tosatosa.net). Ravenscourt Park or Stamford Brook tube. **Lunch served** 12.30-2.30pm Tue-Sun. **Dinner served** 6-11pm Tue-Sat; 6-10.30pm Sun. **Main courses** £5-£12. **Set meals** £20-£25 3 courses. **Credit** MC, V.
The friendliness of the staff and the quality (and value) of the food more than make up for a lack of design credentials at this newcomer. Ask for a seat

Best for Refuelling after shopping on Regent Street.
Babies and children welcome: high chairs. Booking advisable weekends. No smoking. Takeaway service. **Map 17 J6.**

Satsuma

56 Wardour Street, W1D 4JG (7437 8338/ www.osatsuma.com). Piccadilly Circus tube. **Meals served** noon-11pm Mon, Tue; noon-11.30pm Wed, Thur; noon-midnight Fri, Sat; noon-10.30pm Sun. **Main courses** £5.60-£15.90. **Credit** AmEx, DC, JCB, MC, V.
The Royal China Group's take on Wagamama just about qualifies as budget eating.
Best for Bountiful bentos and unexpected toppings.
Babies and children welcome: high chairs. Bookings not accepted. Disabled: toilet. No smoking. Takeaway service. **Map 17 K6.**

Soho Japan NEW

52 Wells Street, W1T 3PR (7323 4661/ www.sohojapan.co.uk). Oxford Circus tube. **Lunch served** noon-2.30pm Mon-Fri. **Dinner served** 6-10.30pm Mon-Sat; 6-9.30pm Sun. **Main courses** (lunch) £5.50-£13; (dinner) £2.50-£10. **Set lunch** £5.50-£6.50. **Set dinner** £9. **Credit** AmEx, JCB, MC, V.
While this former pub still sports many a Guinness poster, the food – from sushi and yakitori to sautéed lotus root and octopus balls – is thoroughly Japanese.
Best for Relative rarities such as yama imo (mountain yam) and ginkgo nuts.
Babies and children admitted. Booking advisable. No smoking. Tables outdoors (3, pavement). Takeaway service. **Map 9 J5.**

Taro

10 Old Compton Street, W1D 4TF (7439 2275). Leicester Square or Tottenham Court Road tube. **Lunch served** noon-2.50pm Mon-Fri; 12.30-3.15pm Sat, Sun. **Dinner served** 5.30-10.30pm Mon-Sat; 5.30-9.30pm Sun. **Main courses** £5.90-£8.80. **Set meal** £8.50-£14. **Credit** JCB, MC, V.
Sushi, sashimi, tempura, noodles? Check. Cream walls? Check. Blond wood? Check. Attractive waiters? Taro does hold some surprises. The original is on Brewer Street.
Best for Space to breathe in the double-height basement, and utterly moreish tori kara age (deep-fried chicken chunks).
Booking advisable. No smoking. Separate room for parties, seats 30. Takeaway service. **Map 17 K6.**
For branch see index.

Tokyo Diner

2 Newport Place, WC2H 7JP (7287 8777/ www.tokyodiner.com). Leicester Square tube. **Meals served** noon-midnight daily. **Main courses** £3.90-£12.90. **Set lunch** (noon-5pm Mon-Fri) £4.40-£8.80. **Set dinner** £5.40-£9.80. **Credit** JCB, MC, V.
Food can be erratic, but we had decent nigiri and great chicken katsu on our last visit. The stools really are titchy, though.
Best for Being open every day all year, and a no-tipping policy.
Babies and children admitted. Bookings not accepted Fri, Sat. No smoking (ground floor and basement). Takeaway service. **Map 17 K7.**

Zipangu

8 Little Newport Street, WC2H 7JJ (7437 5042). Leicester Square tube. **Meals served** noon-11pm Mon-Sat; noon-10.30pm Sun. **Main courses** £4.50-£14. **Set lunch** (noon-5.30pm) £6-£12.50. **Set dinner** £9.50-£14. **Credit** AmEx, MC, V.
No smoking, few frills and little space – but plenty of value in the modest menu and daily set special.
Best for A bargain quick lunch.
Bookings not accepted Fri, Sat. No smoking. Separate room for parties, seats 15. Takeaway service. **Map 17 K7.**

THE SPECIALISTS

Abeno Too

17-18 Great Newport Street, WC2H 7JE (7379 1160/www.abeno.co.uk). Leicester Square tube. **Meals served** noon-11pm Mon-Sat; noon-10.30pm Sun. **Main courses** £6.95-£18.50. **Set lunch** £7.80-£12.80. **Credit** AmEx, DC, JCB, MC, V.
A neat little provider of okonomiyaki, cooked on hot-plates set into the window tables and the main counter.
Best for Warming winter fare.
Babies and children admitted. Bookings not accepted. Disabled: toilet. No smoking. Takeaway service. **Map 18 K6.**
For branch (Abeno) see index.

Kulu Kulu

51-53 Shelton Street, WC2H 9HE (7240 5687). Covent Garden tube. **Lunch served** noon-2.30pm Mon-Fri; noon-3.30pm Sat. **Dinner served** 5-10pm Mon-Sat. **Dishes** £1.20-£3.60. **Credit** JCB, MC, V.
The newest of the three Kulu Kulus, this branch offers the same simple formula: a conveyor-belt carrying sushi, sashimi and Japanese cakes; a few hot dishes; and seating at stools.

Best for The cheapest kaiten plate tariff (£1.20-£3.40).
Babies and children admitted. Bookings not accepted. No smoking. Takeaway service. **Map 18 L6.**
For branches see index.

Ryo

84 Brewer Street, W1F 9UB (7287 1318). Piccadilly Circus tube. **Meals served** 11.30am-midnight Mon-Wed, Sun; 11.30am-1am Thur-Sat. **Main courses** £5-£10. **Set meal** £5.50-£10. **No credit cards**.
Pay-first, eat-later Ryo (formerly Hamine) is still going strong and is home to the best pork gyoza in town. Some dishes, however, aren't what they sound like (yakisoba, for instance).
Best for Late-night noodle cravings.
Babies and children admitted. Disabled: toilet. Separate room for parties, seats 25. Takeaway service. **Map 17 J7.**

Yazu Sushi NEW

46 Curzon Street, W1J 7UH (7491 3777). Green Park tube. **Lunch served** noon-3pm, **dinner served** 6-10.30pm Mon-Fri. **Dishes** £1.80-£4. **Credit** AmEx, MC, V.
Located in the alley connecting Curzon Street with Shepherd Market, this compact kaiten offers tiny premises, sizeable prices, several kinds of fresh fish and no hot options – unless you count miso soup.
Best for A quickie snack and dining solo.
Bookings not accepted (lunch). No smoking. Takeaway service. **Map 9 H8.**

Yo! Sushi

Myhotel, 11-13 Bayley Street, Bedford Square, WC1B 3HD (7636 0076/ www.yosushi.com). Tottenham Court Road tube. **Lunch served** noon-11pm Mon-Sat; noon-10.30pm Sun. **Dishes** £1.50-£5. **Credit** AmEx, DC, JCB, MC, V.
One of dozens of branches in the Yo! chain, which stretches across London and beyond. Tables are provided, as well as stools in front of the long and winding conveyor-belt. Not the cheapest kaiten joint (plates £1.60-£4), but the menu is always an interesting read.
Best for A healthy break from haggling in the hi-fi shops of Tottenham Court Road.
Babies and children welcome: high chairs. Bookings not accepted. Disabled: adapted tables; toilet. No smoking. Tables outdoors (3, terrace). Takeaway service (0870 190 8040). Vegetarian menu. **Map 10 K5.**
For branches see index.

RESTAURANTS

---

at the front by the robata grill and choose from daily specials (ox tongue with ponzu, and grilled saury fish with salt were among those offered on our visit) or go with the general menu. But don't miss out on the grilled dishes – a set selection is a good place to start. Ours comprised: yakitori with chicken and onion; shiso and pork loin (highly recommended); asparagus and pork belly; shiitake; and atsuage tofu. Starters such as hijiki (seaweed) salad and small dishes like maguro natto (tuna and fermented soy beans) are nicely presented and seasoned. Cold beef salad (a neat mound of meat, small potatoes and red onion) had a good sharp flavour. We were impressed with the house tosa maki, containing avocado, shiso leaf and cucumber, with thinly sliced salmon on the outside. Service is charm personified, so feel free to ask questions and let staff guide you through the menu; you can't go far wrong.

Babies and children admitted. Booking advisable. No smoking. Tables outdoors (3, terrace). Takeaway service. Vegetarian menu. **Map 20 4A.**

Ladbroke Grove

Mika NEW

78 Tavistock Road, W11 1AN (7243 8518/ www.mikalondon.com). Ladbroke Grove or Westbourne Park tube. **Lunch served** noon-5pm daily. **Dinner served** 6-10pm Mon-Thur, Sun; 6-10.30pm Fri, Sat. **Main courses** £2.50-£20. **Set lunch** £5.50-£8.50. **Credit** AmEx, MC, V.
Edamame arrived hot and sprinkled with salt, but a little underboiled, followed by satisfyingly thick slices of salmon sashimi and a good dollop of ikura on a shiso leaf. Yakitori was nicely cooked, though no bargain at £4.75 for two skewers. Chicken udon boasted a generous array of toppings

and a gentle stock, but failed to ring true. So, good news and bad news from the menu at Mika. The decor couldn't be more basic at this box of a café, with matt black floor tiles, white breeze-block walls, stainless-steel counters and a matt black ceiling. The tables and benches are regulation pine. Nevertheless, Mika achieves a welcoming ambience with a floor-to-ceiling glass façade, plenty of space and a helpful, very relaxed manageress. It was pouring with rain on our visit, but there are plastic round tables and folding chairs outside for more clement weather, making good use of the restaurant's location on the pedestrianised end of Tavistock Road where it meets Portobello Road.
Babies and children welcome: children's menu. Booking advisable. No smoking. Tables outdoors (8, pavement). Takeaway service; delivery service (noon-3pm, 6-10pm; within 2-mile radius). **Map 19 B2.**

Notting Hill

Feng Sushi
101 Notting Hill Gate, W11 3JZ (7727 1123/ www.fengsushi.co.uk). Notting Hill Gate tube. **Meals served** 11.30am-10pm Mon-Wed; 11.30am-11pm Thur-Sat; noon-10pm Sun. **Main courses** £2.50-£10. **Set meal** £8 bento box. **Credit** AmEx, DC, MC, V.
Branches of this expanding chain stick to what seems a successful formula, offering eat-in dining alongside a busy takeaway business. Feng Sushi is notable for a couple of reasons: it takes sourcing seriously (the salmon is sustainably farmed in Loch Duart, for instance); and its menu has enough dishes to satisfy vegetarians – even vegans won't go hungry. We tried dishes with a 'new' symbol next to them, including 'new-style' sea bass sashimi, which came dressed with chilli oil, sesame oil and fresh coriander: it was both pretty and flavourful. Sushi of line-caught Cornish mackerel was super-fresh, and a salad of cold soba noodles topped with pine nuts was enlivened by peppery rocket leaves and yuzu. Worth a taste are the seasonal dishes, such as (winter) soft-shell crab and chilli tempura, and (summer) sweet shrimp ceviche with chilli and pomegranate. This branch occupies a corner site. We've found staff here more attentive than at other Feng Sushis. A drawback, though, is the Lilliputian seating (on tiny rattan stools) of the upstairs dining room.
Babies and children admitted. Bookings not accepted. No smoking. Takeaway service; delivery service (within 2-mile radius). Map 7 A7.
For branches see index.

Paddington

★ Yakitoria NEW
2006 WINNER BEST DESIGN
25 Sheldon Square, W2 6EY (3214 3000/ www.yakitoria.co.uk). Paddington tube/rail. **Lunch served** noon-3pm Mon-Fri; 11am-3pm Sun. **Dinner served** 6-11pm Mon-Sat. **Main courses** £13.50-£35. **Set lunch** £13-£14.50. **Credit** AmEx, DC, JCB, MC, V.
Though only a year old, Yakitoria has a chequered history. Owned by Moscow-based restaurant group Vesta-Centre International, it opened in the very much work-in-progress Paddington Basin development with quite some fanfare, only to put off customers and critics with a tricky location, long, confusing carte and breathtakingly bad service. Fortunately, the food has been glitch-free. Our dishes – classic (tofu, gyoza, sashimi) and modern (chilled green vegetable soup with crab) – ranged from good to sublime. Some were expensive (lamb chops smoked over Japanese tea leaves, £18), some not (spicy red-eye roll, £8.50). In addition, the management has taken on board early criticisms by slimming down the menu and bringing staff up to speed with the adventurous cuisine (pizza sushi, anyone?) and fancy electronic till system. Dark wood tables, lime-washed wooden banquettes, a cherry blossom mural, and black, sharply tailored waiters uniforms mix with a playful colour scheme of cerise pink and wasabi green. Surreal touches such as the giant Ingo Maura domed black light lined in shocking pink, the quirky green Maxima chairs, the cerise padded wall, the diamante curtain masking an intimate dining room, and the hilarious wonky glasses make a meal at Yakitoria feel like an experience. What's more, the narrow bar to the rear serves a mean Mojito (though, alas, no more Ninja Ale).
Babies and children welcome: high chairs. Booking advisable. Disabled: lift; toilet. Dress: smart casual. Tables outdoors (15, terrace). Takeaway service. Vegetarian menu. Map 7 C6.

South West
Putney

Chosan
292 Upper Richmond Road, SW15 6TH (8788 9626). East Putney tube. **Lunch served** noon-2.30pm Sat, Sun. **Dinner served** 6.30-10.30pm Tue-Sat; 6.30-10pm Sun. **Main courses**

Yakitoria

£3.30-£25. **Set lunch** £7.90-£13.90 incl miso soup, rice. **Set dinner** £18.90-£20.90; £19.90-£24.90 bento box. **Credit** MC, V.
Unless you make the mistake of coming for a weekday lunch, when the place is closed, you're sure of a warm welcome from Chosan's friendly mama-san and her partner behind the sushi bar. Daily specials are written in elegant kanji on wooden boards above the bar. Good food comes from both the kitchen and the fish-chiller. Ohitashi, a starter of parboiled spinach, was superlative, and glistening slices of tai (sea bream) were the highlight of a sushi plate whose salmon and toro were also perfectly judged. Chosan's speciality is a range of bento boxes. These include sushi, sashimi, salad and vegetables, plus other titbits that can be more hit and miss (the tempura was fine, the chicken teriyaki less so). Given its diminutive size, perhaps Chosan tries to do too much with such a long menu. The restaurant's busy decor, which now looks tired, could also do with stripping back. Nevertheless, the black cod with miso here is nearly as good as Nobu's, and costs half the price.
Babies and children admitted. No-smoking tables. Separate area for parties, seats 25. Takeaway service.

Wimbledon

Makiyaki
149 Merton Road, SW19 1ED (8540 3113). South Wimbledon tube. **Lunch served** noon-3pm Mon-Sat. **Dinner served** 6-10.30pm Mon-Thur; 6-11pm Fri, Sat. **Main courses** £6-£11.50. **Set lunch** £7.50-£11.50. **Credit** JCB, MC, V.
As the astute will have gathered from the name, Makiyaki's main reason for being is maki. There

are 45 different, fancifully named sushi rolls on the menu, running from Crazy Monkey (tuna, yellowtail, salmon, eel, tobiko caviar and cucumber) to Red Dragon (deep-fried prawn, tuna and avocado). Our more conventional california roll of crab and avocado was well put together, but let down by the crab, which appeared to be more seafood stick than the real thing. The rest of the meal worked well enough, including a tangy wakame seaweed salad that crunched like jellyfish, and a sustaining bowl of udon topped with pumpkin, aubergine and prawn tempura. But are we the only ones to question the wisdom of a cuisine in which you go to all the trouble of battering and frying food until perfectly golden and crisp, only to throw it into hot soup to go soggy? With its cared-for dining room, Makiyaki serves the neighbourhood with good cheer. Sit in the smaller back room if you want more of a sushi-bar atmosphere.
Babies and children welcome: high chairs. Booking advisable dinner Fri, Sat. No-smoking tables. Takeaway service.
For branches see index.

South
Battersea

Tokiya
74 Battersea Rise, SW11 1EH (7223 5989/ www.tokiya.co.uk). Clapham Junction rail. **Lunch served** 12.30-3pm Sat, Sun. **Dinner served** 6.30-10.30pm Tue-Sun. **Main courses** £7-£15. **Set dinner** £16-£28 5 courses. **Credit** AmEx, JCB, MC, V.
Tokiya is a fine neighbourhood restaurant: small, friendly and reasonably priced. It's a down-to-

RESTAURANTS

earth, welcoming spot, decorated with hanging kimonos and fans, and was bustling with diners on a Friday night. Tables are packed close, so perhaps it isn't an ideal venue for an intimate date. Despite calling itself a sushi bar, the place has a fairly limited sushi menu – but what was lacking in quantity was made up for in quality. A plate of avocado and salmon maki fairly burst with freshness and flavour; dobin mushi was fragrant and delicate; grilled eel on rice oozed warm, meaty flavours. Other dishes were less successful: grilled salmon was only just saved from blandness by a zesty citron sauce; vegetable tempura was too floury; and deep-fried aubergine in tsuyu was unpleasantly oily. Chestnut ice-cream – with a nutty flavour and fantastic woody texture – gave a final lift to the meal.
Babies and children admitted. Booking essential weekends. No smoking. Takeaway service; delivery service (over £20). **Map 21 C4.**

Clapham

★ Tsunami

5-7 Voltaire Road, SW4 6DQ (7978 1610). Clapham North tube. **Dinner served** 6-11pm Mon-Fri. **Meals served** 12.30-11.30pm Sat; 1-9.30pm Sun. **Main courses** £6.95-£20. **Credit** AmEx, MC, V.
Tsunami has fallen off the foodie radar of late. When it first opened in 2001 to a barrage of salivating reviews, chef Singi Nakamura was the new saviour of Japanese food, and half of London headed to Clapham. Nakamura has long since moved on, and these days it's Claphamites who come here for a medium-to-big night out. We can't blame them. The menu still has that Nobu-esque blend of old and new, and the food is as good as ever. The Tsunami special roll of tuna, snow crab, salmon, sweet shrimp and egg is like an entire sushi counter wrapped in nori. 'Sunkiss' salmon sashimi combines furls of lush, velvety salmon seared in olive oil with a drizzle of ponzu. And oyster tempura is the epitome of great Japanese deep-frying: the batter (egg, flour, iced-water) light, crisp and oil-free. Meat lovers will adore the gyu niku: perfectly rare, sliced rib-eye arranged in two hefty layers and served with chef's special sauce. It can be only a matter of time before the rest of the known world discovers Tsunami all over again.
Babies and children welcome: booster chairs. Booking advisable weekends. No-smoking tables. Takeaway service (before 7.30pm). **Map 22 B1.**

Waterloo

Ozu

County Hall, Westminster Bridge Road, SE1 7PB (7928 7766/www.ozulondon.com). Embankment tube/Charing Cross or Waterloo tube/rail. **Lunch served** noon-3pm, **dinner served** 5.30-10.30pm Mon-Sat. **Main courses** £12-£15. **Set lunch** £14.50-£32.50. **Set dinner** £34.50-£45.50. **Credit** AmEx, MC, V.
Ozu is a classy purveyor of classic Japanese fare. On our lunchtime visit the vibe was polite but easy-going, the clientele mostly execs in assertive suits along with a smattering of tourists. We went for the beef and salmon teriyaki menus. These both started in the same manner – first-rate sashimi and tempura – before the respective main attractions arrived. The beef was generously served and faultlessly tender, the sauce just right; the salmon was a hit too. Nice touches in presentation included small chrysanthemums on the side of the dishes bearing the sashimi. Service was somewhat shambolic, if well meaning: our waiter cleared one person's plate away while the other was still eating. This trifling glitch aside, the meal was a success. The restaurant is moving across County Hall at the end of summer 2006 – to a much nicer riverside location (once occupied by Chinese restaurant Four Regions). So expect dramatic views of the Thames and the Palace of Westminster, from virtually every table, they say. There are also plans to add teppanyaki tables and a sushi bar and, eventually, to commandeer the coveted outdoor terrace.

Babies and children welcome: high chair. Booking advisable. Disabled: toilet. No smoking. Vegetarian menu. **Map 10 M9.**

South East
Catford

★ Sapporo Ichiban

13 Catford Broadway, SE6 4SP (8690 8487). Catford rail. **Lunch served** noon-3pm Mon-Fri; noon-4pm Sat, Sun. **Dinner served** 6-11pm daily. **Main courses** £5.50-£16. **Set meal** £8.50 per person 2 courses (minimum 2), £12 sushi per person (minimum 2). **Credit** MC, V.
Faced with a lurid cascade of oriental knick-knackery out front – there's even an ornamental fish pond – we were pleasantly surprised by the simple white interior here. Sapporo Ichiban seems like a fish out of water, peddling sashimi, tempura, yakitori and soba on Catford Broadway. However, for a Monday night, business didn't look bad at all. And, heaven knows, south London's crying out for more decent Japanese restaurants. Most of the rear is taken up by sunken tables in pseudo-tatami style. Ordinary white tables for two or four people and a sushi prep area occupy the rest of the space. Although our dishes didn't always look the part (agedofu cut into minuscule cubes and scattered over a plate, salmon and avocado sushi made to look triangular, quaintly English crustless sandwiches), they did taste Japanese. Everything was generously portioned, at skinflint prices. Service might be termed erratic: the waiter asked to take our order three times before we'd decided; once ready, we couldn't get eye contact for love or money.
Babies and children welcome: high chair. Booking advisable. Disabled: toilet. Takeaway service.

North
Camden Town & Chalk Farm

★ Asakusa

265 Eversholt Street, NW1 1BA (7388 8533/ 8399). Camden Town or Mornington Crescent tube. **Dinner served** 6-11.30pm Mon-Fri; 6-11pm Sat. **Main courses** £5.50-£12. **Set dinner** £5.20-£19. **Credit** MC, V.
Combine your local pub with a sushi bar and what do you get? Camden neighbourhood haunt Asakusa. With its flock wallpaper, swirly carpet, wooden bar and unpretentious atmosphere, you half expect Dot Cotton to come through the restaurant's doors bearing a platter of sushi. Ordering from the massive menu, we kicked off with the nigiri moriawase, which included luscious portions of all the regulars: mackerel, tuna, salmon, prawn, ikura. But the fresh, glistening fish and satisfyingly sticky rice were anything but run of the mill. Unagi (grilled eel) was also a winner; restaurants often slip up with eel, leaving it too soft after cooking or drowning it in overly sweet sauce, but this was firm yet tender, suffused with smoky flavour and drizzled with a sauce that didn't overwhelm. Mackerel simmered in miso was similarly impressive, the nutty soy flavours infusing the flesh. Service was pleasant and unobtrusive and the bill was extremely reasonable. Asakusa was packed to its fake-Tudor rafters with Japanese customers – who clearly know when they're on to a good thing.
Babies and children admitted. Booking essential Fri, Sat. Separate room for parties, seats 20. Takeaway service. Vegetarian menu. **Map 27 D3.**

Holloway

Hana

150A Seven Sisters Road , N7 7PL (7281 2226). Finsbury Park tube/rail/4, 29, 253, 254 bus. **Lunch served** noon-3pm Mon-Sat. **Dinner served** 6-11pm daily. **Main courses** £2.50-£10.50. **Set lunch** £2.90-£14.50. **Set dinner** £16.50-£23 4 courses. **Credit** MC, V.

Hana blooms like a flower in an otherwise sullen stretch of Seven Sisters Road. It's a tiny place with just a sushi counter and some chunky wooden tables. Service, from possibly The Cheeriest Person in Seven Sisters, is a delight. The menu is to the point, consisting of donburis, noodles, teriyaki, deep-fried dishes and sushi. The Korean ownership is evident from the inclusion of bibimbap and bulgogi. Nasu dengaku (aubergine topped with sweetened miso and grilled) was deliciously sweet and savoury. Japanese pickles featured a green tangle of seaweed, a purplish mound of cucumber and yellow slices of radish, making a crunchy counterpoint to the fresh, tender sea bream sashimi and slender tuna nigiri. Hana is big on maki, proffering jokily titled rolls such as the Cherry Blossom (tuna, salmon and avocado) and – wait for it – Rock 'n' Roll (crabstick and avocado). Arranged in a wavy pattern on the plate and topped with slices of grilled eel, our Rock 'n' Roll looked like a swimming sea creature. A homely place with a sense of humour and appetising, affordable food.
Babies and children welcome: high chairs. Booking advisable. Takeaway service; delivery service (within 2-mile radius). Vegetarian menu.

Islington

Itsuka NEW

54 Islington Park Street, N1 1PX (7354 5717). Highbury & Islington tube/rail. **Dinner served** 6-10.30pm Mon-Thur, Sun; 6-11pm Fri, Sat. **courses** £9-£22. **Set meals** £8.50-£17.50 2 courses; £22 per person 3 courses (minimum 2). **Credit** MC, V.
Beneath the ukiyo-e prints and plasma screen showing CGI cherry blossom, there's no mistaking this venue was once something quite un-Japanese. The Buddha Bar and Primo's Lounge, in fact. Not sure which one bequeathed its decor, but the long, long room is dominated by a crimson bar and precarious-looking high stools fashioned out of tangled metal, while there's a low stage at the back. Strung between them are a dozen or so tables, some bearing chess or backgammon markings. The food, at least, is definitely Japanese, and decent ingredients are in evidence. However, presentation was a bit half-baked on our visit: the sashimi assortment sounded good (13 pieces featuring salmon, tuna, sea bass, prawn and eel for £14) and tasted good, yet it looked measly and haphazard on a mock-lacquer platter. Likewise, teriyaki beef was nicely cooked, but appeared stranded on a clumsily strewn sea of lettuce. The menu is limited yet holds surprises: there is no noodle category; you can have cheesecake tempura (!) for dessert; and the chef seems to like shiitake with everything in the tempura section. Sweet service, though.
Babies and children admitted. Booking advisable. Entertainment: musicians monthly (phone for details). Takeaway service.

North West
Golders Green

Café Japan

626 Finchley Road, NW11 7RR (8455 6854). Golders Green tube/13, 82 bus. **Lunch served** noon-2pm Sat, Sun. **Dinner served** 6-10pm Wed-Sat; 6-9.30pm Sun. **Main courses** £8-£9. **Set lunch** £8.50. **Set dinner** £12-£17. **Credit** MC, V.
You can tell a lot about a restaurant at last orders, and when we squeaked in one Saturday evening minutes before the sign on the door was flipped to 'Closed', the welcome was warm: none of the tetchiness sometimes shown to late-comers elsewhere. From the long menu our excellent and varied nigiri selection was 14-strong, each topped with a large piece of fish; of the à la carte nigiri specials, we had a brace of grilled unagi with caramelly sauce, which was lovely, and tako (octopus), which was tough – a rare event here. King crab tempura was airy and delicious. All present were in a good mood. Cheerful banter bubbled away behind the counter between the

RESTAURANTS

master chef and his assistants as they prepared dishes and, later, packed away ingredients and diligently cleaned work surfaces. The cosmopolitan crowd of diners – largely eastern around the counter, largely western in the narrow, yellow-walled room to the rear – was plainly enjoying the food. Little wonder Café Japan has been one of north London's most popular Japanese joints for so long.

Babies and children admitted. Booking advisable. No smoking. Takeaway service.

Eat Tokyo NEW

14 North End Road, NW11 7PH (8209 0079). Golders Green tube. **Lunch served** noon-3pm Tue-Sun. **Dinner served** 5.30-11pm Mon-Sat; 5.30-10pm Sun. **Main courses** (lunch) £2.50-£10; (dinner) £7-£18. **Set lunch** £5.80-£13. **Set dinner** £7-£25. **Credit** MC, V.

Although there are several Japanese restaurants between Swiss Cottage and Golders Green, few equal the might of Café Japan (*see p195*). But each time a new establishment opens in the area, the local Japanese community rushes over. And the food in this red, black and white eaterie – festooned with bright kimonos and pictures of geisha – is worth rushing over for. Potato croquettes were little more than mashed potato patties (studded with peas, dipped in breadcrumbs), but packed more flavour than anything made with such prosaic ingredients had a right to. Steak teriyaki was as glossy, tender and muscular as a sumo wrestler. Agedofu was pale, delicate and quivery: like female characters in a Murakami novel. The only dud was stir-fried vegetables, which were reminiscent of something you'd get in a Chinese takeaway, and arrived with unannounced chicken and pork pieces that had less flavour than the tofu. The food here doesn't quite measure up to that of Café Japan, but the Café is sometimes closed (often for several days and at short notice), so Eat Tokyo is a reliable alternative.

Babies and children welcome: high chairs. Booking advisable dinner. No smoking. Takeaway service.

Hampstead

Jin Kichi

73 Heath Street, NW3 6UG (7794 6158/ www.jinkichi.com). Hampstead tube. **Lunch served** 12.30-2pm Sat, Sun. **Dinner served** 6-11pm Tue-Sat; 6-10pm Sun. **Main courses** £5.50-£12.70. **Set lunch** £7.30-£13.80. **Credit** AmEx, DC, JCB, MC, V.

This dinky, two-level izakaya-style restaurant (there are three tables in the tiny basement) seats about 50. With just a fraction of its capacity taken, a pleasant calm prevailed on our Sunday lunchtime visit (though we've known the place humming on other Sundays). The speciality is sumiyaki, or char-grilled food, yet the long menu covers plenty of other bases: from standard starters like hiyayakko (chilled tofu) and wakame kyuri-su (vinegared seaweed and cucumber) via sashimi, sushi and udon to less common dishes like sake kama (grilled salmon jaw with salt). We ordered two set meals (with the usual bowl of rice and miso soup included): the seven-piece nigiri and the tempura teishoku, beefed up with a dish of sunagimo (tender and tasty fried chicken gizzards in a ponzu and grated daikon dressing). Japanese beers were our whistle-wetters, though the drinks menu also has a good-looking selection of shochu and umeshu (plum liqueur). Service is relaxed, friendly and efficient, and the food is served on nice homely tableware.

Babies and children welcome: booster seats. Booking advisable Fri-Sun. Takeaway service. **Map 28 B2.**

Swiss Cottage

Benihana

2006 WINNER BEST FAMILY RESTAURANT
100 Avenue Road, NW3 3HF (7586 9508/ www.benihana.co.uk). Swiss Cottage tube. **Lunch served** noon-3pm daily. **Dinner served** 5.30-10.30pm Mon-Sat; 5-10pm Sun.

Set lunch £11-£15. **Set dinner** £17-£55. **Credit** AmEx, DC, JCB, MC, V.

This is one of three London branches of the global teppanyaki chain, founded in 1964 by ex-Olympic wrestler Rocky Aoki; it's the smallest and oldest (opened in 1986) of the trio. Decor-wise, the restaurant is very much of its era, but the whole point of coming to Benihana is the hot-plate in front of you. Choose one of the set meals, and the food is prepared and cooked before your eyes by red-toqued chefs who arrive like gunslingers, with low-riding belts, and knives instead of six-shooters. They're performance artists as much as chefs, and conversation around the table stops as they get to work with a flamenco rat-a-tat of metal on metal. If you come with children, they'll be wide-eyed; our eight-year-old squealed with delight as an onion 'volcano' doused in soy sauce burst into flames. Youngsters also get spring-loaded chopsticks – a nice touch. And the food is good: the beef in our hearty chateaubriand menu was copious and tender, as was the delicious tuna steak with a gingery teriyaki sauce. Onion soup, rice and appetisers are served with each meal; you can also order sushi and sashimi.

Babies and children welcome: children's menu (Sun); high chairs. Booking advisable; essential weekends. No smoking. Tables outdoors (6, garden). Takeaway service. Vegetarian menu. **Map 28 B4.**
For branches see index.

★ Wakaba

122A Finchley Road, NW3 5HT (7586 7960). Finchley Road tube. **Lunch served** noon-3pm, **dinner served** 6.30-11pm Mon-Sat. **Main courses** £4.50-£19.80. **Set buffet** £6.60 (lunch). **Set dinner** £22.50-£34. **Credit** AmEx, DC, JCB, MC, V.

Originally designed by minimalist architect John Pawson, this white-out oasis on grey Finchley Road had been looking tatty for several years. But a recent wash and brush-up has restored its former space-shuttle-white glory. The curved façade of

Menu

For further reference, Richard Hosking's *A Dictionary of Japanese Food: Ingredients & Culture* (Tuttle) is highly recommended.

Agedashidofu: tofu (qv) coated with katakuriko (potato starch), deep-fried, sprinkled with dried fish and served in a shoyu-based broth with grated ginger and daikon (qv).

Amaebi: sweet shrimps.

Anago: saltwater conger eel.

Bento: a meal served in a compartmentalised box.

Chawan mushi: savoury egg custard served in a tea tumbler (chawan).

Daikon: a long, white radish (aka mooli), often grated or cut into fine strips.

Dashi: the basic stock for Japanese soups and simmered dishes. It's often made from flakes of dried bonito (a type of tuna) and konbu (kelp).

Dobin mushi: a variety of morsels (prawn, fish, chicken, shiitake, ginkgo nuts) in a gently flavoured dashi-based soup, steamed (mushi) and served in a clay teapot (dobin).

Donburi: a bowl of boiled rice with various toppings, such as beef, chicken or egg.

Dorayaki: mini pancakes sandwiched around azuki bean paste.

Edamame: fresh soy beans boiled in their pods and sprinkled with salt.

Gari: pickled ginger, usually pink and thinly sliced; served with sushi to cleanse the palate between courses.

Gohan: rice.

Gyoza: soft rice pastry cases stuffed with minced pork and herbs; northern Chinese in origin, cooked by a combination of frying and steaming.

Hamachi: young yellowtail or Japanese amberjack fish, commonly used for sashimi (qv) and also very good grilled.

Hashi: chopsticks.

Hiyashi chuka: Chinese-style (chuka means Chinese) ramen (qv noodles) served cold (hiyashi) in tsuyu (qv) with a mixed topping that usually includes shredded ham, chicken, cucumber, egg and sweetcorn.

Ikura: salmon roe.

Izakaya: 'a place where there is saké'. An after-work drinking den frequented by Japanese businessmen, usually serving a wide range of reasonably priced food.

Kaiseki ryori: a multi-course meal of Japanese haute cuisine, first developed to accompany the tea ceremony.

Kaiten-zushi: 'revolving sushi' (on a conveyor belt).

Katsu: breaded and deep-fried meat, hence **tonkatsu** (pork katsu) and **katsu curry** (tonkatsu or chicken katsu with mild vegetable curry).

Maki: the word means 'roll' and this is a style of sushi (qv) where the rice and filling are rolled inside a sheet of nori (qv).

Mirin: a sweetened rice spirit used in many Japanese sauces and dressings.

Miso: a thick paste of fermented soy beans, used in miso soup and some dressings. Miso comes in a wide variety of styles, ranging from 'white' to 'red', slightly sweet to very salty and earthy, crunchy or smooth.

Miso shiru: classic miso soup, most often containing tofu and wakame (qv).

Nabemono: a class of dishes cooked at the table and served directly from the earthenware pot or metal pan.

Natto: fermented soy beans of stringy, mucous consistency.

Nimono: food simmered in a stock, often presented 'dry'.

Noodles: second only to rice as Japan's favourite staple. Served hot or cold, dry or in soup, and sometimes fried. There are many types, but the most common are **ramen** (Chinese-style egg noodles), **udon** (thick white wheat-flour noodles), **soba** (buckwheat noodles), and **somen** (thin white wheat-flour noodles, usually served cold as a summer dish – hiyashi somen – with a chilled dipping broth).

Nori: sheets of dried seaweed.

Okonomiyaki: the Japanese equivalent of filled pancakes or a Spanish omelette, whereby various ingredients are added to a batter mix and cooked on a hotplate, usually in front of diners.

Ponzu: usually short for ponzu joyu, a mixture of the juice of a Japanese citrus fruit (ponzu) and soy sauce. Used as a dip, especially with seafood and chicken or fish nabemono (qv).

Robatayaki: a kind of grilled food, generally cooked in front of customers, who make their selection from a large counter display.

Saké: rice wine, around 15% alcohol. Usually served hot, but may be chilled.

Sashimi: raw sliced fish.

Shabu shabu: a pan of stock is heated at the table and plates of thinly sliced raw beef and vegetables are cooked in it piece by piece ('shabu-shabu' is onomatopoeic for the sound of washing a cloth in water). The broth is then portioned out and drunk.

Shiso: perilla or beefsteak plant. A nettle-like leaf of the mint family that is often served with sashimi (qv).

Shochu: Japan's colourless answer to vodka is distilled from raw materials such as wheat, rice and potatoes.

Shoyu: Japanese soy sauce.

Sukiyaki: pieces of thinly sliced beef and vegetables are simmered in a sweet shoyu-based sauce at the table on a portable stove. Then they are taken out and dipped in raw egg (which semi-cooks on the hot food) to cool them for eating.

Sunomono: seafood or vegetables marinated (but not pickled) in rice vinegar.

Sushi: combination of raw fish, shellfish or vegetables with rice – usually with a touch of wasabi (qv). Vinegar mixed with sugar and salt is added to the rice, which is then cooled before use. There are different sushi formats: **nigiri** (lozenge-shaped), **hosomaki** (thin-rolled), **futomaki** (thick-rolled), **temaki** (hand-rolled), **gunkan maki** (nigiri with a nori wrap), **chirashi** (scattered on top of a bowl of rice), and **uramaki** or **ISO maki** (more recently coined terms for inside-out rolls).

Tare: general term for shoyu-based cooking marinades, typically on yakitori (qv) and unagi (qv).

Tatami: a heavy straw mat – traditional Japanese flooring. A tatami room in a restaurant is usually a private room where you remove your shoes and sit on the floor to eat.

Tea: black tea is fermented, while green tea (**ocha**) is heat-treated by steam to prevent the leaves fermenting. **Matcha** is powdered green tea, and has a high caffeine content. **Bancha** is the coarsest grade of green tea, which has been roasted; it contains the stems or twigs of the plant as well as the leaves, and is usually served free of charge with a meal. **Hojicha** is lightly roasted bancha. **Mugicha** is roast barley tea, served iced in summer.

Teishoku: set meal.

Tempura: fish, shellfish or vegetables dipped in a light batter and deep-fried. Served with tsuyu (qv) to which you add finely grated daikon (qv) and fresh ginger.

Teppanyaki: 'grilled on an iron plate' or, originally, 'grilled on a ploughshare'. In modern Japanese restaurants, a chef standing at a hotplate (teppan) is surrounded by several diners. Slivers of beef, fish and vegetables are cooked with a dazzling display of knifework and deposited on your plate.

Teriyaki: cooking method by which meat or fish – often marinated in shoyu (qv) and rice wine – is grilled and served in a tare (qv) made of a thick reduction of shoyu (qv), saké (qv), sugar and spice.

Tofu or dofu: soy beancurd used fresh in simmered or grilled dishes, or deep-fried (agedashidofu), or eaten cold (hiyayakko).

Tokkuri: saké flask – usually ceramic, but sometimes made of bamboo.

Tonkatsu: see above katsu.

Tsuyu: a general term for shoyu/mirin-based dips, served both warm and cold with various dishes ranging from tempura (qv) to cold noodles.

Umami: the nearest word in English is tastiness. After sweet, sour, salty and bitter, umami is considered the fifth primary taste in Japan, but not all food scientists in the West accept its existence as a basic flavour.

Unagi: freshwater eel.

Uni: sea urchin roe.

Wafu: Japanese style.

Wakame: a type of young seaweed most commonly used in miso (qv) soup and kaiso (seaweed) salad.

Wasabi: a fiery green paste made from the root of an aquatic plant that belongs to the same family as horseradish. It is eaten in minute quantities (tucked inside sushi, qv), or diluted into shoyu (qv) for dipping sashimi (qv).

Yakimono: literally 'grilled things'.

Yakitori: grilled chicken (breast, wings, liver, gizzard, heart) served on skewers.

Zarusoba: soba noodles served cold, usually on a bamboo draining mat, with a dipping broth.

Zensai: appetisers.

Eat Tokyo. See p196.

frosted glass and seamless panelled interior certainly has a calming effect. Yet perhaps potential customers were having trouble noticing such minimalist surroundings; we were the only diners for most of our midweek evening meal. Oshibori (hot wet flannels) got the meal off to an authentic start, and the food that followed didn't disappoint. Superb crab tempura hosomaki, chosen from the huge sushi menu, arrived featherlight and crispy, with beautifully juxtaposed flavours and textures. From the impressive specials list, halibut kazu zuke boasted slightly bitter charcoal flavours offset by a sweet saké glaze. Dobin mushi was fragrant, delicate and citrusy, while crunchy broccoli with a gooey sesame paste was gorgeous – the bright, fresh vegetable flavours perfectly partnering the warm, woody sesame. Although Wakaba is pricey, such fine contrasts of flavours make it well worth hunting down.
Babies and children admitted. Booking advisable Fri, Sat. Restaurant available for hire. Takeaway service. **Map 28 B3**.

Willesden

★ Sushi-Say
33B Walm Lane, NW2 5SH (8459 2971). Willesden Green tube. **Lunch served** noon-2.30pm Tue-Fri; 1-3.30pm Sat, Sun. **Dinner served** 6.30-10.30pm Tue-Fri; 6-11pm Sat; 6-10pm Sun. **Main courses** £6.30-£19.50. **Set dinner** £19.50-£30.30. **Credit** JCB, MC, V.
A small, friendly place that consistently turns out high-quality, imaginative food, Sushi-Say shines like a beacon amid the myriad depressing fast-food outlets and cheap caffs that line Walm Lane. From the sushi bar at the front of the long, low-ceilinged room came a gleaming plate of sashimi moriawase, bearing thick, luscious slices of tuna, salmon, sea bass and mackerel, and neat, precise natto maki. Raw fish dressed with ponzu is a speciality. Our sliced turbot wing and sunomono had the right combination of chewy texture and sharp flavours. A star dish was squid and cod roe in ponzu: thin, white ribbons of squid with pink pearls of roe. From the list of daily specials, rich, pâté-like slices of monkfish liver were served with grated radish and sliced spring onion. Yasai ten don (vegetable tempura on rice) seemed pedestrian in comparison, but a dessert of wasabi ice-cream – a palate-bending combination of hot and cold – marked a return to form. Book ahead; this place is deservedly popular with locals.
Babies and children welcome: high chairs. Booking advisable dinner. No smoking. Takeaway service.

Outer London
Richmond, Surrey

Matsuba
10 Red Lion Street, Richmond, Surrey TW9 1RW (8605 3513). Richmond tube/rail. **Lunch served** noon-3pm, **dinner served** 6-11pm Mon-Sat. **Main courses** £10-£30. **Set lunch** £9-£20. **Set dinner** £35-£40. **Credit** AmEx, JCB, MC, V.
Neat and petite, Matsuba oozes sophistication with its low-slung lighting, dark wood panelling and slate floors. The space consists of just seven tables and a small sushi bar tended by a white-hatted chef; friendly service adds to this intimacy. The restaurant is Korean-run, so alongside the Japanese food, you'll find Korean specialities such as a fine version of fiery kimchi (pickled chinese cabbage). One of the best dishes we tried was spicy cod's roe nigiri (the roe mixed with bright red chilli then perched on a finger of rice), a Korean twist that worked a treat. Also enjoyable was courgette iridashi: five thick deep-fried discs served with tsuyu. Uni nigiri was fresh as a sea breeze and a Florida maki (with yellowtail, tuna and spring onion wrapped in nori) was full of colour and flavour. At lunch most dishes cost less than £12, though a wider, pricier menu is offered in the evening. Prices can be steep, particularly for sashimi, but quality (apart from some tough toro on our visit) is generally high. It's wise to book.
Babies and children admitted. Booking advisable. No smoking. Takeaway service.

Jewish

The laws of kashrut (what defines food as kosher) can be briefly summarised: meat from a pig and all shellfish are forbidden; cows, sheep and poultry must be killed in accordance with strict rules; no dairy products are served with, or for some hours after, meat. The restaurants that follow these rules are supervised. A few others listed here, offering Jewish-style food, are designated 'not kosher'.

There are two Jewish restaurants in central London that aim high, with inventive, changing menus and creative chefs in the kitchen. Both **Six-13** and **Bevis Marks Restaurant** specialise in excellent desserts, but though they are ideal places for entertaining clients or friends, occasional lapses in the cooking deprive them of top billing. North-west London is bustling with kosher restaurants and bakeries. Of the eight establishments newly listed here, **Novellino**, a fish and dairy restaurant, offers style, good service and fresh, modern food; and **Kavanna** is the first kosher-supervised restaurant in the capital to venture into Indian cuisine. Also worth a mention is **Penashe** in Edgware. Although small, it continues to provide grilled meats of a consistently high standard, and is well worth the journey.

Central
City

Bevis Marks Restaurant
Bevis Marks, EC3A 5DQ (7283 2220/www.bevis markstherestaurant.com). Aldgate tube/Liverpool Street tube/rail. **Lunch served** noon-3pm Mon-Fri. **Dinner served** 5.30-9pm Mon-Thur. **Main courses** £11.50-£18.90. **Credit** AmEx, MC, V.
Through the windows of London's most stylish kosher venue you can see the chandeliers of the adjoining 18th-century synagogue. Lunch is served in the courtyard or upstairs, where there's elegant napery and spot-lit modern art. Despite such surroundings, both the food and service can be erratic and lackadaisical. On one occasion, attentive waiters brought well-executed dishes. Another time, thai beef was too heavily spiced and duck confit was crisp but overcooked. Plus points include an extensive wine list and an inventive menu; starters (pâté de foie gras, and sorrel-cured salmon) came with well-judged accoutrements. A chilled pea soup was refreshingly creamy. Next, rack of lamb and ribeye beef steak were both tender and rich, though the sauces needed more care in their construction. Roast cod fillet or vegetable linguini were the non-meat options. Desserts are unusually good: pears and fresh figs served with rosewater or almond macaroons; cherry tarte tatin; and gooseberry crumble with more than passable ice-'cream', the parev ingredients well disguised with vanilla, cinnamon or chocolate.
Babies and children admitted. Booking advisable lunch. Disabled: toilet. Kosher supervised (Sephardi). Restaurant available for hire. Tables outdoors (4, courtyard). Takeaway service. Vegetarian menu. **Map 12 R6**.

Marylebone

Reuben's
79 Baker Street, W1U 6RG (7486 0035). Baker Street tube.
Deli/café **Open** 11.30am-4pm, 5-10pm Mon-Thur; 11.30am-1hr before Sabbath Fri; 11.30am-10pm Sun.
Restaurant **Meals served** 11.45am-4pm, 5-10pm Mon-Thur; 11.45am-1hr before Sabbath Fri; 11.30am-10pm Sun. **Main courses** £9-£22. **Minimum** £10 per person. **Credit** MC, V.
Currently the only kosher deli in the West End, Reuben's is bustling at lunchtime when it's popular with those wanting a kosher sandwich. In the evening the basement restaurant offers more adventurous dishes, but simple grills are probably the best choice. Chicken wings on a skewer came pleasantly spiced, and grilled steak (or lamb chops) with chips were competently cooked. But although portions are generous and the chopped liver was meaty and smooth, it's hard to get excited about the menu. Anyone expecting a New York deli, with a bright and appealing cafeteria-style display, will be disappointed. Soups are served from covered containers; barley soup, though thick and comforting, had the unmistakable smell of a stock cube. Latkes, as large as a fried fillet of fish, were solid and greasy. Salt beef won the day: richly flavoured, succulent and of a good texture. A full serving is so generous that, even if you fancy one of the cakes on display, you won't have room.
Babies and children welcome: high chairs. Booking advisable (restaurant). Kosher supervised (Sephardi). No-smoking tables. Tables outdoors (3, pavement). Takeaway service. **Map 3 G5**.

Six-13
19 Wigmore Street, W1U 1PH (7629 6133/ www.six13.com). Bond Street or Oxford Circus tube. **Lunch served** noon-2.30pm Mon-Fri. **Dinner served** 5.30-10.30pm Mon-Thur. **Main courses** £17-£24. **Set lunch** £20 2 courses, £24.50 3 courses. **Credit** AmEx, MC, V.
Businessmen who want attractively presented kosher food in pleasant, if unspectacular, surroundings have found the perfect venue here. Each dish has been devised with care, though sometimes the unusual combinations are less successful than the traditional recipes. Is chicken soup with a julienne of smoked chicken an improvement on soft knaidlach? Are chicken liver croquettes better than real chopped liver? True, the croquettes came with a confit of red onion and a saffron poached pear, but our choice seemed less appealing than the beef carpaccio or futomaki sushi. Main courses were equally hit and miss. A medallion of beef with mushroom duxelle, roasted butternut squash and red wine jus was rare and tender. Yet tagine of lamb came with a bland, roasted fennel mash and cold apple sultana compote; there were no visible pieces of meat and the flavour was too sweet. Service was sluggish; it would have been wise to warn customers of the 20-minute wait for the hot chocolate fondant. Never mind – the excellent dessert menu offered white chocolate amaretto crème brûlée, and a smooth mocha parfait with vanilla crème pâtissière and crisp cinnamon tuile. Altogether, though, Six-13 provides pretty food that just misses star quality.
Babies and children welcome: high chairs. Kosher supervised (Sephardi). Separate room for parties, seats 22. Takeaway service; delivery service. **Map 9 H6**.

North
Finchley

The Burger Bar [NEW]
110 Regents Park Road, N3 3JG (8371 1555). Finchley Central tube. **Meals served** noon-midnight Mon-Thur, Sun. **Main courses** £6.95-£7.95. **Set lunch** (noon-4pm) £9.95 1 course incl soft drink. **No credit cards**.
This US-style diner, decorated with photos of 1960s America, is lit by eight large copper globes. The look is an unusual mixture, and such a description could also be applied to the food. The establishment is under the same Israeli ownership as Café Orli next door. Nineteen types of burger are offered, but no starters or desserts (unless you count non-dairy milkshakes in three colours). The meat is of a high quality, stacked into toasted sesame buns with a choice of additions. We tried the sweet chilli (with red pepper and a pleasantly spicy sauce), the avocado (a thick slice of the cool pear with mayonnaise) and the Mediterranean (tasty aubergine with a smear of houmous). The beef was grilled to order (meaning a fairly long wait) and was served garnished with lettuce, red onion and tomato. Some other choices (salmon or goose liver and the advertised fresh juices) were unavailable. You expect to pay more for kosher meat, and a hefty one-course burger with chips or onion rings will cost about £10. Not cheap if you're taking the family, but the novelty of a kosher hamburger will make this a popular venue.
Babies and children welcome: children's menu; high chairs. Booking advisable. Kosher supervised (Federation). No smoking. Tables outdoors (8, pavement). Takeaway service.

Olive Restaurant [NEW]
224 Regents Park Road, N3 3HP (8343 3188). Finchley Central tube. **Meals served** 11am-midnight Mon-Thur, Sun; 11am-2pm Fri. **Main courses** £10-£18. **Set meal** £37 2 courses (serves 2). **Credit** AmEx, MC, V.
A new venture into Persian kosher cuisine deserves more than one visit to test the sauces and herbs. In the first weeks the service and food at Olive were a bit haphazard. A month on, both had improved and the place was buzzing. Start the meal with squares of freshly made flatbread and sabzi: fresh herbs that have a pleasant menthol-like effect on the palate. The vegetarian meze includes salads and vine leaves stuffed with rice and raisins. Main courses are centred around various types of choresht: an Iranian stew with a thick sauce of pulses, vegetables, fruit, nuts and herbs. The version with lamb had aubergines and split lentils, but the vegetarian option, with parsley, coriander and spring onions, lacked body and complexity of flavour. Both these came with a lot of plain white rice, rather than more interesting 'polov' (with saffron, vermicelli or pistachios). Grilled lamb chops and barbecued chicken are also available, but these were unexceptional. Prices are reasonable and the takeaway menu of kebabs in pitta or laffa seems good value. For dessert there's well-made baklava, but more unusual is 'faloodeh shirazo' (ice noodles): a lemony sorbet with white vermicelli and frozen berries.

*Babies and children welcome: children's menu;
high chairs. Booking advisable. Disabled: toilet.
Kosher supervised (Sephardi). No-smoking tables.
Restaurant available for hire. Tables outdoors
(3, pavement). Takeaway service.*

North West
Golders Green

Bloom's

*130 Golders Green Road, NW11 8HB (8455
1338/www.blooms-restaurant.co.uk). Golders
Green tube.* **Lunch served** noon-3pm Fri. **Meals
served** noon-10.30pm Mon-Thur, Sun. **Main
courses** £10-£20. **Credit** AmEx, MC, V.

The menu, and many of the waiters, seem not to
have changed for around 40 years at Bloom's
(which originally had premises in the East End).
Yet perhaps there's a new chef, as the traditional
Ashkenazi cooking has improved of late. Well-
flavoured soups and meats are now a highlight.
Service is not only swift, but comes with a joke and
a smile. Portions are generous. There are no
delicate starters; go for the hefty mounds of
chopped liver or herring served with fresh rye
bread. Soup can be a meal in itself: haimishe barley
or chicken soup with lockshen, light knaidlach and
meat-filled kreplach. The best main courses are the
old favourites: cold fried haddock or salt beef. Ask
staff to leave the fat on the beef and you'll get
delicious, succulent slices. Meat lovers should also
try the mixed grill: tender steak, lamb chop,
sausage and chicken or liver. Good chips, passable
latkes or rice are included in the price. Vegetarians
are less well served, with little in the way of fresh
vegetables. Wine (just Israeli red or white, no
details) is available but rarely ordered. To end the
meal, lemon tea is probably a wiser choice than
apple strudel or lockshen pudding.
*Babies and children welcome: children's menu;
high chairs. Kosher supervised (Beth Din).
No smoking. Tables outdoors (2, pavement).
Takeaway service.*

★ Coby's Café & Flowers [NEW]

*115A Golders Green Road, NW11 8HR (3209
5049/5054). Golders Green tube.* **Meals served**
8am-11pm Mon-Thur, Sat, Sun; 8am-2pm Fri.
Main courses £4-£8. **Set breakfast** £6.80
1 course & soft drink. **Credit** AmEx, DC, MC, V.

Golders Green is bursting with eateries, so a new
one needs an angle; this one has flowers. Coby's is
divided into two: a flower shop on one side and a
café with an espresso machine and fresh juices on
the other. In the back are tables where you can
enjoy an Israeli-style lunch – light food, nicely
presented. The menu gives new meaning to the
word 'inventive'. Dishes are named after flowers,
with apparently little connection between the
names and flavours. There's a pizzanillus omelette
(new potatoes and mozzarella) served with a
pyramid of Israeli salad and a ball of soft cheese;
bonsai (fried mushrooms); and freesia pizza (sweet
potato and leek). The bird of paradise sandwich
boasted fried smoked salmon. There are crêpes,
fresh fruit shakes and nice-sounding cakes too; the
cheesecake was light and not oversweet. Pick up a
bunch of gerberas as you leave.
*Babies and children welcome: high chairs.
Booking advisable. Kosher supervised (Beth Din).
No smoking. Tables outdoors (3, pavement).
Takeaway service.*

Dizengoff's

*118 Golders Green Road, NW11 8HB (8458
7003/www.dizengoffkosherrestaurant.co.uk).
Golders Green tube.* **Meals served** *Summer*
noon-midnight Mon-Thur, Sun; noon-3.30pm Fri.
Winter noon-midnight Mon-Thur, Sun; noon-
3.30pm Fri; 7pm-midnight Sat. **Main courses**
£12-£18. **Credit** AmEx, MC, V.

This busy Israeli restaurant, with pictures of the
eponymous street in Tel Aviv, has peaks of
excellence and disappointing troughs. Free pickles
contained poor-quality olives, but the little latkes,
offered with the menu, are the best in Golders
Green. For meat lovers there are hearty soups such
as chicken or kooba (the patties bobbing in a
tomato- and lemon-based stock). Vegetarians will

be pleased with the wide choice of houmous –
creamy and delicious, with either chickpeas, tahina
or aubergine. Inventive dishes include an excellent
stuffed artichoke starter with a lemon and
mushroom sauce. Grilled meats are usually the
best choice for main course. Chicken kebabs or a
flattened thigh were tasty and tender. On one visit,
however, and for the first time ever, we found the
lamb cubes on a skewer to be tough. Mains come
with good thin chips, but an indifferent salad often
arrives too. Service is swift and pleasant, and there
are nice touches such as the offer of cut-up oranges
before dessert. A warm apple strudel had flaky
pastry and a pleasantly spiced fruity filling. More
attention to detail would help Dizengoff's regain
its star quality.
*Babies and children welcome: high chairs. Book
weekends. Kosher supervised (Sephardi). Tables
outdoors (3, pavement). Takeaway service.*

La Fiesta

*239 Golders Green Road, NW11 9PN (8458
0444). Brent Cross tube.* **Lunch served** noon-
3pm, **dinner served** 6-11pm Mon-Thur.
Meals served noon-11pm Sun. **Main courses**
£7.50-£45. **Set lunch** £15.50 3 courses. **Credit**
AmEx, MC, V.

Choose a table overlooking the street and watch the
bustling life in the orthodox section of Golders
Green. No place for vegetarians, La Fiesta is
primarily a steak restaurant, and this it does well:

'as good as kosher meat gets' according to some.
Cooked over hot coals, asado ribs (marbled with
fat), brochettes and lamb chops were succulent and
flavoursome. If you like beef rare, order a thick cut
and remember it continues to cook on the sizzling
hot-plate left on the table. Our entrecôte (1kg
shared between three) was juicy and tender. Huge
plates of chips or saltenia (sautéed potatoes with
garlic and parsley) made up for the slightly bland
chimichurri sauce. French wines, beer and soft
drinks can accompany the meal. Starters –
chorizo, meat or mushroom empanada pastry, or
a slightly under-grilled vegetable brochette – were
acceptable, but it's better to save your appetite for
such main courses as char-grilled chicken or three
hefty lamb cutlets. Fish, such as grilled sea bass
or salmon, is another alternative. Most desserts
rely on faux cream and ice-cream (more fruit would
be nice), so it's best to finish with an espresso or a
glass of fresh mint tea.
*Babies and children welcome: high chairs. Booking
advisable dinner. Kosher supervised (Beth Din).
No-smoking tables. Separate area for parties, seats
90. Takeaway service.*

★ Kinnor David [NEW]

*119 Golders Green Road, NW11 8HR (8455
7766). Golders Green tube.* **Meals served** noon-
11pm Mon-Thur, Sun. **Main courses** £7-£13.50.
Set lunch £8.99 2 courses, £11.95 3 courses.
Credit AmEx, MC, V.

Novellino

Menu

There are two main strands of cooking: Ashkenazi from Russia and eastern Europe; and Sephardi, originating in Spain and Portugal. After the Inquisition, Sephardi Jews settled throughout the Mediterranean, in Iraq and further east. London used to contain mainly Ashkenazi restaurants, but now Hendon and Golders Green are full of Sephardi bakeries and cafés, specialising in the Middle Eastern food you might find in Jerusalem. You can still get traditional chicken soup and knaidlach or fried latkes, but these are never as good as you'll find in the home. Nor will you find the succulent, slow-cooked Sabbath dishes that are made in many homes every Friday. The Israeli-type restaurants are strong on grilled meats and offer a range of fried or vegetable starters.

Since most kosher restaurants serve meat (and therefore can't serve dairy products), desserts are not a strong point. Rather than non-dairy ice-cream, it's better to choose baklava or chocolate pudding. Though, by the time you've got through the generous portions served in most places, you may not have room for anything more than a glass of mint or lemon tea.

Bagels or **beigels**: heavy, ring-shaped rolls. The dough is first boiled then glazed and baked. The classic filling is smoked salmon and cream cheese.
Baklava: filo pastry layered with almonds or pistachios and soaked in scented syrup.
Blintzes: pancakes, most commonly filled with cream cheese, but also with sweet or savoury fillings.

Borekas: triangles of filo pastry with savoury fillings such as cheese or spinach.
Borscht: a classic beetroot soup served hot or cold, often with sour cream.
Challah or **cholla**: egg-rich, slightly sweet plaited bread for Sabbath.
Chicken soup: a clear, golden broth made from chicken and vegetables.
Chopped liver: chicken or calf's liver fried with onions, finely chopped and mixed with hard-boiled egg and chicken fat. Served cold, often with extra egg and onions.
Chrane or **chrain**: a pungent sauce made from grated horseradish and beetroot, served with cold fish.
Cigars: rolls of filo pastry with a sweet or savoury filling.
Falafel: spicy, deep-fried balls of ground chickpeas, served with houmous and tahina (sesame paste).
Gefilte fish: white fish minced with onions and seasoning, made into balls and poached or fried; served cold. The sweetened version is Polish.
Houmous: chickpeas puréed with sesame paste, lemon juice, garlic and oil.
Kataifi or **konafa**: shredded filo pastry wrapped around a nut or cheese filling, soaked in syrup.
Kibbe, kuba, kooba, kubbeh or **kobeiba**: oval patties, handmade from a shell of crushed wheat (bulgar) filled with minced meat, pine nuts and spices. Shaping and filling the shells before frying is the skill.
Knaidlach or **kneidlach**: dumplings made from matzo meal and eggs, poached until they float 'like clouds' in chicken soup. Also called matzo balls.

Kreplach: pockets of noodle dough filled with meat and served in soup, or with sweet fillings, eaten with sour cream.
Laffa: large puffy pitta bread used to enclose falafel or schwarma.
Latkes: grated potato mixed with egg and fried into crisp pancakes.
Lockshen: egg noodles boiled and served in soup. When cold, they can be mixed with egg, sugar and cinnamon and baked into a pudding.
Matzo or **matzah**: flat squares of unleavened bread. When ground into meal, it is used to make a crisp coating for fish or schnitzel.
Parev or **parve**: a term describing food that is neither meat nor dairy.
Rugelach: crescent-shaped biscuits made from a rich, cream cheese pastry, filled with nuts, jam or chocolate. Popular in Israel and the US.
Salt beef: pickled brisket, with a layer of fat, poached and served in slices.
Schnitzel: thin slices of chicken, turkey or veal, dipped in egg and matzo meal and fried.
Schwarma or **shwarma**: layers of lamb or turkey, cooked on a spit, served with pitta.
Strudel: wafer-thin pastry wrapped around an apple or soft cheese filling.
Tabouleh: cracked wheat (bulgar) mixed with ample amounts of fresh herbs, tomato and lemon juice, served as a starter or salad.
Viennas: boiled frankfurter sausages, served with chips and salt beef.
Worsht: beef salami, sliced thinly to eat raw, but usually cut in thick pieces and fried when served with eggs or chips.

The bright, welcoming interior was full on our early visit to this recently opened restaurant. The name is reflected in pictures of David's harp on one wall. Opposite this, a juicy looking shwarma was rotating in the stainless-steel cooking area. The food is predominantly North African: harira soup, couscous served in terracotta tagines, merguez sausages and Moroccan 'cigars'. But as well as a spicy white bean soup, you can have the traditional chicken broth with lockshen and knaidlach – well flavoured and served in deep chunky bowls. From the grill there's chicken with honey mustard sauce, fresh tuna or steaks. A veal escalope was crisply breaded and served with decent chips. Competing with three established kosher restaurants a stone's throw away, Kinnor David has attractively low prices: a salt beef sandwich for £4, main courses at £10. Service was swift, with complimentary pickles brought with a smile. The waiter even offered an opinion on the desserts, recommending the crème caramel. Wanting to leave on a happy note, we didn't mention the mounds of faux cream that came with this and wished we had chosen a fried pastry and glass of mint tea instead.
Babies and children admitted. Booking advisable. No smoking. Kosher supervised (Federation). Tables outdoors (3, pavement). Takeaway service.

Madison's Deli

1-4 Belmont Parade, NW11 6XP (8458 8777). Golders Green tube.
Deli **Open** 11am-10pm daily.
Restaurant **Lunch served** noon-3pm, **dinner served** 5.30-10pm daily. **Main courses** £5-£14.
Both **Credit** MC, V. Not kosher

Photos of New York yellow cabs decorate this new offshoot of the successful Stanmore deli. It's a noisy place and during busy lunchtimes the sound bounces off the grey tables and plastic chairs. Service is fast and smiling. The menu has been extended to include ciabatta sandwiches, wraps and melts. There's also more choice for vegetarians, but still a big selection of deli favourites such as Reuben sandwiches (corned beef, cheese and sauerkraut on rye bread), gefilte fish and burgers. The food was hit and miss on our visit: cold borsht resembled a beetroot cordial with little depth of flavour, but vegetable spring rolls were crisp and tasty. We also enjoyed a large portion of smooth chopped liver. Main courses were similarly variable. An unexceptional plate of salt beef and a poor meat loaf with watery mashed potatoes came from the same kitchen as a fresh grilled sole with crisp, dry chips and a just-right liver and fried onions. Desserts (mostly dairy, as Madison's doesn't follow kashrut rules) are appealing and inexpensive. The cheesecake and carrot cake looked good, and from past experience we can recommend the delicious lockshen pudding and chocolate fudge cake.
Babies and children welcome: children's menu; high chairs. Booking advisable weekends. Disabled: toilet. No-smoking tables. Restaurant available for hire. Takeaway service.
For branch see index.

Met Su Yan

134 Golders Green Road, NW11 8HB (8458 8088/www.metsuyan.co.uk). Golders Green tube.
Lunch served noon-2.15pm Mon-Thur; noon-2.30pm Sun. **Dinner served** 6-11pm Mon-Thur,

Sun. **Main courses** £12.95-£15.95. **Set meal** £19.50 2 courses, £25-£29.50 3 courses, £39.50 4 courses. **Credit** AmEx, MC, V.
The name of this kosher oriental restaurant means 'excellent' and the bright, spacious interior and elegant china promise high standards. The menu is adventurous – from sushi and a wide selection of fish to an extensive choice of lamb, beef, duck and chicken. To get an idea of the variety, we chose a set menu and started with the impressive imperial hors d'oeuvres. Apart from a heavy spring roll, the dishes were faultless, if predictable: chicken satay, seaweed, sticky spare ribs and crisp triangles of sesame chicken. To follow, crispy aromatic duck could have done with some crunchy skin as the meat was dry. The hoi sin sauce and vegetable sticks were fine, but as the pancakes were cold the overall taste was disappointing. Main courses were generous. Beef (rather large pieces) in a mild sauce with spring onion and pak choi was less enjoyable than the lamb satay (a repeat of the spicy peanut sauce featured in the starters). The rice was good, but the tasteless stir-fried vegetables could have done with a splash of soy sauce. Service comes with a smile, but, like the food, doesn't reach heights of excellence.
Babies and children welcome: high chairs. Booking advisable. Kosher supervised (Federation). No smoking. Takeaway service; delivery service (over £30 within 2-mile radius).

★ Novellino NEW

103 Golders Green Road, NW11 8EN (8458 7273). Golders Green tube. **Meals served** 8.30am-midnight Mon-Thur, Sun; 8.30am-4pm Fri. **Main courses** £8-£16.50. **Credit** MC, V.

The display of fresh country breads in the window is a forerunner of good things to come. Novellino's tables are wide enough apart to be comfortable, and service is attentive and cheerful. The specialities are fish and vegetarian dishes, with the emphasis on Italian pastas and salads. For a quick lunch you could simply have soup of the day with freshly cut slices of raisin or ciabatta bread (plus good oil or tapenade in which to dip them), but it's hard to resist going through a full three courses. Light starters include the likes of roasted vegetables (properly cooked aubergines, courgettes, sweet potato and tomato), goat's cheese and feta salad, or tuna carpaccio. Fish comes in various forms: grilled, in tempura, with a cream sauce or with Moroccan seasoning. It also features in some pasta dishes; our fresh cod with fettuccine and green vegetables had tender white flakes. Another main course, salmon fish cake with chips, was crisp without a trace of grease. More unusual was the mushroom ragout and salsify, cooked in sweet red wine and cream. The seriously hungry can linger over coffee with chocolate cheesecake, or a custardy apricot tart with perfect pastry, while they make a date to return here.
Babies and children welcome: children's menu; high chairs. Booking advisable. Disabled: toilet. Kosher supervised (Beth Din). No smoking. Tables outdoors (5, pavement). Takeaway service.

Solly's

148A Golders Green Road, NW11 8HE (ground floor & takeaway 8455 2121/first floor 8455 0004). Golders Green tube.
Ground floor **Lunch served** 11.30am-4pm Fri. **Meals served** *Summer* 11.30am-11pm Mon-Thur, Sun. *Winter* 11.30am-11pm Mon-Thur, Sun; 1hr after Sabbath-1am Sat.
First floor **Dinner served** *Summer* 6.30-11.30pm Mon-Thur; noon-11pm Sun. *Winter* 6.30-11.30pm Mon-Thur; 1hr after Sabbath-midnight Sat; noon-11pm Sun.

Both **Main courses** £10-£15. **Set dinner** £24 3 courses. **Credit** MC, V.
The ground floor has wooden tables; upstairs in the 'Exclusive' restaurant, there are paper tablecloths. The menu is the same in both areas, and there's an oven turning out perfect hot and puffy pitta bread. We found that the cold starters were the best: a lemony tabouleh full of herbs; grilled aubergines chopped with either tahina or garlic and tomato; and creamy houmous with a slick of peppery olive oil. Hot hors d'oeuvres are more variable. Kibbe had a crisp, thin crust around a meat filling that was moist and tasty. Yet the other fried dishes were less appetising: tough falafel balls and vegetarian cigars that weren't as good as the meat version. And for some reason the chicken wings were served cold. Main courses included chunky chips or rice and the usual Israeli salad. Grills were reliably cooked; chicken, lamb shish kebab or schwarma were tender but sometimes over-seasoned. For dessert, baklava, turkish delight or halva are a better choice than the parev ice-cream. The menu mentions 'fine old Lebanese traditions', but Solly's needs more staff to cope with the number of tables; currently, it is let down by lapses in service.
Babies and children welcome: high chairs. Booking advisable (first floor). Disabled: toilet. Kosher supervised (Beth Din). No smoking. Separate room for parties, seats 100. Takeaway service.

Hendon

Eighty-Six Bistro Bar

86 Brent Street, NW4 2ES (8202 5575). Hendon Central tube. **Lunch served** noon-3pm, **dinner served** 6-11pm Mon-Thur. **Meals served** noon-11pm Sun. **Main courses** £9.95-£22.95. **Credit** MC, V.
A year after opening, Eighty-Six still offers an original and appealing menu, but whereas the service has improved, some dishes are disappointing.

Slices of challah were brought to the table with tapenade, pesto and vegetable sticks. Starters of calvados foie gras and salad of roast tongue both offered tender meat and well-judged, if slightly sweet sauces. Main-course grills include T-bone steak, veal or lamb chops and poussin, but one of the most frequently ordered dishes is the '86 burger', a juicy chunk of minced beef topped with smoked goose breast. Prices are higher than average, but the standard of food doesn't always meet expectations. Roast duck fillet with noodles turned out to be a leg (apparently pre-cooked) on a bed of spaghetti with a jammy sauce and prunes. Steamed vegetables also seemed tired, with little flavour. Our spirits were restored with a half bottle of full-flavoured Baron David Bordeaux and an excellent sirloin steak salad. Portions are generous so desserts aren't essential. Nevertheless, we plumped for chocolate fondant; it wasn't available, and a heavy slab of chocolate cake was offered as an alternative.
Babies and children welcome: high chairs. Booking advisable. Kosher supervised (Federation). No smoking. Takeaway service.

Isola Bella Café

63 Brent Street, NW4 2EA (8203 2000/ www.isolabellacafe.com). Hendon Central tube. **Meals served** 8am-11pm Mon-Thur, Sun; 8am-4pm Fri. **Main courses** £10-£18. **Set lunch** £15-£18 3 courses. **Credit** AmEx, DC, MC, V.
How do you approach a menu offering 314 dishes? Vegetables, fish, pasta and pizza come in a multitude of combinations – and now sushi has been added to the mix. Can there possibly be a Thai, Italian, Israeli and Japanese chef in the kitchen? Mushrooms, tomatoes, french beans and sweetcorn are served in many guises: tossed in a sauce with potatoes, or added to noodles or rice. But when fusion takes over, as with pesto and salsa, the results are less successful. While the

Bakeries

Here we've listed the best of London's kosher bakeries – along with the non-kosher Brick Lane Beigel Bake – offering hot-from-the-oven bread and pastries. The standard is consistently high, especially for the smoked salmon bagels. It's hard to believe that the flaky croissants don't come from Paris or the borekas from a market in Jerusalem.

Bonjour

84 Brent Street, NW4 2ES (8203 8848). Hendon Central tube. **Open** 5am-11pm Mon-Wed, Sun; 5am Thur-6pm Fri. **No credit cards.**
A small shop where the sweet smell of baking bursts out into the street. Breads include a puffy pitta and a crusty rye loaf. Best cakes: small danish pastries, a light and fruity blueberry muffin, and a warm chocolate soufflé.
Kosher supervised (Beth Din). Takeaway service.

Brick Lane Beigel Bake

159 Brick Lane, E1 6SB (7729 0616). Liverpool Street tube/rail/8 bus. **Open** 24hrs daily. **No credit cards.** Not kosher
The competitor two doors down does better sausage rolls, but this charismatic, 24-hour East End institution – all human life is here – wins out in every other regard: perfect bagels both plain and filled (egg, cream cheese, herring, mountains of salt beef), superb breads and magnificently moreish cakes.
Takeaway service. **Map 6 S4.**

Carmelli

128 Golders Green Road, NW11 8HB (8455 2074/www.carmelli.co.uk). Golders Green tube. **Open** 6.30am-1am Mon-Wed; 6am Thur-1hr before Sabbath Fri; 1hr after Sabbath Sat-1am Mon. **No credit cards.**
The best of all the displays can be ogled here: challahs and rolls on the left, creamy gateaux in the centre, and hot borekas and pizza on the right. The range is huge, including a good nutty baklava and well-filled sweet cheese buns. In the evenings, Carmelli is popular with the young crowd.
Kosher supervised (Beth Din and Kedassia).

Daniel's Bagel Bakery

12-13 Hallswelle Parade, Finchley Road, NW11 0DL (8455 5826). Golders Green tube. **Open** 7am-9pm Mon-Wed; 7am-10pm Thur; 7am-1hr before Sabbath Fri. **No credit cards.**
Daniel's knows how to bake: biscuits are crisp and not oversweet; bagels, plain or filled with smoked salmon, have the right chewiness. Don't miss the fresh breads behind the counter, especially the rye. Crumbles and pies are also served to customers at Café Dan next door.
Kosher supervised (Beth Din).

M&D Grodzinski

223 Golders Green Road, NW11 9ES (8458 3654). Golders Green tube. **Open** 6am-11pm Mon-Thur, Sun; 6am-5pm Fri. **Credit** MC, V.
Once a large chain of bakers, dating back to 1888, Grodzinski's specialises

in traditional festival cheese- and honey-cakes. The style is old-fashioned: sandwiches, doughnuts, jam tarts, gingerbread men and, from the yeast cakes, a delicious currant loaf.
Kosher supervised (Beth Din and Kedassia). Takeaway service.

Hendon Bagel Bakery

55-57 Church Road, NW4 4DU (8203 6919/9866). Hendon Central tube. **Open** 7am-11pm Mon-Wed; 7am midnight Thur; 7am-6pm Fri; 11pm Sat-11pm Sun. **No credit cards.**
These folk bake challah and rolls of superlative quality, lightly glazed and perfect in texture. Sweet cheese danish and plain croissants are crisp and light too. An interesting takeaway menu for parties offers platters of mini borekas and bagels, along with tiny pizzas and quiches, and fish balls or goujons.
Kosher supervised (Federation).
For branches (Orli) see index.

Mr Baker

119-121 Brent Street, NW4 2DX (8202 6845). Hendon Central tube. **Open** 7am-midnight Mon-Thur, Sun; 1hr after Sabbath-3am Sat. **No credit cards.**
In the year since it opened, Mr Baker's café has expanded into the light airy space of the bakery display. Have a cappuccino and a sweet cinnamon or custard croissant. Then take home a few mushroom borekas and pizza rounds.
Babies and children admitted. Tables outside (4, pavement). Takeaway service.

flavour of many of the dishes is appealing, if not quite authentic, the plates are uncomfortably over-filled. A starter of california roll sushi (raw tuna and avocado in nori cones) was generous, but the mozzarella salad (white balls on a mountain of greens) would have been enough for four. Main courses are equally hearty. From the Thai section a grilled St Denis (sea bream) arrived fragrantly charred. With salad and stir-fried vegetables, there wasn't an inch of space on the plate. Droolingly creamy dessert cakes are flown in from Israel: layers of white chocolate, meringue, tiramisu, mousse and ganache (aptly named Himalaya or Storm). The waitresses (cheerful but mainly non-English speaking) are many sizes thinner than those enjoying the food.

Babies and children welcome: high chairs. Booking advisable. Kosher supervised (Beth Din). No smoking. Separate room for parties, seats 70. Takeaway service. Vegetarian menu.

Kavanna NEW

60 Vivian Avenue, NW4 3XH (8202 9449). Hendon Central tube. **Meals served** 5.30-11pm Mon-Thur, Sun. **Main courses** £10.50-£15.50. **Set meal** £22 per person (minimum 2); £20 per person (minimum 4). **Credit** MC, V.

The thick carpet, crisp linen tablecloths and chandeliers look like those at many a high-street Indian restaurant, but Kavanna is kosher-supervised: a first for London. Within days of opening, with no advertising, the place was already full of customers eager to try its tandoori delicacies. Onion bhajis were crisp and perfectly fried; charred chicken wings came mildly spiced and attractively presented with a cucumber flower. From a wide choice of dishes (birianis, baltis, grills that arrive sizzling from the kitchen), it was hard to make decisions. Chicken tikka masala was cooked with almonds, 'cream' and spices – but of course real cream wasn't used, and though the sauce was rich and smooth, it wasn't quite authentic. Lamb biriani had cubes of tender lamb mixed with basmati rice and was served with a vegetable sauce. Bombay aloo was altogether hotter on the spice scale, the potatoes coated in a golden sauce. Peshwari nan (filled with coconut, sultanas and almonds) was puffy and totally delicious. Service on our visit was pleasant, if a bit languid. Perhaps as the staff settle in they'll be more welcoming.

Babies and children welcome: children's menu. Booking advisable. Kosher supervised (Beth Din and Kedassia). No smoking. Takeaway service. Vegetarian menu.

St John's Wood

Harry Morgan's

31 St John's Wood High Street, NW8 7NH (7722 1869/www.harryms.co.uk). St John's Wood tube. **Meals served** 11.30am-10pm Mon-Fri; noon-10pm Sat, Sun. **Main courses** £8.95-£11.50. **Credit** AmEx, MC, V. Not kosher

The St John's Wood ladies who lunch seem to have gone elsewhere, so the sound of a radio, rather than fashion gossip, fills the air at Harry's. The 'kosher style' food is reliable as ever: smooth, creamy chopped liver with sweet and sour cucumbers; and boiled gefilte fish that is soft and 'grandma-like'. On a cold day you might choose hungarian goulash or fried chicken livers, but in summer a plate of tongue with coleslaw was more appealing. We've had perfect haddock in the past here – crisply fried and flaky inside – but choosing it grilled was a mistake, and it seemed less fresh this time. A smoked salmon bagel or mozzarella salad might have been better. Desserts are a strong point, with good cheesecake and lockshen pudding, but our cheese blinz had been overheated so the filling was too set and the sauce jammy. The wine list includes a Jean Lafitte white Burgundy and an Australian shiraz by the glass. Few people seem to order wine, however, preferring to get stuck into the traditional Jewish food. Presentation is appealing and service pleasant, but perhaps the portions are too big if you're intent on hitting the boutiques afterwards.

Babies and children welcome: high chairs. Booking advisable (taken on weekdays only). Tables outdoors (5, pavement). Takeaway service. **Map 2 E2. For branch see index.**

Outer London

Edgware, Middlesex

Aviv

87-89 High Street, Edgware, Middx HA8 7DB (8952 2484/www.avivrestaurant.com). Edgware tube. **Lunch served** noon-2.30pm Mon-Thur, Sun. **Dinner served** *Winter* 5.30-11pm Mon-Thur, Sat, Sun. *Summer* 5.30-11pm Mon-Thur, Sun. **Main courses** £9.95-£13.95. **Set lunch** (noon-2.30pm Mon-Thur) £9.95 2 courses. **Set meals** £15.95, £19.95, 3 courses. **Credit** AmEx, MC, V.

The high standard of service and the reliability of the food don't change at Aviv. You never have to wait; staff are keen and attentive. But either the tables have shrunk or the plates have grown, because the eating space seemed a little cramped. Starters ranged from an acceptable chicken soup to a good, smooth chopped liver and an excellent chicken satay (tender and mildly spiced with a creamy peanut sauce). Grills – burgers and steaks – came with very good chips and fresh courgettes and mangetout. The duck was less appealing, slightly overcooked with a sticky plum sauce that masked the flavour of the meat. In contrast, hungarian goulash was superb: melt-in-the-mouth tender and full of flavour. Barbecued rack of ribs was tasty and, of necessity, quite fatty. Portions are more than generous. For dessert, the chocolate coffee mousse was smooth and rich, but it's less wise to choose the meringue roulade or tiramisu: both are made with a non-dairy alternative to cream and mascarpone. The best way to end a satisfying meal here is with Aviv's fruit salad: a refreshing mix of at least eight fruits.

Babies and children welcome: children's portions; high chairs. Booking essential. Kosher supervised (Beth Din). No smoking. Tables outdoors (14, patio). Takeaway service.

★ B&K Salt Beef Bar

11 Lanson House, Whitchurch Lane, Edgware, Middx HA8 6NL (8952 8204). Edgware tube. **Lunch served** noon-3pm, **dinner served** 5.30-9.15pm Tue-Sun. **Main courses** £4.80-£11. **Unlicensed. Corkage** no charge. **Credit** MC, V. Not kosher

B&K has been going for years. Possibly the locals visit as much for a chat as for the rib-sticking kosher-style food; the decor isn't much of a draw. On a recent visit, the owner was welcoming and cheerful and quick to bring bread and a menu. The traditional starters were all good: chopped liver, a hearty bean and barley soup, and gefilte fish that might have come straight from grandma's kitchen. Worsht (salami) and eggs were competently cooked, but it's the salt beef that's the star of the show: a massive, warming, comforting plate of tender slices. The mixed salad could be a course on its own, but the latke, as is often the case in restaurants, was poorly cooked. Desserts aren't a highlight; you might do better to pass up the lockshen pudding and the apple strudel (the latter was rather overheated). Instead, sit with a glass of lemon tea, watch the busy takeaway counter and listen to the banter.

Babies and children admitted. Bookings not accepted. No smoking. Takeaway service (11.30am-9.30pm).

Kinneret NEW

313 Hale Lane, Middx HA8 7AX (8958 4955). Edgware tube. **Meals served** 2-10pm Mon-Thur, Sun. **Main courses** £10.95-£17.95. **Set lunch** £11.95, £14.95, 3 courses. **Set dinner** £16.95, £19.95, 3 courses. **Credit** MC, V.

First impressions of Kinneret's new owners are good: tablecloths are linen, and the complimentary nibbles include garlicky tomatoes and olives with warm pitta. The menu is extensive, with the chef offering a wide variety of cuisines. Yet we have doubts whether he can pull off lamb kleftiko, thai beef salad and aubergine baba ganoush in addition to the more standard salt beef, grills and kebabs. Starters included a creamy houmous with perfect falafel balls. A rather opaque chicken soup with lockshen and soft knaidlach was less appealing. The good-value set menu included starters of chopped liver, barbecued ribs, spring rolls or a mushroom pancake, followed by an acceptable grilled steak. Chicken couscous with flavoursome vegetables (carrots, sweet potato, celery) was served with a fillet of char-grilled chicken on top, instead of the expected sauce: not authentic, but a pleasing combination of textures. All main courses include chips or basmati rice and fresh chopped salad on the side. Save room for dessert: warm, flaky apple strudel or deliciously soft lockshen pudding (sweet with a hint of lemon). Service was attentive. Soft Brazilian music and watercolours on the walls added to an enjoyable experience.

Babies and children welcome: children's menu; high chairs. Booking advisable. Kosher supervised (Federation). No smoking. Takeaway service.

★ ★ Penashe

60 Edgware Way, Mowbray Parade, Edgware, Middx HA8 8JS (8958 6008/www.penashe.co.uk). Edgware tube. **Lunch** noon-3pm, **dinner served** 5-10pm Mon-Thur. **Meals served** 1hr after Sabbath-midnight Sat (winter only); noon-10pm Sun. **Main courses** £3.10-£8.45. **Credit** MC, V.

With small tables surrounded by photos of New York, there is little space to sit while you wait for the best takeaway in kosher London. Young people watch the TV. Oldies read copies of the *Jewish Chronicle* and while away time with a carton of 'Booba's homemade soup': as good a chicken soup and matzo ball as you'll find in many Jewish homes. Each item on the small menu is cooked to order. Penashe offers just one type of burger, but that (like the scrumptious barbecued chicken wings) is grilled and temperature-checked to ensure perfect cooking. The salt beef – cut American-style with layers of thinly sliced meat piled into rye or white bread – was succulent and fresh. Chips arrived thick and crisp, though latkes were less successful. In winter try the hot goulash. Otherwise go for a grilled steak sandwich, with the meat cut from the ball of the rib: satisfying down to the last tender bite. Standards are equally high at Penashe's catering service, where the firm provides Fun Stalls for bar- and batmitzvahs.

Babies and children welcome: children's menu; high chairs. Kosher supervised (Beth Din). No smoking. Takeaway service.

Sheva & Sheva NEW

311 Hale Lane, Edgware, Middx HA8 7AX (8905 4552). Edgware tube. **Lunch** noon-3pm, **dinner served** 6-11pm Mon-Fri. **Meals served** 11am-11pm Sun. **Main courses** £8.95-£14.95. **Set lunch** £12.99 2 courses incl coffee. **Credit** AmEx, MC, V.

The name Seven & Seven has a biblical significance, the two numbers meaning good luck. This is certainly a buzzing venue, with an illuminated tree on display and old Italian songs on the sound system. Clearly, from the packed room, there's a demand for a kosher pizzeria. Ceilings are low and noise-levels are high, so waiters can hardly hear your orders. Classic Italian food is on the menu: pizzas, pasta and a good choice of fish (but no meat as this is a dairy/vegetarian establishment). Roasted red pepper and plum tomato salad, or cannellini carciofo (with artichokes) sound good, but the appeal doesn't always transfer to the plate. The fish section is imaginative, yet though the sauces are inventive, it's the freshness of the cod or tuna that ought to stand out. Pizzas were as they should be: large, crisp crust, generous filling. The pasta 'al forno' section offered generous, bubbling portions of lasagne, baked aubergines or stuffed mushrooms, but the pastas with a cream sauce could do with stronger seasoning. Before you leave, have a cup of real Italian coffee and try a chocolate kiss from the choice of lush-looking cakes.

Babies and children welcome: high chairs. Booking advisable. Disabled: toilet. Kosher supervised (Sephardi). No smoking. Takeaway service.

RESTAURANTS

Korean

K orean food is not, as you might expect, some halfway house between Chinese and Japanese. It has surprisingly vibrant flavours, mainly derived from chillies, garlic, fermented soy bean pastes, and sesame oil. The staples of the cuisine are more predictable – rice and noodles – but when they are used with barbecues, hot-pots and sizzling dishes, you get something uniquely Korean.

Much like Japanese food in London 15 years ago, Korean restaurants are undergoing a rapid evolution. A mere decade ago, Korean establishments were divided between a few central restaurants catering for mainly Japanese customers, and small neighbourhood cafés and eateries where London's main Korean community is based – New Malden in Surrey (on the edge of south-west London). New Malden remains a prime destination for Korean food, and is the location for star choices such as **Asadal** (which now has a branch in Holborn) and **You-Me**. However, in the past couple of years, a dozen new low-priced Korean restaurants have sprung up in the heart of the West End. These were originally aimed at Korean students, but some restaurateurs have realised that adventurous non-Koreans also make good customers, and have been gearing their menus accordingly. Budget pit-stops **Woo Jung** and **Myung Ga** have recently been joined by **Dong San**, **Bi Won** and the smarter **Jindalle**.

If you're not familiar with Korean food, try a set lunch, which makes a good entry point to the cuisine. These meals not only allow you to experience some of the signature dishes of Korean food, they are also terrific value; even in the smartest places you can usually eat for under a tenner.

Central
Bloomsbury

★ Bi Won NEW
24 Coptic Street, WC1A 1NT (7580 2660). Russell Square or Tottenham Court Road tube. **Meals served** noon-11pm daily. **Main courses** £5-£8. **Set meal** £17-£25 per person 2 courses (minimum 2). **Credit** MC, V.
Tucked away in a backstreet near the British Museum, this neat, cosy café, with cream walls and wooden floor, was packed with Korean students during our lunchtime visit. The place is poorly ventilated, so was rather smoky, but the food more than made up for it. Tasty kimchi was brought over as soon as we'd ordered our meal, and included piquant, long-fermented cabbage and freshly pickled grated radish. Mandu kuk was a generous bowlful of dumpling soup; the translucent dumplings featured good pastry that tasted own-made, and had a delicate pork and spring onion stuffing. They came in a light, refreshing chicken broth, punctuated with sliced rice cakes and egg whites. Vegetable tolsot bibimbap was packed with shredded carrots, spring onions, mushrooms and peppers, and topped with raw (rather than the more usual fried) egg; mixed with fiery koch'ujang, the dish was a delight. Porich'a was free, but we had to ask for it. The lunchtime set meals are exceptionally good value, particularly for central London; an à la carte menu is served only in the evenings.
Babies and children welcome: high chairs. Separate room for parties, seats 30. Tables outdoors (2, pavement). **Map 18 L5.**

Chinatown

Corean Chilli NEW
51 Charing Cross Road, WC2H 0NE (7734 6737). Leicester Square tube. **Meals served** 11am-11pm daily. **Main courses** £4.50-£20. **Credit** JCB, MC, V.
For an unassuming Korean rice and noodle bar, this small venue, set over two floors, is pleasantly decorated with colourful murals, clipped plants, and grey cement tongue-and-groove walls. The menu is also more adventurous than other Korean eateries in the area. Among the array of pancakes, rice and noodle dishes and a few Japanese items, you'll find seldom-seen ingredients such as sea slugs, ox bones and turban shells. We liked the crisp fried pork dumplings, and slender pancakes of candyfloss-light silken tofu, prettily studded with green chillies and mild, musky, bright red Korean chilli threads. Also satisfying was vegetable bibimbab: choy sum, bamboo shoot slivers, cucumber slices and beansprouts arranged like spokes of a wheel on plain rice, topped with a fried egg and nori seaweed strips, and mixed at the table with red chilli sauce. Stir-fried pork and 'vegetables' (in fact, half a leaf of pak choi) were also tasty, especially after we livened them up with extra dollops of gochu chang (fermented soy bean and red chilli paste). Cabbage, radish and stuffed cucumber kimchis were very fresh, and assertively flavoured with ginger and red chilli flakes. For an inexpensive, no-frills venue, Corean Chilli is much better than it needs to be.
Babies and children welcome: high chairs. Booking advisable. No-smoking tables. Restaurant available for hire. Takeaway menu. **Map 17 K6.**

Covent Garden

★ Woo Jung
59 St Giles High Street, WC2H 8LH (7836 3103). Tottenham Court Road tube. **Meals served** noon-1am Mon-Sat; 5pm-midnight Sun. **Main courses** £6-£8. **Set lunch** £6.50-£10 1 course incl soup. **Set meal** £17-£30 2 courses incl soup. **Credit** MC, V.
This tiny no-frills eaterie does a brisk lunchtime trade. We started with kimchi and freshly grated radish namul: both were too chilled, lacked the traditional fieriness, and the flavour was a little thin. In contrast, yuk hwe was a refreshing, generous portion of high-quality raw beef strips, with crunchy pear slices, raw egg yolks and pine nuts. Vegetable bindaedok, cooked with carrots and spring onions, had a lovely crisp texture yet was made with an egg and flour batter rather than the traditional mung beans: more p'ajeon than bindaedok. Vegetable tolsot bibimbap – containing round-grain rice, carrots, spring onions and mushrooms, topped with a fried egg – didn't come with koch'ujang as it should, and wasn't mixed at the table by the waiter. Instead, a squeezy plastic bottle of chilli sauce was plonked near us. Service could be more attentive. Woo Jung keeps its prices down by using cheaper ingredients (the dipping sauce and soy sauce were of inferior quality, for instance), but at least the porich'a is free. Come for a filling budget meal in central London.
Babies and children admitted. Takeaway service. **Map 18 K6.**

Holborn

★ Asadal
227 High Holborn, entrance on Kingsway, WC1V 7DA (7430 9006). Holborn tube. **Lunch served** noon-3pm Mon-Sat. **Dinner served** 6-11pm Mon-Sat; 5-10pm Sun. **Main courses** (lunch) £6-£8.90; (dinner) £5-£20. **Set lunch** £12.50 1 course. **Set dinner** £17.50 3 courses, £25-£30 4 courses. **Credit** MC, V.
This smart, spacious, subterranean venue next to Holborn tube station is a branch of the popular, long-established restaurant of the same name in New Malden. The dining area is pleasantly decorated in earthy tones, with walls covered in wooden panels and blocks of wood, a partially tiled wooden floor, cream leather banquettes, judiciously placed tasteful antiques and artefacts, and several nooks, crannies and group dining rooms for privacy. The food was sublime. We were blown away by the kimchi – especially crunchy radish and fiery stuffed cucumber. Tender pieces of scallops and tofu added interest to a flavoursome soup. Yuk hwe was a generous tangle of top-quality matchsticks of beef and crisp pear slices mixed at the table with raw egg. We also enjoyed succulent, though somewhat under-seasoned bulgogi cooked on a portable barbecue at our table. Vegetable japch'ae was a little mundane, and contained too much sesame oil, but light, fluffy tofu jeon (pancake), featuring silky-soft tofu, was a moreish dish prettily studded with colourful peppers. A lively fresh fruit platter, and own-made green tea ice-cream (not on the menu, but suggested by our waitress) rounded off a highly enjoyable meal.
Babies and children welcome: high chairs. Booking advisable. Disabled: toilet. Separate rooms for parties, seating 6 and 10. Takeaway service. Vegetarian menu. **Map 18 L5.** **For branch see index.**

Mayfair

★ Kaya
42 Albemarle Street, W1S 4JH (7499 0622/ 0633/www.kayarestaurant.co.uk). Green Park tube. **Lunch served** noon-3pm, **dinner served** 6-11pm Mon-Sat. **Main courses** £9-£18. **Set lunch** £12-£15 1 course. **Credit** JCB, MC, V.
There's a branch of Tiffany & Co almost opposite and a Paul Smith boutique down the road, which may give you certain preconceptions about this elegant Korean restaurant in the middle of

RESTAURANTS

Asadal

Mayfair. Don't panic: prices aren't much higher than you'd pay in Soho and the food is worth the extra investment. Unlike most West End Koreans, Kaya has gone for a bright, airy interior, with lots of intriguing Korean knick-knacks on the walls. At the back, hidden behind a mock-up of a Korean temple, are two private banquet rooms. There's also a cosy karaoke bar in the basement. The menu features the usual Korean repertoire – meaty barbecues, hot soups and rice hot-pots – plus an impressive selection of set lunches. We plumped for kalbi, a delicious mound of smoky, sweet-soy marinated beef spare ribs, with grilled spring onions, lettuce leaves and koch'ujang for wrapping, served with rice, salad and a tasty spring onion and bean-paste soup on the side. A selection of namul and panch'an arrived as part of the deal, including strongly fermented kimchi and cold steamed pumpkin. Our conclusion? Good value and more atmospheric than most of the central London competition.

Booking advisable. Separate rooms for parties, seating 8 and 12. Takeaway service. Vegetarian menu. **Map 9 J7.**

Piccadilly

Jindalle NEW

6 Panton Street, SW1Y 4DL (7930 8881). Piccadilly Circus tube. **Meals served** noon-11pm daily. **Main courses** £6.50-£21.90. **Credit** AmEx, MC, V.

What used to be a Korean-run Japanese restaurant called Samurai has morphed into a full-blown Korean eaterie, with an extensive menu and an emphasis on table-top barbecues. Waitresses are clad in cherry blossom-hued traditional dress, and the decor is smart and contemporary, with white walls and comfy black chairs. The food pulls no punches. Our kimchi had a kick like a startled mule. Seafood p'ajeon was hot and fresh and tasted 'like posh fish fingers' according to a novice to the cuisine. Likewise, a homely casserole dish of

potatoes and chicken cooked in a chilli-spiced bean paste chased away the cold weather outside. Choosing from among the barbecue dishes, which range from seafood to pork, beef and, unusually, duck, isn't easy. We took the road less travelled with marinated duck in Jindalle sauce. Duck breast, strips of carrot and spring onion had been marinated in a sweet and spicy sauce that was cooked to smoky, caramelised richness on the barbecue: delicious. At lunch, there are 20 dishes for under £6, from soup to meat and rice ensembles – not bad in a part of London that's better known for tourist traps than Korean treats.

Babies and children welcome: high chairs. No-smoking tables. Takeaway service. **Map 17 K7.**

Soho

Dong San NEW

47 Poland Street, W1F 7NB (7287 0997). Oxford Circus tube. **Lunch served** noon-3pm, **dinner served** 6-11pm daily. **Main courses**

£6-£12. **Set lunch** £6-£10 2 courses. **Set dinner** £28 3 courses. **Credit** AmEx, DC, MC, V.

One of the new crop of Korean-run restaurants that's aiming beyond the confines of oriental customers, Dong San is helped in this task by an appealing menu of Japanese dishes. We stuck to the Korean food, and were pleased with the results. Dish presentation, mirroring the the pleasingly simple but bold colours of the brightly lit interior, is a strong point. Yuk hwe was geometrically arranged around its plate like a Buddhist mandala, with matchsticks of nashi pear, cucumber, thin strips of cold raw beef and a raw egg, mixed at table by the waitress. Staff were concerned and keen to help. 'Do you know what to do?' enquired our waitress as a cold platter of pork belly, cut like fat bacon, arrived with an array of pickles. You take one of the cold, boiled chinese cabbage leaves, and use it as a wrap with some pork, kimchi and the chilli pastes. As with many Korean restaurants, the lunch deals here are great value. We tried a satisfying bowl of rice and abalone porridge aimed at oriental customers, but there are many other dishes with a broader, more occidental appeal. *Babies and children admitted. Booking advisable. Takeaway service.* **Map 17 J6.**

Jin

16 Bateman Street, W1D 3AH (7734 0908). Leicester Square or Tottenham Court Road tube. **Lunch served** noon-3pm, **dinner served** 6-11pm Mon-Sat. **Main courses** £8-£15. **Set lunch** £7.50-£10 lunchbox. **Set dinner** £30-£35 6 courses. **Credit** AmEx, MC, V.
Jin espouses the austere styling typical of Korean restaurants in Soho: dark furniture, white walls and Formica-topped tables with embedded hot-plate barbecues. Waiters and waitresses buzz around in all-black uniforms; curls of cigarette smoke waft up from the tables towards the extractor fan. The overall effect is slightly 1980s, but the welcome is friendly and the menu covers a broad range of Korean staples and some interesting-sounding drinks, including fruity cocktails made with soju. Our dinner started with a flavoursome bowl of yukkaejang, spicy egg-drop soup with beef shreds and Korean vegetables, and a plate of fiery kimchi on the side. Cooked at the table, sizzling bulgogi had plenty of flavour, but you have to order lettuce leaves and garnishes separately, which isn't pointed out on the menu. Chicken and ginseng soup was less successful. It sounded more intriguing than it tasted, though the pulpy ginseng root added some interest to an otherwise bland, watery broth. Still, waiters and waitresses were very attentive, returning regularly to stir the barbecue. Prices are unlikely to break the bank. So, not bad, but make sure you know what you're getting when you order.
Babies and children admitted. Booking advisable weekends. Separate room for parties, seats 10. Takeaway service. **Map 17 K6.**

★ Myung Ga

1 Kingly Street, W1B 5PA (7734 8220/ www.myungga.co.uk). Oxford Circus or Piccadilly Circus tube. **Lunch served** noon-3pm Mon-Sat. **Dinner served** 5.30-11pm Mon-Sat; 5-10.30pm Sun. **Set dinner** £25-£35 3 courses. **Credit** AmEx, DC, MC, V.
Instead of the usual dark wood and minimalist styling, Myung Ga has gone for light wood and minimalist styling. It pays off: the dining room feels bright and airy and the atmosphere is more cosy and friendly than at most of the competition. There are few surprises on the menu, but everything we tried surpassed our expectations. Despite the café vibe, food is beautifully presented. Fried, wun tun-style goonmandu (meat dumplings) arrived on a flat basket with carved vegetable garnishes, as did the oyster pancake (a dense, doughy omelette infused with the flavour of cooked oysters). Of the mains, yukkaejang was sublime – a complex, spicy soup with layers of chilli heat and tender strips of shredded sirloin beef. Spicy daeji bulgogi (barbecued pork) was prepared behind the scenes, but arrived on a sizzling platter in a thick spicy sauce; the flavours worked brilliantly, but we missed the ritual of cooking it ourselves at the table. For our money, this is the best Korean in Soho for an post-work dinner: prices are fair, food is excellent and there are numerous pubs along Kingly Street for a drink before or after.
Babies and children welcome: high chair. Booking advisable. Separate room for parties, seats 14. **Map 17 J6.**

Nara

9 D'Arblay Street, W1F 8DR (7287 2224). Oxford Circus or Tottenham Court Road tube. **Lunch served** noon-3.30pm Mon-Sat. **Dinner served** 6-11pm daily. **Main courses** £6.50-£45.50. **Set lunch** £6.50 1 course. **Set dinner** £7.50 1 course. **Credit** AmEx, MC, V.
Good-value lunches are the big draw here. The menu features dozens of Japanese and Korean meals, available as cheap lunches or slightly more expensive dinners. Inside, Nara looks like every other Korean restaurant in Soho (black tables and chairs, potted palms), but we defy anyone to find a cheaper Korean barbecue. Everything is freshly prepared, often right at the table. The place is understandably popular. When we visited, people were still trying to gain entrance after the kitchen had closed at 3pm. We decided against the Japanese menu and went for a Korean set lunch of

RESTAURANTS

Menu

Chilli appears at every opportunity on Korean menus. Other common ingredients include soy sauce (different to both the Chinese and Japanese varieties), sesame oil, sugar, sesame seeds, garlic, ginger and various fermented soy bean pastes. Until the late 1970s eating meat was a luxury in Korea, so the quality of vegetarian dishes is high.

Given the spicy nature and overall flavour of Korean food, drinks such as chilled lager or vodka-like soju/shoju are the best matches. A wonderful non-alcoholic alternative that is always available, although not always listed, is barley tea (porich'a). Often served free of charge, it has a light dry taste that perfectly matches Korean food. Korean restaurants don't usually offer desserts (some serve half an orange or some watermelon with the bill).

Spellings on menus vary hugely; we have given the most common.

Bibimbap or **pibimbap**: rice, vegetables and meat with a raw/fried egg dropped on top, often served on a hot stone.
Bindaedok, **bindaedoek** or **pindaetteok**: a mung bean pancake.
Bokum: a stir-fried dish, usually including chilli.
Bulgogi or **pulgogi**: slices of marinated beef barbecued at the table, then sometimes rolled in a lettuce leaf; eaten with vegetable relishes.
Chang, **jang** or **denjang**: various fermented soy bean pastes.

Chapch'ae or **chap chee**: mixed vegetables and beef cooked with transparent vermicelli or noodles.
Cheon, **jeon** or **jon**: the literal meaning is 'something flat'; this can range from a pancake containing vegetables, meat or seafood, to thinly sliced vegetables, beancurd and so on, in a light batter.
Chigae or **jigae**: a hot stew containing fermented bean paste and chillies.
Gim or **kim**: dried seaweed, toasted and seasoned with salt and sesame oil.
Gu shul pan: a traditional lacquered tray with nine compartments containing individual appetisers.
Hobak chun or **hobak jun**: sliced marrow in a light egg batter.
Japch'ae or **jap chee**: alternative spellings for chapch'ae (qv).
Jjim: fish or meat stewed for a long time in soy sauce, sugar and garlic.
Kalbi, **galbi** or **kalbee**: beef spare ribs, marinated and barbecued.
Kimchi, **kim chee** or **kimch'i**: pickled vegetables, usually chinese cabbage, white radishes, cucumber or greens, served in a small bowl with a spicy chilli sauce.
Kkaktugi or **kkakttugi**: pickled radish.
Koch'ujang: a hot, red bean paste.
Kook, **gook**, **kuk** or **guk**: soup. Koreans have an enormous variety of soups, from consommé-like liquid to meaty broths of noodles, dumplings, meat or fish.
Ko sari na mool or **gosari namul**: cooked bracken stalks dressed with sesame seeds.
Mandu kuk or **man doo kook**: clear soup with steamed meat dumplings.

Namul or **na mool**: vegetable side dishes.
P'ajeon or **pa jun**: flour pancake with spring onions and (usually) seafood.
Panch'an: side dishes; they usually include pickled vegetables, but possibly also tofu, fish, seaweed or beans.
Pap, **bap**, **bab** or **pahb**: cooked rice.
Pokkeum or **pokkm**: stir-fry. For example, **cheyuk pokkeum** (pork), **ojingeo pokkeum** (squid) **yach'ae pokkeum** (vegetable).
Porich'a: barley tea.
Shinseollo, **shinsonro**, **shinsulro** or **sin sollo**: 'royal casserole'; a meat soup with seaweed, seafood, eggs and vegetables, all cooked at the table.
Soju or **shoju**: a strong Korean vodka, often drunk as an aperitif.
Teoppap or **toppap**: 'on top of rice'. For example, **ojingeo teoppap** is squid served on rice.
Toenjang: seasoned (usually with chilli) soy bean paste.
Tolsot bibimbap: tolsot is a sizzling hot stone bowl that makes the bibimbap (qv) a little crunchy on the sides.
Tteokpokki: bars of compressed rice (tteok is a rice cake) fried on a hot-plate with veg and sausages, in a chilli sauce.
Twaeji gogi: pork.
T'wigim, **twigim** or **tuigim**: fish, prawns or vegetables dipped in batter and deep-fried until golden brown.
Yuk hwe, **yukhoe** or **yukhwoe**: shredded raw beef, strips of pear and egg yolk, served chilled.
Yukkaejang: spicy beef soup.

dol bibimbap, a crucible-like hot-pot filled with rice, vegetables and seasoned beef, topped with an egg and folded together at the table with hot chilli sauce. This is probably the most filling dish on the menu, so we were quite happy with the small size of the side dishes: a fairly plain spring onion soup and several small bowls of panch'an and namul. Sit at the front: the back room has disco-blue spotlights and the downstairs dining room feels cramped and remote.

Babies and children admitted. Booking not accepted Fri, Sat. Takeaway service. **Map 17 J6**.

South West
Parsons Green

Wizzy
616 Fulham Road, SW6 5PR (7736 9171/ www.wizzyrestaurant.co.uk). Parsons Green tube. **Lunch served** noon-3pm, **dinner served** 6-11.30pm daily. **Main courses** £8.50-£15. **Credit** AmEx, MC, V.
This small neighbourhood restaurant opened in a blaze of publicity in 2005, not least because it has a Korean woman chef, and serves Korean food with a contemporary twist. Some dishes work, but others miss the mark. Naju pear (one of the fragrant varieties of pears from South Korea) and mango salad arrived looking like a window box; there were so many mixed salad leaves that we had to play 'spot the pear and mango' (four or five pieces were eventually uncovered). The sesame-mandarin dressing was delicious, though, and this same dressing also featured in a starter of filo-wrapped king prawns, prettily served in a Martini glass. But the prawns tasted dry, and, topped with a yoghurt and yuzu-fruit sauce, there was too much going on in the dish. Spring onion pancake resembled a thick, deep-fried quiche, yet was packed with fresh vegetables and so tasted better than it looked. Beef stew was scrumptious; the meat had been slow-cooked and was exceptionally tender, and the gravy, flavoured with bone marrow, was rich and caramel-like. Despite our caveats, we rate Wizzy as a wonderful local eaterie – as opposed to a wonderful Korean restaurant.
Babies and children welcome: high chairs. Booking advisable.

Raynes Park

★ ★ Cah Chi
34 Durham Road, SW20 0TW (8947 1081). Raynes Park rail/57, 131 bus. **Lunch served** noon-3pm, **dinner served** 5-11pm Tue-Fri. **Meals served** noon-11pm Sat; noon-10.30pm Sun. **Main courses** £4.50-£14. **Set dinner** £18 3 courses. **No credit cards**.
This is easily the most accessible Korean restaurant in south-west London, particularly for newcomers to the cuisine. Staff are happy to explain the ins and outs of Korean cooking and waitresses cut seamlessly from speaking Korean to Home Counties English. Inside, Cah Chi feels more like a nursery school than a restaurant. Children's drawings adorn the walls, and menus are handwritten in chunky Korean script on coloured cards in the window. The liberal use of varnished pine only adds to the kindergarten feel. Soups are a big hit. Seaweed broth with bean paste resembled a more complicated miso, while maeun jang (spicy fish soup) had plenty of chilli heat but was refreshingly clean on the palate. Even barbecues are done with imagination. Marbled medallions of beef tenderloin were lightly grilled at the table, dipped in seasoned sesame oil, then popped hot on to the plate, ready to wrap in lettuce leaves with koch'ujang and tangy shreds of marinated spring onion. All meals come with a selection of namul and panch'an, including cabbage, radish and cucumber kimchi and delicious honey-marinated soy beans. You can bring your own wine too (10% corkage). Payment is by cash or cheque.
Babies and children welcome: high chairs. Booking essential. Separate room for parties, seats 18. Takeaway service.

North West
Golders Green

Kimchee
887 Finchley Road, NW11 8RR (8455 1035). Golders Green tube. **Lunch served** noon-3pm Tue-Fri; noon-4pm Sat, Sun. **Dinner served** 6-11pm Tue-Sun. **Main courses** £6.50-£8.50. **Set lunch** £6.50 1 course incl soup. **Credit** JCB, MC, V.
Since our last visit, the long-established Kimchee has been redecorated. Busy wallpaper covered with blocks of oriental line prints is now a feature, as are wall-mounted wooden cupboards with bamboo screens, and ceramic Korean masks. The distinctive wood, glass and rope dining tables with built-in barbecues are the same, and the young Korean waitresses dressed in hanbok continue to smile. Very few Korean restaurants get their barbecue dishes just right, and Kimchee is no exception. Our waitress placed unmarinated mussels, squid and mixed vegetables on to the barbecue all at once; as these ingredients require different cooking times, the dish wasn't a success. Moreover, it was bland. Much more flavoursome was yuk hwe – here flecked with lots of parsley. The best dishes were vegetarian. Delicate, spongy bindaedok (made from fermented yellow mung-bean flour batter) came studded with an array of colourful vegetables; and fried tofu cubes and seaweed squares added texture and interest to vegetable tolsot bibimbap. Disappointingly , the kimchi and fresh radish namul lacked a kick. If the staff and kitchen went that extra mile, Kimchee could be one of the best Koreans in town.
Babies and children admitted: high chairs. Booking essential Fri-Sun. Takeaway service.

Outer London
New Malden, Surrey

★ Hamgipak
169 High Street, New Malden, Surrey KT3 4BH (8942 9588). New Malden rail. **Meals served** 11am-10pm Mon, Tue, Thur-Sun. **Main courses** £5-£20. **Credit** MC, V.
Only 12 people can squeeze into this tiny Korean café on busy New Malden High Street, but locals drift in all day for authentic Korean food served in double-quick time. Don't be put off by the Lilliputian dimensions of the dining room; the menu runs for pages and pages, with all the expected barbecues, hot-pots and stir-fries. Quite how the cooks manage to prepare all this in the tiny kitchen at the back is one of life's mysteries. Dishes are divided into plate meals (with rice or noodles) and main courses, which are normally big enough to share. Our lunch began with pickled cucumbers stuffed with shredded radish, which seemed slightly superfluous to the free kimchi that arrived on the side. Spicy fried chicken on rice melted in the mouth; it came with a thick, chilli-speckled sauce full of broccoli and beansprouts. We didn't, however, warm to the cha jang myun (white noodles with caramelised onions in black bean sauce). Our fellow diners seemed to adore the pungent flavour and gloopy consistency, but we found it slightly overpowering. In all, we feel that Hamgipak is more suitable for a lunchtime snack than a slap-up dinner.
Babies and children admitted. No smoking. Takeaway service.

Han Kook
Ground floor, Falcon House, 257 Burlington Road, New Malden, Surrey KT3 4NE (8942 1188). Raynes Park rail. **Lunch served** noon-3pm Mon, Tue, Thur, Fri. **Dinner served** 6-11pm Mon-Fri. **Meals served** noon-11pm Sat, Sun. **Main courses** £5.90-£27.90. **Set meal** £20 3 courses (minimum 2). **Credit** MC, V.
Spacious and homely, Han Kook has many charms – but, unfortunately, its food is not one of them. The dining room, with traditional low seating on one side, is pleasantly decked out with paper and bamboo screens. Free porich'a and panch'an were

brought as soon as we sat down. The panch'an included tangy, long-fermented cabbage kimchi, omelette squares, caramelised barley, and cucumber kimchi so garlicky that we felt self-conscious on our train journey home. Sashimi was a mixed bag: very fresh salmon, but mundane turbot. Other dishes were similarly variable. Bibimbap was tasty, but bulgogi lacked flavour; it was cooked on a portable barbecue with lots of watery gravy and heaps of vegetables, then mixed with cellophane noodles into an odd japch'ae-like concoction. In other words, the dish was all wrong. The menu is a carnivore's delight (there's little for vegetarians), with many rarely seen dishes, the majority of which serve two. The drinks list features traditional cinnamon and persimmon tea, and various types of soju flavoured with citrus, cucumber and bamboo. Service from hanbok-clad waitresses was delightfully attentive.
Babies and children welcome: high chairs. Booking essential dinner Fri-Sun.

★ Jee Cee Neh
74 Burlington Road, New Malden, Surrey KT3 4NU (8942 0682). New Malden rail. **Lunch served** noon-3pm, **dinner served** 5-11pm Tue-Sun. **Main courses** £6.50-£8. **Credit** MC, V.
Previously known as Jee's, this smart café has been refurbished. It now boasts stripy coloured panels running down one wall, framed Korean paintings, polished dark wood furniture and grey tiled floor. The food was spankingly fresh and exquisitely flavoured, and service was helpful. We were wowed by namul; Korean greens, beansprouts with shredded cucumber, and grated radish featured just-picked freshness married with the crunch of roasted sesame seeds. Yet we needn't have ordered this; free kimchi arrived unbidden (along with malted tea), and included long-fermented cabbage, fresh hispi cabbage in red-pepper sauce, bracken stalks, and chilli-spiked potato with Korean leeks. Japch'ae is difficult to get right; the slipperiness of translucent sweet potato noodles doesn't make for easy cooking. Here, the noodles were mixed with red and green peppers, dried and fresh mushrooms, shredded carrots and rectangular, wafer-thin omelette strips: one of the most flavoursome versions we've tasted. Young yang sot bab was a 'healthy' casserole cooked in an earthenware pot, a wholesome and delicious dish crammed with white, black and wehani rice (a type of brown rice), red millet, black-eye beans, red kidney beans, chestnuts, pine nuts, gingko nuts, whole ginseng, dried red dates and cubes of sweet potato and kabachi pumpkin.
Babies and children welcome: high chairs. Takeaway service.

★ You-Me
96 Burlington Road, New Malden, Surrey KT3 4NT (8715 1079). New Malden rail. **Meals served** 11.30am-10.30pm Mon, Wed-Sun; 6-10.30pm Tue. **Main courses** £5.90-£13. **Set lunch** £8.90 2 courses. **Credit** MC, V.
This home-style family restaurant could have been plucked straight from a suburban street in Seoul. Game shows babble on a TV in the corner, Korean magazines lie in piles around the dining room, and families feast at low tables in the banquet room at the back. Despite the casual surroundings, the menu is huge, with plenty of barbecue dishes and some interesting hot-pots and chigaes. We began with warm saké and a satisfying bean-flour pancake, stuffed with spring onions and tiny morsels of pork. We also enjoyed the hot chilli chicken, rolled in batter in a tongue-searing sauce infused with the flavour of dried chillies. Portion sizes vary; the prawn barbecue was big on flavour, but quite small for the money. Free namul and panch'an were provided without prompting (the kimchi and mung-bean jelly were particularly good). A tin pot of Korean tea arrived as soon as we sat down, and the delightful staff tripped over themselves to please (our waitress even popped around the corner to buy more saké when the kitchen ran out). One of our favourites.
Babies and children welcome: high chairs. Separate room for parties, seats 10. Takeaway service.

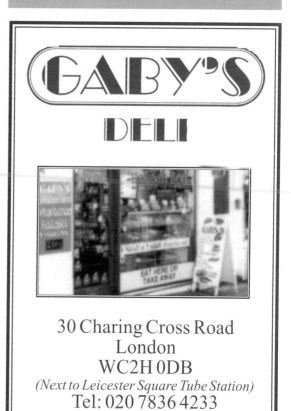

Malaysian, Indonesian & Singaporean

Back in the early days of London's restaurant revolution, food from Malaysia, Indonesia and Singapore had a moment in the fashion spotlight. Its celebrity was brief (we had a world to discover in the early 1990s, and the next new cuisine duly came along), but it was marked enough to convince several Chinese-owned restaurants to conjure up a list of Malaysian specials, and rustle up a satay stick or two. Such venues still exist – and Chinese-Malay amalgams are indeed a notable part of Malaysian and Singaporean cookery – but restaurants serving food from these countries are mostly low-profile affairs. In the past year, however, the cuisine's standing in London gained a major fillip with the opening of **Awana**, dedicated to Malaysian fine dining. This high-flying establishment joins another star, **Champor-Champor** (with its modern, innovative angle on the cuisine), and two top-notch old-stagers: **Satay House** (great for more than just meat on sticks) and, fresh from its recent makeover, **Singapore Garden**. Perhaps the intriguing, full-flavoured food of the region is due another turn in the limelight.

Central
City

Singapura
1-2 Limeburner Lane, EC4M 7HY (7329 1133/ www.singapuras.co.uk). St Paul's tube/Blackfriars tube/rail. **Lunch served** 11.30am-3.30pm, **dinner served** 5-10.30pm Mon-Fri. **Main courses** £8.25-£13.75. **Set lunch** £10-£15 2 courses. **Set meal** £20-£25 per person (minimum 2). **Credit** AmEx, DC, MC, V.
In summer, it's the sunny outdoor terrace that lures the suit-and-tie crowd to this businesslike restaurant tucked under a modern City block. In winter, it's the bargain-priced set lunches. The dining room is spacious and starkly plain; the most colourful things are the waitresses' red silk blouses and the fresh rosebuds on each white-clothed table. In spite of Singapura's name, the food is a mix of Thai, Chinese and Malaysian cuisines. Nearly everyone starts with a mixed platter of satay, spring rolls, prawn toast and Thai fish cakes. This is generally followed by orders of Thai soups and Thai curries – which is probably more a reflection of the popularity of Thai food in this country than the quality of Malaysian cooking here. We'd have let the uninspired presentation of the food pass if the dishes had tasted better. Our chicken satay had an almost fried, greasy quality; nasi goreng was thrown askew by odd, chlorine-tasting shrimps and grey egg; a house special of ayam tempra (stir-fried chicken) was little more than buffet food; and the prawns in the sambal udang had no flavour to match the overwhelming sweetness of the sauce. *Babies and children admitted. Booking advisable lunch. Disabled: toilet. Tables outdoors (15, terrace). Takeaway service; delivery service. Vegetarian menu. Vegan dishes.* **Map 11 O6**.
For branches see index.

Edgware Road

Mawar
175A Edgware Road, W2 2HR (7262 1663). Edgware Road tube.
Buffet **Meals served** noon-10.30pm Mon-Sat; noon-10pm Sun. **Set meal** £4-£5 1 course.
Restaurant **Lunch served** noon-3pm daily. **Dinner served** 6-10.30pm Mon-Sat; 6-10pm Sun. **Main courses** £3.30-£18. **Unlicensed**. **Corkage** no charge.
Both **Credit** (over £10) AmEx, MC, V.
An anonymous, unpromising stairway leads down to this subterranean halal cafeteria, where you'll find easy-wipe tables, plain green walls and a steamy bain-marie counter. But who needs designer niceties when you can queue at the counter and get rice and vegetables with three dishes of your choice for a mere £5? For a little more refinement, there's a separate restaurant area with clothed tables, fanned serviettes and long-stemmed (fabric) roses. Here you get waiter service, an à la carte menu, and your bottle of wine expertly opened – if you brought one (Mawar is unlicensed). But even in the restaurant, you'd be hard pressed to spend more than £25 for two. Ayam perduk, with its grilled pieces of very firm chicken in a thick sauce, was one-dimensional; the sweetness of a sambal sumis sotong (squid with flat green petai beans) overshadowed the tender squirls of squid; and the bendi goreng belada (okra fried with chilli) was a glugfest. The food is sustaining enough for the price, but it's a shame so much of it looks like indecipherable chunks in a thick brown sauce. *Babies and children welcome: high chair. Booking essential weekends. No-smoking tables. Takeaway service (on orders over £30).* **Map 8 E5**.

Marylebone
Rasa Singapura
Regent's Park Hotel, 154-156 Gloucester Place, NW1 6DT (7723 6740/www.regentspk hotel.com). Baker Street tube/Marylebone tube/rail. **Lunch served** noon-3pm, **dinner served** 6-11.30pm daily. **Main courses** £5.50-£25. **Set meal** £16-£30 3 courses. **Credit** AmEx, DC, JCB, MC, V.
Upstairs is a cheap and cheerful tourist hotel. The ground floor provides a little taste of the colonies in a quaint conservatory room complete with hanging baskets of fake plants. Lionel Ritchie is incongruously singing 'Hello. Is it me you're looking for?' At the next table, two Chinese women bow their heads and say grace. It's an odd setting for some good home-style Malaysian cooking. Hainanese chicken rice worked well, with its warm, tender chicken breast, full-flavoured chicken rice and light chicken soup. Assam curry fish – redolent with the citric notes of tamarind – was full of meaty chunks of fish, green pepper, pineapple and aubergine. Even a hawker noodle dish of char kueh teow had just the right balance of flat rice noodles to prawns and fish cake, plus an appealingly scorchy flavour. Only an oyster omelette failed to deliver, being heavy on the oil. Throw in an ice-cold Tiger beer, and maybe another bowl of chicken rice, and we'll even put up with the rest of the Lionel Ritchie. *Babies and children welcome: high chairs. Booking advisable. No-smoking tables. Takeaway service; delivery service (over £15 within 2-mile radius). Vegetarian menu.* **Map 2 F4**.

Soho
Melati
21 Great Windmill Street, W1D 7LQ (7437 2745). Piccadilly Circus tube. **Meals served** noon-11.30pm Mon-Thur, Sun; noon-midnight Fri, Sat. **Main courses** £6.75-£10.95. **Set meals** £20-£23.50 per person (minimum 2). **Credit** AmEx, MC, V.
Not to be confused with the nearby Peter Street restaurant of the same name, this long-established three-storey restaurant also stands erect in a street lined with sleazy strip bars and clip joints. It makes sitting at a window seat a novel form of entertainment, but tear your eyes away from the nervous men and scantily clad touts and you'll find an extensive menu of classic dishes. Portions are large; a bowl of gado gado was generously filled, albeit with a high ratio of beansprouts. Char kway teow also contained plenty of tasty morsels such as tempeh among the stir-fried noodles, with the flavour of shrimp paste-accented soy sauce not too dominant. Only the fried flatbread of the roti canai was disappointing; the real thing should be multi-layered, but this one bore a striking resemblance to the Malaysian-style frozen parathas you can buy in Asian supermarkets. At one time Melati led the way as one of London's best Indonesian and Malaysian restaurants. Although it has lost some of that edge, it's still a reliable place for a good meal with friendly service in a Soho backstreet. *Babies and children admitted. Book dinner Fri, Sat. Separate rooms for parties, both seating 30. Takeaway service. Vegetarian menu.* **Map 17 K7**.

South Kensington
★ Awana NEW
85 Sloane Avenue, SW3 3DX (7584 8880/ www.awana.co.uk). South Kensington tube.
Bar **Open** noon-11.30pm Wed-Sun.
Restaurant **Lunch served** noon-3pm daily. **Dinner served** 6-11pm Mon-Wed; 6-11.30pm Thur-Sat; 6-10.30pm Sun. **Main courses** £9.50-£25. **Set lunch** £12.50 2 courses, £15 3 courses. **Set dinner** £36 tasting menu.
Both **Credit** AmEx, DC, MC, V.
Awana has made headlines in Malaysia for having the chutzpah to charge eyebrow-raising prices for common dishes that cost pennies in Kuala Lumpur.

True enough, but the food at London's first Malaysian fine-dining restaurant is in an entirely different league to that served at your average KL street stall. Plump, juicy, corn-fed chicken satay skewers were accompanied by a delicious house-made peanut sauce into which we also dunked slithers of flaky roti canai. Nasi goreng was beautifully presented, with a fan of ripe pineapple slices and peppery shiso leaves dressing the fried egg; so packed was it with prawns that we gave up counting. Salad sajian laut was a refreshing mix of prawns, crab meat, tart pomelo and green mango. The generously portioned ten-course degustation menu included the flavoursome ikan panggang: melt-in-the-mouth butterfish cooked in a banana leaf with lemongrass, coriander and chilli. Awana's sleek teak fit-out is reminiscent of a Malaysian plantation house. Stylised clouds drift across a deep-blue wall, a visual interpretation of the restaurant's name (Awana is Malay for 'in the clouds'). Service was excellent.
Babies and children welcome: high chairs. Booking advisable Fri, Sat. **Map 14 E10.**

West
Notting Hill

★ Nyonya

2A Kensington Park Road, W11 3BU (7243 1800/www.nyonya.co.uk). Notting Hill Gate tube. **Lunch** served 11.30am-2.45pm, **dinner** served 6-10.30pm Mon-Fri. **Meals served** 11.30am-10.30pm Sat, Sun. **Main courses** £5.50-£8.50. **Set lunch** £8 2 courses. **Credit** AmEx, DC, MC, V.
Sitting at the curved modern communal table looking out of the fishbowl window at red double-decker buses and black cabs surging past is like watching a rerun of *Notting Hill.* Nyonya is as close as Malaysian dining gets to groovy: a bright, light dining room with moulded stools, and young, good-natured staff. The menu offers a variety of dishes based on the uniquely fused cooking style of Straits-born Chinese-Malay (Peranakan) families. Some servings are quite small, and dishes tend to come in a rush, but the food is well put together, and flavours are bright, snappy and not overly sweet. Star of the night

was nasi lemak, an uncharacteristically large serving of steamed coconut rice, moist curried chicken, crisply fried mackerel and chilli-laden sambal sauce. We also liked the soft crunch of beansprouts with salted fish, and the scorchy, earthy flavour of the Penang char kway teow noodles with lup cheong and prawns (made with rice sticks instead of fresh kway teow rice noodles). Kuih are another highlight: multi-layered, multicoloured Malaysian jellies.
Babies and children welcome: high chair. Booking advisable. No smoking. Takeaway service. **Map 7 A7.**

Paddington

★ Satay House

13 Sale Place, W2 1PX (7723 6763/www.satay-house.co.uk). Edgware Road tube/Paddington tube/rail. **Lunch** served noon-3pm, **dinner** served 6-11pm daily. **Main courses** £5-£18.50. **Set meal** £13.50, £18, £25 per person (minimum 2). **Credit** AmEx, MC, V.
It's the aromas that get you. At regular intervals, highly enticing spice-laden smells drift out from the semi-open kitchen of this 33-year-old veteran, giving fragrant reassurance that your food is being cooked to order. Satay House occupies a neat, tidy, cottage-like space and is populated by regulars who make themselves at home with newspapers and favourite dishes. As you would hope, the satays are the real thing: sizzling, scorchy and hot off the grill, served with a killer peanut sauce. With every dish, our meal got better. Begedil (spicy meat and vegetable balls) were soft and squidgy inside, crisp outside; a whole grilled mackerel with a tamarind sauce was firm, fat and flavour-packed; and kangkong belacan (water spinach with shrimp paste) was a crunchy green pleasure to eat. Then came the best nasi lemak we've had in London – a bowl-shaped mound of perfect coconut rice with crunchy little ikan bilis, roasted peanuts, hard-boiled egg, and an extremely good, dark chilli-laden sambal featuring fresh, bouncy prawns. What a treat.
Babies and children welcome: high chairs. Book weekends. Separate room for parties, seats 35. Takeaway service. **Map 8 E5.**

Westbourne Grove

C&R Café

52 Westbourne Grove, W2 5SH (7221 7979). **Meals served** noon-11pm Mon-Thur, Sun; noon-11.30pm Fri, Sat. **Main courses** £6-£15. **Set meal** £14.50 vegetarian, £17 per person (minimum 2). **Credit** MC, V.
We're trying to work out what C&R stands for. Clean & Respectable? Curry & Roti? The unprepossessing exterior of this plain, shopfronted Westbourne Grove newcomer belies the prepossessing interior with its moody downlights, clothed tables, tall blond chairs and folded napkins. Although the place does a roaring trade in familiar Chinese favourites such as crispy duck, crab and sweetcorn soup, and lemon chicken, there is also a large selection of Malaysian hawker market dishes. Best was a generous serving of Singaporean-style spicy chilli crab, which was gloriously gloopy, sticky, spicy and sweet – eat now, bathe later. Other dishes paled in comparison. Flat roti bread served with a good curry sauce was excessively oily; lamb satays had flavour aplenty but were tough; and the Indian mee goreng (traditionally consisting of thick hokkien noodles, potato, tomato and prawns) was made with thin egg noodles and no potato. Still, we'll be back for that crab, with plenty of C&R's impressively fluffy coconut rice on the side. Ah, that's what it means: Crab & Rice.
Babies and children welcome: high chairs. Takeaway service. **Map 7 B6.**
For branch see index.

South East
London Bridge & Borough

★ Champor-Champor

62-64 Weston Street, SE1 3QJ (7403 4600/ www.champor-champor.com). London Bridge tube/rail. **Lunch** served by appointment Mon-Sat. **Dinner** served 6.15-10.15pm Mon-Sat. **Set meal** £22.50 2 courses, £26.90 3 courses, £41 tasting menu. **Credit** AmEx, JCB, MC, V.
'Probably the best Thai food I've had since Thailand,' is among the many appreciative reviews scribbled in the guest book here. The confusion is

Awana. See p209.

understandable. Champor-Champor means 'mix and match' in Malay and the description applies both to the restaurant's exotic and inventive decor – African masks and beadwork, Indian wood carvings, découpage on the walls beside the papier mâché head of a crimson holy cow – and the modern and innovative interpretation of Malaysian cuisine on the seasonally changing menu. Hence the satay is of very tender ostrich, and nasi goreng comes with a crocodile fillet. Some dishes work: we loved the deep-fried soft-shell crab salad, for example, the tart calamansi lime dressing bringing it alive. Others don't: the meat in the beef sirloin masak kichap was tough and smothered in a bland sauce, while the accompanying pear and pumpkin-seed salsa was bland. Highlights included the green curried frogs' legs congee served with an earthy steamed peanut salsa, a comforting dish of subtle flavours and textures; and the lovely smoked banana ice-cream. Service was courteous and attentive. No wonder the place was full on a midweek night.
Babies and children welcome: high chair. Booking essential. Separate room for parties, seats 8.
Map 12 Q9.

Georgetown

10 London Bridge Street, SE1 9SG (7357 7359/ www.georgetownrestaurants.co.uk). London Bridge tube/rail. **Lunch served** noon-2.30pm, **dinner served** 5.30-11pm daily. **Main courses** £7.75-£12.95. **Set lunch** £10 2 courses, £12.50 3 courses. **Credit** AmEx, DC, MC, V.
Named after the capital of Penang (from where, incidentally, the restaurant's chef hails), Georgetown is next to London Bridge Hotel and promises a colonial Malaysian 'experience'. What you get is an ersatz Raffles-on-the-Thames where the dining room has a parquet floor, mini-chandeliers, polite, smartly dressed waiters and soothing classical music in the background. Often there's a pianist at the grand piano, but not on our visit. The menu dips into the Malay, Chinese and Indian cultures of Malaysia for its inspiration and includes a good selection for vegetarians. Our best choices were from the Malay section: udang bakar kering, four jumbo prawns pan-fried in an appealing red onion sauce; and ikan kurau, a very tasty slab of threadfin fish beautifully cooked and

robustly spiced. Presentation of the latter dish, with neat piles of sauté potatoes, mangetout and carrots, exhibited the prissy English side of the colonial theme. Similar politeness diluted the authentic punch of the otherwise competent captain's curry and laksa lemak, although the lemak did come with a side of chilli sauce to spice it up.
Babies and children welcome: high chairs. Booking advisable. Disabled: toilet. No-smoking tables.
Map 12 Q8.

North

Crouch End

★ Satay Malaysia

10 Crouch End Hill, N8 8AA (8340 3286). Finsbury Park tube/rail then W7 bus. **Dinner served** 6-10.45pm Mon-Thur, Sun; 6-11.45pm Fri, Sat. **Main courses** £5.50-£9. **Set dinner** £12-£14 per person (minimum 2). **No credit cards**.
This small, friendly Chinese-Malay restaurant, sweetly decorated with batik and framed orchid prints, is a world away from formulaic, high-style dining. More than 120 dishes are on the menu, so perhaps it's not surprising that the cooking can be slightly patchy. Beef satay – served authentically with onion, cucumber and compressed rice – had an appetising flavour, but the accompanying peanut sauce was disappointing, merely sweet and sticky. A generous portion of sambal prawns in a sweet chilli sauce went down well, as did sayur lemak (spinach in coconut sauce). Our favourite dish was shien ba, tender aromatic pork in soy sauce gravy, but the pa tai mee (stir-fried noodles) was distinctly dull. Nonetheless, banana fritters with ice-cream and golden syrup rounded off the meal nicely. Diners on our Saturday night visit ranged from a mother and daughter enjoying a treat, to a couple of loud-voiced male musicians pontificating on the music scene. Others dropped by to pick up takeaways. As we left, a large party arrived for a birthday dinner, practically filling the restaurant. Homely and hospitable, Satay Malaysia is a relaxed local offering good-value grub.
Babies and children admitted. Book weekends. Takeaway service. Vegetarian menu.

Turnpike Lane

★ Penang Satay House

9 Turnpike Lane, N8 0EP (8340 8707). Turnpike Lane tube/29 bus. **Dinner served** 6-11pm daily. **Main courses** £4-£8.50. **Set meal** £11.90, £13.50 per person (minimum 2) 3 courses. **Credit** MC, V.
With its bright green neon sign adding a dash of colour to a rather scruffy stretch of Turnpike Lane, the veteran Penang Satay House has built up a firm local following. Its spacious dining room, complete with bar and lashings of batik, makes a pleasantly mellow setting. On our weekday visit the place was filled with various, multicultural parties of diners, chatting over their food. After this promising first impression, however, things went downhill. House special satay (chicken, prawns and beef) was rather dry, served with a sweet and coconutty sauce. Main courses too were a let-down. Chicken curry in coconut milk – rather than the richly spiced Malay dish we were hoping for – was so salty as to be inedible, and yet curiously flavourless. Twice-cooked pork turned out to be very dull indeed, complete with leathery strips of meat. Only the chinese spinach with blachan (prawn paste) was a pleasant dish to eat. In the past, the kitchen here has performed to a much higher standard, so we left disappointed, hoping our latest experience was caused by a temporary glitch.
Babies and children welcome: high chairs. Booking essential. Takeaway service; delivery service (over £10 within 2-mile radius). Vegetarian menu.
For branch (Penang Express) see index.

North West

Swiss Cottage

★ Singapore Garden

83A Fairfax Road, NW6 4DY (7624 8233). Swiss Cottage tube. **Lunch served** noon-3pm Mon-Sat; noon-5pm Sun. **Dinner served** 6-11.30pm daily. **Main courses** £5.50-£9. **Set meal** £23.50-£38.50 per person (minimum 2). **Minimum charge** £15 per person. **Credit** AmEx, DC, MC, V.

The retirement of Singapore Garden's founder, Mrs Toh, has led to her daughter Lin Toh and two new investors making some dramatic changes. A stunning new 'modern oriental' look has been assisted by two rooms being knocked into one, and a plate-glass front now opens on to the street. The waitresses have also had a makeover, and sport stunningly patterned cheongsams and flattering dresses in bold batik. The bulk of the menu is still more Sino than Malay, but there's also a score of Singaporean and Malaysian specialities. The breakfast dish roti canai was an excellent version, with pleasingly stretchy roti and a full-flavoured curry sauce dip. Assam prawns, big fellas in a moreish tamarind sauce, were also a hit. But Singapore laksa tasted curiously mild and bland; it could have done with more shrimp paste and chilli. Our waitress might have pointed out that the rojak and tahu goreng we ordered were near-identical dishes, both smothered in the same spicy peanut sauce; a few more smiles from her wouldn't

have hurt either. We were also disappointed to see that a card of bought-in frozen ices has crept into the dessert options.
Babies and children admitted. Booking advisable. Tables outdoors (3, pavement). Takeaway service; delivery service (within 1-mile radius). Map 28 A4.

Outer London
Croydon, Surrey

★ **Malay House**
60 Lower Addiscombe Road, Croydon, Surrey CR0 6AA (8666 0266). East Croydon rail then 197, 312, 410 bus. **Dinner served** 6-11pm Tue-Sat. **Meals served** 1-9pm Sun. **Main courses** £7.50-£9. **Buffet** (Sun) £7. **Unlicensed. Corkage** £1 per person. **Credit** MC, V.
This simple little caff is still going strong after nearly a decade, despite its curious location on a corner site of a traffic-laden Croydon road. For

most of the week there's a classically Malaysian à la carte menu: real Malay food, not the Sino-suburban norm, with dishes such as murtabak, rendangs, sambals and rice meals. On Sundays, though, there's only a buffet of dishes kept warm on hot-plates. Making the best of the unfortunate timing of our Sunday visit, we nonetheless enjoyed many dishes; it's clear someone in the kitchen is an excellent cook. A lamb stock soup was scented with cinnamon and star anise, among other deftly blended spices. Beef rendang was also a stunning dish, with a clear lemongrass flavour. The least impressive dishes were those that don't take well to being kept at serving temperature for hours, such as the vegetable stir-fries or fried chicken. Our late arrival sent the sweet staff scurrying into the kitchen to add fresh banana fritters and a coconut milk and sweetcorn pudding to the selection.
Babies and children welcome: high chairs. Booking advisable Fri, Sat. Takeaway service. Vegetarian menu.

Menu

Here are some common terms and dishes. Spellings can vary.

Acar: assorted pickled vegetables such as carrots, beans and onions, which are often spiced with turmeric and pepper.
Assam: tamarind.
Ayam: chicken.
Bergedel: a spiced potato cake.
Blachan, belacan or **blacan:** dried fermented shrimp paste; it adds a piquant fishy taste to dishes.
Char kway teow or **char kwai teow:** a stir-fry of rice noodles with meat and/or seafood with dark soy sauce and beansprouts. A Hakka Chinese-derived speciality of Singapore.
Chilli crab: fresh crab, stir-fried in a sweet, mild chilli sauce.
Daging: beef.
Ebi: shrimps.
Gado gado: a salad of blanched vegetables with a peanut-based sauce on top.
Galangal: also called lesser ginger, Laos root or blue ginger, this spice gives a distinctive flavour to many South-east Asian dishes.
Goreng: wok-fried.
Hainanese chicken rice: poached chicken served with rice cooked in chicken stock, a bowl of light chicken broth and a chilli-ginger dipping sauce.
Ho jien: oyster omelette, flavoured with garlic and chilli.
Ikan: fish.
Ikan bilis or **ikan teri:** tiny whitebait-like fish, often fried and made into a dry sambal (qv) with peanuts.
Kambing: actually goat, but in practice lamb is the usual substitute.
Kangkong or **kangkung:** water convolvulus, often called water spinach or swamp cabbage – an aquatic plant often steamed and used in salads with a spicy sauce.
Kecap manis: sweet dark Indonesian soy sauce.
Kelapa: coconut.
Kemiri: waxy-textured candlenuts, used to enrich Indonesian and Malaysian curry pastes.
Kerupuk: prawn crackers.
Laksa: a noodle dish with either coconut milk or (as with penang laksa) tamarind

as the stock base; it's now popular in many South-east Asian cities.
Lemang: sticky Indonesian rice that is cooked in bamboo segments.
Lengkuas or **lenkuas:** Malaysian name for galangal (qv).
Lumpia: deep-fried spring rolls filled with meat or vegetables.
Masak lemak: anything cooked in a rich, red spice paste with coconut milk.
Mee: noodles.
Mee goreng: fried egg noodles with meat, prawns and vegetables.
Mee hoon: rice vermicelli noodles.
Murtabak: an Indian-Malaysian pancake fried on a griddle and served with a savoury filling.
Nasi goreng: fried rice with shrimp paste, garlic, onions, chillies and soy sauce.
Nasi lemak: coconut rice on a plate with a selection of curries and fish dishes topped with ikan bilis (qv).
Nonya or **Nyonya:** the name referring to both the women and the dishes of the Straits Chinese community. *See below* Peranakan.
Otak otak: a Nonya (qv) speciality made from eggs, fish and coconut milk.
Pandan leaves: a variety of the screwpine plant; used to add colour and fragrance to both savoury and sweet dishes.
Panggang: grilled or barbecued.
Peranakan: refers to the descendants of Chinese settlers who first came to Malacca (now Melaka), a seaport on the Malaysian west coast, in the 17th century. It is generally applied to those born of Sino-Malay extraction who adopted Malay customs, costume and cuisine, the community being known as 'Straits Chinese'. The cuisine is also known as Nonya (qv).
Petai: a pungent, flat green bean used in Malaysian cooking.
Poh pia or **popiah:** spring rolls. Nonya or Penang popiah are not deep-fried and consist of egg or rice paper wrappers filled with a vegetable and prawn medley.
Rempah: generic term for the fresh curry pastes used in Malaysian cookery.
Rendang: meat cooked in coconut milk, a 'dry' curry.
Rijsttafel: an Indonesian set meal of several courses; it means 'rice table' in Dutch.

Rojak: raw fruit and vegetables in a spicy sauce.
Roti canai: a South Indian/Malaysian breakfast dish of fried round, unleavened bread served with a dip of either chicken curry or dahl.
Sambal: there are several types of sambal, often made of fiery chilli sauce, onions and coconut oil; it can be served as a side dish or used as a relish. The suffix 'sambal' means 'cooked with chilli'.
Satay: there are two types – terkan (minced and moulded to the skewer) and chochok ('shish', more common in London). Beef or chicken are the traditional choices, though prawn is now often available too. Satay is served with a rich spicy sauce made from onions, lemongrass, galangal (qv), and chillies in tamarind sauce; it is sweetened and thickened with ground peanuts.
Sayur: vegetables.
Soto ayam: a classic spicy Indonesian chicken soup, often with noodles.
Sotong: squid.
Tauhu goreng: deep-fried beancurd topped with beansprouts tossed in a spicy peanut sauce, served cold.
Tempeh or **tempe:** an Indonesian fermented soy bean product; similar to tofu, it has a more varied texture and can look like peanut butter.
Udang: prawns.

DESSERTS
Bubor pulut hitam: black glutinous rice served in coconut milk and palm sugar.
Cendol or **chendol:** mung bean flour pasta, coloured and perfumed with essence of pandan leaf (qv) and served in a chilled coconut milk and palm sugar syrup.
Es: ice; a prefix for the multitude of desserts made with combinations of fruit salad, agar jelly cubes, palm syrup, condensed milk and crushed ice.
Es kacang: shaved ice and syrup mixed with jellies, red beans and sweetcorn.
Gula melaka: palm sugar, an important ingredient with a distinctive, caramel flavour added to a sago and coconut-milk pudding of the same name.
Kueh or **kuih:** literally, 'cakes', but used as a general term for many desserts.
Pisang goreng: banana fritters.

RESTAURANTS

Middle Eastern

There are two main strands to Middle Eastern food in London. The first – and the dominant one – is Lebanese. Other Levantine and Arab countries have their own variations on meze dishes and grilled meats, but essentially, throughout the Middle East good restaurant food means Lebanese food. The roots of this go back to the age when the Ancient Phoenicians were in a pivotal position for seafaring trade and the spice routes. Many centuries later the region we now call Lebanon was occupied by the Ottomans, who introduced courtly cooking. Although the ingredients and techniques are essentially simple, relying on the freshness of ingredients and herbs or familiar spices for flavour, the results can be remarkably refined. Restaurants such as **Noura**, **Al Hamra**, **Fairuz** and **Al Waha** are good places to see just how it should be done.

The other, distinctly different, culinary strand in the Middle East is Iranian food, more usually referred to as Persian food. The cooking techniques and flavours are very different to Lebanese food. Rice dishes will often have layered spice flavours, the meats are invariably marinated, nuts and berries are frequently used. London's Persian restaurants tend to cluster around Olympia, and even the simplest restaurants such as **Alounak** and **Mohsen** produce dishes fit for banquets.

Central

Belgravia

★ Noura
16 Hobart Place, SW1W 0HH (7235 9444/ www.noura.co.uk). Hyde Park Corner tube/ Victoria tube/rail. **Meals served** noon-midnight daily. **Main courses** £10-£23. **Set lunch** (noon-6pm) £16.50 2 courses incl coffee. **Set meals** £29-£38 per person (minimum 2) 3 courses incl coffee. **Credit** AmEx, DC, MC, V. Lebanese
Sister restaurant Noura Central was the winner in the Best Vegetarian Meal category in 2005's *Time Out* Eating & Drinking Awards. And although, as the judges cited, it is a godsend to find fine Levantine cooking at reasonable prices just off the fast-food ghetto of Piccadilly Circus, we'd recommend you travel just that little bit further – to the back of Buckingham Palace, in fact – to the Hobart Place branch. This was the first of the London Nouras and it still has dash and class. A wholly modern and light interior references traditional Levantine architecture, providing a stylish setting for smartly suited waiters to whisk between buzzing tables of equally smartly attired diners (it's the sort of place you'll wish you'd made more of an effort to dress for). Vegetarians will still appreciate the range of meatless meze, while omnivores can opt for the likes of makanek (pungent Lebanese sausage flambéed in lemon and garlic) and kebbeh nayeh (lamb tartare, the raw mince as smooth as pâté), as well as the ubiquitous grills that constitute the bulk of the mains. Desserts are the best we've ever come across in a Middle Eastern restaurant, particularly aish assaraya, a caramelised bread pudding with clotted cream. Own-made ice-creams also impress.
Babies and children welcome: high chairs. Booking advisable; essential dinner. Disabled: toilet. Takeaway service; delivery service (over £25 within 2-mile radius). **Map 15 H9.**
For branches see index.

Edgware Road

★ Kandoo
458 Edgware Road, W2 1EJ (7724 2428). Edgware Road tube. **Meals served** noon-midnight daily. **Main courses** £6-£11.50. **Unlicensed. Corkage** no charge. **Credit** MC, V. Iranian
The heart seems to have gone out of Kandoo. Despite a grim location at the spot where Edgware Road departs the West End for the middle of nowhere, we've found in the past that it has always managed to transcend the sombre surrounds and offer warmth and welcome. No more. On a recent visit the place was bare, harshly lit and not at all comfortable. Cooking, though, remains pretty solid. Aside from a Saturday special of duck breast cooked in a walnut and pomegranate sauce, it's a standard mix of starters and kebabs. The meat in the kebabs had been nicely marinated (in, so we were told, a concoction of lime juice, olive oil, vegetable oil and yoghurt) and we asked for the rice with a sprinkling of sumac berries, which adds a bit of a tang. The masto musir was nicely thick and creamy and the kashk-e bademjan, a purée of aubergine in yoghurt, came with a swirl of runny goat's cheese and a sprinkling of fried onions. Bread was delivered hot from the tiled oven in the corner of the room. While the food is enjoyable, this is not a restaurant to travel far to. Though if you do happen to find yourself north of the Marylebone flyover and in need of a kebab…
Babies and children welcome: high chairs. Tables outdoors (10, garden). Takeaway service. **Map 2 D4.**

Maroush Gardens
1-3 Connaught Street, W2 2DH (7262 0222/ www.maroush.com). Marble Arch tube. **Meals served** noon-midnight daily. **Main courses** £13-£16. **Set dinner** £45 per person (minimum 2) 3 courses. **Credit** AmEx, DC, MC, V. Lebanese

You may not have heard of him, but Marouf Abouzaki is the biggest name in Middle Eastern dining in London. He launched Maroush back in 1981 and since then has opened a further five restaurants under the same name, as well as four Ranoush Juice Bars and a Beirut Express. While the original restaurant, at 21 Edgware Road, remains popular for its belly dancing and cabaret, we like the atmosphere at this branch, which is just up the street. We appreciate the large airy dining room, which most evenings buzzes like a mainline train station with troops of waiters serving dozens of big round tables. The menu runs to about 60 meze plus mixed grills, and is strong on offal and preparations involving raw minced meat. We've always been impressed by the quality of the dishes, although on a recent visit the chicken livers were made unbearably tart through the use of too much pomegranate juice, and the amount of meat on the plate in a lamb meshwi was a bit on the mean side. These are minor blips, we're sure, and it's our experience that Maroush usually delivers a quality Lebanese dining experience.
Babies and children admitted. Booking advisable. **Map 8 F6.**
For branches (Beirut Express, Maroush) see index.

★ Meya Meya
13 Bell Street, NW1 5BY (7723 8983). Edgware Road tube. **Meals served** 9am-11pm daily. **Main courses** £3.10-£8.50. **Unlicensed. Corkage** £5. **No credit cards.** Egyptian
The ground-floor room, with nothing but a pizza furnace, counter and one table, appears to be a takeaway. But look closely and you'll see that freshly made rounds of hot fiteer (Egyptian pizza) are being whisked downstairs to a busy room with several tables. There is an extensive menu at Meya Meya, but the fiteer is the draw: envelopes of filo pastry filled with all manner of ingredients. The Cairo fiteer, with slices of basturma, tomato, pepper and olives, was a generous portion of smoked beef with fresh veg. The Masria packed a real punch, with spicy mince, sausage and melting cheese. The menu also includes Egyptian staples such as fuul and taamaya (aka falafel). These were almost perfect: fuul was well seasoned and the taamaya were crunchy on the outside, and grease-

BEST MIDDLE EASTERN

For an alternative to Lebanese
Ali Baba (see p214) and **Meya Meya** (see above) are authentic Egyptian; **Abu Zaad** (see p218) offers Syrian specialities; while **Mesopotamia** (see p219) is Iraqi.

For smoking sheesha
Almost every Middle Eastern restaurant offers sheesha these days, but **Lebanese Lounge** (see p218) has a dedicated smoking room. **Levant** (see p215) and **Fakhreldine** (see p216) have smoking areas.

For non-meat eaters
Every Lebanese restaurant majors in meze, the majority of which are vegetarian. It's common practice to fill the table with these and never order any meat. Try **Maroush Gardens** (see left), **Al Fawar** (see p214), **Fairuz** (see p214), **Al Waha** (see p216) and especially **Noura** (see left).

For a taste of Iran
London's Iranian community is centred on Kensington, which is where you'll find **Alounak** (see p217), **Mohsen** (see p217) and **Yas** (see p218). Also highly recommended is **Patogh** (see p214) on Edgware Road.

Menu

See also the menu boxes in **North African** and **Turkish**. Note that spellings can vary. For more information, get hold of a copy of *The Legendary Cuisine of Persia*, by Margaret Shaida (Grub Street).

MEZE

Baba ganoush: Egyptian name for moutabal (qv).
Basturma: smoked beef.
Batata hara: potatoes fried with peppers and chilli.
Falafel: a mixture of spicy chickpeas or broad beans ground, rolled into balls and deep fried.
Fatayer: a soft pastry with fillings of cheese, onions, spinach and pine kernels.
Fattoush: fresh vegetable salad containing shards of toasted pitta bread and sumac (qv).
Fuul or **fuul medames:** brown broad beans that are mashed and seasoned with olive oil, lemon juice and garlic.
Kalaj: halloumi cheese on pastry.
Kibbeh: highly seasoned mixture of minced lamb, cracked wheat and onion, deep-fried in balls. For meze it is often served raw (**kibbeh nayeh**) like steak tartare.
Labneh: Middle Eastern cream cheese made from yoghurt.
Moujadara: lentils, rice and caramelised onions mixed together.
Moutaba: a purée of char-grilled aubergines mixed with sesame sauce, garlic and lemon juice.
Muhamara: spiced and crushed mixed nuts.
Sambousek: small pastries filled with mince, onion and pine kernels.
Sujuk: spicy Lebanese sausages.
Sumac: an astringent and fruity-tasting spice made from dried sumac seeds.
Tabouleh: a salad of chopped parsley, tomatoes, crushed wheat, onions, olive oil and lemon juice.
Torshi: pickled vegetables.
Warak einab: rice-stuffed vine leaves.

MAINS

Shawarma: meat (usually lamb) marinated then grilled on a spit and sliced kebab-style.
Shish kebab: cubes of marinated lamb grilled on a skewer, often with tomatoes, onions and sweet peppers.
Shish taouk: like shish kebab, but with chicken rather than lamb.

DESSERTS

Baklava: filo pastry interleaved with pistachio nuts, almonds or walnuts, and covered in syrup.
Konafa or **kadayif:** cake made from shredded pastry dough, filled with syrup and nuts, or cream.
Ma'amoul: pastries filled with nuts or dates.
Muhallabia or **mohalabia:** a milky ground-rice pudding with almonds and pistachios, flavoured with rosewater or orange blossom.
Om ali: bread pudding, often made with filo pastry, also includes nuts and raisins.

IRANIAN DISHES

Ash-e reshteh: a soup with noodles, spinach, pulses and dried herbs.
Halim bademjan: mashed char-grilled aubergine with onions, herbs and walnuts.
Kashk-e bademjan: baked aubergines mixed with herbs.
Kuku-ye sabzi: finely chopped fresh herbs mixed with eggs and baked in the oven.
Masto khiar: yoghurt mixed with finely chopped cucumber and mint.
Masto musir: shallot-flavoured yoghurt.
Mirza ghasemi: crushed baked aubergines, tomatoes, garlic and herbs mixed with egg.
Sabzi: a plate of fresh herb leaves (usually mint and dill) often served with a cube of feta.
Salad olivieh: a bit like a russian salad, with chopped potatoes, chicken, eggs, peas and gherkins, plus olive oil and mayonnaise.

---

free and an authentic green on the inside. Cakes included a lovely moist konafa (shredded filo with pistachios and fragrant syrup).
Babies and children admitted. No-smoking tables. Tables outdoors (2, pavement). Takeaway service. Map 2 E5.

★ Patogh
8 Crawford Place, W1H 5NE (7262 4015). Edgware Road tube. **Meals served** 1pm-midnight daily. **Main courses** £6-£12. **Unlicensed. Corkage** no charge. **No credit cards.** Iranian
The all-over rag-rolled shade of nicotine brown is overwhelming in this little space, but while Patogh may be a loser in the style stakes, it's an effortless winner when it comes to the food. This is in authentic Persian kebab restaurant vein: a few yoghurty starters plus sabzi; enormous discs of warm, house-baked flatbread; and great platters of meat served with Iranian-style rice. We have to confess we usually stick to our favourite – a boneless chicken kebab – which was as good as always. The meat had been marinated with saffron to a yellowish colour and a tender consistency, and grilled without charring. Some of

the rice had been cooked with saffron too, giving a distinctive white and yellow effect on the plate. Iranians have real skill with rice. Patogh's version was light and fluffy, and – as per tradition – was served with a knob of butter in the middle. Add some lemony red sumac spice (on hand on the table), and you have all the ingredients of a classic Persian eating experience.
Book weekends. Takeaway service. Map 8 E5.

★ Ranoush Juice Bar
43 Edgware Road, W2 2JR (7723 5929). Marble Arch tube. **Meals served** 8am-3am daily. **Main courses** £3-£10. **No credit cards.** Lebanese
This is the fast-food component of the many-tentacled Maroush empire. Bains-marie behind a long glass counter that runs the length of the room contain a variety of warm meze, including stuffed vine leaves and falafel, and there are trays of fresh tabbouleh and green salads – but a likely eight-out-of-ten customers are here for the shawarma. Eaten in at one of a handful of tables or taken out, this is possibly the best shawarma in town. Whether lamb or chicken, both come with sliced pickle, sliced tomatoes, chopped lettuce and onion, and a garlic sauce. Ranoush also does good squeezed-to-

order fruit juices – choose your combination from the array of fruit piled behind the counter. As much social centre as eaterie, the place is busy throughout the day with local, expat and visiting Middle Easterners. It remains buzzing through to the early hours of the morning, when it becomes a West London alternative to Soho's Bar Italia for coffee and something decent to eat.
Babies and children admitted. Takeaway service; delivery service. Map 8 F6.
For branches see index.

Marylebone

Al Fawar
50 Baker Street, W1U 7BT (7224 4777/ www.alfawar.com). Baker Street tube. **Meals served** noon-11pm daily. **Main courses** £12.50-£13.90. **Set meal** £25 3 courses incl coffee and dessert. **Cover** £2 (à la carte). **Credit** AmEx, DC, JCB, MC, V. Lebanese
This is the place with the big picture windows that always looks completely empty and soulless if you happy to glance in from Baker Street. Don't be put off – it's an excellent restaurant. It is a massive room with acres of plush maroon carpet, white tableclosths and a ceiling hung with cut-glass chandeliers. The nearest fellow diners will likely be a brisk ten-minute walk away and it's necessary to communicate with the waiters by semaphore. It always puts us in mind of dining rooms in the sort of grand old hotels that crop up in Agatha Christie novels. There are no fewer than 84 varieties of meze to choose from. We were really impressed by a crisp, tangy fattoush (a very fresh salad with crisp bread pieces, doused in a vinaigrette) and a plate of crisp-skinned, smoky quail, which are listed as meze but make a substantial main dish. The mains are all grilled meats and come unapologetically unadorned – hunks of meat on a plate with a few triangles of flatbread as the only dressing. However, the meat is beautifully spiced and done to perfection. Service throughout is smooth and polished.
Babies and children welcome: high chairs. Book dinner. Dress: smart casual. Restaurant available for hire. Takeaway service; delivery service (within 3-mile radius). Map 9 G5.

★ Ali Baba
32 Ivor Place, NW1 6DA (7723 7474/5805). Baker Street tube/Marylebone tube/rail. **Meals served** noon-midnight daily. **Main courses** £6-£8. **Unlicensed. Corkage** no charge. **No credit cards.** Egyptian
Minutes away from the hubbub of Marylebone Road is this one-of-a-kind restaurant offering nothing but fresh Egyptian food. In the evenings, the restaurant at the back is often buzzing with lively Arabic chatter, although on our visit there were plenty of non-Egyptians enjoying the warm welcome and home-style cooking. Vine leaves stuffed with fluffy, flavoursome rice are a must, and a far cry from the gloopy degraded specimens found in tins. Houmous with warm pitta was equally good, and we could have ordered another bowl easily. Mains were even more impressive. Shish kebab delivered succulent char-grilled chunks of lamb cooked to absolute perfection. Moussaka, made with tender pieces of aubergine, oozed béchamel and gently spiced meaty juices. A scorchingly hot om ali, a creamy filo pastry version, crammed with sultanas, is plenty for two. Service was attentive, prices are reasonable and you get baklava on the house after your meal.
Babies and children welcome: high chairs. Booking advisable. Takeaway service; delivery service. Map 2 F4.

★ Fairuz
3 Blandford Street, W1U 3DA (7486 8108/ 8182/www.fairuz.uk.com). Baker Street or Bond Street tube. **Meals served** noon-11.30pm Mon-Sat; noon-11pm Sun. **Main courses** £10.95-£18.95. **Set meal** £18.95. **Set meze** £26.95 3 courses. **Cover** £1.50. **Credit** AmEx, MC, V. Lebanese
Fairuz represents the more casual face of Lebanese dining in the London. Its fold-back frontage with pavement seating and Mediterranean-flavoured

interior of lemon yellow and duck-egg blue are sufficiently welcoming that the place is always busy. It's a big favourite with groups, which can make for a noisy dining experience. However, the quality of food is consistently excellent. The menu is standard Lebanese with an expansive offering just short of 50 hot and cold mezes. Standouts include light, fluffy falafel that come with a little pot of tahina, and houmous strongly flavoured with tahina and decorated with diamonds of red pepper. You could gorge on meze, but that would be a shame because the mains are unusually good for a Lebanese restaurant. Farouj musakhan was a duvet of flatbread filled with chicken pieces smothered in fried onions and parsley and baked in the oven, while the 'knuckle of lamb' was more like a fist of the most tender meat, served on vermicelli rice topped with chopped almonds. Fairuz also has a more style-conscious namesake over on Westbourne Grove (itself is a homage to Lebanon's most popular diva), but there is no longer a connection between the two restaurants.
Babies and children welcome: high chairs. Booking essential dinner. No-smoking tables. Separate room for parties, seats 25. Takeaway service; delivery service. **Map 9 G5.**

Levant

Jason Court, 76 Wigmore Street, W1U 2SJ (7224 1111/www.levant.co.uk). Bond Street tube. *Bar* **Open** noon-2.30am Mon-Sat; noon-1am Sun. *Restaurant* **Meals served** noon-midnight daily. **Main courses** £12.50-£26. **Set lunch** (noon-5.30pm Mon-Fri) £8-£15 2 courses. **Set dinner** £26.50-£42 3 courses. **Cover** £2. *Both* **Credit** AmEx, DC, JCB, MC, V. Lebanese
It's full theme ahead at Levant – a concept restaurant par excellence. Diners head down a candlelit, rose petal-strewn staircase, and pull open the heavy wooden door at the bottom to reveal an oriental wonderland. First comes an attractive bar area with low tables. Beyond is the restaurant, decorated with earth colours and eastern lamps. There's non-stop Arabic music, you can guarantee

an appearance by at least one belly dancer – and some of the best Lebanese food in London. On a recent visit we opted for a 'Levant feast': multiple little bowls of meze followed by a huge plateful of various top-quality grilled meats with rice. Many of the dishes were superb and none was below par. Best was muhamara – this version had a depth and subtlety of warm, nutty flavour we've never found before – but the likes of smooth houmous, smoky baba ganoush, barbecued chicken wings and crunchy falafel were way up there. Service was a problem. A two-hour-per-sitting policy is annoying in principle, even more so as we couldn't actually escape for three and a half, with dishes going astray and it being impossible to attract the attention of overstretched staff above the loud music. A free cognac helped, but if this is a recurring problem the restaurant needs to sort it out.
Booking advisable. Entertainment: belly dancer 8.30pm. Separate area for parties, seats 12. Takeaway service. **Map 9 G6.**
For branch (Levantine) see index.

Mayfair

★ Al Hamra

31-33 Shepherd Market, W1Y 7HR (7493 1954/ www.alhamrarestaurant.com). Green Park or Hyde Park Corner tube. **Meals served** noon-11.30pm daily. **Main courses** £14-£22.50. **Minimum** £20. **Cover** £2.50. **Credit** AmEx, DC, JCB, MC, V. Lebanese
Nothing less than an institution, Al Hamra has been a purveyor of top-class Lebanese food to an international Mayfair clientele for decades. Snowy white tablecloths and sparkling glassware greet diners, along with a menu that includes more than 50 meze dishes and plenty of meat grills. Service is of the formal, traditional variety, although these days besuited staff are more likely to lighten up with the odd flash of friendliness. Like most trad Lebanese places, it's child-friendly – we were struck on a recent evening visit by the number of families enjoying a lateish dinner. Quality rarely

slips here, and our dinner was no exception. We stuck to vegetarian standards: houmous was even-textured; falafel was crusty on the outside, oil-free on the inside and served with a delicate tahina sauce; sambousek came as dainty cheese cigars wrapped in filo pastry; fuul moukala (green beans cooked with lemon juice and coriander in olive oil) was tangy and fresh; tabouleh had a lemony bite; and muhamara contained finely chopped nuts and was warmly spiced. Prices are at the top of the range for upper-level Lebanese places, but this doesn't deter the wealthy citizens of the world who make Al Hamra their regular haunt.
Babies and children welcome: high chairs. Book dinner. Tables outdoors (24, terrace). Takeaway service; delivery service (over £20). **Map 9 H8.**

Al Sultan

51-52 Hertford Street, W1J 7ST (7408 1155/ 1166/www.alsultan.co.uk). Green Park or Hyde Park Corner tube. **Meals served** noon-midnight daily. **Main courses** £12-£13.50. **Minimum** £20. **Cover** £2. **Credit** AmEx, DC, MC, V. Lebanese
Al Sultan has long attracted a well-heeled clientele who keep on coming back for the extensive (but expensive) trad Lebanese menu of two-score-and-more meze dishes plus grilled meat main courses. On past visits we've sometimes found the resolutely old-school atmosphere translating into stuffy, less-than-friendly service. This time, though, we couldn't have asked for a warmer welcome – an Arabic speaker and a nine-year-old in tow may have helped, our waiters finding time for many a quip to keep our young friend amused. Heavy cutlery, pristine starched tablecloths, pastel decor and soothing Arabic music provide that international, slightly bland sense of luxury. Our meze choices were anything but bland: lemony, herby foul moukala (fresh broad beans); lightly sautéed beid ghanam (lambs' testicles) and crunchy kibbeh were faultless – each was simply, freshly delicious. Main courses can sometimes take

a back seat in places like this, but moistly tender shish taouk and farruj meshwi (grilled baby chicken with chilli and garlic sauce) also shone. Mint tea and complimentary pastries rounded off a truly satisfying feast.

Babies and children welcome: high chairs. Book dinner. Tables outdoors (4, pavement). Takeaway service; delivery service (over £35 within 2-mile radius). Vegetarian menu. **Map 9 H8.**

Piccadilly

Fakhreldine

85 Piccadilly, W1J 7NB (7493 3424/www. fakhreldine.co.uk). Green Park tube. **Meals served** noon-midnight Mon-Sat; noon-11pm Sun. **Main courses** £13-£23. **Set lunch** £17 2 courses, £22 3 courses. **Credit** AmEx, DC, JCB, MC, V. Lebanese

One of the less Lebanese of London's top Lebanese restaurants, Fakhreldine opted a few years ago for a sleek modern take on food and decor. We like its look, especially the central sofa-filled bar area, not to mention the magnificent views over Green Park from the first-floor dining room. Dishes are mainly delicate, painstakingly prepared versions of classics – with occasional 'creative' use of ingredients (the set lunch menu on a recent visit included meat cooked with grapefruit). We opted for mezes for a summer lunch, and everything was top quality, as one might expect from a £5-£10.50 price tag: smoky and sensual baba ganoush; tabouleh with a lemony bite; prawns fried in a lovely light batter; firm little falafels; and dinky discs of mana'eesh zaatar that bore only a distant relationship to the usually heftier chunks of pitta grilled with olive oil and zaatar spice. We also shared a main-course lamb kebab. It was a decent-sized portion of the very best lamb, perfectly grilled – but we wonder who is happy to pay £18 for grilled meat. The care taken with the cooking, along with the sense of style, lend a sense of occasion to a visit here. Service, from mainly European staff, was pleasant and professional.

Babies and children welcome: high chairs. Booking advisable. Takeaway service; delivery service. **Map 9 H8.**

West

Bayswater

★ Al Waha

75 Westbourne Grove, W2 4UL (7229 0800/ www.waha-uk.com). Bayswater or Queensway tube. **Meals served** noon-midnight daily. **Main courses** £9.50-£18.50. **Set lunch** £12.50 5 dishes. **Set dinner** £21 (minimum 2) 3 courses, £25 (minimum 2) 4 courses. **Cover** £1.50. **Minimum** £12.50 (dinner Fri & Sat). **Credit** MC, V. Lebanese

Al Waha has had a face-lift since our last visit; it's now brown and cream of hue, but has kept a traditional feel with the usual white tableclothes and sparkling glassware. It's quite an intimate space that majors in relaxed ambience over cosmopolitan glitz – and has good food into the bargain. A recent dinner on a quiet weekday evening featured such lovely dishes as fatoush salad, warmly spiced with sumac; a citrusy salatate al rahib (mashed aubergine with lemon juice, plus chopped peppers and onions); makdous (little pickled aubergine with walnuts); and a firm, slinky houmous. Only tabouleh – comprising rather soggy, vinegary chopped leaves with no bulgar wheat to bulk it out or add flavour – disappointed. The mixed meat grill was superb: perfectly grilled and juicy cubes of lamb and chicken. There have been complaints about the new £12.50 minimum charge for food, but it only operates on Friday and Saturday evenings, and we exceeded it without effort. Service is low-key and professional and, despite that pesky charge, prices remain lower than in the Edgware Road/Mayfair epicentre of Lebanese dining.

Babies and children welcome (until 7pm): high chairs. Booking advisable; essential dinner. Tables outdoors (4, patio). Takeaway service; delivery service (over £20 within 3-mile radius). **Map 7 B6.**

Beity NEW

92 Queensway, W2 3RR (7221 8782/ www.beity.co.uk). Bayswater tube. **Meals served** 9am-1.30am Mon-Sat; 9am-midnight Sun. **Main courses** £9.75-£15.75. **Set lunch** £12.75 2 courses incl coffee or tea. **Set dinner** £16.50-£21.50 4 dishes incl coffee or tea; £23.50 10 dishes incl coffee or tea. **Credit** MC, V. Lebanese

This new Lebanese café seems to appeal to everyone: families with teens, couples, grandparents, as well as the men out front sharing a sheesha pipe. Past the smart chilled counter lined with meze and fruit is a smart yet casual dining area with wooden chairs and granite-look tables. The menu lists over 30 of the most familiar hot and cold starters and 16 mains, though many customers were ordering the cheaper, modestly sized wraps rather than overflowing plates of shawarma, kibbeh and the like. Moutabal had the requisite smoky flavour acquired by char-grilling the aubergine. An appetising dish of little Lebanese lamb sausages came with finely chopped fresh lemon and shards of pine kernels. Mixed shawarma of finely sliced chicken and lamb was deliciously moist. With a light banana milkshake and freshly squeezed mango juice from the juice bar, there was no room for desserts such as mohalabia (milk pudding) or sha'aybiyat (pastries with clotted cream). Fortunately, brisk service allowed us to quickly make way for more customers, and stop a queue forming.

Babies and children welcome: high chairs. Restaurant available for hire. Tables outdoors (5, pavement). Takeaway service; delivery service (over £20 within 2-mile radius). **Map 7 C6.**

★ Fresco

25 Westbourne Grove, W2 4UA (7221 2355/ www.frescojuices.co.uk). Bayswater or Royal Oak tube. **Meals served** 8am-11pm daily. **Main courses** £5.95-£7.95. **Set meze** £9.95. **Credit** MC, V. Lebanese

The juicer's constantly on the go at Fresco, squeezing all manner of produce for the single juices, combos, vegetable juices and fruity milkshakes that are at the heart of Fresco's winning formula. The cheery yellow decor and buzz of activity only adds to the sense of health and vitality. Portions are generous: £2.95 bought a huge sundae-style glass of tropical-tasting banana, strawberry and orange juice. Serious juice fans might enjoy the 'energisers', such as the carrot, broccoli and beets combination. At lunchtime, queues form at the counter for takeaways: on display are Lebanese vegetarian meze dishes (many of which can be served in pitta bread as a sandwich). Grilled chicken kebab and western-style sandwiches are also on the menu. There is a table-service café if you want to eat in; we've always found the waitresses pleasant and efficient. On our last visit we ordered a selection of meze: falafel, houmous, tabouleh and batata hara. It was nicely presented on one plate – not the kind of food you get in upmarket restaurants, but everything was tasty (and the bill was far lower). The juice was the star of the show, though.

Babies and children welcome: high chairs. Bookings not accepted. Takeaway service; delivery service (within 3-mile radius). Vegetarian menu. **Map 7 B6. For branches see index.**

Hafez

5 Hereford Road, W2 4AB (7221 3167/7229 9398/www.hafez.com). Bayswater tube/328 bus. **Meals served** noon-midnight daily. **Main courses** £6-£14.50. **No credit cards.** Iranian

Outdoor tables make this Persian restaurant, in a quiet street off Westbourne Grove, a particularly apt choice for dinner on a balmy summer night. We've had the odd bad experience here in the past, so were pleasantly surprised by the quality of the food on this visit. A plate of sabzi with a mound of fragrant mint and tarragon sprigs, delightfully creamy feta and radishes for crunch made a good

start, and kashk-e bademjan – baked aubergine purée, here mixed with yoghurt, walnuts and olive oil – was a richly flavoured accompaniment to the warm Iranian bread. Then came the kebabs. A twinning of lamb and minced lamb comprised beautiful juicy meat, cooked to perfection, served with the traditional buttery rice (and, on this occasion, some salad too). Poussin wasn't so special: the perky notes we had been expecting from the saffron-tinged bird marinated in lime juice were hard to detect; and an overly fragrant yet strangely flavourless rosewater ice-cream didn't improve things. Some duff dishes, then, but Hafez provided us with a pleasant taste of Persian cooking in tranquil surroundings.
Babies and children welcome: high chairs. Tables outdoors (4, pavement). Takeaway service; delivery service. **Map 7 B6**.
For branch see index.

Kensington

★ Randa NEW
23 Kensington Church Street, W8 4LF (7937 5363). High Street Kensington tube. **Meals served** noon-midnight daily. **Main courses** £11.95-£16. **Set lunch** £12 2 courses. **Set dinner** £45 (2 people), £90 (4 people) tasting menu. **Credit** MC, V. Lebanese
The newest venture from the Maroush stable, Randa occupies a former corner pub site. The mode of conversion is a clue as to who the new restaurant is aimed at – we guess it's non-Arabs or perhaps trendy younger Lebanese. On two floors, it's a rather clumsy effort at steel, glass and breeze-block modernism. Design values aside, the Maroush à la mode concept seems to be working: a midweek visit found Randa doing a roaring trade, and the clientele was younger, more western and louder than at other branches. The food was very good indeed. Highlights of our meat-free meze feast included melt-in-the-mouth cheese sambouseks with lovely light pastry, dense falafel

with a good crunch to the outside served with a light tahina sauce, and a well-seasoned fuul that made a gloriously tasty mess when mashed up with olive oil. Add smooth, mellow houmous and citrusy tabouleh into the mix and you have a pretty faultless Lebanese meal. A shame that the staff hadn't quite got it together – service veered between slightly frosty Lebanese and slightly inefficient European.
No-smoking tables. Separate room for parties, seats 40. Takeaway service; delivery service (over £25 within 1-mile radius). **Map 7 B8**.

Olympia

★ ★ Alounak
10 Russell Gardens, W14 8EZ (7603 7645). Kensington (Olympia) tube/rail. **Meals served** noon-midnight daily. **Main courses** £5.60-£11.10. **Unlicensed. Corkage** no charge. **Credit** MC, V. Iranian
Alounak impresses with its consistency. We've been eating here since at least the early 1990s, when the restaurant was a prefab cabin beside the railway tracks, and we've yet to come away less than 100% satisfied. Except perhaps for the marinated grilled sea bass (served with head and tail intact), the menu has little to differentiate it from London's other Iranian restaurants. Starters include the usuals, such as mirza ghasemi, halim bademjan and salad olivieh, while the mains are kebabs. But when the food arrives the rice is always light and fluffy, and the meat always tender and flavourful. On such things as Iranian restaurants judged. Additionally, Alounak scores highly for its bright, cheerful and family-friendly air, although the cosy front area with its rusticated brickwork and hanging bauble lights is far preferable to the rear part of the restaurant, which is slightly gloomy and often filled with large parties.
Babies and children welcome: high chairs. Booking advisable. Takeaway service; delivery service.
For branch see index.

★ Chez Marcelle
34 Blythe Road, W14 0HA (7603 3241). Kensington (Olympia) tube/rail. **Meals served** 5-10pm Tue-Thur; noon-10pm Fri-Sun. **Main courses** £8-£10.50. **No credit cards**.
Lebanese
Marcelle has been running her restaurant for 13 years now. It is still very much a one-woman show, with this formidable Lebanese lady doing all the cooking herself in the large kitchen that occupies the rear of the one modest room. Not only is the bustling Marcelle visible, she's also audible, singing as she works. She frequently escapes the kitchen to warmly greet arriving customers, and seemed to know all of them by name on a recent visit. The menu is a laminated card of 36 meze, plus standard grilled meat mains. Portions are generous: the falafel are the size of tennis balls; the batata hara comes in a mountainous heap; similarly the chicken livers, which swim in a rich gravy far too good to leave, so the dish comes with a heap of bread to mop up with. Three or four meze make more than a meal for two, so order sparingly. Mains include a highly recommended 'stuffed lamb', which isn't stuffed but baked, cut thinly, layered on cinnamon rice and topped with sliced pistachios and almonds. The restaurant is cash or cheque only, with the nearest ATM a 20-minute walk away on Kensington High Street.
Babies and children admitted. Booking advisable. Separate room for parties, seats 40. Takeaway service. **Map 20 C3**.

★ Mohsen
152 Warwick Road, W14 8PS (7602 9888). Earl's Court tube/Kensington (Olympia) tube/rail. **Meals served** noon-midnight daily. **Main courses** £12-£15. **Unlicensed. Corkage** no charge. **No credit cards**.
Iranian
Located on the busy Warwick Road with an inescapable view of a Homebase hoarding, Mohsen may at first appear unpromising, but on a

Randa

RESTAURANTS

Saturday lunchtime, spruce after a recent refurbishment, it was heaving with a mainly Iranian crowd spreading into the conservatory-style back room. Charming 3-D pictures of village houses break up the plain decor. The enticing aroma of featherlight bread baking on the wall of a stainless-steel oven sets the appetite racing. Everything seemed fresher than fresh – from a dazzling range of 14 starters, pert tarragon and parsley with feta; masto musir; and char-grilled aubergines with walnut and mint made our tastebuds sing. Each day there's a different stew, but we were delighted with kebabs served on huge mounds of fluffy rice with a saffron-yellow topping. Barg was a long, thin and gloriously tender slice of lamb fillet; joojeh was butter-soft chicken marinated in lime juice and saffron. There's no licence – most of our fellow diners were drinking doogh (a Persian yoghurt drink), but one group wanting wine were encouraged to pop to the bar next door and bring back a bottle. Finish with aromatic tea.
Babies and children welcome: high chairs. Tables outdoors (2, yard) Delivery service. **Map 13 A10.**

Yas

7 Hammersmith Road, W14 8XJ (7603 9148/ www.yasrestaurant.co.uk). Kensington (Olympia) tube/rail. **Meals served** noon-4.30am daily. **Main courses** £7-£12. **Credit** MC, V. Iranian
Yas is an unassuming Iranian neighbourhood eaterie with sunny yellow walls and a blue-tiled clay oven fulfilling the promise of delicious, puffy, fresh-baked Iranian bread. Midweek it was empty and draughty, with pleasant but casual service. The modest menu offers the usual Iranian staples: kashk-e bademjan (aubergine purée with mint and goats cheese); good salad olivieh, like a Persian version of russian salad, with chicken, eggs, peas, potatoes and gherkins bound in thick, creamy mayonnaise; and our favourite, sabzi-e paneer – a

pile of mouth-tingling fresh herbs (predominantly tarragon) with salty feta. The chicken kebab was OK, but lacked the soft-as-butter tenderness we usually associate with the Iranian saffron-marinated version. A lamb, aubergine and split pea stew with dried limes is a revelation for tastebuds unaccustomed to Iranian flavours – a deliciously robust sauce with the sharp hook of the limes tempered by a certain mustiness. The lamb itself, though, was rather meagre and tired-tasting. Mains all come with huge mounds of the fluffiest, lightest chello rice with a characteristic crunchy crust. It's worth a visit just for this. The exceptionally late opening hours are also a real plus when you're hungry at 4am.
Babies and children welcome: high chairs. Booking advisable. Takeaway service.

Shepherd's Bush

★ Abu Zaad

29 Uxbridge Road, W12 8LH (8749 5107). Shepherd's Bush tube. **Meals served** 11am-11pm daily. **Main courses** £4.50-£11. **Credit** MC, V. Syrian
A rather forbidding corner site, complete with barred windows, gives way to a far cheerier interior at Abu Zaad, with artefacts and blown-up photographs of Damascus on the walls, a central juicing and coffee-making area, and a grill station at the back. It has the air of a well-established local: there's a warm welcome for all and customers – a mixed bunch of nationalities, many of whom know the staff – share the confident air of those who realise are getting something good. The menu is more or less identical to those at snazzy uptown Lebanese joints, at about half the price. A long list of juices, and sharwerma sandwiches, complete the picture. Some of the dishes in our meze lunch may have lacked the precision and vivid colours of the Edgware Road versions, but nearly everything was full of taste. Batata hara had plenty of bite, fattoush was crunchy and spicy. Fatayer bi lahm

(meat parcels) were little canoes of soft pastry filled with delicately spiced minced lamb. Only foul makala (broad beans with coriander and lemon, cooked in olive oil) was a disappointment, featuring flavourless beans with chewy skins. Sweet own-made lemonade was a good accompaniment to a happy meal.
Babies and children welcome: high chairs. Book weekends. No-smoking tables. Separate room for parties, seats 30. Takeaway service. **Map 20 B2.**

East
Brick Lane

Lebanese Lounge NEW

50-52 Hanbury Street, E1 5JL (7539 9200/ www.lebaneselounge.com). Aldgate East tube/ Liverpool Street tube/rail. **Meals served** noon-11pm daily. **Main courses** £9-£15. **Set lunch** (noon-5pm Mon-Fri) £9.90 2 courses incl drink. **Set dinner** £18 3 courses. **Credit** MC, V. Lebanese
This Middle Eastern incursion into the Bangladeshi heartland is a welcome respite from the 20%-off school of restaurantry that dominates the Brick Lane area. It's understated – almost hidden, in fact – employs no touts and is an all-round classy affair. The restaurant wraps around three sides of a small courtyard off Hanbury Street. On one side is a convivial smoking lounge, scattered with throw cushions for slothful reclining and shisha. On the other side is the main dining room, which is old-school formal (red cloths over white on the tables, single carnations in vases) with stiff but courteous service from besuited staff. The menu offers the standard mix of hot and cold meze and meat dishes. Our grilled meat dish was terrific: farouj meshwi was a boneless baby chicken served with an eye-watering garlic sauce, served with rice peppered with sultanas and cashews. Kafta

Lebanese Lounge

yogurtlieh was good too: three torpedos of spicy minced lamb baked in a dish of yoghurt and sprinkled with paprika. Food and service are far superior to that found in many of the restaurants in the traditional Middle East End of Queensway and the Edgware Road, but whether the idea of nipping down to Brick Lane for a kofta rather than a curry will ever catch on remains to be seen. *Babies and children admitted. Booking advisable Fri, Sat. Disabled: toilet. No-smoking tables. Separate room for parties, seats 20. Takeaway service.* **Map 12 S5.**

North
Camden Town & Chalk Farm

Le Mignon
98 Arlington Road, NW1 7HD (7387 0600). Camden Town tube. **Lunch served** noon-3pm, **dinner served** 6pm-midnight daily. **Main courses** £9.50-£18.50. **Credit** MC, V. Lebanese

It's a sign of Le Mignon's success that this restaurant, on a side street off Camden's main drag, was doing a healthy trade on a weekday lunchtime. It's unlikely customers are here for the decor: the little corner space is dominated by multicoloured brick cladding, and the tablecloths are pink. But what Le Mignon lacks in looks it makes up for in food. It provides a welcome chance to sample the best of Lebanese food in a small owner-run restaurant a million miles from the glitz of some central London venues. We couldn't find anything to fault on a recent visit. We loved the fried chicken livers (sawda dajaj), with a sharp lemony tang; fuul moukala were a cooked to perfection with coriander and lemon; a fattoush salad was fresh and colourful, with lots of warm sumac spice and crisp little squares of toasted pitta; batata hara had plenty of flavour. Perfect food for a summer lunch. We appreciate the quiet style of service too.
Babies and children admitted (daytime). Booking advisable. Tables outdoors (4, pavement). Takeaway service. **Map 27 D3.**

Outer London
Wembley, Middlesex

Mesopotamia NEW
115 Wembley Park Drive, Wembley, Middx HA9 8HG (8453 5555/www.mesopotamia.ltd.uk). Wembley Park tube. **Dinner served** 6pm-midnight Mon-Sat. **Main courses** £11-£14.50. **Set meal** 3 courses £23. **Credit** AmEx, DC, MC, V. Iraqi

Iraqi menus read like a greatest hits compilation of Middle Eastern dishes. Skim through the appetisers and you may be left thinking: 'Now That's What I Call Meze'. But a closer look at the menu will reveal that along with the houmous and fattoush salad so typical of Lebanese cuisine, the dolma and baklava that Iraqis embraced enthusiastically from Turkey, and the fesanjun (chicken stew featuring a delicious sauce of pomegranate juice and walnuts) shared with Iran, there are some unique dishes. Beef is more common in Iraq than other parts of the Middle East. Here it was offered as a special dish of dhob: a lean prime cut braised in a mild spice gravy. It came with a side plate containing both rice pilaf and bulgur wheat. Beef was also combined with sultanas and onion in fried kubbah – similar to Lebanese kibbeh (minced lamb meze), but often made with rice or potato in place of bulgur wheat. Iraq is a prolific date producer and while this intensely flavoured fruit is typically served as a post-prandial refreshment, you may also find them in a sweetly savoury starter dip with walnuts, onion and yoghurt. With its tented ceiling and friendly atmosphere, Mesopotamia makes a refreshingly different night out in Wembley Park. *Babies and children admitted. Booking advisable. No smoking. Restaurant available for hire. Vegetarian menu.*

Modern European

Ask any Londoner where they'd most like to eat, and chances are it will be one of the restaurants in this chapter. Yet the expression Modern European is a term many diners still don't recognise. It means dishes in the European tradition, but not necessarily attributable to any one region or country. Twenty years ago the predecessors of this magpie style of cooking were termed Modern British, but gradually menus, ingredients and techniques shifted south to the Mediterranean and even further afield, so the terminology shifted to 'European'. In Australia and the US, this type of cooking would simply be called 'contemporary', but we like to recognise its European roots. It's one of the most dynamic sectors of London dining, and still tends to be the cuisine of choice in see-and-be-seen restaurants. This year we're pleased to welcome another wave of excellent new openings, including **Arbutus**, **The Ambassador**, **11 Abingdon Road**, **The Terrace** and **Upstairs**.

Central
Barbican

Searcy's
Level 2, Barbican, Silk Street, EC2Y 8DS (7588 3008/www.searcys.co.uk). Barbican tube. **Lunch served** noon-2.30pm Mon-Fri. **Dinner served** 5-10.30pm Mon-Sat. **Main courses** £11.95-£19.50. **Set dinner** (5-7.30pm) £22.50 2 courses, £26.50 3 courses. **Credit** AmEx, DC, JCB, MC, V.

This smart venue – with black leather furnishings, primrose-yellow walls, and a quiet bar – curves around the second level of the Barbican Centre. The Centre was undergoing refurbishment on our visit, but the restaurant was as hushed, sparsely elegant and corporate-looking as ever. On a hot, sultry day, we sat by a window overlooking the terrace and the lakeside, glasses of chilled rosé in hand: summertime bliss. From a seasonal menu with eastern accents, chilled minted pea soup was lively, although its garnish of crunchy spätzle (German pasta, here made with broad-bean flour) was odd. Rich, velvety foie gras pâté was more enjoyable. Next, a somewhat brittle parmesan tart filled with baba ganoush (grilled, mashed aubergine), topped with herby polenta, was a weird combination. Beautifully cooked scallops arrived with smoked mackerel ravioli that dominated the dish; it was like two main courses on one plate. Puddings such as red chilli-flecked pineapple carpaccio with basil sorbet, and honeydew melon and pink grapefruit terrine were refreshing. Stick to the simpler, less ambitious dishes and you won't go wrong.
Booking advisable. Disabled: toilet. Dress: smart casual. No smoking. **Map 11 P5.**

City

The Chancery
9 Cursitor Street, EC4A 1LL (7831 4000/ www.thechancery.co.uk). Chancery Lane tube. **Meals served** noon-2.30pm, **dinner served** 6-10.30pm Mon-Fri. **Set menu** £32 3 courses incl coffee. **Credit** AmEx, DC, JCB, MC, V.

The Chancery was fairly empty on our last visit; the place is notable for its absence of pulling-power. The interior, with white walls, black leather chairs, and copper tones (courtesy of the wall art), reeks of sobriety. This is perhaps appropriate, given the lawyer-heavy clientele, but makes for a dull atmosphere. The menu, although ambitious, is composed of robust dishes that tend to lack cohesion. Pan-fried mackerel with pancetta crisp and lentils made a heavy starter, the spiced lentils being more than a match for the strong flavour of the fish. For main courses, fillets of red mullet came with a spiced orange and cardamom couscous that was tasty but let down by the proliferation of cucumber and by the dish's overall lack of vibrancy. A duo of braised beef fillets with Madeira jus was of a high quality – shame, then, that it was accompanied by a virtually potato-free, excessively oily gratin dauphinois. For dessert, iced tiramisu with Kahlúa ice-cream was sweet and rich, yet not especially memorable. Still, the fixed-price menu is reasonably good value (for £32 you'll get three courses plus appetisers, palate-refreshers, coffee and petits fours). Service is well judged.
Babies and children welcome: high chairs. Booking essential. No smoking. Separate rooms for parties, both seating 25. **Map 11 N6.**

The Don
The Courtyard, 20 St Swithin's Lane, EC4N 8AD (7626 2606/www.thedonrestaurant.com). Bank tube/DLR.
Restaurant **Lunch served** noon-2.30pm, **dinner served** 6.30-10pm Mon-Fri. **Main courses** £12.95-£23.95.
Bistro **Lunch served** noon-3pm, **dinner served** 6-10pm Mon-Fri. **Main courses** £8.95-£14.95.
Both **Credit** AmEx, DC, MC, V.

Graced with an epic wine list and formal, attentive staff, the Don's restaurant and bistro are designed to impress City folk. The austere modern art and high ceilings may not be to everyone's taste, but the food is solid Mod Euro fare, served in well-measured portions. A starter of scallops baked en croûte with lime and vanilla was dramatically

presented in a scallop shell sealed with pastry (cut apart with pageantry by the waiter); the cream of the surrounding sauce contrasted nicely with wilted rocket and spinach. We also sampled a rich gateau of lamb sweetbreads with lamb fillet and morel mushrooms, and a pressed foie gras and confit of duck with Sauternes jelly on toasted brioche – both of which matched the elegance of the cavernous room. Mains of lamb chops with shallots, and duckling with confit of savoy cabbage and celeriac (essentially, sauerkraut), were hearty, delicious and perfectly cooked. However, the fat of a suckling pig was disappointingly soft. The Don is a good place for food, but a great place to splurge on a choice bottle; vintage port is decanted daily.
Booking essential. Children over 10 years welcome. Dress: smart casual. Separate room for parties, seats 24. **Map 12 Q7.**

Lanes

East India House, 109-117 Middlesex Street, E1 7JF (7247 5050/www.lanesrestaurant.co.uk). Liverpool Street tube/rail.
Bar **Open** 10am-11pm Mon-Wed; 10am-1am Thur, Fri; 6pm-midnight Sat. **Main courses** £8-£17.
Restaurant **Main courses** £12.50-£24.95. **Set dinner** £15 2 courses, £21.50 3 courses.
Both **Lunch served** noon-3pm Mon-Sat.

Dinner served 5.30-10pm Mon-Fri; 6-10pm Sat. **Credit** AmEx, DC, JCB, MC, V.
Judging by the familiarity of the greetings exchanged between staff and clientele, Lanes draws a good deal of repeat business. The regulars like the location (on the fringe of the City but isolated from its bustle) and the decor (that of an approachable 21st-century gentlemen's club – though diners, mostly City workers, seem an equal mix of men and women). And they clearly like the staff, who exude a natural bonhomie without ever once taking their collective eye off the ball. Yet the imbalance between the quality and the price of the food is a little too great to ignore. Save for an asparagus starter let down by poorly sourced ingredients, nothing we ate was bad; indeed, our other starter, duck served with a beetroot carpaccio, was quite impressive. But a beautifully presented fillet of monkfish, served with tomatoes and a little spinach patty, was marginally overcooked, and a portion of pork tenderloin, with carrot, cabbage and extremely slender potato gratings, was very plain. Neither dish did anything like enough to justify its £18 price tag. Even if money is no object, you can get more bang for your buck just a short walk away.
Bar and restaurant available for hire. Booking essential lunch. Disabled: toilet. Separate room for parties, seats 28. **Map 12 R6.**

★ Prism

147 Leadenhall Street, EC3V 4QT (7256 3875/ www.harveynichols.com). Monument tube/Bank tube/DLR.
Bar **Open** 11am-11pm Mon-Fri. **Meals served** 11am-3pm, 6-10pm Mon-Fri. **Main courses** £4-£10.
Restaurant **Lunch served** 11.30am-3pm, **dinner served** 6-10pm Mon-Fri. **Main courses** £15-£23.
Both **Credit** AmEx, DC, MC, V.
Prism is one of many City banking halls that have been converted to the cause of fine dining – by Harvey Nichols, in this case. It's a lovely room, white and airy, combining a huge bar (you can snack and drink at low tables in the centre of the room) and linen-decked tables along one wall. We visited on a hot night; the restaurant was nearly empty, and some senior staff were off-duty. This probably explains the slightly uncoordinated service. But we can offer nothing but raves about the food. It's ambitious, elaborate and, at its best, extraordinary. Shellfish bisque, profound in flavour, bathed a succulently seared scallop. A ballottine of rabbit and dates was wrapped in a thick slice of prosciutto and served with celeriac remoulade and a little cup of creamy rabbit soup. Star of the meal: a roast quail with cabbage, foie gras and a marinated fig – one of the best dishes

Sam's Brasserie & Bar. See p227.

we've ever had. Presentation is artful but purposeful, and ingredients are top-notch. The huge wine list, though best suited to those with deep pockets, offers fair choice under £30. Prices are pretty fancy (as you'd expect when most customers are City folk), but not out of line. If you want stunning food in a lovely setting, Prism deserves attention.

Babies and children admitted. Booking advisable. Disabled: toilet. Separate rooms for parties, seating 20 and 40. Vegetarian menu. **Map 12 Q6.**

Clerkenwell & Farringdon

★ Ambassador NEW

2006 RUNNER-UP BEST NEW RESTAURANT
55 Exmouth Market, EC1R 4QL (7837 0009/ www.theambassadorcafe.co.uk). Angel tube/ Farringdon tube/rail/19, 38 bus. **Meals served** 8.30am-10.15pm Mon-Fri; 11am-4pm Sat, Sun. **Main courses** £9.50-£17. **Set lunch** (noon-3pm Mon-Fri) £12.50 2 courses, £16 3 courses. **Credit** AmEx, MC, V.
This easy-going incarnation of an idealised bistro is the perfect addition to Exmouth Market's restaurant roster. You can just drink, or add a bar plate or two to the equation (san daniele ham or chicken rillettes with cornichons and toast, both £4), or order a meal from the short but tempting menu. Everything we sampled was good, with the exception of a workaday macaroni and red pepper gratin (a main course that just didn't meld). Starters of tomato salad with goat's cheese cream, and confit of salmon with dill and pickles melted in the mouth. And fillet of gilthead bream in spring vegetable broth was a sensational piece of fish, beautifully cooked. Puds are worth ordering: play safe with raspberry cheesecake, or go for the sweet challenge of poached rhubarb with sweet bread sauce (an unusual, headily flavoured dessert that won us round). The menu is matched by an interesting wine list, with plenty by the glass. Breakfast is also served, plus brunch at weekends. Service is very friendly; first-timers here won't need any persuading to become regulars – especially when the weather allows the restaurant to extend on to the pavement, continental style.
Babies and children welcome: children's menu; high chairs; toys. Booking advisable. Disabled: toilet. No-smoking tables. Tables outdoors (5, pavement). Map 5 N4.

Clerkenwell Dining Room

69-73 St John Street, EC1M 4AN (7253 9000/ www.theclerkenwell.com). Barbican tube/ Farringdon tube/rail. **Lunch served** noon-2.30pm Mon-Fri; **Dinner served** 6-11.30pm Mon-Fri; 7-11.30pm Sat. **Main courses** £12-£16. **Set meal** £14.50 2 courses, £19.50 3 courses. **Credit** AmEx, DC, JCB, MC, V.
A Saturday night saw the Clerkenwell Dining Room pretty empty, devoid of atmosphere and sepulchrally quiet, save for our fellow diners' gratingly snooty conversation. The impressive sculptural floristry looked a touch faded round the edges. That said, the restaurant is seriously smart, with cream leather banquettes and dark blue upholstery, thick linen tablecloths and weighty tableware. The menu is a mixed bag. We couldn't fault scrumptious starters of sea-fresh seared scallops with curry spices and potato pakoras, and an excellent seared yellow-fin tuna niçoise salad. But mains were uneven. A trio of grilled salmon, tiger prawns and squid, stingy on the seafood, was artfully arranged with pools of pesto and piperade around a large melting piece of mozzarella buried under grilled courgettes – why? Decent pink canon of lamb served atop minted tagliolini with peas felt it deserved more robust accompaniment. This left room for delectable puds like rich hot chocolate fondant with moreish malt ice-cream. Service, a touch stiff at first, mellowed as the evening progressed. The fairly pricey carte is mitigated by a reasonably pitched wine list. We left feeling that a much better all-round experience could probably be had here midweek. We'll happily try again.
Babies and children welcome: high chair. Booking advisable. No-smoking tables. Separate room for parties, seats 40. Map 5 O4.

Portal

88 St John Street, EC1M 4EH (7253 6950/ www.portalrestaurant.com). Barbican tube/ Farringdon tube/rail. **Lunch served** noon-3pm Mon-Fri. **Dinner served** 6-10.15pm Mon-Sat. **Main courses** £9.50-£32. **Credit** AmEx, MC, V.
The name of this spacious Portuguese restaurant is a homage to winemakers Quinta da Portal. There's no official collaboration, but Portal's owner is a friend and a fan of the critically acclaimed Douro-based winery. A selection of the company's bottles appear on the restaurant's unusual, Iberian-leaning wine list. Food is equally imaginative. A starter of crab carpaccio, served as numerous wafer-thin discs under lines of a dark sauce, was a light, tasty opener. Then came an onslaught of flesh for mains: three enormous hunks of salted, braised pork (from the semi-wild Bisaro pig) that fell apart perfectly at the fork; and an ample john dory, delicately grilled. The restaurant's design is appealingly casual. Exposed brickwork and trendy curved chairs look sleek and relaxed, belying the relative smartness of the clientele; and there's a wonderful glass-roofed dining room at the back. Set behind the stylish, dark bar at the entrance, this room brings customers as close to alfresco dining as possible in the winter months. In summer, brightly lit and airy, it is one of the nicest spaces we've eaten in.
Babies and children welcome: high chairs. Disabled: toilet. No-smoking tables. Separate room for parties, seats 10. Map 5 O4.

Smiths of Smithfield

67-77 Charterhouse Street, EC1M 6HJ (7251 7950/www.smithsofsmithfield.co.uk). Farringdon tube/rail.
Cocktail bar **Open** 5.30-10.30pm Mon-Wed; 5.30pm-1.30am Thur-Sat.
Dining room **Lunch served** noon-2.45pm Mon-Fri. **Dinner served** 6-10.45pm Mon-Sat. **Main courses** £11.50.
Ground floor bar/café **Meals served** 7am-4.30pm Mon; 7am-5pm Tue-Fri; 10am-5pm Sat; 9.30am-5pm Sun.
Both **Credit** AmEx, DC, MC, V.
One of London's most ambitious eating and drinking projects of the past decade has developed into an unstoppably successful operation, over four floors and 15,000sq ft (around 1,400sq m) of converted warehouse. It has been claimed that the perpetually packed ground-floor bar serves more beer per square foot than any other in London (you can also eat breakfast, brunch and lunch down here); on super-busy nights, the first-floor cocktail bar fills apace. Like the spaces below it, the second-floor Dining Room carries an artfully industrial look, bare brick walls contributing to a (deliberately?) terrible acoustic. Still, the City workers and Clerkenwell thirtysomethings who make up an agreeably mixed clientele don't mind (those that do have the smarter, calmer, British-slanted Top Floor). A starter of bucatini pasta with tender crab had its subtleties overwhelmed by a creamy chilli sauce; grilled mushrooms and poached egg on sourdough toast also disappointed, the bread slightly old and the egg overcooked. Happily, the mains were better: a generous, succulent portion of duck with pak choi; and cannelloni with a velvety blend of butternut squash and buffalo ricotta. The old meat marketeers look on bemusedly from their trucks and trailers, but the beat goes on.
Babies and children welcome (restaurant). Disabled: toilet. Entertainment: DJs 7pm Thur-Sat (ground floor). Separate room for parties, seats 26. Tables outdoors (4, pavement; 6, terrace). Takeaway service (café). Map 11 O5.

The Trading House NEW

12-13 Greville Street, EC1N 8SB (7831 0697/ www.thetradinghouse.net). Chancery Lane tube/ Farringdon tube/rail.
Bar **Open** noon-midnight Mon-Fri. **Main courses** £4.25-£8.75.
Restaurant **Main courses** £9.70-£16.95.
Both **Meals served** noon-9pm Mon-Fri. **Credit** AmEx, MC, V.
Sadly, this understated bar-restaurant has yet to grow into its name. Evening trade can feel

desperately slow – but not because there's anything wrong with the food. If anything, chef Tim Haigh's Modern European menu is a little too good, with dishes such as pot-roasted chicken breast with fondant leeks, celeriac rösti and tarragon jus sounding more polished than most of the gems dealt in neighbouring Hatton Garden. A starter of risotto nero proved the best dish: rich and satisfying with two curls of citrusy squid on top. A main of chateaubriand – served for a minimum of two and indeed as monumental as a castle – was meaty and bloody, with watercress salad and decent fries on the side. On occasion, though, dishes are ill-judged. Are veal brain beignets really their by overwhelming demand, or more a case of culinary posturing? Besides, the slapdash service was a let-down. Surrounded by wholesalers and rag traders, this location is not, perhaps, in need of highfalutin cuisine. With less fussy food and more attention front of house, perhaps the diamond would begin to shine.
Babies and children welcome. Booking advisable. No smoking (restaurant). Map 11 N5.

Vivat Bacchus

47 Farringdon Street, EC4A 4LL (7353 2648/ www.vivatbacchus.co.uk). Chancery Lane tube/ Farringdon tube/rail.
Bar **Open/snacks served** noon-10.30pm Mon-Fri. **Snacks** £6-£9.
Restaurant **Lunch served** noon-2.30pm, **dinner served** 6.30-9.30pm Mon-Fri. **Main courses** £13.50-£18. **Set meal** £15.50 2 courses, £17.50 3 courses.
Both **Credit** AmEx, DC, MC, V.
There's a theory that some white wines are better warm, and our sommelier at this restaurant (now with a wine bar of the same name) was insistent that such was the case with Jordan's 2002 chardonnay (£7.90 for a 175ml glass). But after finally letting us have a new glass at a cooler temperature, the wine came out with all its ripe melon, peach and mineral scents. Vivat Bacchus is the sister restaurant of Browns in Johannesburg, and wine is the forte. So the staff should know better. The firm has around 40,000 bottles, some in a cellar viewable through a glass wall in the restaurant. But in focusing on the grape so much, the management has ignored the other components that go to make a restaurant. The main room is more student cafeteria than fine-dining restaurant, with polyester squares on the ceiling, and brickwork that looks accidentally exposed rather than deliberate. On the plate, an amuse-bouche of fried gnocchi was followed by springbok meat coated in mustard and breadcrumbs. This was dry and came with overcooked butternut, although the pinotage (a grape much-planted in South Africa) sauce was a pleasant reduction. The wine list is a delight, but don't expect food of the same standard.
Babies and children admitted. Bar available for hire. Booking advisable. Disabled: toilet. No-smoking tables. Off-licence. Wine club (7pm Mon; £15). Map 11 N5.

Covent Garden

Axis

One Aldwych, 1 Aldwych, WC2B 4RH (7300 0300/www.onealdwych.com). Covent Garden or Embankment tube/Charing Cross tube/rail. **Lunch served** noon-2.45pm Mon-Fri. **Dinner served** 5.45-10.45pm Mon-Fri; 5.45-11.30pm Sat. **Main courses** £14.95-£22.50. **Set meal** £17.50 2 courses, £20.50 3 courses. **Credit** AmEx, DC, JCB, MC, V.
Located in the spacious basement of the stylish One Aldwych hotel, Axis remains a reliable bet for a sophisticated meal in comfortable, central London surrounds. Critics may lament its demise in the cutting-edge style stakes, yet the place is still undeniably impressive, with its huge Big Bang-like mural and its white linen-covered tables and black leather chairs. The kitchen delivers too, with a focus on high-quality, seasonal British ingredients and a varied choice of simple, well-executed dishes from an inventive Modern European menu. Our meal got off to a good start with a choice of artisan breads. Next, we exploited the menu's grill-

emphasis with a flavourful char-grilled asparagus starter followed by mains of Scottish beef fillet and spanking-fresh organic salmon, both of which were perfectly cooked. Grills are served with a sauce and garnish of your choice; other main courses might include porcini risotto, gruyère and parmesan soufflé or hay-baked leg of lamb. The high standards are maintained for dessert; a chocolate fondant with caramel ice-cream was delicious. Service is knowledgeable, attentive, restrained, yet completely unhaughty – perfectly pitched to the smart, business clientele.
Babies and children welcome: high chairs. Booking advisable. Disabled: toilet. Entertainment: jazz 8pm Tue, Wed. Restaurant available for hire. Vegetarian menu (book in advance). **Map 18 M7.**

Bank Aldwych

1 Kingsway, WC2B 6XF (7379 9797/ www.bankrestaurants.com). Holborn or Temple tube.
Bar **Open** 11.30am-11pm Mon-Sat; 11.30am-4.30pm Sun.
Restaurant **Lunch served** noon-2.45pm, **dinner served** 5.30am-11pm Mon-Sat. **Meals served** 11.30-4.30pm Sun. **Main courses** £18-£22. **Set meal** (5.30-7pm, 10-11pm Mon-Sat) £13.50 2 courses, £16 3 courses.
Both **Credit** AmEx, DC, MC, V.
Our latest meal here was a sorry affair, with lumpen food and a hefty bill providing a sting in the tale. We can only hope that this once-sparkling, supersized dining room was suffering a temporary lapse and that normal service will shortly be resumed. Only the waiting staff lacked fault this time. The once-innovative Modern European menu (cutting-edge in the restaurant's 1990s heyday) has been rehashed into a crowd-pleasing mix of breakfast, brunch, children's and time-limited prix fixe options, ranging from croque monsieur or cumberland sausages and mash to a truly horrible, sickly-sweet take on seared tuna with miso dressing. Grilled venison steak with ceps, fig chutney and a red wine jus wasn't much better, the meat served too rare and chewy, the whole incongruously accompanied by roasted winter vegetables on a supposedly summer menu. An indelicate chunk of raspberry and passionfruit roulade was a pretty dismal finish. We look forward to a return to happier days.
Babies and children welcome: high chairs. Booking advisable; essential weekends. Disabled: toilet. Dress: smart casual. Entertainment: jazz musician 1.30-4pm Sun. Separate rooms for parties, both seating 40. **Map 10 M6.**

The Ivy

1 West Street, WC2H 9NQ (7836 4751/ www.caprice-holdings.co.uk). Leicester Square tube. **Lunch served** noon-3pm Mon-Sat; noon-3.30pm Sun. **Dinner served** 5.30pm-midnight daily. **Main courses** £9.75-£38.50. **Set lunch** (Sat, Sun) £21.50 3 courses. **Cover** £2. **Credit** AmEx, DC, JCB, MC, V.
'Is that someone from children's TV?' It's easy to become entangled by the Ivy's mystique, created by the opaque, stained-glass latticed windows and the legend of impossible-to-book tables groaning with celebs. Yet after several abortive phone calls, we eventually phoned at 11am and bagged two same-day lunchtime seats. Once ensconced on the banquettes, try to ignore the flummery and simply relish the surroundings (wooden panelling and flooring, monochrome photos of old film stars), the vivacity (a roomful of excitable people) – and the food, which is better than you'd imagine. Correct, sparklingly eyed staff bring a menu of enticing, if mainstream, Mod Euro classics, augmented by a satisfying dose of earthiness and laudable seasonality. To start, sashimi (strips of three raw fish) edged out an oblong meld of potted ham and (minimal) foie gras. Neither of these thrilled like the main courses: a summery ensemble of lamb's sweetbreads, broad beans and peas in profound gravy; and an immaculately cooked chunk of cod on a modicum of mouth-watering saffron risotto with gremolata, topped with crunchy samphire. Scandinavian iced berries with hot white chocolate sauce was the pick of the puds. Wait until coffee

before allowing your eyes to wander. Yes, that's Antonia Fraser and Harold Pinter in the corner.
Babies and children welcome: high chairs. Booking essential, several weeks in advance. Separate room for parties, seats 60 (minimum 25). Vegetarian menu. Vegan dishes. **Map 18 K6.**

Fitzrovia

Villandry

170 Great Portland Street, W1W 5QB (7631 3131/www.villandry.com). Great Portland Street tube.
Bar **Open** 8am-11pm Mon-Fri; 9am-11pm Sat. **Breakfast served** 8-11.45am Mon-Sat. **Lunch served** noon-3.30pm Mon-Fri; noon-3pm Sat. **Dinner served** 5-10pm Mon-Fri; 7-10pm Sat. **Main courses** £9.50-£17.50. **Set dinner** (7-10pm Sat) £20 3 courses.
Restaurant **Lunch served** noon-3pm Mon-Fri; 11.30am-4pm Sat, Sun. **Dinner served** 6-10.30pm Mon-Sat. **Main courses** £9-£19.50.
Both **Credit** AmEx, MC, V.
Bar, restaurant, shop and lunch takeaway rolled into one: Villandry has brought a welcome breath of life to an otherwise dead part of town for nearly ten years. The whole place was bustling on a recent lunchtime visit, but we opted to eat in the large dining room. The carefully sourced, high-quality ingredients in the shop are also present on the restaurant's menu. Refreshingly, the list isn't dominated by meat, so vegetarians have some decent choices. We dived straight into the main courses. Linguine with wild garlic, scallops and parsley was brimming with fresh ingredients. Salmon fish cake with spinach and herb sauce, in contrast, was heavy-going and stodgy after just a few mouthfuls; it wasn't aided by accompanying Jersey royals that were a little underdone. Service (by several young lads) was well meaning but amateurish; there was a distinctive hard sell on the booze too. Still, amends were made with desserts. There's no point resisting the likes of apple crumble or sticky toffee pudding, though it's equally hard to turn down Villandry's justly renowned cheese plate. Wines don't have to break the bank – prices start at £13.75 a bottle. Not spectacular then, but still a worthwhile option.
Babies and children welcome: children's menu; high chairs. Bar & restaurant available for hire. Booking advisable. Entertainment: jazz 7.30pm Sat (bar). No smoking (restaurant). Tables outdoors (13, pavement). Takeaway service. **Map 3 H5.**

BEST MODERN EUROPEAN

For wine lovers
Ambassador (see p221), **The Avenue** (see p226), **Bibendum** (see p227), **The Don** (see p219), **Orrery** (see p225), **Ransome's Dock** (see p233), **Redmond's** (see p231), **Vivat Bacchus** (see p221).

For the scene
The Ivy (see left), **Embassy** (see p225), **Fifth Floor** (see right), **The Wolseley** (see p225).

For alfresco dining
Bank Westminster (see p227), **Babylon** (see p229), **Hoxton Apprentice** (see p236), **The Island** (see p236), **Oxo Tower** (see p234), **Petersham Nurseries Café** (see p237), **Phoenix Bar & Grill** (see p232), **Plateau** (see p235), **Le Pont de la Tour** (see p235), **The Terrace** (see right), **Wapping Food** (see p236).

For romance
L'Etranger (see right), **Lamberts** (see p232), **Oxo Tower** (see p234), **Fifth Floor** (see right), **Upstairs** (see p233).

Gloucester Road

L'Etranger

36 Gloucester Road, SW7 4QT (7584 1118/ www.etranger.co.uk). Gloucester Road tube. **Lunch served** noon-3pm Mon-Fri. **Dinner served** 6-11pm Mon-Sat. **Main courses** £12-£20. **Set meal** (noon-3pm, 6-6.45pm Mon-Fri) £14.50 2 courses, £16.50 3 courses. **Credit** AmEx, MC, V.
L'Etranger has a beautiful storm-cloud coloured interior, offset by architectural flower displays. There's an understated sense of occasion about the place, making it ideal for a special date. However, it serves equally well as a casual drop-in for the well-heeled locals. Staff are attentive but unobtrusive; the sommelier soon worked out our price range, helping us choose a surprisingly nice Greek Santorini. Head chef Jerome Tauvron has created an inventive and accomplished menu that shows a healthy respect for fine ingredients. Presentation and preparation are scrupulous. A delicately flavoured starter of lobster ravioli with lemongrass was equalled by the subtle and crisp yuba (beancurd skin) tempura with king crab and seaweed, burdock and sancho pepper. To follow, one taste of the succulent caramelised black cod was enough to emphasise why this simple fish is so popular; when cooked to perfection it is head and gills above the rest. Toro sashimi and tartare served with seaweed salad further exhibited Tauvron's command of eastern craft. Dessert was an almost perfect crème brûlée trio; saffron and lavender lived up to our high expectations, but the wasabi was altogether jarring. Still, it'll take more than one misplaced horseradish to dampen our enthusiasm for this lovely venue.
Babies and children welcome. Booking advisable. Restaurant available for hire. Vegetarian menu. **Map 13 C9.**

Holborn

The Terrace   NEW

Lincoln's Inn Fields, WC2A 3LJ (7430 1234/ www.theterrace.info). Holborn tube. **Breakfast served** 8-11am Mon-Fri. **Brunch served** 11am-5.30pm Sat. **Lunch served** noon-3pm Mon-Fri. **Dinner served** 5.30-8.30pm Mon-Sat. **Main courses** £8.50-£16.50. **Set lunch** £10.50 2 courses, £12.75 3 courses. **Credit** AmEx, MC, V.
On approaching the Terrace in Lincoln's Inn Fields you'd be forgiven for thinking you were looking at a large contemporary garden shed, a notion not dispelled on entering the sleek, light-filled wood and glass structure. There's a touch of greenhouse too on sunny days, when it's best to head out to the terrace tables and watch the tennis players. The menu is Modern European with hints of Caribbean, thanks to head chef and proprietor Patrick Williams' hybrid influences: Caribbean cooking from his mother, sous cheffing at the Ivy, and an apprenticeship with Gary Rhodes. All this results in a wide-ranging and tantalising menu that takes in everything from light and refreshing – smoked salmon and spring onion potato cake, or fresh pea and asparagus salad – to heartier starters like chorizo sausage and poached egg salad, or caramelised onion tart. Mains are equally eclectic. Jerk chicken, roast snapper or bream accompanied by sautéed plantain, sweet potato or mango salad all bear the Terrace signature: huge portions of well-cooked food that is usually as mouth-watering as it looks. The one vegetarian main course (spinach, mushroom and herb pancakes) was disappointing, but failed to spoil our enjoyment of a nicely different meal in a nicely different setting.
Babies and children welcome: high chairs. Booking advisable. Disabled: toilet. No smoking. Tables outdoors (15, terrace). **Map 10 M6.**

Knightsbridge

★ Fifth Floor

Harvey Nichols, Knightsbridge, SW1X 7RJ (7235 5250/www.harveynichols.com). Knightsbridge tube.

Café **Breakfast served** 8am-noon, **lunch
served** noon-3.30pm, **dinner served** 6-10.30pm
Mon-Sat. **Brunch served** 11am-5pm Sun.
Tea served 3.30-6pm Mon-Sat; 3.30-5pm Sun.
Main courses £9.50-£15.
Restaurant **Brunch served** noon-4pm Sat, Sun.
Lunch served noon-3pm Mon-Fri. **Dinner
served** 6-11pm Mon-Sat. **Main courses**
£15-£24. **Set dinner** £34.50 2 courses, £39.50
3 courses incl unlimited house wine. **Set meal**
£19.50 2 courses, £24.50 3 courses.
Both **Credit** AmEx, DC, JCB, MC, V.
Five floors above the workaday life of street level,
there's something otherworldly about Fifth Floor.
Perhaps it's the feminine decor: blue walls, rounded
corners, with unusual vertical lighting tubes
casting a glamorous glow across the spacious
dining area. Food can be on the ethereal side too.
Carpaccio of scallops, capers, toasted almonds and
sevruga caviar was tiny, delicate slivers and blobs
artistically arranged on a large oblong plate – all
very Victoria Beckham, but it was a wonderful
medley of tastes. It's the same with much of the
cooking (overseen by executive chef Helena
Puolakka); it's so sympathetic, with such vivid
flavour combinations, that small portions are
enough. Take English lamb, baby artichoke and
chickpeas, with cardamom-infused jus. A light
Moroccan touch, it seemed – and to prove it there
were flashes of spice from nuggets of merguez
beneath the tender meat. And for pudding? To
confound expectations, the kitchen had gone retro
with chocolate fondue: marshmallows, cherries,
toasted brioche and lashings of warm chocolate
sauce. A memorable meal, and it could have been
a boozy one: Harvey Nichols' own-label wine came
in unlimited quantities as part of a set-meal deal
that allowed us to order from the carte.
*Babies and children welcome: children's menu;
high chairs. Disabled: toilet.* **Map 8 F9**.

Marble Arch

The Crescent

*Montcalm Hotel, Great Cumberland Place,
W1H 7TW (7402 4288/7723 4440/www.
montcalm.co.uk). Marble Arch tube.* **Lunch
served** 12.30-2.30pm Mon-Fri. **Dinner
served** 6.30-10.30pm daily. **Set lunch** (incl
half bottle of wine) £21 2 courses, £26 3 courses.
Set dinner (incl half bottle of wine) £24.50
2 courses, £29.50 3 courses. **Credit** AmEx, DC,
JCB, MC, V.
Hidden from West End bustle in a leafy, tree-
shaded crescent off Great Cumberland Place, the
Montcalm Hotel is indeed a calming place to be.
One end of the building houses the restaurant,
which continues the serene, tree theme via a soft-
hued mural of a topiary garden covering one entire
wall, and comfortable, muted colours elsewhere.
Interesting dishes are cooked with confidence yet
avoid over-embellishment and represent money
well spent; around £25 buys a three-course lunch
or two-course dinner, with half a bottle of perfectly
decent red or white wine included in the price.
Lobster bisque opened our meal, a deeply fragrant
and flavoursome red broth completed with a few
spoonfuls of lobster meat as a nice surprise
lurking in the base of the tureen. Next came
expertly cooked supreme of chicken, featuring
unusually crispy and honestly appetising skin,
plus an elegant filling of mushroom and tarragon
mousse; these subtle tastes were heightened by a
smudge of star anise and black pepper in the
accompanying Madeira jus. Generous portions,
quietly efficient staff, a shrine to peace – the
Crescent is an asset to the area.
*Babies and children welcome: high chairs.
Booking advisable. Dress: smart casual.
No-smoking tables. Separate rooms for parties,
seating 20 and 60.* **Map 8 F6**.

Marylebone

★ Blandford Street

*5-7 Blandford Street, W1U 3DB (7486 9696/
www.blandford-street.co.uk). Baker Street
or Bond Street tube.* **Lunch served** noon-
2.30pm Mon-Fri. **Dinner served** 6.30-
10.30pm Mon-Sat. **Main courses** £11-£17.50.

Ambassador. See p221.

Set lunch £19.95 2 courses, £22.95 3 courses.
Credit AmEx, MC, V.
Blandford Street's smart look blends in well with the dapper surroundings of Marylebone village. The decor is classy in a simple way – no gimmicks here – and the table service is managed with cheerful charm. Most of the energy is channelled precisely where it should be: into the food. The kitchen uses prime ingredients from named sources and excels at bringing exciting secondary flavours to a Modern European menu (a fig vinaigrette here, a coconut rice there) without detracting from the coherence of the dish. Fine examples on our latest visit included a delicate, super-fresh crab salad (subtly enhanced by a saffron jelly and watercress velouté) and roast breast of barbary duck served with juicy roast pineapple and a delicately nutty wild-rice griddle cake. A creamy side of potato with spring onions went well beyond the call of duty. By this stage, we were expecting nothing less than excellence from our espresso vanilla parfait. It didn't disappoint. If we have one gripe, it is that our pinot grigio might have had a more zesty flavour. Nevertheless, Blandford Street is an extremely accomplished restaurant that (though certainly not cheap) offers value for money.
Babies and children admitted. Booking advisable. Dress: smart casual (dinner). No-smoking tables. Separate area for parties, seats 18. Tables outdoors (3, pavement). **Map 9 G5.**

★ Orrery

55 Marylebone High Street, W1U 5RB (7616 8000/www.orrery.co.uk). Baker Street tube.
Bar **Open** 11am-11pm daily.
Restaurant **Lunch served** noon-2.30pm daily. **Dinner served** 6.30-10.30pm Mon-Wed, Sun; 6.30-11pm Thur-Sat. **Main courses** £16-£28. **Set lunch** £23.50 3 courses. **Set meal** (noon-1.30pm, 6.30-9.30pm) £58 6 courses; £96 6 courses incl wine. **Credit** AmEx, DC, JCB, MC, V.
We didn't immediately like Orrery, the most ambitious restaurant in the Conran group. We entered the long, cool dining room to an atmosphere of churchyard seriousness. A few men in suits sat around eating business lunches, while our waiter greeted us coldly and superciliously. But something happened during the meal. Perhaps the staff melted a little in the summer heat. Perhaps they were just pleased by our interest in the food, but by the end of lunch they had won us over. They were helped, of course, by the excellence of the food (now under new chef Allan Pickett). An amuse-bouche of celeriac foam dressed in truffle oil and chives awakened our taste buds. A delicious velouté of white onion and thyme, served in a copper pan, was poured over croûtons and crispy shallots, while bocconcini of mozzarella were served with a stimulating array of wild rocket leaves, toasted pine kernels, and beetroot slices, with dots of aged balsamic vinegar. We found a main course of grilled rump of veal comforting but lacking in pzazz, though another main of hake was charming with its beautiful halo of beans and sun-dried piquillo pepper. Desserts were summery and picture-perfect. In all, our meal seemed stupendously good value at £23.50 a head for the three-course set lunch; dinner is quite another matter.
Babies and children welcome: high chairs. Booking essential. Disabled: toilet. No-smoking tables. Tables outside (12, bar roof terrace). Vegetarian menu. **Map 3 G4.**

Mayfair

Embassy

29 Old Burlington Street, W1S 3AN (7851 0956/www.theembassygroup.co.uk). Green Park or Piccadilly Circus tube. **Dinner served** 6-11.30pm Tue-Sat. **Main courses** £14.50-£25. **Set meal** (6-8pm) £17 2 courses, £20 3 courses. **Credit** AmEx, MC, V.
Embassy is one of the few Mayfair restaurants with appealing outdoor tables, something we took advantage of on a balmy evening. By chance, we sat next to one of the owners, Mark Fuller. He spent the evening talking loudly on his mobile phone, in between greeting and vetting new arrivals, and directing the bouncers of the basement nightclub: 'They can go to the bar, but not downstairs, right?' A procession of boy-band lookalikes, music biz blokes, *Big Brother* wannabes and surgically enhanced women were given the yeah or nay by our host. At our table, Garry Hollihead's cooking was as refined as ever, from a perfectly cooked roast breast of duck and confit leg with thyme-flavoured dauphinois, to a perfectly cooked lemon sole; only a white gazpacho disappointed, as it lacked a distinctive almond flavour. Prices are high, but diners are ensured free entry to the nightclub, where a wet T-shirt competition was jiggling along on our visit. An impenetrable throng of men left us with a view of the on-stage shower fixtures and a succession of peroxide-blonde glamour models towelling themselves. As we were leaving, a taxi driver pulled up alongside a gaggle of primped women, enquiring 'Which one's the chihuahua?' – presumably a reference to the lap dog cowering in someone's handbag.
Booking advisable. Dress: smart casual. Restaurant available for hire. Tables outdoors (6, terrace). **Map 9 J7.**

Langan's Brasserie

Stratton Street, W1J 8LB (7491 8822/ www.langansrestaurants.co.uk). Green Park tube. **Meals served** 12.15-11.45pm Mon-Fri. **Dinner served** 7pm-midnight Sat. **Main courses** £12.50-£18.50. **Cover** £1.50. **Credit** AmEx, DC, JCB, MC, V.
Portraits of original owners Peter Langan, Michael Caine and Richard Shepherd still top the Hockney-designed menu at this Mayfair institution, though it's years since that's been the set-up. The dining room is a morass of expensive art and haphazard decadence, dickie-bowed waiters strut between the tables, and the menu is packed with comfort food for the chattering classes. One such dish was a 'croustade' of quails' eggs – a rustic pastry tart filled with mushrooms and dripping with warm eggy sauce – while the crunchy greens and tangy feta of a greek salad made a satisfyingly summery starter. For mains, roast saddle of lamb was tender, despite arriving closer to well done than the medium rare requested. Pan-fried halibut with peppers and onions was an enormous chunk of fish that was filling yet ultimately forgettable. We just managed to finish our bottle of house red (an unremarkable vin de table); for those with bigger appetites, puddings include childhood favourites such as treacle tart, and strawberries and cream. Given London's current climate of gastronomic innovation, Langan's feels like an anomaly, but with a bar full of permatans and sports jackets, it remains an entertainingly unique destination.
Babies and children welcome: booster chairs. Booking advisable; essential dinner. Entertainment: jazz 10.30pm Wed-Sat. No-smoking tables. Separate room for parties, seats 50. **Map 9 H7.**

Nicole's

158 New Bond Street, W1F 2UB (7499 8408). Bond Street or Green Park tube.
Bar **Open** 10am-6pm Mon-Sat. **Meals served** 11.30am-5.30pm Mon-Sat. **Main courses** £9-£13.50.
Restaurant **Breakfast served** 10-11am Mon-Fri; 10-11.30am Sat. **Lunch served** noon-3.30pm Mon-Fri; noon-4pm Sat. **Afternoon tea served** 3-6pm Mon-Sat. **Main courses** £15.50-£25. **Cover** (noon-4pm Mon-Sat) £1. **Minimum** £15.
Both **Credit** AmEx, DC, JCB, MC, V.
Situated in the basement of Nicole Farhi's fashion store, this restaurant has all the makings of a haute-couture eaterie. Brown leather banquettes combine with starched white tablecloths to give an upmarket feel. The atmosphere, though, is far from stuffy. On a recent visit – albeit a quiet Monday lunchtime – we were practically welcomed with open arms by the charming staff. Starters include at least one soup (such as vichyssoise: too thick and bland on this occasion), while mains feature steaks, a risotto and pasta dish of the day, plus lots of fish, including an excellent swordfish with Indian spicing (the spicing perfectly judged, the accompanying basmati rice and chickpea salad light and moreish). Desserts encompass tiramisu, fresh fruit salad and tarts. In fact, our only gripe is with the prices: starters rise to £10.95, mains average £20 and desserts are £7. That said, bargains can't be expected on New Bond Street, and portions aren't massive; you wonder where the ladies who lunch put it all, or how anyone can make it back up the stairs after three courses.
Babies and children admitted: booster seats. Booking advisable. Disabled: toilet. No-smoking (lunch). Restaurant available for hire. **Map 9 H7.**

Sotheby's Café

Sotheby's, 34-35 New Bond Street, W1A 2AA (7293 5077). Bond Street or Oxford Circus tube. **Breakfast served** 9.30-11.30am, **lunch served** noon-3pm, **afternoon tea served** 3-4.45pm Mon-Fri. **Main courses** £12.50-£17. **Set tea** £5.25. **Credit** AmEx, DC, MC, V.
Considering the pedigree of this world-famous auction house, the in-house café is surprisingly low key and unintimidating. It's open shopping-friendly hours (serving breakfast through to afternoon tea) and is staffed by a cheery but polite, well-turned-out crew. Diners tend to be exactly what you'd expect on Bond Street: beautifully attired young men from local galleries, well-heeled tourists, and a sprinkling of shoppers. A short lunch menu lists one extravagance – lobster sandwich – but otherwise is a reasonably priced list of undemanding but pleasant dishes. Chilled pea soup and potted salmon with toast made a good start. Mains were more mixed: fillet of cod with a lightly spiced bean sauce gained more approval than a delicate goat's cheese soufflé rather overwhelmed by tapenade and artichoke hearts. The restaurant is on the ground floor and makes the best of a space seemingly carved out of a grand hallway; black and white photos provide the eye candy. One to remember when stuck for somewhere civilised but acceptably priced in the centre of town.
Babies and children admitted. Booking essential lunch. Disabled: toilet. No smoking. **Map 9 H6.**

Piccadilly

★ The Wolseley

2006 RUNNER-UP BEST PATISSERIE
160 Piccadilly, W1J 9EB (7499 6996/www.the wolseley.com). Green Park tube. **Breakfast served** 7-11.30am Mon-Fri; 9-11.30am Sat, Sun. **Lunch served** noon-3pm daily. **Tea served** 3-5.30pm Mon-Fri; 3.30-6pm Sat, Sun. **Dinner served** 5.30pm-midnight Mon-Sat; 5.30-11pm Sun. **Main courses** £6.75-£28.50. **Cover** £2. **Credit** AmEx, DC, JCB, MC, V.
It's a shame the Wolseley has gone the way of the Ivy (the owners' previous establishment) in terms of booking policy. Phone even for Monday lunch several weeks in advance and you're likely to be told to come at 12.15pm and leave by 1.45pm – like it or lump it. It seems people like it (and walk-ins are welcomed). We had a very pleasant lunch, though never escaped the feeling of being churned through a glamorous machine. This is one of the loveliest-looking restaurants in London, with a high, multi-domed ceiling and a sleek black and cream colour scheme, right down to the tiled floor. Cutlery, tablecloths and coffee pots all have an old-fashioned charm. There's a £2 cover charge – unusual in restaurants opened in the past ten years – yet the wide-ranging menu isn't greedily priced. The inspiration is a grand Viennese café, so there are dishes such as wiener schnitzel or soufflé suisse (a cheesy comfort-food treat, served with green salad). But you'll also find classics such as steak tartare, or roast skate with capers and lemon; omelettes and salads (both panzanella and crayfish salad were summery hits); and modern must-haves such as seared scallops with pancetta. There are fabulous cakes and ices too; tea-time is important, and possibly the most relaxed hour to experience the Wolseley.
Babies and children welcome: crayons; high chairs. Disabled: toilet. No-smoking tables (no bookings). Takeaway service. **Map 9 J7.**

RESTAURANTS

Pimlico

Rex Whistler Restaurant at Tate Britain

Tate Britain, Millbank, SW1P 4RG (7887 8825/ www.tate.org.uk). Pimlico tube/87 bus. **Breakfast served** 10-11.30am Sat, Sun. **Lunch served** 11.30am-3pm, **afternoon tea served** 3-5pm daily. **Main courses** £14.95-£18.45. **Credit** AmEx, DC, MC, V.

Every gallery deserves a restaurant like this. Wrapped in Rex Whistler's exuberant mural *In Pursuit of Rare Meats*, the buzzy room is matched by a punchy menu that combines the best of British flavours with the occasional international twist. So, a starter of rare sirloin of Oxfordshire beef was a carpaccio-like plateful of delicious slivers of meat topped with rocket, beetroot and – best of all – a mouth-watering dollop of horseradish-tinged sour cream. Seared scallops came coated in a rich lobster sauce that brought extra exotica to the tastiest of seafoods. For mains, roasted rump of Welsh lamb was given a distinctly Tuscan twist by a warm bean salad, while a hearty haddock and salmon fish cake came perched on a lovely spinach and pea purée. Plum sorbet with thyme-roasted plums felt like a Willy Wonka pudding designed to induce idyllic English country garden dreamstates in the darkest depths of winter; dark chocolate tart was a plateful of sticky hedonism. When food this good is matched by an award-winning wine list and friendly, efficient service, you can forget Constable landscapes and Turner Prize controversy – this restaurant is reason enough to visit Tate Britain. The wine list also attracts serious oenophiles.
Babies and children welcome: high chairs. Booking advisable. Disabled: toilet. No smoking. Tables outdoors (8, terrace). **Map 16 L11.**

St James's

★ The Avenue

7-9 St James's Street, SW1A 1EE (7321 2111/ www.egami.co.uk). Green Park tube. *Bar* **Open** noon-11pm Mon-Fri; 6-11pm Sat. *Restaurant* **Lunch served** noon-3pm Mon-Fri. **Dinner served** 5.45pm-11.30pm Mon-Thur; 5.45pm-12.30am Fri, Sat. **Main courses** £12.50-£18. **Set meal** £17.95 2 courses, £19.95 3 courses.
Both **Credit** AmEx, DC, MC, V.

Our lunch at Avenue came close to achieving perfection. The vast all-white room, unchanged after 12 years of trading, is classy without being intimidating – an important consideration if you're not accustomed to eating amid the wealthy of St James's. Distinctly un-St-Jamesian are the prices, which allow you to eat three courses for around £20 (though à la carte dinner prices are higher). We had five dishes, all intelligently conceived, generously portioned and expertly cooked. Chef Rino Scalco goes for robust flavours, exemplified in a starter of perfectly sautéed chicken livers with black pudding and a poached egg. Attention to detail extends to points that other restaurants neglect: a wonderful side salad was just one such example. Service is friendly and welcoming, but has a standard of professionalism you'd expect to find only in much more expensive places. And the crowning glory is the well-chosen wine list, which starts at around £20 but doesn't impose greedy mark-ups. Wines by the glass are a strong point. We were finished in an hour and a quarter, perfect for a weekday lunch, but no one hurried us and we dawdled happily over good espresso and a pot of peppermint tea made from fresh leaves. For value, quality and service, Avenue is a star.
Babies and children welcome: high chairs. Disabled: toilet. Booking advisable. **Map 9 J8.**

Le Caprice

Arlington House, Arlington Street, SW1A 1RJ (7629 2239/www.caprice-holdings.co.uk). Green Park tube. **Lunch served** noon-3pm Mon-Sat; noon-5pm Sun. **Dinner served** 5.30pm-midnight Mon-Sat; 6pm-11pm Sun. **Main courses** £14.25-£26.50. **Cover** £2. **Credit** AmEx, DC, MC, V.

For no particular reason, it seems, Le Caprice has become what the media like to refer to as a 'celebrity haunt'. On our visit, there were no 'slebs', but there were plenty of swivel-headed tourists hoping to spot an A- or B-lister. To its credit, Le Caprice's menu has appealing seasonal specials, and the restaurant is one of the few places to sell gulls' eggs in season. Most of the menu, though, is simple comfort food. A starter of deep-fried courgette flower with goat's cheese and beetroot overdid the deep-frying. A main course of loin of tuna served with rocket and spiced lentils, although based on a lovely piece of tuna, lacked the flavour that searing or marinating might have given it. Lobster salad was 'perfectly nice', though not over-endowed with crustacean. There's little to challenge the sensibilities of the mature, largely monied clientele. Service, unfortunately, is of the sort that likes to get you in and out as quickly as possible. We felt so rushed that leaving after our strict two-hour slot was a relief. And how's this for cheek: a £2 cover charge per person?
Babies and children welcome: high chairs. Booking essential, several weeks in advance. Entertainment: pianist 6.30pm-midnight daily. Vegetarian menu. Vegan dishes. **Map 9 J8.**

Quaglino's

16 Bury Street, SW1Y 6AJ (7930 6767/ www.conran.com). Green Park tube. *Bar* **Open** 11.30am-1am Mon-Thur; 11.30am-2am Fri, Sat; noon-11pm Sun. *Restaurant* **Lunch served** noon-3pm daily. **Dinner served** 5.30-11.30pm Mon-Thur; 5.30pm-12.30am Fri, Sat; 5.30-10.30pm Sun. **Main courses** £12.50-£22.50. **Set meal** (noon-3pm, 5.30-6.30pm daily) £16.50 2 courses, £19 3 courses.
Both **Credit** AmEx, DC, JCB, MC, V.

When it opened in 1993, Quaglino's was the hottest ticket in town – a bold, theatrical statement from Conran that kick-started a mega-restaurant trend for the rest of that decade. It's still a spectacle, with a central stairwell fit for a screen goddess to descend, and serried ranks of tables busier than a beehive. But the reservation line has cooled off; you can now book a table at a time of your choice the same evening, as we did. We found the restaurant only two-thirds full at 9pm, yet the noise was just as overwhelming as ever. We strained to hear above shouting groups from the Home Counties, many of whom were taking advantage of the frequent and good-value meal-deal offers. Our pricier à la carte dishes failed to sparkle: from a cold little crêpe made from chickpea flour, to the scallop dish with mean-sized slivers of white asparagus. Even the oysters tasted insipid. The meringue posturing as a pavlova and a feeble orange millefeuille suggested the pastry counter is not a strong point either. The procession of impersonal waiting staff also left us wondering where Quag's went wrong.
Babies and children welcome: children's menu; high chairs. Booking advisable. Disabled: toilet. Entertainment: musicians 7pm daily; phone for details. Separate room for parties, seats 44 (7389 9619). **Map 17 J7.**

Soho

Alastair Little

49 Frith Street, W1D 4SG (7734 5183). Leicester Square or Tottenham Court Road tube. **Lunch served** noon-3pm Mon-Fri. **Dinner served** 6-11.30pm Mon-Sat. **Main courses** £19.50 (lunch); £24.50 (dinner). **Set lunch** £33 3 courses. **Set dinner** £38 3 courses. **Credit** AmEx, JCB, MC, V.

As much a fixture of the Soho landscape as its neighbour, jazz club Ronnie Scott's, this unassuming little restaurant was at the forefront of the British cooking revolution 20 or so years ago. Chef Alastair Little was a key figure in introducing the style of cooking we now term Modern European, and the minimalist design of his restaurant – pale floorboards, cream walls offset by bright abstract paintings – has become so common as to seem almost dated. Little is no longer connected with the operation, but the basics remain the same: high-quality seasonal ingredients cooked simply and with aplomb. The short menu

– with, rather oddly, more choices for starter or dessert than main course – mixes straightforward dishes (parma ham and charentais melon) with more complicated ones (Japanese-inspired tuna tataki and spinach oshitashi with soy, ginger and hot mustard). A main of organic salmon with wood sorrel, broad beans, celeriac remoulade and truffle was a fabulous, summery creation, while a dessert of own-made vanilla ice-cream in a pool of Pedro Ximenez sherry – a menu stalwart – made a classic finish. The price of dining out on history isn't cheap – but we think it's worth it.
Babies and children admitted. Booking advisable. No-smoking tables. Separate room for parties, seats 25. **Map 17 K6.**

Andrew Edmunds

46 Lexington Street, W1F 0LW (7437 5708). Leicester Square, Oxford Circus or Piccadilly Circus tube. **Lunch served** 12.30-3pm Mon-Fri; 1-3pm Sat; 1-3.30pm Sun. **Dinner served** 6-10.45pm Mon-Sat; 6-10.30pm Sun. **Main courses** £7.95-£15. **Credit** MC, V.

There's a distinctive air of the gentlemen's club about Andrew Edmunds. First, there's the dark-wood decor, combined with cream walls on the ground floor and green walls in the basement. Then there's the menu: starters include the likes of English asparagus with lemon oil and parmesan, or dressed crab, while mains might be pan-fried calf's liver, bacon and mash. Teetotallers and vegetarians get short shrift (non-alcoholic drinks comprise just water or elderflower or ginger pressé, and there's only one veggie main course). A starter of crispy duck salad with egg noodles, julienne vegetables and peanut dressing was pretty but flavourless, the dressing barely detectable. Out of curiosity we also tried a gull's egg, but it had little flavour. Roast cod with saffron and caper rice, steamed courgettes, and tomato and olive salsa was generously sized and deftly cooked, though, again, flavours were muted. More interesting was beetroot tarte tatin, though the portion was a bit meagre for a main course. Even chocolate mousse cake was a tad dry. Nonetheless, we can't help but like this place: service is friendly, and prices are very reasonable (a two-and-a-half course meal for two, albeit sans alcohol, came to £40 with service).
Babies and children admitted. Booking essential. No-smoking tables. Tables outdoors (2, pavement). **Map 17 J6.**

★ Arbutus NEW

2006 WINNER BEST NEW RESTAURANT
63-64 Frith Street, W1D 3JW (7734 4545/ www.arbutusrestaurant.co.uk). Tottenham Court Road tube. **Lunch served** noon-2.30pm Mon-Sat; 12.30-3.30pm Sun. **Dinner served** 5-11pm Mon-Sat; 6.30-9.30pm Sun. **Main courses** £12-£15.50. **Set meal** (lunch daily, 5-7pm Mon-Sat) £13.50 2 courses, £15.50 3 courses. **Credit** AmEx, MC, V.

For the prices alone, Arbutus deserves to succeed. The set lunch/pre-theatre menu is a steal for cooking of this imagination and flair, and the wine prices are almost shockingly diner-friendly, as is the choice by 250ml carafe; around 60 wines, including dessert, are available this way. The quality of our meal was signalled early with starters of salad with fresh sheep's ricotta and summer vegetables (a pretty dish that tasted even better than it looked), and squid and mackerel 'burger' with barbecue sauce (texture-wise, this was reminiscent of a Thai fish cake; flavour-wise, it was sensational). What followed – bavette of beef persillade with exquisite dauphinois potatoes, and gnocchi (in thin blocks) with parmesan and vegetables – maintained the high standard. Crème brûlée with langue de chat was pudding perfection. The only off-note was sounded by panna cotta scented with gentian and pistachio; the flavour just wasn't to our taste, though the accompanying cherries and biscotti were lovely. Staff are easy-going but professional. The room is attractive in a bland, minimal kind of way, yet lack of soft furnishings means that noise levels can be high. But these are minor niggles – this is an impressive operation with real heart and verve.
Babies and children welcome: high chairs. Booking essential. No smoking. **Map 17 K6.**

South Kensington

★ Bibendum

Michelin House, 81 Fulham Road, SW3 6RD (7581 5817/www.bibendum.co.uk). South Kensington tube. **Lunch served** noon-2.30pm Mon-Fri; 12.30-3pm Sat, Sun. **Dinner served** 6.30-11.30pm Mon-Fri; 7-11.30pm Sat; 7-10.30pm Sun. **Main courses** £19-£42. **Set lunch** £28.50 3 courses. **Credit** AmEx, DC, MC, V.

Never mind an odd entrance through the ground-floor Oyster Bar in the art deco Michelin building, and never mind that grey-carpeted floors and upholstery detract from stunning stained-glass windows depicting the tyre-clad Michelin man – Bibendum remains one of the classiest joints in town. Chef Matthew Harris gives clever spins to pan-European dishes familiar from many a Conran outlet. Starters range from a Bovril-like fish soup, via lobster with broad bean purée and truffle vinaigrette, to perhaps the single most challenging dish: 'warm salad of calf's brain with mustard, cucumber and chervil'. Squeamish customers may be consoled by fish and chips or a gorgeous wild sea bass with artichokes à la barigoule (in this case a broth of carrots interleaved with paper-thin slices of garlic and basil leaves). Roast quails with porcini mushrooms and foie gras weighed in at the other end of the cholesterol scale, among meat dishes that are as classic and imaginative as desserts. Service is excellent: a waiter for every course and not too stuffy or too casual. The 23-page wine list is a corker, including a house Burgundy that's as good a house wine as you'll get anywhere – and not unreasonably priced at £18.

Babies and children welcome: high chair. Booking essential; 2 weeks in advance for dinner. Dress: smart casual. **Map 14 E10.**

Trafalgar Square

The Portrait Restaurant

National Portrait Gallery, St Martin's Place, WC2H 0HE (7312 2490/www.searcys.co.uk). Leicester Square tube. *Bar* **Open** 10am-5pm Mon-Wed, Sat, Sun; 10am-10pm Thur, Fri. *Restaurant* **Lunch served** 11.45am-2.45pm Mon-Fri; 11.30am-3pm Sat, Sun. **Tea served** 3-5pm daily. **Dinner served** 5.30-8.30pm Thur, Fri. **Main courses** £11.95-£24.95. *Both* **Credit** AmEx, JCB, MC, V.

Given the wonderful setting – overlooking Trafalgar Square, with views that encompass Big Ben and the Palace of Westminster – it's a shame that the food at the Portrait Gallery rarely rises above average, but hardly a surprise, given that it's produced by the catering firm Searcy's. While dishes sound tempting, the execution lacks conviction. A starter of roasted king scallops with bacon, cabbage and onion potato cake was adequate, though the cake was overwhelmed by the bacon. A special of cod and smoked haddock fish cake on a bed of wilted salmon with lemon and herb sauce was also fine, if a little too salty. Desserts veer from the prosaic (ice-creams, sorbets) to classics with a twist, such as eton mess with blackberries, banana, ginger, passionfruit and lime. Prices are on the high side, the most expensive main costing nearly £25. Working in the restaurant's favour is the relaxed atmosphere (though diners are probably talking about the art they've just seen, rather than the food on their plate).

Babies and children welcome: children's menu; high chairs. Booking advisable. Disabled: lift; toilet. No-smoking tables. **Map 18 K7.**

Westminster

Bank Westminster

45 Buckingham Gate, SW1E 6BS (7379 9797/ www.bankrestaurants.com). St James's Park tube. *Bar* **Open** 11am-11pm Mon, Tue; 11am-1am Wed-Fri; 5pm-1am Sat. *Restaurant* **Lunch served** noon-3pm Mon-Fri. **Dinner served** 5.30-11pm Mon-Sat. **Main courses** £10.95-£25. **Set meal** £15.95 2 courses, £17.95 3 courses. *Both* **Credit** AmEx, DC, MC, V.

If you refocus your eyes after gazing along the Zander Bar to the horizon's vanishing point (it is reputedly the UK's longest bar), you'll settle on Bank Westminster's elegant conservatory with its huge picture windows. The venture is part of a mini chain – along with Bank Aldwych (the smaller original, *see p223*), Bank Birmingham, and now the Zinc Bar & Grill chain (*see p47*) – all serving straightforward dishes. Kitchen staff take care over the kind of robust mainstays too often skipped over by the healthy living brigade. 'Cod and chips' produced cod fillet deep-fried in dripping and served with own-made tartare sauce, mushy peas and thick-cut chips – lovely. Spring vegetable risotto was an unctuous swamp of mint, peas and asparagus, garnished with a quail's egg poached just so. Factor in the other savouries that fatten up head chef Stuart Dring's lengthy menu, like Gloucester Old Spot sausages and roast rump of lamb; add the sticky tarts, courteous service and a grand Victorian courtyard for alfresco dining – and Bank Westminster might lend itself to leisurely suppers more readily than snappy lunches. Yet, as this is a business district, trade can be quiet in the evenings.

Babies and children welcome: children's menu; high chairs. Booking advisable. Disabled: toilet (hotel). Separate room for parties, seats 50. Tables outdoors (15 , courtyard). **Map 15 J9.**

West

Bayswater

Island Restaurant & Bar

Royal Lancaster Hotel, Lancaster Terrace, W2 2TY (7551 6070/www.islandrestaurant. co.uk). Lancaster Gate tube. *Bar* **Open** noon-11pm daily. *Restaurant* **Lunch served** noon-3pm, **tea served** 3-6pm, **dinner served** 6-11pm daily. **Main courses** £12.50-£18. **Set meal** (noon-7pm) £13.50 2 courses, £16.50 3 courses. *Both* **Credit** AmEx, DC, MC, V.

A few steps from the tube station exit and across the road from the Italian fountains of Kensington Gardens, Island has its own entrance separate from the Royal Lancaster Hotel. Inside, the modern dark woods and picture windows are comfortable and solid, if a bit bland. But the shortish menu, full of good British ingredients treated with a French flair, is anything but. A clean-tasting asparagus soup was puréed smooth, with a cooling blob of lemon-flavoured yoghurt. A tiny 'bloc' of perfect foie gras scented with sherry was intensely rich, and accompanied by a grape and raisin chutney and a neat little salad dressed with walnut oil and garnished with purple basil. For mains, a small but perfectly cooked slice of brill came with borlotti beans, artichokes, dandelion leaves and preserved lemon. Cheese soufflé was flavoured gently with stilton and topped with pine nuts. An unctuous crème brûlée dessert came with raspberries and mascarpone hidden under the glazed caramel top; and strawberries were surrounded by a delicious balsamic caramel and a scoop of extraordinarily light goat's cheese ice-cream. Service, delivered by a mostly French team, was exemplary; bread, cutlery, linen and glass were all first-class. Island deserves to be better known.

Babies and children welcome: high chairs. Booking advisable. Disabled toilet. No-smoking tables. **Map 8 D6.**

Chiswick

★ Sam's Brasserie & Bar

2006 WINNER BEST LOCAL RESTAURANT
11 Barley Mow Passage, W4 4PH (8987 0555/ www.samsbrasserie.co.uk). Chiswick Park or Turnham Green tube. *Bar* **Open** 9am-midnight Mon-Thur, Sun; 9am-12.30am Fri, Sat. *Restaurant* **Brunch served** 9am-noon Mon-Fri; 9am-4pm Sat, Sun. **Lunch served** noon-3pm Mon-Fri. **Dinner served** 6.30-10.30pm Mon-Sat; 6.30-10pm Sun. **Main courses** £8.95-£16.50. **Set lunch** (Mon-Fri) £11.50 2 courses, £15 3 courses. **Set dinner** (6.30-7.30pm) £13.50 2 courses. *Both* **Credit** AmEx, MC, V.

Interview

SAM HARRISON

Who are you?
Owner-operator of **Sam's Brasserie & Bar** (*see left*).

Eating in London: what's good about it?
Range and diversity – the number of cuisines available – and the competition that drives up standards.

What's bad about it?
London is slightly dominated by chains. Other cities still tend to have good independent neighbourhood restaurants. A lot comes down to high rent and landlords' demands.

Which are your favourite London restaurants?
J Sheekey (*see p83*) is everything a restaurant should be. It's old-school in style without being old-fashioned. The food and service are fantastic. At **Fino** (*see p252*) every mouthful is a complete pleasure. Their sourcing of ingredients is extraordinarily good. I also like **Tartine** (114 Draycott Avenue, SW3 3AE, 7589 4981), just because it's great comfort food.

What single thing would most improve London's restaurant scene?
The cult of the celebrity chef may have detracted from how important good service is. The English are often not very good at service and other countries can put us to shame.

How does being outside central London affect your business?
Places like Chiswick still have a villagey, community feel and, to me, a big part of owning a restaurant is getting to know the customers and building a relationship with them. About 90% of our customers walk to the restaurant, and that's important. It takes longer to build up that kind of relationship in the West End. That wouldn't appeal to me.

Any hot tips for the coming year?
I do think independent restaurants are making a comeback, and it's very nice to see.

RESTAURANTS

Fifth Floor. See p223.

Now into its second year of operation, Sam's has obviously plugged a gap in Chiswick's dining options. Locals have taken the place to heart: it was packed on our midweek visit. The large space (formerly a paper factory) has been modishly converted, with grey paintwork, giant lampshades and higgledy-piggeldy shelving units/waiters' stations set against industrial piping and bare brickwork. The lively bar to one side is worth a visit in its own right for decent cocktails and an impressive, globe-trotting wine list that offers plenty of choice for under £20, as well as Krug champagne at £120. The menu mixes brasserie classics with more elaborate dishes. A starter of white peaches, tomatoes, rockets and basil featured fantastically intense peach chunks – too strong, in the end, for the insipid tomatoes. For mains, smoked haddock and cheese omelette with crunchy chips was comfort food of the highest order, while snow-white plaice sprinkled with tiny grey shrimp, in a light garam masala sauce, worked well – though the portion was huge. Summery puds ranged from prosecco and mint jelly with raspberries to crème caramel. Friendly, on-the-ball staff keep the place ticking over nicely. Casual yet smart, Sam's ticks all the right boxes.
Babies and children welcome: children's menu; high chairs; toys. Booking advisable Thur-Sat. Disabled: toilet. Entertainment: jazz band 7pm occasional Sun. No smoking (restaurant).

Kensington

Babylon

Seventh floor, The Roof Gardens, 99 Kensington High Street, W8 5SA (7368 3993/www.virgin.com/roofgardens). High Street Kensington tube. **Lunch served** noon-3pm daily. **Dinner served** 7-11pm Mon-Sat. **Main courses** £15.50-£26.50. **Set lunch** (Mon-Fri) £16 2 courses, £18 3 courses; (Sat) £16.50 2 courses, £19.50 3 courses; (Sun) £18.50 2 courses, £21.50 3 courses. **Credit** AmEx, DC, JCB, MC, V.
Looking out over the lush roof-garden tree-tops at the south London cityscape, Richard Branson's Babylon has instant dramatic appeal. Inside, the chic but understated design (with features like leather booths and white walls) provides a stylish backdrop for view-gazing. Service during our visit was attentive and friendly; the laid-back atmosphere was enhanced (on a Thursday night) by low-key live music. Oliver Smith's brasserie-style menu works well. A starter of scallops subtly flavoured by shallot purée and a tomato and vanilla vodka compote that tasted creamy without overwhelming the dish. Asparagus with chive oil was done to a turn. To follow, succulent red mullet arrived with a perfectly cooked rich saffron risotto, while soft rump of lamb was equally well-complemented by aubergine purée and a red chard and beetroot salad. Strawberry and vanilla crème brûlée with hazelnut shortbread held no surprises, but made a pleasant enough finish to a well-constructed meal. The wine list contains a few pricey numbers, but choices such as the 2004 pinot grigio will please those on a smaller budget. The no-smoking policy is an added bonus.
Babies and children welcome: children's menu; entertainer (Sun); high chairs. Booking advisable. Disabled: lift; toilet. Entertainment: musicians Thur. No smoking (restaurant). Separate room for parties, seats 12. Tables outdoors (15, balcony). **Map 7 B9.**

Clarke's

124 Kensington Church Street, W8 4BH (7221 9225/www.sallyclarke.com). Notting Hill Gate tube. **Brunch served** 11am-2pm Sat. **Lunch served** 12.30-2pm Mon-Fri. **Dinner served** 7-10pm Tue-Sat. **Main courses** (lunch) £14-£16. **Set dinner** £39.75 3 courses; £49.50 4 courses incl coffee. **Credit** AmEx, JCB, MC, V.
Since she returned from a stint at California's legendary Chez Panisse in the 1980s and opened her own place, Sally Clarke has been at the cutting edge of London's culinary trends. Her famous no-choice evening menu of char-grills and salads – made up of the freshest seasonal ingredients, carefully sourced and put together with the minimum of fuss – has been gaining praise for

more than 20 years. However, although wondrous, simple but intensely flavoured dishes continue to emerge from the kitchen, the restaurant is in danger of seeming dated. The Kensington-dinner-party decor is badly in need of a revamp and fails to lend that desired sense of occasion that a bill for £70 a head demands. In a bid, we presume, to regain lost popularity, Clarke has recently introduced a set four-course dinner offering a choice of dishes. Whatever the outcome, we'll continue to be grateful for dishes such as char-grilled Welsh lamb served with black olive, red pepper and celery relish; lightest-ever duck liver mousse with grilled ciabatta, san daniele ham, radishes and pickles; or sublime maple syrup ice-cream with warm chocolate sauce and brown sugar palmier. The drinks list has one of Europe's best selections of unusual wines from California and the Antipodes.
Babies and children welcome: high chair. Booking advisable; essential weekends. No smoking. **Map 7 B7.**

11 Abingdon Road NEW

11 Abingdon Road, W8 6AH (7937 0120/www.abingdonroad.co.uk). High Street Kensington tube. **Lunch served** noon-2.30pm Mon-Sat; noon-3pm Sun. **Dinner served** 6.30-10.45pm Mon-Sat; 6.30-10.30pm Sun. **Main courses** £11.95-£17.50. **Set dinner** £17.50 2 courses. **Credit** MC, V.
This sophisticated new operation just off High Street Ken shares owners with Sonny's (*see p231*) in Barnes and the Phoenix (*see p232*) in Putney: a fine pedigree, as both are exemplary neighbourhood restaurants. It also shares an aesthetic – restrained but stylish, with pale green walls, soothing lighting and plenty of original modern art on the walls – and a Mediterranean-slanted cooking style that emphasises seasonality. To start, red, pink and golden beetroot, broad beans, purslane and goat's curd – almost too pretty to eat – was a lovely summery creation; risotto of courgette and brown shrimp, scented with basil and lemon, was also a subtly flavoured dish. Seared calf's liver is always a good test of a restaurant – here it came as a main course with onion soubise, peas, pancetta and sage, and passed with flying colours. Pigeon and lamb were also available, but the focus was on fish and seafood (sea bass, salmon, lemon sole, sardines, crab). For dessert, grappa-scented panna cotta, flecked with vanilla seeds, was light and wobbly, just as it should be. Polished and charming service, and a wine list that allows for splurging added to the feel-good factor. The plummy crowd at the next-door table seemed very happy with their new local.
Babies and children welcome: high chairs. Booking advisable. Disabled: toilet. No-smoking tables. **Map 7 A9.**

Kensington Place

201-209 Kensington Church Street, W8 7LX (7727 3184/www.egami.co.uk). Notting Hill Gate tube. **Lunch served** noon-3.30pm daily. **Dinner served** 6.30-11.15pm Mon-Thur, Sun; 6.30-11.45pm Fri, Sat. **Main courses** £14-£22.50. **Set lunch** (Mon-Fri) £19.50 3 courses; (Sun) £21.50 3 courses. **Set dinner** £24.50 3 courses, £39.50 3 courses incl a glass of wine for each course. **Credit** AmEx, DC, JCB, MC, V.
Large, cool blue and with a picture-window frontage, Kensington Place is not an intimate restaurant. But it is a modern and relaxed one, with reliable cooking. A starter featured soft-as-butter char-grilled squid matched with a chilli dressing where little specks of chilli gave just the right degree of bite. That kind of accuracy was missing from a borscht, which was thick but a little sweet, and rather too large a portion. Meat, generally simply cooked, is the best bet. Roast lamb emerged as gorgeous pinkish chunks, served with summer vegetables (peas, broad beans and baby carrots). Steak with béarnaise and chips was a yardstick of what this classic should be: a thick slab of protein with chunky golden fries. Service was never less than polite and professional, but overwrought – our main courses got lost en route. Staff, however, were apologetic and we were

rewarded with free puds: a dense panna cotta speckled with vanilla and served with strawberries, and a selection of own-made ice-creams. By late evening the space had filled up, and a vibe had got going. We began to understand why this 1980s veteran has such staying power.
Babies and children welcome: high chairs. Booking advisable; essential weekends. Disabled: toilet. Separate room for parties, seats 45. **Map 7 B7.**

Launceston Place

1A Launceston Place, W8 5RL (7937 6912/www.egami.co.uk). Gloucester Road or High Street Kensington tube. **Lunch served** noon-2.30pm Mon-Fri, Sun. **Dinner served** 6-11pm Mon-Sat; 6-10.30pm Sun. **Main courses** £17.50-£19.50. **Set lunch** (Sun) £24.50 3 courses. **Set meal** (lunch, 6-7pm Mon-Fri) £16.50 2 courses, £18.50 3 courses. **Credit** AmEx, DC, JCB, MC, V.
There's an atmosphere of welcoming hospitality at Launceston Place, and the layout lends itself to cosy dinners in quiet corners. On the night we visited the clientele mostly comprised well-heeled regulars and love-struck couples. A menu full of tempting options was executed with differing degrees of success. Chicken and leek terrine with gewürztraminer and summer truffles sounded delicious, but was a little too dry and bland. Roasted foie gras with confit duck salad was tasty save for being scattered with burnt pine nuts. In contrast, we loved our main courses. These included slices of juicy pork fillet wrapped in parma ham and paired with meaty black pudding and apple sauce. Our order of monkfish arrived perfectly cooked, cloaked with nutty brown butter and laid over a bed of fragrant risotto dotted with mussels and clams. Dessert was less impressive; apricot baked alaska featured doughy meringue that overwhelmed its sweet fruit core.
Babies and children welcome: admitted. Booking advisable. Separate rooms for parties, seating 14 and 30. **Map 7 C9.**

The Terrace

33C Holland Street, W8 4LX (7937 3224/www.theterracerestaurant.co.uk). High Street Kensington tube. **Brunch served** noon-3pm Sat; noon-3.30pm Sun. **Lunch served** noon-2.30pm Mon-Fri. **Dinner served** 6.30-11pm Mon-Sat. **Main courses** £11-£19. **Set brunch** (Sat, Sun) £17.50 2 courses, £21.50 3 courses. **Set lunch** £14.50 2 courses, £17.50 3 courses. **Credit** AmEx, JCB, MC, V.
There's something quintessentially Kensington about the Terrace. Small and low key, it occupies a corner site on a quiet side street. Outdoor tables surrounded by hedges – perhaps the restaurant's best asset – make it a fine spot for summer dining. The two waiting staff, enough to take care of the few tables, were professional but informal. But it's the clientele that really mark the place out: American bankers with their well-behaved families; middle-aged Kensington couples. One almost expects to see Hugh Grant, in character, dining with the parents of the bride. Cooking is solid, if not especially adventurous. To start, a Terrace salad was ordinary (especially for £7.25); big, juicy prawns in their shell came with a sparky sauce, bringing a little flash of fusion flair. Mains benefited from the best ingredients. Tender pieces of roast duck came with a thick, cranberry-infused gravy, plus peas and cherry tomatoes, while a rare steak was served with a delicately frothed béarnaise. A Côtes du Rhone was a good, full-bodied accompaniment, though pricey at £19.50 – but the Terrace is the kind of place that creates a comfort zone for a brand of customer who would rather pay more than go elsewhere.
Babies and children welcome: children's portions; high chairs. Booking advisable. Restaurant available for hire. Tables outdoors (8, terrace). **Map 7 B8.**

Whits

21 Abingdon Road, W8 6AH (7938 1122/www.whits.co.uk). High Street Kensington tube. **Bar Open** noon-11pm Tue-Fri; 5-11pm Sat. *Restaurant* **Lunch served** 12.30-2.30pm Tue-Fri. **Dinner served** 7-10.30pm Tue-Sat.

THE ULTIMATE GUIDES TO LIVING IN LONDON

Main courses £11.50-£17.95. **Set lunch** (express menu) £12.95 2 courses incl wine; £14.50 2 courses, £17.50 3 courses. **Set dinner** (7-8pm) £15 3 courses; £22.50 3 courses. **Credit** AmEx, MC, V.

In a sidestreet that's had a recent influx of exciting new restaurants, Whits seems very old guard. In fact, chef-patron Steve Whitney took over the former Goolies wine bar as recently as 2004, though you'd not know it from the timeless decor of white walls, wooden floors and original artworks. Staff are delightfully welcoming, and service is attentive throughout our meal. Whitney trained under Swiss chef Anton Mosimann – evident in the Swiss precision of the dishes, but also in the 1980s presentation and touches such as a tower of vegetable mousse. A starter of lobster and scallop ravioli was light, but paired with an intensely flavoured lobster sauce. Chicken liver and foie gras parfait was a generous slab with a light brioche. Monkfish came tightly wrapped in parma ham, then so perfectly cut that its carefully arranged sections looked like red-skinned potato resting in a tomato and saffron sauce. Our only quibble was that although tournedos of fillet steak were perfectly rare and tender, they rested on a shallot and red wine jus that smothered a potato rösti, giving the base a muddy effect. Desserts include hot soufflés, chocolate trios and a black forest roulade. It's possible simply to have a drink in the front bar area, though the wine list is utterly pedestrian.
Babies and children admitted. Booking advisable. No-smoking tables. Restaurant available for hire. **Map 7 A9.**

Shepherd's Bush

Brackenbury

129-131 Brackenbury Road, W6 0BQ (8748 0107). Goldhawk Road or Hammersmith tube. **Lunch served** 12.30-2.45pm Mon-Fri; 12.30-3.30pm Sun. **Dinner served** 7-10.45pm Mon-Sat. **Main courses** £9-£18. **Set lunch** (Mon-Fri) £12.50 2 courses, £14.50 3 courses. **Credit** AmEx, MC, V.

A neighbourhood restaurant that's full on a Monday night has to be doing something right, and it seems the Brackenbury is doing most things right. The new paint job works a treat, the dark green shades adding an air of gravitas; service is friendly, even when stretched; and the wine list is short but sweet. The best tables are those on the pavement terrace, but you won't feel short-changed if you end up in the comfortable interior. Foodwise, the only real gripe we have is that some of the dishes are a bit too fussy. Mains of roast cod with lobster and tarragon risotto, shellfish and lemon cream sauce and basil oil, and char-grilled tuna with sweet potato, spicy cherry tomato chutney, petit salad and raita, could both have done with fewer ingredients. Starters were straightforward and better: sauté chicken livers with poached egg, croûtons and confit red onion; and a salad of pousse, balsamic red onion, butternut squash and pine nuts. In fairness, we could have plumped for gruyère omelette with sauté potatoes, or char-grilled ribeye with sauté potatoes, confit shallot jus and béarnaise sauce. Do order a pud – chocolate and vanilla cookies with raspberry ice-cream went down a storm.
Babies and children welcome: high chair. Booking advisable. No smoking (dinner). No-smoking tables (lunch). Tables outdoors (7, patio). **Map 20 B3.**

Bush Bar & Grill

45A Goldhawk Road, W12 8QP (8746 2111/ www.bushbar.co.uk). Goldhawk Road tube. *Bar* **Open** noon-11pm Mon-Wed, Sun; noon-midnight Thur; noon-1am Fri, Sat. **Meals/snacks served** noon-11pm Mon-Wed, Sun; noon-midnight Thur-Sat. **Snacks** £2-£10. *Restaurant* **Lunch served** noon-3pm, **dinner served** 5.30-11.30pm Mon-Sat. *Both* **Main courses** £9.50-£14.50. **Credit** AmEx, MC, V.

From the alleyway entrance, Bush Bar & Grill looks like somewhere you'd come to have your Hoover repaired. Once through the courtyard, though, the spare modernist design of the place –

with its soaring ceiling and earthy terracotta and green colours – is fresh and inviting. On the night we visited, the place was (unusually) nearly empty: just four customers and six chefs. Given such a ratio, we pondered why two of our dishes arrived at the table tepid. Soggy deep-fried whitebait with aïoli (actually bog-standard mayonnaise) had none of the crunch and sizzle we'd been craving. A much more accomplished main course of pan-fried monkfish with crushed potatoes, caperberries and walnut dressing was also tepid, yet the flavours were zingy, the textures worked and the plate was appealingly presented. Also passing muster was a starter of pan-fried scallops with pancetta and a red onion and caper dressing. 'Caramelised' red onion and balsamic tart with goat's cheese and sage was less successful. The pastry, thin and crisp, was delectable, but the onions were simply slow-cooked, with none of the soft, sweet 'meltingness' we wanted. A bit up and down, then, but the Bush is still a popular, fashionable hangout (most nights at least).
Babies and children welcome: children's portions; high chairs. Booking advisable. Disabled: toilet. No smoking (restaurant). Separate room for parties, seats 40. Tables outdoors (16, patio). **Map 20 B2.**

South West

Barnes

★ Sonny's

94 Church Road, SW13 0DQ (8748 0393/ www.sonnys.co.uk). Barnes or Barnes Bridge rail/33, 209, 283 bus. *Café* **Open** 10.30am-6pm Mon-Sat. **Lunch served** noon-4pm Mon-Sat. **Main courses** £3.95-£9. *Restaurant* **Lunch served** 12.30-2.30pm Mon-Sat; 12.30-3pm Sun. **Dinner served** 7.30-11pm Mon-Sat. **Main courses** £10.75-£16. **Set lunch** (Mon-Sat) £13.50 2 courses, £16.50 3 courses; (Sun) £21 3 courses incl coffee. **Set dinner** (Mon-Thur) £16.50 2 courses, £19.50 3 courses. *Both* **Credit** AmEx, MC, V.

Sister restaurant to the Phoenix (*see p232*) and new arrival 11 Abingdon Road (*see p229*), Sonny's makes the art of running a successful neighbourhood restaurant look easy. It helps to have an attractive space – white, clean-lined and softly lit, but enlivened by plenty of original modern art – a well-heeled local clientele (this is Barnes) and 20 years of experience. And then there's the cooking. The menu focuses on top-notch seasonal ingredients, with both British and Mediterranean influences in evidence. A main of fillet of wild halibut, with a crispy herbed crust and mushroom linguine, was a lovely combination, while Burleigh Estate venison with braised red cabbage and juniper jus majored in rich, earthy flavours. There are occasional lapses: a starter of sardines with sweet and sour dressing, raisins and pine nuts just didn't work. Desserts are straightforward – panna cotta, own-made sorbets, crème brûlée. The set menu is good value, especially for cooking of this calibre, though limited in choice. Pluses include a carefully chosen wine list and assiduous staff. A new head chef arrived as we went to press: Ed Wilson, who has worked at the Almeida, the Wolseley and, most recently, the much-lauded Galvin Bistrot de Luxe – so Sonny's star looks as if it can only get brighter.
Babies and children welcome: high chairs. Booking advisable (restaurant). No-smoking tables. Restaurant available for hire. Separate room for parties, seats 22.

Chelsea

Bluebird

350 King's Road, SW3 5UU (7559 1000/ www.conran.com). Sloane Square tube then 11, 19, 22, 49, 319 bus. *Bar* **Open** noon-midnight Mon-Thur; noon-1am Fri, Sat; noon-11.30pm Sun. *Restaurant* **Brunch served** noon-3.30pm Sat, Sun. **Lunch served** 12.30-2.30pm Mon-Fri. **Dinner served** 6-11pm Mon-Sat; 6-10pm Sun. **Main courses** £13.50-£25.

Set lunch £12.95 2 courses, £15.95 3 courses. **Credit** AmEx, DC, JCB, MC, V.

The ground-floor shop has gone through more incarnations than Madonna (these days it's a gourmet food store), but the food in the first-floor Bluebird restaurant – not to be confused with the Bluebird Dining Rooms in the same complex – is as inconsistent as ever. The room is cavernous, but at least it's light and airy, with touches of colour provided by beautiful flower arrangements. Service is hit and miss; our heavily pregnant companion was completely ignored at the bar. Still, even the fussiest of eaters will be accommodated, the menu encompassing roasts, soups, grills, pies and, in particular, fish and seafood. But you wouldn't know the latter was a forte judging by our lacklustre starter of smoked salmon. In contrast, a wedge of montgomery cheddar and leek tart was lusciously light, still wobbling as it was served. Main courses were another mixed bunch: Bluebird fish pie was infallible, while chicken with mustard and buttered crumbs was overpowered by the mustard. Desserts include some standard comfort options. Charging £6 for three scoops of (albeit great) chocolate ice-cream seems plain wrong, though the same price tag was justified when it came to apple crumble, presented in an individual pan. The wine list includes some pricey stunners, but the set meals are good value.
Babies and children welcome: children's menu (weekends); high chairs. Disabled: toilet. Entertainment: DJs/musician 8pm Fri, Sat; phone to check. Separate rooms for parties, both seating 30. **Map 14 D12.**

East Sheen

Redmond's

170 Upper Richmond Road West, SW14 8AW (8878 1922/www.redmonds.org.uk). Hammersmith tube then 33 bus/Mortlake rail then 337 bus. **Dinner served** 6.30-10pm Mon-Thur; 7-10pm Fri, Sat. **Set lunch** (Sun) £18.50 2 courses, £23 3 courses. **Set dinner** (6.30-7.45pm Mon-Thur) £14.95 2 courses, £16.95 3 courses; (Mon-Sat) £27.50 2 courses, £32 3 courses. **Credit** JCB, MC, V.

You really want to like this suburban dining room, because all the right things appear to be in the right places. However, like the ingredients in some of Redmond's more ambitious dishes, somehow the parts don't quite form a perfect whole. Scallop tortellini (yellow pasta sporting a striking stripe of squid's ink), floating in a subtle lobster broth, made an ideal start to a meal. Twice-cooked belly pork came with a rich mash, high-quality black pudding and chorizo; everything except the centrepiece was fine, but during the second cooking, the pork had been robbed of its skin, the meat dried unforgivably, and the three matchsticks of crackling sticking out of the mash, while pretty, were meagre. Roast cod with sweet potato mash and minted peas was plain and unsophisticated. For dessert, proportions were off-kilter in a millefeuille, where too much pastry completely overpowered the peach and mascarpone nestled within. The owners' interest in wine has given Redmond's an impressive list, with strengths in all the classic French regions including some interesting choices from the Loire, a good house champagne, and a few splurge options, such as Château Lagrange from Pomerol.
Babies and children welcome: children's portions; booster seat. Booking advisable; essential weekends. No smoking. Restaurant available for hire.

★ Victoria

10 West Temple Sheen, SW14 7RT (8876 4238/ www.thevictoria.net). Mortlake rail. **Open** 8am-11pm Mon-Sat; 8am-10.30pm Sun. **Breakfast served** 7-9.30am Mon-Fri; 8-10am Sun. **Lunch served** noon-2.30pm Mon-Fri; noon-3pm Sat; noon-4pm Sun. **Dinner served** 7-10pm Mon-Sat; 7-9pm Sun. **Main courses** £8.95-£19.95. **Credit** AmEx, MC, V.

The Victoria has a hugely loyal and regular clientele, from yummy mummies and lunching ladies, to evening diners happy to slope off to the

The Terrace. See p223

hotel rooms upstairs. The decor shows an inspiring use of space. With its windowed ceiling, the place feels enormous and is flooded in light. From an excellent wine list, we chose a light, refreshing rosé (2005 Domaine Montrose vin de pays d'Oc). Service is bend-over-backwards accommodating, without being cloying. The menu takes pride in its seasonality; it comes complete with extensive notes and suggested ingredient substitutions (shaved pecorino instead of parma ham with asparagus, for example). Many starters also come as mains. To start, spanish salad of salt cod, Ortiz white tuna and boquerones was a mouth-watering pile of delicacies, drenched in excellent vinaigrette. Charolais ribeye steak with wild garlic butter, chips and salad was superb. Delicious too were the wild boar and apple sausages ('from a specialist game dealer in Berkshire') with mash and onion gravy. Desserts deserve special mention: the malted chocolate ice-cream is sublime. The Victoria is exceptionally child-friendly, with a safe play area outside visible from the restaurant. It could be the ultimate Sunday lunch venue.
Babies and children welcome; children's menu; high chairs; play area (garden). Booking essential. No-smoking tables. Restaurant available for hire. Separate area for parties, seats 40. Tables outdoors (10, garden). Vegan dishes.

Fulham

The Farm
18 Farm Lane, SW6 1PP (7381 3331/ www.thefarmfulham.co.uk). Fulham Broadway tube/11, 14, 211 bus.
Bar **Open** noon-midnight Mon-Fri; 10am-midnight Sat; 10am-11.30pm Sun. **Meals served** 10am-10.30pm Sat, Sun. **Main courses** £3.95-£9.95.
Restaurant **Brunch served** 10am-3pm Sat; 10am-3.30pm Sun. **Lunch served** noon-3pm Mon-Fri. **Dinner served** 6-10.30pm Mon-Sat; 6-10pm Sun. **Main courses** £9.95-£15.95.
Both **Credit** AmEx, MC, V.
Located on a side street just off Fulham Broadway, this smart bar/restaurant has been under new management since April 2006. No much has

changed in terms of decor: the front bar has lost a few leather sofas, but is otherwise the same attractive space in dark polished wood, while beyond the central square bar lies the stylish dining room. It's got the same oak tables, black leather chairs, and a glass back wall behind which lies a white-painted, trellis-covered brick wall: an ingenious use of a difficult feature. The menu is longer and slightly pricier than before, with much emphasis placed on sourcing (Elwy Valley lamb, USDA ribeye, Rare Breed Survival Trust beef, day boat-caught cod). The standard of the cooking varied. A main of strikingly pink beetroot and ricotta ravioli with poppy seeds and balsamic butter was a winner, as was a dessert of grenadine-soaked pineapple 'carpaccio' with a stunning basil and lemon sorbet. But a starter of crab, avocado, pickled ginger and pink grapefruit was marred by chunks of tasteless tomato, and a chocolate fondant was too small to have a properly gooey centre. The young staff were very personable if inexperienced (recommending one wine as 'good value'), but overall we like the place.
Babies and children welcome: children's menu; high chairs. Booking advisable. Disabled: toilet. No smoking (restaurant). Tables outdoors (4, pavement; 4, terrace). Map 13 A13.

Putney

Phoenix Bar & Grill
162-164 Lower Richmond Road, SW15 1LY (8780 3131/www.sonnys.co.uk). Putney Bridge tube/22, 265 bus. **Lunch served** 12.30-2.30pm Mon-Sat; 12.30-3pm Sun. **Dinner served** 7-11pm Mon-Thur; 7-11.30pm Fri, Sat; 7-10pm Sun. **Main courses** £9.50-£16.50. **Set lunch** (Mon-Sat) £13.50 2 courses, £15.50 3 courses. **Set meal** (dinner Mon-Thur, Sun) £15.50 2 courses, £17.50 3 courses. **Credit** AmEx, MC, V.
The Phoenix is part or Rebecca Mascarenhas' restaurant stable, which includes nearby Sonny's (*see p231*) and newcomer 11 Abingdon Road (*see p229*). The trio have some common themes: they're great neighbourhood spots, with imaginative and appealing menus, and wine lists that are far from

pedestrian. The Phoenix attracts a loyal local (and, this being the Putney/Barnes borders, well-heeled) clientele. Dishes are modish without being scarily trendy and are, for the most part, well executed. Pan-fried lamb's liver, with plump raisins and a sweetish sherry sauce, was cooked just-so, the sauce suitably piquant. Wild sea bass cooked en papillote with mussels, clams and artichokes was the sort of imaginatively constructed, seasonally inspired dish at which the Phoenix excels: it was succulently spot-on. Desserts span the likes of ultra-English eton mess to iconically Italian Vin Santo with cantuccini. The wine list is notable for its good value as well as its impeccable choice. Service is well intentioned, but waits can be long during busy times. A bonus is the enchanting front terrace, lit with fairy lights and kept toasty, if necessary, with patio heaters.
Babies and children welcome: children's menu (Sun); crayons; high chairs. Booking essential summer; advisable winter. Disabled: toilet. No-smoking tables. Tables outdoors (19, terrace).

South

Balham

★ Lamberts
2 Station Parade, Balham High Road, SW12 9AZ (8675 2233/www.lambertsrestaurant.com). Balham tube/rail. **Lunch served** noon-3pm Sat. **Dinner served** 7-10.30pm Tue-Sat. **Meals served** noon-9pm Sun. **Main courses** £13-£17.50. **Set meal** (Tue-Thur) £15 2 courses, £18 3 courses. **Credit** AmEx, JCB, MC, V.
Many would kill to have a place like this on their high street. The menu's short yet enticing, the service polite and professional, the drinks list alluring, and the prices wallet-friendly. Seasonal ingredients are chosen with care and prepared with respect. Our starter of brown shrimp 'cocktail' was blissfully free of pink marie-rose dressing. The shrimps' sea-salty flavour sang through the light mayonnaise sauce: just right for scooping up with crisp leaves of little gem lettuce. The chef's skill was evident in the veggie choice: smoked

aubergine, wild mushroom and spinach layers with roasted beetroot and a port reduction. The plate looked gorgeous with its blobs of magenta beet and red tomato, and the smoky, mushroomy flavours were complex without being confusing. We couldn't resist the mutton, wether and lamb cooked three ways (rack, slow-roast shoulder and rump, respectively). The sumptuously flavoured meat rested on a precise circle of boulangère potatoes sliced so thinly we could have read the wine list through them. A dessert of raspberry, crème pâtissière and glazed meringue tart looked almost too good to eat. You don't come across cooking so precise – and consistent – every day. Easily one of the best places to dine in south London (lucky old Balham).
Babies and children welcome: children's menu (weekends); high chairs. Booking advisable. No smoking. Restaurant available for hire.

Battersea

Louvaine

110 St John's Hill, SW11 1SJ (7223 8708/ www.louvaine.co.uk). Clapham Junction rail. **Brunch served** 10.30am-3pm Sat; 10.30am-4pm Sun. **Dinner served** 6-10.30pm Tue-Fri; 7-10.30pm Sat. **Main courses** £8.50-£14. **Set dinner** (Tue, Wed) £15 2 courses, £20 3 courses. **Credit** AmEx, MC, V.
A small corner bar/bistro, Louvaine has a real neighbourhood feel. It's a double-decker set-up – the ground floor is for smokers, downstairs can be a bit cramped, and there are some tables outside. Chef-proprietor Robin Priestley conjures up a short, simple menu with daily specials. Prices are pleasing: a 7oz burger, own-made chips and salad (on the weekend brunch menu) costs just £8. Delicious freshly baked bread helps to fill hungry, impatient mouths – especially useful when the place is busy (expect a bit of a wait, as the staff can struggle to cope). On our most recent visit all the daily specials had already been scoffed, but an asparagus and pea risotto was delicious; the freshness of the ingredients shone through and illuminated the dish. Cod had also been cooked

with care. For dessert, a fruit sorbet was memorable for the veracity of its flavour. On Tuesday and Wednesday Louvaine offers a fairly priced set menu. The wine list is short but wide-ranging, with plenty of decent choices for under £20. A great-value, friendly establishment.
Babies and children admitted: high chair. Booking advisable. Tables outdoors (5, pavement). **Map 21 B4.**

Niksons

172-174 Northcote Road, SW11 6RE (7228 2285/www.niksons.co.uk). Clapham Junction rail. *Bar* **Open** 5-11pm Mon; noon-11pm Tue-Thur; noon-midnight Fri, Sat; noon-10.30pm Sun. *Restaurant* **Lunch served** noon-3pm Tue-Fri. **Dinner served** 6-10pm Mon-Sat. **Meals served** 11am-10.30pm Sun. **Main courses** £10-£20. **Cover** £1.
Both **Credit** AmEx, DC, MC, V.
In a street thick with low-budget eating places, Niksons distances itself at the smarter end – that is, well away from Clapham Junction. There's a smarter, quieter, conservatory-like dining room at the back, but the front – a mix of bar and more boisterous eating area – tends to be much busier. Despite the always-on TV screen in the bar, this is a surprisingly convivial and relaxing place to eat. The menu is one of the most interesting in Battersea, with dishes such as 'wholemeal orecchiette' (actually more like spaetzle) mixed in with pancetta, olives, anchovy, pecorino and broccoli – unsurprisingly, this was on the salty side. Char-grilled paillarde (thin, flattened escalope) of veal had flavours and textures that were perfectly judged: the veal was served with olive oil, grilled lemons, rocket and frisée leaves. Desserts included appealing choices such as pear and almond tart, or there's a good-looking cheeseboard. Some of the wines by the glass are excellent, such as the Kiwi sauvignon blanc (South Bank Estates from Marlborough) at £5.50. Behind us a loud group were discussing forthcoming wedding arrangements before roaring off in their Porsche – heading away from Clapham Junction, obviously.

Babies and children welcome: high chairs. Booking advisable. Disabled: toilet. Entertainment: jazz 6pm 2nd Sun of mth. No-smoking tables. Separate room for parties, seats 30. Tables outdoors (4, pavement). **Map 21 C5.**

Ransome's Dock

35-37 Parkgate Road, SW11 4NP (7223 1611/ www.ransomesdock.co.uk/restaurant). Battersea Park rail/19, 49, 319, 345 bus. **Brunch served** noon-3.30pm Sun. **Meals served** noon-11pm Mon-Fri; noon-midnight Sat. **Main courses** £10.50-£21.50. **Set meal** (noon-5pm Mon-Fri) £15 2 courses. **Credit** AmEx, DC, JCB, MC, V.
Not much has changed over the years at this likeable local. The interior could do with a bit of a wash and brush-up, but Ransome's Dock is a good place to have on your doorstep, with friendly staff and a flexible Modern European menu made up of fresh, seasonal ingredients put together with the minimum of fuss or frills. To start, there might be Norfolk eel fillets served warm, with a beetroot and herb salad and horseradish cream, or courgette fritters with feta, mint and dill. To follow, choose calf's liver with red wine and bacon, or perhaps some slow-roasted pork belly with sherry, lentils and green beans. We enjoyed a salad of grilled quail matched with tangy orange and watercress, followed by slices of pink duck breast served with peas, baby carrots and a rich red wine jus. A fruity trio of own-made sorbets made a suitably refreshing finish. Alongside the monthly carte and daily specials, there's a two-course set lunch to keep the local office workers happy, and an unusually wide-ranging, eclectic wine list.
Babies and children welcome: high chairs. Booking advisable. Disabled: toilet. No-smoking tables. Tables outdoors (12, terrace). **Map 21 C1.**

Brixton

Upstairs [NEW]

2006 RUNNER-UP BEST LOCAL RESTAURANT
89B Acre Lane, entrance on Branksome Road, SW2 5TN (7733 8855/www.upstairslondon.com). Clapham Common tube/Brixton tube/rail.

Lunch served 12.30-3pm Sun. **Dinner served** 6.30-10.30pm Tue-Sat. **Set meal** £13 2 courses, £23 3 courses. **Credit** MC, V.

Upstairs has the vibe of an exclusive private dinner party rather than a restaurant. It's the setting, for a start. Access is via a discreetly marked door with a buzzer, up a narrow staircase to the first-floor bar (all tan leather banquette seating and mushroom walls), then up more stairs to the restaurant itself. Which is tiny, seating no more than 25 in a low-key style (white-leather chairs, dark wood tables twinkling with glassware and candles, a turquoise wall). The fixed-price menu offers just three choices per course, plus a couple of specials. Portions are small – no side dishes – but the cooking shows ambition and finesse, even if it doesn't always pull together. Rump of lamb came with an overflavoured jus and underflavoured couscous, but the meat was tender, including two excellent merguez sausages. Home-cured salmon was rubbery, though the cherry tomatoes on the side were bursting with sweetness. Best was a creamy coconut crème brûlée with sugar-coated banana beignets. The bar does cocktails for a fiver (London Exotic gin, lychee, lime, cranberry juice), while the wine list has bottles ranging from £11 to well over £100. Our fellow diners – more Clapham than Brixton – seemed well pleased with their find.
Babies and children welcome: high chair.
No smoking. **Map 22 C2.**

Clapham

Morel

14 Clapham Park Road, SW4 7BB (7527 2468/ www.morelrestaurant.co.uk). Clapham Common tube. **Dinner served** 6-10.30pm Tue-Sat. **Meals served** noon-4pm Sun. **Main courses** £11-£17. **Set meal** (Tue-Fri, Sun) £13 2 courses. **Credit** MC, V.

Morel aims high, offering formal, old-school – if a mite pretentious – dining. At the front is a small bar and a red banquette area where patrons can drink aperitifs and peruse the menu. Slanted glasses set the design tone. We were treated to unexpected but welcome appetisers and friendly, attentive service as we chose our food. Chef-proprietor Jean Chaib cooks in a modern French style and adds twists to familiar dishes. Our gazpacho starter was upped a couple of notches by a lovely Bloody Mary jelly in the middle; red mullet with saffron was flavourful and well presented. Our waiter went into great detail about the half-lobster salad main course, which lived up to its verbose description. But our other choice, pork loin and black pudding, was dry and overcooked. Palate-cleansing pear sorbet was another unexpected treat, though a white chocolate, almond and coconut soup dessert lost marks for still having ice in the middle. Put the glitches down to a slightly off night in the kitchen. Morel has an excellent wine list, and there are also more straightforward set meals.
Babies and children welcome: high chairs.
Booking advisable. No smoking. **Map 22 B2.**

Tooting

Rick's Café

122 Mitcham Road, SW17 9NH (8767 5219). Tooting Broadway tube. **Lunch served** noon-3pm daily. **Dinner served** 6-11pm Mon-Sat; 6-10pm Sun. **Main courses** £6-£12. **Credit** MC, V.

The first time we visited Rick's, on a Wednesday (without booking, we admit), the place was full to bursting. It was 'Spanish night', with a flamenco guitarist and all. The next time, on a Monday, the restaurant was busy again. Something good must be happening here. Our starter of haddock chowder bore this out, delivering a perfect balance of smoked fish and hot peppers. A dish of asparagus was slightly overcooked, but flavoursome nonetheless. Both main courses were excellent. Pork fillet was presented in bite-size portions charred round the edges, with a fried egg on top that oozed into the tasty, chunky chips. Ribeye steak wasn't as thick as most, but had a heart of fat that spread flavour

to all its edges. On the waitress's recommendation, we shared a summer pudding; the fruity interior was sharp and fresh, but the dish lacked a further layer of sweetness to bring it to life. Two excellent wines are available by the glass. Service – divided between a sole chef, a laid-back maître d' and a friendly young woman – was fast and efficient.
Babies and children welcome: children's portions; high chairs. Booking advisable dinner and weekends. Disabled: toilet. No smoking.

Waterloo

Oxo Tower Restaurant, Bar & Brasserie

Eighth floor, Oxo Tower Wharf, Barge House Street, SE1 9PH (7803 3888/www.harvey nichols.com). Blackfriars or Waterloo tube/rail. **Bar Open** 11am-11pm Mon-Sat; noon-10.30pm Sun.
Brasserie **Lunch served** noon-3.15pm Mon-Sat; noon-3.45pm Sun. **Dinner served** 5.30-11pm Mon-Sat; 6-10.15pm Sun. **Main courses** £10.25-£17. **Set meal** (lunch, 5.30-6.45pm Mon-Fri) £16.50 2 courses, £21.50 3 courses.
Restaurant **Lunch served** noon-2.30pm Mon-Sat; noon-3pm Sun. **Dinner served** 6-11pm Mon-Sat; 6.30-10pm Sun. **Main courses** £17.50-£26. **Set lunch** £29.50 3 courses.
All **Credit** AmEx, DC, JCB, MC, V.

This landmark restaurant, brasserie and bar commands striking aerial views across the Thames – as long as you book a seat on the terrace. Seated further in, you miss out. Peak dinner times are very busy, so you're likely to be offered a 6.30pm or 9.30pm slot. Lunch is easier, when it's often possible to book the same day. Both brasserie and restaurant have terrace seats; one has an expensive menu, the other a very expensive menu. We opted for the brasserie, with its oriental-slanted Modern European dishes ranging from roasted salmon on soba noodles to osso bucco: both perfectly good dishes. Food was of a consistently high standard, though an ambitious home cook could produce it. Chicken saltimbocca, for example, was sautéed thin slices of breast with sage and prosciutto, hastily assembled on a panzanella (bread and tomato) salad. It's the more imaginative combinations in the puddings that steal the show, such as the rhubarb fool served with gingerbread. We found the service charming, polite and professional. Two consecutive glasses of wine from a very tempting list were corked, and both were replaced graciously. 'It's terribly Conran isn't it,' opined a fellow diner: presumably unaware Oxo Tower is a Harvey Nichols-run restaurant, but perhaps touching on a deeper truth.
Babies and children welcome: children's menu; high chair. Booking advisable. Disabled: lift; toilet. Entertainment: pianist/singer 7.30pm daily (brasserie). No smoking. Restaurant available for hire. Tables outdoors (34, brasserie terrace; 27, restaurant terrace). Vegetarian menu.
Map 11 N7.

South East

Blackheath

Chapter Two

43-45 Montpelier Vale, SE3 0TJ (8333 2666/ www.chaptersrestaurant.co.uk). Blackheath rail. **Lunch served** noon-2.30pm Mon-Sat; noon-3pm Sun. **Dinner served** 6.30-10.30pm Mon-Thur; 6.30-11pm Fri, Sat; 6.30-9pm Sun. **Set lunch** £15.95 2 courses, £19.95 3 courses. **Set dinner** (Mon-Thur, Sun) £18.45 2 courses, £23.95 3 courses; (Fri, Sat) £24.50 3 courses. **Credit** AmEx, DC, JCB, MC, V.

Chapter Two is split between two floors, with a spacious, nondescript 1990s feel and good acoustics. The menu is very seasonal, and the food has a French feel to its presentation, with neat, well-portioned piles of vegetables around the main attraction. A starter tournedo of salmon was seared, then served cold with a refreshing cucumber and coriander dressing and a small salad of baby spinach on the side. Another starter, of pressed terrine of foie gras with toasted brioche and strawberry chutney, was a good, generously

sized dish. From the main-course choices, slow-roast belly of pork arrived in a shallow pool of cider jus with small piles of braised white cabbage and lentils, and was meltingly tender. Desserts were impressive creations, with at least three components to each selection. Coffee panna cotta came in a demi-tasse with a cappuccino foam on the top and a cute little pile of doughnuts and an oval of whisky ice-cream as accompaniments. The interesting choice of wines ranges from French to German, plus a few New World bottles, all reasonably priced.
Babies and children welcome: high chairs.
Booking advisable. Disabled: toilet. No-smoking. Restaurant available for hire.

Greenwich

Greenwich Park Bar & Grill NEW

1 King William Walk, SE10 9JY (8853 7860/ www.thegreenwichpark.com). Greenwich rail/ Cutty Sark DLR/108, 177, 180, 472 bus. **Bar Open** 11am-11pm daily. **Lunch served** 11am-4pm, **dinner served** 6-9.30pm daily. **Main courses** £6-£7.95.
Restaurant **Lunch served** noon-4pm Mon-Fri; 11am-4pm Sat, Sun. **Dinner served** 6.30-10pm daily. **Main courses** £7.95-£15.95.
Both **Credit** MC, V.

The meal began with bread so deliciously fresh we had to wait for it to come out of the oven. A starter of thickly cut, almost meaty smoked salmon with asparagus spears followed, equally fresh and worth savouring. Sea bass (more appealing to us than the T-bone or lamb cutlets from the grill), baked with carrots and celery and served with green vegetables, was simple, substantial and cooked to perfection. The quality of ingredients was high (some rocket exploded on the tongue), but cooking was not without slips. A baked crème brûlée cheesecake was sickly, and not helped by the sweetness of its accompanying mango salsa. Portions were uneven (a measly two scallops comprised one main). We also resented having to go downstairs to the bar to toilets that were in a bad state. Otherwise, the first-floor restaurant is a restful retreat with its cool, light open decor, an impressive, colourful mural on one wall and large windows with great views of the park. The bar has sofas, a patio and better than average bar food, a fine children's menu, and a large open frontage. Attention to detail and a little work on the rough edges would do wonders.
Babies and children welcome (until 7pm); children's menu; high chairs. Disabled: toilet. No-smoking tables. Separate room for parties, seats 50. Tables outdoors (6, courtyard; 4, pavement).

Inside

2006 RUNNER-UP BEST LOCAL RESTAURANT
19 Greenwich South Street, SE10 8NW (8265 5060/www.insiderestaurant.co.uk). Greenwich rail/DLR. **Brunch served** 11am-2.30pm Sat. **Lunch served** noon-2.30pm Tue-Fri; noon-3pm Sun. **Dinner served** 6.30-11pm Tue-Sat. **Main courses** £10.95-£16. **Set lunch** £11.95 2 courses, £15.95 3 courses. **Set dinner** (6.30-8pm) £15.95 2 courses, £19.95 3 courses. **Credit** AmEx, MC, V.

Set in an uninspiring parade of run-down shops near the train station, Inside is a little gem among Greenwich's paltry eating options. The single room is minimally decorated, with wooden floorboards, white and dark brown walls hung with small bright pictures, and linen-covered tables; it's a soothing space, but can be a little bleak if customers are few. There's care behind the operation, from the way the food is arranged neatly on white plates to the sole waitress's attentive service. On our visit, chef Guy Awford's menu offered plenty of spring-like flavours alongside Middle Eastern and oriental influences; lamb kofte kebab with spiced couscous rubbed up against pea and spinach samosa with red lentil dahl (both main courses). Less exotic fare included roast corn-fed chicken: pleasant if a little dull, but nicely balanced with garlicky spinach, mash and a fragrant thyme jus. Dinner party-style desserts (chocolate brownie with ice-cream, pavlova with mixed berries) make a rich finish. The set menu is a better deal than in many places in that it offers very similar dishes to the carte, with only slightly few options – and for a good price. Classic brunch dishes (eggs benedict, smoked salmon) are available on Saturday.

Babies and children admitted. Booking advisable. Disabled: toilet. No smoking.

London Bridge & Borough

Bermondsey Kitchen

194 Bermondsey Street, SE1 3TQ (7407 5719/ www.bermondseykitchen.co.uk). Borough tube/ London Bridge tube/rail. **Brunch served** 9.30am-3.30pm Sat, Sun. **Lunch served** noon-3pm Mon-Fri. **Dinner served** 6.30-10.30pm Mon-Sat. **Main courses** £9-£13. **Credit** AmEx, DC, MC, V.

Although the Bermondsey Kitchen's menu finds room on a single sheet for lunch, brunch (several ways with eggs, most in concert with Tamworth bacon) and soft drinks, it makes pretty good reading. Smoked chicken with cos lettuce and anchovy mayonnaise arrived as a starter, even though our breezily charming waitress had asked whether we wanted it as a main, but our authentic starter – grilled asparagus with poached egg and orange hollandaise – was a fresh and snappy triumph. The rhubarb was too bashful in a stolid main of roast duck breast with spiced cannellini beans, lime and rhubarb sauce, and, while the pickled red cabbage side dish was excellent, harissa new potatoes had heat without power. For afters, we left the well-heeled families in the crisply modern dining area and moved to the loungeable window seats of the quiet front bar. Passionfruit cream tart might have been a better choice than an unexpectional hot chocolate pudding with crème fraîche, but we were delighted with the dessert wines (Rutherglen Muscat, a red Tokaji) and ample cheese (Quick's cheddar and Strathdon blue with oatcakes and apple). Spanish tapas bar snacks are on hand, should you get peckish over a drink. The menu clearly indicates the service policy (optional 12.5%, going 'entirely to our staff').

Babies and children welcome: high chairs. Booking advisable. No-smoking tables. Restaurant available for hire. Tables outdoors (1, terrace). **Map 12 Q9.**

Delfina

50 Bermondsey Street, SE1 3UD (7357 0244/ www.delfina.org.uk). London Bridge tube/rail. **Lunch served** noon-3pm Mon-Fri. **Dinner served** 7-10pm Fri. **Main courses** £9.95-£12.95. **Credit** AmEx, DC, MC, V.

The stripped-down aesthetic of this restaurant and art gallery is appealing; the white warehouse space is light and bright, and the tables are so widely spaced you could drive a car between them. A shame, then, that the food is better on the page than in the mouth. Unusual ingredient combinations and inventive spicing show that the kitchen is ambitious, but execution tends to fall short. A main of tender braised kangaroo rump with jasmine rice, watercress and shiitake mushrooms was overpowered by a too-salty soy sauce, while red sea bream with cuttlefish chunks and parmesan polenta croûtons came with a dull tomato sauce. A side salad of charentais melon, artichoke and mint with lemon dressing sounded intriguing – but in reality, melon and artichoke don't mix (and why add unannounced grapefruit?). The best dish was a starter of radicchio and strawberry risotto with balsamic reduction. Even a panna cotta trio for dessert disappointed: the three flavours (star anise, cinnamon, cardamom) were indistinguishable, and the accompanying spiced green tomatoes tasted of nothing but cinnamon. Still, service was friendly – staff were happy to accommodate an extra diner who arrived just for pudding – and the wine list is decent. We've enjoyed Delfina in the past, so hope it returns to form.

Babies and children admitted. Booking advisable. Disabled: toilet. Separate rooms for parties, seating 12, 30 and 260 (7564 2400). **Map 12 Q9.**

Tower Bridge

Blueprint Café

Design Museum, 28 Shad Thames, SE1 2YD (7378 7031/www.conran.com). Tower Hill tube/Tower Gateway DLR/London Bridge tube/rail/47, 78 bus. **Lunch served** noon-3pm Mon-Sat; noon-4pm Sun. **Main courses** £12.50-£22. **Set meal** £22.50 2 courses incl glass of wine & museum entrance. **Credit** AmEx, DC, MC, V.

The Blueprint Café's breathtaking view of Tower Bridge and the Gherkin, from enormous windows right on the riverfront, never fails to elicit a gasp. On a hot night, windows slide open, giving a great outside feel without the chilly breeze that's prone to blow on the diminutive terrace. Regrettably, both food and service failed to match the surroundings on our last visit. Robust and simple can be carried too far. Starters of smoked fish and pickles, and pickled herrings with mustardy potato salad made an overpowering assault on the taste buds, leaving us reeling and unenthusiastic about mains. Halibut with peas and bacon was fairly insipid, reminiscent of dull nursery food; rabbit with fennel was average gastropub fare, all unappealing beige. Even a bottle of Austrian grüner veltliner lacked its usual pzazz. Only a heavenly rich chocolate and macaroon pud, Saint Emilion au chocalat, saved the day. Dining à deux, we sometimes had to shout over the din of big parties amplified by unsympathetic acoustics. Service was inattentive. Trying to attract the attention of waiters, even to pour the wine (placed beyond our reach), was tiresome. Diners will continue to come here for the brilliant location, but the Blueprint can't forever rest on its laurels.

Babies and children welcome: high chair. Booking advisable dinner. Disabled: toilet (in Design Museum). Restaurant available for hire. Tables outdoors (4, terrace). **Map 12 S9.**

Le Pont de la Tour

Butlers Wharf Building, 36D Shad Thames, SE1 2YE (7403 8403/www.conran.com). Tower Hill tube/rail/47, 78 bus. **Bar & grill Lunch served** noon-3pm, **dinner served** 6-11pm daily. **Main courses** £11.50-£22. **Set lunch** £12.50 2 courses, £14.95 3 courses. **Restaurant Lunch served** noon-3pm, **dinner served** 6-11pm daily. **Main courses** £11.50-£35.50.

Both **Credit** AmEx, DC, JCB, MC, V.

This smart Conran restaurant has a terrace that makes a lovely spot for outside dining on summer evenings. The restaurant is an elegant room with river-facing windows: a fitting venue for cooking that's in the French tradition. The bar and grill is a more informal space and specialises in seafood; it also boasts a cheesy, middle-aged crooner on the piano. Choosing what to slurp from the immense, pricey wine list might take a few minutes. Food is presented in an unfussy yet appetising way. Before choosing our mains, we ate starters of beef carpaccio and smoked eel – both excellent. We then ordered lobster and chips, but our waiter returned five minutes later to inform us there were no chips. It was 7pm on a Sunday. Vegetables were proffered as an alternative, but instead we opted for wood pigeon stew; it was delicious, but needed accompanying carbs. Red mullet was fresh, meaty and garnered no such complaints. You can choose a matching cocktail with dessert, but we went for a no-frills strawberry feuilleté. The location and class of Le Pont push up the prices – starters and desserts cost around £8; main courses £20. Staff can be over-attentive or may studiously ignore you.

Babies and children welcome: high chairs. Booking advisable. Entertainment: pianist 7pm daily (bar & grill); duos/trios 7pm Thur-Sat. Separate room for parties, seats 20. Tables outdoors (22, terrace). **Map 12 S8.**

East

Docklands

Plateau

Canada Place, Canada Square, E14 5ER (7715 7100/www.conran.com). Canary Wharf tube/DLR. **Bar & grill Meals served** noon-10.45pm Mon-Sat; noon-4pm Sun. **Main courses** £10-£18.75. **Set meal** £17 2 courses, £21 3 courses. **Restaurant Lunch served** noon-3pm Mon-Fri. **Dinner served** 6-10.15pm Mon-Sat. **Main courses** £17.50-£27.50. **Set dinner** £24.75 3 courses, £29.75 4 courses.

Both **Credit** AmEx, DC, MC, V.

With dramatic floor-to-ceiling windows running the length of the fourth floor of Canada Place, Conran's Plateau lets its location do the talking. The architectural interior (white curves, statement lighting, big slabs and spaces) beautifully complements the steel-and-glass views across Canada Square. It's a vast place, running from bar to grill to restaurant to open-roofed terrace (not

Wapping Food. See p236.

always the coolest spot on a summer's night), through varying degrees of formality, none of them particularly casual. The visual drama combines with super-attentive service, rigorous attention to detail and an economically unfettered menu and wine list to give a distinct note of glamour, which the food usually lives up to. In the restaurant, the food is creative but safely so, with clear seasonal influences. Wild sea bass with jerusalem artichokes, walnuts and chanterelles might be preceded by pumpkin risotto with mascarpone and marjoram. We could cavil over a couple of off-key dishes (the salmon wrapped in rice paper, with wasabi mash, begged the question, 'why'?), but in general ingredients were high quality and flavours well defined. In the large bar things are more in the comfort-food zone, with gastropub and light Italian classics. One of Docklands' best restaurants, but expensive.
Babies and children welcome: high chairs. Booking advisable. Disabled: toilet. Dress: smart casual. Separate rooms for parties, seating 12 and 24. Tables outdoors (17, terrace). Vegetarian menu.

Shoreditch

Cru Restaurant, Bar & Deli
2-4 Rufus Street, N1 6PE (7729 5252/ www.cru.uk.com). Old Street tube/rail.
Bar **Open/tapas served** 11am-11pm Tue-Sun.
Tapas £2-£15.
Deli **Open/meals served** 11am-11pm Tue-Sun.
Main courses £4-£15.
Restaurant **Brunch served** noon-3.30pm Sat, Sun. **Lunch served** noon-3pm Tue-Fri. **Dinner served** 6-11pm Tue-Sat; 6-10.30pm Sun. **Main courses** £9.50-£15.50.
All **Credit** AmEx, MC, V.
This fairly plain space off Hoxton Square is made to feel bigger thanks to gentle distinctions between three dining areas: a buzzy section at the front (by windows that open on to the street in summer), a quieter bit at the back, and a positively cosy corner to the right partitioned off by curtains. The menu proudly declares that all the meat is organic, but on our visit the cooking was hit and miss. While the lamb shanks were delightfully tender (if slightly stringy), the roast chicken was surprisingly tough. No complaints about the sides, mind: the lamb came with a pleasingly creamy mash (why do so few restaurants get it right?), and the chicken with an immaculate potato gratin. An order of asparagus showed that the restaurant takes care sourcing its ingredients. Prior to this, we'd started with an agreeable sharing platter of prawns, parmesan croquettes, wafer-thin beetroot slices and, best of all, tender chorizo atop a moreish red pepper marmalade. It was just as well we skipped the uninspiring list of desserts; moments after our bill arrived, a scary-looking fire in the open-plan kitchen resulted in the restaurant's evacuation.
Babies and children welcome: high chairs. Booking advisable. Disabled: toilet. No-smoking tables. Takeaway service (deli). **Map 6 R4.**

Hoxton Apprentice
16 Hoxton Square, N1 6NT (7739 6022/ www.hoxtonapprentice.com). Old Street tube/rail.
Bar **Open** noon-11pm Mon-Sat; noon-10pm Sun.
Restaurant **Lunch served** noon-4pm daily. **Dinner served** 7-10.30pm Mon-Sat; £10pm Sun. **Main courses** £9.90-£16.75. **Set lunch** (Mon-Fri) £6.99 2 courses, £9.99 3 courses.
Both **Credit** MC, V.
Described as a training restaurant, Hoxton Apprentice was set up to provide unemployed people with the skills to find work. It's unreasonable to expect perfection, but on our last visit we felt the charity was running too much in one direction. For a start, prices are what you expect from a bar/restaurant in Shoreditch (though the atmosphere's mellower). Fillet of beef with dark ale jus, roast new potatoes, plum tomatoes and red onions was the most expensive dish at just under £17. Cheaper meals can be had by snacking on the likes of baba ganoush or houmous with grilled nan bread (excellent flavours). Yet the two main dishes we tried didn't taste great. Pan-fried halloum was tarnished by a tabouleh accompaniment with the tang of a supermarket salad. An acceptable tomato

risotto was sprinkled with completely out-of-place popcorn. We couldn't be tempted by pudding, not even that day's special, figs and mascarpone. We sat outside on the pleasant terrace that overlooks Hoxton Square; inside is softly lit, high-ceilinged and filled with black wood furniture. Service is super-attentive and the global wine list has something for everyone. This place has a lot going for it, and we'd like to be more generous in our praise, but a steadier hand in the kitchen is needed.
Babies and children admitted: high chairs. Disabled: toilet. Separate room for parties, seats 40. Tables outdoors (9, pavement). **Map 6 R3.**

Wapping

★ Wapping Food
Wapping Hydraulic Power Station, Wapping Wall, E1W 3ST (7680 2080/www.thewapping project.com). Wapping tube/Shadwell DLR.
Brunch served 10am-12.30pm Sat, Sun.
Lunch served noon-3.30pm Mon-Fri; 1-4pm Sat, Sun. **Dinner served** 6.30-11pm Mon-Fri; 7-11pm Sat. **Main courses** £11-£19. **Credit** AmEx, MC, V.
There can be few more unusual spots to eat out in London than Wapping Food, housed in a former hydraulic power station. The dramatic conversion of this vast space into a restaurant/gallery/ community centre makes little effort to hide its origins, with the rusting and peeling pumps, chains and giant hooks still firmly in place. Set against the fading mint-green paint of the industrial equipment, the trendy orange chairs, silver chandeliers and crisp white linen at the restaurant achieve a quite stunning brand of industrial chic. On our last visit, the menu – which changes daily and includes a couple of cocktails (we were tempted by a rhubarb Bellini) – was a tremendous success. We sampled a wonderfully strong wild garlic soup with melting mascarpone on top; a sensationally mushroomy sformato (akin to a soufflé, but less airy); a melt-in-the-mouth lamb shank served, unusually, with creamy semolina; and coconut, pineapple and chilli sorbet. Waiting staff struck just the right note between casual and formal. Atmosphere wasn't lacking on a weekday, even given the cavernous space. After our meal, we looked around an avant-garde art exhibition next door – which only added to a dining experience that was truly out of the ordinary.
Babies and children welcome: high chairs. Disabled: toilet. Entertainment: performances and exhibitions (phone for details). No-smoking tables. Tables outdoors (20, garden).

North West
Kensal Green

The Island **NEW**
2006 RUNNER-UP BEST LOCAL RESTAURANT
123 College Road, NW10 5HA (8960 0693/ www.islandpubco.com). Kensal Green tube/rail/ Kensal Rise rail.
Bar **Open** 5-11pm Mon; noon-11pm Tue-Sat; noon-10.30pm Sun. **Lunch served** 12.30-3pm Mon-Fri; 12.30-3.30pm Sat; 12.30-4pm Sun.
Dinner served 7-10pm Mon-Sat; 7-9.30pm Sun. **Main courses** £5.75-£13.
Restaurant **Dinner served** 7-10pm Mon-Sat.
Main courses £8.50-£14.50.
Both **Credit** MC, V.
It may be located on a nondescript residential road in Kensal Rise, but the Island is obviously a huge success: less than six months after opening, it was buzzing with locals on a midweek night. Once an ugly 1970s pub, the building has been transformed inside and out. A huge bamboo-screened terrace runs around the sandy-coloured exterior; the ground floor and basement are now a bar (also serving food), while the first floor is a light, bright dining room with colonial-style dark wooden furniture. The kitchen and more tables occupy a mezzanine above that. A jumble of decorative elements (a large world map, sheets of matchbox covers, eclectic artworks) add to the casual, holiday vibe, as do the charming staff. A

shame, then, that the menu is shorter and less ambitious then when the place first opened, though it must suit the clientele. A starter of smoked salmon with baby beetroot, spinach and (undetectable) horseradish was generous if unremarkable. Large ravioli were stuffed with a tasty mix of ricotta, spinach and oyster mushrooms, but the pasta was tough. Sea bass (two nicely cooked fillets) came with ratatouille that had a charred aftertaste; and a caramelised orange tart was too dry. So, flaws in the kitchen, but the operation is still a definite hit.
Babies and children welcome: children's menu; high chairs. Booking essential (restaurant). Disabled: toilet. No smoking (restaurant). Tables outdoors (21, terrace).

West Hampstead

Walnut
280 West End Lane, NW6 1LJ (7794 7772/ www.walnutwalnut.com). West Hampstead tube/rail. **Dinner served** 6.30-11pm Tue-Sun.
Main courses £9.50-£14. **Credit** DC, JCB, MC, V.
Despite its stylish interior, there's something vaguely disconcerting about Walnut's oddly shaped corner location. Don't let that put you off. Neither should you worry unduly about the worn menus, which might indicate the place is getting a little tatty. OK, so you're unlikely to find dishes on the menu (or bottles on the reasonably priced, though uninspiring wine list) to rock your world – but the bill won't either. Friendly service, good fresh flavours and generally accurate cooking ensure Walnut is what you want from a neighbourhood restaurant. A relaxed 'come-as-you-are' atmosphere pervades the place. To start, a thick and smoky Mediterranean fish soup made up in flavour what it lacked in authenticity. Juicy, nicely seared scallops were accompanied by a roast garlic and balsamic dressing that could have done with considerably more punch. Mains were generally more successful: a hunk of perfectly cooked halibut with a crisp, almost perfumed sorrel rösti; and a delicately creamy crayfish risotto. There's also a good choice of vegetarian dishes, including aubergine and sorrel sausages.
Babies and children welcome: children's portions; high chairs. Booking advisable weekends. No-smoking tables. Restaurant available for hire. Tables outdoors (4, pavement). **Map 28 A2.**

Outer London
Barnet, Hertfordshire

Dylan's Restaurant
2006 RUNNER-UP BEST LOCAL RESTAURANT
21 Station Parade, Cockfosters Road, Barnet, Herts EN4 0DW (8275 1551/www.dylans restaurant.com). Cockfosters tube. **Lunch served** noon-2.30pm Mon-Sat; noon-3pm Sun.
Dinner served 6-10pm Mon-Sat; 6-9pm Sun.
Main courses £12.50-£17.50. **Set lunch** £18.50 2 courses, £22.50 3 courses. **Set meal** (lunch Mon-Sat, 6-7pm daily) £12.50 2 courses, £15.50 3 courses. **Credit** AmEx, JCB, MC, V.
It's quite a shock to find this smart, modern restaurant tucked into an unspired 1930s parade of shops at the very end of the Piccadilly line. The look is sleek and clean-lined, in a palette of grey, white, black and hot pink; it's a touch '80s, but not in a bad way. Manager Dylan Murray and chef Richard O'Connell (both ex-One Aldwych hotel) have put their West End experience to good use: the black-clad staff are courteous and efficient, and the menu mixes Mod Euro classics with a jaunty fusion twist. We visited for Sunday lunch; a jazz trio played in one corner as a stream of well-dressed locals arrived. Good-quality ingredients are deftly used, whether in a simple starter of mozzarella, tomato and rocket with sweetish balsamic, or in more elaborate creations, such as crispy-skinned salmon atop a pile of Asian vegetables (bok choi, nashi pear, shiitake mushrooms) in a sweet-sour broth. The broth was too sweet, but the fish was perfect. Traditionalists could opt for Sunday roast (beef or lamb). Desserts

veer towards comfort territory: chocolate fondant, perhaps, or vanilla ice-cream sprinkled with amaretti crumbs and drizzled in toffee sauce. The global wine list has plenty of choice under £25.
Babies and children admitted: children's menu; high chairs. Booking essential Fri, Sat lunch. Entertainment: jazz 1-4pm Sun. No smoking.

Kew, Surrey

The Glasshouse
14 Station Parade, Kew, Surrey TW9 3PZ (8940 6777/www.glasshouserestaurant.co.uk). Kew Gardens tube/rail. **Lunch served** noon-2.30pm Mon-Sat; 12.30-2.45pm Sun. **Dinner served** 7-10.30pm Mon-Thur; 6.30-10.30pm Fri, Sat; 7.30-10pm Sun. **Set lunch** (Mon-Fri) £23.50 3 courses; (Sat) £25 3 courses; (Sun) £29.50 3 courses. **Set dinner** £35 3 courses, £50 7 courses. **Credit** AmEx, MC, V.
A light, bright, wedge-shaped room in the middle of Kew village, the Glasshouse continues to be a major local attraction – somewhere that reflects back to diners their own good feelings about life. It's owned by the people behind the equally consistent French restaurants La Trompette and Chez Bruce. On our visit, most tables were taken by double-dating fortysomethings, younger romantics and European businessmen cementing deals. Some dishes have been evolving on the menu for several years. Our food was largely excellent. In a warm salad of wood pigeon with deep-fried truffled egg, the meat was as tender and the egg as fragrant as ever. There was a hint of *Ready Steady Cook* about a salad of skate pieces with beetroot, pea shoots, capers and horseradish (what happened to the rest of the skate wing?), though it went down well. A main course of slow-roast pork belly was delicious, with crispy crackling and salty choucroute on sharp apple tart, as was roast rump of lamb with provençal vegetables, the rump soft and pink. There was no rush to the evening; service was unusually slow and forgetful, unlike the normal high standard.
Babies and children welcome (lunch): children's menu; high chairs. Booking essential dinner and Sun lunch. No smoking.

Richmond, Surrey

★ Petersham Nurseries Café
Church Lane, off Petersham Road, Petersham, nr Richmond, Surrey TW10 7AG (8605 3627/ www.petershamnurseries.com). Richmond tube/ rail then 30min walk or 65 bus.
Café **Lunch served** 12.30-3pm Tue-Sun.
Main courses £14-£22.
Tea house **Tea served** 11am-4.30pm Mon, Sun; 10am-4.30pm Tue-Sat.
Both **Credit** MC, V.
For the ultimate *rus in urbe* experience, head to the café at Petersham Nurseries. The setting is idyllic, with wonky garden furniture either inside one of the artfully distressed greenhouses or outside, beneath rustic sunscreens, surrounded by colour-coordinated plant displays. Success has led to expansion, so there's also a tea house for soup and own-made cakes. The café is open only for lunch and is very popular with Richmond's well-to-do mums, so you'll have to book. The daily changing menu is short, and expensive – starters around a tenner, mains twice that – but ingredients are impeccably sourced and the cooking, under Skye Gyngell, shows real panache. A fritto misto starter comprised courgettes and flowers (from the nursery) in a delicate, tempura-like batter. For mains, tea-smoked trout, served cold and smeared with sauce vert, sat atop a pile of spinach, samphire, peas and flavour-rich beef tomatoes; and meen moilly was a lightly spiced Indian 'stew' of monkfish and tomatoes. Finish with a chocolate pot or sherry-soaked apricot ice-cream. To drink, there's wine, Bellinis, elderflower cordial or own-made lemonade. There's a small car park, but complaints by residents about overcrowding and lack of parking make it an even better idea to arrive on foot across the riverside meadows.
Babies and children welcome: high chairs. Booking essential. Disabled: toilet. No-smoking. Tables outdoors (15, garden).

North African

Two ambitious new restaurants have upped the ante on Moroccan frills in the West End, which now has more brass platters, Berber rugs and filigree lanterns than the souk in Fez. We've always been a bit dismissive about these kinds of places, the ones that lavishly decorate their dining rooms like some Indiana Jones fantasy and then spend nothing in the kitchen. But that's changing, as **Souk Medina** and **Zaytouna** prove that it is possible to have not only sequinned throw cushions and hookahs, but good food too. Both restaurants ape the trend begun by Marylebone's **Occo** a couple of years back of taking the North African staples – the tagine (a slow-cooked stew) and couscous – and introducing new flavours, textures and snazzy ways of presentation. The results aren't always successful, but we're just happy to be presented with North African menus that offer a choice beyond lamb or chicken, chicken or lamb.

Meanwhile, **Momo** manages to remain one of the capital's most exciting restaurants of any kind, not so much for the food but because, after all these years, on the right night it still feels like the most glamorous, sexy, happening place in town. Founder Mourad 'Momo' Mazouz once said his ambition was to have the 'best little couscous house in town', a modest aim,f but one that, despite all his successes, we feel he has yet to achieve. That particular accolade goes to **Moroccan Tagine**, a humble café that's pretty much a one-man show, but which serves one of the best tagines north of the Straits of Gibraltar. Mind you, it is in the heartland of London's North African community, and if you can't find a good tagine on Golborne Road, where are you going to find one?

Central
Covent Garden

Souk Medina NEW
1A Short's Gardens, WC2H 9AT (7240 1796/ www.soukrestaurant.co.uk). Covent Garden tube. **Meals served** noon-midnight daily. **Main courses** £8.50-£12.95. **Set lunch** £15 4 courses. **Set dinner** £17.95 4 courses. **Credit** AmEx, DC, MC, V.
Sister restaurant to the original Souk just round the corner on Litchfield Street, this newcomer is a far larger and more professional affair. Arches, sand-coloured rusticated plasterwork and burnt-earth tiles, with a minimum of ethnic knick-knackery, give it that ersatz kasbah look. There's a long bar doing cocktails and a loungey salon open all day for tea and sheesha. It's like a Momo for *Heat* readers. The menu expands the usual limited line-up of tagines to include such intriguing choices as chicken with feta cheese and spinach, and a beautifully done lamb with prune, apple and almonds. Where most North African restaurants tend to palm off non-meat eaters with a take-it-or-leave-it vegetable tagine, here there are no less than eight veggie options. And if the choice of meze is less exciting than in some other restaurants, at least what we tried was good: falafel on a bed of crisp, fresh, chopped mixed peppers and lettuce, and some fiery little lamb merguez smothered in a chopped tomato and parsley sauce. Effort has gone into the desserts too, with the likes of crêpes and apple tart with rosewater in addition to the standard baklava.
Babies and children welcome: high chairs. Booking advisable Fri, Sat. Disabled: toilet. Entertainment: belly dancer, DJ 9pm Fri, Sat. Separate rooms available for parties, seating 45 and 100. Takeaway service; delivery service (within 2-mile radius). Vegetarian menu. Vegan dishes. **Map 18 L6.**
For branch (Souk Bazaar) see index.

Gloucester Road

★ Pasha
1 Gloucester Road, SW7 4PP (7589 7969/ www.pasha-restaurant.co.uk). Gloucester Road tube/49 bus. **Meals served** noon-midnight daily. **Main courses** (noon-5pm) £6 4 dishes, £8-£15 6 dishes. **Set dinner** £30-£32 per person (minimum 2) tasting menu. **Credit** AmEx, DC, MC, V.
Pasha was always a bit of a looker, but since being taken over by Tony Kitous of Levant it's positively ravishing. The street level has become a bar and hookah lounge that is so wantonly seductive you may never make it downstairs to the restaurant proper. This is also totally luscious, all glowing and twinkling in golden reds and copper tones, with fine patterning and textures courtesy of the work of Moorish artisans. There is artistry in the food too. In Morocco the little pastry triangles known as briouettes typically come in lamb or cheese flavours, but at Pasha (where the spelling is anglicised to the clumsy 'briwats') they do them in combinations of scallops and red pepper, cod and paprika, chicken and lemon, green olive and tomato, cheese and mint, and lamb and prunes. You can try all six for £12 – and we recommend

that you do. The superior tagines and couscous are served with style and flair, and lots of little extras such as dishes of sultanas and tongue-scorching harissa paste. Prices on the high side, but this is a restaurant that exudes a sense of occasion, and many of the customers dress accordingly.
Babies and children welcome: high chairs. Look weekends. Separate room for parties, seats 18. Vegetarian menu. **Map 7 C9**.

Leicester Square

Saharaween
3 Panton Street, SW1Y 4DL (7930 2777). Leicester Square or Piccadilly Circus tube.
Meals served noon-11.30pm daily. **Main courses** £8-£14. **Unlicensed. Corkage** no charge. **Credit** MC, V.
What at first impression seems a definite no-hoper of a restaurant delivers a pleasant surprise. The main entrance is framed by two columns that look as though they're made of painted cardboard; and the ground-floor and basement are both more Portobello knick-knack emporium than serious dining venue (appropriately, everything you can see is for sale, according to a note on the menu). It is only when it comes to the kitchen that Saharaween displays some serious good taste(s). The menu is short to the point of abruptness, but among its handful of standard tagines are a couple of unusual items, including a tagine sfira of slow-cooked chicken with 'cheesey bread balls' and a tagine mhama of lamb with glazed apple, plum, pine nuts and 'lamb juice'. The latter dish was terrific, with the fruit reduced to a soft gooiness that beautiful complimented the generous hunk of tender, almost flaky meat. Desserts are worth trying, particularly the Berber pancakes, which are thick and spongy like American breakfast pancakes, and come with honey and ice-cream. The 'bar man' mixes some excellent fresh fruit cocktails that make good use of Maghrebi flavours such as pomegranate, lemon, mint and ginger.
Babies and children admitted. Separate rooms for parties, seats 35 and 40. Tables outdoors (2, pavement). Takeaway service. **Map 17 K7**.

Marylebone

Occo
58 Crawford Street, W1H 4NA (7724 4991/ www.occo.co.uk). Edgware Road tube. **Lunch served** noon-3pm Mon-Sat. **Dinner served** 6.30-10pm daily. **Main courses** £11.75-£14.25. **Credit** AmEx, MC, V.

BEST NORTH AFRICAN

For a big night out
Office parties and large groups are well catered for at **Souk Medina** (*see p237*), which has a variety of rooms and screened spaces including a private mezzanine area.

For Marrakech-style chic
It may be old news, but **Momo** (*see right*) remains one of London's best-looking restaurants, with the best-looking staff and the best-looking clientele.

For great food and no frills
The colour and flair is all in the kitchen at always reliable **Original Tagines** (*see above*), but for the absolute best North African it has to be **Moroccan Tagine** (*see p239*).

For something other than Moroccan
Adam's Café (*see p239*) has a menu of excellent Tunisian specialties, in addition to being one of the friendliest restaurants in town.

Both a popular cocktail bar that attracts a noisy happy-hour crowd and a proper restaurant, our one gripe at Occo is the loud music – be warned if you're planning to whisper sweet nothings to a date. That said, the multi-level approach looks good; eating in the soothingly neutral and airy conservatory we could see up to an opulent dark red sheesha lounge through open ironwork grilles. Great cocktails such as Malika Mary (Bloody Mary with chermoula spices) set the theme: fusion-style dishes with a Moroccan twist. Pastry cigars stuffed with sea bass, cod, crevettes and vermicelli with tomato salsa were a heavenly take on traditional briouats. Calamari in featherlight smoky paprika and herb batter with fennel and garlic aïoli were just as good. Lamb brochettes with mouth-watering pineapple salsa and pomegranate dressing, and roast duck stuffed with pistachio and prunes in a rich sauce were both top-notch. And who can resist puds such as date and coconut tart with roasted apricots and coconut ice-cream? With friendly but proper service, it's all very Moor-ish.
Babies and children admitted. Disabled: toilet. Separate rooms for parties, seats 20 and 50. No-smoking tables. Tables outdoors (4, pavement). **Map 8 F5**.

Original Tagines
7A Dorset Street, W1U 6QN (7935 1545/ www.originaltagines.com). Baker Street tube.
Lunch served noon-3pm Mon-Fri. **Dinner served** 6-11pm daily. **Main courses** £9.50-£11.95. **Set lunch** £9.50 2 courses.
Credit MC, V.
Original Tagines offers refreshing relief from the average Moroccan local packed with over-the-top ethnic tat. A lighter hand is evident in the clean, bright decor: yellow walls, sparingly decorated with gold calligraphy. Bright mosaic tables bring extra colour, and soothing Arabic music plays in the background. There's a more enterprising range of starters here than is often found: try gently braised kidneys, broad beans in a garlicky cumin-infused tomato sauce or briouats – filo-type pastry parcels filled with cheese or kefta (minced lamb). Mains don't diverge from the standard selection of tagines and couscous, but there's a pleasing lightness of touch, which means you don't end up feeling stuffed to the gunnels. Gently spiced with cinnamon, cumin and paprika, lamb tagine with almonds and prunes could have been a touch more intense. Chicken kedra with caramelised onions and raisins in a delicate broth with ginger and cinnamon and fluffy couscous was light and subtle. You'll also find an enticing range of puds – try rice pudding with orange-flower water or a briouat stuffed with almonds. With a good range of wines including Moroccan bottles, Original Tagines is a cut above its competitors. Here's hoping the style might catch on.
Babies and children welcome: high chairs. Booking advisable. Tables outdoors (5, pavement). Takeaway service. **Map 3 G5**.

Mayfair

★ Momo
25 Heddon Street, W1B 4BH (7434 4040/ www.momoresto.com). Piccadilly Circus tube.
Lunch served noon-2.30pm Mon-Sat. **Dinner served** 6.30-11.30pm Mon-Sat; 6.30-11pm Sun. **Main courses** £9.75-£19.50. **Set lunch** £11 1 course, £13 2 courses, £16 3 courses. **Credit** AmEx, DC, MC, V.
Momo is not for the faint-hearted. We've heard moans about diners being hurried to vacate tables and haphazard service from those oh-so attractive waiting staff, but where else is dancing on the table quite so chic? Dining à deux, it's hard not to make new friends as you cosy up on long canteen-like tables (albeit with proper starched tablecloths). Provided you're in the mood, this adds to the fun. Every so often, the fine mix of North African sounds ratchets up and you're encouraged to down cutlery and get grooving. Naff? No way – a sense of 'le cool' pervades as the truly cosmopolitan crowd gyrates to the beat. And the food? The usual North African crowd-pleasers shine here, with some modern twists: try crispy gambas with an

avocado gateaux or a traditional, subtly smoky mechouia (roast pepper salad). Lamb couscous was sublime: melting shank, chewy char-grilled chunks, wonderfully natural merguez (minus the scary red food colouring), a vat of earthily spiced broth with tender veg and a massive bowl of fluffy couscous. Drinks are great too, if pricey. Try Mô Tea Room next door for something lighter. All this in beautiful, artfully lit surroundings with delicate filigree window screens. A unique experience.
Babies and children admitted. Booking advisable weekends. Dress: smart casual. Tables outdoors (6, terrace). Vegetarian menu. **Map 9 J7**.
For branch (Mô Tea Room) see index.

Soho

Zaytouna NEW
45 Frith Street, W1D 4SD (7494 9008/ www.zaytouna.co.uk). Tottenham Court Road tube. **Meals served** noon-1am Mon-Sat; noon-midnight Sun. **Main courses** £9.95-£15.95.
Set dinner vegetarian £29.95 per person (minimum 2); £32.95 per person (minimum 2). **Credit** MC, V.
Money has been spent turning three floors of this Soho townhouse into a Moroccan fantasia, complete with carpets and cushions from Tangier and crockery and polychromic tiling from Fez, all pulled together by a designer from Rabat. The cook is from Casablanca, where things are a little more restrained though never dull; tastes here are strong but well defined. Bread came topped by slivers of fried garlic, chicken briouettes were sprinkled with lemon juice, and an otherwise simple green Moroccan salad contained a pound's worth of orange segments. Similarly, the mains: a couscous royale of lamb, chicken and fiery little red merguez (spicy sausage) had a sweet, near-caramelised topping of sultanas and onions. Another plus is that the tagines come with a complimentary side of couscous – many places charge extra for it. Desserts are surprisingly good for a North African restaurant; we enjoyed an excellent ginger brûlée. The main dining room is on the first floor, sandwiched between a street-level café-cum-bistro and the upper floor, which is is set to open as a hookah lounge.
Booking advisable. Children over 5 years admitted. Entertainment: belly dancer 10pm Fri, Sat. No-smoking tables. Separate room for parties, seats 50. Tables outdoors (2, pavement). **Map 17 K6**.

West

Bayswater

Couscous Café
7 Porchester Gardens, W2 4DB (7727 6597). Bayswater tube. **Meals served** noon-11pm Mon-Thur, Sun; noon-midnight Fri, Sat. **Main courses** £9.95-£15.95. **Corkage** no charge. **Credit** AmEx, MC, V.
The Couscous Café is a good little local with the typical souk look – red rugs, mosaic tables and lots of Moroccan lamps and beaten copper knick-knacks. It's cosy, but wasn't oppressive on a hot evening. Service is friendly and accommodating – knowing the chef to be a bit of a smen (Moroccan clarified butter) fiend, we asked for couscous without any. Although this request was then forgotten, our butter-phobe was able to reject the buttered dish and pick something else. This is one of few Moroccan restaurants in London to offer own-made bread, which we enjoyed in abundance with our meze: pretty un-Moroccan houmous and feta, rich garlicky zaalouk, salata mechouia (grilled peppers and tomatoes) and chakchouka (tomatoes with peppers and eggs). All the usual tagines are here. Lamb with prunes and almonds wasn't quite rich and gloopy enough. Both our chicken tagines (one with apricots, the other with olives and preserved lemons) were fine, if a little watery. All lacked the rich flavours of reduction achieved by long, slow cooking. Alcohol is served, but diners can bring their own – there's a well-stocked off-licence round the corner. Finish with fresh, fragrant mint tea, theatrically poured.

Menu

North African food has similarities with other cuisines; see the menu boxes in **Middle Eastern** and **Turkish**.

Bastilla or **pastilla**: an ouarka (qv) envelope with a traditional filling of sliced or minced pigeon, almonds, spices and egg, baked then dusted with cinnamon and powdered sugar. In the UK chicken is often substituted for pigeon.

Brik: minced lamb or tuna and a raw egg bound together in paper-thin pastry, then fried.

Briouats, briouettes or **briwat**: little envelopes of deep-fried, paper-thin ouarka (qv) pastry; these can have a savoury filling of ground meat, rice or cheese, or be served as a sweet flavoured with almond paste, nuts or honey.

Chermoula: a dry marinade of fragrant herbs and spices.

Chicken kedra: chicken stewed in a stock of onions, lemon juice and spices (ginger, cinnamon), sometimes with raisins and chickpeas.

Couscous: granules of processed durum wheat. The name is also given to a dish where the slow-cooked grains are topped with a meat or vegetable stew like a tagine (qv); couscous royale usually involves a stew of lamb, chicken and merguez (qv).

Djeja: chicken.

Harira: thick lamb, lentil and chickpea soup.

Harissa: very hot chilli pepper paste flavoured with garlic and spices.

Maakouda: spicy potato fried in breadcrumbs.

Merguez: spicy, paprika-rich lamb sausages.

Ouarka: filo-like pastry.

Tagine or **tajine**: a shallow earthenware dish with a conical lid; it gives its name to a slow-simmered stew of meat (usually lamb or chicken) and vegetables, often cooked with olives, preserved lemon, almonds or prunes.

Zaalouk or **zalouk**: a cold spicy aubergine, tomato and garlic dip.

Babies and children admitted. Booking essential. Tables outdoors (2, pavement). Vegetarian menu. **Map 7 C6**.

Hammersmith

Fez

58 Fulham Palace Road, W6 9BH (8563 8687). Hammersmith tube. **Dinner served** 6pm-midnight daily. **Main courses** £7.95-£11.95. **Set meze** £22.95-£24.95 per person (minimum 2). **Credit** MC, V.

Surprisingly for a name that suggests you're walking into a Moroccan restaurant, most of the dishes on the menu at this restaurant just off Hammersmith Broadway are Lebanese. Take the starters. There's not a single Moroccan item on the list – although the spinach fatayer were delicious, with a satisfying shortcrust pastry and just a hint of cinnamon. There is, however, a slight nod to North African cuisine in the mains. The couscous options are always a safe bet, but, disappointingly, the pastilla comes with chicken rather than the traditional pigeon. The pastry envelope, despite being on the dry side, was a good combination of savoury (onions and chicken) and sweet (spices, apricots and sultanas). If you ignore the black forest gateau and cheesecake for dessert, there are still a few authentic touches, including a perfectly drinkable fruity house red from Morocco and a refreshing, albeit very sweet, mint tea. Our advice to Fez? Tone down the overdone coral and blue interior and the gimmicky tinsel, and don't be afraid to give Londoners a real flavour of Morocco.

Babies and children admitted. Booking advisable weekends. Entertainment: belly dancers Fri, Sat. Takeaway service. **Map 20 C4**.

Ladbroke Grove

★ ★ **Moroccan Tagine**

95 Golborne Road, W10 5NL (8968 8055). Ladbroke Grove or Westbourne Park tube/23 bus. **Meals served** noon-11pm daily. **Main courses** £4.90-£8.90. **Unlicensed**. No alcohol allowed. **Credit** MC, V.

Despite being a no-frills street café in a relatively insalubrious area of west London, the cooking at Moroccan Tagine puts to shame almost every other North African restaurant in town. It's the work of the genial, bearded Hassan, a Berber from the Rif Mountains, who prepares his tajines according to family recipes. Mama must have had an extensive repertoire because Hassan's menu boasts no less than six kinds of lamb tajine alone, including with artichokes, with prawns and boiled egg, and with okra and tomatoes. With one of London's best fishmongers up the street, it's not surprising that there's also a good showing of seafood: sardines stuffed or grilled, calamari, fish tajine and a fish platter with salad. Our only complaint is that it's really messy trying to debone sardines when they sit on top of a mound of unnecessary salad. We're told all the herbs are organic and imported from Morocco, as is the olive oil and the complimentary olives, marinated to Hassan's own recipe. There's no alcohol, but there are fruit cocktails, such as a 'Berber cooler' of raspberries, strawberries and blackberries shaken with lemon, apple and fresh orange juice.

Babies and children welcome: high chairs. Book weekends. No-smoking tables. Tables outdoors (4, pavement). Takeaway service; delivery service (within W10). **Map 19 B1**.

Shepherd's Bush

★ ★ **Adam's Café**

77 Askew Road, W12 9AH (8743 0572). Hammersmith tube then 266 bus. **Dinner served** 7-11pm Mon-Sat. **Set dinner** £10.50 1 course, £13.50 2 courses, £15.50 3 courses. **Credit** AmEx, MC, V.

Local restaurants don't get much better than this, with its friendly service, cheerful buzz of diners of all ages and lovingly prepared, strikingly fresh food. The owner hails from the island of Djerba, so fish is a speciality, and you'll get the rare chance

Souk Medina. See p237.

RESTAURANTS

Zaytouna. See p238.

to try a few Tunisian dishes from the all-purpose North African menu. Complimentary rustic bread, fiery harissa with olive oil (a Tunisian essential), pickled veg and tiny herby meatballs appear as if by magic. Do try a Tunisian brik au thon to start: a lovely thing to behold, it's a fragile shell of crisp, deep-fried ouarka pastry that breaks to reveal a yummy egg, potato and tuna filling. Couscous royale was a good version: a succulently delicious mix of grilled and stewed meat served with a huge vat of pungently spiced broth, tender veg and harissa on the side. Our neighbours tucked into a baked whole mullet, four-year-old and 74-year-old alike. With a three-course deal for £15.50 and fairly priced drinks, Adam's Café remains a winner.
Babies and children admitted. Book weekends. Separate room for parties, seats 24. Vegetarian menu. **Map 20 A1.**

South

Balham

★ Tagine

1-3 Fernlea Road, SW12 9RT (8675 7504). Balham tube/rail. **Dinner served** 5-11pm Mon-Fri. **Meals served** noon-11pm Sat, Sun. **Main courses** £8-£12. **Set dinner** (Mon-Wed) £11.99 2 courses. **Unlicensed. Corkage** no charge. **Credit** MC, V.
Balham's bustling dining strip, based on Bedford Hill, also spills into side streets. Tagine faces the famous Bedford pub across a traffic-choked tributary, but the noise doesn't deter the restaurant's owners from opening the French doors and putting out pavement tables. The interior is more enticing, with Moroccan-style chandeliers, low brass tables and heaps of other kasbah tat to give it a louche Marrakech look. The empty wine glasses on the tables stay empty though, as Tagine doesn't serve alcohol; the Moroccan tea is a good substitute. Corners are sometimes cut with dishes – the pitta bread is a cheap version, for example – but other dishes are pleasingly fresh, such as zaalouk salad with an appealing tang of cumin. Among all the usual starters, couscous dishes, grills and tagines are a few dishes that stand out. Couscous zizou gives you the full Moroccan monty: a herb-rubbed brochette of lamb, a little merguez sausage, some well-cooked chickpeas and mushy vegetables, all capped with a dome of turmeric-stained cabbage leaf. Service was willing, bit not very informed. Our waiter hesitated before telling us our fish tagine was made with 'cod' – even though it clearly wasn't.
Babies and children welcome: high chairs. Booking advisable. No-smoking tables. Tables outdoors (6, pavement). Entertainment: music 8pm Sun.

North

Islington

Fez

70 Upper Street, N1 0NU (7359 1710/ www.fez-islington.co.uk). Angel tube. **Meals served** noon-11pm Mon-Wed; noon-2am Thur-Sat; noon-midnight Sun. **Main courses** £6.95-£23.95. **Credit** MC, V.
Changes at Fez since our last visit mean that the upstairs room now has a slightly barn-like feel with heavy wooden tables in serried ranks against the walls, rather than the previous intimate arrangement with decorative ironwork furniture. Is the restaurant possibly becoming more of a fuelling stop for the small disco bar downstairs? The menu has been watered down to include many more international dishes such as deep-fried camembert, and steak and chips. There's still a reasonable range of Moroccan fare, though fewer choices than before. Zaalouk (served warm here) was garlicky and packed quite a punch with rich chilli undertones; light crispy briouat came stuffed with goat's cheese. Couscous was served as a one-plate dish with no extra broth or harissa to add, and was consequently a touch too dry. That said, tender well-cooked lamb and vibrantly spiced merguez sitting atop juicy squash, courgettes, carrots and chickpeas was very tasty indeed. We always enjoy the wide range of cocktails and beers including Moroccan Casablanca. Finishing with fragrant mint tea, poured slightly gingerly from on high by our sweetly charming waitress, we were pleasantly surprised by the all-round experience.
Babies and children admitted. Booking advisable. Tables outdoors (3, pavement). Vegetarian menu. **Map 5 O2.**

Maghreb

189 Upper Street, N1 1RQ (7226 2305/ www.maghrebrestaurant.co.uk). Highbury & Islington tube/rail. **Meals served** 6-11.30pm daily. **Main courses** £7.95-£12.95. **Set dinner** (Mon-Thur, Sun) £9.95 2 courses. **Credit** AmEx, JCB, MC, V.
Maghreb's bright yellow walls and glowing, jewel-rich silk lanterns against red and blue upholstery give an opulent, exotic feel without any 'road to Morocco' overload. Traditional Moroccan fare is cooked with a delicate hand, along with some fusion-style dishes. On our latest visit we weren't so pleased with the starters – sardines with chermoula tasted rather tired, and good garlicky zalouk was served too cold – but the mains were spot-on. Chicken tagine with olives and preserved lemons was tender and flavoursome, the liquor cooked just to the right point of reduction. Mixed

grill couscous also impressed: tender char-grilled lamb and chicken with feistily spiced merguez and kefta sat on a pile of light, fluffy couscous, with an aromatic vegetable stew. We particularly enjoyed the friendly, attentive but unobtrusive service from the owner. He's rightly proud of his well-priced wine list, with many more Moroccan choices than is usually found in London. There's a good range of puds: baghrir are rich, yeasty pancakes with an irresistible honey and butter sauce. Given its Islington location, Maghreb is a very good-value local, with an upmarket but pleasantly relaxing feel and better than average food.
Babies and children welcome: high chairs. Booking advisable. No-smoking tables. Restaurant available for hire. Separate areas available for parties, seating 38 and 44. Takeaway service. **Map 5 O1.**

North West

Hampstead

Safir

116 Heath Street, NW3 1DR (7431 9888/ www.safir-restaurant.co.uk). Hampstead tube. **Dinner served** 6pm-midnight Mon-Thur. **Meals served** noon-midnight Fri-Sun. **Main courses** £8.85-£17.50. **Set meal** £12.95 2 courses, £17.95 3 courses. **Credit** MC, V.
London's Moroccan restaurants really need to get with it. Eat at some of the latest additions to the Casablanca or Marrakech dining scene and you'll be sitting on Eames chairs using Philippe Starck tableware while poking at dishes that Heston Blumenthal might have created. An interior like Safir's – walls hung with red and green tent material, star-shaped lanterns, painted table tops, and seats cloaked in satiny red and gold covers – is the stuff of tourist fantasias. Which isn't to say it's not attractive and very arresting. The menu is, for the most part, totally traditional, other than the occasional item such as prawn briouettes, which are more like South-east Asian spring rolls. The couscous was some of the best we've had, incredibly fine and light, and the vegetables in the couscous dishes also avoid the overcooking that is common in so many North African kitchens. Tagine of lamb with prunes was excellent too; the chef achieves that reduced, sweet, gloopy sauce that is often too watery elsewhere. With food this good, it's easy to forgive the hackneyed decor, although avoid Safir at the end of the week unless you're happy to be subject to the attentions of a belly dancer.
Babies and children welcome: high chairs. Booking essential Fri, Sat, dinner Sun. Entertainment: belly dancer 8pm Thur-Sat; band 7.30pm Fri. Restaurant available for hire. Separate room for parties, seats 25. Takeaway service. **Map 28 C1.**

Oriental

Just as Modern European food has been forged out of the flavours and cooking styles of a bagful of countries, so too with Oriental cuisine. Singapore is the best recent example of a crucible creating eastern-fusion food, melding the flavours of Indonesian, Malaysian, Tamil and Chinese settlers. Cities such as Sydney and London are newcomers at dabbling with Oriental food, perhaps adding Japanese culinary techniques to Thai spicing – plus the occasional European pudding for afters. In this 'new' cuisine there are no rules, and as a result, depths can occasionally be plumbed as well as new heights reached.

Success has come in two distinct segments of the market. **Wagamama** single-handedly created the demand for fashionable noodle bars that are low-budget but wholesome; it continues to thrive, as do many of its imitators. The other London trailblazer for Oriental cooking has been restaurateur Will Ricker. His restaurants are big on stylish design, and also serve innovative and often memorable food. **Great Eastern Dining Room** and **E&O** are our current favourites from the Ricker stable, though their hip new rival **Cocoon** (in a similar mould but under different ownership) also takes some beating. The problem with the upmarket trendy Oriental restaurants is that they don't seem to last long: since the 2006 edition of this guide the short-lived Taman Gang, Grocer on Warwick Café and Pengelley's have all closed – though chef Ian Pengelley can now be found at newcomer **Gilgamesh**.

Central

Bloomsbury

Wagamama
4A Streatham Street, WC1A 1JB (7323 9223/ www.wagamama.com). Holborn or Tottenham Court Road tube. **Meals served** noon-11pm daily. **Main courses** £5.95-£9.95. **Credit** AmEx, DC, MC, V.
Wagamama has stood the test of time well. The 1992 Rick Mather minimalist interior still looks contemporary, and despite founder Alan Yau's early loss of the company to other investors, the business stays close to its original ethos of providing wholesome fast food at a fair price. The menu is more extensive than in the beginning, when it focused on Japanese-style noodle dishes with South-east Asian flavours. You can now follow the filling main courses with desserts such as tamarind and chilli pavlova. By Japanese standards, the basics are, indeed, basic. Yaki soba was no better than Japanese motorway service-station food: a heap of egg noodles with bits of pork, chicken, red ginger and odd slivers of red and green raw capsicum pepper seemingly included for their dramatic colour. The gyoza (steam-fried dumplings) had a curiously dry filling; chicken is substituted for the more usual and more moist pork mixture. But there are a great many things Wagamama does right – from the Henry Ford-like efficiency of the service, to the always-reasonable bill – that will ensure the chain continues to expand even beyond its current reach (which includes cities such as Dubai and Auckland). *Babies and children welcome: high chairs. No smoking. Takeaway service. Vegan dishes.* **Map 10 K5.**
For branches see index.

City

Silks & Spice
Temple Court, 11 Queen Victoria Street, EC4N 4UJ (7248 7878/www.silksandspice.com). Mansion House tube/Bank tube/DLR. **Meals served** 11.30am-10.30pm Mon-Fri. **Main courses** £6.75-£13.75. **Set meal** £15.95 (vegetarian) 3 courses, £16.95 (meat) 3 courses, £19.95-£25.95 4 courses (minimum 2). **Credit** AmEx, MC, V.
You get the feeling there has been a hurried, low-cost refurbishment here. The result is a dining area that lacks character, decorated with mismatched furniture. At least the cosy horseshoe booths we opted for were as comfy as they looked. The three-star system used to indicate levels of chilli heat on the menu seemed entirely inaccurate. Our hottest dish, named 'Weeping Tiger', was also the worst, comprising chewy charred sirloin steak served with a lip-searing soy-based sauce. It was only given one star. In contrast, a mild, creamy Thai duck red curry with soft meat, crunchy bamboo shoots and pea aubergines was given three. Tempura vegetables had been perfectly cooked, leaving them with soft centres and a crisp, if slightly oily, coating. Pla la prik (crispy cod fillet in a spicy sweet and sour sauce) also went down well. Despite this, we reckoned that, given the City prices charged, Silks & Spice's cooking didn't represent great value. *Babies and children admitted. Booking advisable; essential for parties of 10 or more. Disabled: toilet. Entertainment: DJs 10.30pm Thur, Fri. Separate room for parties, seats 20. Takeaway service. Vegetarian menu.* **Map 11 P6.**
For branches (Ekachai, Pacific Spice, Silks & Spice) see index.

Clerkenwell & Farringdon

Cicada
132-136 St John Street, EC1V 4JT (7608 1550/www.cicada.nu). Farringdon tube/rail. **Bar Open** noon-11pm Mon-Sat. **Restaurant Lunch served** noon-3pm Mon-Fri. **Dinner served** 6-10.30pm Mon-Sat. **Dim sum served** noon-3pm, 6-10pm Mon-Fri; 6-10pm Sat. **Dim sum** £3-£6. **Main courses** £8-£16.50. **Both Credit** AmEx, DC, MC, V.
This slick, modishly designed outfit from the Will Ricker stable attracts local after-work drinkers seeking cocktails and Asian-influenced nibbles. The menu is divided into small plates, salads, sushi, roasts and main courses, with the cuisine being inspired by anywhere from Japan to Java. On the night we visited the most enjoyable dish was a pretty soft-shell crab and pomelo salad that also featured slivers of sharp green mango, crunchy roasted peanuts, sliced shallots and chopped mint and coriander. Sesame spring rolls were fine, if a little oily, with a filling of glass noodles, carrots and shiitake mushrooms that tasted more of soy than sesame. Our crispy pork belly was crisp, but let down by meat that was tough. Main courses were the most disappointing, comprising a chewy steak with bulgogi sauce, and an aubergine and gingko nut red curry that suffered from an overload of extra ingredients and a sludgy sauce. Our advice is to stick to light bites and long drinks. *Babies and children admitted. Booking advisable lunch. No-smoking tables. Separate room for parties, holds 65. Tables outdoors (5, pavement).* **Map 5 O4.**

Fitzrovia

Bam-Bou
1 Percy Street, W1T 1DB (7323 9130/ www.bam-bou.co.uk). Goodge Street or Tottenham Court Road tube. **Bar Open** 6pm-midnight Mon-Sat. **Restaurant Lunch served** noon-3pm Mon-Fri. **Dinner served** 6-11pm Mon-Sat. **Main courses** £9.75-£18. **Set meal** (lunch, 6-7.30pm Mon-Fri) £12.50 2 courses. **Both Credit** AmEx, JCB, MC, V.
Bam-Bou's teak, bamboo and eastern artwork, together with its occupation of an entire Georgian house (complete with dim, narrow corridors), lend the restaurant the feel of a pre-war colonial club somewhere in the French Far East. To match, the food produces some finely honed pan-oriental flavours. Among the starters, we particularly enjoyed bo la lot (little rolls of delicately spicy ground beef wrapped in wild betel leaves) and har gau prawn dumplings (a dim sum staple with prawns tucked inside a slippery casing). Other starters include some unusual ingredients (crispy beef with asian pear and chickweed salad, for example). A main course of green curried chicken might sound standard, but care and precision in cooking made for a subtle combo of vivid flavours and texture, with crunchy winter shoots meeting smooth, aromatic green curry sauce enhanced with thai basil. In contrast, caramelised ginger chicken with cashews and water chestnuts didn't quite do it for us; we found it too sweet. Puddings are fun: the likes of banana and pistachio fritters or crispy chocolate orange spring rolls. Service is pleasant and efficient. *Babies and children admitted. Booking advisable. Separate rooms for parties, seating 12, 14 and 20. Tables outdoors (4, terrace).* **Map 10 K5.**

Crazy Bear
26-28 Whitfield Street, W1T 2RG (7631 0088/ www.crazybeargroup.co.uk). Goodge Street or Tottenham Court Road tube. **Bar Open** noon-10.45pm Mon-Fri; 6-10.45pm Sat. **Restaurant Meals served** noon-10.45pm Mon-Fri. **Dinner served** 6-10.45pm Sat. **Dim sum** £2.50-£3.50. **Main courses** £10-£28. **Set lunch** £7.50-£8 1 course. **Set meal** £25-£38 tasting menu. **Both Credit** AmEx, DC, MC, V.

Even if you can navigate your way to this almost unmarked restaurant with its nightclub looks (part of a growing chain branching from an Oxfordshire gastropub-hotel), you may be stumped by the toilets, whose location behind a fake wall is indicated by only a spotlight. The disco decor alone (shiny silvery floors, invisible electronic taps and waterfall urinals) is worth a journey, as is the gorgeously dramatic basement bar. On a lunchtime visit, starter salads chosen from the ambitiously long menu were underpowered. Crispy duck salad could have been more moist and better flavoured; a crustacean equivalent lacked the vividness of truly fresh seafood – and both contained unexciting greens sprinkled with a chilli-flavoured Japanese dressing. Mains were better: grilled sea bass fillet; and a tremendous little pot of casseroled ox cheek, with a delicious sweet gravy spiked with Asian spices, coriander and chilli. Vegetables of grilled asparagus and wok-fried morning glory were fresh and flavoursome. Staff may have been friendly and well informed, but service was slow. The separate pricing of side dishes can make the bill add up too. *Babies and children admitted (lunch). Booking advisable.* **Map 4 K5.**

★ dim T café

32 Charlotte Street , W1T 2NQ (7637 1122). Goodge Street or Tottenham Court Road tube. **Meals served** noon-midnight daily. **Dim sum** £2.50-£2.75. **Main courses** £6.85-£8.95. **Credit** MC, V.

Fashionably styled pan-oriental eateries may be two a penny in London these days, but the small dim T chain is nonetheless a fine example of a winning formula – and after recently raising impressive investment capital, the company has plans for expansion outside London to prove it. Baskets of fresh and flavoursome dim sum at affordable prices are the main event here. The steamed soupçons won't necessarily win any prizes for authenticity when pitted against Chinatown's best, but the parcels are prepared with

care and – in an unconventional but canny twist – they are served all day. The menu uses English translations instead of the Chinese names, which can be confusing. The create-your-own-dish noodle menu lets you customise your meal, or you can play safe with one of the handful of reliable Asian mains: Indonesian satay, Singaporean fried noodles, pad Thai, Japanese teriyaki. The decor is gently modish, with its lilac banquettes and eastern design touches, and the service consistently friendly. Dim T scores well for affordable glamour: if you're careful (tap water, no puds), you can eat here for a tenner. With puddings as tempting as banana fritters with ginger and chocolate sauce, you may want to consider blowing the extra £3.95.

Babies and children welcome: children's portions; high chairs. Booking advisable lunch. No-smoking tables. Tables outdoors (2, pavement). Takeaway service. **Map 9 J5.**
For branches see index.

Piccadilly

★ Cocoon

65 Regent Street, W1B 4EA (7494 7609/ www.cocoon-restaurants.com). Piccadilly Circus tube. **Lunch served** noon-3pm Mon-Fri. **Dinner served** 5.30pm-1am Mon-Sat. **Main courses** £9-£23. **Set meal** (lunch, 5.30-7pm daily) £17-£20 per person (minimum 2). **Credit** AmEx, MC, V.

Hailed as a memorable new restaurant design when Cocoon opened last year, Stephanie Dupoux's cool mixture of colourful kitsch and sinuous minimalism continues to pick up awards. The bar is an increasingly popular and stylish hangout. What's more (and somewhat surprisingly), Cocoon's food is seriously good. Seated in our circular bucket chairs at a table topped with rose petals, we tried two different bento lunches, each made up of seven little items. The highlights were a soft-shell crab tempura with yuzu aïoli, and two kinds of delicious steamed dim sum. The only

disappointment was the foie gras gyoza, the dumplings being a little leathery. Separate dishes that worked particularly well included the chilli prawns, the mussels with lemongrass and coconut, and some exquisitely crisp and well-seasoned salt-and-pepper squid. For pudding, the tropical fruit plate contained a generous selection of perfectly ripe fruit; and the creamy lemon nai-won with cinnamon ginger doughnuts – a kind of Chinese crème caramel flavoured with vanilla and limoncello – was one of the best desserts we've had in months. Service was attentive and prompt, and coffee modestly priced. Not a cheap meal, but an unforgettable one.

Babies and children admitted. Booking advisable. Disabled: toilet. No-smoking tables. Separate room for parties, seats 14. **Map 17 J7.**

Soho

★ Itsu

103 Wardour Street, W1F 0UQ (7479 4790/ www.itsu.com). Piccadilly Circus tube. **Meals served** noon-11pm Mon-Thur; noon-midnight Fri, Sat; 1-10pm Sun. **Main courses** £1.95-£6.95. **Credit** AmEx, MC, V.

The long line of Soho regulars queuing up outside these premises at lunchtime for takeaway sushi gives advance notice that Itsu offers better Japanese food than the average conveyor-belt sushi bar. Enter the buzzy, colourful interior and you discover a creditable range of pan-Asian dishes too, some passing on the belt and others to be ordered from the friendly staff. Seared beef with a sweet dipping sauce was served in generously thick, tender slices, each given a kick by a dab of mustard. Salmon sashimi came new-style – part-seared, thinly sliced and dressed with lemon and oil – and also traditional, cut into thicker squares but absolutely fresh. The chilli crystal crab rolls burst with crunchy, finely chopped vegetables and crab meat with the smell of the sea. Sesame-encrusted vegetable rolls with cooked carrot and

Crazy Bear. See p241.

avocado were less exciting, but the chinese broccoli came with a sauce that perfectly balanced sweet and salty flavours. Desserts were less promising: crème brûlée arrived warm rather than chilled; and a Valrhona chocolate mousse was merely good rather than spectacular. Our lunch for two cost £45; refraining from pudding will keep the bill as well as your waistline trim.

Babies and children admitted. Bookings not accepted. No smoking. Takeaway service.
Map 17 K6.
For branches see index.

West

Bayswater

I-Thai

The Hempel, 31-35 Craven Hill Gardens, W2 3EA (7298 9001/www.the-hempel.co.uk). Lancaster Gate tube/Paddington tube/rail. **Dinner served** 7-10.30pm Mon-Sat. **Main courses** £15.95-£29.95. **Credit** AmEx, DC, JCB, MC, V.

Set inside the entrance to the dramatically minimalist Hempel hotel, I-Thai sits in a spacious dining room filled with candles and orchids. The menu used to focus on fusion cuisine alone, but now starts with Modern European, has a page of unusual sushi platters, and ends with a traditional Thai section. We tried a coconut chicken soup from the Thai menu and found it too heavy on the coconut, and marred by tough fragments of lemongrass. From the fusion menu, duck with hoi sin sauce maki was better. To follow, a lobster salad was generous, with the crustacean dramatically arranged in its shell. Tuna came seared to perfection with an aubergine pâté in a bath-sized pool of tomato sauce. Extras were dotted throughout the meal – edamame; a tomato, mozzarella and basil amuse-gueule; and a spoonful of lemon and star anise sorbet – but service was clumsy. The romantic atmosphere is more of a draw than the food, so it's probably no loss that I-Thai now opens only for dinner. Hotel guests are much in evidence among the diners; this is no place for the price-sensitive.

Babies and children welcome: high chairs. Booking advisable. Disabled: toilet. No-smoking tables. Separate room for parties, seats 35. Tables outdoors (50, terrace). **Map 7 C6.**

Ladbroke Grove

★ E&O

14 Blenheim Crescent, W11 1NN (7229 5454/ www.eando.nu). Ladbroke Grove or Notting Hill Gate tube. **Bar Open/dim sum served** noon-midnight Mon-Sat; noon-11.30pm Sun. **Dim sum** £3-£6.50. *Restaurant* **Lunch served** noon-3pm Mon-Sat; 12.30-3.30pm Sun. **Dinner served** 6-10.30pm Mon-Sat; 6-10pm Sun. **Main courses** £6-£21.50. *Both* **Credit** AmEx, DC, MC, V.

Often lauded as the star of the group of restaurants owned by Will Ricker – which include the Great Eastern Dining Room (*see p245*), Eight Over Eight (*see below*) and Cicada (*see p241*) – E&O boasts a dark wood and fuchsia-walled bar that's usually filled with gorgeous people sipping delicious cocktails. The calmer, cream-walled dining room offers a pan-Asian fusion menu so full of exotic names that a glossary is enclosed. When we visited, the most notable dish was a peppered tuna with miso aïoli that paired thick rounds of sweet, fresh fish (wrapped in wafer-thin spinach and beancurd skin) with an unctuous mayonnaise sauce. We also loved black cod glazed with sweet miso paste (melt-in-the-mouth tender), and crisp-skinned chicken served in a pool of intensely savoury shiitake stock. The big disappointment was a salad of rare salmon, ikura and green papaya, which was overpowered by slices of salty, mushy-textured fish. We've a slight worry that unusual ingredients are being used to mask a lack of skill in the kitchen. Nevertheless, the perfect sweet finish was provided by a dessert of strawberries and other treats dipped in a dark chocolate fondue.

Babies and children welcome: high chair. Booking essential. Separate room for parties, seats 10-18. Tables outdoors (5, pavement). Vegan dishes. **Map 19 B3.**

★ Uli

16 All Saints Road, W11 1HH (7727 7511). Ladbroke Grove or Westbourne Park tube. **Dinner served** 6.45-11.15pm daily. **Main courses** £6.75-£9. **Credit** MC, V.

This sweetly decorated eaterie boasts an outdoor patio where Salman Rushdie was dining on the night of our visit. Little touches such as cushioned seats and an abundance of potted plants convey a feeling of comfort and attention to detail. The menu offers standard pan-Asian staples interspersed with several intriguing choices for those who feel adventurous. We opted for more unusual dishes, and these were executed with differing degrees of success. Both fried oysters and salt-and-pepper frogs' legs were juicy and tender, but their flavour was overwhelmed by overly thick batter. A plate of mildly hot chillies stuffed with prawns and served with black bean sauce went down a treat, but our final dish of squid with sweet chillies took an unreasonably long time to arrive and even then was undercooked. The alfresco eating is a bonus, but we'd advise ordering carefully and sticking to tried-and-tested favourites.

Babies and children admitted. Booking essential. Restaurant available for hire. Tables outdoors (6, patio). Takeaway service. Vegan dishes. **Map 19 B2.**

South West

Chelsea

Eight Over Eight

392 King's Road, SW3 5UZ (7349 9934/ www.eightovereight.nu). Sloane Square tube then 11, 22 bus. **Lunch served** noon-3pm Mon-Fri; noon-4pm Sat. **Dinner served** 6-11pm Mon-Sat; 6-10.30pm Sun. **Main courses** £7-£24. **Set lunch** £15 2 courses. **Credit** AmEx, DC, JCB, MC, V.

Chelsea cocktail lovers come in droves to gossip, drink and nibble edamame and dim sum. Lamps that look like upside-down paddyfield hats create an oriental feel to the decor. So does a petal-patterned woodcut screen, which separates the bar from the dark wood and leather-upholstered dining room. A short but sweet Asian-fusion menu, divided into compact sections, encourages diners to deviate from the three-course standard and opt for ordering a selection of dishes to share. Our outright favourite was a lobster laksa that was both spicy and soothing, and rich with savoury shellfish flavour. Also delicious was a salad of sliced duck cloaked in hoi sin sauce and tossed with cashew nuts and cubes of sweet watermelon. We were less impressed by a stodgy butternut squash and water chestnut gyoza. Likewise with a sweet potato and mangosteen mussaman curry, which lacked depth of flavour and variation of texture. Puddings were enticingly described, yet, when tasted, not much to sing about. Perhaps it would be better to order a sweet concoction from the tempting cocktail list.

Babies and children admitted. Booking advisable. Dress: smart casual. No-smoking tables. Separate room for parties, seats 12. **Map 14 D12.**

Fulham

★ Zimzun

Fulham Broadway Retail Centre, Fulham Road, SW6 1BW (7385 4555/www.zimzun.co.uk). Fulham Broadway tube. **Meals served** noon-10pm Mon, Sun; noon-10.30pm Tue-Thur; noon-11pm Fri, Sat. **Main courses** £5.50-£7.95. **Set lunch** £5.95 1 course. **Credit** AmEx, MC, V.

A location in the shopping centre above Fulham Broadway tube station ensures that this sleekly decorated den is often full of young locals tucking into generous portions served by friendly staff. Clear beaded curtains hang down over large, square communal tables, softly lit by floating candles intermingled with brightly coloured flowers. The cooking is mainly Thai-inspired, with

Chinese and Japanese influences. We began with battered squid with ginger, garlic, coriander and young peppercorns; it was tasty but arrived cold. Deep-fried garlic prawns were better, though marred by its sweet sauce. Our lamb red curry was the biggest disappointment, consisting of chewy, overcooked meat coated in a sauce that was too creamy. Things improved with a crunchy, spicy and sour som tam (green papaya) salad, and a grilled duck noodle salad that combined soft slices of duck with cherry tomatoes, lettuce and mung bean noodles plus a dressing of chilli, lime and garlic. Large one-plate dishes seem the best value here; come for the noodle salads.

Babies and children admitted. Booking advisable weekends. Disabled: toilet. No-smoking tables. Takeaway service. **Map 13 B13.**

South

Battersea

★ Banana Leaf Canteen

75-79 Battersea Rise, SW11 1HN (7228 2828). Clapham Junction rail. **Lunch served** noon-3pm, **dinner served** 6-11pm Mon-Fri. **Meals served** noon-11pm Sat, Sun. **Main courses** £5.95-£9.20. **Credit** AmEx, MC, V.

Basic canteen-style decor coupled with a colourful Battersea clientele creates the vibe of an urban traveller's café here. This is in keeping with a menu that leans towards Malaysian food, but also includes other South-east Asian dishes. A starter of 'stuffed beancurd filo pastry with whole tiger prawns' was not quite crisp enough to be called filo, but contained a fresh and bouncy filling, and the portion was generous for its price. Char-grilled chicken bakar jawa, described as being marinated in Javanese aromatic spices, was tender and full of big flavours when drizzled with the wedge of sour lime and sweet chilli salsa that accompanied it. We also enjoyed our seafood kari santan melayum: a comforting red coconut curry with a surprisingly large melange of ingredients, including prawns, baby squid, salmon, shiitake and bamboo shoots. This is a perfect place for meeting friends before a night out, or grabbing a quick bite while catching up with a mate. Fast service, hearty portions and low prices keep customers coming back.

Babies and children welcome: children's menu; high chairs. Booking advisable. Disabled: toilet. No-smoking tables. **Map 21 C4.**

Brixton

★ New Fujiyama

7 Vining Street, SW9 8QA (7737 2369/ www.newfujiyama.com). Brixton tube/rail. **Meals served** noon-11pm Mon-Thur, Sun; noon-midnight Fri, Sat. **Main courses** £5.10-£6.70. **Credit** MC, V.

Tucked into a backstreet off Atlantic Road, Fujiyama provides decent music, long shared tables, and a lengthy menu of large, well-priced dishes. No wonder the locals appreciate it. We arrived for a late weekday lunch, and the place only began to quieten down at 3pm. The menu ranges widely (perhaps alarmingly for such a small place) across China, Japan and Thailand, with stops for noodle soup, rice plates, sushi and dumplings. We dined well. An order of regular sashimi included prawns and ark shell, yellowtail and bass, and salmon. According to an American visitor, it was as good as you'd find in New York. The centrepiece of a bento meal was a comfort-food pair of tofu and vegetable croquettes. The beef in karai ramen (a spicy noodle dish) was of a grey hue but tender, though the dish was let down by a curious seafood taste. Gyoza (steamed and fried dumplings stuffed with crispy vegetables) were a triumph of bright flavours. And a big helping of spinach ohitashi was good, though more Chinese than the traditional Japanese rolled greens because it arrived in a sea of sweet sauce, like a Cantonese stir-fry.

Babies and children welcome: high chairs. Booking advisable. No-smoking tables. Separate rooms for parties, seating 14-35. Takeaway service; delivery service (7737 6583; over £10 within 3-mile radius). **Map 22 E2.**

Waterloo

Inshoku

*23-24 Lower Marsh, SE1 7RJ (7928 2311).
Waterloo tube/rail.* **Lunch served** noon-3pm
Mon-Fri. **Dinner served** 5.30-10.30pm
Mon-Sat. **Main courses** £6-£15. **Set lunch**
£4-£8.40. **Set meal** £6 bento box. **Credit**
AmEx, MC, V.
Before Yo! turned sushi into a mass-market budget
meal – and at the same time improved the eating
options at several of London's railway stations –
this was the kind of place you went to if desperate
for Japanese food but not too picky about the
standard. Inshoku isn't in Waterloo station itself;
you walk a few hundred yards, and find it among
a parade of shops in the street market of Lower
Marsh. Most of the lunchtime clientele seems to
come from the immediate locality, rather than from
the station. The interior, furnished with worn-
looking parasols and ukiyoe prints, needs
redecorating, and both lighting and the cleanliness
of the dining area could be improved. We sampled
some good gyoza, some acceptable miso soup, and
enjoyed the comfort-food taste of oyako-don
(chicken pieces on rice). Service was friendly too.
However, our sushi, though copious, was mostly
left on the plate; it just didn't seem to have that
zinging-fresh quality of the best fish. Prices are
modest, but the standard of food seems similarly
low instead of better than expected.
*Babies and children welcome: high chairs.
Booking advisable Thur, Fri. Takeaway service;
delivery service (over £15 within 3-mile radius).*
Map 10 M9.

South East

Gipsy Hill

Mangosteen

*246 Gipsy Road, SE27 9RB (8670 0333).
Gipsy Hill rail/322 bus.* **Lunch served**
11am-3pm, **Dinner served** 6-11pm Mon-Sat.
Main courses £8.50-£10.50. **Set lunch**
£5.95 1 course. **Credit** JCB, MC, V.
Mangosteen has a clean, subdued interior with
neatly arranged cushions lining the walls.
Contemporary photographs make a subtle
reference to Vietnamese culture. There's a decent-
sized terrace too, although busy traffic and a
teenage gang hanging around outside on our visit
were offputting. The food, like the decor, is nicely
presented and combines simple pan-oriental
flavours and textures. To start, juicy pork wun tun
parcels and prawn crackers came with the usual
hot chilli and soy dipping sauces. Mains were more
experimental, but less consistent. Appetising mild
coconut and lime sea bream came topped with an
attractive nest of crispy leeks. However,
caramelised ginger chicken had a very watery and
lacklustre texture – despite being strongly
flavoured. Portions are generous. The desserts
were most tempting, with moreish chocolate
almond pancakes and banana tempura to fight
over. Although Mangosteen isn't in the most
accessible of locations, its impeccable service and
beautifully arranged food deserve to attract a
wider clientele than just local devotees.
*Babies and children welcome: children's menu;
high chairs. Booking advisable weekends.
No smoking. Tables outdoors (5, terrace).
Takeaway service.*

Herne Hill

Lombok

*17 Half Moon Lane, SE24 9JU (7733 7131).
Herne Hill rail/37 bus.* **Lunch served** noon-3pm
Tue-Sun. **Dinner served** 6-10.30pm Tue-Thur,
Sun; 6-11pm Fri, Sat. **Main courses** £6-£8.50.
Credit MC, V.
This compact eaterie has long-standing popularity
among Herne Hill's residents, who are drawn to its
high-quality and, in places, unusual Vietnamese
and Thai cuisine. The service was polite and
efficient on our visit, despite a small child
constantly tugging on the waitress's apron strings.
A few wooden spirit houses provide the decoration,

and the seating is quite closely packed in – not so
comfortable when the place is busy, although fine
during weekend afternoons when it's virtually
empty. For starters, steamed lemongrass mussels
sounded tempting but were unavailable, so we
opted for an enjoyable chicken satay alongside
crispy chilli corn and okra fritters with a spicy
dipping sauce. There are several seafood options
for the main course, and the generous serving of
stir-fried scallops with pak choi and wild
mushrooms was perfect. Various curries, given
names like 'Thai', 'Rangoon' and 'Bangkok' sit
alongside subtle, simple dishes such as a chilli-
laced chicken, scattered with thai basil leaves.
Desserts encompass the usual frozen offerings, not
necessarily oriental, although the mango sorbet
soothed the palate nicely. Chang, Singha and Tiger
beers are also available.
*Babies and children admitted. Booking essential
weekends. Takeaway service.* **Map 23 A5.**

East

Shoreditch

★ Great Eastern Dining Room

*54-56 Great Eastern Street, EC2A 3QR
(7613 4545/www.greateasterndining.co.uk).
Old Street tube/rail/55 bus.*
Below 54 bar **Open/meals served** 7pm-1am
Fri, Sat. **Main courses** £6.50-£10.50.
Ground-floor bar **Open/meals served**
noon-midnight Mon-Fri; 6pm-midnight Sat.
Main courses £8.50-£10.50.
Restaurant **Lunch served** 12.30-3pm Mon-Fri.
Dinner served 6.30-10.45pm Mon-Sat.
Main courses £7-£18.50.
All **Credit** AmEx, DC, MC, V.
What's not to like about a place that serves
beautifully presented pan-Asian food in
comfortable, cool surroundings? Start with a
seductively strong cocktail before moving on to a
menu full of tempting dishes that arrive looking
like jewels. Our only let-down was a plate of dry
slices of pork laid over green papaya slivers,
soaked in an overly sweet dressing. We loved the
Japanese newspaper cone that enveloped our chilli
salt squid. Tuna tartare, enriched with lemon oil
and chives, was delicious and came nestled in a
ring of ice studded with frozen flowers. Soft-shell
crab with Thai asparagus combined delicate meat
in a crisp shell with a salad that was full of
crunch and flavour. Our favourite dish was the
aubergine and lychee green curry – a fabulous
marriage of sweet juicy lychees with hot chilli
and comforting coconut cream. Desserts were
delicious, but didn't quite hang together. A lovely
coconut and pandan panna cotta didn't need the
accompanying minted pineapple chunks; and a
moreish sweet-sour tamarind ice-cream seemed a
strange partner for passionfruit pavlova. Still,
we'd be pleased to return for the unusual food and
the exhilarating vibe. Great Eastern is part of the
Will Ricker group.
*Babies and children admitted (restaurant). Bar
available for hire. Booking advisable; essential
Fri, Sat. Entertainment: DJs 9pm Fri, Sat.
No-smoking tables.* **Map 6 R4.**

North East

Stoke Newington

★ Itto

*226 Stoke Newington High Street, N16 7HU
(7275 8827). Stoke Newington rail/67, 73,
76, 149, 243 bus.* **Meals served** noon-11pm
daily. **Main courses** £3.90-£6.20. **Credit**
MC, V.
Itto is the perfect little local to satisfy a craving for
Asian cuisine. The food is straightforward and
honest, and the prices won't hurt your wallet.
The lilac and deep pink interior has a DIY quality
about it. There are no surprises in the mixed-Asian
menu, which sticks to anglicised Chinese, Japanese
and Thai tried-and-tested favourites. Nevertheless,
everything we requested was freshly cooked to
order. We started with agedashi tofu that was
nicely crisp on the outside, soft on the inside, and

bathed in a soy and mirin sauce. The batter in the
king prawn and vegetable tempura was of the
right kind though a little too thick, and the
vegetables were slightly undercooked. A mild Thai
green chicken curry was fine, while egg-fried rice
was simple and faultless, containing wisps of egg
and lightly oiled grains of rice. Best of all was the
Itto chicken noodle spicy soup: a large steaming
bowl of rice noodles with slices of fried fish cake
and beancurd, crab sticks, pak choi, eggs, prawns
and soft juicy morsels of chicken. Every
neighbourhood should have a local like this.
*Babies and children welcome: high chairs.
No smoking. Takeaway service; delivery service
(over £10 within 2-mile radius).* **Map 25 C1.**

North

Camden Town & Chalk Farm

Gilgamesh NEW

2006 RUNNER UP BEST BAR
*Camden Stables Market, Chalk Farm Road,
NW1 8AH (7482 5757/www.gilgameshbar.com).
Chalk Farm tube/rail.*
Bar **Open/snacks served** noon-2.30am
Mon-Sat; noon-1.30am Sun.
Restaurant **Lunch served** noon-3pm Fri; noon-
6pm Sat, Sun. **Dinner served** 6pm-midnight
daily. **Main courses** £10-£46. **Set lunch**
(Sat, Sun) £15 3 courses.
Tea house **Open/snacks served** noon-3pm
Mon-Thur.
All **Credit** AmEx, MC, V.
Gilgamesh was an ancient Babylonian king in
southern Mesopotamia. What he's doing presiding
over a bar-restaurant with food from the Far East
and wood carvings from India is anyone's guess.
However, at least he's used his superhuman powers
to make its bizarre location, above the higgledy-
piggledy stalls of Camden Stables Market, rather
soothing. He also has the magical ability to make
the roof disappear, so that a meal here feels like
sitting in Indiana Jones's outdoor lounge room.
Everything we tried from head chef Ian
Pengelley's menu was exquisitely fresh, the
flavours beautifully balanced. The fire of
Thailand's deceptively hot green papaya salad was
cleverly offset with a soothing mound of coconut-
flavoured rice. The Japanese chefs at the sushi
counter constructed an impressive raw vegetable
roll, wrapped in uniform ribbons of crisp daikon.
Thai beef salad, duck spring rolls, and black bean
ribs were so tasty we ordered another round.
However, the tedious, confused service made us
feel mummified. And when Gilgamesh summoned
the forces of evil by asking for a tip via the card
reader, in addition to the 12.5% service charge
already on the bill, he went from hero to zero.
*Babies and children admitted. Booking esssential.
Disabled: lift; toilet. Dress: smart casual; no flip-
flops or shorts. Restaurant for hire.* **Map 27 C1.**

★ Lemongrass

*243 Royal College Street, NW1 9LT (7284 1116).
Camden Town tube.* **Dinner served** 5.30-11pm
daily. **Main courses** £5.40-£8.60. **Set dinner**
£16.60-£18.80 per person (minimum 2). **Credit**
JCB, MC, V.
A flashing neon yellow sign hanging above the
door marks out this quirky Cambodian/Indo-
Chinese restaurant. Diners can watch the chef at
work with his wok cooker, so huge it dominates the
tiny kitchen. We liked our 'leek cake' starter, a fried
glutinous rice pancake with chopped chinese leeks
sealed inside. Also enjoyable was a soft, sweet
mango salad dressed with salty fish sauce, hot red
onions and shreds of crunchy pickled cucumber
and carrot. Other dishes were less successful.
Garlic lemon mushrooms and fresh asparagus
were both let down by being drenched in too much
seasoning that tasted as if it had come from a
Maggi seasoning sauce bottle (similar to soy
sauce); it was also covered with tasteless, coarse
pre-ground pepper. Monivong whisky prawns
suffered from a sickly-sweet sauce heady with
alcohol that hadn't been burned off. The meal was
saved by tender lok luk beef: cubes of seared rare

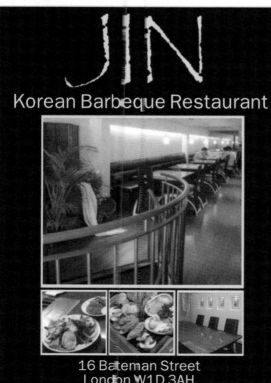

fillet in a black peppercorn sauce. We wouldn't recommend going out of your way to eat here. *Babies and children admitted. Booking advisable weekends. No smoking. Restaurant available for hire. Takeaway service. Vegetarian menu.* **Map 27 D1.**

Primrose Hill

★ Café Maya

38 Primrose Hill Road, NW3 3AD (7209 0672). Chalk Farm tube/31 bus. **Dinner served** 6-11pm Tue-Sun. **Main courses** £4.95-£6.50. **Credit** MC, V.

Memories of restaurants that cater to western travellers backpacking across Asia came rushing back with our visit here. There are wind chimes over the door, book shelves stuffed with all manner of travel memorabilia, and hundreds of CDs stacked in precarious towers. The cooking is mostly Malaysian or Thai and the quality is hit and miss. We enjoyed starters of spare ribs in a sweet sticky sauce, and spicy/salty battered squid. Similarly, singapore laksa was a good combination of thin silky rice noodles with strips of chicken and egg in a gentle coconut and chilli broth. Other dishes were less successful. Malay fish curry featured overcooked fried cod in a sauce that tasted uncannily like the instant curries sold in Japanese supermarkets, while nuggets of deep-fried chicken came in a syrupy-sweet hoi sin sauce instead of the yellow bean sauce described on the menu. Generous portions and friendly service made for a nice meal, but not one to go out of the way for. *Babies and children welcome: high chairs. Booking advisable weekends. No-smoking tables. Restaurant available for hire. Takeaway service; delivery service (over £15 within 3-mile radius).* **Map 28 C5.**

Outer London
Barnet, Hertfordshire

★ Emchai

78 High Street, Barnet, Herts EN5 5SN (8364 9993/www.emchai.co.uk). High Barnet tube. **Lunch served** noon-2.30pm Mon-Thur; noon-3pm Fri-Sun. **Dinner served** 6-11pm Mon-Thur; 6pm-midnight Fri, Sat; 5-10pm Sun. **Main courses** £4.20-£7.90. **Set meal** £14.50 2 courses. **Credit** AmEx, JCB, MC, V.

Adding a contemporary note to High Barnet's high street, this roomy restaurant was buzzing with a youthful crowd of diners on our Friday night visit. Emchai is run by Chinese Malaysians. Its reasonably priced menu offers both Chinese and Malay dishes, from crispy duck to mee goreng (fried noodles), cooked by industrious chefs on show in the open-plan kitchen. Our meal got off to a good start with sticky pork ribs, and some tasty salt-and-spicy prawns with a garlic and chilli kick. To follow, a delicate stir-fry of prawns with lily bulbs and asparagus; honey-roast duck; and gai lan with ginger were all nicely executed. Our sweet tooth was satisfied by melon pudding in palm sugar syrup and (a retro classic) banana fritters. Serving staff were excellent (polite, friendly and efficient), bringing us complimentary prawn crackers. A ten-year-old boy in our party was made to feel as welcome as the grown-ups, and requests for tap water were dealt with as courteously as those for beer. No wonder Emchai has built up an appreciative following in Barnet. *Babies and children welcome: high chairs. Disabled: toilet. No-smoking tables. Restaurant available for hire. Takeaway service.*

Kingston, Surrey

Cammasan

8 Charter Quay, High Street, Kingston upon Thames, Surrey KT1 1NB (8549 3510/ www.cammasan.co.uk). Kingston rail.
Meinton noodle bar **Lunch served** noon-3pm, **dinner served** 5.30-11pm Mon-Fri. **Meals served** noon-11pm Sat, Sun. **Main courses** £5.50-£8.90.
Chaitan restaurant **Lunch served** noon-3pm, **dinner served** 5.30-11pm Mon-Fri. **Meals served** noon-11pm Sat, Sun. **Minimum** £15. **Main courses** £5.50-£30. **Set meal** £14.90-£20.90 per person (minimum 2).
Both **Credit** AmEx, MC, V.

When Kingston was having its mini-renaissance a few years back, two-floor oriental joint Cammasan was one of the first businesses to set up shop in the sought-after riverside location of Charter Quay. It has been bustling ever since. Ascend to the first floor for a little formality; here you'll find tasteful pastel walls, starched tablecloths and sweet-tempered service. The menu is divided into 'little plates' and 'big bowls'. The former consist mostly of deep-fried titbits (Thai fish cakes with satay sauce, vegetable spring rolls with chilli sauce); the latter include curries (duck red curry, say), stir-fries (cod sweet and sour) and salads (gado gado). We weren't disappointed with the tasty loh hon chai stir-fry (Chinese vegetable stir-fry, with chinese mushrooms and glass noodles). There's a canteen on the ground floor that serves a shorter, simpler version of what's offered upstairs. *Babies and children welcome: high chairs. Booking advisable. Disabled: toilet. Restaurant available for hire. Tables outdoors (12, terrace). Takeaway service.*
For branch (China Royal) see index.

Great Eastern Dining Room. See p245.

RESTAURANTS

Portuguese

For the geographical core of eating the Portuguese way, head to Ladbroke Grove for a trio of cafés, and to Vauxhall and Stockwell for half a dozen restaurants that give you a street-level flavour of the community and cuisine in act on. If it's finely tuned tradition that takes your fancy, then Knightsbridge's **O Fado** still stands tall, but what's exciting is the consolidation, or emergence, of restaurants elsewhere that know what they're doing. Camden's **Pescador** is on a seafood roll, and Chelsea's **Tugga** is marking out its own territory in a stylish, mixed-menu way. As always with the Portuguese, atmosphere and accessibility figure highly alongside the great fish and meat dishes, and vibrant, diverse wines.

PASTELARIA

West
Ladbroke Grove

★ Lisboa Pâtisserie
57 Golborne Road, W10 5NR (8968 5242).
Ladbroke Grove or Westbourne Park tube/23,
52 bus. **Open** 8am-7.30pm daily. **Credit** MC, V.
Ladbroke Grove is the only area north of the river that can boast a Portuguese centre of gravity anywhere like the Vauxhall and Stockwell hubs. A claim for greater attention lies in this café (named after Portugal's capital city), which epitomises much of Golborne Road, where life is lived indoors and out by a multicultural population. If any decent weather shows, you can be sure of a lively gathering on the pavement, but inside is where the main event plays out. Lisboa feels like the west London equivalent of Brick Lane's bagel bars. Portuguese classics – pasteis de nata, fish and prawn pasties, rice cakes and more – occupy the glass-fronted counter display, alongside filled rolls, pastries and tarts. Turnaround is fast, with the strengths definitely in the home players. Add in a milky galão (why exactly did the latte become the shorthand dairy coffee experience internationally?) and you've got an instantly authentic moment from the motherland. Perfect for a pit-stop, Lisboa stands proud around its core concerns, and if it ain't broke…
Babies and children admitted. Tables outdoors
(3, pavement). Takeaway service. **Map 19 B1.**
For branches see index.

★ Oporto Pâtisserie
62A Golborne Road, W10 5PS (8968 8839).
Ladbroke Grove or Westbourne Park tube/23,
52 bus. **Open** 8am-7pm daily. **No credit cards.**
With the case made for Lisboa Pâtisserie (*see above*), it's hard to give pole position to this second Portuguese café on Golborne Road – just as, back in Portugal, Lisbon tends to win out over the city of Oporto. This similarly busy, similarly intentioned outfit does what it sets out to do, providing a range of generic and nation-specific snacks and drinks, though the quality is very variable, and it's not the case that the Portuguese pastries and fritters are always the best choice. A chicken fritter was especially disappointing. Pasteis de nata always work – but it would be time to pack up and head for the port if you were of Portuguese persuasion and couldn't deliver a good pastel. On one level, it doesn't matter; prices are low and nobody's expecting fireworks, but choose carefully. Stick to what looks good on the

outside, because the interior is sometimes an unknown, and even unappealing, country.
Babies and children admitted. Tables outdoors
(3, pavement). Takeaway service. **Map 19 B1.**

Tea's Me
129A Ladbroke Grove, W11 1PN (7792 5577).
Ladbroke Grove tube. **Open** 7.30am-7pm Mon-Sat; 10am-4pm Sun. **No credit cards.**
This is one of the most unusual makeovers in the London Portuguese landscape. What used to be Café Algarve, bringing a coastal brightness to Ladbroke Grove, is now a chic, kitsch, design-driven microspace. The outdoor tables were occupied on our visit, so we stepped inside to discover immaculately groomed trustafarians whiling away the hot afternoon around the large central table, with a stack of the latest high-end glossies. On the food and drink front, the attention to detail continues, and there's no doubting the quality of the product. You know you're not on Golborne Road anymore when a largely organic breakfast line-up includes a £7 white omelette with spinach and salmon. There's a lunch special, smart sandwiches, and salads of the feta and avocado variety. Hot and cold drinks are standard stuff – with latte, not galão – but what matters are the Portuguese cakes, which really deliver. Beautifully presented and dense with flavour and texture, the almond and bean cakes, pasties and brownies all hit the mark. The only downside was the service; good-natured but seriously erratic, and the place was far from busy.
Babies and children admitted. Tables
outdoors (4, pavement). Takeaway service.
Map 19 B3.

South
Vauxhall

★ Café Madeira
46A-46B Albert Embankment, SE1 7TN (7820 1117). Vauxhall tube/rail. **Open** 6am-9pm daily. **Credit** (over £10) MC, V.
Anyone who knows Albert Embankment will appreciate that this major thoroughfare is not best suited to an intimate tête-à-tête over coffee and cake, or to the family food run when the fridge is bare and the kids are demanding sustenance. More suited to exhaust repair and (wholesale) bathroom sales, it does, however, contain a short stretch of converted arches where the pace chills dramatically. Several eateries are dominated by the Madeira operation, with bakery, deli and café, and an easy-going atmosphere. There's a mixture of Portuguese talent – fish pasties and fritters, pasties and rice cakes – alongside all the usual suspects on the sandwich and sweet front. Hot mains,

including paella and curry, also appear. Tasty, friendly, relaxed; these are important qualities. Close your eyes a minute while you eat: the rich texture of flavours and voices will work its magic and you will find yourself somewhere else than grimy Vauxhall.
Babies and children admitted. Disabled: toilet.
No-smoking tables. Tables outdoors
(10, pavement). Takeaway service. **Map 16 L11.**

RESTAURANTS

Central
Knightsbridge

★ O Fado
49-50 Beauchamp Place, SW3 1NY (7589 3002/
www.restauranteofado.co.uk). Knightsbridge or
South Kensington tube. **Lunch served** noon-3pm daily. **Dinner served** 6.30pm-1am Mon-Sat; 6.30pm-midnight Sun. **Main courses** £10.95-£17.50. **Cover** £1.50. **Credit** AmEx, JCB, MC, V.
Dining at O Fado, the oldest Portuguese dining establishment in London, is a dignified and rewarding experience. Stepping off the designer pavements of Knightsbridge into this quietly neat basement restaurant, there is no sense of subterranean gloom, or of the melancholy so attached to the titular music (which seems to play only once the pop hits tape has finished). Careful, attentive staff and neatly laid tables set the mood. If the menu is traditional, it is also extensive and subtly varied in its sauces, associations and flavouring. Meats and fish dominate, as expected, but the vegetables are flavoursome and not the watery stand-ins so common elsewhere. Starters of grilled sardines and squid (both large portions) were as tasty as desired. Satisfying mains included deliciously soupy arroz de tamboril and fresh fish fillets. By this stage, dessert was not an option, if only because of earlier generosity. The wine list is, as you might expect, very decent. Given its location, prices are extremely reasonable. O Fado remains the best place in town for an authentic taste of Portugal.
Babies and children admitted. Booking
advisable; essential dinner weekends.
Entertainment: guitarists 8pm Wed-Sun.
Separate room for parties, seats 35. Takeaway
service. **Map 14 F9.**

South West
Chelsea

★ Tugga
312 King's Road, SW3 5UH (7351 0101/
www.tugga.com). Sloane Square tube then 11,
19, 22 bus. **Meals served** 4pm-midnight Tue-Fri; 12.30pm-midnight Sat, Sun. **Main courses** £17.50. **Set meal** £32 tasting menu. **Credit** AmEx, MC, V.
The very smartly dressed (newish) kid on the block, Tugga is doing for Portuguese cuisine what has happened with other national menus: shaking up ingredients, combinations and presentation, and stirring in a modern Mediterranean flavour with a zest and invention that yields real results. From the moment you enter the place, it's clear that the game has changed. The stylish bar and dining area is decorated with deep reds and bold patterns, with not a fishing net in sight. There's also a lounge and cocktail bar downstairs. Starters – delicately sauced octopus, and a fine bean/prawn concoction – worked very well, as did main courses of salt cod and sea bass, which showed real delicacy and attention to detail. Prices tend to be high in such an environment and on such a street, of course, with mains coming well into double figures. The lively wine list covers the length of Portugal, and a new development is the well-priced tasting menu. A major addition to London's Portuguese dining scene.

RESTAURANTS

Babies and children admitted. Booking advisable. Disabled: toilet. Entertainment: DJs 9pm Thur-Sat. Separate rooms for parties, seating 12 and 40. Tables outdoors (3, pavement). **Map 14 D12.**

South

Brixton

The Gallery

256A Brixton Hill, SW2 1HF (8671 8311). Brixton tube/rail/45, 109, 118, 250 bus. **Dinner served** 7-9.30pm Thur, Sun; 7-10pm Fri, Sat. **Main courses** £7-£13.50. **Credit** AmEx, MC, V.
Don't be deterred by the Gallery's takeaway chicken 'n' chips shopfront; slip through the back door and you enter another culinary world altogether. Within lies a highly convivial Portuguese restaurant, with gallery seating above a ground-floor dining area decorated with murals. A chorizo starter was served flaming. For main courses, we opted for fish. Seafood and monkfish kebab was fresh, tasty and came with boiled potatoes and a slightly miserly green salad. The real discovery was the acorda de marisco. A Portuguese version of paella, with bread and eggs replacing rice – and giving the dish its pleasantly gluey texture – it was leavened by coriander and plentifully populated by prawns, mussels and slabs of fish. Eaten with a sweet-dry Portuguese white wine such as Bucelas, it was uncommonly flavoursome. And the meal was good value at around £25 a head. Clearly our favourite local restaurant for families, the Gallery is worth a visit for its friendly service and slightly clandestine location, but, above all, for that marvellous fish stew.
Babies and children welcome: high chairs. Book weekends. Takeaway service. **Map 22 D3.**

Stockwell

Bar Estrela

111-115 South Lambeth Road, SW8 1UZ (7793 1051). Stockwell tube/Vauxhall tube/rail. **Breakfast served** 8am-noon, **meals served** noon-11pm daily. **Main courses** £5-£12.50. **Credit** AmEx, MC, V.
We'd tried to get into this hub of the Portuguese community in Lambeth on the evening of their World Cup win over England: it seemed to make sense, riding the wave. The huge, good-natured throng around the numerous pavement tables made that impossible, so a sweltering weekday afternoon visit took its place. This lively and easy-going bar/restaurant is all you would expect from a breakfast-till-late venue, with a few regulars and assorted others dropping in for a cold drink or a cake, and all the staples in place. Given the time and the heat, we snacked – on fish cakes and pasteis de nata – with several beers to ease things forward. It was all perfectly enjoyable, but not about to shake the world (and we weren't expecting it to). We checked the main courses of our neighbours – squid and bacalhau – and they were complimentary on these Portuguese standards. If you're in the area, do stop by.
Babies and children welcome. Tables outdoors (10, pavement). **Map 16 L13.**

O Cantinho de Portugal

135-137 Stockwell Road, SW9 9TN (7924 0218). Stockwell tube/Brixton tube/rail/2, 322, 325, 355 bus.
Bar **Open** 11am-11pm daily.
Restaurant **Meals served** noon-11.30pm daily. **Main courses** £7-£11.
Both **Credit** AmEx, MC, V. Closed 1st 3wks Aug.
A short walk from Stockwell tube station, this friendly local restaurant sits among a row of competing local eateries. A prawn cocktail starter was uninspiring, tasting as if the prawns had come straight from the freezer and the sauce from a tube. We fared better with the main courses. Grilled red snapper in butter sauce came with boiled potatoes, fresh runner beans and a salad: all tasty, and good value at under a tenner. We also opted for that national staple of salted cod (bacalhau), beaten with eggs and thin potato strips into a kedgeree-

like concoction. Wholesome and flavoursome, it went well with a bottle of house white and was one of several bacalhau-based specials, which, judging from ours, would be well worth sampling. Two courses, including dessert, coffee and a bottle and half of wine, came to around £25 a head.
Babies and children welcome: high chairs. Booking advisable weekends. Disabled: toilet. Takeaway service. **Map 22 D1.**

Grelha D'Ouro

151 South Lambeth Road, SW8 1XN (7735 9764). Stockwell tube/Vauxhall tube/rail. **Meals served** 7am-11pm daily. **Main courses** £4.50-£12. **Credit** MC, V.
On the night of our visit (following Portugal's win over England in the World Cup), this typical bar-café-restaurant was absolutely packed, but we managed to squeeze past the spilling pavement tables and pull up a couple of chairs alongside a young Portuguese welder enjoying his few months in London, and his steak. The place was too full for us to make it into the wood- and wine bottle-lined main dining area at the back, but the determined waiters meant all meals flowed freely though the space. This was a truly democratic night, with maybe 20 nationalities all enjoying themselves – with all the energy you could want

from a venue clearly important to both the Portuguese and the wider community. Given the pressure on the kitchen, we went straight to sardines: grilled and tasty, a generous helping, with straightforward, but perfectly edible vegetables. The house white went down very easily. A fine example of what London and the Portuguese can do when at their best.
Babies and children welcome: children's portions. Booking advisable weekends. No-smoking tables. Separate room for parties, seats 60. Takeaway service. **Map 16 L13.**

O Moinho

355A Wandsworth Road, SW8 2JH (7498 6333). Stockwell tube/Vauxhall tube/rail/77, 77A bus. **Meals served** 10am-11pm daily. **Main courses** £6.50-£9.50. **Credit** MC, V.
It was hotter than July when we dropped into this cool and airy café/restaurant on the steaming Wandsworth Road. With all the doors open, we headed to a quieter location at the back near the bar. Service was swift and friendly, and the cover elements, delivered unprompted, were extensive, with fish pâtes in addition to olives. We opened with grilled squid (slightly tough), then followed with an excellent mixed fish and grilled vegetable kebab. We ended up taking the latter away – no

Menu

If you think the cooking of Portugal is just poor man's Spanish cuisine, you haven't eaten enough Portuguese food. Despite sharing the Spanish love for chorizo-style sausages (chouriço), dry cured ham (presunto) and salt cod (bacalhau), the Portuguese have developed a cooking style that has a character, a culture and a cachet all its own. Take the famous arroz (rice) dishes that appear on practically every Portuguese menu. While they are often compared to paella, they are, in fact, far soupier, with the rice used almost as a thickening agent.

Portuguese cooking is in essence a peasant cuisine: the food of farmers and fishermen. Pork, sausages and charcuterie figure prominently, as does an abundance of fresh fish and seafood and olive oil (azeite). There's a strong tradition of charcoal-grilled fish and meats. The hearty bean stews from the north and the thick bready soups (açordas) are also worth trying, as is the coastal speciality of caldeirada, Portugal's answer to bouillabaisse. Garlic, lemon juice, wine and wine vinegar are much used in marinades, with favoured spices being piri-piri (hot peppers, often used to flavour oil in which chicken is basted) and, for the cakes, cinnamon – both the latter showing the culinary influence of Portugal's colonial past.

To finish, there is always a lush arroz doce (rice pudding), a wobbly pudim flan (crème caramel) or the world's most loved custard tart, the deliciously scorched pastel de nata.

Açorda: a bread stew, using bread that's soaked in stock, then cooked with olive oil, garlic, coriander and an egg. Often combined with shellfish or bacalhau (qv).
Amêijoas à bulhão pato: clams with olive oil, garlic, coriander and lemon.

Arroz de marisco: soupy seafood rice.
Arroz de tamboril: soupy rice with monkfish.
Arroz doce: rice pudding.
Bacalhau: salt cod; soaked before cooking, then boiled, grilled, stewed or baked, and served in myriad variations; Portugal's national dish.
Bifana: pork steak, marinated in garlic, fried and served in a bread roll.
Caldeirada: fish stew, made with potatoes, tomatoes and onions.
Caldo verde: the classic soup of finely sliced spring cabbage in a potato stock, always served with a slice of chouriço (qv).
Canela: cinnamon; a favourite spice, used in sweet and savoury dishes.
Caracois: boiled snails, eaten as a snack with beer.
Carne de porco alentejana: an Alentejo dish of fried pork, clams and potato.
Cataplana: a special copper cooking pan with a curved, rounded bottom and lid.
Chouriço assado: a paprika-flavoured smoked pork sausage cooked on a terracotta dish over burning alcohol.
Cozido à portuguesa: the traditional Sunday lunch of Portugal – various meats plus three types of sausage, cabbage, carrots, potatoes and sometimes white beans, all boiled together.
Dobrada: tripe stew.
Espadarte: swordfish.
Feijoada: bean stew, cooked with pork and sausages.
Pastel de bacalhau (plural **pasteis**): salt cod fish cake.
Pastel de nata: a rich egg custard tart made with crisp, thin, filo pastry.
Piri-piri or **peri-peri:** Angolan hot red pepper.
Pudim flan: crème caramel.
Queijo: cheese.
Sardinhas assadas: fresh sardines, roasted or char-grilled.

problem at all, it was packed well and stayed hot – because the youngest in our party decided he needed to hit the swings once the starter had been dealt with. He had been excellently accommodated, with a high chair and sensitive clearing of the table immediately in front of him. We would happily return to O Moinho for both the food and the intuitive understanding on the part of the staff as to parents' and children's needs – a combination rarely found in London restaurants.
Babies and children admitted. Booking advisable. Separate area for parties, seats 50. Tables outdoors (5, pavement). Takeaway service.

North East
Dalston

★ Nando's
148 Kingsland High Street, E8 2NS (7923 3555/ www.nandos.co.uk). Dalston Kingsland rail/38, 76, 149, 236, 243 bus. **Meals served** noon-11.30pm Mon-Thur, Sun; noon-midnight Fri, Sat. **Main courses** £5.25-£7.75. **Credit** AmEx, JCB, MC, V.
The only chain restaurant in this chapter, this chicken emporium is an international brand that plays hot with its spicy peri-peri sauce and its laid-back, brightly coloured cabin vibe. Equal parts Brazilian, southern African and Portuguese in its atmosphere, Nando's is very much at the top end of the fast-food spectrum. It offers fresh ingredients, a decent wine list, plenty of pluses including endless soft drinks, and a spirited humour (with a gentle touch of innuendo in the sloganeering around birds and all that). The Dalston branch is one of the biggest in London, playing well to the taste demands of the locals, and pretty busy throughout the day. This is really an assembly operation, where you choose the part of chicken you fancy, then add the extras (fries and so on), alongside the crucial element: the sauce and its degree of fire. For vegetarians, the bean burger is perfectly serviceable, and the coffee and pasteis are as good as anywhere. Cheap and genuinely cheerful, in its core concerns Nando's delivers well.
Babies and children welcome: children's menu; crayons; high chairs. Booking advisable. Disabled: toilet. No-smoking tables. Takeaway service.
Map 25 C4.
For branches see index.

North
Camden Town & Chalk Farm

Pescador
23 Pratt Street, NW1 0BG (7482 7008). Camden Town or Mornington Crescent tube/24, 29 bus. **Dinner served** 6-11pm Mon-Fri. **Meals served** 1-11pm Sat; 1-10pm Sun. **Main courses** £8.50-£19. **Credit** JCB, MC, V.
This seafood-focused eaterie, one of very few Portuguese venues outside the west and south London heartlands, has been up and down in recent years. There's no denying its extensive menu offering a full range of fish and seafood specialities, but something in the slight blandness of the decor seemed mirrored in the meals and presentation in years past. The walls decked with standard prints might remain unchanged, but clearly a lot else has: this was one of the most enjoyable outings of the year. We started with sardines and squid, testing the basics, and they came up well above last year's poor experience. For mains, we sampled two tried and very trusted deliveries: the seafood rice stew that is arroz de marisco, and tuna steak. Coffees and brandy worked well to finish the meal. We talked towards the witching hour with no pressure from the staff, who had been attentive throughout the evening. With very welcome developments in quality all round, Pescador is one we'll be back to.
Babies and children welcome: high chair. Booking advisable; essential weekends. Takeaway service.
Map 27 D2.
For branch (Pescador Two) see index.

Spanish

Spanish food – particularly tapas – has been undergoing a remarkable renaissance in Spain for more than decade, not just in the hallowed ground of Ferran Adrià's El Bulli or in San Sebastián, but even in neighbourhood tapas bars across the country. Food and travel magazines have been describing Spanish food as the hot new cuisine of Europe. This new wave of interest has had a knock-on effect in London, with many wonderful places such as **Fino**, **Salt Yard** and **Cigala** leading the way, while more orthodox but high-quality produce eminates from **Tapas Brindisa**. 'Moorish food' is still largely confined to the restaurant that coined the phrase, namely **Moro**. Otherwise, London's Spanish restaurant scene seems very conservative when compared to Spain, and has been moving in slo-mo this year, with no significant openings. Although the restaurants reviewed here are the best London has to offer, there are still far too many other places – not listed here – that seem to think that just being a tapas bar and offering a list of classics is all that's needed, without any requirement for an original, individual approach. We suggest avoiding these. With excellent tapas bars such as **Tendido Cero** to go to, there's no need to settle for the merely adequate.

Central
Bloomsbury

★ Cigala
54 Lamb's Conduit Street, WC1N 3LW (7405 1717/www.cigala.co.uk). Holborn or Russell Square tube.
Bar **Open/tapas served** 5.30-10.45pm Mon-Sat. **Tapas** £2-£8.
Restaurant **Meals served** noon-10.45pm Mon-Fri; 12.30-10.45pm Sat; noon-9.45pm Sun. **Main courses** £11-£19.50. **Set lunch** (noon-3pm Mon-Fri) £15.50 2 courses, £18 3 courses. **Set meal** (Sun) £10.50 1 course.
Both **Credit** AmEx, DC, MC, V.
Enter the front door of Cigala and you catch the whiff of wood smoke. Welcome to Spain, in London. Chef-proprietor Jeff Hodges is an aficionado of classic Spanish cooking and it certainly shows on the plate – although not (thankfully) in the decor, which is all clean lines, white wall and bare boards, blissfully free of tacky Costa memorabilia. Some of the dishes, such as grilled razor clams – three large, tender (if slightly gritty) clams with lashings of olive oil, garlic and slices of fresh lemon – are served purely, simply, traditionally. Others get a twist of innovation. Roasted belly of pork with big white judión beans was difficult to fault, with succulent, flavourful pork and creamy beans, all topped with a 'quince alioli', which brought a welcome sharpness. A dressed baby vegetable salad with romesco sauce was perfectly nice (particularly the flavourful, nutty, peppery sauce), but the fish and meat dishes are inevitably the stars here, much as they are in Spain. The set lunch offers limited choice, but some interesting dishes such as roasted wood pigeon with potato and artichoke gratin. The drinks are as true to the Spanish roots as the food. The wine list goes well beyond providing just basic Rioja, with fine examples from regions on the rise, such as Txacoli and Toro, plus some excellent sherries.
Babies and children welcome: high chairs. Bar available for hire. Booking advisable. Tables outdoors (10, pavement). **Map 4 M4.**

City

Barcelona Tapas Bar y Restaurante
15 St Botolph Street, entrance at 1 Middlesex Street, EC3A 7DT (7377 5222/www.barcelona-tapas.com). Aldgate tube/Liverpool Street tube/ rail. **Tapas served** 11am-11pm Mon-Fri. **Tapas** £2.95-£13.95. **Credit** AmEx, DC, MC, V.
We are happy to report that the food here seems to have improved in the last year. That's not to say that miracles have been worked, but what we ate was reasonable. Octopus with paprika was soft and sweet; pincho del diablo, pork in a hot chilli marinade, had a satisfying kick; chicken with garlic was fine too. Some of the dishes had too much oil – but that's as common in Spain as it is in London. Another oil-related complaint is more serious. We were bemused to discover that we had been charged 75p for the inadequate amount of olive oil served with our bread (which was itself unrequested and cost another 75p per person). Bemusement became displeasure when we were handed the credit card machine and pointedly asked to add a tip if we wished, even though a 12.5 per cent service charge had already been included. Barcelona might be in the shadow of the City's skyscrapers, but that's no excuse for such foul play. The food isn't actually expensive per se, and it will serve you well for a wholesome scoff; just beware the offputting tactics.
Babies and children welcome: high chair. Booking advisable lunch. Restaurant available for hire. Mezzanine floor for parties, seats 80.
Map 12 S6.
For branches see index.

Mesón Los Barriles
8A Lamb Street, E1 6EA (7375 3136). Aldgate East tube/Liverpool Street tube/rail. **Tapas served** 11am-11pm Mon-Fri; noon-4pm Sun. **Closed** 3 wks Aug. **Tapas** £3-£8.90. **Credit** AmEx, JCB, MC, V.
The exposed bricks, unvarnished wood floors, open kitchen and suspended serrano hams all suggest a taberna you might find in deepest old

RESTAURANTS

Tapas Brindisa. See p258.

Castile. We were attentively showr to our seats and informed of the specials. Oysters wrapped in bacon sounded so good we ordered a plate before we had even got our menus. These bivalves were delicious; the excellent, fruity house Rioja readied our tastebuds for the next round – we were really starting to like the place. But then things went unexpectedly downhill. Service slowed down, and many of the remaining dishes tasted as if they'd been pre-cooked and reheated (and our proximity to the open kitchen helped us verify the theory). Lardons of jamón were served with some tough artichokes; prawns in a gambas pil pil were overdone. Ham croquettes weren't so bad. Perhaps we were unlucky. We really wanted to like Mesón Los Barriles. Stay safe (in other words, order dishes that need to be freshly prepared), and just hope that the food doesn't let the surroundings down.

Babies and children welcome: high chairs. Booking advisable. Tables outdoors (5, market). **Map 12 R5.**
For branch see index.

Clerkenwell & Farringdon

Anexo

61 Turnmill Street, EC1M 5PT (7250 3421/ www.anexo.co.uk). Farringdon tube/rail/55, 243 bus.
Bar **Open** 11am-1am Mon-Thur; 11am-2am Fri; 4pm-2am Sat.
Restaurant **Lunch served** 11.30am-2.30pm Mon-Fri. **Dinner served** 6-11pm Mon-Sat.
Tapas served 11am-11pm Mon-Sat. **Main courses** £6.50-£12.50. **Tapas** £2.50-£5.25.
Set lunch £6.50 2 courses, £8 3 courses.
Set dinner £10 2 courses, £12 3 courses
Both **Credit** AmEx, MC, V.
Wedged into the Turnmills building, Anexo offers a dark space heaving with office workers celebrating the home time bell; in summer the open frontage adds traffic noise to the already loud soundtrack. The ideal night here is a chat over jugs of cocktails with some food thrown in; the

Gaudiesque decor captures well the feel of a Spanish bar. We went on a weekday lunchtime when there are fewer customers and more emphasis on food, and grabbed the last of the rickety pavement tables – the dark interior being a little too *triste* on a sunny day. In general, we had above-par tapas. You can usually get a pretty good handle on a tapas restaurant from its patatas bravas, and Anexo delivered a creditable version, along with meaty albóndigas, odd-looking but tasty spinach fritters, and a rich, spicy chorizo dish. The weakest links were tired sardines, and gambas a la plancha, which were poor value at £10.50. The wine list is perfunctory, but staff get full marks.
Babies and children admitted (lunch only). Booking advisable dinner. Entertainment: DJs (top floor) 8pm Thur-Sat. Restaurant available for hire. Separate floor available for parties. Tables outdoors (10, pavement). **Map 5 N4.**

★ Moro

34-36 Exmouth Market, EC1R 4QE (7833 8336/www.moro.co.uk). Farringdon tube/rail/ 19, 38 bus.
Bar **Open/tapas served** 12.30-11.45pm Mon-Sat (last entry 10.30pm). **Tapas** £2.50-£12.
Restaurant **Lunch served** 12.30-2.30pm, **dinner served** 7-10.30pm Mon-Sat. **Main courses** £13.50-£17.50.
Both **Credit** AmEx, DC, MC, V.
These days, few London restaurant-goers need ask 'What's Moorish food?'. Thanks to chef-proprietors Sam and Sam Clark, the Spanish-North African nexus on the menu at Moro is part of the restaurant lexicon. A decade after it opened, Moro's still going strong; expect to wait for up to three weeks for a booking. Refreshingly, though, Moro doesn't have the snooty attitude of other in-demand restaurants. There's an air of bustle from the open kitchen at the back and the long zinc bar at the side (you can eat tapas here throughout the day). Plain decor and high ceilings mean that the acoustics are rattly; when this place is busy it's very, very noisy. But the weekly changing menu reads like a dream.

Baby artichokes stuffed with fresh cheese and nutmeg were served with flatbread and a tangy red onion and black olive salad. Roast pork, from the wood-fired oven, was cooked to tender perfection, served with sautéed chard with pine nuts and raisins. Chocolate and apricot tart was enveloped by the thinnest, flakiest pastry. The only off-note was turbot with salmorejo and chopped jamón, which was slightly undercooked. Wines are from some of Spain's best forward-looking producers, and you'd be a fool to pass up the sherries.
Babies and children welcome: high chairs. Booking essential. Disabled: toilet. No smoking (restaurant). Tables outdoors (6, pavement). **Map 5 N4.**

Fitzrovia

★ Fino

33 Charlotte Street, entrance on Rathbone Street, W1T 1RR (7813 8010/www.finorestaurant.com). Goodge Street or Tottenham Court Road tube.
Lunch served noon-2.30pm Mon-Fri; 12.30-2.30pm Sat. **Dinner served** 6-10.30pm Mon-Sat.
Tapas £4-£15.50. **Credit** AmEx, MC, V.
One of a new breed of restaurants serving updated Spanish food in chic settings, Fino is comfortably maintaining high standards three years after bursting on the scene to rapturous applause. The draw here is a bountiful, daily changing tapas menu that reworks the old school with a dash of the new; and a smart, buzzing basement setting that cleverly plugs the gap in atmosphere between bar and restaurant. With prices edging towards £10 for all but the most basic of tapas – and luxurious ingredients such as lobster, foie gras and jamón gran reserva pushing the bill higher still – you expect a near-impeccable dining experience. And that, in the main, is exactly what Fino delivers. Waiting staff are practised and pleasant (if a touch too busy to provide that personal touch), and you can bank on culinary highs of the ilk of a beautifully creamy ajo blanco soup, a platter of supremely moreish wind-dried beef, or tiger

prawns grilled to perfection. Dud dishes are rare (we were served an unusually runny tortilla on our latest visit), the quality of the ingredients way above average and the presentation alluringly simple. We just hope Fino keeps its eye firmly on the ball, so that it can justify its steep prices against an expanding army of 'new Spanish' competition. *Babies and children welcome: high chair. Booking advisable. Disabled: lift; toilet.* **Map 9 J5.**

Navarro's
67 Charlotte Street, W1T 4PH (7637 7713/ www.navarros.co.uk). Goodge Street or Tottenham Court Road tube. **Lunch served** noon-3pm Mon-Fri. **Dinner served** 6-10pm Mon-Sat. **Tapas** £1.50-£15.50. **Credit** AmEx, MC, V.
Navarro's two floors of closely packed tables is so convincingly decorated with Spanish tiles, wrought iron and hand-painted chairs you'd swear you were in Spain. As with many Charlotte Street restaurants, the central location means that this tapas bar is perpetually packed. We waited so long for both our menus and to order that only the threat of walking out prompted speedy service. When the food did arrive, we were pleased with it, from the Galician-style hot octopus to the lentejas, a rich lentil stew with chorizo and vegetables. Piquillo peppers stuffed with crab were fresh and well made, and the salmorejo sauce with the grilled lamb cutlets was as deliciously garlicky as you'd find in Cordoba. Some dishes also made good conversation pieces for the many groups of office colleagues who patronise the place, such as the spectacular-looking bombas de patatas y verduras which at first glance look like paprika-dusted poached eggs, but are in fact curiously textured deep-fried creamed potatoes with an alioli dressing. This place bustles, but for a more relaxed meal with better food, go to nearby Salt Yard (*see below*). *Babies and children welcome: high chairs. Booking essential dinner.* **Map 9 J5.**

★ Salt Yard
54 Goodge Street, W1T 4NA (7637 0657/ www.saltyard.co.uk). Goodge Street tube. **Open** noon-11pm Mon-Fri; 5-11pm Sat. **Tapas served** noon-3pm, 6-11pm Mon-Fri; 5-11pm Sat. **Tapas** £2.75-£8.50. **Credit** AmEx, MC, V.
This is one of those places that proves emphatically that less can be more. It's a compact space deftly furnished with a sleek, pared-down aesthetic of steely greys, chocolatey browns and well-chosen design accents (a striking wooden bar top, a mirrored stairwell). More crucially, the brief menu – divided into cold meats, bar snacks and tapas – and wine list demonstrate superb attention to detail. Unwilling to be cornered geographically, Salt Yard gathers together the very best of Spain and Italy; so wooden boards of corn-fed jamón ibérico and tangy chorizos face off against delicate prosciuttos from Alto Adige and herb-flecked Tuscan salami, while on the cheese front three pecorinos with truffle honey takes on manchego with quince. The classic tapas (padrón peppers, patatas bravas, tortilla) are beautifully turned out, but Salt Yard also excels in more innovative dishes, such as crisp squid and braised octopus with cauliflower purée and pink grapefruit and – our highlight – the sublime courgette flower stuffed with gooey Monte Enebro cheese and drizzled with honey. In an area that's thick with good restaurants, Salt Yard manages to be continuously busy – and for all the right reasons: serious ingredients prepared with passion and care, and served with enthusiasm and efficiency. *Babies and children admitted. Booking advisable. No-smoking tables. Tables outdoors (3, pavement).* **Map 9 J5.**

Mayfair

El Pirata
5-6 Down Street, W1J 7AQ (7491 3810/ www.elpirata.co.uk). Green Park or Hyde Park Corner tube. **Meals served** noon-11.30pm Mon-Fri; 6-11.30pm Sat. **Main courses** £10.50-£16. **Tapas** £3.95-£9. **Set lunch** (noon-3pm) £9 2 dishes incl glass of wine. **Set meal** £13.95-£17.75 per person (minimum 2) 8 dishes. **Credit** (over £10) AmEx, DC, JCB, MC, V.

Café Garcia. See p255.

As one of the few affordable, not to mention upbeat, dining options in this plush neighbourhood of hotels, private clubs and expense accounts, El Pirata enjoys immense popularity with local business folk. It provides a reliable lunch or after-work spot in which to knock back a decent, reasonably priced house tempranillo along with a few tapas dishes. It's spread over two floors; the ground-floor bar is nicer than the basement, offering walls cheerfully decorated with Picasso and Miró reproductions, close-packed tables and unflaggingly amiable waiters adding to the buzzy atmosphere. We eschewed the specials – a good-looking parallida of fish and shellfish among them – for a mix of classics from the long tapas menu. Standouts were gambas al pil pil; a rich, cheesy dish of aubergines; and montaditos (slices of bread) topped with first-class jamón serrano, but we also enjoyed a tasty fabada (bean stew), meatballs, and fair renditions of arroz negro and patatas bravas. With Spanish spoken at several tables around us, we felt we had stepped off a Mayfair street straight into the Plaza Mayor. *Babies and children admitted. Booking advisable dinner. Separate room for parties, seats 65. Tables outdoors (4, pavement). Takeaway service.* **Map 9 H8.**

Pimlico

Goya
34 Lupus Street, SW1V 3EB (7976 5309/ www.goyarestaurant.co.uk). Pimlico tube. **Lunch served** noon-3pm, **dinner served** 6-11.30pm daily. **Main courses** £10.90-£16.95. **Tapas** £1.80-£6.85. **Credit** AmEx, DC, JCB, MC, V.
A splendid setting amid the glinting white porticos of Pimlico (with alfresco pavement space to boot), a smart blond wood interior, and a healthy complement of diners already in situ when we arrived tempted us to suppose that the cooking at Goya might be a cut above the decidedly average standard of most of the capital's Hispanic restaurants. But we shouldn't have been quite so optimistic. A dish such as kidneys in sherry needs precise treatment – but ours were overdone, and the sauce might have been punchier. More straightforward tapas dishes could also have been better: pincho moruno (pork kebab, described on the menu as 'tender') was also dry from overcooking, while fried calamares weren't at all crispy. A main-course platter of grilled seafood (cod, mussels, octopus and so on) was far better, and a plate of jamón ibérico, the expensive top-

class Spanish cured ham, was excellent (but then it's difficult to ruin good cured ham). The patchy cooking is a let-down, but the surroundings are very pleasant, and if you play it safe with your menu selections you might not do too badly.
Babies and children admitted. No-smoking tables Mon-Fri. No-smoking tables. Tables outdoors (7, pavement). Takeaway service. **Map 15 J11**. **For branch see index.**

Soho

★ Meza
100 Wardour Street, W1F 0TN (7314 4002/ www.conran.com). Tottenham Court Road or Leicester Square tube. **Open** noon-2.30pm, 5pm-2am Mon-Thur; noon-2.30pm, 5pm-3am Fri, Sat. **Tapas served** noon-2.30pm, 5pm-1.30am Mon-Thur; noon-2.30pm, 5pm-2.30am Fri, Sat. **Tapas** £1.50-£8.50. **Credit** AmEx, MC, V.
The latest incarnation of this flagship Conran venue (formerly Mezzo), Meza occupies the upper floor of the premises, while the Cuban-themed Floridita fills the basement. Meza is suitably sleek, with soft blue banquettes and booths, armchairs for more louche lounging, subtle colours, and partitions that artfully divide up the big space. As often in Conran restaurants, there seem to be quite a lot of staff who meet, greet and stand around looking corporate rather than doing anything more obviously useful, but our waiter was friendly, charming and very professional. And the food was lovely. The menu – mostly tapas, with a few larger options – is based on classic Spanish favourites. Such dishes, often simply (and, here, stylishly) prepared, depend above all on first-rate ingredients, and nothing we tried disappointed in any way. Steamed asparagus with shaved manchego cheese was beautifully fresh; ham and cheese croquettes were crisp and creamy; octopus served with sautéed potatoes was expertly well hammered to a perfect texture; and soft goat's cheese with dried figs was exquisitely refreshing. Subtle desserts such as lemon sorbet with cava are a tempting follow-up, and the drinks lists – including a connoisseur's sherry selection – are equally refined. A very superior, but not snooty take on the tapas bar.
Babies and children welcome: high chairs. Booking advisable. Disabled: lift; toilet. Separate room for parties, seats 38. **Map 17 K6**.

South Kensington

Cambio de Tercio
163 Old Brompton Road, SW5 0LJ (7244 8970/ www.cambiodetercio.co.uk). Gloucester Road or South Kensington tube. **Lunch served** 12.30-2.30pm Mon-Sat, Sun. **Dinner served** 7-11.30pm Mon-Sat; 7-11pm Sun. **Main courses** £13.50-£16.75. **Credit** AmEx, DC, MC, V.
With orange-painted walls and matador paintings, Cambio de Tercio may be proud of its Spanish roots, but don't expect paella and sangria – this restaurant has long been considered one of the leading exponents of modern Spanish cooking. It was a surprise, then, that none of our choices really shone. Thinly sliced foie gras with 'cabernet' vinaigrette and apple salad was creamy with well-balanced acidity, but the coffee breadcrumbs scattered over the dish were unpleasant. Assorted potatoes with octopus, sweet paprika and olive oil, Galician-style, must be the most refined version of pulpo a la gallega ever produced, but it lacked seasoning. Mains were acceptable, but no more; a plate of oxtail caramelised in red wine was dry; better was slow-roasted leg of baby lamb with confit potatoes, though that harked back to the hefty, never subtle, London-Spanish dishes of the old school. Service, however, is charming, the bread and espresso first rate, and the wine list a textbook on modern Spanish wines. Since we've previously been very impressed by the cooking, we're adopting the charitable view that there was trouble in the kitchen on our visit.
Babies and children admitted. Booking advisable dinner. Restaurant available for hire. Separate room for parties, seats 22. Tables outdoors (4, pavement). **Map 13 C11**.

★ Tendido Cero
174 Old Brompton Road, SW5 0BA (7370 3685/www.cambiodetercio.co.uk). South Kensington tube. **Tapas served** noon-11pm daily. **Tapas** £4-£14. **Credit** AmEx, MC, V.
As befits its Brompton Road locale, Tendido Cero is smart and sophisticated, although the real swankiness belongs to sister restaurant Cambio de Tercio (*see above*) across the road. This bright star in the restaurant firmament leaves Tendido Cero to offer a menu of traditional tapas – with a few bold flourishes. We were highly impressed. Standards at all its albóndigas, marinated anchovies, and octopus with paprika are as good as any we've had in London. The more innovative menu entries were even better: seared tuna steak with an avocado dressing was first class; deep-fried filo pastry parcels filled with Mallorcan sobresada sausage and soft cheese were wonderfully indulgent, as was deep-fried arzua cheese. Splendid food was matched by extremely attentive and accommodating service. Our only caution is financial: the tapas are very reasonably priced, but alcohol (on a licence that was only recently acquired) could send your bill into orbit if you're not careful: our 'house red' (at least, that's what we requested) was £17.50, which is just a little over the odds.
Babies and children admitted. Booking advisable dinner Tue-Sat. Restaurant available for hire. Tables outdoors (5, pavement). **Map 13 C11**.

West

Hammersmith

Los Molinos
127 Shepherd's Bush Road, W6 7LP (7603 2229). Hammersmith tube. **Lunch served** noon-3pm Mon-Fri. **Dinner served** 6-10.45pm Mon-Sat. **Tapas** £3.50-£6.50. **Credit** AmEx, DC, MC, V.
A perennial favourite with local diners on account of its welcoming atmosphere, cheerful and attentive service and accomplished kitchen. The small main dining room is done out sweetly – peach walls, blond wood, a little garden visible out back – and despite its size it manages not to feel overcrowded even when packed, as it was on the weeknight when we visited. The quality of our tapas, chosen from an impressive list that mixes classic dishes with the less well-known, ranged from reasonable to excellent. Highlights were squid in its own ink, and veal in a cream and brandy sauce; grilled sardines were also good. Two textbook tapas choices – albóndigas and patatas bravas – were not prepared to the classic recipe. Both came in very thin – almost watery – sauces. Originality is laudable, but we're not sure it's a good idea in these cases: these dishes are old favourites. But they certainly weren't bad, and didn't detract from a very pleasant meal, including some bottles of the Spanish lager Estrella.
Babies and children welcome: high chair. Booking advisable dinner Fri, Sat. Separate room for parties, seats 50. **Map 20 C3**.

Ladbroke Grove

★ ★ Café García
248-250 Portobello Road, W11 1LL (7221 6119). Ladbroke Grove tube. **Tapas served** 9am-5pm Mon-Thur; 8am-11pm Fri, Sat; 10am-7pm Sun. **Tapas** £1.50-£5. **Credit** AmEx, MC, V.
Annexed to the veteran Spanish supermarket/ importers R Garcia & Son, this place is just what its name suggests: a café. There is no table service: you point out your tapas choices from under the glass counters at the front and then take a seat; your selections are unceremoniously dished out, warmed up (if necessary) and brought over. It's a straightforward, no-frills set-up – and a tremendous success. The selection of dishes available at any time is not huge, but everything is freshly prepared. We picked a faultless tortilla with chorizo, some albóndigas in a nice, rich ragú, a fine salt-cod empanada and some asparagus wrapped in jamón serrano. A vast paella was hauled out just as we finished eating; it looked fantastic. It was a perfect

Saturday lunchtime refuelling experience – and the clean, classy and bright interior wasn't even that busy though it was market day at Portobello Road. We noted that every other table was populated by Spaniards, which we took as a positive sign. The other remarkable thing was our bill: £21 covered all the food, plus a fantastic dessert (chestnut-cream cake), two espressos and two beers. Top marks.
Babies and children admitted. No-smoking tables. Takeaway service. **Map 19 B2**.

Galicia
323 Portobello Road, W10 5SY (8969 3539). Ladbroke Grove tube. **Lunch served** noon-3pm Tue-Sun. **Dinner served** 7-11.30pm Tue-Sat; 7-10.30pm Sun. **Main courses** £7.90-£13.95. **Tapas** £2.95-£6.50. **Set lunch** £7.50 3 courses; (Sun) £8.50 3 courses. **Credit** AmEx, DC, MC, V.
Most of the restaurants in this section try – with varying degrees of success – to emulate a Spanish tapas bar or taberna; Galicia, on the other hand, is the real thing. The staff are Spanish, the restaurant forming the social hub of upper Portobello's little Hispanic ghetto, the clientele is largely Spanish, and the cooking is convincingly, authentically Spanish. And you might say that the occasionally slow service and the odd substandard plate show a stereotypically Spanish laxness of approach. Our misgivings are minimal, however. Every element of our most recent meal was in order: excellent tapas, such as fried whitebait (fresh fish, crispy batter), chorizo al vino (rich, succulent chunks) and garlic prawns (enormous and perfectly cooked) were followed by substantial, hearty mains. Both hake with clams, prawns and asparagus, and veal escalope with mushrooms boasted large, tender cuts of fish and meat dressed in first-rate sauces. Prices are relatively low; there's a good wine list, including a large cache of Riojas; and an unremarkable list of desserts does nothing to overshadow the rest of the menu.
Babies and children admitted. Booking essential weekends. **Map 19 B1**.

Maida Vale

Mesón Bilbao
33 Malvern Road, NW6 5PS (7328 1744). Maida Vale tube. **Lunch served** noon-3pm Mon-Fri. **Dinner served** 6-11pm Mon-Thur; 7-11.30pm Fri; 6-11.30pm Sat. **Main courses** £9.95-£12.95. **Tapas** £3.50-£6.95. **Credit** MC, V.

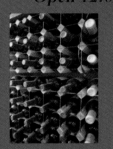

Malvern Road is not the smartest part of NW6, and Mesón Bilbao's dark-beamed decor doesn't aspire to trendiness, but nevertheless this snug little Basque restaurant remains a favourite with a widely varied clientele. The big draw is outstanding fresh fish and seafood, expertly prepared and sourced from the best available in London, with an eye to quality that puts many more celebrated (and more expensive) venues to shame. It pays to follow staff recommendations on what's best that day: our star tapa of fresh squid, simply grilled a la plancha with a slice of lemon, was delicious – first-rate seafood perfectly tenderised. Others, such as octopus a la gallega (with olive oil, rock salt and paprika), lentils with chorizo, and a salty salpicón of braised hake were not quite so special, but still very enjoyable. For mains, the highlights are the classic Basque fish dishes, from sea bream or monkfish simply grilled to merluza a la koskera (hake simmered with olive oil, onions and clams). Mesón Bilbao has its eccentricities – some meat and veg tapas can be disappointingly ordinary – but its pluses make up for them. Service is charming, and wines include quality Spanish labels at very friendly prices.
Babies and children welcome: high chairs. Booking advisable dinner Fri, Sat. Tables outdoors (2, pavement). **Map 1 A3**.

South West
Putney

Olé
240 Upper Richmond Road, SW15 6TG (8788 8009/www.olerestaurants.com). East Putney tube/Putney rail. **Bar Open/tapas served** noon-midnight Mon-Sat; noon-11pm Sun. **Restaurant Meals served** noon-11pm Mon-Sat; noon-10.30pm Sun. **Main courses** £11.50-£14.75. **Tapas** £2.50-£5.55. **Set meal** (noon-6pm Sun) £9.95 2 tapas and glass of wine. **Both Credit** AmEx, DC, JCB, MC, V.
So many Spanish eateries in London are painfully clichéd – whether in their unadventurous menus or their kitsch, touristy interiors. And too often the token clichés mask a mediocre kitchen. So it's refreshing to see new ventures making deliberate departures from convention. Olé – the name is a cliché, but that's as far as it goes – is one such establishment. Recently moved to Putney, it features white walls, floor-to-ceiling windows, blond wood furniture and floors, and no reference whatsoever to tacky pseudo-tabernas. Cooking is Spanish with some Modern European twists. Everything we tried was above average: octopus with paprika was astonishingly tender; prawns in garlic were nice and juicy, as was the pork fillet in a rich, stocky mushroom sauce. Main courses too were good, a fillet steak being particularly notable. On a weeknight the spacious dining room was empty and hushed. This meant it didn't have the bustling warmth of a neighbourhood hangout, but it did get busier as the evening progressed, And with food of this standard it should begin to gain a new loyal following.
Babies and children welcome: high chairs. Book weekends. Disabled: toilet. Restaurant/bar available for hire.

South
Clapham

El Rincón Latino
148 Clapham Manor Street, SW4 6BX (7622 0599). Clapham Common tube. **Dinner served** 6.30-11.30pm Tue-Fri. **Meals served** 11am-11.30pm Sat; 11am-10.30pm Sun. **Main courses** £9.95-£14.95. **Tapas** £3.20-£5.40. **Credit** AmEx, MC, V.
The look here is old-school taberna (terracotta paint, dark wooden furniture, trinkets on the walls). Low lighting and a warm atmosphere make it a popular destination for couples in the evening, but the crowd was fairly mixed on our weeknight visit. And although the place was almost full, service was exceptionally quick and attentive. We

have found the cooking here patchy, and this visit was no exception. Of our choices from the long menu, vegetable and meat tapas were better than seafood options: pincho de cordero (lamb skewer) was delicious, while white asparagus croquettes were fluffy and creamy. But peppers stuffed with salt cod were a bit gloopy, and prawns in garlic were overcooked and lacked flavour (perhaps the alternative, shell-off option is better). It's a crime to get the tapas cliché of calamares wrong, but the verdict was guilty: the squid itself was fine, but the batter was limp and soggy, suggesting the frying had taken place long before. The ambience might draw us back; it's just a shame the cooking is a bit of a lucky dip.
Babies and children welcome: high chairs. Booking essential dinner. Disabled: toilet. Vegetarian menu (tapas). **Map 22 B1**.

Vauxhall

★ Rebato's
169 South Lambeth Road, SW8 1XW (7735 6388/www.rebatos.com). Stockwell tube. **Tapas bar Open** 5.30-10.45pm Mon-Fri; 7-11pm Sat. **Tapas** £3.25-£5.50. **Restaurant Lunch served** noon-2.30pm Mon-Fri. **Dinner served** 7-10.45pm Mon-Sat. **Main courses** £11.95. **Both Credit** AmEx, DC, MC, V.
The lone Spanish establishment in the otherwise predominantly Portuguese enclave of South Lambeth Road, Rebato's makes no attempt to jostle territorially. With net curtains and a front door that remains closed, it keeps a low profile while its neighbours spill out on to the pavement in European alfresco style. The high quality of its cooking means it can afford to maintain an air of quiet dignity without having to worry about filling tables. Plumping for tapas in the front-of-house room (we could have also eaten in the restaurant at the back, where a larger à la carte menu is offered), we enjoyed some superb dishes from a compact but intelligent selection, including baby squid with garlic, sautéed oyster mushrooms and grilled langoustines; best of all was a (tapas-sized) lamb shank. Only kidneys in sherry weren't up to the standard of everything else (they were overdone), but that was the exception in an otherwise faultless line-up. With expert, committed service and good wines and sherries to boot, this remains one of the finest tapas restaurants in town.
Babies and children admitted. Booking essential (restaurant). **Map 16 L13**.

South East
Herne Hill

Number 22
22 Half Moon Lane, SE24 9HU (7095 9922/www.number-22.com). Herne Hill rail/ 3, 37, 68 bus. **Meals served** noon-11pm Mon-Sat; noon-10.30pm Sun. **Tapas** £3-£8. **Credit** MC, V.
Having established itself as Herne Hill's best (OK, only) restaurant for Mediterranean food, Number 22's Hispanophile owner-chef Chris Adnitt now focuses on tapas. The bar is more than an adjunct, so the cocktails are great. But if you're here for dinner, try a palate-soothing manzanilla and then choose from an extensive menu whose highlights include pan-fried artichokes, couscous with sun-dried tomatoes and a sampler of seafood with harissa that featured luscious king prawns but slightly chewy squid. Other favourites were padrón peppers, and halloumi, beetroot and pine-nut salad (really lovely, though it could have done with a bit more halloumi). If you want a substantial meal, the paella (for two) is made to a very high standard. Several desserts are chocolate-heavy, but for those not so keen on chocolate, mil hoja (millefeuille) with sambayon cream and fresh oranges, and a regional cheese platter were both good. The wine list features some interesting bottles: our £20 Syrah from La Mancha was superb. Busy on a drizzly Monday evening, Number 22 has found a slot among the new gastropubs and cafés in the area.

Interview
SAM HART

Who are you?
Co-owner of **Fino** (*see p252*), and co-author of *Modern Spanish Cooking* (Quadrille) – both with brother Eddie.

Eating in London: what's good about it?
You can eat fantastic food of every possible different sort, from the smartest classic French or traditional British to Thai and Chinese. It's so varied – particularly if you're used to living in a place like Spain, where all the local restaurants would be Spanish except for one greasy Chinese.

What's bad about it?
There is no relation between price and quality. You can go to a restaurant and pay £60-£70 per head and be looked after badly, or go to a gastropub and pay £10-£15 per head and it will be brilliant.

Which are your favourite London restaurants?
I love the food at **Yauatcha** (*see p70*) and think they're the best at that type of Chinese cooking. I also love **Esarn Kheaw** (*see p263*) – a great cheap and cheerful Thai restaurant.

What single thing would most improve London's restaurant scene?
More 'everyday' restaurants. A lot of restaurants are really ripping people off. For £50-£60 per head you have unbelievable choice, but London needs more good places for £30 a head.

What's your advice on choosing sherry to go with food?
The easiest sherries are the lighter styles (Manzanilla, Manzanilla Pasada and Fino). These are wonderful with cold meats, olives, almonds, fish and seafood of every kind. The heavier sherries are harder to pair, but great combinations are Amontillado with rice dishes, game and lean pork; Oloroso with cheese, foie gras or nutty tarts; and Pedro Jiménez with chocolate.

Any hot tips for the coming year?
Bar eating is the next big thing.

RESTAURANTS

Babies and children admitted. No smoking. Tables outdoors (4, patio; 2, pavement). **Map 23 A5**.

London Bridge & Borough

★ Tapas Brindisa
18-20 Southwark Street, SE1 1TJ (7357 8880/ www.brindisa.com). London Bridge tube/rail. **Tapas served** noon-11pm Mon-Thur; 9am-11am, noon-11pm Fri, Sat. **Tapas** £3-£8. **Credit** MC, V.

The interior is basic and hard-edged and you can't book, but this class act on the edge of Borough Market packs them in, with credit going to the owners' vision to showcase quality Spanish imports beyond their Borough Market stall and Exmouth Market shop. Our most recent meal was superb. Even when just opening tins, say for a selection of cured fish (sardines, tuna loin smoked mackerel, anchovies), the result is fat, succulent and of the highest quality. Portions are small plates rather than tiny dishes and choosing three or four will provide an enjoyable mix of vibrant tastes. A nicely done classic Catalan dish of spinach with pine nuts and raisins teamed well with first-class chorizo cooked in cider, while pan-fried asparagus with fried duck egg and serrano ham was perfect, full of rich, multi-layered flavours – such cooking manages to be distinctive and original yet true to its roots. The same attention to detail is applied to the drinks, with a sound selection of sherries and a wine list that includes many recent Spanish labels. The service is delightful.
Babies and children admitted. Booking not accepted. Disabled: toilet. No smoking. Tables outdoors (6, pavement). **Map 11 R8**.

East

Bethnal Green

Laxeiro
93 Columbia Road, E2 7RG (7729 1147). Bethnal Green tube/Liverpool Street tube/rail/8, 26, 48, 55 bus. **Tapas served** noon-3pm, 7-11pm Tue-Sat; 9am-3pm Sun. **Tapas** £2.95-£9.50. **Credit** AmEx, DC, MC, V.

A visit to this bright café on Columbia Road, named after Galician avant-garde artist Laxeiro, is always a treat, but on a sunny Sunday, when the flower market is in full swing, getting a table here is the equivalent to winning El Gordo (you can't book on Sundays). A splendid job has been done of fashioning a small space into a cosy, welcoming place to eat. We enjoyed our dinner, but this perhaps had more to do with the environs than the cooking, which was reasonable but could have been better. Freshness of fish and meat was our biggest misgiving. The albóndigas didn't taste freshly prepared and the calamares, though battered well, were a bit chewy. 'BBQ' marlin seemed a bit dry, but the flavour was fine. On the other hand, chorizo in red wine was spot-on, as were the simple vegetable dishes we tried, such as asparagus and pea revuelto (in other words, jazzed-up scrambled eggs), and broad beans with manchego cheese. Portions are generous; advice not to order more than five dishes between two proved to be sound. The wine list is extensive and reasonably priced, covering sherries, Malagan wine and cavas, though most opt for Rioja.
Babies and children welcome: booster seats. Booking advisable; not accepted Sun. Tables outdoors (3, pavement). Takeaway service. **Map 6 S3**.

Victoria Park

Mar i Terra
223 Grove Road, E3 5SN (8981 9998/ www.mariterra.co.uk). Mile End tube then 277 bus. **Meals served** 6-11pm Tue; noon-11pm Wed-Sat; noon-10pm Sun. **Tapas** £3.50-£8.75. **Credit** MC, V.

Aside from the addition of loud paint and cheapish furniture, this airy space looks much as it did when it was still an organic gastropub called the Crown, with picture windows looking towards Victoria Park and a few tables out front. And the tapas menu, an appetising jumble of dishes ancient and modern, will be familiar to anyone who's visited any of the other restaurants in the Mar i Terra group. The pimientos de padron (small green peppers) were greasy and the higadillos de pollo (chicken livers) lacked texture, but everything else was successful; we especially enjoyed a zingy portion of grilled chorizo, a creamily moreish rice dish arroz a banda and some good quality boquerones. Desserts too were a treat; none was better than the turron de jijona (almond nougat), served with a small glass of moscatel dessert wine. Service was seemingly available only in Spanish, but we pointed and mimed and eventually got what we wanted. The wine list includes some wonderfully enthusiastic descriptions; our bottle of red was pinned as like 'Ornette Coleman suddenly appearing at a chamber concert', but was almost smooth enough to remind us of the peerless 1955 album *Clifford Brown with Strings*.
Babies and children welcome: high chairs. Disabled: toilet. Separate room for parties, seating 20 and 30. Tables outdoors (5, terrace). **For branches (Mar i Terra, 'Za London) see index**.

North

Camden Town & Chalk Farm

★ El Parador
245 Eversholt Street, NW1 1BA (7387 2789). Mornington Crescent tube. **Lunch served** noon-3pm Mon-Fri. **Dinner served** 6-11pm Mon-Thur; 6-11.30pm Fri, Sat; 6.30-9.30pm Sun. **Tapas** £3.30-£6. **Credit** MC, V.

A full house by 7pm on a Monday has got to bode well. We hadn't expected much from this place: the location is unremarkable, the decor unassuming (though not unpleasant). It's only when you read the menu that things get interesting. The list of dishes and choice of ingredients reflect a grown-up, forward-thinking approach to tapas cooking that is painfully scarce in the capital. There are a few classics to please the unadventurous – calamares, albóndigas, chorizo, and so on, all of which are done very well. But the treats are elsewhere, in some delicious, creative combinations. Things were good from the start: our bread was served with a wonderfully aromatic hot paste of broad beans, rosemary and roast garlic. And it got better. Slow-roasted pork belly was thick and sticky. Morcilla with chestnut mushrooms, green beans, feta and toasted pine nuts was superb. A roast beetroot, feta and rocket salad was a revelation. And the list goes on. Virtually

Cambio de Tercio. See p255.

everything we tried was top-notch. Yes, a chicory salad was overdressed and our espressos weren't great, but by that point we were well and truly sold.
Babies and children admitted. Bookings accepted for 3 or more only. Separate room for parties, seats 30. Tables outdoors (10, garden). Vegetarian menu. **Map 27 D3**.

★ Jamón Jamón

38 Parkway, NW1 7AH (7284 0606). Camden Town tube. **Meals served** noon-11.30pm Mon-Thur, Sun; noon-12.30am Fri, Sat. **Tapas** £3.25-£6.95. **Set meal** (noon-5pm Mon-Fri) 2 dishes for the price of 1. **Credit** AmEx, DC, MC, V.
Although the updated decor of this comfortable, cheery neighbourhood tapas joint aspires towards the sophisticated, the menu promises nothing spectacular (mostly standards like calamares and chorizo al vino). But reliable simplicity is precisely the appeal of this kind of cooking. We enjoyed jamón serrano, its salty, succulent slices still glistening from fresh carving. Pollo al ajillo (chicken in white wine and garlic sauce) was also respectable, the meat tender, the broth assertive, while bacalao con tomate was fresh, flaky chunks of cod fillet in a straightforward but authentic sauce. But there were some notable disappointments, proving that a modest remit still leaves plenty of room for mediocre execution. Stuffed peppers (baked with cheese) were poor: multiple stages of cooking had robbed the ingredients of texture and taste. And the diced potatoes that came with various dishes (such as the ubiquitous patatas bravas) had a starchy bite that bespoke a frozen past. Still, our house Rioja was enjoyable, the service was attentive, and this remains a shrewd choice for a cheap, hearty meal.
Babies and children welcome: high chairs. Booking advisable dinner and weekends. Vegetarian menu. **Map 27 C2**.
For branches (La Siesta, Sangria, Tapeo) see index.

Crouch End

La Bota

31 Broadway Parade, Tottenham Lane, N8 9DB (8340 3082). Finsbury Park tube/rail then 91, W7 bus. **Lunch served** noon-2.30pm Mon-Sat. **Dinner served** 6-11pm Mon-Thur; 6-11.30pm

Fri, Sat. **Meals served** noon-11pm Sun. **Main courses** £7.50-£11.95. **Tapas** £2-£4.50. **Credit** MC, V.
Tapas aren't complicated, but it's still a surprise to find a restaurant that does them consistently well and with panache. La Bota is a paragon of the genre. The Spanish proprietor has opted for authenticity, decorating the two-tiered dining room with rustic furniture and repro Spanish artwork. Service was exceptionally attentive on a recent visit, even though the place filled up quickly. And most importantly, the food, though not dazzling, ticked all the relevant boxes: what we ate was hearty, fresh and tasty. We couldn't fault our selection of rape al pisto (monkfish in a tomato and vegetable sauce), chistorra (sausage in cider), tortilla de patatas, and spinach with raisins and pine nuts. Unusually, kidneys in sherry was done well, while grilled sardines were some of the best we've had on these shores. We didn't care much for our house red (opt for the Rioja instead, though it's little more expensive), but that is a minor gripe. If you don't expect surprises or sophistication, just good food, you'll leave satisfied.
Babies and children welcome: high chairs. Booking advisable dinner Fri, Sat. Takeaway service.

Harringay

La Viña

3 Wightman Road, N4 1RQ (8340 5400). Harringay rail/29, 341 bus. **Meals served** 5pm-midnight Mon-Sat. **Main courses** £8.95-£10.95. **Tapas** £3-£5. **Credit** MC, V.
This unpretentious and highly amenable neighbourhood tapas joint, tucked away just north of Finsbury Park, continues to do a successful line in classic Spanish comfort food. There's little to dislike: the trad two-tiered dining space, with the odd splash of decorative authenticity, is comfortable; staff are attentive; and the cooking, while not spectacular, is reliable. The menu is largely a line-up of old favourites, but what we ate was tasty and fresh: grilled sardines; a well-dressed salad of green beans with red onion and raw garlic; a fabada of chorizo and beans. Cod with chickpeas would have benefited from a bit more fish, but it was still good; lamb in a lamb stew (estofada) could have been a little bit juicier. A tapa

of quails sounded interesting, but was no longer available (although perhaps a silver lining can be found in the fact that they had recently been fresh, rather than dragged from the freezer). However, none of these quibbles spoiled the experience. The house Rioja was decent, and a moist tarta de santiago (almond cake) wrapped things up nicely. Not a destination venue, but a very sound choice should you find yourself in the neighbourhood.
Babies and children welcome: high chairs. Booking advisable. No-smoking tables. Restaurant available for hire (Sun). Takeaway service.

Muswell Hill

Café Loco

266 Muswell Hill Broadway, entrance on Muswell Hill, N10 2QR (8444 3370). Highgate tube then 43, 134 bus. **Open** 6pm-2am Mon-Wed; 6pm-3am Thur-Sat; 4.30pm-1am Sun. **Dinner served** 6-10.30pm Mon-Sat; 4.30pm-1am Sun. **Main courses** £7-£10.50. **Tapas** £2.50-£5.95. **Credit** AmEx, DC, MC, V.
Dining is only half the equation at this lively bar-restaurant: drinking and dancing are given just as much attention (half the floor space has bar seating rather than dining tables, and a DJ plays most nights). So our culinary expectations were not very high. Yet there were some pleasant surprises. Albóndigas – large, freshly made meatballs – were moist, expertly seasoned and dressed in a mellow tomato sauce. Calamares, so often either chewy or deep-fried to destruction, were very good, their tender flesh coated in a crisp and light (in both colour and texture) batter. A surprise menu entrant – scallops with prawns in a rich fish sauce – arrived sans prawns, but was tasty nevertheless. Other things were more as predicted: some jamón serrano looked as if it came from a packet (it tasted OK, though), and a tapa of garlic chicken was unnecessarily oily. But the odd culinary shortfall doesn't detract from what is, all in all, a successful formula: this is an unpretentious local hangout that is first and foremost about having fun. The decent grub is a bonus.
Babies and children admitted (until 9.30pm). Booking essential dinner Fri, Sat. Dress: no tracksuits or caps. Entertainment: DJ 10.30pm Mon, Wed-Sun. Restaurant available for hire.

RESTAURANTS

Thai

With the explosion of Thai food in pubs and bars, red and green curries are now as familiar as roghan gosht and vindaloo. But there's a difference between good Thai food and great Thai food. Plenty of neighbourhood Thais serve a perfectly decent meal, so we've pulled these into a separate box (see p269 **Local Thais**), but the venues given a main listing are where to find the complex flavours and spicing that characterise the best Thai cuisine. As well as familiar faces such as **Nipa**, **Nahm** and **Blue Elephant** – all still serving excellent food in classy surroundings – there are some impressive newcomers. **Isarn** in Islington (which opened in 2005) and **Sukho** in Fulham (2004) are already making waves with their innovative cooking. Then there's the handful of family-run neighbourhood Thais with a truly inspired chef in the kitchen; **Laicram**, **Mantanah** and **Esarn Kheaw** deserve special mention.

Central

Belgravia

★ Nahm

The Halkin, Halkin Street, SW1X 7DJ (7333 1234/www.nahm.como.bz). Hyde Park Corner tube. **Lunch served** noon-2.30pm Mon-Fri. **Dinner served** 7-11pm Mon-Sat, 7-10pm Sun. **Main courses** £11-£16.50. **Set lunch** £26 3 courses. **Set dinner** £49.50 4 courses. **Credit** AmEx, DC, JCB, MC, V.

A visit to Nahm is loaded with high expectations. Australian-born founder David Thompson is the world's most renowned Thai chef, is the author of the award-winning cookbook and magnus opus *Thai Food*, and is so well regarded in Bangkok that he teaches Thai cooking to chefs there. Although not present often at this London restaurant, every dish from this menu of recreated Thai courtly cooking was faultless. The dining room, a sophisticated, stone-lined space in Belgravia's sleek Halkin hotel, has annoying acoustics, but this seems a minor complaint if you are here for the food. As in Thailand, the savoury dishes arrive at the same time, so there are no starters or main courses. Patient waiters will steer you through a menu that strays far from the familiar. Jungle curry with prawns and heart of coconut palm was full of steamy, other-worldly flavours, but quite incendiary. We were glad to have the soothing fresh coconut creaminess of dtom kek (an aromatic, lemony soup with smoked red mullet) to douse the flames. Trout and pomelo salad came with a hidden nugget of trout caviar. Highly palatable wines from the Halkin estate in Australia's Hunter Valley accompanied the feast. Yes, prices are high, but it's worth splashing out if you have a serious interest in Thai cooking.
Book dinner. Disabled: toilet. Dress: smart casual. No smoking. Separate room for parties, seats 36. Vegetarian menu. **Map 9 G9.**

City

Nakhon Thai

10 Copthall Avenue, EC2R 7DJ (7628 1555/ www.nakhonthai.co.uk). Moorgate tube/rail. **Meals served** 11.30am-10pm Mon-Fri. **Main courses** £5-£19. **Set meal** £22.95 3 courses. **Credit** AmEx, MC, V.

We were the only diners not in suits at lunchtime at this popular City restaurant, which should give you some idea of what to expect. Food is well above average, served in a spartan dining room

with a thatched bar and flat-faced Buddha carvings on the walls. The interior looks as if it might once have been a dance studio, with its long wall mirror, the raised floor at the back, and the intriguing scuffs on the walls; in fact, it was previously an Indian restaurant. Although the menu meanders through familiar royal Thai territory, it contains some adventurous flourishes, including scallops in the shell with prawn and chilli paste, and a beautifully presented lobster yellow curry. Of the dishes we sampled, the tom kha gai was excellent, a perfectly judged mix of kaffir lime leaves, galangal, chicken, chilli and coconut cream. Thai fish cakes were given extra zing by thin slices of lime zest. Our favourite main course was moo tod prik khing: lean pork and crisp green pea pods fried with lime leaves and a tasty, but mild, red curry paste. A satisfying experience, but a bit more fire in the chilli dishes would have been nice.
Babies and children admitted. Booking advisable. No-smoking tables. Separate room for parties, seats 16. Takeaway service; delivery service (7-10pm within 3-mile radius). **Map 12 Q6.** **For branch see index.**

Marylebone

★ Busaba Eathai

8-13 Bird Street, W1U 1BU (7518 8080). Bond Street tube. **Meals served** noon-11pm Mon-Thur; noon-11.30pm Fri, Sat; noon-10pm Sun. **Main courses** £5.50-£9. **Credit** AmEx, MC, V.

Style is paramount at this mini-chain (three outlets in central London), where the hand of Alan Yau is evident in the streamlined, precisely designed interior. People share the chunky wooden tables, food arrives in a trice, it is consumed quickly, then customers move on, making space for the next wave of diners. Huge lanterns create pools of light over each table (set with place mats, chopsticks, Thai sauce bottles and not much else), and theatrical waiters buzz around like black-clad hoverflies. With the fast-food concept, there's always a risk that cooking gets rushed, and this is what we found with the stir-fry of cod fillet and krachai (galangal, aka thai ginger): it was dry and lacking in flavour or identity. Khanom jin noodles was a big improvement, drenched in a subtle and savoury green curry sauce. Probably the biggest hits were kwiatew pad thai – an upmarket version with smoked chicken and holy basil – and an inspired fruit smoothie with jasmine, passionfruit and yoghurt.

Babies and children admitted. Bookings not accepted. Disabled: toilet. No smoking. Takeaway service. **Map 9 G6.** **For branches see index.**

★ Eat-Thai.net

22 St Christopher's Place, W1U 1NP (7486 0777/www.eatthai.net). Bond Street tube. **Lunch served** noon-3pm, **dinner served** 6-10.30pm daily. **Main courses** £8.25-£15.95. **Set lunch** £8.95 2 courses. **Set dinner** £25-£35 per person (minimum 2) 3 courses. **Credit** AmEx, MC, V.

For consistency, this has to be one of our favourite Thai restaurants; every time we visit, the food is exemplary. Hidden away on a tiny alley off Oxford Street, Eat-Thai has two dining rooms – a narrow strip of tables for couples at street level, and a bistro-like area downstairs with tables set into booths under the arches of an old wine cellar. Chef Nipon Senkaewsai, a veteran of the Bangkok five-star hotel circuit, has produced a huge menu of royal Thai classics. Esarn dishes from north-east Thailand and intriguing Thai-fusion creations. In the first wave of food, moo muk kha was sublime: flavoursome strips of crispy fried pork with a sweet chilli dip and golden balls of deep-fried rice. Duck spring rolls, bound with seaweed, were tastier without the slightly overpowering plum sauce. To follow, honey-marinated Esarn-style pork was grilled to perfection, just as it would be on the hawker stands on the banks of the Mekong. Chicken jungle curry (the one without coconut milk) was also well-judged and searingly hot, just as it should be. Factor in prompt service and faultless presentation (on angular pieces of Thai porcelain) and Eat-Thai scores top marks.
Babies and children welcome: high chairs. No smoking. Takeaway service. **Map 9 G6.**

Soho

Patara

15 Greek Street, W1D 4DP (7437 1071/ www.pataralondon.com). Leicester Square or Tottenham Court Road tube. **Lunch served** noon-2.30pm Mon-Sat. **Dinner served** 6.30-10.30pm daily. **Main courses** £12.95-£15.50. **Set lunch** £11.95 2 courses, £14.95 3 courses. **Set dinner** (6.30-7.30pm) £13.95 2 courses. **Credit** AmEx, DC, JCB, MC, V.

'A triumph of style over content' was the verdict after our latest visit to this exquisitely designed restaurant in the post-production quarter of Soho. With its moody lighting and Zen-inspired interior, Patara promises a lot, but we found good ingredients swamped by heavy-handed sauces. It's a shame, as the interior is a stunning piece of design – friezes of lotus-blossom tiles, flickering tealights, a teak spirit house in the centre of the room, and pin-sharp spotlights creating small pools of intimacy at each table. Dinner began with grilled prawns and beef in betel leaf parcels, nicely presented but rather insipid. Prawn and duck paper rolls were better, with an unusual selection of stuffings and a tangy lime and chilli dip. The menu makes a big deal of gourmet ingredients; red curry with Gressingham duck was enlivened by zingy little slices of kumquat. However, pad po tak (mixed seafood curry) was a disappointment: mussels, scallops and cod drowning in a syrupy, over-sweet sauce. Presentation was beautiful, but overall we expected more for our money. We've heard that standards are higher at the three branches, in South Kensington, Knightsbridge and near Oxford Circus.
Booking advisable. No-smoking tables. Vegetarian menu. **Map 17 K6.** **For branches see index.**

West

Bayswater

★ Nipa

Royal Lancaster Hotel, Lancaster Terrace, W2 2TY (7262 6737/www.royallancaster.com). Lancaster Gate tube.

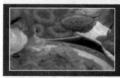

Bar **Open** 11am-11pm Mon-Sat; 11am-10.30pm Sun.
Restaurant **Lunch served** noon-2pm Mon-Fri. **Dinner served** 6.30-10.30pm Mon-Sat. **Main courses** £7.85-£14. **Set meal** £25-£28 4 courses.
Both **Credit** AmEx, DC, MC, V.
A tiny jewel-box of a restaurant, hidden behind the concrete façade of the iconic 1960s Royal Lancaster Hotel. Like many hotel restaurants, Nipa feels a little trapped in time, but the food is artfully prepared and full of flavour. The dining room is decked out with gaudy Benjarong china and Thai-style scroll-work. A plate-glass window looks out over the Hyde Park fountains. The menu doesn't try to be too ambitious; most dishes are familiar royal Thai standards. However, all the ingredients are impressively fresh and the combinations of spices are inspired. For starters, yum nuea (spicy beef salad) had plenty of punch, courtesy of some strips of very hot green chilli, while the simple glass noodle soup was perked up by garlic and coriander-scented chicken meatballs. Green curry with chicken had just the right level of chilli zip, and was well complemented by creamy coconut rice. The best came last: pla nueng ma nuo, a steamed fillet of white fish, swimming in a deliciously zesty lemon and chilli sauce. A feast and worth every penny.
Babies and children welcome: high chairs.
Booking essential Fri, Sat. Disabled: toilet (hotel). Dress: smart casual. Takeaway service. Vegetarian menu. **Map 8 D6**.

Tawana
3 Westbourne Grove, W2 4UA (7229 3785/ www.tawana.co.uk). Bayswater tube. **Lunch served** noon-3pm, **dinner served** 6-11pm Mon-Sat. **Meals served** noon-10pm Sun. **Main courses** £5.75-£17.95. **Set meal** £15.95 2 courses. **Minimum** £10 per person. **Credit** MC, V.
With dinky tables covered in white tablecloths, and a glass display case full of fruit, Tawana could easily have been an English teashop in a former life. But that was before the potted palms and Thai wood carvings arrived. These days, the place feels quite upmarket for a neighbourhood Thai, but without being snooty (quite an achievement for this part of London). Dinner kicked off with intriguing moo sarong, little birds' nests of fried yellow noodles with a hidden payload of minced pork with garlic and coriander. Tom yam goong (lemongrass-scented prawn soup) was less successful – just too much going on with the flavours. Curries restored our confidence. Green curry with chicken was just-so: complex, exotic and full of va-va-voom. We were also impressed by hor mok pla: white fish in a red curry sauce, steamed into a moist cake in a parcel of banana leaves. The food is highly authentic and the menu covers all the bases, but the small portions may disappoint big eaters. And be wary of the tables in the window, where you can feel like an exhibit for passing tourists.
Babies and children admitted. Booking advisable. Separate room for parties, seats 50. Takeaway service. Vegetarian menu. **Map 7 B6**.
For branches (Thai Hut, Thai Kitchen) see index.

Shepherd's Bush

★ ★ Esarn Kheaw
314 Uxbridge Road, W12 7LJ (8743 8930/ www.esarnkheaw.com). Shepherd's Bush tube/207, 260, 283 bus. **Lunch served** noon-3pm Mon-Fri. **Dinner served** 6-11pm daily. **Main courses** £5.95-£8.95. **Credit** AmEx, DC, MC, V.
Pastel green is the dominant colour at small, completely authentic Esarn Kheaw. The walls are green, the ceiling is green, so are the napkins and plates – but this is no great failing, as food takes priority over the interior design. The owner, the ever-formal Mr M Puntar, moved to London from north-east Thailand, cooking for the Intercontinental in Park Lane before branching out on his own in 1993. Since then, he has never strayed far from his roots; food here tastes exactly as it does along the Thai-Laos border. We could tell

from the first bite that everything was own-made. Esarn-style sausage was delicious, with a subtle sour flavour that really grew on us. Likewise, the sweet, crisp spring rolls were some of the best we've tried. With the mains, we could have been more adventurous (there's Esarn-style catfish, for instance). 'Tiger Cry' (Thai-style steak) had a fine marinade and a fiery sauce, but at the end of the day, it was just a steak. In contrast, the house pad thai was spectacular: sweet, flavoursome and full of peanuts, egg and fresh spring onion.
Babies and children welcome: high chairs. Booking advisable. Takeaway service. **Map 20 B1**.

South West
Fulham

Blue Elephant
4-6 Fulham Broadway, SW6 1AA (7385 6595/ ww.blueelephant.com). Fulham Broadway tube. **Lunch served** noon-2.30pm Mon-Fri; noon-3pm Sun. **Dinner served** 7pm-midnight Mon-Thur; 6.30pm-midnight Fri, Sat; 7-10.30pm Sun. **Main courses** £10.60-£28. **Set meal** £33-£39 3/4 courses. **Set buffet** (lunch Sun) £22 adults, £11 children. **Credit** AmEx, DC, MC, V.
A carnival atmosphere pervades at this well-known and lavish restaurant. The interior is a rainforest of palms, ferns and topiary, with artificial waterfalls, ponds full of koi carp and

flourishes of orchids. It's good fun, in a Las Vegas floorshow kind of way – and the greenery creates a sense of privacy in what would otherwise be an aircraft hangar of a dining room. As with other branches of the chain (in Paris, Bangkok, Moscow), the menu is well thought out, though some of the more exotic-sounding items are actually familiar Thai favourites dolled up with flashy names. Chillied lamb turned out to be a variation on pad kraprow (a spicy stir-fry with basil leaves and green peppercorns): tasty, but not as interesting as it sounded. Nevertheless, the flavours were well crafted, as they were in the orange prawn curry (a creamy, tamarind-flavoured concoction full of cherry tomatoes and sweet strips of jackfruit). Both these main courses built on competent starters: moist prawns in sweetcorn batter; and a tart, fragrant salad with roasted coconut, tamarind, prawns and crunchy banana blossom. Service is friendly but brisk – leave a dish unattended and you might lose it.
Babies and children welcome: colouring books; face painting (Sun); high chairs. Booking advisable. Disabled: toilet. Dress: smart casual; no shorts. Takeaway service; delivery service (over £30 within SW6). Vegetarian menu. **Map 13 B13**.

Saran Rom NEW
Waterside Tower, The Boulevard, Imperial Wharf, Townmead Road, SW6 2UB (7751 3111/ www.saranrom.com). Fulham Broadway tube

Saran Rom

RESTAURANTS

then *391, C3 bus.* **Meals served** noon-11.30pm daily. **Main courses** £6.50-£18.95. **Set lunch** £10 2 courses. **Set dinner** £25 per person (minimum 2) 2 courses. **Credit** AmEx, MC, V.
Inspired by Bangkok's Vimanmek palace, Saran Rom rolls out a princely design aimed at a wealthy clientele. Most impressive is the main bar, a long, high space with flamboyant teak carvings and panelling (created in Thailand by master craftsmen), hanging silks, a statement staircase and oriental lanterns. It occupies a prime site on the lower floors of a riverside apartment building – complete with outdoor terrace – but the food doesn't quite live up to the sumptuous surroundings. At these prices we were hoping for more than solid yet unremarkable cooking. Nevertheless, the decor alone warrants a visit. Wooden staircases spiral up from the lobby, lights are shaded by strings of faux jasmine blossoms and the wood-panelled bar looks out over the Thames. Our starters were tiny but tasty; khanom jeeb (steamed Thai dumplings stuffed with chicken, peanuts and tamarind) and chor ladda (flower-shaped dumplings with chicken and prawn, dyed a striking eggshell blue) were both competently rendered. Mains were more variable. Orange curry with pork was pleasantly infused with the scent of lime leaves, but venison stir-fry was bland and insipid, closer to Chinese boiled beef than Thai game. Good service, however, was a plus. Order the £8 Irish coffee just to see it prepared, flamed at the table in a wine glass frosted with caramelised sugar.
Babies and children welcome: high chairs. Disabled: lift; toilet. No-smoking tables. Separate rooms for parties, seating 8, 25, 35 and 110. Tables outdoors (28, riverside patio). Takeaway service. **Map 21 A2.**

★ Sukho NEW

855 Fulham Road, SW6 5HJ (7371 7600). Parsons Green tube. **Lunch served** noon-3pm, **dinner served** 6.30-11pm daily. **Main courses** £8.95-£12.95. **Set lunch** £7.95 1 course, £10.95 2 courses. **Credit** MC, V.
For once, here's an upmarket Thai restaurant that places as much emphasis on flavour as on appearance. Located at the Putney Bridge end of Fulham Road, Sukho serves food that could hold its own in any five-star hotel in Bangkok – which is appropriate, as the chef used to cook at the famous Oriental hotel in the Thai capital. The dining room has moody colonial overtones, with lots of dark wood and starched linen, and presentation is exquisite; the psychedelic, salt-glazed porcelain is particularly striking. The menu steps outside the usual Thai comfort zone, and diners are well rewarded for trying new things. Thai tuna salad was a stunning carpaccio of raw tuna in a spicy, mint-scented dressing; crispy vegetable tempura came topped with sweet, tangy tamarind and roast coconut chutney. All mains were excellent, but nothing really matched the moo ping: long skewers of moist, marinated pork, char-grilled and rolled in crushed coriander seeds. The wine list rarely exceeds £25, yet comprises a grown-up selection of New and Old World bottles. A treat.
Babies and children admitted. Booking advisable. Takeaway service.

Putney

Thai Square

Embankment, 2 Lower Richmond Road, SW15 1LB (8780 1811/www.thaisq.com). Putney Bridge tube/14, 22 bus.
Bar Open/snacks served noon-midnight Mon-Thur; noon-2am Fri, Sat; noon-10.30pm Sun. **Restaurant Lunch served** noon-2pm daily. **Dinner served** 5.30-11pm Mon-Sat; 5.30-10.30pm Sun. **Main courses** £7.95-£23. **Set dinner** £35 per person (minimum 2) 3 courses, £40 per person (minimum 2) 4 courses. *Both* **Credit** MC, V.
The flagship branch of the Thai Square chain features postcard-perfect views of Putney Bridge (during the Boat Race, you won't stand a chance of getting a table). It's a strikingly designed building (it used to house fine-dining establishment

Menu

We've tried to give the most useful Thai food terms here, including variant spellings. However, these are no more than English transliterations of the original Thai script, and so are subject to considerable variation. Word divisions vary as well: thus, kwaitiew, kwai teo and guey teow are all acceptable spellings for noodles.

Thailand abandoned chopsticks in the 19th century in favour of chunky steel spoons and forks. Using your fingers is usually fine, and essential if you order satay sticks or spare ribs.

USEFUL TERMS

Khantoke: originally a north-eastern banquet conducted around a low table while seated on traditional triangular cushions – some restaurants have khantoke seating.
Khing: with ginger.
Op or **ob:** baked.
Pad, pat or **phad:** stir-fried.
Pet or **ped:** hot (spicy).
Prik: chilli.
Tod, tort, tord or **taud:** deep-fried.
Tom: boiled.

STARTERS

Khanom jeep or **ka nom geeb:** dim sum. Little dumplings of minced pork, bamboo shoots and water chestnuts, wrapped in an egg and rice (wun tun) pastry, then steamed.
Khanom pang na koong: prawn sesame toast.
Kratong thong: tiny crispy batter cups ('top hats') filled with mixed vegetables and/or minced meat.
Miang: savoury appetisers with a variety of constituents (mince, ginger, peanuts, roasted coconut, for instance), wrapped in betel leaves.
Popia or **porpia:** spring rolls.
Tod mun pla or **tauk manpla:** small fried fish cakes (should be lightly rubbery in consistency) with virtually no 'fishy' smell or taste.

SOUPS

Poh tak or **tom yam potag:** hot and sour mixed seafood soup.
Tom kha gai or **gai tom kar:** hot and sour chicken soup with coconut milk.
Tom yam or **tom yum:** a hot and sour soup, smelling of lemongrass. **Tom yam koong** is with prawns; **tom yam gai** with chicken; **tom yam hed** with mushrooms.

RICE

Khao, kow or **khow:** rice.
Khao nao: sticky rice.
Khao pat: fried rice.
Khao suay: steamed rice.
Pat khai: egg-fried rice.

SALADS

Laab or **larb:** minced and cooked meat incorporating lime juice and other ingredients like ground rice and herbs.
Som tam: a popular cold salad of grated green papaya.
Yam or **yum:** refers to any tossed salad, hot or cold, but it is often hot and sour,

flavoured with lemon and chilli. This type of yam is originally from the north-east of Thailand, where the Laotian influence is greatest.
Yam nua: hot and sour beef salad.
Yam talay: hot and sour seafood salad (served cold).

NOODLES

Generally speaking, noodles are eaten in greater quantities in the north of Thailand. There are many types of **kwaitiew** or **guey teow** noodles. Common ones include **sen mee:** rice vermicelli; **sen yai** (river rice noodles): a broad, flat, rice noodle; **sen lek:** a medium flat noodle, used to make pad Thai; **ba mee:** egg noodles; and **woon sen** (cellophane noodle): transparent vermicelli made from soy beans or other pulses. These are often prepared as stir-fries.

The names of the numerous noodle dishes depend on the combination of other ingredients. Common dishes are:
Khao soi: chicken curry soup with egg noodles; a Burmese/Thai dish, referred to as the national dish of Burma.
Mee krob or **mee grob:** sweet crispy fried vermicelli.
Pad si-ewe or **cee eaw:** noodles fried with mixed meat in soy sauce.
Pad Thai: stir-fried noodles with shrimps (or chicken and pork), beansprouts and salted turnips, garnished with ground peanuts.

CURRIES

Thai curries differ quite markedly from the Indian varieties. Thais cook them for a shorter time, and use thinner sauces. Flavours and ingredients are different too. There are several common types of curry paste; these are used to name the curry, with the principal ingredients listed thereafter.
Gaeng, kaeng or **gang:** the generic name for curry. Yellow curry is the mildest; green curry (**gaeng keaw wan** or **kiew warn**) is medium hot and uses green chillies; red curry (**gaeng pet**) is similar, but uses red chillies.
Jungle curry: often the hottest of the curries, made with red curry paste, bamboo shoots and just about anything else to hand, but no coconut cream.
Massaman or **mussaman:** also known as Muslim curry, because it originates from the area along the border with Malaysia where many Thais are Muslims. For this reason, pork is never used. It's a rich but mild concoction, with coconut, potato and some peanuts.
Penang, panaeng or **panang:** a dry, aromatic curry made with 'Penang' curry paste, coconut cream and holy basil.

FISH & SEAFOOD

Hoi: shellfish.
Hor mok talay or **haw mog talay:** steamed egg mousse with seafood.
Koong, goong or **kung:** prawns.
Maw: dried fish belly.
Pla meuk: squid.

Putney Bridge) with an exterior lit up in rainbow colours at night. Inside, a wave-like white wall of moulded plaster sweeps upstairs from the ground-floor bar to a sophisticated split-level dining room with starched white tablecloths and floor-to-ceiling windows. Unusually for a chain restaurant, the food we tried was better than expected. The menu is extensive, yet holds few surprises (though rambutan- and lychee-flavoured cocktails sounded interesting). We started with a convincing portion of tod mun pla (fish cakes) that came, disappointingly with a side salad topped with french dressing. 'Koh Samui-style' fish salad was better: crisp deep-fried fish, cashew nuts and fresh pineapple in a tart, spicy dressing. We were also lucky with the mains. Drunken duck was a stimulating, peppery stir-fry of duck, bamboo shoots, chilli and peppercorns. Puddings consist of some distinctly un-Thai desserts – ice-cream, tiramisu and banoffi pie.
Babies and children welcome: high chairs. Bar available for hire. Disabled: lift; toilet. No-smoking. Takeaway service; delivery service (within 3-mile radius). Vegetarian menu.
For branches see index.

South East
Blackheath

★ ★ Laicram
1 Blackheath Grove, SE3 0DD (8852 4710). Blackheath rail. **Lunch served** noon-2.30pm, **dinner served** 6-11pm Tue-Sun. **Main courses** £4.50-£13.90. **Credit** MC, V.
Blackheath residents would rather you didn't know about Laicram. There are barely enough tables to go around on weekday nights as it is. All the food at this bistro-like restaurant is exactly as you might find in Koh Samui, Bangkok or Chiang Mai. A certain chintziness prevails in the decor (wooden trellises covered in plastic flowers and bright pictures of Thai royalty on the walls), but

the space is surprisingly intimate, with an intriguing dessert trolley near the door. We ordered everything together, from a familiar royal Thai menu, and were bowled over. Tom kha soup was full-flavoured and fabulously spicy, while the Thai fried rice was sweet and moreish – best with a sprinkling of prik nam (fish sauce with chillies). Mee krob (spicy deep-fried noodles) was nicely presented, but an acquired taste. In contrast, red curry with beef was an unalloyed delight, full of bamboo shoots and moist aubergines that radiated chilli heat. It would be foolhardy to leave without trying a dessert: Thai egg custard was firm and drenched in sweet syrup, while the banana-leaf parcels of coconut cream contained a hidden layer of crisp water chestnut.
Babies and children admitted. Booking essential Fri, Sat. Takeaway service. Vegetarian menu.

London Bridge & Borough

Kwan Thai
The Riverfront, Hay's Galleria, Tooley Street, SE1 2HD (7403 7373/ www.kwanthairestaurant.co.uk). London Bridge tube/rail. **Lunch served** 11.30am-3pm Mon-Fri. **Dinner served** 6-10.30pm Mon-Sat. **Main courses** £9.50-£15. **Set lunch** £7.95-£8.95 2 courses. **Set dinner** £21-£30 per person (minimum 2) 3 courses. **Credit** AmEx, DC, MC, V.
Kwan Thai has much in its favour, including good food and a riverside vista that takes in HMS *Belfast*, St Paul's and Norman Foster's 'Gherkin'. No surprise then that it is packed at lunchtimes with City workers and ladies who lunch. Inside there's a vague Malacca Straits theme – lots of pale wood and green upholstery – and you can sit half below street level, or half above, in the mezzanine. The kitchen excels in cooking meat. We began with an expertly seasoned chicken satay and a melt-in-the-mouth moo yang: skewers of sublimely tender pork loin, marinated in spices and honey, then char-grilled and served with a fiery chilli-flake dipping sauce. Suea rong hai (marinated steak with the same chilli-flake sauce) was another fine

cut of meat, but didn't taste particularly Thai. More impressive was the chicken with cashew nuts, one of the few we've found in London prepared the authentic Thai way, with big strips of dried red chilli. Portions are massive. One criticism: service was slow, particularly as we were among the last diners at lunchtime.
Babies and children welcome: high chairs. Booking advisable. No-smoking tables. Tables outdoors (40, riverside terrace). Takeaway service. Vegetarian menu. **Map 12 Q8.**

New Cross

★ Thailand
15 Lewisham Way, SE14 6PP (8691 4040). New Cross or New Cross Gate tube/rail. **Lunch served** noon-2.30pm Mon-Fri. **Dinner served** 5-11.30pm daily. **Main courses** £4.95-£10. **Set meal** (noon-2.30pm, 5-7pm) £3.95 2 courses; £10 2 courses incl glass of wine. **Credit** MC, V.
This reliable Thai and Laotian canteen near New Cross station has been around for an age, but standards are as high as ever. A discerning clientele of Asian exchange students from Goldsmiths College keeps it that way. The dining room is tiny, and unadorned apart from a few Thai prints on the walls. In contrast, the menu is vast, with pages of Thai and Laotian delights at prices that will leave change for the journey home. At lunchtime, most customers order the standards: green and red curries, pad kaprow (stir-fries with basil, chilli and green peppercorns) and the like. We tucked in to some deliciously tender pork spare ribs, marinated in honey and coriander and incredibly moreish. The follow-up, chicken stir-fried with cashew nuts, was also well seasoned, but a little dry and lacking in chilli punch. We added extra heat in the form of nam prik (fish sauce with chopped chillies). Given more time, or an evening visit, we would put the Laotian menu through its paces; 'angry lamb' sounded particularly intriguing. In all, this is a solidly authentic local Thai, but the food outweighs the atmosphere.

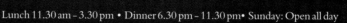

Babies and children admitted. Booking essential Fri, Sat. No smoking. Takeaway service; delivery service (over £10 within 3-mile radius). Vegetarian menu.

South Norwood

★ ★ Mantanah

2 Orton Building, Portland Road, SE25 4UD (8771 1148/www.mantanah.co.uk). Norwood Junction rail. **Lunch served** noon-3pm Sat, Sun. **Dinner served** 6-11pm Tue-Sun. **Main courses** £5.75-£8.50. **Set dinner** £16 per person (minimum 2) 3 courses, £22 per person (minimum 2) 4 courses. **Set buffet** (lunch Sun) £7.95 adults, £3.50 children. **Credit** AmEx, DC, MC, V.

People in Norwood Junction don't realise the treasure they have on their doorstep. No matter that Mantanah looks like any other neighbourhood Thai, it serves better food than many places charging three times as much. Depth of flavour is what really stands out here. No dish is predictable and you can ruminate for hours trying to work out the combinations of spices and flavours. Vegetarians do particularly well: meat-free dishes are prepared with pumpkin, aubergine, nuts, tofu, or a very convincing mock-duck made from textured beancurd (just look for the quirky names on the menu). Pork satay was tasty and nicely presented, but it faded into insignificance with the arrival of the yum lanna – an intoxicating mix of banana blossom, dried chilli and shredded chicken in a sweet, tart dressing, dusted with roasted coconut. We followed this with the intriguing-sounding 'Copy Cat', a rich and complex red curry with pineapple, cherry tomatoes and mock-duck, served with fragrant coconut rice (with the unusual addition of lemongrass). A fabulous meal, served quickly and with real style, complete with purple orchids on every plate. Simply one of the best Thai restaurants in London.

Babies and children admitted. Booking advisable. Takeaway service; delivery service (within 2-mile radius). Vegetarian menu.

East

Docklands

Elephant Royale

Locke's Wharf, Westferry Road, E14 3AN (7987 7999/www.elephantroyale.com). Island Gardens DLR. **Lunch served** noon-3pm, **dinner served** 5.30-10.30pm Mon-Fri. **Meals served** noon-midnight Sat; noon-10.30pm Sun. **Main courses** £4.90-£38. **Set meal** £20.50-£30.50 4 courses. **Set buffet** (noon-4pm Sun) £14.50. **Credit** AmEx, DC, MC, V.

We've twice sampled the popular Sunday buffet in this big, modern restaurant at the tip of the Isle of Dogs. Based on the latest experience, we recommend sticking to the à la carte. Although several dishes were pretty good, Thai food benefits from being served fresh from the wok and only the salads showed the potential of the kitchen. Elephant Royale's dining room and terrace overlook the Thames, which helps attract a mix of Docklands loft-dwellers and locals from across the river. The interior is full of foliage, water features and Thai statuary. As for the food, som tam (green papaya salad) was hot and full-flavoured, with a punchy lime and chilli dressing and plenty of pounded dried shrimp. Stir-fried beef with asparagus also showed potential: sweet soy, beef and asparagus was a surprisingly complementary set of flavours. On the downside, the satay was dry, pandanus chicken was only so-so, and most of the curries failed to excite. Best was the massaman curry, with a pleasing level of spice and big hunks of lamb and potatoes. The buffet is an 'all you can eat' deal, but a smaller meal from the menu would probably be more satisfying.

Children over 2 years admitted (Sun buffet). Booking essential. Disabled: toilet. Entertainment: band 7pm Thur-Sat. No-smoking tables (Mon-Thur). Tables outdoors (19, patio). Takeaway service. Vegetarian menu.

For branches see index.

Laicram

Nipa. See p260.

North

Archway

★ Charuwan

110 Junction Road, N19 5LB (7263 1410). Archway or Tufnell Park tube. **Lunch served** noon-3pm Mon-Fri. **Dinner served** 6-11pm daily. **Main courses** £4.95-£8.95. **Set dinner** £18 per person (minimum 2) 4 courses. **Credit** AmEx, MC, V.

Though in the neighbourhood-Thai mould, Charuwan has built a reputation by steadfastly refusing to water down its food to appeal to the masses. This is Thai cooking the way the Thais like it: homely, hot and unashamedly authentic. Furnishings are typical of the local Thai. Walls are covered in oriental bric-a-brac, while framed portraits of the Thai king and queen hang proudly over the bar. Service is friendly but ponderous: things can slow to a crawl at busy times. The menu offers familiar royal Thai dishes and a handful of surprises from the south and north-east of the country. To start, house laab (spicy mince salad) was formidable – red hot and lemon-tangy with the flavour of coriander shining through. Beef penang curry was replete with chilli and lime leaves and reminiscent of late-night meals in Bangkok street cafés. As on our last visit, pla lad prik stole the show: crispy hunks of white fish with a scorching sweet sauce packed with bird's-eye chillies.
Booking advisable. Children over 5 years admitted. Takeaway service. Vegetarian menu. **Map 26 B2**.

Islington

★ Isarn

119 Upper Street, N1 1QP (7424 5153). Angel tube/Highbury & Islington tube/rail. **Lunch served** noon-3pm, **dinner served** 6-11pm Mon-Fri. **Meals served** noon-11pm Sat; noon-10.30pm Sun. **Main courses** £6.50-£14.50. **Set lunch** £5.90 3 courses. **Credit** AmEx, MC, V.

This elegant restaurant only opened in 2005, but it's already turning out imaginative food with more confidence and flair than some of London's most established Thai names. Much of the credit goes to Tina Juengsoongneum, younger sister to Alan Yau of Hakkasan and Busaba Eathai (*see p260*) fame. Here she provides a boutique dining experience instead of gourmet fast food. The interior is futuristic without being spartan, with plenty of dark wood, cloth canopies and giant lampshades. Every dish served is distinctive. A main course of char-grilled lamb chops in a thick, spicy red curry sauce was one of the best Thai dishes we've found in London: a symphony of lime leaves, chilli and tender rare lamb. Green curry with monkfish and krachai (galangal in English) was also well flavoured, with a zingy, coarse curry paste that tasted fresh from the pestle and mortar. Of the starters, duck and pomelo salad was the most compelling: crisp duck, lime zest, coconut and ginger in a betel leaf wrap. Isarn is a real find Note you only get an hour to eat on weekend evenings.
Babies and children admitted. No smoking. Tables outdoors (2, garden). Takeaway service. **Map 5 O1**.

Local Thais

In the second edition of this guide, published in 1984, we proudly announced that London had ten Thai restaurants. It wasn't until the beginning of the 1990s, when cheaper flights to the Far East became a reality, that the food gained widespread popularity across the capital. Returning backpackers were eager to re-acquaint themselves with the hot, sour, pungent flavours they had encountered while travelling across Thailand. What's more, Londoners whose experience of the mysterious East stretched no further than Dagenham also fell for the food. Unlike many other cuisines whose moment in the fashion limelight was brief and involved just a few West End restaurants, Thai cooking went out into the suburbs and beyond. The phenomenon of the 'neighbourhood Thai' took root.

Several of these restaurants formed a partnership with London boozers – a trend started in 1988 when the manager of the Churchill Arms on Kensington Church Street, who enjoyed holidaying in Thailand, recruited a Thai chef to cook in the pub. It was a big success, and other pubs in the same chain began offering Thai food too. More followed suit. Perhaps the reason lay behind the link between spicy food and a healthy thirst; perhaps pub landlords wanted to provide their drinkers with an alternative to the 'local Indian'.

You won't find all the subtleties of first-rate Thai cuisine in these venues, and ingredient-substitution is common (garden peas instead of pea aubergines is a favourite), but they provide a reliable source of inexpensive meals where you can sample at least some of the stimulating flavours of South-east Asia.

Ayudhya

14 Kingston Hill, Kingston upon Thames, Surrey, KT2 7NH (8546 5878/www.ayudhya.co.uk). Norbiton rail. **Lunch served** noon-2.30pm Tue-Sun. **Dinner served** 6.30-11pm Mon-Sat; 6.30-10.30pm Sun. **Main courses** £5.95-£9.95. **Set meal** £20.95 per person (minimum 2) 3 courses incl tea or coffee. **Credit** MC, V.

Babies and children admitted. Booking advisable. Separate rooms for parties, both seating 30. Takeaway service. Vegetarian menu.

Bangkok Room

756 Finchley Road, NW11 7TH (8731 7473/www.bangkokroom.co.uk). Golders Green tube. **Lunch served** noon-3pm, **dinner served** 6-11pm daily. **Main courses** £6.95-£11.50. **Set lunch** (1 course) £3.50 vegetarian, £3.95 meat, £4.95 seafood. **Set dinner** (incl tea or coffee) £17.50 3 courses, £20.50 4 courses. **Credit** AmEx, MC, V.

Babies and children welcome: high chairs. Booking advisable. Tables outdoors (4, courtyard). Takeaway service; delivery service (within 2-mile radius). Vegetarian menu.

★ Ben's Thai

Above the Warrington, 93 Warrington Crescent, W9 1EH (7266 3134). Maida Vale or Warwick Avenue tube. **Lunch served** noon-2.30pm, **dinner served** 6-10.30pm daily. **Main courses** £5-£7.50. **Set dinner** £13.95-£15.95 per person (minimum 2) 3 courses. **Credit** MC, V.

Babies and children welcome: high chairs. Booking advisable; essential dinner. No-smoking tables. Takeaway service. Vegetarian menu. **Map 1 C4**.

★ Churchill Thai Kitchen

Churchill Arms, 119 Kensington Church Street, W8 7LN (7792 1246). High Street Kensington or Notting Hill Gate tube. **Meals served** noon-10pm Mon-Sat; noon-9.30pm Sun. **Main courses** £6. **Credit** MC, V.

Babies and children admitted. Book evenings. No-smoking tables. **Map 7 B7**.

★ Nid Ting

533 Holloway Road, N19 4BT (7263 0506). Archway or Holloway Road tube. **Dinner served** 6-11.15pm Mon-Sat; 6-10.15pm Sun. **Main courses** £5-£9.50. **Set dinner** £15 2 courses incl coffee. **Credit** AmEx, DC, JCB, MC, V.

Babies and children admitted. Booking essential Fri, Sat. Separate room for parties, seats 25. Takeaway service. Vegetarian menu. **Map 26 C2**.

★ Paolina

181 King's Cross Road, WC1X 9BZ (7278 8176). King's Cross tube/rail. **Lunch served** noon-3pm Mon-Fri. **Dinner served** 6-10pm Mon-Sat. **Main courses** £3.95-£7.90. **Set dinner** £11.95-£15.95 3 courses. **Unlicensed. Corkage** 50p. **No credit cards.**

Babies and children admitted. Booking advisable dinner. Takeaway service. Vegetarian menu. **Map 4 M3**.

Papaya Tree

209 Kensington High Street, W8 6BD (7937 2260). High Street Kensington tube. **Lunch served** noon-3.30pm, **dinner served** 6-11pm daily. **Main courses** £7.95-£9.95. **Set lunch** £5-£7 1 course. **Set dinner** £18-£24 3 courses. **Credit** AmEx, JCB, MC, V.

Babies and children admitted. Booking advisable. No-smoking tables. Takeaway service; delivery service (7644 6666). Vegetarian menu. **Map 7 A9**.

★ Pepper Tree

19 Clapham Common Southside, SW4 7AB (7622 1758/www.thepeppertree.co.uk). Clapham Common tube. **Lunch served** noon-3pm Mon-Fri. **Dinner served** 6-10.30pm Mon; 6-11pm Tue-Fri. **Meals served** noon-11pm Sat; noon-10.30pm Sun. **Main courses** £4-£6. **Credit** MC, V.

Babies and children welcome: high chairs. Bookings not accepted dinner. No smoking. Takeaway service. **Map 22 A2**.

★ Soho Thai

27-28 St Anne's Court, W1F 0BN (7287 2000/www.thaisq.com). Tottenham Court Road tube. **Lunch served** noon-3pm, **dinner served** 6-11.30pm Mon-Sat. **Main courses** £6.25-£9.95. **Credit** AmEx, MC, V.

Booking essential weekends. No-smoking tables. Takeaway service. Vegetarian menu.

★ Talad Thai

320 Upper Richmond Road, SW15 6TL (8789 8084). Putney Bridge tube/Putney rail. **Lunch served** 11.30am-3pm, **dinner served** 5.30-10.30pm Mon-Sat. **Meals served** 12.30-8.30pm Sun. **Main courses** £5.50-£7.95. **Set lunch** (Mon-Fri) £5.50 1 course. **Credit** MC, V.

Babies and children admitted. No-smoking tables. Takeaway service; delivery service (over £15 within 2-mile radius). **Map 17 K6**.

★ Thai Café

12 Mason's Avenue, Harrow, Middx HA3 5AP (8427 5385). Harrow & Wealdstone tube/rail. **Dinner served** 6-11pm Tue-Sat. **Main courses** £4.50-£5.50. **Unlicensed. Corkage** no charge. **No credit cards.**

Babies and children admitted. Booking advisable Fri, Sat. No-smoking tables. Takeaway service. Vegetarian menu.

Turkish

Slowly but surely Londoners are coming to realise that Turkish food is a cuisine to be reckoned with and ill deserves its British reputation, earned by the greasy late-night döner kebab. Many of the restaurants and cafés in the capital cook on large open grills called ocakbaşı. These are usually positioned in the main part of the restaurant, so it's possible to see how fresh the ingredients are as you watch the food prepared. In London the term 'mangal', which traditionally means a smaller brazier, refers to the same thing.

The spread of good authentic local restaurants beyond their previous heartlands in Hackney and Harringay continues. In addition, several more upmarket modern Turkish establishments have appeared closer to the centre of town, whether in the form of chains like Tas (*see* **EV**) or individual restaurants such as **Kazan** and **Ishtar**.

It is good to see that exceptional own-made pide bread is being served at an increasing number of places. Unfortunately, the habit of some central London restaurants to charge for pide also continues. This may seem a small point, but once the bread is seen as a side order rather than a general accompaniment its role in a meal changes. In contrast, there's an encouraging tendency among local restaurants to supply more freebies for diners, such as extra starters and salad.

Central

City

Haz

9 Cutler Street, E1 7DJ (7929 7923/www.haz restaurant.com). Liverpool Street tube/rail. **Meals served** 11.30am-11.30pm daily. **Main courses** £7-£13. **Set meal** £8.45 2 courses, £18.45 3 courses incl coffee. **Set meze** £12.95. **Credit** AmEx, MC, V.

Sitting in the buzzing and busy interior of Haz can feel like being in a posh office canteen or a fish tank. The floor is several feet below the pavement outside, so passers-by tower over your table – an odd experience. Outside, queues of people waited patiently for admission. As we surveyed the menu we were supplied with great fat olives and good warm pide – though later arrivals were given pitta. For starters, midye tava came in lovely fresh doughy batter, but rather too much of it, so the flavour of the mussels was overpowered. In contrast, zeytinyagli dolma were perfect, with the vine leaves firm and the rice fresh and sharp. Haz lamb stew arrived on a bed of smoky mashed aubergine with rice; it was very tasty, but somewhat small. Kalamar was a large portion of exquisitely tender battered squid rings served with very nice walnut 'butter' (not liquid enough to be called a sauce). Unusually for a Turkish restaurant, salads and vegetables must be ordered separately. Service was amenable but impersonal, and slowed down once our order was placed. Nonetheless, the standard of food was high and we can recommend Haz as a City haunt.
Babies and children welcome: high chair. Booking advisable Mon-Fri. Takeaway service. **Map 12 R6.**

Edgware Road

Safa

22-23 Nutford Place, W1H 5YH (7723 8331). Edgware Road or Marble Arch tube. **Meals served** noon-midnight daily. **Main courses** £5.50-£16. **Set meal** £10.50-£14.50 meat, £19.50 fish, 2 courses. **Credit** MC, V.

Its choice of Iranian and Turkish dishes makes Safa unusual, even in a district famed for Middle Eastern cuisine. A starter of lentil soup was exemplary – not too salty, with a hint of cumin. The uncommon adayes pitta, stuffed with minced lamb and pine nuts, was also pleasing. To follow, şiş kebab came with lots of rice, but the lamb itself was rather dry. Baghali polo (salmon) was presented buried under a great mound of rice, its exterior somewhat overcooked. One unequivocal delight is the beautiful crispy, wafer-thin Iranian bread – usually, but not always, baked in an oven by the entrance. When the oven is in use, it fills the place with a beautiful countryside smell. Desserts too are excellent, including ice-cream flavoured with saffron. Safa is a small, busy spot; for the most part it succeeds as a Turkish restaurant, and adds variety with its Iranian repertoire, but it would benefit from more consistency in the cooking.
Booking advisable weekends. Tables outdoors (4, pavement). Takeaway service; delivery service. **Map 8 F5.**

Fitzrovia

Istanbul Meze

100 Cleveland Street, W1P 5DP (7387 0785/ www.istanbulmeze.co.uk). Great Portland Street or Warren Street tube. **Meals served** noon-11pm Mon-Thur; noon-midnight Fri, Sat. **Dinner served** 5-11pm Sun. **Main courses** £7-£12. **Set lunch** £7.90 2 courses. **Set dinner** £10.90 2 courses. **Set meze** £20. **Credit** AmEx, MC, V.

Turkish musicians play in the basement wine bar here at weekends; as we ate, the unobtrusive rhythms could be heard through the floor. Istanbul Meze's popularity with Turks is a good sign. To start, our houmous was well presented, while börek was slightly overcooked but still enjoyable. Plenty of warm pitta bread accompanied both dishes (though pide would have been preferable). For mains, karni yarik (a large aubergine stuffed with diced lamb) produced a delicate fusion of flavours. Lokma kebab (wrapped lamb fillet with rice and salad) was fresh and tender: first rate. As is the norm here, freshly made chilli sauce was brought round in a saucepan (and we wouldn't have it any other way). Most Turkish restaurants will display distinctive turquoise-eye (nazar boncuk) amulets to ward off the evil eye. Here, not only do the charms adorn the walls, they have been added to the staff uniforms. Istanbul Meze has much of the appeal of a local restaurant, but is just around the corner from Great Portland Street. Well worth a visit.
Babies and children admitted. Book weekends. Separate room for parties, seats 40. Tables outdoors (4, pavement). Takeaway service. Vegetarian menu. **Map 3 J4.**

★ Özer

5 Langham Place, W1B 3DG (7323 0505/ www.sofra.co.uk). Oxford Circus tube. *Bar* **Open** noon-11pm daily. *Restaurant* **Meals served** noon-midnight daily. **Main courses** £8.70-£15.70. **Set lunch** (noon-6pm) £8.95 2 courses. **Set dinner** (6-11pm) £10.95-£16.45 2 courses. *Both* **Credit** AmEx, DC, MC, V.

First you enter a bustling bar, with a striking scarlet decor and an enormous display of brightly coloured artificial flowers. Shisha pipes are on view, but weren't in use on a recent visit. The bar offers the usual range of drinks, but is mainly a staging area for the large restaurant behind. Here we were supplied with beautiful pide bread, houmous and enormous olives. Service was efficient, friendly and helpful. The wine list is varied and extends beyond the common selection of Turkish wines, including a cabernet sauvignon/ gamay blend that's worth trying. Özer's menu is broad in scope (including several fish and vegetarian dishes) and unafraid to stray from the traditional. Chicken and leek börek with Thai-style sweet chilli sauce, for example, was an interesting diversion from the norm, looking more like a spring roll. For mains, lamb fillet with a small portion of rice was excellent, and well-spiced köfte came with lightly cooked rice and a small portion of steamed vegetables, including broccoli. The meat in both main courses was perceptibly fresh and tender. Özer deserves its status as one of the leading Turkish restaurants in London.
Babies and children welcome: children's menu; high chairs. Disabled: toilet. No-smoking tables. Tables outdoors (5, pavement). Takeaway service. **Map 9 H5.**

Marylebone

Grand Bazaar

42 James Street, W1U 5HS (7224 1544/ www.grand-bazaar.co.uk). Bond Street tube. **Meals served** noon-11pm Mon-Thur, Sun; noon-midnight Fri, Sat. **Main courses** £9-£10. **Set lunch** £6.50 2 courses. **Set meze** £8.95. **Credit** AmEx, MC, V.

The interior is shadowy and cluttered with twinkling lamps and incense burners – aiming to recreate the feel of the Grand Bazaar in Istanbul, we presume. The restaurant is popular with groups of young people, and there's often a party atmosphere. For starters, houmous kavurma combined very smooth houmous with olive oil and bite-size chunks of lamb. Sucuk izgara, grilled spicy sausage on lettuce, was also up to standard, though it lacked the subtle taste gradations of some starters. Accompanying pide was puffy, inflated like a balloon. Imam bayıldı was offered as a main course: an aubergine stuffed with vegetables and oven-cooked. It was a satisfying dish, though the veg stuffing was surprisingly heavy on the peas. As a meaty alternative, köfte in sauce with yoghurt was very good. We have a gripe that the tables here are tiny for the number of plates needed for a Turkish meal; that aside, Grand Bazaar has been tightening up on the details. Service was noticeably more attentive than on previous visits, contributing towards an enjoyable evening.

Troia. See p272.

Babies and children admitted. Booking advisable.
Tables outdoors (16, pavement). Takeaway
service. **Map 9 G6**.

Ishtar NEW

10-12 Crawford Street, W1U 6AZ (7224 2446/
www.ishtarrestaurant.com). Baker Street tube.
Meals served noon-11pm Mon-Thur, Sun; noon-
11.30am Fri, Sat. **Main courses** £7.95-£13.50.
Set lunch (noon-6pm) £6.95 2 courses. **Set meal**
£16.95 3 courses. **Set meze** £9.95. **Credit** MC, V.
The decor at Ishtar is pleasingly modern: muted
lighting emanates from bulbs set in copper
chandeliers; a spiral staircase leads down to a
basement bar. Starters of long thin sigara böreği
(feta-filled filo pastries) were properly textured, light
and crispy. Patlıcan soslu, with aubergine and green
peppers, was also a good choice, almost puréed in
fine olive oil. The pide bread was first-rate. Next,
lamb with apricot and pear came with plenty of
meltingly tender lamb, which had a sweet, intense
flavour; it was worth ordering extra rice to stop the
dish becoming overpowering. Chicken with
asparagus was also delicious, though the dish
contained surprisingly little potato in relation to the
other ingredients. In good weather it's possible to sit
out on the pavement (the road's not busy), at tables
that incline at a gentle angle. On our visit, the black-
clad staff were very helpful. Ishtar is part of the
growing band of restaurants moving Turkish
cuisine in London upmarket. Well worth visiting.
Babies and children welcome: high chairs. Booking
advisable Fri, Sat. Entertainment: musicians
Tue-Sat; belly dancer Fri, Sat. No-smoking tables.
Separate room for parties, seats 150. Tables
outdoors (6, pavement). Takeaway service.
Vegetarian menu. **Map 2 F5**.

Mayfair

Sofra

18 Shepherd Street, W1Y 7HU (7493 3320/
www.sofra.co.uk). Green Park tube. **Meals**
served noon-11pm daily. **Main courses** £8.45-

£15.95. **Set lunch** £8.95 2 courses. **Set dinner**
£11.95 2 courses. **Set meze** £12.95-£15.95 per
person (minimum 2). **Cover** £1.50. **Credit**
AmEx, MC, V.
An upmarket chain with branches around London,
Sofra follows the basic formula developed at this
original restaurant in posh Shepherd Market: food
made from top-quality ingredients, served quickly
and efficiently. The main section of the dining
space has large windows and a pleasant view and
is far preferable to the cramped and enclosed
basement; there are also tables outside. Wherever
you eat, the food is excellent. We kicked off with
spinach and feta börek, featuring very crisp filo
pastry and crumbling, but not melted feta. Another
starter, melon and feta, was a good contrast of
textures. A main-course mixed grill came with
tender chicken, lamb and köfte plus vegetables and
large potato chips. Our other choice, honey-glazed
shoulder of lamb (with mashed potatoes and rich
gravy) melted in the mouth. Notable too are the
juicy olives, houmous and extremely good pide
provided as nibbles before the starters.
Babies and children welcome: high chairs.
Booking advisable. Separate room for parties,
seats 14. Tables outdoors (10, pavement).
Takeaway service. Vegetarian menu. **Map 9 H8**.
For branches see index.

Pimlico

★ Kazan NEW

93-94 Wilton Road, SW1V 1DW (7233 7100/
www.kazan-restaurant.com). Victoria tube/rail.
Meals served noon-11pm daily. **Main courses**
£9.95-£17. **Set lunch** (noon-6pm) £9.99 per
person (minimum 2). **Set meze** £19.99 per
person (minimum 2); £29.99 per person
(minimum 4). **Credit** MC, V.
Kazan's restaurant and adjoining bar aim to
provide a comfortable environment and a modern
slant on Turkish cooking. For starters, courgette
fritters were light, deep-fried balls, also containing
diced onion and cheese. Sardines wrapped in vine

---

leaves were of a similarly high standard. To follow,
fistik kebab (a minced lamb kebab with pistachio)
was subtly spiced, not overwhelmed by pistachio,
and accompanied by good rice with chickpeas and
salad, plus great Turkish sweet chilli sauce. We
can also vouch for the excellent poussin with
yoghurt, lemon and chilli; the chicken had a
lemony tang, but left a memory of chilli in the
mouth. Our only gripe is with the rectangular
plates, which may look stylish but are hard to eat
from. A range of vegetarian meals is available and
shisha pipes are offered. Poached pears made a
first-rate dessert. Kazan deserves its success.
Babies and children welcome: high chairs.
Booking advisable dinner. Disabled: toilet.
Entertainment: belly dancers; phone for details.
No-smoking tables. Separate rooms for parties,
seating 40 and 60. Tables outdoors (3, pavement).
Takeaway service. **Map 15 J11**.

West

Notting Hill

★ Manzara

24 Pembridge Road, W11 3HL (7727 3062).
Notting Hill Gate tube. **Meals served** 7.30am-
midnight Mon-Wed; 7.30am-1am Thur, Fri;
8am-1am Sat; 9am-11.30pm Sun. **Main courses**
£6.75-£9.85. **Set meze** £5.95. **No credit cards**.
At heart, Manzara is a Mediterranean takeaway. The
cuisine is essentially Turkish, with a good selection
of Turkish pizzas. Otherwise, there's an emphasis
on char-grilling and on healthy food, much of it
organic. Ingredients may be fresh, but our spinach
börek was heavy; rather than being wrapped and
fried, it had been thickly layered and cut in triangles
like a sandwich. Next, the mixed kebab contained a
good selection of meat, along with a fair helping of
rice and a heavily dressed salad. Köfte was bland,
but chicken and lamb shish were faultless. Service
was friendly if vague. MOR music seeped out of the
sound system over tables that were reminiscent of a

fast-food joint – despite their tablecloths. Such an ambience might explain why the restaurant was two-thirds empty on a Saturday night. A pity, as we reckon that for all its faults Manzara is worth a visit, providing the best food of its type for miles.
Babies and children welcome: high chair. Booking advisable. Tables outside (2, pavement). Takeaway service. **Map 7 A7**.

West Kensington

Best Mangal II

66 North End Road, W14 9ET (7602 0212). West Kensington tube. **Meals served** noon-1am daily. **Main courses** £7-£16. **Set meal** £18 3 courses incl drink. **Credit** MC, V.
This second branch of the renowned Mangal mini-chain is ever so slightly more upmarket than the original further along the road and tends to be less crowded. Certainly, the interior is less cramped and rather more impersonal, dominated by Victorian-style paintings of Ottoman life. Occasional live music warms the atmosphere. Best Mangal remains a good source of ocakbaşı cooking. A starter of muska böreği came in a sizeable portion, with a tangy cheese. To follow, kariski kebab offered a selection of grilled meat dishes all had a hearty smoked flavour, though the pirzola chop and kaburga rib were particularly impressive. The dish was served with an enjoyable mix of thin saç and fat pide bread, as well as a fresh salad – but no rice. All portions were enormous and in danger of spilling from the plate. The range of desserts is limited, but what there is is good; we had a thoroughly satisfying baklava. Staff were friendly and attentive.
Babies and children welcome: high chair. Booking advisable. Takeaway service. Vegetarian menu. **For branch see index.**

South West

Earlsfield

Kazans

607-609 Garratt Lane, SW18 4SJ (8739 0055/ www.kazans.com). Earlsfield rail/44, 77, 270 bus. **Dinner served** 6-11pm Mon-Fri **Meals served**

11am-11pm Sat, Sun. **Main courses** £7.50-£14.95. **Credit** AmEx, MC, V.
The double frontage at Kazans opens on to a restaurant and a bar. When it began trading a couple of years ago, this family-run enterprise seemed very cagey about its Turkish heritage. As Earlsfield has come to love it, such reticence has disappeared. Dishes now have their Turkish names on the menu, and a wider range of Turkish cooking is available. Drinks are also multifarious, including cocktails, spirits, beers and wines: Turkish and otherwise. The interior is decorated with stylish enlargements of family photos from Turkey in the 1960s, and the black-topped tables are covered with wooden-slat mats. Our mixed cold meze came with the usual dips of houmous, tarama and cacik, but also more adventurous choices including enginar (artichokes) and fava bean purée. To follow, we were pleased to have ordered a large fillet of grilled snapper from the daily specials. Another main course, kuzu shish, featured tender chunks of meat. Couples like Kazans, and the restaurant is usually busy.
Babies and children welcome: high chairs. Booking advisable weekends. Disabled: toilet. Separate rooms for parties, seating 30 and 50. Tables outdoors (4, decking). Takeaway service.

South

Waterloo

★ EV Restaurant, Bar & Delicatessen

The Arches, 97-99 Isabella Street, SE1 8DA (7620 6191/www.tasrestaurant.com). Southwark tube/Waterloo tube/rail.
Bar **Open/meze served** noon-11.30pm Mon-Sat; noon-10pm Sun. **Meze** £3.55-£8.95.
Deli **Open** 7am-10pm Mon-Sat; 9am-10pm Sun.
Restaurant **Meals served** noon-11.30pm Mon-Sat; noon-10.30pm Sun. **Main courses** £5.45-£12.45. **Set meal** £8.25 2 courses, £18.25 3 courses person (minimum 2). **Set meze** £8.25-£10.25 per person (minimum 2).
All **Credit** AmEx, MC, V.
The upmarket Tas chain has expanded along the southern bank of the Thames from London Bridge

to Waterloo, and up into the West End. The restaurants have many features in common, despite being called variously Tas, Tas Café, Tas Pide and EV (which means 'home' in Turkish). Fittings are lush and chefs would rather mix intense flavours than risk blandness. Set in three old railway arches, EV has a large bar next to an equally capacious restaurant, plus a bakery/deli. For starters, balik böreği was gorgeous: filo pastry filled with mixed seafood, mushrooms and cashar cheese. Although not as exciting, çilbir (fried egg and sun-dried tomato, served with yoghurt and olive oil) was also good. Mains kept up the quality with notably tasty balik köftesi (fish cakes in a fresh tomato and coriander sauce). Portakal soslu tavuk (grilled chicken) veered away from the traditional too, being served with an appetising orange and mustard sauce. For dessert, sütlaç, flavoured with rosewater and orange peel, was excellent, but kaymakli patlıcan (honeyed aubergine) wasn't a success. In general, though, the inventiveness of EV's menu pays off.
Babies and children welcome: high chairs. Booking advisable Tue-Sat. Disabled: toilet. Entertainment: guitar player 7.30pm. No smoking. Tables outdoors (50, pavement). Takeaway service. Vegetarian menu. Vegan dishes. **Map 11 N8**.
For branches (Tas, Tas Café, Tas Pide) see index.

Troia NEW

3F Belvedere Road, SE1 7GQ (7633 9309). Waterloo tube/rail. **Meals served** noon-midnight daily. **Main courses** £8.25-£12.95. **Set lunch** (noon-4pm) £7.95 2 courses. **Set meze** £9.95 per person (minimum 2). **Credit** AmEx, DC, JCB, MC, V.
This pleasing restaurant is situated behind County Hall and a stone's throw from the London Eye. It has yet to create much of its own atmosphere, but the location on a traffic-free street, under a covered walkway, makes sitting outside more enjoyable than is the London norm. The walls are decorated with mosaics of Homeric characters such as Helen of Troy. In these days of excellent pide, we would rate the bread here as merely very good. There's a sizeable selection of meze, including outstanding dolma with fresh, zesty vine leaves wrapping the

rice and pine nuts. Pear and lamb stew made a slightly offbeat main course, very tasty yet with neither flavour overpowering the other; it came with notably good rice. An order for iskender produced mixed chicken and lamb shish pieces (rather than the traditional döner) on a bed of tomato sauce and a small base of pide. At the moment, Troia doesn't get the business it deserves: once tempted in, customers are likely to be impressed.
Babies and children welcome: children's menu; high chairs. Booking advisable. Disabled: toilet. Tables outdoors (14, pavement). Takeaway service. Vegetarian menu. **Map 10 M9.**

South East

Lewisham

Meze Mangal

245 Lewisham Way, SE4 1XF (8694 8099/ www.meze-mangal.co.uk). Lewisham or St John's rail. **Meals served** noon-2am daily. **Main courses** £7-£14. **Set meze** £10 per person (minimum 2), £14.50 per person (minimum 4). **Credit** MC, V.
In an area starved of good Turkish food, Meze Mangal has a menu containing all the basic grills, but also vegetarian and Turkish pizza dishes. For starters, kalamar was slightly stringy, but arrived with a decent tarator walnut sauce. Filo pançanka böreği parcels filled with spicy sausage and peppers were a decent choice. To follow, çop şiş came very well done, but the lamb was tender and the salad crisply fresh. An order for bıldırcın produced two plump quails, though they weren't as overflowing with gamey flavours as this dish can be when at its best. Nevertheless, Meze Mangal is an authentic and traditional ocakbaşı: a good-quality local restaurant that is deservedly crowded. Our basket of pide was frequently replenished and we were offered complimentary Turkish tea and coffee. The place was filled with staff and students from the college across the road. Its popularity suggests there is room for many more such establishments south of the river.
Babies and children welcome: high chair. Booking advisable. No-smoking tables. Takeaway service. Vegetarian menu.

East

Shoreditch

Han of Nazz NEW

4 Calvert Avenue, E2 7JP (7033 3936/ www.hanofnazz.co.uk). Liverpool Street tube/rail then 47, 149 bus. **Meals served** noon-midnight daily. **Main courses** £7.50-£14. **Set meal** £22.95 3 courses. **Set meze** £17.50 per person (minimum 2). **Credit** MC, V.
Much effort has been put into the decor of this new, long, thin restaurant. Han of Nazz has been filled with swags and drapes of chiffon and velvet in shades of tangerine and plum. It resembles a series of tents. In the basement a 'Harem room' has hubble-bubble pipes. We've found the food here variable: from excellent to dull. Starters have generally been top-notch: kizartma made with chunky sliced aubergines and roast vegetables; a layered, but crisp sigara böreği; spicy and beefy sucuk (presented on sautéed cubed potatoes). On one visit, we also relished the lamb shish: half a dozen pieces that had an almost feral taste, and the tenderness of chicken livers. However, main courses on another trip were lacklustre: iskender lacked pzazz; and Nazz chicken was bland in its white sauce with mushrooms. After learning that the chef comes from the Black Sea region, we wish we'd gone for one of the many fish dishes. Perhaps the hit-and-miss food explained the lack of many diners on a Friday evening. It's not easy to survive simply on Turkish exoticism. Han of Nazz has the skill in its kitchen, but needs to become more consistent.
Babies and children admitted. Booking advisable. Disabled: toilet. No-smoking tables. Separate room for parties, seats 80. **Map 6 R4.**

★ Savarona

66 Great Eastern Street, EC2A 3JT (7739 2888/ www.savarona.co.uk). Old Street tube/rail. **Meals served** 11am-midnight Mon-Sat. **Main courses** £8-£14. **Set lunch** £11.95 2 courses, £13.95 3 courses. **Set meal** £12.99-£20.99 2 courses. **Credit** MC, V.
Rakı-fired halloumi makes an interesting, tasty and spectacular start to a meal at Savarona. A dish of

cheese was brought to our table, rakı poured over it and set alight, infusing the slightly singed cheese with the flavour of the aniseed spirit. Patlıcan salatası was less dramatic, but had a beautiful garlic flavour. Pide bread came with a small dish of fine olive oil for dipping. For mains, the vegetable moussaka was very hot and flavoursome. Special mixed grill arrived with a nice mixed leaf salad and excellent rice; the meat was tender in the extreme, and was tinged with the aroma of the wood grill. Both the upstairs bar and downstairs restaurant were very quiet on a Friday evening, although the waiter assured us it had been busy at lunchtime. Perhaps the management should have placed the bar beneath the restaurant, rather than the other way around. At present, the Shoreditch crowd doesn't know what it's missing.
Babies and children admitted. Booking advisable. Disabled: toilet. No-smoking tables. Vegetarian menu. **Map 6 Q4.**

North East

From around Dalston Kingsland station northwards up the A10 roughly to Stoke Newington Church Street, you are in the Turkish and Kurdish heart of Hackney. The Turkish food sold in this area is more authentic and varied than anywhere else in London. The intense competition means that restaurants and cafés come and go at a dizzying rate, and there's a constant race to provide different services and dishes. More and more places now serve small starters, often izğara sogan (grilled onion with pomegranate sauce), without charge. None of the following gets a full review, but only because the area is a cornucopia of choice: **Bodrum Café** (61 Stoke Newington High Street); **Dem** (18 Stoke Newington High Street); **Dervish Bistro** (15 Stoke Newington Church Street); **Evin** (115 Kingsland High Street); **Şölen** (84 Stoke Newington High Street); **Şomine** (131 Kingsland High Street), for stews; **Tava** (17

Özer. See p270.

RESTAURANTS

Stoke Newington Road); **Testi** (36 Stoke Newington High Street); and **Turku** (79 Stoke Newington Road), for meze with folk music. Also worth a visit is the pâtisserie **Öz Antepliler** (30 Stoke Newington Road), which sells perfect baklava.

Dalston

★ ★ 19 Numara Bos Cirrik

34 Stoke Newington Road, N16 7XJ (7249 0400). Dalston Kingsland rail/76, 149, 243 bus. **Meals served** noon-midnight daily. **Main courses** £5-£8. **Credit** MC, V.

Still our favourite on this stretch, the original 19 Numara remains pretty much perfect. It's a small restaurant, with a café-like feel. The pale walls are decorated with reliefs of Egyptian and Greek scenes. Across the back runs the ocakbaşı grill. When a main course is ordered it comes preceded by a range of starters, usually including grilled onion in a sharp pomegranate and turnip sauce, and chilli onion. The sauces are far subtler in taste than in competing restaurants that have started providing similar additional dishes. Portions are sizeable and enticing enough for us no longer to order any other starters – a pity, in a way, as there's a wide variety on the menu and quality is beyond reproach. A main course of spicy adana yoğhurtlu came with a minty yoghurt sauce, as did the tavuk yoğhurtlu; both also featured succulent, well-grilled meat. The bıldırcın was outstanding, with ridiculously plump quail, tasty and tender. Salads were large and fresh, if not very varied, and pide was warm and frequently replenished. If grills don't take your fancy, try something from the wide range of Turkish pide pizzas.
Babies and children admitted. Booking advisable. Takeaway service. **Map 25 C4.**
For branch see index.

★ Istanbul Iskembecisi

9 Stoke Newington Road, N16 8BH (7254 7291). Dalston Kingsland rail/76, 149, 243 bus. **Meals served** noon-5am daily. **Main courses** £8-£12.95. **Set lunch** (noon-5pm) £5 2 courses. **Set meal** (from 5pm) £11.50 2 courses; £16 per person (minimum 2) 2 courses. **Credit** MC, V.

Once the flagship restaurant of the area, Istanbul's main claim to fame now is that it stays open until 5am, and there's permanently something of the early hours about it. The tripe soups that give the place its name (literally 'Istanbul Tripe House') are still on the menu, but otherwise most of the dishes are available elsewhere in the area. Starters of mitite köfte were small meatballs, overcooked so that the taste was mostly of frying. They were presented with wonderful pide, though. Houmous kavurma was superb, with crispy nibblets of lamb in the houmous. To follow, the mixed grill showed that the chefs still know how to cook meat, with pirzola, adana, tavuk and shish all being fine. Iskender (a mix of adana and shish kebabs on a bed of bread, yoghurt and rich tomato sauce) was quite acceptable, but lacked a certain magic. There are still some nice touches, such as the plate of complimentary watermelon, yet service is literally distant, as the staff congregated by the bar at the far end of the restaurant. It's a pity to see what was once one of the best Turkish restaurants in London adrift.
Babies and children welcome: high chairs. Book Fri, Sat. Takeaway service. **Map 25 B4.**

Mangal II

4 Stoke Newington Road, N16 8BH (7254 7888). Stoke Newington rail/76, 149, 243 bus. **Meals served** noon-1am daily. **Main courses** £7-£12. **Set meal** £14.50 per person (minimum 2) 2 courses. **Credit** MC, V.

The three related Mangal restaurants in this area are so different that their link isn't immediately obvious. The original (Mangal Ocakbaşı; *see below*) is a café offering straightforward grills and the third is a specialist pide pizza stop, while Mangal II is a bustling high-street restaurant, popular with a broad spectrum of Stoke Newington and Dalston locals, including many Turkish families. Service is friendly, attentive and efficient. Lighting, in the

blue and yellow interior, is rather bright. While the menu isn't particularly adventurous, neither is it conservative. To begin our meal, we mixed a standard but very pleasant ispanak salad with a less common dish of lightly fried diced lambs' kidneys. Both were very fresh and perfectly prepared. For mains, an adana kebab was top-notch, as one would expect from this chain. Patlıcan kebab, alternating patties of minced lamb and slices of aubergine grilled on a skewer, was also excellent, the flavour of each ingredient infusing the other. A constant stream of diners came and went during our meal, but staff put us under no pressure to leave.
Babies and children welcome: high chairs. Book weekends. Takeaway service. **Map 25 C4.**

Mangal Ocakbaşı

10 Arcola Street, E8 2DJ (7275 8981/ www.mangal1.com). Dalston Kingsland rail/76, 149, 243 bus. **Meals served** noon-midnight daily. **Main courses** £7-£12.50. **No credit cards.**

A queue could be seen emerging from the door as we approached the restaurant down the side street on which it is hidden. Mangal does have a takeaway service, but the queue was made up of people waiting for seats. It says something about its legendary reputation that, amid London's densest concentration of Turkish restaurants, people are prepared to queue to squeeze past the takeaway counter and be crushed into a plain, grey-tiled café where they will have to endure curt service. There are no menus, so we chose our dishes from the stacks of raw kebabs on display at the front. Basic starters such as houmous and lentil soup are often available if you ask. Our grills were wonderful, though no longer exceptional – quality has not fallen, but the competition has caught up, particularly in the provision of starters and other comforts. Unless it is midwinter, diners are better off seated away from the heat of the fiery grill. Still, it doesn't do to be uncharitable. All fans of Turkish food (other than vegetarians) should visit Mangal at some point.
Book weekends. Takeaway service. **Map 25 C4.**

Hackney

★ Anatolia Ocakbaşı

253 Mare Street, E8 3NS (8986 2223). Hackney Central rail/48, 55, 253, 277, D6 bus. **Meals served** 11am-midnight daily. **Main courses** £4.90-£9.10. **Corkage** £3.50. **Credit** MC, V.

Both the somewhat barn-like restaurant and the takeaway at the front are usually busy, with a fast turnover of customers. This could explain why Anatolia had run out of soup in the early evening, though it might be because the restaurant is popular with local Turks who see soup as primarily a lunchtime dish. A substituted haydari (a mix of fresh yoghurt, garlic, chilli and, in this case, grated carrot) made an invigorating starter. For mains, an enormous dish of halep kebab was served bubbling hot. A thick, buttery, tomatoey sauce – containing a mix of peppers and other vegetables – enveloped lamb döner kebab and pide bread, drenching the bread to the point of disintegration. As ever, it was good to see the kebabs and salad being prepared behind the bar. Anatolia could offer more for vegetarians, but remains a decent local ocakbaşı.
Babies and children welcome: high chair. Booking advisable weekends. Takeaway service. Vegetarian menu.

Newington Green

★ Beyti

113 Green Lanes, N16 9DA (7704 3165). Manor House tube then 141, 341 bus. **Meals served** noon-midnight daily. **Main courses** £4.50-£10. **No credit cards.**

In addition to the expected Turkish restaurant food, Beyti offers a number of northern Anatolian and Black Sea dishes, which have an interestingly different flavour. This alone is enough to make the restaurant worth finding, even though its location is far from the main drag of Green Lanes. Beyti also provides a varied range of fish dishes. For

starters, we enjoyed some subtly spiced deep-fried meatballs (misket köfte). Kalamar arrived piping hot in fine batter, with well-flavoured squid that wasn't the least bit rubbery. As a main, we can also vouch for the very tasty grilled salmon. Pirzola (grilled lamb chops) were also fine, though ours were too well done. It's also worth checking for the daily specials. Food is hearty rather than subtle, and the atmosphere is akin to that of a café – but these aren't criticisms. Photos of staff and regulars smile down from the walls, giving the place the feel of a local. For aficionados jaded with the uniform menus of many otherwise excellent cafés, Beyti is an intriguing alternative.
Babies and children admitted. Booking advisable. Restaurant available for hire. Tables outdoors (2, pavement). **Map 25 A3.**

★ ★ Sariyer Balik

56 Green Lanes, N16 9NH (7275 7681). Manor House tube then 141, 341 bus. **Meals served** 5pm-1am daily. **Main courses** £6.50-£10. **No credit cards.**

First-time visitors must peer into the rather shabby, black-painted interior of Sariyer Balik and wonder if they have come to the right place. They shouldn't worry, as things haven't changed here for years. A new menu has been printed, but the basic dish is still char-grilled fish – the species dependent on what's fresh at the market. The expanding collection of paintings and oddities in the fishing nets that adorn the walls is merely an added bonus. For starters, the mixed hot meze showed how much can be achieved on a relatively small canvas. Prawns in chilli sauce, kalamar marinated in vodka, and mussels in batter and beer are all simple dishes, but were flawlessly executed. The alcohol theme continues during the meal, as many diners like to order rakı with their grills. Lightly battered anchovies were a melting delight as a main course. True, the bass was full of bones, but the flesh was moist and just right. A single bite-sized honey dessert (seker pare) was brought as a complimentary offering. The obscure location and wacky decor may put off some, but for those in the know Sariyer Balik is a treasure.
Babies and children welcome: high chairs. Booking advisable. Separate room for parties, seats 60. Takeaway service. **Map 25 A3.**

Stoke Newington

★ Café Z Bar

58 Stoke Newington High Street, N16 7PB (7275 7523). Stoke Newington rail/73, 76, 149, 243 bus. **Meals served** 8am-11pm daily. **Main courses** £4.50-£7.50. **Set meal** £4.95 2 courses. **No credit cards.**

A standard café menu is complemented by a fair choice of Turkish mezes and grills. Muhamarra (a paste made from red peppers, walnuts and pomegranate syrup) made a very fresh, spicy starter. There's also a number of specials and special offers to be tried. Our main course, a juicy çöp şiş, was served on wooden skewers, with a salad of grated lettuce, carrot and red cabbage. Several vegetarian and fish dishes are available, as well as a selection of Turkish pizzas. You can also order Turkish all-day breakfasts, together with great freshly squeezed apple, orange and carrot juices. We've always found the service to be excellent. Mixing elements of café, bar, gallery and restaurant, Z Bar has become something of a local cultural centre, with occasional evening concerts and events in the basement. The relaxed vibe keeps a constant stream of locals coming and going.
Babies and children welcome: high chairs. Book weekends. Entertainment: jazz workshop 8pm Thur; phone for details. Separate room for parties, seats 50. Tables outdoors (4, pavement). Takeaway service. **Map 25 C2.**

North

Finchley

There's a growing number of perfectly acceptable Turkish restaurants in Finchley, not reviewed here, including long-established

Menu

It's useful to know that in Turkish 'ç' and 'ş' are pronounced 'ch' and 'sh'. So şiş is correct Turkish, shish is English and sis is common on menus. Menu spelling is rarely consistent, so expect wild variations on everything given here. See also the menu boxes in **Middle Eastern** and **North African**.

COOKING EQUIPMENT
Mangal: brazier.
Ocakbaşı: an open grill under an extractor hood. A metal dome is put over the charcoal for making paper-thin bread.

SOUPS
İşkembe: finely chopped tripe soup, an infallible hangover cure.
Mercimek çorba: red lentil soup.
Yayla: yoghurt and rice soup (usually) with a chicken stock base.

MEZE DISHES
Arnavut ciğeri: 'albanian liver' – cubed or sliced lamb's liver, fried then baked.
Barbunya: spicy kidney bean stew.
Börek or böreği: fried or baked filo pastry parcels with a savoury filling, usually cheese, spinach or meat. Commonest are muska (cheese) and sigara ('cigarette' so long and thin).
Cacik: diced cucumber with garlic in yoghurt.
Çoban salatası: 'shepherd's' salad of finely diced tomatoes, cucumbers, onions, perhaps green peppers and parsley, sometimes with a little feta cheese.
Dolma: stuffed vegetables (usually with rice and pine kernels)
Enginar: artichokes, usually with vegetables in olive oil.
Haydari: yoghurt, infused with garlic and mixed with finely chopped mint leaves.
Hellim: Cypriot halloumi cheese.
Houmous: creamy paste of chickpeas, crushed sesame seeds, oil, garlic and lemon juice.
Houmous kavurma: houmous topped with strips of lamb and pine nuts.
Imam bayıldı: literally 'the imam fainted'; aubergine stuffed with onions, tomatoes and garlic in olive oil.
İspanak: spinach.
Kalamar: fried squid.
Karides: prawns.

Kısır: usually a mix of chopped parsley, tomatoes, onions, crushed wheat, olive oil and lemon juice.
Kizartma: lightly fried vegetables.
Köy ekmeği: literally 'village bread'; another term for saç (qv).
Lahmacun: 'pizza' of minced lamb on thin pide (qv).
Midye tava: mussels in batter, in a garlic sauce.
Mücver: courgette and feta fritters.
Patlıcan: aubergine, variously served.
Patlıcan esme: grilled aubergine puréed with garlic and olive oil.
Pide: a term encompassing many varieties of Turkish flatbread. It also refers to Turkish pizzas (heavier and more filling than lahmacun, qv).
Pilaki: usually haricot beans in olive oil, but the name refers to the method of cooking not the content.
Piyaz: white bean salad with onions.
Saç: paper-thin, chewy bread prepared on a metal dome (also called saç) over a charcoal grill.
Sucuk: spicy sausage, usually beef.
Tarama: cod's roe paste.
Tarator: a bread, garlic and walnut mixture; havuç tarator adds carrot; ıspanak tarator adds spinach.
Yaprak dolması: stuffed vine leaves.
Zeytin: olive.

MAIN COURSES
Alabalik: trout.
Balik: fish.
Güveç: stew, which is traditionally cooked in an earthenware pot.
Hünkar beğendi: cubes of lamb, braised with onions and tomatoes, served on an aubergine and cheese purée.
İçli köfte: balls of cracked bulgar wheat filled with spicy mince.
İncik: knuckle of lamb, slow-roasted in its own juices. Also called kléftico.
Karni yarik: aubergine stuffed with minced lamb and vegetables.
Kléftico: see incik.
Mitite köfte: chilli meatballs.
Sote: meat (usually), sautéed in tomato, onion and pepper (and sometimes wine).
Uskumru: mackerel.

KEBABS
Usually made with grilled lamb (those labelled **tavuk** or **piliç** are chicken), served with bread or rice and salad.

Common varieties include:
Adana: spicy mince.
Beyti: usually spicy mince and garlic, but sometimes best-end fillet.
Bıldırcın: quail.
Böbrek: kidneys.
Çöp şiş: small cubes of lamb.
Döner: slices of marinated lamb (sometimes mince) packed tightly with pieces of fat on a vertical rotisserie.
Halep: usually döner (qv) served over bread with a buttery tomato sauce.
İskender: a combination of döner (qv), tomato sauce, yoghurt and melted butter on bread.
Kaburga: spare ribs.
Kanat: chicken wings.
Köfte: mince mixed with spices, eggs and onions.
Külbastı: char-grilled fillet.
Lokma: 'mouthful' (beware, there's a dessert that has a similar name!) – boned fillet of lamb.
Patlıcan: mince and sliced aubergine.
Pirzola: lamb chops.
Şeftali: seasoned mince, wrapped in caul fat.
Şiş: cubes of marinated lamb.
Uykuluk: sweetbread.
Yoğhurtlu: meat over bread and yoghurt.

DESSERTS
Armut tatlısı: baked pears.
Ayva tatlısı: quince in syrup.
Baklava: filo pastry interleaved with minced pistachio nuts, almonds or walnuts, and covered in sugary syrup.
Kadayıf: cake made from shredded pastry dough, filled with syrup and nuts or cream.
Kazandibi: milk pudding, traditionally with very finely chopped chicken breast.
Kemel pasha: small round cakes soaked in honey.
Keşkül: milk pudding with almonds and coconut, topped with pistachios.
Lokum: turkish delight.
Sütlaç: rice pudding.

DRINKS
Ayran: refreshing drink made with yoghurt.
Çay: tea.
Kahve (aka Turkish coffee): a tiny cup half full of sediment, half full of strong, rich, bitter coffee. Offered without sugar, medium or sweet.
Rakı: a spirit with an aniseed flavour.

Izgara (11 Hendon Lane, 8371 8282), **Durum** (119 Ballards Lane, 8346 8977), **Merlot** (145 Ballards Lane, 8346 8089) and also **Divan** (163 Ballards Lane, 8346 4414). All are worth a visit.

The Ottomans
118 Ballards Lane, N3 2DN (8349 9968). Finchley Central tube. **Meals served** noon-10.30pm daily. **Main courses** £5.90-£12.90. **Set lunch** £5.95 2 courses. **Set dinner** £14.50-£15.90 3 courses incl coffee. **Credit** JCB, MC, V.
Original paintings of Ottoman scenes decorate the fashionably distressed walls here, with a large waterside mural dominating one side. Diners eat at wooden tables, most of which have room for two people. The fussy knick-knacks common in

Turkish eateries are present and correct, but overall there's an airy, cool feel to the place. In a nice touch, each table has a different fresh flower in a vase. For starters, houmous kavurma came with beautifully textured houmous and unusually large chunks of lamb – nice, though £4.90 seems a little steep for such a relatively simple dish. There was nothing to complain about in our main course. Külbasti consisted of two slices of extra-tender fillet lamb, with rice and a salad of grated carrot, lettuce and onion. Ask for the garlic and chilli sauces as an accompaniment. The Ottomans seems to be maturing, becoming more of a restaurant than a café.
Babies and children welcome: children's portions; high chairs. Booking advisable weekends. No-smoking tables. Takeaway service. Vegetarian menu.

Finsbury Park

★ Yildiz
163 Blackstock Road, N4 2JS (7354 3899). Arsenal tube. **Meals served** noon-11.30pm daily. **Main courses** £4-£12.65. **Set lunch** £6 1 course incl soft drink. **Credit** MC, V.
Though Yildiz's menu ranges around the Mediterranean, Anatolian food remains very much its focus. Behind the ocakbaşı at the front of the restaurant, the lighting is subdued and the atmosphere scented by the smoke from the open grill. Among the mats decorating the walls are a couple of toy lambs on little shelves, their wool tinged grey with the smoke. Turkish pop accompanied our meal. A starter of patlıcan kizartma (slices of fried aubergine with thick yoghurt and tomato) was hearty but unsubtle. It

also proved unnecessary, as Yildiz will supply nibbles while the main course is being prepared. We were given grilled onion in spicy turnip and pomegranate sauce, onion with chilli, and a salad. All this came with fine, slim pide bread. The recipe for iskender varies from place to place; the version here had the usual base of pide, a layer of meat (köfte kebab) covered in sauce, and yoghurt. The sauce was almost Italian in its infusion of tomatoes, and contained a range of vegetables including peppers and even mushrooms. Despite these touches of inauthenticity, the dish was large, filling and highly satisfying. Yildiz remains a good, solid local restaurant.
Babies and children welcome: high chair. Takeaway service.

Harringay

Green Lanes in Harringay has the most intense concentration of Turkish cafés and restaurants in London. It also features a wide range of Turkish grocers, pâtisseries, greengrocers and butchers. The restaurants may lack the variety found in the cluster around Dalston and Stoke Newington in Hackney, but many of the ocakbaşı cafés are well worth a visit. Few are licensed for alcohol, but most will let you bring your own. The following is a non-exhaustive selection of some of the better choices (street numbers are given in brackets, any numbers under 100 are on Green Lanes Grand Parade): **Ari** (7 Salisbury Promenade), a Turkish café and pâtisserie; **Bingöl** (No.551); **Damak** (No.395); **Diyarbakır** (No.69); **Gaziantep** (No.52); **Gökyüzü** (No.27); **Harran** (No.399); **Mangal** (No.443), with a wonderful psychedelic sign; **Öz Sofra** (No.421), open 24 hours; **Köz** (No.64), which is licensed; **Selale** (2 Salisbury Promenade); **Tara** (No.6), which has a more Middle Eastern feel; and **Yayla** (No.429). The menus rarely stray from the standard grills, guveç and pide (both bread and pizza), but the food is good quality, fresh and very cheap.

★ Antepliler

46 Grand Parade, Green Lanes, N4 1AG (8802 5588). Manor House tube/29 bus. **Meals served** 11.30am-11.30pm daily. **Main courses** £5-£8.50. **Credit** MC, V.
Antepliler is a little more adventurous than most Turkish restaurants on this relatively conservative strip. For instance, çig köfte is among the cold starters – spicy raw mince balls served with lettuce leaves. In Turkey this is a popular dish in the home, but rarely found in restaurants (where it's harder to judge the freshness of the meat). The dish is certainly worth trying, but eight patties was too much for a starter and the spicing was a little too crude. There was a considerable delay before kaburga lamb ribs arrived, but the wait was eased by a fresh onion salad and a mixed salad. The portion of lamb was plentiful, though the meat was quite rare and the accompanying rice with chickpeas a little overdone. However, the pide was excellent, and useful for handling the hot bones. The restaurant space is dominated by a large wall painting of food preparation; brick ovens at the front and rear provide further entertainment. A Turkish pâtisserie is attached to the premises, which explains the restaurant's name (roughly meaning pâtisserie). Antepliler is well worth visiting for the scope and experimentation of its menu, but some added subtlety wouldn't go amiss.
Babies and children welcome: high chairs. Takeaway service.

Mizgîn Restaurant NEW

485 Green Lanes, N4 1AJ (8340 8965). Manor House or Turnpike Lane tube. **Meals served** 7am-midnight daily. **Main courses** £5-£10. **Set meze** £4.50. **Unlicensed. Corkage** no charge beer, £3 wine. **No credit cards.**

Fresh fish displayed in its window make Mizgîn stand out from the other cafés lining this street. The marine life is there to be grilled, and most of the usual Turkish meat grills can also be ordered. No starters are listed on the menu, though standards like houmous and cacik are available on request. Appetisers are hardly necessary, however, as a large fresh salad with tomato, lots of cucumber and olives soon appears, along with a small chilli salad, once the meal is ordered. The pide bread was fine, though it didn't taste own-made. The range of fish on the menu is limited and varies daily depending on what's available. On our visit, only sea bream was offered. Each selection is £10, which perhaps may seem expensive for this kind of no-frills café, but ours was a good-sized fish very satisfactorily cooked.
Babies and children welcome: high chairs. Booking advisable. Takeaway service.

Highbury

★ İznik

19 Highbury Park, N5 1QJ (7354 5697). Highbury & Islington tube/rail/4, 19, 236 bus. **Lunch served** 10am-4pm, **dinner served** 6.30pm-midnight daily. **Main courses** £7.50-£9.50. **Credit** MC, V.
This is a wonderful place to sample the wide range of Turkish dishes based on oven cooking rather than grilling. The atmosphere is cosy; the walls are cluttered with an array of tiles from the city of İznik, lamps, candles and even a finely embroidered Ottoman jacket. For starters, mücver was excellent, not in the least oily (as this dish can sometimes be), and served with chilli sauce. Fava beans came with rich, high-quality olive oil, a reminder that the simplest starters are often among the most flavoursome. It's a minor disappointment that İznik still serves warm pitta, rather than the range of pide offered at most other restaurants of similar quality. For mains, kadin budu (literally 'ladies' thighs') was a dish of succulent lamb patties fried in egg and flour. Our other choice was a marvellous beykoz kebab: a soft hunk of lamb in aubergine. Both mains came with a small portion of rice with diced aubergine and a very fresh salad with olives. To finish, ayva tatlısı (baked, honeyed quince with cream) was a memorably tasty dessert.
Babies and children admitted. Booking essential weekends. Takeaway service.

Islington

★ Gallipoli

102 Upper Street, N1 1QN (7359 0630/ www.cafegallipoli.com). Angel tube/Highbury & Islington tube/rail. **Meals served** noon-11pm Mon-Thur; noon-midnight Fri; 10am-midnight Sat; 10am-10.30pm Sun. **Main courses** £6.50-£10. **Set lunch** £7.95 1 course. **Set dinner** £9.95 1 course. **Set meze** £11.95. **Credit** AmEx, MC, V.

Han of Nazz. See p273.

The Gallipoli restaurants remain the most popular Turkish eateries in Islington, despite stiff competition. A sign on the wall in this, the original branch, proclaims 'Tis the season to be jolly, bring your friends to Gallipoli' – which, even read during May, comes close to summing up the place; it's relaxed and a great favourite among young Islingtonians. The standard of food is generally very high. We started with a mixed meze, which included cacik, a most enjoyable patlican salata and black-eyed beans. A large meze is also offered as a full meal and makes a good choice, especially for vegetarians. Unfortunately, Gallipoli maintains its bothersome habit of charging for bread, even when bread is served with a meze. For mains we chose imam bayıldı, a pleasant mix of vegetables and chickpeas: oven-baked aubergine stuffed with various vegetables and chickpeas. Sucuk kebab (spicy sausage, yoghurt and bread) was a bit heavy and monotonous as a main course or its own. There's a cluster of small tables on the pavement outside during the summer.
Babies and children welcome: high chairs.
Booking advisable. Tables outdoor (8, pavement).
Takeaway service.
For branches see index.

★ Gem

265 Upper Street, N1 2UQ (7359 0405/
www.gemrestaurantbar.co.uk). Angel tube/
Highbury & Islington tube/rail. **Meals served**
noon-11pm Mon-Sat; noon-10.30pm Sun **Main courses** £5.95-£8.50. **Set lunch** £5.95 3 courses, £7.95 4 courses. **Set dinner** £8.50 3 courses, £11.45 4 courses, £22.45 5 courses incl house wine or beer. **Credit** MC, V.
It is worth travelling further along Upper Street than the average punter to visit this charming Kurdish restaurant. Diners sit at heavy wooden tables; farming implements adorn the walls. The complimentary qatme – Kurdish flatbread, made in the open restaurant – is beautiful. It came stuffed with cheese, though it's also available with other fillings, such as spinach. The portion was small enough for us to be eager to sample another starter. For this, we can recommend the exceptionally fresh and tangy yaprak dolma with rice and pine nuts. A main course of minced beyti kebab was accompanied by dishes of fresh yoghurt and chilli sauce, as well as rice, bread and salad. There's also a selection of vegetarian dishes. A complimentary baklava, served with ice-cream, made an ideal dessert. Gem continues to provide varied, well-produced food at reasonable prices and deserves more custom.
Babies and children admitted. Booking advisable
weekends. Separate room for parties, seats
80. Takeaway service. Vegetarian menu.
Map 5 O1.

Mem & Laz NEW

8 Theberton Street, N1 0QX (7704 9089).
Angel tube/Highbury & Islington tube/rail.
Meals served 11.30am-11.30pm Mon-Thur, Sun; 11.30am-midnight Fri, Sat. **Main courses** £5.95-£11.95. **Set meal** (11.30am-6pm) £6.95 2 courses, £8.95 3 courses. **Credit** AmEx, MC, V.
A 'Mediterranean restaurant' based on Turkish cuisine with a largely Turkish staff, Mem & Laz feels no great pressure from its heritage. Turkish dishes are offered alongside Italian and chips, but the decor is all Anatolian. Dark wood and clusters of lamps dominate. While we were ordering, sun-dried tomato bread and olive bread arrived: good, if not quite traditional. Two large grilled sardines made an excellent starter. We also enjoyed an obviously freshly made pepper dolma, with sweet rice and raisins stuffed in a green pepper. To follow, a sizeable portion of grilled halibut was served with boiled potatoes and a very lettuce-oriented salad. Köfte meatballs were well spiced (though arguably undercooked), and came with thick yoghurt and a salad. A separate menu offers daily changing specials. The atmosphere and mix of dance and Turkish music seemed to please the customers, most of whom were couples. Service was friendly, if a little over-attentive at times. Islingtonians must like the place: Mem & Laz has already opened a second branch on Upper Street.

Babies and children welcome: children's
portions; high chairs. Booking advisable dinner.
No-smoking tables. Separate room for parties,
seats 50. Tables outdoors (15, pavement).
Takeaway service; delivery service (over £20
within 1-mile radius). Vegetarian menu.
Map 5 O1.
For branch see index.

★ Pasha

301 Upper Street, N1 2TU (7226 1454/
www.pasharestaurant.co.uk). Angel tube/
Highbury & Islington tube/rail. **Meals served**
noon-11.30pm Mon-Thur; noon-midnight Fri-Sat; noon-11pm Sun. **Main courses** £7.50-£13.95. **Set meze** £13.95-£19.95. **Cover** £1. **Credit** (over £20) AmEx, MC, V.
Traditionally, all Turkish restaurants had a blue and white charm on the wall to fend off the evil eye. Pasha may well have the biggest in London, and it seems to be effective: the place is usually buzzing. On a recent visit, we began with a highly satisfactory mücver and salad, and a spinach-packed börek. Our meal continued with a surprisingly compact rack of lamb, which turned out to be a substantial piece of meat of melting tenderness. It came with a square of layered gratin potato. Dolma ordered as a main course includes a pepper, an aubergine and a courgette – each stuffed with mince and rice. Desserts were memorable too, both the intensely dense and rich chocolate mousse and the subtly flavoured sütlaç. The restaurant's orange walls are decorated with large mirrors, candles and great lanterns, together with paintings of Ottoman scenes. Waiting staff buzz around the interior incessantly, collecting large trays of food from downstairs and being – if anything – over-attentive on the tables. Pasha still reigns supreme over the Turkish restaurants in Angel.
Babies and children admitted. Booking advisable
weekends. Tables outdoors (3, pavement).
Separate room for parties, seats 20. Takeaway
service. **Map 5 O1.**

Sedir

4 Theberton Street, N1 0QX (7226 5489).
Angel tube/Highbury & Islington tube/rail.
Meals served 11am-11.30pm Mon-Thur;
11.30am-midnight Fri, Sat; 11.30am-11.30pm Sun. **Main courses** £6.95-£11.95. **Set lunch** £6.50-£7.95 2 courses. **Set meal** £16.50 per person (minimum 2) 3 courses. **Credit** AmEx, JCB, MC, V.
Spread over two floors, Sedir's pastel walls are decorated with large Victorian orientalist images of the Ottoman Empire, favouring naked harem women. In good weather a few tables are placed outside on the quiet street. Both our starters were first class on a recent visit: dolma were delicious, crisp on the outside and fresh; patlıcan salata, with puréed aubergine, had a pleasing rough texture. They were served with good pide bread, though it's irksome that Sedir charges extra for this. Main courses were excellent. Kilyos fish stew – named after the Black Sea resort near Istanbul – contained a delicious mix of squid, mussels, large unshelled prawns and hunks of salmon, their flavours blended in a thick sauce. Külbasti (grilled fillet of lamb) came with good rice and a side salad. Sedir has found a good niche in the market in offering variations on the traditional Turkish canon, and food is cooked to a high standard. An evening here can be pleasant, but we often feel that Sedir isn't quite achieved the relaxed ambience that is the hallmark of some of its competitors.
Babies and children welcome: children's menu;
high chair. Booking essential dinner. Separate
room for parties, seats 50. Tables outdoors
(4, pavement). Takeaway service. **Map 5 O1.**

Muswell Hill

Bakko

172-174 Muswell Hill Broadway, N10 3SA
(8883 1111/www.bakko.co.uk). Highgate tube
then 43, 134 bus. **Meals served** 11.30am-10.30pm daily. **Main courses** £8.90-£16.90. **Set lunch** (11.30am-4pm Mon-Fri) £8.90 3 courses. **Set meal** £17.90 per person (minimum 2) 3 courses. **Credit** MC, V.

The atmosphere is relaxed and friendly at Bakko, and the waiting staff are very attentive (making up an ayran yoghurt drink for us, though it was not on the menu). A large front window opens on to Muswell Hill Broadway, and big potted plants have been added to many of the tables, giving a pleasing green feel to the place. Unfortunately, the food was not what we have come to expect. Prawn guveç was neither very flavoursome nor bubbling hot. Similarly, patlıcan salata (usually one of the most reliably tasty staples of Turkish cuisine) was rather bland. Although the walls are covered in pictures of Kurdish women baking bread, the restaurant resolutely maintains its habit of only serving pitta, and appears to be reducing the Kurdish element in the food. A main course of ali nazik (lamb with yoghurt and mashed aubergine) was better, and a basic shish kebab was fine, though the rice was overcooked. We hope this apparent drop in standards was a hiccup, but are worried that Bakko has decided to tone down its cooking to please a less adventurous crowd.
Babies and children welcome: high chairs. Book
weekends. No smoking. Vegetarian menu.

North West
Golders Green

★ Beyoglu

1031 Finchley Road, NW11 7ES (8455 4884).
Golders Green tube/82, 160, 260 bus. **Meals served** noon-midnight daily. **Main courses** £6.50-£10. **Set dinner** £12-£13.75 3 courses incl coffee. **Credit** MC, V.
While there is nothing especially noteworthy about the food here – though the ingredients and presentation are commendable – this is a fine local restaurant that deserves support. For starters, both patlıcan salata and fava beans were faultless, the quality of the olive oil being noticeable. They came with wafer-thin saç bread as well as a warm pide. Main courses kept up the quality. Chicken shish was tender, while inegol köfte were luscious lamb patties spiced with cumin, parsley and pepper. Accompanying rice was light and fluffy. Desserts don't venture much beyond baklava and sütla, but both these were excellent. The mock-Tudor beams that cross the wide interior are decorated, like the walls, with patterned Turkish plates, bags and tiles, but the restaurant retains a light, spacious feel. Service was friendly and attentive. This is still the best of the Turkish restaurants in the area.
Babies and children welcome: high chairs. Book
weekends. No-smoking tables. Tables outdoors
(2, pavement). Takeaway service. Vegetarian menu.

Hampstead

★ Zara

11 South End Road, NW3 2PT (7794 5498).
Belsize Park tube/Hampstead Heath rail. **Meals served** 11.30am-11.30pm daily. **Main courses** £7.50-£10.50. **Credit** MC, V.
Cushioned benches run along the walls of Zara's compact interior, which is divided into smoking and non-smoking areas. In summer the glass front opens up and a few tables are placed on the wide pavement. The mixed cold meze gives a good idea of the range of starters, including houmous, tarama, börek, cacik and kısır. Each had a pleasing texture and was distinctly fresh. The pide was fine – though not, alas, baked in-house – and staff happily replenished it on request. Zara's menu is not extensive, but covers all the bases (apart from Turkish pizza). A basic lamb shish kebab made an excellent main course, accompanied by rice and salad. Kuzu firin consisted of a melting knuckle of lamb from the oven, cooked in a thick gravy with vegetables and potato, and also served with rice and salad. The pale walls are decorated with beautifully coloured and patterned tiles, together with summery paintings. Zara is popular with local diners and is usually busy. It makes an ideal end to a day out in Hampstead.
Babies and children welcome: high chairs. Book
weekends. No-smoking tables. Tables outdoors
(3, pavement). Takeaway service. Vegetarian
menu. **Map 28 C3.**

Vegetarian

London's vegetarian dining scene is in a state of flux. With the exception of the consistently reliable **Manna**, cooking at the top end has slipped a notch or two, whereas the food at the lower end has improved dramatically – thereby levelling out the overall meat-free dining experience. **222 Veggie Vegan** wowed us this year with its highly accomplished cooking. Moreover, many long-established vegetarian restaurants are modernising, getting refurbished or launching new menus.

You'll also find plenty of vegetarian dishes in Indian restaurants: try newcomers such as **Sanghamam** or **Satya**. Italian establishments, such as **Carluccio's Caffè** and **Locanda Locatelli**, offer excellent vegetarian dishes; and Middle Eastern eateries, including **Al Sultan**, **Noura** and the **Maroush** chain, serve a wonderful selection of meat-free meze and hot dishes. Thai restaurant **Mantanah** has a notable vegetarian menu, while other Thai establishments **Blue Elephant** and **Patara** have impressive meat-less menus that are suitable for special occasions. You'll also find a reasonable choice in Ethiopian, Greek and some Oriental restaurants.

For a few special occasion restaurants that offer good vegetarian set menus, *see right* **Set menus**.

Central
Barbican

Carnevale
135 Whitecross Street, EC1Y 8JL (7250 3452/ www.carnevalerestaurant.co.uk). Barbican tube/Old Street tube/rail/55 bus. **Lunch served** noon-3.30pm Mon-Fri. **Dinner served** 5.30-10.30pm Mon-Sat. **Main courses** £11.50. **Minimum** (noon-2.30pm Mon-Fri) £5.50. **Set meal** (lunch Mon-Fri, 5.30-7pm Mon-Sat) £13.50 courses. **Credit** MC, V.
Starters were the most promising course at this tiny, vanilla-hued Mediterranean restaurant, which houses a deli and a conservatory. They included roast jerusalem artichoke and pumpkin salad, and soft-poached egg atop a slab of toasted brioche (the egg was so intensely flavoured it tasted like duck egg). Both dishes came with a thatch of overdressed wild rocket – as did all the other dishes we tried. A main course of roast pear caponata (Italian sweet-sour aubergine casserole) wasn't a successful combination of flavours; the accompanying chilli polenta fritters, though unstodgy, were lacking in chilli. Breaded aubergine stuffed with smoked mozzarella and ricotta was better; the combination of the vegetable and smoked cheese gave the dish an unexpectedly meaty taste and texture. White chocolate pudding and chocolate rum pudding were both disappointing. They had a overly dense, gluey texture (perhaps caused by using too much agar-agar as a substitute for gelatin), and came with marinated plums and berries overwhelmed by the muskiness of cloves. Carnevale's menu is short and repetitive in its use of ingredients, and lacks the true sunshine flavours of the Mediterranean. *Babies and children admitted. Booking advisable. Tables outdoors (3, conservatory). Takeaway service. Vegan dishes.* **Map 5 P4.**

Covent Garden

★ Food for Thought
31 Neal Street, WC2H 9PR (7836 9072). Covent Garden tube. **Meals served** noon-8.30pm Mon-Sat; noon-5pm Sun. **Main courses** £3-£6.70. **Minimum** (noon-3pm, 6-7.30pm) £2.50. **Unlicensed. Corkage** no charge. **No credit cards.**
A compact subterranean café, Food for Thought is furnished with chunky wooden furniture and a small service counter crammed with friendly staff. On our summer visit we were told the area had just been struck by a power cut. The venue was being run on emergency electricity supplies, but the oven wasn't working so no hot dishes were available, only food that could be served at room temperature (quiche, salads, bread and cakes). The staff, despite having to work in hot, sweaty conditions, coped with aplomb, and their smiles never wavered. It's a testimony to how well loved this café is that the customers patiently remained, unfazed and uncomplaining. The result was a somewhat surreal sight of groups of hungry people happily munching away on quiche and salad in an intimate space. The quiche was delicious: the custard filled with fresh leeks, the pastry substantial without being stodgy. Salads were made from seasonal summery ingredients such as new potatoes, broad beans and fresh mint. This Covent Garden institution continues to dish up old-school veggie food with 21st-century zest and verve – with or without electricity. *Babies and children admitted. Bookings not accepted. No smoking. Takeaway service. Vegan dishes.* **Map 18 L6.**

Marylebone

Eat & Two Veg
50 Marylebone High Street, W1U 5HN (7258 8595/www.eatandtwoveg.com). Baker Street tube. **Meals served** 9am-11pm Mon-Sat; 10am-10pm Sun. **Main courses** £8-£10.25. **Credit** AmEx, MC, V.
This hip venue, furnished with red leather banquettes and pale turquoise Formica-topped tables, looks like an American-style diner. There's a small cocktail bar at the front. Tiles, bricks, wooden panels, industrial pipes, painted surfaces and suspended lamps give plenty of character to floors and walls – and the latter are decorated with framed adverts from the 1950s. So how's the food? Fine, as long as you like meat substitutes, or 'analogue meats' as they're sometimes known, such as TVP, quorn and tofu. Nevertheless, it's the dishes cooked without these that work the best. We started with good cocktails and smoky, lemony roasted almonds. Grilled halloumi salad was made with top-quality cheese, and fresh, zestily dressed leaves. Beetroot and goat's cheese croquettes were bland, as was schnitzel, though this did have a good crisp texture. It came with watercress sauce, silky mash and vibrant spinach. Thai green curry, made with sweet potatoes, had a lively, assertive flavour and was accompanied by vegetable rice. To finish, chocolate mousse cake was as rich and dense as a millionaire celebrity without a pre-nup on the brink of a divorce settlement. *Babies and children welcome: high chairs. Booking advisable. Disabled: toilet. No-smoking tables. Takeaway service; delivery service (7644 6666). Vegan dishes.* **Map 3 G4.**

Soho

Mildred's
45 Lexington Street, W1F 9AN (7494 1634/ www.mildreds.co.uk). Oxford Circus or Piccadilly Circus tube. **Meals served** noon-11pm Mon-Sat. **Main courses** £6.50-£7.95. **No credit cards.**
Now a leading contender for 'Soho's buzziest restaurant' award, were there indeed such a thing, this long-established venue has recently undergone a complete overhaul. It has a new layout and decor, and has become a totally different type of restaurant altogether. Gone are the wheatgrass and cranberry juices of yesteryear, replaced by

Set menus

The best vegetarian meals are found in the most unlikely places. Try these for a special treat.

HAUTE CUISINE
Gordon Ramsay Restaurants are the unexpected champions of vegetarian haute cuisine in London. **Gordon Ramsay at Claridges** is arguably the most impressive place for a vegetarian meal, though six courses will set you back £75 per head. Marcus Wareing's **Pétrus** is even pricier at £80 per head, while **Angela Hartnett at the Connaught** costs £55 for three courses or £70 for the tasting menu. **The Savoy Grill** – also a Ramsay outpost – has a three course vegetarian menu (£55, though the price was changing as we went to press). Shane Osborn's **Pied à Terre** is also a stunning restaurant with stunning food – £49.50 for two courses, or £75 for the eight-course vegetarian menu.

ELEGANT FRENCH
The euphemism 'garden menu' tends to be used in French restaurants (as the vegetarian concept is virtually unknown in France). The seven-course menu at the excellent **Roussillon** costs £55, while **Morgan M** offers a six-course garden menu for £36.

AUTHENTIC ROYAL THAI
A Buddhist tradition and courtly cooking are combined on the vegetarian menus at **Nahm**, where lunch costs £26 and dinner £49.50.

RESTAURANTS

Green Note. See p283.

fabulous Kir Royales in the tiny, vibrant bar at the front. The bright, cheery dining room at the back – filled with beautifully clad, hip twenty- and thirtysomethings – is decorated with witty contemporary art. Vegetable gyoza were feather-light and delicately flavoured, and a slightly sweet, tangy Hyderabad-style aubergine curry was robustly spiced. Mushroom and ale pie wasn't a success, however; the pastry was stodgy, the filling bland and sloppy, and the accompanying chunky chips and mushy peas were dry and grainy. To finish, mascarpone-stuffed figs poached in red wine and orange juice were fine, but the real show-stopper was the stunning chocolate, raspberry and roasted hazelnut trifle from the specials board. Mildred's doesn't take bookings, so be prepared to wait your turn at the bar.
Babies and children admitted. No smoking. Tables outdoors (2, pavement). Takeaway service. Vegan dishes. **Map 17 J6**.

West
Hammersmith

The Gate
51 Queen Caroline Street, W6 9QL (8748 6932/ www.thegate.tv). Hammersmith tube. **Lunch served** noon-2.45pm Mon-Fri. **Dinner served** 6-10.45pm Mon-Sat. **Main courses** £8.50-£13.50. **Credit** AmEx, MC, V.
This smart, artistically decorated venue, leased from a church on its premises, is one of the capital's leading vegetarian restaurants. However, our visit this year was a disappointment. We phoned to book a table for 7pm, and were told that there was a turnaround on tables, so we'd have to finish by 9.30pm – 'or 9.45pm at a push'. Throughout our meal, the restaurant remained half empty and, come the appointed time, there was no pressure for us to leave. So why the fuss? 'We tell the customers that they'll have to give up their tables in case there's a late rush from nearby theatres,' said the manager when we asked. Service, from slightly scatty staff with attitude, started off rushed, but relaxed as the evening wore on. Food is based on the Mediterranean repertoire, but the menu also incorporates the likes of Caribbean curry and aubergine teriyaki. Some of our dishes, notably raw shiitake mushroom cake, and spicy halloumi kebabs, were delicious; others, like wild mushroom galette, and feta and avocado-stuffed artichoke on a too-hefty slab of lemongrass polenta, worked less well, as the dishes were misjudged and the flavours askew. We hope that this long-time favourite isn't becoming complacent.

Babies and children welcome: high chairs. Booking essential. No smoking. Tables outdoors (15, courtyard). Vegan dishes. **Map 20 B4**.

Shepherd's Bush

Blah Blah Blah
78 Goldhawk Road, W12 8HA (8746 1337). Goldhawk Road tube/94 bus. **Lunch served** 12.30-2.30pm, **dinner served** 6.30-10.30pm Mon-Sat. **Main courses** £9.95. **Unlicensed**. **Corkage** £1.45 per person. **No credit cards**.
Something of a gem on an insalubrious stretch of Goldhawk Road, Blah Blah Blah has been recently refurbished. It now boasts attractive cream and maroon walls festooned with large tribal artefacts. The menu seems to have taken a more Mediterranean stance. Asparagus tartlets were made with extremely good flaky pastry and filled with deliciously light, creamy béarnaise sauce flavoured with the sweet spikiness of tarragon and dill. A Mediterranean terrine layered with grilled aubergines, courgettes, green beans, new potatoes, roast peppers and goat's cheese, served with sun-dried tomato toast, epitomised the flavours of southern France on a (very pretty) plate. Less pleasing was a slightly 'so-what' dish of roulade made from paper-thin potato slices stuffed with ricotta, tomatoes, basil and pine nuts, served with slightly odd sauces and salad garnishes. However, we enjoyed tackling a tall tower of tostada, somewhat awkwardly layered with punchily flavoured refried beans, sweetcorn and avocados. Don't miss the puddings: warm rhubarb and apple charlotte boasted wonderfully light sponge; and the strawberry and chocolate meringue was simply divine. Service is matey and unruffled.
Babies and children admitted. Booking advisable. Separate room for parties, seats 35. Vegan dishes. **Map 20 B2**.

West Kensington

★ 222 Veggie Vegan
222 North End Road, W14 9NU (7381 2322/ www.222veggievegan.com). West Kensington tube/28, 391 bus. **Lunch served** noon-3.30pm, **dinner served** 5.30-10.30pm daily. **Main courses** £7.50-£10.50. **Set buffet** (lunch) £5.95. **Credit** MC, V.
Since our visit last year, this vegan eaterie – with cream walls, wooden furniture, potted plants and funky pictures of seashells – has been spruced up. The cooking has also risen several notches. Every dish we sampled was carefully and competently cooked by Ghanaian-born head chef Ben Asamani, beautifully presented, and packed with flavour, texture and colour. It's difficult to make good vegan pancakes, and in the past we've found the pancakes here leathery; this time, however, we were impressed by their soft and velvety texture, and the lightness of the tofu and black-eye bean filling. The restaurant's signature dish, '222 Gardens', combines Afro-Caribbean-style plantain and okra with Middle Eastern falafel, oriental-style soy-marinated aubergines and courgettes, and Mediterranean-style tomato sauce. It is deeply delicious. Rich, creamy stroganoff made from mushrooms and seitan (wheat gluten) was given a thumbs-up by our Hungarian guest. A customer at the next table, cheered on by fellow diners, lifted up her plate and licked it clean. We didn't go quite that far, but we knew what she meant.
Babies and children welcome: high chairs. Booking advisable. No smoking. Takeaway service. Vegan dishes. **Map 13 A12**.

South
Streatham

★ Wholemeal Café NEW
1 Shrubbery Road, SW16 2AS (8769 2423). Streatham Hill rail. **Meals served** noon-10pm daily. **Main courses** £2.60-£6.95. **Credit** MC, V.
Popular with locals, this small no-frills caff serves hefty old-fashioned veggie staples such as stews, casseroles, bakes, quiches, jacket potatoes and

cakes. There's a blackboard of daily changing specials, but no written menu. Garlic mushrooms and pitta bread came with fresh mixed salad; a carrot, celery and aubergine stew was pleasantly flavoured with coriander and cumin. Homity pie, once a hugely popular dish at the now-defunct chain of Cranks restaurants, had all but disappeared from London's vegetarian dining scene. Here it makes a nostalgia-inducing appearance and is at least as good as the classic version (but with thinner pastry). We recommend the desserts; own-made carrot cake is a veggie restaurant cliché, but here it was beautifully moist and topped with a simple drizzle of sugar syrup, rather than the more ubiquitous calorific icing. It's cheeky for an unassuming local café to name its signature dessert 'world famous banoffi pie', but do try the dish. Thick, rich, dense, yet somehow light and tasting of buttery caramel – if it's not world-famous, it certainly ought to be. *Babies and children admitted. No smoking. Takeaway service. Vegan dishes.*

South East
Crystal Palace

★ Spirited Palace NEW
105 Church Road, SE19 2PR (8771 5557/ www.spiritedpalace.com). Crystal Palace or Gipsy Hill rail. **Meals served** 11am-9.30pm Tue-Fri;

2-9.30pm Sat, Sun. **Main courses** £3.50-£5. **Set meal** £5.50 1 course. **No credit cards.**
A vegan restaurant with a health food shop attached, the Spirited Palace offers holistic therapies, and hosts everything from raw food demonstrations to drumming workshops. It has a Caribbean chef cooking Ital food (meaning 'vital, healthy and natural' in Rastafarian patois). The Ital dietary laws forbid the use of meat, poultry, fish, alcohol, cow's milk, coffee and sometimes even added salt. Despite these restrictions, our food was delicious. Tofu was sliced in wafer-thin squares, fried in tempura-like batter and topped with herbs and spices. Kale in coconut milk was creamy, with mineral overtones. Even the brown rice was plump, shiny and well seasoned. Tangy barbecued strips of gluten were particularly tasty. For dessert, apple roly-poly, with a crust somewhere between pastry and sponge, was scrumptious, and arrived with superlative soy milk custard. As a restaurant, though, the place doesn't work. The chef, 'Auntie', was out catering for a party on our visit. The dining area consists of two poky rooms in the basement. We were the only customers on a Friday night – although any more, and it would have been crowded. We're told the owners are looking for larger premises.
Babies and children welcome: high chairs. Booking advisable. No smoking. Separate room for parties, seats 32. Vegan dishes.

North
Camden Town & Chalk Farm

Green Note NEW
106 Parkway, NW1 7AN (7485 9899/ www.greennote.co.uk). Camden Town tube. **Bar Open** 6-10.30pm Tue; 6-11pm Wed, Thur; 6pm-midnight Fri; noon-midnight Sat; noon-10.30pm Sun. *Restaurant* **Dinner served** 6-9.30pm Tue-Thur; 6-10pm Fri. **Meals served** noon-10pm Sat; noon-9.30pm Sun. **Tapas** £2.95-£4.95. **Main courses** £7.95-£9.95. **Admission** varies; check website. **Credit** MC, V.
When this lively venue, which has a tiny dining room at the front and a more spacious music club with bar at the back, opened in 2005, it served a full menu alongside a list of global tapas. It no longer offers the full menu – only a fairly wide selection of tapas (platters of 'small eats' designed to be shared). The focus of the venture seems to be very much its live folk, blues and country. We enjoyed mango, halloumi and fresh mint salad: an excellent, summery combination of flavours. Another salad was more prosaic, but nonetheless contained well-flavoured chunks of marinated tofu. Aloo tikki (Indian potato patties)

Budget cafés

For a cheap, tasty and healthy alternative to the lunchtime sandwich, try one of these budget cafés. Most are open during the daytime only, though Beatroot, Red Veg and Wild Cherry serve into the early evening.

★ Beatroot
92 Berwick Street, W1F 0QD (7437 8591). Oxford Circus, Piccadilly Circus or Tottenham Court Road tube. **Meals served** 9.15am-9.30pm Mon-Sat. **Main courses** £3.50-£5.50. **No credit cards.**
Small, medium and large containers are filled to the brim at this compact, wholesome eaterie, which is also popular as a takeaway. Daily specials include salads, snacks, bakes, quiches, tagines, vegan cakes, organic juices and smoothies.
Babies and children admitted. No smoking. Tables outdoors (4, pavement). Takeaway service. Vegan dishes. **Map 17 J/K6.**

★ Gallery Café
21 Old Ford Road, E2 9PL (8983 3624). Bethnal Green tube/8, 388 bus. **Meals served** 9am-4pm Tue-Sat. **Main courses** £3.50-£4.80. **Credit** MC, V.
Now under new management, this café is no longer owned by the London Buddhist Centre. The focus is on a changing seasonal menu; in summer, for instance, there's a wide range of salads, plus stir-fries and cakes.
Babies and children welcome: high chairs. No smoking (indoors). Tables outdoors (14, patio/conservatory). Takeaway service. Vegan dishes.

★ The Place Below
St Mary-le-Bow, Cheapside, EC2V 6AU (7329 0789/www.theplacebelow.co.uk). St Paul's tube/Bank tube/DLR. **Breakfast served** 7.30-11am, **lunch served** 11.30am-2.30pm, **snacks served** 2.30-3.30pm Mon-Fri. **Main courses** £5.50-£7.50. **Unlicensed. Corkage** no charge. **Credit** MC, V.

Vegetarian cookery writer Bill Sewell's smart canteen inside the Norman crypt of St Mary-le-Bow church continues to offer tasty breakfasts, salads, bakes and quiches, along with fresh juices and coffee. The Place is worth a visit for its singular atmosphere.
Babies and children admitted. No smoking. Tables outdoors (24, churchyard). Takeaway service (7.30am-3pm). Vegan dishes. **Map 11 P6.**

★ Red Veg
95 Dean Street, W1V 5RB (7437 3109/ www.redveg.com). Tottenham Court Road tube. **Meals served** noon-9.30pm Mon-Sat; noon-6.30pm Sun. **Main courses** £3.15-£4.35. **No credit cards.**
Specialising in a variety of burgers, this tiny café and takeaway also sells falafels, hot dogs and (chicken-less) nuggets. Hot pasta dishes – including one with own-made pesto – have also been introduced to the menu.
Babies and children admitted. Takeaway service. Vegan dishes. **Map 17 K6.**

★ Service-Heart-Joy
191 Hartfield Road, SW19 3TH (8542 9912). South Wimbledon tube/Wimbledon tube/rail. **Meals served** 8am-4.30pm Mon-Fri; 9am-4.30pm Sat. **Main courses** £1.95-£6.95. **Credit** MC, V.
There's more emphasis on cakes now at this café, run by followers of Indian spiritual leader Sri Chinmoy. The menu boasts 47 varieties of own-made cakes, including blueberry, mango, cardamom and chocolate truffle, as well as breakfast dishes and hot savouries.
Babies and children admitted. No smoking. Tables outdoors (2, pavement). Takeaway service. Vegan dishes.

★ Wheatley's NEW
33-34 Myddleton Street, EC1R 1UR (7278 6662). Angel tube/Farringdon tube/ rail. **Lunch served** 11am-3pm Mon-Fri. **Main courses** £3.50-£5.50. **Set lunch** £3-£5 1 course. **No credit cards.**

Wheatley's, a wholesome café, is tucked in a sidestreet near Sadler's Wells and City University. Sweet potato and carrot soup was deliciously garlicky, and came with chunky wholemeal bread on our visit. Other dishes included roasted vegetable lasagne, potato and red pepper curry, sandwiches and wraps.
Babies and children admitted. Disabled: toilet. No smoking. Tables outdoors (10, garden). Takeaway service; delivery service (within EC1). Vegan dishes. **Map 5 N3.**

★ Wild Cherry
241-245 Globe Road, E2 0JD (8980 6678). Bethnal Green tube/8 bus. **Meals served** 10.30am-7pm Tue-Fri; 10.30am-4.30pm Sat. **Main courses** £3.25-£5.95. **Unlicensed. Corkage** £1. **Credit** MC, V.
Run by women from the local London Buddhist Centre, this sparse, somewhat scruffy canteen offers a daily changing selection of hearty casseroles, soups, pastas, baked potatoes, risottos, pies, curries and salads. Portions are generous, and there are queues at lunchtimes. Unlike many veggie caffs, it's okay to bring in your own alcohol.
Babies and children welcome: high chairs. No smoking. Tables outdoors (9, garden). Takeaway service. Vegan dishes.

★ World Food Café
First floor, 14 Neal's Yard, WC2H 9DP (7379 0298). Covent Garden tube. **Meals served** 11.30am-4.30pm Mon-Fri; 11.30am-5pm Sat. **Main courses** £6.50-£7.95. **Minimum** (noon-2pm Mon-Fri; 11.30am-5pm Sat) £6. **Credit** MC, V.
Meze, thalis, platters of tapas, and other set meals – as opposed to individual dishes – from around the globe (Japan, Mexico, Turkey, Africa) are the USP here. The small first-floor café overlooks Neal's Yard; world music provides the soundtrack.
Babies and children welcome: high chairs. No smoking. Takeaway service. Vegan dishes. **Map 18 L6.**

were delicious and served with chili-spiked coconut and coriander chutney. In contrast, a trio of Greek-style dips disappointed, as their texture was too dense and dry. Puddings are a strong point: vegan tofu cheesecake topped with strawberries was very light; and warm chocolate brownie was deliciously rich. Although the food is freshly cooked on the premises and is, on the whole, of a high standard, the venue works better as a music club.

Babies and children admitted (restaurant). Booking essential. Entertainment: folk, blues, country Wed-Sun. No-smoking tables. Vegan dishes. **Map 27 C3.**

★ Manna

4 Erskine Road, NW3 3AJ (7722 8028/ www.manna-veg.com). Chalk Farm tube. **Brunch served** 12.30-3pm Sun. **Dinner served** 6.30-11pm daily. **Main courses** £9.50-£12.95. **Credit** MC, V.

An ideal venue to impress a vegetarian date or a guest from overseas. The menu is spankingly modern and imaginative, using fashionable ingredients little seen in London's other vegetarian restaurants. Manna is an intimate yet spacious affair, with two dining rooms, a small conservatory at the front, plus tables outside for alfresco dining. The floor, furniture and ceilings are all made from wood, so the effect is akin to sitting inside a box – albeit a smart one, and with friendly, professional staff on hand. Potato böreks boasted tasty fillings inside excellent pastry. Celeriac and blue cheese roulade with watercress pesto was perfectly cooked, with strong, sharp flavours. Also impressive were tortillas, rendered smoky with the addition of smoked tofu and chipotle chili. Nettle ravioli (more like pasties), served with wild garlic pesto, gained plaudits too. There's a marvellous drinks list (encompassing organic beer and cider, organic teas and coffees and a notable wine list) along with a beautifully executed selection of desserts, such as pistachio and date chocolate brownie. Set amid the leafy environs of Primrose Hill, Manna is in a class – and world – of its own.

Babies and children welcome: high chairs. Booking advisable. No smoking. Tables outdoors (2, pavement; 2, conservatory). Takeaway service. Vegan dishes. **Map 27 A1.**

Outer London

Kingston, Surrey

Riverside Vegetaria

64 High Street, Kingston upon Thames, Surrey KT1 1HN (8546 0609/www.rsveg.plus.com). Kingston rail. **Meals served** noon-1pm Mon-Sat; noon-10.30pm Sun. **Main courses** £6.95-£8.50. **Credit** MC, V.

This cosy restaurant offers an unusual juxtaposition of substantial old-school winter fare and summery views of the river bedecked with ducks, swans and boats. Owned by Sri Lankan-born Ritchie Sakthivel, a follower of the Sai Baba religious sect which originated in India, the venue prides itself on offering additive-free, mainly organic and vegan dishes in keeping with Sakthivel's religious beliefs. There's a long international menu, plus a very extensive specials board. The selection of mostly spicy dishes could easily be entitled 'around the world in 80 stews'. We liked the hearty Jamaican stew: it was made with sweet potatoes, carrots, green and red peppers, and a plethora of freshly cooked (not tinned) beans such as black-eye, red kidney, butter and chickpeas – in chilli- and turmeric-flecked coconut sauce. The drinks list contains many organic and vegan wines; we recommend the golden apple wine from Sedlescombe Organic Vineyard in Sussex, which was refreshing and not too sweet. We'd love to see more local English wines like this, including aromatic fruit and herb wines from the south of England, on more restaurant menus.

Babies and children welcome: children's portions; high chairs. Book weekends. No smoking. Tables outdoors (7, riverside terrace). Takeaway service. Vegan dishes.

Vietnamese

Hackney is home to one of the largest Vietnamese communities in Britain: up to 4,000 at the last count. The majority arrived in 1979, when the British government offered homes to 20,000 Vietnamese boat people from Hong Kong. Some are ethnic Chinese who left northern Vietnam after the 1979 Sino-Vietnamese war; others are southern Vietnamese who fled the communist takeover in 1975. It took some 15 years after their arrival for a Vietnamese culinary enclave to become established in Hackney. The seeds were sown when the An-Viet Foundation, a charity helping the boat people adjust to their new lives in London, opened a very basic canteen in a residential street in Dalston; **Huong-Viet** quickly became known for its fresh, authentic food. Some of the staff at Huong-Viet later opened **Viet Hoa** (at the southern end of Kingsland Road), which first appeared in this guide more than a decade ago. Nowadays, Viet Hoa is surrounded by Vietnamese restaurants of varying quality; of these, **Sông Quê** is particularly recommended. This year we're also pleased to welcome an upmarket restaurant that fuses French culinary traditions with those of Vietnam (Vietnam was, after all, a French colony for nearly a century until 1954) – **Xích Lô,** which has arrived in London via a first branch in Oslo.

Central

Clerkenwell & Farringdon

★ Pho

86 St John Street, EC1M 4EH (7253 7624). Barbican tube/Farringdon tube/rail. **Lunch served** noon-3pm, **dinner served** 6-10pm Mon-Fri. **Main courses** £5.95-£7.45. **Credit** MC, V.

The English owners of this appealing and modern little café have taken a few Vietnamese street snacks, and turned them into a 'concept'. Pho, the beef broth and noodle soup, is the mainstay of the menu, coming in more than a dozen variations. The stock of ours was sublime: aromatic and richly flavoured yet clear, such that the accompanying seasonings (a little plate of fresh herbs, red chillies, beansprouts, squeeze of lime) were barely needed. The flat rice noodles also had a perfectly elastic texture, and both the meatballs and slices of steak were top quality. Much less impressive was a starter of summer rolls; most of the filling was bland rice noodles with hardly any prawn or herbs, so that not even the accompanying nuoc cham sauce could pep it up. There's a handful of other Vietnamese dishes too, and an extensive drinks list that includes decent wines, Vietnamese-style iced coffee, and the expensive so-called 'weasel coffee'. The gimmick is that the coffee beans have supposedly been through the alimentary tract of an Asian rodent – but in reality this is a myth perpetuated by the canny Vietnamese makers.

Babies and children admitted. Bookings not accepted. No smoking. Takeaway service. **Map 5 O4.**

★ Xích Lô NEW

103 St John Street, EC1M 4AS (7253 0323/ www.xichlorestaurant.com). Barbican tube/ Farringdon tube/rail. **Lunch served** noon-3pm Mon-Fri. **Dinner served** 6-11pm Mon-Sat. **Main courses** £11.50-£17.50. **Set lunch** £6 1 course. **Set dinner** £24.95 3 courses. **Credit** MC, V.

The menu at the big new Xích Lô ('cycle rickshaw') takes its inspiration from the French colonial period of Indochina, resulting in a successful mix of French restaurant technique and Vietnamese flavours. Every dish is paired with a recommended wine, and some food, such as beef tenderloin with sautéed mushrooms and red wine sauce, is distinctly European. Yet the Norwegian and Vietnamese owners have the sense to leave classic Vietnamese dishes alone. Vietnamese chicken salad (goi ga) is an excellent version of shredded white meat, green papaya, carrot and lotus root, given piquancy with nuoc cham and Vietnamese herbs (rau thom). The Norwegian chef-proprietor, Odd Arne Braute, used to run a party-catering business; order the tasting menu and you'll get a succession of pretty plates and morsels of food that resemble canapés. There are amuse-bouches such as a little soup spoon appetiser of beef stir-fried with tamarind; this combination of ingredients is usually used in soups and sauces, not in stir-fries. Vietnamese desserts include banana with sweet potato and tapioca pearls; or there's passionfruit crème brûlée, which is exceptional even by smart French restaurant standards.

Babies and children admitted. Disabled: toilet. No-smoking tables. Separate room for parties, seats 50. **Map 5 O4.**

West

Hammersmith

Saigon Saigon

313-317 King Street, W6 9NH (0870 220 1398/www.saigon-saigon.co.uk). Ravenscourt Park or Stamford Brook tube. *Bar* **Open/snacks served** 6-11.30pm Thur-Sun. *Restaurant* **Lunch served** noon-3pm Tue-Sun. **Dinner served** 6-11pm Mon-Thur, Sun; 6-11.30pm Fri, Sat. **Main courses** £6-£13. **Set meal** £22-£30 3 courses. *Both* **Credit** MC, V.

The dark wooden floors, the thick bamboo shoots and the engraved decor here make for a tasteful, minimalist interior reminiscent of Indochina. The menu promises to be similarly traditional, with such dishes as lau hai sun (Vietnamese fondue),

classic pho soup, and the banh xeo (pancake). As a starter, the friendly waiter brought us deep-fried prawns in a wonderful crusty batter, served with a flavoursome salt, lime, pepper and chilli dip. Canh khoai mo was a tasty thick soup containing fleshy pieces of yam and delightful morsels of shrimp, all topped with aromatic parsley. We continued with ga xao lang, a chewy and bland turmeric chicken, stir-fried with vermicelli, black fungus and onion. Grilled salted mackerel (ca nuc uop xa muoi nuong la chuoi) arrived neatly arranged on banana leaves; it was crunchy yet juicy on the inside, and the aromas of the chopped fresh lemongrass and chilli sprinkled on top worked extremely well with the salty fish. Overall, a satisfying example of Vietnamese cooking.
Babies and children welcome: high chairs. Bar available for hire. Booking advisable. No smoking (restaurant). Tables outdoors (4, pavement).
Map 20 A4.

South East
Deptford

★ West Lake
207 Deptford High Street, SE8 3NT (8465 9408). Deptford rail. **Meals served** 11.30am-10pm daily. **Main courses** £3-£6. **Unlicensed. Corkage** no charge. **No credit cards.**
Amid Asian supermarkets, African food shops and 99p stores, you'll find this small Vietnamese café. The dim lighting and wooden decoration exude an oriental ambience. West Lake is popular among local Vietnamese, and serves many specialities that you wouldn't find in restaurants aimed at westerners. Aside from the usual pork, beef, seafood and vegetarian dishes, there are less common ingredients on the menu such as squid tentacles, quail and jellyfish. We tried the frogs' legs with onions, seasoned with pepper and salt. Dunked in a sauce made of salt, lime and chillies, these lean, little legs were delightful. The beef in 'lot' leaves that followed was too greasy, however, with tough and unpleasant-tasting meat. Sour soup with tomatoes, spring onions, beansprouts, taro stem and fish cake was dominated by lime juice, though dill and the chewy fish cake produced added flavour. Greasy pork with onions, supposedly in a Vietnamese-style curry sauce, was simply displeasing, tasting of soy sauce and MSG, with the curry powder barely noticeable. A decidedly mixed experience, then.
Babies and children admitted. Book weekends. Takeaway service.

East
Shoreditch

★ Au Lac
104 Kingsland Road, E2 8DP (7033 0588/ www.aulac.co.uk). Old Street tube/rail/26, 48, 55, 67, 149, 242, 243 bus. **Lunch served** noon-3pm Mon-Fri. **Dinner served** 5.30-11.30pm Mon-Thur; 5.30pm-midnight Fri. **Meals served** noon-midnight Sat; noon-11.30pm Sun. **Main courses** £4.50-£8.50. **Set dinner** £12-£15.50 per person (minimum 2) 7 courses. **Credit** JCB, MC, V.
Isn't it always the way? Just when you feel like eating crispy eels with betel leaf, the waiter informs you that they've run out. This was the only disappointment at Au Lac, a classy standout among the Kingsland Road Vietnamese brigade. No Formica table-tops or plastic flowers here: real white linen tablecloths rest beneath paper coverings; real plants decorate the spacious room; there are real fish in the aquarium; and orange silk lanterns and colourful paintings add an authentic touch too. We ordered the set dinner for two and found it enough for four. The golden pancake was excellent: the batter light and crisp; the filling bursting with fresh beansprouts, chicken and prawns. Grilled monkfish on noodles was equally accomplished. The tactile pleasure of using these ingredients to create our own rice starch rolls was enhanced by the wonderful combination of tastes. Among the mains, spicy chicken was packed with chilli yet wasn't so hot as to ruin our palate for the tender stir-fried beef with ong choi (a crunchy green vegetable). Service was friendly, reasonably prompt and unobtrusive, though we've also experienced total collapse on busy nights. The former branch in Highbury (82 Highbury Park, N5 2XE, 7704 9187) is now run entirely separately, though shares the same name.
Babies and children welcome: high chairs. Booking advisable weekends. Entertainment: pianist 8-10pm Fri. Takeaway service.
Map 6 R3.

★ Cây Tre
301 Old Street, EC1V 9LA (7729 8662). Old Street tube/rail. **Lunch served** noon-3pm Mon-Sat. **Dinner served** 5.30-11pm Mon-Thur; 5.30-11.30pm Fri, Sat. **Meals served** noon-10.30pm Sun. **Credit** AmEx, MC, V.
Bright little Cây Tre is set amid the hustle and bustle of Old Street. Its menu offers some rarely seen (even in Shoreditch) Vietnamese dishes that,

to indicate their authenticity, are marked with small smiley faces. Particularly exceptional is the range of typical herbs used. The speciality of the house, cha ca la vong (sliced monkfish with fennel and dill, marinated in galangal and saffron), was fried at the table for us by the friendly, helpful waitress. Combined with rice vermicelli and fermented shrimp sauce (pungent and sour), this appetiser for two produced a luscious fusion of different, typically Vietnamese aromas. Then the meal went downhill. Canh chua soup (spicy and sour, with beansprouts, pineapple, celery and taro stems) was refreshing yet unspectacular. The traditional tamarind flavour was barely detectable and the white fish had an unpleasant rubbery texture. Sliced fried tofu garnished with herbs in a sweet tomtaot broth was simply unsatisfactory, as the unusually thick and sweet tomato sauce was reminiscent of a cheap Chinese takeaway.
Babies and children admitted. Booking advisable. Takeaway service.
For branch (Viet Grill) see index.

★ Hanoi Café
98 Kingsland Road, E2 8DP (7729 5610/ www.hanoicafe.co.uk). Old Street tube/rail/26, 48, 55, 67, 149, 242, 243 bus. **Meals served** noon-11.30pm daily. **Main courses** £3.50-£6.90. **Set lunch** £3.80 1 course. **Credit** (over £10) AmEx, MC, V.
It's disconcerting to sit down in an empty restaurant and even more so if you hear what appears to be a brawl coming from the direction of the kitchen. But the screeching soundtrack of a kung fu movie was soon turned down and this unassuming café, decorated with arty photos and jaunty green table-tops, attracted a steady stream of customers during the course of our meal. So it should, for the food here is highly appealing. The low point was a king prawn bun devoid of taste – weird, as our other dishes sparkled with flavour. Three dainty sticks of prawn mousse on sugar cane made a great appetiser, leaving plenty of room for the huge serving of lime chicken roll-it-yourself summer rolls. There was probably little actual chicken in the crispy fried strips, but the whole thing tasted pretty good. Even better was caramelised ginger duck: tender chunks of meat in a luscious, not overly sweet sauce. The high point was a whole king fish, fried to perfection, covered with fresh mango slices and a tangy sauce.
Babies and children welcome: high chairs. Restaurant available for hire. Takeaway service; delivery service (within 3-mile radius).
Map 6 R3.

★ Loong Kee

134G Kingsland Road, E2 8DY (7729 8344). Old Street tube/rail/26, 48, 55, 67, 149, 242, 243 bus. **Lunch served** noon-3pm Mon-Fri. **Dinner served** 5-11pm Mon-Thur; 5pm-midnight Fri. **Meals served** noon-midnight Sat; noon-11pm Sun. **Main courses** £3.50-£5.50. **Unlicensed. Corkage** no charge. **No credit cards.**

Just past the clutch of Vietnamese restaurants on Kingsland Road, you'll find this inconspicuous little spot. Although Loong Kee is somewhat run down (the toilet was in a state, and a bucket full of musty water functioned as a sink), the Vietnamese community and other locals appreciate its northern Vietnamese specialities. Noodle soups, vermicelli dishes and salads make up the genuine Vietnamese section of the Sino-dominated menu. Banh cuon (steamed rice pasta filled with minced pork and cloud-ear fungus), served with lettuce and sweet-sour nuoc cham, was a treat for the taste buds. Chicken feet and lotus stem salad with herbs and peanuts, on the other hand, was less delightful. The chicken feet, though stimulating in texture, simply soaked up the uninteresting vinegar dressing, while the pickled lotus stems tasted of nothing but sour preservatives. The unusually small and flappy goi cuon (rice-paper rolls filled with shrimp, lettuce and vermicelli) were also disappointing. Bun bo xao xa, a rice vermicelli dish on a bed of shredded lettuce, beansprouts and deliciously lemongrass-flavoured beef, saved the dinner. Loong Kee lacks consistency in quality, but at least the service was friendly and attentive.
Babies and children welcome: high chairs. Booking advisable. Separate room for parties, seats 30. Takeaway service. **Map 6 R3.**

★ ★ Sông Quê

134 Kingsland Road, E2 8DY (7613 3222). Old Street tube/rail/26, 48, 55, 67, 149, 242, 243 bus. **Lunch served** noon-3pm, **dinner served** 5.30-11pm Mon-Sat. **Meals served** noon-11pm Sun. **Main courses** £4.40-£5.60. **Credit** AmEx, MC, V.

The interior of Sông Quê may be kitsch – flaky pale green paint covers the walls, along with plastic lobsters and fake ivy – but don't be put off. Here you'll find delicious and authentic Vietnamese food. The menu can be overwhelming, offering over 170 dishes, including a great range of regional specialities, and roughly 20 variations of pho. There are also rarities such as tre ba mau (three-coloured pudding, a dessert consisting of red beans, mung beans, tapioca and coconut milk) or ca kho to (snapper cooked in brine). Bi cuon were luscious rice-paper rolls with lettuce, vermicelli, mint and chives. Banh xeo (a bright yellow pancake filled with beansprouts, onions, chicken and prawns) was a bit greasy, yet still delicious; coriander, sweet basil and mint brilliantly complemented the salty filling and the sweet and sour sauce. Sông Quê is particularly good for soups. Pho rice noodle soup was full of aromatic nuances; hints of star anise, cinnamon, coriander and sweet basil unfolded in our mouths. From central Vietnam, bun bo hue (vermicelli topped with beef and Vietnamese sausage) was also scrumptious.
Babies and children welcome: high chairs. Booking advisable. No-smoking tables. Takeaway service. **Map 6 R3.**

★ Tay Do Café

65 Kingsland Road, E2 8AG (7729 7223). Old Street tube/rail/26, 48, 55, 67, 149, 242, 243 bus. **Lunch served** 11.30am-3pm, **dinner served** 5-11.30pm daily. **Main courses** £4-£8.50. **Set lunch** £3.30 1 course. **Unlicensed. Corkage** 50p. **Credit** (over £10) MC, V.

This little café on Kingsland Road is certainly a hit with Hoxton hipsters and Vietnamese locals. At weekends it can be hard to find a table; often you'll have to sit bum to bum with other guests. The popularity is understandable, as the food is simply outstanding. Rich minced eel and onions on crunchy prawn crackers had the sweet and spicy taste of Vietnamese curry, as well as a lovely velvety texture. Combined with fresh and crisp papaya salad (papaya, carrot, prawn, pork and rau ram herbs), this made a perfect start to our meal. To follow, we ordered gilthead snapper in fish sauce with mango. This deep-fried delicacy was extremely crisp and yet tender on the inside. The sour unripe mango strips harmonised wonderfully with the salty taste of the fish sauce. Bun bi cha gio (a combination of vermicelli, shredded pork and traditional Vietnamese spring rolls) was blissful, fresh and filling. The only downside to Tay Do is the service. The waiters rush from one table to another, keeping conversations with the diners brusque; they often have trouble understanding food orders too.
Babies and children welcome: high chairs. Booking advisable. Disabled: toilet. Takeaway service. **Map 6 R3.**
For branch see index.

★ Viet Hoa

70-72 Kingsland Road, E2 8DP (7729 8293). Old Street tube/rail/26, 48, 55, 67, 149, 242, 243 bus. **Lunch served** noon-3pm Mon-Fri; 12.30-4pm Sat, Sun. **Dinner served** 5.30-11pm daily. **Main courses** £3.50-£8.50. **Credit** AmEx, MC, V.

Spread over two floors, Viet Hoa is much bigger than most of the Viet eateries along Kingsland Road. But even if it outdoes local competitors in size, it doesn't quite reach their culinary standards. Apart from the usual rice vermicelli dishes and noodle soups, the main courses sound like Sino-Viet combos rather than Vietnamese specialities. Disappointingly, the spring rolls were made with Chinese dough wrappers instead of Vietnamese rice paper. At least they contained the Vietnamese filling of carrots, glass noodles, minced pork and black fungus – but wrapped in lettuce and dipped in nuoc cham (sour fish sauce with chilli), they were merely adequate. Cha ca ha noi (Hanoi-style fried fish fillets), a northern Vietnamese recipe, arrived in a small iron dish still sizzling, the dill

and turmeric producing an appetising aroma. The fish rested atop lettuce, cucumber, coriander and rice vermicelli, and was more evocative of the herbal experience that is Vietnamese cuisine. There's some authenticity in the drinks list. To quench your thirst, choose from a small selection of Asian beers, including Tiger, Tsingtao or, more interestingly, the Vietnamese Hue beer.

Babies and children welcome: high chairs. Booking advisable; essential dinner. No-smoking tables. Takeaway service. **Map 6 R3.**

Victoria Park

★ ★ Namo NEW

178 Victoria Park Road, E9 7HD (8533 0639). Mile End tube then 277 bus. **Lunch served** noon-3.30pm Thur-Sun. **Dinner served** 5.30-11pm Tue-Sun. **Main courses** £3.90-£8.50. **Credit** DC, JCB, MC, V.

Namo fits perfectly into the small cluster of shops and restaurants bordering Victoria Park. A moody black frontage opens on to a bright interior full of neatly laid square tables, 1950s-style chrome chairs and Vietnamese bric-a-brac. Table settings are centred on posies from Columbia Road flower market and out the back is a deck full of potted bamboo and palms, shaded by a retractable canvas canopy. It's definitely trendy, but with a bohemian edge that marks it out as Victoria Park rather than Shoreditch or Hoxton. More surprise, then, to find out that this is an affiliate of Huong-Viet (*see below*), the much-loved canteen inside the offices of Dalston's Vietnamese charity. Namo takes a familiar menu of Viet favourites and modernises it. We started with the traditional – a piping hot bowl of bun Hue noodle soup with tender beef, chilli and lemongrass – then moved on to an inspired creation of char-grilled pork, marinated in five-spice, smeared with sweet chilli jam and served on a bed of sweet, gingery pickles, vermicelli noodles and black-eyed beans. This was among the most imaginative Vietnamese cooking we've sampled in London, and service was zippy, even on a busy Sunday lunchtime.

Babies and children welcome: children's menu; high chairs. Booking essential. No smoking. Tables outdoors (6, garden). Takeaway service.

North East

Dalston

★ ★ Huong-Viet

An Viet House, 12-14 Englefield Road, N1 4LS (7249 0877). Bus 67, 149, 236, 242, 243. **Lunch served** noon-3.30pm Mon-Fri; noon-4pm Sat. **Dinner served** 5.30-11pm Mon-Sat. **Main courses** £3.30-£12. **Set lunch** £6 2 courses incl soft drink. **Credit** JCB, MC, V.

Huong-Viet gets ever better with age. Tucked away behind the nondescript doors of the An-Viet Foundation, a charity devoted to giving practical help to Vietnamese refugees, the canteen on this site has been serving fabulous Vietnamese food since the early 1990s. The current staff run a popular takeaway service for local Vietnamese people; most of the eat-in diners are young, trendy and self-employed. The dining room is cavernous; tables are lit by tiny spotlights, and photos of South-east Asia hang in every spare space on the walls. The menu offers a huge selection of salads, stir-fries, grills, noodle soups and spring rolls, and the food more than lives up to its reputation. Spare ribs came as bite-sized morsels, encrusted with chilli, ginger and lemongrass. We also rated the crispy Vietnamese pancake, stuffed with beansprouts, onions and tender prawns, and served with a divine sweet dip. Tofu with green leaves was slightly bland, but soft noodles with chicken went perfectly with a giant slice of kingfish, grilled to smoky brilliance in a wrapper of banana leaves. When you remember speedy service and low prices, it's easy to see why people keep coming back.

Babies and children welcome: high chairs. Booking advisable; essential weekends. Disabled: toilet. Separate room for parties, seats 25. Takeaway service. Vegetarian menu.

Namo

Hackney

★ Green Papaya

191 Mare Street, E8 3QE (8985 5486/ www.greenpapaya.co.uk). Bus 48, 55, 253, 277, D6. **Meals served** 5-11pm Tue-Sun. **Main courses** £5-£8. **Credit** DC, JCB, MC, V.

Green Papaya firmly targets the Hackney middle classes with Hoxton-style modernist decor and a thought-provoking menu, selected to appeal to adventurous western palates. All the Vietnamese favourites are here (pho, spicy stir-fries, meats and seafood encrusted in salt, pepper, garlic and chilli), but the dishes are described only in English, so you might not immediately recognise familiar items. No matter: everything we tried was delicious. Tangy banana flower salad with shredded chicken was crisp and full of texture, while crispy battered squid was brought to life by a zesty purple basil dip. Mains were distinguished by sophisticated flavours. Slow-cooked lamb was tender, with a complex lemongrass, coconut and galangal sauce, and stir-fried beef with asparagus had an almost Chinese quality, full of pepper and chilli punch and piled with tender asparagus spears. We ordered rice noodles with barbecued pork on the side, but it could easily have been a meal in itself – Lao-style grilled pork with a hint of lemongrass, served on a huge mound of steamed vermicelli with a sweet dip and peppery Vietnamese herbs. A feast.

Babies and children welcome: high chairs. Booking advisable. No-smoking tables. Tables outdoors (5, garden). Takeaway service.

★ Tre Viet

251 Mare Street, E8 3NS (8533 7390). Hackney Central rail/48, 55, 253, 277, D6 bus. **Meals served** 11am-11pm daily. **Main courses** £4-£10. **Unlicensed. Corkage** no charge. **No credit cards.**

Tre Viet serves Vietnamese food to Vietnamese locals, using brilliantly fresh ingredients from the Vietnamese wholesalers along Mare Street. Diners eat at glass-topped tables beneath a bamboo trellis hung with faux leaves and red Chinese lanterns, surrounded by chintzy mother-of-pearl collages; still, the focus is on the inexpensive and thoroughly authentic food. We started with a tasty plate of bo la lot, a north Vietnamese staple of five-spiced beef wrapped in peppery betel leaves and grilled on skewers (it's the Vietnamese equivalent of Greek stuffed vine leaves). Goi cuon rolls were also as authentic as anything we've had in Hue or Hoi An: soft steamed prawns, vermicelli, coriander and mint, rolled up in freshly steamed, semi-transparent rice paper. Mains were more hit and miss. A huge pile of soft noodles with sliced chicken was delicious, perked up by crisp pieces of water chestnut, but sizzling lamb with coconut,

chilli and lemongrass had a distracting medicinal flavour. It looked great, though, arriving in a huge cloud of white steam. This is solid and tasty food, but it's best to opt for familiar Vietnamese standards over exotic-sounding specials.

Babies and children welcome: high chairs. Booking advisable weekends. Disabled: toilet. Separate room for parties, seats 30. Takeaway service.

Wanstead

★ Nam An

157 High Street, E11 2RL (8532 2845). Wanstead tube. **Lunch served** noon-2.30pm Wed-Sun. **Dinner served** 6-11.30pm daily. **Main courses** £4-£6. **Set meal** £20-£35 per person (minimum 2). **Credit** AmEx, JCB, MC, V.

The fact that on our midweek visit the waiter was leisurely mopping the floor of this deserted restaurant perhaps indicates that lunchtime trade hasn't picked up since last year – though evenings are much busier for the 50-plus table settings. It wasn't long after our arrival before synthesised Vietnamese music parped into action, with the waiter not far behind. A couple of Halida beers later, we were transported, via the vivid sepia photographs on the wall, to colonial-era Saigon. Ornate dark wood screens, plastic bamboo, and a carp pond complete the old-school oriental set-up. Given the size of the menu (much of which betrays a strong Chinese influence), it's debatable how much market-fresh produce makes it on to the plate. Nevertheless, soft-shell crab deep-fried with chilli and salt had a clean, nutty crunch; and a zingy soup with prawns and tamarind was crammed with crisp beansprouts and juicy straw mushrooms. An unctuous main course of duck with aubergine cooked in a clay pot resounded with subtle aromatic spices. Undoubtedly worth a return visit.

Babies and children welcome: high chairs. Booking advisable. Disabled: toilet. No smoking. Separate room for parties, seats 26. Takeaway service. Vegetarian menu.
For branch see index.

North

Camden Town & Chalk Farm

★ Viet Anh

41 Parkway, NW1 7PN (7284 4082). Camden Town tube. **Lunch served** noon-4pm, **dinner served** 5.30-11pm daily. **Main courses** £3.95-£7.95. **Credit** MC, V.

When we arrived for lunch, Viet Anh was packed – always a good sign. The light turquoise walls and painted clouds across the ceiling provide an airy atmosphere and keep this compact place from

Although most Vietnamese restaurants in London offer a range of Chinese dishes, it's best to ignore these and head for the Vietnamese specialities. These contain fresh, piquant seasonings and raw vegetable ingredients that create a taste experience entirely different from Chinese cuisine. Vietnamese cookery makes abundant use of fresh, fragrant herbs such as mint and Asian basil, and refreshing, sweet-sour dipping sauces known generically as nuoc cham. Look out for spices such as chilli ginger and lemongrass, and crisp root vegetables pickled in sweetened vinegar.

Some dishes are steamed or stir-fried in the Chinese manner; others are assembled at the table in a way that is distinctively Vietnamese. Order a steaming bowl of pho (rice noodles and beef or chicken in an aromatic broth), and you'll be invited to add raw herbs, chilli and citrus juice as you eat. Crisp pancakes and grilled meats are served with herb sprigs, lettuce leaf wraps and piquant dipping sauces. Toss cold rice vermicelli with salad leaves, herbs and hot meat or seafood fresh from the grill. All these dishes offer an intriguing mix of tastes, temperatures and textures.

Aside from the pronounced Chinese influence on Vietnamese culinary culture, there are hints of the French colonial era (in sweet iced coffee, for example, and the use of beef), and echoes of neighbouring South-east Asian cuisines. Within Vietnamese cooking itself there are several regional styles; the mix of immigrants in London means you can sample some of them here. The food of Hanoi and the north – try **West Lake** (see p285) and **Loong Kee** (see p286) – is known for its plain, no-nonsense flavours and presentation. The former imperial capital Hue and its surrounding region are famed for a royal cuisine and robustly spicy soups; look out for Hue noodle soups (bun bo hue) on some menus. The food of what used to be called Saigon (now Ho Chi Minh City) and the south is more elegant and colourful in style, and makes great use of fresh herbs and vegetables.

Below are some specialities and culinary terms; spellings can vary. For recipes and info about Vietnamese food culture, look for *Pleasures of the Vietnamese Table* by Mai Pham. It's published in the US by HarperCollins, but is available in the UK.

Banh cuon: pancake-like steamed rolls of translucent fresh rice pasta, sometimes stuffed with minced pork or shrimp (reminiscent in style of Chinese cheung fun, a dim sum speciality).
Banh pho: flat rice noodles used in soups and stir-fries, usually with beef.
Banh xeo: a large pancake made from a batter of rice flour and coconut milk, coloured bright yellow with turmeric and traditionally filled with prawns, pork,

beansprouts and onion. To eat it, tear the pancake apart with your chopsticks, roll the pieces with sprigs of herbs in a lettuce leaf, and dip in nuoc cham (qv).
Bun: rice vermicelli, served in soups and stir-fries. These are also eaten cold, with raw salad vegetables and herbs, with a nuoc cham (qv) sauce poured over, and a topping such as grilled beef or pork, all of which are tossed together at the table.
Cha gio: deep-fried spring rolls. Unlike their Chinese counterparts, the wrappers are made from rice paper rather than sheets of wheat pastry, and pucker up deliciously after cooking.
Chao tom: grilled minced prawn on a baton of sugar cane.
Goi: salad. There are many types in Vietnam, but they often contain raw, crunchy vegetables and herbs, perhaps accompanied by chicken or prawns, with a sharp, perky dressing.
Goi cuon (literally 'rolled salad', often translated as 'fresh rolls' or 'salad rolls'): cool, soft, rice-paper rolls usually containing prawns, pork, fresh herbs and rice vermicelli, served with a thick sauce similar to satay sauce but made from hoi sin mixed with peanut butter, scattered with roasted peanuts.
Nem: north Vietnamese name for cha gio (qv).
Nom: north Vietnamese name for goi (qv).
Nuoc cham: the generic name for a wide range of dipping sauces, based on a paste of fresh chillies, sugar and garlic that is diluted with water, lime juice and the ubiquitous fish sauce, nuoc mam (qv).
Nuoc mam: a brown or pale liquid derived from fish that have been salted and left to ferment. It's the essential Vietnamese seasoning, used in dips and as a cooking ingredient.
Pho: the most famous and best-loved of all Vietnamese dishes, a soup of rice noodles and beef or chicken in a rich, clear broth flavoured with aromatics. It is served with a dish of fresh beansprouts, red chilli and herbs, and a squeeze of lime; these are added to the soup at the table. Though now regarded as quintessentially Vietnamese, pho seems to have developed as late as the 19th century in northern Vietnam, and may owe its origins to French or Chinese influences. Some restaurants, such as **Sông Quê** (see p286), offer many versions of this delicious, substantial dish.
Rau thom: aromatic herbs, which might include Asian basil (rau que), mint (rau hung), red or purple perilla (rau tia to), lemony Vietnamese balm (rau kinh gioi) or saw-leaf herb (ngo gai).
Tuong: a general term for a thick sauce. One common tuong is a dipping sauce based on fermented soy beans, enlivened with hints of sweet and sour, and often garnished with crushed roasted peanuts.

feeling too cramped. The menu lists over 250 items (but no desserts), though many are variations on similar themes and the helpful waitress was happy to make recommendations. Starters of a golden pancake with prawns and beansprouts, and minced beef wrapped in betel leaf, both came with quarters of crisp iceberg lettuce and sprigs of coriander for wrapping. All the ingredients couldn't have been fresher, and the own-made dipping sauce was a delightful sweet-sour accompaniment. Succulent lemongrass chicken on egg fried rice arrived in an enormous portion: more than we could manage. Best of all was the galangal monkfish, meaty pieces of fish with a delicate ginger flavour. We were in and out within the hour, making this an ideal pit-stop for a speedy lunch, although the inexpensive wine list is temptation enough to return for a more lingering dinner.
Babies and children admitted. Booking advisable. No-smoking tables. Tables outdoors (2, pavement). Restaurant available for hire. Takeaway service. **Map 27 C2.**

Crouch End

★ Khoai Café
6 Topsfield Parade, N8 8PR (8341 2120). Finsbury Park tube/rail then W3, W7 bus or Archway tube then 41, W5 bus. **Lunch served** noon-3.30pm, **dinner served** 5.30-11.30pm daily. **Main courses** £3.60-£8.50. **Set lunch** £7.45 2 courses. **Credit** MC, V.
Khoai Café's pared-down, Formica-happy interior is never going to win any design awards, but that doesn't bother the Crouch End locals who have thronged to the place since it opened early in 2005. The lure is easy to understand: deftly handled Vietnamese dishes, at distinctly wallet-friendly prices. A starter of sautéed squid was tender, and fragrant with chilli and garlic fried to toffee-like nuggets. The clean flavour of the summer rolls – stuffed fat with prawn, crab, mint and cucumber – was deepened by a savoury dipping sauce. Main courses displayed the same sense of flavour balance: fried catfish was served whole, with slivers of punchy ginger; beef pho was assertively spicy; a pork stir-fry featured tender broccoli that even George Bush Sr wouldn't refuse; and a side-dish of just-wilted greens came in a delicate, liquor-like oyster sauce. It's a good idea to book.
Babies and children welcome: high chairs. No bookings taken 8-10pm Fri, Sat. Takeaway service. Restaurant available for hire.

Islington

★ Viet Garden
207 Liverpool Road, N1 1LX (7700 6040/ www.vietgarden.co.uk). Angel tube. **Lunch served** noon-3.30pm daily. **Dinner served** 5.30-11pm Mon-Thur, Sun; 5.30-11.30pm Fri, Sat. **Main courses** £4.50-£8.50. **Set lunch** (Mon-Fri) £6 2 courses. **Set dinner** £15 2 courses. **Credit** MC, V.
Well away from Islington's main drag, and with suburban-style half-timber and plaster walls, Viet Garden is unlikely to stop trendsters in their tracks. There's a pleasant courtyard that would make a great outdoor dining setting, but local authority permission is slow coming, so the garden theme is evoked by fresh pink rosebuds on every table. We were charmed by the friendly service from one of the two sisters who run the restaurant. She recommended the pork kho, and when it came we could see why the flavoursome, slow-cooked meat is a winner with regulars. However, the deep-fried duck egg that accompanied it was way too rubbery. The golden pancake starter, while obviously made with plenty of fresh ingredients, lacked flavour. Compensating, though, was the salt and pepper fish: crisply fried chunks of cod given ample zing by a sprinkle of dill and chilli. Bun xa noodles, quick fried with lemongrass and tossed with salad and chicken, was also a winner, as was beef in tamarind sauce, which got the sweet-sour balance just right.
Babies and children welcome: high chairs. Booking advisable weekends. No-smoking tables. Restaurant available for hire. Takeaway service. Vegetarian menu. **Map 5 N1.**

Cheap Eats

Budget

There are plenty of low-cost dining options in the capital that are more appealing, adventurous and healthy than the typical standby kebab house, greasy spoon or high-street curry house: we've listed the best below. Some of these deal mainly in takeaways or are casual, café-like affairs, others are full-blown restaurants. Most serve food into the evenings; for daytime operations, see the **Cafés** section, starting on p297. For cooking tied to a particular country, turn to the relevant chapter elsewhere in this guide (not just Indian, but Thai, Chinese, Turkish, Korean...) where you'll find cheap options indicated by a ★.

For even more choice, *Time Out's Cheap Eats in London* is the most comprehensive guide to wallet-friendly dining in the capital, covering more than 700 eateries where you can dine for under £20 a head.

Central
Clerkenwell & Farringdon

Little Bay
171 Farringdon Road, EC1R 3AL (7278 1234/ www.little-bay.co.uk). Farringdon tube/rail. **Meals served** noon-midnight Mon-Sat; 10am-11pm Sun. **Main courses** £5.95-£7.95. **Credit** MC, V.
The eccentric surroundings and the menu where all starters, mains and desserts are grouped in equal price brackets (first and last courses £2.95, mains £7.95 – or £1.95/£5.95 noon-7pm) mark Little Bay out as a relative of Le Mercury and LMNT (for both, *see p295*). With branches in Battersea, Fulham, Kilburn and Croydon, Little Bay's formula of quality dishes at knockdown prices is popular all over town. The space looks like a home makeover-show – faux Renaissance prints laminated on to sprayed-gold tabletops, bead-and-wire lampshade decorations – but the gaudiness is soon overlooked when the food arrives. To start, duck terrine with figs and cranberries was rich and feast-like, while a plate-sized mushroom topped with blue cheese and spinach was meaty and earthily juicy. A special of sea bream on crushed potatoes made a satisfying main, but vegetarian options are a little uninspired (you're in trouble if you don't like goat's cheese). Our order was delivered speedily and the house white was an excellent bottle for the price.
Babies and children admitted. Booking advisable. Disabled: toilet. Separate room for parties, seats 120. **Map 5 N4.**
For branches see index.

Covent Garden

★ Canela
33 Earlham Street, WC2H 9LS (7240 6926/ www.canelacafe.com). Covent Garden tube. **Meals served** 9.30am-10pm Mon-Sat; 10am-8pm Sun. **Main courses** £6.50-£7.90. **Credit** MC, V.
Covent Garden doesn't have enough in the way of unusual and appealing cafés, which makes this one particularly worth seeking out. It's a hole in the wall of the Thomas Neal Building, a high-ceilinged room with lots of natural light that reminds you of its warehouse origins. This makes an attractive showcase for the interesting mix of Portuguese and Brazilian snacks and dishes. Customers wanting something hearty can opt for the excellent baked dishes, such as bacalhau à brás, made with salt cod, potatoes, eggs, onion and parsley; or the

classic Brazilian black bean and pork stew, feijoada. If you're in the mood for a lighter snack, the Brazilian cheese bread now comes in flavoured versions: with chorizo, basil, olives or just plain. The cakes are a high point: the quindim is a little cake rich in yellow egg yolk, upturned to show the grated coconut base. Drinks range from galão (Portuguese cappuccino) through Portuguese wines to Caipirinha cocktails. Never before has popping into town for a Brazilian been such an attractive prospect.
Babies and children admitted. No smoking. Tables outdoors (4, pavement). Takeaway service; delivery service (within 1-mile radius). **Map 18 K6.**

Leicester Square

Gaby's
30 Charing Cross Road, WC2H 0DB (7836 4233). Leicester Square tube. **Meals served** 11am-midnight Mon-Sat; noon-10pm Sun. **Main courses** £3.80-£9. **No credit cards.**
On our most recent visit, we bumped into friends from the Bromley synagogue. Gaby's is that sort of place, a clean little café patronised since 1965 by London Jews who pop in for a gossip as much as for the mix of Eastern Mediterranean, heimische (home-style eastern European), and New York Jewish dishes. It's non-kosher, so you can mix cheesecake with salt beef, cappuccino with chopped liver sandwich. Some dishes are better bets than others: the salt beef special has a generous filling. But the latka was disappointing: a huge, soggy, flaccid potato cake that had been sitting around for too long in the window display. It's better to stick to the wide range of salads, or the bowls of straightforward soups (lentil, bean and barley). Gaby's isn't just for aficionados of Jewish food (though this undoubtedly helps): there's a laminated menu showing colour photos of the main dishes, in case you're not sure what falafel with pitta or couscous royale might be.
Babies and children admitted. No-smoking tables. Takeaway service. **Map 18 K7.**

Piccadilly

New Piccadilly
8 Denman Street, W1D 7HQ (7437 8530). Piccadilly Circus tube. **Meals served** noon-8.30pm daily. **Main courses** £4.50-£7.50. **Unlicensed. No corkage. No credit cards.**
Periodic tales of the imminent demise of this archetypal caff – propagated by the owner himself – seem overstated, as it's still going strong years after we first heard the rumours. New Piccadilly

has hardly altered since it opened in the 1950s, with white-tunicked staff, ceiling fans, plastic flowers, Formica tables and glass cups and saucers evocative of post-war Soho. The menu also transports you straight back to Arthur Askey's Britain, with many very dated Brit-Ital dishes, such as steak with risotto, chicken casserole, or semolina pudding. While our mixed salad was fine, the ravioli was overcooked, the filling a mystery sludge, and the only flavour came from added hot tomato sauce and tablespoon of pesto. The cappuccino was disappointingly watery. We had a soft spot for the peach melba, though, made from condensed milk and tinned peaches with scoops of ice-cream and a 'raspberry' (gloopy and red) sauce. Come here for the retro decor and atmosphere, complete with soothing classical music on the radio – not for the food and drink.
Babies and children admitted. No-smoking tables. Takeaway service. **Map 17 J7.**

Soho

Breakfast Club NEW
33 D'Arblay Street, W1F 8EU (7434 2571). Oxford Circus or Tottenham Court Road tube. **Meals served** 8am-6pm Mon-Fri; 9.30am-5pm Sat. **Main courses** £3.50-£5. **No credit cards.**
As the name suggests, this caff does a decent line in breakfast dishes that aren't the usual fry-ups: you could have Special K with toast and Marmite or jam, plus tea/coffee and fresh orange juice. Or get in touch with your inner sybarite and have the peanut butter and banana toasties, or even a Nutella toastie. It's a nice place for lunch too: the split-level room is quiet, and attractively decorated in a decidedly uncorporate, renovated-warehouse kind of way. The young staff are friendly, and the range of food includes toasted sandwiches such as tuna melts, prettily presented on a plate with lots of salad garnish. The espresso-based coffees are decent, and there are iMacs on a counter that allow customers free internet access. It's a good place to rest up for a while in busy Soho.
Babies and children admitted. Bookings not accepted. Takeaway service. Tables outdoors (3, pavement). Vegan dishes. **Map 17 J6.**

★ Hummus Bros NEW
2006 RUNNER-UP BEST CHEAP EATS
88 Wardour Street, W1F 0TJ (7734 1311/ www.hbros.co.uk). Oxford Circus or Tottenham Court Road tube. **Meals served** 11am-10pm Mon-Wed; 11am-11pm Thur, Fri; noon-11pm Sat. **Main courses** £2.50-£5. **Credit** AmEx, MC, V.
At this small, stylish fast-food café and takeaway in busy Soho, houmous – that ever-present dip, that perennial garnish – is upgraded and given main event status. It works. The eponymous chickpea and tahini purée is served in shallow bowls with a hollow in the middle that is filled with Levantine-inspired extras, such as chicken in tomato sauce, chunks of stewed beef, fava beans, guacamole or a mushroom mix, plus one or two daily changing specials. The resultant combo is then scooped up with warm white or brown pitta bread. No forks, no fuss, no cucumber sticks. Excellent side dishes such as tabouleh, roasted aubergine and vegetable salads (plus Innocent smoothies, herbal teas and a handful of desserts) complete an ultra-compact menu. Diners pack in to sit at the long shared tables and benches, but most seem to take away in tubs. It's such a simple, effective idea, 'tis a wonder such 'hummus bars' haven't popped up before.
Babies and children welcome: children's menu. Bookings not accepted. No smoking. Takeaway service; delivery service (7644 6666). Vegetarian menu. Vegan dishes. **Map 17 K6.**

Leon NEW
35-36 Great Marlborough Street, W1F 7JE (7437 5280/www.leonrestaurants.co.uk). Oxford Circus tube. **Meals served** 8am-10pm Mon-Fri; 9.30am-10pm Sat; 10.30am-6.30pm Sun. **Main courses** £4.20-£11. **Credit** AmEx, MC, V.

Breakfast Club

Gourmet burger bars

The rise of London's upmarket burger chains started with the Kiwi-run Gourmet Burger Kitchen in Battersea, itself an idea borrowed and adapted from somewhere else – New Zealand, where gourmet burger bars are almost as commonplace as sheep. Two years after GBK flipped their first patty and topped it with beetroot (to make a kiwiburger, of course), several other entrepreneurs were putting their MBAs to good use in me-too operations.

What is most striking about this new wave – apart from how much better they are than the fast-food burger chains – is how similar they are. Dark wood interiors with wipe-clean tables, counter ordering but table service, and good quality meat and other fillings between big buns: it's the new burger bar cliché, but one that we're always happy to get our teeth into.

Burger Shack

14-16 Foubert's Place, W1F 7JH (7287 6983/www.burgershack.co.uk). Oxford Circus tube. **Meals served** 11am-9pm Mon-Wed; 11am-10pm Thur-Sat; 11am-5pm Sun. **Main courses** £5.45-£7.40. **Credit** AmEx, MC, V.

Burger Shack, just off Carnaby Street, produces perfectly good food that differs little from the other gourmet burger chains: decent fries, burgers, good buns – with nothing too outre on the menu that might scare off the tourists. The differences to the competition are largely cosmetic: walls adorned with photographs of the gods of rock music, plus a few rock dinosaurs and some fossils. It seems well targeted at its customers, who include one-visit shoppers, tourists and slackers passing through west Soho. There is one more contemporary brush with glamour: Burger Shack shares its loos with the neighbouring Attica nightclub. At the end of 2005 this outlet was

taken over by Smollensky's, which has now added two more branches in the West End – by transforming what had been Smollensky's Metro sites into Burger Shacks.
Babies and children welcome: children's menu; high chairs. Disabled: toilet. No smoking. Tables outdoors (30, pavement). Takeaway service. **Map 17 J6.**
For branches see index.

Fine Burger Company

37 Bedford Hill, SW12 9EY (8772 0266/ www.fineburger.co.uk). Balham tube/rail. **Meals served** noon-11pm Mon-Sat; noon-10pm Sun. **Main courses** £5.95-£8.95. **Set lunch** (Mon-Fri) £5.95 burger and drink. **Credit** AmEx, DC, MC, V.

FBC is the first of the gourmet burger chains to diversify significantly from its core products. The new menu introduced in 2006 includes unusual variations on beefburgers such as teriyaki sauce or stilton cheese, but you can also order chicken breast six ways, falafel, minced lamb, even a salmon fish cake in a burger bun. But have they lost their way on the path to hamburger heaven? Not in our experience, as the medium-cooked patty is still just right, the bun's firm, and details such as the cheese and lettuce leaves are top quality. The chips are made from real potatoes (you can see the skins) and are cooked just-so. We're less sure about some of the side orders, though: the onion rings are the size and colour of doughnuts, while the 'sweet chilli and sour cream' dip is no more than a dollop of sour cream with a squirt of sweet chilli sauce on top. Don't lose your way, FBC: keep your burgers in order, and you'll not need to jerk those chicken breasts.
Babies and children welcome: children's menu; high chairs; toys. Booking advisable weekends. No smoking. Tables outdoors (2, pavement). Takeaway service. Vegetarian menu.
For branches see index.

★ Gourmet Burger Kitchen

44 Northcote Road, SW11 1NZ (7228 3309/www.gbkinfo.com). Clapham Junction rail/49, 77, 219, 345 bus. **Meals served** noon-11pm Mon-Fri; 11am-11pm Sat; 11am-10pm Sun. **Main courses** £5.45-£7.40. **Credit** MC, V.

GBK was the first, and remains our favourite gourmet burger chain. Its purchase at the end of 2004 by Clapham House (an umbrella company that runs a few restaurant chains) and GBK's subsequent rapid expansion has seen no dip in standards – or, at least, none that we've noticed. The sesame-flecked buns still have firm texture, the tasty fillings are prime quality, and you'll find no finer Aberdeen Angus beef patties. Portions are huge, the fat chips are golden and just right, and the extras are no-corners-cut. Among the many fabulous variations is the beetroot- and pineapple-layered kiwiburger – much better than it sounds, honest. And the service at this (the original) branch is as friendly and welcoming as ever. Their secret? We think it's due in part to the strong Kiwi influence; the three founders and many of the current upbeat staff are from New Zealand, as is their inspiration (NZ's excellent gourmet burger bars). Renowned Kiwi chef Peter Gordon was also the menu consultant.
Babies and children welcome: children's portions; high chairs. No smoking. Tables outdoors (4, pavement). Takeaway service. **Map 21 C4.**
For branches see index.

Haché

24 Inverness Street, NW1 7HJ (7485 9100/www.hacheburgers.com). Camden Town tube. **Meals served** noon-10.30pm Mon-Sat; noon-10pm Sun. **Main courses** £4.95-£10.95. **Credit** AmEx, MC, V.

Haché eschews the utilitarian aesthetic of most burger bars, instead resembling a bijou modern bistro with its fairy lights and fey art. The dishes also take a slightly more sophisticated approach than you might expect: the Ayrshire steaks are chopped (haché, in French) and seasoned before being grilled medium, or cooked as requested. The toppings are excellent: bacon dry-cured in brine, proper cheese, huge portobello mushrooms. Haché also wins our best buns award: the ciabatta buns don't just look good, they also have an appealing chewy texture. Chips are frites-style, skinny or fat. Non-beef burgers include tuna steak, chicken, and three veggie variations. Another sure sign that this is no ordinary burger bar: three salad main courses, including tuna niçoise and chicken caesar. There's a decent selection of wines, and crêpes have recently been added to the dessert options. This is somewhere you can go with a date, family or friends, and feel that you're treating yourselves.
Babies and children welcome: high chairs. No smoking. Tables outdoors (4, pavement). Takeaway service.
Map 3 H1.

Hamburger Union

23-35 Dean Street, W1D 3RY (7437 6004/www.hamburgerunion.com). Tottenham Court Road tube. **Meals served** 11.30am-9.30pm Mon; 11.30am-10.30pm Tue-Fri; 12.30-10.30pm Sat; 1-8pm Sun. **Main courses** £3.95-£9.95. **Credit** DC, MC, V.

The Soho location ensures that this diner gets more than its share of people tapping into BlackBerries, arranging the slope of their jeans and wearing hats indoors. Self-regard apart, the Soho bohos know a good thing when they see it. The drinks list is a cut above other burger bars, from Hook Norton bitter through fresh and fruity wines to Chegworth Valley pear juice; the chips are properly chunky; and the hamburgers are made from happy cows, we don't doubt. Homage is paid to the chorizo bun pioneered by the Brindisa stall at Borough Market with the chorizo sausage with olive oil, piquillo pepper and rocket in a bun, but otherwise there's little funny stuff, just well-textured beef patties cooked medium and served in a good-looking bun. Only a few details disappoint, such as the plasticky-textured cheese. But after one of their malts (vanilla, chocolate, strawberry or banana) you'll forgive them anything.
Babies and children welcome: high chairs. Disabled: toilet. No smoking. Takeaway service. **Map 17 K6. For branches see index.**

Ultimate Burger

34 New Oxford Street, WC1A 1AP (7436 6641/www.ultimateburger. co.uk). Holborn tube. **Meals served** noon-11.30pm daily. **Main courses** £5.55-£6.95. **Credit** MC, V.

Handy for the British Museum, this small chain (with three other branches in London) gives you no starters, but four variations on burgers of beef, chicken, lamb or vegetarian (mushroom, aubergine or veggie burgers). The toppings and treatments tend towards the classic rather than the outlandish – barbecue sauce, crisp bacon, satay sauce. The beef comes cooked medium as standard, and we couldn't complain about the big sesame seed bun or the quality of the extras (the cheese was real cheese). Chips? Medium-cut, nicely fried until light golden, not too heavily salted. To drink: four flavours of milkshake, two choices each of red or white wine, two bottled lagers. Ultimate may not be the ultimate, but it does everything well, and leaves little room for complaint.
Babies and children welcome: high chairs. Disabled: toilet. No smoking. Takeaway service. **Map 18 L5. For branches (Immo, Ultimate Burger) see index.**

Leon caused a big splash when it opened in 2003 – more to do with canny design and marketing than intrinsic excellence, we can't help feeling. Despite our reservations, it's a good little café-restaurant (now a chain of four branches, serviced by a central kitchen) that serves interesting dishes with an 'Eastern Mediterranean' slant. The queue to order and the frequently disorganised and rushed service at this original Carnaby Street branch can discourage, but the wait is rewarded with healthy salads such as peas, broccoli, quinoa, alfalfa and fresh herbs: no problem getting your five-a-day with this boxed lunch. Other dishes are less impressive: a roasted sweet potato 'falafel' was nothing like a falafel, it was stodge in a wrap. We think Leon is best outside of the lunch scrum; at breakfast, for example, it does decent porridge and fry-ups. Prices tend to be on the high side if you're used to paying Pret a Manger prices (hardly the budget option themselves), but it makes a refreshing change from endless sandwiches. So Leon's good – it's just not *that* good.
Babies and children admitted. Disabled: toilet. No smoking. Tables outdoors (7, pavement). Takeaway service. **Map 17 J6. For branches see index.**

Maoz Vegetarian

43 Old Compton Street, W1D 6HG (7851 1586/ www.maozveg.com). Leicester Square or Tottenham Court Road tube. **Meals served** 11am-1am Mon-Thur; 11am-2am Fri, Sat; 11am-midnight Sun. **Main courses** £2.50-£3.50. **Unlicensed. No credit cards.**

This fast-food falafel place is the best option for healthy and inexpensive nosh on Old Compton Street. It's a simple formula, first perfected at this chain's many outlets in the Netherlands: brown or white pitta bread, a filling of small fried falafels, the option of houmous and/ or fried aubergine, then your pick from a well-stocked salad bar that includes dairy-free coleslaw, couscous salad, pickled chillies and – our favourite – baby pickled aubergines that are stained purple with beetroot juice. The meal deals are great value, such as the £4.20 meal, which includes a soft drink and nice fat English chips, not the Low Countries frites you might expect. It's mainly a takeaway place; seating is spartan and limited. Not only delicious, Maoz is also kosher and vegan, and open late: useful for late-night Soho revellers in search of sustenance. There's also a new branch in nearby Brewer Street.
Babies and children admitted. No alcohol allowed. No smoking. Tables outdoors (2, pavement). Takeaway service. **Map 17 K6. For branch see index.**

Stockpot

18 Old Compton Street, W1D 4TN (7287 1066). Leicester Square or Tottenham Court Road tube. **Meals served** 11.30am-11.30pm Mon, Tue; 11.30am-midnight Wed-Sat; noon-11.30pm Sun. **Main courses** £3.40-£5.50. **Set meal** (Mon-Sat) £4.95-£6.50 2 courses; (Sun) £6.50 2 courses. **No credit cards.**

It serves popular British and continental dishes at rock-bottom prices, yet it's sited in the prime central London locations that the big chains usually gobble up. Just how does the Stockpot do it? Not by cutting corners with the food, in our experience; the dishes always pass muster. Penne pasta was perfectly al dente, with generous amounts of ham and spinach for £3.95. Green salad at £1.85 was as pert and well dressed as the young men strolling past the Old Compton Street branch's french windows and outdoor tables. We love the retro feel of the Stockpot's menu: maybe egg mayonnaise as a starter, vegetarian moussaka to follow, jelly and cream for pudding. It might remind some of school dinners, but then school didn't sell bottles of wine at £7.60. Sponge pudding, with golden syrup and lashings of custard, costs a mere £1.50 – heck, you can barely buy a cappuccino that little these days. For reliably good, affordable food right in the heart of Soho, the Stockpot has no peers.
Babies and children admitted. Tables outdoors (2, pavement). Takeaway service. **Map 17 K6. For branch see index.**

Trafalgar Square

Café in the Crypt

Crypt of St Martin-in-the-Fields, Duncannon Street, WC2N 4JJ (7839 4342/www.stmartin-in-the-fields.org). Embankment tube/Charing Cross tube/rail. **Lunch served** 11.30am-3pm Mon-Sat; noon-3pm Sun. **Dinner served** 5-7.30pm Mon-Wed, Sun; 5-10.15pm Thur-Sat. **Main courses** £5.95-£7.50. **Set meal** £5.25 soup and pudding. **Credit** MC, V.

Have you ever received a present that looks amazing – ribbons, glitter, the whole shebang – but turns out to be a bit disappointing? Well, that's the Café in the Crypt. A fantastic location off Trafalgar Square, one of the most whimsical addresses in London and the dim-lit crypt itself, complete with curved stone pillars, combine to have you rubbing your hands with glee at what's ahead. Unfortunately, the food is rather school-dinnerish, as well as being cheekily priced – £6.95 for half an avocado stuffed with tuna, anyone? The changing menu offers salad platters (read: lettuce, a bit of cucumber and a slab of quiche) as well as a hot option (lamb casserole with tomato and mint, say) and old-fashioned puds. We still like this café, though, because it's a fair bet there aren't many places in London where you can eat your lunch decorously while reading the epitaph on a gravestone. Plus the afternoon tea (with no less than three cakes) for £4.95 is a winner, and the regular jazz evenings sound rather pleasant too.
Babies and children welcome: high chairs. Disabled: toilet. Entertainment: jazz 7.30pm alternate Tue; check website for details. No-smoking tables. Restaurant available for hire. Separate room for parties, seats 70. **Map 18 L7.**

West
Ladbroke Grove

Babes 'n' Burgers

275 Portobello Road, W11 1LR (7229 2704). Ladbroke Grove tube. **Meals served** 10am-11pm daily. **Main courses** £3.50-£8.95. **Credit** MC, V.

The transformation of the dedicated children's room into an eating area dominated by a large screen shows that B&B has grown up a little. Not too many, there are still toys, children's meals and high chairs, but the kids aren't the only pebbles on this beach. The front area of the café is presided over by a perspiring chef and sidekicks, flipping organic hamburgers, constructing salads, whizzing smoothies and shouting at the waiting staff. On market days, a busy atmosphere means that staff can be prone to confusion, but they're friendly. As 'healthy' fast food is the selling point, we opted for the 'halloumicado' burger, a toasted bun filled with seared halloumi cheese, avocado and plenty of sliced salad items, washed down with a smoothie (the orange and strawberry was very refreshing). The classic beef burger (organic meat, juicily grilled), comes in small sizes for the £4.95 kids' meal (which could also be organic chicken goujons or tofu in a bun with fries and a drink). We passed on side orders of lecithin granules in favour of marinated olives and guacamole, enjoyed a £3.95 glass of Prosecco and felt all the healthier for it.
Babies and children welcome: children's menu; crayons; high chairs; toys. Disabled: toilet. No smoking. Separate room for parties, seats 30. Tables outdoors (2, pavement). Takeaway service. **Map 19 B2.**

South
Battersea

Fish in a Tie

105 Falcon Road, SW11 2PF (7924 1913). Clapham Junction rail. **Lunch served** noon-3pm, **dinner served** 6pm-midnight Mon-Sat. **Meals served** noon-11pm Sun. **Main courses** £5.95-£10.50. **Set meal** £6.50 3 courses. **Credit** MC, V.

You know a place is popular when the tables are packed so tight that anyone who has overindulged

CHEAP EATS

Pie & mash

As London's white working-class communities continue to sell up and shift out to outer boroughs, so the eateries that nourished them must transform, relocate or die. London's boozers have in the main trodden the transformation route, making the most of their Victorian interiors, yet jettisoning their pickled eggs for parma ham, their Ben Truman for Bourgogne Aligoté.

No such compromise has, and perhaps can, be made by London's time-honoured caterers to the workers: the pie and mash shops. They stick resolutely to providing food that has altered little since the middle of the 19th century: potatoes (a wedge of glutinous mash), pies (minced beef and gravy in a watertight crust), eels (jellied and cold, or warm and stewed) and liquor (an unfathomable lubricant loosely based on parsley sauce). Escalating eel prices mean that many places only serve pie and mash. Vinegar and pepper are the preferred condiments, a fork and spoon the tools of choice.

A choice bunch of these establishments remains – resplendent with tiled interiors, marble-topped tables and worn wooden benches. The oldest and most beautiful pie and mash shop is **M Manze** on Tower Bridge Road, established in 1902, though **F Cooke** of Broadway Market, the **Kellys'** and the **Harrington's** shops all date from the early 20th century. Visit these family-run businesses while you can, for each year another one closes and with it vanishes a slice of old London. Relish the food, the surroundings, the prices (you'll rarely pay more than a fiver) and also your dining companions: Londoners to the core, not yet seduced by the trashy allure of the international burger chains.

None of these shops serves alcohol or accepts payment by credit card; all offer takeaways. They're often a family-friendly lot too.

WJ Arment
7 & 9 Westmoreland Road, SE17 2AX (7703 4974). Elephant & Castle tube/rail/12, 35, 40, 45, 68A, 171, 176, 468 bus. **Open** 10.30am-5pm Tue, Wed; 10.30am-4.30pm Thur; 10.30am-5.30pm Fri, Sat.

Bert's
3 Peckham Park Road, SE15 6TR (7639 4598). Bus 21, 53, 78, 172, 177, 381. **Open** 11.30am-1.30pm, 4.30-6.30pm Tue, Thur, Fri; 11.30am-1.30pm Wed; 11.30am-1.30pm, 4.30-6pm Sat.

Castle's
229 Royal College Street, NW1 9LT (7485 2196). Camden Town tube/Camden Road rail. **Open** 10.30am-3.30pm Tue-Fri; 10.30am-4pm Sat. **Map 27 D1**.

Clark's
46 Exmouth Market, EC1R 4QE (7837 1974). Farringdon tube/rail. **Open** 10.30am-4pm Mon-Thur; 10.30am-5.30pm Fri, Sat. **Map 5 N4**.

Cockneys Pie & Mash
314 Portobello Road, W10 5RU (8960 9409). Ladbroke Grove tube. **Open** 11.30am-5.30pm Tue-Thur, Sat; 11.30am-6pm Fri. Tables outdoors (2, pavement). **Map 19 B1**.

F Cooke
150 Hoxton Street, N1 6SH (7729 7718). Old Street or Liverpool Street tube/rail/48, 55, 149, 242, 243 bus. **Open** 10am-7pm Mon-Thur; 9.30am-8pm Fri, Sat. **Map 6 R2**.

F Cooke
9 Broadway Market, E8 4PH (7254 6458). Liverpool Street tube/rail then 26, 48 or 55 bus/London Fields rail. **Open** 10am-7pm Mon-Thur; 10am-8pm Fri, Sat. No-smoking tables.

AJ Goddard
203 Deptford High Street, SE8 3NT (8692 3601). Deptford rail/Deptford Bridge DLR/1, 47 bus. **Open** 9.30am-3pm Mon-Fri; 9am-3pm Sat. No-smoking tables.

Harrington's
3 Selkirk Road, SW17 0ER (8672 1877). Tooting Broadway tube. **Open** 11am-9pm Tue, Thur, Fri; 11am-2pm Wed; 11am-7.30pm Sat. No smoking.

G Kelly
414 Bethnal Green Road, E2 0DJ (7739 3603). Bethnal Green tube/rail/8 bus. **Open** 10am-3pm Mon-Thur; 10am-6.30pm Fri; 9.30am-4.30pm Sat.

G Kelly
600 Roman Road, E3 2RW (8983 3552). Mile End tube. **Meals served** 10am-2.30pm Tue, Thur, Fri; 10am-5pm Sat. No smoking.

S&R Kelly
284 Bethnal Green Road, E2 0AG (7739 8676). Bethnal Green tube/rail/8 bus. **Open** 9am-2.30pm Mon-Thur; 9am-5.30pm Fri; 10am-3.30pm Sat. No smoking. **Map 6 S4**.

Manze's
204 Deptford High Street, SE8 3PR (8692 2375). Deptford rail/Deptford Bridge DLR/1, 47 bus. **Open** 9.30am-1.30pm Mon, Thur; 9.30am-3pm Tue, Wed, Fri, Sat. No-smoking tables.

L Manze
76 Walthamstow High Street, E17 7LD (8520 2855). Walthamstow Central tube/rail. **Open** 10am-4pm Mon-Wed; 10am-5pm Thur-Sat. For branch see index.

M Manze's
87 Tower Bridge Road, SE1 4TW (7407 2985/www.manze.co.uk). Bus 1, 42, 188. **Open** 11am-2pm Mon; 10.30am-2pm Tue-Thur; 10am-2.15pm Fri; 10am-2.45pm Sat. No-smoking tables. For branches see index.

will have difficulty squeezing back to their seat. At this endearingly named bistro, prices are so darned low that it is regularly crammed to the rafters. The homely interior, with candles precariously stuck into bottles, only adds to the atmosphere. From an expansive menu, we had the very shareable pasta of the day starter for a wallet-friendly £3.95, then moved on to main courses that were equally good: rack of lamb, and chicken with stilton and pears were straightforward plates of fab food for less than a tenner. Our neighbour's swordfish provoked cries of delight too. FT's not going to win acclaim as a fine dining venue, but if it's a fantastic local or chilled night with friends you're after, pop along. For pudding, a pancake concoction enigmatically titled 'Black Tulip', was tasty, and there's a decent wine list. And if that's not enough, they give you a free slice of watermelon at the end. Bless 'em. *Babies and children welcome: high chairs; children's portions. Booking advisable. No-smoking tables. Separate rooms for parties, seating 25 and 40.* **Map 21 C3**.

East
Bethnal Green

E Pellicci
332 Bethnal Green Road, E2 0AG (7739 4873). Bethnal Green tube/8 bus. **Meals served** 6.30am-5pm Mon-Sat. **Main courses** £4.60-£7.60. **Unlicensed. Corkage** no charge. **No credit cards.**
This proper East End greasy spoon has been in the same family since Edwardian times, but the remarkable art deco marquetry interior – now grade II listed by English Heritage – was created in 1946 under the supervision of Elide Pellicci, the current owner's mother. Its friendly service and neighbourly feel made it the favourite caff of those loveable East End rogues, the Krays. The same qualities now make it a popular spot for all manner of local heroes, plus the occasional interloping design students admiring the primrose-coloured Vitrolite frontage. Yet it's still a proper caff, serving fry-ups (including some unusual ones – you might have ham off the bone instead of bacon, say), salads, grills, chops and sarnies. A much-loved institution, and long may it remain so. *Babies and children welcome: children's menu.*

Brick Lane

★ Story Deli
3 Dray Walk, The Old Truman Brewery, 91 Brick Lane, E1 6QL (7247 3137). Liverpool Street tube/rail. **Meals served** 9am-6pm daily. **Main courses** £6.50-£9.50. **Unlicensed. Corkage** no charge. **Credit** AmEx, MC, V.
With its distressed floorboards, huge butcher-block tables and cardboard packing case seats creating a strangely uncafé-like appearance, you could easily overlook this 100% organic café and pizzeria. But on a Tuesday evening, Story Deli was packed to its shabby-chic rafters, and on tasting the food it's easy to see why. The pizzas are amazing, a cross between classic thin Neapolitan dough and the delicate pastry of Egyptian fatirs, topped with an inventive range of ingredients – prawns and peppers; ham, aubergine and olive; and rosemary and garlic among them. But other dishes are equally good. A prawn kebab came laden with sweet, fat prawns, grilled with juicy chunks of courgette, aubergine and onion; and the small but excellent range of mains includes steak sandwich, the Story burger, roasted cod and aïoli chips, and bowls of salad. And if you've room after the huge portions, a nice selection of cakes is complemented by excellent coffee. *Babies and children welcome: children's portions; high chairs; toys. No smoking. Restaurant available for hire. Tables outdoors (10, pavement). Takeaway service. Vegan dishes.* **Map 6 S5**.

Shoreditch

Premises Café/Bistro
209 Hackney Road, E2 8JL (7684 2230/ www.premisesstudios.com). Old Street

tube/rail/26, 48, 55 bus. **Meals served** 8am-11pm Mon, Wed, Thur, Sun; 8am-5.30pm Tue; 8am-midnight Fri, Sat. **Main courses** £4.95-£10.95. **Credit** (over £10) AmEx, MC, V.

The music studios attached to this café-bistro have seen everyone from Nina Simone to Spiritualized go through the mixing desk, though an appetite-dampening picture of Jamie Cullum features on the café's wall of fame. The rock 'n' roll ethos snakes through to the eating section, where breakfast is served until 5.30pm in a head-spinning number of combos. Choose from meaty or veggie sausages, bubble and squeak, hash browns and thick bacon on a man-sized platter surrounding a lake of beans, or have them fill a sandwich. It's predictably greasy grub, great for filling a hangover hole. In the evening a bistro menu is offered, a mixed, loosely Mediterranean bag of meze dishes, pastas and grilled meats. There's even beef stroganoff; incredibly tempting, if only because the last time it was an option was at a friend's mum's house. The dining space is titchy, though not overbearingly cramped. Chummily bustling service and a lively clatter emanating from the kitchen add to the fun.
Babies and children welcome: high chairs. Disabled: lift; toilet. No-smoking tables. Tables outdoors (6, pavement). Takeaway service. **Map 6 S3.**

North East
Hackney

LMNT

316 Queensbridge Road, E8 3NH (7249 6727/ www.lmnt.co.uk). Dalston Kingsland rail/236 bus. **Meals served** noon-11pm Mon-Sat; noon-10.30pm Sun. **Main courses** £6.95-£8.95. **Credit** MC, V.

An urn-shaped dining pod, tables in raised cubbyholes, stone sphinxes and a candelit Zeus-like mask – the boldfaced decor at LMNT is one of its principal draws. The food, however, is less reliable. Crisp-skinned sea bream was overpowered by badly judged, oddly tangy braised fennel. Beetroot and horseradish risotto was an intriguing idea, though instead of a dish with cohesive creaminess we got separate rice grains in a watery background sauce. It was offputtingly lukewarm in places too. Some of this was forgiven with the arrival of a delectable pistachio crème brûlée. At £8.95 or less for mains, £3.45 for starters and desserts, too much griping would be coarse – especially given that on a repeat visit everyone in the party was more than satisfied with the food. Whether it's the corny recorded guitar strummings or the unabashed kitsch decor, LMNT pulls off a surprisingly authentic Mediterranean tourist-joint vibe, in the nicest, most convival way.
Babies and children admitted. Entertainment: opera 8pm Sun. Tables outdoors (6, garden). **Map 25 C5.**

North
Camden Town & Chalk Farm

Marine Ices

8 Haverstock Hill, NW3 2BL (7482 9003). Chalk Farm tube. **Lunch served** noon-3pm, **dinner served** 6-11pm Mon-Fri. **Meals served** noon-11pm Sat; noon-10pm Sun. **Main courses** £6.10-£13.75. **Credit** MC, V.

Designed on a naval theme (hence the name) over 70 years ago, this gelateria/eaterie has been run by the same family since its inception, and occupies a soft spot in the heart of many locals, particularly families who bring successive generations to continue dearly held traditions. You'll want to join in with the uninhibited nippers screaming for ice-cream – which has its own menu and is available in grown-up, liqueur-soaked combos. Or go with the kiddie flow and invent your own sundae with an assortment of sauces and teeth-aching toppings. The pizza and pasta aren't gourmet by any means, but are immensely hearty, as our tomato and cream gnocchi and chilli scampi linguine coated in identical fluoro-orange sauces attested. Good feeling towards the place had already been engendered with a starter of ridiculously fresh tomatoes topping thick bruschetta. Try to bag a window table, from where you can watch the motley passers-by, a mix of oddball Camden and genteel Chalk Farm.
Babies and children welcome: children's portions; high chairs. No smoking. Takeaway service. **Map 27 B1.**

Islington

Candid Arts Café NEW

Candid Arts Trust, 3 Torrens Street, EC1V 1NQ (7837 4237/www.candidarts.com). Angel tube. **Meals served** 11am-10pm Mon-Sat; noon-5pm Sun. **Main courses** £4-£8. **Credit** AmEx, MC, V.

The café of the Candid Arts Trust has a stylishly dishevelled feel about it. Artwork from the studios next door is on display, with purchase info tacked beneath on scraps of paper. There are two spaces in which to partake of your health-conscious meals. Up the rickety stairs is a room that's beyond bohemian, with red velvet chairs, battered floorboards, a vaguely pornographic Rubenesque painting and seemingly 100 years' worth of spookily shaped candle wax drippings. The long, stately home-like central table is ideal for large groups. This room overlooks a pretty, plant-filled courtyard, popular in warmer months. Languid French 1920s jazz played on our visit. You order from a blackboard by the till (there is no table service). Meals could include tuna steak with guacamole, spicy vegetable stew, pinto bean pie or a good greek salad. Own-made cakes come in numerous homely permutations, including marble, ginger, and apple – one serving of deliciously nutty banana bread produced three generous slices. Staff were welcoming, helpful and laid-back, which added to the feel-good vibe.
Babies and children welcome; children's portions. Booking advisable. Separate room for parties, seats 30. Tables outdoors (8, courtyard). Takeaway service. **Map 5 O2.**

Flaming Nora

177 Upper Street, N1 1RG (0845 835 6672/ www.flamingnora.com). Highbury & Islington tube/rail. **Meals served** 11am-midnight Mon-Thur, Sun; 11am-2am Fri, Sat. **Main courses** £3.75-£7.75. **Credit** MC, V.

Here's a novel concept: seeing inside the kitchen of a kebab joint. Normally, the idea would have you running for the hills, but funky Flaming Nora is not your normal kebab house. From the arty decor on the walls to the 'lo-carb' options on the menu, it is a different beast to the average fast-food grease palace. The service is friendly, the burgers and kebabs come in wrappers saying things like 'luvvly lamb', and – a boon for the health-conscious – the meat, from beef to salmon, is grilled. There are even puddings, such as the delectable fruit kebab, and a huge selection of sauces; you don't find many kebab vendors selling mint and coriander dressing. Nora is let down by not having quite enough seats for eating in, but then it is primarily a takeaway. And, should you forget that, just take a look at the ingenious 'extras' they sell: from condoms to breath freshener to alcohol, they provide all the accoutrements late-night revellers are likely to need.
Babies and children welcome: children's menu; high chairs; toys. Disabled: toilet. No smoking. Takeaway service; delivery service (over £10 within 4-mile radius). **Map 5 O1.**

Le Mercury

140A Upper Street, N1 1QY (7354 4088). Angel tube/Highbury & Islington tube/rail. **Meals served** noon-1am Mon-Sat; noon-11.30pm Sun. **Main courses** £5.95. **Credit** AmEx, JCB, MC, V.

Situated as it is on the corner of Almeida and Upper Streets, French-leaning Le Mercury is ideally suited for a meal before or after a show at the Almeida theatre opposite. The constant stream

Interview
HUMMUS BROS

Who are you?
Christian Mouysset (left) and Ronen Givon, founders of the **Hummus Bros** (*see p290*).
Eating in London: what's good about it?
Diversity. London, and Soho in particular, always astonish us with new places offering food we've never seen before, that are packed. Londoners always seem to be happy to embrace something new as if it were part of their own culture.
What's bad about it?
A very limited choice of quality food after 11pm. Late-night food options consist mainly of cheap, low-quality takeaway joints that survive because of lack of competition. By issuing a limited number of extra late licences councils could increase competition, which would lead to a rise in the overall quality of the food on offer.
Which are your favourite London restaurants?
Brunch at the **Providores & Tapa Room** (*see p161* – poached eggs with whipped yoghurt and hot chilli), lunch at **Ottolenghi** (*see p167* – seven-hour cooked lamb), dinner at **Café Japan** (*see p195* – salmon salad and salt-grilled yellowtail neck) and, of course, **Hummus Bros** (houmous with the guacamole topping).
What single thing would most improve London's restaurant scene?
More places catering for people with food allergies. Between five and ten per cent of the population have a food allergy, and their choice of eating places is limited.
Any hot tips for the coming year?
Keep an eye on the breakfast market. There is wide scope for innovation in this time slot. Also, more restaurants should realise the adverse effects they have on the environment and take steps to compensate for this, for example, carbon offsetting.

our pet chickpeas

Hummus Bros. See p290.

of patrons only lulled at curtain-time. The wraparound windows give the welcome illusion of space, but once inside, the tables are a little cramped. Waiting staff are aware of this and at pains to step aside to let customers through en route to the toilets. On the food front, aubergine pithivier resembled an upmarket version of a pie, though the pastry was a little burned. Mackerel with rhubarb, beetroot and lime was a sort of fishy fruit salad, but much more appetising than that sounds. A thoroughly British treacle sponge pudding with a continental blob of chantilly cream made a comfortingly dense and syrupy finish. A long-standing low-cost spot in pricey Islington. *Babies and children admitted. Booking advisable weekends. Separate room for parties, seats 50.* **Map 5 O1.**

S&M Café
4-6 Essex Road, N1 8LN (7359 5361/ www.sandmcafe.co.uk). Angel tube. **Meals served** 7.30am-11pm Mon-Thur; 7.30am-midnight Fri; 8.30am-midnight Sat; 8.30am-10.30pm Sun. **Main courses** £5.95-£6.95. **Credit** DC, MC, V.
Ordering at this breezy, friendly café is as slick and painless as it gets. Choose three key components from a simple menu plus a daily changing specials board: first your sausage, then your mash, then your gravy. Decide whether you want peas, whether you want them mushy, and the job's done. You might end up ordering two pork bangers in cheesy mash with house gravy, or a lamb sausage and a chicken one in bubble-and-squeak mash with mushy peas, or veggie sausages in 'virgin' mash (no butter) with a neapolitan tomato sauce on top. There are other options – a few pies, some sausage-themed salads, old-fashioned desserts such as spotted dick – but, unless opting for one of the excellent fried breakfasts, stick to the speciality S&M as it's too good to miss. This Essex Road branch is a particular treat: the art deco shopfront of bygone greasy spoon Alfredo's has been preserved in all its chrome and Vitrolite glory. Inside, simple decor follows the retro lead, making the space an attractive place to linger.
Babies and children welcome: children's menu; high chair. Booking advisable; not accepted before 4pm weekends. Tables outdoors (5, pavement). Takeaway service. **Map 5 O1.**
For branches see index.

Outer London
Richmond, Surrey

Stein's
55 Richmond Towpath, west of Richmond Bridge, Richmond, Surrey TW10 6UX (8948 8189/www.stein-s.com). Richmond tube/rail then 20min walk or 65 bus. **Meals served** Easter-Christmas 11am-dusk Mon-Fri; 10am-dusk Sat, Sun. **Main courses** £2.50-£16.90. **Set lunch** (noon-3pm Mon-Fri) £5.99 1 course and soft drink. **Credit** MC, V.
Bavarian-themed Stein's is one of several quaint eateries along the Richmond riverside walkway. It has outside seating of trestle tables and benches, so doesn't operate in winter. There is a small kiosk where the food is prepared, and orders are taken and served. If you're unfamiliar with Bavarian dishes, Stein's offerings may seem hilariously limited. It's mainly three sausages: bratwurst (veal, pork and spices, fried), currywurst (frankfurter coated in curry powder) or weisswurst (white veal sausage, boiled). These are served accompanied by a sizeable heap of sauerkraut, and sautéed potatoes. Dunk your wurst in sweet mustard and munch with a brezen (bready pretzel). There's also wiener schnitzel and spetzl (thick noodles), served with bacon and sauerkraut. A wedge of apple strudel, and a refreshing Erdinger, Paulaner or Löwenbräu beer will leave you replete. Unfortunately, Stein's isn't a beer garden – you can only have one alcoholic drink per meal, which is maybe why you'll see most punters going for a hefty litre of beer. *Prost!*
Babies and children welcome: high chairs. Tables outdoors (28, towpath). Takeaway service

Cafés

Not 'caffs', mind – you'll find a selection of the best caffs in our **Budget** chapter (starting on p290) – but characterful cafés that express excellent espresso, brew brilliant tea, or cater well for kids. In this chapter we also recognise the resurgence of fine pâtisserie in London with several new entries. We even created a new Best Pâtisserie category for the 2006 Time Out Eating & Drinking Awards. It was a tough job, but our experts left no choux untried, no handsome profiterole unkissed in our quest to to find fairy-tale pâtisserie; check out the **Wolseley**, **Yauatcha** and newcomers **Hummingbird**, **Ladurée** and **Macaron** to see the results. The **Table** is also worth noting for its imaginative yet low-cost take on self-service food.

Central
Clerkenwell & Farringdon

De Santis
11-13 Old Street, EC1V 9HL (7689 5577). Barbican tube/Old Street tube/rail/55 bus. **Open** 8.30am-11pm Mon-Fri. **Main courses** £5-£10. **Licensed. Credit** MC, V.
A little piece of Milan (home of the original De Santis) in Clerkenwell. This paninoteca is a sleek-looking joint with a smooth concrete floor, and is bigger that it first appears – as well as the bustling room on the ground floor, there's a quiet terrace at the back and a more loungey room downstairs. As in Italy, not much is made of breakfast here (coffee and a croissant about covers it); the action starts at lunch. Paninis are the backbone of the menu, and come with a wide variety of fillings: meats (speck, mortadella, bresaola, prosciutto), vegetables, cheese or fish. The bread is baked on the premises, and is light and delicious. Piattini (cold platters) and tartine (open sandwiches) also make a showing, as do hot dishes. These included lentil stew with garlic bruschetta and penne arrabiata, perhaps followed by pear and yogurt cake or tiramisu. The wine list – 30 reds, 30 whites – comes into its own as day turns to night. A popular local with a justified sense of confidence.
Babies and children admitted. Restaurant available for hire. Separate room for parties, seats 45. Tables outdoors (14, courtyard). Takeaway service; delivery service (within 3-mile radius). **Map 5 O4.**

Kipferl NEW
70 Long Lane, EC1A 9EJ (7796 2229/ www.kipferl.co.uk). Barbican tube. **Open** 8am-7pm Mon-Fri; 9am-5pm Sat. **Main courses** £3-£5.80. **Unlicensed. No credit cards.**
The only Austrian café in town – but Kipferl has more to offer than novelty value. A handful of tables are squeezed into the small room, alongside shelves holding a limited selection of Austrian wines and a range of deli items. Highlights include that great Styrian treasure, pumpkin seed oil, plus Zotter chocolate bars, Staud's pickles and jams, and a small choice of breads. A packed cold cabinet holds savoury filled rolls and open sandwiches, cheeses, meats, and cakes such as sachertorte, linzertorte and apple cake. More substantial lunchtime options include sausages and sauerkraut, salads, goulash soup and a hot dish of the day. Coffee is good – it comes with a chocolate or a cookie – and we're big fans of the melange (coffee with milk), though in summer you may be tempted by the Viennese iced coffee. Service comes with a smile from a bunch of enthusiastic young Austrians.

Babies and children admitted. No smoking. Takeaway service. **Map 11 O5.**

Covent Garden

Kastner & Ovens
52 Floral Street, WC2E 9DA (7836 2700). Covent Garden tube. **Open** 8am-5pm Mon-Fri. **Main courses** £4.25-£4.75. **Unlicensed. No credit cards.**
Located in central Covent Garden (at the Opera House end of Floral Street), K&O remains surprisingly unknown to tourists and consequently feels like a locals' takeaway lunch joint, especially as the quality is evident and prices keen. Cooks emerge via a spiral staircase from the basement kitchen with freshly prepared, daily changing dishes, displayed buffet-style on huge tables (savouries to the left, sweets to the right). Staff serve customers with impressive efficiency – and a smile. It's uncomplicated, comfortable fare, well done. Sandwiches, soup (butternut squash and ginger, for example) and salads (tabouleh, cabbage and apple) appear alongside pastries (spinach and feta filo, smoked chicken and thyme pie), quiche (aubergine, spring onion and goat's cheese) and heartier specials. Pork and chorizo casserole featured generous chunks of meat and spicy sausage; no tiny cubes of token meat here. Make space for desserts – the apple pie and carrot cake shouldn't be missed. Drinks are largely bottled organic juices.
Babies and children admitted. No smoking. Takeaway service. **Map 18 L6.**

Fitzrovia

Squat & Gobble NEW
69 Charlotte Street, W1T 4RJ (7580 5338/ www.squatandgobble.co.uk). Goodge Street or Warren Street tube. **Open** 7am-5pm Mon-Fri; 9am-5pm Sat. **Main courses** £3.25-£4.95. **Unlicensed. No credit cards.**
This no-frills café sits at the unfashionable northern end of Charlotte Street. Its tightly packed tables – chunky wood inside the café, metal outside – overflow at lunchtime, so time your visit if you don't want to queue (there's a roaring takeaway trade too). The unfeasibly long menu covers almost every conceivable option from breakfast items (porridge, steak and eggs) through to soup, salads, jacket potatoes, daily specials and sandwiches (the 'posh' fish fingers, served on thick white bread with own-made tartare sauce, has achieved classic status). Cakes and old-school puddings are also available. Prices are a steal – you'll be hard-pressed to spend more than a fiver – and plates are piled high. Fluffy, full-flavoured tuna, dill and spring onion fish cakes were better than you'd find in many smarter establishments, and came with new

CHEAP EATS

potatoes and five different salads including a rich coleslaw and mixed beans. There's no alcohol, but plenty of coffee, teas, milkshakes, smoothies and juices. A real treasure.
Babies and children admitted. No smoking. Tables outdoors (10, pavement). Takeaway service. **Map 3 J5.**
For branch see index.

Knightsbridge

★ Ladurée NEW

2006 RUNNER-UP BEST PATISSERIE
2006 RUNNER-UP BEST DESIGN
Harrods, entrance on Hans Road, SW1X 7XL (7893 8293/www.laduree.com). Knightsbridge tube. **Open** *Shop* 9am-9pm Mon-Sat; noon-6pm Sun. **Lunch served** 11.30am-3.30pm Mon-Sat; noon-3.30pm Sun. **Tea served** 3.30-6.30pm Mon-Sat; 3.30-6pm Sun. **Main courses** £15-£27.50. **Set lunch** £29 2 courses, £34 3 courses. **Set tea** £21. **Licensed.** **Credit** AmEx, DC, JCB, MC, V.
Bringing Parisian café culture bang up to date, the London branch of Ladurée (inside Harrods) boasts a wealth of delicate dainties for shoppers with sweetly indulgent tastes. Right at the cutting edge of food fashion, this elegant café borrows from the Parisian trend of launching pâtisserie collections in much the same way as clothes designers showcase a new season's line. We're talking the likes of liquorice macaroons, orange blossom creams, and Arabica coffee mousses. The decor is as ornate as the wares on offer: weighty chandeliers, pastel-shaded pâtisserie boxes and streams of colourful ribbons complement rows of perfectly executed pâtisserie, lush chocolates and a magnificent choice of macaroons. Bag a table in the light and airy café area for the closest seats to the impressive display counter. The religieuse – choux pastry, crowned with a swathe of rose-scented rosettes of cream – is an outstanding version. Traditionalists can take their pick from éclairs, millefeuilles and elegant meringues. If you've time for just one quick bite, make it a macaroon – they're to die for.
Babies and children welcome: high chairs. Bookings not accepted tea. Disabled: toilet. No smoking. Takeaway service. **Map 14 E10.**

Marylebone

Apostrophe

23 Barrett Street, W1U 1BF (7355 1001/ www.apostropheuk.com). Bond Street tube. **Open** 7.30am-8pm Mon-Fri; 9am-8pm Sat, Sun. **Main courses** £3.50-£5. **Unlicensed.** **Credit** MC, V.
Apostrophe is a small chain of boulangerie-pâtisseries that stocks excellent continental-style breads, pâtisserie and sandwiches, plus top-notch coffee. The branches vary, but this St Christopher's Place corner site is one of the best, with a score of seats outside and friendly, prompt service. The sandwich fillings are French-inspired, and include goat's cheese with tapenade or tuna mayonnaise with green beans in different breads. Pastries extend beyond light croissants and danish pastries to quiche-like onion tarts and vegetable strudels. Prices are on the high side, but quality is also high; the pear or lemon tarts are especially good. Still, it's best to not come here if you're too ravenous, as the bill can quickly pass the £10 threshold – quite a lot for a sandwich bar. The takeaway breads include Poilâne sourdough, plus various first-rate loaves from Apostrophe's own central bakery.
Babies and children admitted. Disabled: toilet. No smoking. Tables outdoors (8, pavement). Takeaway service. **Map 9 H6.**
For branches see index.

★ La Fromagerie

2-4 Moxon Street, W1U 4EW (7935 0341/ www.lafromagerie.co.uk). Baker Street or Bond Street tube. **Open** 10.30am-7.30pm Mon; 8am-7.30pm Tue-Fri; 9am-7pm Sat; 10am-6pm Sun. **Main courses** £6.50-£13.50. **Licensed.** **Credit** AmEx, MC, V.
The 'tasting café' in the back of this popular, rustic-style deli offers the opportunity to sample some of the shop's carefully sourced foodstuffs. It's a simple set-up: one large communal wooden table, flanked by benches, plus three small satellite tables. Unsurprisingly (given the cheese room's 100-plus artisanal varieties), the daily cheese plate takes centre stage, and a ploughman's is raised above pub-lunch status with Montgomery cheddar and a pork and veal pie from the Ginger Pig gourmet butcher next door. The fish plate is a flavour-packed medley of smoked trout and mackerel pâtés, gravadlax and black rice and crab salad. Hearty soups, cured and roast meats, and inventive salads dressed with rarefied oils and vinegars are also on the lunch menu. Breakfast (including a full spanish featuring a selection of cheeses and charcuterie) is accompanied by excellent Florentine espresso, while superior cakes – Valrhona chocolate brownies or cheesecake made from Corsican soft cheese, for example – are served at teatime. The place is mobbed at weekend lunchtimes and staff can veer from offhand to charmingly solicitous.
Babies and children admitted. Bookings not accepted. Café available for hire (evenings).

Ladurée

No smoking. Takeaway service. Map 3 G5.
For branch see index.

Garden Café
Inner Circle, Regents Park, NW1 4NU (7935 5729/www.thegardencafe.co.uk). Baker Street or Regents Park tube. **Open** *9am-dusk daily.* **Main courses** £4.25-£12.50. **Licensed.** **Credit** MC, V.
Lunch in the park should be a relaxed affair, but perhaps more for those eating it than for those serving it. The Garden Café – part full restaurant, part service-counter offering sandwiches and salads – has a smashing location, its 300 seats split between its recently rejuvenated 1964 building and the lawns and patios outside. So far, so delightful, but service in the restaurant can be muddled – you may be forgotten about if you sit at the outside tables on the raised area slightly removed from restaurant. Pity: the food is pretty impressive. A cauliflower and cumin soup came with an appealing tang, while a fullish plate of nicely sourced asparagus polonaise (with a breadcrumb-based topping) was excellent value at £5.50. A plump portion of baked haddock was soaked in a creamily moreish parsley sauce; linguine with herbs and parmesan, although it was on the cold side of lukewarm, had the makings of a smashing summer dish. Ice-cream is sourced from the estimable Marine Ices, and tends to be a better bet than the other desserts: a slightly tired gooseberry and elderflower pavlova and a positively exhausted banana split.
Babies and children welcome: children's menu; high chairs. Booking advisable (online booking only). Disabled: toilet. No smoking (indoors). Restaurant available for hire. Tables outdoors (35, garden). Takeaway service. Map 3 G3.

Le Pain Quotidien
72-75 Marylebone High Street, W1U 5JW (7486 6154/www.lepainquotidien.com). Baker Street or Bond Street tube. **Open** *7am-7pm Mon-Fri; 8am-6pm Sat; 9am-6pm Sun.* **Main courses** £5.75-£7.95. **Unlicensed. Credit** MC, V.
A popular chain in Belgium and France, LPQ's ethos of a good, daily handmade bread is accented in its menu; delicious slabs of chewy organic sourdough accompany soups, salads and platters, or star as the base for tartines. Breakfast baskets include brioche and croissants served with butter and moreish own-made jams and praline spreads. Tartines (French open sandwiches) feature largely Mediterranean ingredients (prosciutto with artichoke paste, Milano salami, gruyère with cornichons) and soup of the day might be pea and mint. Huge salads (Fourme D'Ambert cheese, pear, rocket and walnuts, for example) and platters (smoked salmon with prawns and guacamole, houmous, baba ganoush and tabouleh) are appealing lunchtime dishes. With rustically exposed brick, a large communal table (surrounded by numerous smaller ones) and floor-to-ceiling windows, the spacious interior exudes light and warmth – an ambience enhanced by the smell of fresh baked goods from the shop at the front. A delightfully welcoming, child-friendly place to eat or just to enjoy great coffee and waffles.
Babies and children welcome: high chairs.
No-smoking tables. Takeaway service. Map 9 G5.

Paul
115 Marylebone High Street, W1U 4SB (7224 5615/www.paul.fr). Baker Street or Bond Street tube. **Open** *7.30am-8pm Mon-Fri; 8pm-8pm Sat, Sun.* **Main courses** £3.50-£7.50. **Unlicensed. Credit** (over £10) MC, V.

Founded in Lille in 1889, this stylish chain – at last count with 13 branches in London – focuses on high-quality, attractive pâtisserie, sweet and savoury tarts and artisan breads. The café's grandiose decor may seem exclusive, but the French staff are welcoming and the menu uncomplicated. Light lunches include quiche (lorraine, trois fromages), salads (chicken, smoked salmon, cured ham) and paillasson – grated potato pancakes. Ours, topped with mushrooms and a fried egg, was delicious; an omelette complet (ham, emmental, bacon and mushrooms) was equally good, although – puzzlingly – it arrived sitting in water. For desserts, bourbon vanilla crème brûlée was perfect: smooth, rich and creamy. Cheesecake was nicely light but dull; it would have benefited from some fruit for flavour, interest and colour. Great service, relaxed surroundings and good food: Paul is deservedly popular, so visit in quieter times to enjoy a lingering latte and macaroon.
Babies and children welcome: high chairs.
Bookings not accepted. No smoking. Takeaway service. Map 9 G5.
For branches see index.

Quiet Revolution
28-29 Marylebone High Street, W1V 4PL (7487 5683). Baker Street or Bond Street tube. **Open** *9am-6pm Mon-Sat; 11am-5pm Sun.* **Main courses** £5.95-£9.95. **Unlicensed. Credit** MC, V.
Locating an organic café within eco-chic Aveda is inspired. Slate-tiled and calm, Quiet Revolution's healthy, largely vegetarian menu appeals to its green-leaning clientele. Well-groomed model-types sip wheatgrass shots and shuffle shopping bags at communal tables to make space for yummy mummies wise to the fact that, while the prices

reflect its Marylebone address, the portions – especially from the kids' menu – are huge, and go far. Market availability dictates the freshly prepared daily menu: chunky soups (pea and mint, beetroot and horseradish), salads (lentil with feta, roast salmon), stews served with brown rice (Thai-style pumpkin curry, lamb with parsnips) and specials (chilli con carne, pasta, frittata). We've always found the food to be fresh, wholesome and well presented, though occasionally uninspiring (houmous with greek salad – again?). Fantastic freshly made juice combos and smoothies are a bonus, as is the pleasant service.
Babies and children welcome: children's menu. No smoking. Tables outdoors (4, pavement). Takeaway service. Vegetarian menu. Vegan dishes. **Map 9 G5.**

Mayfair

Cibo NEW

Mamas & Papas, 256-258 Regent Street, W1B 3AF (01484 438376/www.mamasandpapas.com). Oxford Circus tube. **Open** 10am-8pm Mon-Wed, Fri; 10am-9pm Thur; 9am-8pm Sat; noon-6pm Sun. **Main courses** £4.50-£9.75. **Licensed**. **Credit** AmEx, DC, JCB, MC, V.
This Italian café is on the first floor of the swish Mamas & Papas nursery shop on Regent Street. Cibo is a symphony in coffee and cream, with glass-topped tables set with wine glasses and gleaming cutlery. It looks a mite too posh to stagger into laden with mewling babies, but Cibo is aimed specifically at young parents and infants. The menu runs through an appealing breakfast section to lunchtime smoothies, paninis, salads and hot dishes. Children's dishes include raw vegetables and dips, Heinz organic tomato soup, organic hamburgers and ice-creams. Everything is presented with a flourish, as if to remind customers that new parenthood doesn't mean compromising on style. We made short work of the organic salmon fish cakes, but were taken aback by the price of the adult mains – a mozzarella and tomato salad was £8.75; the same items in a panini £7.25. Cibo does a good job of spoiling its customers, both young and older, but be prepared to pay for it.
Babies and children welcome: children's menu; high chairs. Disabled: lift; toilet. No smoking. **Map 9 J6.**

Sketch: The Parlour

9 Conduit Street, W1S 2XJ (0870 777 4488/ www.sketch.uk.com). Oxford Circus tube. **Open** 8am-9pm Mon-Fri; 10am-9pm Sat. **Tea served** 3.30-7.30pm Mon-Sat. **Main courses** £7-£10. **Set tea** £7.50-£18.50; £30 incl glass of champagne. **Licensed**. **Credit** AmEx, DC, MC, V.
In the past, we've relied on Parlour to soothe away our city stresses; the quiet clink of china and the sophisticated selection of pâtisserie have won it many loyal fans. A recent makeover has bulldozed away the wispy curtains and elegant sitting room atmosphere, and in its place installed a rough-edged den for clinching business deals. Even the lengthy cake counter has been truncated. Most of the pâtisserie remains on a par with previous visits. Top marks to the pistachio nut-filled éclair – its pastel-hued filling and silky texture makes it a real treat. It's hard to fault the nutty blackcurrant meringue discs, sandwiched with violet-scented buttercream: utterly delicious. Cracks are beginning to show though – one of our pastry tarts had a burnt base, and the strawberry compote in a shot glass was too syrupy for its own good. Parlour is living on past glories, and needs to address its shortfalls if it's to regain its position as one of the best pâtisseries in London.
Babies and children admitted. Bookings not accepted. Café available for hire, seats 35. Takeaway service. **Map 9 J6.**

Piccadilly

Nouveauté NEW

Habitat, 121-123 Regent Street, W1B 4HX (7287 6525). Oxford Circus or Piccadilly Circus tube. **Open** 8.30am-6.30pm Mon-Wed, Fri; 8.30am-7.30pm Thur; 10am-6.30pm Sat; 11.30am-5.30pm Sun. **Main courses** £4-£8. **Licensed**. **Credit** MC, V.
The new Regent Street Habitat store is inside a grade II-listed building that has seen £4.5 million invested in its restoration. Beautiful original features sit well around Tom Dixon's dark wood and metal stairway and mezzanine. At the top you will find a cream-coloured cafeteria with monastic resin tables, a few lounge chairs, and trays that look like pretty floral plates. Customers serve themselves from a neat display of salads, plump rolls and cakes. Respectable tortilla was offered with a choice of six or so salads for £7.50. We liked the Mediterranean-style mix of aubergine, yellow pepper, red onion and tomatoes, the herby new potato salad, and bowl of sprightly undressed leaves. The filled rolls looked excellent and were generously portioned. Only the cakes were a let-down. The bright Australian service and classy vibe make this a tempting retreat from the thoroughfare outside. Come for a light, healthy lunch and you won't be disappointed.
Babies and children welcome: children's portions; high chairs. Disabled: toilet. No smoking. Restaurant available for hire. Takeaway service; delivery service (over £20 within 2-mile radius). **Map 17 J7.**

★ The Wolseley

2006 RUNNER-UP BEST PATISSERIE
160 Piccadilly, W1J 9EB (7499 6996/ www.thewolseley.com). Green Park tube. **Open** 7am-midnight Mon-Fri; 9-11.30am Sat, Sun. **Tea served** 3-5.30pm Mon-Fri; 3.30-6pm Sat, Sun. **Licensed**. **Credit** AmEx, DC, JCB, MC, V.
Dining at the Wolseley is a big-budget affair, but an affordable afternoon tea offers a taster of the splendour and elegance of this landmark venue. For less than a tenner, you can indulge in a plate of freshly baked scones, complete with own-made jam, clotted cream and a pot of tea – we've tried the afternoon tea here and rate it one of London's best. Renowned pastry chef Claire Clark left her post at the Wolseley in 2005, but her legacy lives on with a superlative mix of English cakes and French pâtisserie. From homely victoria sponges sandwiched with jam, to fondant-topped coffee éclairs, moist rum babas and creamy fruit tartlets, this place makes stylish cakes with flair, commitment and good taste. On our last visit, we tucked into a mouth-watering pastry tart, filled with a deep layer of rich chocolate mousse and topped with the sharp bite of whole raspberries – a match made in heaven. Next time, we'll plump for the vanilla cheesecake, which also has a reputation among London's cake aficionados.
Babies and children welcome: crayons; high chairs. Disabled: toilet. No-smoking tables (no bookings). Takeaway service. **Map 9 J7.**

Soho

★ Amato

14 Old Compton Street, W1D 4TH (7734 5733/ www.amato.co.uk). Leicester Square, Piccadilly Circus or Tottenham Court Road tube. **Open** 8am-10pm Mon-Sat; 10am-8pm Sun. **Main courses** £3.95-£8.25. **Licensed**. **Credit** AmEx, DC, MC, V.
Step back in time at this delightful Italian brasserie – everything about it has a charmingly old-fashioned vibe, from the art deco posters to the dark wood-panelled walls. But it's the lavish display of pâtisserie that lures shoppers and Soho bohos. Cakes topped with ruffled chocolate fans; whipped whirls of cream, rising like beehive hair-dos from pastry tartlets; and individual mousses: they all tempt lovers of naughty-but-nice. Before diving straight into chocolate profiteroles, take the edge off your appetite with a simple, homely pasta dish – we're always satisfied with the pasta sauces. Other recommendations include a light sponge, stacked with lush layers of zabaglione cream, and wobbly mounds of profiteroles filled with whipped cream and topped with a dab of chocolate fondant. Service, like the cooking, is friendly and informal.
Babies and children welcome: high chairs. Takeaway service. **Map 17 K6.**

Bar Italia

22 Frith Street, W1D 4RT (7437 4520). Leicester Square, Piccadilly Circus or Tottenham Court Road tube. **Open** 24hrs Mon-Sat; 7am-4am Sun. **Main courses** £3.20-£8. **Licensed**. **Credit** (noon-3am) AmEx, DC, MC, V.
If you haven't 'done' coffee at Bar Italia, you haven't 'done' Soho. Or so the regulars who dominate the outdoor tables here will tell you. In honesty, neither the bitter coffee, nor the pre-prepared ciabatta sandwiches, nor the unexciting pizzas are that special: what Bar Italia oozes is aged, authentic character. The red leather stools, ancient till and enormous Rocky Marciano poster behind the counter are the stuff of Soho legend, unchanged for decades. Uniformed staff aren't the types to stop for a chat (at least, not with casual visitors), but orders arrive swiftly and with a minimum of fuss. Prices are high (about £6 for a parma ham and mozzarella ciabatta) and are only justified if you nab an outdoor seat: there are few better people-watching spots in London. Inside, a huge TV screen on the back wall plays pop videos; the channel is only switched on for Italian football matches. When these occur, the place is vibrant with vocal nationals. During Italy's winning run in the World Cup, parts of Frith Street had to be closed down due to the weight of the crowd around Bar Italia's window.
Babies and children welcome: high chairs. Tables outdoors (4, pavement). Takeaway service. **Map 17 K6.**

Maison Bertaux

28 Greek Street, W1D 5DQ (7437 6007). Leicester Square, Piccadilly Circus or Tottenham Court Road tube. **Open** 8.30am-11pm daily. **Main courses** £1.50-£4.50. **Unlicensed**. **No credit cards**.
Opened in 1871, Maison Bertaux's charms have remained unchanged for decades: rickety tables (some of these on the pavement), pink taffeta tacked to the ceiling, and Gallic tat decorating an interior straight out of *Monsieur Hulot's Holiday*. The staff are characters too, led by the eccentric owner, Michelle Wade. The range of drinks and baked goods also seem to have changed little over the decades. With no espresso machine, the main alternative to café crème is pots of tea. The savoury pastries are, frankly, not terribly good: perhaps broccoli quiche, or a disappointing 'pizza' made, bizarrely, with a puff pastry base. The pâtisserie just saves the day. The best include the lemon tarts, with their thin crust and tangy filling; the fruit tarts, éclairs and various permutations of cream and choux pastry are also fine. Maison Bertaux is charming, but with lots of competition from the likes of the new Paul branch just down

BEST CAFES

For cakes from around the world
Visit **Hummingbird** (*see p301*) for US-style baking, **Kipferl** (*see p297*) for a taste of Austria, and **Yauatcha** (*see p301*) for Asian delights.

For drinking tea
Tea Palace or **Yauatcha** (for both, *see p301*) have scores of teas to choose from. For old-fashioned high tea, *see p303* **Hotel teas**.

For alfresco eating
Try the upmarket **Garden Café** (*see p299*) or head to one of London's green open spaces (*see p305* **Park cafés**).

For families
You can't get more child-friendly than **Boiled Egg & Soldiers** (*see p302*), **Brilliant Kids Café** (*see p304*), **Bush Garden Café** (*see p301*), **Cibo** (*see left*), **Crumpet** (*see p302*), **Frizzante@City Farm** (*see p303*) and **Gracelands** (*see p305*).

the road – not to mention longtime rival Pâtisserie Valerie (*see below*) – it really needs to make more effort with its food and drink.
Babies and children admitted. No-smoking tables. Tables outdoors (5, pavement). Takeaway service. **Map 17 K6**.

Pâtisserie Valerie
44 Old Compton Street, W1D 4TY (7437 3466/ www.patisserie-valerie.co.uk). Leicester Square, Piccadilly Circus or Tottenham Court Road tube. **Open** 7.30am-8.30pm Mon, Tue; 7.30am-9pm Wed-Fri; 8am-9pm Sat; 9.30am-7pm Sun. **Main courses** £3.75-£8.25. **Licensed**. **Credit** (over £5) AmEx, DC, MC, V.
We keep returning to this branch of Pâtisserie Valerie, but more for its quirky atmosphere and first-floor views on to the Old Compton Street life than for its pâtisserie. If appearances mean anything, it delivers the goods with an impressive glass counter crammed with sumptuous gateaux, flans, tartlets, mousse cakes and cute little marzipan figurines. Decor is appealingly old-school, and a tribute to 1920s Parisian café culture. If you're a late riser, this spot serves breakfast until 4pm, and the lunch menu – although hardly outstanding – offer salads, quiches, omelettes and light bites. The ground floor tends to be a bit gloomy for our taste; we always head upstairs to the light and breezy first floor. On our last visit, afternoon tea was a combination of hits and misses: a wedge of tiramisu gateau delivered the goods, but a strawberry cheesecake was let down by cream that was anything but fresh. Good service made up for shortfalls on the table.
Babies and children welcome: high chairs. No-smoking tables. Takeaway service. **Map 17 K6**.
For branches see index.

★ Yauatcha
2006 RUNNER-UP BEST PATISSERIE
15 Broadwick Street, W1F 0DL (7494 8888). Leicester Square, Oxford Circus or Tottenham Court Road tube. **Open** *Tea house* noon-11pm Mon-Fri; 11.45am-11pm Sat; 11.45am-10.30pm Sun. **Dim sum served** £3-£14.50. **Licensed**. **Credit** AmEx, JCB, MC, V.
Yauatcha's tea room is unrivalled for its stylish good looks and marriage of east-meets-west pâtisserie. The space occupied exclusively by the tea room has shrunk since the place first opened, as dim sum is now also served here: a new partition corrals tea-drinkers next to the entrance, where you can admire rows of cakes perfectly aligned in pristine glass display cabinets. Top choices include the violetta, a light-as-air violet-scented mousse, topped with a shimmering heap of blackcurrants – top marks for its intense fruity flavour. Asian flavours also frequent the pâtisserie: a richly decadent chocolate mousse was lightened with a hit of floral-scented jasmine cream. For aficionados of high-quality teas, this place offers around 150 varieties. Our favourite, though, was a tall glass of refreshing passionfruit and lime iced tea. Recent additions include nibbles for adventurous tastes, such as apricot and wasabi truffles, or green tea macaroons. The waitresses are gracious and courteous, but not always attentive.
Babies and children admitted. Booking advisable (restaurant). Disabled: toilet. No smoking. Takeaway service (tea house). **Map 17 J6**.

West
Ladbroke Grove

Armadillo Café
11 Bramley Road, W10 6SZ (7727 9799/ www.armadillocafe.co.uk). Latimer Road tube. **Open** 8am-4.30pm Mon-Fri; 10am-3pm Sat. **Main courses** £2-£6. **Unlicensed**. **Corkage** no charge. **No credit cards.**
This small café caters mainly to people working at the Chrysalis offices next door, and there are lots of pavement tables in summer where you can sit and spot Heart FM's presenters on their way to work. High-class coffee is a speciality, and food comes from the attached Armadeli, which has links to Wiltshire farms and organic suppliers. A

selection of tasty ready-made sandwiches with good bread includes classics such as Wiltshire ham and farmhouse cheddar, made with excellent-quality ingredients. A Mexican tuna baguette was disappointingly low on the Mexican, with just a bit of sorry sweetcorn to justify the name. Still, own-made brownies were deliciously moist and sold out by early afternoon. Stock up on cured meats, smoked fish, sausage rolls and ready-made shepherd's pie at the deli – but don't get there too late, or the Chrysalis lot will have eaten everything.
Babies and children admitted. No smoking. Tables outdoors (10, pavement). Takeaway service. Vegetarian menu.

Books for Cooks
4 Blenheim Crescent, W11 1NN (7221 1992/ www.booksforcooks.com). Ladbroke Grove tube. **Open** 10am-6pm Tue-Sat. **Set lunch** £4 1 course, £5 2 courses, £7 3 courses. **Licensed**. **Corkage** no charge. **Credit** MC, V.
This iconic bookshop is a treasure-trove for cookery book collectors, but the café at the back of the shop is much more hit and miss. The cooks are amateurs, and every day prepare a handful dishes from the shop's thousands of books. There are only six small tables, yet even by 1.30pm the café can often run out of dishes; on our most recent visit they could offer only an (excellent) bruschetta starter and a choice of cakes for afters. Had we arrived earlier we might have been able to enjoy chicken pasta with green beans and goat's cheese from Peter Gordon's *Salads* book. The café is licensed, but as wine is served in squat tumblers don't expect to be able to discern any subtle aromas. The cappuccino was merely adequate, with no decaff option. Despite its shortcomings – you can't even book a table – the Books for Cooks café is an institution we're happy to return to, as long as we can be there early enough.
Bookings not accepted. Disabled: toilet. No smoking. **Map 19 B3**.

★ Hummingbird [NEW]
2006 RUNNER-UP BEST PATISSERIE
133 Portobello Road, W11 2DY (7229 6446/ www.hummingbirdbakery.com). Ladbroke Grove or Notting Hill Gate tube. **Open** 10am-5.30pm Tue-Sat; 11am-5pm Sun. **Main courses** £1.45-£3.45. **Unlicensed**. **Credit** AmEx, MC, V.
A grotto for cup cakes, frostings and icings, Hummingbird celebrates the Stateside version of sweet extravagance with aplomb, self-assurance and bling. Forget delicate new-wave flavours – this spot delivers a mean wedge of devil's food cake, the best blueberry cake in town, and lemon pie crowned with a mile-high duvet of meringue. It's a homely set-up, just a couple of stools and a few tables outside the café, but it's the cake and cup cake display that really impresses. On our visit, two staff members, armed with palette knives, a tray of cup cakes and a cavernous bowl of icing, were slathering on the frosting, then selling them on within minutes. We struck gold with our choice: a dreamy match of chocolate sponge and caramel frosting – at less than £2 each, they're a bargain. Other top-drawer classics include pumpkin, pecan and mississippi mud pies. This is a patch of Portobello Road that will be forever America.
Babies and children admitted. No smoking. Tables outdoors (2, pavement). Takeaway service. **Map 19 B3**.

Maida Vale

Raoul's
13 Clifton Road, W9 1SZ (7289 7313). Warwick Avenue tube/6 bus. **Open** 8.30am-10.15pm Mon-Sat; 9am-10pm Sun. **Main courses** £8.50-£15. **Minimum** £3.95. **Licensed**. **Credit** MC, V.
This long-established Maida Vale staple is a favourite with well-dressed locals. The menu rarely changes and offers a reliable selection of all-day breakfasts, hearty sandwiches, burgers, salads and full-blown meals. Highly recommended are the smoothies, which are huge, fabulously frothy and packed with fruit. Foodwise, eggs benedict is a good choice, but you could also, more unusually, have a kipper or (our favourite) a smoked chicken,

avocado and rocket baguette. The slick interior features luxurious leather banquettes, chic black and white photography on the walls, and a gleaming chrome coffee machine, and this, along with super-smooth service, is what makes the place such a classic. Plenty of tables outside attract a huge crowd on sunny days, and the attached deli opposite is worth a visit too. A sister restaurant recently opened in Notting Hill with the same menu and an extra dose of glamour in the decor, but it's the Maida Vale original that packs in the crowds.
Babies and children welcome: high chairs. No smoking. Tables outdoors (13, pavement and patio). Takeaway service (6-10pm). **Map 2 D4**. **For branches see index.**

Notting Hill

★ Tea Palace
175 Westbourne Grove, W11 2SB (7727 2600/ www.teapalace.co.uk). Bayswater or Notting Hill Gate tube. **Open** 10am-7pm, **tea** served 3-7pm daily. **Main courses** £8-£13. **Set tea** £15-£22. **Licensed**. **Credit** AmEx, MC, V.
Half teashop, half smart café, this peaceful, white tableclothed sanctuary specialises in the kind of prim and pretty afternoon teas so beloved of big London hotels. The event is a little less starchy and expensive here, though the tiered trays filled with scones, cakes and finger sandwiches should satisfy any critical-eyed regular at the Dorchester. There are also brunch and lunch menus (offering the likes of buttered muffins and salad dishes, respectively), but the majority of menu space is dedicated to tea. The tea selection, all 16 pages of it, might seem bewildering, but staff are happy to advise and the quality of the tea is such that adventure will be rewarded. We tried a variety: excellent oolongs, tasty fruit blends, and a house creation called Mint Breeze, which turned out to be a liquorish-mint-lime brew that was so good that we bought a bag of it from the shop on our way out.
Babies and children welcome: high chairs. Booking advisable. Disabled: toilet. No smoking. **Map 19 C3**.

Shepherd's Bush

Bush Garden Café
59 Goldhawk Road, W12 8EG (8743 6372). Goldhawk Road tube. **Open** 7.30am-7pm Mon-Fri; 8am-5pm Sat. **Main courses** £4-£5. **Licensed**. **Credit** (over £10) MC, V.
Situated right next to Goldhawk tube, this organic, veggie haven is a chilled café frequented by all types, from suits in need of some vitamins to mothers and children in need of a bit of a treat (there is children's menu and a garden/play area). Standard café fare sits next to more exotic options, such as the refreshing acerola (a Brazilian fruit rich in vitamin C) smoothie or the Heidi pie, made with sweet potato, spinach and goat's cheese. The bohemian atmosphere is welcome, as are the heaving shelves of organic produce available for you to purchase, take home and try for yourselves. The plain white walls and chalked menu boards show just what a thoroughly unpretentious and pleasant place Bush Garden Café is. Well worth a visit if you're in the area and in need of some café-based R&R.
Babies and children welcome: children's menu; high chairs; toys. No smoking. Tables outdoors (10, garden). Takeaway service. Vegetarian menu. **Map 20 B2**.

Westbourne Grove

Tom's Delicatessen
226 Westbourne Grove, W11 2RH (7221 8818). Notting Hill Gate tube. **Open** 8am-6.30pm Mon-Sat; 9am-6.30pm Sun. **Main courses** £6.95-£9.75. **Unlicensed**. **Credit** MC, V.
This Westbourne Grove favourite has had a bit of a refurb, but its quirky, stylish feel hasn't changed. Display cases show 1950s products with a bit of tongue-in-cheek nostalgia and new booths are made from old public transport seats. Downstairs there's a big table and new breakfast bar in the deli, providing a welcome bit of extra seating (you'll be tempted by the look and smell of the pizza slices),

while the menu still offers all the old American-style favourites. A posh toasted muffin with scrambled eggs and smoked salmon came with a dollop of caviar, while eggs benedict featured perfect poached eggs and proper hollandaise. There are club sandwiches, salads and smoothies, as well as cup cakes, beautifully packaged sweets and classy sandwiches to take away. With tables in the garden, clever clip-on high chairs and very tasty coffee, Tom's is still getting it right in its second decade.
Babies and children welcome. high chairs. No smoking. Tables outdoors (6, garden; 2, terrace). Takeaway service. Map 7 A3.

South West
Chelsea

Daylesford Organic Café NEW
Bamford & Sons, The Old Bank, 3 Sloane Square, SW1W 8AG (7881 8020/www. daylesfordorganic.com). Sloane Square tube. **Open** 8am-6pm Mon-Fri; 10am-6pm Sat; noon-5pm Sun. **Main courses** £8-£14. **Licensed. Credit** AmEx, DC, MC, V.
Tucked away in the basement of her Sloane Square clothes shop, this London branch of Lady Bamford's award-winning Daylesford farm shop in the Cotswolds has a lot going for it – not least the food. A chicory, pear and walnut salad with blue cheese was beautifully presented, the crisp texture of the chicory and fresh roasted walnuts a good match for the soft, succulent pear and creamy Harbourne blue, an award-winning British goat's milk cheese. The ploughman's platter was also superior, with own-made condiments of chutney and piccalilli that complemented a meaty pork pie. A leg of air-dried and aged jamón ibérico from Brindisa sits proudly on the counter, in front of the Daylesford organic food range (which is also sold in Selfridges). Everything is tastefully arranged, with soft beige furnishings and a careful attention to detail. The result is a new lunching destination for the Chelsea set that's pricey, but worth it.
Babies and children welcome. Disabled: toilet. No smoking. Takeaway service. Vegan dishes. Map 15 G11.

South
Battersea

Boiled Egg & Soldiers
63 Northcote Road, SW11 1NP (7223 4894). Clapham Junction rail. **Open** 8am-6pm Mon-Sat; 9am-4pm Sun. **Main courses** £4.95-£9.95. **Licensed. No credit cards.**
Northcote Road's well-heeled twentysomethings come here for the hangover breakfasts and comfort food that takes them back to their childhoods. But those who aren't suffering will also enjoy the slap-up all-day specials, which include the usual fried/scrambled favourites as well as less common smoked haddock and poached egg combos, plus the eponymous boiled egg and soldiers (served in comedy chicken eggcups). There's also a 'posh breakfast' that comes with a glass of fizz. The nursery nostalgia theme continues with Marmite on toast, baked potatoes filled with baked beans and grated cheese, various salads, lots of ice-cream and tasty cakes (we liked the fruity flapjacks). There are Bloody Marys and Virgin Marys, smoothies, milkshakes and even cool jugs of Pimm's for hot days. It's a small, squashed space with laid-back (well, a bit haphazard) service and child's bedroom-style bright decor. Battersea's young crowd love it.
Babies and children welcome: children's menu; high chairs. Tables outdoors (2, pavement; 8, garden). Takeaway service. Map 21 C4.

Crumpet
66 Northcote Road, SW11 6QL (7924 1117/ www.crumpet.biz). Clapham Junction rail. **Open** 9am-6pm Mon-Sat; 10am-6pm Sun. **Main courses** £3.95-£14.95. **Licensed. Credit** AmEx, MC, V.

This place is all about children. Bright, airy and uncluttered, it has ample space for buggies, plenty of high chairs, a special play den at the back and a serious focus on simple, healthy fare. A tempting assortment of old-fashioned cakes is on display, and the menu offers a good range of sandwiches, salads, snacks and smoothies. We didn't doubt that our tasty goat's cheese and onion marmalade sandwich was 'hand-cut' – its doorsteppy nature gave it away. A long tea list is accompanied by cutesy descriptions: decaff is 'the pregnant one' and Darjeeling 'the posh one'. The soft drinks (ginger beer or traditional lemonade, for example) are all organic. There's a separate children's menu full of healthy options including cottage pie, sausages and nursery specials, as well as wholesome breakfasts of the porridge/fruit/muesli variety. Slightly austere classroom furniture adds to the sensible nature of the place, which is fantastic for families but just pointless for those without small children.
Babies and children welcome: children's menu; high chairs; toys. No smoking. Tables outdoors (2, pavement). Takeaway service. Map 21 C5.

Clapham

★ Macaron NEW
2006 WINNER BEST PATISSERIE
22 The Pavement, SW4 0HY (7498 2636). Clapham Common tube. **Open** 7.30am-8pm Mon-Fri; 9am-8pm Sat, Sun. **Main courses** £2.75-£3.50. **Unlicensed. No credit cards.**
Picture-perfect and charmingly old-fashioned, Macaron looks as if it has been lifted from a 1930s French film set. It's a celebration of nostalgia – lovely china cake plates, flowery cups and saucers, and jars filled with loose leaf teas complement a fabulous array of pâtisserie and freshly baked bread. The creative head pâtissier, Nicolas Houchett, lines up classic French pastries alongside heavenly new-wave numbers, and does it all in impressive style. Our current raves include Le Lingot; topped with glistening apricot glaze, this deliciously light apricot mousse gives way to a sheet of coconut cream – making a marvellous match with the buttery crunch of its biscuit base. Other treats include the Paris-Brest (choux pastry rings, crammed with praline and custardy cream), tangy lemon tarts, and scrumptious mini macaroons. Don't miss out on the fine range of carefully chosen teas, including top-end Japanese, Chinese and Indian choices. Staff are helpful and utterly charming, adding to the informal, laid-back set-up. Customers sit around a big communal table and soak in the spectacle of chefs whipping icings and piping rosettes on to pastries, visible through the kitchen window. Sweet temptation doesn't get better than this.
Babies and children admitted. No smoking. Tables outdoors (2, pavement). Takeaway service. Map 22 A2.

South East
Bankside

★ The Table NEW
2006 WINNER BEST CHEAP EATS
2006 RUNNER-UP BEST DESIGN
83 Southwark Street, SE1 0HX (7401 2760/ www.thetable.co.uk). Southwark tube/London Bridge tube/rail. **Open** 8am-6pm Mon-Thur; 8am-11pm Fri. **Licensed. Corkage** £2.50. **Main courses** £3.50-£8. **Credit** MC, V.
On an otherwise grim stretch of Southwark Street hides this gem of a café, on the ground floor of the offices of architects Allies and Morrison – who designed the space. It features raw concrete walls, chunky wooden tables and benches, an outdoor courtyard with wooden decking, an open kitchen and plate-glass windows. A long table by the front window displays sandwiches and a wonderful, Mediterranean-inspired salad bar. Selections such as a baby shrimp pasta salad or roasted pumpkin with spinach leaves are charged by weight and change weekly. Dishes like minute steak, chicken breast and tuna are ordered at a different counter,

then supplemented with your choice of pre-prepared Italian 'garnishes', such as stewed aubergine with capers and pine nuts. At breakfast, this counter dishes out porridge and bacon sarnies. There are plans to expand evening dining once the huge Bankside 1-2-3 development opens across the road in 2007. We can't wait. Once, words like 'salad bar' and 'pre-prepared' suggested unimaginative, dingy food. Not here: meat is grilled to order, pasta is made on the premises, and salads are assembled from nearby Borough Market. This is self-service food, elevated to a new level. Wonderful.
Babies and children admitted. Disabled: toilet. No smoking. Separate room for parties, seats 50. Tables outdoors (8, terrace). Takeaway service. Map 11 O8.

Dulwich

Au Ciel
1A Carlton Avenue, SE21 7DE (8488 1111/ www.auciel.co.uk). North Dulwich rail/37 bus. **Open** 8.30am-5.30pm Mon-Sat; 10am-5.30pm Sun. **Main courses** £1.50-£2.95. **Unlicensed. Credit** DC, MC, V.
The refinement of this classy little pâtisserie suits its genteel Dulwich Village location to a tee. While partaking of a silver pot of the unusual infusions (Golden Flowers, Royal Plum, White Tangerine or Dragon Eye Oolong) and gorging on a moist slab of Belgo cake (truffle base, whipped cream and thick chocolate icing), your eyes will feast on the vast array of be-ribboned bonbons, beautifully packaged teas and gilded biscuit boxes stacked on the shelves, or the handmade chocolates adorning the counter. While there are antique brass chandeliers on walls and ceiling, and marble-topped tables, the banquettes are made from slightly tatty leatherette and the lino floor now bears signs of age – but it all works, in an insouciant, Parisian sort of way. Stick to the cakes, breads or divine Di Sotto's ice-creams, however. A leaden slab of quiche arrived microwaved and unadorned by even the teeniest salad garnish.
Babies and children admitted. No smoking. Tables outdoors (2, pavement). Takeaway service. Map 23 B5.

London Bridge & Borough

★ Konditor & Cook
10 Stoney Street, SE1 9AD (7407 5100/ www.konditorandcook.com). London Bridge tube/rail. **Open** 7.30am-6pm Mon-Fri; 8.30am-5pm Sat. **Main courses** £2.10-£4.95. **Unlicensed. Credit** AmEx, MC, V.
Locals flock here for a daily changing selection of appealing lunches: soups and salads supplemented with well-filled sandwiches, smoked salmon frittata, spinach and ricotta tartlets, plus hot meals and daily specials (gnocchi in fresh tomato and basil sauce with black olives, for example). Dieters beware: we've yet to witness the most nonchalant of browsers leave without some heavenly orange lavender slab cake or a dark chocolate-chip brownie. K&C's commitment to high-quality ingredients is evident in their baked goods; even the humble flapjacks taste deliciously indulgent. Breakfast baking (scones, croissants, buns) includes deliciously savoury spinach parmesan muffins (so filling we had no room left for coffee). K&C's speciality cakes are justifiably legendary – the Curly Whirly double-layer chocolate cake with real vanilla bean frosting is eye-closingly good.
Babies and children admitted. No smoking. Tables outdoors (1, pavement). Takeaway service. Map 11 P8.
For branches see index.

Peckham

Petitou
63 Choumert Road, SE15 4AR (7639 2613). Peckham Rye rail. **Open** 9am-5.30pm Tue-Sat; 10am-5.30pm Sun. **Main courses** £5.95-£6.45. **Licensed. Credit** AmEx, DC, MC, V.
Great coffee, generous portions of good, fresh-cooked food and the gentle, unstinting courtesy of its staff has turned Petitou into the thriving, chocolate-sprinkled hub of Peckham's chattering

classes. Situated down a tree-lined avenue off Bellenden Road, its shaded, mosaic-floored front patio quickly fills up in summer. But the cool, pale green interior, with its scuffed wood floor and furniture, is a year-round haven for lunching mums, earnest couples, solitary news perusers and young families. There's a quiet buzz from 10am on, as locals drift in for a coffee or one of the wide range of teas, fresh juices or gooey almond croissants. Huge slabs of toasted granary bread cost £1 for two slices with butter (40p extra for jam, Marmite or peanut butter). A choice of own-made quiches with salad, plus fresh soups, form the bulk of the lunch menu. Well-priced organic wine, cider and beer are now available. And the cakes are a must: a daily changing menu of moist, calorie-laden treats are homemade by a rota of three local domestic goddesses.
Babies and children welcome: children's portions; high chairs. No smoking. Tables outdoors (6, patio). Takeaway service. **Map 23 C3.**

East
Shoreditch

Frizzante@City Farm
Hackney City Farm, 1A Goldsmith's Row, E2 8QA (7739 2266/www.frizzanteltd.co.uk). Liverpool Street tube/rail then 26, 48 bus. **Open** 10am-4.30pm Tue-Sun. **Main courses** £5-£7. **Unlicensed. Corkage** no charge. **Credit** MC, V.
Being situated within Hackney City Farm might explain the noisy 'herd of animals' atmosphere. Happily, the food is so good you won't care. Yellow-painted walls are covered in children's paintings, while the oilcloth-covered tables are heaving with parents and their offspring tucking into healthy foods chosen from the chalkboard, and made in the open-plan kitchen. There's own-made lasagne, pastas, herb-crusted chicken and – big on Sundays – Frizzante's big farm breakfasts. Prices are reasonable and portions large. Our juicy burgers came with delicious roasted potatoes and a big salad, while barbecued chicken had a tangy thai dipping sauce. Orders are taken at the deli counter, where you can also buy goods such as olives, artichokes, cheese and salami, as well as scrumptious-looking cakes and own-made biscuits. Drinks include smoothies, tea, coffee and juices. If you can still move after your food-fest, check out the noticeboard – there's always something going on at Frizzante. On our visit it was breastfeeding classes (thankfully, taking place next door), as well as pottery, upholstery and knitting classes, and even Patty's singing class.
Babies and children welcome: children's menu; high chairs; toys. Bookings not accepted weekends. Disabled: toilet. No smoking. Separate room for parties, seats 40. Tables outdoors (12, garden). Takeaway service. Vegetarian menu. Vegan dishes. **Map 6 S3.**
For branch (Frizzante@Unicorn Theatre) see index.

Jones Dairy Café
23 Ezra Street, E2 7RH (7739 5372/www. jonesdairy.co.uk). Liverpool Street tube/rail then 26, 48 bus/Old Street tube/rail then 55 bus. **Open** 9am-3pm Fri, Sat; 8am-3pm Sun. **Main courses** £2-£5. **Unlicensed. No credit cards.**
It's been almost 70 years since this dinky Dickensian-looking café last housed a cow, but it still pays homage to its roots with a fine selection of English and continental cheeses in its tiny shop. Regrettably, none of these is available in the attached café, which instead serves up huge bagels and excellent mugs of coffee during the Sunday Columbia Road flower market, when numbers dictate that only cold foods are available. Come on a Friday or Saturday and it's a very different matter. Then the quietness of the old cobbled streets gives an eerie sense of being on an empty film set, and it's delightful to while away an hour tucking into a hearty all-day breakfast or omelette, or a massive bowl of mixed salad, featuring egg, cheese, smoked salmon, olives and delicious dressed organic leaves. Finish with a slice of welsh fruit cake and you'll be set up for the day.
Babies and children welcome: high chair. No smoking. Tables outdoors (2, pavement). Takeaway service. **Map 6 S3.**

North East
Stoke Newington

Blue Legume
101 Stoke Newington Church Street, N16 0UD (7923 1303). Stoke Newington rail/73 bus. **Open** 9.30am-11pm Mon-Sat; 9.30am-6.30pm Sun. **Main courses** £4.95-£17.95. **Licensed. Credit** (after 6pm) MC, V.
If you want a cake that will brighten your day, and possibly your entire life, try the lemon cheesecake at this Stokey stalwart. It's also the place if you like veggie food; they have an extensive and tasty selection, as well as smoothies, a good range of teas and coffees, and breakfast options such as organic honey waffles with fresh fruit, maple syrup and yogurt. At night, it transforms into a restaurant,

---

Hotel teas

For a quintessential English experience, head to one of London's posher hotels to indulge in the ritual of a formal afternoon tea. It can be an expensive business, and you'll have to dress smartly, but when everything is as it should be – fresh and interesting sandwiches, hot crumpets, rivers of refreshing teas, and extravagant cakes – this is a great way to spend an afternoon. Do book well in advance.

The Bentley
27-33 Harrington Gardens, SW7 4JX (7244 5555/www.thebentley-hotel.com). Gloucester Road tube. **Tea served** 3-5.30pm daily. **Set tea** £24-£30. **Credit** AmEx, DC, JCB, MC, V.
Babies and children welcome: children's menu; high chairs. Disabled: toilet. Dress: smart casual. No-smoking tables. **Map 13 C10.**

The Berkeley
Wilton Place, SW1X 7RL (7235 6000/ www.the-berkeley.co.uk). Knightsbridge tube. **Tea served** 2-6pm daily. **Set tea** £31-£39.50 incl glass of champagne. **Credit** AmEx, DC, MC, V.
Babies and children welcome: high chairs. Booking essential. Disabled: toilet. Dress: smart casual. No-smoking tables. **Map 9 G9.**

The Capital
22-24 Basil Street, SW3 1AT (7589 5171/7591 1202/www.capitalhotel.co.uk). Knightsbridge tube. **Tea served** 3-5.30pm daily. **Set tea** £15.50; £26.50 incl glass of champagne. **Credit** AmEx, DC, MC, V. Booking advisable; essential weekends. Children over 12 admitted. Dress: smart casual. Separate rooms for parties, seating 10, 12 and 24. **Map 8 F9.**

Claridge's
55 Brook Street, W1K 4HA (7409 6307/ www.claridges.co.uk). Bond Street tube. **Tea served** 3-5.30pm daily. **Set tea** £30.50-£38.50. **Cover** (if not taking set tea) £3. **Credit** AmEx, DC, MC, V. *Babies and children welcome: high chairs. Disabled: toilet. Entertainment: musicians 3-6pm daily. No smoking. Vegetarian menu. Vegan dishes.* **Map 9 H6.**

The Connaught
16 Carlos Place, W1K 2AL (7499 7070/ www.theconnaught.com). Bond Street or Green Park tube. **Tea served** 3-5.30pm daily. **Set tea** £18-£24. **Credit** AmEx, DC, JCB, MC, V.
Babies and children welcome: high chairs. Disabled: toilet. No smoking. **Map 9 H7.**

The Dorchester
53 Park Lane, W1K 1QA (7629 8888/ www.thedorchester.com). Hyde Park Corner tube. **Tea served** 2.30pm, 4.30pm Mon-Fri; 2.30pm, 4.45pm Sat, Sun. **Set tea** £28.50; £34.50 incl glass of champagne; £38.50 high tea. **Credit** AmEx, DC, JCB, MC, V.
Babies and children welcome: high chairs. Disabled: toilet. Entertainment: pianist 3-11pm Mon-Sat; 3-7pm Sun. **Map 9 G7.**

Fortnum & Mason
181 Piccadilly, W1A 1ER (7734 8040/ www.fortnumandmason.co.uk). Green Park or Piccadilly Circus tube. **Tea served** noon-5.15pm Mon; 3-5.15pm Tue-Sat. **Set tea** £24; £26 high tea; £29-£34 incl glass of champagne. **Minimum** £4.50. **Credit** AmEx, DC, JCB, MC, V.
Babies and children welcome: high chairs. Disabled: lift; toilet. Dress: smart casual; no shorts or sandals. **Map 17 J7.**

The Lanesborough
Hyde Park Corner, SW1X 7TA (7259 5599/www.lanesborough.com). Hyde Park Corner tube. **Tea served** 3.30-6pm Mon-Sat; 4-6.30pm Sun. **Set tea** £28-£37. **Minimum** £9.50. **Credit** AmEx, DC, MC, V.
Babies and children welcome: high chairs. Disabled: toilet. Dress: smart casual. Entertainment: pianist 3.30-6pm Mon-Sat; 4-6.30pm Sun. No smoking. **Map 9 G8.**

The Ritz
150 Piccadilly, W1J 9BR (7493 8181/ www.theritzhotel.co.uk). Green Park tube. **Tea served** (reserved sittings) 11.30am, 1.30pm, 3.30pm, 5.30pm, 7.30pm daily. **Set tea** £35. **Credit** AmEx, MC, V.
Babies and children welcome: high chairs. Disabled: toilet. Booking essential. Dress: jacket and tie; no jeans or trainers. **Map 9 J7.**

The Savoy
Strand, WC2R 0EU (7836 4343/www.the-savoy.com). Covent Garden or Embankment tube/Charing Cross tube/rail. **Tea served** 2-5.30pm Mon-Fri; noon-5.30pm Sat, Sun. **Set tea** (Mon-Fri) £24; (Sat, Sun) £27. **Credit** AmEx, DC, JCB, MC, V.
Babies and children welcome: high chairs. **Map 18 L7.**

The Soho Hotel
4 Richmond Mews, W1D 3DH (7559 3007/ www.firmdale.com). Tottenham Court Road tube. **Tea served** 3-5pm daily. **Set tea** £17.50-£25. **Credit** AmEx, JCB, MC, V.
Babies and children welcome: high chairs. Booking advisable. Disabled: toilet. Dress: smart casual. Tables outdoors (2, pavement). **Map 17 K6.**

Threadneedles
5 Threadneedle Street, EC2R 8AY (7657 8080). Bank tube/DLR. **Tea served** 3-5.30pm Mon-Fri. **Set tea** £8-£16. **Credit** AmEx, DC, MC, V.
Booking advisable. Disabled: toilet. Dress: smart casual. **Map 12 Q6.**

Macaron. See p302.

serving wine and Turkish-inspired food such as the trademark Blue Legume, an aubergine parcel of roasted vegetables topped with goat's cheese. The surroundings are very pleasant: green walls and a quirky cloud-covered ceiling in the front room, and an airy mini conservatory at the back. And the low points? The attractive mosaic tables are somewhat crammed together and the service was a little lackadaisical on our visit. But after you've sampled the cakes, you probably won't care.
Babies and children welcome: high chairs.
Booking advisable dinner. No-smoking tables.
Tables outdoors (5, pavement). Takeaway service.
Map 25 B1.

North
Highgate

Kalendar
15A Swains Lane, N6 6QX (8348 8300).
Gospel Oak rail/214, C2, C11, C12 bus.
Open 8am-10pm Mon-Fri; 9am-10pm Sat, Sun.
Main courses £7-£12. **Licensed. Credit**
AmEx, DC, JCB, MC, V.
Situated in a slice of affluent suburbia of the kind that provides the blueprint for Working Title film sets, Kalendar is that rare thing – an open-all-hours café that manages to be all things to all people. The menu, like the boho-country decor, is eclectic: along with a stellar all-day breakfast, there are fresh juices, char-grills, and sandwiches and salads with a Mediterranean bias. Much of the produce used is available from the on-site deli, and sourcing is careful: meat from Elite Meats next door, cakes from Konditor & Cook, cheeses from Neal's Yard (including, on our visit, an oozily ripe brie the size of a hubcap). Come the evening, the line-up is gastropub in all but name – our salad of smoky duck breast came with a beautifully judged dressing, and salmon fish cakes were crisp without, sweetly flaky within. There's also a short but well-chosen wine list. A Nesquik-like scoop of strawberry ice-cream struck the only discordant note of our meal.
Babies and children welcome: children's menu;
high chairs. Bookings not accepted lunch.
No smoking. Tables outdoors (10, pavement).
Takeaway service.

North West
Hampstead

Maison Blanc
62 Hampstead High Street, NW3 1QH (7431 8338/www.maisonblanc.co.uk). Hampstead tube.
Open 8am-7pm Mon-Sat; 9am-7pm Sun. **Main courses** £2.50-£6. **Unlicensed. Credit** MC, V.
A recent refit has given this branch of Maison Blanc a new sparkle, and even its range of gateaux, rich mousse cakes and cheesecakes looks fresher than in previous years. On a Saturday morning visit, the baguettes were particularly quick to disappear from the shelves. However, the all-day menu remains largely unchanged from before and could do with sprucing up – though it does offer an affordable option to pricier venues (such as the recently opened Paul, located just down the road). A dense and seductive chocolate mousse cake flecked with the crunch of crisp flecks of ground praline will satisfy any chocolate cravings, while lovers of fruity flavours will be buoyed by the satisfyingly tangy lemon tarts. Savouries are less appealing. Tarte provençale, a pastry flan lined with mustard and emmental cheese and topped with sliced tomatoes, had a soggy texture and tasted as if it had been reheated in a microwave. Service is bright and breezy.
Babies and children admitted. Disabled: toilet.
No smoking. Takeaway service. **Map 28 B2**.
For branches see index.

Kensal Green

★ **Brilliant Kids Café** NEW
8 Station Terrace, NW10 5RT (8964 4120/ www.brilliantkids.co.uk). Kensal Green tube/ Kensal Rise rail. **Open** 8am-6pm Mon-Fri; 9am-

5pm Sat; 10am-2pm Sun. **Main courses**
£5.50-£7.50. **Unlicensed. Corkage** no charge.
Credit MC, V.
Already a mummy magnet, the new Brilliant café
and arts centre sits next to the kids' clothing and
equipment store of the same name. Crisply turned
out, the bright, polished café with airy art rooms
at the back, beyond which blossoms a lovely
garden, is a ray of sunshine among the dowdy
shopfronts of Kensal Rise. The feel-good factor
extends way beyond fresh paint and flowery
pergolas, however, thanks to a thrifty, sustainable
theme. Ingredients are wholesome and locally
sourced where possible. Baked goods come from
various artisan bakeries nearby; Karma cakes is a
favourite source. Savoury dishes might include
tomato and mozzarella quiche or balsamic chicken
with lentils, while own-made elderflower cordial
might complete a virtuous, good-value light lunch.
It can be lovely eating in the garden, watching
a pair of toddlers demolishing flapjacks on the
large, sunny deck. Places such as Brilliant suffuse
parenthood with a rosy glow, which, when you're
bringing up babies in the flinty heart of the city,
can be no bad thing.
Babies and children welcome: children's portions;
high chairs; play area; supervised activities.
Booking advisable. Disabled: toilet. No smoking.
Restaurant available for hire. Tables outdoors
(2, garden). Takeaway service.

Gracelands
118 College Road, NW10 5HD (8964 9161).
Kensal Green tube. **Open** 8am-5pm Mon-Fri;
9am-4pm Sat; 9.30am-3pm Sun. **Main courses**
£4-£7. **Unlicensed. Corkage** no charge.
Credit MC, V.
For local parents, Gracelands is almost too good to
be true. Children can entertain themselves in a
designated play corner while their parents drink
coffee and take advantage of the wireless internet
connection to work on their laptops. There's a
friendly local feel, highlighted by a noticeboard
where people give away outgrown baby stuff,
advertise local yoga classes and look for childcare.
Art, clothes and jewellery by local designers are
displayed for sale on the walls. The food is healthy
and delicious. Creative quiches (goat's cheese and
sweet potato is a favourite) and salads show a
loving touch – we enjoyed generous helpings of
lemon-infused courgettes and a herby lentil and
beetroot combo. A good selection of sandwiches,
panini and breakfasts is boosted by heftier daily
specials such as meatballs. Staff are a tad chaotic,
in a charming way. The café shuts early, so don't
leave it too late.
Babies and children welcome: children's menu;
high chairs; toys. No smoking. Tables outdoors
(4, pavement; 3, garden). Takeaway service.

Queen's Park

★ Baker & Spice
75 Salusbury Road, NW6 6NH (7604 3636/
www.bakerandspice.com). Queen's Park tube.
Open 7am-7pm Mon-Sat; 8am-5pm Sun.
Licensed. Credit MC, V.
What a place. Brilliant breads, cakes and
pâtisserie, excellent coffee, a counter spilling over
with colourful and interesting salads, and a big
shared table with customers loitering over the
colour supplements – the appeal is obvious. The
dishes are excellent quality and hard to resist, even
at their inflated prices (£5.50 for a croque monsieur
– *mon dieu!*). Behind the glass display case is a
cornucopia of Mediterranean-style lunch dishes:
globe artichoke hearts in olive oil with fresh chives,
garlic and rosemary; grilled aubergine with
pomegranate sauce and parsley; sphere-shaped
courgettes filled with bechamel sauce, then grilled.
The lumpenproletariat of Queen's Park occupy the
shared table most of the day, so getting a takeaway
can make more sense if you live locally (the giant
meringues make excellent pavlova). Be warned
that when they say the café shuts at 7pm, you
shouldn't turn up at 6.55pm expecting to be let in.
Babies and children admitted. No smoking.
Tables outdoors (1, pavement). Takeaway service.
Map 1 A2.
For branches see index.

PARK CAFÉS

The popular image of park cafés –
sticky seats, weak tea, curled-up
sandwiches – is becoming a thing of
the past, at least in London. While
a handful of the capital's cafés have
always bucked the trend, several
others have spruced themselves up
in recent years. There's also the
Garden Café (*see p299*) in Regent's
Park, and **Inn The Park** (in the
British chapter) in St James's Park.

West
Kensington

Kensington Palace Orangery
The Orangery, Kensington Palace, Kensington
Gardens, W8 4PX (7376 0239/www.digby
trout.co.uk). High Street Kensington or
Queensway tube. **Open** Mar-Oct 10am-6pm
daily. *Nov-Feb* 10am-5pm daily. **Main courses**
£7.95-£11.50. **Set tea** £7.95-£16.95. **Licensed.**
Credit DC, MC, V.
The vast, cool interior is minimally decorated with
all focus going on the vast table display of piles of
fresh scones, generously iced chocolate, coffee and
sponge cakes, lemon and strawberry tarts, and
shortbread, all with a magnificent backdrop of
lilies. Fresh, fragrant freesias on each plain white
table add a simple and delightful garden feel. Table
service on this visit was excellent, though has been
known to deteriorate on summer weekends when
queues stretch out on to the veranda. A hearty
ploughman's, or tarragon, broad bean and bacon
salad with cherry tomatoes, mint and rocket, are
light lunch options, and could be followed by iced
mango brûlée. Most visitors go for afternoon tea,
complete with delicate cream cheese and cucumber
sandwiches, scones with clotted cream and jam,
slices of cake, loose-leaf teas – or champagne if you
feel like an upgrade. Children were easily
accommodated on our visit.
Babies and children welcome: children's menu;
high chairs. Disabled: toilet. No smoking. Tables
outdoors (12, terrace). **Map 7 C8.**

South West
Wandsworth

Common Ground
Wandsworth Common, off Dorlcote Road,
SW18 3RT (8874 9386). Wandsworth Common
rail. **Open** 9am-5.30pm Tue-Fri; 10am-5.30pm
Sat, Sun. **Main courses** £3.50-£9. **Licensed.**
Credit MC, V.
A shady patio area overlooks a cricket ground. It's
a great place to relax with a fresh sandwich
(chicken, rocket and lemon mayonnaise, for
instance) or a savoury tart. Inside, the seating area
is charming, with local art-for-sale adorning the
walls, lots of community notices, and fresh flowers
on the tables. The back parlour has comfortable
sofas, a play area and toys. The own-made cakes
are always delightful. Common Ground isn't cheap
and we had to ask for table service outside, but it
is relaxed and relaxing. A popular spot for yummy
mummies, it balances a very child-friendly
approach (there's a decent kids' menu) with a
perfectly comfortable environment for child-free
visitors. Indulge in a beer while you tempt the
children with a babycino and a fairy cake, or while
away hours with the newspaper in the
conservatory. Even a dog can have a cool drink.
Babies and children welcome: children's menu;
high chairs. No-smoking tables. Separate room
for parties, seats 100. Tables outside (15, patio).
Takeaway service.

South East
Camberwell

Chumleigh Gardens Café
Chumleigh Gardens, Burgess Park, SE5 0RJ
(7525 1070). Elephant & Castle tube/rail then
12, 42, 63, 68, 171, 343, P3 bus. **Open** 9am-
5pm Mon-Fri; 10am-5pm Sat, Sun. **Main courses**
£3-£5. **Licensed. Credit** (80p charge) JCB, MC, V.
It is a very pleasant surprise to come upon the
quaint Chumleigh almshouses and magnificent
gardens in rather barren Burgess Park. The café,
situated between the compact Mediterranean and
Islamic Gardens, is a cheerful and unpretentious
place, with its incongruous mix of bright, plastic
tablecloths, samba music and peaceful outdoor
seating around a fountain and tiled pond. You'll
find gorgeous, hearty salads, a huge array of
sandwiches made to order, all-day breakfasts,
omelettes, baked potatoes and individually
wrapped cakes. The coffee is Fairtrade. Our only
grumble was that meals were literally served one
at a time, and a 20-minute wait for a sandwich on
a quiet weekday lunchtime was a little frustrating.
Parents beware – there are some (signposted)
poisonous plants at toddler level.
Babies and children welcome: high chairs.
Disabled: toilet. Entertainment: jazz 1pm Sun.
No smoking. Tables outdoors (9, garden).
Takeaway service.

Dulwich

Pavilion Café
Dulwich Park, SE21 7BQ (8299 1383).
West Dulwich rail/P4 bus. **Open** *Summer*
8.30am-6pm Mon-Fri; 9am-6pm Sat, Sun.
Winter 8.30am-4.30pm Mon-Fri; 9am-4.30pm
Sat, Sun. **Main courses** £4.50-£6.50. **Licensed.**
No credit cards.
The child-free zone here is calm and cool, and feels
nicely distanced from the rest of this otherwise
bustling cafe by the lake in seemingly well-to-do
Dulwich Park. Little ones have toys to play with
and ice-creams and fairy cakes to consume.
Watermelon and feta cheese salad, and asparagus
and salmon quiche topped the bill, which also
features sandwiches (that usually run out by 3pm)
and all-day breakfasts. Lemon poppy seed cake
was made on the premises and, having just come
out of the oven, was warm, light and delicious.
Militant red signage (multiplied since 2005, due to
a regrettable increase in vandalism) makes the
atmosphere slightly uncomfortable, but the staff
are relaxed and the operation runs like clockwork.
Large french windows keep the interior airy and
the simple pale walls are perfect for displaying
work by local artists.
Babies and children welcome: children's menu;
high chairs; toys. Disabled: toilet. No smoking.
Tables outdoors (12, park). Takeaway service.

Greenwich

Pavilion Tea House
Greenwich Park, Blackheath Gate, SE10 8QY
(8858 9695). Blackheath rail/Greenwich rail/
DLR. **Open** 9am-6pm Mon-Fri; 9am-7pm Sat,
Sun. **Main courses** £2.50-£7.25. **Licensed.**
Credit MC, V.
This is a consistently lovely lunch place, situated
alongside the Royal Observatory (due to reopen
in 2007 following major redevelopment). A big
draw is the enclosed lawn, with its lovingly
tended flower beds, large, part-shaded eating area
and fab views over Greenwich Park and
Docklands, with the dome of St Paul's in the
distance. Visitors are welcome to relax and eat on
the lawns. Inside, the operation is well organised,
with appetising wall-mounted pictures of the
mains; it's a cosy refuge in winter. Staff are
friendly and helpful. Hot food has a British bent,
and includes smoked salmon and scrambled eggs,
welsh rarebit or smoked chicken and asparagus
salad. Sandwiches are chunky and fresh, and
classic dishes such as bread pudding, trifle,
scones and rock cakes feature for dessert. The
decor incorporates features of the original

CHEAP EATS

refreshment house, built in 1909, with a more modern, sleek look, making this a pleasantly individual spot.

Babies and children welcome: high chairs. Disabled: toilet. No smoking. Tables outdoors (20, garden). Takeaway service.

For branch (Cow & Coffee Bean) see index.

North

Highgate

Pavilion Café

Highgate Woods, Muswell Hill Road, N10 3JN (8444 4777). Highgate tube. **Open** *Summer* 8.30am-8.30pm Mon-Wed; 8am-8.30pm Thur-Sun. *Winter* 9am-dusk daily. **Main courses** £5-£8.95. **Licensed. Credit** AmEx, JCB, MC, V.

The Pavilion is located on the edge of the cricket ground in the middle of Highgate Woods. Grilled salmon on puy lentils with salsa verde was tasty and a chunky Pavilion burger with big chips, salad and chilli dip was satisfying. The simple menu features good-quality ingredients sourced locally; there's a wide selection for kids who are made welcome into the evening. We ate listening to energetic live jazz, surrounded by sprawling and beautiful flowering greenery. Unfortunately, our visit was marred by disorganised and uninterested service (with one charming exception). The mains arrived before we'd finished our starters (delicious own-made houmous and a white bean and garlic dip), a glass of water took four requests to materialise, and quibbling about an overcharge on the bill was unpleasant. On top of this, a sneaky cover charge and £1 for extra flatbread left us feeling unimpressed.

Babies and children welcome: children's menu; high chairs. Entertainment: jazz 6pm Thur, Fri (June-Aug). No smoking. Tables outdoors (27, terrace; 8, veranda). Takeaway service.

Stamford Hill

Springfield Park Café

White Lodge Mansion, Springfield Park, E5 9EF (8806 0444/www.sparkcafe.co.uk). Stamford Hill or Stoke Newington rail. **Open** *Apr-Oct* 10am-6pm daily. *Nov-Mar* 10am-4pm daily. **Main courses** £3.90-£5.90. **Unlicensed. No credit cards.**

The outdoor seating – white plastic tables and chairs set on a lawn in front of the café – offers a quiet green panorama of north-east London, with willows and a pond close by. The interior is spacious and welcoming, with bright yellow walls packed with fantastic photos. The service was genuinely lovely, and this alone would tempt us back. The menu is quite substantial, including panini, sandwiches, salads and breakfasts, with plenty of options for children. The Absolute Mediterranean Platter was substantial and delicious, containing stuffed vine leaves, houmous, olives, tomato salsa, falafel and flatbread. A huge chunk of thickly iced coffee and walnut cake was irresistible. Ingredients are organic where possible, and there's lots of choice for the health-conscious.

Babies and children welcome: children's menu; high chairs. Disabled: toilet. No smoking. Tables outdoors (20, garden; 6, pavement). Takeaway service.

North West

Golders Green

Golders Hill Park Refreshment House

Off North End Way, NW3 7HD (8455 8010). Golders Green tube. **Open** *Summer* 10am-7pm daily. *Winter* 10am-4.30pm daily. **Main courses** £6-£7. **Licensed. No credit cards.**

On a hot day you can spot the queues for the excellent own-made gelati from the entrance of the park, just round the corner from the Refreshment House. The glasshouse interior is spacious, and cafeteria-like, with good-value self-service salads, sandwiches and scones, croissants, muffins and a few own-made cakes and flans. Pasta features heavily, and children's portions are available. Chunks of watermelon were appetising, and made a healthy alternative to ice-cream. However, service is consistently mediocre and the cold food did not look very appetising. It's a good snack spot, but even without the signs encouraging you to move on as soon as you are finished, it's not a place at which you'd feel inclined to linger. The sunny terrace is large and looks over the tended undulating grounds of the park, but there were no sun-shades on our visit on a hot day.

Babies and children welcome: children's menu; high chairs. Disabled: toilet. Entertainment: brass band 3-5pm Sun (May-Sept); jazz & folk Tue evenings (June-Aug); children's entertainers weekly (Aug). No smoking. Tables outdoors (60, terrace). Takeaway service.

Hampstead

Brew House

Kenwood, Hampstead Lane, NW3 7JR (8341 5384/www.companyofcooks.com). Archway or Golders Green tube then 210 bus. **Open** *Apr-Sept* 9am-6pm (7.30pm on concert nights) daily. *Oct-Mar* 9am-4pm daily. **Main courses** £3.95-£9.95. **Licensed. Credit** MC, V.

Set in the beautiful English-country-garden surroundings of Kenwood House, the Brew House is geared for the masses, rather than for the individual's enjoyment. The interior is self-service, but hovers on the brink of chaos with hot and bothered people milling about each island where desserts are piled high, hot food is served or drinks are dispensed. The servers are unsure of ingredients (though signs suggest otherwise) and you get what you're given – there's no room for variations on dishes. Farmhouse sausages, roasted veg and onion gravy was the special on our visit. Free-range produce is sourced locally. The cakes are fabulous – a lavender and orange sponge, and a gooseberry and elderflower cheesecake were imaginative options. There is little shade in the outdoor seating area, so it is best avoided on a busy day in high summer. The same outfit runs the new café in the reopened Roundhouse in Camden.

Babies and children welcome: children's menu; high chairs. Disabled: toilet. No-smoking tables. Restaurant available for hire. Separate room for parties, seats 120. Tables outdoors (100, garden and terrace). Takeaway service. Vegetarian menu. **Map 28 C1.**

For branch (The Broadwalk Café) see index.

The Table. See p302.

Fish & Chips

The exact origins of this peculiarly British ensemble – fried fish with chipped potatoes – have been all-but lost in the murk of myriad deep-fat fryers. In London, it's likely that the eat-in chippie began life in the mid 19th century, propelled into being by the same imperative that helped create pie and mash shops: a vast increase of the urban working class, whose members needed a cheap, filling lunch. Today, it's still possible to find a budget meal of fish and chips, but as the world's stocks of cod and haddock plummet, prices look set to rise, and judicious species-swapping seems the only ethical option. You should also choose your chippie with care; only a tiny proportion of London's practitioners gets it right. Timing, oil temperature and ultra-fresh ingredients are what's needed to produce fragile, crisp batter; flaky, succulent fish; and golden-brown chips. The city's top chip shops are fairly evenly split between long-time operators such as **Sea Shell**, **Brady's** and **Fryer's Delight** and newer ventures like **Olley's**, **Sea Cow** and **Fish Club** (London's most fashionable chippie). For restaurants specialising in a wider variety of marine life (not necessarily served with chips), *see p81* **Fish**.

Central

Barbican

★ Fish Central
149-155 Central Street, EC1V 8AP (7253 4970).
Old Street tube/rail/55 bus. **Lunch served**
11am-2.30pm Mon-Sat. **Dinner served**
5-10.30pm Mon-Thur; 5-11pm Fri, Sat. **Main courses** £5.45-£14.50. **Credit** AmEx, MC, V.
The word is out: this once-popular haunt of cabbies and tradesmen is now heaving with suits and affluent pensioners. Oddly located in the middle of a council estate, Fish Central is light and airy, with white walls, wooden flooring and IKEA-style plastic tables and chairs. On the sunny Friday lunchtime of our visit, the large front windows were open out on to the street, providing a pleasant breeze. The extremely friendly staff immediately made an extra area of the restaurant non-smoking when they ran out of tables, and swiftly presented us with metre-long menus. These list a wide selection of shellfish and steak, as well as various fish: deep-fried, grilled or cooked in matzo meal. The haddock was perfectly steamed, with thick, chunky flakes encased in a thin, crisp batter. Servings are huge; one portion of chips or mushy peas will easily stretch to two people. The wine selection is diverse and the mark-ups are refreshingly low. Next door, the firm operates a standard takeaway offering a much-reduced menu.
Babies and children welcome: children's portions; high chairs. Booking advisable. No-smoking tables. Separate room for parties, seats 60. Takeaway service. **Map 5 P3.**

Bloomsbury

North Sea Fish Restaurant
7-8 Leigh Street, WC1H 9EW (7387 5892).
Russell Square tube/King's Cross tube/rail/68, 168 bus. **Lunch served** noon-2.30pm, **dinner served** 5.30-10.30pm Mon-Sat. **Main courses** £7.90-£16.95. **Credit** AmEx, MC, V.
Reminiscent of *Coronation Street*'s Rover's Return pub, North Sea's salmon velvet chairs, dark-wood tables and threadbare carpet give the place a near-comical look in this up-and-coming part of town.

Academics and reserved over-60s dine here; the restaurant is located just down the road from the British Library, yet is tricky to find. We arrived to see three groups of people waiting outside for tables – a good sign. The starters of own-made fish cakes are definitely worth trying, as is the fish soup. The 'normal sized' portions are massive, so skip at least breakfast (and possibly lunch) before attempting the 'jumbo'. Be sure to sample the tartare sauce, which is made in-house (almost unheard of these days), and comes with quite a kick. The ideal accompaniment is a glass of St Peter's ale from Suffolk. If you can handle a pudding, go for the sherry-heavy trifle.
Babies and children welcome: high chairs. Booking essential weekends. No-smoking tables. Separate room for parties, seats 40. Takeaway service (until 11pm). **Map 4 K4.**

Covent Garden

Rock & Sole Plaice
47 Endell Street, WC2H 9AJ (7836 3785/
www.rockandsoleplaice.com). Covent Garden tube. **Meals served** 11.30am-11pm Mon-Sat;
noon-10pm Sun. **Main courses** £8-£14.
Credit JCB, MC, V.
Rows of sturdy wooden tables, fairy-lights on trees, and a maître d' dressed in Bavarian garb give Rock & Sole Plaice the feel of a beer garden rather than a chippie. Yet this is supposedly London's oldest surviving chip shop, with a history dating back to 1871. Tourists and suit-wearers beat a path here, ready to wait for the super-sized fish suppers. The chips are hand-cut and wide, lightly fried and potatoey in flavour. The same balance of moisture and crispiness was exhibited in the fried fish, while the own-made mushy peas were of a perfect consistency – thick enough to stand your spoon in. For an alternative British experience, order one of the chunky own-made pies, with choices of steak and mushroom, chicken and mushroom, and beef and onion. Finish off with either spotted dick, sticky toffee pudding or syrup sponge, all 'as cheap as chips' at £2.50.
Babies and children welcome. Booking advisable. Separate room for parties, seats 36. Tables outdoors (20, pavement). Takeaway service. **Map 18 L6.**

Fitzrovia

★ Fish Bone
82 Cleveland Street, W1T 6NF (7580 2672).
Great Portland Street or Warren Street tube.
Meals served 11am-11pm Mon-Fri; 5-11pm Sat.
Main courses £6-£10. **Credit** MC, V.
Our visit to Fish Bone found the restaurant full of men sitting alone, heads down, furiously tucking into colossal steaming portions of Friday lunch magic. The male staff were over the moon to see some women enter this haunt of cabbies and lone-ranger office workers. Their shoebox-sized restaurant is a bit of a squeeze inside, but the premises are clean and well decorated in dark red and brown. Fish comes grilled or fried in peanut oil, and is served with enough hand-cut chunky chips to make a family feast. The mushy peas, although suspiciously bright in colour, were addictively sweet, and made a fine accompaniment to a perfect cup of tea. If you feel like something a little stronger to drink, choose from the wide selection of bottled lagers or one of the few standard bottles of wine.
Babies and children admitted. No-smoking tables. Tables outdoors (3, pavement). Takeaway service. **Map 3 J4.**

Holborn

★ Fryer's Delight
19 Theobald's Road, WC1X 8SL (7405 4114).
Holborn tube/19, 38, 55 bus. **Meals served**
noon-10pm Mon-Sat. **Main courses** £2.10-£6.70. **Minimum** £2.10. **Unlicensed. Corkage** \no charge. **No credit cards.**
You'll probably smell Fryer's Delight before you see it, and the greasy smell will linger in your clothes, hair and skin. But this café, decked out in 1950s diner decor, is exactly what a chippie should be: no-frills. You'll feel like you've stepped back 50 years, with black and white photographs of London lining the walls – not to mention the bafflingly low bill. The fried plaice was the best we've tasted this side of Scarborough, which must have something to do with being double fried in beef dripping. The chips were equally good: chunky, moist, and loads of them. Team your fish and chips with a big mug of sweet tea, two paving-stone thick slices of bread and butter, and a pot of thick, sweet mushy peas. It's sad to see Fryer's so empty these days, so enjoy its proper fish suppers while you can.
Babies and children admitted. Takeaway service (until 11pm). **Map 4 M5.**

Marylebone

Golden Hind
73 Marylebone Lane, W1U 2PN (7486 3644).
Bond Street tube. **Lunch served** noon-3pm
Mon-Fri. **Dinner served** 6-10pm Mon-Sat.
Main courses £5-£10.70. **Minimum** (lunch)
£4, (dinner) £5. **Unlicensed. Corkage** no charge. **Credit** AmEx, JCB, MC, V.
Run by a dishy set of tough-looking Greek men, the Golden Hind oozes character. It was operated by Italians from 1914 until 1994, when the Greeks moved in, bringing with them calamares and Greek pickles. Portion sizes are fairly variable, as are the opening hours, but don't let this put you off – the food is top notch. Fish, fresh as a daisy, comes coated in a batter second to none. Chips have a tendency to be slightly undercooked, but you'll soon forgive this once you try the creamy own-made tartare sauce. The Hind is packed most evenings, so arrive early. Its BYO alcohol option is also worth taking advantage of. The atmosphere is fun, young and friendly, offset by a soundtrack of light American jazz. Signed celebrity photos and faded framed newspaper cuttings form part of the decorations, but the biggest draw for fish and chip junkies is the decommissioned art deco fryer by F Ford of Halifax, now displayed in the dining room.
Babies and children welcome: children's portions. Booking advisable. No smoking. Separate room for parties, seats 28. Takeaway service. **Map 9 G5.**

★ Sea Shell

49-51 Lisson Grove, NW1 6UH (7224 9000/ www.seashellrestaurant.co.uk). Marylebone tube/rail. **Lunch served** noon-2.30pm, **dinner served** 5-10.30pm Mon-Fri. **Meals served** noon-10.30pm Sat. **Main courses** £6.75-£16. **Credit** AmEx, JCB, MC, V.

Located just around the corner from Marylebone station, Sea Shell draws a plummy crowd of well-dressed professionals. The walls are covered in Cubist-style artwork from Icelander Harry Bilson (think George Braque). Prices have stayed low since the refurbishment last year, making the range of fresh fish taste that much better. Haddock was perfectly steamed, wrapped in a thin, nutty batter, and arriving with chunky chips. Mushy peas are an essential choice: thick, flavoursome, and of a natural green hue (compared to the neon-tinted industrial version). A tasty alternative to fish is the corn-fed chicken, which came with a small mountain of roasted Mediterranean vegetables. Portion sizes are immense, so swap your chips for a side salad if you're feeling calorie-conscious. With keen waitresses, speedy service and toilets clean enough to eat in, Sea Shell has little to fault it. *Babies and children welcome: children's menu; high chairs. Booking advisable Thur-Sat. Disabled: toilet. No-smoking tables. Separate room for parties, seats 25. Takeaway service.* **Map 2 F4.**

Victoria

Seafresh Fish Restaurant

80-81 Wilton Road, SW1V 1DL (7828 0747). Victoria tube/rail/24 bus. **Lunch served** noon-3pm, **dinner served** 5-10.30pm Mon-Fri. **Meals served** noon-10.30pm Sat. **Main courses** £5.50-£16.95. **Credit** AmEx, DC, MC, V.

Five minutes' walk from Victoria station, this central chippie attracts a mismash of customers, from noisy suits to lost-looking tourists. Run by Greek Marius Leonidou, and previously owned by his father, Seafresh achieves the balance between family-run intimacy and modern sophistication. The recently refurbished dining room is bright and airy, with light wooden tables and picture windows. All the fish is fried or grilled, and the portions are generous. One serving of chips does for two, especially as they can be a bit dry. Worthwhile alternatives are the own-made fish pie, and the fisherman's platter that comes with haddock, cod, lemon sole, skate wing, king prawns and calamares. The only downside is that food is a little expensive. Then again, you can order much of the menu at the significantly cheaper takeaway next door. Steer clear of the spam fritters. *Babies and children welcome: high chairs. Booking advisable. Restaurant available for hire. Takeaway service.* **Map 15 J10.**

West

Bayswater

Mr Fish

9 Porchester Road, W2 5DP (7229 4161/ www.mrfish.uk.com). Bayswater or Queensway tube. **Meals served** 11am-11pm daily. **Main courses** £5.95-£11.95. **Set lunch** £4.99 cod & chips incl soft drink, tea or coffee. **Credit** AmEx, MC, V.

Walk through the takeaway area at Mr Fish and you'll find a restaurant that looks like a 1950s ice-cream parlour, with a black and white tiled floor, pink and lime coloured chairs, and wooden walls painted aquamarine. We were almost taken aback when our waitress didn't arrive on roller skates, chewing bubblegum. There's much more on the menu than the restaurant's name would suggest, with chicken (southern-fried or barbecue roasted), hamburgers, beanburgers, and wraps, as well as various fish. To drink, you can choose from 18 wines, beers, spirits and liqueur coffees. The starters are fabulously cheap; seafood chowder cost only £2.20, and was thick and flavoursome. The haddock was a little skinny, but came in a delicious golden crispy batter. The mushy peas are

a must: rich in flavour and thick and gloopy in texture (although ours were served lukewarm). To round things off, we surrendered to a scoop of subtly flavoured vanilla ice-cream. *Babies and children welcome: children's menu; high chair. No-smoking tables. Takeaway service (until midnight).* **Map 7 C5.**

Notting Hill

★ Costas Fish Restaurant

18 Hillgate Street, W8 7SR (7727 4310). Notting Hill Gate tube. **Lunch served** noon-2.30pm, **dinner served** 5.30-10.30pm Tue-Sat. **Main courses** £4.70-£7.40. **No credit cards.**

Some of the best fish and chip shops in London are run by Greek-Cypriots, and Costas is the textbook example. It is tucked away off the noisy main road, and at first sight looks like a simple takeaway. But a half-hidden restaurant right of the counter offers a private, quiet sanctuary. The staff here are lovely to the point of becoming your new best friends. Costas has Greek-Cypriot starters of pitta bread with houmous or taramasalata, and avocado in a number of styles. Main-course choices are more limited, with the standard fish you'd expect, as well as chicken goujons. On our last visit the haddock tasted a little sour, but this was not in keeping with the usual high standards. The hand-cut chips were as good as ever. To finish, there's baklava, banana fritters and super-strength Greek coffee. *Babies and children admitted. Booking advisable dinner. Tables outdoors (2, pavement). Takeaway service.* **Map 7 A7.**

Geales

2 Farmer Street, W8 7SN (7727 7528). Notting Hill Gate tube. **Lunch served** noon-3pm Mon-Fri. **Dinner served** 6-11pm Mon-Fri; 6-10.30pm Sun. **Meals served** noon-11pm Sat. **Main courses** £8.50-£11.50. **Cover** 50p. **Credit** AmEx, MC, V.

Subtle touches of class can be spotted at Geales: the royal-blue tablecloths, the sparkling wine glasses, the fresh flowers. Notting Hill sophisticates are well catered for with starters of crab and leek tart, oscietra Iranian caviar with toast and chopped egg, and grilled goat's cheese salad. But no trip to Geales is complete without trying the own-made fish soup; it starts off well, but becomes heavenly with the addition of the rouille and cheese provided. Fish and chips arrive in enormous portions, with moist, juicy flakes of cod inside a crispy batter, and chips thin yet potato-packed. If at all possible, leave room for the own-made sticky toffee pudding with caramel sauce. To drink, stick with a traditional London Pride on tap, or try one of the 15 wines, 11 of which are available by the glass – a tell-tale sign you're in Notting Hill. *Babies and children welcome: children's menu; high chairs. Booking advisable. No-smoking tables. Tables outdoors (4, pavement). Takeaway service.* **Map 7 A7.**

South West

Wandsworth

★ ★ Brady's

513 Old York Road, SW18 1TF (8877 9599). Wandsworth Town rail/28, 44 bus. **Lunch served** 12.30-3pm Wed-Fri; 12.30-4pm Sat, Sun. **Dinner served** 6.30-10pm daily. **Main courses** £6.60-£9.75. **Credit** MC, V.

Now something of a local landmark, Brady's continues to serve reasonably priced fish and chips to the well-fed burghers of Wandsworth. The slightly faded lime green decor is reminiscent of a mid 1980s wine bar, but there's nothing old or run-down about the food – excellently sourced fresh fish with beautifully cut golden chips. It's simple fare with none of the pretension you might expect to find in a sit-down chipper this far into south-west London. Only the extensive wine list reinforced our prejudices. The haddock arrived tenderly cooked in a batter light enough to sleep a baby in. Tuna was juicy and well done: a shame since we'd ordered it medium rare. Alongside the

ketchup and tartare sauce are dill, tarragon, and tomato and basil mayonnaises for dipping chips into. A takeaway menu caters for locals wanting their Brady's fix in the comfort of their own homes. *Babies and children welcome: children's portions. Bookings not accepted. Takeaway service.* **Map 21 A4.**

South

Battersea

★ Fish Club

189 St John's Hill, SW11 1TH (7978 7115/ www.thefishclub.com). Clapham Junction rail. **Meals served** noon-10pm Tue-Sat; noon-9pm Sun. **Main courses** £4.50-£12. **Credit** AmEx, JCB, MC, V.

The guys at Fish Club have put in the effort and it has paid off handsomely. The stylish modern furnishings (curvy mirrors, and running water under a Perspex floor), attract a young, trendy crowd – not the sort of folk often seen in your average chippie. There's a broad range of high-quality fish, which changes seasonally. Fresh mackerel, red mullet and razor clams have all made appearances, displayed in a wet counter so you can specify how you'd like them cooked. You'll find many other interesting options too; prepare yourself for prawn and chorizo kebabs, trays of fresh sushi, and chips made from sweet potato. Potatoes also come boiled, mashed or chipped. Fish Club's dedication to own-made dishes stretches from its condiments to its seasonal English puds. The high prices might startle punters used to cheap fish suppers, though. *Babies and children welcome: children's menu; high chair. Bookings not accepted. Disabled: toilet. No smoking. Tables outdoors (3, courtyard; 2, pavement). Takeaway service.* **Map 21 B4.**

Clapham

Sea Cow

57 Clapham High Street, SW4 7TG (7622 1537/ www.theseacow.co.uk). Clapham Common or Clapham North tube. **Meals served** noon-11pm Tue-Sat; noon-9pm Sun. **Main courses** £7-£9. **Credit** JCB, MC, V.

Sea Cow is one of the few chippies to offer some organic food (organic salmon, for instance). This Clapham branch remains somewhat in the shadow of the original restaurant in East Dulwich, but appears to be popular nonetheless (there's a branch in Fulham too). Its über-trendy minimal decor is a hit with Clapham's fashion-conscious twenty-somethings, who banter with the fun, friendly staff. The menu is short but to the point – as it should be. Fish, fresh from Billingsgate Market, is displayed like pieces of art in the wet counter. There has been recent criticism of slipping standards, and our fried cod came in slightly soggy batter, but the minted mushy peas were so flavourful we could have eaten them on their own. Variations include crab cakes, which are served with a sharp lime mayonnaise. The tuna steak is also a favourite with customers, many of whom come here to people-watch. *Babies and children welcome: children's menu; high chairs. Bookings not accepted for parties of fewer than 6. No smoking. Takeaway service.* **Map 22 B1.** **For branches see index.**

Waterloo

Masters Super Fish

191 Waterloo Road, SE1 8UX (7928 6924). Waterloo tube/rail. **Lunch served** noon-3pm Mon-Sat. **Dinner served** 5.30-10.30pm Mon; 4.30-10.30pm Tue-Thur, Sat; 4.30-11pm Fri. **Main courses** £7-£16.50. **Credit** JCB, MC, V.

With its brick walls painted green and brown, glaring lighting and plastic furnishings, Masters resembles a motorway services café. A heavy smell of batter and vinegar permeates the room; why not open a window? But what this place lacks in sophistication, it makes up for in the food. Three complimentary shell-on prawns and a basket of baguette arrive at the table seconds after you do.

The extensive menu offers everything from Cromer crab to hamburgers. You can even have your fish grilled if you're willing to wait 30 minutes. The piled-high plates are memorable. Not one of our fellow diners – cabbies and pensioners – could manage the portions. The fried plaice was vast, but tasted exceptionally light and came in a thin moist batter. The scampi was the biggest and juiciest we've tasted to date. There are drawbacks, though: the mushy peas were embarrassingly watery, and the chips, although hand-cut, seemed a bit soggy.
Babies and children welcome: high chair.
Booking advisable Fri, Sat. Takeaway service.
Map 11 N9.

South East

Herne Hill

★ Olley's

65-69 Norwood Road, SE24 9AA (8671 8259/ www.olleys.info). Herne Hill rail/3, 68, 196 bus.
Dinner served 5-10.30pm Mon. **Meals served** noon-10.30pm Tue-Sun. **Set lunch** £5 1 course incl soft drink. **Main courses** £7.65-£18.25.
Credit AmEx, MC, V.
Rightly well-known south of the river, Olley's attracts a healthy mix of customers – including sophisticated suits and well-heeled pensioners. The restaurant occupies two old railway arches knocked together. Inside, there's plenty of bare brick and heavy wooden beams. Olley's fried fish never seems to stop winning awards. It might be something to do with owner Harry Niazi's not-so-secret formula of chilling the batter before frying it, or perhaps it's due to the consistently fresh fish. The likes of mahi mahi and halibut fillet also come steamed or grilled. The creamy mushy peas are 'the best in London' (as we said in 1999), and the chips also deserve a mention, being blanched before frying. Don't overlook the Neptune's Punchbowl starter: a creamy own-made soup that's something of a luxury lucky dip, packed with various fish. And anywhere that offers a 'Lord Archer Experience – tart not included' surely deserves a visit.
Babies and children welcome: children's menu; high chairs. Disabled: toilet. No-smoking tables. Tables outdoors (6, pavement). Takeaway service.
Map 23 A5.

Lewisham

★ Something Fishy

117-119 Lewisham High Street, SE13 6AT (8852 7075). Lewisham rail/DLR. **Meals served** 9am-5.30pm Mon-Sat. **Main courses** £4.95-£5.95. **No credit cards.**
You can get fed for a fiver at this well-loved chip shop close to Lewisham market. Something Fishy's plastic seating and Formica tables might sport a greasy film on occasion, but when it comes to the food there's nothing fishy going on. Some of London's finest fish and chips are served here. Huge portions of flaky fish come in crispy light batter, complemented by tartare sauce (bought in, but of a high quality). The mushy peas were a little sweet, but the hand-cut chips are as big as fish fingers. Pie and mash and saveloys are further options. To finish, push the boat out and enjoy a time-honoured dessert like jam roly-poly or knickerbocker glory. Staff are friendly enough, but don't expect them to waste time discussing the weather. The posher first-floor restaurant is now open only on Fridays and Saturdays.
Babies and children welcome: children's menu; high chairs. Bookings not accepted. No-smoking tables. Tables outdoors (5, pavement). Takeaway service.

North East

Dalston

Faulkner's

424-426 Kingsland Road, E8 4AA (7254 6152). Dalston Kingsland rail/67, 76, 149, 242, 243 bus. **Lunch served** noon-2.30pm Mon-Fri.
Dinner served 5-10pm Mon-Thur; 4.30-10pm

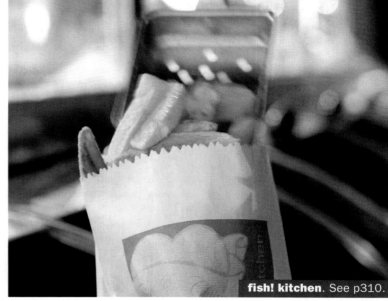
fish! kitchen. See p310.

Fri. **Meals served** 11.30am-10pm Sat; noon-9pm Sun. **Main courses** £8.50-£13. **Minimum** £4.
Credit AmEx, JCB, MC, V.
Faulkner's is probably the only place you'll find tablecloths in this run-down neighbourhood. And you don't only get a bit of linen: think fresh flowers, heavy well-polished cutlery, and beautifully groomed waitresses. Starters highlight the new Turkish ownership, with houmous, taramasalata and tender fried calamares, all served in main-course portions. A specials board offers whole sea bass and halibut at reasonable prices. We enjoyed a fabulous fried lemon sole, so fresh it could have leapt straight from the Thames, with a batter crisp in some places, moist in others. Only the chips let the side down, being pale in colour, soft and very dried out. Tartare sauce and ketchup came in the sort of stainless-steel pots you find in Indian restaurants. Own-made desserts of cakes and cherry tart, and an impressive fish tank provide the finishing touches. Lucky Dalston.
Babies and children welcome: children's menu; high chairs. Bookings not accepted. Disabled: toilet. No-smoking tables. Separate room for parties, seats 25. Takeaway service. **Map 6 R1.**

North

Finchley

Two Brothers Fish Restaurant

297-303 Regent's Park Road, N3 1DP (8346 0469). Finchley Central tube. **Lunch served** noon-2.30pm, **dinner served** 5.30-10.15pm Tue-Sat. **Main courses** £9-£18.15. **Minimum** £9.95. **Credit** AmEx, MC, V.
The glass front of this friendly place is generously sprinkled with stickered recommendations and clippings from far and wide, but don't bother with any of that: just look through the glass. The place is packed, as it always is – there's your recommendation. Brothers Leon and Tony Manzi have been reeling in the punters to their clean, smart eaterie for years, with reliably excellent chips and a decent range of traditional (and fresh) fish. The top-selling cod and haddock are firm, flavourful and large, but the menu also offers jellied eels, cod's roe in batter, delicious salmon fish cakes, rock eel, skate wing, whole sea bream, sea bass, and, on occasion, plaice on the bone. You can have your fish steamed, battered or coated in matzo. There's a minimum charge of £9.95 a head, but vacate your table by 7pm and you'll qualify for a 15% discount; alternatively, the adjoining takeaway

counter will sell you copious portions of the same chips and the classic fish options for less than half the price you'd pay in the restaurant.
Babies and children welcome: high chairs. Bookings accepted lunch only. No-smoking tables (daytime); no smoking (evenings). Takeaway service (until 10pm).

Muswell Hill

Toff's

38 Muswell Hill Broadway, N10 3RT (8883 8656). Highgate tube then 43, 134 bus. **Meals served** 11.30am-10pm Mon-Sat. **Main courses** £8.95-£17.50. **Set meal** (11.30am-5.30pm) £7.95 1 course incl soft drink. **Credit** AmEx, DC, JCB, MC, V.
When you first step foot in Toff's you could be forgiven for thinking it was any other chippie. Behind the takeaway counter, staff in white smocks toss chips into sizzling fryers as they cater for the constant queue of customers. But behind the bustling shop front, a restaurant offers more serenity. Mock-Tudor wood panelling and mirrors provide a homely atmosphere better suited to the Muswell Hill clientele. Signed photographs of famous customers line the walls. Victoria Wood and Iron Maiden have chomped chips here. The generously portioned haddock was tender, flaky and encased in a delicate batter. The melt-in-your-mouth chips were light and fluffy, but the mushy peas tasted slightly bland. Toff's wide range of fish, from dover sole to sea bass, can also be ordered in matzo-meal batter, or grilled for a healthier alternative. There's a short, modestly priced wine list and, for those with stamina, a dessert menu offering the likes of own-made tiramisu and crème caramel.
Babies and children welcome: children's menu; high chairs. No-smoking tables. Separate room for parties, seats 20. Takeaway service.

North West

Golders Green

★ Sam's

68-70 Golders Green Road, NW11 8LM (8455 9898/7171). Golders Green tube. **Meals served** noon-10pm daily. **Main courses** £6.50-£12.50. **Set lunch** (noon-4pm) £6.95 1 course incl tea or coffee. **Credit** MC, V.
This must be the friendliest chippie in London. It's the sort of place where the waiters are on first-name terms with almost everybody. Sam's has

established legendary status among Golders Greeners, and is frequented by glamorous grandmas and smart middl-aged couples. The nautical decor is taken seriously, with fishing nets, stone fish hanging from fishing lines, and pictures of ships on every wall. At lunchtime the place fills with pensioners taking advantage of a deal where fried cod and chips with a drink and dessert cost £6.50. Fish can be fried, grilled or steamed with onions and tomato. Every main course comes with a salad that's much more than decoration, with heaps of red cabbage, tomatoes, cucumber and lettuce. There's also a wide choice of vegetarian dishes, including moussaka and aubergine salad, and an interesting selection of starters, such as kisir (cracked wheat, celery, hazelnut, parsley and tomato), and pickled herrings.

Babies and children welcome: children's menu; high chairs. Booking advisable. Disabled: toilet. No-smoking tables. Takeaway service.

West Hampstead

Nautilus

27-29 Fortune Green Road, NW6 1LT (7435 2532). West Hampstead tube/rail then 328 bus. **Lunch served** 11.30am-2.30pm daily. **Dinner served** 4.30-10pm Mon-Sat; 5–10pm Sun. **Main courses** £9.50-£19.50. **Credit** JCB, MC, V.

Don't be put off by the gaudy blue and white exterior – inside is a much better story. Wooden tables and chairs, white tablecloths, wine glasses holding napkins, and well-dusted fake flowers give Nautilus a homely, thoughtful touch. The owners are Greek-Cypriot, but this influence only gets as far as the starters (with rather predictable houmous and taramasalata options) and Keo lager on the drinks list. At first sight the fish may seem a little expensive, but when a specimen of *Jaws*-like proportions arrives, you'll appreciate that you get what you pay for. Batter is among the most delicious and crispy to be found this side of Scunthorpe. The fish is equally laudable, steamed to perfection in its hardened jacket. It's just a shame that whoever mushed the peas was far too enthusiastic, and that the tartare sauce tasted mass-produced. The only other drawback is the all-singing, all-flapping, Big Mouth Billy Bass fish at the bar, perfectly positioned for anyone measuring under a metre.

Babies and children welcome: high chairs. No-smoking tables. Takeaway service. **Map 28 A1.**

Outer London

Kingston, Surrey

★ fish! kitchen NEW

2006 RUNNER-UP BEST CHEAP EATS
58 Coombe Road, Kingston, Surrey KT2 7AF (8546 2886/www.fishkitchen.com). No-biton rail/57, 85, 213 bus. **Meals served** noon-10pm Tue-Sat. **Main courses** £8.95-£13.95. **Credit** AmEx, MC, V.

This smart little fish and chip joint has been added by owner Tony Allan (of the 2003 BBC cookery show 'Tony & Giorgio') to his wet fish shop, Jarvis, next door. With expansive outdoor decking, shiny black tiles inside and uniformed staff, the new restaurant annex certainly looks the part – we'd call it a 'gourmet' chippie if we weren't so sick of the word being tagged on to prole food. Though fishy dishes such as king prawn kebab and fish pie appear on the menu, the main focus is battered fish: five varieties plus daily specials, served with chips, mushy peas and tartare sauce. Portions aren't too huge, and the tartare sauce is own-made; otherwise, there are few surprises. Nevertheless, our cod dinner was excellent: an enormous door-stop fillet, thinly layered with batter and beautifully fleshy within, served atop ungreasy, hand-cut chips and decent mushy peas. A starter of 'smoked haddock rarebit' was an interesting combination of ideas, the smoked flavour of the fish well offset by a mustardy cheese topping. A wonderful boon for locals.

Babies and children welcome: children's menu; high chairs. Disabled: toilet. No smoking Tables outdoors (12, terrace). Takeaway service.

Pizza & Pasta

When it comes to a quick, cheap, cheerful meal out, London's pizza and pasta joints are an obvious choice. The scene is invariably dominated by the chains (which we've reviewed together, to make comparison easier – *see p314* **Chain gang**), but there are plenty of independent operations too, offering a serving of individuality along with your pizza fiorentina and tiramisu. For more restaurants serving pizza and pasta, see **Italian**, starting on p168, and **The Americas**, starting on p33.

Central

Euston

Pasta Plus

62 Eversholt Street, NW1 1DA (7383 4943/ www.pastaplus.co.uk). Euston Square tube/Euston tube/rail. **Lunch served** noon-3pm Mon-Fri. **Dinner served** 5.30-10.30pm Mon-Sat. **Main courses** £6.50-£15.50. **Credit** AmEx, DC, MC, V.

The grimy surroundings of Euston station are unlikely to whet the appetite, but if you find yourself in the area this cheerful, air-conditioned restaurant offers a welcome refuge. Staffed by Italians and populated by regulars, it has a friendly family feel. Tables in the conservatory space at the rear look out on a tiny garden bursting with geraniums. A complimentary bowl of fat green and black olives was supplied while we scanned a menu big on Italian classics and, of course, pasta. We started with a refreshing plate of parma ham and melon, and a gossamer-light beef carpaccio. A main dish of tagliatelle and huge prawns looked rather better than it tasted (the prawns were on the tough side), but another dish of tagliatelle with saffron, cream, bacon and mushrooms was deliciously fragrant, and left only just enough room for a generous dollop of rich tiramisu. The wine list is also surprisingly good – although you have to wonder how many people spend £52 on an Antinori red on a night out in Euston.

Babies and children welcome: high chairs. No-smoking tables. Tables outdoors (26, conservatory). Takeaway service. **Map 4 K3.**

Fitzrovia

Cleveland Kitchen

145 Cleveland Street, W1T 6QH (7387 5966). Great Portland Street or Warren Street tube. **Lunch served** noon-3pm Mon-Fri. **Dinner served** 6-10.30pm daily. **Main courses** £9.50-£14. **Set lunch** £6 1 course incl drink, £11 2 courses. **Credit** AmEx, MC, V.

There's only a handful of crammed-in tables in this laid-back restaurant, but that – along with its imaginative, great-value menu – is part of the charm. There are daily changing set-price lunches, each including wine, beer or coffee. Starters are huge, so choose wisely. After a creamy asparagus risotto, we barely had room for pan-fried sea bass, accompanied by nicely wilted spinach and spot-on mashed potatoes. Other tempting starters include chilli and garlic squid with rocket salad, and tagliatelle with wild boar ragout. Mains tend to be meaty (veal escalope, pan-fried duck breast), but of the dozen classic pizzas on offer, half are vegetarian, and the pasta dishes include wonderfully fresh, own-made potato gnocchi and mushroom ravioli. The food is nicely presented and competently cooked, though on this visit the kitchen seemed overly generous with its seasoning as both the sea bass and risotto verged on salty. And size isn't everything; we'd prefer smaller

pizzas, more generously topped. Still, pleasant service and a relaxed atmosphere make this a popular choice with local workers.

Babies and children admitted. Booking advisable lunch. No-smoking tables. Tables outdoors (2, pavement). Takeaway service. **Map 3 J4.**

Marylebone

Spighetta

43 Blandford Street, W1U 7HF (7486 7340/ www.spighetta.co.uk). Baker Street or Bond Street tube. **Lunch served** noon-3pm daily. **Dinner served** 6.30-11pm Mon-Sat; 6.30-10.30pm Sun. **Main courses** £10.30-£14. **Credit** AmEx, MC, V.

At first glance, this looks like a cosy neighbourhood eaterie, its basic decor enlivened by original artworks and – on the quiet Saturday night of our visit – a mellow jazz soundtrack. The ground floor is deceptive, however, as most of the seating is in the substantial subterranean space that also houses a wood-fired pizza oven and small bar. Cooking is competent, and the relaxed vibe makes this a better bet than the chain pizzerias in the area. We enjoyed a starter of polenta topped with oyster mushrooms, the mild flavours sharpened by melted taleggio cheese. A vegetable pizza, featuring a somewhat sparse selection of sliced grilled aubergine, courgette, marinated red pepper and artichokes, was palatable but lacked oopmph; char-grilled sardines with large-grained, Sardinian couscous salad was a more flavoursome choice. However, at time of writing the Sardinian owner had just sold up and there will probably be changes to the menu – although pizzas will still figure prominently.

Babies and children admitted. No-smoking tables. Separate room for parties, seats 80. Tables outdoors (4, pavement). Takeaway service. **Map 9 G5.**

Mayfair

Rocket

4-6 Lancashire Court, off New Bond Street, W1Y 9AD (7629 2889/www.rocketrestaurants. co.uk). Bond Street or Oxford Circus tube. **Bar Open** noon-11pm, **meals served** noon-10pm Mon-Sat. **Main courses** £9-£12. *Restaurant* **Lunch served** noon-3pm, **dinner served** 6-11pm Mon-Sat. **Main courses** £8-£14. *Both* **Credit** AmEx, MC, V.

Hidden in a cobbled alley behind New Bond Street, Rocket is evidently popular with local office workers, who spill out of the ground-level bar on fine evenings. In contrast to the intimate den below, the first-floor restaurant is an airy space whose soaring proportions are enhanced by a massive skylight. The relaxed yet lively atmosphere is well suited to after-work parties, and comfy red plush armchairs make it a pleasure to linger at table. The large gas-fired oven takes centre stage, but the pizzas are somewhat eclipsed by the inventive (and enormous) salads.

A salad of succulent marinated 'Thai bourgois fish' (as they call it: it's similar to red snapper), with bok choi, roasted pineapple and cucumber ribbons trounced an unremarkable aubergine pizza. While starters such as deep-fried baby squid with a sweet chilli, plum and lemon dip looked inviting, we found our choice – roquefort on a 'carpaccio' of beetroot and rather chewy kohlrabi – rather hard work. A globe-spanning wine list is helpfully divided into such categories as 'light aromatic' and 'medium-bodied fruity'. Despite being rushed off their feet, the fresh-faced waiting staff were charming.

Babies and children welcome: high chairs. Booking advisable. No smoking. Separate rooms for parties, seating 10 and 28. **Map 9 H6.**
For branch (Rocket Riverside) see index.

Piccadilly

Frankie's Italian Bar & Grill NEW

2006 RUNNER-UP BEST FAMILY RESTAURANT
224 Piccadilly, W1J 9HP (7930 0488/ www.frankiesitalianbarandgrill.com). Piccadilly Circus tube. **Meals served** noon-11pm Mon-Sat; noon-10pm Sun. **Main courses** £12-£16.50. **Set meal** (noon-7pm) £14.95 2 courses, £17.95 3 courses. **Credit** AmEx, DC, JCB, MC, V.

In a typically flamboyant gesture, Frankie Dettori opened this venture on horseback, back in January 2006 – although our waiter commented that the former jockey-turned-restaurateur hasn't been back since. The famously jaw-dropping, neo-Byzantine interiors of the Criterion make a stunning setting, drawing plenty of attention from passers-by on Piccadilly Circus. The food is undramatic, but efficiently produced and presented. A generous starter of calf's tongue was thinly sliced and perfectly tender. 'Frankie's pizza', crispy-based and garlanded with prosciutto and tomatoes, should have been the size of a tractor wheel for its £12.50 price tag. We loved the creamy pumpkin risotto dressed with candied fruit, but were charged for a large plateful when we'd asked for the small. Sides of tomato bread and a rather flimsy green salad consisting chiefly of flat-leaf parsley and bitter endive proved a little dull. Children get an own-made cheeseburger (very good) and fries, followed by chocolate cake and ice-cream, for £7.50 – plus the attention of a roving magician who entertains on Saturday and Sunday lunchtimes.

Babies and children welcome: children's menu; high chairs. Booking advisable. Dress: smart casual. Restaurant available for hire. Separate room for parties, seats 70. **Map 17 K7.**
For branches see index.

Soho

★ Italian Graffiti

163-165 Wardour Street, W1F 8WN (7439 4668/www.italiangraffiti.co.uk). Oxford Circus tube. **Lunch served** 11.45am-3pm, **dinner served** 5.45-11.30pm Mon-Fri. **Meals served** 11.45am-11.30pm Sat. **Main courses** £7-£14. **Credit** AmEx, DC, MC, V.

Run by the same family for two decades, this cosy trattoria is a Soho gem: unpretentious and reasonably priced, with roaring fires or air-con for comfortable year-round ambience. Simple is sometimes best; the kitchen produces good basic Italian cooking in vast amounts, but the wood-fired oven-baked pizzas are what most people come for. Tasty vegetarian and seafood toppings balance out meaty favourites such as americana and speck; the bases are authentically thin and crispy. Just-right fettuccine with a rich, tomatoey sauce, was good. Ravioloni al porcini, generously stuffed with flavoursome mushroom and shallots, and gnocchi with mozzarella and tomato sauce are other options. Heartier dishes include steak, veal and spinach-stuffed chicken breast. For seafood fans, swordfish is recommended: two large slabs, grilled with olive oil, herbs and garlic, and served with potatoes and beans – simple and delicious. Banoffi pie makes a popular sweet conclusion. Book at peak times; this place has many fans.

Rocket

Babies and children welcome: booster seat; children's portions. Booking advisable. **Map 17 K6.**

Kettners

29 Romilly Street, W1D 5HP (7734 6112/ www.kettners.com). Leicester Square or Piccadilly Circus tube.
Bar **Open** 11am-midnight Mon-Wed; 11am-1am Thur-Sat; 11am-10.30pm Sun.
Restaurant **Meals served** noon-midnight Mon-Wed; noon-1am Thur-Sat. **Main courses** £8.95-£16. **Credit** AmEx, DC, MC, V.

Kettners was founded in 1867 as a highfalutin French restaurant by the former chef to Napoleon III, Auguste Kettner. By the 1970s it had been taken over by Pizza Express; the result was like a pizzeria wearing a posh but tattered frock. A refurb in 2002 spruced it up considerably, though it retains the Edwardian look of dusty pinks and still has the air of a faded English seaside resort. The menu has also modernised and expanded, with the addition of grills and contemporary Italian dishes such as lemon polenta cake, but the pizzas are still a big draw. They are thin-crust, piping hot and with tasty, good-quality toppings – reliably better than some branches of Pizza Express, then. Instead of 25p going to save Venice, ordering the Kettners Soho pizza will donate 25p to the Soho Community Environment Fund (to help clean up pavement pizzas, perhaps). The dish quality here is more than decent, and the civilised atmosphere remarkable for the centre of Soho. The champagne list is vast, with low mark-ups; if you're celebrating something with bubbly, this or the adjoining champagne bars are ideal.

Babies and children welcome: high chairs. Entertainment: pianist 12.30-2.30pm, 7-10pm daily. No-smoking tables. Separate rooms for parties, seating 12, 16, 20, 35, 50 and 85. **Map 17 K6.**

★ Spiga

84-86 Wardour Street, W1V 3LF (7734 3444/ www.vpmg.net). Leicester Square, Piccadilly Circus or Tottenham Court Road tube. **Meals served** noon-11pm Mon, Tue; noon-midnight Wed-Sat. **Dinner served** 6-11pm Sun. **Main courses** £8.90-£19.50. **Set meal** £17.95 2 courses, £21.95 3 courses. **Credit** AmEx, MC, V.

Spiga's stablemates in the Vince Power Music Group include a clutch of style bars and music venues; while there's no live music or DJs here, a light jazz soundtrack accompanies casual daytime dining, and picks up when the buzzier evening crowd arrives. Contemporary decor, booth seating, a small bar and smart, black-clad Italian staff provide the good looks; the food is similarly well presented and competent. Pizzas are consistently faultless, with fresh-tasting, interesting toppings and thin bases. Our mediterraneo (taleggio, courgettes, anchovies, sweet chilli) was first-rate; a starter of own-made, three-colour taglierini with mixed mushrooms was also delicious. Other pasta dishes include eggless strozzapreti with duck confit; oxtail-filled ravioli; and linguine with lobster. Main courses are heartily meaty (pan-fried duck breast with spinach, say, or grilled fillet beef with pecorino cheese and shallots), with tuna steak and roasted sea bass as alternatives. Asparagus risotto was the sole vegetarian option. From the set menu, rabbit leg comfit was beautifully tender and fell from the bone, accompanied simply by new potatoes, olives and sun-dried tomatoes. Hot chocolate soufflé with excellent vanilla ice-cream (pod-flecked and melting into the chocolate) and professional service completed an enjoyable meal.

Babies and children welcome: high chairs. Booking advisable. Disabled: toilet. Restaurant available for hire. Takeaway service. **Map 17 K6.**

SPAGHETTIHOUSE

RISTORANTE · PIZZERIA

Passione e Gusto d'Italia a Londra dal 1955

Visit our website
to find your nearest restaurant

www.spaghetti-house.co.uk

West

Maida Vale

★ Red Pepper

8 Formosa Street, W9 1EE (7266 2708).
Warwick Avenue tube. **Dinner served** 6.30-
11pm Mon-Fri. **Meals served** noon-11pm Sat;
noon-10.30pm Sun. **Main courses** £10-£16.
Credit JCB, MC, V.

'The best pizza I've had outside Italy,' declared a
British-Italian friend after a single bite of the
basilico pizza: a thin, elastic crust topped with
tomato sauce, fresh tomato, gorgeously textured
mozzarella and basil oil. Red Pepper is packed
every night of the week (so do book), but diners
definitely come for the food, not the atmosphere.
The place is tiny, the tables are cramped, the
acoustics are lousy, and service can be scatty (five
waiters tried to give us a bottle of wine when we'd
asked for a glass). The food, however, makes up for
all shortcomings. A starter of deep-fried baby
squid tempura, surrounding a pile of thin threads
of deep-fried courgette, fresh, crisp and cloud-
light, received a rapturous response. Likewise,
spaghetti with crab, tomatoes and rocket couldn't
be faulted. Daily specials include the likes of sea
bass with wild mushrooms and artichokes, or a
starter of thinly sliced smoked duck served with
castelluccio lentils and red onion marmalade. For
those with healthy appetites, desserts such as
tiramisu or pears poached in red wine keep to the
Italian theme, as does the short, all-Italian wine list.
Babies and children admitted. Booking advisable.
Separate room for parties, seats 25. Tables
outdoors (5, pavement). Takeaway service.
Map 1 C4.

South West

Fulham

Napulé

585 Fulham Road, SW6 5UA (7381 1122).
Fulham Broadway tube. **Lunch served** 1.30-
3.30pm Sat, Sun. **Dinner served** 6.30-11.30pm
Mon-Sat; 6.30-10.30pm Sun. **Main courses**
£8-£16. **Credit** MC, V.

Napulé appears small from the outside, but it
stretches back. En route to your table you pass
mouth-watering antipasti, which looked so
delicious we ordered a platter. Grilled carrots,
roasted fennel, parma ham and broad bean salad
didn't disappoint and were bursting with
Mediterranean flavour. A Bufalina pizza (tomato
sauce, mozzarella and buffalo mozzarella) had a
thin, crispy base and, although pricey, the toppings
were of the best quality. A special of linguine with
prawns, courgette and asparagus with white wine
boasted juicy prawns and was a very tasty, decent-
sized portion. Tiramisu rounded off the meal
nicely. In summer, the conservatory roof is pulled
back to give an outdoorsy feel; inside, the brick-
lined walls create a rustic atmosphere, and there's
a lower ground floor that's ideal for parties. Service
was relaxed and friendly .
Babies and children welcome: high chairs.
Booking advisable. Separate room for parties,
seats 40. Takeaway service. **Map 13 A13.**
For branches (Luna Rossa, Made in Italy,
Santa Lucia) see index.

★ Rossopomodoro NEW

214 Fulham Road, SW10 9NB (7352 7677).
South Kensington tube then 14 bus. **Meals**
served 11.30am-midnight Mon-Sat; 11.30am-
11.30pm Sun. **Main courses** £8.60-£16.
Set lunch £10 2 courses. **Credit** AmEx, MC, V.

Rossopomodoro Neapolitan Pizzeria may not quite
trip off the tongue, but the recently opened London
branch of this well-known Italian chain is proving
a tasty culinary mouthful with punters. Colourful
pop-art canvases and woven cane chairs lend a
retro flourish, but it's the gleaming open kitchen
that holds the attention. Watch the chefs as they
whip out pizzas from the traditional wood-fired
oven, toss pasta with practised ease, and season
their act with Neapolitan-style theatrics. Yes, it's
noisy and sometimes chaotic, but the marketplace

vibe seems appropriate (the first floor is quieter).
Although there are Neapolitan grills, salads and
seafood choices, the pizzas and pasta are the best
bets. Our pizza looked pretty much like a regular
margarita, but on cutting, its crisp, golden-edged
base yielded to a deliciously creamy ricotta cheese
filling, flecked with garlicky salami shreds. Richly
indulgent, this was our star dish. Paccheri pasta
tubes, scattered with peas and beefy meatballs,
worked well with herby tomato sauce, but was
marred by a shortfall of meat. Still, at a mere £6.50
a plate, it was good value. Despite a few gripes,
this place brims with energy, boasts a great laid-
back atmosphere and the pizzas are a real treat.
Babies and children welcome: high chairs. Booking
advisable. Separate room for parties, seats 50.
Map 13 C12.

Putney

Il Peperone

26 Putney High Street, SW15 1SL (8788 3303).
Putney Bridge tube/Putney rail. **Lunch served**
11am-4pm, **dinner served** 6-11.30pm Tue-Sun.
Main courses £6.50-£10.95. **Set lunch** £5
1 course. **Set dinner** £10 3 courses. **Credit**
AmEx, DC, MC, V.

This family-run pizzeria occupies a prime site on
bustling Putney High Street, a stone's throw from
the river and many bars. A bruschetta starter
arrived on untoasted bread and with a less-than-
generous topping of tomatoes and sliced olives.
Pizza mains were variable. A proscuitto and rucola
version was mediocre; it was slightly overcooked,
but, more disappointingly, the rocket had been
cooked beneath the ham. Formaggio di capra
(goat's cheese, roast aubergine and mozzarella) was
more successful, with a generous serving of
cheese. The menu also offers pastas, fish and meat
dishes. On the plus side, the service was some of
the most genuinely friendly we've experienced in
London, and the house wine, at £9.95, was both
good value and drinkable. A choice of more than
two desserts would have been appreciated. With a
little more attention to food preparation and
cooking, this could be a reliable local restaurant.
Babies and children welcome: high chairs. Booking
advisable. Separate room for parties, seats 50.
Tables outdoors (4, pavement). Takeaway service.

South

Balham

Ciullo's

31 Balham High Road, SW12 9AL (8675 3072).
Clapham South tube/Balham tube/rail. **Dinner**
served 6-11pm Mon-Thur; 6-11.30pm Fri, Sat.
Meals served 1-10.30pm Sun. **Main courses**
£5.50-£12.50. **Credit** MC, V.

Other places come and go, but this old-fashioned
pizzeria and ristorante in Balham sets the standard
by which pizza and pasta can be measured. The
starters are fine and the meat and fish dishes
mostly live up to expectations, but it's the pizza and
pasta dishes that the Ciullo family excel at. The
pastas are always al dente, the pizzas thin and
crisp. The sauce of penne all'arrabiata was
agreeably spicy, and at only £4, no more expensive
than at a budget caff. The topping of a pizza
fiorentina was perfect: not enough to make the base
soggy, but enough to cover it to the edges. The
wine list isn't exactly modern, and the choices by
the glass are very limited, but at least it's cheap.
Our only caveat is that while the rest of Balham's
new restaurants have invested in stylish interior
design, Ciullo's (est. 2004) has an amateurish and
rather naff 1970s look, complete with dodgy art on
the walls and twinkling fairy lights at the entrance.
Babies and children welcome: high chairs.
Booking advisable. No-smoking tables. Tables
outdoors (3, terrace).

Battersea

Donna Margherita

183 Lavender Hill, SW11 5TE (7228 2660/
www.donna-margherita.com). Clapham Junction
rail. **Lunch served** noon-3pm Fri, Sat.

Dinner served 6-10.30pm Mon-Thur; 6-11pm
Fri, Sat. **Meals served** 12.30-10.30pm Sun.
Main courses £6.90-£16. **Credit** AmEx, DC,
JCB, MC, V.

Donna Margherita is proud of its good press, to the
extent that it decorates the cubicles of the ladies'
loos with reviews. This could be annoying and
attention-seeking (and perhaps still is), but the fact
remains, their pizzas are first-rate. The crust has
excellent flavour, imparted by the wood oven in
which they are cooked. The toppings on the Donna
Margherita pizza featured a light tomato sauce,
buffalo mozzarella, whole leaves of basil, and
cherry tomatoes – all fine examples of the fresh
ingredients used. The kitchen also makes its own
pasta; fusilli with ricotta, peppers and basil was a
bit rich on a warm day, but the quality of the pasta
was good. The outside tables are a great place to
watch Battersea walk by, while the indoor dining
room is wonderfully eclectic, with an enormous
Nativity scene on display in June, and other Italian
kitsch dotting the walls.
Babies and children welcome: high chairs. Booking
essential. Separate room for parties, seats 18.
Tables outdoors (18, terrace). Takeaway service;
delivery service (over £10 within 1-mile radius).
Map 21 C3.

Pizza Metro

64 Battersea Rise, SW11 1EQ (7228 3812/
www.pizzametro.com). Clapham Junction rail.
Dinner served 6-11pm Tue-Fri. **Meals**
served noon-11pm Sat; noon-10.30pm Sun.
Main courses £7-£15. **Credit** MC, V.

Pizza Metro is a good argument for never having
to eat at high-street pizza chains again. Service is
cheerful, friendly and Italian. Framed tarot cards,
a funny market mural and cheerful checked
tablecloths conspire to make you feel you're in Italy
– or perhaps a Disney version of Italy. Appealing
starters, including meatballs and refreshing cold
courgettes fried and marinated in olive oil, lemon,
balsamic vinegar and mint, were a warm-up for
the job at hand: ploughing through a platter of
pizza. Metro bakes its pizzas in an oblong shape,
serving them on a huge metal tray, which stretches
from across the table. While this might be a bad
idea for allergy sufferers (there is some cross-
contamination of toppings), it is rather fun and
makes this a popular place for parties. The crusts
of the pizzas are perfectly thin and crisp and the
menu lists typical classic fresh Italian toppings.
Babies and children welcome: high chairs.
Booking advisable. No smoking. Tables outdoors
(10, pavement). Takeaway service; delivery service
(within 1-mile radius). **Map 21 C4.**

Clapham

Eco

162 Clapham High Street, SW4 7UG (7978
1108/www.ecorestaurants.com). Clapham
Common tube. **Lunch served** noon-4pm, **dinner**
served 6.30-11pm Mon-Fri. **Meals served** noon-
midnight Sat; noon-11pm Sun. **Main courses**
£5.40-£10.50. **Credit** AmEx, MC, V.

This split-level space is dominated by an elongated
counter where pizzas are made and money is taken
by a team of well-choreographed staff. Tables,
particularly in the front of the restaurant, are close
enough for you to compare your meal with your
neighbours. Sculpted metal features and a winding
staircase to the upstairs toilets give a sense of
'grown-up' style in comparison to the bijou branch
in Brixton. Of the list of 30 pizzas, a fine choice is
the vegetarian option with huge porcini
mushrooms, fontina cheese and truffle oil. A spicy
chicken pizza came with chilli sauce, courgette,
onion, mozzarella, tomato sauce, garlic and olive
oil. This was another bumper offering, although a
slightly crispier base would have been better.
Among the non-pizza options worth trying is
penne with mushrooms, cream sauce and fresh
basil. Or there are large fresh salads with own-
made dressings, such as gorgeous crab meat and
smoked salmon with fresh herbs and capers, or a
parma ham and bresaola platter. Classic desserts,
all served with mascarpone or fresh cream, include
tiramisu, baked cheesecake, and a rich maraschino
black forest gateau.

CHEAP EATS

Babies and children welcome: high chairs. Booking advisable; essential weekends. No-smoking tables (daytime). Tables outdoors (3, pavement). Takeaway service.
Map 22 A2.
For branch see index.

Verso
84 Clapham Park Road, SW4 7BX (7720 1515/ www.versorestaurant.co.uk). Clapham Common tube. Dinner served 6-11.30pm Mon-Fri; 4-11.30pm Sun. Meals served noon-11.30pm Sat. Main courses £7.50-£13.90. Set meal (Mon-Thur, Sun) £10 2 courses. Credit AmEx, DC, MC, V.

Great for intimate meals or ful -blown party specials, Verso is a bit more than a straightforward pizza joint. It offers a versatile menu that features such options as a wonderfully creamy and well-spiced risotto with pancetta and fresh herbs, and monkfish with asparagus and spinach. The pizza choices are fairly straightforward, but well made and very generous. Most are vegetarian, although you can mix and match your toppings to create your ideal pizza. The calzone goloso was a wonderful (and filling) choice featuring tomato, mozzarella, gorgonzola, asparagus, courgette and rocket, while a weighty pizza imperiale came with pancetta, bacon, spinach and egg. Own-made desserts include panna cotta and comforting tiramisu, which is generously sized and suitably fluffy. Golden walls and dark wood tables neatly dressed with deep orange tablecloths and sparkling wine glasses give the place a cosy feel.

Wines are predominantly Italian, and staff manage laid-back friendliness with ease.
Babies and children admitted. Disabled: toilet. Restaurant available for hire. Tables outdoors (8, pavement). Takeaway service; delivery service (orders over £7.50 within 2-mile radius).
Map 22 B2.

South East
Camberwell

★ Mozzarella e Pomodoro
21-22 Camberwell Green, SE5 7AA (7277 2020). Elephant & Castle tube/rail then 12, 35, 45, 68, 176, 185 bus. Lunch served noon-3pm Mon-Fri. Dinner served 6-11.30pm Mon-Sat; 5-11pm Sun. Main courses £5.25-£23.95. Set lunch (Mon-Fri) £7.50 2 courses. Credit AmEx, JCB, MC, V.
The sign outside – 'pastas and pizzas half-price Tuesday' – looks distinctly downmarket, which suits this ugly patch of Camberwell. But once inside this diner-like Italian restaurant, all is serene and strangely sophisticated. It was good to see the same waiters still here after many years, and the usual classics on offer: veal milanese, gnocchi, mushroom risotto, and basic but brittle-based pizzas decorated with fresh rocket and anchovies. It's all very mouth-watering and the extensive menu is worth a browse before you order. Whitebait came crunchy and nicely charred, with an optional mayo dip, while a side salad of caprese with avocado was a smallish but tasty appetiser. If there are two of you, a good approach is to share

a pizza and one of the wonderful mains, such as tender, rosemary-scented sea bream in white wine and brandy sauce. Desserts are displayed on a 'point here' menu with photos, but a torta della nonna was fresh and tasty; have a sharp espresso with it as Italian pastries tend to be as dry as dust. Service was Mediterranean, so efficiency was softened by jokes and decorum.
Babies and children welcome: high chairs. Booking advisable Fri, Sat. Separate room for parties, seats 120. Takeaway service. Map 23 A2.

Elephant & Castle

Pizzeria Castello
20 Walworth Road, SE1 6SP (7703 2556). Elephant & Castle tube/rail. Dinner served 5-11.30pm Sat. Meals served noon-11pm Mon-Thur; noon-11.30pm Fri. Main courses £5-£12. Credit AmEx, MC, V.
Rumours of a change of management here whistled around Elephant & Castle's high-rises, and, what's worse, that the bread had got soggy. Or rather, soggier, as Castello was never a true boutique pizzeria doing delicate bases. In fact, only the boss has changed and the pizzas remain tastily tomatoey, and the better toppings – rocket, four seasons, pepperoni – as generous as they have always been. Anchovies and capers liven up the medium-grade mozzarella, and fresh leaf salads provide roughage. Service is as fast, warm and welcoming as you'd expect in an authentic neighbourhood Italian. The upstairs, decorated in bright reds with local art photos on the wall, is very

CHEAP EATS

Chain gang
Think that one pizza chain is like any other? Think again. Here's the lowdown on the strengths and weaknesses of the main London chains.

★ ASK
160-162 Victoria Street, SW1E 5LB (7630 8228/www.askcentral.co.uk). Victoria tube/rail. Meals served noon-11pm Mon-Sat; noon-10.30pm Sun. Main courses £5.25-£7.95. Credit AmEx, DC, JCB, MC, V.
Although it can sometimes seem to be cut from the same cloth as Pizza Express, ASK does have its own style. Namely, a slightly breezier atmosphere and a willingness to offer pizzas at which others might balk, such as the Huz-a-rie (spicy sausage, roast pepper, roast onions) or tropicale (ham and pineapple) – the latter, these days, being rarely seen outside Domino's. The vibe is friendly, the food is usually good, and ASK appears to be pitched one notch above Zizzi, its sister chain. Service can slow when things get busy, but this is a safe bet in the unlikely event of there being no Pizza Express in the vicinity.
What's available 20 pizzas, 16 pastas, 8 salads.
How does the pizza rate? Generally good, although a recent napoletana was surprisingly bland given it included anchovies, olives, onion, capers and dill.
Total number of branches 23.
Best for A quick and simple meal.
Babies and children welcome: high chairs. Booking advisable. No-smoking tables.
Map 15 H10.
For branches see index.

★ Pizza Express
316 Kennington Road, SE11 4LD (7820 3877/www.pizzaexpress.co.uk). Oval or Kennington tube. Meals served

11.30am-11.30pm Mon-Fri, Sun; noon-11.30pm Sat. Main courses £5.25-£8.25. Credit AmEx, MC, V.
London, and the UK's, most famous pizza chain (as long as you don't count Pizza Hut). Pizza Express started in Wardour Street, spread to Coptic Street and from there has all but taken over the country. Restaurants tend to be uniformly styled in a tasteful, Habitat way, and food is similarly enjoyable – always good but never outstanding. In summer 2006 the company added a 'Sicilian Passion' element to the menu, with starters, pizzas and salads inspired by the Mediterranean island. While there are pasta and salad dishes on the menu, you'd be well advised to stick to the pizzas. The clue is in the name.
What's available 23 pizzas, 5 pastas, 6 salads.
How does the pizza rate? Perfectly good.
Number of branches 96.
Best for When you don't want to have to think too hard.
Babies and children welcome: high chairs. No-smoking tables. Separate room for parties, seats 25. Takeaway service.
For branches see index.

★ Pizza Paradiso
61 The Cut, SE1 8LL (7261 1221/ www.pizzaparadiso.co.uk). Southwark tube/Waterloo tube/rail. Meals served noon-midnight Mon-Sat; noon-11pm Sun. Main courses £6-£15.95. Credit AmEx, DC, JCB, MC, V.
From its base in Store Street, where it set root as the Ristorante Olivelli in 1934, Pizza Paradiso has (very) slowly grown into a mini-chain of six branches, each of which still manages to retain the feel of a neighbourhood trattoria through

strategic use of floral displays and signed photographs. Although pizza is the standby option, Pizza Paradiso also has a number of steak and fish dishes on the menu, which help to elevate it above the chain norm, while the pasta dishes are more than just an afterthought. We've never had bad meal here. Still the most individually appealing of London's chain pizzerias.
What's available 15 pizzas, 15 pastas, seven salads.
How does the pizza rate? Consistently good, with fine, fresh toppings and a solid base.
Total number of branches 6.
Best for Second dates, when you're not quite sure if they're worth the money but don't want to completely blow it.
Babies and children welcome: high chairs. Booking advisable Wed-Fri. Tables outdoors (4, pavement). Takeaway service.
Map 11 N8.
For branches (Pizza Paradiso, Ristorante Olivelli Paradiso) see index.

★ La Porchetta
141 Upper Street, N1 1QY (7288 2488/ www.laporchetta.co.uk). Angel tube. Dinner served 5.30pm-midnight Mon-Fri. Meals served noon-midnight Sat, Sun. Main courses £5.10-£7.50. Credit DC, MC, V.
This north London stalwart started in Stroud Green and now has four branches, the most southerly being in Holborn and the best known in Upper Street. The latter branch is by far the best, occupying two roomy floors and serving a budget, choice-heavy menu. In the Holborn restaurant they have a habit of cramming in at least half a dozen more tables than space suggests. Food is fresh and filling: pretty much what you'd expect for the price.

busy most nights, and the cosy basement gets a few drinkers and diners too. Steak, seafood and fish dishes are offered, but neither these nor the pastas are as good as the pizzas: the bolognese was simply too bland and seemed bereft of the wine reduction that usually gives the sauce its glory. Desserts (gelatos and pastries) are rather dull, but the coffee is excellent. Castello continues to be a bastion of good eating amid the Elephant's Latino snack bars and run-down malls.
Babies and children welcome: high chairs. Booking advisable. No-smoking tables. Separate room for parties, seats 100. Tables outdoors (4, pavement). Takeaway service. **Map 24 O11.**

Peckham

★ The Gowlett NEW

62 Gowlett Road, SE15 4HY (7635 7048/ www.thegowlett.com). East Dulwich or Peckham Rye rail/12, 37, 40, 63, 176, 185, 484 bus. **Open** noon-midnight Mon-Thur; noon-1am Fri, Sat; noon-11.30pm Sun. **Lunch served** 12.30-2.30pm Tue-Fri. **Dinner served** 6.30-10.30pm Mon-Fri. **Meals served** noon-10.30pm Sat; noon-9pm Sun. **Main courses** £7-£8. **Credit** MC, V.
Real ale and fresh stone-baked pizzas form the backbone of this thriving, and still relatively undiscovered, local – despite the awards from CAMRA. Tucked down a Peckham backstreet, it attracts a dedicated core of locals who relish the mellow atmosphere, the eclectic soul and reggae soundtrack and the evident enjoyment with which the owners, Johnny and Claire Henfrey, and their

staff serve up this winning formula. Pizzas are super-thin and loaded with premium-quality toppings (Gowlettini, the house special, features goat's cheese, pine nuts, prosciutto and rocket). Plate-sized discs of Tuscan anchovy or garlic bread are very moreish. If you have room for pud, the double choc brownie with ice-cream is divine. All wines are organic and well priced at between £10 and £30. An ever-changing cast of guest ales, in addition to the house Adnams, keep the taps flowing – a dozen different barrels are ordered at a time, so there's a new beer to discover most days.
Babies and children admitted (until 9pm). Disabled: toilet. Entertainment: quiz 8.30pm Mon; DJs 4pm Sun. Tables outdoors (3, heated terrace; 4, pavement). **Map 23 C3.**

East

Bethnal Green

★ StringRay Globe Café Bar & Pizzeria

109 Columbia Road, E2 7RL (7613 1141/ www.stringraycafe.co.uk). Bethnal Green tube. **Meals served** 11am-11pm daily. **Main courses** £4.50-£9.95. **Credit** MC, V.
The dark converted pub interior will never garner any design awards, but this laid-back pizzeria wins over a young clientele with friendly, helpful staff and cheap and cheerful prices geared towards providing an enjoyable night. A nicely varied menu includes english breakfast (served until 5pm), braised rabbit, Basque-style cod, veggie risotto and

19 huge pizzas, from a simple margherita to a vegetarian calzone. Everything here is huge; a salad tricolore starter was big enough to be a hearty lunch; a plate of tender fried liver was turned into a Desperate Dan cartoon by a pile of creamy mash and perfectly cooked cabbage. At the pricier end of the menu, ingredients aren't top-notch, but adventurous sauces make many of them work, against the odds: red pepper and red wine sauce, white wine and prune sauce, and even an own-made tomato sauce smothering the (huge) calzone. About the only small thing here is the selection of desserts, which we passed over happily, too stuffed to even debate the merits of white peach and redcurrant sorbet over cherry cheesecake.
Babies and children welcome: children's menu; high chairs. Booking advisable. Disabled: toilet. Tables outdoors (7, pavement). Takeaway service. **Map 6 S3.**
For branches (Shakespeare's, StringRay Café) see index.

Shoreditch

★ Furnace NEW

1 Rufus Street, N1 6PE (7613 0598). Old Street tube/rail. **Lunch served** noon-3pm Mon-Fri. **Dinner served** 6-11pm Mon-Sat. **Main courses** £7-£11. **Credit** MC, JCB, V.
Tucked away off Hoxton Square, this neat, exposed-brick restaurant serves the best pizza in the area. We opted for asparagus salad with quail's eggs and asiago cheese sauce, a swanky combination that worked very well. The main menu

What's available 26 pizzas, 35 pastas, 5 salads.
How does the pizza rate? Good. Spills over the edge of the planet, with decent toppings and a solid base. Impressive pasta dishes too.
Total number of branches 5.
Best for Couples saving some pounds during an exhausting afternoon shopping on Upper Street.
Babies and children welcome; high chairs. Bookings accepted only for parties of 5 or more. Disabled: toilet. No-smoking tables. Separate room for parties, seats 80. Takeaway service. Vegan dishes.
Map 5 O1.
For branches see index.

★ Prezzo
17 Hertford Street, W1J 7RS (7499 4690/www.prezzoplc.co.uk). Green Park or Hyde Park tube. **Meals served** noon-11.30pm Mon-Sat; noon-11pm Sun.
Main courses £5.75-£8.95. **Credit** AmEx, DC, JCB, MC, V.
Prezzo has only three outlets in London and presents itself as a slightly better class of pizza chain, something epitomised by the grandeur of the Mayfair branch – all dark wooden panelling and English country house art (offset somewhat by what appears to be an inflatable nun in one corner). Similarly, the nosh is a cut above, flirting with a standard that could be termed 'gourmet'. In our experience, the pizzas and pastas are uniformly excellent, while the mains also stretch into more imaginative territory – such as a fine mozzarella and red pesto burger, and various (free-range) chicken dishes.
What's available 13 pizzas, 19 pastas, 6 salads.
How does the pizza rate? Very decent.

We particularly like the lip on the crust, which provides a smidgeon more crunch.
Total number of branches 3.
Best for Business lunches of low-level importance.
Babies and children welcome: high chairs. Booking advisable. Takeaway service.
Map 9 H8.
For branches see index.

Strada
Riverside, Royal Festival Hall, Belvedere Road, SE1 8XX (7401 9126/www.strada. co.uk). Embankment tube or Waterloo tube/rail.
Meals served noon-11pm Mon-Fri; 11am-11pm Sat; 11am-10.30pm Sun.
Main courses £6.50-£16.50. **Set meal** (5.30-7.30pm Mon-Fri) £10.95 2 courses.
Credit AmEx, MC, V.
Strada has managed to kid everybody into thinking it's a superior sort of pizza chain by the simple method of associating itself with a superior sort of London locale – Blackheath, Islington, Marylebone, Exmouth Market – and banging on about wood-burning ovens. In reality, our experiences here have been mixed; some fine pizzas, but also a couple so bad that they couldn't even be finished, suggesting it is not quite the middle-class pizza-topia that its cheerleaders proclaim. That didn't stop them receiving the lucrative new Royal Festival Hall franchise, which suggests Strada is impressing some of the right people. However, we do like the way they put free bottles of water on every table – without us even having to ask.
What's available 13 pizzas, 9 pastas, 4 salads.
How does the pizza rate? Sometimes excellent, sometimes very poor. A recent fiorentina was overcooked, rendering

the spinach damp and tasteless and the base limp. They must do much better.
Total number of branches 25.
Best for When next door's Wagamama is full.
Babies and children welcome: high chairs. Disabled: toilet. No smoking. Tables outdoors (22, terrace). Takeaway service (pizza). **Map 10 M8.**
For branches see index.

Zizzi
33-41 Charlotte Street, W1T 1RR (7436 9440/www.zizzi.co.uk). Goodge Street or Tottenham Court Road tube. **Meals served** noon-11.30pm daily. **Main courses** £8-£10.
Set meal £15.95 2 courses. **Credit** AmEx, DC, JCB, MC, V.
Owned by the same people who run ASK – clearly a clever bid to corner the A and Z of the telephone directory – Zizzi is a slightly downmarket version of its sister chain. Restaurants tend to be large and homogeneous, though the logs around the wood-fired pizza oven offer a pretence of authenticity. Zizzi can be hit and miss; we've had passable meals here, but also some that were pretty dire. The size of the Charlotte Street branch makes it ideal for group outings, although don't come if you're in a hurry as the service can be a little slack.
What's available 16 pizzas, 19 pastas, 7 salads.
How does the pizza rate? Adequate. Decent size and taste, but nothing to write home about.
Total number of branches 16.
Best for Groups with time on their hands.
Babies and children welcome: high chairs. Booking advisable. Disabled: toilet. No-smoking tables. Tables outdoors (4, pavement). Takeaway service. **Map 9 J5.**
For branches see index.

lists only pizzas, but there are also daily pasta specials such as spinach and ricotta tortellini. The monster-sized pizzas, however, are what everyone comes for (including a constant stream of patient take-away customers). You could opt for gorgonzola with poached pears or a funghi feast of wild, porcini and large flat mushrooms on truffle paste. Our porchetta topping was thinly cut and generously piled on to a base topped with sour cream and fennel. The crusts are artfully thin and slightly crunchy rather than stretchy. Tiramisu doesn't go out of fashion in Italian restaurants – good job too when it's as gratifying as it is here. *Babies and children admitted. No-smoking tables. Takeaway service. Separate room for parties, seats 40.* **Map 6 R4.**

Wapping

Il Bordello

81 Wapping High Street, E1W 2YN (7481 9950). Wapping tube/100 bus. **Lunch served** noon-3pm Mon-Fri. **Dinner served** 6-11pm Mon-Sat. **Meals served** 1-10.30pm Sun. **Main courses** £7.75-£22.95. **Credit** AmEx, DC, MC, V.
Il Bordello is a classy joint, its brushed copper walls about as far as you can get from the checked tablecloths of Italian restaurant cliché. The food, while not earth-shattering, was fresh and enjoyable: linguine with scallops in a cream and brandy sauce was a particular highlight, although (as it seemed for some of our fellow diners) too rich for anyone to be able to finish such a large portion. The whole endeavour has an element of style over substance, but it's obviously going down well with Wapping diners, as it was almost alarmingly busy for a Sunday night. Luckily, the smoothly professional waiting staff ensured that our meal went off without a hitch. Prices are on the high side, but you get what you pay for.
Babies and children welcome: high chairs. Booking advisable. Disabled: toilet. Takeaway service. **For branch (La Figa) see index.**

North East

Stoke Newington

Il Bacio

61 Stoke Newington Church Street, N16 0AR (7249 3833). Stoke Newington rail/73 bus. **Dinner served** 6-11.40pm Mon-Fri. **Meals served** noon-11.15pm Sat, Sun. **Main courses** £6.50-£15.95. **Credit** MC, V.
Bring a good appetite to Il Bacio: the pizzas are seriously large, at least a foot and a half in diameter. We made the mistake of having one each. At around £9.50 each, they'd have been a steal if we'd shared, but as it was it was up to the staff cheerfully to doggie-bag what we couldn't finish. Quality is high: bases were light and crisp, the toppings fresh, tasty and wide-ranging – including a special selection with extra buffalo mozzarella. The meat and fish dishes looked good too, and were almost as large. A salad with mushrooms in a spicy dressing was a zingy starter, but alas for the bought-in puds displayed on a laminated card. The atmosphere is authentically Italian (maybe too authentic – we had to repeat our orders) and the decor endearing, from classic prints to paintings of big-bottomed ladies climbing into baths. It's no surprise the place is buzzing with all sorts of people every night.
Babies and children welcome: high chairs. Booking advisable. Separate room for parties, seats 50. Tables outdoors (3, pavement). Takeaway service; delivery service (over £10). **Map 25 B1.**
For branches see index.

North West

Hampstead

Fratelli la Bufala

45A South End Road, NW3 2QB (7435 7814/ www.fratellilabufala.com). Belsize Park tube/ Hampstead Heath rail. **Lunch served** noon-3pm, **dinner served** 6-11pm Mon-Fri. **Meals served** noon-11pm Sat; noon-10.30pm Sun.

Main courses £6-£13.50. **Set lunch** (Mon-Fri) £10 2 courses. **Credit** AmEx, MC, V.
This friendly Italian offers good-value Neapolitan grub and has a pleasant local vibe. A traditional brick oven takes centre stage, with tables arranged in two surrounding dining areas. The restaurant makes a fuss of using mozzarella di bufala, but many ingredients – sausages, steaks burgers, cheeses – also derive from buffalo. To start, Il Tortino (potato cake with aubergines and mozzarella) had a perfectly light, fluffy texture and oozed with cheese; La Filatina (melted mozzarella with fresh tomato sauce) was plainer but tasty. Mains were less consistent: one pizza was too oily and sauce-laden, although a buffalo burger arrived tender and rare as requested. Desserts include various buffalo cheesecakes, ice-creams and fruity puds. Staff were friendly, but the star of the occasion was the flamboyant owner who spent the evening jollying up to the waitresses and guests.
Babies and children welcome: high chairs. Booking advisable. No-smoking tables. Separate room for parties, seats 20. Tables outdoors (2, pavement). Takeaway service. **Map 28 C3.**

Kilburn

Osteria del Ponte

77 Kilburn High Road, NW6 6HY (7624 5793). Kilburn Park tube. **Lunch served** noon-3.30pm Mon-Thur; noon-4.30pm Fri-Sun. **Dinner served** 6.30-11pm Mon-Sat; 6.30-10.30pm Sun. **Main courses** £9-£12. **Credit** MC, V.
Were it not for the brightly painted central oven and a pizza maker hard at work, you'd be hard-pressed to distinguish this Italian 'restaurant and bar' from a normal pub. Yes, there are high-backed brown leather chairs surrounding dining tables, and a plush sofa area with a low coffee table, but also a row of sad old men holding up the bar while reading the *Mirror*. Surly staff actively encouraged us not to eat in the restaurant section – mainly, it seemed, because they didn't want to walk over there. The menu features 18 varieties, including classic fiorentina, quattro formaggi and an osteria special of spicy sausage, rocket, mozzarella, tomato, roast peppers and onions. Damn, those pizzas were good: wide, thin, crispy bases overshooting the rims of the plates, fresh tasty toppings, and sprightly leaves scattered over the top. Osteria del Ponte is a handy joint to have at the end of your road, but it's not worth a tube ride.
Babies and children welcome: high chairs. Booking advisable. No-smoking tables. Restaurant available for hire. Tables outdoors (5, pavement). **Map 1 B1.**

West Hampstead

La Brocca

273 West End Lane, NW6 1QS (7433 1989). West Hampstead tube/rail/139, C11 bus. **Bar Open** noon-11pm Mon-Thur, Sun; noon-1am Fri, Sat. **Lunch served** noon-4pm Mon-Fri; noon-4.30pm Sat, Sun. **Main courses** £5.95-£10.95. *Restaurant* **Dinner served** 6.30-10.30pm Mon, Sun; 6.30-11pm Tue-Sat. **Main courses** £7.95-£14.50. *Both* **Credit** AmEx, JCB, MC, V.
Walking into La Brocca, a man outside (who, on further reflection, may or may not have been connected to the restaurant) cried, 'It's bloody good in there!' And you know what? He was right – up to a point. From the young, vibrant atmosphere to the pleasant, leafy conservatory that houses most of the tables in summer, it was good, but not amazing. The tempting menu includes the usual pizzas and pastas, as well as more adventurous dishes such as veal ravioli with pine nuts. The starters were nicely cooked and there is a good selection of fairly priced wines. But the cost of the dishes seemed a shade steep: £14.95 for lamb shank with roasted veg and marscapone, and over a tenner for many of the pizzas. The service was a bit 'am I bovvered?', and the place is so popular with locals that it was occasionally a little difficult to hear oneself think.
Babies and children welcome: high chairs. Booking advisable. **Map 28 A2.**

Outer London

Kingston, Surrey

★ Terra Mia

138 London Road, Kingston upon Thames, Surrey KT2 6QJ (8546 4888/www.terra-mia. co.uk). Kingston rail. **Lunch served** noon-2.30pm, **dinner served** 6-11.30pm Mon-Sat. **Main courses** £4.90-£8.90. **Set lunch** (Mon-Fri) £5.90 1 course incl soft drink; £6.90 1 course incl alcoholic drink. **Credit** MC, V.
Terra Mia retains the decor of the previous pizzeria on this site, including knick-knacks on the walls, and an enormous mural of the Pont du Gard. The menu offers 20 or so pizzas, including all the classic versions you'd expect. The pizzas are a touch smaller than you'd find in most chains, but that's no bad thing if you're saving room for a sorbet later. But it's the pick-and-mix pasta choices we like best; there are ten or so pasta sauces and seven types of pasta available.
Babies and children welcome: children's portions; high chairs. Booking advisable. Tables outdoors (6, garden). Takeaway service.

Mozzarella e Pomodoro. See p314.

Sarastro Restaurant "The Show After The Show"

A sumptuous treasure trove hidden within a Grade II listed Victorian
townhouse, Sarastro is perfectly located in the heart of London's Theatreland.

A wide selection of delicious Mediterranean dishes are served with theatrical flair and
passion against the elaborate backdrop of golden drapes and decorative frescoed walls.

Every Sunday matinee and Sunday and Monday evenings there are live performances from up
and coming stars of the Royal and National Opera houses and all over the world.
Sarastro is ideal for pre- and post-theatre dining and perfect for red carpet parties and
celebrations with a menu available at £12.50.

Also available for lunch every and all day.

A private function room is available for corporate and red carpet occasions (for up to 300 guests).

**126 Drury Lane, London WC2 Tel: 020 7836 0101 Fax: 020 7379 4666
www.sarastro-restaurant.com E: reservations@sarastro-restaurant.com**

Papageno Restaurant & Bar "Seeing is believing"

Nestling in the heart of London's bustling Covent Garden, Papageno is
dedicated to pre- and post-theatre dining.

Open all day, seven days a week, guests are invited to eat from
an exclusive a la carte menu or choose from special set theatre meals available from £12.50.

Available for private functions, weddings, parties and other events for up to 700 guests,
Papageno has one of London's most exquisite rooms with its own private entrance and bar.

**29-31 Wellington Street, London WC2 Tel: 020 7836 4444 Fax: 020 7836 0011
www.papagenorestaurant.com E: reservations@papagenorestaurant.com**

Drinking

Bars

Here we list a few of our favourites from London's ever-growing, ever-changing bar scene, from louche cocktail lounges to swanky hotel bars, some attached to restaurants. For pubs serving good food, *see* **Gastropubs**, starting on p102. For the best boozers, *see* **Pubs**, starting on p327. And for hundreds and hundreds of drinking options across the capital, see the annual *Time Out Bars, Pubs & Clubs* guide.

Central
Belgravia

Blue Bar
The Berkeley, Wilton Place, SW1X 7RL (7235 6000/www.the-berkeley.co.uk). Hyde Park Corner tube. **Open/snacks served** 4pm-1am Mon-Sat; 4-11pm Sun. **Snacks** £6-£11. **Credit** AmEx, DC, MC, V.
This deeply stylish venue is located by the lobby of the Berkeley hotel. It's decorated by David Collins in a striking 'Lutyens blue' colour scheme, with a white onyx bar with seats, a black crocodile-print leather floor and a sunken seating area. Juicy olives and caramelised nuts are brought by polite staff as soon as you're seated. To drink, there's a large selection of high-end Champagnes, classic and contemporary cocktails, wines by the glass, and 50 whiskies. There's also a Grape & Smoke menu that enables the many business clients to match cigars with wines. Bar snacks include such upscale 'oriental tapas' as lime leaf and chicken on coconut crisp with citrus coulis and rice paper. Little wonder the bar is enduringly popular with designers and fashionistas.
Disabled: toilet (hotel). Dress: no shorts or caps. **Map 9 G9.**

City

★ Hawksmoor
2006 RUNNER-UP BEST BAR
2006 RUNNER-UP BEST STEAK RESTAURANT
157 Commercial Street, E1 6EJ (7247 7392/www.thehawksmoor.com). Liverpool Street tube/rail. **Open** 5pm-1am Tue-Sat; 4pm-midnight Sun. **Meals served** 6-11pm Tue-Sat; 6-10pm Sun. **Main courses** £14-£22. **Credit** AmEx, DC, MC, V.
Named after the baroque architect whose masterpiece Christ Church is just down the road, this is an understated American restaurant (see *p33*) with a bar dedicated to the art of fine cocktail making. With the same owners as nearby Mexican tequila bar/restaurant Green & Red (see *p326* and *p43*) and the Marquess Tavern in Islington (see *p114*), the joint fizzes with bonhomie and the strains of Johnny Cash and Jason King calypsos. From a cocktail menu that covers juleps, aromatic cocktails, sours, fizzes, daisies, punches, tikis and 'expat' classics (including the Scoff Law cocktail from Prohibition days), the crew mix up an explosion of fabulous, well-tempered flavours. Own-designed R&R Sour (redcurrant-infused rum with Aperol, redcurrant purée, lime, sugar and egg white) was delicious, and a Sidecar made with Armagnac, was one of the best we've had. From a library of Mai Tai recipes we also tried a delicious concoction that included yellow Chartreuse. Some fine po'boys snacks included scampi and tartare. Hawksmoor is friendly, fun, professional and distinctly un-posey. A delight.
Babies and children admitted. Disabled: toilet. Restaurant available for hire. Separate room for parties, seats 30. **Map 6 R5.**

Covent Garden

Lobby Bar
One Aldwych, 1 Aldwych, WC2B 4RH (7300 1070/www.onealdwych.com). Covent Garden or Embankment tube/Charing Cross tube/rail. **Open** 8am-midnight Mon-Sat; 8am-10.30pm Sun. **Snacks served** noon-midnight Mon-Sat. **Snacks** £1-£13.75. **Credit** AmEx, DC, MC, V.
This large, buzzy bar inside One Aldwych is one of the most stylish hotel bars in London. It has huge picture windows, contemporary sculptures (including a strange rowing scene) and high-backed chairs. Fashionable and smartly attired young professionals come here to sip top-notch cocktails (including 22 imaginative varieties of Martini), gins and vodkas. Drinks are served with spicy warm nuts, and bar snacks range from sushi to oscietra caviar. Food, including continental breakfast, organic cakes and sandwiches – is served in the bar throughout the day. Cold food only (antipasti) is available on Sunday.
Babies and children welcome: high chair. Disabled: toilet. Separate rooms for parties, seating 30-100. **Map 18 M7.**

Edgware Road

Salt Whisky Bar
82 Seymour Street, W2 2JB (7402 1155/www.saltbar.com). Marble Arch tube. **Open** 2pm-1am Mon-Sat; 5pm-1am Sun. **Meals served** 2-11pm Mon-Sat; 5-11pm Sun. **Main courses** £10-£16. **Credit** MC, V.
Whisky, erroneously viewed as the tipple of the roué and the Shadow Cabinet grandee, has an image problem. Thankfully, Salt comes to the rescue, dedicated to the pleasure of whisky in an ultra-modern environment. This sleek, dark wood bar has ample floor space and perches for a quick stopover, and comfy sofas upon which to set the world to rights – for, according to writer William McIlvanney, if wine is for seduction, then whisky surely is for philosophy. The classic cocktails are here, impeccably mixed (an excellent Rob Roy features an interesting soupçon of dry vermouth), with Glenfiddich as the house standard. Of the fun signature cocktails, go for a Honey Old Fashioned, mixed with ginger and the peaty-fruity delights of the Islay malt Bowmore. Staff are no less expert when juggling the flavoured vodkas, but with more than 200 whiskies on offer – Scotch, American, Irish and Japanese – why diversify?
Booking advisable. Entertainment: DJs 8pm Wed-Sat; jazz 8-11pm Sun. Separate room for parties, seating 50. Tables outdoors (3, pavement). **Map 8 F6.**

Fitzrovia

Hakkasan
8 Hanway Place, W1T 1HD (7907 1888). Tottenham Court Road tube.
Bar **Open** noon-12.30am Mon-Wed; noon-1.30am Thur-Sat; noon-midnight Sun.

Restaurant **Lunch/dim sum served** noon-3pm Mon-Fri; noon-4pm Sat, Sun. **Dinner served** 6-11.30pm Mon, Tue, Sun; 6pm-12.30am Wed-Sat. **Dim sum** £3.50-£16. **Main courses** £12.50-£48.
Both **Credit** AmEx, MC, V.
Ensconced in a basement on an unassuming 'blink-and-you'll-miss-it' side street, Hakkasan is probably the capital's most glamorous, must-visit Chinese restaurant (see *p66*). Walk past the extravagant floral arrangements by the reception to reach the Ling Ling bar at the far side of the restaurant, where you'll find a moodily brooding space lit with flickering candles. Designed by Christian Liaigre, the stained oak bar is decked out with colourful backlit panels and richly embroidered oriental fabrics. There's a complex cocktail list that was put together by legendary London barman Dick Bradsell. It boasts oriental-themed cocktails (around £8 each) made from saké, oriental spirits and fresh exotic fruit. Try Kumquat Javu (Appleton rum, Mandarine Napoléon, Southern Comfort and kumquats) or Plum Sour (Chinese plum brandy, Chivas Regal and sours). Impeccable dim sum is served as bar snacks, and service from elegantly attired staff (uniforms by Hussein Chalayan, no less) is seamlessly efficient.
Babies and children admitted. Disabled: toilet. Entertainment: DJs 9pm daily. Restaurant available for hire. Separate room for parties, seats 65. **Map 17 K5.**

Long Bar
The Sanderson, 50 Berners Street, W1T 3NG (7300 1400). Oxford Circus or Tottenham Court Road tube. **Open** noon-12.30am Mon-Sat; noon-10.30pm Sun. **Lunch served** noon-2.30pm daily. **Dinner served** 6-11pm Mon-Sat; 6-10pm Sun. **Main courses** £10-£15. **Credit** AmEx, DC, MC, V.
The bright, stylish bar next to the lobby in Philippe Starck's Sanderson hotel used to attract a fashionable young crowd, but nowadays the hipsters seem to have moved on – on our visit, the place was packed with tourists, older fellows in suits and gaggles of giggly girls. Service can be snooty, but the long onyx bar remains attractively hip, surrounded by bar stools with Dali-esque eyeball motifs on the back. There are a dozen Martinis, Champagne cocktails and highballs (around £10), plus wines by the glass. A seasonally changing food menu includes burgers, charcuterie, meze platters, cheesecake and cookies. Food and drink can be consumed in the bar or in the courtyard overlooking a modern oriental garden.
Babies and children admitted (terrace). Disabled: toilet (hotel). Tables outdoors (20, terrace). **Map 17 J5.**

Shochu Lounge
Basement, Roka, 37 Charlotte Street, W1T 1RR (7580 9666/www.shochulounge.com). Goodge Street or Tottenham Court Road tube. **Open/meals served** 5.30-11pm Mon, Sat; noon-11pm Tue-Fri; 5.30-10.30pm Sun. **Main courses** £9.90-£55. **Credit** AmEx, DC, MC, V.
The alluring basement bar below award-winning Japanese restaurant Roka (see *p185*) won Time Out's Best Bar award in 2005, and it's still a hit: the crowd of customers at 7pm on a midweek evening proved that. It has a lot going for it, from the louche yet sociable mood conferred by dim lighting and a low ceiling to the pioneering focus on Japan's vodka-like spirit shochu. Here, you can enjoy it tinctured with items like cinnamon ('for joy of life') or lemon ('for virility'), served neat or in cocktails by Tony Conigliaro – a Hello Kitty of shochu, rasperries, rose, lemon and sparkling water, perhaps. The wooden vats and rustic bar counter, low tables and plush, boxy red seats in enclaves make for a setting that's half 21st-century style bar, half film set for *Zatoichi*. It's a shame, then, that the service was by turns edgy and distracted – an off-note we felt the more keenly for the near-note-perfect location, food (you can order anything on Roka's menu) and drinks.
Entertainment: DJs 8pm Thur-Sat. **Map 9 J5.**

DRINKING

Donovan Bar

Holborn

Pearl Bar & Restaurant

Chancery Court Hotel, 252 High Holborn, WC1V 7EN (7829 7000/www.pearl-restaurant.com). Holborn tube.
Bar **Open** 11am-11pm Mon-Fri; 6-11pm Sat. *Restaurant* **Lunch served** noon-2.30pm Mon-Fri. **Dinner served** 6-10pm Mon-Sat. **Set lunch** £23.50 2 courses, £26.50 3 courses. **Set dinner** £45 3 courses, £55 5 courses (£10 incl wine). *Both* **Credit** AmEx, DC, MC, V.
This glamorous bar and restaurant is part of the luxurious Chancery Court Hotel, with a separate courtyard entrance through revolving doors. The bar area has a tiled monochrome floor and stunning lampshades decorated with strings of real pearls. It's furnished with leather chairs and banquettes in a neutral colour scheme, with further (velvet) banquettes inside cosy walnut-wood alcoves and hand-made tables inlaid with mother-of-pearl. The main draw is the wine list, which is one of the best in town. There are over 40 by the glass (priced between £4.50 and £39) kept fresh by the Cruvinet System (which pumps nitrogen into the airspace above the wine), and several 'wine flights' are available at any given time. Martinis and other cocktails cost around £9, and Champagne cocktails such as the exquisite Pink Pearl (Rémy Martin, elderflower and spiced berry cordials, brown sugar and pink Champagne) will set you back £10.50. Olives and sugared almonds are complimentary with the drinks, which also include blended Scotches, single malts and Canadian whiskies.
Babies and children welcome (if dining). Disabled: toilet. Entertainment: pianist 6pm daily. No smoking (restaurant). **Map 10 M5.**

Knightsbridge

Mandarin Bar

Mandarin Oriental Hyde Park, 66 Knightsbridge, SW1X 7LA (7235 2000/www.mandarinoriental. com). Knightsbridge tube. **Open/meals served** 10.30am-2am Mon-Sat; 10.30am-1.30pm Sun. **Main courses** £10-£15. **Admission** £5 after 11pm Mon-Sat. **Credit** AmEx, DC, MC, V.
Walk through the glossy marble lobby of the classic but contemporary hotel, past the beautiful fresh flower arrangements, and you'll reach a surprisingly cool bar that's not only ideal for an early evening cocktail or a post-prandial cigar and brandy, but also a destination in its own right. The centrepiece is a wall of frosted backlit glass panels, behind which you can see shadows theatrically shaking and mixing. The bar is furnished with leather armchairs and decorated with mohair, marble, glass, mirrors and wood. Cream silk walls are lined with handcrafted cocktail glasses and

ornamental bar paraphernalia. A selection of 45 cigars is offered in an enclosure where international businessmen enjoy single-malt Scotch and complimentary bar snacks.
Disabled: toilet (hotel). Entertainment: jazz trio 9pm Mon-Sat; 8pm Sun. **Map 8 F9.**

Zuma

5 Raphael Street, SW7 1DL (7584 1010/ www.zumarestaurant.com). Knightsbridge tube.
Bar **Open** noon-11pm Mon-Fri; 12.30-11pm Sat; noon-10pm Sun.
Restaurant **Lunch served** noon-2.15pm Mon-Fri; 12.30-3.15pm Sat; 12.30-2.45pm Sun. **Dinner served** 6-10.45pm Mon-Sat; 6-10.15pm Sun.
Main courses £3.80-£65.
Both **Credit** AmEx, DC, MC, V.
Situated at the front of one of London's hippest restaurants (*see p187*), this contemporary venue attracts a steady stream of A-list celebrities. Zuma offers traditional Japanese izakaya-style informal eating and drinking. The bustling cube-shaped bar is decked out in green, with a spacious counter surrounded by high seats that are hard to come by in the evenings. The bar area is surrounded by granite-like walls and prettily lit with candles. The drinks list features more than 30 types of saké, shochu and cocktails made from fresh fruit and Japanese spirits. We loved Rubabu (rhubarb-infused Ozeki saké, 42 Below vodka, fresh passionfruit). The oriental bar snacks include freshly rolled sushi.
Babies and children welcome: high chairs. Booking advisable. Disabled: toilet. No smoking (restaurant). Separate rooms for parties, seating 12 and 14. Tables outdoors (4, garden).
Map 8 F9.

Marylebone

Annex 3

2006 RUNNER-UP BEST BAR
6 Little Portland Street, W1W 7JE (7631 0700/ www.annex3.co.uk). Oxford Circus tube. **Open** 5pm-midnight Mon-Fri; 6pm-midnight Sat. **Meals served** 6.30-11pm Mon-Sat. **Main courses** £9.95-£17.95. **Credit** AmEx, MC, V.
You either love it or you hate it. Fans of Loungelover (*see p326*) and Les Trois Garçons restaurant (*see p99*) – run by the same people – adore the over-the-top conflation of styles: retro wallpaper, antique furniture, chandeliers, a working Meccano model, all mixed up and masked in glitter, gold and glamorous high camp. Others complain of sensory overload, surly staff (wearing horrible outfits), ear-piercing music and uninspiring food. No one argues about the drinks. With a menu covering 16 pages, including a page of punches, it's unlikely you'll want for inspiration. The Bengal Lancer, adapted from a recipe used when the British

Empire extended to the East Indies, certainly packs a punch (and being the size of a small goldfish bowl, it's big enough for two). Dr Strangelove is a delicious explosion of Querville calvados, Prosecco, pear, cinnamon and caramel). On our visit the service (from a waitress enveloped in a cool wrapover number) was charming and attentive, the pan-Asian bar food was delicious, and the music (Moroccan-tinged, Nitin Sawhney, Gorillaz) was conversation-friendly. As a bar, it is far more hit than miss.
Bar available for hire. Disabled: toilet. Entertainment: 8pm Fri, Sat. **Map 9 J5.**

Mayfair

China Tang

The Dorchester, Park Lane, W1K 1QA (7629 9988/www.thedorchester.com). Green Park or Hyde Park Corner tube.
Bar **Open/dim sum served** 11am-1am Mon-Sat; 11am-midnight Sun.
Restaurant **Meals/dim sum served** 11am-midnight Mon-Sat; 11am-11pm Sun. **Main courses** £10-£45.
Both **Dim sum** £4-£22. **Credit** AmEx, DC, MC, V.
The bar adjacent to the sumptuous Chinese restaurant (*see p69*) in the basement of the Dorchester shimmers with the rich and famous: Kate Moss, for instance, has been a frequent visitor. Decked out in chocolate and cream, the smart room looks like an old-fashioned cruise liner, with a few comfortable bar stools and luxurious leather chairs scattered around the thick patterned carpet. There's great range of Champagnes (from £45) and the wines (from £25) include a spice-friendly selection from Alsace and Bordeaux, and aromatic New World varieties.
Babies and children welcome: high chairs. Disabled: lift; toilet. Separate rooms for parties, seating 18-50. Vegetarian menu. **Map 9 G7.**

Donovan Bar

2006 RUNNER-UP BEST BAR
Brown's Hotel, 33-34 Albemarle Street, W1S 4BP (7493 6020/www.roccofortehotels.com). Green Park tube. **Open/snacks served** 11am-midnight Mon-Sat; noon-midnight Sun. **Snacks** £10-£15. **Credit** AmEx, MC, V.
Named after celebrated 'Swinging Sixties' photographer Terence Donovan, and apparently inspired by the Helmut Newton Bar in Berlin, the refurbished Brown's Hotel bar is certainly a classy (if small and slightly corporate) affair. Drinks are mixed behind a Bill Amberg-designed black leather bar with a stained-glass window backdrop; little zinc tables nestle between fabric tub chairs and banquettes, and putty-coloured walls are hung with an array of Donovan's iconic images.

Continuing the photographic theme, the drinks list includes a delicious Box Brownie (strawberries infused for 12 hours with a secret combo of liqueurs and topped with Champagne), as well as more familiar Martinis, Slings, Margaritas and Old-Fashioneds (slightly too much soda in the one we tried). Bar snacks include langoustine tails with spicy tomato sauce. From around 8pm you'll be joined by a Spanish guitar-player. Prices are a little sharp, starting at £12 for a basic cocktail, but then you are surrounded by some of the world's most beautiful faces (albeit in black and white).
Disabled: toilet. Entertainment: jazz musicians 7.30pm Mon-Sat. **Map 9 J7.**

Dorchester Bar

The Dorchester, Park Lane, W1K 1QA (7629 8888/www.thedorchester.com). Green Park or Hyde Park Corner tube. **Open** noon-1am Mon-Thur; noon-2am Fri, Sat; noon-midnight Sun. **Meals served** noon-11.30pm Mon-Sat; noon-10.30pm Sun. **Main courses** £12-£30. **Credit** AmEx, DC, JCB, MC, V.

The new-look Dorchester bar is elaborate, with plush purple and gold swirly banquettes and red glass spikes fringing the room like extra-terrestrial bulrushes. The effect is a little Eurotrashy, but fun and luxurious; and while the decor suggests modernity, a sense of grand tradition is still conveyed through the impressive drinks list. The staff are keen to show off their knowledge and enjoy engaging customers in conversation about the drinks, their history and their ingredients. A flight of vermouths intended for sharing showcases the hotel's selection (said to be the largest in the UK) and highlights the distinct flavours from light and dry to intensely sweet and herbal. Or there are flights of Martinis, served in modern cone-shaped glasses set in tumblers of ice.
Disabled: toilet (hotel). **Map 9 G7.**

Polo Bar

Westbury Hotel, New Bond Street, W1S 2YF (7629 7755/www.westburymayfair.com). Bond Street or Oxford Circus tube. **Open** 11am-1am daily. **Meals served** 11am-11pm daily. **Main courses** £10.50-£22.50. **Credit** AmEx, DC, MC, V.

It may occupy some dead space at the front of a hotel, but Polo beats many West End bars hands down for a pre-dinner drink. They're catering for the big spenders, with only six wines by the glass but oodles by the bottle – in fact, even spirits are offered by the bottle, with a Wray & Nephew rum for £120 if you feel the need to crash and burn. The classic cocktails include a stunning Martini made with Tanqueray Ten at £11, while the attention to detail even extends to soft drinks, with apple juice laced with gorgeous hints of cinnamon. The unobtrusive beats provide a gentle, tick-tock backdrop, while the teal velour and art deco motifs of the bar lead you further down the road to relaxation. Ideal for a midweek treat.
Babies and children admitted. Bar available for hire. Disabled: toilet (hotel). No-smoking tables. **Map 9 H7.**

Trader Vic's

The London Hilton, 22 Park Lane, W1K 4BE (7208 4113/www.tradervics.com). Hyde Park Corner tube.
Bar **Open/meals served** noon-1am Mon-Thur; noon-3am Fri; 5pm-3am Sat; 5-1am Sun. **Main courses** £8.50-£12. **Admission** £7 after 11pm Mon-Sat.
Restaurant **Lunch served** noon-5pm Mon-Fri. **Dinner served** 6pm-12.30am daily. **Main courses** £18-£22.
Both **Credit** AmEx, DC, MC, V.

This chain of bars extends from Atlanta to Taiwan, and makes its London home in the basement of the Hilton hotel. If you haven't been, you should – if only to tick it off your list of preposterous sights in the capital. It's an absurd Polynesian theme bar, framed by bamboo trellis-work from which dangle large glass baubles and, er, a canoe. Rum-drenched cocktails with names like 'Suffering Bastard' are around £7 each, while bar snacks consist of such unlikely dishes as morel mushrooms en croûte, a snip at £8.50. So, it's

something of a financial challenge to get drunk here, but there are lots of laughs: the Hawaiian entertainer and his preposterous banter, the background music playing 1980s classics slightly too fast, and wealthy businessmen attempting to impress pouting girlfriends with a faceful of smoke from a fat cigar. Warning: attempting to get in after 11pm will incur a £7 cover charge.
Babies and children welcome: high chairs. Booking advisable (restaurant). Disabled: toilet (hotel). Entertainment: musicians 10.30pm daily. No-smoking tables (restaurant). Separate room for parties, seats 50. **Map 9 G8.**

Piccadilly

Cocoon

65 Regent Street, W1B 4EA (7494 7609/ www.cocoon-restaurants.com). Piccadilly Circus tube.
Bar **Open/snacks served** 5.30pm-midnight Mon-Wed; 5.30pm-3am Thur-Sat.
Restaurant **Lunch served** noon-3pm Mon-Fri. **Dinner served** 5.30pm-midnight Mon-Sat. **Main courses** £10-£25. **Set meal** (lunch, 5.30-7pm) £17-£19.50 per person (minimum 2).
Both **Credit** AmEx, MC, V.

Designed by American designer Stéphane Dupoux, this oriental restaurant (*see p242*) has six round dining rooms lined up vertically, decorated in the style of the six-stage life cycle of a butterfly, with subtle cocoon motifs throughout. The circular bar counter, surrounded by bar stools, is located between the third and fourth dining rooms. Friendly, flirty mixologists shake oriental-style cocktails with a theatrical flourish. Watermelon Martini (fresh watermelon, Stolichnaya vodka, shochu, vanilla and honey, £7.50) was fruity and refreshing; many other cocktails are muddled with fresh fruit and come heavily perfumed with

rosewater and rose petals. The drinks list also boasts an exquisite selection of saké and shochu, which are used liberally in many of the cocktails. Champagnes, spirits, a couple of Japanese beers, wines by the glass and interesting alcohol-free cocktails are also available. Bar snacks are oriental. A great spot in central London for meeting friends, perfect if you want to impress a date.
Babies and children admitted (restaurant). Booking advisable. Disabled: toilet. Entertainment: DJs 11pm Thur-Sat. No-smoking tables. Separate room for parties, seats 14. **Map 17 7J.**

St James's

Duke's Hotel Bar

Duke's Hotel, 35 St James's Place, SW1A 1NY (7491 4840/www.dukeshotel.co.uk). Green Park tube. **Open** noon-11pm Mon-Sat; noon-10.30pm Sun. **Snacks served** noon-3.30pm daily. **Snacks** £15-£20. **Credit** AmEx, DC, MC, V.

What's the secret of a good Martini? The bar of the Duke's Hotel is known worldwide for mixing the best Martinis in London, and the secret seems to be this: use only Tanqueray or Bombay Sapphire gin and Cristal or Smirnoff Black vodka, freeze them for 24 hours, and serve in a cocktail glass that's been frozen before use. Little wonder that the relaxing, comfortable bar of this elegant, privately owned hotel is popular with American visitors. The drinks list also offers Champagne, Pimm's and classic cocktails such as Bloody Marys. The extraordinary cognac selection includes vintages from the 19th century; some dated to mark particular birthdays or anniversaries are available for the aficionado.
Disabled: toilet (hotel). Dress: smart casual. No-smoking area. Tables outdoors (1, garden). **Map 9 J8.**

DRINKING

Annex 3

Soho

Astor Bar & Grill
20 Glasshouse Street, W1B 5DJ (7734 4888/ www.astorbarandgrill.com). Piccadilly Circus tube.
Bar **Open** 5pm-1am Mon-Wed; 5pm-3am Thur-Sat.
Restaurant **Dinner served** 6-11pm Mon-Sat.
Main courses £17-£27.50. **Set dinner** £32.50-£50 3 courses incl coffee. **Admission** £10 after 10pm Thur; £15 after 10pm Fri, Sat.
Both **Credit** AmEx, MC, V.
Until very recently, this was the landmark Atlantic, a bar that made its name as a celeb hangout in the mid 1990s, a sought-after venue of VIP ropes and excellent cocktails. Now renamed the Astor, it needs to regain its cachet. Decor-wise, it has put up a couple of unusual works of art – flattened, crinkly cigarette packets of Gauloises and Belga, a photo of two old drunks snogging over a bottle of cider. Drinks-wise, mixer-meister Mario has added zings of ginger, fresh passionfruit and figs to a new selection of contemporary cocktails (£7.50), such as a Headhunter with Havana 3 or Make It Last Forever with Zubrowka vodka. Lychee liqueur features in the signature Lady Astor with Wyborowa Orange. The classics have also been slightly twisted – perhaps an Astor Champagne cocktail with 42 Below and passionfruit. Superior bar food comes courtesy of the French restaurant (*see p95*) that shares the same expansive basement, and exhibitions and DJs are promised at weekends, as well as some unusual shock cabaret on Saturdays.
Entertainment: musicians 10.30pm Thur; DJs 10.30pm Thur-Sat. Separate rooms for parties, seating 60 and 80. **Map 17 J7.**

Floridita
100 Wardour Street, W1F 0TN (7314 4000/ www.floriditalondon.com). Tottenham Court Road tube.
Bar **Open** 5.30pm-2am Mon-Wed; 5.30pm-3am Thur-Sat. **Admission** (after 6.30pm Thur-Sat) £10.
Restaurant **Meals served** 5.30pm-1am Mon-Wed; 5.30pm-1.30am Thur-Sat. **Main courses** £13.50-£35.
Both **Credit** AmEx, DC, MC, V.
Constante was the bartender who ran Havana's El Floridita of Hemingway lore. London's Floridita is an equally upscale operation – contemporary restaurant upstairs (*see p41*), fashionable nightspot Bar Constante below – that recreate the glitz and high-level gluttony of those pre-Castro days. Enjoy faithful renditions of Daiquiris (£6.50-£7.50) with Havana Club Añejo Blanco, limes and soda, some Maraschino here, some orange Curaçao there, the New Cuban counterparts involving pomegranate, passionfruit and fig purée. Martinis (£13-£25) are made with large measures of Grey Goose, Tanqueray Ten and, fashionably, Kauffman vodka. All are impeccably mixed at an extensive bar counter that runs the length of a large basement space sparkling with decorative bling. The food is good – tiny bar snacks of octopus and ceviche, red snapper or warm Brazilian cheesebreads, serious and authentic mains of charcoal-grilled lobsters. Cuban musicians and professional dancers create post-midnight entertainment, and this being a Conran enterprise, there's an extensive cigar menu.
Booking advisable. Disabled: toilet. Entertainment: DJ/band 8pm Mon-Sat. Separate rooms for parties, seating 6 and 56. **Map 17 K6.**

Lab
12 Old Compton Street, W1D 4TQ (7437 7820/ www.lab-townhouse.com). Leicester Square or Tottenham Court Road tube. **Open** 4pm-midnight Mon-Sat; 4-10.30pm Sun. **Snacks served** 6-11pm Mon-Sat; 6-10.30pm Sun. **Snacks** £5-£14. **Credit** AmEx, MC, V.
Founded by Douglas Ankrah, Lab has long been at the forefront of the capital's cocktail scene. Set over two compact floors decorated with a tinge of retro, Lab operates on a huge range of original cocktails, its list recently reinvented. All are £7 or as near as dammit. The Streets Ahead range features twisted concoctions such as a KFC

Sazerac, using Buffalo Trace with fig jam and caramel liqueur in an absinthe-washed glass; a Plata Passion with Gran Centenario Plata tequila, own-made honey water and passionfruit, served frappé; and a Saga Branca, Sagatiba Velha cachaça, Fernet-Branca and egg white. The Hall of Fame offers further apothecary (Absolut Citron muddled with fresh kumquats in an Absolutely Crushed) – and these are only the tip of a very tasty iceberg. Bar snacks are Thai, a platter for two including prawn sarong, salt and pepper squid, dim sum and dips. Outstanding.
Bar available for hire. Dress: no ties. Entertainment: DJs 8pm Mon-Sat. **Map 17 K6.**

Milk & Honey
61 Poland Street, W1F 7NU (7292 9949/0700 655 469/www.mlkhny.com). Oxford Circus tube. **Open** *Non-members* 6-11pm Mon-Fri; 7-11pm Sat. *Members* 6pm-3am Mon-Fri; 7pm-3am Sat. **Snacks served** 6pm-2am Mon-Sat. **Snacks** £3-£14. **Credit** AmEx, DC, MC, V.
With the cachet of a members' bar, but without pretension of complete exclusivity, the London incarnation of Manhattan's legendary referral-only destination is a place that takes its drinks seriously. It isn't just the 40-odd cocktails (although they are exquisitely concocted with just the right touch of Maraschino or egg white, chilled with hand-cut jagged chunks of ice, and surprisingly reasonably priced at £7-£8.50), it's the service that brings them to your own snug booth, one of six in the main Red Room. Numbers are best comfortable by the house policy of booking in a limited number of non-members, generally at the start of the week and always before 11pm – always phone ahead. Monthly changing amuse-bouches include luxuries such as griddled pheasant skewers and wild mushroom and walnut strudel, some turning up on the two- and four-person platters (£16-£30). Fittingly for the Prohibition-era inconspicuous door entry, jazz plays equally subtly in the background. Members (£300 a year) have access to the private bar and games room upstairs.
Booking essential for non-members. Dress: smart casual; no sportswear. Separate rooms for parties, seating 20 and 60. **Map 17 J6.**

South Kensington

190 Queensgate
The Gore Hotel, 190 Queensgate, SW7 5EX (7584 6601/www.gorehotel.co.uk). Gloucester Road or South Kensington tube.
Bar **Open** 5pm-2am Mon-Thur; 5pm-4am Fri, Sat; 5pm-1am Sun. **Snacks served** 5-11pm daily. **Snacks** £7.50-£10.50.
Bistro **Meals served** 7am-10.30pm daily. **Main courses** £10.50-£26.50.
Both **Credit** AmEx, DC, MC, V.
Far from the South Ken hub and ideal for combining with a visit to the Royal Albert Hall is this cool and quirky bar. Quite what it is doing out here is a mystery, but one definitely worth a visit to puzzle over. Old paintings, blue, brown and maroon leather sofas and a wood-panelled ceiling suggest an old-style members' club, but the blue-lit spirit bar running the length of the room introduces a sense of cutting-edge sophistication mirrored in the cocktail list. Try the Geisha Girl (rum, fraise des bois, vanilla sugar, strawberries, guava juice and passionfruit, £8.50) or Gingingermon (infused gin and ginger lemongrass cordial, Champagne and a sloe gin float, £10.50). The spirit list is spectacularly extensive, with 24 rums and 12 tequilas. The crowd comprises dazzled hotel guests and the beautiful set, complementing the idiosyncratic old and new setting.
Babies and children welcome (bistro only). Entertainment: DJ 10pm Fri, Sat. Separate room for parties, seats 60. **Map 8 D9.**

Strand

American Bar
The Savoy, Strand, WC2R 0EU (7836 4343/ www.fairmont.com/savoy). Covent Garden or Embankment tube/Charing Cross tube/rail. **Open** noon-1am Mon-Sat; noon-10.30pm Sun.

Meals served noon-10.30pm Mon-Sat; noon-10pm Sun. **Main courses** £12-£14. **Cover charge** £5 after 8pm. **Credit** AmEx, MC, V.
Tucked inside the elegant art deco Savoy hotel, the American Bar is steeped in history (Harry Craddock of the legendary *Savoy Cocktail Book* introduced cocktails to the UK from Prohibition-era America). This once talked-about and much-imitated bar is lined with monochrome pictures of Hollywood stars – although on our visit, we had to make do with Martin Clunes. Smartly attired drinkers like to congregate here for well-regarded Martinis (made from Ketel One, Grey Goose or Plymouth, £11.50) and other classic cocktails, wines and Champagnes. Service is unfailingly polite, and olives and nuts are brought to the table as soon as you take your seat. The tinkling piano music in the evenings gives the place a sense of Old Hollywood timelessness.
Disabled: toilet (hotel). Entertainment: pianist/singer 7pm-midnight Mon-Thur; 7pm-1am Fri, Sat. No-smoking tables. **Map 18 L7.**

West

Ladbroke Grove

Ruby & Sequoia
6-8 All Saints Road, W11 1HH (7243 6363/ www.ruby.uk.com). Ladbroke Grove or Westbourne Park tube.
Bar **Open** 6pm-12.30am Mon-Thur; 6pm-2am Fri; 11am-2am Sat; 11am-12.30am Sun. **Snacks served** 6-11pm Mon-Fri; 11am-11pm Sat, Sun. **Snacks** £2.50-£13.
Restaurant **Brunch served** 11am-4pm Sat, Sun. **Dinner served** 6pm-11pm daily. **Main courses** £8-£15.
Both **Credit** AmEx, MC, V.
This latest bar and restaurant from the Ruby Lounge folks is ace. The ground floor is impressive enough, with friendly bar staff, modish cocktails and a fun interior that mixes diner-style booth seating with silver and white flock wallpaper in a retro-funky way. The dining area has an ambitious menu, ranging from escabeche of prawns to braised rabbit with mustard, tarragon and bacon, at proper restaurant prices. But it's as a bar that Ruby & Sequoia is best: after 9pm, DJs work the decks in the bigger and more elegant Sequoia basement, which gets busy on Friday and Saturday nights (a doorman, and door policy of sorts, appears on those nights). Sequoia is a great place to spread out on leather banquettes, admire the studied cool of the Perspex lights, and wonder what the beautiful young people of Notting Hill actually do for a living.
Babies and children welcome (restaurant until 6pm). Bar available for hire. Disabled: toilet. Entertainment: DJs 9pm Thur-Sun. Tables outdoors (2, pavement). **Map 19 B2.**

Trailer Happiness
177 Portobello Road, W11 2DY (7727 2700/ www.trailerhappiness.com). Ladbroke Grove or Notting Hill Gate tube. **Open** 5-10pm 1st Mon of mth; 5pm-midnight Tue-Fri; 6pm-midnight Sat; 6-10.30pm Sun. **Snacks served** 6-10.30pm Tue-Sat. **Snacks** £6-£11. **Credit** AmEx, MC, V.
This little basement bar resembles an Austin Powers shag pad (plenty of smoked glass, thick carpet, retro paintings of dusky Tahitian maidens gazing down from the wall), but is looking more dated than tongue in cheek these days. Happily, the clientele are more likely to be here for a good range of cocktails that can be sipped in a cosy atmosphere. House favourites (£7-£15) include a Mitch Martini (Zubrowka with passionfruit, peach, apple and Champagne) and a Mojito Especial (with Havana Club Añejo Especial), while authentically 1950s-style Tikis include a Zombie (five rums, juices, absinthe, syrups, bitters) – which is limited to two per person, for obvious reasons. Food – or rather 'TV Dinners' – covers anything from finger fare such as chips to something more substantial along the lines of lamb and lemon racks.
Entertainment: DJs 8pm Wed-Sat. Tables outdoors (5, pavement). **Map 19 B3.**

DRINKING

South

Clapham

★ Lost Society

2006 WINNER BEST BAR

697 Wandsworth Road, SW8 3JF (7652 6526/ www.lostsociety.co.uk). Clapham Common tube/ 77, 77A bus. **Open** 5pm-1am Tue-Thur; 4pm-2am Fri; 11am-2am Sat; 11am-1am Sun. **Meals served** 5-11pm Tue-Thur; -11pm Fri; 11am-11pm Sat, Sun. **Main courses** £3.50-£12.95. **Admission** £3 after 9.30pm Fri; £5 after 9.30pm Sat. **Credit** AmEx, MC, V.

Lucky Battersea. This two store/ bar/restaurant serves great cocktails made with well-sourced spirits, and high-quality food. On the ground floor there's a number of differently styled bar areas, plus a little garden terrace – perfect for summer drinking. Upstairs, the pitched roof with exposed columns and beams is hung with an enormous chandelier, giving the space a slightly louche feel. Deep-turquoise leather banquettes and cubes line bare brick walls decorated with painted peacocks (the live ones can preen themselves before the numerous mirrors). A new drinks menu has a fine global choice of bottled beers, but it's the cocktails that demand special attention. An Amaretto Sour was a perfectly blended combo of Di Saronno shaken with lemon juice, sugar, bitters and egg white, while a vodka Martini (Grey Goose, with a twist of lemon) was top-notch. Wines are good too. Food-wise, ribeye – with peppercorn sauce and chunky chips – was perfectly tender and juicy. Table service is friendly, knowledgable and (almost over) attentive, and there are DJ sets at the end of the week. A fantastic addition to an area lacking in original concept bars; long may it last.
Entertainment: burlesque show 9pm 1st Thur of mth; DJs 9pm Thur-Sat, jazz/funk 7.30pm Sun. No-smoking tables. Separate room for parties, seats 60. Tables outdoors (20, garden; 10, terrace).

East

Bethnal Green

Bistrotheque Napoleon Bar

23-27 Wadeson Street, E2 9DR (8983 7900/ www.bistrotheque.com). Bethnal Green tube/rail/ Cambridge Heath rail/55 bus.
Bar **Open** 5.30pm-midnight Mon-Sat; 1pm-midnight Sun.
Restaurant **Lunch served** 11am-4pm Sat, Sun. **Dinner served** 6.30-10.30pm daily. **Main courses** £10-£21. **Set lunch** £21 3 courses. **Set dinner** (6.30-7.30pm Mon-Fri) £12 2 courses, £15 3 courses.
Both **Credit** AmEx, MC, V.

Bistrotheque is infused with the sort of effortless cool that wouldn't look out of place in New York's meatpacking district. The venue incorporates a bar (Napoleon) and a cabaret room on the ground floor, and a rustic Anglo-French bistro (see p99) on the first. The dimly lit bar is furnished with comfortable grey seats and banquettes, and has exposed brick walls, opulent chandeliers and a large etched-glass mirror on dark-wood panelling behind the counter. Champagnes, wines and draught beer are available, but the hip and beautiful from the fashion, media, music and design industries that flock to the place prefer to sip the exquisite cocktails, meticulously blended by the friendly barman. All the cocktails are reasonably priced between £5 and £8.50, with most costing around £6.50. Our favourite is the simply sensational Passionfruit Caipirinha, which is made with Germana cachaça, fresh passionfruit, passionfruit syrup and lime.
Babies and children admitted. Booking advisable. Disabled: toilet. Entertainment: cabaret 10pm Tue-Sat; pianist noon-4pm Sun. Separate room for parties, seats 50.

Green & Red

51 Bethnal Green Road, E1 6LA (7749 9670/ www.greenred.co.uk). Liverpool Street tube/rail. **Open** 5.30pm-midnight Mon-Fri; noon-midnight Sat; noon-11.30pm Sun. **Lunch served** noon-5pm daily. **Dinner served** 6-11pm Mon-Sat; 6-10.30pm Sun. **Main courses** £9.40-£14.50. **Credit** AmEx, MC, V.

Well conceived and well run, Green & Red combines an almost evangelical commitment to fine tequila with a kitchen that produces great Mexican drinking food (tacos de carnitas; chorizo asado); it works equally well whether you're drinking or eating (see p43) or just killing time with the papers. They take themselves seriously enough to offer tasting flights (three tequila shots, £12-£59.40), but not too seriously to have fun – witness the El Burro ('Moscow Mule Mexican-style') or Lager-ita ('Two of our favourite drinks in one glass'). We enjoyed a couple of different Margaritas (from £6) over a leisurely brunch in the ground floor Cantina Bar, where decor is a slightly odd combination of Spaghetti Western and industrial chic. Staff are charming, knowledgeable and enthusiastic. Impressive.
Babies and children welcome: high chair. Disabled: toilet. Entertainment: DJs 8pm Fri, Sat. Tables outdoors (6, terrace). **Map 6 S4**.

Shoreditch

Loungelover

1 Whitby Street, E2 7DP (7012 1234/www.lounge lover.co.uk). Liverpool Street tube/rail. **Open** 6pm-midnight Tue-Thur, Sun; 6pm-1am Fri; 7pm-1am

Sat. **Snacks served** 6-11.30pm Tue-Fri, Sun; 7pm-11.30pm Sat. **Snacks** £8-£18. **Credit** AmEx, DC, MC, V.

Under the same owners as the celebrated Les Trois Garçons French restaurant (see p99) around the corner, Loungelover shares its taste in divinely decadent decor. A wealth of extravagantly theatrical fixtures, fittings and accessories – fabulous chandeliers, a stuffed hippo head, hot-house plants, a replica religious fresco adorning one wall, glass-topped tables, coloured Perspex lighting, red velveteen stools and faux Regency chairs, giant green coach lamps and candles – create a uniquely swish ambience. Mock croc-bound menus list cocktails by genre (Flower Power, Herbal Lover, Hot Lover, Virgin) and range between £7 and £11, but make no mention of the 12.5% service charge added to your bill. If you want to impress a date, Loungelover is perfect, but its attitude (unnecessarily snooty and superior, you sit where you're told, the necessity of having to book in advance for a timeslot) and inflated prices rather spoil the effect.
Booking advisable. Disabled: toilet. Entertainment: DJs 7pm Fri, Sat. **Map 6 S4**.

Sosho

2 Tabernacle Street, EC2A 4LU (7920 0701/ www.sosho3am.com). Moorgate or Old Street tube/rail. **Open** noon-midnight Tue; noon-1am Wed, Thur; noon-3am Fri; 7pm-4am Sat; 9pm-6am Sun. **Meals served** noon-10.30pm Tue-Fri; 7-11pm Sat. **Main courses** £7.50-£9. **Admission** £3-£10 after 9pm Thur-Sun. **Credit** AmEx, DC, MC, V.

As part of the Match chain, Sosho shares its mission statement: 'To fix great drinks for a mixed crowd of grown-ups.' The emphasis is thus very much on cocktails (as selected by celebrated mixologist Dale DeGroff) and there are just three (bottled) beers on offer, although the wine list is quite respectable. Once hip, Sosho's look – dark floor, red walls with exposed brickwork, squashy leather sofas and low lighting in the street-level bar – is now penny plain, but it's an agreeable enough space, with a raised dais providing seating at black lacquered tables. Downstairs, there's a smaller lounge area, where brown leatherette banquettes and violently patterned wallpaper suggest 1970s après ski. Not that this bothers the City types who pour in from Moorgate to sup fancy cocktails on a Thursday and Friday, or maybe cut some rug under the glitterball.
Babies and children welcome (daytime). Disabled: toilet. Entertainment: DJs 9pm Wed-Sun. Separate room for parties, seats 150. **Map 6 Q4**.

North

Camden Town & Chalk Farm

Bullet

147 Kentish Town Road, NW1 8PB (7485 6040/ www.bulletbar.co.uk). Camden Town tube/Kentish Town tube/rail. **Open** 7pm-midnight Mon-Wed; 7pm-1am Thur; 7pm-2am Fri, Sat; 6pm-midnight Sun. **Admission** £3-£5 Mon-Fri; £5 after 9pm Sat; £3 Sun. **Credit** MC, V.

This corner bar wouldn't turn too many heads in Soho, but tucked away on a junction between Kentish Town and Camden, it's a marvel. The wide, bare brick and wine-red space, once a grim rockers' joint, has been transformed into a low-key cocktail bar, with stylish (if predictable) retro furniture and lamps. Pints seem to be the poison of choice for the mix of grown-up indie kids and office types hanging about on the sofas. Although the beer on tap is nothing remarkable, bottles include Cobra, Peroni and Mort Subite Framboise, and the good list of classic cocktails are handled competently by the swish bar staff. Musicians are a big draw, with popular nights run by indie45, plus acoustic sets and open-mic nights.
Disabled: toilet. Entertainment: bands 7pm Mon, Tue, Thur, Fri; acoustic/open-mic 7pm Wed; DJ 7pm Sat; musicians 7pm Sun. Tables outdoors (5, garden). **Map 27 D1**.

Ruby & Sequoia. See p325.

Gilgamesh
2006 RUNNER-UP BEST BAR
Camden Stables Market, Chalk Farm Road,
NW1 8AH (7482 5757/www.gilgameshbar.com).
Chalk Farm tube/rail.
Bar **Open/snacks served** noon-2.30am
Mon-Sat; noon-1.30am Sun.
Restaurant **Lunch served** noon-3pm Fri;
noon-6pm Sat, Sun. **Dinner served** 6pm-
midnight daily. **Set lunch** (Sat, Sun) £15
3 courses. **Main courses** £10-£46.
All **Credit** AmEx, MC, V.
The story goes that Gilgamesh (an ancient
Babylonian king, since you ask) once went to the
cedar forest in search of timber. Head up the
escalator to Ian Pengelley's restaurant (*see p245*)
and you'll see where most of it ended up. The
enormous space (surely the biggest bar/restaurant
in London) was apparently inspired by the British
Museum, and is variously panelled, decorated,
bedecked and draped in intricately carved wood
depicting Babylonian battles, super-sized statuary,
inlaid tables and friezes, and – just when you think
you've seen it all – a 40ft glass ceiling opens up and
you're suddenly on a roof terrace. The drinks list
continues the Assyrian/Babylonian theme, so you
might sip on an Ishtar (Mount Gay Rum, raspberry
and Champagne) or a Kish Martini (lychee, rose,
apple and cranberry with Smirnoff Black and
Nijizaki lime saké), but wines are also reasonably
priced, and there's even a saké sommelier. The bar
food is impressive (duck spring rolls were superb).
Babies and children admitted. Booking esssential.
Disabled: lift; toilet. Dress: smart casual; no flip-
flops or shorts. Restaurant available for hire.
Map 27 C1.

Peachykeen
112 Kentish Town Road, NW1 9PX (7482 2300/
www.peachy-keen.com). Camden Town tube.
Open noon-3pm Mon-Fri; 5-11.30pm Mon-Thur;
noon-3pm, 5pm-midnight Fri; 5pm-midnight Sat.
Snacks served noon-3pm, 5-9pm Mon-Fri.
Snacks £3-£5. **Credit** AmEx, MC, V.
'Rizzo, how are you?' asks Sandy in *Grease*. 'Peachy
keen, jelly bean,' replies Rizzo. Quite some way
from the cheer of Rydell High, there's thankfully
no memorabilia pinned to the walls and no ageing
T-Birds at the bar. White-walled and high-
ceilinged, upstairs is mainly for standing and
enjoying the cocktails; vodka and muddled
passionfruit went together like ramalama in a
refreshing Pink & Fluffy. Downstairs is cosier:
twinkling fairy lights illuminate low tables and
comfortable beanbag stools. Cocktails are around
£5, as are shareable snack platters. Most wines are
available by the glass. Peachykeen deserves some
custom, so get down there like greased lightni…
you get the idea.
Bar available for hire. Entertainment: DJs
8pm occasional Fri, Sat. Tables outdoors
(2, pavement). Separate room(s) for parties,
seats 35. **Map 27 D1**.

Islington

Anam
3 Chapel Market, N1 9EZ (7278 1001/
www.anambar.com). Angel tube. **Open** 6pm-
midnight Tue, Wed; 5pm-2am Thur-Sat; noon-
11.30pm Sun. **Credit** AmEx, MC, V.
You've got to move slowly in this smart, Chapel
Market retreat. And not just to appreciate its
impeccably stylish, retro-inspired decor – nice
though it is. This jazzy DJ/cocktail bar is so small
and gets so crammed that you have no choice.
Unsurprisingly, there's an intimate party vibe to
the place – but this is not just down to the lack of
space. There's finger food (veggie spring rolls,
mixed charcuterie) on the menu and free popcorn
at the bar, but it's the tantalising liquid concoctions
courtesy of mixologists Simon Sheena and Filippo
Lari that fuel the funky atmosphere. At around £8
each, they don't come cheap, but made with
premium brand spirits and unusual ingredients
(fresh chillies, fig liqueur) they're a decadent treat.
Basement bar available for hire. Booking
advisable. Disabled: toilet. Dress: smart
casual. Entertainment: DJs 8pm Thur-Sat.
Map 5 N2.

Pubs

The big news in 2006 was that Young's Brewery in Wandsworth, which has been on the same site since the 19th century, is to close and relocate to Hertfordshire in a merger with another brewer (Charles Wells). This leaves only one large brewery still operating in London, namely Fuller's, in Chiswick. There's no need to despair, though: Young's pubs will continue to be Young's pubs, microbreweries are thriving, and you can still get a good pint of real ale in hundreds of boozers across London. Here is a choice selection of some of the best; for more, grab a copy of the latest edition of the *Time Out Bars, Pubs & Clubs*. For pubs that specialise in food, see **Gastropubs**, starting on p102.

Central

Aldwych

Seven Stars
53 Carey Street, WC2A 2JB (7242 8521).
Chancery Lane, Holborn or Temple tube. **Open**
11am-11pm Mon-Fri; noon-11pm Sat; noon-
10.30pm Sun. **Lunch served** noon-3pm, **dinner**
served 5-10pm Mon-Fri. **Meals served** 1-10pm
Sat; 1-9pm Sun. **Credit** AmEx, MC, V.
Roxy Beaujolais' fabulous little pub manages to
squeeze the best ales, wines and food into an
interior whose compactness is dictated by the
constraints of its 1602 construction. It's low-
ceilinged and cramped around the main bar
counter, but nobody seems to mind, certainly not
the jolly clientele from the Royal Courts of Justice
across the road. Decent Australian shiraz, house
Duluc and draught Dark Star Hophead, Adnams
Bitter and Broadside, and Bitburger lager, are
consumed with gusto through the afternoon. The
blackboard of gastronomic fare (perhaps featuring
mixed game stew and char-grilled ribeye steak),
and checked tablecloths in the dining areas at
either end, lend a rustic, French touch. There is just
enough room for a decor theme to emerge, as all
the film stills and posters on display are of Hovis-
era British courtroom dramas. The knocked-
through alcove has a framed collection of cigarette
cards, portraits of the 'Seven Stars': pre-war
actresses who lent this fine venue its name.
No piped music or jukebox. No-smoking tables.
Map 10 M6.

Belgravia

Thomas Cubitt NEW
44 Elizabeth Street, SW1W 9PA (7730 6060/
www.thethomascubitt.co.uk). Victoria tube/rail.
Open 11am-11pm daily. **Meals served** noon-
10pm daily. **Credit** AmEx, MC, V.
If you want to see how a pub renovation should be
done, pop along to the Thomas Cubitt. At first
glance it looks like just another old pub that's been
tarted up, but, as your eyes adjust to the low light,
you appreciate the thought and expense that's gone
into this subtly rendered Georgian and Regency
look. Although new, the oak panelling, wooden
floors, fireplaces and sturdy bar are perfectly in
keeping with this grade II-listed building. The
pub's new name is also a homage to the master
builder who created much of Belgravia and
Pimlico in the second quarter of the 19th century;
this pub lies on one of the many streets Cubitt
built. This place is no museum piece, though. The
ground floor bustles with people enjoying Adnams
and Theakston's Lightfoot, or bar snacks such as
oysters or posh sausage and mash. The first floor

is occupied by a more ambitious dining room,
serving British-accented Modern European food;
but the real draw of the place is the understated
beauty of the interior.
Babies and children admitted. No-smoking tables.
Separate room for parties, seats 18. Tables
outdoors (8, pavement). **Map 15 G10**.

Bloomsbury

Lamb
94 Lamb's Conduit Street, WC1N 3LZ (7405
0713/www.youngs.co.uk). Holborn or Russell
Square tube. **Open** 11am-midnight Mon-Sat;
noon-10.30pm Sun. **Meals served** noon-9pm
daily. **Credit** AmEx, MC, V.
For a taste of old Bloomsbury – and slow-roast
lamb shank, pan-seared lamb's liver or prime
Scotch beefburgers – the near 300-year-old Lamb
is for you. Founded in 1729, a date celebrated in
the naming of its own-made steak and mushroom
pie, this beautifully restored etched glass and
mahogany masterpiece is class itself. Today the
snob screens have a decorative role above the
horseshoe island bar, but, back in the days when
music hall stars were regulars here, they were used
to deflect unwanted attention. The stage stars are
remembered with two rows of small, gilt-framed
portraits running around the walls, and other
vintage theatrical touches are provided by a
polyphon (the old mechanical musical instrument
in the corner), dinky brass balustrades around the
bar tables and the Pit, a sunken back area that
gives access to a summer patio. The beer is
Young's, the wines a well-chosen half-dozen of
each colour from Cockburn and Campbell, and the
menu seasonal, with most mains under a tenner.
No piped music or jukebox. No-smoking table.
Separate room for parties, seats 32. Tables
outdoors (3, patio; 3, pavement). **Map 4 M4**.

Clerkenwell & Farringdon

Jerusalem Tavern
55 Britton Street, EC1M 5UQ (7490 4281/
www.stpetersbrewery.co.uk). Farringdon tube/
rail. **Open** 11am-11pm Mon-Fri. **Lunch served**
noon-3pm, **dinner served** 5-10pm Mon-Fri.
Credit AmEx, MC, V.
As the only London pub associated with the
Suffolk-based St Peter's Brewery, the Jerusalem
serves exemplary booze: Mild, Old-Style Porter,
Bitter and Golden Ale, as well as Bitburger and
Suffolk Cyder, on draught, plus a full range of
other St Peter's beers in bottles and a reasonable
wine list. But the beer isn't left in the hands of
middle-elderly beards. The place was so packed on
a clement evening that people were sitting on the
window sills and minuscule tables outside, the
clientele a fine mix of nationalities, genders, ages

and professions. The pub divides into three areas: a benched front section is partitioned from the bar (whose happily wonky feel is exemplified by a single table isolated on a kind of balcony), then a bit of table space at the back. It's all pretty tight and cosy, the green-painted wood, chipped walls and candles working well with original tiles and a shopfront that dates back to 1810.
Babies and children admitted. Bar available for hire (weekends only). No piped music or jukebox. Tables outdoors (2, pavement). **Map 5 O4.**

Pakenham Arms

1 Pakenham Street, WC1X 0LA (7837 6933). Russell Square tube/King's Cross tube/rail. **Open** 9am-1am Mon-Thur, Sat; 9am-1.30am Fri; 9am-10.30pm Sun. **Lunch served** noon-2pm, **dinner served** 6-10pm Mon-Fri. **Meals served** 10am-6pm Sat; noon-6pm Sun. **Credit** MC, V.
Opposite Mount Pleasant sorting office lies this freehouse. If real ale is your thing, you're sorted. You'll find Charles Wells Bombardier, Fuller's London Pride and Adnams Broadside, and more are promised soon. Most of the posties seemed to plump for an after-shift pint of lager on our last visit, with eyes down for a perusal of the day's papers or glued to the TV above the door beaming in Sky Sports. Banquettes line the edge of the main bar area, leaving a mildly disconcerting amount of empty space in the centre of the pub. Food is of the burgers and baguettes variety.
Babies and children admitted. Tables outdoors (7, pavement). **Map 4 M4.**

Covent Garden

Lamb & Flag

33 Rose Street, WC2E 9EB (7497 9504). Covent Garden tube. **Open** 11am-11pm Mon-Sat; noon-10.30pm Sun. **Lunch served** noon-3pm Mon-Fri, Sun; noon-4.30pm Sat. **Credit** MC, V.
By far the best pub in tourist-ridden Covent Garden. The problem is that everyone knows it and consequently most evenings, especially in warmer weather, you'll be hard pushed to get anywhere near its 350-year-old (or more) interior. Besides bags of wooden-framed, low-ceiling history, it's got the most picture-perfect location at the head of a narrow cobbled lane off Garrick Street, with an ancient tunnelled passageway squeezing down one side. It has a staff that have remained loyal and capable for seemingly decades now, and a great line-up of mainly Young's ales supplemented by guests that include the likes of Courage Best. There are ploughman's lunches and doorstop sandwiches downstairs, and full pub grub on red checked tablecloths in the Dryden room upstairs, which is also where a bunch of elderly but lively trad jazzers play every Sunday evening.
Babies and children admitted (lunch only). Entertainment: jazz 7.30-10.15pm Sun. No piped music or jukebox. **Map 18 L7.**

Holborn

Princess Louise

208 High Holborn, WC1V 7EP (7405 8816). Holborn tube. **Open** 11am-11pm Mon-Fri; noon-11pm Sat; noon-10.30pm Sun. **Lunch served** noon-2.30pm, **dinner served** 6-8.30pm Mon-Fri. **Credit** MC, V.
One of the better Sam Smith's pubs in central London, the Princess Louise is spacious and ornate, with intricate woodwork, tall engraved mirrors and a moulded ceiling. Much is made of the food, although it's standard fare – basket meals such as jumbo sausages, scampi and so on, served in the upstairs bar (open only at mealtimes). Sandwiches and baguettes are served in the main bar – avocado and bacon, roast beef and horseradish – as are the ploughman's lunches with a choice of four cheeses and soup of the day. Not sumptuous enough to attract tourists, too staid to bring in young nine-to-fives, the pub mainly lives from a middle-aged, male clientele who lend the place a somewhat sad air during the day. After work (for want of better, perhaps), it's packed.
No piped music or jukebox. **Map 18 L5.**

Seven Stars. See p327.

Ye Old Mitre

1 Ely Court, Ely Place, at the side of 8 Hatton Gardens, EC1N 6SJ (7405 4751). Chancery Lane tube/Farringdon tube/rail. **Open** 11am-11pm Mon-Fri. **Meals served** 11am-9.30pm Mon-Fri. **Credit** AmEx, MC, V.
Deliciously hidden (the tiny alley is marked by a little pub sign between jewellers' shops), this charming pub dates back to 1546. A gruffly cheerful and efficient Scottish barman with a fierce military haircut now runs it on properly old-fashioned lines. The draught line-up is quality stuff, changing weekly and featuring the likes of Deuchars IPA, Adnams Bitter and Broadside (plus Carling, Carlsberg and Guinness if you must). Wood panels, exposed beams and a gas-powered hearth fire make for a toasty little lounge bar. Off to one side there's a snug, sized for half a dozen close friends without fears for their knees, and you can nip outside to a second small bar. Up a tricky staircase past the ladies', the Bishop's Room has the least character and the most room. Gents have an outside facility, off a concrete courtyard with big barrels, to stand in in summer. The bar menu runs to toasties, pork pies and even scotch eggs.
No piped music or jukebox. Tables outdoors (10 barrels, pavement). **Map 11 N5.**

West

Hammersmith

Dove

19 Upper Mall, W6 9TA (8748 5405). Hammersmith or Ravenscourt Park tube. **Open** 11am-11pm Mon-Sat; noon-10.30pm Sun. **Lunch served** noon-3pm Mon-Fri; noon-5pm Sun. **Dinner served** 5-10pm Mon-Fri. **Meals served** noon-9pm Sat. **Credit** AmEx, MC, V.
Selling drinks since Hammersmith was a dozy hamlet, this 17th-century masterpiece started out as a coffee shop before moving on to bigger things. William Morris lived next door, Hemingway and Graham Greene both drank here, and the *Guinness Book of Records* bestowed an award on the microscopic front bar (127cm x 239cm) back in 1989. Today's Dove comes with three additional sections, all sumptuously scruffy, plus an outdoor Thames-side terrace. A Fuller's pub, the bar stocks the usual dark suspects; Budweiser in the fridge supplements a dismal range of draught lagers, but there's a refreshingly well-stocked selection of wines, and a good supply of pub grub. On top of its lovely river view, the Dove keeps the eyes and minds busy with a superb selection of old photos of the locality.
No piped music or jukebox. Tables outdoors (15, riverside terrace). **Map 20 A4.**

Ladbroke Grove

Elgin

96 Ladbroke Grove, W11 1PY (7229 5663). Ladbroke Grove tube. **Open** noon-11pm Mon-Thur; noon-11.30pm Fri; 11am-11.30pm Sat; noon-10.30pm Sun. **Meals served** noon-9pm daily. **Credit** AmEx, MC, V.
This is a mother of a pub. Everything is enormous, from the height of the ceilings and size of the rooms – three of them – to the huge bar that services them all. It was built back in 1853 by Dr Samuel Walker, a property-speculating clergyman. The original Victorian bevelled glass screen set with chunks of coloured glass, and the wall tiles and carved mahogany are, however, the work of William Dickinson, who acquired the pub in 1892. On our visit no one was here for the beer (of three rotating real ales, one was off). There's a small range of spirits, wine by the glass, bottles of alcopops, and a range of 'Best of British' pub grub that ranges from pie of the day to egg and chips. What we all wanted, and got, was football on the telly, and plenty of it. There is a fitting huge screen in each room, where assorted sofas, tables and chairs provide accommodation.
Babies and children admitted. Entertainment: DJs 9pm alternate Fri; karaoke 8.30pm alternate Sat; quiz 6pm Sun. No-smoking tables. Tables outdoors (12, pavement). **Map 19 B2.**

South West

Colliers Wood

Sultan

78 Norman Road, SW19 1BT (8542 4532).
Colliers Wood or South Wimbledon tube. **Open**
noon-11pm Mon-Thur; noon-midnight Fri, Sat;
noon-11pm Sun. **Credit** MC, V.
Proud and deserved winner of the Time Out Best
Pub award in 2005, the Sultan (named after the
great racehorse of the 1830s) is a magnet for lovers
of real ale. It's a place that has no truck with
modern fripperies, focusing instead on great beer
and the provision of a warm and comfortable
environment in which to sup it. The only Hop Back
Brewery pub in London, you'll find Entire Stout,
GFB and Summer Lightning on draught. To tempt
non-beeros there are four reds, four whites and a
rosé, or house-spirit doubles. Two fires kept the
busy saloon bar cosy, but the larger public bar
(named after an actor from *The Archers*) was also
full on a Friday night. A cabinet of trophies and
picture of famous darts' dieter Andy 'The Viking'
Fordham suggest darts are taken seriously here,
but otherwise the entertainment is all down to you.
Disabled: toilet. Entertainment: quiz 8.30pm Tue
(Sept-June). Tables outdoors (8, garden).

Parsons Green

White Horse

1-3 Parsons Green, SW6 4UL (7736 2115/
www.whitehorsesw6.com). Parsons Green tube.
Open 11am-midnight Mon-Thur; 11am-1am Fri,
Sat. **Meals served** noon-10.30pm Mon-Fri;
11am-10.30pm Sat, Sun. **Credit** AmEx, MC, V.
If you're in the Parsons Green area and looking for
top-quality beer, the White Horse is a godsend. A
freehouse, it serves Harveys Sussex Best Bitter,
Adnams Broadside and Fuller's ESB, plus a huge
variety of other draught and bottled British and
international beers (20 on draught and another 139
in bottles, according to the landlord – and we're in
no position to gainsay him). Wine is also a strong
point, with a choice of 130 or so. The kitchen
places an emphasis on British fare such as hot
smoked pheasant, and steak and ale pie. Prices are
not especially low, but quality is good. The place
is large and generally very crowded, so you
sometimes have to wait a time to get served at the
bar. Also known as the 'Sloaney Pony', it can be
something of a hang-out for hoorays. The space
outside sometimes hosts barbecues in summer.
Babies and children admitted. Disabled: toilet.
No piped music or jukebox. Tables outdoors
(50, garden).

South

Greenwich

Greenwich Union

56 Royal Hill, SE10 8RT (8692 6258). Greenwich
rail/DLR. **Open** noon-11pm Mon-Fri; 11am-11pm
Sat; noon-10.30pm Sun. **Meals served** noon-
10pm Mon-Fri; noon-9pm Sat, Sun. **Credit** MC, V.
Ray Richardson's bright artwork of the footballer
looking heavenward is as iconic a Greenwich
landmark as the beers at this Meantime Brewery
flagship. Alistair Hook, who learned his age-old
trade in Munich, has made a wonderful success of
this bar since it opened in 2001. The house draught
beers are proudly named in block capitals over the
small rectangle of bar counter: Pilsener, Kölsch,
Wheat, Union, Raspberry and Indian Pale Ale
(£2.70-£3.80), each with its own fresh, tangy
flavour. But it's not just that – there's a relaxed,
enjoyable, unsnobby atmosphere throughout.
Richardson aside, decor is kept to a few framed
copies of the *Picture Post* in the comfortable back
area. There are foreign bottled beers too (Westmalle
Trippel and US microbrews such as Sierra
Nevada), wines and well-conceived dishes, either
mains (sea bass and tuna seafood velouté) or tapas
(golden chicken breast skewer). Even the coffee is
well sourced.
Babies and children admitted (until 9pm).
No-smoking tables. Tables outdoors (12, garden).

South East

Deptford

Dog & Bell

116 Prince Street, SE8 3JD (8692 5664/
www.thedogandbell.com). New Cross tube/rail/
Deptford rail. **Open** noon-11pm Mon-Sat;
noon-10.30pm Sun. **Lunch served** noon-3pm
Mon-Fri; 2-4pm Sun. **Dinner served** 6-9pm
Mon-Fri. **Credit** AmEx, MC, V.
Now decorated with some unusual art in stone
tablets in the busy side room, the landmark Dog &
Bell – sat in a dark passage between Deptford and
Greenwich – is still best known for its eclectic
beers and cheap prices. Frequently changing guest
beers come from Larkin, Pitfield and Dark Star
breweries; there's also Fuller's ESB and London
Pride. Running round the walls an unusual
collection of plates decorated with caricatures of
famous chefs keeps watch over proceedings, but
don't worry: no nouvelle cuisine here. Honest, well-
turned-out pub grub keeps honest, well-turned-out
regulars happy. There are authentic retro touches
(the political map of India, the bar billiards table),
but, this being Deptford, nobody pays much
attention. There's drinking to be done.
Bar available for hire. Disabled: toilet.
Entertainment: quiz 9pm Sun. Tables outdoors
(4, garden).

London Bridge & Borough

Royal Oak

44 Tabard Street, SE1 4JU (7357 7173).
Borough tube. **Open** 11am-11pm Mon-Fri;
6-11pm Sat; noon-6pm Sun. **Lunch served** noon-
3pm Mon-Fri; noon-5pm Sun **Dinner served**
5-9.30pm Mon-Fri; 6-9.30pm Sat. **Credit** MC, V.
No wonder this place is a popular location for real-
ale get-togethers. Tight and exclusive links to the
Sussex brewery Harveys guarantee imbiber-
friendly quality, as much as the welcoming service
and surroundings prompt devotion. Multiple
awards jostle for position with framed theatre
posters, old photos of moustachioed bartenders
and traditional prints on the maroon mock-flock
walls in two bijou bars, furnished with chunky
tables, green leather settees and several rocking
chairs. Space is so tight the latest accolade for
the Society for the Preservation of Beers as the
Wood's Greater London Pub of the Year 2006 has
yet to find a permanent location. Perhaps the
unpretentious and cheery atmosphere was
encapsulated in the following exchange: [Bar lady]
'D'you want ice wiv that, gel?' [Regular] 'Oh yer, I
larve all the trimmins!' Special.
Disabled: toilet. No piped music or jukebox.
Separate room for parties, seats 20. **Map 11 P9**.

East

Bethnal Green

Camel NEW

277 Globe Road, E2 0JD (8983 9888). Bethnal
Green tube. **Open** noon-11pm Mon-Sat; noon-
10.30pm Sun. **Meals served** noon-9pm daily.
Credit MC, V.
This pub has been sensitively renovated by co-
owners Matt Kenneston and Joe Hill, who have
retained its original brown-tile exterior and dark-
wood bar while updating it with retro lighting,
striking wallpaper and chairs covered with fabric
designed by Kenneston's girlfriend. Since they're
not tied to a brewery, the owners source their
drinks from a range of independent companies.
You'll find Adnams Broadside and Southwold real
ales, Bitburger and Amstel lagers, and Guinness,
as well as six rums, five whiskies, nine decent red
wines and the same number of white (all served
by the glass). Food is pie and mash, but these are
hand-made gourmet pies – such as steak and
chorizo or wild mushroom and asparagus – served
with a pile of mint, buttery mash and minty mushy
peas. Tea, coffee and cakes are also available and,
to top it all, the pub is a smoke-free zone.
Babies and children admitted. No smoking.
Tables outside (4, pavement).

Limehouse

Grapes

76 Narrow Street, E14 8BP (7987 4396).
Westferry DLR. **Open** noon-3pm, 5.30-11pm
Mon-Fri; noon-11pm Sat; noon-10.30pm Sun.
Lunch served noon-2pm Mon-Fri; noon-2.30pm
Sat; noon-3.30pm Sun. **Dinner served** 7-9pm
Mon-Sat. **Credit** AmEx, MC, V.
Were you to imagine a historic riverside pub, this
would be it: handsome etched-glass and greenery
frontage; a wood-beams interior on the small side
of cosy; model ships, a barometer, sea charts and
porcelain plates as decoration; enjoyably old-
fashioned Sunday roasts and quality beer (Marston
Pedigree, Timothy Taylor Landlord, Adnams
Bitter). There's even a pretty reliable Dickens
connection: this could very well have been the
model for the Six Jolly Fellowship Porters in *Our*
Mutual Friend. The current premises date from
1720, although signs of modern life include a
notice asking that mobile phones be switched off,
and a no-smoking area. The latter is in the riverside
half of the bar, and has an open fire. A rickety
balcony extends over the Thames, equally rickety
stairs lead up to a middling seafood restaurant, and
board games await those who forgot the papers.
Booking advisable (restaurant). No piped music
or jukebox. No-smoking tables.

North

Harringay

Salisbury Hotel

1 Grand Parade, Green Lanes, N4 1JX (8800
9617). Manor House tube then 29 bus. **Open**
5pm-midnight Mon-Wed; 5pm-1am Thur; noon-
2am Fri, Sat; noon-11.30am Sun. **Lunch served**
noon-3pm Fri, Sat; noon-6pm Sun. **Dinner**
served 6-10pm Mon-Sat. **Credit** MC, V.
If this former hotel turned pub/restaurant were
located in Notting Hill it would be nationally
famous, but its remote Green Lanes location keeps
it at local-celebrity level. The grand decor is
reminiscent of a Victorian gentlemen's club, with
chequered marble flagstones, ornate woodwork
over the enormous bar, and ceilings festooned with
evidence of a craftsman's touch. The dining room's
bar has been converted into an open-plan kitchen
serving adventurous pub fare (vanilla chicken and
an excellent burger were two highlights) and
diners can admire the leaded skylight as they tuck
in. Elsewhere punters converse by the fire or take
one of the more secluded leather booths at the back.
The excellent range of beers – two Litovels, and
several Fuller's ales on tap – is the icing on the cake.
Babies and children admitted (restaurant).
Disabled: toilet. Entertainment: jazz 8.30pm Sun
mthly; phone to check. No-smoking (restaurant);
no smoking tables (bar). Separate room for
parties, seats 75.

Holloway

Swimmer at the Grafton Arms

13 Eburne Road, N7 6AR (7281 4632).
Holloway Road tube/Finsbury Park tube/rail.
Open 5-11pm Mon; 1-11pm Tue-Fri; noon-11pm
Sat; noon-10.30pm Sun. **Lunch served** 1-3pm
Tue-Fri; noon-4pm Sat, Sun. **Dinner served**
6-9pm Mon-Sat. **Credit** MC, V.
On a residential street opposite the Odeon cinema,
this bijou pub is a real find. It's a long and narrow
space done up in creamy yellow and black,
modernised yet still retaining original features,
such as the ornate surround behind the bar and the
high-backed wooden booths. The choice of lagers
is a revelation, with unusual Czech brew Litovel in
the line-up, and there's BelleVue Kriek as well as
home-grown ESB and London Pride. A dozen
wines by the glass go with a decent but not
excessively gastro menu, cooked up in the open
kitchen. Games are popular too – ask for Scrabble
and chess from the bar – but the real passion is
reserved for the pub quiz; the winners can make
off with over £100 if there's a rollover.
Entertainment: quiz 9pm Mon. No-smoking
tables. Tables outdoors (15, garden).

DRINKING

Wine Bars

Perhaps the dreadful image of the London wine bar is changing at last – something we recognised in the 2006 Time Out Eating & Drinking Awards, with our first-ever award for London's Best Wine Bar. Three new places, **Negozio Classica**, **Vinoteca** and **Green & Blue**, have arrived in the capital in the last two years and all three are variants on the Italian enoteca concept – you can buy wines in the bar, or from a shop in the same building. The recent appearance of **Bedford & Strand**, with its short list of well-sourced bottles, is encouraging too. Such venues haven't sprung from nowhere – the way was paved by the excellent, stylish **Cellar Gascon** near Smithfield Market, bravely focusing on wine from the south-west of France. And old-timers such as **Albertine** and **Shampers** show that quality wasn't entirely lacking amid the welter of 1980s openings.

Maybe the stranglehold of the big chains on London's wine bars, with more than 100 venues owned by just four companies, is finally being broken. The best thing about wine bars in the capital has always been cost: the price of a bottle is often much lower than in a restaurant. The problem was that the food and surroundings often didn't match up. Now, a dozen decent wine bars in a city of eight million people still isn't enough – but it's an improvement.

Central

Bloomsbury

Grape Street Wine Bar

222-224A Shaftesbury Avenue, WC2H 8EB (7240 0686). Holborn or Tottenham Court Road tube. **Open** noon-11pm Mon-Fri. **Lunch served** noon-3.30pm, **dinner served** 5-10pm Mon-Fri. **Main courses** £6.95-£13.95. **House wine** £11.50 bottle, £2.95 glass. **Credit** AmEx, MC, V.

The 1980s are back! This place has the orange-pinky walls and pearl-wearing clientele that seemed just right – 20 years ago. The basement room is an odd wedge shape, with space behind the bar to escape loud parties that sometimes cram into the main area. Alternatively, you can head upstairs to a room with high ceilings and big windows. Prices have moved on since the 1980s, but they're still keen – a bottle of passable French vin de pays costs £11.50. The excellent 2004 Santorini Sigalas from Greece (£21.50) is a good step up in quality, as is a fine, minerally riesling kabinett from Schloss Johannisberger (£25) or a 2004 grüner veltliner 'Breiter Rain' from Sepp Moser in Austria (£25) – all drinkable options from unusual regions. Food isn't great, with marmalade and Cointreau ice-cream tasting as if it had sat around a bit. Nonetheless, Grape Street is a good place to take a group of friends or to throw an office party.
Babies and children admitted (restaurant). Bar available for hire. Booking advisable. Separate room for parties, seats 18. Tables outdoors (2, pavement). **Map 18 L6.**

Vats Wine Bar & Restaurant

51 Lamb's Conduit Street, WC1N 3NB (7242 8963). Holborn or Russell Square tube. **Open** noon-11pm Mon-Fri. **Lunch served** noon-2.30pm, **dinner served** 6-9.30pm Mon-Fri. **Main courses** £11.50-£17. **House wine** £13.95 bottle, £3.95 glass. **Credit** AmEx, DC, MC, V.

With its dark-panelled walls and old prints, Vats looks like a boarding house from the *Pickwick Papers*, but in typical London style it has a fashionable edge too, thanks to its young, sparky and briskly efficient staff. You'll need to get here early to beat the crowds, especially if you want to bag the comfortable thick-cushioned window seats, or the few tables outside. The bar has a core of regulars, which it maintains with reliable if not wonderfully exciting food; a plate of tasty haddock and prawn fish cakes was served with an average chardonnay and cream sauce. Pork belly arrived slightly dry, but sat upon delicious mash and buttery savoy cabbage, with a lightish white wine and stock sauce. The French-heavy wine list contains some good second-rank Bordeaux, along with bottles from the lovely South African estate of Thelema, in both white and red. A 2004 Louis Latour Macon-Lugny Les Genevrières is the best by-the-glass selection, served properly cold, though there should be more choice in the 175ml size to attract those who shun a whole bottle for lunch.
Babies and children admitted. Separate room for parties, seats 50. Tables outdoors (4, pavement). **Map 4 M5.**

City

Bar Bourse

67 Queen Street, EC4R 1EE (7248 2200/2211/ www.barbourse.co.uk). Mansion House tube. **Open** 11.30am-11pm Mon-Fri. **Lunch served** 11.30am-3pm, **dinner served** 5-10pm Mon-Fri. **Main courses** £15-£23. **House wine** £14 bottle, £5 glass. **Credit** AmEx, MC, V.

The clash of styles at this basement bar brings together 1980s jazz café (black and white photos plus mirrors) and '90s style venue (wacky zigzag gold leaf-style roof), a melange that's close in years but far apart in taste. If you can cope with this assault on the eyeballs, there's plenty for the taste buds, such as halibut with sautéed Jersey royals and fennel (£20.50) at lunchtime. This is way superior to the evening food – £9 was a high price to pay for squid with from-the-bottle chilli sauce.

Claude Michot's 2004 Pouilly-Fumé (£6.50 for 175ml glass) was also something of a let-down, lacking in fruit, but with a hint of caramel and apricots, a good sign in a sweeter drink, but not in a straightforward sauvignon blanc. At least service is friendly, and the list warms up past the £27 mark with Alois Lageder's pinot grigio from Alto Adige in Italy (£27.50) a more interesting example of that grape than many. A jackets-off, ties-loosened clientele seems to appreciate some of the bar's latter qualities, and not be bothered by the foremost, its madcap decor.
Booking advisable. Off-licence. **Map 11 P7.**

Corney & Barrow

10 Paternoster Square, EC4M 7DX (7618 9520/ www.corney-barrow.co.uk). St Paul's tube. **Open** 7.30am-11pm Mon-Fri. **Breakfast served** 7.30am-noon, **lunch served** noon-3pm, **snacks served** 3-10.30pm Mon-Fri. **Main courses** £7.95-£14.95. **House wine** £13.95 bottle, £3.95 glass. **Credit** AmEx, DC, MC, V.

Prince Charles played a role in the redevelopment of this square next to St Paul's and, while it didn't please many at the time, he's partly to thank for creating an area that bustles with people. Corney & Barrow is happy too, with rows of outside tables at its new branch filled with men and women down from an important meeting. HRH would approve of a dish of Hampshire white pork, well flavoured, and with mash and a sauce of stock and meat juices, although ours came with far too much sloppy apple sauce. It was bravely paired on the menu with a 2003 Eagle Vale's merlot from Western Australia (£5.95 for 175ml), a strange-looking combination, but one that worked; sometimes weedy, the grape is made here in a ballsy, fruit-filled fashion, and was able to stand up to the food. A flavourful, if oily piece of salmon lay on a pile of roasted beetroot, spring onions and fennel, with shrimps scattered around. This is an excellent place for the summer; with a less heavy hand in the kitchen it would be almost perfect.
Booking advisable lunch. Disabled: toilet. No-smoking tables. Off-licence. Separate rooms for parties, seating 14 and 40. Tables outdoors (22, terrace). **Map 11 O6.**
For branches see index.

El Vino

47 Fleet Street, EC4Y 1BJ (7353 6786/ www.elvino.co.uk). Chancery Lane or Temple tube/Blackfriars tube/rail. **Open** 8.30am-9pm Mon; 8.30am-11pm Tue-Fri. **Breakfast served** 8am-11.30am, **meals served** noon-9pm Mon-Fri. **Main courses** £8.75-£12.95. **House wine** £14.40 bottle, £3.60 glass. **Credit** AmEx, MC, V.

Much is made at El Vino of its inclusion in Rumpole of the Bailey, a fictitious account of court life centred on the Inns of Court. Amazingly, the types you might find in that collection of novels sometimes turn up in this original branch of the wine bar, by London's law district. It must be the Oxbridge common-room look – dark wood-panelled walls and high-backed leather chairs – that brings in men with tall quiffs, handkerchiefs and clipped accents talking loudly about plea bids. Surprisingly, Sky Sports burbles away in the background too, but it's a small screen, and you can escape to the back room to sample the reasonable wine list. This includes good bottles from the excellent Viu Manent winery in Chile. Kiwi winemaker Grant Phelps has a parcel of old malbec vines in the Colchagua region, which in 2005 produced refined, juicy, plummy flavours (£15.75 a bottle). The food is not nearly as appetising; a steak sandwich featured a dull baguette surrounding bland button mushrooms and onions, plus stringy skirt steak.
Booking advisable. No-smoking tables. Separate room for parties, seats 50. Tables outdoors (4, courtyard). **Map 11 N6.**
For branches see index.

La Grande Marque

47 Ludgate Hill, EC4M 7JU (7329 6709/ www.lagrandemarque.com). St Paul's tube/ Blackfriars tube/rail. **Open/snacks served**

11.30am-11pm Mon-Fri. **Snacks** £3-£6.50.
House wine £14.50 bottle, £4.25 glass.
Credit AmEx, DC, MC, V.
Walking into Grand Marque makes you feel that you've just missed out on a very good party. Groups of insurance brokers and bankers congregate in the back area, where ice buckets and empty bottles of Champagne rest atop small tables. Like any wedding buffet the food is quickly gone – even at lunch you can only order sandwiches (such as our tasty honey-roast ham with mustard). As for the wine, there's not much choice by the glass, but a 2004 Southbank riesling from New Zealand could be safely drunk at midday, with only 10.5% abv; thankfully there are still some winemakers who aren't obsessed with high alcohol content. The property dates back to 1871 and is one of many banks converted into a bar in the past ten years. The interior is suitably lavish; intricate plasterwork covers the ceiling over the central bar. Nevertheless, this is a place for lunchtime refuelling, rather than for a long after-work session.
No-smoking tables. Off-licence. Separate room for parties, seats 25. **Map 11 O6.**

Jamies

107-112 Leadenhall Street, EC3A 4AA (7626 7226/www.jamiesbars.co.uk). Bank tube/DLR.
Bar **Open/snacks served** 11am-11pm Mon-Fri.
Snacks £2-£6.
Restaurant **Meals served** noon-4pm Mon-Fri.
Main courses £11-£18.
Both **House wine** £15.50 bottle, £4.75 glass.
Credit AmEx, MC, V.
By far the best food in the Jamies chain is served in the restaurant upstairs at this City bar. Talented chef Matt Potts makes adventurous, well-executed dishes, with tasting menus involving game and top-quality meat: marinated venison, roasted vegetables, braised red cabbage and chocolate

BEST WINE BARS

Bottled out?
Sample the fine by-the-glass selections at **Albertine** (see p334), **Cellar Gascon** (see right) and **Vinoteca** (see right).

First growth
Children are welcome at **Green & Blue** (see p335), **Vinoteca** (see right) and **Wine Wharf** (see p335).

Case history
Bars with a decent wholesale business or shop attached include **Green & Blue** (see p335), **Negozio Classica** (see p334) and **Vinoteca** (see right).

Brave New World
For wines from Australia, South Africa and the Americas, head to **Cork & Bottle** (see p332), **Corney & Barrow** (see p330), **Green & Blue** (see p335) and **Wine Wharf** (see p335).

Vintage chart
For top names from classic years, visit **Corney & Barrow** (see p330), **Vivat Bacchus** (see right) and **Wine Wharf** (see p335).

Well aged
Fashion stands still at **Ebury Wine Bar** (see p333), **El Vino** (see p330), **Gordon's** (see p333) and **Skinkers** (see p335).

Vinous value
For wine bars with sensible mark-ups, try **Albertine** (see p334), **Shampers** (see p333), **Vinoteca** (see right) and **Wine Wharf** (see p335).

sauce, for instance. Curvaceous windows offer fine views past the Lloyds building. Downstairs it's rather different. The ground-floor bar has a choice of sandwiches and platters, including an oriental version that was dry, flavourless and dominated by a pile of huge prawn crackers – at £7.50 it seemed a complete waste of money. The wine list has quality amid the branded names, such as the Winemaker's syrah viognier blend reserve from Babich in New Zealand (£24.50 a bottle) offering not wholly ripe tannins, but a delicious, scented peach and plum aroma. A bar for those few City workers that still eat well in the middle of the day.
Babies and children welcome (restaurant): high chair. Booking advisable. No-smoking tables. Separate room for parties, seats 32. **Map 12 R6.**
For branches see index.

Clerkenwell & Farringdon

Bleeding Heart Tavern

Bleeding Heart Yard, off Greville Street, EC1N 8SJ (7242 8238/www.bleedingheart.co.uk). Farringdon tube/rail.
Tavern **Open** 7.30am-11pm Mon-Fri. **Lunch served** noon-3pm, **snacks served** 3-6pm, **dinner served** 6-10.30pm Mon-Fri. **Main courses** £7.95-£12.95. **House red** £11.75 bottle, £2.95 glass. **House white** £14.45 bottle, £3.60 glass.
Bistro **Lunch served** noon-3pm, **dinner served** 6-10.30pm Mon-Fri. **Main courses** £7.45-£14.95. **House red** £13.50 bottle, £3.10 glass. **House white** £14.25 bottle, £3.65 glass.
Restaurant **Lunch served** noon-2.30pm, **dinner served** 6-10.30pm Mon-Fri. **Main courses** £11.95-£21.50. **House red** £19.95 bottle, £4.95 glass. **House white** £16.45 bottle, £4.15 glass.
All **Credit** AmEx, DC, MC, V.
With an owner who has shares in a New Zealand winery, and a sister restaurant in the City that specialises in port, this small bar with exposed brickwork has a good choice of drink. More than 450 wines are stocked, but you'll need to request the full list to see them. The mind that devised the shorter list seems willing, with Santa Rita's cool-climate Casablanca a good choice of Chilean chardonnay (£18.25). But the wallet tends to dominate, with a few too many big brand wines. The Tavern has switched to well-sourced British food rather than the classical French of its other sibling, the neighbouring Bleeding Heart restaurant. Fine-tasting dishes include spit-roast, ale-fed suckling pig, served with black pudding and apple stuffing. Go when the bar quietens down, after the hordes of lawyers have left for home, to try wines from the Bleeding Heart's part-owned wine estate Trinity Hill, particularly the sauvignon blanc (£4.50 125ml).
Booking advisable. Dress: smart; no shorts, jeans or trainers (restaurant). Separate rooms for parties, seating 30-40. Tables outdoors (22, terrace). **Map 11 N5.**

★ Cellar Gascon

2006 RUNNER-UP BEST WINE BAR
59 West Smithfield, EC1A 9DS (7600 7561/ 7796 0600). Barbican tube/Farringdon tube/rail.
Open noon-midnight Mon-Fri. **Tapas served** noon-11.30pm Mon-Fri. **Tapas** £3.50-£6.
House wine £15 bottle, £4.50 glass. **Credit** AmEx, MC, V.
Like its elder sibling Club Gascon, Cellar Gascon has a louche, clubby feel: all leather banquettes and polished wood with polished steel touches. At the back, a map of south-west France sets the scene. The wine here – and the food, for that matter – is proudly and patriotically south-west in feel (Club Gascon chef Pascal Aussignac is from the region, and wines here are sourced from Caves de Pyrene, which specialises in the area). Black-clad waiting staff are largely Francophone and most seem well versed in the styles and flavours of the wines served. The selection of about 120 wines is one that you won't find elsewhere. For each familiar region such as Languedoc-Roussillon or Bergerac, there's a Côtes du Marmandais or Gaillac waiting to be discovered. Our Irouléguy Xuri d'Ansa (£7 a glass) was creamy yet fresh, complex and compelling; a

more pedestrian rosé from Bergerac was just the thing for a warm evening. Food-wise, look out for imaginative, well-executed tapas-sized dishes such as tourte gasconne (a gorgeously soft-textured terrine-like 'pie' with wild mushrooms), or barley 'risotto' with tiny clams, dusted with hot paprika.
Bar available for hire. Tables outdoors (3, pavement). **Map 11 O5.**

★ Vinoteca NEW

2006 WINNER BEST WINE BAR
7 St John Street, EC1M 4AA (7253 8786/ www.vinoteca.co.uk). Farringdon tube/rail.
Open 11am-11pm Mon-Sat. **Lunch served** noon-2.45pm Mon-Fri. **Dinner served** 6.30-10pm Mon-Sat. **Main courses** £7.50-£12.50.
House wine £11.80 bottle, £2.95 glass.
Credit MC, V.
Vinoteca has 'wine lover' written all over it. Just one look at the list and you can tell it has been put together by folk who certainly know their La Chapelle from their Chapel Down. The venture was set up in autumn 2005 by a group of young, enthusiastic refugees from the wine and catering trades. In going from the frying pan to the fire, they've created one of London's hottest wine bars. The 200-bin list champions the lesser-known and largely underrated wine regions of Spain (Txacoli, Calatayud, Cigales and Toro), France (Savoy, Gascony and Jura, plus sensible selections from Burgundy and Bordeaux) and Italy (Campania, Alto Adige, plus well-chosen bottles from Tuscany and Piedmont). Mark-ups are commendably low. By-the-glass selections (about £2.95-£8) might include a supple, lightly herbaceous Lagrein from northern Italy or a peppery, intense Estecillo Garnacha from Spain's Calatayud. The menu is an enticing read, with modish combinations such as a Spanish-influenced sauté of squid, chorizo, peppers and white beans, or a meaty 'six-bird terrine' that tasted anything but foul. If you fall in love with any of the bottles, take them home, as Vinoteca has a licence for off-trade sales too.
Babies and children admitted. Bookings not accepted for dinner. No smoking. Off-licence. Tables outdoors (4, pavement). **Map 11 O5.**

★ Vivat Bacchus NEW

2006 RUNNER-UP BEST WINE BAR
47 Farringdon Street, EC4A 4LL (7353 2648/ www.vivatbacchus.co.uk). Chancery Lane tube/ Farringdon tube/rail.
Bar **Open/snacks served** noon-10.30pm Mon-Fri. **Snacks** £6-£9.
Restaurant **Lunch served** noon-2.30pm, **dinner served** 6.30-9.30pm Mon-Fri. **Main courses** £13.50-£18. **Set meal** £15.50 2 courses, £17.50 3 courses.
Both **House red** £19.95 bottle, £6.90 glass. **House white** £15.50 bottle, £4.90 glass.
Credit AmEx, DC, MC, V.
Vivat Bacchus restaurant, long known as a place that takes its wine seriously, has extended its premises to house this light, spacious new wine bar. The firm originated in Johannesburg, so there's a fine selection of South African wines from producers such as Martin Meinert (maker of possibly South Africa's best merlot, available here by the glass for £6.70) and Paul Cluver, but you'll find plenty more; the full list runs to 250 bins. The by-the-glass selection is relatively small, but if you show a keen interest, the manager might take you on a guided tour of one of the five wine cellars and let you choose your bottle. The food's much more than an afterthought, with 'daily dishes' such as citrus chicken and set lunches for about a tenner. Our cheeseboard was impressive – ripe, smelly, and piquant in all the right places. The new premises also incorporate tasting and teaching rooms; on our visit an introductory class on wine appreciation was in full swing. A wine club meets here on Monday evenings and there's also occasional tutored tastings and wine dinners with wine producers. This is one of the most ambitious wine operations in the capital.
Babies and children admitted. Bar available for hire. Booking advisable. Disabled: toilet. No-smoking tables. Off-licence. Wine Club (7pm Mon; £15). **Map 11 N5.**

DRINKING

Covent Garden

★ Bedford & Strand `NEW`

1A Bedford Street, WC2E 9HD (7836 3033).
Covent Garden tube/Charing Cross tube/rail.
Open noon-midnight Mon-Sat. **Lunch served**
noon-3pm, **dinner served** 6.30-11pm Mon-Sat.
Main courses £7.95-£14.95. **Set meal** £10.95
2 courses, £12.95 3 courses. House wine £12
bottle, £3 glass. **Credit** AmEx, MC, V.
Though it opened in summer 2006, Bedford &
Strand looks as if it has been around for ages with
its French bentwood chairs, cream walls and long
zinc bar. Much of this basement room is devoted
to the bistro side of the operation with a French-
oriented menu of popular classics, from steak
tartare through niçoise salad to lemon tart. All the
dishes we tried were more than competent, but it's
the wine list that shines. The list is brief, but
carefully chosen, with good producers and some
unexpected bottles. There's a pinot gris from
Stoneleigh Vineyard in New Zealand, which is
stylistically midway between the Alsace and
Italian versions of this grape: fermented fully dry
(unlike most Alsatian pinot gris), yet with plenty
of character (unlike much Italian pinot grigio),
with the aroma and flavour of a freshly cut juicy
pear. Or there's an Argentinian viognier from Altas
Cumbres, which has a very New World style – rich,
concentrated, high in alcohol and peachy. There
are under 50 wines currently available, with fewer
than ten sold by the glass, but the wines are all to
be savoured and enjoyed. Service is jolly and
chipper, as you might expect when the people who
own the wine bar also work there.
Babies and children admitted. Booking advisable.
No-smoking tables. **Map 18 L7.**

Café des Amis

11-14 Hanover Place, WC2E 9JP (7379 3444/
www.cafedesamis.co.uk). Covent Garden tube.
Bar **Open** 11.30am-1am Mon-Sat.
Restaurant **Meals served** 11.30am-11.30pm
Mon-Sat. **Main courses** £11.50-£20.50. **Set**
meal (11.30am-7pm, 10-11.30pm Mon-Sat) £14.50
2 courses, £16.50 3 courses.

Both **House wine** £15.75 bottle, £4.05 glass.
Credit AmEx, DC, MC, V.
Head into a small alleyway, down some stone steps
and through a glass door – hidden-away Café des
Amis is free of the hordes in white T-shirts in
nearby Covent Garden Piazza. Groups of smart
women perch around small tables and bottles of
chilled white, while chaps in open-necked shirts
chat volubly atop tall stools. It could be the circle
bar at the nearby Royal Opera House, especially
as there are pictures of ballet dancers in various
painful-looking poses covering the walls,
illuminated by spotlights shining down from the
low ceiling. The wine list contributes to a Gallic
theme, dominated by French fare such as Domaine
Botti's 2005 Macon-Villages (£5.85 a glass, £22.50
a bottle), a good value Burgundy with pleasant
lime, peach and mineral hints. The barman
commendably poured a small amount to try, a rare
thing indeed in London, before we accepted a
whole glass. Food also has a cross-Channel flavour
with a tasty plate of moules marinières (£7.50
small, £12.50 large). This place has style, and is
very popular with opera and ballet buffs. There's
also a brasserie on the ground floor.
Babies and children admitted. Booking advisable
Thur-Sat. No-smoking. Separate room for
parties, seats 80. Tables outdoors (12, terrace).
Map 18 L6.

King's Cross

Smithy's `NEW`

15-17 Leeke Street, WC1X 9HY (7278 5949/
www.smithyslondon.com). King's Cross tube/rail.
Open noon-11pm Mon-Wed; noon-midnight
Thur; noon-1am Fri; 11am-1am Sat; 11am-6pm
Sun. **Lunch served** noon-3pm, **dinner served**
6-10.30pm Mon-Fri. **Meals served** 11am-5pm
Sat; 11am-6pm Sun. **Main courses** £7.75-£13.50.
House wine £11.50 bottle, £2.90 glass. **Credit**
AmEx, MC, V.
Smithy's has been under new ownership since
May 2006, but remains a soft-furnishings-free
zone. With its metal pillars and cobbled floor, this
former blacksmith's yard looks more akin to the
chill-out room at a nightclub than a wine bar.

However, after 5pm the place is full of designers
and men with computer bags, many trying out the
food under new head chef Memo Boukerma. A
lamb shank cooked for eight hours in veal stock,
rather than doused in red wine, was light and
delicate as opposed to dark and rich. It came with
buttery mash and large pieces of smoked
pancetta, and matched well with a clove-scented,
redcurrant-flavoured Rioja, from Bodegas Urbina
(£16 a bottle). Not over-oaked as some Riojas can
be, this youthful crianza (that is, a wine that's aged
for around one year in a barrel rather than the two
or three of reservas), is just one example of how
the excellent wine list beats the dire choice of
beers (Budvar on tap being the best option).
Smithy's is a fine, hidden venue: somewhere to lose
yourself for a night.
Babies and children admitted. Booking advisable.
Entertainment: jazz 1pm Sun. Separate rooms
for parties, seating 60 and 120. **Map 4 M3.**

Leicester Square

Cork & Bottle

44-46 Cranbourn Street, WC2H 7AN (7734
7807/www.donhewitson.com). Leicester Square
tube. **Meals served** 11am-11.30pm Mon-Sat;
noon-10pm Sun. **Main courses** £11-£13.50.
House wine £14.95 bottle, £3.75 glass. **Credit**
AmEx, DC, MC, V.
This basement bar is easy to spot, thanks to its
flashing red lights and red velvet advertising
Mumm Champagne. Downstairs there's a
blackboard full of wine offers and 1920s posters.
It's all a bit 1970s, with caked-on painted decor and
a buffet selection that needs a makeover. The
cheese and ham pie is 'legendary' according to the
menu, but ours was more like a kebab in pastry
plus cheese. Staff run around serving such
delights to businessmen, women from the shires
and Americans tipped off that this is the place to
go in central London after the theatre. That would
be true if the Cork & Bottle were judged on its
wine list alone. South Africa's Hamilton Russell,
Joseph Phelps from California and Jim Barry in
Australia are some of the wonderful producers

listed at length. Hamilton Russell's 2004 chardonnay (£35) is particularly worth drinking. But don't be tempted to eat as well.
Booking advisable. Disabled: toilet. No-smoking tables. **Map 18 K7.**

Soho

Shampers
4 Kingly Street, W1B 5PE (7437 1692/ www.shampers.net). Oxford Circus or Piccadilly Circus tube. **Open** 11am-11pm Mon-Sat *(Aug closed Sat).* **Meals served** noon-11pm Mon-Sat. **Main courses** £8.75-£15. **House wine** £11.75 bottle, £3.50 glass. **Credit** AmEx, DC, MC, V.
Amid all the shiny sports-shoe shops around Carnaby Street, this bar comes as a welcome relief. The 1980s-style shopping centre behind it has taken some of the character from the area, but the development hasn't impinged on Shampers' more basic charms. Exposed ducts and dark green walls provide the backdrop for a quiet drink by the bar. The wine list is excellent, with keen prices to boot. A bottle of 1998 Les Terrasses from the highly rated Priorat region in Spain (£28), or the over-performing Bordeaux Cru Bourgeois, Château Potensac (£30), stand out. The by-the-glass list of 27 is commendably extensive, although more wines like Bordeaux's 1998 Haut-Beauséjour ought to be included. The expectation here is that you'll have food with your wine, as most of the bar is taken up by dining tables. Low lighting and candles create a bistro feel to the place. We enjoyed a well-flavoured if slightly oily salmon, plus crunchy purple-sprouting broccoli. With nearby bars serving ropey beer at £4 a bottle, Shampers beats local competition at a canter.
Babies and children admitted. Bar available for hire. Separate room for parties, seats 45. Tables outdoors (3, courtyard). **Map 17 J6.**

South Kensington

The Oratory
234 Brompton Road, SW3 2BB (7584 3493/ www.brinkleys.com). South Kensington tube. **Bar Open** noon-11pm daily.

Restaurant **Meals served** noon-11pm Mon-Sat; noon-10.30pm Sun. **Main courses** £7-£16.
Both **House wine** £7.50 bottle, £3 glass. **Credit** AmEx, MC, V.
Few bars get it as right as the Oratory, a delightful place for a drink where the chef turns out restaurant-standard food. Far enough from Harrods to miss the tourist hordes, it is close to expensive Georgian villas that provide a pleasant backdrop amid rustling trees. Take a pavement table to get a better view, and you'll be joined by groups of Americans in Ralph Lauren shirts and braying local art dealers. The interior is a more challenging sight, just the right side of camp with gold paint swirls on blue walls around fish-eye mirrors and multicoloured chandeliers. Despite being part of the Brinkleys group, which owns five other venues, the Oratory has its own identity. Staff are well trained, bringing plates of beautifully char-grilled lamb, plus fast-fried spinach and long-cooked puy lentils promptly and without fuss. The wine list has some quality morsels too, such as Masi's sweet-sour 2004 Valpolicella (£7.50 for a half bottle). While the clientele may not be to everyone's taste, everything else about this bar comes highly recommended.
Babies and children admitted (restaurant). Booking advisable. No smoking. Tables outdoors (6, pavement). **Map 14 E10.**
For branches see index.

Strand

Gordon's
47 Villiers Street, WC2N 6NE (7930 1408/ www.gordonswinebar.com). Embankment tube/Charing Cross tube/rail. **Open** 11am-11pm Mon-Sat; noon-10pm Sun. **Meals served** noon-10pm Mon-Sat; noon-9pm Sun. **Main courses** £7.25-£9.75. **House wine** £11.95 bottle, £3.40 glass. **Credit** AmEx, MC, V.
Some things, like Frankie Howerd, are so old-fashioned that they become trendy again, and that's the case with Gordon's, one of London's oldest wine bars. It has gained a cult appeal among youngsters in Paul Smith tops, where once it was the haunt of pinstriped port drinkers. This is

despite sycophantic newspaper articles on the Royal Family taking pride of place, and a large picture of Lord Kitchener urging support for the war effort. Bar staff struggle to keep up with the demand from drinkers outside by Embankment Gardens, or inside at tables among low, dark arches. The wine list is no better than average. It has a spread that covers the globe, but fails to contain the best examples – New Zealand's 2005 Tuatara Bay sauvignon blanc (£20.35) apart. You'd be far better opting for a port, sherry or madeira, such as the brick-red, savoury 10-Year-Old Tawny from Messias. This went well with two big chunks of cheese plus salad from the buffet menu. Don't expect a classic, old-fashioned wine bar experience: rather an all-too-familiar, very busy London one.
Bookings not accepted dinner. Tables outdoors (20, terrace). **Map 18 L7.**

Victoria

Ebury Wine Bar & Restaurant
139 Ebury Street, SW1W 9QU (7730 5447/ www.eburywinebars.co.uk). Sloane Square tube/Victoria tube/rail.
Bar **Open** 11am-11pm Mon-Sat; 6-10.30pm Sun.
Restaurant **Lunch served** noon-2.45pm Mon-Sat. **Dinner served** 6-10.15pm Mon-Sat; 6-9.45pm Sun. **Main courses** £10-£19.50. **Set meal** (noon-2.45pm, 6-7.30pm) £14.50 2 courses, £17.50 3 courses.
Both **House wine** £12.70 bottle, £3.35 glass. **Credit** AmEx, MC, V.
Glance and you could mistake this bar for a members' club, with its dark panelled walls and deferential staff. Intricately painted scenes of temples and ivy-clad pillars look old-fashioned rather than exotic, but lend the Ebury a jauntiness that's absent from wine bar chains. The promptly served European food puts many glass-and-zinc temples to shame – though the array of dishes hasn't changed much of late. Rabbit terrine came with spikily dressed salad leaves that cut through the darkish flesh. Pork was stuffed with apricot and sat alongside bacon mash. But on another occasion we found roasted beetroot and pine nut

Vinoteca. See p331.

risotto violently coloured and oversalted. The list of drinks indicates a buyer who knows where to look in better-known wine producing countries. Sicily's Planeta chardonnay 2003 (£30.20) is a ripe, sunny expression of the grape with some delicate minerality. In the far southern Chilean region of Bio Bio, a pinot noir from Agustinos showed freshness rather than jamminess, as is sometimes the case with warmer climate examples of this grape. It's filled with sociable business types (men sporting slicked-back hair, women in thick jackets). *Babies and children admitted. Booking advisable. No-smoking tables.* **Map 15 H10.**

Tiles

36 Buckingham Palace Road, SW1W 0RE (7834 7761/www.tilesrestaurant.co.uk). Victoria tube/rail.
Bar **Open** noon-11pm Mon-Fri.
Restaurant **Lunch served** noon-2.30pm, **dinner served** 5.30-10pm Mon-Fri. **Main courses** £8.75-£13.50.
Both **House wine** £12.95 bottle, £3.75 glass.
Credit AmEx, MC, V.
It may look more like an old-fashioned tea room than a wine bar, but the paucity of choice around Victoria makes Tiles seem heaven-sent. The name comes from the attractive stone flooring, which you can view from tables spread out in the narrow main room, or even via the pavement outside. Strangely, most people seem to opt for the basement bar, with its IKEA-like tall paper lamps, cork colours and average food. Fish cakes were rusky and lacking in flavour, though they came with decent chips and a tasty salad. Casa do Lago Trincadeira from Portugal is the pick of the wines-by-the-glass, with creamy oak and blackcurrant fruit, though our sample seemed to have lost its acidic edge. The petit syrah grape has made inroads in California, and further down the road in Mexico it exhibits strong spice and nutmeg flavours in a 2002 example from LA Cetto (£5.95). Don't come here expecting the best, but the said you could do a great deal worse.
Babies and children admitted. Booking advisable. Separate room for parties, seats 50. Tables outdoors (5, pavement). **Map 15 H10.**

West
Holland Park

Julie's

135 Portland Road, W11 4LW (7229 8331/ www.juliesrestaurant.com). Holland Park tube.
Bar **Open** 9am-11pm Mon-Sat; 9am-10pm Sun. **Lunch served** noon-3pm Mon-Sat; 12.30-3pm Sun. **Afternoon tea served** 3-7pm daily. **Dinner served** 7-11pm Mon-Sat; 7-10pm Sun.
Restaurant **Lunch served** 12.30-3pm Sun. **Dinner served** 7-11.30pm Mon-Sat.
Both **Main courses** £10-£17. **House wine** £17 bottle, £4 glass. **Credit** AmEx, JCB, MC, V.
A Gothic-Moroccan melange of a toffs' bar, Julie's is a Holland Park institution. Locals have been coming back for more since the 1970s. The wooden partitions, carved into intricate patterns, provide useful screens for watching the local crowd: a cross-section of ladies who lunch, wealthy Americans, and well-dressed older gents. Bearing in mind the market the bar is aiming at, it's best to hit the wine list at around the £25 mark, trying out Morton's very serviceable 2004 pinot noir (£25) or Brocard's lovely, minerally Chablis from the Montmains vineyard (£35). There are 11 wines by the glass, including Mitchells cabernet sauvignon from the Clare Valley (ripe blackcurrant fruit and spice). Surprisingly, ales from the Sam Smith brewery are also available, by the bottle. In summer the ample pavement space is filled with tables, ideal for tucking into the likes of grilled swordfish with turmeric, pickled vegetables and sesame lime mayonnaise. Unusual y, you can book a table outside too.
Babies and children welcome; children's set meal Sun; crèche (1-4pm Sun); high chairs. Booking advisable. Separate rooms for parties, seating 12, 16, 24, 35 and 45. Tables outdoors (10, pavement). **Map 19 B5.**

Shepherd's Bush

Albertine

1 Wood Lane, W12 7DP (8743 9593/ www.gonumber.com/albertine). Shepherd's Bush tube. **Open** 10am-11pm Mon-Thur; 10am-midnight Fri; 6.30pm-midnight Sat. **Meals served** noon-10.30pm Mon-Fri; 6.30-10.30pm Sat. **Main courses** £5.90-£8.50. **House wine** £11.20 bottle, £2.90 glass. **Credit** MC, V.
It looks like a gastropub, but the wooden tables and blackboards shouldn't blind you to the fact that there's outstanding drinking to be had here. A waiter helpfully moved the list (it was about to be set on fire by a stray candle), allowing us to take in a shocking sight: the fantastic Cullen Ellen Bussell from Western Australia, 2003, by-the-glass at £4.85 (£18.90 a bottle). A blend of cabernet sauvignon and merlot from one of the world's outstanding wineries, this bottle oozed fruit and finesse. The fact that the wine had kept so much of its fruit is evidence that Albertine is looking after its bottles properly too. Another truly outstanding winemaker from further east in Australia, Jeffrey Grosset, is listed via his 1999 riesling from Polish Hill (£30). The food is less impressive, party buffet fare. Small sausages were lost in a swath of gravy, plus mash; and a french onion tart surrounded by green leaves was merely average. Come here to drink some outstanding wines at a great price, but treat the food as fuel for the endeavour.
Bookings not accepted evenings. Off-licence. Separate room for parties, seats 25. **Map 20 B2.**

Westbourne Grove

Negozio Classica NEW

283 Westbourne Grove, W11 2QA (7034 0005/ www.negozioclassica.co.uk). Ladbroke Grove or Notting Hill Gate tube. **Open** 11am-11pm Mon-Thur, Sun; 11am-midnight Fri; 9am-midnight Sat. **Meals served** noon-10.30pm Mon-Thur, Sun; noon-11.30pm Fri, Sat. **Snacks** £2.50-£12. **House wine** £5.99 bottle, £3 glass. **Corkage** £4.50. **Credit** AmEx, MC, V.
This Italian bar and wine shop looks like yet another small, boutique store in this photogenic part of west London, but it's actually part of a large company with outlets across the world, and arrived in London in 2004. Rows of bottles are the main attraction covering one wall, but thankfully without mass-produced factory brands from the Veneto and the south of Italy. You can take wine away, but a few seats and tables allow you to enjoy a glass of decent northern Italian fare such as Agriano's delightful, grippy Brunello di Montalcino (£7.25 for a 125ml glass) and a light, delicate pinot noir prosecco from Coisel (£3.25 for a 125ml glass). If you want to drink a whole bottle, there's a flat rate corkage (£4.50) on the shelf prices. A dish of thick cut parma ham came with slices of mozzarella and mushy fig and was pricey at £12.95, but sweet and delicious, while courgettes were thin cut and tasty, with rather too many parmesan chunks (£6.50). Over-keenness with this aged cheese aside, it's a great place for a long afternoon's drinking and snacking.
Babies and children admitted. Bookings not accepted. No smoking. Off-licence. Tables outdoors (2, pavement). Takeaway service. **Map 7 A6.**

South West
Earlsfield

Willie Gunn

422 Garratt Lane, SW18 4HW (8946 7773/ www.williegunn.co.uk). Earlsfield rail/bus 44, 77, 270. **Open** 11am-11pm Mon-Sat; 11am-10.30pm Sun. **Meals served** 11am-10.30pm Mon-Sat; 11am-10pm Sun. **Main courses** £9.50-£15. **Set lunch** £6.50 1 course. **House wine** £12.50 bottle, £3.25 glass. **Credit** AmEx, MC, V.
The front room of this Earlsfield wine bar is a bare boards, loud muzak, sports on the telly kind of place with a heavy pall of cigarette smoke. The dining room through the back is where to head if you're eating (though you may still have the inane

canned music to contend with). Whichever side you're in, you'll be treated to a good range of wine styles, regions and grapes, though the list itself is hard to decipher – producer, grape variety and country are mixed and muddled. For some bottles ('Avant Garde Merlot', for instance) you are left guessing both the country and producer. Still, the prices are agreeably low, with quite a few decent bottles at under £15 (no mean feat), and plenty under £20; the wines by the glass tend to be cheaper, less interesting choices. The globally inspired menu ranges from pan-fried lemon sole (cooked too long at too low a temperature, we suspect, but otherwise OK), through thai green curry to weiner schnitzel. The best dish was globe artichoke hearts with a stuffing of provençal vegetables. A warning: we were still humming *Hot Stuff* the following day.
Babies and children welcome (until 6pm): high chairs. Booking advisable dinner. Tables outdoors (3, pavement).

Parsons Green

Amuse Bouche NEW

51 Parsons Green Lane, SW6 4JA (7371 8517/ www.abcb.co.uk). Parsons Green tube. **Open** noon-11pm Mon, Sun; noon-midnight Tue-Thur; noon-12.30am Fri, Sat. **Lunch served** noon-3.30pm Sat. **Dinner served** 6-11pm Tue-Sat; 6-10.30pm Mon, Sun. **Main courses** £4-£8.25. **House wine** £15 bottle, £5.50 glass. **Credit** AmEx, DC, MC, V.
A hop and skip from Parsons Green tube, Amuse Bouche is a new Champagne bar that sticks to a simple formula: Champagne, lots of it, at low mark-ups. It draws a well-dressed, attractive crowd of thirtysomethings. Noisy groups cluster around the taller tables, while couples have intense conversations on the lower, black leather seats. You'll find all the usual brands, but owner Charles Adams (formerly at wine merchants Lea & Sandeman) offers some less well-known names too. A lovely non-vintage rosé from Ayala (£7 a glass, £35 a bottle) had fresh strawberry flavours with sharp, mouth-cleansing acid; Lacombe Brut NV (£4.50, £20) was limey and delicious. There could be more from smaller growers, but with a choice of 26 Champagnes by the bottle, eight by the glass, and ten Champagne cocktails, you'd be a mug asking for bottled lager (though the bar does stock some). The cocktails are hit and miss; a watery Mojito was constructed with whole ice cubes instead of crushed, and seemingly just one mint leaf, though the Champagne cocktails are much better. Bar food comprises a long list of canapés based on miniaturised classics such as shots of soup, fish and chips and a trio of mini-burgers.
Babies and children admitted. Booking advisable. Off-licence. Separate room for parties, seats 40. Tables outdoors (6, courtyard).

Putney

Putney Station

94-98 Upper Richmond Road, SW15 2SP (8780 0242/www.brinkleys.com). East Putney tube.
Bar **Open** 11am-11pm Mon-Sat; 11am-10.30pm Sun.
Restaurant **Meals served** noon-11pm Mon-Sat; noon-10.30pm Sun. **Main courses** (lunch) £4.50-£12.50; (dinner) £7-£15.50.
Both **House wine** £7.50 bottle, £3 glass.
Credit MC, V.
A departure for the Brinkley's chain, which runs more traditional-looking venues in Chelsea and Knightsbridge, Putney Station is half Shoreditch warehouse, half *The Office*. Venetian blinds are drawn over stark metal-framed windows, with the odd pot plant providing the decoration. Drinkers rattle around the minimalist interior: a crowd of suits at lunchtime, and gaggles of local girls in the evening. To eat, we sampled nicely char-grilled strips of calf's liver upon gluey mash, with a sauce made from delicious meat juices and stock lightened up by the use of white wine and finished off by fried sage leaves. Next, toffee cake was tasty (even though it seemed rather quickly reheated) and came with vanilla-flecked ice-cream. The wines are virtually the same in all Brinkley's

outlets – decent enough, with a good global spread to the list, but without anything truly exciting. Esk Valley's 2005 sauvignon blanc from Hawkes Bay in New Zealand (£4.50 for a 250ml glass) is a big, tropical version of the grape, but is one of only seven by-the-glass options: a rare example of where this bar is missing its market.
Babies and children welcome: high chairs. Disabled: toilet. No-smoking tables. Separate room for parties, seats 40. Tables outdoors (3, pavement).

South

Waterloo

Archduke
Concert Hall Approach, SE1 8XU (7928 9370/ www.thearchduke.co.uk). Waterloo tube/rail.
Bar **Open** 8.30am-11pm Mon-Fri; 11am-11pm Sat. **Meals served** 11am-11pm Mon-Sat. **Main courses** £4-£9.
Restaurant **Lunch served** noon-2.15pm Mon-Fri. **Dinner served** 5.30-11pm Mon-Sat. **Main courses** £10-£16. **Set meal** (lunch, 5.30-7.30pm) £14 2 courses, £17.25 3 courses incl coffee.
Both **House wine** £12.25 bottle, £3.10 glass. **Credit** AmEx, DC, MC, V.
Converted railway arches were all the rage back in the 1980s – and this bar was laid out by an enthusiast. Every corner of the curved space has floors, corners and different levels, bricked-in on one side, and with panes of glass on the other and lots of live greenery. This has left the top-floor restaurant with a cosy atmosphere, but no great views; it looks out towards the commuter walkway to Waterloo rather than the nearby London Eye. People are drawn up here by the set meals, but these don't always deliver. Caesar salad had too few pieces of lettuce, as if thrown on to the plate from the said Eye, and the sauce was creamy and mayonnaise-like. Duck leg was slightly dry, but came with well-flavoured, rich puy lentils. Wines are great value, including the competent efforts of the A Mano winery in southern Italy (2003 Primitivo de Puglia, £21.50) and Picpoul de Pinet from Languedoc (2004 Château de Beranger, £17). Considering the location, the food should be better.
Babies and children admitted. Booking advisable dinner. Entertainment: jazz 8.30pm Tue-Sat. No smoking (restaurant). Tables outdoors (4, garden; 10, terrace).
Map 10 M9.

South East

East Dulwich

★ Green & Blue
2006 RUNNER-UP BEST WINE BAR
38 Lordship Lane, SE22 8HJ (8693 9250/ www.greenandbluewines.com). East Dulwich rail/37, 40, 176, 185 bus. **Open/tapas served** 5-11pm Tue-Fri; 11am-11pm Sat; noon-8pm Sun. **Tapas** £6-£6.50. **House wine** £11.50 bottle, £3.20 glass. **Credit** MC, V.
Part wine shop, part wine bar, Green & Blue has more than one way to please local oenophiles. Proprietor Kate Thal is a champion of small-scale, high-quality wineries. Many of those on the list are family-run and many are organic or biodynamic operations. The list is broad-ranging, with fine pickings from all around the world, from Lugana in Italy to Swartland in Thal's native South Africa. These are hand-selected wines, a far cry from the sort of bottles found in supermarkets. You can buy a wine to take home or you can drink it on the premises for a modest mark-up. In the room at the back (which doubles as a tasting room) you'll find some cracking wines by the glass, such as a fresh summery rosé from Pic-St-Loup in France and a crisp, vibrant Frankland Estate Rocky Gully riesling from Australia. For food, there's a selection of cold platters, meats and cheeses (our 'superior' pork pie was quite so). G&B also runs regular tasting evenings.
Babies and children welcome (until 7pm). No smoking. Off-licence. Takeaway service.
Map 23 C4.

London Bridge & Borough

Balls Brothers
Hay's Galleria, Tooley Street, SE1 2HD (7407 4301/www.ballsbrothers.co.uk). London Bridge tube/rail.
Bar **Open** *June-Sept* 11am-11pm Mon-Fri; 11am-6pm Sat, Sun. *Oct-May* 11am-11pm Mon-Fri.
Restaurant **Meals served** noon-3pm Mon-Fri. **Lunch served** noon-3pm, **dinner served** 5.30-9pm Mon-Fri. **Main courses** £4.50-£12.50. **Main courses** £8.95-£16.
Both **House wine** £14 bottle, £3.50 glass. **Credit** AmEx, DC, MC, V.
One of the company's newer wine bars, this branch is located in a 19th-century former wharf building. Inside, exposed brick walls are lit by spot shades. It's a middle-aged man's idea of a trendy bar, but at least the crowd is younger than in some Balls Brothers – many are in their early thirties talking against a background of loudish dance music. A separate restaurant area, with black leather-backed seats and cubist-style paintings, attracts fewer folk. Monkfish with spinach and potato rösti had decent texture, but not much flavour. It came in a much-reduced red wine sauce, which meant the sweet, oaky fruit of the 2000 Môreson Magia (from the Coastal Region in South Africa; £25 a bottle) worked better than a white Burgundy recommended by the staff. Dining in an outside area is described as alfresco, but as you're beneath the huge, arching roof of the Hay's Galleria shopping area, that's not strictly correct. Only a hint of the Thames can be discerned, on one side of the tall building. Service is as prompt and attentive as advertised.
Booking advisable. Dress: smart casual. No-smoking tables. Tables outdoors (20, pavement).
Map 12 Q8.
For branches see index.

Skinkers
42 Tooley Street, SE1 2SZ (7407 9189/ www.davy.co.uk). London Bridge tube/rail.
Bar **Open** 10am-11pm Mon-Fri. **Snacks served** 10am-10pm Mon-Fri. **Snacks** £4.50-£10.
Restaurant **Meals served** 10am-10pm Mon-Fri. **Main courses** £8.95-£22.95.
Both **House wine** £13.95 bottle, £3.75 glass. **Credit** AmEx, DC, MC, V.
Next to the Hammer House of Horrors that is the London Dungeon, this branch of the Davy's chain makes a stab at getting in on the scary act. Butchers' hooks hang over the bar next to blackened chains. But perhaps the most terrifying sight is the wall of suits gathered by the door as you walk in. Break through them, and you're into quieter territory: two rooms at the back where eating is more the norm. As a concession to the Pitcher & Piano-isation of the pub world, a stray sofa lingers in the hallway. This same process has coloured the food too, as parmesan and lemon-flavoured oil have been added to the asparagus. Far better to opt for the more traditional, excellently cooked char-grilled ribeye steak (served with potatoes and salad), though ours didn't arrive rare as requested. The 2004 Domaine des Billards, Saint-Amour, Loron made a good match: a posh Beaujolais with some blackcurrant flavours that were brought out by the food. Glass in hand, Skinkers is far better than it first looks.
Babies and children admitted (lunch). Booking advisable. No-smoking tables. Separate rooms for parties, seating 50 and 70. **Map 12 Q8.**
For branches (Davy's) see index.

★ Wine Wharf
2006 RUNNER-UP BEST WINE BAR
Stoney Street, Borough Market, SE1 9AD (7940 8335/www.winewharf.com). London Bridge tube/rail. **Open** 11.30am-11pm Mon-Sat. **Meals served** noon-10pm Mon-Sat. **Main courses** £4.50-£9. **House wine** £14 bottle, £3 glass. **Credit** AmEx, DC, MC, V.
Located just a Champagne cork's pop from the Vinopolis wine museum and across the road from Borough Market, Wine Wharf's position in London's throbbing new gastro-heart could hardly be better. The decor is 1990s-style loft chic: bare

Interview
KATE THAL

Who are you?
Owner of **Green & Blue** shop and wine bar (*see left*) in East Dulwich, and wine buyer for RTL hotels and **Cru** restaurant (*see p236*) in Hoxton.
Drinking in London: what's good about it?
The places that get it spot-on: quality of drinks, service and ambience, in a range of styles from intimate spaces for a quiet chat to livelier places for a big night out. And they're not as self-conscious as they tend to be in New York or Paris. The London crowd is a relaxed, very eclectic mix, which in the right environment makes for a fantastic night (or day) out.
What's bad about it?
The relative scarcity of places that get it spot-on, and the absolutely appalling service in so many places. I'm turning into a grumpy old trout about it, but too many staff deliberately avoid your eye, have absolutely no sense of urgency and know little and care less about what they're serving.
Which are your favourite London restaurants?
J Sheekey (*see p83*), **Randall & Aubin** (*see p47*), **Galvin Bistrot de Luxe** (*see p93*), **Sea Cow** (*see p308*) on Lordship Lane, **The Wolseley** café (*see p300*), **Maison Touaregue** (22-23 Greek Street, W1D 4DZ, 7439 1063).
What single thing would most improve London's wine lists?
Less ridiculous mark-ups, more thought and effort put into the choice, and better trained staff who are capable of properly selling it.
Any hot tips for the coming year?
I don't have any specific tips, only an enduring dream – for more places that let you bring your own wine and serve good, fresh, simple food for realistic prices. I'd like more restaurants like the **Ambassador** (*see p221*): relaxed and completely unpretentious, serving delicious, rustic food at great prices.

DRINKING

brick, stainless steel and pale wood, with the odd wine barrique here and there to drive home the wine theme. The wine list is superb, with more than 100 wines by the glass, and plenty for under £5 (for 125ml). On our visit a glass of Austrian grüner veltliner from Dr Unger (£5.75) was in top shape – crisp, delicate and mineral ly – but a glass of Nasiakas white from Greece wasn't as fresh as it should have been. The broad ranging list is balanced between the Old and New Worlds and manages to wave a flag for lesser-known regions and producers (try a glass of Saperavi from Georgia if you get bored of Aussie shiraz). The food is less impressive; dishes such as welsh rarebit and veggie enchiladas seem to be designed mainly for soaking up alcohol. For beer lovers, Beer Wharf is next door; Mod Euro restaurant Cantina Vinopolis is in the same complex.
Babies and children welcome (before 8pm): high chairs. Booking advisable. Disabled toilet.

Entertainment: jazz 7.30pm Mon. Off-licence. Venue available for hire. **Map 11 P8.**

North West
West Hampstead

No.77 Wine Bar
77 Mill Lane, NW6 1NB (7435 7787). West Hampstead tube/rail. **Open** 6-11pm Mon; noon-11pm Tue; noon-midnight Wed-Sat; noon-10.30pm Sun. **Meals served** 6-10.30pm Mon; noon-10.30pm Tue-Sat; noon-10pm Sun. **Main courses** £8.75-£9.95. **House wine** £12.10 bottle, £2.90 glass. **Credit** MC, V.
In what estate agents would describe as West Hampstead borders, this bar on the road to Cricklewood is a cut above local drinking holes, with big double doors opening out on to pavement tables, and a wood-panelled interior with large tables for eating. No.77 opened in the 1980s heyday for wine bars. You can date it by a bowed olive tree taking up one section. This makes up for a lack of greenery on the plate, at least. A thick patty in the bar's classic beefburger was cooked as requested – rare with some deliciously smoked cheese on a decent bun – but arrived with just a few leaves of frisée. A moist chunk of Icelandic redfish was served with a tasty sauce of mussels, cream and white wine. To accompany it, a glass of wine made by a friend of the owner (Astley Vineyards 2005 from Severn Vale in England) exhibited a mix of apple and lime flavours. A major drawback was that the food took nearly an hour to arrive. This was particularly annoying as we were able to watch all the buses we needed to catch go past.
Babies and children admitted. Bar available for hire. Booking advisable. No-smoking tables. Tables outdoors (8, pavement). **Map 28 A1.**

The big four

There are four main wine bar chains in London, together responsible for almost 100 outlets. Each chain offers its own approach to the pleasures of the grape – but which to choose? Read on.

Balls Brothers
The heyday of this chain was during the 1980s when an Olde World Dickensian style – hunting prints, brass lamps and polished wood panelling – was rolled out. The Broadgate branch shows this off well, but recently there has been a change of approach, with light wood (in the new chain-bar image) filling new, plate-glass fronted rooms, as at the Victoria branch. Yet a wine list heavily skewed towards the classic regions prevents anyone from viewing this chain in a dramatically new light.
Outlets 18 (seven have restaurants).
Best venue Hay's Galleria has a permanent pétanque site and a terrace by the Thames. It's not quite the south of France, but good fun nonetheless.
What's to drink? Some excellent Bordeaux such as the 1995 Ducru-Beaucaillou (£39) is balanced by cursory selections from Austria, Germany, Alsace, Rhône, the Loire and California. Surely one of these regions could have been included at greater length?
Home shopping Stick to classic France; Balls Bros is excellent for those favourites in Oxbridge cellars such as 1993 Château Cissac (£16.25), or Chablis from the great Montmains vineyard, by JM Brocard 2002 (£13.50). Choice in New World wines has been improved, but still lags way behind the Old. And take the note with a pinch of salt: there's no way that 2003 Bordeaux was a 'great vintage'.

Corney & Barrow
The directors had a big flop on their hands when a new bar was tried on St Martin's Lane in the West End, so they've gone back to what they know: the City, in almost brutal, modernist style. Aimed at the City boy who likes a bit of sport but buys the odd case too, Corney & Barrow bars also attract a surprising number of women (who are presumably relieved not to have to go to a dark pub or dingy basement wine bar – the norm in this part of town). Slick and modern, these venues are an office from office for many City workers. As befits the surroundings, C&B's wine list leans more to the New World than is the case at many of its competitors.
Outlets 11.
Best venue The Exchange Square branch on the roof of Liverpool Street station has a croquet lawn for summer games, and a large outside terrace so you can laugh at your friends as they mess up the play.
What's to drink? Good, if not outstanding New World growers such as Nelson's Creek in South Africa, plus just a few from France. Olivier Leflaive dominates the finer whites section with some of his well-made Burgundy.
Home shopping In existence since 1780, the wholesale business has the better selection by far. It includes the outstanding Burgundy winemaker Anne-Claude Leflaive with her 1998 Puligny-Montrachet Les Pucelles (£690 a case). Also listed are Domaine de la Romanée-Conti and Bonneau du Martray.

Davy's
Now on the fifth generation of family owners since opening its first wine bar in 1870, this company has the motto 'Service, Service, Service'. Until very recently, however, Davy's seemed to be governed by the maxim 'Old, old and older hat'. Despite the changes in London's bars in the past 15 years, the firm had been adhering to the formula of dark wood surrounds and floors occasionally scattered with sawdust. Some bars go under the Davy's name, yet many do not. The bars – scattered all over London but particularly in the financial district – are popular with an after-work crowd. A new, glass-fronted bar on the Euston Road and another by St Paul's hint at a change of approach.
Outlets 37 (plus one shop).
Best venue Heeltap & Bumper, Cannon Street, has a clean, light interior and lots of outside seating. It also has a great view of St Paul's and serves breakfast from 8am.
What's to drink? Fine wines include the lovely Gruaud Larose, from the underrated 1997 vintage (£58), plus Cockburn's 1963 vintage port (£98). But on the main list there's too much Davy's own-label and, Josef Leitz's 2003 riesling kabinett (£19.95) aside, few thrilling examples outside France.
Home shopping Some great second labels from Bordeaux provide the best value. These are wines made by the top châteaux, but with slightly less rigorous grape selection – in other words, they're still high quality. Les Fiefs de Lagrange – from Château Lagrange – is a good example of such wines, and for £15.95 a bottle from the outstanding 2000 vintage, shouldn't be missed.

Jamies
Attempting to take over the City with soft furnishings rather than urban chic, Jamies wine bars have partly worked, thanks to a crowd aged 35-55 who are keen on the scrubbed-up approach. Rapid expansion was halted when the two entrepreneurs behind the business sold out, but the trendy King's Road style bar Apartment 195, Canyon restaurant in Richmond and Henry J Bean's are now part of the same company. Outlets vary from almost pub-like, as at Philpot Lane (dark wood with low lighting), to continental café with spotlights, in the case of the Orangery, opposite Liverpool Street station.
Outlets 18.
Best venue It's called Pavilion and looks like changing rooms for the local village cricket club. But located inside Finsbury Circus Gardens, this hideaway overlooks gardens and a bowling green. A restaurant seats 20.
What's to drink? 'We think we have rather an exciting list,' says the publicity, but in fact, more expensive Aussie shiraz apart, this selection isn't going to inflame any passions. Arranging the choice by grape rather than country doesn't help when Cycles Gladiator Merlot 2004 from California and Château du Plantier Bordeaux Rouge 2002 taste very different. Lists in West End Jamies bars are much shorter than their City counterparts.
Home shopping Not available.

Eating & Entertainment

Comedy

It's difficult to find a comedy venue that serves food and laughs of equal standard. There are, however, a few places that offer dishes of a higher quality than standard old-style pub grub. In south London, **Up the Creek** (302 Creek Road, SE10 9SW, 8858 4581, www.up-the-creek.com) is well worth a visit. Over in Maida Vale there's the **Canal Café Theatre** (first floor, The Bridge House, on the corner of Westbourne Terrace Road and Delamere Terrace, W2 6ND, 7289 6056, www.canalcafetheatre.com; map 1 C5), while Shoreditch has the **Comedy Café** (66-68 Rivington Street, EC2A 3AY, 7739 5706, www.comedycafe.co.uk; map 6 R4).

The best-known comedy club in London is probably Leicester Square's **Comedy Store** (1A Oxendon Street, W1Y 4EE, bookings Ticketmaster 0870 060 2340, www.the comedystore.co.uk; map 17 K7). Another favourite is **Jongleurs Camden Lock** (Middle Yard, Camden Lock, Chalk Farm Road, NW1 8AD, 0870 787 0707, www.jongleurs.com; map 27 C1) – which has two other London branches, in Battersea and Bow.

For up-to-date information on the capital's comedy clubs, see the Comedy section in the weekly *Time Out London* magazine.

Dining afloat

Vessels for hire include canal cruisers from the **Floating Boater** (Waterside, Little Venice, Warwick Crescent, W2 6NE, 7266 1066, www.floatingboater.co.uk; map 1 C5); the **Leven is Strijd** (West India Quay, Hertsmere Road, West India Docks, E14 6AL, 7987 4002, www.theleven.co.uk), a classic Dutch barge, for views of Canary Wharf; and the **Elizabethan** (8780 1562, www.thames luxurycharters.co.uk), which is a replica of a 19th-century Mississippi paddle steamer that cruises from Putney to beyond the Thames Barrier.

The **Sunborn Yacht Hotel ExCeL** (Royal Victoria Dock, E16 1SL, 0870 040 4100, www.sunbornhotels.com) has good food, but a conference-centre vibe, while the **RS Hispaniola** next to Hungerford Bridge (Victoria Embankment, WC2N 5DJ, 7839 3011, www.hispaniola.co.uk; map 10 L8) is a popular party venue with tapas bar, cocktail lounge and a large restaurant.

DIY

Blue Hawaii
2 Richmond Road, Kingston upon Thames, Surrey KT2 5EB (8549 6989/www.bluehawaii. co.uk). Kingston rail. **Dinner served** 6pm-1am Mon-Sat. **Meals served** noon-1am Sun. **Set meal** £8.95-£11.95 unlimited barbecue. **Set dinner** £15 2 courses; (Fri, Sun) £19.50 3 courses; (8pm-1am Sat) £21.50 3 courses. **Credit** AmEx, DC, MC, V.

Surrey's own slice of Hawaii sees flowery-garbed waiting staff carrying cocktails back and forth to a multitude of party bookings in this restaurant-cum-Hawaiian-hut. Chefs cook the ingredients you choose on the big teppanyaki grilling area at the front. While it's more a restaurant than a bar, it's not unheard of for diners to end up dancing around the tables towards the end of the evening, waving their tiki drinks in the air. Sundays are geared towards families.
Babies and children welcome: children's menu; high chairs; supervised play area (noon-5pm Sun). Booking essential weekends. Entertainment: musicians 10pm Fri, Sat, occasional weekdays.

Mongolian Barbeque
12 Maiden Lane, WC2E 7NA (7379 7722/ www.themongolianbarbeque.co.uk). Covent Garden tube. **Meals served** noon-11pm Mon-Fri, Sun; noon-11.30pm Sat. **Set meal** £7.95 1 bowl, £9.95 starter & 1 bowl, £13.95 unlimited buffet. **Credit** AmEx, JCB, MC, V.

Genghis Khan and his Mongolian warriors may have been a fearsome bunch, but after a hard day's fighting, they knocked up a mean stir-fry. This venue takes inspiration from the technique of throwing whatever ingredients that can found into metal 'shields' to create an impromptu meal. Diners pick ingredients, sauces and spices from the buffet, and chefs fry it in front of them on a metal hot plate. Recipes on the wall help to guide you on taste combinations. Popular with party groups.
Babies and children welcome: children's menu; high chairs. Booking advisable. Tables outdoors (10, patio). Map 18 L7.

Tiger Lil's
270 Upper Street, N1 2UQ (7226 1118/ www.tigerlils.com). Highbury & Islington tube/ rail/4, 19 bus. **Lunch served** noon-3pm Fri. **Dinner served** 6-11pm Mon-Fri. **Meals served** noon-midnight Sat, Sun. **Set lunch** £5.35 1 course. **Set dinner** £11.90 3 courses, £12.65 unlimited buffet. **Credit** AmEx, DC, JCB, MC, V.

It's food as entertainment at this oriental-inspired restaurant. Tables are clustered around the chefs, who cook diners' food in a large wok, sending up frequent bursts of flame. It's a family-friendly spot, with badges and mini chopsticks for children, plus a monthly changing menu of cocktails for older members of the group. The buffet selection of vegetables is good, but try not to overdo it as too many ingredients spoil the dish.
Babies and children welcome: children's menu; high chairs. Booking advisable. Disabled: toilet. Separate room for parties, seats 40. Vegan dishes. **For branch see index.**

Dogs' dinners

Walthamstow Stadium
Chingford Road, E4 8SJ (8531 4255/www.ws greyhound.co.uk). Walthamstow Central tube/rail then 97, 97A, 215, 357 bus. **Meals served** 6.30-9.30pm Tue, Thur, Sat. **Set meal** £19 3 courses. **Admission** *Popular enclosure* £1 Tue, Thur; £3 Sat. *Main enclosure* £6 Tue, Thur, Sat. Free under-15s. **Credit** MC, V.

There are dining options a-plenty at north-east London's favourite greyhound racing destination. You'll need to book three or four weeks in advance to get into the two restaurants proper: the Paddock

Grill offers à la carte dining; the Stowaway Grill does a three-course set menu for £19. If you want a cheaper option, there's also the Classic Diner, offering burgers, chicken and chips.
Booking essential. Disabled: toilet. Private boxes for parties, seating 25-200.

Wimbledon Stadium
Plough Lane, SW17 0BL (8946 8000/www.love thedogs.co.uk/wimbledon). Tooting Broadway tube/Earlsfield rail then 44, 270, 272 bus. **Meals served** 7-9.30pm Tue, Fri, Sat. **Set meal** £20-£25 3 courses (Tue, Fri, Sat), £25-£30 3 courses incl half bottle of wine and racecard. **Admission** £5.50 grandstand. **Credit** AmEx, MC, V.

Make the most of a night out at the dogs by having dinner while you're there. Star Attraction offers long rows of benches overlooking the finish line, or there's Broadway restaurant's more intimate layout, with TVs nearby so that you needn't miss any of the action. Both eateries serve a range of internationally inspired dishes.
Babies and children admitted. Booking essential. Disabled: lift; toilet. Separate rooms for parties, seating 28-120.

Jazz & soul

Dover Street
8-10 Dover Street, W1S 4LQ (7629 9813/ www.doverstreet.co.uk). Green Park or Piccadilly Circus tube. **Open** noon-3.30pm, 5.30pm-3am Mon-Thur; noon-3.30pm, 7pm-3am Fri; 7pm-3am Sat. **Lunch served** noon-2.30pm, **dinner served** 7-11.30pm Mon-Sat. **Main courses** £13.95-£21.95. **Set lunch** £7-£10 1 course, £18.95 2 courses. **Set dinner** (Mon-Wed) £24.95-£38 3 courses; (Thur-Sat) £32.50-£45 3 courses. **Music** *Bands* 9.30pm Mon; 10.30pm Tue-Sat. *DJs* until 3am Mon-Sat. **Admission** £6 after 10pm Mon; £7 after 10pm Tue; £8 after 10pm Wed; £12 after 10pm Thur; diners only until 10pm, then £15 Fri, Sat. **Credit** AmEx, DC, MC, V.

Is it a music venue or a restaurant? Well, it's both. A lounge jazz trio tootle away as waiters serve a Modern European menu created by ex L'Aventure chef Laurent Pichaureaux. Black-and-white fashion and jazz prints adorn the walls, and there are three bars, all set around the stage. After dinner, jazz bands prompt diners to take to the dancefloor.
Booking advisable. Dress: no jeans or trainers. Separate room for parties, seats 23. Map 9 J7.

Jazz After Dark
9 Greek Street, W1D 4DQ (7734 0545/ www.jazzafterdark.co.uk). Leicester Square or Tottenham Court Road tube. **Open** 2pm-2am Mon-Thur; 2pm-3am Fri, Sat. **Meals served** 2pm-midnight Mon-Sat. **Music** 9pm Mon-Thur; 10.30pm Fri, Sat. **Main courses** £5-£10. **Set menu** £10.95 3 courses. **Admission** £3 Mon-Wed; £5 Thur; £10 Fri, Sat. **Credit** AmEx, DC, JCB, MC, V.

Jazz After Dark is a jazz club of the old school. It's small, dark and smoky, and the walls are adorned with the works of artists who drink there. To add to the laid-back jazz atmosphere, some nights see impromptu sets by Amy Winehouse and Pete Doherty, who are both regulars. The cuisine is international, ranging from tapas to Tex-Mex.
Booking essential Fri, Sat. Dress: smart casual; no trainers. Restaurant available for hire. Tables outdoors (2, pavement). Map 17 K6.

Jazz Café
5-7 Parkway, NW1 7PG (7916 6060/ www.meanfiddler.com). Camden Town tube. **Open** 7pm-1am Mon-Thur; 7pm-2am Fri, Sat; 7pm-midnight Sun. **Meals served** 7.30-9.30pm daily. **Music** 8.30pm daily. **Club nights** 11pm-2am Fri, Sat. **Main courses** £16.50. **Set meal** £25 3 courses. **Admission** £15-£30. **Credit** MC, V.

The Jazz Café's line-up of soul, R&B, jazz and acoustic rock acts often attracts slightly more mature music fans. When buying your gig ticket, you can opt to book a table at the balcony restaurant overlooking the stage. Club nights start when the musicians stop, and continue on into the

Octave – the Live Music Supper Club...

Octave

....a new generation of RESTAURANT offering LIVE MUSIC and a VIBRANT BAR environment

Try a cocktail created by our resident mixologist at our stylish bar or dine at Octave's restaurant where you can choose from a modern European style menu created by our head chef Greg Blampied using only the freshest ingredients. All whilst enjoying mesmerising live music performed by some of Europe's top jazz musicians.

Octave is available for exclusive or part hire and can cater for press/product launches, media events, private dining, breakfast/lunch events and parties

Opening hours:
Mon - Wed: 5pm - 11pm
Thurs - Sat: 5pm - 2am
Sun: Closed - available for private hire

For all reservations, listings and enquiries contact:
27-29 Endell St., Covent Garden, London, WC2H 9BA
Tel: 020 7836 4616 Fax: 020 7836 2608
www.octave8.com • email: office@octave8.com

WINEWHARF

NOMINATED FOR BEST WINE BAR IN LONDON TIMEOUT AWARD 2006!

The Wines: Hand picked by wine experts, there are over 400 wines to choose from (over 100 of which is by the glass) and our wine list also starts at very affordable prices, and then ascends to our fantastic fine wine selection.

Atmosphere: Our bar is informal and relaxed, with leather sofas, soft lighting and eclectic music.

Position: Situated next to Borough Market, close to the City and South Bank, we're two minutes walk from London Bridge station, so finding us is never a problem.

Simple Sumptuous Food: food to accompany the wine, not wine to accompany fancy food – we are a wine bar after all! Food is served from Midday – 10pm.

Special Events: include regular public wine tastings and regular live music.

Wine Wharf also provides the perfect setting for your private or corporate function. We offer a range of menu options and custom made wine tastings.

But don't just take our word for it - give us a try!
For more information please go to www.winewharf.com or call us on 02079408335

For more fabulous venues at Vinopolis, please check out our sister venues below:

BREW WHARF
www.brewwharf.com 02073786601

CANTINA
www.cantinavinopolis.com 02079408333

BAR BLUE
www.barbluevinopolis.com 02079408333

early hours during weekends. Check the website for listings of who's playing when.
Booking advisable. Disabled: toilet. No-smoking tables. **Map 27 D2.**

Pizza Express Jazz Club

10 Dean Street, W1D 3RW (7439 8722/ www.pizzaexpress.com/jazz). Tottenham Court Road tube. **Meals served** noon-midnight daily. **Music** 9pm daily. **Main courses** £4.95-£8.25. **Admission** £15-£20. **Credit** AmEx, DC, MC, V.
Crowds have been loyally flocking to the basement club of this pizzeria since it opened in 1965. Acts have varied from Van Morrison to Jamie Cullen, and up-and-coming stars often make the line-up. Pizza Express standards make the eating part of the equation perfectly pleasant, and the atmosphere is always friendly. Musicians play seven nights a week; check the website for details.
Babies and children welcome: high chairs. Booking advisable. Disabled: toilet. No-smoking tables. Takeaway service. **Map 17 K6.**

Ronnie Scott's

47 Frith Street, W1D 4HT (7439 0747/ www.ronniescotts.co.uk). Leicester Square or Tottenham Court Road tube. **Open/music** 6pm-3am Mon-Thur; 6-10.30pm, 11pm-3am Fri, Sat; 6pm-midnight Sun. **Meals served** 6pm-1am Mon-Sat; 6-11pm Sun. **Main courses** £9-£29.50. **Set meal** £23 2 courses. **Admission** (non-members) £25-£45. **Membership** £165/yr. **Credit** AmEx, DC, MC, V.
Opened in 1959, Ronnie Scott's is one of the UK's oldest venues for top jazz and jazz fusion acts. A refurbishment in early 2006 included a much-needed overhaul of the menu, which now features internationally flavoured dishes ranging from Welsh lamb to sweet and sour battered lobster tail, and organic beefburgers. Check the website for details of forthcoming acts.
Booking advisable. No smoking. **Map 17 K6.**

606 Club

90 Lots Road, SW10 0QD (7352 5953/ www.606club.co.uk). Earl's Court tube. **Open** 8pm-1am Mon; 7.30pm-1am Tue, Wed; 8pm-1am Thur; 8pm-1.30am Fri, Sat; 8pm-midnight Sun. **Meals served** 7.30pm-midnight Mon-Wed; 8pm-12.30am Thur; 8pm-1am Fri, Sat; 8-11.15pm Sun. **Music** 9pm Mon, Thur, Sun; 8pm Tue-Wed; 9.30pm Fri, Sat. **Main courses** £8.95-£18.45. **Admission** (non-members) £8 Mon-Thur; £10 Fri, Sat; £9 Sun. **Membership** £95 first yr; £60 subsequent yrs. **Credit** AmEx, MC, V.
This candle-lit, Parisian-style jazz club dishes up a contemporary European menu, which changes every week. There's live music every night, and the number of musicians that hang out here after work give it some serious muso credibility. The second Sunday of every month sees 606's gospel brunch, where diners enjoy their meals to the sound of a four-piece gospel band. Note that if you're not a member, you have to dine.
Babies and children admitted. Booking advisable weekends. **Map 13 C13.**

Latin

Cuba

11-13 Kensington High Street, W8 5NP (7938 4137/www.cubalondon.co.uk). High Street Kensington tube. *Club* **Open** noon-2.30am Mon-Sat. *Restaurant & Bar* **Open** noon-2.30am Mon-Sat; 1pm-12.30am Sun. **Meals served** noon-1am Mon-Sat; 1-11.30pm Sun. **Main courses** £7.95-£14.95. **Set dinner** £23.95 3 courses. **Admission** £3 after 10pm Wed; £5 after 10pm Thur; £5 after 9.30pm, £8 after 11pm Fri, Sat. **Credit** AmEx, MC, V.
Despite feeling a little like a Cuban revolutionary hall of fame (pictures of Che and Castro adorn the walls), there's nothing communist regime about this place. The friendly waiting staff dance the Latin cuisine over to tables in time to the samba music, and the 12.30-7pm happy hour often sees the place rammed. There are also regular salsa classes, and the last Monday of each month is Mexican party night.

Babies and children admitted (noon-5pm Fri, Sat). Booking advisable weekends. Entertainment: salsa classes 7.30-9.30pm Mon-Sat, 6.30-8.30pm Sun; Latin singer 8.30pm Wed; jazz 8.30pm Sun; DJs 9.30pm daily. **Map 7 C8.**

Nueva Costa Dorada

47-55 Hanway Street, W1T 1UX (7636 7139/ www.costadoradarestaurant.co.uk). Tottenham Court Road tube. **Open/meals served** 6pm-3am Mon-Sat. **Main courses** £12.50-£16.50. **Credit** AmEx, DC, MC, V.
With its nightly flamenco shows (Tuesday through Saturday), colourful decor and a late-night licence, an evening at Costa Dorada can be a fun night out and is a popular choice for office parties. New management and a recent makeover have refreshed its look, emphasising the cocktail bar with cosy leather booths. Food remains Spanish.
Entertainment: DJ 8.30pm Fri, Sat; flamenco shows 9.30pm Tue-Sat. **Map 17 K6.**

Salsa!

96 Charing Cross Road, WC2H 0JG (7379 3277/www.barsalsa.info). Leicester Square or Tottenham Court Road tube. *Bar* **Open** 5.30pm-2am Mon-Sat; 6pm-1am Sun. *Café* **Open** 9am-5.30pm Mon-Sat. **Snacks served** noon-5.30pm Mon-Sat. **Set buffet** (noon-6pm Mon-Sat) 99p per kilo. *Restaurant* **Meals served** 5.30-11pm daily. **Main courses** £4.75-£11.50. *Bar & Restaurant* **Admission** £4 after 9pm Mon-Thur; £2 after 7pm, £4 after 8pm, £8 after 9pm, £10 after 11pm Fri, Sat; £3 after 7pm, £4 after 8pm Sun. *All* **Credit** AmEx, MC, V.
Dance classes are held in the bar most evenings, followed by bands and DJs so that you can practise your moves into the night. Free sessions are offered on Fri (6.30-8.30pm) and Sun (7-8pm) for beginners. Latin American fare and a substantial cocktail list add to the spirit of the place. During the week the Brazil café offers a buffet, charged by weight.
Booking advisable. Dress: no sportswear or trainers. Entertainment: DJs 9.30pm daily; dance classes 7pm Mon, Wed-Sun; bands 9.30pm Tue, Thur-Sat. Tables outdoors (10, pavement). Takeaway service (café). **Map 17 K6.**

Music & dancing

Camden newcomer **Green Note** (*see p283*) is a music club and vegetarian restaurant.

Pigalle Club NEW

215-217 Piccadilly, W1J 9HN (7734 8142/ www.thepigalleclub.com). Piccadilly Circus tube. **Open** 7pm-2am Mon-Wed; 7pm-3am Thur-Sat. **Dinner served** 7-11.30pm Mon-Sat. **Set meal** £29 2 courses, £35 3 courses. **Music** 8.30pm, 9.45pm, 10.45pm daily. *DJs* midnight Thur-Sat. **Admission** £10 after 10pm Mon-Thur; £15 after 10.30pm Fri, Sat. **Credit** AmEx, DC, MC, V.
Part of the Vince Power stable, this 1940s-style supper club is a great music venue, with retro-swanky furnishings, low lighting and tables with good views of the stage. It's a shame, then, that the food (competently prepared, but mean on accompaniments) is not as successful as the decor. Some aspects of the set-up are annoying (high prices for extras, nothing on the wine list under £25 a bottle, inconsistent service, for instance), but with a decent house band and headline acts such as Van Morrison featuring from time to time it's a pretty good formula.
Booking advisable. Disabled: toilet. No-smoking tables. **Map 17 K7.**

Roadhouse

35 The Piazza, WC2E 8BE (7240 6001/ www.roadhouse.co.uk). Covent Garden tube. **Open** 4.30pm-3am Mon-Sat; 3pm-1am last Sun of mth. **Meals served** 4.30pm-1.30am Mon-Sat. **Main courses** £6.50-£13.90. **Admission** £3 after 10.30pm Mon-Wed; £5 after 10pm Thur; £10 after 9pm Fri, Sat; £5 after 7pm Sun. **Credit** AmEx, MC, V.
The Roadhouse is a prime target for beery lads and riotous hen bashes, with the attractions of happy-hour cocktails, DJs and rock/pop cover bands playing party anthems. There's also an open-mic session on Mondays. You'll find comfort food such as chicken wings, steaks and nachos on the American diner menu.
Booking advisable. Dress: smart casual. Entertainment: bands/DJs 7pm Mon-Sat. **Map 18 L7.**

Lucky Voice. See p341.

DRINKING

The Spitz

109 Commercial Street, E1 6BG (7392 9032/ www.spitz.co.uk). Liverpool Street tube/rail. Bar/Bistro **Open** 10am-midnight Mon-Wed, Sun; 10am-1am Thur-Sat. **Meals served** 10am-10.30pm daily. **Main courses** £10.95-£14.95. **Set lunch** (noon-2pm Mon-Sat) £8.95 2 courses, £10.95 3 courses. **Music** 8pm Mon, Tue, Fri, Sat. *Venue* **Open** 7pm-midnight Mon-Wed, Sun; 7pm-1am Thur-Sat. **Music** 7pm daily. **Admission** varies. *Both* **Credit** MC, V.
The Spitz is a chilled bar/bistro/music venue, with a diverse programme covering all genres from jazz to electronica. The bar has a terrace overlooking Spitalfields Market, while the bistro offers an international menu with a decent vegetarian section. Dishes currently include roast salmon, flame-grilled burgers and salads. Check the website for listings, including photography exhibitions at the art gallery.
Art gallery. Babies and children welcome (bistro): high chairs. Booking advisable Fri, Sat; bookings not accepted Sun lunch. Disabled: toilet. Art gallery and venue available for hire. Tables outdoors (12, terrace). Vegetarian menu. **Map 12 R5.**

Tiroler Hut

27 Westbourne Grove, W2 4UA (7727 3981/ www.tirolerhut.co.uk). Bayswater or Queensway tube. **Open** 6.30pm-1am Tue-Sat; 6.30pm-midnight Sun. **Dinner served** 6.30pm-midnight Tue-Sat; 6.30-11pm Sun. **Main courses** £10.90-£16.90. **Set menu** (Fri, Sat) £21.50 3 courses. **Credit** AmEx, DC, MC, V.
This lively, family-run basement restaurant is a breath of fresh air in otherwise staid Bayswater. The interior is decorated like a traditional alpine ski lodge, the waiting staff are all clad in lederhosen and there's a a good selection of German and Austrian beers and wines. The performance of Tirolean music (Wednesday to Sunday), ranging from accordions to cowbells, often gets customers on their feet, singing along with the act.
Babies and children admitted. Booking essential. Entertainment: cowbell show 9pm Wed-Sun. Restaurant available for hire. Vegan dishes. **Map 7 B6.**

One-offs

Dans Le Noir NEW

30-31 Clerkenwell Green, EC1R 0DU (7253 1100/www.danslenoir.com/london). Farringdon tube/rail. **Lunch served** by appointment. **Dinner served** (fixed sittings) 7pm, 9pm Tue-Sat. **Set dinner** £27-£29 2 courses, £34-£37 3 courses. **Credit** AmEx, MC, V.
Launched in Paris in 2004, Dans Le Noir's pitch black interior has diners literally left in the dark, guessing what their surroundings – and dishes – are like. It's remarkably disconcerting. Food is Mod Euro and competently prepared (if a bit expensive), but the 'sensory culinary experience' gimmick does offer, as intended, a remarkable glimpse into what life is like if you are blind. Napkin up; you'll leave with plenty of dropped food down your front.
Booking essential. Disabled: toilet. No-smoking tables. Separate room for parties, seats 60. **Map 5 N4.**

Lucky Voice NEW

52 Poland Street, W1F 7NH (7439 3660/ www.luckyvoice.co.uk). Oxford Circus tube. **Open/meals served** 6pm-1am Mon-Thur; 3pm-1am Fri, Sat. **Main courses** £7-£19. **Credit** AmEx, MC, V.
This small, stylish karaoke bar, decorated in contemporary red and black Japanese design motifs, offers reasonably priced, if rather weak, oriental cocktails such as green tea Bellini for £6. Saké and shochu (Japanese vodka) is sold only by the bottle, making them much more expensive. The karaoke pods have no stage and are very cramped, but there's a comprehensive playlist and friendly waitress service. Oriental snacks (bento boxes, veg gyoza) are not sensational, but work well.
Bar available for hire. Entertainment: karaoke pods for hire; £5-£10 per person per hr. Over-21s only. **Map 17 J6.**

Rainforest Café

20 Shaftesbury Avenue, W1D 7EU (7434 3111/ www.therainforestcafe.co.uk). Leicester Square or Piccadilly Circus tube. **Meals served** noon-10pm Mon-Thur, Sun; noon-7.30pm Fri, Sat. **Main courses** £10.25-£16. **Credit** AmEx, DC, MC, V.
The ultimate themed restaurant, designed to thrill children with animatronic wildlife, cascading waterfalls and jungle sound effects. The menu has plenty of family-friendly fare, from 'paradise pizza', and 'Bamba's bangers' for kids to a host of amusingly named dishes for the grown-ups – 'Major Mojo Bones,' for instance.
Babies and children welcome: bottle-warmers; children's menu; crayons; high chairs; nappy-changing facilities. No smoking. Separate rooms for parties, seating 11-100. **Map 17 K7.**

Twelfth House

35 Pembridge Road, W11 3HG (7727 9620/ www.twelfth-house.co.uk). Notting Hill Gate tube. Bar **Open/snacks served** noon-11pm Mon-Fri; 10am-11pm Sat; 10am-10.30pm Sun. *Restaurant* **Meals served** noon-10pm Mon-Fri; 10am-10pm Sat, Sun. **Main courses** £9.50-£11. *Both* **Credit** MC, V.
Emulating the 18th-century tradition of discussing life and horoscopes in coffee shops, this mystical- and magical-themed café/restaurant offers 'astrological chart sessions' with owner Priscilla for £30. You can also just have your basic chart printed for £5, or select a 'tarot card of the day' for £3. The restaurant on the ground floor serves a selection of international dishes.
Babies and children admitted (restaurant). Booking advisable. Restaurant available for hire, seats 25. Tables outdoors (4, garden). **Map 7 A7.**

Volupté NEW

9 Norwich Street, EC4A 1EJ (7831 1622/ www.volupte-lounge.com). Chancery Lane tube. **Open** 11.30am-1am Tue-Thur; 11.30-2am Fri; 7.30pm-3am Sat. **Lunch served** noon-3pm Tue-Fri. **Dinner served** 6-10pm Tue-Fri; 7.30-10.30pm Sat. **Main courses** £8-£12. **Set menu** £24 2 courses, £30 3 courses. **Tapas** £10-£18. **Credit** MC, V.
London's latest neo-burlesque bar is dedicated to feather-fan dancing and the erotic removal of an elbow-length glove. Visit on Wednesdays and Fridays; it's less impressive on no-show nights. Decently priced retro cocktails are served in the upstairs bar, warming up a louche crowd before the glittery show in the fabulous Moulin Rouge-style stage room downstairs.
Booking advisable. Dress: smart casual. Entertainment: cabaret 8pm Tue-Sat. No-smoking tables. Restaurant available for hire. Vegan dishes. **Map 11 N5.**

Opera

Mamma Amalfi's

45 The Mall, W5 3TJ (8840 5888). Ealing Broadway tube/rail. **Meals served** 9.30am-11pm Mon-Sat; 9.30am-10.30pm Sun. **Main courses** £4.95-£12.95. **Credit** AmEx, MC, V.
Along with a traditional Italian menu, this family-friendly trattoria dishes up free jazz shows on Thursdays, and opera on Sundays. The menu includes thin-crust pizzas from a wood-fired oven, pastas and salads. The Croydon branch (Bella Italia) offers operatic recitals on Friday evenings.
Babies and children welcome: children's menu; high chairs. Entertainment: jazz 8pm Thur; opera 8pm Sun. No-smoking tables. Tables outdoors (8, pavement). Takeaway service. **For branches (Bella Italia, Mamma Amalfi's) see index.**

Sarastro

126 Drury Lane, WC2B 5QG (7836 0101/ www.sarastro-restaurant.com). Covent Garden or Holborn tube. **Meals served** noon-11.30pm daily. **Main courses** £8.50-£17.50. **Set lunch** (noon-6.30pm Mon-Fri) £12.50 2 courses. **Set meal** £23.50 3 courses incl coffee. **Credit** AmEx, DC, MC, V.
Individually styled opera boxes line the sides of this flamboyantly designed restaurant; velvet

drapes, statues and other colourful frippery provide a theatrical backdrop for the opera-based entertainment (performed by singers from the nearby opera houses). The food is Mediterranean/Turkish fare. Sister establishment Papageno is similarly showy.
Babies and children welcome: high chairs. Booking advisable. Disabled: toilet. Entertainment: opera, string quartet 1.30pm, 8.30pm Sun; 8.30pm Mon. No-smoking tables. **Map 18 M6. For branch (Papageno) see index.**

Sports bars

All Star Lanes NEW

Victoria House, Bloomsbury Place, WC1B 4DA (7025 2676/www.allstarlanes.co.uk). Holborn tube. **Open/meals served** 5-11.30pm Mon-Wed; 5pm-midnight Thur; noon-2am Fri, Sat; noon-11pm Sun. **Main courses** £9-£30. **Bowling** (per person per game) £7.50 before 5pm Mon-Fri; £8.50 after 5pm Mon-Fri; £7.50 all day Sat, Sun. **Credit** MC, V.
Styling itself on Stateside 'boutique' bowling alleys – darker, with modishly decorated bars and dining areas – All Star Lanes offers an adult alternative to retail park bowling clubs filled with children's parties. There are four bowling lanes (plus two private lanes upstairs) and sleek diner-style booths at which to enjoy (pricey) burgers and steaks and the spectacle of players bowling gutterballs. Cocktails cost £6.60-£7.90.
Babies and children admitted (until 6pm). Booking advisable. Disabled: toilet. Separate room for parties, holds 75. **Map 10 L5.**

Bloomsbury Bowling Lanes NEW

Basement, Tavistock Hotel, Bedford Way, WC1H 9EU (7691 2610/www.bloomsbury bowling.com). Russell Square tube. **Open/meals served** noon-2am Mon-Wed; noon-3am Thur-Sat; noon-midnight Sun. **Main courses** £6.75-£9.95. **Bowling** before 4pm £3-£5.50 per person per game; after 4pm hourly rates from £36/hr 1 lane. **Credit** MC, V.
With twice as many lanes and hire costs almost half the price of All Star Lanes, bowling here is a less flashy affair. The low-key decor and worn booths in the restaurant (burgers £6.75) seem to offer a more authentic representation of Americana. There are also two karaoke rooms (seating 12 and 20) plus a film-screening room (seating 40) for hire.
Booking advisable; essential weekends. Disabled: toilet. No under-18s after 4pm. **Map 4 K4.**

Elbow Room

89-91 Chapel Market, N1 9EX (7278 3244/ www.theelbowroom.co.uk). Angel tube. **Open** 5pm-2am Mon; noon-2am Tue-Thur; noon-3am Fri, Sat; noon-midnight Sun. **Meals served** 5-11pm Mon; noon-11pm Tue-Sun. **Main courses** £5-£8. **Pool table hire** £6-£9 per hour. **Admission** £5-£6 after 8pm Thur; £2 9-10pm, £5 after 10pm Fri, Sat. **Credit** MC, V.
This popular, retro-chic bar has ten pool tables on which to rack up some frames. Evenings and weekends are lively; there can be a long wait for your turn on a table. Ping-pong, live bands and a dancefloor provide distractions for a trendy, clubby crowd. Drinks feature fluorescent cocktails and lager; bar food is of the burger variety. Club nights are posted on the website.
Disabled: toilet. Entertainment: DJs 9pm Wed-Sat; bands 9pm Thur. Separate room for parties, seats 30. **Map 5 N2. For branches see index.**

Sports Café

80 Haymarket, SW1Y 4TE (7839 8300/ www.thesportscafe.com). Piccadilly Circus tube/ Charing Cross tube/rail. **Open** 11.30am-3am Mon, Tue, Fri, Sat; 11.30am-2am Wed, Thur; 11.30am-midnight Sun. **Meals served** noon-11pm daily. **Main courses** £8.95-£13.95. **Admission** £5 after 11pm Mon, Tue, Fri, Sat. **Credit** AmEx, DC, MC, V.
Beer, bar food and TV sports are the raison d'être at this US-styled bar: more than 100 TVs screen

DRINKING

All Star Lanes. See p341.

non-stop international sporting events from football and rugby league to Formula One and tennis. During big matches or tournaments it can become uncomfortably busy and loud; escape for a game of pool (there are 12 tables) or food (buffalo wings, burgers, ribs, steaks) in the dining areas. DJs play from 10pm most nights.
Children admitted (until 6pm, dining only). Disabled: toilet. Entertainment: DJs 10pm Mon-Sat. Restaurant available for hire. Takeaway service. **Map 17 K7**.

24-hour eats

Tinseltown
44-46 St John Street, EC1M 4DT (7689 2424/ www.tinseltown.co.uk). Farringdon tube/rail. **Open** 24hrs daily. **Main courses** £3.50-£10. **Set lunch** (noon-5pm Mon-Fri) £5 2 courses incl soft drink. **Credit** AmEx, DC, MC, V.
Late-night clubbers waiting for the first tube home, cabbies and general stop-outs frequent this US-styled basement diner and milkshake bar near Smithfield Market. Booth seating, music-TV and thick peanut butter and banana shakes should help to keep you going until sunrise. The sister restaurant in Hampstead is open until 3am on Friday and Saturday nights.
Babies and children welcome: children's menu; high chair. Takeaway service. **Map 5 O5**.
For branch see index.

Vingt-Quatre
325 Fulham Road, SW10 9QL (7376 7224). South Kensington tube. **Open/meals served** 24hrs daily. **Main courses** £6.95-£11.75. **Credit** AmEx, MC, V.
No 24-hour greasy spoon, this. V-Q is licensed until midnight, and as befits its Chelsea location, smart French staff serve classy versions of late-night fare to a well-to-do crowd in search of post-clubbing sustenance. A full english starts at £6.95; the menu also features fish and chips, steak, posh pasta, club sandwiches with fries, and more adventurous options such as crayfish spring rolls. **Map 14 D12**.

Views & victuals

The Tenth
Royal Garden Hotel, 2-24 Kensington High Street, W8 4PT (7361 1910/www.royalgarden hotel.co.uk). High Street Kensington tube. **Lunch served** noon-2.30pm Mon-Fri. **Dinner served** 5.30-10.30pm Mon-Sat. **Main courses** £18.50-£36. **Credit** AmEx, DC, MC, V.
The last Saturday of the month is Manhattan Night, when the Gary Williams Orchestra evokes New York's glamorous dinner-dance scene, with 1950s big band classics. The evening costs £60 per person for a five-course dinner (better value than dining à la carte) and the views over Hyde Park from the tenth-floor windows are impressive. The Modern European menu includes dishes such as lobster cannelloni.
Babies and children welcome: high chairs. Disabled: lift; toilet. Dress: smart casual. No-smoking tables. **Map 7 B8**.

Vertigo 42
Tower 42, 25 Old Broad Street, EC2N 1HQ (7877 7842/www.vertigo42.co.uk). Bank tube/ DLR/Liverpool Street tube/rail. **Open** noon-3pm, 5-11pm Mon-Fri. **Lunch served** noon-2.15pm, **dinner served** 5-9.30pm Mon-Fri. **Main courses** £9.50-£15.50. **Set lunch** £15 3 courses. **Credit** AmEx, DC, MC, V.
Situated on the 42nd floor, this bar has a truly breathtaking panorama. Seats are arranged so everyone gets a view; no bad thing since the interior is less impressive, with the feel of an upmarket airport lounge. Gary Rhodes' restaurant, Rhodes Twenty Four, serves classic British fare some 18 floors down. Security arrangements mean that prior booking is essential for both bar and restaurant; diners must obtain a pass and walk through an X-ray machine. The last admission time – 9.45pm – is strictly followed.
Bar available for hire. Dress: smart casual. No cigars or pipes. **Map 12 Q6**.

Shops & Courses

Food Shops

This is only a small selection of some of our favourite food shops in London; for a bigger choice, get a copy of the latest Time Out *Shopping* guide, published annually.

Food halls

Four of London's department stores have fabulous food halls, stocked with a huge range of fresh and preserved foodstuffs.

Fortnum & Mason
181 Piccadilly, W1A 1ER (7734 8040/www. fortnumandmason.co.uk). Green Park or Piccadilly Circus tube. **Open** 10am-6.30pm Mon-Sat; noon-6pm Sun. **Credit** AmEx, DC, JCB, MC, V.

Harrods
87-135 Brompton Road, SW1X 7XL (7730 1234/www.harrods.com). Knightsbridge tube. **Open** 10am-8pm Mon-Sat; noon-6pm Sun. **Credit** AmEx, DC, MC, V.

Harvey Nichols
109-125 Knightsbridge, SW1X 7RJ (7235 5000/www.harveynichols.com). Knightsbridge tube. **Open** 10am-8pm Mon-Fri; 10am-7pm Sat; noon-6pm Sun. **Credit** AmEx, DC, MC, V.

Selfridges
400 Oxford Street, W1A 1AB (0870 837 7377/www.selfridges.com). Bond Street or Marble Arch tube. **Open** 9.30am-8pm Mon-Wed, Fri, Sat; 9.30am-9pm Thur; noon-6pm Sun. **Credit** AmEx, DC, MC, V.

Markets

Borough Market
Between Borough High Street, Bedale Street, Stoney Street & Winchester Walk, SE1 1TL (7407 1002/www.boroughmarket.org.uk). London Bridge tube/rail. **Open** 10am-5pm Thur; noon-6pm Fri; 9am-4pm Sat. **No credit cards.**
Borough Market has become one of London's top tourist attractions, as well as a place to buy excellent food from first-rate producers. As a result it can be stupidly busy, so try not to visit on a Saturday. There are fewer stalls on Thursday. Many stalls offer tastings, and quality is high – as are prices. There are around 100 stalls, selling everything from burgers to saffron. Among the most popular are: Brindisa (artisanal Spanish produce); Cool Chile Co (chillies and Mexican foodstuffs); Elsey & Bent (unusual vegetables); Flour Power City (breads); Ginger Pig (butcher); Northfield Farm (butcher); Silfield Farm (butcher); Wyndham House Poultry (poultry). There are also numerous stalls selling all manner of snacks and drinks, plus free tastings. Be warned there is nowhere nearby to park, so serious shopping trips need to be planned with military precision.

Farmers' markets

London now has dozens of farmers' markets, most of which appear (and change) on a weekly basis. Some are well established, others last only a few trial weeks. The best way to keep track of them is via websites. The original and best is the London Farmers' Markets website – **www.lfm.org.uk** – though there are a few markets not under the LFM banner. Also useful is Big Barn's site **www.bigbarn.co.uk/rivercottage.php**, as it shows the markets and local food producers in your area (just enter your postcode).

Bakeries & pâtisseries

& Clarke's
122 Kensington Church Street, W8 4BU (7229 2190/www.sallyclarke.com). Notting Hill Gate tube. **Open** 8am-8pm Mon-Fri; 8am-4pm Sat. **Credit** AmEx, DC, MC, V.
Sally Clarke's renowned shop sells aromatic and voluptuous breads, pastries and cakes baked without artificial colours and preservatives. Fig and fennel, and rosemary and raisin breads are the most famous, but there are also horseshoe-shaped loaves studded with apricots, cornmeal bread shaped like ears of corn, round hazelnut and raisin loaves, walnut bloomers, and parmesan bread scented with sage, rosemary and thyme. Fruit tarts, cakes, focaccias, pizzas, brioches, newly fashionable cheese straws, and sweet pastries made from unsalted Normandy butter are also available. The casual, prettily laid-out shop also stocks Neal's Yard cheeses, Monmouth House coffee, fresh fruits and vegetables, olive oils, chocolates, and own-made pickles, jams and chutneys – all enticingly packaged.

De Gustibus
53 Blandford Street, W1U 7HL (7486 6608/www.degustibus.co.uk). Baker Street tube. **Open** 7am-4pm Mon-Fri. **No credit cards.**
Set up by Dan and Annette Degustibus, this iconic company has become one of the most acclaimed artisan bakers in Britain. Old recipes are used from the US, Britain and Ireland, and across Europe. There are five changing ranges: American (wholegrain graham bread, fresh pumpkin bread, wild rice and lentil sourdough, apricot nut bread, desem); British (granville sour, millers cob, eight grain, rustique wholemeal); east European (Latvian, Ukrainian, Polish and Russian rye, potato bread with courgettes and buttermilk); continental (alpine muesli bread, parisienne, potato and yoghurt bread, boule, paysan, kaiser bread, German Sunday stuten); and Mediterranean (mozzarella and dill bread, spinach ciabatta, Tuscany bread, pane milanese, tortino, fig and rosemary). All varieties are made with natural ingredients, using long fermentation processes. **For branches see index.**

Lighthouse Bakery
64 Northcote Road, SW11 6QL (7228 4537/www.lighthousebakery.co.uk). Clapham Junction rail. **Open** 8.30am-5pm Tue-Sat. **Credit** MC, V.
This small artisan bakery specialises in American, British and continental breads, cakes and pastries – all baked daily on the premises. Every loaf is hand-moulded, after long fermentation to achieve a fuller flavour. No artificial additives or flour improvers are used, and the breads are low in salt, sugar and fat. Flour is from Shipton Mill in the Cotswolds. There are three ranges of breads: speciality (apricot and walnut crown, chocolate bread, sweet pepper bread), traditional English wheat breads (London bloomer, cottage loaf, split tin), and wholemeal and malted (country malt, honey wholewheat, wholemeal walnut). Seasonal bakes include hot cross buns and mince pies. New for 2006 are opera gateau, croquembouche, new york cheesecake and some wheat-free breads.

Old Post Office Bakery
76 Landor Road, SW9 9PH (7326 4408/www.oldpostofficebakery.co.uk). Clapham North tube. **Open** 10.30am-7pm Mon, Wed-Fri; 10.30am-5.30pm Tue; 10am-5pm Sat. **No credit cards.**
The much-loved Old Post Office Bakery has been making handmade, hand-kneaded breads for nearly two decades, and is a favourite with the capital's master bakers as well as home cooks. It specialises in organic breads that are certified by the Soil Association, and made without additives and improvers. The bakery is best known for its sourdough, but also sells other varieties such as sunflower, malted grain, and wholemeal loaves. There's a yeast-free range too. Cakes (a huge hit with the locals) are baked daily, and come in flavours like banana and walnut, carrot, chocolate, apple, and almond.

Poilâne
46 Elizabeth Street, SW1W 9PA (7808 4910/www.poilane.fr). Sloane Square tube/Victoria tube/rail. **Open** 7.30am-7.30pm Mon-Fri; 7.30am-6pm Sat. **Credit** MC, V.
Set up by Pierre Poilâne in 1932 in Paris, Poilâne is best known for its round sourdough loaves. These are widely available in delis and restaurants, and taste great with soups and in sandwiches. The bread is made using a modernised version of an ancestral recipe. Pesticide-free, stone-ground wheat and spelt flour is mixed with salt; then, after the addition of natural leavening and long fermentation, the loaves are baked in a wood-fired oven for an hour. The bakery also sells rye breads, walnut bread, currant and raisin loaves, butter cookies, and sourdough loaves decorated with seasonal, bespoke designs for special occasions.

Cheese

The Cheeseboard
26 Royal Hill, SE10 8RT (8305 0401/www.cheese-board.co.uk). Greenwich rail/DLR. **Open** 9am-5pm Mon-Wed; 9am-1pm Thur; 9am-5.30pm Fri; 8.30-4.30pm Sat. **Credit** AmEx, MC, V.
For more than two decades, this shop has been selling 100 varieties of cow's, buffalo's, goat's and ewe's milk cheeses. It specialises in farmhouse, artisan-produced varieties, many of them unpasteurised. The selection encompasses cheeses from Britain (cotherstone, smoked cumberland, lanark blue), Holland (extra-matured gouda, leiden), France (boulette d'avesnes, camembert au calvados, clacbitou), Germany (cambozola), Greece (feta in olive oil and oregano), Ireland (gubbeen, cooleeney, cashel blue), Italy (torta basilico, taleggio, pecorino nero), Norway (gjetost, jarlsberg), Spain (idiazabal, zamorano, picos blue), and Switzerland (appenzell, tête de moine). There are also, wines, chutneys, olives, Seggiano olive oils, vinegars and honeys from Tuscany, Cavalieri pasta, breads, dairy products (cream from Jersey, butter from France), and handmade sweet, savoury, and water biscuits. The shop has recently introduced three-tiered cheesecakes for weddings.

La Fromagerie
2-4 Moxon Street, W1U 4EW (7935 0341/www.lafromagerie.co.uk). Baker Street or Bond Street tube. **Open** 10.30am-7.30pm Tue-Fri; 9am-7pm Sat; 10am-6pm Sun. **Credit** AmEx, MC, V.
Patricia Michelson's iconic cheese boutique is one of the best in London, and this Marylebone branch is very attractively laid out, with a temperature-controlled cool room. Michelson travels extensively around Britain and the continent, selecting cheeses from small artisan cheesemakers. The result is unusual cheeses, such as, on our visit in July, lingot de la monastere, a thyme-scented goat's cheese from the Dalmeyrie monastry in Herault; limited-supply Devon blue from Robin Congden's dairy in Totnes; and Venetian cheeses like vezzena. The shop also sells speciality seasonal produce such as Amalfi lemons, white nectarines and Saturn peaches, along with own-made jams and chutneys. There's a lovely café (*see p298*) with a daily changing menu. Look out for special events, such as dinners centred around regional or seasonal cheeses, tutored tastings, cheese and wine pairing evenings, picnics in farms and orchards, and visits to local beehives. **For branch see index.**

Hamish Johnston

48 Northcote Road, SW11 1PA (7738 0741).
Clapham South tube/Clapham Junction rail.
Open 9am-6pm Mon-Sat. **Credit** MC, V.
There's a huge selection of goat's and sheep's milk
cheeses at this friendly cheesemonger's, sited on
one of south London's principal food streets.
Approximately 150 cheeses are stocked. Most are
British, Irish or French, but there are some Spanish
and Italian varieties too. You'll also find terrines,
preserves, olive oils and vinegars, as well as
pickles, chutneys and jams, traditionally cured
bacon, speciality foods from Gascony, eggs (from
ducks, quail and free-range hens), dried fruits, a
small selection of fish (smoked salmon, potted
shrimps) and a range of organic produce.

Neal's Yard Dairy

17 Shorts Gardens, WC2H 9UP (7240 5700).
Covent Garden tube. **Open** 11am-6.30pm Mon-
Thur; 10am-6.30pm Fri, Sat. **Credit** MC, V.
In business for over 25 years, Neal's Yard Dairy
began by making its own cheeses, but then started
buying them from small artisan cheesemakers in
Britain and Ireland. Cheeses are matured in the
cellars beneath the shop, and sold in peak
condition. Customers are given tastings, and their
feedback is actively sought. Knowledgeable staff
are on hand to advise on care and storage. There
are over 50 seasonal varieties sold at any given
time, some of the more unusual being ardrahan
(creamy, pungent Irish cow's milk cheese),
crockhamdale (sweet, sharp sheep's cheese from
Kent) and harbourne (crumbly goat's cheese from
Devon). Ingredients are clearly listed, including
whether animal or vegetable rennet was used. The
company also has a stall at Borough Market.
Related items such as breads, pickles, crackers,
fruit pastes, and olives are sold too.
For branch see index.

Paxton & Whitfield

93 Jermyn Street, SW1Y 6JE (7930 0259/
www.paxtonandwhitfield.co.uk). Green Park tube.
Open 9.30am-6pm Mon-Sat. **Credit** MC, V.
Established in 1797, Britain's oldest cheesemonger
has been a favourite of the royal family, Winston
Churchill and Sophie Grigson, among others.
Artisan cheeses are sourced from the UK, France
and Italy, and allowed to mature. The range
includes individual and cut cheeses, such as
Cornish capra, brillat savarin, epoisses de
bourgogne, celtic promise and ticklemore. Pickles,
biscuits, cakes, charcuterie, deli products, relishes,
preserves, pâtés, terrines, wines and ales are also
available, as are cheese knives, cheeseboards and
tableware. A monthly cheese club delivers cheeses
to members' homes. The friendly staff's knowledge
of their subject is second to none. Watch out for
long queues at Christmas.

Confectioners

Chocolate

L'Artisan du Chocolat

89 Lower Sloane Street, SW1W 8DA (7824
8365/www.artisanduchocolat.com). Sloane
Square tube. **Open** 10am-7pm Mon-Sat.
Credit MC, V.
Owned by Belgium-trained ex-pastry chef Gerard
Coleman, this cosy glass-fronted shop has enticing
displays of chocolate sculptures, and is a favourite
of food writers and top chefs (to whom he
supplies). Coleman makes small quantities of very
fresh chocolates (to be eaten within two weeks),
using additive-free ingredients and small amounts
of sugar. Flavours are daring and innovative, and
include green cardamom, lemon verbena, lapsang
souchong, basil and lime, sichuan pepper, banana
and thyme, lavender bud, red wine and tobacco.
The salt caramels are internationally famous.
Coleman also holds chocolate-tasting evenings.

Choccywoccydoodah

47 Harrowby Street, W1H 5EA (7724 5465/
www.choccywoccydoodah.com). Edgware Road
or Marble Arch tube. **Open** 10am-2pm, 3-6pm
Tue-Fri; 11am-6pm Sat. **Credit** MC, V.

Damas Gate. See p349.

Choccywoccydoodah specialises in extravagant bespoke and designer chocolate cakes, covered in flowers, leaves, gems, and other romantic and pretty motifs – ideal for weddings. Rich, dark chocolate cake is used as a base, layered with chocolate truffles or chunks, whole cherries, almonds, brazil nuts, vine fruits and spices, and sloshed with French brandy. The bespoke range has a wide variety of pretty and colourful designs, such as 'buxom ballerinas' and 'Belgian boudoir', while the designer range comes in five elegant choices (country rose, cherubic, kiss, lily, and orchid), and are large enough for 40 people. The house-style cakes are the cheapest (from £25), and are will serve up to ten people.

The Chocolate Society

36 Elizabeth Street, SW1W 9NZ (7259 9222/ www.chocolate.co.uk). Sloane Square tube/Victoria tube/rail. **Open** 9.30am-5.30pm Mon-Fri; 9.30am-4pm Sat. **Credit** MC, V.
This company sells mainly own-label chocolates, along with Valrhona, and a carefully chosen artisan range. Stock includes fresh handmade Yorkshire truffles, French chocolate bonbons, aromatic Eastern Promise bars (with saffron, rose oil and cardamom), Chiman's spice bars (in flavours such as cardamom and blue poppy seed, and allspice and sesame), chocolate honeycombs, nougat, sugared almonds, chocolate dragées, edible gold leaf (used in Middle Eastern and Indian cookery, and in baking) and novelty items such as chocolate pigs. At the front is a small café area with tables, where you can indulge in chocolate brownies, ice-creams and milkshakes.
For branch see index.

Montezuma's Chocolates

51 Brushfield Street, E1 6AA (7539 9208/ www.montezumas.co.uk). Liverpool Street tube/ rail. **Open** 10am-6pm daily. **Credit** MC, V.
What sets Montezuma's apart from other chocolatiers? The fact that much of its chocolate is organic, additive-free, gluten-free, fair-traded (the bars are made from organic cocoa from the Dominican Republic) and suitable for vegans. Chocolate varieties include bars (weighing up to 1kg), truffles, buttons, a drinking and cooking range, and a selection in fish and turtle shapes designed for children. Wedding 'favours' – bespoke truffles given to guests – are also made to order. It also specialises in unusual flavours, such as sweet paprika and strawberry, orange and geranium, three peppers, and even lime pickle.

Rococo

321 King's Road, SW3 5EP (7352 5857/ www.rococochocolates.com). Sloane Square tube then 11, 19, 22 bus. **Open** 10am-6.30pm Mon-Sat; noon-5pm Sun. **Credit** MC, V.
This fabulous shop sells a range of imaginative chocolates to tempt and seduce adventurous palates. How about some fruit and flower fondants, caramels, gingers, chilli and passionfruit chocolate, saffron and ginger fudge, or Islay single-malt whisky truffles? Chocolate bars are flavoured with orange and geranium, rosemary, lavender or Arabic spices. Cuban chocolate cigars, and cinnamon granduja almonds are also sold. Shelf space is found for sugar-free, dairy-free and organic ranges too.
For branch see index.

International

Ambala Sweet Centre

112-114 Drummond Street, NW1 2HN (7387 3521/www.ambalasweets.com). Euston Square tube. **Open** 9am-9pm daily. **Credit** MC, V.
This Indian confectioner was set up in 1965 by Mohammed Ali Khan, who named the shop after his birthplace in India. The business now has branches all over the UK, but this is the flagship. It's pristinely clean, with shiny glossy surfaces, and efficient, professional staff. Beautifully displayed, colourful Indian sweets – made from various flours, condensed milk, dried fruit, nuts and saffron – include barfi (in chocolate, almond and pistachio flavours), halwa made from figs and

Rococo

carrots, vermicelli-like nests of suter pheni, ras malai, jalebi and Bengali specialities such as gulab jamun and cham cham. Attractively packaged sweetmeats in boxes and jars make ideal gifts. The shop also sells pickles and savouries such as bombay mix, spiced nuts and lentils, and salty chickpea-flour vermicelli in various shapes. Ambala is always busy, but especially so at Diwali, when long queues snake out of the door.

Minamoto Kitchoan

44 Piccadilly, W1J 0DS (7437 3135/ www.kitchoan.com). Piccadilly Circus tube. **Open** 10am-7pm Mon-Fri, Sun; 10am-8pm Sat. **Credit** AmEx, MC, V.
This gorgeous shop, with charming and helpful staff, has neat displays of wagashi that look like rows of semi-precious jewellery. Wagashi are Japanese confectionery made from a combination of rice flour, aduki bean paste, nuts and seasonal fruit. They're eaten as afternoon snacks, given as gifts, and used in tea ceremonies. Varieties here include kurikissho (chestnut-bean jam wrapped in aduki bean and rice-flour pastry), saisaika (Japanese loquat marzipan), tousenka (white peach stuffed with baby green peach, covered in jelly), oribenishiki (chestnut and aduki bean paste wrapped in Japanese crêpe), kohakukanume (whole plum encased in plum wine jelly, decorated with gold powder), and honey and green tea sponge cakes. They're healthy, low in fat and rich in vitamins and minerals.

Retro sweets

Hope & Greenwood

20 North Cross Road, SE22 9EU (8613 1777/ www.hopeandgreenwood.co.uk). East Dulwich rail/12, 40, 176, 185 bus. **Open** 10am-6pm Mon-Sat; 10am-5pm Sun. **Credit** AmEx, MC, V.
In premises styled like a 1950s sweet shop, a Miss Hope and a Mr Greenwood (dressed in vintage clothes) sell old-fashioned sweeties over an old-fashioned marble-topped counter. There are 175 glass jars of retro confectionery, including cola cubes, Tunnocks tea cakes, refreshers, drum sticks, acid drops, sweet tobacco, flying saucers, cough candy, sarsaparilla tablets and sherbet lemons. You can also buy 24 varieties of liquorice (ranging from pontefract cakes to Bassetti wands), as well as handmade chocolates in rose, violet, damson and plum flavours that would no doubt thrill your granny. Hope & Greenwood arguably kicked off the current fashion for nostalgic confectionery, and there are now many imitators in London.

Lollipop

201 St John's Hill, SW11 1TH (7585 1588). Clapham Common tube then 37 bus/Clapham Junction rail then 39, 170, 337 bus. **Open** 10am-6.30pm Tue-Sun. **Credit** MC, V.
The Italian owners of La Gastronomia deli in West Dulwich recently sold up and opened a sweet shop in Clapham. They found they were selling more confectionery than any other item, and were determined not to resort to flogging sandwiches and coffee. This shop stocks 140 classic sweets from around the UK (mainly Scotland, Lancashire and Birmingham), plus a small selection from the US, including Bazooka bubble gum and Vimto lollies. Other offerings include gobstoppers, sugar mice, marshmallows and, of course, lollipops, and there's various kinds of rock from Blackpool in summer. Also available are natural sweets without artificial colours and flavours (from a firm called the Natural Candy Shop), plus a sugar-free range. Ice-cream from Sub Zero in Wales is a bestseller.

Delicatessens

East Dulwich Deli

15-17 Lordship Lane, SE22 8EW (8693 2525). East Dulwich rail. **Open** 9am-6pm Mon-Sat; 10am-4pm Sun. **Credit** MC, V.
This friendly deli specialises in handmade Italian and Spanish products, such as pastas, sauces, olives, jams, cheeses, charcuterie, beverages and fresh-roasted coffee beans. Savouries such as tarts, pies and stuffed vegetables are also available, and

there's a selection of Born & Bread loaves, including wholemeal, white, ciabatta, black olive and the delicious kentish flute.

Elizabeth King
34 New King's Road, SW6 4ST (7736 2826/ www.elizabethking.com). Parsons Green tube. **Open** 9am-8pm Mon-Sat; 9.30am-6pm Sun. **Credit** AmEx, MC, V.
Popular with local office workers, this specialist store holds a vast range of products from Italy, France and the UK. There is cheese (more than 100 varieties), Monmouth Coffee, bakery products (delivered daily), Chegworth Valley juices, free-range meat, fresh fish from Cornwall, Vallebona products from Sardinia, fresh pasta, soups, herbs and spices, chocolates, wines and liqueurs. Many items are organic, including bread, fruit and vegetables, and an own-made frozen meal range. Lengthy queues form at lunchtimes for freshly filled sandwiches, hot meals, salads and soups, cooked by the shop's on-site chef.

Flâneur Food Hall
41 Farringdon Road, EC1M 3JB (7404 4422/ www.flaneur.com). Farringdon tube/rail. **Open** 8.30am-10pm Mon-Sat; 10am-6pm Sun. **Credit** AmEx, JCB, MC, V.
Dominated by blond wood shelves stacked to the ceiling – every inch of wall space is crammed – this deli-cum-restaurant looks impressive. In the centre is a large serving area, surrounded by high stools. There are a few seats at the front by the window, and a cosy, almost hidden restaurant (*see p46*) at the back. An extensive selection of flavoured oils (in unusual varieties like pistachio and melon seed) is stocked, along with breads, Neal's Yard cheeses, jams, pickles, pasta, preserves, wines, pastries, fresh fruit and vegetables. There's also a daily changing restaurant-standard menu for eating in or to take away, which includes quiches, sausage rolls, salads and cakes.

Mr Christian's
20 Camden Passage, N1 8ED (7359 4103/ mrchristians.co.uk). Angel tube. **Open** 8am-6pm Tue, Thur, Sat; 8am-7pm Wed, Fri; 10am-6pm Sun. **Credit** MC, V.
This second branch of Mr Christian's (now part of the Jeroboams Group), located among the antique shops of Camden Passage, opened at the end of 2005. It sells a large selection of cheeses, charcuterie, pastas, fruit juices, olives, oils, ready-cooked meals, gourmet snacks, freshly baked breads, bottled sauces and own-made chutneys, mustards and jellies. A lovely café area at the back (with a communal wooden table) serves salads, cheese and meat platters, soups, pies and tarts, and brunch dishes. Everything is cooked daily on the premises in the roomy basement kitchen. As at the Notting Hill original, a popular weekend stall outside sells a seasonal, weekly changing selection of breads, pastries, cookies, fruit tarts, muffins and desserts. Expect to find Ukranian kolos bread, buttermilk loaves, and fig baguette.
For branch see index.

Mortimer & Bennett
33 Turnham Green Terrace, W4 1RG (8995 4145/www.mortimerandbennett.com). Turnham Green tube. **Open** 8.30am-6pm Mon-Fri; 8.30am-5.30pm Sat. **Credit** MC, V.
Forget the current buzz words 'local' and 'British': M&B's USP is speciality foods from around the world, sourced during travels by owners Dan Mortimer and Di Bennett. Small, artisan family producers are championed, so many products are not seen elsewhere in the UK. Newly introduced this year is rare-breed salami from Tuscan company Macalleria Falorni, made from Siena white-belted pig, perhaps, or Chianino beef. Other meaty items include duck pâté in gewürztraminer, and Spanish foie gras macerated in grape juice. The mind-boggling selection of preserves includes Austrian thayatal honey and Lebanese mulberry and wild rose jams. Oils come in fashionable flavours like argan and pumpkin seed, and balsamic vinegars may be flavoured with blackcurrants or blueberries.

Panzer's
13-19 Circus Road, NW8 6PB (7722 8596/ www.panzers.co.uk). St John's Wood tube. **Open** 8am-7pm Mon-Fri; 8am-6pm Sat; 8am-2pm Sun. **Credit** MC, V.
This family-run deli has been around for more than 50 years, and is best known for its excellent range of high-quality fruit and vegetables. If you're looking for rare wild mushrooms, little-seen fresh herbs, miniature vegetables or white truffles at Christmas, you'll find them here. Another notable aspect is the large choice of American products (home baking mixes, cookies, condiments, snacks, candy, cereals, beers and sodas). Other groceries come from France, Germany, Greece, Italy, Japan, Mexico, Morocco, Spain and South Africa. There are over 50 varieties of breads (some supplied by & Clarke's and Poilâne), plus wines, champagnes and soft drinks. A large delicatessen counter at the back sells smoked salmon, vacherin and st marcelin cheeses, charcuterie (including bresaola and biltong), caviar and freshly made salads. A kosher section offers meat, poultry, cakes, cheese, wine and foie gras. Service is friendly, but can be a little rushed.

Trinity Stores
5-6 Balham Station Road, SW12 9SG (8673 3773/www.trinitystores.co.uk). Balham tube/rail. **Open** 8am-8pm Mon-Fri; 9am-6.30pm Sat; 10am-4pm Sun. **Credit** MC, V.
This cosy, inexpensive new deli is a welcome addition to Balham's burgeoning food scene. It sells Mediterranean and British products sourced from small, regional suppliers that favour traditional methods. Glass counters display cheeses from Britain (via Neal's Yard) and Italy, alongside olives, dips, antipasti and freshly made salads. Dairy products are from Cornwall, and the organic fruit and vegetables come from Kent. Breads, chelsea buns and eccles cakes are from Breads Etc and Flour Station. Spanish salamis and hams are supplied by Brindisa; meats, olive oils, organic pastas and wines are imported from Italy. The neatly stacked shelves also hold Luscombe soft drinks, British beers and a range of preserves and condiments. A café area has a short menu of sandwiches, soups, and salads.

Truckle
349 Fulham Palace Road, SW6 6TB (7736 2727). Putney Bridge tube. **Open** 9am-7.30pm Mon-Fri; 9am-4.30pm Sat. **Credit** MC, V.
An offshoot of the popular Blue Mountain café in Dulwich, this smart, compact deli is owned by Jamaican-born Mel Nugent. Carefully selected, mostly organic and fairtrade items from small producers include Blue Mountain coffee. The main emphasis is on a changing selection of cheeses, including comte d'estive and lingot geant supplied by La Fromagerie. Meats include finocchiona salami and Alderton ham. Bread is from Born & Bread, and includes unusual varieties such as paillassou (a type of white) and pain de meteil (a mixture of rye and white). Other goods include organic Italian pasta and risotto rice, and Jamaican hot sauces. Fresh food, such as seafood and spinach pasta, is made in the café and brought over daily. Sandwiches (on weekdays) and fresh Monmouth Coffee are also available.

International
African & Caribbean

Blue Mountain Peak
2A Craven Park Road, NW10 4AB (8965 3859). Willesden Junction tube. **Open** 7am-6pm Mon, Thur; 7.15am-6pm Tue, Wed; 6.30-6pm Fri, Sat. **Credit** MC, V.
Owned by well-informed Indians, this enormous shop is well stocked with African and Caribbean foods. At the entrance is a large display of fresh fruit and veg, such as white and yellow yams, tannias (Caribbean root vegetable), sugar cane, mustard leaves, callaloo (Caribbean greens), aloe vera leaves (used as medicine), fresh pinto beans, white maize, jackfruit, breadfruit, young green coconuts and Jamaican mangoes. Pulses include East African maganjo beans, Nigerian brown beans, and white-eyed black beans. There's also maganjo and soy flour, gari (cassava flour) and fufu (vegetable starch). Small cassava bread and large Caribbean roti are kept in the chiller, and the freezer stocks fresh cassava and cornmeal doughs. Seasonings include hot and mild chilli sauces, pepper sauces, jerk seasonings, hot African yellow chilli powder, ground egusi (melon seeds), ground egobono (large white and brown beans), dried bitter leaves and many little-seen herbs. Drinks include herbal bitters and fruit syrups in flavours like cherry and guava.

British

A Gold, Traditional Foods of Britain
42 Brushfield Street, E1 6AG (7247 2487/ www.agold.co.uk). Liverpool Street tube/rail. **Open** 11am-8pm Mon-Fri; 10am-6pm Sat; 11am-6pm Sun. **Credit** AmEx, MC, V.
Resembling a village shop from a bygone era, A Gold sells traditional and speciality British foods from small UK suppliers. The baked goods look like they're straight out of Jane Grigson's kitchen: Cornish saffron cakes, Welsh cakes and currant shrewsburys. Confectionery ranges from forgotten classics such as Farrah's Harrogate toffee to Romney's Kendal mint cake – either sold loose or in attractive packaging fashioned out of, say, rationing boxes. Drinks include English mead, and

Fishy business
Decent displays of fresh fish can be found at many London **food halls** (*see p344*), and there are also several outstanding stalls at **Borough Market** (*see p344*). The **FishWorks** (*see p88*) restaurant chain has ten branches around London, all with fishmonger counters. The following shops are all reliable:

B&M Seafood *258 Kentish Town Road, NW5 2AA (7485 0346). Kentish Town tube/rail.* **Open** 8am-6pm Mon-Sat. **Credit** MC, V.
Chalmers & Gray *67 Notting Hill Gate, W11 3JS (7221 6177). Notting Hill Gate tube.* **Open** 8am-7pm Mon-Fri; 8am-6pm Sat; 8am-4pm Sun. **Credit** MC, V.
Covent Garden Fishmongers *37 Turnham Green Terrace, W4 1RG (8995 9273). Turnham Green tube.* **Open** 8am-5pm Tue, Sat; 8am-5.30pm Wed-Fri.* **Credit** MC, V.
France Fresh Fish *99 Stroud Green Road, N4 3PX (7263 9767). Finsbury Park tube/rail.* **Open** 9am-6.45pm Mon-Sat; 11am-5pm Sun. **No credit cards.**
Golborne Fisheries *75 Golborne Road, W10 5NP (8960 3100). Ladbroke Grove tube.* **Open** 8am-6pm Mon-Sat. **No credit cards.**
Moxon's *Westbury Parade, Shop E, Nightingale Lane, SW4 9DH (8675 2468). Clapham South tube.* **Open** 9am-8pm Tue-Fri; 9am-6pm Sat. **Credit** MC, V.
Sandy's *56 King Street, Twickenham, Middx TW1 3SH (8892 5788/www. sandysfish.net). Twickenham rail.* **Open** 8am-6pm Mon-Sat. **Credit** MC, V.
Steve Hatt *88-90 Essex Road, N1 8LU (7226 3963). Angel tube.* **Open** 7am-5pm Tue-Sat. **No credit cards.**
Walter Purkis & Sons *17 The Broadway, N8 8DU (8340 6281/www.purkis4fish. co.uk). Finsbury Park tube/rail then W7 bus.* **Open** 8am-5pm Tue-Sat. **Credit** AmEx, MC, V.

wines evocative of the English countryside made from elderflower and gooseberries. Other items include Cornish pilchards, teas, chutneys, cheeses and meats – including Richard Woodall's bacon, widely used in modern British restaurants.

Chinese

Wing Yip
395 Edgware Road, NW2 6LN (8450 0422/ www.wingyip.com). Cricklewood rail/16, 32, 316 bus. **Open** 9.30am-7pm Mon-Sat; 11.30am-5.30pm Sun. **Credit** MC, V.
This spacious, family-run oriental supermarket sells 2,500 items of mainly Chinese products, but also many Japanese, Malaysian, Vietnamese, Korean and Singaporean foods. You'll find well-regarded own-label sauces and curry pastes, as well as noodles, rice, herbs and spices, fresh fruit and vegetables, fresh and frozen seafood, cooking wines, soups, oils, vinegars, tofu, seaweed, dried mushrooms, kitchenware, tableware, and speciality items such as chicken feet. There's a vast choice of teas including green jasmine, Chinese oolong and Korean ginseng, alongside saké, liqueurs and beers. An enticing range of desserts and sweet snacks features sweet aduki bean pastries, sesame seed cookies, grass jelly, moon cakes, fortune cookies, sweet coconut gel and prepared fresh fruit such as durian. As we go to press, this Cricklewood branch is undergoing a massive refurbishment, scheduled to be completed by the end of 2006 – however, the shop remains open for business as usual.
For branch see index.

East European

Fortune Foods
387-389 Hendon Way, NW4 3LP (8203 9325). Hendon Central tube. **Open** 10am-10pm daily. **No credit cards.**
This new deli sells imported foods from Lithuania, Russia, Poland and Slovakia. Neat rows of shelves are lined with jams, syrups, condiments, biscuits, honeys, savoury snacks, pastas, soup mixes, beans and grains, and soft drinks. Chiller cabinets stock Polish meats and sausages, Russian smoked fish, caviar, a large range of dairy products such as ketyras (drinking yoghurt), and ready meals like shish kebabs and fresh sauerkraut. Frozen foods include Lithuanian cepelina dumplings, Polish pierogi dumplings and a variety of ice-creams. Baked goods feature Polish chleb bread, Lithuanian black rye loaf with caraway, Russian honey muffins, and sakotisx cakes. Staff speak Russian, Polish, Lithuanian and English. Jewish locals drop by for salted herrings and pickles, and the confectionery is popular with the English. There's a notable range of Germans loose tea: try the aromatic blueberry and rose petal tea with Slovakian porridge, and breakfast will never be the same again.

German

German Wurst & Delicatessen
127 Central Street, EC1V 8AF (7250 1322/ www.germandeli.co.uk). Barbican tube/Old Street tube/rail. **Open** 10am-7pm Mon-Fri; 10am-6pm Sat. **No credit cards.**
This tiny shop has gone from strength to strength, and now has a stall at Borough Market. The product range has increased, and many items now list ingredients in English alongside cooking instructions and recipes. You can buy rollmops in vinegar with gherkins and onions and spätzle dough, as well as condiments such as sweet Bavarian mustard, garlic ketchup, concentrated vinegar, and horseradish with apples. Pickles range from spiced pumpkin to barrel-fermented sauerkraut, and preserves include rosehip jam and black sour cherries in syrup. The meat selection is particularly impressive, encompassing sliced hams, sausages, frankfurters, wurst and salamis. Also available are rye breads and sourdoughs, cheeses, cereals, snacks, confectionery and

beverages. Tinned soups, stews and casseroles abound, in varieties such as curly kale with knacker sausages and potatoes.

Indian

Fruity Fresh
111-113 Ealing Road, Wembley, Middx HA0 4BP (8902 9797). Alperton tube. **Open** 9am-11pm daily. **No credit cards.**
Around half a dozen Indian greengrocers are clustered along the stretch of Ealing Road near Alperton tube. All sell sparklingly fresh fruit and vegetables, piled high on pavement tables. Prices are generally rock bottom; three large bunches of fresh fenugreek leaves can cost as little as 50p. This neat, spacious greengrocer is one of the best: fruit and veg are delivered daily, and service is excellent. You'll find parwal and tindora (striped Indian baby marrows), jelly-like palm nuts (eaten as snacks), chowra (fresh green blackeye beans), boxes of Indian and Pakistani mangoes (alphonso, rajapuri, kesar and chauso during our midsummer visit), raw green mangoes used in pickles and salads, 'frog melons' (so called because of their mottled skin), marble-bright white aubergines and fragrant pink guavas. Groceries such as beans, lentils, pickles, spices and rice are also sold.

Ganapathy Cash & Carry
34-38 Ealing Road, Wembley, Middx HA0 4TL (8795 4627). Wembley Central tube/rail. **Open** 6am-midnight Mon-Sat; 8am-midnight Sun. **Credit** MC, V.
An enticing array of fresh fruit and veg greets you at the entrance of this Sri Lankan shop. There are purple banana blossoms, large jackfruits, marble-like jackfruit seeds, little Sri Lankan shallots, club-shaped green and yellow Sri Lankan cucumbers, stripy lilac aubergines, yams, mangoes and intriguing-looking hard brown woodapples and elongated vegetable drumsticks. Inside, the good-sized venue is packed with catering-size bags of rice – in particular, different shades of Sri Lankan red rice – and a huge selection of dried and frozen fish. Spices include roasted Colombo curry powder and dried green chillies preserved in salt and buttermilk. There are also many pickles and condiments. Ready-cooked meals like curries, idiappa and kothu roti come frozen or in tins. At one side of the shop a counter sells snacks, sweets and takeaway meals like kuttu with fish curry.

VB & Sons
147 Ealing Road, Wembley, Middx HA0 4BU (8795 0387). Alperton tube. **Open** 9.30am-7pm Mon-Sat; 10.30am-5pm Sun. **Credit** MC, V.
At the centre of this popular, Gujarati-owned Indian food shop is a pickle cart that holds around a dozen freshly made pickles in buckets, sold by weight. The range includes variations on chillies, raw green mangoes, lemons and Indian berries. Elsewhere, there are unusual dried herbs and spices rarely found in London, such as cobra saffron, soapnuts, malucca nuts, mango-ginger and lotus seeds. Snacks and savouries include handmade spiced cassava popadoms from Kenya, and Indian noodles. Other items include a variety of homemade paneer, freshly sprouted beans, flour made from different types of grains, unusual oils (such as mustard and almond), frozen undhiyu (Gujarati vegetable casserole) mix, and heaps of beans, lentils, rice, breads and sweets.

Italian

Carluccio's Delicatessen
28A Neal Street, WC2H 9QT (7240 1487/ www.carluccios.com). Covent Garden tube. **Open** 8am-8pm Mon-Fri; 10am-7pm Sat; noon-6pm Sun. **Credit** AmEx, MC, V.
Priscilla and Antonio Carluccio set up this Italian deli 15 years ago. Since then, the couple have opened an ever-expanding chain of caffès (*see p171*) all over London. There's no café area at this original deli, but there is a fantastic selection of Italian sandwiches, freshly cooked hot meals such as tarts, bakes and roast meats, and breads, cakes and pastries to take away. Products are sourced

from different regions of Italy, and include rice, polenta, pastas, sauces flavoured with cuttlefish ink and wild boar, antipasti such as char-grilled artichokes and organic capers, herbs and spices, vinegars including a ten-year old balsamic, and regional olive oils sourced from small suppliers. Sweet treats include honey cantucci, fresh amaretti, and gelati in flavours such as Amalfi lemons or arabica coffee. Preserves range from fig jam and quince cotognata from Piedmont, to mostarda (preserved fruit) and agrumi (solid citrus fruit preserve) from Sicily. The deli is renowned for its delicious emerald green pesto and, in particular, sublime fresh and dried mushrooms in season.

Japanese

Japan Centre
212 Piccadilly, W1J 9HG (7255 8255/ www.japancentre.com). Piccadilly Circus tube. **Open** 10am-7pm Mon-Fri; 10.30am-8pm Sat; 11am-7pm Sun. **Credit** JCB, MC, V.
This 30-year-old venue sells books, magazines, CDs and over 1,000 Japanese food items in its shop. The centre is a focal point for London's Japanese community, and also houses a restaurant (*see p190*), bookshop, travel agency and recruitment

agency. Over 20 types of rice and rice cakes are stocked (including the highly regarded kokuhou rose rice), plus an array of soba, udon, somen, harusame and hiyamugi noodles. Soy sauces, soup bases and stocks come in many organic and reduced-salt varieties. You'll also find packets of powdered sushi vinegar among bottles of rice vinegars, cooking saké and mirin. Condiments and seasonings include shiso leaf salad dressing, ume paste, ponzu citrus-flavoured soy sauce, seaweed paste, pickle granules with yuzu, eel sauce and the excellent Bulldog vegetable and fruit tonkatsu sauce – the Japanese equivalent of brown sauce, but tastier. There's also a large range of flours, instant meals, miso, tofu, seaweed, curry and stew mixes, pancake and tempura mixes, green and barley tea, and kitchenware. Snacks include bestselling wasabi peas.

Korean

Korea Foods

Unit 5, Wyvern Industrial Estate, Beverley Way, New Malden, Surrey KT3 4PH (8949 2238/ www.koreafoods.co.uk). Raynes Park or New Malden rail. **Open** 9am-8pm daily. **Credit** MC, V.

London's largest and best-stocked Korean supermarket also sells a few Japanese, Chinese and Thai products. To one side are the fresh meat and fish counters. Here, butchers and fishmongers are on hand to offer advice, and to wrap up ready-prepared and marinated products that are ideal for quick meals after work. Meat, seafood and dumplings are also stored in the many freezers and chiller cabinets. Packs and jars of fresh kimchi (Korean pickles) abound. There are enormous bags of rice, grains and beans everywhere, plus smaller packs of noodles, tofu, confectionery, snacks and rice cakes. Homewares include cooking pans, chopsticks and bamboo mats. The vegetable section contains some fresh produce such as beansprouts, taro, kabocha pumpkins and fragrant Korean greens. The friendly staff are happy to offer tastings, especially at weekends.

Middle Eastern

Damas Gate

81-85 Uxbridge Road, W12 7NR (8743 5116). Shepherd's Bush tube. **Open** 9am-10pm daily. **Credit** MC, V.

A favourite of such foodies as Joanna Blythman and Nigella Lawson, this enormous, bustling, inexpensive Middle Eastern supermarket is central to life in Shepherd's Bush. There's a vast display of fresh vegetables, fruit and herbs outside. Inside, a butcher's counter offers halal meat, and a fast-food section sells own-made falafels, kebabs and shawarma sandwiches to take away. Long aisles are stacked with aromatic spices, flatbreads, olives, Lebanese pastries, soft drinks and wines. Blocks of feta and fresh pickles are laid out in buckets, and there's an enormous selection of high-quality nuts (don't miss the bright green sliced pistachios – handy for sprinkling on everything from pasta dishes to home-made cakes).

Maroush Deli

45-49 Edgware Road, W2 2HZ (7723 3666). Marble Arch tube. **Open** 8am-midnight daily. **Credit** AmEx, MC, V.

Lebanese entrepreneur Marouf Abouzaki owns the acclaimed Maroush chain of restaurants (*see p213*) and fast-food cafés – but this is the only delicatessen in the chain. It's a handsome place, set over two floors, and packed with fresh fruit and veg, confectionery, breads, sweet and savoury pastries, pickles, preserves, rice, dried beans, ice-creams, soft drinks, chocolates and freshly ground Lebanese coffee. A number of deli counters on both floors sell olives, cheeses, dairy products and prepared meats such as kebabs. There's also a separate wine vault that displays wines from Lebanon and the Middle East. Designated counters deal in halal meat and fish – all very high quality (this is among the best halal butchery in London). Delicious hot snacks such as pizza and falafel are also sold. Staff are friendly and eager.

Oriental

Oriental City

399 Edgware Road, NW9 0JJ (8200 0009). Colindale tube/32, 142, 204, 303 bus. **Open** 10am-9pm Mon-Fri, Sun; 10am-6pm Sat. **No credit cards**.

This spacious mall is similar to shopping centres you'd find in Tokyo. It no longer caters only for the Japanese community, although the Japanese influence is the strongest. There's Yamazaki, a well-stocked Japanese supermarket that sells fresh fish flown in daily from Japan, plus ready-cooked meals and speciality items such as kobe beef. In the crowded Food Court, a dozen shops sell very cheap Japanese, Chinese, Malaysian, Indonesian, Korean, Thai, Vietnamese and even South Indian street food. There are also two inexpensive Chinese restaurants, plus a café selling Japanese crêpes, ice-cream, cakes and tapioca 'bubble tea'. A small bakery stocks wonderfully fluffy Japanese bread, melon buns and a variety of sweet and savoury doughnuts. Other delights include a fresh fruit stall (selling durian in season), karaoke bar, video game arcade, and shops full of clothes, kitchenware, pottery, herbal medicine, furniture and gifts. Many of the shops open later, and close earlier, than the centre's official opening hours.

South African

St Marcus Fine Foods

1 Rockingham Close, SW15 5RW (8878 1898/ www.stmarcus.equology.com). Barnes rail/337 bus. **Open** 9am-6pm daily. **Credit** MC, V.

Set up more than 20 years ago, this friendly shop is the largest importer of South African foods in the UK, and supplies to a number of restaurants, pubs and delis. Meat includes a very wide selection of sausages, droewors, boerewors, biltong and sosaties. There are also tasty condiments to liven up the meat, such as flavoured salts, barbecue rubs, hot chakalaka sauces, marinades and Mrs Ball's chutneys and cooking sauces. Even crisps come in flavours such as smoked beef, and there's a selection of outdoor cooking equipment. Confectionery, such as Wilson cola-flavoured toffee and Safari fig rolls, is always popular with expats. Lagers (including iconic Castle lager), liqueurs such as Mainstay International cane spirit, ciders, brandies, wines, sours, sambuca, fruit juices, tea and coffee, and popular soft drinks such as Rose Kola Tonic are part of the extensive drinks range.

Trinity Stores. See p347.

Spanish

Brindisa
32 Exmouth Market, EC1R 4QE (7713 1666/ www.brindisa.com). Angel tube/Farringdon tube/rail/19, 38 bus. **Open** 11am-6pm Mon; 9.30am-6pm Tue-Sat. **Credit** MC, V.
This highly respected company was set up by Monika Linton and her brother Mark Lavery nearly 20 years ago. It imports foods from some of Spain's best producers, supplies to restaurants and delis, and has two shops (the other is in Borough Market) and a tapas bar (*see p258*). This shop does a brisk trade in takeaway sandwiches and salads. Wooden shelves are stacked to the ceiling with superior tinned fish, dried beans and chickpeas, chocolates, confectionery, wines, sherries, paella pans and Spanish cookery books. The deli counter sells olives, regional cheeses, sauces, dips, snacks, charcuterie, chorizo and morcilla (black pudding). Spices include smoked paprika, wood-smoked piquillo peppers, and saffron from La Mancha. There's an unrivalled selection of iberico and serrano hams, which can be carved on site (carving sets are also sold). New for 2006 is a range of charcuterie, goats' cheeses, oils, vinegars and cheeseboard extras (such as quince paste).
For branch see index.

Thai

Tawana Oriental Supermarket
18-20 Chepstow Road, W2 5BD (7221 6316). Notting Hill Gate tube. **Open** 9.30am-8pm daily. **Credit** MC, V.
In business for more than 20 years, Tawana is one of London's leading Thai supermarkets. As one of the largest importers of Thai produce, it supplies many of the capital's oriental restaurants. Fresh fruit and veg are flown in twice a week, and include young bamboo shoots, miniature aubergines, mangosteen, longan and durian, plus fragrant fresh herbs such as holy basil and lime leaves. There's an outstanding selection of regional Thai sauces, curry pastes, condiments, fish sauces and shrimp pastes. A few Chinese, Japanese and Filipino products are also sold. Also available are fresh flowers, garlands (used during festivals and in religious ceremonies), magazines, newspapers, videos and CDs. The company also owns three restaurants, and two Thai shops a few doors away.

Vietnamese

London Star Night Supermarket & Video
213 Mare Street, E8 3QE (8985 2949). Hackney Central or London Fields rail/bus 48, 55, 253. **Open** 10am-10pm daily. **Credit** MC, V.
London's Vietnamese community is clustered around Hackney; of the many Vietnamese food shops in the area, this large supermarket is the pick of the bunch. There's a fresh seafood counter offering razor shell clams and cuttlefish, and a wide range of condiments like fermented shrimp paste and regional curry pastes. You can pick up large bunches of fragrant Vietnamese herbs, plus tropical fruits such as dragon fruit, durian and mangosteen. Other items include crackers, cookies, rice, noodles, confectionery, snacks and banh (rice cakes wrapped in banana leaves). Rice cookers, woks, chopsticks and decorative serving bowls are also sold, and during the Têt festivities miniature Buddhist altars, incense sticks and paper money to burn are also available.

Health food & organic

Fresh & Wild
208-212 Westbourne Grove, W11 2RH (7229 1063/www.freshandwild.com). Notting Hill Gate tube. **Open** 8am-9pm Mon-Fri; 8am-8pm Sat; 10am-7pm Sun. **Credit** AmEx, DC, V.
Fresh & Wild was pretty radical when it first opened its Camden store in 1999. Since then, the company has been sold to Whole Foods Market – the world's largest and most famous organic retail chain, based in Texas (which is set to open its own-

brand store in London at the end of 2006). Products are sourced from small suppliers all over the world, and include own-baked breads (many of them gluten-free), cheese, coffee, meat, everyday groceries like toothpaste, natural remedies, vitamin supplements and skincare products. Staff are informed and perky.
For branches see index.

Planet Organic
42 Westbourne Grove, W2 5SH (7221 7171/ www.planetorganic.com). Bayswater tube. **Open** 9.30am-8.30pm Mon-Sat; noon-6pm Sun. **Credit** AmEx, MC, V.
This organic supermarket was set up in 1995 and has since grown into a mini chain. The original branch has a tempting cake counter, and a popular juice bar that sells freshly pressed juices. There's a range of cereals and other products from Rude Health, flours from the acclaimed Doves Farm, Tofurky and Turtle Island meat substitutes, Green & Black chocolate, and other health-food shop regulars like spelt bread, hemp pasta, brown basmati rice, quinoa black sesame snacks, and vegan-friendly Japanese products ranging from kuzu root (used for adding starch and body to food) to rice cakes.
For branches see index.

Honey

The Hive Honey Shop
93 Northcote Road, SW11 6PL (7924 6233/ www.thehivehoneyshop.co.uk). Clapham Junction rail. **Open** 10am-5pm Mon-Sat. **Credit** MC, V.
This charming specialist shop, owned by professional beekeeper James Hamill, sells honey, pollen, propolis, beeswax and royal jelly. The most fascinating aspect of the premises is the 5ft high beehive at the back, where it's possible to see 20,000 bees in action. The wide range of honeys includes single-floral varieties like linden blossom, hawthorn and sweet chestnut. Honey-based sauces, chocolates, relishes, conserves, mustards, and mead and honey liqueurs are also sold, alongside handmade candles, cosmetics, health products and tableware.

Meat & game

Independent butchers have been hit hard by the rise of supermarkets. We couldn't list all the places in London that do a brilliant job, but here's a small selection of top places.

A Dove & Son
71 Northcote Road, SW11 6PJ (7223 5191/ www.doves.co.uk). Clapham Junction rail. **Open** 8am-4pm Mon; 8am-5.30pm Tue-Sat. **Credit** MC, V.
In business since 1889, Dove's sells prime Scottish beef, grass-fed English lamb, pedigree pork and own-made sausages. Free-range bronze turkeys are available at Christmas. This is one of the few butchers in south London – or anywhere in the capital, in fact – where you can regularly find game when it's in season. The staff are particularly helpful and will cut your meat to order.

Ginger Pig
8-10 Moxon Street, W1U 4EW (7935 7788). Bond Street or Baker Street tube/Marylebone tube/rail. **Open** 8.30am-6pm Mon-Thur; 8.30am-6.30pm Fri, Sat; 9am-3pm Sun. **Credit** MC, V.
This celebrated butcher's is owned by Tim Wilson and his business partner Anne Wilson (no relation), who have their own organic, sustainable farm in the Yorkshire Moors. They raise longhorn cattle, Swaledale and Black Face sheep, and rare-breed Gloucester Old Spot and Tamworth pigs. It's from the latter's ginger-hued coat that the company takes its name. Much of the meat comes from the company's own farm, and the shop is famous for its pork, bacon and sausages. The 25 varieties of sausages include chorizo, merguez, herb, roasted apple, and toulouse. The shop also sells black puddings, hamburgers, raised pork pies, foie gras,

sausage rolls, pâtés and terrines. Properly hung lamb, beef, venison, rose veal, free-range chicken (and free-range eggs) can be bought here, and Ginger Pig cures and smokes its own bacon. Order the cut of meat you want, and the carving and butchery is done in front of you.
For branch see index.

C Lidgate
110 Holland Park Avenue, W11 4UA (7727 8243). Holland Park tube. **Open** 7am-6pm Mon-Fri; 7am-5pm Sat. **Credit** MC, V.
One of the most highly respected butchers in London, this 150-year-old business has been owned by four generations of Lidgate family, and is currently overseen by David Lidgate. It specialises in organic, free-range meat, some of which is reared to the company's specifications. Indeed, there's a very strong emphasis on sourcing. Much of the meat comes from the prestigious Gatcombe, Goodwood and Highgrove royal estates, and lamb suppliers change according to seasons. Beef is reared on Duchy of Cornwall land, and comes in the form of steaks and roasts – with beef dripping, casseroles and newly introduced home-cured pastrami from Highgrove beef all proving to be runaway successes. Sausages are made on site, and include smoked bratwurst, chipolatas and boudin blanc. Gourmet pies, such as coq au vin and boeuf en croute, are hugely popular. Staff can give advice on the differences between American and British cuts of meat, and provide cooking instructions and recipes. Celeb fans include Michael Winner and Egon Ronay.

M Moen & Sons
24 The Pavement, SW4 0JA (7622 1624/ www.moen.co.uk). Clapham Common tube. **Open** 8am-6.30pm Mon-Fri; 8am-5pm Sat. **Credit** MC, V.
Moen specialises in organic and free-range meats, but it's not only a butcher – it's a food hall too, selling related products sourced from 60 top suppliers. In addition to lamb, beef, pork, bacon and chicken, there's game in season, ranging from wood pigeons to hare. Four large counters display own-made sausages (wild boar, merguez), prepared meats (stuffed quail, veal meatballs), seasonal specialities (gulls' eggs, haggis) and offal. You can order meat prepared to your requirements at a day or two's notice. Shelves at the back are lined with pickles, chutneys, sauces, mustards, jams and preserves, and confit, pâtés, rillettes, goose fat and cassoulet are delivered weekly from France. Deli items to complement the meats include cheeses, breads, fresh pesto, olives, herbs and seasonal vegetables.

GG Sparkes
24 Old Dover Road, SE3 7BT (8355 8597). Blackheath or Westcombe Park rail. **Open** 8.30am-5.30pm Mon-Fri; 8am-5pm Sat. **Credit** MC, V.
Established in 1952, this traditional, family-run butcher, one of the best in south London, specialises in rare breed, free-range meat – around 75% of which is organic. Pork is from the UK or Sweden, and veal from Sussex. Beef and lamb come from Scotland, Wales, the West Country and the Midlands, and there's also game in season. You can also buy acclaimed Label Anglais chicken, burgers, kebabs and free-range sausages. A comprehensive range of grocery and deli items includes organic pasta, herbs and spices, cheese, sauces, dips and cereals. Staff are very friendly.

Wyndham House Poultry
2-3 Stoney Street, SE1 9AA (7403 4788). London Bridge tube/rail. **Open** 8.30am-4.30pm Mon-Fri; 8.30am-4pm Sat. **Credit** MC, V.
This family-owned butcher specialises in free-range corn-fed chicken, plus duck, game birds, goose and turkey. Most of the chickens are supplied by the company's own farm. Wyndham also sells Label Anglais chicken: a cross between two traditional British chickens, Red Cornish and White Rock, the birds are raised on a farm in Essex. Also from Essex are flavoursome Golden Promise turkeys. Pâtés and terrines are also sold.
For branch see index.

Drink Shops

Beer

Real Ale Shop

*371 Richmond Road, Twickenham, Middx TW1
2EF (8892 3710/www.realale.com). Twickenham
rail.* **Open** noon-8pm Mon-Thur; 11am-9pm Fri;
10am-9pm Sat; 11am-7pm Sun. **Credit** MC, V.
High-quality, lesser-known British ales – bottle-
conditioned, with no or minimal preservatives –
are championed at this newish shop. Most of the
diverse, 70-plus ales were previously available
only in the locality of their breweries: from south-
west England to the Orkney Islands. They are
graded from light to dark in colour and body.
Draught ale and a new, irregularly changing mini-
cask are also offered. Don't miss the ciders and
perries (pear cider), such as New Forest Perry
(£2.75 a bottle). Monthly tastings are held.

Wine

Wine merchants

Bedales

*5 Bedale Street, SE1 9AL (7403 8853/
www.bedalestreet.com). London Bridge tube/rail.*
Open 11.30am-8.30pm Mon-Thur; 11am-9.30pm
Fri; 9am-5pm Sat. **Credit** AmEx, DC, MC, V.
Marked by barrels outside, Bedales is packed with
bottles from around the world. As well as
examples from Bordeaux, Burgundy, Tuscany and
Spain, there are exceptional New World bottles,
fabulous kosher wines (Galil Mountain and
Domaine du Castel from Israel), and some of
Luxembourg's best (Mathis Bastian pinot gris,
£12.50). European nibbles complement the
selection. At the bar, you can have a bite and a
drink from any bottle on the shelves (£5 corkage).
Weekly wine tastings are held. There's also a small
but well-chosen range of spirits, such as local gin
Jensen's Bermondsey. A Spitalfields branch (12
Market Street, E1 6DT, 7375 1926) opened in 2006.

Berry Bros & Rudd

*3 St James's Street, SW1A 1EG (7396 9600/
www.bbr.com). Green Park tube.* **Open** 10am-
6pm Mon-Fri; 10am-4pm Sat. **Credit** AmEx,
DC, MC, V.
In 2004 Britain's oldest wine merchant merged
with the Burgundy- and California-led agency
Morris & Verdin. BB&R's formidable heritage
(trading here since 1698) is reflected in its panelled
sales and tasting rooms. Among the French-heavy
selection, which includes many old and rare
bottles, are 2005 Château Haut-Brion (£387.50 a
bottle) and its US counterpart Ridge Monte Bello
2005 (£52), but house wines cost under a fiver.
There are some 20,000 bottles in the vaulted
Georgian cellars; knowledgeable (if occasionally
pompous) staff are on hand to advise. The website
is among the best of its kind.

Corney & Barrow

*194 Kensington Park Road, W11 2ES (7221
5122/head office 7265 2400/www.corneyand
barrow.com). Ladbroke Grove tube.* **Open**
10.30am-9pm Mon-Fri; 10.30am-8pm Sat.
Credit AmEx, MC, V.
The shop may be small, but behind it is a large City
agency that supplies classy French wines, along
with many other European and New World
selections. Top Argentinian producer Achaval
Ferrer's Quimera (£23) sits aside biodynamic
producer Dom AP de Villaine's Bourgogne Aligoté
de Bouzeron (£11.67). The knowledgeable staff
organise weekly shop-floor tastings. Ticketed
monthly events cover themes such as vintage

Champagne. C&B also runs a series of wine bars
(see p330) in the Square Mile. The website
provides useful tips.

Fortnum & Mason Food Hall

*181 Piccadilly, W1A 1ER (7734 8040/
www.fortnumandmason.co.uk). Green Park
or Piccadilly Circus tube.* **Open** 10am-6.30pm
Mon-Sat; noon-6pm Sun. **Credit** AmEx,
DC, JCB, MC, V.
Celebrating its tercentenary in 2007, this tourist
magnet stocks over 1,000 wines. Highlights include
Champagne, Bordeaux, Burgundy, sweet wines,
port, sherry and wines from Germany and Austria.
F&M boasts an impressive own-label range; buyer
Tim French's ethos is to source individual,
expressive wines from small producers, such as
Germany's Horst Sauer, France's Philippe
Delesvaux (with a gorgeous Coteaux du Layon
SGN), Tokaji's Istvan Szepsy, Australia's Torbreck
estate, and rare sherries from Bodegas Tradición.
A wine bar is due to open in October 2006.

Friarwood

*26 New Kings Road, SW6 4ST (7736 2628/
www.friarwood.com). Parsons Green tube.* **Open**
10am-7pm Mon-Sat. **Credit** AmEx, DC, MC, V.
An independent wine merchant since it was
established in 1967 by Peter Bowen, Friarwood is
a retail/wholesale outlet with a branch in London
and another in Edinburgh. Its portfolio leans
heavily towards French wines (including en
primeur Bordeaux offerings), but balances the
revered wines of the Old World with innovators
from the New. The shops often have wines open
for casual sampling, and informal courses are
offered. Buying online from the user-friendly
website couldn't be easier.

Green & Blue

*38 Lordship Lane, SE22 8HJ (8693 9250/
www.greenandbluewines.com). East Dulwich
rail/37, 40, 176, 185 bus.* **Open** 5-11pm Tue-Fri;
11am-11pm Sat; noon-9pm Sun. **Credit** MC, V.
One of a handful of wine shop/bar hybrids, G&B
makes wines accessible, alongside a bar menu of
dishes at £6.50 or under. There's an interesting on-
shelf selection from smaller producers, such as
Napa Valley's playfully named Leapfrogmilch
2004 (£14). In the relaxed, clean-lined space, wines
(from £5) are divided into easily understood
style/flavour categories. The South African owner,
wine consultant and former sommelier Kate Thal,
and her husband, host tasting evenings to
introduce customers to lesser-known regions and
grape varieties. *See also p333.*

Handford Wines

*105 Old Brompton Road, SW7 3LE (7589
6113/www.handford.net). South Kensington
tube.* **Open** 10am-8.30pm Mon-Sat. **Credit**
AmEx, MC, V.
Master of Wine James Handford has been selling
fine wines from his Holland Park shop since 1992,
and opened a second, smaller outpost in South
Kensington in 2004. Additions to the globe-
spanning stock include Ksara Blanc de Blancs
2004 from Lebanon's Bekaa Valley (£9.50), and
Mulderbosch Chardonnay 2004 from South
Africa's Stellenbosch region (£11.99). Handford
and his relaxed, friendly staff host twice-weekly
customer tastings (£30-£150) from wineries such
as La Spinetta of Piedmont.

Jeroboams

*6 Pont Street, SW1X 9EL (7235 1612/
www.jeroboams.co.uk). Knightsbridge or Sloane*

Square tube. **Open** 10am-8pm Mon-Fri; 10am-
7pm Sat. **Credit** AmEx, MC, V.
Jeroboams (and its wine-shipping arm, Laytons)
continues to grow, recently taking on the small
chain of La Reserve shops, including Milroy's of
Soho (see p353), and the Mr Christian's delis.
Autumn 2005 saw the opening of two additional
shops, bringing the number of central London
locations to 13. Stock is largely French-focused and
particularly strong on Bordeaux, Burgundy and
southern France. Jeroboams also stocks the
excellent Manzanilla La Gitana sherry in a
convenient 50cl size (£4.95). The selection of fine
spirits (£10-£10,000) is extensive.

Majestic Wine Warehouse

*63 Chalk Farm Road, NW1 8AN (7485 0478/
www.majestic.co.uk). Chalk Farm tube.* **Open**
10am-8pm Mon-Fri; 9am-7pm Sat; 10am-5pm Sun.
Credit AmEx, MC, V.
Although you must commit to a minimum
purchase of 12 bottles (any mix of wines and/or
spirits), you can't fault Majestic on price. The 129
stores offer free delivery in the UK. Fast, friendly
service adds to the appeal. Special deals, although
confusingly arranged, are ridiculously good value.
Selections are better balanced than at most shops,
with equally good European and New World
offerings. Buyers aim to source large quantities of
passable wine at low prices. Small but good-value
high-end buys are scattered throughout Majestic's
stores, based on local affluence.

Oddbins

*57 Lombard Road, SW11 3RX (7738 1029/
www.oddbins.com). Clapham Junction rail.*
Open 10am-9pm Mon-Thur; 10am-10pm Fri, Sat;
10am-8pm Sun. **Credit** AmEx, MC, V.
With 270 branches, Oddbins is a major force in
UK wine retailing – although it's now owned by
France's Castel wine group. Current policy is to
offer 20% discount across 90% of the wine stock,
highlighting seasonal themes. Regular informal
in-store tastings are supplemented by annual
large gatherings in London and Edinburgh. Staff
were famously among the most knowledgeable
enthusiasts in retail, but the recent changes have
slightly diminished this. The website is extremely
user-friendly. There's a nice selection of malt
whiskies too.

Philglas & Swiggot

*21 Northcote Road, SW11 1NG (7924 4494/
www.philglas-swiggot.co.uk). Clapham Junction
rail.* **Open** 11am-7pm Mon-Sat; noon-5pm Sun.
Credit AmEx, MC, V.
P&S has built a strong reputation by offering some
of the finest New World wines to wash up on these
shores. Australia, New Zealand and the Americas
are the specialities, but top selections from
England's bubbly king Nyetimber, and Alsace's
overlooked Rolly Gassmann, dot the list. The
eclecticism embraces Charles Melton Sparkling
Shiraz and Villa Wolf's pinot blanc from
Germany's Pfalz region. There are also more
standard offerings from Chianti Classico's leading
light Felsina (£14.95-£27.95). The firm now has
branches in Richmond and Marylebone.

Roberson

*348 Kensington High Street, W14 8NS (7371
2121/www.robersonwinemerchant.co.uk).
High Street Kensington tube/ Kensington
(Olympia) tube/rail.* **Open** 10am-8pm Mon-Sat.
Credit AmEx, MC, V.
The well-balanced choice of wine here comes from
across the world, including lesser-known regions
such as Bordeaux's Lalande-de-Pomerol, and
Lebanon, plus an excellent selection of fine spirits
(the brooding, autumnal 20-year-old Baron de
Sigognac Armagnac costs £39.95). The monthly
tasting schedule features such winemakers as
Anne-Claude Leflaive of Burgundy, and Robyn
and Mike Tiller (the proprietors of New Zealand's
Isabel Estate). Staff are genuine, knowledgeable
and efficient. A 10% discount for 12-bottle cases
(5% for Champagne) is a further perk.

Thameside

265 Putney Bridge Road, SW15 2PT (8788 4752/www.thamesidewines.com). East Putney tube. **Open** 10am-9pm Mon-Sat; 11am-9pm Sun. **Credit** MC, V.

Run by Master of Wine Stephen Skelton, this newcomer has polished oak floors that lend an aura of distinction. Bottles from all major wine-producing countries are represented, including quality £8-plus options from Australia and the US. Skelton is the foremost expert on English wines, so home-produced bottles are well represented. Especially intriguing are the eight vintages of West Sussex's Nyetimber Première Cuvée. Portugal, New Zealand, Champagne and other bubblies are well covered too. Both the 1994 and 1996 vintages of the ultra-rare Château de Valandraud Bordeaux are here, as is the elusive Château d'Yquem Sauternes.

Wimbledon Wine Cellar

8 The Boulevard, Imperial Wharf, SW6 2UB (7097 5090/www.wimbledonwinecellar.com). Fulham Broadway tube then 391, C3 bus. **Open** 10am-9pm Mon-Sat; 11am-7pm Sun. **Credit** AmEx, MC, V.

Owner Andrew Pavli opened his Wimbledon shop in 1986, hence the company name; of the three branches, this new riverside outpost is the largest. You'll find one of London's most extensive ranges of wines from Burgundy, Bordeaux and Italy, with a fair holding of Californian bottles from Duckhorn, Robert Craig and Stags' Leap. Stock also includes spirits, cigars and Riedel glassware.

Mail order & internet

Adnams Wines

Southwold, Suffolk IP18 6JW (01502 727 222/www.adnamswines.co.uk). **Open** phone enquiries 9am-6.30pm Mon-Fri; 9am-5pm Sat. **Credit** MC, V.

The ales of this excellent regional merchant are available throughout the south-east. The business delivers wines anywhere in mainland UK at no charge. There's plenty of good southern Burgundy 'away from the region of premier cru egos', as senior wine-buyer Alastair Marshall puts it. A fine example of the many special offerings is a three-bottle-each sampling of four different pinot noirs from Domaines Sarrazin and Marechal in Burgundy, Forrest Estate in New Zealand, and Yarra Valley Australia's Backridge Estate – at the ridiculously low price of £115.

Domaine Direct

6-9 Cynthia Street, N1 9JF (7837 1142/www.domainedirect.co.uk). **Open** phone enquiries 8.30am-6pm Mon-Fri. **Credit** MC, V.

In business since 1981, Domaine Direct offers an outstanding choice of wines from Burgundy, along with something from Bordeaux south-west France and the Loire, as well as a few good buys from the New World (especially top-end California and Oz), on a very well-designed website. Pommard's Roblet-Monnot's village wine from the mature 2000 vintage is a relative snip at £13.50, and Western Australia's Leeuwin Estate Chardonnay 2001 is gorgeous for now or the next five years at £35.

Farr Vintners

220 Queenstown Road, SW8 4LP (7821 2000/www.farr-vintners.com). **Open** phone enquiries 9am-6pm Mon-Fri. **Credit** MC, V.

The largest en primeur (new release) merchant of Bordeaux wines also lists some fine producers from Burgundy and the Rhône, plus a few more from around the globe, including Italy, Australia, New Zealand and the US. There's still plenty of 2000 claret, including the majestic Latour (£5,000 for a case of 12), overseen by director Frédéric Engérer in Pauillac. Minimum order is £500; delivery for up to 14 cases costs £15 in London and £25 for the rest of the UK.

Justerini & Brooks

61 St James's Street, SW1A 1LZ (7493 8721/www.justerinis.com). **Open** phone enquiries 9am-5.30pm Mon-Fri. **Credit** AmEx, MC, V.

In premises looking more like an office than a shop (complete with computers and curvy desks), J&B's staff wheel and deal in premium wines. Much of their sales come from broking, and here they will only sell wines by the case (and only if the stock is on site). Beware the vintage reports, which can be overly positive. Tasting notes are concise, useful and the website is easy to use. Great wines include those by maverick Loire and Jurançon producer Didier Dagueneau, and Germany's star Mosel winery JJ Prüm.

Lay & Wheeler

Holton Park, Holton St Mary, Suffolk CO7 6NN (01473 313 233/www.laywheeler.com). **Open** phone enquiries 9am-6pm Mon-Fri; 9am-1pm Sat. **Credit** MC, V.

This well-respected East Anglian company, dating back to 1854, has recently followed the long-established trend of wine merchants opening wine bars in London, with two outlets in the City (one on Cornhill and the other in Leadenhall Market). The merchant list contains interesting bottles from New Zealand, supplemented by plenty from Bordeaux and Burgundy. Unfortunately, you can't view the full list on the website. L&W is also the force behind Vinopolis's wine selection and its October Wine Festival.

Stone, Vine & Sun

13 Humphrey Farms, Hazeley Road, Twyford, Winchester, Hants SO21 1QA (01962 712 351/www.stonevine.co.uk). **Open** phone enquiries 9am-5pm Mon-Fri; 9.30am-4pm Sat. **Credit** MC, V.

This newish outfit has a name that fashionably suggests an emphasis on small, family-owned estates rather than industrial wine production. The inclusion of the voluptuous 2002 Lequin-Colin, Bâtard-Montrachet (£67.10), confirms that individuals and not factories are behind most of the list; it has nervosité and is one to lay down. Regional France is emphasised, especially Languedoc-Roussillon, Rhône and the Loire (where the extensive range includes some great examples from Chinon). All wines listed are duty-paid and so can be delivered within two working days.

Vinceremos Wines & Spirits

74 Kirkgate, Leeds, West Yorks LS2 7DJ (0113 244 0002/www.vinceremos.co.uk). **Open** phone enquiries 8.30am-5.30pm Mon-Fri. **Credit** AmEx, MC, V.

Organic specialist Vinceremos offers 300 wines from across the globe, as well as beer, cider, spirits, cordials and olive oil. From the US, the Fetzer sub-brand Bonterra is a good starting point. It's a reliable, succulent, peachy take on the unusual southern French grape roussanne. France has led the way with organics and while it's a shame not to see pioneers like Nicolas Joly from the Loire or Jean Meyer from Alsace here (due to their deals with other importers), you will find biodynamic producer Huet's Vouvray, Le Haut Lieu Sec Huet 2004 (minerally and long on the finish).

Vintage Roots

Farley Farms, Reading Road, Arborfield, Berks RG2 9HT (0118 976 1999/www.vintageroots.co.uk). **Open** phone enquiries 8.30am-5.30pm Mon-Fri. **Credit** MC, V.

The best-known organic wine merchant is owned by Neil Palmer, a man committed to the cause of naturally made wine. Many top organic winemakers are stocked at other merchants without being flagged up as such, but at least Vintage Roots guarantees that its wines won't contain a concoction of chemicals. It's an odd fact that some wines are filtered using gelatin, cow's bladder, fish scales or egg whites; Vintage Roots sells wines produced using none of these processes. Certain bottles are suitable for vegetarians and vegans, such as Châteauneuf-du-Pape's Domaine Jacqueline André 1999 at £16.75.

The Wine Society

Gunnels Wood Road, Stevenage, Herts SG1 2BG (01438 740 222/www.thewinesociety.com). **Open** phone enquiries 8.30am-9pm Mon-Fri; 9am-5pm Sat. **Credit** MC, V.

The Society buys 1,500 different wines direct from suppliers from across the world, including 100 own-label wines such as J-Marc Brocard's chablis (£8.95) and Concha y Toro's Rapel Valley merlot (£5.50). Storage facilities are extensive. A total of 45 special offers are made annually. The Society has opened a second outlet in northern France. Membership costs £40, but this gives access to 133 tastings and events at 74 locations around the country. The good-to-average 2005 Burgundy vintage is offered in bond, so you can buy it without paying VAT, have it stored, then pay up when it comes out of the warehouse.

Yapp Bros

The Old Brewery, Mere, Wilts BA12 6DY (01747 860 423/www.yapp.co.uk). **Open** phone enquiries 9am-6pm Mon-Sat. **Credit** MC, V.

This firm majors in two areas of France that the British wine trade once neglected – the Loire and the Rhône. The latter has gained in popularity and price in recent years, but few can match the outstanding selections here from Jean-Louis Chave, including his 1996 Hermitage at £75. Yapp also stocks vinous oddities such as Saint Joseph's Grippat 1976 (£8.50), and the oft-overlooked southern Rhône sparkler Clairette de Die. The remainder of France is covered fairly well, and some Australian bottles are thrown in the mix.

Spirits

Gerry's

74 Old Compton Street, W1D 4UW (7734 4215). Leicester Square or Piccadilly Circus tube. **Open** 9am-6.30pm Mon-Fri; 9am-5.30pm Sat. **No credit cards.**

Displaying a quirky jumble of unusual and novelty bottles in the window, Gerry's lays claim to the widest range of spirits in London. It specialises in vodka, offering 150 varieties – including a cannabis-flavoured one and a bottle containing a scorpion. Also crowding the shelves of the small premises are 90 tequilas and 80 rums. Lots of miniatures are available. There's also an interesting assortment of liqueurs and bitters, such as the Czech Republic's Becherovka (£19.75) and Gorkilist liqueur from Serbia (£15), along with grape distillates such as piscos (from £18). The wine selection is mediocre.

Milroy's of Soho

3 Greek Street, W1D 4NX (7437 9311/www.milroys.co.uk). Tottenham Court Road tube. **Open** 10am-8pm Mon-Fri; 10am-7pm Sat. **Credit** AmEx, MC, V.

Now part of the expanding Jeroboams group (see p351), with access to the group's entire catalogue of wines, Milroy's sells its own-brand whiskies alongside favourites such as the complete Macallan vintage series. Stock embraces rare whiskies from around the world (including Japan, Canada and India), as well as limited-release distillery bottlings that will impress aficionados: for example, Springbank 21-year ceramic jug (£350) and Isle of Pillaged (a blend of all seven Islay distilleries) at £900. The shop also hosts an evening programme in its tasting cellar.

The Vintage House

42 Old Compton Street, W1D 4LR (7437 2592/www.vintagehouse.co.uk). Leicester Square or Piccadilly Circus tube. **Open** 9am-11pm Mon-Fri; 9.30am-11pm Sat; noon-10pm Sun. **Credit** MC, V.

In business for over 50 years, the Vintage House has an impressive display of more than 1,400 malt whiskies, with nearly as many miniatures. The emphasis is on Scottish malts, but there are also whiskies from other parts of the world. New independent bottlings include an eight-year Argyll malt, Smoking Islay (predominantly Laphroaig with a bit of Bunnahabhain), at £14.95 for 20cl – and you can put your own label on it. It's cask strength, so will need diluting to taste. Other spirits, including 80 vodkas and a similar number of bourbons, and a globe-spanning range of wines, are also on offer. For online ordering, visit www.sohowhisky.com.

At last, a
Club on
St James's
where
everyone's
welcome.

Berrys'
Wine Club

Tea & coffee

Algerian Coffee Stores

52 Old Compton Street, W1V 6PB (7437 2480/www.algcoffee.co.uk). Leicester Square or Piccadilly Circus tube. **Open** 9am-7pm Mon-Sat. **Credit** AmEx, MC, V.

This Soho institution has been selling coffee and tea since 1887. The atmospheric, aromatic little shop, which retains its original wooden counter and display case, manages to pack in more than 140 coffees roasted to order twice weekly, such as the exotic Chinese Yiedusuo (£3.50/250g) and Sulawesi Kalossi Estate from Indonesia (£3.72/250g), with an upsurge of Fairtrade varieties. The choice of teas embraces the classics as well as flower petal teas and rare Chinese greens (Keemun Mao Feng, £4.60/125g). Superior drinking chocolate comes from the US and Europe.

Drury Tea & Coffee Company

3 New Row, WC2N 4LH (7836 1960/ www.drury.uk.com). Leicester Square tube. **Open** 9am-6pm Mon-Fri; 11am-5pm Sat. **Credit** MC, V.

Established in 1936, Drury is a specialist roaster supplying a selection of 40 ground and whole bean coffees such Jamaican Blue Mountain (£72/kg) and Old Brown Java (£13.20/kg), as well as 12 flavours of coffee syrup. Espresso machines, coffee makers and other accessories are sold too. There are also more than 100 different teas including Chinese whites Jasmine Pearl and Jade Pillar.

HR Higgins

79 Duke Street, W1K 5AS (7629 3913/ www.hrhiggins.co.uk). Bond Street tube. **Open** 9.30am-5.30pm Mon-Fri; 10am-5pm Sat. **Credit** AmEx, MC, V.

When HR Higgins opened his business in an attic on South Molton Street in 1942, he delivered his imported coffees to customers by bicycle-cart. More than 60 years on, the family-run business has a royal warrant. Expert staff will guide you through the excellent coffees from the company's own roasters, including the popular Creole Blend (£20.32/kg), rare, organically grown San Cristobal from the Galapagos Islands (£36.96/kg), and the organic, Fairtrade Colombian Kachalu (£24.40/kg). Self-blended and rare individual-leaf teas are also sold. Prices aren't cheap, but you can try before you buy in the café downstairs.

Monmouth Coffee House

27 Monmouth Street, WC2H 9EU (7379 3516/ www.monmouthcoffee.co.uk). Covent Garden tube. **Open** 8am-6.30pm Mon-Sat. **Credit** MC, V.

Monmouth sources and roasts beans directly, rather than buying on the open market, from single farms, estates and co-operatives around the coffee-growing world. Its three London locations – Covent Garden and two Borough Market outposts – double as shop and café. Featured coffees include such exotics as the Biti Estate (£15/kg) from Karnataka in India, and a full-flavoured Sumatran Lintong (£16/kg). Cakes and pastries from Villandry accompany the java. Staff are young and upbeat.

Postcard Teas NEW

9 Dering Street, W1S 1AG (7629 3654/ www.postcardteas.com). Bond Street or Oxford Circus tube. **Open** 10.30am-6.30pm Tue-Sat. **Credit** MC, V.

An exquisite selection of black, white, green and oolong teas is kept here. Some varieties, such as Tea Flower Tea, made from the leaves of a camellia at Sri Lanka's Handunugoda Tea Estate, are as evocative of exotic places as postcards (and downstairs, indeed, you'll find an exhibition of vintage postcards). Prices for the pretty tins start at a very reasonable £2.95 for 50g. At the sole shared table, you can sample the wares for just £1.50 a pot, with well-matched nibbles such as chocolate cake (£2.50 a slice), medjool dates or almonds. Delightful tea-making accessories are sold too: tiny bamboo strainers, Japanese and Korean pottery, red lacquer trays, pottery chai cups and tea glasses from India.

Postcard Teas

Courses

Several restaurants have jumped on the cookery school bandwagon. These can be fun, but be warned: if you want to learn to cook, restaurant chefs can be some of the worst teachers, not least because pro methods and equipment do not translate readily to the home kitchen. London restaurants offering cookery classes include **Almeida** (*see p100*), **Amici** (*see p181*), **Chutney Mary** (*see p142*), **Feng Sushi** (*see p193*), **Floridita** (*see p41*), **One-O-One** (*see p127*), **Pearl Bar & Restaurant** (*see p126*), **Saki** (*see p185*), **Tom Aikens** (*see p133*) and **Umu** (*see p188*). Contact the restaurants directly for more information.

Before booking a course, consider what you want from it: a few tips and an evening's entertainment, new recipes for your repertoire, or skills that will last a lifetime? All are offered below.

Cookery

The Avenue Cookery School
74 Chartfield Avenue, SW15 6HQ (8788 3025/ www.theavenuecourses.co.uk). East Putney tube. **Open** phone enquiries 8am-7.30pm Mon-Fri. **No credit cards.**
Based in a large family home on a leafy street in Putney, classes at the Avenue are nevertheless held in purpose-built, well-equipped kitchens. The four-week Complete Cooking Course (£500 per week) takes you from chopping an onion to planning a party. On the evening courses (six classes for £280), which are aimed at young newcomers to London, students cook a three-course meal, then sit down together to eat it. Wine is included, as is another dish that is taken home to eat later in the week. There's also a singles-only Cooking for Crumpet option (£65). One-day sessions with lunch cover subjects such as Entertaining with Ease and Christmas cookery.

Billingsgate Seafood Training School
28 Billingsgate Market, Trafalgar Way, E14 5ST (7517 3548/www.seafoodtraining.org). Blackwall DLR. **Open** phone enquiries 9am-5pm Mon-Fri. **No credit cards.**
Born of the need to encourage more young people to enter the fish trade, the training school at Billingsgate Market runs courses for school kids and professionals, as well as interested members of the public. New kitchens mean director teacher CJ Jackson (author of *Leith's Fish Bible*) can lead practical classes as well as demonstration sessions. Some begin with tours of the fish market below. Fish & a Dish evening sessions on themes such as 'scallops' or 'squid and octopus' start at £35; one-day courses are £150-£170 per person.

Books for Cooks
4 Blenheim Crescent, W11 1NN (7221 1992/ www.booksforcooks.com). Ladbroke Grove tube. **Open** 10am-6pm Tue-Sat. **Credit** MC, V.
This riotous cooking studio above the famous Notting Hill speciality bookshop/café (*see p301*) is cramped but friendly. You can book for evening and morning demonstration sessions, as well as one-day hands-on workshops for a smaller number of students. The wide variety of tutors includes Celia Brooks Brown for vegetarians, eastern European specialist Silvena Rowe, Indian cookery writer Manju Mahli, Lebanese food writer Nada Saleh, plus French chef Eric Treuille, who owns the business. Literary Lunches see well-established, respected or hip authors and chefs cooking a three-course meal from their latest book. There's something to suit all pockets too: prices range from £15 to £90.

Cookery School
15B Little Portland Street, W1W 8BW (7631 4590/www.cookeryschool.co.uk). Oxford Circus tube. **Open** phone enquiries 9am-5pm Mon-Fri. **Credit** MC, V.
The inconspicuous front door to Cookery School on Little Portland Street gives no hint of the enchanted world within. Run by Rosalind Rathouse, it has a large kitchen with cooking equipment galore, and a tilted mirror hung at an angle above the long work surface so that you don't miss any of the culinary action. Saturday hands-on workshops (£150) are run in conjunction with the Wine & Food Academy. Evening sessions for beginners and generally competent cooks are based on a tasty menu, and cost £60 for a single session or £300 for a full course. Intermediate evening classes (at the same price) focus on specific subjects such as fish and shellfish, or pastry.

Le Cordon Bleu
114 Marylebone Lane, W1U 2HH (7935 3503/ www.lcblondon.com). Bond Street tube. **Open** phone enquiries 8.30am-7.30pm Mon-Fri. **Credit** MC, V.
This year has seen the introduction of several new one-day courses for 'gifted amateurs' at this internationally renowned French cooking school. Seasonal sessions, canapés and other dishes for entertaining, plus viennoiserie and boulangerie, are some of the subjects covered, with fees from £130. Alternatively, contact the school to see about sitting in on one of the demonstration courses for the diploma students – a limited number of places are regularly available.

La Cucina Caldesi
118 Marylebone Lane, W1U 2QF (7487 0750/ 0759/www.caldesi.com). Bond Street tube. **Open** phone enquiries 9am-5pm Mon-Fri. **Credit** AmEx, MC, V.
A welcoming studio kitchen in a mews off Marylebone Lane, La Cucina Caldesi offers novices and accomplished cooks a splendid guide to Italy's gastronomic offerings. It is run by Giancarlo and Katie Caldesi (who you may have seen on BBC2's *Return to Tuscany*), and the homespun dishes are testament to their culinary passion. Quality guest teachers and children's classes also feature. Expect to pay £50-£120 depending on the session.

Denise's Kitchen
PO Box 83, Northwood, Middx HA6 2HD (836456/www.jewishcookery.com). **Open** phone enquiries 9.30am-10pm Mon-Fri, Sun. **No credit cards.**
Denise Phillips runs courses in her own home specifically for Jewish adherents, but this doesn't mean sessions are limited to themes such as Pesach baking. East meets West, alfresco dining, tapas and mezze are just some of the topics covered in the morning classes (limited to 12 participants). Hen night cooking sessions are also available; like the classes, these are £50 per person.

Divertimenti
33-34 Marylebone High Street, W1U 4PT (7935 0689/www.divertimenti.co.uk). Baker Street or Bond Street tube. **Open** 9.30am-6pm Mon-Wed, Fri; 9.30am-7pm Thur; 10am-6pm Sat; 11am-5pm Sun. **Credit** AmEx, DC, MC, V.
You can now book online for classes held in the plush cooking studios of Divertimenti's two London stores. Such is the reputation of the kitchenware outlet that they have no trouble attracting culinary stars such as Henry Harris, Gennaro Contaldo, Tom Aikens and Skye Gyngell for promotional sessions, but the lesser-known teachers are worth seeing too. Topics include knife skills, healthy Chinese cooking, and sessions designed to make you the hostess with the mostest. Lunchtime classes are £25, evenings from £50.

Eat Drink Talk NEW
Unit 102, 190 St John Street, EC1V 4JY (7689 6693/www.eatdrinktalk.co.uk). Farringdon tube/rail. **Open** 9.30am-6pm Mon-Fri. **Credit** MC, V.
Well-travelled Jennifer Klinec has recently launched this new school in a Clerkenwell loft demonstration kitchen. Sunday Brunch, Delicious Ways with Vegetables, Modern Japanese, and Roasting & Braising are just some of the subjects covered in hands-on and pure demo sessions. Klinec also organises tailor-made classes on themes such as vegan cooking, Thai food, cocktails and canapés, and leads tours of Borough Market, Edgware Road and Chinatown to help participants achieve a better understanding of ingredients.

FishWorks Cookery School NEW
13-19 The Square, Old Market, Richmond, Surrey TW9 1EA (07913 093 088/ www.fishworks.co.uk). Richmond tube/rail. **Open** phone enquiries 9am-9pm daily. **Credit** AmEx, MC, V.
FishWorks' Richmond outpost is the only one to incorporate a purpose-built cookery school, in a sleek loft-style setting overlooking the restaurant (though cookery classes are available at all the chain's branches). Courses aim to put you at ease when buying fresh fish, and emphasise simple recipes. Prices range from £150-£225. If you've got £1,500 to spare, you can treat yourself and up to seven guests to a private course with tuition, dinner and wine.

Japan Centre Sushi Academy NEW
Restaurant Toku, Japan Centre, 212 Piccadilly, W1J 9HX (7255 8255/www.sushi-courses.co.uk). Piccadilly Circus tube. **Open** phone enquiries 10am-8pm daily. **Credit** JCB, MC, V.
We've all heard how sushi chefs have to apprentice for years before they're even allowed to pick up a knife – it's no wonder making maki and slicing sashimi can be intimidating for non-Japanese. However, once a month the Japan Centre offers two-hour classes for amateurs, with Japan-trained chefs from the centre's Toku restaurant. Prices start at £100.

The Kids' Cookery School
107 Gunnersbury Lane, W3 8HQ (8992 8882/ www.thekidscookeryschool.co.uk). Acton Town tube. **Open** phone enquiries 9am-5.30pm Mon-Fri. **No credit cards.**

Children as young as three can join in the classes at this charitable school, which aims to promote cookery skills, healthy eating and food awareness among children of all social backgrounds. Established food writers such as Barney Desmazery, Alex Mackay and Sri Owen lead sessions, in addition to the school's own team headed by Fiona Hamilton-Farley. Subjects range from baking and barbecues to Thai and Caribbean cooking. Classes cost £15 for one-hour, workshops £30 for two-hours, study day £50 for five hours. There are a number of assisted places available to children whose parents are in receipt of income support or state benefits.

Leiths School of Food & Wine
21 St Alban's Grove, W8 5BP (7729 0177/ www.leiths.com). High Street Kensington tube. **Open** phone enquiries 9am-5pm Mon-Fri. **Credit** AmEx, DC, JCB, MC, V.
Some of the food industry's leading names first trained at Leith's (not Prue Leith – she went to Cordon Bleu), and you can too, even if you're not up for the cost or commitment of a year-long diploma course. Leith's Saturday morning hands-on sessions for 'enthusiastic amateurs' include dinner party menus and recipes from Ottolenghi chefs. Winter sees workshops devoted to Christmas preparations and game skills such as plucking birds and skinning rabbits. Evening classes cost £50, half-day workshops £65-£110 and full days from £110.

À Table
7 Arlington Road, Richmond, Surrey TW10 7BZ (8940 9910/www.atable.info). Richmond tube/rail. **Open** phone enquiries 9am-5pm Mon-Fri. **No credit cards.**
Martina Lessing is a professional event caterer based in south-west London who also leads cookery courses with the aim of giving students the confidence to entertain dinner guests. The inexpensive classes (£28 each with discounts for multi-booking) are limited to six to eight people and cover subjects such as fish and Italian classics. Lessing also runs sessions especially for men.

Tasting Places
PO Box 38174, W10 5ZP (8964 5333/ www.tastingplaces.com). **Open** phone enquiries 10am-5pm Mon-Fri. **Credit** AmEx, DC, MC, V.
You'll pay from £140-£220 to participate in one of Tasting Places' masterclasses, which are held primarily in London restaurants. Most take the form of a morning demo followed by lunch. Highly popular are sessions with Jeremy Lee, who teaches the Blueprint Café's classic dishes, plus some of his personal faves. Other respected chefs include Sam Clarke of Moro, Eric Chavot of the Capital, and David Thompson and Matthew Albert of Nahm.

Underground Catering & Cookery School NEW
4-5 Eldon Street, EC2M 7LS (7426 2171/ www.undergroundcatering.com). Liverpool Street tube/rail. **Open** phone enquiries 8am-5pm Mon-Fri. **No credit cards.**
Amid an air of organised chaos, Matt Kemp leads informal, hands-on, group cooking sessions in the professional kitchen of a City church basement. Kemp (who's worked at the River Café, Bibendum and Le Pont de la Tour), loves improvising, adding, say, dark chocolate to meatballs, and tomato sauce at the last minute. Most students are staff from nearby blue-chip companies, who take home in foil trays three-course meals for two that they've helped prepare. An entertaining, informative and inspiring way to spend an evening (and £50).

Vegetarian Society
Citrus House, mews entrance, 70 Fortune Green Road, NW6 1DS (925 2014/www.vegsoc.org). West Hampstead tube. **Open** phone enquiries 9am-5pm Mon-Fri. **Credit** MC, V.
Chef Chico Francesco leads the classes at the West Hampstead offshoot of Cheshire's Vegetarian Society. One-day and half-day sessions cover subjects such as Thai, Lebanese and North African cuisines – completely vegetarian, of course – with

students limited to six for workshops and ten for watch-and-lunch sessions. Although small, the shiny new kitchen benefits from video facilities. Prices are £105-£163.

Wine, beer & cocktails

Leiths (*see above*) also also offers one-off wine and food matching evenings and wine tasting events. A two-hour class costs £70.

Beer Academy
01206 752 212/www.beeracademy.org. **Open** phone enquiries 9am-5pm Mon-Fri. **Credit** MC, V.
This not-for-profit organisation aims to help people deepen their understanding and appreciation of beer. Its courses are run at various venues around the UK, including the estimable White Horse pub in Parsons Green. Prices start at £145 for the one-day foundation course, and there are also occasional intermediate courses and half-day food matching events. Beer Academy will also arrange bespoke tastings for 15 or more people at a venue of your choice.

Connoisseur
Marlborough Hotel, 9-13 Bloomsbury Street, WC1B 3QE (07956 870772/www.connoisseur. org). Tottenham Court Road tube. **Open** phone enquiries 9am-6pm Mon-Fri. **Credit** AmEx, DC, JCB, MC, V.
These informal tasting classes for groups of ten to 25 are run by Margaret Silbermann, who has more than 15 years' experience in the wine import trade. Each class examines a range of good-quality, readily available wines, from classic regions and lesser-known areas. Courses cater for beginners and the more advanced, with prices starting at £75 for a basic one-day course, moving up to £169 for a series of five evening classes. Silbermann also runs one-off food matching events and tastings themed around particular countries, styles or grape varieties. A full list can be found on the website.

Shaker BarSchool NEW
Hollywell Centre, 1 Phipp Street, EC2A 4PS (18707 202 877/www.shaker-uk.com). Old Street tube/Liverpool Street tube/rail. **Open** phone enquiries 9am-5pm Mon-Fri; 10am-2pm Sat. **Credit** MC, V.
As well as training professional bartenders, this upbeat company also offers a one-day introduction to cocktail-making for enthusiasts, presented by the likes of mixologist Jamie Stephenson. After an introduction to the history of cocktail-making, participants get down to the business of shaking, muddling and straining and learn to make such classics as the Martini, Mojito and Cosmopolitan. You can also experiment with developing your own recipe. The five-hour course (£149) and includes a cocktail shaker or recipe book to take home.

Sotheby's
Grosvenor Galleries, Bloomfield Place, W1X 9HX (7293 5727/www.sothebys.com/wine). Bond Street tube. **Open** phone enquiries 9am-5pm Mon-Fri. **Credit** AmEx, DC, MC, V.
Places on Sotheby's prestigious six-week wine courses are much sought after. As befits the firm's position as auctioneers, fine wines are the main focus, yet the 90-minute classes aim to be informal and friendly. The Varietal course (held on Monday evenings in January/February and September/October) looks at major grape varieties, including cabernet sauvignon, merlot, pinot noir, shiraz, chardonnay, riesling and sauvignon blanc. The Regional course (May/June and November/December) emphasises French territories, but also touches on Spain, Italy and the New World. If you take the courses consecutively, you pay £450 for both, instead of £240 per course.

Tim Atkin's Wine 'Uncorked' Series
Bank Aldwych, 1 Kingsway, WC2B 6XF (7379 5088/www.bankrestaurants.com). Holborn or Temple tube. **Credit** AmEx, DC, MC, V.

Master of Wine and *Observer* columnist Tim Atkin runs entertaining and instructive six-week courses at Bank Aldwych restaurant for beginners and intermediates. The courses are designed to be taken consecutively, but those with a basic knowledge of tasting and major wine styles can sign straight up for the intermediate course. Classes can also be taken individually. You'll learn how to navigate supermarket wines, and decipher restaurant wine lists. The beginners course runs from September to November 2006, while the intermediate one starts in January 2007. Cost is £270 per course or £45 per session.

Vinopolis, City of Wine
1 Bank End, SE1 9BU (0870 241 4040/ www.vinopolis.co.uk). London Bridge tube/rail. **Open** noon-9pm (last tour 7pm) Mon, Fri, Sat; noon-6pm (last tour 4pm) Tue, Wed, Thur, Sun. **Credit** MC, V.
Wine museum Vinopolis is a tourist attraction that is open daily, but it also has a Wine School that runs one-off masterclasses and tastings for enthusiastic beginners. The changing schedule of two-hour evening tastings covers themes such as 'Riesling: Old World versus New' and 'Syrah or Shiraz'? The £50 price includes a set of six professional tasting glasses. Otherwise, there are monthly evening classes (£49) in cocktail-making, whisky or wine, which include a 10% discount at the neighbouring Wine Wharf bar and restaurant. Vinopolis is also a venue for Wine & Spirit Education Trust (*see below*) advanced courses – open to those with a WSET intermediate certificate.

Wine & Food Academy
93 Hazelbourne Road, SW12 9NT (8675 6172/ www.winefoodacademy.com). Clapham South tube. **Open** phone enquiries 8.30am-6pm Mon-Sat. **Credit** AmEx, MC, V.
Past and present students are able to buy all wines tasted at wholesale prices from the Wine & Food Academy, which hosts workshops at various London locations. 'Harmonising Wines & Food' (from £285) is an informal ten-week evening course with supper included, while 'Know your Wine' is a five-week evening class for beginners (£155). Champagne tastings, connoisseur classes and corporate events are also available. The academy is also a certified to offer WSET intermediate and advanced certificate courses.

Wine & Spirit Education Trust
39-45 Bermondsey Street, SE1 3XF (7089 3800/ www.wset.co.uk). London Bridge tube/rail. **Open** phone enquiries 9am-5pm Mon-Fri. **Credit** MC, V.
WSET is a popular training ground for drinks industry professionals, but you don't have to aspire to Master of Wine status to take classes here – though note that they do involve homework and an exam at the end. Courses from beginner to diploma level are available in wine, spirits and bartending. A one-day foundation course costs £140; the nine-week series of intermediate evening classes is £325. For something a bit more laid-back, there are after-work tastings (from £35) on topics including rosé and sparkling wine, going up to £250 for first-growth Bordeaux.

WineWise
107 Culford Road, N1 4HL (7254 9734/ www.michaelschusterwine.com). Highbury & Islington tube/rail/21, 30, 38, 73, 76, 141 bus. **Open** phone enquiries 8.30am-8.30pm Mon-Fri. **No credit cards.**
Michael Schuster is one of Britain's best wine educators, with long experience of the wine retail trade. He now focuses on writing and teaching, with Sotheby's (*see above*) among his clients. His WineWise school – which takes place in the basement of his Islington house – offers beginners and fine wine courses, as well as tutored tastings for the more experienced. On the beginners course (£185 for six two-hour sessions), you can expect to sample wines costing £4-£25 per bottle, while the fine wine course focuses on wines up to around £150 per bottle – so at £285 for six classes it's pretty good value. One-off tastings looking at particular regions or chateaux start at £59.

Maps

The following maps highlight London's key restaurant areas – the districts with the highest density of good places to eat and drink. The maps show precisely where each restaurant is located, as well as major landmarks and underground stations. For an overview of every area, see **Key to Maps** below; this shows which areas are covered, and places them in context.

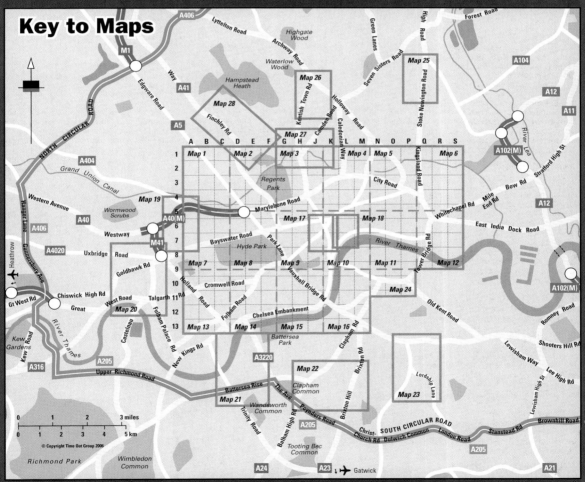

Key to Maps

In association with

Queen's Park & Maida Vale

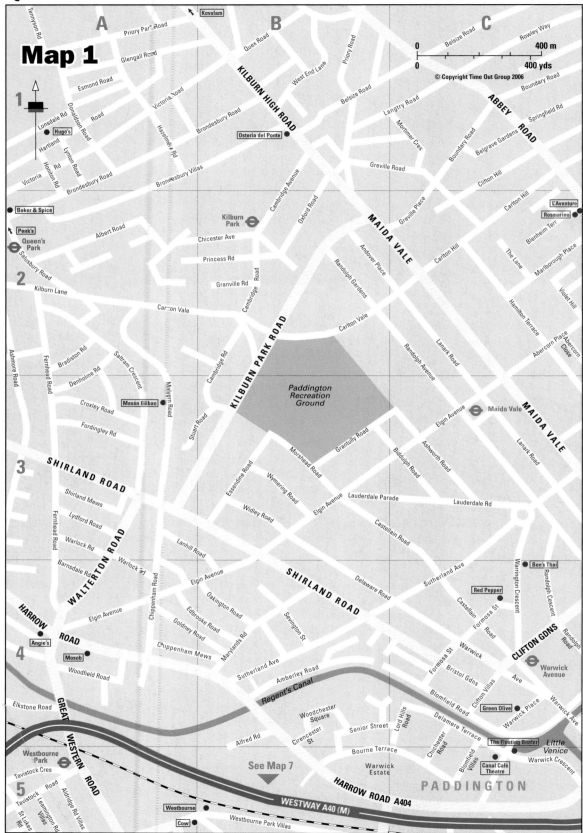

Map 1

Kovalam

A

B

C

Belsize Road

Rowley Way

0   400 m

0   400 yds

© Copyright Time Out Group 2006

Tennyson Rd

Priory Park Road

Quex Road

West End Lane

Priory Road

Belsize Road

Boundary Road

ABBEY ROAD

Glengall Road

Langtry Road

Springfield Rd

KILBURN HIGH ROAD

Mortimer Cres

Boundary Road

Belgrave Gardens

Esmond Road

Brondesbury Road

Greville Road

Clifton Hill

Hugo's

Victoria Road

Hazelmere Rd

Osteria del Ponte

Greville Place

Carlton Hill

L'Aventure

Lonsdale Rd

Hartland

Lynton Road

Donaldson Road

Cambridge Avenue

Oxford Road

Greville Road

MAIDA VALE

Carlton Hill

Rosmarino

Victoria

Homton Rd

Rd

Brondesbury Villas

Blenheim Terr

Carlton Hill

The Lane

Baker & Spice

Albert Road

Kilburn Park

Chicester Ave

Andover Place

Carlton Hill

Marlborough Place

Penk's

Princess Rd

Randolph Gardens

Violet Hill

Queen's Park

Salusbury Road

Granville Rd

Cambridge Road

Hamilton Terrace

Abercorn Place

Kilburn Lane

Carlton Vale

Carlton Vale

Randolph Avenue

Lanark Road

Abercorn Close

Ashmore Road

Fernhead Road

Bradiston Rd

Saltram Crescent

Cambridge Rd

KILBURN PARK ROAD

Randolph Avenue

Lanark Road

MAIDA VALE

Denholme Rd

Mesón Bilbao

Malvern Road

Elgin Avenue

Maida Vale

SHIRLAND ROAD

Croxley Road

Stuart Road

Paddington Recreation Ground

Grantully Road

Ashworth Road

Lanark Road

Fordingley Rd

Shirland Mews

Essendine Road

Morshead Road

Wymering Road

Elgin Avenue

Lauderdale Parade

Lauderdale Rd

Lydford Road

Fernhead Road

Widley Road

Biddulph Road

Castellain Road

Warlock Rd

WALTERTON ROAD

Lanhill Road

Warlock Rd

Delaware Road

SHIRLAND ROAD

Sutherland Ave

Ben's Thai

Warrington Crescent

Randolph Cresent

Barnsdale Rd

Chippenham Road

Elgin Avenue

Red Pepper

Castellain Road

HARROW ROAD

Elgin Avenue

Oakington Road

Sevington St

Castellain Road

Formosa St

CLIFTON GDNS

Randolph Road

Angie's

Edbrooke Road

Marylands Rd

Formosa St

Warwick

Warwick Avenue

Mosob

Goldney Road

Sutherland Ave

Bristol Gdns

Clifton Villas

Warwick Ave

Woodfield Road

Chippenham Mews

Amberley Road

Blomfield Road

Green Olive

Warwick Place

Elkstone Road

Regent's Canal

Woodchester Square

Lord Hills Road

Delamere Terrace

The Floating Boater

Little Venice

GREAT WESTERN ROAD

Alfred Rd

Cirencester St

Senior Street

Bourne Terrace

Blomfield Villas

Chichester Road

Warwick Crescent

Westbourne Park

See Map 7

Canal Café Theatre

Tavistock Cres

Warwick Estate

PADDINGTON

Tavistock Road

Aldridge Rd Villas

Leamington Rd Villas

St Lukes Rd

Westbourne

HARROW ROAD A404

WESTWAY A40 (M)

Cow

Westbourne Park Villas

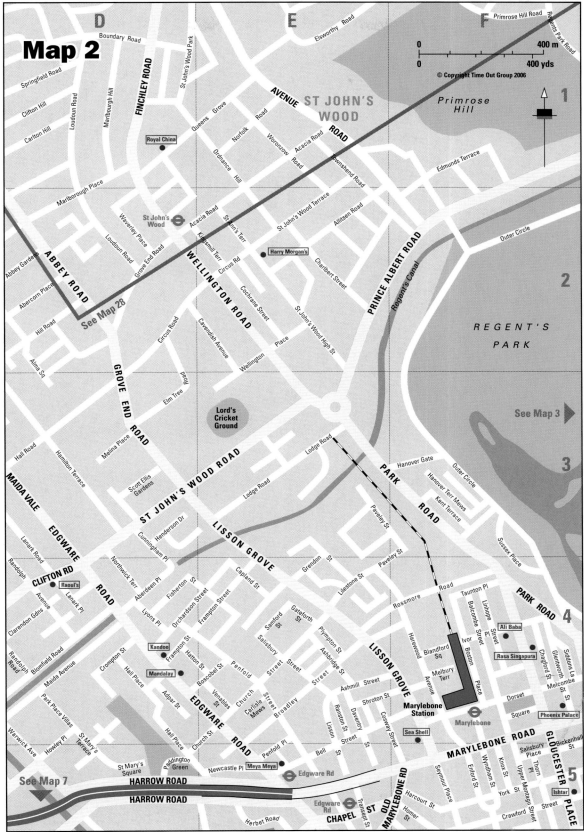

Map 2

St John's Wood Park
Boundary Road
Springfield Road
Clifton Hill
Carlton Hill
Loudoun Road
Marlbourgh Hill
Marlborough Place
Maida Vale
Abbey Gardens
Abercorn Place
Hill Road
Alma Sq
Hall Road
Hamilton Terrace
Melina Place
Scott Ellis Gardens

FINCHLEY ROAD
Queens Grove
Norfolk Road
Ordnance Hill
Acacia Road
Waverley Place
Loudoun Road
Grove End Road
WELLINGTON ROAD
Circus Road
Elm Tree Road
Cavendish Avenue
GROVE END ROAD
ST JOHN'S WOOD ROAD

Royal China

St John's Wood
Kingsmill Terr
St John's Terr
Circus Rd
Cochrane Street
Wellington Place
Henderson Dr
Cunningham Pl

AVENUE
ST JOHN'S WOOD
ROAD
Acacia Road
Woronzow Road
Townshend Road

Harry Morgan's
St John's Wood Terrace
Allitsen Road
Charlbert Street
St John's Wood High St

PRINCE ALBERT ROAD
Regent's Canal

Elsworthy Road
Primrose Hill Road
Regents Park Road

Primrose Hill

Edmunds Terrace

Outer Circle

REGENT'S PARK

See Map 3

Lord's Cricket Ground

Lodge Road
Lodge Road
Hanover Gate
Hanover Terr Mews
Kent Terrace
Outer Circle
Sussex Place

PARK ROAD
Paveley St
Paveley St

Grendon St
Lilestone St
Rossmore Road
Taunton Pl

MAIDA VALE
EDGWARE ROAD
Lanark Road
Randolph Avenue
Clarendon Gdns
Randolph Road
Biomfield Road
Maida Avenue
Park Place Villas
Warwick Ave
Howley Pl
St Mary's Terrace
St Mary's Square

CLIFTON RD
Raoul's
Lanark Pl
Northwick Terr
Aberdeen Pl
Lyons Pl
Crompton St
Frampton St
Hatton St
Hall Place
Adpar St
Church St
Hall Place

Fisherton
Orchardson Street
Frampton Street
Boscobel St
Venables
Carlisle Mews
Church St
Kandoo
Mandalay

Sanford St
Salisbury Street
Penfold St
Capland St
Gateforth St
Plympton St
Ashbridge St
Broadley Street
Ashmill Street
Shroton St

LISSON GROVE
Harewood Avenue
Blandford Sq
Melbury Terr
Ivor
Boston Place

Linhope Street
Balcombe Street

PARK ROAD
Ali Baba
Rasa Singapura
Chagford St
Glentworth St
Melcombe St
Dorset Square
Siddons La
Bickenhall St

Marylebone Station
Marylebone
Sea Shell

Cosway Street
Daventry Street
Ranston St
Lisson Street
Bell Street
Penfold Pl

MARYLEBONE ROAD
Phoenix Palace
Salisbury Place
Knox St
Wyndham St
Enford St
York St
Upper Montagu Street
Crawford Street
Thorn St
GLOUCESTER PLACE
Ishtar

Harcourt St
Homer St
Seymour Place

See Map 7
Paddington Green
Newcastle Pl
Meya Meya
Edgware Rd

HARROW ROAD
HARROW ROAD
Edgware Rd
Transept St
CHAPEL ST
OLD MARYLEBONE RD
Herbet Road

MAPS

Camden Town & Marylebone

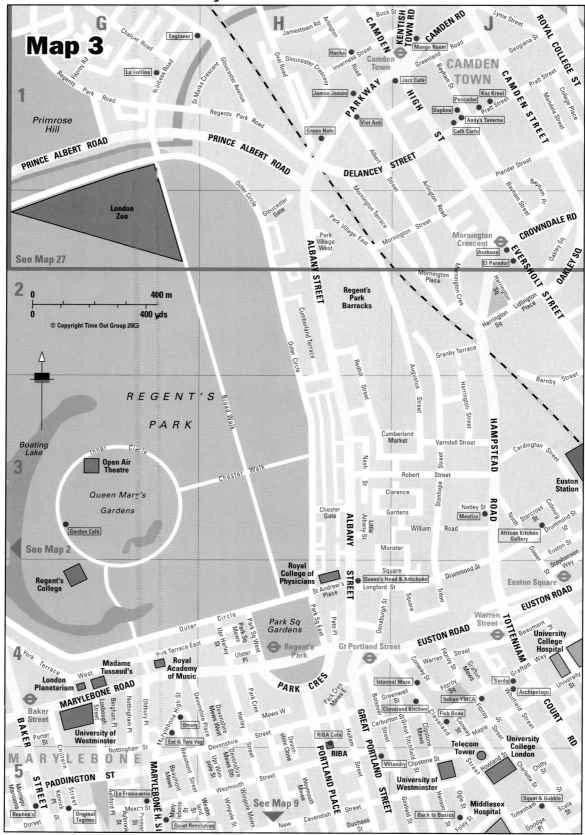

Map 3

G **H** **J**

Chalcot Road
Engineer
La Collina
Fitzroy Rd
Outram Road
St Marks Crescent
Gloucester Avenue
Regents Park Road
Jamestown Rd
Arlington
Oval Road
Gloucester Crescent
Inverness Street
Haché
Buck St
Mango Room
KENTISH TOWN RD
CAMDEN RD
Lyme Street
ROYAL COLLEGE ST
Geogiana St
Road
Greenland
Bayham St
CAMDEN TOWN
Pratt Street
College Place
Mandela Street
CAMDEN STREET

Regents Park Road
PARKWAY
Jamón Jamón
Jazz Café
HIGH
Pescador
Kaz Kreol
Daphne
Pratt Street
Andy's Taverna
Café Corfu
Viet Anh
Green Note
Plender Street
Bayham Street
Bayham Pl

Primrose Hill

PRINCE ALBERT ROAD
PRINCE ALBERT ROAD
DELANCEY STREET
Albert
STREET
Arlington Road
Mornington Terrace
Mornington Place
Mornington
Street
Mornington Cres
CROWNDALE RD
Mornington Crescent
Asakusa
El Parador
EVERSHOLT STREET
OAKLEY SQ
Oakley Sq
Harrington Sq
Lidington Place
OAKLEY SQ

London Zoo
Outer Circle
Gloucester Gate
Park Village East
Park Village West
ALBANY STREET
Regent's Park Barracks
Harrington Sq
Barnby Street
HAMPSTEAD ROAD

See Map 27

2
0   400 m
0   400 yds
© Copyright Time Out Group 20□

Cumberland Terrace
Outer Circle
Redhill Street
Augustus Street
Granby Terrace
Harrington Street
Cardington Street
Cobourg St
Drummond St
Euston Station

R E G E N T ' S P A R K
Broad Walk
Cumberland Market
Varndell Street
Stanhope Street
Robert Street
Clarence Gardens
William Road
Munster Square
Drummond St
Triton
Nash St
Little Albany St
ALBANY
STREET
Netley St
Mestizo
African Kitchen Gallery
North
Starcross
St
Gower St
Stephenson Way
Euston St

Boating Lake
Inner Circle
Open Air Theatre
Queen Mary's Gardens
Garden Café
Chester Walk
Chester Gate
St Andrew's Place

3

See Map 2

Regent's College

Royal College of Physicians
Queen's Head & Artichoke
Longford St
Euston Square
EUSTON ROAD
TOTTENHAM

Outer Circle
York Terrace East
Upr Harley St
Ulster Pl
Park Sq West
Park Sq Mews
Park Sq East
Peto Pl
Regent's Park
Park Sq Gardens
Gt Portland Street
Warren Street
Euston Road
Beaumont St
University College Hospital

4
York Terrace West
Madame Tussaud's
Royal Academy of Music
PARK CRES
Park Cres Mews E
Park Cres Mews W
Maws W
Warren
Fitzroy St
Conway
Gt Portland
Grafton
Way
Istanbul Meze
Sarda
University St
Archipelago
COURT RD

MARYLEBONE ROAD
London Planetarium
Luxbough Street
Bingham Pl
Nottingham Pl
Oldbury Pl
Marylebone High St
Devonshire Place
Devonshire Mews West
Devonshire Street
Greenwell
Bolsover
Indian YMCA
Cleveland Kitchen
Fish Bone
Conway
Maple
Whitfield Street
University College London
Chitty St

Baker Street
BAKER STREET
Porter St
University of Westminster
Orrery
Eat & Two Veg
Devonshire Mews South
Harley
Upr Wimpole St
Devonshire Street
RIBA Café
RIBA
Hallam
GREAT PORTLAND STREET
Carburton St
Gt Titchfield
Clipstone Mews
Clipstone
Fitzroy
Conway St
Telecom Tower
Howland
Charlotte Street

5
MARYLEBONE
PADDINGTON ST
Chiltern
Paddington
Kenrick
Ashford Pl
Moxon
Marylebone Mews
Beaumont Mews
Marylebone H. St
Weymouth Mews
Wimpole Mews
Wimpole St
Weymouth Mews
Villandry
University of Westminster
Squat & Gobble
Middlesex Hospital
Scala

Montagu Mansions
Reuben's
Original Tagines
La Fromagerie
Dorset
Marylebone
New Cavendish St
Quiet Revolution
Weymouth Street
Weymouth
Mews
See Map 9
PORTLAND PLACE
Duchess St
Back to Basics
Hanson St
Gosfield St
Ogle St
Foley St
Goodge Pl
Tottenham St

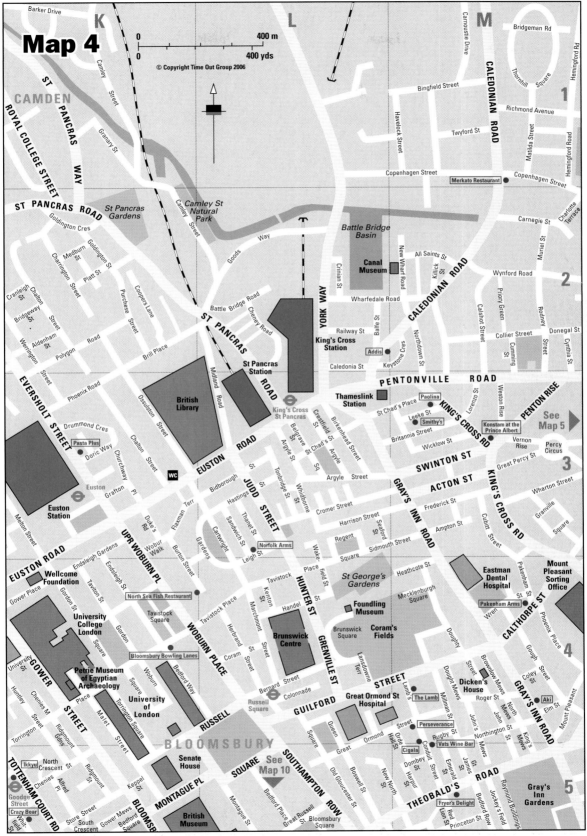

Islington, Clerkenwell & Farringdon

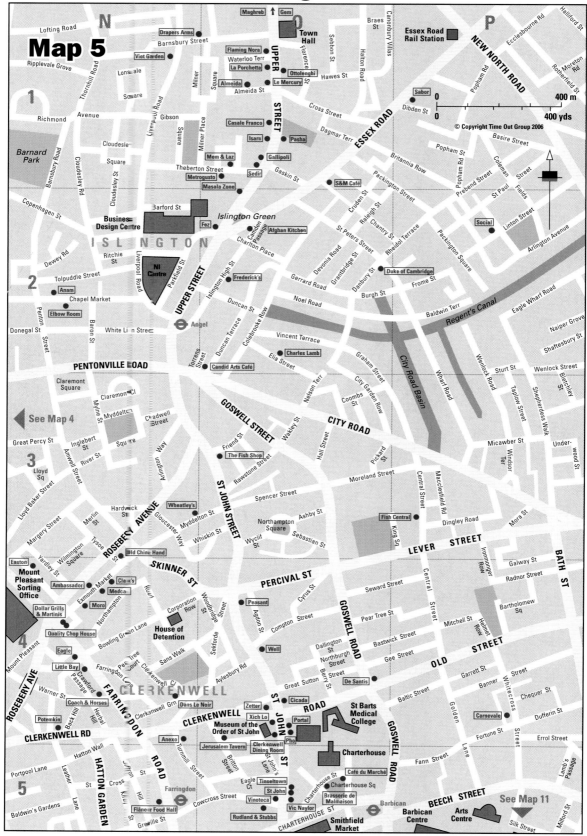

Map 5

Lofting Road
Barnsbury Street
Ripplevale Grove
Richmond
Avenue
Cloudesley
Square
Copenhagen St
Barnard Park
Thornhill Road
Liverpool Road
Milner
Square
Gibson
Square
Milner Place
Theberton Street
Barford St
ISLINGTON
Dewey Rd
Ritchie St
Tolpuddle Street
Anam
Chapel Market
Elbow Room
Penton St
Baron St
White Lion Street
Donegal St

Maghreb Gem
Drapers Arms
Flaming Nora
Waterloo Terr
La Porchetta
Almeida
Almeida St
Casale Franco
Isarn
Mem & Laz
Sedir
Metrogusto
Masala Zone
Fez
Camden
Passage
Charlton Place
Frederick's
Islington High St
Duncan St
UPPER STREET
NI Centre
Angel

UPPER
STREET
Ottolenghi
Le Mercury
Cross Street
Dagmar Terr
Pasha
Gallipoli
Gaskin St
Camden
Afghan Kitchen
Gerrard Road
Noel Road

Town
Hall
Seebon St
Florence St
Hawes St
ESSEX ROAD
S&M Café
Cruden St
Raleigh St
St Peters Street
Devonia Road
Grantbridge St
Danbury St
Burgh St
Duncan Terrace
Colebrooke Row
Vincent Terrace
Elia Street
Charles Lamb
Candid Arts Café
Torrens Street

Braes St
Canonbury Villas
Halton Road
Essex Road
Rail Station
Sabor
Dibden St
Britannia Row
Packington Street
Chantry St
Rheidol Terrace
Packington Square
Duke of Cambridge
Frome St
Baldwin Terr
Regent's Canal
City Road Basin
Wharf Road
Graham Street
City Road Row
Coombs St
City Garden Row
Nelson Terr

NEW NORTH ROAD
Ecclesbourne Rd
Halliford St
Popham Rd
Moreton
Rd
Rotherfield St
Popham St
Basire Street
Popham Rd
Prebend Street
Coleman
St Paul
Linton Street
Social
Arlington Avenue
Eagle Wharf Road
Naiper Grove
Shaftesbury St
Wenlock Rd
Sturt St
Wenlock Street
Taplow Street
Micawber St
Shepherdess Walk
Bletchley St
Windsor Terr
Under-
wood St

400 m
400 yds
© Copyright Time Out Group 2006

See Map 4

PENTONVILLE ROAD
Claremont
Square
Claremont Cl
Myddelton
Chadwell
Street
Great Percy St
Inglebert St
Amwell Street
River St
Lloyd Sq
Lloyd Baker Street
Margery Street
Merlin St
Hardwick St
Yardley St
Wilmington Square
Tysoe St
ROSEBERY AVENUE
Myddelton St
Wheatley's
Gloucester Way
Arlington
Way
Friend St
The Fish Shop
Rawstone Street
Spencer Street
ST JOHN STREET
Whiskin St
Wyclif
St
Northampton
Square
Ashby St
Sebastian St

GOSWELL STREET
Wakley St
CITY ROAD
Hall Street
Moreland Street
Central Street
Pickard
St
Macclesfield Rd
Dingley Road
Fish Central
King St
LEVER STREET
Ironmonger
Row
Galway St
Radnor Street
Bartholomew
Sq
Mora St
BATH ST

Easton
Mount
Pleasant
Sorting
Office
Ambassador
Exmouth Market
Clark's
Medca
Dollar Grills
& Martinis
Moro
Northampton
Quality Chop House
Eagle
Little Bay
ROSEBERY AVE
Mount Pleasant
Warner St
Back Hill
Potemkin
CLERKENWELL RD
Baldwin's Gardens
Portpool Lane
Leather
Lane
HATTON GARDEN
Cross
St
John
St
Hatton Wall
Herbal Hill
CLERKENWELL
Clerkenwell Grn
Dans Le Noir
Anexo
Jerusalem Tavern
Farringdon
St John's
Lane
Benton St
Tinseltown
St John
Vinoteca
Rudland & Stubbs
Flâneur Food Hall
Cowcross Street
Greville St

SKINNER ST
Corporation
Row
Bowling Green Lane
House of
Detention
Sans Walk
Sekforde St
Woodbridge St
PERCIVAL ST
Cyrus St
Agdon St
Peasant
Compton Street
Pear Tree St
Well
Dallington
St
Northburgh
Street
Gee Street
Great Sutton St
Berry St
De Santis
GOSWELL ROAD
Cicada
Zetter
Xich Lo
Portal
Museum of the
Order of St John
Clerkenwell
Dining Room
Pho
Charterhouse
Café du Marché
Charterhouse Sq
Brasserie de
Malmaison
Barbican
CHARTERHOUSE ST
Smithfield
Market
Vic Naylor
St Barts
Medical
College
ST JOHN ST
ROAD
Seward Street
Mitchell St
Helmet
Row
Bastwick Street
OLD
STREET
Garrett St
Banner
Golden
Fortune St
Carnevale
Lamb's
Passage
Whitecross
Chequer St
Dufferin St
Errol Street
Fann Street
BEECH STREET
See Map 11
Barbican
Centre
Arts
Centre
Silk Street
Milford St

MAPS

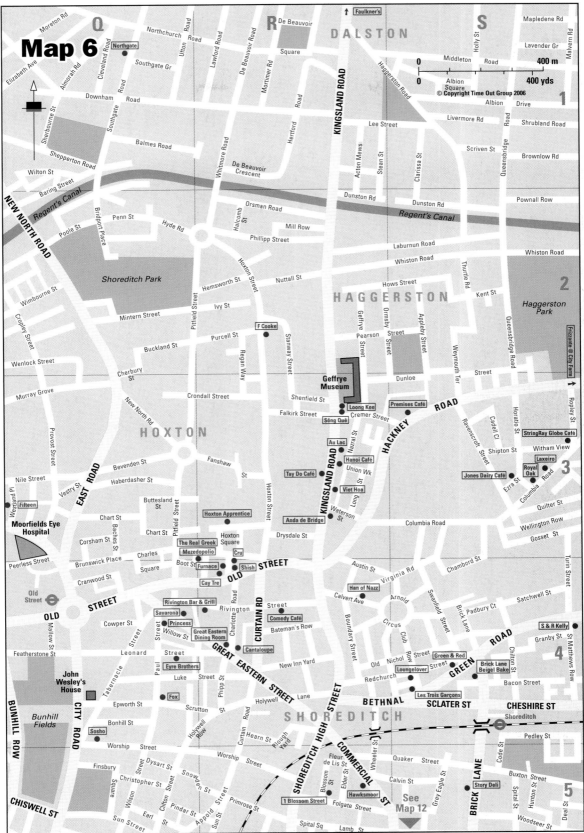

Notting Hill, Bayswater & Kensington

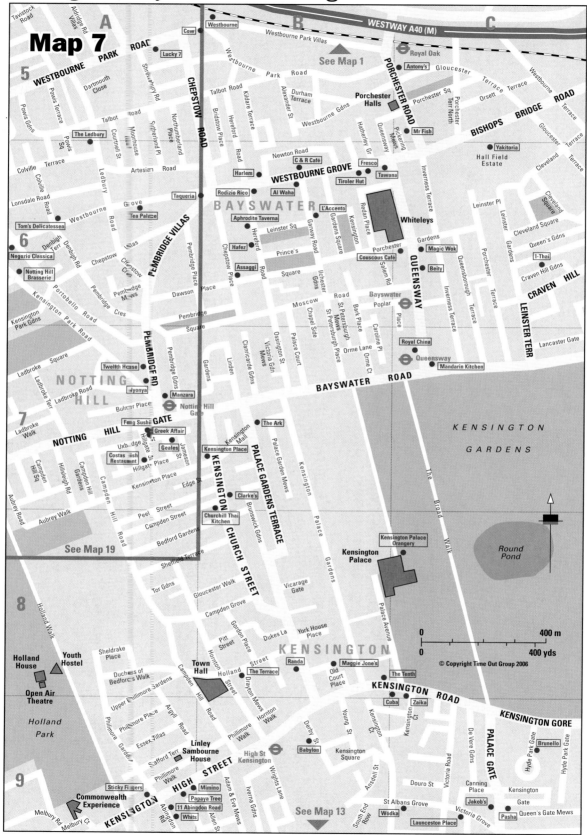

Map 7

WESTBOURNE PARK ROAD
A
Cow
Westbourne
Lucky 7
WESTWAY A40 (M)
B
Westbourne Park Villas
See Map 1
PORCHESTER ROAD
Royal Oak
Antony's
Gloucester
C
BISHOPS BRIDGE ROAD
Westbourne Terrace
Orsett Terrace
Gloucester Terrace

5
WESTBOURNE
Aldridge Rd Villas
Tavistock Road
Dartmouth Close
Powis Terrace
Powis Gdns
Shrewsbury Rd
Talbot Road
Northumberland Place
Moorhouse Road
Talbot Road
Westbourne Park Road
Westbourne Gdns
Durham Terrace
Alexander St
Hereford Road
Bridstow Place
Kildare Terrace
Porchester Halls
Porchester Sq
Porchester Terr North
Hatherley Mews
Pickering Mews
Queensway
Mr Fish
Yakitoria
Hall Field Estate
Cleveland Terrace

The Ledbury
Powis Sq
Colville Terrace
Courtnell St
Artesian Road
Newton Road
C & R Café
Harlem
WESTBOURNE GROVE
Fresco
Tiroler Hut
Tawana
Inverness Terrace
CHEPSTOW ROAD
CHEPSTOW ROAD

Colville Road
Lonsdale Road
Ledbury Road
Westbourne Road
Grove
Tea Palace
Taqueria
Rodizio Rico
Al Waha
BAYSWATER
L'Accento
Aphrodite Taverna
Leinster Sq
Hereford Road
Garway Road
Gardens Square
Kensington Gardens
Redan Place
Whiteleys
Leinster Pl
Cleveland Square
Leinster Gardens
Queen's Gdns

6
Tom's Delicatessen
Negozio Classica
Notting Hill Brasserie
Denbigh Rd
Denbigh Rd
Chepstow Villas
Chepstow Place
Hafez
Assaggi
Prince's Square
Porchester Gardens
Couscous Café
Magic Wok
Beity
I-Thai
Queensborough Terrace
Inverness Terrace
Craven Hill Gdns

PEMBRIDGE VILLAS
Portobello Road
Pembridge Villas
Pembridge Cres
Pembridge Mews
Dawson Place
Ilchester Gdns
Moscow Road
Chepstow Place
Ossington St
St Petersburgh Mews
St Petersburgh Place
Bayswater
Poplar
QUEENSWAY
CRAVEN HILL
LEINSTER TERR

Kensington Park Gdns
Kensington Park Road
Pembridge Square
Pembridge Gdns
Gardens
Linden Gdns
Clanricarde Gdns
Victoria Gdn Mews
Palace Court
Bark Place
Caroline Pl
Orme Ln
Orme Ct
Royal China
Lancaster Gate

7
Ladbroke Square
Ladbroke Grove
Ladbroke Road
Twelfth House
PEMBRIDGE RD
Nyonya
Manzara
NOTTING HILL GATE
Bulmer Place
Notting Hill Gate
Feng Sushi
Greek Affair
Geales
Kensington Mall
The Ark
BAYSWATER ROAD
Queensway
Mandarin Kitchen

NOTTING HILL
Ladbroke Terr
Ladbroke Walk
Jmeba Road
Uxbridge Street
Hillgate
Hillgate Place
Jameson St
Costas Fish Restaurant
Kensington Place
Kensington Place
Edge St
Palace Gardens Mews
KENSINGTON
GARDENS

Campden Hill Sq
Hillsleigh Rd
Campden Hill Gardens
Campden Hill Road
Peel Street
Camden Street
Clarke's
Churchill Thai Kitchen
PALACE GARDENS TERRACE
Brunswick Gdns
Bedford Gardens
Kensington Mall
Round Pond
The Broad Walk

8
Aubrey Road
Aubrey Walk
See Map 19
Sheffield Terrace
CHURCH STREET
Palace Gardens
Kensington Palace Orangery
Kensington Palace
Palace Avenue
400 m
400 yds
© Copyright Time Out Group 2006

Holland House
Youth Hostel
Holland Walk
Sheldrake Place
Duchess of Bedford's Walk
Tor Gdns
Gloucester Walk
Campden Grove
Pitt Street
Gordon Place
Dukes La
York House Place
KENSINGTON

Open Air Theatre
Upper Phillimore Gardens
Phillimore Place
Town Hall
Campden Hill Road
Hornton Street
Holland Street
Randa
The Terrace
Maggie Jones's
Old Court Place
The Tenth
KENSINGTON ROAD
Cuba
Zaika
KENSINGTON GORE

Holland Park
Phillimore Gardens
Stafford Terr
Argyll Road
Linley Sambourne House
Phillimore Walk
Drayton Mews
Hornton Walk
Derby St
Young St
Kensington Ct
Kensington Sq
Babylon
High St Kensington
Kensington Square
Ansdell St
Victoria Road
De Vere Gdns
Brunello
Hyde Park Gate
Hyde Park Gate
PALACE GATE

9
Commonwealth Experience
Melbury Rd
Melbury Ct
Sticky Fingers
KENSINGTON HIGH STREET
Mimino
Papaya Tree
11 Abingdon Road
Whits
Abingdon Rd
Adam & Eve Mews
Iverna Gdns
Wrights Lane
See Map 13
Derry St
Iverna Ct
Cheniston Gdns
Wódka
Launceston Place
Douro St
St Albans Grove
Victoria Grove
Jakob's
Canning Place
Kensington Gate
Queen's Gate Mews
Pasha

MAPS

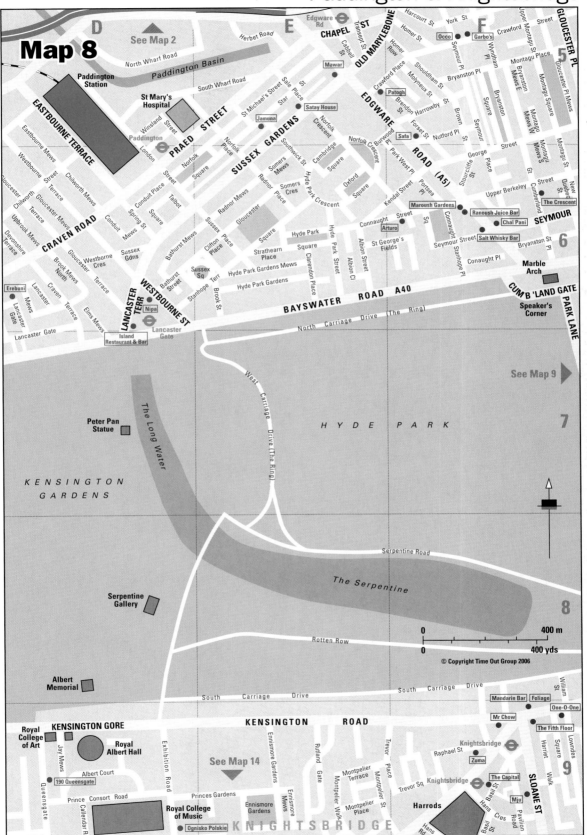

Map 8

See Map 2

D

E

F

5

Edgware Rd

CHAPEL ST

Harcourt St

York St

Upper Montagu St

GLOUCESTER PL

Herbet Road

Transept St

Cabbell St

Old Marylebone

Homer St

Homer Row

Shouldham St

Occo

Garbo's

Crawford St

Wyndham Pl

Upper Montagu St

Montagu Place

Gloucester Pl Mews

North Wharf Road

Mawar

Seymour Pl

Bryanston Pl

Montagu Square

Paddington Basin

Paddington Station

South Wharf Road

Crawford Place

Molyneux St

Bryanston Square

Montagu Mews W

Montagu Mews E

St Mary's Hospital

Windland Street

St Michael's Street

Star St

Sale Place

Patogh

Brendon Place

Harrowby St

Brown St

George Street

Montagu St

Montagu Mews S

Gt Cumberland Street

New Quebec St

Praed Street

Jamuna

Satay House

Norfolk Crescent

EDGWARE

Forset St

Nutford Pl

Seymour Pl

Upper Berkeley St

The Crescent

Paddington

London Street

Norfolk Place

Southwick St

Cambridge Square

Norfolk Crescent

Safa

Park West Pl

Portsea Pl

Kendal Street

Maroush Gardens

Upper Berkeley St

Cumberland

SUSSEX GARDENS

Somers Mews

Oxford Square

ROAD (A5)

Connaught Street

Ranoush Juice Bar

Chai Pani

SEYMOUR

Radnor Mews

Somers Cres

Hyde Park Crescent

Arturo

Connaught Square

Salt Whisky Bar

Bryanston St

6

Conduit Place

Talbot Square

Gloucester Mews

Clifton Place

Square

Hyde Park Square

Hyde Park Street

Albion Street

St George's Fields

Seymour Street

Stanhope Pl

Conaught Pl

Spring St

Bathurst Mews

Strathearn Place

Hyde Park Square

Clarendon Place

Albion Cl

Marble Arch

CRAVEN ROAD

Westborne Cres

Bathurst Street

Sussex Sq

Stanhope Terr

Hyde Park Gardens Mews

CUMB 'LAND GATE

Gloucester Terrace

Westbourne Terrace

Brook Mews North

Elms Mews

Sussex Gdns

Brook St

Hyde Park Gardens

BAYSWATER ROAD A40

Speaker's Corner

PARK LANE

Erebuni

Craven Terrace

Lancaster Mews

WESTBOURNE ST

Nipa

LANCASTER TERR

North Carriage Drive (The Ring)

Lancaster Gate

Lancaster Gate

Island Restaurant & Bar

Lancaster Gate

See Map 9

7

West Carriage Drive (The Ring)

HYDE PARK

Peter Pan Statue

The Long Water

KENSINGTON GARDENS

Serpentine Road

The Serpentine

Serpentine Gallery

8

0 — 400 m

0 — 400 yds

© Copyright Time Out Group 2006

Rotten Row

Albert Memorial

South Carriage Drive

South Carriage Drive

Mandarin Bar

Foliage

William St

KENSINGTON ROAD

One-O-One

Royal College of Art

KENSINGTON GORE

Mr Chow

The Fifth Floor

Jay Mews

Royal Albert Hall

Exhibition Road

See Map 14

Knightsbridge

Raphael St

Zuma

Lowndes Square

Harriet Walk

9

Albert Court

190 Queensgate

Trevor Place

Montpelier Terrace

Montpelier St

Knightsbridge

The Capital

SLOANE ST

Queensgate

Prince Consort Road

Callendar Rd

Princes Gardens

Ennismore Mews

Ennismore Gardens

Montpelier Walk

Montpelier Place

Trevor Sq

Basil St

Mju

Pavilion Road

Royal College of Music

Ennismore Gardens

Harrods

Hans Cres

Basil St

Ognisko Polskie

KNIGHTSBRIDGE

Hans Rd

MAPS

Marylebone, Fitzrovia, Mayfair & St James's

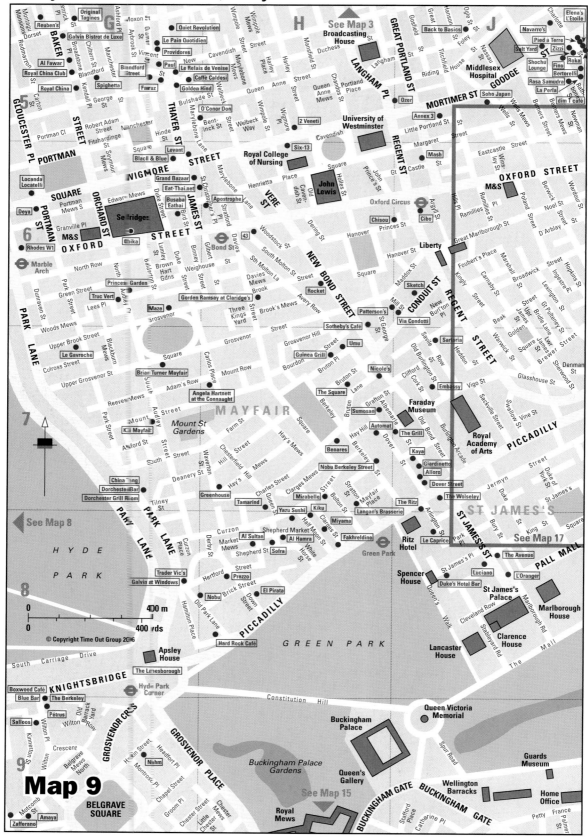

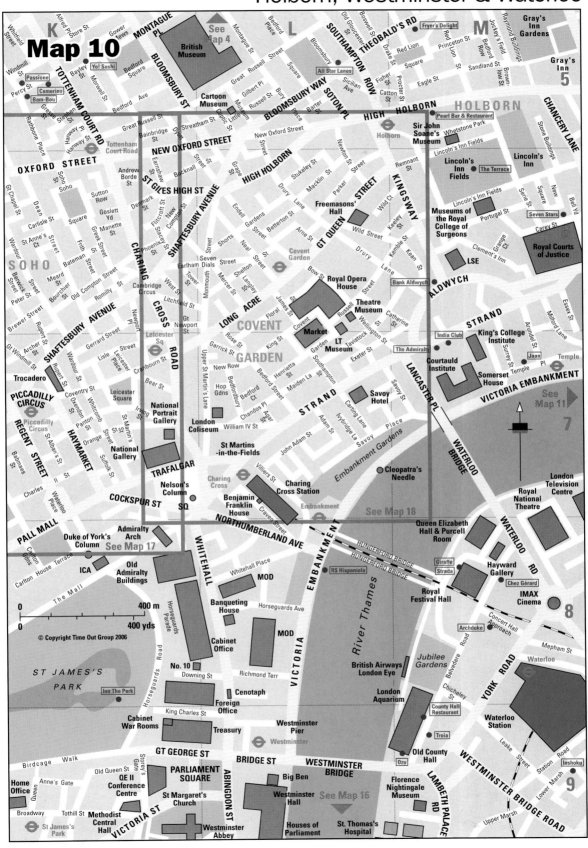

Map 10

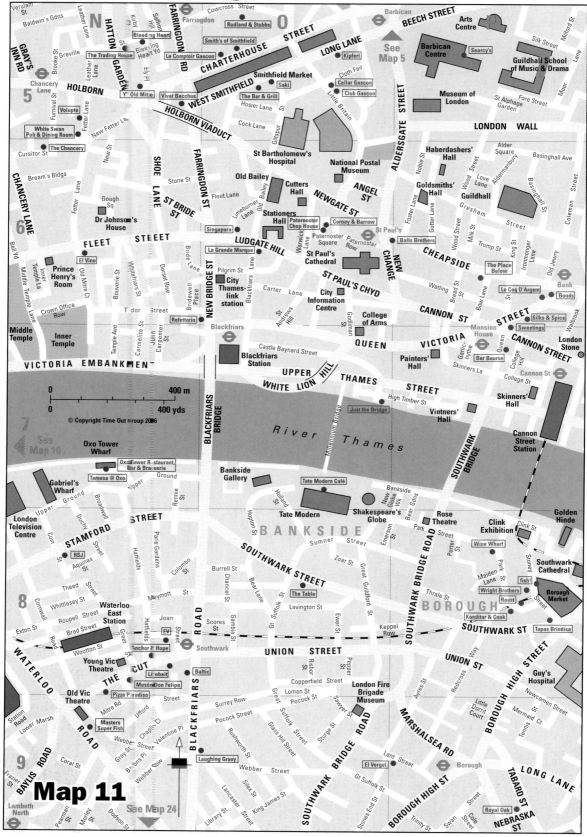

MAPS

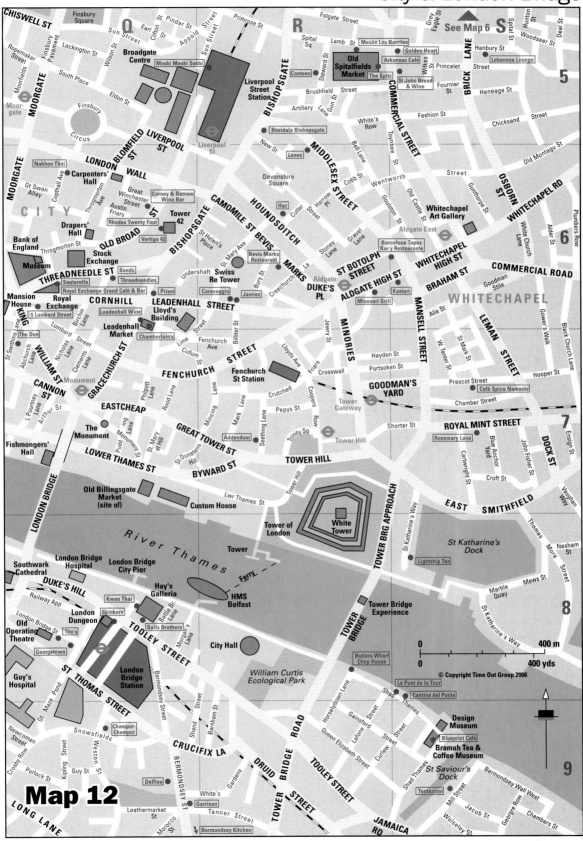

Map 12

MAPS

Earl's Court, Gloucester Road & Fulham

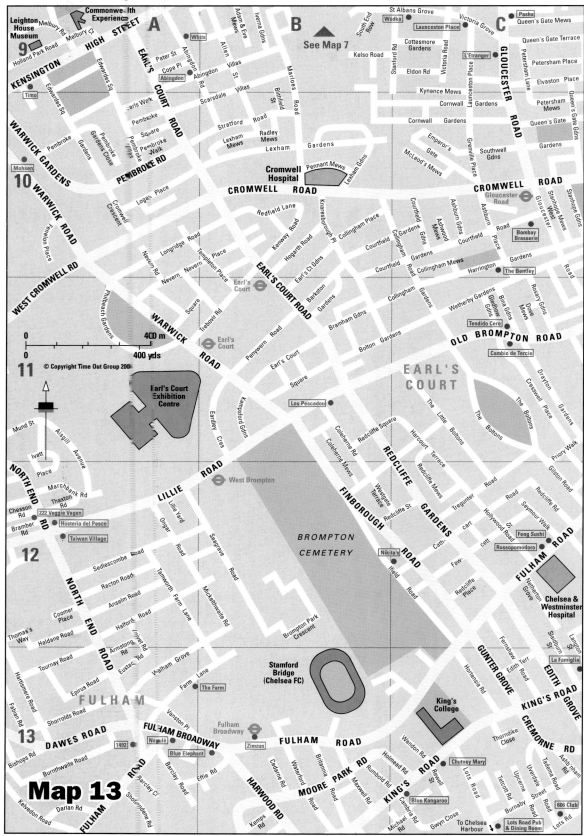

Leighton House Museum

Commonwealth Experience

See Map 7

Whits

Timo

Mohsen

KENSINGTON

HIGH STREET

EARL'S COURT ROAD

WARWICK GARDENS

WARWICK ROAD

WEST CROMWELL RD

PEMBROKE RD

NORTH END ROAD

LILLIE ROAD

WARWICK ROAD

CROMWELL ROAD

Cromwell Hospital

Pasha

Launceston Place

L'Etranger

GLOUCESTER ROAD

CROMWELL ROAD

Gloucester Road

Bombay Brasserie

The Bentley

Tendido Cero

OLD BROMPTON ROAD

Cambio de Tercio

EARL'S COURT

Earl's Court

Earl's Court

Lou Pescadou

The Bentley

REDCLIFFE GARDENS

FINBOROUGH ROAD

West Brompton

222 Veggie Vegan

Hosteria del Pesce

Taiwan Village

BROMPTON CEMETERY

Nikita's

Feng Sushi

Rossopomodoro

FULHAM ROAD

Chelsea & Westminster Hospital

Thomas's Way

Stamford Bridge (Chelsea FC)

The Farm

GUNTER GROVE

La Famiglia

EDITH GROVE

KING'S ROAD

FULHAM

DAWES ROAD

FULHAM BROADWAY

1492

Napulé

Blue Elephant

Fulham Broadway

Zimzun

FULHAM ROAD

King's College

MOORE PARK RD

KING'S ROAD

Chutney Mary

Blue Kangaroo

CREMORNE RD

606 Club

Lots Road Pub & Dining Room

HARWOOD RD

FULHAM ROAD

To Chelsea Harbour

0   400 m
0   400 yds

© Copyright Time Out Group 200

Map 13

A   B   C

9

10

11

12

13

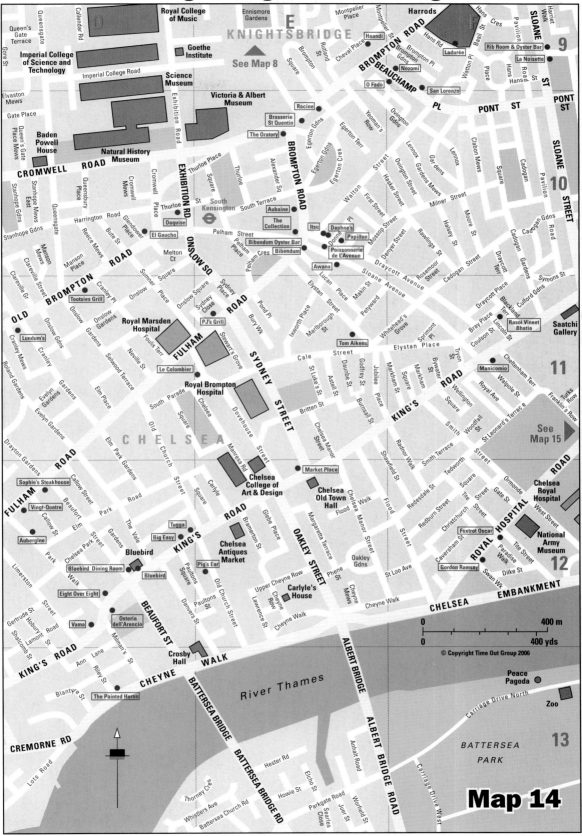

Map 14

Belgravia, Victoria & Pimlico

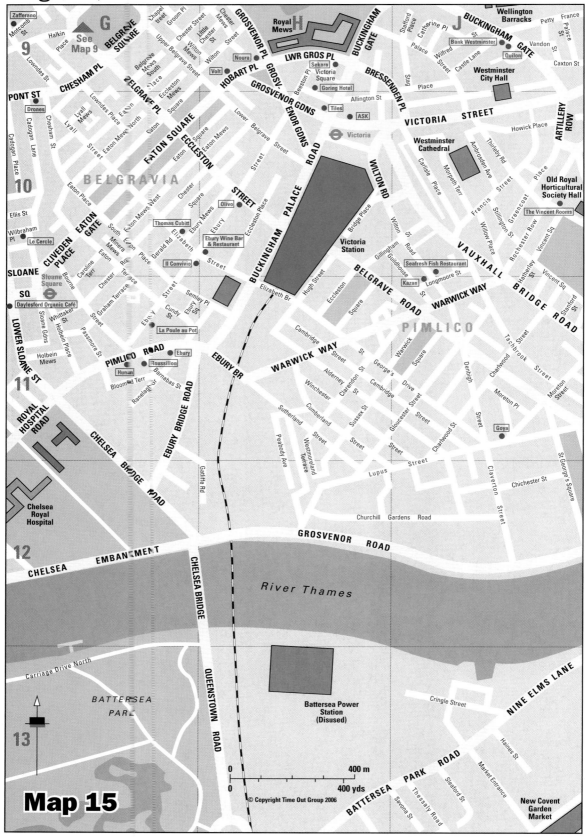

Map 15

© Copyright Time Out Group 2006

0   400 m

0   400 yds

MAPS

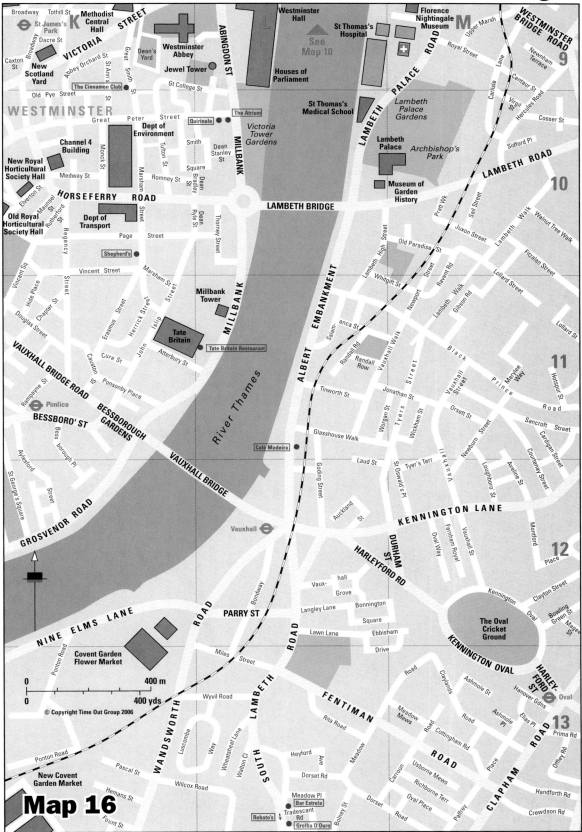

Soho & Piccadilly

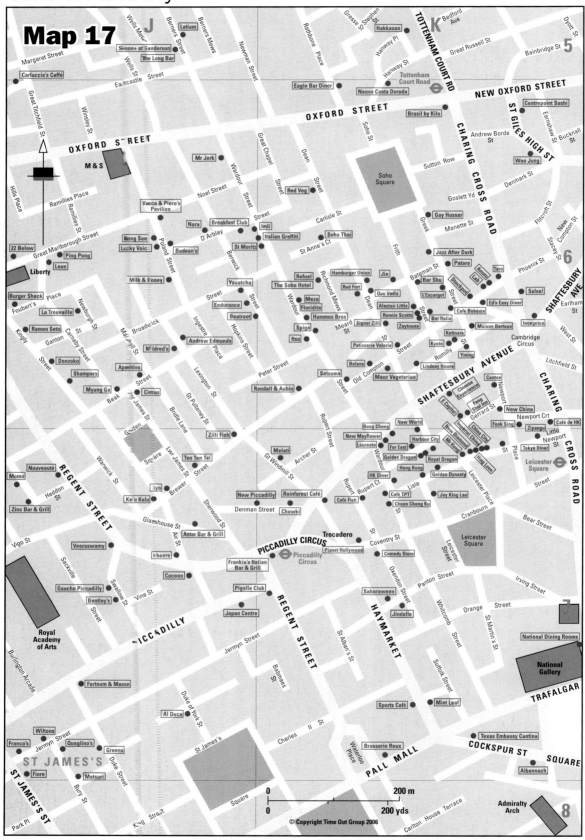

Map 17

J · K · 5 · 6 · 7 · 8

MAPS

Latium · Hakkasan · Bedford Ave · Dyott St · Bainbridge St
Wells Mews · Berners Street · Berners Mews · Grosse St Stephen · Hanway Pl · Great Russell St · 5
Soon+ at Sanderson · Margaret Street · Wells St · Newman Street · Hanway Way · TOTTENHAM COURT RD
The Long Bar · Rathbone Place · Tottenham Court Road · Centrepoint Sushi
Carluccio's Caffé · Eastcastle Street · Eagle Bar Diner · Neuva Costa Dorada · NEW OXFORD STREET · Earnshaw St
Great Titchfield Street · Winsley St · OXFORD STREET · Soho St · Brasil by Kilo · St Giles High St · Bucknall St · Woo Jung
Hills Place · OXFORD STREET · M&S · Ramillies Place · Andrew Borde St · Denmark St · New Compton St
Mr Jerk · Great Chapel Street · Soho Square · Sutton Row · CHARING CROSS ROAD · Fitzroy St · Stacey St
Noel Street · Wardour Street · Dean Street · Red Veg · Goslett Yd · Phoenix St · 6
Ramillies St · Vasco & Piero's Pavilion · Carlisle St · Greek · Gay Hussar · Manette St · SHAFTESBURY AVE
22 Below · Nara · Breakfast Club · Imli · Italian Graffiti · Soho Thai · Jazz After Dark · Patara · Ammo · Taro · Earlham St
Great Marlborough Street · Poland Street · D'Arblay · St Moritz · St Anne's Ct · Frith · Bateman St · Bar Shu · Stockpot · Leb · Salsa! · West St
Ping Pong · Long San · Lucky Voic · Bodean's · Berwick · Refuel · Hamburger Union · Jin · L'Escargot · Café Bohème · Ed's Easy Diner · Incognico
Liberty · Leon · Milk & Honey · Yauatcha · The Soho Hotel · Red Fort · Quo Vadis · Alastair Little · Bar Italia · Maison Bertaux
Burger Shack · Foubert's Place · Endurance · Richmond Mews · Meza · Dean · Ronnie Scotts · Zaytouna · Kettners · Cambridge Circus · Litchfield St
La Trouvaille · Newburgh St · Beatroot · Floridita · Hummus Bros · Meard St · Signor Zilli · Patisserie Valerie · Kyoto · Yming
Ramen Seto · Ganton Street · Ingestre · Spiga · Itsu · Romilly · Lindsay House · Canton
Donzoko · Carnaby Street · Mildred's · Andrew Edmunds · Hopkins Street · Balans · Old Compton · Maoz Vegetarian · SHAFTESBURY AVENUE · Newport · Chinese Experience · CHARING
Shampers · Aperitivo · Broadwick · Lexington St · Peter Street · Satsuma · Canton · Feng Shui Inn · New China · Newport Crt
Myung Ga · Circus · Beak · Gt Pulteney St · Randall & Aubin · Rupert Street · E Capital · Gerrard · China City · Fook Sing · Zipangu · Café de HK · CROSS
Golden Square · Bridle Lane · Zilli Fish · Melati · Archer St · Rong Cheng · New World · Imperial China · Mr Kong · Little Newport · Tokyo Diner
Nouveauté · Warwick St · Lwr James St · Ten Ten Tei · Gt Windmill St · New Mayflower · Laureate · Harbour City · Far East · New Diamond · Hing Loon · ROAD
Momo · Brewer · Rupert St · HK Diner · Golden Dragon · Royal Dragon · Golden Dynasty · Leicester Square
Zinc Bar & Grill · Heddon St · Kulu Kulu · Sherwood St · New Piccadilly · Rainforest Café · Café Fish · Hong Kong · Leicester Place · Leicester Square
REGENT STREET · Glasshouse St · Denman Street · Chowki · HK Diner · Café TPT · Joy King Lau · Bear Street
Vigo St · Air St · Astor Bar & Grill · Chuen Cheng Ku · Cranbourn · Irving Street
Veeraswamy · Sackville · Cheers · Trocadero · PICCADILLY CIRCUS · Planet Hollywood · Coventry St · Comedy Store · 7
Gaucho Piccadilly · Swallow St · Cocoon · Piccadilly Circus · Frankie's Italian Bar & Grill · Oxendon Street · Panton Street · National Dining Rooms
Bentley's · Vine St · Pigalle Club · REGENT STREET · Saharaween · Whitcomb Street · St Martin's St
Royal Academy of Arts · PICCADILLY · Japan Centre · HAYMARKET · Jindalle · Orange Street · National Gallery
Burlington Arcade · Jermyn Street · St Alban's St · Sports Café · Mint Leaf · TRAFALGAR
Fortnum & Mason · Bahmaes St · Texas Embassy Cantina · SQUARE
Al Duca · Duke of York St · Charles II St · Brasserie Roux · COCKSPUR ST · Albannach
Wiltons · Quaglino's · Greens · PALL MALL · Waterloo Place
Franco's · Jermyn Street · St James's St · Admiralty Arch · 8
ST JAMES'S · Fiore · Matsuri · Duke Street · King Street
ST JAMES'S ST · Park Pl · Bury St · Carlton House Terrace

0 ——— 200 m
0 ——— 200 yds

© Copyright Time Out Group 2006

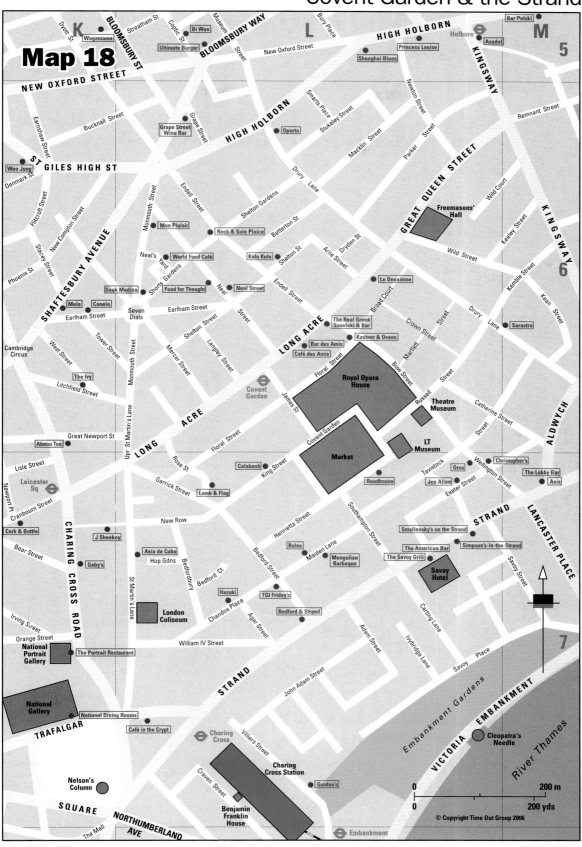

Map 18

MAPS

Discover London's finest Gastropubs with **Leffe** – proud sponsors of the Eating and Drinking Awards 2006

Leffe is a rich complex beer that demands to be savoured, making it the perfect partner to enjoy with any gastropub occasion.

So why not take some time out to savour a Leffe and some gastronomic food for yourself at one of the top five nominations for the Leffe Best Gastropub Award 2006, directions below:

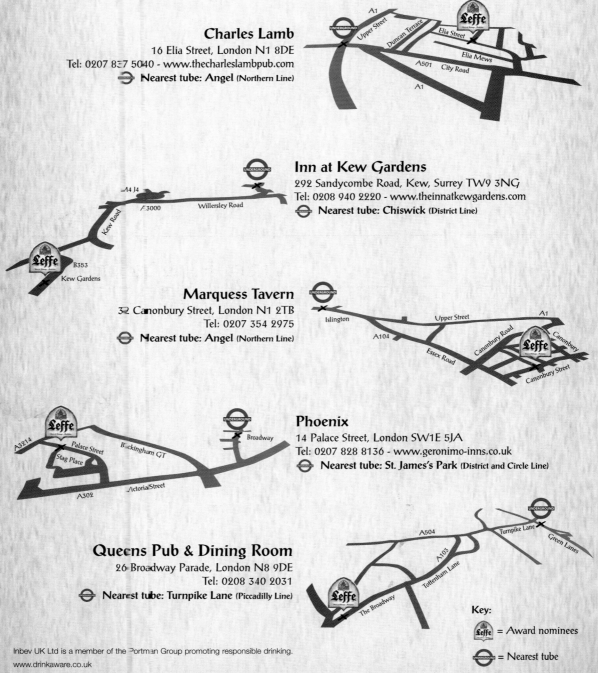

Charles Lamb
16 Elia Street, London N1 8DE
Tel: 0207 837 5040 - www.thecharleslambpub.com
Nearest tube: **Angel** (Northern Line)

Inn at Kew Gardens
292 Sandycombe Road, Kew, Surrey TW9 3NG
Tel: 0208 940 2220 - www.theinnatkewgardens.com
Nearest tube: **Chiswick** (District Line)

Marquess Tavern
32 Canonbury Street, London N1 2TB
Tel: 0207 354 2975
Nearest tube: **Angel** (Northern Line)

Phoenix
14 Palace Street, London SW1E 5JA
Tel: 0207 828 8136 - www.geronimo-inns.co.uk
Nearest tube: **St. James's Park** (District and Circle Line)

Queens Pub & Dining Room
26 Broadway Parade, London N8 9DE
Tel: 0208 340 2031
Nearest tube: **Turnpike Lane** (Piccadilly Line)

Key:
Leffe = Award nominees
UNDERGROUND = Nearest tube

Hammersmith & Shepherd's Bush

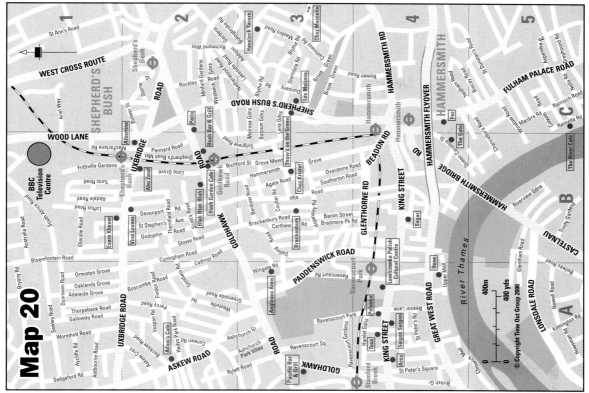

Notting Hill & Ladbroke Grove

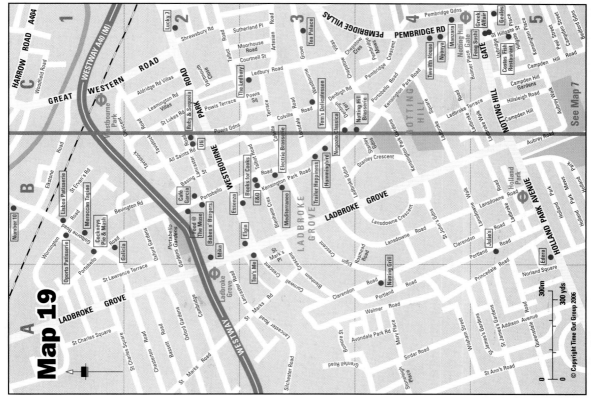

Clapham & Brixton

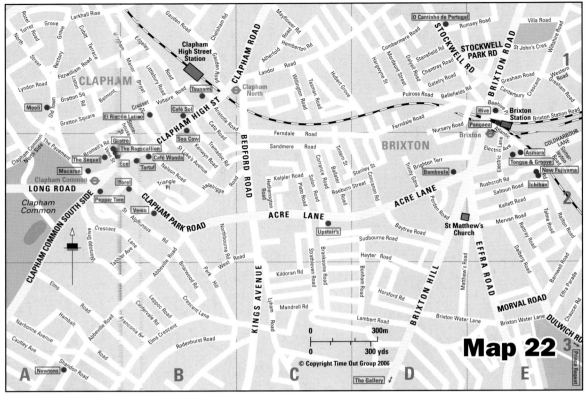

Map 22

Battersea & Wandsworth

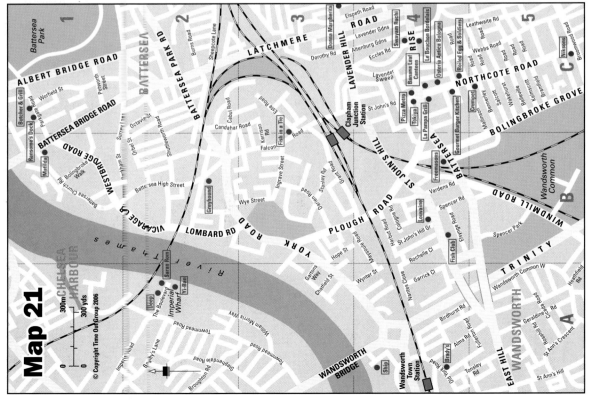

Map 21

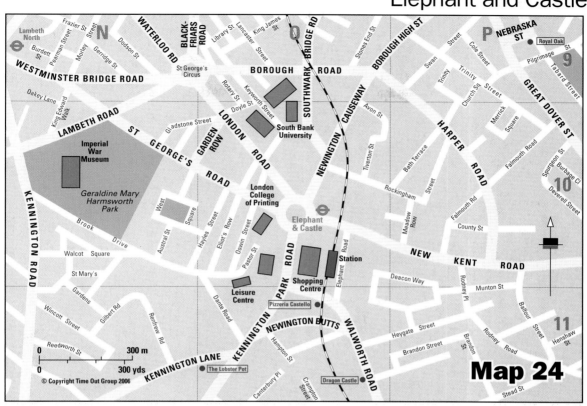

Map 24

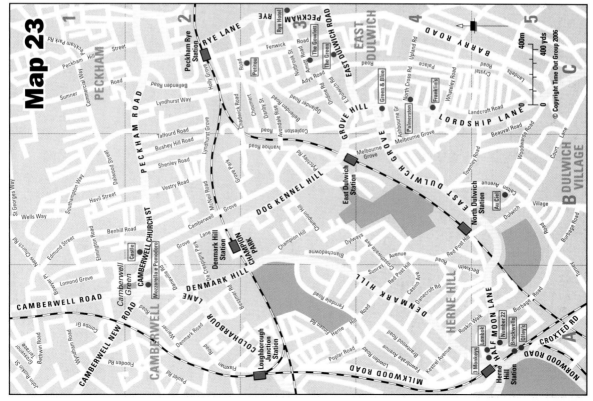

Map 23

Kentish Town to Archway

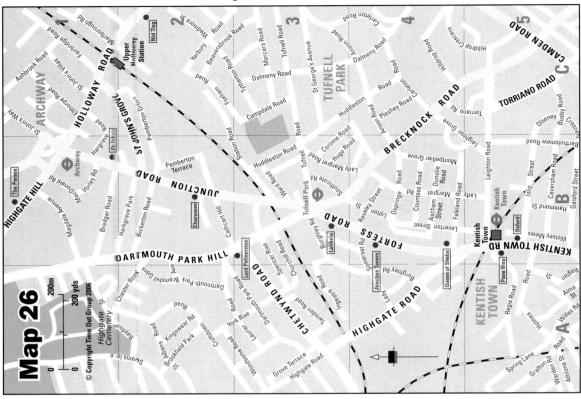

Dalston & Stoke Newington

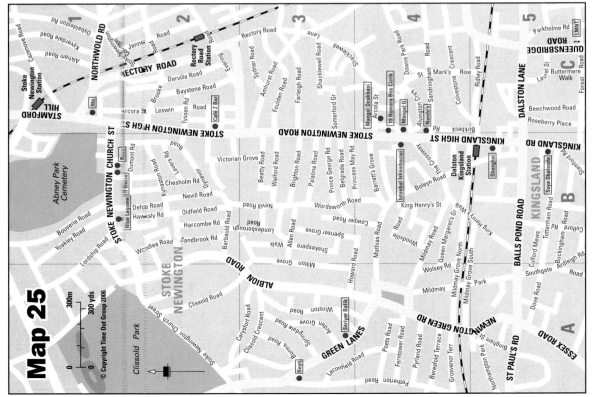

Hampstead to St John's Wood

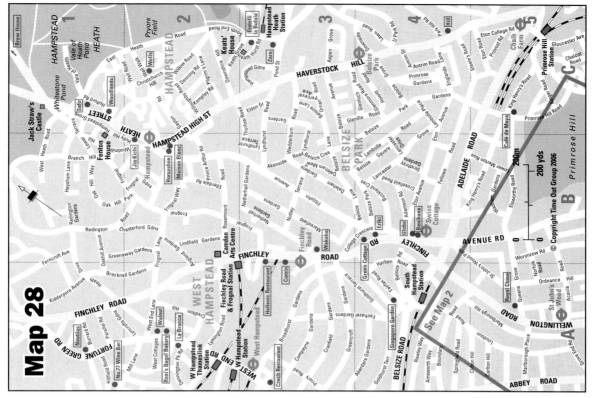

Camden Town & Chalk Farm

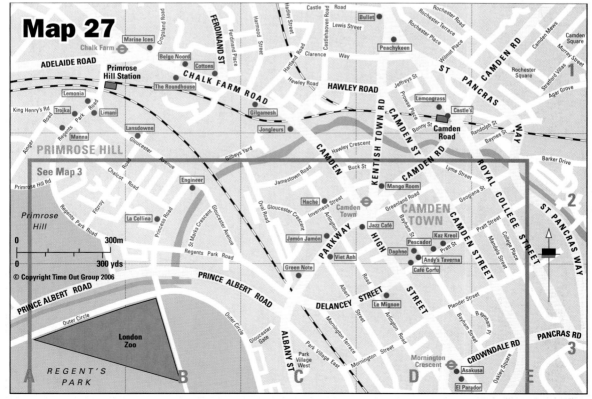

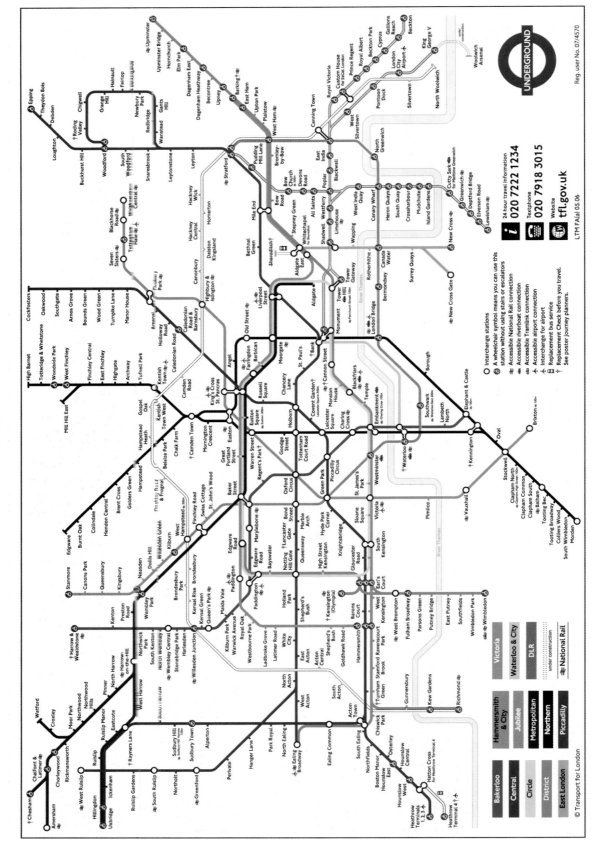

MAPS

Street Index

STREET INDEX

STREET INDEX

Advertiser's Index

Please refer to relevant sections for addresses / telephone numbers

Subject Index

SUBJECT INDEX

Shops A-Z Index

Restaurants Area Index

Definite articles are ignored (The, L',
La, Le, Les, Il, El etc) and names (eg
J Sheekey) are indexed by surname).

Little Bay
228 York Road, SW11 3SJ
(7223 4080)
Nando's
1A Northcote Road, SW11 1NG
(7228 6221)
La Pampa Grill
60 Battersea Rise, SW11 1EG
(7924 4774)
Pizza Express
230-236 Lavender Hill, SW11 1LE
(7223 5677)
Pizza Express
46-54 Battersea Bridge Road,
SW11 3AG (7924 2774)
Strada
11-13 Battersea Rise, SW11 1HG
(7801 0794)
Tootsies
1 Battersea Rise, SW11 1HG
(7924 4935)

British
The Butcher & Grill   p59
39-41 Parkgate Road, SW11 4NP
(7924 3999/www.thebutcherand
grill.com)

Budget
Fish in a Tie   p293
105 Falcon Road, SW11 2PF
(7924 1913)
Gourmet Burger Kitchen   p292
44 Northcote Road, SW11 1NZ
(7228 3309/www.gbkinfo.com)

Cafés
Boiled Egg & Soldiers   p302
63 Northcote Road, SW11 1NP
(7223 4894)
Crumpet   p302
66 Northcote Road, SW11 6QL
(7924 1117/www.crumpet.biz)

Fish & Chips
Fish Club   p308
189 St John's Hill, SW11 1TH
(7978 7115/www.thefishclub.
com)

French
Le Bouchon Bordelais   p98
5-9 Battersea Rise, SW11 1HG
(7738 0307/www.lebouchon.co.uk)
The Food Room   p98
123 Queenstown Road, SW8
3RH (7622 0555/www.thefoodroom.
com)

Gastropubs
Greyhound   p106
136 Battersea High Street, SW11 3JR
(7978 7021/www.thegreyhoundat
battersea.co.uk)
Matilda   p107
74-76 Battersea Bridge Road,
SW11 3AG (7228 6482/
www.matilda.tv)

Indian
Swayam Ruchi   p145
2 Battersea Rise, SW11 1ED
(7738 0038)

International
Cinnamon Cay   p164
87 Lavender Hill, SW11 5QL (7801
0932/www.cinnamoncay.co.uk)

Italian
Osteria Antica Bologna   p181
23 Northcote Road, SW11 1NG
(7978 4771/www.osteria.co.uk)

Japanese
Tokiya   p193
74 Battersea Rise, SW11 1EH
(7223 5989/www.tokiya.co.uk)

Modern European
Louvaine   p233
110 St John's Hill, SW11 1SJ
(7223 8708/www.louvaine.co.uk)
Niksons   p233
172-174 Northcote Road, SW11 6RE
(7228 2285/www.niksons.co.uk)
Ransome's Dock   p233
35-37 Parkgate Road, SW11 4NP
(7223 1611/www.ransomesdock.
co.uk/restaurant)

Oriental
Banana Leaf Canteen   p243
75-79 Battersea Rise, SW11 1HN
(7228 2828)

Pizza & Pasta
Donna Margherita   p313
183 Lavender Hill, SW11 5TE
(7228 2660/www.donna-
margherita.com)
Pizza Metro   p313
64 Battersea Rise, SW11 1EQ
(7228 3812/www.pizzametro.com)

Bayswater
Branches
The Broadwalk Café
Kensington Gardens, W2 4RU
(7034 0722)

The Americas
Harlem   p37
78 Westbourne Grove, W2 5RT
(7985 0900/www.harlemsoulfood.
com)

Branches
ASK
41-43 Spring Street, W2 1JA
(7706 0707)
ASK
17-20 Kendal Street, W2 2AE
(7724 4637)
ASK
Whiteley's Shopping Centre, 151
Queensway, W2 4SB (7792 1977)
Bella Italia
Second floor, Whiteley's Shopping
Centre, Queensway, W2 4SB
(7792 9992)
Fresco
Second floor, Whiteleys Shopping
Centre, W2 4YN (7243 4084)
Gyngleboy
(branch of Davy's)
27 Spring Street, W2 1JA
(7723 3351)
Mr Jerk
19 Westbourne Grove, W2 4UA
(7221 4678)
Nando's
63 Bayswater Grove, W2 4UA
(7313 9506)
Pizza Express
26 Porchester Road, W2 6ES
(7229 7784)
Shish
71-75 Bishops Bridge Road, W2 6BG
(7229 7300)
TGI Friday's
96-98 Bishop's Bridge Road, W2 5AA
(7229 8600)
Thai Kitchen
108 Chepstow Road, W2 5QF
(7221 9984)
Yo! Sushi!
40 Whiteley's Shopping Centre,
Queensway, W2 4YN (7727 9392)

Chinese
Magic Wok   p71
100 Queensway, W2 3RR
(7792 9767)
Mandarin Kitchen   p71
14-16 Queensway, W2 3RX
(7727 9012)
Royal China   p71
13 Queensway, W2 4QJ (7221 2535/
www.royalchinagroup.co.uk)

East European
Antony's   p78
54 Porchester Road, W2 6ET (7243
8743/www.antonysrestaurant.com)
Erebuni   p80
London Guards Hotel, 36-37 Lancaster
Gate, W2 3NA (7402 6067/www.
erebuni.ltd.uk)

Eating & Entertainment
Tiroler Hut   p341
27 Westbourne Grove, W2 4UA
(7727 3981/www.tirolerhut.co.uk)

Fish & Chips
Mr Fish   p308
9 Porchester Road, W2 5DP
(7229 4161/www.mrfish.uk.com)

Greek
Aphrodite Taverna   p121
15 Hereford Road, W2 4AB
(7229 2206)

Italian
L'Accento   p176
16 Garway Road, W2 4NH
(7243 2201)
Assaggi   p176
First floor, 39 Chepstow Place,
W2 4TS (7792 5501)

Middle Eastern
Al Waha   p216
75 Westbourne Grove, W2 4UL
(7229 0806/www.waha-uk.com)
Beity   p216
92 Queensway, W2 3RR (7221 8782/
www.beity.co.uk)
Fresco   p216
25 Westbourne Grove, W2 4UA
(7221 2355/www.frescojuices.co.uk)
Hafez   p216
5 Hereford Road, W2 4AB (7221
3167/7229 9398/www.hafez.com)

Modern European
Island Restaurant & Bar   p227
Royal Lancaster Hotel, Lancaster
Terrace, W2 2TY (7551 6070/
www.islandrestaurant.co.uk)

North African
Couscous Café   p238
7 Porchester Gardens, W2 4DB
(7727 6597)

Oriental
I-Thai   p243
The Hempel, 31-35 Craven Hill
Gardens, W2 3EA (7298 9001/
www.the-hempel.co.uk)

Thai
Nipa   p260
Royal Lancaster Hotel, Lancaster
Terrace, W2 2TY (7262 6737/
www.royallancaster.com)
Tawana   p263
3 Westbourne Grove, W2 4UA
(7229 3785/www.tawana.co.uk)

Belgravia
Bars
Blue Bar   p320
The Berkeley, Wilton Place, SW1X 7RL
(7235 6000/www.the-berkeley.co.uk)

Branches
Baker & Spice
54-56 Elizabeth Street, SW1W 9PB
(7730 3033)
Goya
2 Eccleston Place, SW1W 9NE
(7730 4299)
Ranoush Juice Bar
22 Brompton Road, SW1X 7QN
(7584 6999)

Chinese
Hunan   p61
51 Pimlico Road, SW1W 8NE
(7730 5712)

French
Le Cercle   p88
1 Wilbraham Place, SW1X 9AE
(7901 9999)
La Poule au Pot   p88
231 Ebury Street, SW1W 8UT
(7730 7763)
Roussillon   p89
16 St Barnabas Street, SW1W 8PE
(7730 5550/www.roussillon.co.uk)

Gastropubs
Ebury   p102
11 Pimlico Road, SW1W 8NA
(7730 6784/www.theebury.co.uk)

Indian
Salloos   p134
62-64 Kinnerton Street, SW1X 8ER
(7235 4444)

Italian
Il Convivio   p168
143 Ebury Street, SW1W 9QN (7730
4099/www.etruscagroup.co.uk)
Olivo   p168
21 Eccleston Street, SW1W 9LX
(7730 2505)

Middle Eastern
Noura   p213
16 Hobart Place, SW1W 0HH
(7235 9444/www.noura.co.uk)

Pubs
Thomas Cubitt   p327
44 Elizabeth Street, SW1W 9PA
(7730 6060/www.thethomascubitt.
co.uk)

Thai
Nahm   p260
The Halkin, Halkin Street, SW1X 7DJ
(7333 1234/www.nahm.como.bz)

Belsize Park
Branches
ASK
216 Haverstock Hill, NW3 2AE
(7433 3896)
Black & Blue
205-207 Haverstock Hill, NW3 4QG
(7443 7744)
Gourmet Burger Kitchen
200 Haverstock Hill, NW3 2AG
(7443 5335)
Pizza Express
194A Haverstock Hill, NW3 2AJ
(7794 6777)
Tapeo
177 Haverstock Hill, NW3 4QS
(7483 4242)
Tootsies Grill
196-198 Haverstock Hill, NW3 2AG
(7431 3812)

Gastropubs
Hill   p115
94 Haverstock Hill, NW3 2BD
(7267 0033)

Global
Belgo Noord   p118
72 Chalk Farm Road, NW1 8AN
(7267 0718/www.belgo-restaurants.
com)

Bermondsey
Budget
M Manze's   p294
87 Tower Bridge Road, SE1 4TW
(7407 2985/www.manze.co.uk)

Gastropubs
Garrison   p107
99-101 Bermondsey Street, SE1
3XB (7089 9355/www.thegarrison.
co.uk)
Hartley   p109
64 Tower Bridge Road, SE1 4TR
(7394 7023/www.thehartley.com)

Italian
Arancia   p183
52 Southwark Park Road, SE16
3RS (7394 1751/www.arancia-
uk.co.uk)

Bethnal Green
The Americas
Green & Red   p43
51 Bethnal Green Road, E1 6LA
(7749 9670/www.greenred.co.uk)

Bars
Bistrotheque Napoleon Bar   p326
23-27 Wadeson Street, E2 9DR
(8983 7900/www.bistrotheque.com)
Green & Red   p326
51 Bethnal Green Road, E1 6LA
(7749 9670/www.greenred.co.uk)

Branches
Nando's
366 Bethnal Green Road, E2 0AH
(7729 5783)

Budget
G Kelly   p294
414 Bethnal Green Road, E2 0DJ
(7739 3603)
S&R Kelly   p294
284 Bethnal Green Road, E2 0AG
(7739 8676)
E Pellicci   p294
332 Bethnal Green Road, E2 0AG
(7739 4873)

Fish
Winkles   p87
238 Roman Road, E2 0RY (8880
7450/www.winklesseafood.com)

French
Bistrotheque   p99
23-27 Wadeson Street, E2 9DR
(8983 7900/www.bistrotheque.com)

Pizza & Pasta
**StringRay Globe
Café, Bar & Pizzeria**   p315
109 Columbia Road, E2 7RL
(7613 1141/www.stringraycafe.
co.uk)

Pubs
Camel   p329
277 Globe Road, E2 0JD
(8983 9888)

Spanish
Laxeiro   p258
93 Columbia Road, E2 7RG
(7729 1147)

Vegetarian
Gallery Café   p283
21 Old Ford Road, E2 9PL
(8983 3624)
Wild Cherry   p283
241-245 Globe Road, E2 0JD
(8980 6678)

Blackheath
Branches
'Za London
17 Royal Parade, SE3 0TL
(8318 5333)
Pizza Express
64-66 Tranquil Vale, SE3 0BN
(8318 2595)
Strada
5 Lee Road, SE3 9RQ (8318 6644)

Modern European
Chapter Two   p234
43-45 Montpelier Vale, SE3 0TJ
(8333 2666/www.chapters
restaurants.co.uk)

RESTAURANTS AREA INDEX

Eating & Entertainment
606 Club p339
90 Lots Road, SW10 0QD
(7352 5953/www.606club.co.uk)

French
Papillon p95
96 Draycott Avenue, SW3 3AD
(7225 2555/www.papillonchelsea.
co.uk)

Gastropubs
Lots Road Pub & Dining Room p106
114 Lots Road, SW10 0RJ (7352
6645/www.thespiritgroup.com)
Pig's Ear p106
35 Old Church Street, SW3 5BS
(7352 2908/www.thepigsear.co.uk)

Hotels & Haute Cuisine
Aubergine p133
11 Park Walk, SW10 0AJ (7352
3449/www.auberginerestaurant.
co.uk)
Gordon Ramsay p133
68 Royal Hospital Road, SW3 4HP
(7352 4441/www.gordonramsay.com)

Indian
Chutney Mary p142
535 King's Road, SW10 0SZ (7351
3113/www.realindianfood.com)
Painted Heron p142
112 Cheyne Walk, SW10 0TJ (7351
5232/www.thepaintedheron.com)
Rasoi Vineet Bhatia p142
10 Lincoln Street, SW3 2TS (7225
1881/www.vineetbhatia.com)
Vama p142
438 King's Road, SW10 0LJ
(7351 4118/www.vama.co.uk)

International
Foxtrot Oscar p164
79 Royal Hospital Road, SW3 4HN
(7352 7179)

Italian
Daphne's p179
112 Draycott Avenue, SW3 3AE (7589
4257/www.daphnes-restaurant.co.uk)
Manicomio p179
85 Duke of York Square, SW3 4LY
(7730 3366/www.manicomio.co.uk)
Osteria dell'Arancio p179
383 King's Road, SW10 0LP (7349
8111/www.osteriadellarancio.co.uk)

Modern European
Bluebird p231
350 King's Road, SW3 5UU
(7559 1000/www.conran.com)

Oriental
Eight Over Eight p243
392 King's Road, SW3 5UZ (7349
9934/www.eightovereight.nu)

Portuguese
Tugga p248
312 King's Road, SW3 5UH
(7351 0101/www.tugga.com)

Chinatown

Chinese
Café de HK p65
47-49 Charing Cross Road, WC2H 0AN
(7534 9898)
Café TPT p65
21 Wardour Street, W1D 6PN
(7734 7980)
Canton p65
11 Newport Place, WC2H 7JR
(7437 6220)
Chinese Experience p61
118 Shaftesbury Avenue, W1D 5EP
(7437 0377/www.chineseexperience.
com)
Far East Chinese Bakery p65
13 Gerrard Street, W1D 5PS
(7437 6148)
Feng Shui Inn p61
6 Gerrard Street, W1D 5PG
(7734 6778/www.fengshuiinn.co.uk)
Fook Sing p61
25-26 Newport Court, WC2H 7JS
(7287 0188)
Golden Dragon p61
28-29 Gerrard Street, W1D 6JW
(7734 2763)
Harbour City p62
46 Gerrard Street, W1D 5QH
(7287 1526/7439 7859)
Hing Loon p65
25 Lisle Street, WC2H 7BA
(7437 3602/7287 0419)
HK Diner p65
22 Wardour Street, W1D 6QQ
(7434 9544)
Hong Kong p63
6-7 Lisle Street, WC2H 7BG
(7287 0352/www.london-hk.co.uk)

Imperial China p63
White Bear Yard, 25A Lisle Street,
WC2H 7BA (7734 3388/www.imperial-
china.co.uk)
Joy King Lau p63
3 Leicester Street, WC2H 7BL
(7437 1132/1133)
Laureate p63
64 Shaftesbury Avenue, W1D 6LU
(7437 5088)
Mr Kong p63
21 Lisle Street, WC2H 7BA
(7437 7341/9679)
New China p63
48 Gerrard Street, W1D 5QL
(7287 9889)
New Diamond p65
23 Lisle Street, WC2H 7BA (7437
2517/7221)
New Mayflower p65
68-70 Shaftesbury Avenue, W1D 6LY
(7734 9207)
New World p66
1 Gerrard Place, W1D 5PA
(7734 0396)
Royal Dragon p66
30 Gerrard Street, W1D 6JS
(7734 1388)

Japanese
Tokyo Diner p191
2 Newport Place, WC2H 7JP (7287
8777/www.tokyodiner.com)
Zipangu p191
8 Little Newport Street, WC2H 7JJ
(7437 5042)

Korean
Corean Chilli p204
51 Charing Cross Road, WC2H 0NE
(7734 6737)

Chingford

Branches
Pizza Express
45-47 Old Church Road, E4 6SJ
(8529 7866)

Chiswick

Branches
Balans
214 Chiswick High Road, W4 1PD
(8742 1435)
Carluccio's Caffè
344 Chiswick High Road, W4 5TA
(8995 8073)
The Coyote
2 Fauconberg Road, W4 3JY (8742
8545/www.thecoyote.co.uk)
FishWorks
6 Turnham Green Terrace, W4 1QP
(8994 0086)
Frankie's Italian Bar & Grill
68 Chiswick High Road, W4 1CU
(8987 9988)
Giraffe
270 Chiswick High Road, W4 1PD
(8995 2100)
Gourmet Burger Kitchen
131 Chiswick High Road, W4 2ED
(8995 4548)
Maison Blanc
26-28 Turnham Green Terrace, W4 1QP
(8995 7220)
Nando's
187-189 Chiswick High Road, W4 2DR
(8995 7533)
Pizza Express
252 High Road, W4 1PD (8747 0193)
Silks & Spice
95 Chiswick High Road, W4 2EF
(8995 7991)
Strada
156 Chiswick High Road, W4 1PR
(8995 0004)
Tootsies Grill
148 Chiswick High Road, W4 1PS
(8747 1869)
Woodlands
12-14 Chiswick High Road, W4 1TH
(8994 9333)
Zizzi
231 Chiswick High Road, W4 2DL
(8747 9400)

Brasseries
High Road Brasserie p47
162-166 Chiswick High Road, W4 1PR
(8742 7474/www.highroadhouse.
co.uk)

East European
Garni p76
472 Chiswick High Road, W4 5TT
(8995 5129/www.garni.co.uk)

Fish
Fish Hook p85
8 Elliott Road, W4 1PE (8742
0766/www.fishhook.co.uk)

French
La Trompette p97
5-7 Devonshire Road, W4 2EU (8747
1836/www.latrompette.co.uk)
Le Vacherin p97
76-77 South Parade, W4 5LF (8742
2121/www.levacherin.co.uk)

Modern European
Sam's Brasserie & Bar p227
11 Barley Mow Passage, W4 4PH
(8987 0555/www.samsbrasserie.
co.uk)

City

The Americas
Arkansas Café p33
Unit 12, Old Spitalfields Market,
E1 6AA (7377 6999)
Hawksmoor p33
157 Commercial Street, E1 6BJ (7247
7392/www.thehawksmoor.com)
Missouri Grill p33
76 Aldgate High Street, EC3N 1BD
(7481 4010/www.missourigrill.com)

Bars
Hawksmoor p320
157 Commercial Street, E1 6BJ
(7247 7392/www.thehawksmoor.com)

Branches
Apostrophe
42 Great Eastern Street, EC2A 3EP
(7739 8412)
Apostrophe
10 St Paul's Churchyard, EC4M 8AL
(7248 9100)
Balls Brothers
Gow's Restaurant, 81 Old Broad
Street, EC2M 1PR (7920 9645)
Balls Brothers
11 Blomfield Street, EC2M 1PS
(7588 4643)
Balls Brothers
158 Bishopsgate, EC2M 4LN
(7426 0567)
Balls Brothers
3 King's Arms Yard, EC2R 7AD
(7796 3049)
Balls Brothers
6-8 Cheapside, EC2V 6AN
(7248 2708)
Balls Brothers
5-6 Carey Lane, EC2V 8AE
(7600 2720)
Balls Brothers
Bury Court, 38 St Mary Axe, EC3A 8EX
(7929 6660)
Balls Brothers
52 Lime Street, EC3M 7BS
(7283 0841)
Balls Brothers
Mark Lane, EC3R 7BB (7623 2923)
Balls Brothers
Minster Court, Mincing Lane,
EC3R 7PP (7283 2838)
Balls Brothers
2 St Mary at Hill, EC3R 8EE (7626
0321)
Balls Brothers
Bucklersbury House, Cannon Street,
EC4N 8EL (7248 7557)
Bangers (branch of Davy's)
Eldon House, 2-12 Wilson Street
, EC2H 2TE (7377
6326/www.davy.co.uk)
Bangers Too (branch of Davy's)
1 St Mary at Hill, EC3R 8EE (7283
4443/www.davy.co.uk)
**Bar Under the Clock
(branch of Balls Bros)**
74 Queen Victoria Street (entrance on
Bow Lane), EC4N 4SJ (7489 9895/
www.ballsbrothers.co.uk)
Barcelona Tapas Bar y Restaurante
24 Lime Street, EC3M 7HS
(7929 2389)
Barcelona Tapas Bar y Restaurante
13 Well Court, off Bow Lane,
EC4M 9DN (7329 5111)
Bertorelli
Plantation Place, 15 Mincing Lane,
EC3R 7BD (7283 3028)
Bertorelli
1 Plough Place, EC4A 1HY
(7842 0510)
Bishop of Norwich (branch of Davy's)
91-93 Moorgate, EC2M 6SJ
(7920 0857)
Bishop's Parlour (branch of Davy's)
91-93 Moorgate, EC2M 6SJ
(7588 2581)
Chez Gérard
64 Bishopsgate, EC2N 4AJ
(7588 1200)
Chez Gérard
1 Watling Street, EC4M 9BP
(7213 0540)

City Boot (branch of Davy's)
7 Moorfields High Walk, EC2Y 9DP
(7588 4766)
City Flogger (branch of Davy's)
Fenn Court, 120 Fenchurch Street,
EC3M 5BA (7623 3251)
City FOB (branch of Davy's)
Lower Thames Street, EC3R 6DJ
(7621 0619)
City Miyama
17 Godliman Street, EC4V 5BD
(7489 1937)
City Pipe (branch of Davy's)
33 Foster Lane, off Cheapside,
EC2V 6HD (7606 2110)
Corney & Barrow
5 Exchange Square, EC2A 2EH (7628
4367/www.corney-barrow.co.uk)
Corney & Barrow
19 Broadgate Circle, EC2M 2QS (7628
1251/www.corney-barrow.co.uk)
Corney & Barrow
111 Old Broad Street, EC2N 1AP
(7638 9308/www.corney-barrow.co.uk)
Corney & Barrow
12-14 Mason's Avenue, EC2V 5BT
(7726 6030/www.corney-barrow.co.uk)
Corney & Barrow
1 Ropemaker Street, EC2Y 9HT
(7382 0606/www.corney-barrow.co.uk)
Corney & Barrow
2B Eastcheap, EC3M 1AB (7929
3220/www.corney-barrow.co.uk)
Corney & Barrow
1 Leadenhall Place, EC3M 7DX (7621
9201/www.corney-barrow.co.uk)
Corney & Barrow
37A Jewry Street, EC3N 2EX (7680
8550/www.corney-barrow.co.uk)
Corney & Barrow
16 Royal Exchange, EC3V 3LP (7929
3131/www.corney-barrow.co.uk)
Corney & Barrow
3 Fleet Place, EC4M 7RD (7329
3141/www.corney-barrow.co.uk)
Davy's
2 Exchange Square, EC2A 2EH
(7256 5962)
Davy's
10 Creed Lane, EC4M 8SH
(7236 5317)
Ekachai
9-10 Liverpool Street, EC2M 7PN
(7626 1155)
The Gaucho Grill
1 Bell Inn Yard, off Gracechurch Street,
EC3V 0BL (7626 5180)
Giraffe
Crispin Place, off Brushfield Street,
E1 6DW (3116 2000)
The Habit (branch of Davy's)
Friary Court, 65 Crutched Friars,
EC3M 2RN (7481 1131)
Heeltap & Bumper (branch of Davy's)
2-6 Cannon Street, EC4M 6XX
(7248 3371)
Jamies
155 Bishopsgate, EC2A 2AA
(7256 7279/www.jamiesbars.co.uk)
Jamies
13 Philpot Lane, EC3M 8AA (7621
9577/www.jamiesbars.co.uk)
Jamies
119-121 The Minories, EC3N 1DR
(7709 9900/www.jamiesbars.co.uk)
Jamies
34 Ludgate Hill, EC4M 7DE (7489
1938/www.jamiesbars.co.uk)
Jamies
5 Groveland Court, EC4M 9EH
(7248 5551/www.jamiesbars.co.uk)
Jamies at the Pavilion
Finsbury Circus Gardens, EC2M 7AB
(7628 8224/www.jamiesbars.co.uk)
Leon
3 Crispin Place, E1 6DW (7247 4369)
Leon
12 Ludgate Circus, EC4M 7LQ
(7489 1580)
Maison Blanc Vite
135 Fenchurch Street, EC3M 5DJ
(7929 6996)
Moshi Moshi Sushi
Kiosk 2B, Central Square, Broadgate,
EC2M 2QS (7920 0077)
Number 25 (branch of Jamies)
25 Birchin Lane, EC3V 9DJ (7623
2505/www.jamiesbars.co.uk)
The Orangery (branch of Jamies)
Cutlers Gardens, 10 Devonshire
Square, EC2M 4TE (7623 1377/
www.jamiesbars.co.uk)
Paul
Kiosk, Tower of London, EC3N 4AB
(7709 7300)
Paul
147 Fleet Street, EC4A 2BU
(7353 5874)

RESTAURANTS AREA INDEX

Little Bay p290
171 Farringdon Road, EC1R 3AL
(7278 1234/www.little-bay.co.uk)

Cafés

De Santis p297
11-13 Old Street, EC1V 9HL
(7689 5577)

Kipferl p297
70 Long Lane, EC1A 9EJ (7796
2229/www.kipferl.co.uk)

Chinese

Old China Hand p66
8 Tysoe Street, EC1R 4RQ (7278
7678/www.oldchinahand.co.uk)

East European

Potemkin p79
144 Clerkenwell Road, EC1R 5DP
(7278 6661/www.potemkin.co.uk)

Eating & Entertainment

Dans Le Noir p341
30-31 Clerkenwell Green, EC1R 0DU
(7253 1100/www.danslenoir.com/
london)

Tinseltown p342
44-46 St John Street, EC1M 4DT
(7689 2424/www.tinseltown.co.uk)

Fish

Rudland & Stubbs p81
35-37 Greenhill Rents, Cowcross
Street, EC1M 6BN (7253 0148/
www.rudlandstubbs.co.uk)

French

Café du Marché p91
22 Charterhouse Square,
Charterhouse Mews, EC1M 6AH
(7608 1609)

Club Gascon p91
57 West Smithfield, EC1A 9DS
(7796 0600)

Le Comptoir Gascon p91
61-63 Charterhouse Street, EC1M 6HJ
(7608 0851)

Gastropubs

Coach & Horses p102
26-28 Ray Street, EC1R 3DJ (7278
8990/www.thecoachandhorses.com)

Eagle p103
159 Farringdon Road, EC1R 3AL
(7837 1353)

Easton p103
22 Easton Street, WC1X 0DS
(7278 7608/www.theeaston.co.uk)

Peasant p103
240 St John Street, EC1V 4PH
(7336 7726/www.thepeasant.co.uk)

Well p103
180 St John Street, EC1V 4JY
(7251 9363/www.downthewell.com)

International

Vic Naylor Restaurant & Bar p160
38-42 St John Street, EC1M 4AY
(7608 2181/www.vicnaylor.com)

Italian

Zetter p169
86-88 Clerkenwell Road, EC1M 5RJ
(7324 4455/www.thezetter.com)

Japanese

Saki p185
4 West Smithfield, EC1A 9JX
(7489 7033/www.saki-food.com)

Modern European

Ambassador p221
55 Exmouth Market, EC1R 4QL
(7837 0009/www.theambassador
cafe.co.uk)

Clerkenwell Dining Room p221
69-73 St John Street, EC1M 4AN
(7253 9000/www.theclerkenwell.com)

Portal p221
88 St John Street, EC1M 4EH (7253
6950/www.portalrestaurant.com)

Smiths of Smithfield p221
67-77 Charterhouse Street, EC1M 6HJ
(7251 7950/www.smithsofsmithfield.
co.uk)

The Trading House p221
12-13 Greville Street, EC1N 8SB
(7831 0697/www.thetradinghouse.net)

Vivat Bacchus p221
47 Farringdon Street, EC4A 4LL
(7353 2648/www.vivatbacchus.co.uk)

Oriental

Cicada p241
132-136 St John Street, EC1V 4JT
(7608 1550/www.cicada.nu)

Pubs

Jerusalem Tavern p327
55 Britton Street, EC1M 5UQ (7490
4281/www.stpetersbrewery.co.uk)

Pakenham Arms p328
1 Pakenham Street, WC1X 0LA
(7837 6933)

Spanish

Anexo p252
61 Turnmill Street, EC1M 5PT
(7250 3401/www.anexo.co.uk)

Moro p252
34-36 Exmouth Market, EC1R 4QE
(7833 8336/www.moro.co.uk)

Vietnamese

Pho p284
86 St John Street, EC1M 4EH
(7253 7624)

Xich Lô p284
103 St John Street, EC1M 4AS
(7253 0323/www.xichlorestaurant.
com)

Wine Bars

Bleeding Heart Tavern p331
Bleeding Heart Yard, off Greville Street,
EC1N 8SJ (7242 8238/www.bleeding
heart.co.uk)

Cellar Gascon p331
59 West Smithfield, EC1A 9DS
(7600 7561/7796 0600)

Vinoteca p331
7 St John Street, EC1M 4AA
(7253 8786/www.vinoteca.co.uk)

Vivat Bacchus p331
47 Farringdon Street, EC4A 4LL
(7353 2648/www.vivatbacchus.co.uk)

Colliers Wood

Pubs

Sultan p329
78 Norman Road, SW19 1BT
(8542 4532)

Covent Garden

African & Caribbean

Calabash p28
The Africa Centre, 38 King Street,
WC2E 8JR (7836 1976)

The Americas

Christopher's p34
18 Wellington Street, WC2E 7DD (7240
4222/www.christophersgrill.com)

Joe Allen p34
13 Exeter Street, WC2E 7DT
(7836 0651/www.joeallen.co.uk)

TGI Friday's p38
6 Bedford Street, WC2E 9HZ
(7379 0585/www.tgifridays.com)

Bars

Lobby Bar p320
One Aldwych, 1 Aldwych, WC2B 4RH
(7300 1070/www.onealdwych.com)

Branches

Belgo Centraal
50 Earlham Street, WC2H 9LJ
(7813 2233)

Bertorelli
44A Floral Street, WC2E 9DA
(7836 3969)

Chez Gérard at the Opera Terrace
45 East Terrace, The Market, The
Piazza, WC2E 8RF (7379 0666)

Crusting Pipe (branch of Davy's)
27 The Market, Covent Garden,
WC2E 8RD (7836 1415)

Hamburger Union
4-6 Garrick Street, WC2E 9BH
(7379 0412)

Livebait
21 Wellington Street, WC2E 7DN
(7836 7161)

Loch Fyne Restaurant
2-4 Catherine Street, WC2B 5JS
(7240 4999)

Papageno
29-31 Wellington Street, WC2E 7BB
(7836 4444)

Paul
29 Bedford Street, WC2E 9ED
(7836 3304)

La Perla
28 Maiden Lane, WC2E 7JS
(7240 7400)

Pizza Express
9-12 Bow Street, WC2E 7AH
(7240 3443)

Pizza Paradiso
31 Catherine Street, WC2B 5JS
(7836 3609)

PJ's Grill
30 Wellington Street, WC2E 7BD
(7240 7529/www.pjsgrill.net)

Pâtisserie Valerie
8 Russell Street, WC2B 5HZ
(7240 0064)

**Segar & Snuff Parlour
(branch of Davy's)**
27A The Market, WC2E 8RD
(7836 8345)

Sofra
36 Tavistock Street, WC2E 7PB
(7240 3773)

Souk Bazaar p237
27 Litchfield Street, WC2H 9NJ (7240
1796/www.soukrestaurant.co.uk)

Strada
6 Great Queen Street, WC2B 5DH
(7405 6293)

Thai Pot
1 Bedfordbury, WC2N 4BP (7379
4580/www.thaipot.co.uk)

Wagamama
1 Tavistock Street, WC2E 7PG
(7836 3330)

Zizzi
20 Bow Street, WC2E 7AW
(7836 6101)

Brasseries

Café des Amis p46
11-14 Hanover Place, WC2E 9JP
(7379 3444/www.cafedesamis.co.uk)

British

Rules p53
35 Maiden Lane, WC2E 7LB
(7836 5314/www.rules.co.uk)

Budget

Canela p290
33 Earlham Street, WC2H 9LS
(7240 6926/www.canelacafe.com)

Cafés

Kastner & Ovens p297
52 Floral Street, WC2E 9DA
(7836 2700)

Eating & Entertainment

Mongolian Barbeque p337
12 Maiden Lane, WC2E 7NA (7379
7722/www.themongolianbarbeque.
co.uk)

Roadhouse p339
35 The Piazza, WC2E 8BE (7240
6001/www.roadhouse.co.uk)

Salsa! p339
96 Charing Cross Road, WC2H 0JG
(7379 3277/www.barsalsa.info)

Sarastro p341
126 Drury Lane, WC2B 5QG (7836
0101/www.sarastro-restaurant.com)

Fish & Chips

Rock & Sole Plaice p307
47 Endell Street, WC2H 9AJ (7836
3785/www.rockandsoleplaice.com)

French

Incognico p92
117 Shaftesbury Avenue, WC2H 8AD
(7836 8866/www.incognico.com)

Mon Plaisir p92
19-21 Monmouth Street, WC2H 9DD
(7836 7243/www.monplaisir.co.uk)

Greek

The Real Greek Souvlaki & Bar p121
60-62 Long Acre, WC2E 9JE (7240
2292/www.therealgreek.com)

Indian

Mela p134
152-156 Shaftesbury Avenue, WC2H
8HL (7836
8635/www.melarestaurant.co.uk)

International

Asia de Cuba p160
45 St Martin's Lane, WC2N 4HX
(7300 5588/www.asiadecuba-
restaurant.com)

Le Deuxième p160
65A Long Acre, WC2E 9JH (7379
0033/www.ledeuxieme.com)

Italian

Neal Street p169
26 Neal Street, WC2H 9QW (7836
8368/www.carluccios.com)

Orso p174
27 Wellington Street, WC2E 7DB
(7240 5269/www.orsorestaurant.
co.uk)

Japanese

Abeno Too p191
17-18 Great Newport Street, WC2H
7JE (7379 1160/www.abeno.co.uk)

Centrepoint Sushi (Hana) p190
20-21 St Giles High Street, WC2H 8JE
(7240 6147/www.cpfs.co.uk)

Hazuki p185
43 Chandos Place, WC2N 4HS (7240
2530/www.hazukilondon.co.uk)

Kulu Kulu p191
51-53 Shelton Street, WC2H 9HE
(7240 5687)

Korean

Woo Jung p204
59 St Giles High Street, WC2H 8LH
(7836 3103)

Modern European

Axis p221
One Aldwych, 1 Aldwych, WC2B 4RH
(7300 0300/www.onealdwych.com)

Bank Aldwych p223
1 Kingsway, WC2B 6XF (7379
9797/www.bankrestaurants.com)

The Ivy p223
1 West Street, WC2H 9NQ (7836
4751/www.caprice-holdings.co.uk)

North African

Souk Medina p237
1A Short's Gardens, WC2H 9AT
(7240 1796/www.soukrestaurant.
co.uk)

Pubs

Lamb & Flag p328
33 Rose Street, WC2E 9EB
(7497 9504)

Vegetarian

Food for Thought p279
31 Neal Street, WC2H 9PR
(7836 9072)

World Food Café p283
First floor, 14 Neal's Yard, WC2H 9DP
(7379 0298)

Wine Bars

Bedford & Strand p332
1A Bedford Street, WC2E 9HD
(7836 3033)

Café des Amis p332
11-14 Hanover Place, WC2E 9JP
(7379 3444/www.cafedesamis.co.uk)

Cricklewood

African & Caribbean

Abyssinia p31
9 Cricklewood Broadway, NW2 3JX
(8208 0110)

Crouch End

Branches

The Boom Bar
18 Crouch End Hill, N8 8AA
(8340 4539)

Brasseries

Banners p50
21 Park Road, N8 8TE (8348 2930/
www.bannersrestaurant.com)

French

Les Associés p99
172 Park Road, N8 8JT (8348 8944/
www.lesassocies.co.uk)

Bistro Aix p100
54 Topsfield Parade, Tottenham Lane,
N8 8PT (8340 6346/www.bistroaix.
co.uk)

Gastropubs

Queens Pub & Dining Room p112
26 Broadway Parade, N8 9DE
(8340 2031)

Indian

Aanya Wine Lounge p150
29 Park Road, N8 8TE (8342 8686/
www.aanya.co.uk)

Italian

Florians p183
4 Topsfield Parade, Middle Lane,
N8 8PR (8348 8348/www.florians
restaurant.com)

**Malaysian, Indonesian &
Singaporean**

Satay Malaysia p211
10 Crouch End Hill, N8 8AA
(8340 3286)

Spanish

La Bota p259
31 Broadway Parade, Tottenham Lane,
N8 9DB (8340 3082)

Vietnamese

Khoai Café p288
6 Topsfield Parade, N8 8PR
(8341 2120)

Croydon Surrey

Branches

Bella Italia
18 George Street, Croydon, Surrey
CRO HPA (8688 5787)

Little Bay
32 Selsdon Road, Croydon, Surrey
CR2 6PB (8649 9544)

Nando's
Unit 4, Valley Park Leisure Centre,
Beddington Farm Road, Croydon,
Surrey CRO 4XY (8688 9545)

Nando's
26 High Street, Croydon, Surrey
CRO 1GT (8681 3505)

TGI Friday's
702-704 Purley Way, Croydon, Surrey
CRO 4RS (8681 1313)

Yo! Sushi
House of Fraser, 21 North End
Road, Croydon, Surrey CRO 1RQ
(8760 0479)

RESTAURANTS AREA INDEX

Zizzi
57-59 Southend, Croydon, Surrey
CR0 1BF (8649 8403)

Malaysian, Indonesian & Singaporean

Malay House p212
60 Lower Addiscombe Road, Croydon,
Surrey, CR0 6AA (8666 0266)

Crystal Palace

Branches

Pizza Express
70 Westow Hill, SE19 1SB
(8670 1786)

Brasseries

Joanna's p50
56 Westow Hill, SE19 1RX (8670
4052/www.joannas.uk.com)

Vegetarian

Spirited Palace p283
105 Church Road, SE19 2PR (8771
5557/www.spiritedpalace.com)

Dalston

African & Caribbean

Suya Obalende p30
523 Kingsland Road, E8 4AR (7275
0171/www.obalendesuya.com)

Chinese

Shanghai p75
41 Kingsland High Street, E8 2JS
(7254 2878)

Fish & Chips

Faulkner's p309
424-426 Kingsland Road, E8 4AA
(7254 6152)

Portuguese

Nando's p250
148 Kingsland High Street, E8 2NS
(7923 3555/www.nandos.co.uk)

Turkish

Istanbul Iskembecisi p275
9 Stoke Newington Road, N16 8BH
(7254 7291)

Mangal II p275
4 Stoke Newington Road, N16 8BH
(7254 7888)

Mangal Ocakbasi p275
10 Arcola Street, E8 2DJ (7275 8981/
www.mangal1.com)

19 Numara Bos Cirrik p275
34 Stoke Newington Road, N16 7JU
(7249 0400)

Vietnamese

Huong-Viet p287
An Viet House, 12-14 Englefield Road,
N1 4LS (7249 0877)

Deptford

Budget

AJ Goddard p294
203 Deptford High Street, SE8 3NT
(8692 3601)

Manze's p294
204 Deptford High Street, SE8 3PR
(8692 2375)

Pubs

Dog & Bell p329
116 Prince Street, SE8 3JD (8692
5664/www.thedogandbell.com)

Vietnamese

West Lake p285
207 Deptford High Street, SE8 3NT
(8465 9408)

Docklands

The Americas

Curve p39
London Marriott, West India Quay,
22 Hertsmere Road, E14 4ED
(7093 1000 ext 2622)

Branches

Carluccio's Caffé
Reuters Plaza, E14 5AJ
(7719 1749)

Corney & Barrow
9 Cabot Square, E14 4EB (7512
0397/www.corney-barrow.co.uk)

Davy's
31-35 Fisherman's Walk, Cabot
Square, E14 4DH (7363 6633)

The Gaucho Grill
29 Westferry Circus, Canary
Riverside , E14 8RR (7987
9494/www.gaucho-grill.com)

Itsu
Level 2, Cabot Place East, E14 4QT
(7512 5790)

Jamies
28 Westferry Circus, E14 8RR
(7536 2861/www.jamiesbars.
co.uk)

Moshi Moshi Sushi
Waitrose, Canary Wharf, Canada Place,
E14 5EW (7512 9201)

Nakhon Thai
1 Dock Road, E16 1AG (7474 5510)

Nando's
Unit 25-26, Jubilee Place, E14 4QT
(7513 2864)

Pizza Express
Cabot Place East, Canary Wharf,
E14 4QT (7513 0513)

Smollensky's
1 Nash Court, Canary Wharf, E14 5AG
(7719 0101)

Tootsies Grill
Jubilee Place, 45 Bank Street,
E14 5NY (7516 9110)

Ubon
34 Westferry Circus, Canary Wharf,
E14 8RR (7719 7800/www.nobu
restaurants.com)

Wagamama
Jubilee Place, 45 Bank Street, Canary
Wharf, E14 5NY (7516 9009)

Yi-Ban
London Regatta Centre, Dockside
Road, E16 2QT (7473 6699/
www.yi-ban.co.uk)

Zizzi
33 Westferry Circus, E14 8RR
(7512 9257)

Chinese

Royal China p74
30 Westferry Circus, E14 8RR
(7719 0888/www.royalchinagroup.
co.uk)

Gastropubs

Gun p110
27 Coldharbour, Docklands, E14 9NS
(7515 5222/www.thegundocklands.
com)

Modern European

Plateau p235
Canada Place, Canada Square,
E14 5ER (7715 7100/www.conran.
com)

Thai

Elephant Royale p267
Locke's Wharf, Westferry Road,
E14 3AN (7987 7999/www.elephant
royale.com)

Dulwich

Branches

Barcelona Tapas Bar y Restaurante
481 Lordship Lane, SE22 8JY (8693
5111/www.barcelona-tapas.com)

Pizza Express
94 The Village, SE21 7AQ (8693 9333)

Sea Cow
37 Lordship Lane, SE22 8EW
(8693 3111)

Brasseries

The Green p50
58-60 East Dulwich Road, SE22 9AX
(7732 7575/www.greenbar.co.uk)

British

Franklins p59
157 Lordship Lane, SE22 8HX (8299
9598/www.franklinsrestaurant.com)

Cafés

Au Ciel p302
1A Carlton Avenue, SE21 7DE
(8488 1111/www.auciel.co.uk)

Pavilion Café p305
Dulwich Park, SE21 7BQ (8299 1383)

Gastropubs

Palmerston p109
91 Lordship Lane, SE22 8EP (8693
1629/www.thepalmerston.co.uk)

Wine Bars

Green & Blue p335
38 Lordship Lane, SE22 8HJ (8693
9250/www.greenandbluewines.com)

Ealing

African & Caribbean

BB's p31
3 Chignell Place, off Uxbridge Road,
W13 0TJ (8840 8322/www.bbscrab
back.com)

Branches

Carluccio's Caffé
5-6 The Green, W5 5DA (8566 4458)

Nando's
1-2 Station Buildings, Uxbridge Road,
W5 3NU (8992 2290)

Pizza Express
23 Bond Street, W5 5AS
(8567 7690)

La Siesta
11 Bond Street, W5 5AP
(8810 0505)

Tootsies Grill
35 Haven Green, W5 2NX (8566 8200)

Eating & Entertainment

Mamma Amalfi's p341
45 The Mall, W5 3TJ (8840 5888)

Gastropubs

Ealing Park Tavern p104
222 South Ealing Road, W5 4RL
(8758 1879)

Japanese

Sushi-Hiro p190
1 Station Parade, Uxbridge Road,
W5 3LD (8896 3175)

Earl's Court

Branches

Balans
239 Old Brompton Road, SW5 9HP
(7244 8838)

Masala Zone
147 Earl's Court Road, SW5 9RQ
(7373 0220)

Nando's
204 Earl's Court Road, SW5 0AA
(7259 2544)

Pizza Express
246 Old Brompton Road, SW5 0DE
(7373 4712)

Pizza Express
Philbeach Elbow, Ground Floor, Earl's
Court Exhibition Centre, SW5 9TA
(7386 5494)

Strada
237 Earl's Court Road, SW5 9AH
(7835 1180)

Zizzi
194-196 Earl's Court Road, SW5 9QF
(7370 1999)

East European

Nikita's p81
65 Ifield Road, SW10 9AU (7352
6326/www.nikitasrestaurant.com)

Fish

Lou Pescadou p85
241 Old Brompton Road, SW5 9HP
(7370 1057)

Greek

As Greek As It Gets p121
233 Earl's Court Road, SW5 9AH
(7244
7777/www.asgreekasitgets.com)

Earlsfield

International

Velvet Lounge p164
394 Garratt Lane, SW18 4HP
(8947 5954)

Turkish

Kazans p272
607-609 Garratt Lane, SW18 4SU
(8739 0055/www.kazans.com)

Wine Bars

Willie Gunn p334
422 Garratt Lane, SW18 4HW
(8946 7773/www.williegunn.co.uk)

East Sheen

Branches

Sarkhel's
199 Upper Richmond Road West,
East Sheen, SW14 8QT (8876 6220)

Modern European

Redmond's p231
170 Upper Richmond Road West,
SW14 8AW (8878 1922/
www.redmonds.org.uk)

Victoria p231
10 West Temple Sheen, SW14 7RT
(8876 4238/www.thevictoria.net)

Eastcote Middlesex

Indian

Nauroz p153
219 Field End Road, Eastcote, Middx
HA5 1QZ (8868 0900)

Edgware Middlesex

Branches

Haandi
301-303 Hale Lane, Edgware, Middx
HA8 7AX (8905 4433)

Nando's
137-139 Station Road, Edgware,
Middx, HA8 9JG (8952 3400)

Jewish

Aviv p203
87-89 High Street, Edgware, Middx
HA8 7DB (8952 2484/www.aviv
restaurant.com)

B&K Salt Beef Bar p203
11 Lanson House, Whitchurch Lane,
Edgware, Middx HA8 6NL (8952 8204)

Kinneret p203
313 Hale Lane, Edgware, Middx HA8
7AX (8958 4955)

Penashe p203
60 Edgware Way, Mowbray Parade,
Edgware, Middx HA8 8JS (8958 6008/
www.penashe.co.uk)

Sheva & Sheva p203
311 Hale Lane, Edgware, Middx
HA8 7AX (8905 4552)

Edgware Road

Bars

Salt Whisky Bar p320
82 Seymour Street, W2 2JB
(7402 1155/www.saltbar.com)

Branches

Beirut Express
112-114 Edgware Road, W2 2JE
(7724 2700)

Maroush
21 Edgware Road, W2 2JE (7723 0773)

Maroush IV
68 Edgware Road, W2 2EG (7224 9339)

Ranoush Juice Bar
43 Edgware Road, W2 2JR (7723 5929)

Global

Mandalay p118
444 Edgware Road, W2 1EG (7258
3696/www.mandalayway.com)

Malaysian, Indonesian & Singaporean

Mawar p209
175A Edgware Road, W2 2HR
(7262 1663)

Middle Eastern

Kandoo p213
458 Edgware Road, W2 1EJ
(7724 2428)

Maroush Gardens p213
1-3 Connaught Street, W2 2DH
(7262 0222/www.maroush.com)

Meya Meya p213
13 Bell Street, NW1 5BY (7723 8983)

Patogh p214
8 Crawford Place, W1H 5NE
(7262 4015)

Ranoush Juice Bar p214
43 Edgware Road, W2 2JR (7723 5929)

Turkish

Safa p270
22-23 Nutford Place, W1H 5YH
(7723 8331)

Elephant & Castle

Branches

Nando's
Unit 4, Metro Central, 119 Newington
Causeway, SE1 6BA (7378 7810)

Chinese

Dragon Castle p73
114 Walworth Road, SE17 1JL (7277
3388/www.dragoncastle.co.uk)

Pizza & Pasta

Pizzeria Castello p314
20 Walworth Road, SE1 6SP
(7703 2556)

Embankment

Hotels & Haute Cuisine

Jaan p125
Swissôtel London, The Howard, 12
Temple Place, WC2R 2PR (7300 1700/
http://london.swissotel.com)

Enfield Middlesex

Branches

Nando's
2 The Town, Enfield, Middx EN2 6LE
(8366 2904)

Pizza Express
2 Silver Street, Enfield, Middx EN1 3ED
(8367 3311)

TGI Friday's
Enfield Rental Park, Great Cambridge
Road, Enfield, Middx, EN1 3RZ
(8363 5200)

Euston

African & Caribbean

African Kitchen Gallery p28
102 Drummond Street, NW1 2HN
(7383 0918)

Branches

Davy's of Regent's Place
Unit 2, Euston Tower, Regent's Place,
NW1 3DP (7387 6622)

Paul
Euston Station Colonnade, Euston
Station, NW1 2RT (7388 9382)

Pizza Express
Clifton House, 93-99 Euston Road,
NW1 2RA (7383 7102)

Prezzo
161 Euston Road, NW1 2BD
(7387 5587)
Rasa Express
327 Euston Road, NW1 3AD
(7387 8974)
Pizza & Pasta
Pasta Plus p310
62 Eversholt Street, NW1 1DA
(7383 4943/www.pastaplus.co.uk)

Ewell Surrey
Branches
Sree Krishna Inn
332 Kingston Road, Ewell, Surrey,
KT19 0DT (8393 0445)

Finchley
Branches
ASK
Great North Leisure Park, Chaplin
Square, N12 0GL (8446 0970)
Nando's
Unit 2, Great North Leisure Park,
Chaplin Square, N12 0GL
(8492 8465)
Pizza Express
820 High Road, N12 9QY (8445 7714)
Zizzi
202-208 Regents Park Road, N3 3HP
(8371 6777)
Fish & Chips
Two Brothers Fish Restaurant p309
297-303 Regent's Park Road,
N3 1DP (8346 0469)
Jewish
The Burger Bar p199
110 Regents Park Road, N3 3JG
(8371 1555)
Olive Restaurant p199
224 Regents Park Road, N3 3HP
(8343 3188)
Turkish
The Ottomans p276
118 Ballards Lane, N3 2DN
(8349 9968)

Finsbury Park
African & Caribbean
Senke p31
1B-1C Rock Street, N4 2DN
(7359 7687)
Fish
Chez Liline p87
101 Stroud Green Road, N4 3PX
(7263 6550)
Turkish
Yildiz p276
163 Blackstock Road, N4 2JS
(7354 3899)

Fitzrovia
The Americas
Eagle Bar Diner p34
3-5 Rathbone Place, W1T 1HJ (7637
1418/www.eaglebardiner.com)
Mestizo p43
103 Hampstead Road, NW1 3EL
(7387 4064/www.mestizomx.com)
La Perla p43
11 Charlotte Street, W1T 1RQ (7436
1744/www.cafepacifico-laperla.com)
Bars
Hakkasan p320
8 Hanway Place, W1T 1HD (7907 1888)
Long Bar p320
The Sanderson, 50 Berners Street,
W1T 3NG (7300 1400)
Shochu Lounge p320
Basement, Roka, 37 Charlotte Street,
W1T 1RR (7580 9666/www.shochu
lounge.com)
Branches
Apostrophe
216 Tottenham Court Road, entrance
in 20/20 optical shop or 9 Alfred
Place, W1T 7PT (7436 6688)
Apostrophe
40-41 Great Castle Street, W1W 8LU
(7637 5700)
ASK
48 Grafton Way, W1T 5DZ (7388 8108)
Busaba Eathai
22 Store Street, WC1E 7DS
(7299 7900)
Chez Gérard
8 Charlotte Street, W1T 2LT
(7636 4975)
Fresco
34 Margaret Street, W1G 0JE
(7493 3838)
Harry Morgan's
6 Market Place, W1N 7AH (7580 4849)

Jamies
74 Charlotte Street, W1T 4QH (7636
7556/www.jamiesbars.co.uk)
Lees Bag (branch of Davy's)
4 Great Portland Street, W1N 5AA
(7636 5287)
Nando's
57-59 Goodge Street, W1T 1TH
(7637 0708)
Pizza Express
7 Charlotte Street, W1T 1RB
(7580 1110)
Pizza Paradiso
3 Great Titchfield Street, W1W 8AX
(7436 0111)
Rasa Express
5 Rathbone Street, W1T 1NX
(7637 0222)
Ristorante Olivelli Paradiso
35 Store Street, WC1E 7BS (7255
2554/www.ristoranteparadiso.co.uk)
Squat & Gobble
27 Tottenham Street, W1T 4RW
(7580 5338)
Strada
9-10 Market Place, W1W 8AQ
(7580 4644)
Ultimate Burger
98 Tottenham Court Road, W1T 4TR
(7436 5355)
Brasseries
RIBA Café p46
66 Portland Place, W1B 1AD
(7631 0467/www.riba.org)
Cafés
Squat & Gobble p297
69 Charlotte Street, W1T 4RJ
(7580 5338/www.squatandgobble.
co.uk)
Chinese
Hakkasan p66
8 Hanway Place, W1T 1HD
(7907 1888)
Eating & Entertainment
Nueva Costa Dorada p339
47-55 Hanway Street, W1T 1UX
(7636 7139/www.costadorada
restaurant.co.uk)
Fish
Back to Basics p81
21A Foley Street, W1W 6DS
(7436 2181/www.backtobasics.
uk.com)
Fish & Chips
Fish Bone p307
82 Cleveland Street, W1T 6NF
(7580 2672)
French
Elena's L'Étoile p92
30 Charlotte Street, W1T 2NG
(7636 7189)
Hotels & Haute Cuisine
Pied à Terre p125
34 Charlotte Street, W1T 2NH
(7636 1178/www.pied-a-terre.co.uk)
Indian
Indian YMCA p134
41 Fitzroy Square, W1T 6AQ
(7387 0411/www.indianymca.org)
Rasa Samudra p134
5 Charlotte Street, W1T 1RE (7637
0222/www.rasarestaurants.com)
International
Archipelago p160
110 Whitfield Street, W1T 5ED
(7383 3346)
Mash p160
19-21 Great Portland Street, W1W 8QB
(7637 5555/www.mashbarand
restaurant.com)
Spoon+ at Sanderson p161
The Sanderson, 50 Berners Street,
W1T 3NG (7300 1444/www.spoon-
restaurant.com)
Italian
Bertorelli p174
19-23 Charlotte Street, W1T 1RL
(7636 4174/www.santeonline.co.uk)
Camerino p169
16 Percy Street, W1T 1DT (7637
9900/www.camerinorestaurant.com)
Carluccio's Caffè p171
8 Market Place, W1W 8AG (7636
2228/www.carluccios.com)
Latium p169
21 Berners Street, W1T 3LP (7323
9123/www.latiumrestaurant.com)
Passione p170
10 Charlotte Street, W1T 2LT
(7636 2833/www.passione.co.uk)
Sardo p170
45 Grafton Way, W1T 5DQ (7387
2521/www.sardo-restaurant.com)

Japanese
Ikkyu p190
67A Tottenham Court Road, W1T 2EY
(7636 9280)
Roka p185
37 Charlotte Street, W1T 1RR
(7580 6464/www.rokarestaurant.
com)
Soho Japan p191
52 Wells Street, W1T 3PR (7323
4661/www.sohojapan.co.uk)
Modern European
Villandry p223
170 Great Portland Street, W1W 5QB
(7631 3131/www.villandry.com)
Oriental
Bam-Bou p241
1 Percy Street, W1T 1DB (7323 9130/
www.bam-bou.co.uk)
Crazy Bear p241
26-28 Whitfield Street, W1T 2RG (7631
0088/www.crazybeargroup.co.uk)
dim T café p242
32 Charlotte Street , W1T 2NQ
(7637 1122)
Pizza & Pasta
Cleveland Kitchen p310
145 Cleveland Street, W1T 6QH
(7387 5966)
Zizzi p315
33-41 Charlotte Street, W1T 1RR
(7436 9440/www.zizzi.co.uk)
Spanish
Fino p252
33 Charlotte Street, entrance on
Rathbone Street, W1T 1RR (7813
8010/www.finorestaurant.com)
Navarro's p253
67 Charlotte Street, W1T 4PH
(7637 7713/www.navarros.co.uk)
Salt Yard p253
54 Goodge Street, W1T 4NA
(7637 0657/www.saltyard.co.uk)
Turkish
Istanbul Meze p270
100 Cleveland Street, W1P 5DP (7387
0785/www.istanbulmeze.com)
Özer p270
5 Langham Place, W1B 3DG
(7323 0505/www.sofra.co.uk)

Fulham
The Americas
1492 p43
404 North End Road, SW6 1LU
(7381 3810/www.1492restaurant.
com)
Sophie's Steakhouse & Bar p38
311-313 Fulham Road, SW10 9QH
(7352 0088/www.sophiessteak
house.com)
Branches
ASK
345 Fulham Palace Road, SW6 6TD
(7371 0392)
Bodean's
4 Broadway Chambers, Fulham
Broadway, SW6 1EP (7610 0440)
Brinkley's
47 Hollywood Road, SW10 9HX
(7351 1683/www.brinkleys.com)
Carluccio's Caffè
236 Fulham Road, SW10 9NB
(7376 5960)
Feng Sushi
218 Fulham Road, SW10 9NB
(7795 1900)
Gourmet Burger Kitchen
49 Fulham Broadway, SW6 1AE
(7381 4242)
Joe's Brasserie
130 Wandsworth Bridge Road,
SW6 2UL (7731 7835)
Lisboa Pâtisserie
6 World's End Place, off King's Road,
SW10 0HE (7376 3639)
Little Bay
140 Wandsworth Bridge Road,
SW6 2UL (7751 3133)
Ma Goa
194 Wandsworth Bridge Road,
SW6 2UF (7384 2122)
Nando's
Unit 20, Fulham Broadway Retail
Centre, Fulham Road, SW6 1BY
(7386 8035)
La Perla
803 Fulham Road, SW6 5HE (7471
4895/www.cafepacifico-laperla.com)
Pizza Express
363 Fulham Road, SW10 9TN
(7352 5300)
Pizza Express
895-896 Fulham Road, SW6 5HU
(7731 3117)

Pizza Express
Unit 4, Fulham Broadway Development,
SW6 1BW (7381 1700)
Sea Cow
678 Fulham Road, SW6 5SA
(7610 8020)
Wine Gallery
49 Hollywood Road, SW10 9HX
(7352 7572/www.brinkleys.com)
Yo! Sushi
Fulham Broadway Centre, Fulham
Road, SW6 1BW (7385 6077)
Zinc Bar & Grill
11 Jerdan Place, SW6 1BE
(7386 2250)
Chinese
Taiwan Village p72
85 Lillie Road, SW6 1UD (7381 2900/
www.taiwanvillage.com)
Eating & Entertainment
Vingt-Quatre p342
325 Fulham Road, SW10 9QL
(7376 7224)
Fish
Deep p85
The Boulevard, Imperial Wharf,
SW6 2UB (7736 3337/www.deep
london.co.uk)
Hosteria del Pesce p85
84-86 Lillie Road, SW6 1TL
(7610 0037/www.hosteriadel
pesce.com)
Italian
La Famiglia p179
7 Langton Street, SW10 0JL (7351
0761/7352 6095/www.lafamiglia.
co.uk)
Modern European
The Farm p232
18 Farm Lane, SW6 1PP (7381
3331/www.thefarmfulham.co.uk)
Oriental
Zimzun p243
Fulham Broadway Retail Centre,
Fulham Road, SW6 1BW (7385 4555/
www.zimzun.co.uk)
Pizza & Pasta
Napulé p313
585 Fulham Road, SW6 5UA
(7381 1122)
Rossopomodoro p313
214 Fulham Road, SW10 9NB
(7352 7677)
Thai
Blue Elephant p263
4-6 Fulham Broadway, SW6 1AA
(7385 6595/www.blueelephant.com)
Saran Rom p263
Waterside Tower, The Boulevard,
Imperial Wharf, Townmead Road,
SW6 2UB (7751 3111/www.saran
rom.com)
Sukho p265
855 Fulham Road, SW6 5HJ
(7371 7600)

Gipsy Hill
Global
Numidie p119
48 Westow Hill, SE19 1RX
(8766 6166/www.numidie.co.uk)
Oriental
Mangosteen p245
246 Gipsy Road, SE27 9RB
(8670 0333)

Gloucester Road
Branches
ASK
23-24 Gloucester Arcade, SW7 4SF
(7835 0840)
Black & Blue
105 Gloucester Road, SW7 4SS
(7244 7666/www.blackandblue.biz)
Paul
73 Gloucester Road, SW7 4SS
(7373 1232)
Cafés
The Bentley p303
27-33 Harrington Gardens, SW7 4JX
(7244 5555/www.thebentley-hotel.
com)
East European
Jakob's p76
20 Gloucester Road, SW7 4RB
(7581 9292)
Indian
Bombay Brasserie p135
Courtfield Close, SW7 4QH (7370
4040/www.bombaybrasserielondon.
com)

RESTAURANTS AREA INDEX

RESTAURANTS AREA INDEX

Restaurants A-Z Index

Definite articles are ignored (The, L', La, Le, Les, Il, El etc) and names (eg J Sheekey) are indexed by surname).

A

A Cena p184
418 Richmond Road, Twickenham, Middx, TW1 2EB (8288 0108). Italian

Aanya Wine Lounge p150
29 Park Road, N8 8TE (8342 8686/www.aanya.co.uk). Indian

Abeno
47 Museum Street, WC1A 1LY (7405 3211). Branch

Abeno Too p191
17-18 Great Newport Street, WC2H 7JE (7379 1160/www.abeno.co.uk). Japanese

Abingdon p162
54 Abingdon Road, W8 6AP (7937 3339). International

Abu Zaad p218
29 Uxbridge Road, W12 8LH (8749 5107). Middle Eastern

Abyssinia p31
9 Cricklewood Broadway, NW2 3JX (8208 0110). African & Caribbean

L'Accento p176
16 Garway Road, W2 4NH (7243 2201). Italian

Adam's Café p239
77 Askew Road, W12 9AH (8743 0572). North African

Addendum p125
Apex City of London Hotel, 1 Seething Lane, EC3N 4AX (7977 9500/www.addendumrestaurant.co.uk). Hotels & Haute Cuisine

Addis p28
42 Caledonian Road, N1 9DT (7278 0679/www.addisrestaurant.co.uk). African & Caribbean

The Admiralty p97
Somerset House, Strand, WC2R 1LA (7845 4646/www.somerset-house.org.uk). French

Afghan Kitchen p117
35 Islington Green, N1 8DU (7359 8019). Global

African Kitchen Gallery p28
102 Drummond Street, NW1 2HN (7383 0918). African & Caribbean

Aki p185
182 Gray's Inn Road, WC1X 8EW (7837 9281/www.akidemae.com). Japanese

Al Duca p174
4-5 Duke of York Street, SW1Y 6LA (7839 3090/www.alduca-restaurant.co.uk). Italian

Al Fawar p214
50 Baker Street, W1U 7BT (7224 4777/www.alfawar.com). Middle Eastern

Al Hamra p215
31-33 Shepherd Market, W1Y 7HR (7493 1954/www.alhamrarestaurant.com). Middle Eastern

Al Sultan p215
51-52 Hertford Street, W1J 7ST (7408 1155/1166/www.alsultan.co.uk). Middle Eastern

Al Waha p216
75 Westbourne Grove, W2 4UL (7229 0806/www.waha-uk.com). Middle Eastern

Alastair Little p226
49 Frith Street, W1D 4SG (7734 5183). Modern European

Albannach p57
66 Trafalgar Square, WC2N 5DS (7930 0066/www.albannach.co.uk). British

Albertine p334
1 Wood Lane, W12 7DP (8743 9593/www.gonumber.com/albertine). Wine Bars

Ali Baba p214
32 Ivor Place, NW1 6DA (7723 7474/5805). Middle Eastern

All Star Lanes p341
Victoria House, Bloomsbury Place, WC1B 4DA (7025 2676/www.allstarlanes.co.uk). Eating & Entertainment

Alloro p173
19-20 Dover Street, W1X 4LU (7495 4768). Italian

Almeida p100
30 Almeida Street, N1 1AD (7354 4777/www.conran.com). French

Alounak p217
10 Russell Gardens, W14 8EZ (7603 7645). Middle Eastern

Alounak Kebab
44 Westbourne Grove, W2 5SH (7229 0416). Branch

Amato p300
14 Old Compton Street, W1D 4TH (7734 5733/www.amato.co.uk). Cafés

Amaya p135
Halkin Arcade, SW1X 8JT (7823 1166/www.realindianfood.com). Indian

Ambassador p221
55 Exmouth Market, EC1R 4QL (7837 0009/www.theambassadorcafe.co.uk). Modern European

American Bar p325
The Savoy, Strand, WC2R 0EU (7836 4343/www.fairmont.com/savoy). Bars

Amici p181
35 Bellevue Road, SW17 7EF (8672 5888/www.amiciitalian.co.uk). Italian

Amuse Bouche p334
51 Parsons Green Lane, SW6 4JA (7371 8517/www.abcb.co.uk). Wine Bars

Anam p327
3 Chapel Market, N1 9EZ (7278 1001/www.anambar.com). Bars

Anatolia Ocakbasi p275
253 Mare Street, E8 3NS (8986 2223). Turkish

Anchor & Hope p107
36 The Cut, SE1 8LP (7928 9898). Gastropubs

Anda de Bridge p32
42-44 Kingsland Road, E2 8DA (7739 3863/www.andadebridge.com). African & Caribbean

Andrew Edmunds p226
46 Lexington Street, W1F 0LW (7437 5708). Modern European

Andy's Taverna p122
81-81A Bayham Street, NW1 0AG (7485 9718). Greek

Anexo p252
61 Turnmill Street, EC1M 5PT (7250 3401/www.anexo.co.uk). Spanish

Angela Hartnett at the Connaught p130
The Connaught, 16 Carlos Place, W1K 2AL (7592 1222/www.gordonramsay.com). Hotels & Haute Cuisine

Angeles p75
405 Kilburn High Road, NW6 7QL (7625 2663). Chinese

Angie's p28
381 Harrow Road, W9 3NA (8962 8761/www.angies-restaurant.co.uk). African & Caribbean

Anglesea Arms p105
35 Wingate Road, W6 0UR (8749 1291). Gastropubs

Annex 3 p322
6 Little Portland Street, W1W 7JE (7631 0700/www.annex3.co.uk). Bars

Antepliler p277
46 Grand Parade, Green Lanes, N4 1AG (8802 5588). Turkish

Antony's p78
54 Porchester Road, W2 6ET (7243 8743/www.antonysrestaurant.com). East European

Apartment 195 (branch of Jamies)
195 King's Road, SW3 5ED (7351 5195/www.apartment195.co.uk). Branch

Aperitivo p174
41 Beak Street, W1F 9SB (7287 2057/www.aperitivo-restaurants.com). Italian

Aphrodite Taverna p121
15 Hereford Road, W2 4AB (7229 2206). Greek

Apollo Banana Leaf p145
190 Tooting High Street, SW17 0SF (8696 1423). Indian

Apostrophe p298
23 Barrett Street, W1U 1BF (7355 1001/www.apostropheuk.com). Cafés

Apostrophe
42 Great Eastern Street, EC2A 3EP (7739 8412). Branch

Apostrophe
10 St Paul's Churchyard, EC4M 8AL (7248 9100). Branch

Apostrophe
16 Regent Street, SW1Y 4BT (7930 9922). Branch

Apostrophe
216 Tottenham Court Road, entrance in 20/20 optical shop or 9 Alfred Place, W1T 7PT (7436 6688). Branch

Apostrophe
40-41 Great Castle Street, W1W 8LU (7637 5700). Branch

Apostrophe
215 Strand, WC2R 1AY (7427 9890). Branch

Applebee's p87
17 Cambridge Park, E11 2PU (8989 1977). Fish

Arancia p183
52 Southwark Park Road, SE16 3RS (7394 1751/www.arancia-uk.co.uk). Italian

Arbutus p226
63-64 Frith Street, W1D 3JW (7734 4545/www.arbutusrestaurant.co.uk). Modern European

Archduke p335
Concert Hall Approach, SE1 8XU (7928 9370/www.thearchduke.co.uk). Wine Bars

Archipelago p160
110 Whitfield Street, W1T 5ED (7383 3346). International

The Ark p178
122 Palace Gardens Terrace, W8 4RT (7229 4024/www.theark restaurant.co.uk). Italian

Ark Fish Restaurant p87
142 Hermon Hill, E18 1QH (8989 5345/www.arkfishrestaurant.com). Fish

Arkansas Café p33
Unit 12, Old Spitalfields Market, E1 6AA (7377 6999). The Americas

Armadillo p45
41 Broadway Market, E8 4PH (7249 3633/www.armadillorestaurant.co.uk). The Americas

Armadillo Café p301
11 Bramley Road, W10 6SZ (7727 9799/www.armadillocafe.co.uk). Cafés

WJ Arment p294
7 & 9 Westmoreland Road, SE17 2AX (7703 4974). Budget

Arturo p171
23 Connaught Street, W2 2AY (7706 3388/www.arturorestaurant.co.uk). Italian

As Greek As It Gets p121
233 Earl's Court Road, SW5 9AH (7244 7777/www.asgreekasitgets.com). Greek

Asadal p204
227 High Holborn, WC1V 7DA (7430 9006). Korean

Asadal
180 New Malden High Street, New Malden, Surrey, KT3 4EF (8942 2334/8949 7385). Branch

Asakusa p195
265 Eversholt Street, NW1 1BA (7388 8533/8399). Japanese

Asia de Cuba p160
45 St Martin's Lane, WC2N 4HX (7300 5588/www.asiadecuba-restaurant.com). International

ASK p314
160-162 Victoria Street, SW1E 5LB (7630 8228/www.askcentral.co.uk). Pizza & Pasta

ASK
56-60 Wigmore Street, W1U 2RZ (7224 3484). Branch

ASK
Business Design Centre, 52 Upper Street, N1 0PN (7226 8728). Branch

ASK
43 Muswell Hill Broadway, N10 3AH (8365 2833). Branch

ASK
Great North Leisure Park, Chaplin Square, N12 0GL (8446 0970). Branch

ASK
1257 High Road, N20 0EW (8492 0033). Branch

ASK
197 Baker Street, NW1 6UY (7486 6027). Branch

ASK
216 Haverstock Hill, NW3 2AE (7433 3896). Branch

ASK
Spice Quay, 34 Shad Thames, Butlers Wharf, SE1 2YE (7403 4545). Branch

ASK
85 Kew Green, Richmond, Surrey TW9 3AH (8940 3766). Branch

ASK
Old Sorting Office, Station Road, SW13 0LJ (8878 9300). Branch

ASK
300 King's Road, SW3 5UH (7349 9123). Branch

ASK
345 Fulham Palace Road, SW6 6TD (7371 0392). Branch

ASK
23-24 Gloucester Arcade, SW7 4SF (7835 0840). Branch

ASK
145 Notting Hill Gate, W11 3LB (7792 9942). Branch

ASK
14-16 Quadrant Arcade, 15A Air Street, W1B 5HL (7734 4267). Branch

ASK
121-125 Park Street, W1K 7JA (7495 7760). Branch

ASK
48 Grafton Way, W1T 5DZ (7388 8108). Branch

ASK
41-43 Spring Street, W2 1JA (7706 0707). Branch

ASK
17-20 Kendal Street, W2 2AE (7724 4637). Branch

ASK
Whiteley's Shopping Centre, 151 Queensway, W2 4SB (7792 1977). Branch

ASK
222 Kensington High Street, W8 7RG (7937 5540). Branch

ASK
74 Southampton Row, WC1B 4AR (7405 2876). Branch

Asmara p30
386 Coldharbour Lane, SW9 8LF (7737 4144). African & Caribbean

Assaggi p176
First floor, 39 Chepstow Place, W2 4TS (7792 5501). Italian

Les Associés p99
172 Park Road, N8 8JT (8348 8944/www.lesassocies.co.uk). French

Astor Bar & Grill p325
20 Glasshouse Street, W1B 5DJ (7734 4888/www.astorbarandgrill.com). Bars

Astor Bar & Grill p95
20 Glasshouse Street, W1B 5DJ (7734 4888/www.astorbarandgrill.com). French

The Atrium p162
4 Millbank, SW1P 3JA (7233 0032/www.atriumrestaurant.com). International

Au Ciel p302
1A Carlton Avenue, SE21 7DE (8488 1111/www.auciel.co.uk). Cafés

Au Lac p285
104 Kingsland Road, E2 8DP (7033 0588/www.aulac.co.uk). Vietnamese

Aubaine p47
260-262 Brompton Road, SW3 2AS (7052 0100/www.aubaine.co.uk). Brasseries

L'Auberge p98
22 Upper Richmond Road, SW15 2RX (8874 3593/www.ardillys.com). French

Aubergine p133
11 Park Walk, SW10 0AJ (7352 3449/www.auberginerestaurant.co.uk). Hotels & Haute Cuisine

Automat p34
33 Dover Street, W1S 4NF (7499 3033/www.automat-london.com). The Americas

L'Aventure p101
3 Blenheim Terrace, NW8 0EH (7624 6232). French

The Avenue p226
7-9 St James's Street, SW1A 1EE (7321 2111/www.egami.co.uk). Modern European

RESTAURANTS A-Z INDEX